Community care and the law

sixth edition

University of Liverpool

Withdrawn from stock

Luke Clements is Cerebra Professor of Law and Social Justice at the School of Law, Leeds University and a consultant solicitor with Scott-Moncrieff & Associates LLP.

Luke Clements can be contacted by e-mail at L.J.Clements@leeds.ac.uk

Available as an ebook at www.lag.org.uk/ebooks

The purpose of the Legal Action Group is to promote equal access to justice for all members of society who are socially, economically or otherwise disadvantaged. To this end, it seeks to improve law and practice, the administration of justice and legal services.

Community care and the law

SIXTH EDITION

Luke Clements

with Karen Ashton, Simon Garlick, Carolyn Goodall,
Jean Gould, Edward Mitchell and Alison Pickup

 Legal Action Group
2017

This edition published in Great Britain 2017
by LAG Education and Service Trust Limited
National Pro Bono Centre, 48 Chancery Lane, London WC2A 1JF

First edition 1996
Reprinted with revisions 1997
Second edition 2000
Third edition 2004
Fourth edition 2007
Fifth edition 2011

British Library Cataloguing in Publication Data
A CIP catalogue record for this book is available from the British Library

Crown Copyright material is produced with the permission of the Controller of HMSO and the Queen's Printer for Scotland.

This book has been produced using Forest Stewardship Council (FSC) certified paper. The wood used to produce FSC certified products with a 'Mixed Sources' label comes from FSC certified well-managed forests, controlled sources and/or recycled material.

Print ISBN   978 1 908407 82 5
ebook ISBN   978 1 908407 83 2

Typeset by Regent Typesetting, London
Printed in Great Britain by Hobbs the Printers, Totton, Hampshire

In memory of Pauline Thompson OBE

Pauline read history at the University of East Anglia and then at the University of Kent obtained her diploma in Social Work. Pauline began her social work career in East Sussex before moving to Barnardo's and subsequently to Bolton social services where she became the authority's first welfare rights adviser. Pauline fulfilled the same role for Lancashire's welfare rights service and later as its welfare rights training officer. By this time Pauline had become a leading expert on the detail of welfare rights and advised many national bodies, including the Association of County Councils at the time of the community care reforms.

In 1996, Pauline moved to Age Concern (now Age UK) as its policy adviser on community care finance where she remained until she retired in 2010. On her retirement, tributes were paid in the House of Lords to her outstanding knowledge and her enormous contribution to the development of a better social care system.

Pauline was a long-standing member of the Law Society's mental health and disability committee, she wrote extensively including contributions to the *Disability Rights Handbook* (Disability Rights UK) the *Paying for Care Handbook* (Child Poverty Action Group) and she co-authored the previous two editions of this book.

The value of social justice was hardwired in Pauline, as was incredible generosity, a complete lack of self-pity, a love of her friends and a love of life – virtues that became more evident as her illness demanded more of her attention. Pauline also did 'indignation' – and when confronted by policies that would exacerbate poverty, indignity and social exclusion she became decidedly 'steely' in putting her case. Tenacious but always friendly: she was someone who talked to strangers and had numerous good colleagues in every walk of life.

As the last edition of this book went to print Pauline was told she had inoperable cancer and that she had two years to live. She said she would pack a lifetime into these years and in many respects she did – travelling around the world, performing with her choirs and visiting friends.

Pauline was a wonderful friend and a wonderful example and inspiration to us all. Pauline died on the 13 January 2014.

Preface

This sixth edition has involved a complete rewriting of almost every page of *Community Care and the Law*. It has been a mammoth undertaking that would not have been possible without the major input of the contributors and countless other generous and wise colleagues.

This edition does not cover the law in Wales or the rights of disabled children:

- devolution has created a distinct social care jurisdiction in each of the UKs nations. For this book to cover the Social Services and Well-being (Wales) Act 2014 it would have had to be twice the length; and
- the law detailing the social care rights of disabled children is now so detailed that its analysis warrants a separate text. Happily the Legal Action Group has published a sister volume that covers this in exemplary detail: *Disabled Children: a legal handbook* (2016) by Steve Broach, Janet Read and myself.

For reasons of space, this edition does not consider in detail 'macro' social services planning functions. These include such things as: the preparation of strategic plans; the operation of Health and Well-being Boards; the health/social care 'integration' obligations (including the local operation of the Better Care Fund); and the duty to promote the diversity/quality of care provision and to manage 'provider failure'.

I have tried to keep to a minimum the use of abbreviations, but have had to shorten references to the commonly used statutes. Likewise I have referred throughout to the key policy guidance, *The Care and Support Statutory Guidance*, as the 'Statutory Guidance' (see para 1.41). In several chapters or sections a particular piece of policy or practice guidance is important and in that section I have given it a shortened title, having of course explained what the shortened title refers to.

This edition has only been possible because of the support and patience of Mo. It has involved many late nights, blank weekends and putting up with a great deal of sighing and groaning on my part.

In writing this book very special thanks are due to the key contributors: Karen Ashton, Simon Garlick, Carolyn Goodall, Jean Gould, Edward Mitchell and Alison Pickup – who have taken the lead on revising key chapters – and without whose genius this edition would not have been possible.

Special thanks and very special apologies are due to the wonderful publisher Esther Pilger for the missed deadlines and the support in getting this edition into print.

I have received enormous assistance from countless kind and wise people. Many important concepts have been explained to me by advocates, advisers, social workers and my clients have taught me far more than (I hope) they will ever realise. Special thanks for their support and inspiration are due to my colleagues:

- at the School of Law, Leeds University;
- at the national children's charity Cerebra;
- at Scott-Moncrieff & Associates Ltd;
- John Bangs, Richard Bartholomew, Steve Brett, Steve Broach, David Brooker, Simon Bull, Jamie Burton, Beverley Clough, Stephen Corlett, Julie Doughty, Morag Duff, Rupert Earl, Tracy Elliot, Dave Everatt, Phil Fennell, Michael Furminger, Emily Holzhausen, Carys Hughes, Byron Jones, Stephen Knafler QC, Anna Lawson, Michael Mandelstam, Tim McSharry, Paul Morgan, Brian O'Shea, Camilla Parker, Janet Read, Frank and Sue Redmond, Lucy Series, Glenn Storhaug, Alison Tarrant, Derek Tilley, Kate Whittaker and Mitchell Woolf.

I have almost certainly omitted from this list many who have also assisted me and to them I apologise.

What is wrong in this text is entirely of my own doing and I would welcome any critical feedback.

Luke Clements
March 2017

Contents

APPENDICES

Table of cases

Table of ombudsman complaints and decisions

Local Government Ombudsman decisions

Health Service Ombudsman decisions

Public Services Ombudsman for Wales decisions

Joint investigations

Table of statutes

Table of statutory instruments

Table of European and international conventions and treaties

Abbreviations

AA 2009	Autism Act 2009
ACPO	Association of Chief Police Officers
ADASS	Association of Directors of Adult Social Services Departments
AHP	allied health professional
AIA 1996	Asylum and Immigration Act 1996
AMCP	approved mental capacity professional
AOR	assessment of resources
ASAP	Asylum Support Appeals Project
ASC	altered states of consciousness
ASCOF	Adult Social Care Outcomes Framework
BMA	British Medical Association
BNA 1981	British Nationality Act 1981
CA 1989	Children Act 1989
CA 2014	Care Act 2014
CAMHS	children and adolescent mental health services
CANH	clinically assisted nutrition and hydration
CAS	Central Alerting System
CASSRs	Councils with Adult Social Services Responsibilities
CCA	community care assessment
CCA 1974	Consumer Credit Act 1974
CC(DP)A1996	Community Care (Direct Payments) Act 1996
CCG	clinical commissioning group
C(EO)A 2004	Carers (Equal Opportunities) Act 2004
CFA 2014	Children and Families Act 2014
CIPFA	Chartered Institute of Public Finance and Accountancy
CCJA 2015	Criminal Justice and Courts Act 2015
CJEU	Court of Justice of the European Union
C(LC)A 2000	Children (Leaving Care) Act 2000
CMHT	community mental health team
CPA	care programme approach
CPR	Civil Procedure Rules
CQC	Care Quality Commission
CRAG	Charging for residential accommodation guidance
CRD	Case Resolution Directorate
CRPD	UN Convention on the Rights of Persons with Disabilities
CSCI	Commission for Social Care Inspection
CSDPA 1970	Chronically Sick and Disabled Persons Act 1970
CSIP	Care Services Improvement Partnership
CSO	civil society organisation
CSU	commissioning support units
DAT	drug action and alcohol team
DBS	Disclosure and Barring Service
DCLG	Department for Communities and Local Government
DFG	disabled facilities grant
DH	Department of Health
DHP	discretionary housing payments

DIA	disposable income allowance
DLA	disability living allowance
DOL	deprivation of liberty
DOLS	deprivation of liberty safeguards
DP	deferred payment
DPA	deferred payment agreement
DPA 1998	Data Protection Act 1998
DRE	disability related expenditure
DST	decision support tool
EqA 2010	Equality Act 2010
ECHR	European Convention on Human Rights
EEA	European Economic Area
EEA Regs 2006	Immigration (European Economic Area) Regulations 2006
EHC	education, health and care
EHRC	Equality and Human Rights Commission
EPIOC	electrically powered indoor/outdoor wheelchairs
ESA	employment and support allowance
EU	European Union
FACS	Fair access to care services (Department of Health statutory guidance)
FOIA 2000	Freedom of Information Act 2000
FSMA 2000	Financial Services and Markets Act 2000
GMS	general medical services
GP	general practitioner
HA 1985	Housing Act 1985
HA 1996	Housing Act 1996
HA 1999	Health Act 1999
HA 2009	Health Act 2009
HAC	Home Adaptations Consortium
HASSASSAA 1983	Health and Social Services and Social Security Adjudications Act 1983
HCPC	Health & Care Professions Council
HGCRA 1996	Housing Grants, Construction and Regeneration Act 1996
HOS	housing ombudsman service
HRA 1998	Human Rights Act 1998
HSCA 1993	Health Service Commissioners Act1993
HSCA 2001	Health and Social Care Act 2001
HSCA 2008	Health and Social Care Act 2008
HSCA 2012	Health and Social Care Act 2012
HSC(CHS)A 2003	Health and Social Care (Community Health and Standards) Act 2003
HSCIC	Health and Social Care Information Centre
HSO	health service ombudsman
HSPHA 1968	Health Services and Public Health Act 1968
HTCS	healthcare travel costs scheme
HWB	health and wellbeing boards
IA 1986	Insolvency Act 1986
IA 2014	Immigration Act 2014
IA 2016	Immigration Act 2016
IAA 1999	Immigration and Asylum Act 1999
ICAS	Independent Complaints Advocacy Service
ICO	Information Commissioner's Office
ILF	Independent Living Fund
IMCA	independent mental capacity advocate
IRP	Independent Review Panel
IS	income support
IUT	Independent User Trust
JSA	jobseekers' allowance

LA 2011	Localism Act 2011
LAA	Legal Aid Agency
LAC	local authority circular
LASSL	local authority social services letter
LASSA 1970	Local Authority Social Services Act 1970
LGA	Local Government Association
LGA 1972	Local Government Act 1972
LGA 1974	Local Government Act 1974
LGA 2000	Local Government Act 2000
LGO	local government ombudsman
LGPIHA 2007	Local Government and Public Involvement in Health Act 2007
LPA	lasting power of attorney
LHB	local health board
MAR	Medication Administration Records
MCA 2005	Mental Capacity Act 2005
MDT	multi-disciplinary team
MHA 1983	Mental Health Act 1983
MHRA	Medicines and Healthcare products Regulatory Agency
MIG	minimum income guarantee
NAA 1948	National Assistance Act 1948
NAFAO	National Association of Financial Assessment Officers
NAM	new asylum model
NASS	National Asylum Support Service (now UKIV)
NHE	National Health Executive
NHS	National Health Service
NHS CC	NHS continuing healthcare
NHSA 1946	National Health Service Act 1946
NHSA 1977	National Health Service Act 1977
NHSA 2006	National Health Service Act 2006
NHSCCA 1990	National Health Service and Community Care Act 1990
NHS(CP)A 2006	National Health Service (Consequential Provisions) Act 2006
NHS(W)A 2006	National Health Service (Wales) Act 2006
NIAA 2002	Nationality, Immigration and Asylum Act 2002
NICE	National Institute of Health and Care Excellence
NRPF	no recourse to public funds
NSF	national service framework
NTA	National Treatment Agency for Substance Misuse
OFSTED	Office for Standards in Education, Children's Services and Skills
OFT	Office of Fair Trading
ONS	Office of National Statistics
OPG	Office of the Public Guardian
OT	occupational therapist
PA 1997	Police Act 1997
PACE 1984	Police and Criminal Evidence Act 1984
PALS	patient advice and liaison service
PCO	protective costs order
PCT	primary care trust
PEA	personal expenses allowance
PFA 2012	Protection of Freedoms Act 2012
PHA	Public Health Act (various years)
PHSO	parliamentary and health service ombudsman
PIP	personal independence payment
PSED	public sector equality duty
PSO	parliamentary service ombudsman
PSSRU	Personal Social Services Research Unit
PTS	patient transport service

RADAR	Royal Association for Disability and Rehabilitation
RAS	resource allocation system
RIPA 2000	Regulation of Investigatory Powers Act 2000
RNCC	registered nursing care contribution
RNIB	Royal National Institute of Blind People
RPR	relevant person's representative
RRO 2002	Regulatory Reform Order 2002
SAB	Safeguarding Adults Board
SAR	Safeguarding adults review
SCIE	Social Care Institute for Excellence
SEN	special educational needs
SIA 1946	Statutory Instruments Act 1946
SOA 2003	Sexual Offences Act 2003
SVGA 2006	Safeguarding Vulnerable Groups Act 2006
TLAPP	Think Local Act Personal Partnership
UASC	unaccompanied asylum seeking child/children
UKVI	Home Office UK Visas and Immigration directorate
UTTC	Unfair Terms in Consumer Contracts
WWS Regs 2002	Withholding and Withdrawal of Support (Travel Assistance and Temporary Accommodation Regulations 2002

Introduction

I.1   The pendulum swings – welfare policy changes: there are no straight lines in community care. It has swung ever since Henry VIII's reformation set it in motion. For all their undoubted faults, the monasteries provided significant care for paupers[1] and their dissolution meant that the regal state had to intervene: that poor laws defining parish obligations had to be enacted.

I.2   Monastic support has been described as 'indiscriminate and unorganised'[2] in the sense that it did not distinguish between categories of paupers – for example between the 'impotent' and the 'able-bodied' poor. The universal nature of the support monasteries provided created a political problem, since it undermined the failing feudal system. Ever since the Black Death and the shortage of labourers it created, workers (particularly those able to escape their bonded existence) had started to demand better pay. In an effort to restrict this, laws were enacted to control wages[3] and to criminalise begging and the free movement of workers.[4]

I.3   State concern about the free movement of workers and the availability of 'universal' benefits is a theme that reoccurs throughout the succeeding centuries. We see successive policies on 'settlement' (today we call it 'ordinary residence') and demands that support be less 'indiscriminate' (be more 'targeted' to use today's language). We see this with the emergence of what the Victorian Poor Law system described as 'deserving and undeserving' poor and today we see it in a range of assessment mechanisms including social care 'eligibility criteria': a system for categorising those whom the state decides ought, and ought not, to be supported.

I.4   Henry VIII's first Poor Law in 1531[5] was about social control. Able-bodied unemployed people were to be 'Tyed to the end of a Carte naked

---

1   While emphasising the variability of the support provided, Rushton concludes that it is 'reasonable to assume that monastic charitable provision in the 1530s constituted a considerable social service of sheltered housing as well as poor relief in the form of distributions in money and in kind': N S Rushton, 'Monastic charitable provision in Tudor England' in *Continuity and Change* 16 (1), 2001 pp9–144 at 34.

2   N L Kunze, 'The Origins of Modern Social Legislation: The Henrician Poor Law of 1536' in *Albion* Vol 3, No 1 (Spring, 1971), pp9–20 at p9.

3   See for example 23 Edward III The Statute of Labourers 1349.

4   See for example 12 Richard II c3, 4, and 7.

5   1531 *Concerning Punishments of Beggars and Vagabonds* (22 Henry VIII c12).

and be beten with Whppes'[6] and to this Edward VI added the sanction in
the Poor Law of 1547[7] of branding and slavery.

I.5   Horrendous as the punishments were for defying the Poor Laws, they
were unsuccessful. Social policy may tilt against economic change – the
movement of labour in response to the collapse of feudalism, the rise of
industrialism, the global free movement of capital under neoliberalism: it
may create barbaric punishments; work houses and walls covering contin-
ents – but ultimately it is futile.

I.6   The Poor Law was eventually consolidated into the Poor Relief Act 1601.
While there were many administrative changes to the system over the succeeding centuries, the basic 1601 scheme survived in a recognisable form
until the cataclysmic Poor Law Reform Act 1834 – which Wikeley (citing
Englander)[8] suggests must rank as 'the single most important piece of
social legislation ever enacted'.

I.7   The 1601 'Old Poor Law' scheme was based on parish responsibility
for the poor with whom it had established links (were 'settled') and who
were, for one reason or another, unable to be maintained by their families.
It was a remarkable system. By 1803 over 11 per cent of the population
received poor relief (over one million people) and its cost had risen fivefold
since 1760.[9] Slack[10] suggests that, although by 1800 the Poor Law was considered to be either 'too purposeless or too expensive', it had nevertheless
come to be regarded as a fundamental obligation of the state,[11] observing:

> No other state could do that, though there were attempts in Scandinavian
> countries in the early eighteenth century to emulate it. Equally, no other
> society could so easily have taken on board the notion that the poor had an
> entitlement to subsistence, an assumption which rested as much on the
> Elizabethan statutes as on the writings of John Locke until both were chal-
> lenged by Malthus and a later school of political economy.

I.8   The Poor Law was exported to the UK's colonies[12] and (prior to the eighteenth century) these laws also tended to be open-textured, and to a degree,
'rights based'. In North America for example, the poor laws 'did not
define ... poverty ... as a critical social problem'[13] and there was no precise

6 N L Kunze, 'The Origins of Modern Social Legislation: The Henrician Poor Law of
   1536' in *Albion* Vol 3, No 1 (Spring, 1971), pp9–20 at p10.

7 1547 for the Punishment of Vagabonds and relief of the Poor and Impotent Persons
   (1 Edw. VI c3).

8 J R Poynter, *Society and Pauperism: English Ideas on Poor Relief, 1795–1834*, Routledge
   and Kegan, 1969, p2, cited in N Wikeley *Child Support Law and Policy*, Hart
   Publishing, 2006, p39.

9 N Wikeley, ibid, p49: it has been suggested that by 1750 poor rates amounted to 1%
   of national income; see P Slack *From Reformation to Improvement: Public Welfare in
   Early Modern England*, Clarendon Press, 1999, p163.

10 P Slack, ibid, pp163–164.

11 Wikeley (footnote 8 above) cites Charlesworth who also considered that it was
    'meaningful to speak of a right relief under the poor law' – L Charlesworth, 'The
    Poor Law: a legal analysis' in *Journal of Social Security Law* (1999) 6 79–92 – but then
    suggests that it would be more appropriate to express the duty as being on parishes to
    relieve the deserving poor (at 39).

12 Although it is a mistake to consider that their local versions were 'unthinking
    duplications of English laws' – see David Rothman, *The Discovery of the Asylum*, (Little
    Brown 1971), p20.

13 David Rothman, ibid, p4.

definition of which categories of poor person were eligible: 'ministerial sermons on charity usually set down communal obligations to the poor without bothering to delineate exactly who fell into the category.'[14]

I.9   In the UK, it would be another 150 years before the notion of an entitlement to subsistence returned, with the creation of the Beveridgean welfare state, and the enactment of the National Assistance Act 1948 – a statute whose endurance can be compared to that of the Poor Relief Act 1601. The 1948 Act, like its ancient predecessor, proved to be 'adaptable, permitting diversity of practice in time as well as place'.[15]

I.10   There was, doubtless, an historical inevitability to the Poor Law Reform Act 1834 coming at did at such a turbulent period of British History: at the close of the Napoleonic wars, the rapidly increasing population, the impact of rural Enclosure, the full throttle of the Industrial Revolution and the brutal philosophies of Malthus and Ricardo eclipsing those of Locke and the Enlightenment.

I.11   Social policy has had more than its fair share of highly fashionable but fundamentally mistaken fads – and the views of the reverend Thomas Malthus[16] must certainly fall into this category. Malthus took a pessimistic view of human nature; believed in 'moral decay' and propounded a theory of populations. The theory predicted that populations would grow exponentially and would only be checked by famine and disease. Despite noble dissenters,[17] the theory was widely accepted as a scientific truth in the early 1800s. Malthus was particularly antipathetic towards the old poor laws.

I.12   Against this backdrop and the burgeoning cost of the Poor Law, a Royal Commission reported in 1834 recommending root and branch reform. This included the suppression of subsistence payments (to ensure they were lower than the lowest wages paid to labourers) and that able-bodied poor should no longer be eligible for Outdoor Relief (ie in their own homes) but only for Indoor Relief (ie in the workhouse, a place 'so severe and repulsive as to make them a terror to the poor'[18]). The Act encouraged parishes to combine to form unions to discharge their Poor Law responsibilities, to build a common workhouse and to create a Board of Guardians that would administer the scheme. The institution was therefore to be the default option unless the pauper could establish their deserving status: the antithesis of 'independent living'. In this we see echoes of Henry VIII's policies and of today's sanctions for the unemployed. To give a flavour of the Commission's brutalist/laissez-faire approach Mencher[19] quotes how it believed that the Old Poor Law conflicted with the 'ordinary laws of nature':

> To enact that the children shall not suffer for the misconduct of their parents, the wife for that of the husband … Can we wonder if the uneducated

14   Ibid, p5.

15   N Wikeley (fn 8 above) citing D Englander, *Poverty and Poor Law Reform in Britain: From Chadwick to Booth 1934–1914*, Addison Wesley Longman, 1998, p1.

16   T Malthus, *Essay on the Principle of Population* (1798).

17   See for example the writings of William Hazlitt (*A Reply to the Essay on Population* (1807)) and William Godwin (*Of Population: An Enquiry concerning the Power of Increase in the Numbers of Mankind* (1820)).

18   E P Thomson, *The Making of the English Working Class*, Penguin, 1991, p295.

19   S Mencher, *Poor Law to Poverty Program*, University of Pittsburgh Press, 1967, p104.

are seduced into approving a system which aims its allurements at all the weakest parts of our nature.

I.13   These were the prevalent views of the powerful classes of the time: Benjamin Franklin, for example considered that the poor laws encouraged the poor to be 'idle and dissolute' and that the 'best way of doing good to the poor is not making them easy in poverty'[20] – and even J S Mill supported the Reform of the Poor Laws.[21] There is much in today's debate about social care that echoes the rhetoric of the 1830's: the emphasis on 'supporting hard-working families' (the Poor Law referred to 'aiding the industrious'); the attack on large families (Malthus); the making work pay (the 'Speenhamland System'); the workfare programme (teaching the poor how to work); the 'something-for-nothing culture' (the indolent and the workshy); the denial of poverty (poverty as a personal failing) and the 'entitlement culture' (of the poor – but not of bankers).

I.14   The 1834 Act led to an increase in what were termed 'pauper lunatics' being placed in workhouses (rather than living in the community with outdoor relief) even though the Act (section 45) did not permit the detention in any workhouse of the 'dangerous lunatic, insane person, or idiot for any longer period than fourteen days'. Concern about this trend led to the Lunatic Asylums Act 1845 which resulted in the expansion of the formal asylums.

I.15   The reforms could also be seen as firm evidence that the Government was now governing for the benefit of the emerging middle classes: a major force to be appeased and not merely by the wider enfranchisement.[22] Engels certainly saw it this way, describing the Act as 'the most open declaration of war of the bourgeoisie upon the proletariat'[23] and for EP Thompson as the 'most sustained attempt to impose ideological dogma, in defiance of the evidence of human need'.[24]

I.16   In order to qualify for support under the reformed Poor Law, a person had to establish that they were 'destitute' which was conditional on a 'subjective judgement'[25] of a poor law official. Like social care eligibility decisions today it was a 'gateway decision that has caused much confusion and an emphasis upon conditionality, negotiation and local custom'.[26] Proving destitution required evidence that there was no family member who could provide support (as required by the 1601 Act), no money or assets

20 S Mencher, ibid, p97.

21 Mill, as always, had a complex view on such things – partly influenced by his Malthusian views – although he was by no means antipathetical to the plight of the poor – see for example, O Kurer, 'John Stuart Mill and the Welfare State' in G W Smith (ed) *John Stuart Mill's Social and Political Thought*, Routledge, 1998, pp339–355.

22 The Great Reform Act 1832.

23 F Engels, *The condition of the working class in England*, Panther, 1969, cited by R Means and R Smith, *From Poor Law to Community Care*, Policy Press, 1998, p17.

24 E P Thomson, *The Making of the English Working Class*, Penguin, 1991, p295.

25 Lorie Charlesworth, 'Welfare's forgotten past: a socio-legal history of the poor law' in *Amicus Curiae* Issue 81 Spring 2010 p19 and see also Mrs Sidney Webb, 'The Abolition of the Poor Law', Fabian Society, 1918, p3.

26 L Charlesworth, ibid.

(such as furniture) and indeed no proper outer or undergarments.[27] It is strongly arguable that the creation by the Poor Law Reform Act 1834 of a new dimension of administrative arrangements was the first effective example of modern bureaucratic legislation and that its 'successful innovations [have] influenced the subsequent administrative direction of English public law'.[28]

I.17 The plight of the poor ceased to be a political concern in the early 1800s – indeed it was not until Dickens and Disraeli[29] that poverty was 'rediscovered' mid-century – only for it to be forgotten and rediscovered at the turn of the century by Seebohm Rowntree,[30] and then to be neglected again/rediscovered again by Orwell[31] and then Peter Townsend.[32]

I.18 Notwithstanding the brutalism underpinning the New Poor Law, it appears that its impact on poor people was often blunted by its humane local application[33] and that throughout the Victorian period outdoor relief still predominated.

I.19 Despite increasingly vehement opposition, the system persisted (with minor change) until the end of the nineteenth century. A notable campaigner Beatrice Webb, and her husband Sydney, published a minority report to the Royal Commission on the Poor Laws and Relief of Distress in 1909 which called for the abolition of the Poor Laws and for a national scheme for promoting employment, health and education. Although the report was largely ignored at the time, it was of enormous influence – not least on one of the report's researchers (and close friend of the Webbs) William Beveridge.

I.20 Nearly 40 years later Sir William, as he had then become, declared war on the five giant evils in society – Giant Want; Giant Disease; Giant Ignorance; Giant Squalor and Giant Idleness. At the end of the Second World War legislation was brought forward with the purpose of slaying some of these monsters: the Education Act 1944, the National Insurance Act 1946, the National Health Service Act 1946 and the National Assistance Act 1948. Giant Squalor was to be slain by a concerted programme of slum clearance and the building, within ten years, of three million new houses.[34]

I.21 All this was done at a time when the UK's public sector net debt was over 180 per cent of GDP (it rose to over 250 per cent in the early 1950s).

---

27 '... the regulations of the Poor Law were such that a person had to be destitute, not only from the point of view of cash, but also from the point of view of clothing before he or she was permitted to receive assistance. I have been in a committee where the chairman ... persisted ... in seeing the underclothing of old people before the committee was prepared to give an order that new underclothing should be supplied. These things remain with us. We remember them.' Betty Braddock MP, House of Commons Debate on the Second Reading of the National Assistance Bill, 24 November 1947 vol 444 cc1635.

28 Lorie Charlesworth, *Welfare's forgotten past*, Routledge, 2010, p60.

29 *Sybil, or The Two Nations*, 1845.

30 *Poverty, A Study of Town Life*, 1901.

31 *The Road to Wigan Pier*, 1937.

32 *Poverty in the United Kingdom*, 1979.

33 Of 'subversive decision making' that undermines the authority's dominant agendas – see S Halliday, 'The Influence of Judicial Review on Bureaucratic Decision-Making' in (2000) *Public Law* 110–22, 118.

34 N Timmins, *The Five Giants*, Fontana, 1996.

In 2007, after the credit crisis, public sector net debt stood at 60 per cent of GDP[35] – but of course the public policy reaction was entirely different: the pendulum was moving in a different direction.

1.22   The neglect of disabled, elderly and ill people living in the community was in many respects the forgotten sixth Giant. Part III of the 1948 Act did however contain the means by which Giant Neglect was to be slain, namely the provision of community care services for ill, elderly and disabled people and indeed accommodation for anyone else who was 'in need of care and attention which is not otherwise available'.[36]

1.23   Even today, reading section 1 of the 1948 Act sparks a sense of frisson, stating as it does 'The existing poor law shall cease to have effect … .' The Act came into force on 5 July 1948 as did the NHS Act 1946 and the National Insurance Act 1946.[37] The pendulum had swung to the left and a new welfare state had been created: one where the ultimate responsibility for the needs of elderly ill, disabled and poor people rested with the state and not with families or charities. It marked a turning point: a new settlement that abolished 400 years of poor laws and with it the hated 'destitution' test, the crippling 'liable family rule' and a great deal more. With the abolition, local resources (principally the workhouses) had to be redistributed. The best of these were absorbed into the fledgling NHS and the remainder were put to use in meeting the new obligations created by Part III of the 1948 Act.[38]

1.24   Part II of the Act replaced outdoor relief with a national means tested benefits system known as 'national assistance' administered by the National Assistance Board, rather than by local councils. In due course Part II was repealed and national assistance replaced by supplementary benefit, which itself was replaced by income support, Employment and Support Allowance, Jobseeker's Allowance and the soon to be Universal Credit.

1.25   Part III of the Act tackled the needs of disabled, elderly and ill people for residential accommodation and community or home-based (domiciliary) care services. However, in the context of the rationing and general shortages in the post war years, the provision of residential care together with other social welfare duties (the house building programme, the creation of the new NHS and the education reforms) represented a huge public spending commitment. Perhaps not surprisingly therefore, when it came to the provision of community or domiciliary care services, authorities were not obliged to provide these services, although they were given discretion to do so if they were able. This power was however limited to disabled people. This represented the concern in 1948 to ensure that those people who had sacrificed their health for peace should be given priority when it came to the provision of scarce resources.[39] In 1948 there was in

---

35   Office National Statistics, *Public Sector* 18 March 2010: public sector net debt is a key measure as – crucially – it compares the debt to the size of the economy.

36   National Assistance Act 1948 s21.

37   The Education Act 1944 came into force on 1 April 1945.

38   For an excellent account of the evolution of 'community care' see R Means and R Smith, *Community Care*, Macmillan, 1994.

39   H Bolderson, *Social Security, Disability and Rehabilitation*, Jessica Kingsley Publishers, 1991, p115.

relative terms a greater number of younger disabled people – in the form of wounded soldiers returning home and those injured in the bombing. This legislative prioritisation of the needs of disabled people (as opposed to those of the temporarily ill or elderly) remained anachronistically until the enactment of the Care Act 2014.[40]

I.26 Although the post-war austerity years gave way to the increasingly prosperous 1950s and the relatively affluent 1960s, the provision of community care services remained a Cinderella area in social welfare terms. The mid and late 1960s were also characterised by a change in social philosophical attitudes – with, for instance, the enactment of the Family Law Reform Act 1969, the Children and Young Persons Act 1969 and the creation of social services departments in 1971 consequent upon the Seebohm report.[41]

I.27 On 6 November 1969 it was announced that Alf Morris MP had won first place in the annual ballot for private members' bills. He chose to promote his own bill (which he himself drafted), the Chronically Sick and Disabled Persons Bill. The Act received Royal Assent on 29 May 1970, the day that parliament was dissolved for the 1970 general election.[42] The most important section of that Act proved to be section 2. It was drafted so as to make the provision of domiciliary services under the 1948 Act obligatory (rather than discretionary). The 1970 Act provided disabled people[43] with specifically enforceable legal rights to specific services. It was however never fully funded. In 1970 the pendulum had nearly completed its leftward swing. The 'Golden Phase' of the twentieth century[44] was drawing to the end. The turmoil precipitated by the oil crisis led to a general retreat from such specific and (in budgetary terms) open-ended welfare rights.

I.28 In the 1970s, in the UK, the pendulum began its long rightward swing attracted by the policies of Friedrich von Hayek and Milton Friedman: small government, low taxes and de-regulation. In social policy terms this has been described as workfare, prisonfare, and social insecurity.[45] Ironically, as the prisons expanded in the UK the closure of long-stay mental hospitals gathered pace, such that community care became linked in the public mind with the care of people with mental health difficulties in the community rather than by incarceration in isolated hospitals. The Mental Health Act 1983 s117 accordingly made particular provision for community care services to be provided for certain patients on their discharge from hospital. Section 117 services are only available to a restricted number of

---

40 The Chronically Sick and Disabled Persons Act 1970 s2 converted the power into a duty, but only for disabled people. Section 2 was (in relation to adults) repealed by the Care Act 2014.

41 Report of the Committee on Local Authority and Allied Personal Social Services [chair Frederic Seebohm] (HMSO, 1968).

42 For an account of the passing of the Act, see RADAR, *Be it enacted . . .*, 1995.

43 The domiciliary care support rights under section 2 were limited to disabled people. The Health Services and Public Health Act 1968 s45 provided older people with this right (this section came into force at the same time as section 2 of the 1970 Act – 29 August 1970) and the same right was provided for people who were 'ill' (ie, those not 'chronically sick') in the NHS Act 1977 Sch 8.

44 See E Hobsbawm, *Age of Extremes*, Michael Joseph, 1994.

45 See for example, L Wacquant, 'Crafting the Neoliberal State: Workfare, Prisonfare, and Social Insecurity' in *Sociological Forum*, Vol 25, No 2, June 2010, pp197–220.

people.[46] Most people with a mental health difficulty receive their care and support services under the Care Act 2014.

I.29   The defining neoliberal Act in social care came in 1990 – the National Health Service and Community Care Act. An Act predicated on a policy of privatisation, responsiblisation,[47] commodification, the reification of 'independence' (in the sense of personal self-sufficiency) and choice.[48] When the Act came into force in 1993 over 90 per cent of community care was provided by council employed staff in the community or in council owned care homes or in council owned day centres. In 2014 less than five per cent of care homes were council run and less than eight per cent of domiciliary care was provided by council employed staff.[49] Provision had been privatised and costs cut: generally by significantly reducing the terms and conditions of care staff.

I.30   A major motivation for the 1990 Act was the soaring social security expenditure on private residential care and nursing home accommodation: this had increased from about £10 million per annum in 1979 to £2.5 billion per annum in 1993. Hospitals were closing long-stay geriatric and psychiatric wards and discharging the patients into private nursing homes where the cost could be funded by the Department of Health and Social Security (DHSS), essentially, therefore, transferring the cost from one central government department's budget (the NHS) to another (social security). At the same time social services authorities were doing much the same, by closing their own residential care homes and transferring the residents to independent-sector homes, which again were capable of being funded via the DHSS, thus transferring the cost from local to central government.

I.31   The 1990 Act sought to cap this expenditure by transferring most of the funding responsibility to social services authorities and restricting access to residential and nursing homes if the person was to be supported by public funds. Access to such care was to be conditional on the authority being satisfied that such a placement was appropriate. Social services authorities were provided with a 'Special Transitional Grant' to compensate them for their extra costs in implementing the community care reforms and in particular for assuming responsibility for funding such accommodation. In the first full year of the reforms (1994–95) the Grant amounted to £735.9

---

46 People who are discharged after detention under section 3 or one of the criminal provisions of the Mental Health Act 1983, see para 15.56 below.

47 See for example I Ferguson, 'Increasing User Choice or Privatizing Risk? The Antinomies of Personalization' in *British Journal of Social Work* (2007) vol 37, pp387–403 and K Juhila et al (eds), *Responsibilisation at the Margins of Welfare Services*, Routledge, 2017.

48 These are values, which in Martha Fineman's opinion have attained sacred and 'transcendent' status: but which are a myth: for 'all of us were dependent as children, and many of us will be dependent as we age, become ill or suffer disabilities' – see M Fineman, 'Cracking the Foundational Myths: Independence, Autonomy and Self-Sufficiency', in M Fineman and T Dougherty (eds) *Feminism Confronts Homo Economicus*, Cornell University Press, 2005, at p180.

49 Health and Social Care Information Centre, *Community Care Statistics: Social Services Activity, England 2013–14, Final release* (2014) pp62 and 51 respectively.

million of which 85 per cent was ring-fenced to the extent that it had to be spent on independent sector care services.[50]

1.32 The Act also endeavoured to bring together the disparate statutes which governed individual entitlement to community care services and, by various amendments, create a degree of coherence in this field of law. It was preceded by a white paper, 'Caring for People'[51] which owed much to a report prepared in 1988 by Sir Roy Griffiths for the Secretary of State for Social Services.[52]

1.33 The 1990 Act did not, however, convert into law many of the themes which infused the white paper, the Griffiths report and many of the subsequent practice guides issued by the Department of Health. For example it provided no practical support for carers – this was left to Malcolm Wicks MP and his private member's bill which became the Carers (Recognition and Services) Act 1995. As to the emphasis on individual choice (or 'preferences'), this concept appeared nowhere in any of the legislation, with the exception of a choice of accommodation – if it had been assessed as necessary (a right which continues today – see para 8.241 below).

1.34 The reforms coincided with the emergence, at a national political level, of the disability rights movements. Many disabled people viewed the community care regime as disabling and disempowering and sought greater control, by way of direct payments and involvement at a strategic planning level. Since commodification was also a key principle of neoliberalism this demand was accepted and addressed by the Community Care (Direct Payments) Act 1996.

1.35 In the first decade of the current century, policy initiatives that have come to be called the 'personalisation agenda' sought to create the illusion of radical new thinking and reform. Although branded in terms of maximising personal choice and involvement, in practical terms there is little to suggest that this has transformed the lives of the majority of people in need of community care services.[53] Indeed it could be argued that it was a component of the responsibilisation agenda – making individuals take control and responsibility for their care needs – without providing the financial and advocacy support essential to enable this to become a reality.

1.36 Throughout the last 50 years another social care movement has been gaining momentum – the carers' movement. Deinstitutionalisation has resulted in many elderly, ill and disabled people being cared for in the community but it has not resulted in increased local authority or NHS community support: indeed fewer people are receiving state supported community care today than 25 years ago. These two factors – demographic change and the welfare residualism that comes with neoliberalism – have resulted in a substantial increase in unpaid caring[54] which is nearing the

---

50 For further details see B Meredith, *The Community Care Handbook*, Age Concern England, 1995, p165.

51 Department of Health (1989) *Caring for People: Community Care in the Next Decade and Beyond*, Cm 849.

52 R Griffiths, *Community Care: Agenda for Action*, HMSO, 1988.

53 See L Clements, 'Individual budgets and irrational exuberance' (2008) 11 CCLR 413–430.

54 Carers UK *Policy Briefing*, 2014.

limits of what families can provide.[55] However, at the same time, there has been a significant increase in female employment rates[56] – in part to offset the decline in average household incomes that would have occurred had women not joined 'the workforce alongside their husbands'.[57] Carers (and they are preponderantly working women) 'are the elastic that has accommodated the contradictions in neoliberalism' and they are 'now stretched to breaking point, and ... governments are aware of this'.[58]

I.37   In 2008 the Law Commission produced a scoping paper[59] proposing the codification of adult social care law: the hotchpotch of conflicting statutes, enacted over a period of 60 years. In due course this process produced the Care Act 2014. The Act repealed almost all of the previous adult social care statutes and those that applied to carers. The 2014 Act largely 'rolled over' the duties owed to disabled, elderly and ill people (now referred to as 'adults in need'). The duty under the 2014 Act to assess, care plan, provide care and so on is little different to that under the previous legislation. The Act did however make commodification of care compulsory (with personal budgets) and opened the way for the almost complete privatisation of adult social care, by enabling the delegation of assessments and care planning to the independent sector.

I.38   The Act's treatment of carers was however radically different in that eligible carers became entitled to support (even if the person for whom they care was not eligible for support) and carers were no longer required to provide 'substantial and regular' care to qualify.

I.39   Law reform does not in itself improve anything. For this to happen the law needs to be obeyed (in spirit and in word) and in the current context extra resources need to be provided.[60] Since adult social care accounts for less than two per cent of total public expenditure (for older people it is less than 0.7 per cent)[61] this is not asking for a great deal.

I.40   Funding remains the outstanding problem – and as the King's Fund notes, 'England remains one of the few major advanced countries that has not reformed the way it funds long-term care in response to the needs of an ageing population'.[62] A succession of Commissions have suggested mechanisms for placing the funding of social care on a sustainable footing – most recently the Dilnot Commission[63] – but politically, there appears

---

55 L Pickard, *Informal care for older people provided by their adult children: projections of supply and demand to 2041 in England*, Report to the Strategy Unit, Department of Health, 2008.

56 M Gutiérrez-Domènech et al, *Female labour force participation in the United Kingdom: evolving characteristics or changing behaviour? Working Paper no 221*, Bank of England, 2004.

57 J Stiglitz, *The Price of Inequality*, Allen Lane, 2012, p14.

58 L Clements, 'Does your carer take sugar', *Washington and Lee Journal of Civil Rights and Social Justice* (2013) vol 19 pp397–434 at 432.

59 Law Commission, *Adult Social Care Scoping Report*, 2008.

60 Central government funding to local government reduced by 37 per cent in real terms between 2010/11 and 2015/16 National Audit Office, *Financial sustainability of local authorities 2014*, HC 783, The Stationery Office, 2014.

61 R Humphries et al, *Social care for older people: home truths*, Kings Fund, 2016, p12.

62 R Humphries, ibid, p74–75.

63 Commission on Funding of Care and Support (2011) *Fairer Care Funding: The Report of the Commission on Funding of Care and Support* (the 'Dilnot' Report).

to be little enthusiasm to take action. The 2014 Act ss15–16 contains a mechanism for a 'cap on costs' but this is not to be implemented until 2020 at the earliest. The administrative implications of this provision have not been thought through[64] – and it is to be hoped that the measure (as currently envisaged) will never come into force.

I.41   The only workable solution that has so far emerged for the funding challenge, is that proposed by the Sutherland Commission[65] in 1999: that social care be free at the point of need. It is a proposal that has been largely adopted in Scotland and a report that deserves a reconsideration. Its adoption in England would of course come at a cost (as it has in Scotland) but since 50 per cent of older people (as 'self-funders') personally pay for all their care, it is a cost that is already being born – but unequally. For this to happen of course, the pendulum would have to swing to the left – but change is inevitable: there are no straight lines in community care.

64 The tracking and recording of independent personal budgets (section 28) and the disputes that they will engender would require a large and disproportionately costly bureaucracy.

65 The Sutherland Report, *With Respect to Old Age: A Report by the Royal Commission on Long Term Care*, HMSO, 1999.

CHAPTER 1

The statutory scheme and social services strategic functions

Introduction

1.1   Primary responsibility for the delivery of social care services rests with social services authorities. In a number of instances, however, the obligation is shared with the National Health Service (NHS) and in certain situations it may be the NHS's exclusive responsibility.

1.2   This chapter commences with an outline of the statutory regimes regulating these two bodies in relation to the discharge of their social care responsibilities. It then considers the nature of their public law obligations and Part I of the Localism Act (LA) 2011 which has conferred on local authorities a 'general power of competence'. It concludes with a brief overview of the market oversight duties of social services authorities under Care Act (CA) 2014 s5.

Local authority social services functions

Background

1.3   The state's formal social care obligations have, since the dawn of the poor law, rested with local councils. The Act for the Relief of the Poor 1601 made parishes primarily responsible for the relief of the poverty experienced by their settled parishioners. This basic duty remained into the 20th century, finally being abolished by the National Assistance Act (NAA) 1948. Social care responsibilities under the NAA 1948 remained 'local' but rested, not with the relieving officers and poor law guardians, but with the welfare departments of county and county borough councils.

1.4   In 1968, concern over the effectiveness of these local arrangements culminated in a critical report – the 'Seebohm report'[1] – that led to the enactment of the Local Authority Social Services Act (LASSA) 1970 which required major reform of the way councils dealt with their social care responsibilities, and resulted in the creation of 'social services departments'. LASSA 1970 remains the primary statute governing authorities that discharge social services functions (the material parts of the Act are in appendix A below). These permitted 'functions' are listed in the first schedule to LASSA 1970. The list is regularly updated and comprises a familiar (and long) list, such as provisions within the Mental Health Act (MHA) 1983, the Children Act (CA) 1989, the Mental Capacity Act (MCA) 2005 and so on. The local authorities concerned are county councils, the London and metropolitan boroughs and other unitary authorities, as well as the Common Council of the City of London and the Council of the Isles of Scilly (LASSA 1970 s1).

1.5   LASSA 1970 s6(A1) requires that every social services authority have a director of adult social services and section 6(6) places a duty on the authority to 'secure the provision of adequate staff for assisting' in the exercise of the director's functions. While authorities will be given a wide discretion by the courts in deciding what is an 'adequate' workforce

---

1   *Report of the committee on local authority and allied personal social services* Cmnd 3703, 1968.

(for the purposes of section 6(6)), the question may be raised in judicial review proceedings (or ombudsman complaints[2]) particularly where the applicant is challenging the non-provision of a service dependent upon 'human resources'.[3] Such proceedings are, however, unlikely to be appropriate where the complaint concerns the interruption of services due to unpredictable staff absences,[4] although where the complaint concerns a repeated failure of the service due to predictable interruptions, this would seem at least a matter of maladministration and amenable to remedy via the local authority complaints system.

1.6　　　The Department of Health has issued two guidance documents concerning the role of the director of adult social services,[5] one being statutory guidance under LASSA 1970 s7(1) (see para 1.35 below) and the other being best practice guidance.

1.7　　　The policy guidance requires, among other things, that local authorities ensure that the director is responsible/accountable for:

- the authority's delivery of social services for adults;
- promoting social inclusion and well-being with a view to (among other things) developing sustainable services that promote independence and minimise the need for intensive home care and residential services;
- maintaining clear and effective arrangements to support the joint planning, monitoring and delivery of local authority social services with the NHS, housing authorities, Supporting People programme and other statutory agencies;
- ensuring (with the director of children's services) 'adequate arrangements' are in place 'to ensure that all young people with long-term social care needs have been assessed and, where eligible, receive a service which meets their needs throughout their transition to becoming adults' (see para 15.91 below).

1.8　　The CA 2014 repealed the NAA 1948 in England but maintained the responsibility of social services authorities for the discharge of adult social care responsibilities and retained the role of the LASSA 1970 in defining the various 'functions' of social services authorities.

NHS community care functions

1.9　　At the beginning of the 20th century the majority of institutional health and social care services were provided via the poor law boards. Gradually as the century progressed, local authorities assumed greater responsibilities

---

2　*Report on complaint no 05/C/18474 against Birmingham City Council*, 4 March 2008 which referred to the council's 'corporate failure to ensure adequate resourcing and performance of its services to highly vulnerable people' (para 55).

3　To establish a case under this ground, useful evidence can be obtained from social services committee minutes, which not infrequently record unsuccessful requests by the director for extra staff.

4　*R v Islington LBC ex p McMillan* (1997–98) 1 CCLR 7 at 10, (1995) *Times* 21 June QBD.

5　Department of Health, *Guidance on the Statutory Chief Officer Post of Director of Adult Social Services issued under s7(1) Local Authority Social Services Act 1970*, 2006; Department of Health, *Best practice guidance on the role of the Director of Adult Social Services*, 2006.

for both functions. The 1929 poor law reforms (under the Local Government Act 1929) led to the creation of local authority health committees, which took control of the better poor law hospitals (then known as public health hospitals). The remaining poor law institutions, workhouses and basic poor law hospitals were also transferred from the poor law boards, becoming the responsibility of the county and county borough councils.

1.10   The creation of the NHS in 1948 did not initially wrest responsibility for health services from local authorities. Although today it is convenient to see the National Health Service Act (NHSA) 1946 and NAA 1948 as demarcating the responsibilities of what we now call social services departments and the NHS, this separation of responsibilities has in fact developed largely as a consequence of subsequent legislation. The NHSA 1946 stipulated that many services we would today label as 'health services' – such as ambulances (section 27), midwifery (section 23) and health visitors (section 24) – were to be the responsibility of local authority health committees (called 'local health authorities').[6] Indeed, NAA 1948 s21(7)(b), as originally enacted, authorised the provision by local authorities of 'health services,[7] not being specialist services or services of a kind normally provided only on admission to hospital'.

1.11   While minor changes to the health/social care responsibilities of NHS/ local authorities occurred over the next 25 years,[8] major reform did not take place until 1974, when the Local Government Act (LGA) 1972 and the National Health Service Reorganisation Act (NHSRA) 1973 came into force. The 1973 Act sought to transfer all nursing functions (whether in hospital, at home or elsewhere) to the NHS. It abolished local health authorities (ie local authority health committees) and in their place created free-standing regional, area and district health authorities.

1.12   Since the early 1970s the NHS has been the subject of continual reform – a process that shows no evidence of abating. In 1977 the NHSA 1946 was repealed and replaced by a consolidating Act, the NHSA 1977, and in 2006 this itself was repealed and consolidated – into three Acts: the NHSA 2006, the National Health Service (Wales) Act 2006 and the National Health Service (Consequential Provisions) Act 2006, of which the former is the principal Act (see para 11.16 below).

Clinical commissioning groups and NHS trusts

1.13   The NHS reforms (which have been described elsewhere[9]) led to the creation of primary care trusts (PCTs) with responsibility for commissioning local health services, and in 2013 these were replaced by clinical commissioning groups (CCGs), of which there were 209 (at the time of writing, December 2016). CCGs are responsible for commissioning primary care and hospital services which duty they discharge in large measure by

6   NHSA 1946 Part II Sch 4.
7   Including nursing services by virtue of NHSA 1946 s25.
8   Most notably the Health Services and Public Health Act 1968 which transferred to local health authorities responsibility for health visitors and nursing other than in a person's home; and LASSA 1970 which in its first schedule sought to delineate the responsibilities of local authority social services departments.
9   See eg the third edition of this book at paras 10.3–10.11.

contracting with NHS trusts and NHS foundation trusts (ie hospitals). These NHS bodies and their respective functions are discussed at paras 11.12 and 11.17 below.

Statutory powers and duties

1.14 Social services and NHS functions are normally expressed as being obligatory (ie a statutory duty) or discretionary (ie a statutory power). Accordingly, the use of the words 'can' and 'may' in a statute are interpreted as conferring a permissive power rather than a duty. Conversely, the appearance of the words 'shall' or 'must' are in general construed as creating a duty – an obligation to do or refrain from doing something. This is not, however, always the case. As de Smith pointed out,[10] a local authority empowered to approve building plans has been held to be obliged to approve plans that were in conformity with its bylaws,[11] whereas a local authority required by statute to provide suitable alternative accommodation for those displaced by a closing order has been held not to be obliged to place them at the top of the housing waiting list.[12]

Powers

1.15 Where an authority has a power to act, but not a duty, it must (when the possible use of that power arises) exercise its discretion in each case. Authorities are generally free to refuse to use a power, provided they reach such a decision in accordance with the principles of administrative law (and the refusal does not result in a breach of the European Convention on Human Rights (ECHR) – see para 2.65 below). In reaching their decision, they must not, however, ignore relevant guidance,[13] operate a perverse policy which (in practice) fetters their discretion[14] or in certain situations fail to consult before reaching a decision.[15]

Duties

1.16 Statutory duties owed by public bodies can be divided into two categories: general public law duties (known as 'target' duties) and specific duties owed to individuals. Specific duties are worded in precise and personal terms, so that it is clear that they are intended to confer enforceable rights upon individuals, and also make clear when these rights arise. Accordingly, a failure to comply with a specific law duty may entitle an aggrieved party to a court order compelling the authority to carry out its duty (for

---

10 De Smith, Woolf and Jowell, *Judicial review of administrative action*, 5th edn, Sweet & Maxwell, 1995, p301.
11 *R v Newcastle-upon-Tyne Corporation* (1889) 60 LT 963.
12 *R v Bristol Corporation ex p Hendy* [1974] 1 WLR 498.
13 *R v North Derbyshire Health Authority ex p Fisher* (1997–98) 1 CCLR 150, QBD (see para 20.187 below).
14 *R v North West Lancashire Health Authority ex p A* [2000] 1 WLR 977, (1999) 2 CCLR 419, CA; and see para 20.187 below generally.
15 See eg *R v North West Lancashire Health Authority ex p A* [2000] 1 WLR 977, (1999) 2 CCLR 419, CA and *R (Morris) v Trafford Healthcare NHS Trust* [2006] EWHC 2334 (Admin), (2006) 9 CCLR 648.

instance, an order requiring it to undertake a lawful social care assessment or to provide a specific care service). Such duties do not, in themselves, create a 'duty of care' at common law which could found a claim for damages for injuries sustained due to their non-performance[16] – although the ombudsman may consider non-performance to be maladministration, for which a compensatory payment might be appropriate.

1.17   Duties cannot be frustrated by fixed or 'blanket' policies – for example, by placing an absolute upper limit on the amount of support that will be provided or on the amount of a direct payment, or of never providing small items of equipment. Indeed, rigid policies of this type are not permitted even where the statute provides for a discretion rather than a duty (see para 20.186 below).

1.18   In *R v Gloucestershire CC ex p Mahfood*[17] McCowan LJ held that Chronically Sick and Disabled Persons Act 1970 s2 created specific public law duties. In his opinion, once an authority had decided that it was under a duty to make arrangements under section 2, it was 'under an absolute duty to make them. It is a duty owed to a specific individual and not a target duty'.[18] The duty under Mental Health Act (MHA) 1983 s117 has also been held to be capable of being an individual public law duty;[19] and it is undoubtedly the case that the duty to assess and the duty to meet eligible needs under the CA 2014 are also specific public law duties.

1.19   In contrast, general public law (or 'target') duties are worded in broad and impersonal terms, and contain a 'degree of elasticity'[20] in their interpretation – such that it is generally left to the authority in question to decide when (and to what extent) the duty comes into being. Callaghan[21] argues that target duties are essentially aspirational in nature, requiring an authority to 'do its best',[22] and that 'courts will permit public authorities to take into account practical realities, including budgetary and resource considerations, in determining how best to fulfil the target duty'.

1.20   A notable example of such a general duty is to be found in NHSA 2006 s1,[23] which places a duty on the secretary of state to 'continue the promotion in England of a comprehensive health service'. The duty is not expressed as being owed to any specific individual and it is particularly

---

16 See, for instance, *Sandford v Waltham Forest LBC* [2008] EWHC 1106 (QBD) which concerned a claim for injuries allegedly suffered as a result of the failure of the local authority to provide cot sides for a bed – which it had assessed as being required. The High Court, however, did suggest that there was a common law duty on social workers to use reasonable skill when undertaking a community care assessment. See, however, Helen Blundell 'Case Comment' (*London v Southampton CC* (QBD, May J, 20 May 2016, [2016] EWHC 2021 (QB)) *Journal of Personal Injury Law* 2016 C192.

17 (1997–98) 1 CCLR 7, (1995) *Times* 21 June, QBD.

18 (1997–98) 1 CCLR 7 at 16G, (1995) *Times* 21 June, QBD.

19 *R (IH) v Secretary of State for the Home Department and others* [2003] UKHL 59, [2003] 3 WLR 1278, (2004) 7 CCLR 147.

20 Per Woolf LJ in *R v Inner London Education Authority ex p Ali* (1990) 2 Admin LR 822, p828D.

21 C Callaghan, 'What is a "target duty"?' (2000) 5(3) *Judicial Review* 184–187: In *R (G) v Barnet LBC* [2003] UKHL 57, [2003] 3 WLR 1194, (2003) 6 CCLR 500 Lord Scott (at para 115) referred to such a duty being 'expressed in broad aspirational terms that would not easily lend themselves to mandatory enforcement'.

22 *R v Radio Authority ex p Bull* [1998] QB 294 at 309, CA.

23 In Wales, NHS(W)A 2006 s1.

difficult for a court to decide when it has been breached. To mount a successful action, an aggrieved patient would have to show, not only that he or she failed to receive a health service due to the service not being 'comprehensive' but also that the secretary of state had effectively abandoned any intention of 'promoting' such a service. As the Court of Appeal held in *R v North and East Devon Health Authority ex p Coughlan*:[24]

> 25. When exercising his judgment [the secretary of state] has to bear in mind the comprehensive service which he is under a duty to promote as set out in section 1. However, as long as he pays due regard to that duty, the fact that the service will not be comprehensive does not mean that he is necessarily contravening either section 1 or section 3.

The section 1 duty is considered further at para 11.8 below.

1.21   It is not always clear whether a particular obligation falls into the specific or target category. As Scott-Baker J observed in *R (A) v Lambeth LBC*:[25]

> Community care legislation has grown up piecemeal through numerous statutes over the past half century. There are many statutes aimed at different targets whose provisions are drawn in differing language. Each Act contains its own duties and powers. Specific duties have to be distinguished from target or general duties and duties from discretions. Sometimes a local authority has several ways in which it can meet an obligation. Some provisions overlap with others and the inter-relationship is not always easy.

1.22   A number of social care duties can be characterised as hybrid in nature – that is to say that although drafted in general terms, they can 'crystallise'[26] during the assessment process (see para 4.55) into specific public law duties owed to individual service users. Thus the general duty under CA 2014 s1 to provide the well-being of individuals (see para 2.12) may be converted by a social care assessment into a specific public law duty. In *R (T, D and B) v Haringey LBC*[27] Ouseley J accepted that, in principle, obligations under the Human Rights Act (HRA) 1998 could 'crystallise' target duties into specific law duties.

1.23   Arguments concerning the enforceability of such statutory provisions are becoming increasing rarefied and difficult to follow.[28] In *R (W) v Lambeth LBC*[29] and *R (G) v Barnet LBC*,[30] for example, the Court of Appeal and the House of Lords grappled with the differing phrasing of the obligations to provide care services for disabled children and disabled adults.

24 [2000] 2 WLR 622, (1999) 2 CCLR 285, CA.
25 [2001] EWHC 376 (Admin), [2001] 2 FLR 1201; the quotation also appears in the subsequent Court of Appeal judgment, *R (A) v Lambeth LBC* [2001] EWCA Civ 1624, (2001) 4 CCLR 486 at 499–450.
26 See the comments of Laws LJ in *R (A) v Lambeth LBC* [2001] EWCA Civ 1624, (2001) 4 CCLR 486 at 499D where he adopted Richard Gordon QC's use of this phrasing.
27 [2005] EWHC 2235 (Admin), (2006) 9 CCLR 58 at [142].
28 See eg the comments of Potter LJ in *R v Kensington and Chelsea RLBC ex p Kujtim* [1999] 4 All ER 161, (1999) 2 CCLR 340 at 353J, CA where he admitted to finding difficulty in following the arguments of Sedley J (concerning a parallel set of target duties) in *R v Islington LBC ex p Rixon* (1997–98) 1 CCLR 119, 15 March 1996, QBD.
29 [2002] EWCA Civ 613, [2002] 2 All ER 901, (2002) 5 CCLR 203.
30 [2003] UKHL 57, [2003] 3 WLR 1194, (2003) 6 CCLR 500.

They concluded that although the assessment process for adults[31] could result in specific public law duties, this was not the case in relation to children (whose assessment process was governed by CA 1989 s17). Not only is it difficult to follow the logic of the court's analysis in reaching this conclusion, it is particularly difficult to see the sense in (effectively) prioritising the rights of disabled adults to services over the rights of disabled children.

1.24   It has been argued that what we are seeing in such cases is an 'attempt to shore up the increasingly questionable public policy approach towards the state delivery of community care services'.[32] In effect, that the artificial distinction between target and specific public law duties stems from the judiciary's anxiety over the resource implications of their judgments,[33] and that this entirely artificial construct is proving to be insufficiently flexible to mediate between the complexities of state responsibilities (in a post-HRA 1998 era) and individual need. Increasingly the courts appear to be using the imperative (if not the logic) of the ECHR in determining the enforceability of statutory obligations – and this approach is considered in greater detail at para 2.64 below.

Delegation

1.25   Public bodies are not permitted to delegate their statutory functions, unless specific provisions exist to the contrary.[34] Prior to the implementation of the CA 2014, the main way by which social services authorities were enabled to delegate their adult social care functions to third party organisations was via agreements under NHSA 2006 s75 (see para 11.30).

1.26   CA 2014 s79(1) permits social services authorities to delegate almost all of their functions under Part 1 of the Act and under MHA 1983 s117 to non-NHS bodies.[35] CA 2014 s79(2), however, prohibits delegation in relation to (a) section 3 (promoting integration with health services); (b) sections 6 and 7 (co-operating); (c) section 14 (charges), (d) sections 42–47 (safeguarding adults at risk of abuse or neglect); and section 79 itself. Delegation under CA 2014 s79 must, however, be for a specified term (section 79(5)(a)).

1.27   Many local authorities have already delegated aspects of carers' assessments to local independent carer support groups. This was possible under the pre-Care Act legislation so long as the actual decision on the

---

31   Under what was then National Health Service and Community Care Act 1990 s47 – now CA 2014 s9.

32   L Clements, 'The collapsing duty: a sideways look at community care and public law' [1997] *Judicial Review Journal* 162.

33   Lord Hoffmann put the position frankly when delivering the 2001 Commercial Bar Lecture ('The separation of powers', unpublished) commenting 'even when a case appears to involve no more than the construction of a statute or interpretation of a common law rule, the courts are very circumspect about giving an answer which would materially affect the distribution of public expenditure'.

34   See para 20.167.

35   In anticipation of these reforms all English local authorities were given power to delegate virtually all of their adult social services powers – see the Contracting Out (Local Authorities Social Services Functions) (England) Order 2014 SI No 829 made pursuant to Deregulation and Contracting Out Act 1994 s70(2), (4) and s77(1).

carer's eligibility for support was made/approved by the local authority – the theory being that the carers' group did the data gathering and/or discussions with the carer, and the local authority then signed off their recommendations. This arrangement can of course continue, but the local authority is now able to delegate the 'sign-off' in addition.

1.28   CA 2014 s79(6) makes it clear that ultimate responsibility in such cases will still rest with the local authority (any acts/omissions by the delegated body will be treated as done/omitted to be done by the local authority).[36] Section 79 opens up the possibility for the delegation of the vast bulk of an adult social services department's functions to the independent sector.[37] In such a situation there is potential for a conflict of interest – for example, when the independent organisation carries out both the care and support planning and then provides the necessary care and support. The statutory guidance to the CA 2014[38] advises in consequence that authorities should consider whether the delegation of their functions 'could give rise to any potential conflict and should avoid delegating their functions where they deem that there would be an inappropriate conflict' (para 18.23). It then suggests that (para 18.24):

> Local authorities should consider imposing conditions in their contracts with delegated parties to mitigate against the risk of any potential conflicts. For example, the local authority may choose to delegate care and support planning, but retain the final decision-making, including signing off the amount of the personal budget ... Local authorities should also consider including conditions that allow the contract to be revoked at any time, if having authorised an external party to exercise its functions, a conflict becomes apparent.

Adult social services – the macro legislative context

Local Authority Social Services Act 1970

1.29   LASSA 1970 sets out the broad framework as to how social services departments are to be organised. As with many social welfare statutes, it contains reserve powers enabling the secretary of state to issue directions; however, in the early years of the Act, central government exercised a 'positive philosophy of as little interference as is possible'[39] – or at least a lightness of touch over these levers of control:

> ... there was no notion of a direct line of command from central government dictating either the organisational structure of social work at the local level or the detailed policies to be implemented within and through that structure in response to legislation. Within loose overall financial controls there was room for local authority social services departments to shape structures

---

36   Local authorities would appear to owe a non-delegable duty of care to residents they fund in care homes – see *Woodland v Essex CC* [2013] UKSC 66, (2013) 16 CCLR 532 para 23 per Lord Sumption (with whom the other judges agreed).

37   See, for example, Dennis Campbell, 'Virgin Care wins £700m contract to run 200 NHS and social care services', *Guardian*, 11 November 2016.

38   Department of Health, *Care and support statutory guidance* to support implementation of Part 1 of the CA 2014 by local authorities, 2016 ('the statutory guidance').

39   J Griffith, *Central departments and local authorities*, Allen and Unwin, 1966, p515 cited by R Means and R Smith, *From Poor Law to community care*, Policy Press, 1998, p156.

and policies within the framework of central government's legislation and general policy guidance.[40]

This is no longer the case. The Department of Health has over the last 50 years steadily sought to increase its control over the actions of social services departments. Although there are today fewer 'performance indicators' and 'targets' than under existed ten years ago, the department's main lever of control continues to be the use of 'statutory guidance', discussed below.

1.30   The department has not, however, abandoned the use of benchmarking and other performance indicators. As at January 2017 the Adult Social Care Outcomes Framework (ASCOF) 2015/16 is 'the Department's key tool for measuring the progress of the adult social care system, supporting our understanding of the outcomes and experiences of people who use care and support, and carer'.[41] ASCOF requires local authorities to evaluate their performance by measuring the outcomes and experiences of people who use care and support against six following six key themes:

- I am happy with the quality of my care and support and I know that the person giving me care and support will treat me with dignity and respect
- I am supported to maintain my independence for as long as possible
- I understand how care and support works, and what my entitlements are
- I am in control of my care and support
- I feel safe and secure
- I have as much social contact as I want with people I like

Regulations

1.31   In common with many other Acts, NHS and local authority statutes empower the secretary of state to issue various forms of delegated legislation – most commonly as regulations, rules and orders. These flesh out the bare bones of the duty or power imposed by the primary statute. For example, CA 2014 s14 empowers authorities to charge for most care and support they provide under the Act and section 14(5) authorises the making of regulations detailing how this is to be done. In October 2014 these were laid before parliament and approved as the Care and Support (Charging and Assessment of Resources) Regulations 2014 SI No 2672 (see para 8.8 below).

1.32   When issuing regulations concerning the CA 2014, section 78 requires that the secretary have 'regard' to the general duty to promote individual well-being (see para 2.12 below).

1.33   Such delegated legislation has the force of law, and the procedure by which it is promulgated is set out in the Statutory Instruments Act (SIA) 1946. The SIA 1946 details the requirements for publication and the various types of procedures by which the legislation is laid before parliament. Delegated legislation must not stray outside the ambit of its enabling statutory provision. Judicial review will lie where the statutory instrument

40   J Harris, *The social work business*, Routledge, 2003, p18.

41   Department of Health, *Adult social care outcomes framework (ASCOF)*, November 2014, para 11.

exceeds such limits.[42] In similar terms, delegated legislation must not derogate from provisions in the enabling legislation; thus where rights are conferred by a statute, any subsequent regulations must not detract from those rights.[43]

Directions

1.34   Directions have the force of law.

1.35   LASSA 1970 s7A authorises the secretary of state to issue general directions requiring local authorities to exercise their social services functions in a particular way. Section 7D empowers the secretary of state to issue a specific direction to a local authority that has failed, without reasonable excuse, to comply with any of its social services duties and – if it fails to comply with the direction – to seek to enforce the direction by way of mandamus (see para 20.215 below).

1.36   The pre-CA 2014 legislative scheme made significant use of the general power to issue directions and this reliance was the subject of criticism:[44] directions are not in general subject to parliamentary scrutiny and can be difficult to obtain as they are not always published as statutory instruments. The Law Commission in its 2011 report recommended that the general power to issue directions under LASSA 1970 s7A should be repealed insofar as it concerned the CA 2014. The government agreed that the general power could be 'confusing and lacks transparency', however it considered that there was a role for the specific power 'to deal with issues arising in individual authorities'.[45] Both the general and specific powers to issue directions continue to be available under the LASSA 1970, although the CA 2014 legislative regime has so far, thankfully, eschewed the use of general directions.

Guidance

1.37   The Law Commission in its 2011 report expressed concern about the volume and variety of social care guidance issued by the Department of Health[46] and recommended that in the revised legislative scheme the use of guidance:

> ... should be kept to a minimum and the legal status of the guidance should be clarified and stated clearly in the guidance itself. Future policy documents should state that they are not legal documents and should be understood as indicating the direction of Government policy.[47]

1.38   The Law Commission recommended that a statutory code of practice subject to parliamentary control should be issued along the line of the code

---

42   See eg *Re Ripon* [1939] 2 KB 838 and *Dunkley v Evans* [1981] 1 WLR 1522.

43   See eg *King v Henderson* [1898] AC 720.

44   See the 5th edition of this book at paras 1.38–1.43; and Law Commission, *Adult social care*, Law Com No 326 HC 941, The Stationery Office, 2011, para 3.20.

45   Law Commission, *Adult Social Care*, Law Com No 326 HC 941, 2011, para 3.14.

46   Law Commission, *Adult Social Care*, Law Com No 326 HC 941, 2011.

47   Law Commission, *Adult Social Care*, Law Com No 326 HC 941, 2011, Recommendation 4.

of practice to the MCA 2005.[48] This proposal was endorsed by the Joint Committee in its 2013 report.[49] The government, however, rejected these recommendations, commenting:[50]

> Our view remains that a code of practice would be too inflexible for adult care and support guidance that may quickly become out of date. Our new bank of statutory guidance would have the same legal status and be subject to consultation in the same way as a code of practice. However, because it would not need to be laid before Parliament each time it is amended for any future changes, it could be kept up to date to reflect emerging policy and practice, which would be particularly important in relation to implementing new funding reforms.

1.39   Prior to the CA 2014, social services guidance relating to adults in need and carers was issued under LASSA 1970 s7 which provided that:

> 7(1) Local authorities shall, in the exercise of their social services functions, including the exercise of any discretion conferred by any relevant enactment, act under the general guidance of the Secretary of State.

The CA 2014 amends[51] LASSA 1970 s7 by specifying that in relation to CA 2014 Part 1 the status of guidance is determined by CA 2014 s78. Section 78 in turn provides as follows:

> 78(1) A local authority must act under the general guidance of the Secretary of State in the exercise of functions given to it by this Part or by regulations under this Part.
> (2) Before issuing any guidance for the purposes of subsection (1), the Secretary of State must consult such persons as the Secretary of State considers appropriate.
> (3) The Secretary of State must have regard to the general duty of local authorities under section 1(1) (promotion of individual well-being)–
> (a) in issuing guidance for the purposes of subsection (1);
> (b) in making regulations under this Part.

The effect of this, in relation to local authorities, is that they have the same obligation to act 'under the general guidance of the Secretary of State' when exercising any of their social services functions under the CA 2014 as they had when exercising their community care functions under the pre-CA 2014 regime.

1.40   CA 2014 s78 imposes additional (but in practice very limited) obligations on the secretary of state, in that she or he must consult before issuing guidance and in so doing must have 'regard' to the general duty to promote individual well-being.

Statutory guidance

1.41   A draft of the *Care and support statutory guidance* to the CA 2014 was published by the Department of Health for consultation in June 2014 and

---

48 Law Commission, *Adult Social Care*, Law Com No 326 HC 941, 2011, Recommendation 3.

49 Joint Committee on the Draft Care and Support Bill, 'Draft Care and Support Bill', HL Paper 143 HC 822, The Stationery Office, 2013, para 65.

50 Secretary of State for Health, *The Care Bill explained. Including a response to consultation and pre-legislative scrutiny on the Draft Care and Support Bill* Cm 8627, The Stationery Office, 2013, para 130.

51 By inserting subsection (1A).

the amended formal version was then published in October 2014. The original and subsequent versions have been published online[52] as HTML documents, but only the October 2014 version has been published by the Department of Health as a single PDF document.

1.42   By January 2017 the statutory guidance had been revised on three occasions (in March, November and December 2016) and although the secretary of state may well have consulted on these changes (as required by CA 2014 s78(2)) it is not immediately obvious with whom. In this text, references to the revised statutory guidance are to the version of the guidance that was current on 1 January 2017.

1.43   It is of significant concern that the revised statutory guidance is not available as a hard copy or in PDF format. A statement issued by the Local Government Association (LGA) in March 2016[53] (accompanying the first revision) stated that the 'new format ... is intended to be read online and has improved navigation and search functionality'. It added that 'if a chapter is updated a note will appear under the chapter title indicating when it was last updated'. It is, however, no simple matter to identify the provenance of any part of the revised statutory guidance – when and how it first appeared in its current version – and this difficulty is certain to become more acute with time. Given that significant changes have already been made and that the revised statutory guidance has something approaching the force of law (see para 1.45 below) it is troubling that no official hard copy will exist. This casual approach to statutory formalities (not to say the 'rule of law') should be reconsidered. It certainly adds weight to the recommendations of the Law Commission:[54]

> ... that the guidance should be subject to Parliamentary oversight through the negative resolution procedure. This would mean that any alteration of the guidance, including the issuing of new guidance, would need to be laid before Parliament ... for 40 days and will come into force unless a resolution annulling it is passed. The guidance plays a crucial role in our scheme as it will be the means by which the Secretary of State ... can guide the exercise of local authority functions under the statute, and it will carry substantial legal force. Accordingly, it is important that any changes are given an appropriate degree of scrutiny. This is consistent with the approach adopted by the Mental Health Act 1983 and Mental Capacity Act 2005.

The status of statutory guidance

1.44   As noted above, guidance issued under CA 2014 s78 has the same status as that issued under LASSA 1970 s7(1). It is a higher-status form of guidance and is generally labelled as such – eg 'statutory guidance' or 'issued under section 78 Care Act 2014'. In similar fashion, the equivalent pre-CA 2014 guidance often contained the statement 'this guidance is issued under s7(1) Local Authority Social Services Act 1970'. Unfortunately this was not always the case (especially prior to 2000), although it was generally

52 See www.gov.uk/government/publications/care-act-statutory-guidance/care-and-support-statutory-guidance.

53 LGA, *Care Act statutory guidance*, March 2016.

54 Law Commission, *Adult social care*, Law Com No 326 HC941, 2011, para 3.30 a proposal endorsed by the Joint Committee on the Draft Care and Support Bill, 'Draft Care and Support Bill', HL Paper 143 HC 822, The Stationery Office, 2013, paras 61–66.

accepted that Department of Health 'policy guidance' was 'statutory guidance' under LASSA 1970 s7(1).

1.45   The wording of LASSA 1970 s7(1) and CA 2014 s78 respectively is such that local authorities are not merely required to bear such advice in mind when making decisions – they must 'act under' it, which is a significantly more powerful obligation.

1.46   The question of how far policy guidance must be followed has been the subject of a number of court judgments. In *R v Islington LBC ex p Rixon*[55] Sedley J held:

> In my judgment Parliament in enacting [LASSA 1970] s7(1) did not intend local authorities to whom ministerial guidance was given to be free, having considered it, to take it or leave it. Such a construction would put this kind of statutory guidance on a par with the many forms of non-statutory guidance issued by departments of state. While guidance and directions are semantically and legally different things, and while 'guidance does not compel any particular decision' (*Laker Airways Ltd v Department of Trade* [1967] QB 643, 714 per Roskill LJ), especially when prefaced by the word 'general', in my view Parliament by s7(1) has required local authorities to follow the path charted by the secretary of state's guidance, with liberty to deviate from it where the local authority judges on admissible grounds that there is good reason to do so, but without freedom to take a substantially different course.

1.47   This was also the approach adopted in *R v Gloucestershire CC ex p Barry and others*[56] where Hirst LJ contrasted the binding nature of statutory guidance with other social services guidance which he considered to be merely of 'persuasive authority on the proper construction of the legislation'.[57]

1.48   The consequences of failing to take into account statutory guidance were spelt out by Sedley J in *ex p Rixon* (above):

> ... if this statutory guidance is to be departed from it must be with good reason, articulated in the course of some identifiable decision-making process even if not in the care plan itself. In the absence of any such considered decision, the deviation from statutory guidance is in my judgment a breach of law ...

It follows that if a local authority decides not to follow statutory guidance it must give clear and adequate reasons for its decision and its departure from the guidance must be as limited as is possible in the particular circumstances.[58]

1.49   *R (KM) v Northampton CC*[59] concerned a local authority's domiciliary care charging policy that deviated significantly from relevant statutory guidance issued by the Department of Health.[60] The court struck down

55 (1997–98) 1 CCLR 119 at 123, 15 March 1996, QBD.

56 [1996] 4 All ER 421, (1997–98) 1 CCLR 19 at 24, CA.

57 Hirst LJ's dissenting opinion was approved by the majority in the House of Lords: [1997] 2 WLR 459, (1997–98) 1 CCLR 40.

58 In this respect see, by way of analogy, *B v X Metropolitan Council* [2010] EWHC 467 (Admin) para 29.

59 [2015] EWHC 482 (Admin).

60 Department of Health, *Fairer charging policies for home care and other non-residential social services guidance for councils with social services responsibilities*, 2013.

the policy and in so doing cited the Court of Appeal judgment in *R (X) v Tower Hamlets LBC*:[61]

> The next question was whether there were cogent reasons for departing from the guidance. There was and is no dispute about the relevant legal principles. Having considered *R v Islington Borough Council ex p Rixon* (1998) 1 CCLR 119 and *R (Munjaz) v Mersey Care NHS Trust* [2006] 2 AC 148, together with other authorities, Males J said (at paragraph 35):
>
> > 'In summary, therefore, the guidance does not have the binding effect of secondary legislation and a local authority is free to depart from it, even "substantially". But a departure from the guidance would be unlawful unless there is cogent reason for it, and the greater the departure, the more compelling must that reason be. Conversely a minor departure from the letter of the guidance while remaining true to its spirit may well be easy to justify or may not even be regarded as a departure at all. The Court will scrutinise carefully the reason given by the authority for departing from the guidance. Freedom to depart is not necessarily limited to reasons resulting from "local circumstances" ..., although if there are particular local circumstances which suggest that some aspect of the guidance ought not to apply, that may constitute a cogent reason for departure. However, except perhaps in the case of a minor departure, it is difficult to envisage circumstances in which mere disagreement with the guidance could amount to a cogent reason for departing from it.'

1.50 Although statutory guidance has quasi-legal characteristics, it cannot amend or frustrate primary or subordinate legislation, and can of course be the subject of judicial review if, for example, it contains an error of law[62] or a misleading explanation of the law.[63] It can, in addition, be struck down if its purpose is to circumvent or frustrate a statutory provision[64] or public law requirement (for instance, an affected party's legitimate expectation).[65]

Codes of practice

1.51 Codes of practice are another example of 'guidance'. Many (but not all) codes of practice are 'statutory' in the sense that they are prepared as a result of a statutory requirement. For example, MCA 2005 s42 requires that a code of practice (see para 13.7 below) be prepared and obliges certain persons to have regard to it when discharging their functions and for courts/tribunals to take notice of any material failures in this respect. It follows that the extent to which such guidance is binding will depend upon the specific context of any decision, but in many cases it is likely to have equivalent force to policy guidance.[66] Guidance of similar effect

---

61 [2013] EWCA Civ 904 (per Maurice Kay LJ at para 28 approving the first instance judgment of Males J).

62 See eg *R v North and East Devon Health Authority ex p Coughlan* [2000] 2 WLR 622, (2000) 2 CCLR 285, CA and *Gillick v West Norfolk Area Health Authority* [1986] AC 112, HL.

63 See eg *R (YA) v Secretary of State for Health* [2009] EWCA Civ 225, (2009) 12 CCLR 213.

64 *R v Secretary of State for Health ex p Pfizer Ltd* (1999) 2 CCLR 270, QBD and *R v Worthing BC ex p Birch* (1985) 50 P&CR 53.

65 *R (Bapio Action Ltd) v Secretary of State Home Department* [2008] UKHL 27.

66 See eg *R (Brown) v Secretary of State for Work and Pensions* [2008] EWHC 3158 (Admin).

is to be found in relation to local authorities' duties to house homeless people (see para 14.27 below) and in relation to general obligations under the Equality Act 2010. The code of practice issued under MHA 1983 s118 is guidance to which all professionals working in the mental health field must have regard. In *R (Munjaz) v Mersey Care NHS Trust*[67] the House of Lords concluded that the code was not absolutely binding, but, like policy guidance, could be departed from where justification for the departure was explained in very considerable detail.

Practice guidance

1.52   The majority of social care guidance produced or approved by the Department of Health has not been issued as statutory guidance. Such guidance has a lesser status – and is often referred to as practice or best practice guidance. Such guidance is advice as to how an authority might go about implementing or interpreting a particular statutory responsibility. It is sometimes said that statutory guidance tells an authority what it must do, whereas practice guidance suggests how it might go about doing it. Guidance of this nature is common to other areas of social welfare law – for instance, in relation to children, CA 2004 s10(8) requires children's services authorities to 'have regard to any guidance given to them' by the secretary of state; and Housing Act 1996 s182(1) places a similar obligation on housing authorities when exercising their homelessness functions.[68]

1.53   Historically, concern has been expressed about the abundance and the 'disparate and unconnected'[69] nature of social care guidance of this kind. The Law Commission in its 2011 report hoped that the reformed social care legislative regime would get to grips with this problem and that if it proved necessary to issue 'multiple documents ... then they should be published in a form which allows them to be presented as a coherent whole, and they should be available in a single accessible location, such as on one webpage'.[70]

1.54   Although authorities are not therefore required to 'act under' such guidance, they are required to 'have regard' to it when reaching a decision in respect of which it may be material. It follows that a failure to have regard to it (rather than a failure to follow it) may result in the subsequent decision being quashed by the courts or condemned by the ombudsman. In *R v Islington LBC ex p Rixon*[71] Sedley J referred to practice guidance in the following terms:

> While such guidance lacks the status accorded by s7(1) of Local Authority Social Services Act 1970, it is, as I have said, something to which regard must be had in carrying out the statutory functions. While the occasional lacuna would not furnish evidence of such a disregard, the series of lacunae which I have mentioned does ...[72]

67   [2005] UKHL 58, [2005] 3 WLR 793.
68   See eg *R (Khatun, Zeb and Iqbal) v Newham LBC* [2004] EWCA Civ 55, [2004] 3 WLR 417 at [23].
69   Law Commission, *Adult social care*, Law Com No 326 HC941, 2011, para 3.35.
70   Law Commission, *Adult social care*, Law Com No 326 HC941, 2011, para 3.35.
71   *R v Islington LBC ex p Rixon* (1997–98) 1 CCLR 119, 15 March 1996, QBD.
72   (1997–98) 1 CCLR 119 at 131E, QBD.

1.55 Practice guidance takes many forms. Previously, Department of Health guidance was given a sequential reference number and a status – for instance, some were labelled 'LAC' (local authority circular) which had a higher standing than those identified as 'LASSL' (local authority social services letter). This system was abandoned in 2002,[73] making it more difficult to ascertain the precise status of guidance issued since that time.[74]

Cancelled guidance

1.56 Some guidance issued by the Department of Health has a self-destruct date – ie containing a statement that 'this guidance will be cancelled on' a specified date. This does not, of course, mean that it ceases thereafter to be of relevance, since it will generally remain a statement of good practice (unless specifically contradicted by subsequent guidance).

1.57 This proposition is sometimes expressed in explicit terms: for example, 2001 guidance concerning social care arrangements for 'deafblind people' (LAC (2001)8) states:

> The circular ... will be cancelled on 28 February 2006. Though the Department will not be reissuing this document, councils are reminded that the principles of good practice the Guidance contains continue to be valid.

1.58 The value of previous guidance will be of particular relevance in the early days of the CA 2014 regime. Although the Act has repealed most of the previous adult social care legislation and in consequence led to the withdrawal of almost all of the associated guidance, it does not mean that that guidance has ceased to be of value. Given that the CA 2014 is largely a consolidating statute and that its revised statutory guidance is in general less detailed than that which it replaced – there are many occasions when it is instructive to see what was considered best practice under the previous regime. This is particularly so in relation to questions concerning charging and direct payments (see chapters 8 and 10 respectively).

National minimum standards and national service frameworks

1.59 Some guidance issued by the Department of Health is entitled 'national minimum standards' or 'national service framework' (NSF). NSFs are non-statutory in origin and essentially aspirational – setting out the Department of Health's long-term strategy for improving specific areas of care. They are NHS led but defined both health and social services obligations and detailed measurable goals within set time-frames, generally being ten-year programmes. They cover a wide variety of subjects including services for older people, for children, for people with long-term conditions and for mental health services.

1.60 National minimum standards were the product of Care Standards Act 2000 s23 which authorised the appropriate minister to publish 'national

---

73 As a consequence of Department of Health, *Shifting the balance of power: the next steps*, 2002, which stated that the change was designed to increase local autonomy with the central government adopting a 'a less hands-on approach' – a noble ambition that demonstrably failed.

74 Or indeed to locate it – guidance lacks an easily identifiable reference, and can appear on a range of websites, as the many and varied footnotes to this book testify.

minimum standards' for the provision of care homes and elsewhere. Such standards are no longer of direct relevance in England.[75]

1.61   Such 'standards' and 'frameworks', although not legally binding, must be taken into account by the relevant authorities when making decisions and have been cited by the ombudsmen as benchmarks when seeking to determine whether the actions of a public body have fallen below an acceptable standard.

NHS guidance

1.62   While the 2006 NHS Acts authorise the issuing of directions (see paras 1.34 and 11.10) in much the same way as authorised under CA 2014 s78, there is no specific provision in the 2006 Acts concerning the issuing of guidance.[76] NHSA 2006 s2(1)(b) empowers the secretary of state to do 'anything whatsoever which is calculated to facilitate or is conducive or incidental to, the discharge of' the duty to promote a comprehensive health service. Such a power clearly authorises the issuing of guidance. In all other respects, though, the NHSA 2006 is silent on the effect of such guidance.

1.63   The extent to which NHS guidance is binding on local NHS bodies is therefore a contextual question that will depend in most cases on the wording of the guidance, the nature of the process in question and the particular facts of an individual case. In some situations it would appear that guidance will have the same coercive effect as social services 'statutory guidance' – as indeed Dyson J so concluded in *R v North Derbyshire Health Authority ex p Fisher*.[77] In a similar vein, it would appear that where joint policy guidance is issued to social services and NHS bodies – but is primarily aimed at the latter – it is not unreasonable to assume that its legal force is no less in relation to the NHS than it is for social services.

1.64   The Autism Act 2009 incorporates an innovative device that provides for binding policy guidance to be issued to NHS bodies. Section 3(2) provides that guidance issued under section 2 of the Act 'is to be treated as if it were general guidance of the secretary of state under section 7 of the Local Authority Social Services Act 1970'. Section 3(3) then provides that for the purposes of such guidance NHS bodies are, in essence to be treated as they are local social services authorities.

Localism Act 2011

1.65   LA 2011 s1 empowers local authorities 'to do anything that individuals generally may do'. This 'general power of competence' builds on a similar but less extensive power that existed in the Local Government Act (LGA) 2000, to promote or improve the economic, social or environmental well-

---

75   In relation to adults in England these have been replaced by Health and Social Care Act 2008 (Regulated Activities) Regulations 2014 SI No 2936 – see para 17.7 below.

76   Although by virtue of NHSA 2006 s77(11), care trusts are subject to such section 7 guidance, and LASSA 1970 s75(6) of the same Act empowers the secretary of state to issue guidance concerning consultation processes.

77   (1997–98) 1 CCLR 150, 11 July 1997, QBD.

being of their area. In relation to the scope of the section 1 power, the explanatory note to the LA 2011 states that:

> ... the starting point is that there are to be no limits as to how the power can be exercised. For example, the power does not need to be exercised for the benefit of any particular place or group, and can be exercised anywhere and in any way.

Although the power is designed to give councils 'increased confidence to do creative, innovative things to meet local people's needs'[78] in the social care context it can also act as a safety net: enabling local authorities to support individuals who, for one reason or another, are not entitled to support under the CA 2014.

1.66   Various limits exist to the use of the LA 2011 s1 power. These include:

- the general power cannot override express prohibitions, restrictions and limitations in primary or secondary legislation that existed at the time of the enactment of the LA 2011 (section 2(2)(a));
- prohibitions, restrictions and limitations in primary or secondary legislation created after the enactment of the LA 2011 only impact on the section 1 power where they are expressed to do so (section 2(2)(b));
- a restriction on the power of authorities to charge for services. If no specific charging power exists, authorities can charge up to full cost recovery for discretionary services – ie services not provided as a result of a duty[79] (section 3).

1.67   *R (Khan) v Oxfordshire CC*[80] provides an example of the first restriction (albeit it concerned the LGA 2000 where a similar provision existed). The applicant was excluded from assistance under National Assistance Act 1948 s21 as she was a person to whom Immigration and Asylum Act 1999 applied (see chapter 16 below). On the basis of this explicit prohibition, the court concluded that the LGA 2000 restriction applied and so support could not be provided under that Act.

1.68   Although general empowering provisions of this nature are not new,[81] the LA 2011 (and its predecessor LGA 2000 Part I) provides considerably more freedom for councils than was previously the case.[82] By way of example, *R (J) v Enfield LBC and Secretary of State for Health (intervener)*,[83] (a case under the LGA 2000) concerned an HIV-positive applicant and her child who sought accommodation from the local authority. The applicant was unlawfully within the UK having overstayed her visa, and at the time of the hearing it was considered that there was no power under CA 1989 s17

---

78 Department for Communities and Local Government, *A plain English guide to the Localism Act*, 2011, p4.

79 For example, under CA 2014 s18 or s20.

80 [2004] EWCA Civ 309, (2004) 7 CCLR 215.

81 LGA 1972 s111, for instance, empowers authorities to 'do anything (whether or not involving the expenditure, borrowing or lending of money or the acquisition or disposal of any property or rights) which is calculated to facilitate, or is conducive or incidental to, the discharge of any of their functions'; see eg *R (A and B) v East Sussex CC* [2002] EWHC 2771 (Admin), (2003) 6 CCLR 117, where the use of this power in relation to community care services was considered.

82 See eg *R (Theophilus) v Lewisham LBC* [2002] EWHC 1371 (Admin), [2002] 3 All ER 851 which concerned further education funding.

83 [2002] EWHC 432 (Admin), (2002) 5 CCLR 434.

to provide accommodation.[84] Elias J concluded that in the absence of any express statutory power to provide for the applicant and her daughter, such a power existed under LGA 2000 s2. He further held that if the use of this power were 'the only way in which [the local authority] could avoid a breach of the claimant's Article 8 rights, then … it would be obliged to exercise its discretion in that way'.[85] This analysis was accepted in *R (Grant) v Lambeth LBC*[86] which concerned a family who were unlawfully within the UK and who had no right to be accommodated. The council concluded that to avoid a breach of the family's ECHR rights (within the provisions of Nationality, Immigration and Asylum Act (NIAA) 2002 Sch 3 para 3 – see paras 16.97 below) it would offer to pay for their travel back to their country of origin. The Court of Appeal held that once an authority had reached this conclusion, it was obliged to consider 'whether there was some other power by the exercise of which a breach of Mrs Grant's Convention rights could be avoided' and, in that context, the use of the power conferred by LGA 2000 s2.

1.69   In *R (GS) v LB Camden*[87] the claimant was excluded from CA 2014 support by virtue of the NIAA 2002. LGA 2002 Sch 3, however, enables support to be provided to the extent that it is necessary to avoid breaching the claimant's rights under the ECHR. Given the claimant's particular circumstances (see para 7.101 below), the court held that if she became homeless it would breach her rights under ECHR Article 3 (prohibition on torture or inhuman or degrading treatment or punishment). This in turn meant that the local authority was able to exercise its power under LA 2011 s1 (and the court held that its failure to do this was unlawful).

Market oversight

Overview

1.70   As noted above (see preface), this book is primarily concerned with the individual social care responsibilities that are owed to adults in need and carers rather than the strategic 'macro' obligations of social services authorities. What follows is therefore only an overview of the CA 2014 market-shaping obligations of social services authorities.[88] One aspect of these obligations is also considered in chapter 7 (para 7.114), namely the

---

84 The Court of Appeal having held in *R (A) v Lambeth LBC* [2001] EWCA Civ 1624, (2001) 4 CCLR 486, that no such power existed: this finding was set aside by a differently constituted Court of Appeal in *R (W) v Lambeth LBC* [2002] EWCA Civ 613, [2002] 2 All ER 901, (2002) 5 CCLR 203.

85 [2002] EWHC 432 (Admin), (2002) 5 CCLR 434 at [72]: a view affirmed by the Court of Appeal in *R (W) v Lambeth LBC* [2002] EWCA Civ 613, [2002] 2 All ER 901, (2002) 5 CCLR 203 at paras 74–75.

86 [2004] EWCA Civ 1711, [2005] 1 WLR 1781 at [50].

87 [2016] EWHC 1762 (Admin): the facts of this case are considered at para 7.101 below.

88 A set of 'market shaping' materials, commissioned by the Department of Health, the Local Government Association, the Association of Directors of Adult Social Services and the Care Provider Alliance has been produced by Institute of Public Care Oxford Brookes University (and accessible via their website).

extent to which they constrain local authority power to dictate fee levels to independent sector providers.

1.71   CA 2014 s5(1) places a duty on local authorities to promote an efficient and effective market 'with a view to ensuring that any person in its area wishing to access services in the market':

(a) has a variety of providers to choose from who (taken together) provide a variety of services;
(b) has a variety of high quality services to choose from;
(c) has sufficient information to make an informed decision about how to meet the needs in question.

1.72   The CA 2014 (fleshed out by regulations[89]) contains a range of provisions designed to address the 'supply side' problems of the social care market – ie (a) the problem of large providers collapsing (such as the Southern Cross Healthcare failure in 2011); and (b) the increasing belief that the quality of services is generally poor and deteriorating. These provisions include 'market oversight' arrangements involving the Care Quality Commission (CQC) – among others (CA 2014 ss53–57) and a temporary duty on social services to intervene if a particular provider 'fails' (CA 2014 ss48–52). In 2014 the Public Accounts Committee was of the view that the CQC (which monitors the top 40–50 providers) lacked 'the skills to undertake this expanded level of monitoring'.[90]

1.73   Regulations[91] provide for 11 fundamental standards of safety and quality that should always be met by providers of health and social care (these being: person-centred care; dignity and respect; need for consent; safe care and treatment; safeguarding service users from abuse; meeting nutritional needs; cleanliness, safety and suitability of premises and equipment; receiving and acting on complaints; good governance; staffing; and fit and proper persons employed). The CQC has issued guidance[92] on how this is to be achieved (and policed) in practice.

1.74   A key problem concerning diversity and quality is that councils hold a dominant position in this market and have (due to their chronic underfunding) been requiring providers to deliver the same quantity of services each year while concurrently imposing cuts to the amount paid. The National Audit Office consider that this relentless pressure by local authorities on fee rates is jeopardising financial sustainability of some providers[93] and the Association of Directors of Adult Social Services Departments (ADASS) accept that local authorities do not always consider the profit margins of their suppliers, or the impact that reducing fees will have on

89   These include the Care and Support (Market Oversight Information) Regulations 2014 SI No 2822; and the Care and Support (Market Oversight Criteria) Regulations 2015 SI No 314 (as well as business failure regulations specific to cross-border placements).

90   House of Commons Committee of Public Accounts, *Adult social care in England* HC 518, The Stationery Office, 2014, p8 – it noted, however, that the Department of Health was confident that it would have the necessary skills by April 2015.

91   Health and Social Care Act 2008 (Regulated Activities) Regulations 2014 SI No 2936.

92   CQC, *Guidance for providers on meeting the regulations*, 2015.

93   Report by the Comptroller and Auditor General, *Adult social care in England: overview* HC 1102 Session 2013–14, National Audit Office, 2014, paras 2.11–2.13.

their viability.⁹⁴ The Joint Committee that scrutinised the draft Care and Support Bill considered that there had to be a mechanism that required local authorities to 'properly take into account the actual cost of care when setting the rates they are prepared to pay providers'.⁹⁵ Such a mechanism is not to be found in the Act – but the statutory guidance is surprisingly direct on this question; this is considered further at para 7.114 below.

1.75   The problem, of course, is not merely that of driving down standards as cost reductions are required, but of driving out smaller providers as only the larger corporations are able to compete on cost. The statutory guidance addresses this concern requiring that local authority commissioning procedures 'must encourage a variety of different providers and different types of services' (para 4.37), including 'voluntary and community based organisations, including user-led organisations, mutual and small businesses' (para 4.38) and should support people who 'micro-commission' their own care (para 4.47). While the guidance envisages that local authorities may have 'approved lists and frameworks that are used to limit the number of providers they work with' it requires that they 'must consider how to ensure that there is still a reasonable choice for people who need care and support' (para 4.39).

1.76   The statutory guidance encourages 'outcomes based' commissioning – ie that instead of a local authority simply commissioning 'units of provision to meet a specified need (eg hours of care provided)' it moves towards specified outcomes for the individual which 'emphasise prevention, enablement, ways of reducing loneliness and social isolation and promotion of independence as ways of achieving and exceeding desired outcomes, as well as choice in how people's needs are met' (para 4.16). The guidance cautions, however, that this move should not have the result of disadvantaging or excluding 'smaller, specialist, voluntary sector and community-based providers' (para 4.18).

1.77   The guidance also contains a timely reminder to local authorities that they 'understand relevant procurement legislation' and in particular make themselves aware of the fact that 'there is significant flexibility in procurement practices' which can 'support effective engagement with provider organisations and support innovation in service delivery, potentially reducing risks and leading to cost-savings' (para 4.99) and that this includes an obligation 'to consider added social value when letting contracts' under the Public Services (Social Value) Act 2012⁹⁶ (para 4.105).

Workforce issues

1.78   The social care workforce has been a direct victim of local authority pressure on providers to reduce their fees. The statutory guidance stresses the importance of authorities 'encouraging a workforce which effectively

---

94 House of Commons Committee of Public Accounts, *Adult social care in England* HC 518, The Stationery Office, 2014, p13.
95 Joint Committee on the Draft Care and Support Bill, 'Draft Care and Support Bill', HL Paper 143 HC 822, The Stationery Office, 2013, para 113.
96 For guidance on the application of the Public Services (Social Value) Act 2012 see Cabinet Office, *Procurement policy note 10/12: The Public Services (Social Value) Act 2012*, 2012.

underpins the market' (para 4.21) and encouraging (by, for example, providing funding – para 4.29) 'training and development'. Local authorities
when commissioning services must assure themselves that their fee levels
do not (among other things) compromise the service provider's ability to:
(1) 'meet the statutory obligations to pay at least minimum wages; (2) 'provide effective training and development of staff' (para 4.31); and (3) pay
remuneration that is:

> ... at least sufficient to comply with the national minimum wage legislation
> for hourly pay or equivalent salary. This will include appropriate remuner-
> ation for any time spent travelling between appointments (para 4.30).

1.79   The statutory guidance advises that where a provider has previously been
in breach of national minimum wage legislation it should in general be
excluded from the tendering process (para 4.103).

Underpinning social care principles

Introduction

2.1   This chapter is concerned with underpinning principles: the legal provisions that regulate the way adult social care decisions are made and implemented. It is primarily concerned with three particular provisions: (1) the well-being duty under the Care Act (CA) 2014; (2) the public sector equality duty (PSED) under the Equality Act (EqA) 2010; and (3) the human rights obligations that flow from the Human Rights Act (HRA) 1998.

2.2   These are not, of course, the only underpinning principles of relevance to adult social care. Two other regulatory schemes, although of considerable importance, are not, however, covered in this chapter, namely: (1) the care quality standards to which local authorities and care providers must adhere, and for which the Care Quality Commission (CQC) acts as regulator (see chapter 17 below); and (2) the *Standards of conduct, performance and ethics* published by the Health & Care Professions Council (HCPC) (2016) that apply to social work professionals in England, including the obligation to 'promote and protect the interests of service users and carers'.

The well-being duty

Background to the underpinning principles of adult social care law

2.3   Prior to the enactment the CA 2014, adult social care legislation contained no express statement of underpinning principles. That is not to say that none operated – merely that as a body of law it contained no formal written statement of as to what these were. As with mental capacity law prior to the Mental Capacity Act (MCA) 2005, a large number of principles, inferences, presumptions and aims had been identified within this body of law – they had not, however, been reduced to statutory form. It is tempting to say that this remains the case today, albeit that a cluster of considerations have been herded into section 1 of the CA 2014. The Act (unlike the statutory guidance[1]) does not, however, refer to these as 'principles'.

2.4   It follows that much of the pre-CA 2014 discussion on these considerations remain relevant – not least because these are intertwined with other statutory provisions (for example, the requirements of the EqA 2010 and HRA 1998) as well as international obligations – such as the UN Convention on the Rights of Persons with Disabilities (CRPD).

2.5   The desirability of a statutory code or some form of underpinning statement of the principles concerning the provision of social care services has been accepted for many years.[2] The Law Commission's 2008 scoping report on the potential for the reform of adult social care law[3] noted that:

---

1 Department of Health, *Care and support statutory guidance* to support implementation of Part 1 of the CA 2014 by local authorities, 2016 ('the statutory guidance').

2 See, for example, L Clements, *Community care and the law*, Legal Action Group, 1996, p18; and L Clements 'Community care: towards a workable statute' *Liverpool Law Review* Vol XIX (2) (1997) pp181–191.

3 Law Commission, *Adult social care scoping report*, 2008.

One of the main criticisms of adult social care law is that the lack of a con-solidated statute means there is no coherent set of overarching principles to direct and assist local authorities, courts and others in carrying out their functions in this area (para 4.2).

2.6 In 2010 the Law Commission in its consultation paper[4] accepted that there was a compelling case for a statement of principles on the face of the statute, and put forward eight principles for discussion, namely: (1) decision-makers must maximise the choice and control of service users; (2) person-centred planning; (3) a person's needs should be viewed broad-ly; (4) the need to reduce or remove future need; (5) independent living; (6) an assumption of home-based living; (7) dignity in care; and (8) safeguard-ing adults from abuse and neglect.

2.7 Ultimately in its final report (2011)[5] the Law Commission rejected this approach, considering for example 'concepts such as *dignity* and *independ-ent living* ... too imprecise to be expressed as statutory principles' (para 4.35; emphasis in original). The Law Commission opted instead for a 'pri-mary well-being principle' on the basis that it 'would provide a positive statement about the nature and purpose of adult social care' (para 4.18).

2.8 It is difficult to follow in its entirety the logic of the Commission's rationale for coming to this conclusion. 'Well-being' is not a principle (the CA 2014 does not describe it as such) and as a concept it is contested. 'Dignity' and 'independent living' are principles used in international con-ventions[6] – and indeed 'dignity' has made its way into the CA 2014 and 'independent living' into the statutory guidance (where it is described as 'a guiding principle' (para 1.19)). It appears probable that pragmatism dic-tated the adoption of 'well-being'.[7] As a duty it is best conceptualised as a temporary vehicle designed to display, 'try out' and hopefully deliver more fundamental principles.

Well-being as a concept

2.9 Well-being is a fashionable and politically favoured concept.[8] In November 2010, when the Law Commission was considering the responses to its consultation paper on adult social care,[9] the government announced its

---

4 Law Commission, *Consultation paper no 192. Adult social care*, 2010, Part 3.

5 Law Commission, *Adult social care*, Law Com No 326 HC941, 2011, Part 4 pp17–24.

6 For example, 'dignity' is a fundamental principle of the German constitution, the Constitution South Africa, the UN Convention on the Rights of Persons with Disabilities (CRPD) and the right to independent living is defined in Article 19 of the CRPD.

7 Between the publication of the consultation paper in February 2010 and the publication of its final report in May 2011, the then Prime Minister launched his major 'well-being' initiative (on 25 November 2010).

8 See, for example, I Bache and L Reardon, 'An idea whose time has come? Explaining the rise of well-being in British politics' in *Political Studies* Volume 61, Issue 4, December 2013, pp898–914; and see generally I Bache, *The politics and policy of wellbeing*, Edward Elgar, 2016.

9 Law Commission, *Consultation paper no 192. Adult social care*, 2010 – the consultation period closed on 1 July 2010.

major 'well-being initiative'[10] in which the then Prime Minister noted that although it was not possible to 'legislate for fulfilment or satisfaction ... government has the power to help improve well-being'.

2.10   Well-being has a respectable history, but as a concept it is complex and contested and fragments into several discourses – for example, 'scientific, popular, critical and environmental'.[11] Since the turn of the century a number of studies[12] have developed indicators that measure 'subjective well-being'[13] although these are not without criticism.[14] In terms of philosophy, the concept is often positioned alongside notions of 'flourishing' and 'the good life'.

2.11   For the purpose of this analysis, 'well-being' is considered simply as a conceptual vehicle which is, in itself, of little or no interest. The interest lies in what the term is said, in the CA 2014, to encompass.[15]

Well-being and the CA 2014

2.12   The CA 2014 does not define well-being. Section 1(1) creates a general duty to promote well-being and section 1(2) lists nine 'areas'/'individual aspects of well-being or outcomes'[16] – which on analysis appear to comprise almost every aspect of life. These are things that the local authority must, whenever exercising any function under Part 1 of the CA 2014, endeavour to promote. The statutory guidance advises that there is 'no hierarchy' to these nine factors and that they 'should be considered of equal importance when considering "well-being" in the round' (para 1.6).

2.13   The obligation applies, therefore, to almost every act by a social services authority that relates to an adult in need or a carer – from a telephone conversation to the setting by the authority of its social care budget. It will be maladministration for a local authority to impose 'restrictive

---

10 David Cameron MP, *Transcript of a speech given by the Prime Minister on well-being on 25 November 2010*, Cabinet Office, 2010.

11 S Carlisle and P Hanlon, 'Well-being and consumer culture: a different kind of public health problem?' *Health Promotion International* (2007) 22 (3): 261–268.

12 See, for example, R Cummins and others, 'Developing a national index of subjective well-being: the Australian unity well-being index' *Social Indicators Research* (2003) vol 64, pp159–190; and Office of National Statistics (ONS), *Measuring national well-being: domains and measures*, 2016.

13 Defined as 'a person's cognitive and affective evaluations of his or her life': see E Diener and others, 'Subjective well-being: the science of happiness and life satisfaction' in C Snyder and S Lopez (eds), *Handbook of positive psychology*, OUP, 2002, p63.

14 Sointu, for example, suggests that 'the increasing popularity of the ideal of well-being appears to reflect shifts in perceptions and experiences of individual agency and responsibility. In particular, dominant discourses of well-being relate to changes in subjectivity; they manifest a move from subjects as citizens to subjects as consumers. In a consumer society, well-being emerges as a normative obligation chosen and sought after by individual agents' - see E Sointu, 'The rise of an ideal: tracing changing discourses of well-being' *Sociological Review* (2005) 53(2): 255–274.

15 In *Re G (Children)* [2012] EWCA Civ 1233 Munby LJ appears to have taken a similar line in relation to the specific generic labels 'welfare', 'well-being' and 'interests' which he considered in the context of that case to be synonymous.

16 Statutory guidance, paras 1.5 and 1.6.

interpretations of Care Act outcomes' that fail to take proper account of an adult's well-being.[17]

2.14   The section 1(2) list of areas that an individual's well-being relates to comprises:

    (a) personal dignity (including treatment of the individual with respect);
    (b) physical and mental health and emotional well-being;
    (c) protection from abuse and neglect;
    (d) control by the individual over day-to-day life (including over care and support, or support, provided to the individual and the way in which it is provided);
    (e) participation in work, education, training or recreation;
    (f) social and economic well-being;
    (g) domestic, family and personal relationships;
    (h) suitability of living accommodation;
    (i) the individual's contribution to society.

2.15   Section 1(3) provides a list of eight matters to which a local authority 'must have regard' when exercising a CA 2014 function, namely:

    (a) the importance of beginning with the assumption that the individual is best-placed to judge the individual's well-being;
    (b) the individual's views, wishes, feelings and beliefs;
    (c) the importance of preventing or delaying the development of needs for care and support or needs for support and the importance of reducing needs of either kind that already exist;
    (d) the need to ensure that decisions about the individual are made having regard to all the individual's circumstances (and are not based only on the individual's age or appearance or any condition of the individual's or aspect of the individual's behaviour which might lead others to make unjustified assumptions about the individual's well-being);
    (e) the importance of the individual participating as fully as possible in decisions relating to the exercise of the function concerned and being provided with the information and support necessary to enable the individual to participate;
    (f) the importance of achieving a balance between the individual's well-being and that of any friends or relatives who are involved in caring for the individual;
    (g) the need to protect people from abuse and neglect;
    (h) the need to ensure that any restriction on the individual's rights or freedom of action that is involved in the exercise of the function is kept to the minimum necessary for achieving the purpose for which the function is being exercised.

2.16   The more substantive of these 17 considerations are analysed below. Some, however, are more appropriately addressed elsewhere in this text – for example, 'protection from abuse and neglect' in the safeguarding chapter (chapter 18) and 'delay' is the subject of discussion in the majority of chapters. A number of these considerations resonate with the principles in the MCA 2005 and are considered in the mental capacity chapter (chapter 13) and several are of particular relevance to eligibility determinations and are considered in chapter 4.

---

17 Complaint 15 011 661 against London Borough of Hammersmith & Fulham 21 July 2016 para 25.

The individual presumption

2.17   The assumption in CA 2014 s1(3)(a) 'that the individual is best placed to judge well-being' creates a default position (rather like the presumption of capacity in MCA 2005 s1) which will require specific evidence if it is to be rebutted. The statutory guidance indicates that this 'principle' should be given an expansive interpretation – for example at para 6.35, that inherent with this principle is the wider assumption that individuals must also be 'best placed to understand the impact of their condition(s) on their outcomes and well-being'.

2.18   Potentially this is an assumption that could have wide ranging implications – the extent of which will have to be determined by case-law. Traditionally courts have deferred to both the expertise of social services staff and their role as final arbiters on questions such as 'eligibility'. To what extent does the individual presumption 'that they are best placed to judge' their well-being impact on this deference? *R (McDonald) v Kensington and Chelsea RLBC*[18] illustrates this question. Lord Walker (at para 33) referred to social services evidence that the appellant Elaine McDonald did not want to wear continence pads at night (wanting instead to have help to reach her commode) and that she had:

> ... concerns about privacy and dignity and about the need to maintain her relationship with her partner. It is the council's view that the use of continence products provides greater privacy and dignity than the presence of a carer assisting with personal and intimate functions at night-time.

Lord Walker then observed:

> Miss McDonald strongly differs from this view, and so may others. But I do not see how it could possibly be regarded as irrational.

2.19   It is strongly arguable that this level of deference is, by virtue of CA 2014 s1, no longer acceptable: no longer does the local authority's view on questions of this nature trump that of the individual. A different interpretation might be advanced, however – namely that although the local authority would now have to accept (absent cogent evidence to the contrary) Elaine McDonald's judgment as to the impact of continence pads on her 'personal dignity'; her 'physical and mental health and emotional well-being'; her 'control ... over day-to-day life (including over care and support ...)'; and her '... personal relationships', it could nevertheless decide on cost grounds that it would not meet this need by the provision of support at night to access her commode. Of course, this line of argument is problematic (putting it charitably – see para 4.66 below), but at the very least the local authority would be required to advance compelling reasons why its view on 'well-being' should be preferred and why its view that meeting the need by providing continence pads would not have (for the purposes of the eligibility determination) a significant impact[19] on her well-being. If, contrary to this view, a local authority is able, routinely and formulaically, to use a costs argument to trump the care and support implications of an

18 [2011] UKSC 33 – see also para 4.66 below.
19 Care and Support (Eligibility Criteria) Regulations 2015 SI No 313 regs 2(1)(c) and 3(1)(c) – see para 4.31 below.

individual's assessment of their well-being, then this would render CA 2014 s1(3)(a) devoid of any substantive value (or indeed meaning).

Dignity

2.20 As noted above (para 2.7) the Law Commission did not favour the inclusion of a duty to promote 'dignity' in the reform legislation on the ground that it was 'imprecise'. The Joint Select Committee expressed concern about its absence from the draft Care and Support Bill and the Law Commission's reasoning – observing 'that "dignity" is no less precise than some of the other factors listed, and we support its inclusion'. [20]

2.21 As a consequence, CA 2014 s1(2)(a) lists 'personal dignity (including treatment of the individual with respect)' as a component of the concept of well-being. The statutory guidance provides no substantive advice as to how 'dignity' should be interpreted in the social care context. The local government ombudsman has, however, considered the concept important in a post-CA 2014 report[21] concerning the failure of a local authority to provide support to a visually impaired adult who needed help to sort her clothes so that she did not wear stained or inappropriate clothing. In the ombudsman's opinion, a failure to 'recognise the importance to [an adult's] personal dignity of wearing clean, presentable and appropriate clothes' amounted to maladministration (see also para 4.18 below).

2.22 'Dignity' is engaged not only by a failure to provide support – but also in the way the support is provided. Commonly, a local authority may be able to satisfy a person's assessed needs in a variety of ways, and the question arises as to how austere a care package will have to be before the courts or ombudsmen will intervene. This in turn raises the question as to the standard by which the court or ombudsman would judge 'austerity' or 'disagreeability' or whatever the measure may be.

2.23 By way of example, a local authority might assess as an 'eligible need' the person's need to access the toilet. If the problem is that the existing toilet is upstairs, and the person has mobility difficulties, this 'need' could be addressed by the provision of a stair-lift, or the construction of a downstairs toilet, or merely by the provision of a commode. Likewise, a person who is unable to use his or her bath due to mobility problems may be assessed as needing to have help to keep clean – and this could be addressed by the provision of a wheelchair-accessible shower, or a specially adapted bath, or merely by an occasional 'strip/blanket' wash.

2.24 In assessing the adequacy of the service provision response, the courts and ombudsmen have resorted to the concept of 'dignity' in the context of a state's positive obligations under Article 8 of the European Convention on Human Rights (ECHR) – the duty to ensure 'respect' for individual privacy (see para 2.85 below). Accordingly, in 2003 the local government ombudsman held that the ability properly to manage bathing/washing

---

20 Joint Committee on the Draft Care and Support Bill, *Draft Care and Support Bill* HL Paper 143 HC 822, The Stationery Office, 2013, para 71.

21 Complaint 15 011 661 against London Borough of Hammersmith & Fulham 21 July 2016, para 24.

with dignity is the entitlement of everybody.[22] By this measure, a policy of only doing strip washes would arguably fail the 'dignity threshold' and amount to maladministration.[23] In *R (Bernard) v Enfield LBC*[24] the local authority's failure to act to move a wheelchair-dependent claimant, a mother of a family of six, to suitable accommodation left her (among other things) unable to access the kitchen or bathroom and forced to defecate or urinate on the floor several times a day. Sullivan J awarded damages for breach of Article 8, finding that these conditions were inimical to her family life and to her physical and psychological integrity. Providing the claimant with suitably adapted accommodation 'would have restored her dignity as a human being' (para 33).

2.25   In *R (Burke) v General Medical Council and others*[25] Munby J considered the extent to which it could be argued that the concept of human dignity is now protected by domestic law. In the analysis he cited *Price v UK*,[26] where in her concurring opinion Judge Greve stated:

> In a civilised country like the United Kingdom, society considers it not only appropriate but a basic humane concern to try to improve and compensate for the disabilities faced by a person in the applicant's situation. In my opinion, these compensatory measures come to form part of the disabled person's physical integrity.

In his earlier judgment in *R (A, B, X and Y) v East Sussex CC and the Disability Rights Commission (No 2)*[27] he had observed that the 'protection of human dignity' was a core value that the courts would protect and that in so doing this amounted to a 'solemn affirmation of the law's and of society's recognition of our humanity and of human dignity as something fundamental'.

2.26   Baroness Hale of Richmond has made much the same point:[28]

> [H]uman dignity is all the more important for people whose freedom of action and choice is curtailed, whether by law or by circumstances such as disability. The Convention is a living instrument . . . We need to be able to use it to promote respect for the inherent dignity of all human beings but especially those who are most vulnerable to having that dignity ignored. In reality, the niceties and technicalities with which we have to be involved in the courts should be less important than the core values which underpin the whole Convention.

---

22   Complaint nos 02/C/8679, 8681 and 10389 against Bolsover DC, 30 September 2003: and see also complaint no 07C03887 against Bury MBC, 14 October 2009, para 40 where the ombudsman characterised the council's inaction as 'institutional indifference' (inaction that left a mother with no option but to hose down her disabled children in the garden).

23   See para 4.22 below.

24   [2002] EWHC 2282 (Admin), (2002) 5 CCLR 577.

25   [2004] EWHC 1879 (Admin), [2005] 2 WLR 431, (2004) 7 CCLR 609.

26   (2002) 34 EHRR 1285 at 1296.

27   [2003] EWHC 167 (Admin), (2003) 6 CCLR 194 at [86].

28   'What can the Human Rights Act do for my mental health?', Paul Sieghart Memorial Lecture 2004, accessible at www.northumbriajournals.co.uk/index.php/IJMHMCL/article/viewFile/162/157. Baroness Hale used a 2002 British Institute of Human Rights report as the inspiration for her lecture – namely J Watson, *Something for everyone: The impact of the Human Rights Act and the need for a Human Rights Commission*, British Institute of Human Rights, 2002.

The requirement to make suitable arrangements to ensure the dignity, privacy and independence of service users applies to all persons registered with the Care Quality Commission (CQC) (essentially all service providers – see chapter 17). Baroness Hale referred in the *McDonald*[29] case to the findings of a CQC Review of Compliance at Ipswich Hospital NHS Trust that dignity was not always sufficiently considered because people were not taken to a toilet away from their bed-space and commodes were used all the time.[30]

2.27　　In a time of austerity economics (and in the absence of the government formulating an independent minimum standard of care) it is inevitable that the courts and the ombudsmen will increasingly be called upon to draw the 'dignity line':[31] the line below which care and support arrangements are 'undignified' to the extent that they are not acceptable in a 'civilised society'.[32]

Control and choice

2.28　　In its final (2011) report on adult social care the Law Commission[33] described 'choice and control' as 'important concepts that are relevant to many aspects of our scheme' although it considered 'that it is choice rather than control that is the key principle' (para 4.25). The duty in CA 2014 s1(2)(d) identifies 'control' as a component of 'well-being ' but makes no mention of 'choice'. Section 1(2)(d) refers to 'control by the individual over day-to-day life (including over care and support, or support, provided to the individual and the way in which it is provided)'.

2.29　　There may not be a great deal of distance between 'choice' and 'control'[34] and this is certainly the impression conveyed by the statutory guidance. It refers to 'choice' on more than 100 occasions[35] (compared to 82 references to 'control') and the phrase 'choice and control' appears 30 times and 'genuine choice' on eight occasions. The statutory guidance emphasises that 'choice ... should be interpreted widely' (para 4.42), for example in relation to such things as: the way services are delivered; who is a person's key care-worker; and arranging for providers to collaborate to ensure the right provision is available (para 4.42).

---

29 [2011] UKSC 33, (2011) 14 CCLR 341.

30 CQC, *Dignity and nutrition for older people: review of compliance Ipswich Hospital NHS Trust*, May 2011, p8.

31 '[W]here the permissible amber becomes the impermissible red' – see L Clements, 'Disability, dignity and the cri de coeur' EHRLR [2011] 6, pp675–685.

32 The dissenting speech of Lady Hale in *R (McDonald) v Kensington and Chelsea RLBC* [2011] UKSC 33, (2011) 14 CCLR 341, para 79.

33 Law Commission, *Adult social care*, Law Com No 326 HC 941, 2011.

34 Lydia Hayes, however, argues that the focus on 'control' has the potential to be used as 'tool of regressive employment reform' – see L Hayes 'Care and control: are the national minimum wage entitlements of homecare workers at risk under the Care Act 2014?' *Industrial Law Journal* (2015) 44 (4), pp 492–521.

35 Not including references to 'Choice of Accommodation' regulations (see para 8.243 below) and 'NHS Choices'.

2.30   The debate about choice is not new. In the 1966 Tunstall advocated such an approach:[36]

> An old lady whose arthritis prevents her from cooking should be able to choose between having mobile meals delivered or having her home help cook them or being transported to a club or centre to eat the meals there, or a combination of the three.

The 1989 white paper, *Caring for people*,[37] presaging the community care reforms of the 1990s, gave as one of its six key objectives, to 'increase the available range of options and widen consumer choice'. Respect for service user preferences has remained central to the rhetoric accompanying all major social care initiatives since that time. This is evident in the title of the 2005 adult social care green paper 'Independence well-being and choice'[38] and the 2010 Coalition Government's 'A vision for adult social care'[39] was premised on the idea that 'with choice and control, people's dignity and freedom is protected and their quality of life is enhanced'.[40]

2.31   'Choice' (or more strictly speaking 'preference') is only given statutory expression in the CA 2014 in section 30, which provides for regulations[41] to enable adults to express a preference for particular accommodation. The 'Choice of Accommodation' scheme is considered at para 8.243 below.

2.32   The courts have distinguished between 'preferences' and 'needs'. In *R v Avon CC ex p M*[42] the applicant, because of his learning disabilities, had formed a fixed psychological attachment to a particular home which was more expensive than the alternative proposed by the local authority. A complaints panel heard uncontroverted evidence concerning his psychological needs and unanimously recommended the placement in the more expensive home. The local authority refused. Henry J, in finding for the applicant, stated as follows:

> Here, there was a clear finding by a body set up for detailed fact finding that M's needs included his psychological needs and, unless that finding could be disposed of, the authority was liable to meet those needs. Without that finding being overthrown, there were not two options before the social services committee, as the paper suggests, there was only one: to meet M's needs, including his psychological needs.[43]

M's attachment to the particular home was a 'need' not a 'choice'. This point was picked up in *R (Khana) v Southwark LBC*[44] where the applicants

---

36 J Tunstall, *Old and alone*, Routledge and Kegan Paul, 1966, p296 cited in P Thane, *Old age in English history*, OUP, 2000, pp423–424.

37 Department of Health, *Caring for people: community care in the next decade and beyond* Cm 849, 1989.

38 Secretary of State for Health, *Independence well-being and choice* Cm 6499, TSO, 2005.

39 Department of Health, *A vision for adult social care: capable communities and active citizens*, 2010, para 4.1.

40 Department of Health, *A vision for adult social care: capable communities and active citizens*, 2010, para 4.1.

41 Care and Support and After-care (Choice of Accommodation) Regulations 2014 SI No 2670.

42 (1999) 2 CCLR 185, QBD and see also Complaint no 15 019 312 against London Borough of Barking & Dagenham, 8 June 2016 which concerned a similar fact context.

43 (1997) 2 CCLR 185 at 196E.

44 [2001] EWCA Civ 999, (2001) 4 CCLR 267.

were demanding a care plan that the local authority considered inappropriate. The Court of Appeal dealt with the claim in the following terms:

> In some circumstances, instanced by *R v Avon CC ex p M*[45] ... a person may have a need ... as distinct from a preference, to reside in a particular place. Here, it seems to me that Mrs Khana ... is in reality seeking to insist, as against Southwark, on the – no doubt strongly held – preferences or beliefs of Mrs Khana and her family as to what community services should be provided to Mrs Khana and in what way. Under the relevant legislation and guidance, Southwark must take into account Mrs Khana's and Mr Karim's beliefs and preferences, but the assessment of any needs regarding, *inter alia*, accommodation and how to provide for them rests ultimately with Southwark.[46]

2.33 The courts have, therefore, treated the principle of 'user choice', not as a fundamental right, but as a relevant consideration that must be taken into account by the authority. It is probable that this approach will continue under the CA 2014, albeit that authorities will be expected to provide more detailed reasons and supporting evidence where they decide not to agree to such a course. It follows that the preferences of an individual in relation to his or her care and/or support plan should (except in relation to choice of accommodation placements[47]):

1) be fully taken into account by the authority; and
2) be accommodated in the care and/or support plan, so long as the local authority does not consider it inappropriate or too expensive.

However, if an authority propounds a plan that does not comply with the service user's preferences, the authority must:

3) give cogent reasons for so deciding and highlight those parts of the plan where there is disagreement.

2.34 Choice is assumed here to be an unalloyed good thing, and undoubtedly for many it has proved to be so. However, research has identified two limiting factors: the need for clear information as a precondition for effectively exercising choice,[48] and the fact that increased choice tends to bring with it greater uncertainty and dissatisfaction.[49]

2.35 In relation to the first factor, the statutory guidance advises that (para 3.1):

> Information and advice is fundamental to enabling people, carers and families to take control of, and make well-informed choices about, their care and support and how they fund it. Not only does information and advice help to promote people's well-being by increasing their ability to exercise choice and control, it is also a vital component of preventing or delaying people's need for care and support.

---

45 See para 2.32 above.
46 [2001] EWCA Civ 999, (2001) 4 CCLR 267 at 281H.
47 See para 8.243 below.
48 See, for instance, K Baxter, C Glendinning, S Clarke, 'Making informed choices in social care: the importance of accessible information', *Health and Social Care in the Community* Volume 16, No 2, March 2008, pp197–207 (11).
49 Eg, S Iyengar and M Lepper, 'When choosing is demotivating: can one desire too much of a good thing?' *Journal of Personality and Social Psychology* (2000) 79, pp995–1006.

2.36   The potential for dissatisfaction with the choices available (and made) is addressed by the statutory guidance in its emphasis on adults and carers having access to 'a wide range of service provision' options 'tailored for their situation' so that they are not be faced with limited or inappropriate support choices (para 4.24). Focussing on this issue will, in the government's opinion (para 4.37):

> ... facilitate an effective open market, driving quality and cost-effectiveness so as to provide genuine choice to meet the range of needs and reasonable preferences of local people who need care and support services, including for people who choose to take direct payments, recognising, for example, the challenges presented in remote rural areas for low volume local services.

2.37   The guidance in this respect is directive – authorities (para 4.38):

> ... must encourage a range of different approaches to services to ensure people have a genuine choice of different types of service. This may be achieved by encouraging different types of service provider organisation, for example, independent private providers, third sector, voluntary and community based organisations, including user-led organisations, mutual and small businesses.

Risk management/consequences of choice

2.38   One consequence of user choice is the acceptance of risk – for which a local authority or NHS body might have misgivings, believing that it is unwise and/or likely to expose the authority to a compensation claim if harm results to the user. Guidance issued by the Department of Health in 2007[50] provided a framework aimed at helping professionals to support service users to make decisions about their own lives and manage any consequent risk in relation to such choices. It endorsed Health and Safety Executive guidance that described risk management in terms of taking 'practical steps to protect people from real harm and suffering, not about bureaucratic back covering or hiding behind the legislation when a difficult decision has to be made' (para 2.36). Its statement in relation to the law of negligence in such matters is concise (para 2.26):

> ... an individual who has the mental capacity to make a decision, and chooses voluntarily to live with a level of risk, is entitled to do so. The law will treat that person as having consented to the risk and so there will be no breach of the duty of care by professionals or public authorities. However, the local authority remains accountable for the proper use of its public funds, and whilst the individual is entitled to live with a degree of risk, the local authority is not obliged to fund it.

2.39   Councils will, on occasions, find themselves in disagreement with disabled people and their families over what is an ideal or safe system for care arrangements – such as the use of equipment. The need in such cases is for flexibility of approach so that a solution can be reached – and a failure to do so, will constitute maladministration – particularly if it leaves

---

50 Department of Health, *Independence, choice and risk: a guide to supported decision making*, 2007. See also Adult Services, SCIE Report 36 *Enabling risk, ensuring safety: self-directed support and personal budgets*, 2010.

the disabled person or carers without support.[51] In *R (A and B) v East Sussex CC (No 2)*,[52] a decision not to provide swimming or horse-riding facilities to two young adults with complex disabilities on health and safety grounds[53] because it would have necessitated some lifting, was held to be an unjustifiable breach of the individuals' ECHR Article 8 right to private life.

Independent living

2.40   As noted above, although the promotion of 'independent living' was listed as a possible principle in the Law Commission's 2010 consultation paper,[54] in its final report[55] the Commission rejected it on the basis that it was too imprecise to be expressed as statutory principles'. Although the duty on local authorities to promote 'independent living' does not appear in the CA 2014, the statutory guidance states (para 1.19):

> The well-being principle is intended to cover the key components of independent living, as expressed in the UN Convention on the Rights of People with Disabilities (in particular, Article 19 of the Convention). Supporting people to live as independently as possible, for as long as possible, is a guiding principle of the Care Act.

This affirmation is repeated at para 23.28 where it is asserted that:

> The concept of 'independent living' is a core part of the well-being principle, and is detailed in the requirement to consider the person's control over their day-to-day life, the suitability of their living accommodation and their contribution to society.

Such express statements are of considerable importance – not least because the courts and ombudsmen have shown a surprising willingness to have regard to the CRPD[56] (which the UK ratified in 2009).

2.41   By making it clear that the duty to promote 'independent living' is to be interpreted in accordance with Article 19 of the CRPD, the guidance is making an important point. In many policy documents, 'independence' is conceptualised in terms of 'self-sufficiency': of the disabled person no longer needing support or state subsidy. This is not the Article 19 conception of 'independent living'. Article 19 is predicated on the notion of 'choice' and of disabled people having a range of high-quality community-based care and support arrangements that enable them to be fully included and to fully participate in the community. Article 19 declares:

---

51   See eg Complaint no 07/B/07665 against Luton Borough Council, 10 September 2008 para 35; and see also chapter 18 which considers the associated 'safeguarding' implications of such questions.

52   [2003] EWHC 167 (Admin), (2003) 6 CCLR 194.

53   As Munby J observed in *Re MM (an adult)* [2009] 1 FLR 443, (2008) 11 CCLR 119 at para 120 – 'What good is it making someone safer if it merely makes them miserable?'. See also para 13.42 below.

54   Law Commission, *Consultation paper no 192. Adult social care*, 2010, Part 3.

55   Law Commission, *Adult social care*, Law Com No 326 HC941 2011, para 4.35.

56   See, for example, *Burnip v Birmingham City Council* [2012] EWCA Civ 629; *R (Bracking and others) v Secretary of State for Work and Pensions* [2013] EWCA Civ 1345, (20013) 16 CCLR 479; and *Cameron Mathieson v Secretary of State for Work and Pensions* [2015] UKSC 47.

States Parties to this Convention recognize the equal right of all persons with disabilities to live in the community, with choices equal to others, and shall take effective and appropriate measures to facilitate full enjoyment by persons with disabilities of this right and their full inclusion and participation in the community, including by ensuring that:

a)   Persons with disabilities have the opportunity to choose their place of residence and where and with whom they live on an equal basis with others and are not obliged to live in a particular living arrangement;

b)   Persons with disabilities have access to a range of in-home, residential and other community support services, including personal assistance necessary to support living and inclusion in the community, and to prevent isolation or segregation from the community;

c)   Community services and facilities for the general population are available on an equal basis to persons with disabilities and are responsive to their needs.

2.42   The promotion of independent living has been a core – perhaps *the* core – principle underpinning the community care legislation.[57] References to independence litter the policy documents of the last three decades, and were given quasi-statutory force in the statutory guidance in the pre-CA 2014 regime (as they have now in the statutory guidance). Under the pre-CA 2014 eligibility criteria,[58] the extent to which 'an individual's presenting needs might pose risks to their independence' was a key factor and the overall objectives of the guidance on domiciliary charging was said to be 'to promote the independence and social inclusion of service users'.[59]

2.43   Under the pre-CA 2014 regime the courts and ombudsmen also placed considerable reliance upon the principle that care and support planning should promote independent living.[60] Thus in *R v Sutton LBC ex p Tucker*[61] the fact that there was an 'effective option' for the service user's discharge from long-stay care in hospital was treated as creating an obligation to act purposefully to progress this objective. In *LLBC v TG, JG and KR* McFarlane J observed that:

Before a local authority seeks to invoke the court's powers to compel a family to place a relative in a residential care home, the court is entitled to expect that the authority will have made a genuine and reasonable attempt to carry out a full assessment of the capacity of the family to meet the relative's needs in the community.[62]

2.44   The statutory guidance reference to the key importance of the CRPD Article 19 should remove any impediment to citing decisions, reports and general comments of the Committee on the Rights of Persons with Disabilities. In any event, these will be a valuable when construing ambiguous statutory

---

57   This assertion has been cited with approval, see *R (B) v Cornwall CC* [2009] EWHC 491 (Admin), (2009) 12 CCLR 381, per Higginbottom J at para 6.

58   Department of Health, *Prioritising need in the context of putting people first* (2010) para 59.

59   Department of Health *Fairer charging policies for home care and other non-residential social services* (2003), paras 3 and 15.

60   See eg *R v Islington LBC ex p Rixon* (1997–98) 1 CCLR 119 at 128, QBD, and see also Local Government Ombudsman Complaint no 07/A/01436 against Hillingdon LBC, 18 September 2008, para 31.

61   (1997–98) 1 CCLR 251 at 255H and 274H, QBD.

62   [2007] EWHC 2640 (Fam), (2008) 11 CCLR 161 at [33].

provisions. In *Burnip v Birmingham City Council*[63] the government argued that the CRPD should not be used as an interpretative tool. In the event recourse to the CRPD proved unnecessary, however Maurice Kay LJ held that if it had been he:

> ... would have resorted to the CRDP and it would have resolved the uncertainty in favour of the appellants. It seems to me that it has the potential to illuminate our approach to both discrimination and justification.

2.45   *R (South West Care Homes) v Devon CC*[64] involved a dispute about the rate at which a local authority-funded care homes in its area and the care home owners argued that it was so low as to risk precipitating largescale care home closures. The court considered that this raised issues of fundamental rights, holding that (para 43):

> Rights for people with disability, such as the right to choose where they live and to have support so as to prevent isolation or segregation from the community, are enshrined in the UN and European Conventions. The result of the exercise might affect those rights, and in my judgment should be carried out having regard to the specific provisions of section 149[65] in mind so as to have due regard to the need to eliminate discrimination and to advance equality of opportunity.

Equality Act 2010 and independent living

2.46   The duty to promote independent living has developed to the stage that it can be seen as a core domestic and international human rights obligation. Domestically, EqA 2010 s149[66] places a duty on all public bodies to have due regard to the need to promote equality of opportunity between disabled persons (as well as others sharing a characteristic protected by EqA 2010) and other persons. In furtherance of this duty public bodies must have particular regard to the need, among other things, to 'encourage persons who share a relevant protected characteristic to participate in public life or in any other activity in which participation by such persons is disproportionately low' (EqA 2010 s149(3)(c)).

2.27   The need to promote independent living through the removal of barriers which impede that goal for disabled people is also given statutory expression domestically in EqA 2010, for example, in section 20, the duty to make reasonable adjustments, including where a provision, criterion or practice puts a disabled person at a substantial disadvantage, and in Part III of EqA 2010, dealing with services and public functions.

2.48   Previous comparable duties under the Disability Discrimination Act (DDA) 1995 were considered in *R (Lunt and another) v Liverpool City Council*.[67] In upholding the challenge to Liverpool's decision not to licence a fully wheelchair accessible form of taxi in the city, Blake J held that the duty to make reasonable adjustments to the taxi licensing policy was 'not

---

63 Consolidated appeal with *Trengrove v Walsall MBC* and *Gorry v Wiltshire CC*) [2012] EWCA Civ 629.
64 [2012] EWHC 2967 (Admin) (7 November 2012) His Honour Judge Milwyn Jarman QC (see also para 7.113 below).
65 EqA 2010 s149 – see para 2.60 below.
66 Inserted by Disability Discrimination Act 2005 s3.
67 [2009] EWHC 2356 (Admin).

... a minimal duty, but seeks broadly to put the disabled person as far as reasonably practicable in a similar position to the ambulant user of a taxi'.[68]

Human Rights Act 1998 and independent living

2.49   A powerful argument can be made that the inappropriate institutionalisation of elderly and disabled people may be contrary to the ECHR – contrary to Article 8 (right to privacy) alone or in combination with Article 14 (prohibition of discrimination). This is particularly the case given that the UK ratification of the CRPD means that it is effectively estopped from denying that such a right can be read into analogous binding conventions such as the ECHR (eg Article 8).

2.50   As yet there is no decided case that addresses this question directly, although there is relevant authority for this proposition in the form of a US Supreme Court decision, *Olmstead v LC*.[69] *Olmstead* concerned the Americans with Disabilities Act 1990 which (amongst other things) proscribes discrimination in the provision of public services. While there is no exactly equivalent legislation in England, Part III of the EqA 2010 (services and public functions) is sufficiently similar to permit comparison. *Olmstead* concerned a care planning regime in the state of Georgia, which skewed funding arrangements to favour institutional placements, rather than community based independent living placements. The applicants alleged that this constituted unlawful discrimination and the majority of the Supreme Court agreed. While the court emphasised that the financial resources of States were relevant factors in determining their policies, it stressed the importance of policies being rational and fair and of the basic principle that 'unnecessary institutionalization' should be avoided if possible. In the view of the majority:

> The identification of unjustified segregation as discrimination reflects two evident judgments: Institutional placement of persons who can handle and benefit from community settings perpetuates unwarranted assumptions that persons so isolated are incapable or unworthy of participating in community life ...

and

> ... confinement in an institution severely diminishes the everyday life activities of individuals, including family relations, social contacts, work options, economic independence, educational advancement, and cultural enrichment.

2.51   The US Supreme Court's acknowledgement that financial resources were of relevance in determining the extent of the independent living obligation raises the question of how these competing principles, 'independence' and 'cost effectiveness', should be balanced. The issue was addressed tangentially in *R (Khana) v Southwark LBC*[70] where the applicants, an elderly couple, sought judicial review of the council's decision to meet their care needs by provision of a placement in a residential care home. The

---

68 [2009] EWHC 2356 (Admin), para 59.
69 527 US 581 (1999).
70 [2001] EWCA Civ 999, (2001) 4 CCLR 267.

applicants wanted (for personal and cultural reasons) to live in the community independently in a home of their own with the support of their relatives and the statutory services. The court held that the pre-CA 2014 assessment duty (which was effectively the same as that under the CA 2014):

> ... contemplate[s] an assessment by the local authority of a person's accommodation needs, which takes very full account of their wishes, including the very fundamental aim of preserving the independence of elderly people in the community and in their own homes for as long and as fully as possible. A certain degree of risk-taking is often acceptable, rather than compromise independence and break family or home links. But, where a local authority concludes, as Southwark did here, that 'the only way in which Mrs Khana's needs can properly be met is for her to go into a full time residential home', and makes a corresponding offer, and where this assessment and the reasonableness of the offer made cannot be challenged as such, then the local authority has in my judgment satisfied its duties under the legislation.[71]

2.52   The judgment confirms that the default position for any support plan is the promotion of independent living and that only where the social care authority concludes for professional (ie not solely financial) reasons that independent living is not viable, is it reasonable for it to propound an institutional care plan. The strong presumption in favour of independent living (over and above financial considerations) comes additionally from the positive obligations imposed by ECHR Article 8:[72] to take action to 'the greatest extent feasible to ensure that they have access to essential economic and social activities and to an appropriate range of recreational and cultural activities' to ensure that their lives are not 'so circumscribed and so isolated as to be deprived of the possibility of developing [their] personality'.[73] Such compensatory measures, as Judge Greve observed in *Price v UK*,[74] are fundamental to disabled people's ECHR Article 8 rights.

Cost effectiveness

2.53   While *R (Khana) v Southwark LBC* suggests that the promotion of 'independent living' is a principle to be accorded considerable weight, it is less clear as to how the balance is to be struck between 'cost effectiveness' and 'user preferences'.

2.54   A starting point would appear to be that if an authority is asserting resource constraints as a reason for rejecting a user's preferred option, it cannot assume that the court or ombudsman will accept these as self-evident: in such cases, as Mance LJ has observed,[75] 'any problem

---

71   [2001] EWCA Civ 999, (2001) 4 CCLR 267 at 281K.

72   See, eg, the observations made by Collins J in *Gunter v South West Staffordshire PCT* [2005] EWHC 1894 (Admin), (2006) 9 CCLR 121 at [20].

73   Per Commissioner Bratza (as he then was) in *Botta v Italy* (1998) 26 EHRR 241, (1999) 2 CCLR 53 and cited by Munby J in *R (A, B, X and Y) v East Sussex CC* [2003] EWHC 167, (2003) 6 CCLR 194 at [102] and see also *R (T, D and B) v Haringey LBC* [2005] EWHC 2235 (Admin), (2006) 9 CCLR 58.

74   (2002) 34 EHRR 53.

75   *R (Khana) v Southwark LBC* [2001] EWCA Civ 999, (2001) 4 CCLR 267 at 282I; see also *Sabah Mohamoud v Greenwich LBC* January 2003 *Legal Action* 23 where impatience was expressed concerning unspecified and 'general assertions' of a similar nature (albeit in a housing context).

of resources would require to be made out by evidence, and cannot be assumed to be present'.

2.55   The assessment process may identify needs which are capable of being met by two or more alternative support packages. In such situations it is not unreasonable for the authority to consider the relative cost of each option. However, if objectively the cheaper option does not meet an assessed need (for instance, because it fails to provide for sufficiently skilled support to address the person's need, or is not in a location where the person is assessed as needing to be, or separates spouses/partners against their will etc) then the local authority cannot opt for that placement and cannot ask for 'top-ups' (see para 8.252 below).

2.56   Authorities are not obliged to choose the cheapest care and/or support plan, but if the less expensive plan is favoured, a number of factors must be considered. First, if the choice concerns a care setting covered by the choice of accommodation regulations, then special rules may apply (see para 8.252). Second, if the cheaper option is within an institutional setting, it may be trumped by the 'independent living' obligation. Finally, if in so deciding the authority rejects a user's preferred support package, it is obliged to (a) give cogent reasons for its decision (not least because the authority may have misunderstood the costing implications[76]), and (b) be able to identify its preferred support package – in the sense that such a package must actually exist, rather than being a hypothetical alternative.[77]

2.57   In constructing a support plan, the issue of resources (the 'cheaper option') only arises if there is objectively a real and present choice of care packages available – which was not the case in *R v Avon CC ex p M*[78] (considered above) or indeed in *R v Sutton LBC ex p Tucker*[79] which concerned a Rubella-impaired applicant. The local authority favoured a home in Birmingham run by the specialist charity SENSE, but the applicant's family, clinicians and indeed the SENSE staff considered that this would not be viable since she needed to be close to her family in Sutton, where unfortunately no such facility existed. The authority balked at the cost of commissioning a purpose-created unit solely for the applicant; the net result being that nothing concrete happened and she remained inappropriately placed in short-term NHS accommodation. In the judicial review proceedings, the authority sought to explain their inaction by reference to the family's unreasonable refusal of a care option – namely the placement in Birmingham. Hidden J disagreed. This was not a situation where there was a choice of care plans; indeed this was a case where there was no care plan at all. In his view, the authority's preference for the Birmingham placement was untenable and a local placement was the only option. Since there was no 'choice of care plan' the issue of resources was not relevant and the local authority had to prepare a plan to this effect.

2.58   Another difficulty may concern the question of net versus gross costs. A care option that is more expensive in gross terms (ie to UK plc) may be

76 *R (Alloway) v Bromley LBC* [2004] EWHC 2108 (Admin), (2005) 8 CCLR 61.
77 *R (LH and MH) v Lambeth LBC* [2006] EWHC 1190 (Admin), (2006) 9 CCLR 622 (in this case the choice of the parent carer).
78 (1999) 2 CCLR 185, QBD.
79 (1997–98) 1 CCLR 251, QBD.

less expensive in net cost terms to the authority (because, for example, part of the cost is met by another state funding stream, or by the individual). This difficulty was identified by the Audit Commission in 1996:

> The financial incentive for authorities to use residential care remains strong. In nearly all situations it is substantially cheaper for local authorities to place people in residential care, even where there is no difference between the gross cost of residential care and care at home.[80]

In such an analysis it would presumably be unreasonable for an authority to take into account the service user's likely financial contribution. Although there appears to be no authority on this point, to permit this could have a seriously distorting influence: for instance, the net cost to an authority of placing a person with capital into residential accommodation could in many situations be nil.

Public sector equality duty

2.59 The following paragraphs provide an overview of the key elements of the PSED. Reference to this duty is made throughout this book.

2.60 Section 149 of the EqA 2010 provides:

(1) A public authority must, in the exercise of its functions, have due regard to the need to–
   (a) eliminate discrimination, harassment, victimisation and any other conduct that is prohibited by or under this Act;
   (b) advance equality of opportunity between persons who share a relevant protected characteristic and persons who do not share it;
   (c) foster good relations between persons who share a relevant protected characteristic and persons who do not share it.
(2) A person who is not a public authority but who exercises public functions must, in the exercise of those functions, have due regard to the matters mentioned in subsection (1).
(3) Having due regard to the need to advance equality of opportunity between persons who share a relevant protected characteristic and persons who do not share it involves having due regard, in particular, to the need to–
   (a) remove or minimise disadvantages suffered by persons who share a relevant protected characteristic that are connected to that characteristic;
   (b) take steps to meet the needs of persons who share a relevant protected characteristic that are different from the needs of persons who do not share it;
   (c) encourage persons who share a relevant protected characteristic to participate in public life or in any other activity in which participation by such persons is disproportionately low.
(4) The steps involved in meeting the needs of disabled persons that are different from the needs of persons who are not disabled include, in particular, steps to take account of disabled persons' disabilities.
(5) Having due regard to the need to foster good relations between persons who share a relevant protected characteristic and persons who do not share it involves having due regard, in particular, to the need to–

---

80 Audit Commission, *Balancing the care equation*, HMSO, 1996, para 40.

(a) tackle prejudice, and

(b) promote understanding.

(6) Compliance with the duties in this section may involve treating some persons more favourably than others; but that is not to be taken as permitting conduct that would otherwise be prohibited by or under this Act.

(7) The relevant protected characteristics are–

age; disability; gender reassignment; pregnancy and maternity; race; religion or belief; sex; sexual orientation.

(8) A reference to conduct that is prohibited by or under this Act includes a reference to–

(a) a breach of an equality clause or rule;

(b) a breach of a non-discrimination rule.

(9) Schedule 18 (exceptions[81]) has effect

2.61   The PSED duty is about process. When the duty is engaged, public bodies must genuinely and conscientiously apply their minds to the promotion of equality: to the elimination discrimination, the advancement of equality of opportunity and the fostering of good relations. It is, however, a duty to have 'due regard' to the statutory objectives in EqA 2010 s149 and not a substantive obligation in the sense that this must 'achieve a result'.[82]

2.62   In *R (Brown) v Secretary of State for Work and Pensions*[83] the Administrative Court identified six key principles associated with the PSED. Although these related to a disability discrimination claim (under what was then Disability Discrimination Act 1995 s49A) they read across into discrimination engaging all other 'protected characteristics' under EqA 2010 s149.[84] These key principles can be summarised as follows:

1) **A general obligation.** The duty to have 'due regard' to requirements of EqA 2010 s149 is 'broad and wide ranging' (para 35) and arises in many routine situations, essentially whenever a public body is exercising a public function, including an exercise of judgment that might affect disabled people.[85]

2) **Consideration before decision made.** The consideration of the potential impact of the decision must take place 'before and at the time that a particular policy that will or might affect disabled people is being considered by the public authority in question' and 'involves a conscious approach and state of mind'.[86] As the court noted in *Brown*, 'attempts to justify a decision as being consistent with the exercise of the duty when it was not, in fact, considered before the decision, are not enough to discharge the duty'.[87]

81 These are essentially the English, Welsh and Scottish legislatures, the General Synod , the security/intelligence services, and elements of the armed forces.

82 *R (Karia) v Leicester City Council* [2014] EWHC 3105 (Admin).

83 [2008] EWHC 3158 (Admin) at [84]–[96].

84 For an excellent review of the duty, see J Halford and S Khan, 'The Equality Act 2010: a source of rights in a climate of cuts?' Discrimination Law Association Briefing 584 v42, March 2011, pp11–16; and see also E Mitchell, '*Pieretti v Enfield LBC*', *Social Care Law Today*, Issue 78, December 2010.

85 *Pieretti v Enfield LBC* [2010] EWCA Civ 1104, (2010) 13 CCLR 650.

86 At para 91; and see *R (Elias) v Secretary of State for Defence* [2006] 1 WLR 3213 para 274 and *R (C) v Secretary of State for Justice* [2008] EWCA Civ 882 para 49.

87 See *R (C) v Secretary of State for Justice* [2008] EWCA Civ 882 para 49.

3) **The duty is a substantial one.** The word 'due' is of importance.[88] It is not enough to 'have regard' to the duty – the public body must pay this 'due regard'. This means that it is a duty of 'substance' that must be exercised 'with rigour and with an open mind'; it is 'not a question of "ticking boxes"'.[89] Although the courts will be wary of 'micro challenges' to 'macro decisions',[90] nevertheless, where the impact of the policy is potentially 'devastating' for disabled people, then in order to satisfy the 'due regard' obligation the review process must be more than 'a 'high level and generalised' description of the likely impact of' the policy – it must make 'some attempt at assessment of the practical impact on those' who would be affected.[91] In such cases, even where the council is facing severe resource constraints the adoption of a fixed view that financially there is 'no more room for manoeuvre' might itself be irrational[92] – as Sedley LJ phrased the question in *R (Domb) v Hammersmith and Fulham LBC*[93] 'can a local authority, by tying its own fiscal hands for electoral ends, rely on the consequent budgetary deficit to modify its performance of its statutory duties?'

The duty does not, however, oblige authorities to 'take steps themselves, or to achieve results' (para 84). It is not a duty to eliminate discrimination or to promote equality of opportunity and good relations – but a duty to have 'due regard to the need to achieve these goals'.[94] Where, however, the decision may have an adverse impact on the goals advocated by EqA 2010 s149, then the public body should consider what it can feasibly do to mitigate this negative impact. In such cases it is 'incumbent upon the borough to consider the measures to avoid that impact before fixing on a particular solution'.[95]

---

88 See eg *R (Meany, Glynn and Saunders) v Harlow DC* [2009] EWHC 559 (Admin) where it was held that the word 'due' must 'add something' and that 'a reduction in almost any community services is likely disproportionately to affect minority groups' – and that the equality duty is to pay 'due regard' to the 'need' (amongst other things) to eliminate unlawful discrimination and to promote equality of opportunity: and see also *R (Rahman) v Birmingham CC* [2011] EWHC 944 (Admin) where it was held that 'even where the context of decision making is financial resources in a tight budget, that does not excuse compliance with the PSEDs and indeed there is much to be said for the proposition that even in the straightened times the need for clear, well-informed decision making when assessing the impacts on less advantaged members of society is as great, if not greater'.

89 Para 92; and see *R (Kaur and Shah) v Ealing LBC* [2008] EWHC 2062 (Admin) at paras 24–25; see also *R (Boyejo and others) v Barnet LBC and Portsmouth CC* [2009] EWHC 3261 (Admin), (2010) 13 CCLR 72.

90 *R (W) v Birmingham CC* [2011] EWHC 1147 (Admin), (2011) 14 CCLR 516 para 161.

91 *R (W) v Birmingham CC* [2011] EWHC 1147 (Admin), (2011) 14 CCLR 516 paras 157 and 183.

92 *R (W) v Birmingham CC* [2011] EWHC 1147 (Admin), (2011) 14 CCLR 516 paras 182–183.

93 [2009] EWCA Civ 941 para 80.

94 *R (Baker) v Secretary of State for Communities and Local Government* [2008] EWCA Civ 141.

95 *R (Kaur and Shah) v Ealing LBC* [2008] EWHC 2026 (Admin) para 43.

The court in *R (Bracking) v Secretary of State for Work and Pensions*[96] approved the following summary of the case-law concerning what having 'due regard' to the PSED means:[97]

(a) The promotion of equality is concerned with issues of substantive equality and requires a more penetrating consideration than whether there has been a breach of the principle of non-discrimination.[98]

(b) 'Due regard' means analysis of the material available with the specific statutory consideration in mind.[99] A bare assertion that this has been done may not be sufficient.[100]

(c) The duty must be brought to the attention of decision-makers, and the court must be able to discern that due regard has been had to the specific elements in play.[101]

(d) The nature of the duty is informed by the provisions of the UN CRPD.[102]

(e) Defective information-gathering prior to a decision being made may result in inadequate consideration of the PSED.[103]

(f) An equality impact assessment is neither a necessary measure before due regard is had, or a sufficient one if the particular assessment does not provide the relevant information, but it is likely to be a useful tool as indeed may be consultation.[104]

4) **A non-delegable duty.** In *Brown* the court considered that it would be possible for another body to undertake the 'practical steps to fulfil a policy' but in such cases the relevant public authority would have to maintain 'a proper supervision over the third party to ensure it carries out its 'due regard' duty' (para 94).

5) **It is a continuing duty.**

6) **Duty to record.** Public authorities must keep 'an adequate record showing that they had actually considered their disability equality duties and pondered relevant questions'.[105] In *R (JL) v Islington LBC*[106] the council

---

96 [2013] EWHC 897 (Admin).

97 *R (Bracking and others) v Secretary of State for Work and Pensions* [2013] EWHC 897 (Admin) para 32; and see also [2013] EWCA Civ 1345, 16 CCLR 479.

98 *R (Baker) v Secretary of State for the Environment* [2008] EWCA Civ 141 at [30].

99 *Harris v Haringey LBC* [2010] EWCA Civ 703 at [40].

100 *R (JL) v Islington LBC* [2009] EWHC 458 Admin at [113]–[123]; *R (Equality and Human Rights Commission) v Secretary of State for Justice* [2010] EWHC 147 (Admin) at [48]–[53].

101 *R (Hurley and Moore) v Secretary of State for Business Innovation and Skills* [2012] EWHC 201 Admin at 96; *R (Rahman) v Birmingham City Council* [2011] EWHC 944 Admin at [31], [57].

102 *Burnip v Birmingham CC* [2012] EWCA Civ 629 at [19] to [22]; *AH v West London Mental Health Trust and Secretary of State Justice* [2011] UKUT 74; and see also *R (Carmichael and others) v Secretary of State for Work and Pensions* [2016] UKSC 58.

103 *R (JM) v Isle of Wight Council* [2011] EWHC 2911 (Admin), (2012) 12 CCLR 413 at 118–119, 122, 126, 140; *Lunt v Liverpool City Council* [2009] EWHC 2356 Admin, [2010] 1 CMLR 14.

104 *R (Kaur) v Ealing LBC* [2008] EWHC 2062 Admin.

105 See eg *R (Bapio Action Ltd) v Secretary of State for the Home Department* [2007] EWHC 199 (Admin) para 69; and *R (Eisai Ltd) v National Institute for Health and Clinical Excellence* [2007] EWHC 1941 (Admin), (2007) 10 CCLR 638 paras 92 and 94.

106 [2009] EWHC 458 (Admin) para 121.

claimed it had considered its public sector equality duty but Black J found against it on the grounds (amongst others) that there was 'no audit trail' to establish this and 'no documentation to demonstrate a proper approach to the question'.

2.63 Regulations have been issued detailing the procedural obligations on public bodies concerning (among other things) the content, the nature of the consultation and publication of materials concerning their discharge of their PSEDs.[107] The Equality and Human Rights Commission has published a number of guides on exercise of the duty.[108]

Human Rights Act 1998 duties

2.64 HRA 1998 s6(1) makes it unlawful for a public authority to act in a way which is incompatible with a right under the ECHR.[109] Section 6(3) states that a public authority includes 'any person certain of whose functions are functions of a public nature' and section 6(6) provides that an 'act' (for the purposes of section 6(1)) includes a failure to act – and so inactivity by a public authority can violate a convention right (and see also para 20.144 below). Section 7 provides that a person who claims that a public authority has acted (or proposes to act) in a way which is made unlawful by section 6(1) may take proceedings against the authority, or rely on the convention right or rights concerned in any legal proceedings provided he or she is (or would be) a victim of the unlawful act.

Convention rights

2.65 The ECHR rights of most relevance in the context of social care law are Articles 2 (right to life), 3 (prohibition of torture or inhuman or degrading treatment or punishment), 5 (right to liberty and security), 6 (right to a fair trial), 8 (right to respect for private and family life) and 14 (prohibition of discrimination). These Articles are considered elsewhere in this book and what follows is a brief summary of the general scope of the rights.

2.66 Often a set of facts will suggest a violation of more than one Article of the convention. For instance, a 2008 ombudsmen's complaint[110] concerned mistreatment of a profoundly disabled care home resident, who had been neglected such that he had been left locked in his bedroom overnight, had poor dental health and had been left in a chair for some

---

107 Equality Act 2010 (Specific Duties) Regulations 2011 SI No 2260.

108 These include: *The essential guide to the public sector equality duty: England and non-devolved public authorities in Scotland and Wales* (2014); *Meeting the equality duty in policy and decision-making* (2014); *Engagement and the equality duty: a guide for public authorities* (2014); *Objectives and the equality duty: a guide for public authorities* (2014); *Equality information and the equality duty: a guide for public authorities* (2014); and *Technical guidance on the public sector equality duty England* (2014).

109 The HRA 1998 refers to these as 'Convention rights' which it lists in Schedule 1 – Article 13 is not included for technical reasons in this list.

110 Complaint nos 03/A/04618 and HS-2608 against Buckinghamshire CC and Oxfordshire and Buckinghamshire Mental Health Partnership Trust (respectively) 17 March 2008.

time, cold, unwashed, unshaven and with his clothes covered in faeces and urine – with the staff offering no explanation, apology or help. These facts, in the opinion of the ombudsmen, engaged Articles 3, 8 and 14.

Article 2: the right to life

2.67   ECHR Article 2, although primarily negative in nature (ie requiring the state to refrain from arbitrarily killing people[111]) has also been held to place a positive obligation on the state to protect life.[112] For example, in *Savage v South Essex Partnership NHS Foundation Trust*[113] (a case concerning a claim for damages against the NHS for failing to prevent the suicide of a psychiatric patient) it was held that the duty arose where there was 'a real and immediate risk to life about which the authorities knew or ought to have known at the time' and the duty on the authority was then 'to do all that reasonably could have been expected of them to prevent that risk'.[114]

2.68   Cases also occur concerning actions by health and social services authorities which might be harmful, such as the closure of dementia wards or residential care homes (see para 7.160 below), as well as decisions not to provide treatment for people with serious illness, such as the decision in *R v Cambridge Health Authority ex p B*[115] considered at para 11.19 below.

2.69   The Article 2 obligation extends to a requirement that there is an effective investigation into death where there is arguably a breach of the duty to protect life.[116] Following the increase in the use of Deprivation of Liberty Safeguards (DOLS) as a result of the decision of the Supreme Court in *P v Cheshire West and Cheshire Council*[117] (see para 13.89 below) the Chief Coroner has issued guidance for coroners in which he advises that, subject to consideration by the High Court, he is of the view that deaths while a DOLS authorisation is in force fall within Coroners and Justice Act 2009 s48(2) and therefore that there must be an inquest, although generally not under Article 2: 'The Article 2 procedural duty may, however, arguably arise where the death is not from natural causes and/or the fact of detention under DOLS may be a relevant factor in the cause of death.'[118]

2.70   Violations of the obligations under Article 2 have been found in cases such as the failure to protect a vulnerable prisoner from a dangerous cellmate[119] and may require individuals to be warned if exposed to any serious environmental or health risks.[120] The European Commission of Human Rights has considered the extent of the state's obligation to reduce the risks

---

111 *McCann v UK* (1995) 21 EHRR 97.

112 *Osman v UK*, Application no 23452/94, (1998) EHRR 245 at 305 – and see generally L Clements and J Read, *Disabled people and the right to life*, Routledge, 2007.

113 [2008] UKHL 74, (2009) 12 CCLR 125.

114 [2008] UKHL 74, (2009) 12 CCLR 125 para 100, citing *Keenan v UK* (2001) 33 EHRR 913, 958 para 92.

115 [1995] 1 WLR 898, CA.

116 *R (Middleton) v West Somerset Coroner* [2004] UKHL 10, [2004] 2 AC 182.

117 [2014] UKSC 19, (2014) 17 CCLR 5.

118 HHJ Peter Thornton QC, *Chief Coroners guidance no 16: DOLS* issued 5 December 2014, para 63.

119 *Edwards v UK* (2002) 35 EHRR 19.

120 *LCB v UK* (1998) 27 EHRR 212.

of a vaccination programme[121] or to fund a health service.[122] There are, however, limits to the obligation under Article 2; it cannot, for instance, be construed to provide a right for an incapacitated adult to have another assist her in dying (*Pretty v UK*[123]).

Article 3: degrading treatment

2.71 As with Article 2, ECHR Article 3 is also primarily negative in its scope – requiring states to refrain from subjecting anyone to torture, inhuman and degrading treatment. It too, however, has been held to place a positive obligation on the state to take reasonable measures to ensure no one is subjected to such treatment.

2.72 The court has emphasised that for treatment to be 'degrading' it must reach a minimum threshold of severity,[124] although it has indicated that this may be significantly lower for disabled[125] and elderly people.[126] Arbitrary and gross acts of discrimination may exceptionally be considered to violate Article 3, even in the absence of actual physical or mental harm.[127] The negative obligations under Article 3 are engaged by detention conditions,[128] corporal punishment[129] and poor detention conditions.[130] Extradition may violate Article 3 if the expelled person is thereby put at risk of degrading treatment: even (exceptionally) if solely a consequence of inadequate medical treatment in the receiving country.[131]

2.73 *Đorđević v Croatia*[132] concerned the harassment by school children of an adult with learning disabilities and his mother, with whom he lived. The police and authorities were aware of this harassment, but took no effective action. The court held that for a positive obligation to arise under Article 3, it had to be established that: (1) the authorities knew or ought to have known at the time of the existence of a real and immediate risk of ill-treatment of an identified individual from the criminal acts of a third party; and (2) that the authorities failed to take measures within the scope of their powers which, judged reasonably, might have been expected to avoid that risk. Given the facts and the finding by the court that 'no serious attempt was made to assess the true nature of the situation complained of ... the lack of any true involvement of the social services ... [and that] no counselling has been provided to the [learning disabled] applicant' it found a violation of Article 3.

---

121 *Association X v UK* DR 14/31.
122 *Osman v UK*, Application No 23452/94, (1998) 29 EHRR 245.
123 (2002) 35 EHRR 1; and see also domestic proceedings at [2001] UKHL 61, [2001] 3 WLR 1598.
124 *Costello-Roberts v UK* (1993) 19 EHRR 112.
125 *Price v UK* (2001) 34 EHRR 1285, (2002), 5 CCLR 306.
126 See *Papon v France* [2001] Crim LR 917, an inadmissibility decision.
127 See *Cyprus v Turkey* (2002) 35 EHRR 30 and *Patel v UK* ('the East African Asians' case) (1981) 3 EHRR 76.
128 *McGlinchley v UK* (2003) 37 EHRR 41.
129 *Campbell and Cosans v UK* (1982) 2 EHRR 293.
130 *Napier v Scottish Ministers* (2001) *Times* 15 November; and see also *Price v UK* (2001) 34 EHRR 1285, (2002) 5 CCLR 306.
131 *D v UK* (1997) 24 EHRR 423.
132 Application no 41526/10, (2012) 15 CCLR 657.

2.74   Article 3 has been construed as creating a positive obligation on states to ensure that no one suffers from degrading treatment. The case-law on Article 3 has established that the courts and social services are obliged to use their powers to protect children[133] and vulnerable adults[134] from abuse. Where credible evidence exists that an individual has suffered abuse while in the care of a public authority, a positive obligation arises under Article 3 for an independent and open investigation to be convened[135] and for positive police/prosecution action to bring the perpetrators to justice.[136]

2.75   *Price v UK*[137] concerned a thalidomide-impaired applicant who in the course of debt recovery proceedings refused to answer questions put to her, and was committed to prison for seven days for contempt of court. She alleged that she suffered degrading treatment as a result of the prison's inadequate facilities, but the UK government argued that any discomfort she experienced had not reached the minimum level of severity required by Article 3. The court, however, considered that the threshold depended 'on all the circumstances of the case, such as the duration of the treatment, its physical and mental effects and, in some cases, the sex, age and state of health of the victim', and after a thorough review it concluded:

> ... that to detain a severely disabled person in conditions where she is dangerously cold, risks developing sores because her bed is too hard or unreachable, and is unable to go to the toilet or keep clean without the greatest of difficulty, constitutes degrading treatment contrary to Article 3.

Of particular interest was the concurring opinion of Judge Greve, in which she stated:

> It is obvious that restraining any non-disabled person to the applicant's level of ability to move and assist herself, for even a limited period of time, would amount to inhuman and degrading treatment – possibly torture. In a civilised country like the United Kingdom, society considers it not only appropriate but a basic humane concern to try to ameliorate and compensate for the disabilities faced by a person in the applicant's situation. In my opinion, these compensatory measures come to form part of the disabled person's bodily integrity.

Article 5: detention

2.76   ECHR Article 5(1) places a total prohibition upon a state's power to detain people except in six clearly defined instances, including under Article 5(1)(e) 'the lawful detention of persons for the prevention of the spreading of infectious diseases, of persons of unsound mind, alcoholics or drug addicts or vagrants'. A substantial body of case-law exists concerning the convention requirements that must be satisfied before a mental health service user can be legally detained, and the Mental Health Act (MHA) 1983 was largely a response to a number of adverse Strasbourg

---

133 *Z and others v UK* (2002) 34 EHRR 97.

134 *In re F (adult: court's jurisdiction)* [2000] 3 WLR 1740, (2000) 3 CCLR 210, CA.

135 *Assenov v Bulgaria* (1998) 28 EHRR 652.

136 See eg *R (B) v DPP* [2009] EWHC 106 (Admin) where a decision by the Crown Prosecution Service not to prosecute (because the victim had mental health problems) was held to violate Article 3 (and the court awarded the victim £8,000 compensation).

137 (2001) 34 EHRR 1285, (2002) 5 CCLR 306.

judgments.[138] Increasingly, the court is requiring detention under this ground to be accompanied by a suitably therapeutic environment.[139]

2.77   In *Winterwerp v Netherlands*[140] and a series of subsequent cases,[141] the court has laid down a number of factors which must be satisfied before the detention of a person of unsound mind is lawful within the meaning of the ECHR, including:

1) The mental disorder must be reliably established by objective medical expertise.
2) The nature or degree of the disorder must be sufficiently extreme to justify the detention.
3) The detention should only last as long as the medical disorder (and its required severity) persists.
4) If the detention is potentially indefinite, then there must be a system of periodic reviews by a tribunal that has power to discharge.
5) The detention must be in a hospital, clinic or other appropriate institution authorised for the detention of such persons.[142]

2.78   Anyone detained for the purposes of Article 5 must be so detained 'in accordance with a procedure prescribed by law'. *HL v UK*[143] concerned a challenge to a decision of the House of Lords, known as the *Bournewood* case.[144] The European Court held that the lack of any procedural protection for 'informally detained' patients[145] who lacked the capacity to consent, but were compliant violated Article 5(1) and it rejected the UK's argument that such people were not 'detained', stating:

> ... the right to liberty is too important in a democratic society for a person to lose the benefit of Convention protection for the single reason that he may have given himself up to be taken into detention ... especially when it is not disputed that that person is legally incapable of consenting to, or disagreeing with, the proposed action.

2.79   In the Strasbourg court's opinion, he was detained because he was 'under continuous supervision and control and was not free to leave': it was 'not determinative whether the ward was 'locked' or 'lockable': a person could be detained, 'even during a period when he was in an open ward with regular unescorted access to the unsecured hospital grounds and unescorted leave outside the hospital'.

2.80   The *Bournewood* decision led to the introduction of the DOLS procedure as part of the MCA 2005, and the implications of this judgment are considered further in chapter 13 below.

---

138 See eg *X v UK* (1981) 4 EHRR 188; *Ashingdane v UK* (1985) 7 EHRR 528; and *Winterwerp v Netherlands* (1979) 2 EHRR 387.
139 *Aerts v Belgium* (1998) 29 EHRR 50.
140 (1979) 2 EHRR 387.
141 See eg *X v UK* (1981) 4 EHRR 188; and *Ashingdane v UK* (1985) 7 EHRR 528.
142 *Ashingdane v UK* (1985) 7 EHRR 528 at [44]; and see *Aerts v Belgium* (1998) 29 EHRR 50 where the court found a violation of Article 5(1) in relation to the detention of the applicant in the psychiatric wing of a prison which was not an 'appropriate establishment' in view of the lack of qualified personnel.
143 (2005) 40 EHRR 32.
144 *R v Bournewood Community and Mental Health NHS Trust ex p L* [1998] 3 WLR 107, (1997–98) 1 CCLR 390, HL.
145 Ie detained under MHA 1983 s131.

Article 6: fair hearing

2.81   Article 6(1) entrenches the right of parties to a fair hearing when their civil rights are affected (or when charged with a criminal offence). It requires hearings to be before 'independent and impartial' tribunals and to be held within a 'reasonable time' which may require 'exceptional diligence' to ensure early listing.[146]

2.82   The right to a fair hearing may require the state to take positive action to ensure legal or advocacy assistance is available to a party under a disability. As the court observed in *Airey v Ireland*:[147]

> ... the fulfilment of a duty under the Convention on occasion necessitates some positive action on the part of the State; in such circumstances, the State cannot simply remain passive ... The obligation to secure an effective right of access to the courts falls into this category of duty.

2.83   *Re H*[148] concerned an unrepresented mother who had been refused legal aid and had a hearing, speech and learning difficulties and was opposed in child protection proceedings by the father and local authority who were legally represented. In the court's opinion, the refusal created a clear danger of a breach of Articles 6 and 8 (see below). In a similar vein, in *Re D (a child)*[149] the court considered that the financial rules that made legal aid unavailable for individuals on low incomes (in this case, parents with learning difficulties) who wanted to challenge the permanent removal of their child for adoption. Given their impairments, it held that legal aid was essential in order to satisfy the requirements of Articles 6 and 8 (see below).

2.84   In *R (Beeson) v Dorset CC*[150] the Court of Appeal held that the, then local authority statutory complaints procedure, coupled with the availability of judicial review, satisfied the requirements for impartiality and independence in Article 6(1).

Article 8: private life, family and home

2.85   The court has consistently defined ECHR Article 8 as positive in nature.[151] This arises out of the presence of the word 'respect': rather than obliging states 'not to interfere' with private and family life, Article 8(1) provides that 'everyone has the right to respect for his private and family life, his home and his correspondence'. The demonstration of 'respect' is inherently positive in nature.

2.86   While family life, the home and correspondence have been given their everyday meanings, the concept of 'private life' has acquired an altogether more expansive interpretation, including a 'person's physical and psychological integrity' for which respect is due in order to 'ensure the development, without outside interference, of the personality of each individual

---

146 *H v UK* (1988) 10 EHRR 95; see also *P and D v UK* [1996] EHRLR 526.
147 (1979) 2 EHRR 305.
148 A County Court Family Court Case (Middlesborough No: MB13P01405) Judge Hallam 14/08/2014 (Lawtel).
149 [2014] EWFC 39.
150 [2002] EWCA Civ 1812, (2003) 6 CCLR 5
151 *Marckx v Belgium* (1979) 2 EHRR 330.

in his relations with other human beings'.[152] The reduction of social care support for a disabled person has been held to engage Article 8(1)[153] and accordingly to be subject to the requirement (see below) that it be done 'in accordance with the law' and to be proportionate.[154] Article 8 has also been held to be engaged in cases concerning sexual rights,[155] environmental pollution,[156] physical barriers to movement,[157] access to files[158] and information about one's illness.[159] In the context of the rights of disabled people, in *R (A & B) v East Sussex CC (No 2)*[160] Munby J described the right to private life as involving dignity and:

> ... the right of the disabled to participate in the life of the community and to have what has been described (in the *Botta v Italy* case) as 'access to essential economic and social activities and to an appropriate range of recreational and cultural activities'. This is matched by the positive obligation of the State to take appropriate measures designed to ensure to the greatest extent feasible that a disabled person is not 'so circumscribed and so isolated as to be deprived of the possibility of developing his personality' (para 99).

2.87   Article 8 is a 'qualified right' in that state interference with the right is permitted, but only where the interference is 'lawful' and is done in a proportionate way in pursuance of a legitimate aim. Although Article 8(2) provides an exhaustive list of six legitimate aims, these are so widely drawn (including, for example, action which protects the rights and freedoms of others, action for economic reasons, or to protect morals or to prevent crime) that in general the court will have little difficulty in finding any 'interference' with Article 8(1) pursues a legitimate aim.

2.88   It is, however, in respect of the second limb of the test that public bodies have most difficulty. They must establish that what they did, not only had a legitimate aim, but also that it was 'proportionate'. Although there is substantial jurisprudence concerning the concept of 'proportionality', the key principles of most relevance in a social welfare context concern the need for the action to be 'the least restrictive interference' commensurate with the legitimate aim pursued, and also that overall the action be 'balanced'.

2.89   In *Gaskin v UK*[161] the applicant sought access to his social services records. The request was refused in part on the ground that some of the information had originally been given in confidence and the law at that time did not permit disclosure of information where such third parties had not provided their consent to the disclosure. The information was important to Mr Gaskin as he had spent almost all his life in care and he wanted it for identity purposes. His was a legitimate claim, as indeed was

---

152 *Botta v Italy* (1998) 26 EHRR 241, (1999) 2 CCLR 53.
153 *McDonald v UK* App 4241/12, [2014] ECHR 492, (2014) 17 CCLR 187 at [47].
154 At [47].
155 *Norris v Ireland* (1988) 13 EHRR 186.
156 *Hatton v UK* (2001) 34 EHRR 1.
157 *Botta v Italy* (1998) 26 EHRR 241, (1999) 2 CCLR 53.
158 *Gaskin v UK* (1989) 12 EHRR 36.
159 *McGinley and Egan v UK* (1998) 27 EHRR 1; and *LCB v UK* (1998) 27 EHRR 212.
160 [2003] EWHC 167 (Admin), (2003) 6 CCLR 194.
161 (1989) 12 EHRR 36.

the refusal to divulge the information, which had been given to the local authority in confidence.

2.90   The court considered that the refusal to disclose pursued a legitimate aim (that of protecting the rights and freedoms of others) but was disproportionate. It was not the 'least restrictive interference'. The court considered that some of the 'third party' material could be disclosed without prejudicing the rights of others – for instance, if the person who had given the information had since died, or could not be traced, or if anyone reading the information would be unable to identity its author. It also considered that the blanket refusal was not 'balanced' since it meant that in such cases Mr Gaskin's claim always failed – and the concept of 'balance' requires that in certain situations the balance of interest might come down in favour of the person seeking disclosure. It was as a consequence of the *Gaskin* judgment that the changes in the Data Protection Act 1998 to accessing social services files were introduced (see chapter 19 below).

2.91   For many disabled people, their home is (in one form or another) in an institutional setting. Provided the stay has been for a reasonable length of time,[162] the home or will be deemed the person's 'home' for the purposes of Article 8. Accordingly, any attempt to move the resident will have to be justified as being proportionate. *R v North and East Devon Health Authority ex p Coughlan*[163] concerned an attempt by a health authority to move the applicant from her specialist NHS unit where she had lived for six years. Having regard to all the circumstances (which included the health authority's desire to close the facility for budgetary reasons) the court considered that the authority had failed to establish that such an interference with the applicant's Article 8 right was justified. The *Coughlan* judgment is considered further at para 12.15 below.

2.92   In *Gunter v South West Staffordshire PCT*[164] the court held that the moving the claimant from her home would interfere with her right to respect for family life within Article 8. Collins J at [20] stated that:

> It is apparent that to remove Rachel from her home will interfere with her right to respect for her family life. Mr Wise has also relied on the positive need to give an enhanced degree of protection to the seriously disabled. This is in my view an unnecessary refinement. The interference with family life is obvious and so must be justified as proportionate. Cost is a factor which can properly be taken into account. But the evidence of the improvement in Rachel's condition, the obvious quality of life within her family environment and her expressed views that she does not want to move are all important factors which suggest that to remove her from her home will require clear justification.

2.93   *R (Bernard) v Enfield LBC*[165] (see also para 14.35) concerned a disabled applicant and her family who through the local authority's failure to assess her community care needs properly, and then provide the necessary services, had been forced to live in 'deplorable conditions' for more

---

162 In *O'Rourke v UK*, Application no 39022/97, 26 June 2001 the court doubted that occupation of a hotel room for one month was sufficient and continuous enough to make it his 'home' for the purposes of Article 8.

163 [2000] 2 WLR 622, (1999) 2 CCLR 285.

164 [2005] EWHC 1894 (Admin).

165 [2002] EWHC 2282 (Admin), (2002) 5 CCLR 577.

than 20 months. Although the court held that this level of suffering had not attained the threshold required by Article 3, it considered that the council's failure to act on its assessments had the effect of condemning the applicant and her family to live in conditions which made it virtually impossible for them to have any meaningful private or family life – and on the facts found a violation of Article 8.

2.94 In a series of cases, the Strasbourg court has considered the obligations on local authorities to provide assistance for disabled parents to enable them to discharge their parental roles. The cases have invariably concerned care proceedings initiated by the authorities based on the lack of parental support for their children. In *Kutzner v Germany*[166] for example, the applicants' 5- and 7-year-old daughters had been removed from their care because it was alleged that the parents' 'impaired mental development' rendered them incapable of bringing up their children. In finding a violation of the family's rights under Article 8, the court referred to the state's positive obligation in such cases to take measures to facilitate the family's reunion, as soon as it is practically possible; it considered that these measures included the provision of additional educational and other measures to support the family. In *SH v Italy*[167] (a case concerning a mother whose children were taken into care and placed for adoption due to her depression) the court held that it was the state's responsibility 'to help people in difficulty, to guide them through the process and advise ... on how to overcome difficulties'. As noted at para 14.17(10) below, the CA 2014 eligibility regulations[168] make specific provision for the needs of disabled parents.

2.95 The interplay of Articles 3 and 8 is illustrated by the case of *Đorđević v Croatia*[169] in which, as noted above, the court held that the harassment by school children of an adult with learning disabilities constituted a violation of Article 3. The applicant's mother also suffered as a result of being present when the harassment occurred, and in relation to this the court found a violation of Article 8 – since it placed a 'positive obligation ... upon States to ensure respect for human dignity and the quality of life in certain respects' and that the harassment of her son also affected her.

Article 14: discrimination

2.96 Article 14 can only be invoked in relation to one of the substantive rights set out in Articles 2–12 of the convention and the protocols. Article 14 requires that in the delivery of the substantive rights, there be no discrimination. Discrimination is permissible under Article 14, if it is established that the measure has an objective and reasonable justification and is 'proportionate'.

---

166 Application no 46544/99, 26 February 2002: see also *Moser v Austria* Application no 12643/02, 21 September 2006; *Saviny v Ukraine* Application no 39948/06, 18 December 2008; *Kocherov & Sergeyeva v Russia* Application no 16899/13, 29 March 2016; and *Re C (a child)* [2014] EWCA (Civ Div) 21 January 2014 which concerned a profoundly deaf parent whose child was taken into local authority care.

167 Application no 52557/14, 13 October 2015.

168 Care and Support (Eligibility Criteria) Regulations 2015 SI No 313 (the 'eligibility regulations').

169 Application no 41526/10, (2012) 15 CCLR 657.

2.97   Thus a violation of Article 14 can only occur in combination with another Article;[170] for instance, the inferior education rights of Roma children in the Czech Republic (compared with non-Roma children) were held to violate Article 14 in conjunction with Article 2 of the first protocol[171] (right to education). The court has further held that there is a positive obligation under Article 14 to combat invidious forms of discrimination such as racism.[172]

2.98   Article 14 discrimination must be based on a particular 'status' or characteristic of the person. In *Cameron Mathieson v Secretary of State for Work and Pensions*,[173] when reviewing this question the Supreme Court accepted that 'status' was not limited to innate characteristics such as gender, sexual orientation, pigmentation of skin and congenital disabilities (para 21) – holding that in that case it included 'a severely disabled child who was in need of lengthy in-patient hospital treatment' (para 19). In *Hurley v Secretary of State for Work and Pensions*[174] the status in question was that of a disabled person 'being cared for by a family member' (para 64). The European Court of Human Rights has confirmed that Article 14 is engaged when direct or indirect discrimination occurs.[175]

2.99   In *Hurley* the court held that where adverse indirect discrimination is identified, a fourfold test of its reasonableness is required namely:

> First, is the objective sufficiently important to justify an adverse impact? Second, is it rationally connected with the objective? Third, could a measure with a lesser adverse impact on the disadvantaged group have been used? Fourth, having regard to those matters, has a fair balance been struck between the interests of the community and the rights of those with a protected characteristic? (para 67)

170 It may be that major improvement in this field will more likely flow from EU law, ie the Amsterdam Treaty amendments.
171 *DH v Czech Republic* Application no 57325/00, 13 November 2007.
172 *Timishev v Russia* (2005) Application nos 55762/00 and 55974/00, 13 December 2005.
173 [2015] UKSC 47, [2015] 1 WLR 3250.
174 [2015] EWHC 3382.
175 *Thlimmenos v Greece* (2000) 31 EHRR 411; and see also *R (MA) v Secretary of State for Work and Pensions* [2014] EWCA Civ 13, [2014] PTSR 584 where *Thlimmenos* discrimination was held to be almost indistinguishable from indirect discrimination.

The duty to assess

continued

Introduction

3.1   Assessment is the cornerstone of the process which determines whether an individual has access to social services resources to meet their needs.[1] Not infrequently, flaws in the eligibility decision or care planning can be traced back to deficiencies in that primary process, and the Administrative Court has shown itself willing to strike down decisions which rest on the foundation of an unlawful assessment.[2]

3.2   The major reform introduced by the National Health Service and Community Care Act (NHSCCA) 1990 was the imposition of a clear statutory duty to assess which was triggered when a person with potential needs for community care services came to the attention of the authority[3]. This became known as the 'section 47 assessment'. The proactive nature of the duty and its low trigger threshold were key characteristics of this right, providing some protection against erosion in the face of scarce resources. Carers had to wait a little longer for the benefit of a specific statutory right to an assessment, first found in the Carers (Recognition and Services) Act 1995, but, even then, that right was dependent on a request being made.

3.3   The Care Act (CA) 2014 replaced the previous legislative provisions governing the duties to assess adults who may have care and support needs and their adult carers, save for the assessment of those who appear to be in need of after-care services under section 117 of the Mental Health Act (MHA) 1983. (This group falls to be assessed under the old NHSCCA 1990 s47 regime (see para 15.58 below).[4]) In doing so, it introduced three main sets of reforms: an equivalent proactive duty to assess carers on the appearance of need; detailed mandatory requirements which establish the framework of a lawful assessment; and rights to involvement, advocacy and information to support the underlying policy intention to create a truly personalised process.[5]

Terminology

Adults with care and support needs

3.4   The CA 2014 does not define the group of people intended to benefit from its assessment and support planning provisions in terms of 'disability'. The term makes only a rare appearance, for example in connection with the duty to maintain registers for planning purposes, and here it carries

---

1   The Department of Health's *Care and support statutory guidance* to support implementation of Part 1 of the Care Act (CA) 2014 by local authorities, 2016 ('the statutory guidance') describes assessment as 'one of the most important elements of the care and support system' (para 6.1).

2   See, for example, *R (Clarke) v Sutton LBC* [2015] EWHC 1081 (Admin); and *R v Birmingham City Council ex p Killgrew* (2000) 3 CCLR 109.

3   National Health Service and Community Care Act 1990 s47(1).

4   See Care Act 2014 and Children and Families Act 2014 (Consequential Amendments) Order 2015 Schedule para 51.

5   'The process must be person-centred throughout, involving the person and supporting them to have choice and control' (statutory guidance, para 6.1).

the definition to be found in Equality Act (EqA) 2010 s77. Instead the Act speaks of 'adults with care and support needs'.

3.5   For an adult to be eligible for care and support, the Eligibility Regulations stipulate that his or her need must 'arise from' or be 'related to' 'a physical or mental impairment or illness'.[6] This requirement (considered further at para 4.11) only applies to eligibility and is not therefore relevant in other contexts – for example, in relation to the safeguarding duties (CA 2014 ss42–46; see para 18.13).

3.6   Where the CA 20124 uses the term 'adult', there is a need for caution. An 'adult' is defined as a person over the age of 18 (CA 2014 s2(8)), but when used in the Act it generally refers to an adult with care and support needs and not to a carer. But this is not consistently the case. For example, section 13(5) requires an authority to provide information and advice about prevention where none of the needs of the 'adult' meet the eligibility criteria. It is clear from the contextual detail that it is intended to apply both to an adult with needs for care and support and to a carer.

Carers

3.7   A 'carer' is defined in CA 2014 s10(3) as an adult who provides or intends to provide care for another adult, who, in that context, is an 'adult needing care'. Those who provide or intend to provide care under a contract or as voluntary work are excluded, unless a local authority exercises its discretion to treat that person as a carer (CA 2014 s10(9) and (10)). For example, it might be appropriate to treat a family member who is paid using direct payments for the care he or she provides as a carer (indeed, it will be obligatory if the family member is also providing care on an unpaid basis).

3.8   'Care' expressly includes not only 'practical' but also 'emotional support' (CA 2014 s10(11)), and this definition should alleviate any problems that family members who do not provide personal care have had in maintaining their involvement in the past. This is consistent with, and gives statutory force to, pre-CA 2014 guidance which recognised that in law 'caring' is a much wider concept than simply providing physical or practical care – stating, for example, that care may relate to being 'anxious and stressed waiting for, or actively seeking to prevent, the next crisis'.[7]

3.9   It is perhaps unlikely that disputed cases will arise requiring resort to the *Oxford English Dictionary*.[8] Courts are likely to accept that care has

---

6 Care and Support (Eligibility Criteria) Regulations 2015 SI No 313 reg 2.

7 See, for example, Department of Health, *Carers and Disabled Children Act 2000: carers and people with parental responsibility for disabled children: practice guidance*, 2000, paras 67–68.

8 The *Oxford English Dictionary*'s account of the etymology of the verb 'to care' shows a migration from its Old High German origin 'chara' (trouble, grief, care): from essentially 'grieve' to 'feel concern' and 'look after/take care of' – although the emotional element remained central until the mid-Victorian period. The shift is evident in an 1887 *Manchester Guardian* report, which noted: 'The child had ... been well cared for.' It appears that the first printed use of the word 'carer' in its modern sense is as recent as 1978 when the OED references 'Age & Ageing VII. 107 A much lower proportion of patients with chief carers in social classes one and two were admitted than those in three, four and five'; and even until 1980 the OED notes that the word carer was still put between inverted commas.

a wide meaning – and that people's perception of themselves as 'caring' should in general be accepted and an assessment offered to them (which might be a relatively brief process in some cases).

3.10   The definition of a 'carer' in CA 2014 s10(3) includes those who are not providing care, but who 'intend to'. Neither the Act nor the statutory guidance provide further detail on this point. The provision first appeared in Carers (Recognition and Services) Act 1995 s1 and was largely directed at hospital discharges (see para 5.14 below). The guidance that accompanied the 1995 Act explained:[9]

> By including carers both providing or intending to provide care, the Act covers those carers who are about to take on substantial and regular caring tasks for someone who has just become, or is becoming, disabled through accident or physical or mental ill health. Local and health authorities will need to ensure that hospital discharge procedures take account of the provisions of the Act and that carers are involved once planning discharge starts.

3.11   The CA 2014 uses the phrase 'care and support'[10] to describe the potential needs of disabled, elderly and ill adults. When discussing how local authorities should respond to the needs of carers it uses the word 'support' only, on the basis that carers do not need 'care' but they may require 'support' for their caring role.

Individuals

3.12   In the text that follows the term adult will be used to refer to the adult in need of care as opposed to the adult providing care. Where the term 'individual' is used, it is intended to refer to both adults and carers.

An overview of the new assessment duties

3.13   The duty to carry out what is called a 'needs assessment'[11] of an adult is found in CA 2014 s9(1):

> (1) Where it appears to a local authority that an adult may have needs for care and support, the authority must assess–
> (a) whether the adult does have needs for care and support, and
> (b) if the adult does, what those needs are.

3.14   At first blush the duty appears to be very similar to that found in the pre-CA 2014 scheme. One particular difference is that the new duty is not triggered by an appearance of need for prescribed community care services,[12] but by a need for 'care and support' (which is undefined, but see below at para 3.20). This is consistent with the overall approach in the CA 2014 which does not impose a duty to provide specified types of service, but a

---

9   Department of Health, *Carers (Recognition and Services) Act 1995 practice guidance* LAC (96)7, para 16.
10 See below at para 3.20 for a discussion of the meaning 'care and support'.
11 CA 2014 s9(2).
12 As required by National Health Service and Community Care Act 1990 s47 – and for which community care services were defined in section 46.

duty to meet needs in whatever way is appropriate (as long as it is within the scope of the authority's powers – see below at para 20.176). Section 8 makes this clear, setting out a list of possible ways that needs can be met, but by way of example only (see para 7.18 below). This is intended to underpin in a more personalised approach to social work practice. Fact sheet 2 (published by the Department of Health to accompany the Act as updated) states:

> We wanted to ensure that the law focuses on the needs of people. The old law created responsibilities to provide particular services. That leads to an approach to assessment and support planning that focuses more on services and organisations – the people that provide the care, not the people who receive it. We wanted to change this, so that the person is always at the centre.[13]

3.15   The duty to assess carers is found in CA 2014 s10:

> (1) Where it appears to a local authority that a carer may have needs for support (whether currently or in the future), the authority must assess–
>   (a) whether the carer does have needs for support (or is likely to do so in the future), and
>   (b) if the carer does, what those needs are (or are likely to be in the future).

3.16   Section 10 effected a major reform to the carer assessment and with it significant implications for practice. Carers now have the benefit of a (broadly) equivalent proactive duty to assess once they come to the attention of the authority: a request is no longer necessary.

3.17   Furthermore, a carer no longer has to demonstrate that he or she provides or intends to provide substantial and regular care which was a precondition of the old carer assessment rights.[14] This attracted little court or ombudsman attention,[15] probably because it was difficult to determine the question until an assessment had been undertaken. In one of the few cases reported cases where a local authority did refuse to assess a carer (because it did not consider his care sufficiently 'substantial'), the local government ombudsman observed:[16]

> It should also have been obvious to the Council that a carer's assessment was necessary in order to see (a) how much support [the carer] could reasonably be expected to provide ...; and (b) what practical help could be provided to [the carer] with respite from his caring responsibilities.

3.18   A second significant reform, applicable to both adults and carers, is the extent to which the framework duties are fleshed out in the Act itself, in regulations[17] (the 'assessment regulations') and also in dedicated sections of the statutory guidance.[18] These more detailed requirements on how an

---

13 Department of Health Care Act 2014 Part 1: fact sheets as updated 13 April 2016.
14 Carer (Recognition and Services) Act 1995 s1(1) and Carers and Disabled Children Act 2000 s1(1).
15 See, for example, L Clements *Carers and their rights*, 5th edn, Carers UK, 2012, para 3.30; and Complaint no 02/C/08690 against Sheffield City Council, 9 August 2004; and see also Complaint no 05/C/11921 (Trafford MBC) 26 July 2007.
16 Complaint no 02/C/08690 against Sheffield City Council, 9 August 2004, para 127.
17 Care and Support (Assessment) Regulations 2014 SI No 2827.
18 Statutory guidance, chapter 6.

assessment should be carried out and what it should address, provide useful analytical tools for assessing the legal adequacy of assessments, not only for advocates and advisers of those who are unhappy with the outcome of the process, but for social services authorities seeking to ensure that adequate assessments are undertaken.

The duty to assess: when does it arise?

Individuals who may be in need

3.19　The assessment duties are triggered only when the authority becomes aware that the individual 'may be in need' of care and/or support. 'May be in need' is likely to be interpreted as imposing a low threshold. This was certainly the view of the court when the equivalent phrase in NHSCC 1990 s47 fell to be considered in *R v Bristol CC ex p Penfold*.[19] The statutory guidance[20] is consistent with this approach, stating that decisions about adult or carer eligibility should come after the assessment and must not affect the authority's decision to carry out an assessment (para 6.13):

> Local authorities must undertake an assessment for any adult with an appearance of need for care and support, regardless of whether or not the local authority thinks the individual has eligible needs ...

3.20　The phrase 'care and support' (used in the adult assessment duty) is undefined in the CA 2014. Although unlikely to be controversial in the majority of cases, its use may generate disputes similar to those about the scope of the pre-CA 2014 duty to provide residential accommodation under section 21 of the National Assistance Act 1948. This imposed a duty to provide residential accommodation to adults 'in need of care and attention', by reason of age, disability or other circumstances, that was not otherwise available to them. One of the leading authorities on the meaning of 'care and attention' in this statutory context was *R (M) v Slough BC*.[21] Baroness Hale said:

> The natural and ordinary meaning of the words 'care and attention' in this context is 'looking after'. Looking after means doing something for the person cared for which he cannot or should not be expected to do for himself: it might be household tasks which an old person can no longer perform or can only perform with great difficulty; it might be protection from risks which a mentally disabled person cannot perceive; it might be personal care, such as feeding, washing or toileting. This is not an exhaustive list. The provision of medical care is expressly excluded.

3.21　However, the extent to which this line of case-law will offer assistance in resolving disputes about the new terminology is unclear.[22] The phrase itself is different – 'care and support' rather than 'care and attention' – and

---

19　(1997–1998) 1 CCLR 315, 23 January 1998, QBD.
20　See also para 1.44 below.
21　[2008] UKHL 52 at para 33.
22　In *R (SG) v Haringey LBC* [2015] EWHC 2579 (Admin) the court was presented with question of when the duty to provide accommodation under the CA 2014 arises. It decided that the principles established in the pre-CA 2014 case-law applied, and in doing made no distinction between the phase 'care and attention' used in NAA 1948

it falls to be interpreted in a different statutory context. In the *Slough* case, the issue was the nature of the care which would qualify the person concerned for residential accommodation. In the CA 2014, the phrase 'care and support' is used to identify those who may be in need of any kind of response from the local authority, not a particular kind of service. Furthermore, the CA 2014 is designed to implement changes in approach in adult social care: a shift from paternalism to enablement and from task-based to outcomes-based models of care. The term 'support' rather than 'attention' reflects that move. It would appear to follow, therefore, that the concept of 'care and support' is much broader than that of 'care and attention'.

3.22   Both concepts ('care and support' in relation to adults and 'support' in relation to carers), although broad, are not unlimited – for instance, in relation to the care and support that can be provided. A social services authority is prohibited, for example, from providing a health service that is required to be provided under the National Health Service Act (NHSA) 2006 if it is of a nature that a social services authority could not be expected to provide (CA 2014 s22(1)(b) – see para 12.12 below).[23]

Social services awareness of the individual

3.23   If the assessment duty is to be triggered, the individual who may be in need must come to the attention of the social services authority. This is the same requirement as under the pre-CA 2014 regime[24] and it is likely that old case-law on this issue will be considered relevant to interpreting the scope of the new provision.

3.24   It is the authority that must have the requisite knowledge, not the social services department. By way of example, in the case of a unitary authority (which has responsibility for both housing and social services) the duty to assess may well arise when a 'vulnerable'[25] person presents himself or herself as homeless (see para 14.23 below). In *R (Patrick) v Newham LBC*[26] the applicant, who had physical and mental health difficulties, was living rough after the authority had determined that she was intentionally homeless. Lawyers acting on her behalf wrote to the authority, enclosing a doctor's letter confirming her significant psychiatric problems and requested urgent accommodation. In the subsequent judicial review proceedings it was argued that this should have triggered a social care assessment.[27] Henriques J held:[28]

> I am wholly unable to accept any suggestion that the respondent has discharged its duty [to assess]. The authority has not carried out any assessment of the applicant's needs for community care services. There is no record of any consideration of the applicant's individual circumstances at all ...

s21 and 'care and support' used in the CA 2014, but there is no evidence that it heard argument on the point. See also para 7.101 below.

23 See chapter 4 on care and support planning.
24 NHS and Community Care Act 1990 s47.
25 Under Housing Act 1996 s189.
26 (2000) 4 CCLR 48, QBD.
27 Under NHSCCA 1990 s47 – now replicated in CA 2014 s9.
28 (2000) 4 CCLR 48, QBD at 51–52.

An assessment of needs is a formal task to be carried out in accordance with Central Government Guidance and involves collation of medical evidence, psychiatric evidence etc., with a view thereafter to matching accommodation to needs. I am satisfied that the Council have not complied with their duty [to assess]. That duty plainly accrued [on the date when] the applicant's solicitors wrote to the respondent describing the applicant's circumstances and requesting urgent accommodation.

3.25   It follows that authorities should ensure that they have the necessary internal organisational networks so that referrals are made to the relevant adult social care team when the first contact with the local authority is made. If they do not do so, they risk breaching the duty to assess. In any event, the new general duty to co-operate requires a local authority to make arrangements for ensuring co-operation internally between social services, housing and children's services (CA 2014 s6(4)) – see para 11.43. A failure to make such arrangements may amount to maladministration causing injustice if it results in a delayed assessment.

Future need for care and support

3.26   Although the phrase 'may be in need' is in the present tense, it was interpreted in the old legislative scheme as including some future needs. In *R (B) v Camden LBC*,[29] the court was required to consider the interpretation of the pre-CA 2014 assessment duty (under NHSCCA 1990 s47) in the context of a patient detained under the Mental Health Act 1983 who was seeking discharge. Stanley Burnton J held that the phrase a person who 'may be in need of such services' referred:

> ... to a person who may be in need at the time, or who may be about to be in need. A detained patient who is the subject of a deferred conditional discharge decision of a tribunal, which envisages his conditional discharge once section 117 after-care services are in place, is a person who 'may be in need of such services', since if such services are available to him he will be discharged and immediately need them. Whether a patient who may reasonably be considered to be liable to have such an order made in an impending tribunal hearing is an issue I do not have to decide in the instant case, but I incline to the view that he is (para 66).

3.27   The issue also arose in the context of those seeking to be released from prison on parole. In *R (NM) v Islington LBC*[30] Sales J held:

> 77. ... In my view, on proper interpretation of that phrase, to bring himself within the scope of this section it is necessary for a claimant to show that there is a sufficiently concrete and likely prospect of him being in a position where community care service may need to be provided to him if he has relevant needs which would require to be met by the provision of services ...
>
> ...
>
> 79. ... this interpretation of the words ... as covering both cases of present need and a narrow penumbra of cases of reasonably predictable future need is justified by reference to the statutory purpose of section 47 and of the community care provisions ...

29 [2005] EWHC 1366 (Admin), (2005) 8 CCLR 422.
30 (2012) 15 CCLR 563.

3.28   It seems likely that a similar approach will be taken to interpreting the scope of the phrase in the CA 2014. Arguably, the emphasis on prevention in the new framework would suggest an intention to require assessment at an early stage to support that policy. For example, if an individual is not yet eligible for care and support, the local authority is required to give written information and advice on prevention.[31]

3.29   Interestingly, the carers' assessment duty imposes an express requirement to assess where a carer may have needs in the future.

3.30   The CA 2014 makes specific provision for those in hospital for acute care. A duty to assess is triggered if the hospital serves notice on the relevant local authority that they consider that the patient is not likely to be safe on discharge unless arrangements are put in place to meet his or her care and support needs.[32] 'Acute care' is defined and excludes, for example, mental health care.

The assessment duty when moving to a new area: portability of care

3.31   In the past it has proved difficult to obtain an assessment of 'future' needs in advance of a disabled person's move from one local authority area to another. The CA 2014 imposes specific duties in these circumstances to improve continuity in the provision of care (section 37), but not, necessarily, consistency. The system is intended to work in the following way:

- On receipt of notification that an adult, whose needs are being met by an authority ('the first authority'),[33] intends to move to the area of a new social services authority ('the second authority'), the second authority, subject to being satisfied that the adult's intention is genuine, must assess the needs of the adult and any carer (section 37(6)).
- The second authority must notify the first authority, which must, in turn, make available various documents, including any care and support plan and the support plan for any carer (section 37(4)(b)).
- When undertaking the assessment, the second authority must have regard to the existing care and support arrangements (section 37(4)) and, very importantly, provide written reasons if it comes to a different decision on needs or on the personal budget (section 37(11) and (12)).
- The first authority must monitor progress. Pending the move, it must keep in contact with the second authority for that purpose and keep the adult and carer involved and informed when doing so (section 37(9)).

3.32   The statutory guidance says that to assure itself that the intention is genuine, the second authority should:

- establish and maintain contact with the person and the person's carer to keep abreast of the person's intentions to move;

---

31 CA 2014 s13(5).

32 CA 2014 Sch 3. This is intended to replace the provisions of the Community Care (Delayed Discharges etc) Act 2003.

33 This includes self-funders who have requested that the first authority meet their needs under CA 2014 s18(3).

- continue to speak with the original authority to get their view on the person's intentions;
- ask if the person has any information or contacts that can verify his or her intention (para 20.12).

3.33 Anyone in this situation intending to move will need information about provision in his or her new local area early on. It may even influence the person's decision on whether to move. The general duty to provide information and advice[34] may well be helpful here, but the second authority must also provide any additional information 'as it considers appropriate' (although this specific additional duty only kicks in when the 'genuine intention' condition is met) (CA 2014 s37(4)(a)).

3.34 Where equipment provided by the first authority is needed in the new home, the statutory guidance says it should move with the adult if that is the person's preference and it is the most cost-effective solution, irrespective of the original cost of the item (para 20.35). Money should not be wasted replicating provision, even if it means that the local authority that provided that equipment will not continue to be responsible for the adult concerned.

3.35 The statutory guidance is also very specific about responsibilities on the day of the move (see para 20.30). The first authority should remain responsible for meeting the care and support needs the adult has in the adult's original home and when moving. The second authority is responsible for providing care and support once the adult moves into the new area.

3.36 Provision is made for a default duty. If the second authority has not completed this process by the day of the intended move, it must make arrangements to meet the eligible needs as assessed by the first authority until it has done so (CA 2014 s38(1) and(2)). This does not mean that the second authority must simply adopt the existing arrangements – they may not make much sense in the new circumstances following a move. When deciding how to meet needs in the performance of its 'default' duty, the second authority must involve the adult and any relevant carers and take all reasonable steps to reach agreement (CA 2014 s38(3) and(4)). Regulations[35] set out a list of factors to be taken into account including the current support plans, and the views of the adult and any carer. Unsurprisingly it must also take into account any 'relevant differences'[36] between the circumstances before and after the move, such as access to a carer, suitability of the new accommodation and its proximity to other services and facilities.

3.37 Chapter 20 of the statutory guidance fleshes out how the process should operate – but it signally fails to address what should happen when a person moves and the second local authority fails to act properly – for example, by failing meet the person's needs identified by the first authority until it has completed its assessment. It is certainly not the case that the first authority

---

34 See CA 2014 s4.
35 Care and Support (Continuity of Care) Regulations 2014 SI No 2825.
36 'Relevant difference' is defined as one likely to have a significant effect on the wellbeing of the adult (reg 2(2)).

can simply wash its hands.[37] The first authority would have the power to continue to meet the adult's needs under CA 2014 s19. This confers two relevant powers to meet needs. The first under section 19(2) arises where (1) a local authority has assessed an individual as having eligible needs; (2) the person is ordinarily resident in the area of another local authority; and (3) it has notified that authority of its intention to do so. The second is under section 19(3) and arises where the needs appear to be urgent, irrespective of whether an assessment has been carried out and irrespective of where the person is ordinarily resident. Both discretions must be exercised in accordance with general public law principles, including the requirement to make a rational decision on the basis of the adult's circumstances without the application of a blanket policy. Furthermore, the power would become a duty if a failure to act would breach the requirements of the Human Rights Act 1998 because, for example, the person concerned was left in such conditions that it amounted to inhuman and degrading treatment.

3.38   If the second authority does not complete its assessment or put arrangements in place before the move date, the adult concerned may not move on the intended date. Nonetheless, the second authority would be subject to the default duty and may incur expenditure as a result even though the adult (on the face of it) remains the responsibility of the first authority on ordinary residence principles. CA 2014 s38(7) entitles the second authority to recover those costs from the first authority.

It is not uncommon for someone who was originally 'placed out of area,' by a local social services authority (in a care home, in supported living accommodation or in a shared lives scheme placement) to decide to move into his or her own accommodation in that area. At the point just before the person's move he or she will be deemed to be ordinarily resident in the area of the placing local authority (see chapter 6), but, after the move, will be ordinarily resident in the area in which he or she was placed. Section 37(3) makes it clear that the 'continuity of care' provisions apply in these circumstances, the placing authority being the first authority and the authority for the area in which the person was placed, the second authority.

3.39   Two local government ombudsman cases in 2016 illustrate difficulties that can arise for people moving to new authority areas:

- In the first complaint[38] the council to which the disabled person was moving (ie the 'second authority') claimed that the first authority's notification letter had not been received. When he moved, in the ombudsman's words the 'records held by the councils show a lack of interest in ensuring one or the other took responsibility for Mr Y's care needs ...

---

37 See *R (AM) v (1) Havering LBC and Tower Hamlets LBC*, which concerned the housing and child in need responsibilities of two authorities where a family had been placed by a housing authority in a neighbouring authority. In that context the judge said: 'Even though there was no on-going duty ... [to the family] once it had left its area, it was nonetheless ... an inexcusable failure of good social work practice to "wash its hands" of the family in this way; continuity of social work involvement and practice best meets the obligations under statute and is indeed the most cost-efficient.'

38 Complaint no 15 012 618 against Oxfordshire CC, 16 August 2016.

Both councils lost sight of the key priority which was the well-being of Mr Y. Council A's evidence of attempts to communicate with Council B do not relieve it of the responsibility to fund Mr Y until the dispute was resolved.'

- In the second complaint[39] although the second authority was notified that the family were to move on 31 August, it failed to undertake an assessment until 27 August. This recommended the same direct payments package of care as previously, but on 23 November the council's panel reduced this substantially and the new package was backdated to 31 August. In finding maladministration, the ombudsman noted that there was no evidence the panel considered either: (a) Mr B's previous assessment; or (b) the impact on Mr B's parents and primary carers. The maladministration was compounded by the council's failure to fund Mr B's existing level of care from the date he moved into the area until it made a decision on the level of funding it would provide.

3.40 What the CA 2014 does not do is deal with the issue of portability of care if an adult decides to move to another part of the UK outside England.[40] Discussions between the Department of Health in England, the Department of Health, Social Services and Public Safety in Northern Ireland, the Department of Health and Social Services in Wales and the Scottish Government Health and Social Care Directorate have produced guidance on the approach to be taken, 'Principles for maintaining continuity of care within the United Kingdom'.[41] The agreed principles are:

1. Responsible authorities should ensure a person-centred process and take into account the outcomes an adult wishes to achieve.
2. Responsible authorities should work together and share information about their local care and support system and services.
3. The adult moving should be given relevant information, in an accessible format, about local care and support provision in the authority they are moving to.
4. Responsible authorities should work together to support a move across national boundaries to ensure the adult's care and support is continued during the move.
5. Responsible authorities should share relevant information about the adult's care and support needs and any other information which it believes necessary in a timely manner and with the consent of the adult involved.

3.41 The definition of 'responsible authorities' given in the guidance is 'the local authority, Integration Authority or Health and Social Care (HSC) Trust, responsible for the assessment of an adult's care during the period of their move'.

3.42 The 'ordinary residence' implications for people who move across national borders are considered at para 6.58 below.

---

39 Complaint no 15 019 587 against the Isle of Wight Council, 9 August 2016.
40 If accommodation is arranged for an adult in another of the UK countries by an English local authority, ordinary residence (and therefore responsibility) will be retained in the placing authority: CA 2014 Sch 1.
41 Available at www.gov.uk/government/publications/continuity-of-care-when-moving-across-borders-within-uk.

Financial circumstances are not relevant

3.43 A local authority cannot (lawfully) refuse to assess because a person has sufficient resources to make their own arrangements. The duty to assess arises irrespective of the financial circumstances of the individual concerned. This was made clear in policy guidance in the pre-CA 2014 scheme,[42] but the new legislation goes further and imposes statutory prohibitions on taking the financial circumstances of adults or carers into account (CA 2014 ss9(3)(b) and 10(3)(b)). The entitlement of self-funders to have arrangements for their care and support made by the local authority (see CA 2014 ss18(3) and 20(3)) would not make sense if not accompanied by an assessment duty.

3.44 This is not to say that an authority has to undertake the needs assessment and financial assessment sequentially – the statutory guidance states (para 6.12):

> The financial assessment may in practice run parallel to the needs assessment, but it must never influence an assessment of needs. Local authorities must inform individuals that a financial assessment will determine whether or not they pay towards their care and support, but this must have no bearing on the assessment process itself.

Level of need is not relevant

3.45 The duty to assess is not dependent on the level of the individual's needs for care and support (CA 2014 ss9(3)(b) and 10(3)(b)). In particular, the authority cannot lawfully refuse to assess on the ground that the individual is unlikely to be eligible. This is consistent with the position under the pre-CA 2014 scheme. The case of *R v Bristol CC ex p Penfold*[43] concerned someone who suffered from anxiety and depression. The authority refused to carry out a community care assessment. One of its reasons for doing so was that there was no prospect of meeting any needs that might have emerged in the course of the assessment (because their eligibility criteria were so tightly drawn, only people at considerable risk were likely to be offered services). In upholding the challenge, Scott Baker J looked at whether assessments in these circumstances would have any value and found:[44]

> Even if there is no hope from the resource point of view of meeting any needs identified in the assessment, the assessment may serve a useful purpose in identifying for the local authority unmet needs which will help it to plan for the future. Without assessment this could not be done.

3.46 Although the current legislative scheme is different from that considered in *Penfold*, the value of an assessment even where an individual is found

---

42 Department of Health, *Prioritising need in the context of Putting People First: a whole system approach to eligibility for social care. Guidance on eligibility criteria for adult social care, England*, 2010, para 71.
43 (1997–98) 1 CCLR 315, QBD.
44 (1997–98) 1 CCLR 315, QBD at 322.

ineligible is clearly recognised in the policy context of personalisation and prevention. The statutory guidance sees assessment as (para 6.2):

> ... not just ... a gateway to care and support, but should be seen as a critical intervention in its own right, which can help people to understand their situation and the needs they have, to reduce or delay the onset of greater needs, and to access support when they require it.

3.47   This message is reinforced specifically in the context of providing guidance on undertaking assessment irrespective of level of need (para 6.6):

> The assessment and eligibility process provides a framework to identify any level of need for care and support so that local authorities can consider how to provide a proportionate response at the right time, based on the individual's needs. Prevention and early intervention are placed at the heart of the care and support system, and even if a person has needs that are not eligible at that time, the local authority must consider providing information and advice and other preventative services ...

The duty arises irrespective of residence or presence?

3.48   A social services authority is only required to provide care and support to an adult who is either ordinarily resident in its area or is present in its area, but of no settled residence elsewhere (CA 2014 s18 (1)) – see para 6.49 below). Similarly, in relation to carers, the duty only arises if the adult for whom they provide care meets these residence requirements (CA 2014 s20(1)(a)). However, there are no such residence conditions expressly limiting the duty to assess.

3.49   The pre-CA 2014 duty[45] to assess was triggered only if the person concerned was someone for whom the local authority may have arranged services. This was interpreted in *R v Berkshire CC ex p P*[46] as requiring only that the local authority had the legal power to provide services to that individual and, as there was a discretion to provide services to the person concerned despite not being ordinarily resident in the local authority's area, the duty to assess was triggered. However, in *R (J) v Southend BC*[47] Newman J held that where the 'ordinarily resident' authority had accepted responsibility to assess, the third party authority could not be compelled to undertake an assessment.

3.50   The legislative scheme is different under the CA 2014. There is no equivalent express limitation in sections 9 or 10. The individual just needs to be someone who may have a need for care and support (or, in the case of carers, who may have need for support). The difference would suggest that there are no residence conditions restricting the sphere of operation of the assessment duties. It remains to be seen whether a limitation of the kind imposed in the *Southend* case might in some way be read into the scheme to avoid, what the judge in that case called, the 'extravagance'[48] of duplicate assessment by different authorities.

45 National Health Service and Community Care Act 1990 s47.
46 (1997–98) 1 CCLR 141.
47 [2005] EWHC 3547 (Admin).
48 [2005] EWHC 3547 (Admin) at para 43.

3.51   Returning UK nationals who may have been living for an extended period abroad and who may have needs for care and support will be entitled to an assessment. They may have no settled residence but will be physically present. If they need arrangements for care and support to be in place immediately on arrival, the local authority may have to either undertake the assessment prior to their return on the basis of their likely and imminent need (see para 3.26 above), or consider exercising their discretion under CA 2014 s19(3) to make arrangements in urgent cases before undertaking an assessment. Section 19(3) expressly applies regardless of whether the adult is ordinarily resident in the authority's area – see para 4.68 below.

Refusal of assessment

3.52   Where an individual refuses an assessment, the duty to that individual[49] is dis-applied (CA 2014 s11(1)). However, there are two exceptions in the case of adults. The first is where the adult lacks the necessary capacity to refuse and the authority is satisfied that it would be in his or her best interests to assess; the second is where the adult is experiencing, or at risk of, abuse or neglect.

3.53   However, the duty revives if and when the individual later requests an assessment or where the authority considers there has been a change of circumstance (subject, of course, to any further refusal) (section 11)). Local authorities will need to ensure that staff in relevant departments are aware of this provision. In effect, it imposes an obligation to re-offer the assessment once the authority becomes aware of a change of circumstances such as a deterioration, loss of carer, or even loss of (or change of) accommodation.

3.54   Local authorities will need to be cautious about interpreting a lack of cooperation with an assessment as a capacitated refusal, particularly where there is evidence that the lack of cooperation is related to the need for care and support that has triggered the duty in the first place. For example, a person with Asperger's Syndrome may find the prospect of negotiating the social relationships required in an assessment exercise very daunting indeed.

3.55   The question of whether a local authority is entitled to treat a statutory duty as being discharged by reason of 'non-cooperation' in a care context arose in relation to the duty to provide residential accommodation under National Assistance Act (NAA) 1948 s21 in *R v Kensington and Chelsea RLBC ex p Kujtim*[50] and the Court of Appeal set a high threshold. Potter LJ said (para 32):

> ... when the circumstances warrant, if an applicant assessed as in need of Part III accommodation either unreasonably refuses to accept the accommodation provided or if, following its provision, by his conduct he manifests a persistent and unequivocal refusal to observe the reasonable requirements

---

49   However, where an adult in need refuses, this will not affect any duties owed to his or her carer.

50   (1999) 2 CCLR 340, CA.

of the local authority in relation to the occupation of such accommodation, then the local authority is entitled to treat its duty as discharged and to refuse to provide further accommodation ...

3.56 Given the potentially serious consequences of treating the duty to assess as being discharged, and the proactive duty on local authorities to involve the adult or carer in their own assessment (see below at para 3.86), it seems likely that a court would impose a similarly stringent test for interpreting uncooperative behaviour as constituting a refusal for the purpose of this new provision.

The relationship with NHS continuing healthcare funding

3.57 There is no express disapplication of the duty to assess on the ground that an adult has been assessed as eligible for NHS continuing healthcare (NHS CC) funding.[51] Indeed, the practice guidance accompanying the National Framework for 'continuing care' suggests that such a person may still remain 'in need' of support from social services and, as a consequence, the duty to assess will be triggered.[52] However, it is important that this is not relied upon to undermine the principle that where there has been a determination of 'continuing care' eligibility, it is the responsibility of the relevant health body to provide a package of care to meet both health and social care needs. The issue is most likely to arise where the care and support required is something that is clearly severable, such as adaptations.[53]

Timescales for an assessment

3.58 One of the common problems faced by those owed an assessment duty is ensuring that it is carried out in a timely manner. As with the pre-CA 2014 scheme, there is no general statutory timescale for the completion of the assessment. However, the statutory guidance helpfully says that local authorities should inform the individual of an 'indicative timescale' and keep the individual informed throughout the assessment process (para 6.29).

3.59 Delay in the performance of a statutory duty can amount to a breach of that duty[54] or a breach of the common law principle that a public authority should not act irrationally/unreasonably. This will depend on the facts of the individual case, in particular the length of the delay and the seriousness

---

51 If a person is eligible for NHS CC funding they are eligible to have their whole care package of health and social care provided as NHS services which are of course, (subject to limited exceptions as specified in the NHS Act 2006) provided free of charge.

52 See the practice guidance section of the Department of Health's *National framework for NHS continuing healthcare and NHS-funded nursing care*, November 2012 (revised) at para 79.5; and see para 12.14 below.

53 See para 14.125 below.

54 See, for example, *Lafarge Redland Aggregates Ltd v Scottish Ministers* [2004] 4 PLR 151.

of the potential prejudice if the assessment is not undertaken within a particular timeframe.

3.60   It is important that the individual ensures that the local authority is aware at an early point of all the circumstances of his or her case that are relevant to this issue so that it can be appropriately prioritised. A prioritisation scheme should be able to consider all the circumstances of an individual case. In a 1995 complaint[55] the local government ombudsman criticised a particular scheme for oversimplifying the issue. She stated:

> ... there will be cases which cannot be described as 'emergencies' but need to be dealt with more urgently within the 'complex' category than others. The Council's over-simple system of priorities resulted in a failure to meet [the complainants' disabled daughter's] needs promptly and I consider that to be an injustice resulting in maladministration.

3.61   Whether or not there is a breach of duty, delays may well amount to maladministration causing injustice. When considering complaints about delayed assessments, the local government ombudsman has had regard to the timescales set out in the relevant local authority's own policy.[56] In the ombudsman's opinion, a reasonable time for an assessment should normally be four to six weeks 'although in a complex case it may take a little longer'.[57] Authorities may adopt a prioritisation scheme for assessments, and the local government ombudsman has accepted that such a system 'does not seem unreasonable'.[58] There is no reason to think that the ombudsman would take a different approach to needs and carers' assessments under the CA 2014.

3.62   Where there is delay in assessing, a complaint should resolve the problem quickly, as long as there is no underlying dispute about the duty to assess. If there is, judicial review may be the more appropriate remedy (see para 12.154 on remedies). Judicial review may also be the appropriate course of action if the delay is likely to cause a breach of the duty to meet eligible needs, particularly if there is a need for an injunction to secure interim provision. For example, an adult may have very specialist needs which make it difficult to find a suitable provider, and a vacancy has arisen in a particular facility that can meet his or her needs. If there is a real risk of the placement being lost if not secured promptly, an application for interim relief in judicial review proceedings may well be justifiable.

3.63   In cases of urgency, councils have the power to provide care and support before completing the adult's assessment (CA 2014 s19(3)) (see para 4.68 below). A relevant factor may well be the extent to which the local authority's delay has contributed to the urgent situation arising. There is no equivalent provision for carers, but insofar as the carer's needs may be met by provision to the adult to meet their needs, this will fall within the scope of section 19(3).

---

55 Complaint no 93/C/3660 against Rochdale Metropolitan BC, 26 October 1995.

56 See eg Complaint no 01/C/15434 against South Tyneside Metropolitan BC, 20 January 2003, where the charter stipulated 21 days for the completion of community care assessments.

57 See Report complaint no 13 006 400 against Cornwall Council, 26 February 2015 at para 29.

58 See complaint no 00/B/00599 against Essex CC, 3 September 2001 at para 33.

The assessment requirements

3.64 One of the most significant differences between the old and new assessment regimes is the extent to which the legislative scheme prescribes how an assessment should be carried out and what it should address if it is to be a lawful assessment. There are requirements not only in the Act but in detailed regulations[59] and in the statutory guidance.[60]

Who can assess

3.65 The statutory guidance gives useful emphasis to the need for assessors to be 'appropriately trained', but also states that registered 'social workers and occupational therapists can provide important support and may be involved in complex assessments which indicate a wide range of needs, risks and strengths that may require a coordinated response from a variety of statutory and community services' (para 6.7). In so doing, the implication is that for non-complex cases social workers may not always be necessary. The general (and welcome) tenor of the statutory guidance is, however, that assessors must be 'appropriately trained'. Paragraph 6.86, for example states that if an 'assessor does not have the necessary knowledge of a particular condition or circumstance, they must consult someone who has relevant expertise' and at paragraph 6.86 it requires that:

> ... assessors undergo regular, up-to-date training on an ongoing basis. The training must be appropriate to the assessment, both the format of assessment and the condition(s) and circumstances of the person being assessed. They must also have the skills and knowledge to carry out an assessment of needs that relate to a specific condition or circumstances requiring expert insight, for example when assessing an individual who has autism, learning disabilities, mental health needs or dementia.

3.66 The statutory guidance contains specific advice concerning the assessment of people who are deaf-blind. (See paras 6.91–6.97 of the guidance.) In particular it says, at para 6.92, that a specialist assessment must be carried out 'by an assessor or team that has training of at least QCF or OCN Level 3, or above where the person has higher or more complex needs'.

3.67 Where a local authority delegates its assessment functions to the NHS or a third party (see para 1.25) the duty remains with the authority to ensure that the assessors have the necessary qualifications and competencies.

What the assessment must address

3.68 CA 2014 ss9 and 10 (which impose the duty to assess an adult and carer respectively) require that the assessment must include an assessment of:

- the impact of the needs on all aspects of well-being[61] (sections 9(4)(a) and 10(5)(c));
- the outcomes the person wants to achieve (sections 9(4)(b) and 10(5)(d));

---

59 Care and Support (Assessment) Regulations 2014 SI No 2827.
60 Statutory guidance, chapter 6.
61 CA 2014 s1(2).

- whether and to what extent the provision of care and support would contribute to those outcomes (sections 9(4)(c) and 10(5)(e)).

3.69   These requirements reflect the national eligibility criteria (see para 4.6 below) which make eligibility dependent on an inability to achieve prescribed outcomes[62] which have a significant impact on well-being. At the risk of stating the obvious, in order to apply these eligibility criteria, an authority will need to gather information about outcomes and impact on well-being. If it does not do so, the assessment will be so defective as to be unlawful. The local authority will always be subject to the common law obligation of public bodies to take reasonable steps to inform themselves of relevant information.[63] Nevertheless, this statutory requirement does add something. It ensures a person-centred approach to the assessment – it must identify the outcomes that the individual wishes to achieve and the extent to which care and support/support would help achieve them – ie it personalises the process.

3.70   This is not to say that the authority should limit the assessment to those issues identified by the individual concerned. Not only does the language used in sections 9 and 10 make it clear that the list of considerations is 'non-exhaustive', but the statutory guidance also makes the point that person-centred does not mean the professional assessor's role is limited to considering the problems as articulated by the person being assessed. If it did, those who are unable or less able to do so effectively would be as a serious disadvantage. For example, the statutory guidance says (para 6.14):

> ... the local authority must also consider whether the individual's needs impact upon their well-being beyond the ways identified by the individual.

3.71   CA 2014 s10 adds two important additional requirements in relation to carers' assessments. The first is that these must include an assessment of whether the carer is able and willing (and is likely to continue to be able and willing) to provide care (section 10(5)(a) and (b)). In this context, the statutory guidance re-emphasises the proactive role required of assessors (para 6.18):

> Some carers may need support in recognising issues around sustainability and in recognising their own needs.

3.72   Sustainability is not only about the ability to continue caring, but a willingness to do so. Local authorities have not always fully taken on board the implications of the principle that they can only rely on the contribution of a carer when the carer is willing to provide it. For example, if a carer plans to take a holiday or attend an evening class, the carer will not be 'willing' to be available during that period and replacement care will be needed to meet any eligible needs of the cared-for person that will be unmet during the carer's absence.

---

62 Although carers' eligibility is in large measure determined by their inability to achieve certain 'outcomes', Care and Support (Eligibility Criteria) Regulations 2015 SI No 313 reg 3(2)(a) provides that a carer may be eligible if his or her 'physical or mental health is, or is at risk of, deteriorating'.

63 *Secretary of State for Education and Science v Tameside MBC* [1977] AC 1014.

3.73   A 2016 local government ombudsman report[64] illustrates this point. An adult with significant leaning difficulties, who lived with his parents, had a care package that included 50 days of replacement care to enable his parents to have a break. On review, this was reduced to 14 days, although his needs had not changed and the sustainability of his parents in maintaining their support was recorded as at risk. In finding maladministration the ombudsman held that the council had to provide an explanation as to the reasons for the reduction: that it 'needs to show what circumstances have changed to warrant this reduction in respite provision'. In the ombudsman's opinion it was not acceptable for the council to state that it would offer emergency respite if the need arose:

> The parent's need for 'weekends away and a little social life are not emergencies but part of a planned sustainable support regime'. The Council's assessment does not address these sustainability issues and the guidance says the impact on the carers' daily lives and non caring activities must be included.

3.74   The second additional requirement of carers' assessments, in a sense, reinforces the first. The authority must have regard to whether the carer works or is participating in education, training or recreation or wishes to do so (CA 2014 s10(6)).[65]

'Carer blind' assessments

3.75   One of the most important principles of an adult's needs assessment is that it must disregard carer input. This is clear from the terms of the eligibility criteria which are based on considering the adult's ability to achieve specified outcomes 'without assistance'.[66] If the adult's assessment took into account a carer's contribution, the authority would not be able to make a lawful eligibility decision because it would not have available the necessary information to enable it to do so. It would not know what the adult could do without assistance.

3.76   The statutory guidance explains the purpose of recording needs which are in fact met by a carer (para 6.15):

> During the assessment local authorities must consider all the adult's care and support needs, regardless of any support being provided by a carer ... The local authority is not required to meet any needs which are being met by a carer who is willing and able to do so, but it should record where that is the case. This ensures that the entirety of the adults needs are identified and the local authority can respond appropriately if the care feel unable or unwilling to carry out some or all of the caring they were previously providing.

3.77   There are two other mandatory elements of the assessment process, namely that the authority is required to consider:

64   Complaint no 15 013 201 against Sefton MBC, 23 August 2016.
65   The provision replicates the obligation first introduced via Carers (Equal Opportunities) Act 2004 s2 – and see Public Service Ombudsman (Wales) Complaint no B2004/0707/S/370 against Swansea City Council, 22 February 2007 (see in particular paras 78, 133 and137).
66   See Care and Support (Eligibility Criteria) Regulations 2015 SI No 313 regs 2(3) and 3(3).

- whether something other than the provision of care and support, or support in relation to a carer, would contribute to the achievement of the outcomes the individual wishes to achieve;
- the individual would benefit from provision of prevention services (under CA 2014 s2), information and advice (under section 4) or anything available in the community (sections 9(6) and 10(8)).

3.78   Although the statutory guidance does focus on the 'alternative' solution' aspect of these provisions (paras 6.63–6.64), arguably it would be wrong to interpret this set of requirements as being a narrow exercise of looking for alternative ways of meeting needs.[67] It is significant that the purpose of the exercise is the achievement of the individual's goals or securing benefits for them (not meeting eligible needs, although the two may of course be connected).

A whole family approach

3.79   The 'whole family approach' is gaining traction throughout the social care field, but (as the statutory guidance makes clear) this is not a narrow 'nuclear family' approach to the obligation (para 6.65):

> The intention of the whole family approach is for local authorities to take a holistic view of the person's needs and to identify how the adults needs for care and support impact on family members or others in their support network.

3.80   The obligation imposed by the assessment regulations is to consider the impact of the individual's needs on any carer and any other person the local authority considers to be relevant (reg 4(1)). The statutory guidance explains that this will require that the authority identifies 'anyone who may be part of the person's wider network of care and support' (para 6.66).

3.81   The statutory guidance explains (paras 6.65–6.73) the intention behind the 'whole family approach' and the obligations it places on authorities which are, in summary, to:

- consider the impact of the needs of the person cared for on family members (and others);
- identify any children who are involved in providing care;
- 'where appropriate' consider whether the child or young carer should be referred for a young carer's assessment or a needs assessment under the Children Act 1989, or a young carer's assessment under CA 2014 s63;
- ensure that adults' and children's care and support services work together – for example, by sharing expertise and linking processes;
- (where it appears that a child is involved in providing care) consider:
  - the impact of the person's needs on the young carer's well-being, welfare, education and development;
  - whether any of the caring tasks the child is undertaking are inappropriate, and if they are, should consider how supporting the adult

---

67 See para 3.92 below on the lawfulness signposting to universal services as a referral 'out of' the assessment process.

with needs for care and support can prevent the young carer from undertaking this care.

3.82 Specific guidance has been published on the whole-family approach and the CA 2014.[68] It advises that a 'whole-family approach' would ensure that family-related questions are embedded in processes at first contact. Whatever assessment process is being used/undertaken the question must be asked whether there are any children in the household and if they are undertaking any caring role (page 15). Additional key questions are identified in the guidance as including (page 3):

- Who else lives in your house?
- Who helps with your support and who else is important in your life?
- Is there anyone that you provide support or care for?
- Is there a child in the family (including stepchildren, children of partners or extended family)?
- Does any parent need support in their parenting role?

3.83 The identification of a child providing care will trigger a duty to assess the child as a young carer under Children Act 1989 s17ZA. Although the authority must consider whether a young carer is undertaking any inappropriate caring tasks in their own assessment, this question must also be addressed in the adult's needs assessment. Regulations require, as part of an adult's (or indeed carer's) assessment:[69]

- consideration of the impact on the child's 'well-being, welfare, education and development'; and
- identification of whether any of the caring tasks the child is undertaking are inappropriate.

3.84 In short, it is not sufficient simply to refer the question to children's services: logically this must follow, since if the young carer is carrying out tasks that are inappropriate, adult care and support may well be required to plug the gap that will be left when they stop doing so. The statutory guidance gives possible examples of inappropriate care, which include personal care such as bathing, maintaining the family budget and administering medication (para 6.72).

3.85 The assessment regulations also confer a right on any person to know where he or she can find information and advice, not just about the assessment process, but generally about the care system (reg 4(2)). The duty is triggered when a person comes to the attention of the local authority and it considers that they would benefit from that information and advice. One circumstance in which that is likely to happen is during the assessment of a member of the household. This individual duty complements the authority's general duty to main an advice and information service (see para 19.5 below) and it seems likely that it will be fulfilled in many cases by signposting the person concerned to that service.

---

68 Department of Health (and others), *The Care Act and whole-family approaches*, 2015, pp 8–9.
69 Care and Support (Assessment) Regulations 2014 SI No 2827 reg 4(3).

The assessment process

Involvement

3.86   At the heart of personalisation is 'involvement'. The CA 2014 does not, however, simply confer a right to be involved, but imposes what is arguably to be interpreted as a proactive duty on the local authority 'to involve'. For an adult's assessment, the duty is to involve the adult, any carer and any other person at the request of the adult, or, if the adult lacks sufficient mental capacity to make such a request, any person who appears to be interested in the adult's welfare (CA 2014 s9(5)(a), (b) and (c)). This replaces the obligation to consult as found in the (repealed) Community Care Assessment Directions 2004.[70] In the case of a carer's assessment, the local authority must involve the carer and anyone else the carer wishes to be involved (CA 2014 s10(7)).

3.87   The assessment regulations endeavour to translate this duty into effective practice in two ways, both of which make it clear that the duty is a proactive one. First is the requirement to ensure that the process is such that the individual is able to participate as effectively as possible (reg 3(b)). The statutory guidance says (para 6.30):

> The local authority should have processes in place, and suitably trained staff, to ensure the involvement of the parties so that their perspective and experience supports a better understanding of the needs, outcomes and well-being.

3.88   Second, the assessment regulations create valuable rights to information about the assessment process itself which must be provided before the assessment 'wherever practicable' and in an accessible format (reg 3(4) and (5)). The statutory guidance says, in specific terms, that the list of questions to be covered in the assessment should be provided (para 6.38). A common complaint of those being assessed is that they do not know what to expect and so cannot prepare properly. This can have serious consequences for the adequacy of the assessment. As the statutory guidance stresses, the individual is best placed to understand the impact of his or her situation on his or her well-being.[71] The authority is, in any event, subject to a duty to assume this is the case as part of the overarching well-being duty (CA 2014 s1(3)).

3.89   One of the most significant reforms in this area is the new duty on social services authorities to appoint an independent advocate where the individual would experience 'substantial difficulty' in participating in any of the assessment, care planning and review processes under the CA 2014 (see para 3.117 below). Mental incapacity is not required to trigger the obligation to appoint an independent advocate, but where there is concern about capacity the statutory guidance says that a capacity assessment should be carried out (para 6.32). This may not only provide information about the support needs the individual may have in the assessment

---

70   Department of Health, *The Community Care Assessment Directions 2004*, 26 August 2004, para 2 – for a copy of this, see the 5th edition of this book at p1016.

71   For example, see para 6.35; and see para 2.17 above.

process, but is very likely to be relevant to the substantive needs assessment in any event.

3.90 The statutory guidance also says that consideration should be given at an early stage to whether the individual may need a specialist interpreter to help with communication (para 6.23) and notes the provisions of the EqA 2010, which of course may require reasonable adjustments to be made.

An appropriate and proportionate process

3.91 Appropriateness and proportionality are two key underlying principles when it comes to assessment under the CA 2014, but the general approach is translated into an individual duty in the assessment regulations. The authority must ensure that the process is appropriate and proportionate to the individual's needs and circumstances (reg 3(1)).[72] However, this does not override the other statutory requirements of an assessment, for example, to address outcomes and well-being (see statutory guidance, para 6.4). Even where it is 'appropriate and proportionate' to operate some kind of triage process, if that (and no additional) process is being used, it must itself be compliant to be a lawful assessment. It cannot be used to, in effect, divert someone who is entitled to an assessment out of the assessment process.

3.92 The statutory guidance envisages the possibility that the authority might suggest alternatives that might help address an individual's difficulties, eg universal services that are available to everyone in the community. However, it certainly does not envisage that the individual would simply be signposted out of the assessment process. The statutory guidance speaks of a 'pause in the assessment process to allow such interventions to take place and for any benefit to the adult to be determined' (para 6.25), ie the effectiveness of those interventions must be revisited and the assessment completed at that stage.[73] Systems will need to be put in place to ensure that individuals are not simply 'lost' at the point of signposting and never have the benefit of a proper (ie lawful) assessment.

3.93 The requirement of appropriateness and proportionality will limit the extent to which a local authority can develop standard procedures to be implemented by personnel without the authority to adapt the process to the individual case. When determining what is appropriate and proportionate, the wishes and preferences of the individual, the outcomes the individual is seeking and the severity and overall extent of the individual's needs must all be taken into account (reg 3(2)). It may be obvious that the more complex an individual's needs, the more complex the assessment will generally need to be, but this regulation makes it clear that there are

72 See also Social Care Institute for Excellence (SCIE) online guidance, *Care Act 2014: assessment and eligibility process map – ensuring assessment is appropriate and proportionate*, January 2015 at www.scie.org.uk/care-act-2014/assessment-and-eligibility/process-map/ which stresses that a proportionate assessment will involve (among other things) 'both hearing and understanding the initial presenting problem; not taking this at "face value"; ensuring any underlying needs are also explored and understood'.

73 This is also addressed at para 6.62 of the guidance that considers the importance of considering preventative approaches in the course of the assessment.

other factors to take into account, in particular the individual's desired outcomes. For example, the assessment of an adult who wishes to be able to continue to participate in outdoor adventure activities but whose developing arthritis has compromised his or her physical abilities may require a specialist occupational therapist assessment and identification of, and input from, specialist activity providers.

3.94   If an assessment process limits itself to considering an individual's needs at a particular point in time, there is unlikely to be an adequate assessment of any fluctuating needs. This issue is expressly addressed in the regulations. The assessment must take into account what is happening over a period of time that the authority thinks is sufficient to establish an accurate picture (reg 3(3)).

3.95   The statutory guidance takes the view that the 'appropriate and proportionate' principle means that a face-to-face assessment may not be necessary in every case. Assessments may be:

- face-to-face;
- supported self-assessment (see below at para 3.98);
- online or phone assessment;
- joint assessments; or
- combined with other assessments (see below at para 3.102).

3.96   In relation to the controversial issue of telephone or online assessments, the statutory guidance carries a very clear warning that they should only be used when appropriate, and gives by way of example cases where the person's needs are less complex (para 6.3). Even then, where there is concern about a person's mental capacity, a face-to-face assessment should be undertaken:

> 6.28 ... Where appropriate, an assessment may be carried out over the phone or online. In adopting such approaches, local authorities should consider whether the proposed means of carrying out the assessment poses any challenges or risks for certain groups, particularly when assuring itself that it has fulfilled its duties around safeguarding, independent advocacy, and assessing mental capacity. *Where there is concern about a person's capacity to make a decision, for example as a result of a mental impairment such as those with dementia, acquired brain injury, learning disabilities or mental health needs, a face-to-face assessment should be arranged.* Local authorities have a duty of care to carry out an assessment in a way that enables them to recognise the needs of those who may not be able to put these into words. Local authorities must ensure that assessors have the skills, knowledge and competence to carry out the assessment in question, and this applies to all assessments regardless of the format they take. [Emphasis added.]

3.97   In general terms there is, of course, something problematic about determining over the phone or online that a person's needs are non-complex, and not infrequently it may also be difficult to determine that there is no concern about their capacity to make a decision. The statutory guidance is also silent on the obligation in any such assessment to ensure that any other adults in need or carers (including young carers) who are identified are contacted so that their needs can be assessed.

Supported self-assessment

3.98 The new scheme provides for the option of supported self-assessment. Arguably, it represents a withdrawal from the more radical models of self-assessment that have been used by some authorities in the last few years of the pre-CA 2014 regime. One model has involved the posting out of a multiple choice questionnaire to be completed without assistance and then translated, without any apparent intervening professional check, into a points score and a personal budget. This kind of 'pure' self-assessment was (and under the new statutory scheme will be) unlawful. As Hickinbottom J held in *R (B) v Cornwall CC*,[74] in relation to the pre-CA 2014 duty,[75] an authority (para 68):

> ... cannot avoid its obligation to assess needs etc by failing to make an appropriate assessment themselves, in favour of simply requiring the service user himself to provide evidence of his needs.

That obligation is, of course, retained in the new regime.

3.99 The assessment regulations define a supported self-assessment as one 'carried out jointly by the local authority and the individual to whom it relates' (reg 2(1)), and require the authority 'to ascertain' whether the individual wants one. Arguably, this requires more than a simple 'offer' of a supported self-assessment, and includes an explanation of what this would involve and how it would compare with the alternative. The individual has a right to opt for this process if he or she has the capacity to take part in it (reg 2(3)). However, difficulties in participation should not be confused with incapacity. If the individual has substantial difficulty in undertaking a supported self-assessment but does have the capacity to do so, he or she has a right to that process and to independent advocacy to assist under CA 2014 s67 (see below at para 3.117).

3.100 In order to facilitate a supported self-assessment, the authority must provide the individual with any relevant information it may have about the individual in an accessible format (reg 2(5)). For example, it would not be sufficient to send an untranslated copy of a previous assessment, without more, to someone who has difficulty in reading/understanding English. In the case of a carer's assessment, information about the cared-for person must be provided as well, subject to the cared for adult's consent or, if incapacitated, the local authority's determination that it would be in the adult's best interests (reg 2(5)). This is a significant right for carers, who have often struggled to get relevant and necessary information about the person they care for (see also para 19.39 below).

3.101 The statutory guidance adds significantly to the assessment regulations in a number of ways. For example, it says that similar paperwork to that used in an assessment by a social worker should be used (para 6.48), even though it is to be completed in a supported self-assessment by the individual themselves (para 6.44).[76] Perhaps most importantly, it also makes clear that the authority 'must ensure that the assessment as completed is

---

74 [2009] EWHC 491 (Admin), (2009) 12 CCLR 381.

75 Under NHSCCA 1990 s47.

76 Para 6.48 notes that the paperwork may have to be adapted so that it is easier to understand although it will cover the same questions.

an accurate and complete reflection' of the individual's needs, outcomes and impact (para 6.46). This may involve consulting other relevant professional and people who know the person being assessed with their consent (see para 6.47). The use of the term 'must' in the statutory guidance indicates the view that this is a legal obligation. This is unsurprising. A supported self-assessment is merely a method of delivering on the statutory duty to assess and it is the local authority that carries the legal responsibility to ensure that it is performed. Furthermore, section 12 only permits the making of regulations for the carrying out of a joint assessment with the local authority. If a local authority were to simply accept the adult's own assessment of their needs, it would not in any sense be a joint assessment. The final decision on eligibility rests with the local authority; there is no provision for joint eligibility decision-making under CA 2014 s13.[77]

Joint and combined assessments

3.102   Combining different assessments can contribute to the proportionality of an assessment process, saving those involved from the frustrations and stress of participating in a number of procedures, each of which asks for at least some of the same information. It can also contribute to a more holistic view of the situation. Needs and carers assessments can be combined with other assessments that the authority is carrying out, whether or not the assessment is being carried out under the CA 2014 (CA 2014 s12(5)). So a needs assessment could be combined with a carer's assessment and/or with a young carer's assessment under the Children Act 1989 (as amended by the Children and Families Act 2014) (see para 15.178 below).

3.103   Assessments can also be combined with assessments that are the responsibility of another body if the local authority exercises its power under CA 2014 s12(7) to undertake that other assessment on behalf of that other body. The obvious candidate is an NHS continuing healthcare (CC) assessment that is the responsibility (usually) of a clinical commissioning group (CCG) (see below at para 11.12). Where the assessment being carried out by the other body is of a person other than the individual being assessed, the power is limited to cases where that other person is a 'relevant' person. A person is a 'relevant person' if it would be reasonable to combine an assessment relating to that person with the needs or carer's assessment (CA 2014 s12(11)). This might well be the case if the proposed combination was of a NHS CC assessment and a carer's assessment. The adult is likely to be a relevant person as defined.

3.104   The authority's power to undertake combined assessments is subject to the consent condition being met (CA 2014 s12(5) and (6)). Not only must the individual to whom the needs or carer's assessment relates agree, but also any other person who is the subject of an assessment with which the needs or carer's assessment is being combined. If that other person is a child, but the child does not have the capacity or competence to agree, the authority will need to be satisfied it is in the child's best interests. The CA 2014 contains no explicit requirement that there be a best interests determination for an adult who does not have sufficient capacity to

---

77 See statutory guidance, para 6.53.

consent: presumably this is merely attributable to 'drafting economy' in the sense that the Mental Capacity Act 2005 must in any event require such a determination.

3.105　　The consent condition should not be treated as an unimportant box-ticking exercise. For example, a young carer may wish to discuss his or her unwillingness to continue to provide care when he or she reaches 18. It may in practice be difficult to maintain appropriate confidentiality if assessments are combined (although section 12(9) allows for the combining of parts of assessments which might overcome the problem in some cases).

3.106　　The local authority also has the power to carry out a joint assessment with another body undertaking its own assessment for which it is responsible (CA 2014 s12(7)). On the face of it, the statutory consent condition does not apply to joint assessment although the statutory guidance suggests that agreement is necessary (see para 6.76).

3.107　　The combining of assessments or their joint undertaking does not in any way override the statutory requirements detailed above.

Skilled assessors and expert input

3.108　　The new duty on social services authorities to ensure that assessors have the 'skills, competence and knowledge' to carry out the assessment in question and are appropriately trained (reg 5(1)) is an important safeguard against overly zealous reductions in the relevant budgets. As the statutory guidance puts it (para 6.85):

> It is essential that the assessment is carried out to the *highest* quality. [Emphasis added.]

3.109　　The quality/competence requirement has significant implications for authorities who contract out assessments (see para 3.137). In such cases there would appear to be a need for explicit contractual obligations requiring the assessment provider to ensure that only competent and trained assessors are used and that an appropriate allocation system exists so that assessors have impairment-specific awareness and skills that match the needs of the individuals they assess. It will not be enough simply to have available a workforce which appears competent and suitably trained overall if it is not possible to provide the right assessor in any particular case: the assessment obligation is an individual duty, not a general one.

3.110　　What is required in any particular case will be determined not only by the circumstances of the individual – the requirement is to have the skills, competence and knowledge to carry out the assessment in question and the assessment method will be a relevant factor (see statutory guidance, paras 6.85–6.86). For example, telephone assessments will require particular skills. These assessors will need to be able to identify whether there is any indication of cognitive impairment or mental illness which means that there should be a face-to-face interview.[78] They will also need to be

78 The advice of ADASS in their 2009 publication, *Personalisation and the law: implementing putting people first in the current legal framework* was: Staff dealing with first contact need enough social work skill and experience to recognise indicators of mental impairment which may affect insight and understanding of the options, and

able to explore, without the benefit of clues other than the verbal account given, whether the individual's articulation of his or her problems and wishes is sufficiently comprehensive. First contact with a social services department is often prompted by a specific problem that has arisen which may be the only issue that is raised unless the assessor takes a proactive approach.

3.111   Where the authority considers that specialist expertise is required, it must consult a person who has that expertise (reg 5(2)). This duty may prove to be very helpful in securing an adequate assessment of people with rarer conditions where there have been problems with the adequacy of assessment in the past because assessors did not properly understand their condition.[79]

3.112   Although the statutory guidance replaces the majority of the previous adult social care assessment guidance, there are two material exceptions. The first relates to specific guidance concerning those with autism, and the second relates to deaf-blind people. The statutory guidance (at para 6.89) summarises the 2010 guidance 'Fulfilling and rewarding lives' (as updated by Think Autism 2014)[80] as saying that local authorities should:

- make basic autism training available for all staff working in health and social care;
- develop or provide specialist training for those in roles that have a direct impact on access to services for adults with autism;
- include quality autism awareness training within the general equality and diversity training programmes across public services.

It goes on to say that the CA 2014 strengthens this guidance (para 6.90):

> The Act places a legal requirement on local authorities that all assessors must have the skills, knowledge and competence to carry out the assessment in question. Where an assessor does not have experience in a particular condition (such as autism, learning disabilities, mental health needs or other conditions) they must consult someone with relevant experience. This is so that the person being assessed is involved throughout the process and their needs outcomes and the impact of their needs on their well-being are all accurately identified.

3.113   The statutory guidance at para 6.89 advises that (previously) published guidance relating to deaf-blind people 'should be read with this guidance'. It is, however, unclear whether this is a reference to the 2009 statutory guidance, *Care and support for deafblind children and adults: policy guidance*[81] and/or the best practice guidance published by the Department of Health,

the processes involved in assessment, so that those applicants may be assured of their right to assessment (p5).

79   Or indeed some of the more common impairments – a 2004 local government ombudsman report turned on the inability of the local authority to understand the needs of someone with an autistic spectrum disorder – see Report on an Investigation into Complaint no 02/C/08690 against Sheffield City Council, 9 August 2004.

80   Department of Health, *Fulfilling and rewarding lives: the strategy for adults with autism in England*, 2010; and Department of Health, *Think autism: fulfilling and rewarding lives, the strategy for adults with autism in England: an update*, 2014.

81   Department of Health, *Care and support for deafblind children and adults: policy guidance*, December 2014.

Think dual sensory.[82] In any event, in relation to the assessment process the assessment regulations – require that the assessor has training and expertise in this disability (reg 6(1)). The statutory guidance contains a specific section concerning the needs of deaf-blind people (paras 6.91–6.97) and requires that their assessments must be carried out by assessors with training of at least QCF or OCN level 3 or above where the individual has higher or more complex needs (para 6.92).

Co-operation and integration[83]

3.114 Under the pre-CA 2014 assessment regime,[84] local authorities were subject to a duty to notify relevant health or housing authorities if the adult being assessed had a potential need for services that either of these authorities could provide and to invite them to assist in the assessment process. This was not a signposting duty which alleviated the local authority of any further responsibility once the 'referral' had been made, although it was sometimes treated as such. The duty also required the local authority to take into account any provision to be made by either of these other authorities when making their own service-provision decision, and, by implication, therefore, required the local authority to 'keep the case open' and conclude their own decision-making process once the input from health or housing was available.[85] There is no equivalent duty in the Care Act – and the select committee that scrutinised the Care and Support Bill expressed concern about this omission (from the bill). The committee did, however, note the view of the Department of Health that 'the duty on local authorities to co-operate generally and in specific cases will ensure that they work with partners such as the NHS and housing authorities'.[86] Time will tell whether this confidence is well-founded, although the local authority's common law public law obligation[87] will require it to gather essential information for the purpose of the assessment and the decision of another authority as to whether to provide services will in many cases be of that nature.

3.115 A specific obligation is placed on local authorities by the assessment regulations to refer adults in need for an NHS CC assessment when it appears to an authority, carrying out a needs assessment, that the individual may be eligible (reg 7). The referral must be to whichever body appears to be responsible, which in most cases will be the local clinical CCG[88] – see para 12.52 below. Again, the outcome of that assessment will be relevant

---

82 Department of Health, *Think dual sensory: good practice guidelines for older people with dual sensory loss*, 1997.

83 Note the general duty to promote integration of care and support with health and health-related provision which includes housing in section 3 which may also be relevant.

84 NHSCCA 1990 s47(3).

85 NHSCCA 1990 s47(3).

86 Joint committee on the draft Care and Support Bill, *Draft Care and Support Bill*, HL Paper 143 HC 822, The Stationery Office, 2013, paras 175–176.

87 *Secretary of State for Education and Science v Tameside MBC* [1977] AC 1014.

88 National Health Service Commissioning Board and Clinical Commissioning Groups (Responsibilities and Standing Rules) Regulations 2012 SI No 2996 regs 20(2) and 21(2).

to the local authority's own decisions about whether they need to take action and it would be unlawful to simply refer and then close down the adult's case on the ground that he or she is 'health's responsibility'. The determination of eligibility for NHS CC is one in which the CCG (or NHS England in certain circumstances)[89] has a crucial role and may of course be pivotal in determining the extent of a local authority's corresponding responsibilities.

3.116   In addition to this specific obligation in the assessment regulations, CA 2014 s7 imposes a duty on any 'relevant partner', in response to a request by the local authority, to cooperate in an individual case.[90] The definition of 'relevant partner' is broad, including virtually all NHS bodies in the local authority's area and for example, where the local authority is a county council, its district councils and in consequence making the local housing authority a 'relevant partner'. The duty is not unqualified, but if the partner body refuses the request it must provide written reasons (CA 2014 s7(3)) either explaining why the request is 'incompatible with its own duties' or why it would have 'an adverse effect on the exercise of its functions' (CA 2014 s7(2)). If a local authority is having difficulty securing the cooperation of relevant partners in carrying out its assessment duties, public law principles require that it act decisively ('grasps the nettle' to quote the ombudsman[91]) and this would include the exercise of its power under section 7. It should not see it simply as the problem of the individual concerned. Having said this, the section 7 duty to cooperate is a duty relating to an individual and, in principle, enforceable in judicial review proceedings as such by that individual.

Advocacy support

3.117   Assessment is the first point in the process where the statutory independent advocacy scheme will be engaged (CA 2014 s67) and the statutory guidance states that the issue should be considered at the very early stage of first contact (para 6.23).

3.118   An advocate must be provided if, without support, the individual would experience 'substantial difficulty' in any one of the following:

- understanding relevant information;
- retaining that information;
- using or weighing that information as part of the process of being involved;
- communicating the individual's views, wishes or feelings (whether by talking, using sign language or any other means (CA 2014 s67(4)).

3.119   'Mental incapacity' as defined by the Mental Capacity Act 2005 is not required. There is no requirement here for the cause of the difficulty to be an impairment of, or a disturbance in the functioning of, the mind or

---

89 See para 12.160 below.

90 CA 2014 s7 mirrors a very similar provision in Children Act 1989 s27 – in which respect, see, for example, *R v Northavon DC ex p Smith* [1994] 3WLR 403 HL.

91 Complaint no 96/C/3868 against Calderdale MBC (1998) – and see para 11.42 below.

brain or for there to be an inability to understand information etc. Substantial difficulty is sufficient. It would therefore apply to people who have no formal diagnosis, and those who are easily confused or who are vulnerable due to coercion or duress. The statutory guidance, when providing examples of circumstances in which it would be appropriate to appoint an independent advocate, in each case illustrates an inability to undertake the relevant process (see statutory guidance paras 7.11–7.14). This is misleading and risks social work practitioners imposing an unlawfully high eligibility threshold. If an individual were unable to do one or more of understanding information, retaining it, weighing it or communicating decisions.

3.120 The authority must have 'particular regard to' a number of factors in deciding whether or not the individual would experience 'substantial difficulty':[92]

- any health condition of the individual;
- any learning difficulty the individual has;
- any disability the individual has;
- the degree of complexity of the individual's circumstances, whether in relation to the individual's needs for care and support or otherwise;
- whether the individual has previously refused an assessment; and
- whether the individual is experiencing, or at risk of, abuse or neglect.

3.121 The duty does not apply if the local authority is satisfied that there is an 'appropriate person' available to facilitate the individual's involvement,[93] but the individual must consent to the individual concerned acting in that role, or, in cases of incapacity, the local authority must be satisfied the selected person will act in the individual's best interests (CA 2014 s67(5) and (6)). In effect, the individual with sufficient mental capacity to do so has the right to choose whether to have a statutory advocate because they can veto any local authority choice of an appropriate person.

3.122 The statutory guidance provides case studies to illustrate the kind of circumstances where, it suggests, it would not be appropriate for a family member to act. They include an example (para 7.35) of a young adult with a moderate learning disability (including finding it hard to retain information) who lives in the family home. She wants to move 'to living more independently' but her parents are 'very worried that she won't be able to cope living in her own home and are against her doing so'. In these circumstances the statutory guidance suggests that the parents would not be 'an appropriate person' who could effectively represent and support her. In most situations of this kind, family members will have a view on what is appropriate for their relative. This may make it difficult for them to act as an appropriate person to facilitate the involvement of the adult who needs support, but it would not necessarily mean that they should be excluded from the process (such as the assessment) being undertaken. Indeed if they are a carer the local authority will have a duty to involve them in the assessment of the cared for adult (CA 2014 s9(5)(b) – see para 3.86 above).

3.123   There will undoubtedly be 'hard cases' where it may be difficult to make a judgment as to whether a family member can act as the appropriate person, but it is difficult to see how either the local authority's advocacy budget or their concerns that a family member might challenge its views might be relevant factors when making that judgment.

3.124   There are two sets of circumstances in which, even where there is an appropriate person, an independent advocate must be appointed in any event. The first is where the assessment or support planning is likely to lead to the NHS arranging hospital accommodation of 28 days or more or care home accommodation of eight weeks or more and the local authority thinks appointing an advocate is in the individual's best interests.[94]

3.125   The second is where there is a disagreement on a material issue between the local authority and the appropriate person, but – importantly – the authority and that person must agree it would be in the adult's best interests to appoint an advocate (reg 4(3)). The requirement for consensus is an important protection against the appointment of an advocate in response to a disagreement with a family member in order to try and marginalise their involvement.

3.126   The duty in section 67 is to appoint a person who is independent of the authority. In support of this fundamental aspect of the duty the regulations:

- require the authority to satisfy itself that the person demonstrates the ability to act independently of the authority (reg 2(3)(a));
- prohibit the appointment of someone who works for the authority (reg 2(3)(b)) or for any organisation commissioned to carry out assessment, support planning or reviews (reg 2(5));
- prohibit the use of a person who is providing care or treatment in a professional or paid capacity to that individual or either to their carer or to the adult for whom they are providing care (reg 2(2)).

3.127   The first of these is arguably a proactive obligation. It is not enough for the authority to say that it has no reason to believe that a person will not act independently if it has no system of identifying and protecting against that risk. For example, its contract under which the individual is appointed might require independence and protect the advocate appropriately against discrimination in future appointments if they challenge the authority in their role as advocates.

3.128   The regulations set out requirements additional to independence. A person cannot be appointed unless they have appropriate experience and training, are of good character, and are appropriately supervised. Interestingly, in addition to this, the regulations impose a requirement of competence (to represent and support that particular individual). Having experience, training and supervision does not, of course, guarantee competence, and the requirement to appoint a competent advocate means that the local authority will need to have some means of ensuring competence.

---

94 Assessment regulations reg 4(2) – mirroring the appointment of independent mental capacity advocate requirements of Mental Capacity Act 2005 ss38–39.

For example, when contracting for the service the contract might oblige the provider to operate some kind of system of monitoring the quality of the advocacy provided by individual advocates and reviewing and acting on the results, in addition to employing experienced advocates who are trained and supervised.

3.129 The independent advocate must comply with the regulations governing the manner in which they must undertake their work (reg 5). They must:

- act with a view to promoting the individual's well-being (reg 5(2));
- meet in private with the individual (reg 5(3)(a));
- consult with those who provide care or treatment in a paid or professional capacity subject to the individual's consent or, in the absence of capacity to consent, if it is in the individual's best interests (reg 5(3)(b)(i));
- consult with others who may be in a position to comment on the individual's wishes, beliefs or values, eg family, carers and friends, again subject to consent or best interests (reg 5(3)(b)(ii));
- assist the individual in understanding the process, to communicate their views wishes or feelings, to understand how their needs could be met, and in making decisions in respect of care and support arrangements (reg 5(5)(a));
- so far as practicable, ensure the individual understands the authority's duties and their own rights and obligations (reg 5(5)(b));
- make such representations as necessary to secure the individual's rights (reg 5(5)(c));
- where they have concerns about the way in which the assessment or support planning has been undertaken or the outcomes, prepare a report to the authority (reg 5(5)(d)) and if they do so the authority must provide a written response (reg 6(2));
- where the individual does not have the capacity to communicate his or her views, wishes or feelings, the advocate must do so to the extent that he or she can ascertain them (reg 5(7));
- respond to a local authority's reasonable requests for information (reg 6(3)).

The first three are not absolute requirements, but limited by the extent that it is practicable and appropriate. The authority is subject to the concomitant obligations to assist the advocate in performing the advocacy role and to take into account any representations that the advocate makes (reg 6(1)(a) and (b)).

3.130 The advocate is placed under two very important duties in relation to challenging local authority decisions. The first is to assist the individual to challenge any decision made in the course of assessment and care and support planning, where they wish to do so (reg 5(5)(a)(v)). However, if the individual does not have the capacity to raise his or her own challenge, the advocate must do so on the individual's behalf if they consider the authority's decision to be inconsistent with the well-being principle (reg 5(8)). The statutory guidance points out that the ultimate goal of representation by an advocate is to 'secure a person's rights and ensure that their wishes are taken fully into account' (para 7.52). It goes on: 'The local authority should understand that the advocate's role incorporates 'challenge' on behalf of the individual' (para 7.53).

3.131   The advocate might find it difficult to perform this role if they did not have access to relevant information. Their rights to examine and take copies of 'relevant records' (as defined in CA 2014 s67(9)) are set out in regulation 5(6) and include (in broad-brush terms) health and social services records and records held by a provider. There is a case for saying that, if a family member (or some other person other than a statutory independent advocate) is facilitating the involvement of the individual concerned, they should also have access such information given that they supposed to be performing an equivalent role. If the adult does not have sufficient capacity to consent to this, it is difficult to see how a record-holder could reach any conclusion other than it is their best interests for such disclosure to be provided. If it is not, then, arguably, that person is probably not an appropriate person to act in the advocacy role.

3.132   In addition to their role in assessments, independent advocates must be appointed in the following processes (CA 2014 s67(3)):

- care and support and/or support planning;
- revising the care and support and/or support plan;
- carrying out transition assessment – child's, child's carer or young carer;
- safeguarding enquiries or reviews.

3.133   The statutory guidance also advises that the appointment of an independent advocate should be considered where joint packages of care are being considered between the CCG and social services:

> 7.22 These processes and arrangements have historically been difficult for individuals, their carers, family or friends, to understand and be involved in. Local authorities (with CCGs) will therefore want to consider the benefits of providing access to independent advice or independent advocacy for those who do not have substantial difficulty and/or those who have an appropriate person to support their involvement.

3.134   There is a real risk of discontinuity if different advocates are appointed for different parts of the process, in particular for assessment and care and support planning, and the statutory guidance argues that '[a]dvocacy should be seamless for people who qualify, so that they can benefit from the support of one advocate for their whole experience of care or safeguarding work' (para 7.60). There is a particular risk of discontinuity if the adult might at some point in the process also qualify for an independent mental capacity advocate (IMCA) under the MCA 2005, for example, if long-term accommodation is in issue. The requirements of both schemes have been designed to facilitate an advocate acting in both roles. If the potential need for an IMCA is identified at the start of the process, an advocate who is qualified to act as both should be appointed and local authority commissioning should facilitate this.[95]

---

95 See statutory guidance, para 7.65; and for an analysis of the extent to which the CA 2014 provides support for decision making in compliance with the requirements of the UN Convention on the Rights of Persons with Disabilities, Article 12(3) and General Comment No 1 (2014) on Article 12 (United Nations Committee on the Rights of

3.135   In *R (SG) v Haringey LBC*[96] the court quashed a decision that an adult was ineligible for care and support in part on the ground that the local authority had failed to appoint a statutory advocate in breach of its duty to do so. The council sought to argue that the claimant was not prejudiced by the absence of an advocate. Although the judge, on the one hand, appeared to leave an opening for this argument to be made again, perhaps successfully, on different facts, he also accepted the claimant's submission in this case that it was simply not possible to tell whether an advocacy appointment would have made no difference. Arguably this would be the position in most if not all cases. The council had said that demand for advocates outstripped supply. This did not sway the court which suggests that the judge (albeit implicitly) accepted that lack of resources cannot be a defence to what would otherwise be a breach of this statutory duty.

Written record of the assessment

3.136   CA 2014 s12 imposes a (new) statutory duty on local authorities to provide a copy of the needs assessment to the adult concerned, and any carer or other person as the adult requests, and equivalent rights in respect of carers assessments (s12(3) and (4)). A similar duty exists in relation to care and support plans (see para 4.144 below). The duty to disclose is not triggered by a request – and so would apply regardless of the mental capacity of the adult needing care. However, in such cases – where the adult with needs would be unlikely to fully understand the assessment themselves (for example, to be able to identify any inadequacies) – it will be of particular importance that a copy is given to a person who can consider it on their behalf. It would appear to follow that in such cases, public law principles (in particular the obligation to act fairly) will require that local authorities address this particular question and make a best interests decision as to whom the copy assessment should be given (in addition to the adult in need).

Delegation of the assessment

3.137   Prior to the implementation of the CA 2014, the main way by which local authorities were enabled to delegate their assessment functions to third party organisations was via agreements under the NHSA 2006 s75 (see para 11.130 where this arrangement is considered further).

3.138   In 2011 eight pilot programmes were run to explore the potential for delegation.[97] The programme was adjudged to have been a success, and in April 2014 English local authorities were given wide powers to delegate most of their adult social services functions (including social care

Persons with Disabilities Eleventh session 31 March–11 April 2014), see Lucy Series *Care Act 2014: consultation on draft guidance and regulations*, Small Places, 2014.

96 [2015] EWHC 2579 (Admin).

97 In large measure these involved small-scale projects run by third sector not for profit organisations – see SCIE, *Social work practice pilot sites*, 2011; and C Sutcliffe and others; 'Care coordination in adult social care: exploring service characteristics within the non-statutory sector in England' *Journal of Social Work* (2016) Vol June 20, 18.05.2016.

assessments).[98] CA 2014 s79 reaffirms this situation by providing a clear and specific statutory power to delegate (among other things – see para 1.25 above) the undertaking of an assessment, and, indeed, eligibility decision-making.

3.139   The legal responsibility for carrying out the relevant function still rests with the local authority. CA 2014 s79(6) provides:

> Anything done or omitted to be done by or in relation to a person author-ised under this section in, or in connection with the exercise or purported exercise of the function to which the authorisation relates *is to be treated for all purposes as done or omitted to be done by or in relation to the local authority.* [Emphasis added.]

3.140   Prior to the enlargement of their powers of delegation, many authorities had delegated aspects of carers' assessments to local independent carer support groups. This was possible under the pre-CA 2014 legislation, so long as the actual decision on the carer's eligibility for support was made/approved by the authority: the theory being that the carers' group did the data gathering/discussions with the carer and the local authority then signed off their recommendations.[99] Post April 2015 this arrangement is still permissible, but authorities are now able to delegate the 'sign-off' in addition. This may of course create some conflicts of interest if the carer organisation is also contracted to provide services.

3.141   The weakness inherent in a contracting out model is that it requires the contracted out tasks to be defined so that the boundaries of the con-tractual obligation are known and payments are calculated on that basis. This can lead to fragmentation and overspecialisation which may not only undermine the effectiveness of the social work service to individuals but ultimately prove more expensive. The statutory guidance warns (para 18.3):

> Local authorities should not delegate its [sic] functions simply to gain effi-ciency where this is to the detriment of the well-being of people using care and support.

---

98 Contracting Out (Local Authorities Social Services Functions) (England) Order 2014 SI No 829 made pursuant to Deregulation and Contracting Out Act 1994 s70(2), (4) and s77(1).

99 The evidence suggests that local authorities were delegating carers' assessments before the law permitted this – see W Mitchell, 'How local authorities allocate resources to carers through carer personal budgets', *Research Findings*, NIHR School for Social Care Research, London, 2014.

Eligibility and care planning

continued

Introduction

4.1 This chapter discusses eligibility criteria for both adults in need of care and support, and for carers; the eligibility decision; the duty to meet needs, including discussions of which needs need to be met as well as discretionary needs and exceptions; through to the actual meeting of needs. The chapter then turns to care and support planning.

Eligibility

Introduction: a brief history of eligibility criteria

4.2 The use of eligibility criteria is the main lawful mechanism by which local authorities can seek to control adult social care expenditure. There was no express provision for their use in the pre-Care Act (CA) 2014 legislative scheme, although early practice guidance suggested that such criteria might play a helpful role. In 1992, the *Laming Letter*[1] suggested that:

> 14. Authorities can be helped in this process by defining eligibility criteria, i.e. a system of banding which assigns individuals to particular categories, depending on the extent of the difficulties they encounter in carrying out everyday tasks and relating the level of response to the degree of such difficulties. Any 'banding' should not, however, be rigidly applied, as account needs to be taken of individual circumstances. Such eligibility criteria should be phrased in terms of the factors identified in the assessment process.

4.3 In the landmark case, *R v Gloucestershire CC ex p Barry*, on the meaning of 'need' for the purpose of Chronically Sick and Disabled Persons Act (CSDPA) 1970 s2, the majority in the House of Lords approved this approach.[2] Lord Clyde explained his view that eligibility criteria were required to make the system work in practice and were, in that sense, inherent in the statutory scheme:

> In deciding whether there is a necessity to meet the needs of the individual some criteria have to be provided. Such criteria are required both to determine whether there is a necessity at all or only, for example, a desirability, and also to assess the degree of necessity. Counsel for the respondent suggested that a criterion could be found in the values of a civilised society. But I am not persuaded that that is sufficiently precise to be of any real assistance ... The determination of eligibility for the purposes of the statutory provision requires guidance not only on the assessment of the severity of the condition or the seriousness of the need but also on the level at which there is to be satisfaction of the necessity to make arrangements. In the framing of the criteria to be applied it seems to me that the severity of a condition may have to be to be matched against the availability of resources.[3]

---

1 Formal advice letter issued by Herbert Laming (the then Chief Inspector of the Social Services Inspectorate) concerning the implementation of the 1993 community care reforms CI (92) 34 (Department of Health).
2 [1997] 2 WLR 459, (1997–98) 1 CCLR 40, HL.
3 [1997] 2 WLR 459, (1997–98) 1 CCLR 40, HL at para 54. The *Barry* judgment was by a 3:2 majority and has not been without criticism – see, for example, Lord Wilson (who gave the majority judgment) in *R (KM) v Cambridgeshire CC* [2012] UKSC 23 at para 5

4.4   In 2002, the Department of Health published detailed statutory guidance on eligibility criteria: *Fair access to care services* (FACS).[4] It applied to some but not all community care services; in particular, it did not apply to residential care provided under National Assistance Act (NAA) 1948 s21.[5] *Prioritising needs*[6] replaced FACS in 2010, although it simply adopted the FACS approach to eligibility. Although the 2010 guidance contained a framework for grading the risk to the sustainability of the caring role (at para 99), this generated (according to the guidance) only a right for carers to a decision on whether services would be provided, not a right to that support. In any event, the guidance appeared to be largely ignored – possibly because carers support services were considered to be 'discretionary' under the pre-CA 2014 regime.[7]

4.5   In the pre-CA 2014 scheme, *Prioritising needs* allowed local authorities to set their own eligibility threshold, but within the framework laid out in that statutory guidance. The framework was prescriptive; local authorities were not permitted to introduce amendments which would make the criteria more onerous.[8] However, the scheme lacked detail in parts which left it vulnerable to inconsistent application and more restrictive interpretation at times when budget savings were a particular priority. The scheme operated by categorising the risk(s) that would arise if no services were provided to meet each presenting need. The four categories were critical, substantial, moderate or low, and the guidance specified the consequences that would place the need in a particular category. For example, if the consequence was that life would be threatened, the need (perhaps the inability to prepare food independently) giving rise to this risk would fall into the critical category. Each local authority was permitted to make its own decision where to set its eligibility threshold, based in part on its financial resources. Immediately before the implementation of the CA 2014 the vast majority of local authorities had fixed their eligibility threshold at the substantial level ie all critical and substantial level needs under such a policy were eligible needs.

4.6   The introduction of national statutory minimum eligibility criteria is one of the major reforms introduced by the CA 2014. The eligibility criteria are not to be found in the Act itself, but in regulations made under section 13(7) and (8): the Care and Support (Eligibility Criteria) Regulations 2015 SI No 313, referred to in this chapter as the 'eligibility regulations'. There are two sets of eligibility criteria – one for adults who need care and support, and one for carers. The consequence of moving to a national scheme is that social services authorities have lost control over a key mechanism

where he noted that, if the judgment intended to say that resources are relevant in the assessment of need, as opposed to later stages such as determining the necessity of meeting needs, 'there are arguable grounds for fearing' that the judgment was in error. See also the judgment of Baroness Hale at para 48.

4 Department of Health, *Fair access to care services – guidance on eligibility criteria for adult social care*, 2003.
5 *R (De Almeida) v Kensington and Chelsea RLBC* (2012) 15 CCLR 318; and see *Prioritising needs*, para 71.
6 Department of Health, *Prioritising need in the context of Putting People First: a whole system approach to eligibility for social care England*, 2010.
7 See L Clements, *Carers and their rights*, 5th edn, Carers UK, 2011, paras 4.86–4.91.
8 *R (JM and NT) v Isle of Wight Council* (2012) 15 CCLR 167 at 66–68.

for reconciling demand with the resources made available in its adult social care budget. It is now under the centralised control of the secretary of state, who can tighten (or loosen) the criteria by amendments to the eligibility regulations.[9]

4.7   Once an individual has been found to have needs that meet the eligibility criteria, the local authority is subject to an individually enforceable duty to meet those needs (CA 2014 ss18 and 20) and to draw up a care and support plan for an adult, or a support plan for a carer. Both of those stages in the process are examined below.

The eligibility criteria for adults needing care and support

4.8   An adult in need of care and support will meet the eligibility criteria if and only if he or she meets three conditions (eligibility regulations reg 2(1)):

1) The **needs** 'arise from or are related to' a physical or mental impairment or illness.
2) As a result of the adult's needs, the adult is unable to achieve *two or more* of the specified **outcomes** (see below).
3) As a consequence, there is, or is likely to be, a significant impact on the adult's **well-being**.

'Needs'

4.9   The duty on the local authority is to meet eligible needs. The way that needs are described can have a critical impact on the nature of the care and support (or support) provided (discussed further at para 4.66 below).

4.10   The statutory guidance to the CA 2014[10] stresses that there is no hierarchy of needs (or of areas of well-being) (para 6.114). It is, however, not uncommon for this principle to be overlooked by financially-squeezed authorities who distinguish, unlawfully,[11] between 'essential' needs (often meaning needs which impact on activities of daily living such as eating, toileting and washing) and 'non-essential' needs (those connected with social contact, community participation and occupation).

Physical or mental impairment or illness

4.11   The first of the criteria in effect limits entitlement to adult social care provision to those with a disability or illness. The purpose of the condition is to exclude needs caused by 'other circumstantial factors'.[12] The statutory guidance states (para 6.104):

> The local authority must consider at this stage if the adult has a condition as a result of either physical, mental, sensory, learning or cognitive disabilities or illnesses, substance misuse or brain injury.

---

9   Subject to the affirmative resolution procedure provided for in CA 2014 s125.
10   Department of Health, *Care and support statutory guidance* to support implementation of Part 1 of the CA 2014 by local authorities, 2016 ('the statutory guidance').
11   Such decisions would be vulnerable to being set aside in judicial review proceedings on the basis that they rest on an error of law.
12   See statutory guidance, para 6.104.

This is broader in scope than the definition of the group who could poten-tially qualify under the pre-CA 2014 scheme for non-residential services under NAA 1948 s29(1):

> ... persons who are blind deaf or dumb or who suffer from mental disorder of any description, and other persons aged 18 or over who are substantially and permanently handicapped by illness, injury, or congenital deformity ...

For example, there is no need under the CA 2014 for the adult to be 'sub-stantially and permanently handicapped'. This change may have a materi-al impact in relation to such matters as hospital discharge responsibilities or pooled community equipment stores and is considered separately at chapter 5 and para 7.71 below.

4.12   However, on the face of it, there appears to be at least one group of beneficiaries of the pre-CA 2014 scheme who no longer qualify – namely pregnant women and nursing mothers, for whom local authorities had a power to provide residential care to regardless of whether they had a phys-ical or mental impairment or an illness. On closer analysis there is, argu-ably, little difference between the two legislative schemes in this respect. Local authorities simply had a power to make this provision under the NAA 1948.[13] Under CA 2014 s19, local authorities have the power to meet the needs of anyone who does not satisfy the eligibility criteria, which would arise in respect of pregnant women and nursing mothers in the same way as it does for anyone else (see para 4.74 below).

4.13   In the past, individuals have had difficulty accessing adult social care because of the lack of a diagnostic label. Those with a cognitive and/or mental health disability who could not be neatly categorised as having a learning disability or a mental illness were particularly vulnerable to this problem. The statutory guidance is helpful here (para 6.104):

> The authority should base their judgment on the assessment of the adult and a formal diagnosis should not be required.

Achieving outcomes

4.14   The second eligibility condition requires that the adult is unable to achieve two or more of the outcomes[14] specified in eligibility regulations reg 2. These 'outcomes' (and the explanation of each outcome by the statutory guidance) are considered below – see para 4.17.

4.15   The version of the eligibility criteria on which the Department of Health consulted required an inability to meet only one outcome. In its response it explained why it had settled on two: the intention was to try to develop criteria that most closely replicated the pre-CA 2014 substantial threshold.[15] Research carried out by the Personal Social Services Research Unit 'concluded that the version that was outcomes-focused and set the

---

13 NAA 1948 s21 and the Secretary of State's Approvals and Directions under section 21(1) National Assistance Act 1948, LAC(93)10, appendix 1 para 3.

14 See para 4.67 below for a discussion of the relationship between an 'outcome' and a 'need'.

15 Department of Health, *Response to the consultation on draft regulations and guidance for implementation of Part 1 of the Care Act 2014* Cm 8955, October 2014, p22.

minimum level at two or more outcomes was the version that came closest to current practice'. Although that may be the case when measured in terms of the overall numbers qualifying, it is possible that some who would have qualified under the old scheme might fall through the new minimum safety net. For example, a need would have fallen into the critical (and therefore eligible) category, if a 'vital' personal care routine would not have been carried out.[16] While the same person may be unable to achieve the outcome of maintaining personal hygiene under the new scheme, if they cannot demonstrate an inability to achieve a second listed outcome, they will not be eligible under CA 2014 s18 even if it is accepted that there will be a significant impact on well-being (the third criterion).

4.16   However, the local authority has a power to meet ineligible needs under CA 2014 s19 and, arguably, given the express policy intention, a local authority should consider whether to exercise this discretion where it is clear that the individual concerned would have been eligible under an old-style 'substantial' eligibility policy. Where the failure to meet a need would breach the individual's rights under the European Convention on Human Rights (ECHR) (such as the right not to be subjected to inhuman and degrading treatment), the discretion would be transformed into duty by virtue of Human Rights Act (HRA) 1998 s6 (see below at para 2.71).

The specified outcomes for adults in need

4.17   Eligibility regulations reg 2 details ten specified outcomes. The statutory guidance (at para 6.106 – which is expressly intended not to be 'exhaustive'[17]) and guidance issued by the Social Care Institute for Excellence (SCIE)[18] both comment on the nature and scope of each. In the following section, the outcome specified in reg 2 is in bold type, with the comments and examples provided by the statutory guidance and the SCIE guidance below.

(1) Managing and maintaining nutrition

Comments in the statutory guidance:

> Local authorities should consider whether the adult has access to food and drink to maintain nutrition, and that the adult is able to prepare and consume the food and drink.

Comments in the SCIE guidance:

> What to consider
> - Does the adult have access to food and drink to maintain nutrition and are they able to access, prepare and consume food and drink?
>
> Examples of circumstances affecting the ability to achieve the outcome
> - If the adult is eating a restricted or unhealthy diet (e.g. only eats toast):
>   - they may have difficulty in getting to the shops to buy food;
>   - they may be able to prepare food but have swallowing problems.

---

16 *Prioritising need*, p21.
17 See statutory guidance, para 6.107.
18 SCIE, *Care Act 2014: eligibility outcomes for adults with care and support needs under the Care Act 2014*. This is not guidance issued by the Department of Health –the SCIE is a registered charity.

(2) Maintaining personal hygiene

Comments in the statutory guidance:

Local authorities should, for example, consider the adult's ability to wash themselves and launder their clothes.

Comments in the SCIE guidance:

What to consider:
- What is the adult's ability to wash themselves and launder their clothes?

Examples of circumstances affecting the ability to achieve the outcome:
- If the adult cannot reach to wash themselves all over, this is not hygienic.
- If the adult does not have access to a washing machine and their mobility is poor, clothes and linen may not be properly clean.
- If the adult cannot buy cleaning products, or cognitively understand how to operate a washing machine, their clothes and linen may not be properly clean.

(3) Managing toilet needs

Comments in the statutory guidance:

Local authorities should consider the adult's ability to access and use a toilet and manage their toilet needs.

Comments in the SCIE guidance:

What to consider:
- Is the adult able to access and use the toilet and manage their own toilet needs?

Examples of circumstances affecting the ability to achieve the outcome:
- If the toilet is no longer accessible due to mobility problems or if the adult takes too long to get to the toilet, they may not be managing their toilet needs.
- If the adult is unable to maintain their night-time continence, they may not be managing from a dignity-of-life point of view.

(4) Being appropriately clothed

Comments in the statutory guidance:

Local authorities should consider the adult's ability to dress themselves and to be appropriately dressed, for instance in relation to the weather to maintain their health.

Comments in the SCIE guidance:

What to consider:
- Is the adult able to dress themselves and be appropriately dressed, that is, in relation to the weather or the activities they are undertaking, which could include work/volunteering?

Examples of circumstances affecting the ability to achieve the outcome:
- If the adult cannot put on or fasten their clothes, they are unlikely to be appropriately dressed.
- If the adult cannot acquire new clothes when needed, they may not be appropriately dressed e.g. for the change in seasons.
- The adult may be able to dress themselves in casual clothes unaided but may not be able to dress themselves in more formal work clothes eg put on a tie, zip up a dress or clean their shoes, and so would not be appropriately dressed for their circumstances.

- If they are severely visually impaired, for example, they may be able to dress themselves but not know if clothes are appropriate or clean.
- Note: This may also affect another outcome in relation to accessing work or volunteering.

(5) Being able to make use of the adult's home safely

Comments in the statutory guidance:

Local authorities should consider the adult's ability to move around the home safely, which could for example include getting up steps, using kitchen facilities or accessing the bathroom. This should also include the immediate environment around the home such as access to the property, for example steps leading up to the home.

Comments in the SCIE guidance:

What to consider:
- Is the adult able to move around the home safely, including climbing steps, using kitchen facilities and accessing the bathroom/toilet?
- This includes their immediate environment e.g. access and steps to the home.

Examples of circumstances affecting the ability to achieve the outcome:
- If the adult cannot reach certain rooms, they may not be using the home safely or be unreasonably confined e.g. having to spend all day in bed.
- If the adult cannot get in or out of the front door (e.g. because they cannot manage the steps), they are unlikely to be using the home safely or have proper access to it.
- If the adult is unable to use home appliances properly and safely (eg cooker, heater), they may not be meeting this outcome.

(6) Maintaining a habitable home environment

Comments in the statutory guidance:

Local authorities should consider whether the condition of the adult's home is sufficiently clean and maintained to be safe. A habitable home is safe and has essential amenities. An adult may require support to sustain their occupancy of the home and to maintain amenities, such as water, electricity and gas.

Comments in the SCIE guidance:

What to consider:
- Is the adult's home sufficiently clean and maintained to be safe, including essential amenities?
- Does the adult require support to sustain the home or maintain amenities such as water, electricity and gas or pay their rent or mortgage?

Examples of circumstances affecting the ability to achieve the outcome:
- If the adult is unable to pay their rent or utility bills (eg due to mental or physical incapacity), they will not be able to sustain their home.
- It may not be a habitable home environment if:
  - the home is damp or in very poor repair;
  - the adult is unable to clean their kitchen, leading to infestation;
  - the adult is hoarding excessively (note: hoarding per se does not determine eligibility; however, the impact of excessive hoarding on the individual's ability to achieve their outcomes, and thereby on their well-being, will affect eligibility).

(7) Developing and maintaining family or other personal relationships

Comments in the statutory guidance:

Local authorities should consider whether the adult is lonely or isolated, either because their needs prevent them from maintaining the personal relationships they have or because their needs prevent them from developing new relationships.

Comments in the SCIE guidance:

What to consider:
• Is the adult lonely or isolated?
• Do their needs prevent them from maintaining or developing relationships with family and friends?

Examples of circumstances affecting the ability to achieve the outcome:
• The adult's physical or psychological state may prevent them from making or maintaining relationships e.g. mental ill-health, autism.
• If the adult is unable to communicate easily and regularly – eg they may not have, or be able to use, a phone or computer, they may be unable to leave their home safely, they may be unable to communicate successfully or interact with others – this may prevent them from maintaining or developing relationships with family, friends and others.

(8) Accessing and engaging in work, training, education or volunteering

Comments in the statutory guidance:

Local authorities should consider whether the adult has an opportunity to apply themselves and contribute to society through work, training, education or volunteering, subject to their own wishes in this regard. This includes the physical access to any facility and support with the participation in the relevant activity.

Comments in the SCIE guidance:

What to consider:
• Does the adult have the opportunity and/or wish to apply themselves and contribute to society through work, training, education or volunteering?
• This includes physical access to any facility and support with participation in the relevant activity.

Examples of circumstances affecting the ability to achieve the outcome:
• If the adult is unable to leave their home safely, or communicate successfully, or interact with others, they may not be able to access work, training, education or volunteering.
• If the adult is unable to access information about opportunities available to them, they are unlikely to be able to engage in activities.

(9) Making use of necessary facilities or services in the local community including public transport, and recreational facilities or services

Comments in the statutory guidance:

Local authorities should consider the adult's ability to get around in the community safely and consider their ability to use such facilities as public transport, shops or recreational facilities when considering the impact on their well-being. Local authorities do not have responsibility for the provision of NHS services such as patient transport, however they should consider needs for support when the adult is attending healthcare appointments.

Comments in the SCIE guidance:

> What to consider:
> *   Is the adult able to get around in the community safely and able to use facilities such as public transport, shops and recreational facilities?
> *   This includes the need for support when attending healthcare appointments.
>
> Examples of circumstances affecting the ability to achieve the outcome:
> *   If the adult is unable to walk, or to use public transport unattended or to organise alternative transport (e.g. someone giving them a lift), or does not have money for a taxi, they may not be able to access services locally.
> *   As well as formal appointments e.g. healthcare appointments, this could include informal appointments e.g. being able to go to the library or to meet a friend in a cafe or pub.

(10) Carrying out any caring responsibilities the adult has for a child

Comments in the statutory guidance:

> Local authorities should consider any parenting or other caring responsibilities the person has. The adult may for example be a step-parent with caring responsibilities for their spouse's children.[19]

Comments in the SCIE guidance:

> What to consider:
> *   Does the adult have any parenting or other caring responsibilities eg as a parent, step-parent or grandparent?
>
> Examples of circumstances affecting the ability to achieve the outcome:
> *   If the individual is not able to take care of others, or feels overwhelmed because of their condition, they may not be able to carry out their caring responsibilities for a child.

The reference to the needs of disabled parents in the regulations represents a considerable advance on the arrangement in the previous legislation, where this important question was left to guidance[20] – guidance which it appears was often overlooked,[21] not least due to the administrative separation of children and adult social care services. The eligibility criteria highlight the importance of recognising that the needs of disabled parents include the need to discharge their parental responsibilities.

Disabled parents have in the past often complained that what is in reality their need for support to undertake parenting tasks is addressed as a need for children's services. This requires treating their child falling within the definition of a 'child in need' under Children Act 1989 s17, but often the only reason for a child doing so is because the disabled parent's needs are not met to enable them to parent. Research[22] suggests that addressing

---

19   This confirmation is to be welcomed.

20   Department of Health, *Good practice guidance on working with parents with a learning disability*, 2007; and see J Morris and M Wates *Supporting disabled parents and parents with additional support needs*, Adult Services Resource Guide 9, SCIE, 2007.

21   Commission for Social Care Inspection, *Supporting disabled parents: a family or fragmented approach?* 2009.

22   R Olsen and H Tyers, *Think parent: disabled adults as parents*, National Family and Parenting Institute, 2004.

such needs, goes at least some way to safeguarding and promoting the welfare of the child.[23]

Bristol City Council v C[24] concerned care proceedings that resulted from a mother's inability to provide the necessary care for her two children due to her mental health difficulties and uncontrolled epilepsy. Although the children had been accommodated for an extended period prior to the care proceedings, the authority had failed to arrange multi-disciplinary meetings/assessments involving Children's Services and Adult Services. The judge was trenchant in his criticisms of the authority's failure and 'profound lack of knowledge of the responsibilities that arise under the Care Act 2014'.

Interpreting the scope of the statutory outcomes

4.18   The scope of the statutory outcomes is a critical issue. A restrictive interpretation could lead to a very different eligibility determination or care package. This is well-illustrated by the complaint against the London Borough of Hammersmith & Fulham, investigated by the local government ombudsman.[25] Ms J had a visual impairment. On review, the council concluded that she had no unmet eligible needs. In relation to getting dressed and preparing food, they said that the CA 2014 outcomes did not require that clothes match or be clean, and that she could make use of long-life food, frozen and ready meals. The ombudsman concluded that the reassessment was flawed for a number of reasons, including the fact that it failed to recognise the importance to Ms J's personal dignity of wearing clean, presentable and appropriate clothes and that fresh food is essential to meeting nutritional needs:

> … the Council's restrictive interpretation of Care Act outcomes did not take proper account of Ms J's well-being. This was fault.

4.19   If the ombudsman's approach (in which well-being can impact on the scope of the outcome) were applied to the interpretation of the scope of other outcomes, it could have interesting consequences. The well-being principle 'is intended to cover the key components of independent living as expressed in the UN Convention of the Rights of People with Disabilities (in particular Article 19 of that Convention)' (statutory guidance, para 1.19). An outcome that was interpreted with this in mind could look very different. For example, the promotion of independent living requires, where possible, that adults are enabled to purchase, prepare and cook food themselves rather than having to rely on meals being cooked for/delivered to them, and to enable them to wash themselves rather than rely on a care worker to do so. Such an approach will also often be more consistent with the statutory duty on local authorities to provide support that will prevent or delay the development of needs (CA 2014 s2).

23 *Prioritising needs*, para 26.
24 *Bristol City Council v S* (2015) 20 May 2015, BS15C00174 before His Honour Judge Wildblood, QC, para 10.
25 Complaint no 15 011 661 against Hammersmith & Fulham LBC, 21 July 2016, para 25.

4.20   Furthermore, on this approach, different 'standards' of outcome could be applied to different individuals. For example, a 'habitable' home for an individual with an obsessive compulsive disorder may be a home maintained to a much higher standard of cleanliness than would ordinarily be the case.

4.21   It must not be forgotten that ultimately the scope of the prescribed outcomes is a matter of statutory interpretation – they are statutory constructs. If the *Hammersmith & Fulham* case is approached in this way, it leads to the same conclusion. The first relevant outcome was 'Being *appropriately* clothed' (emphasis added). The council appear to have omitted the reference to 'appropriately' when determining what the outcome required, thereby reaching a decision based on a misinterpretation of the statutory provision. 'Managing and maintaining *nutrition*' (again emphasis added) means not just eating, but having food which contains the nutrients needed to maintain health (in the short and long term). Again the council fell into error because it failed to appreciate the distinctions made in the concepts used in the statutory language.

4.22   Further 2016 ombudsman reports have commented on local authority decision-making which has impacted on the scope of outcomes. For example, a complaint[26] concerning a council's decision that a person had a need for help with dressing but not for an evening visit to help undress. The report held that it was logical to expect a person who needs assistance with dressing to need assistance with undressing. Being appropriately dressed for bed is equally as important as being dressed in day clothes.

The 'missing' outcomes

Safeguarding

4.23   The list of statutory outcomes does not include 'maintenance of personal safety', ie there is no specific 'safeguarding'-related outcome. However, it is likely that most forms of neglect or abuse would, in effect, come within the scope of one or more of those outcomes. For example, some safeguarding issues will mean that the individual is not able to make use of his or her home safely and others might mean that the adult is unable (safely) to make use of facilities in the community. If the risk of abuse is as a result of difficulties recognising or managing inappropriate behaviour of 'friends' or family this may fall within the scope of 'Developing and maintaining family or other personal relationships'.

4.24   Concerns were raised about the omission of a specific safeguarding outcome by respondents to the government's consultation on the proposals for the criteria, but these did not persuade the Department of Health to make amendments prior to submitting the draft regulations to the affirmative resolution procedure:

> Local authorities ... almost unanimously supported the Department's policy to keep safeguarding separate to the eligibility decision , ensuring that there is a quick and appropriate response when the adult is at risk. We have therefore retained the separation of safeguarding from other needs

26 Complaint no 15 014 893 against Dorset County Council, 1 September 2016.

and strengthened the guidance on both assessment and safeguarding in response to the comments received.[27]

It is very difficult to see how the inclusion of personal safety as an outcome in the eligibility scheme could have prevented a local authority responding appropriately and promptly – and indeed the Welsh legislation deals with this explicitly by making a risk of 'abuse or neglect' a distinct ground for eligibility.[28] One potential consequence of the Department of Health's decision is that those experiencing (or at risk of) abuse or neglect may find themselves having to seek the assistance of the court to resolve a dispute about whether or not the local authority is under a duty to provide care and support for protective purposes.

4.25   As we note elsewhere (see para 2.73 above) there is a positive obligation on local authorities under the Human Rights Act 1998 to protect vulnerable adults from abuse and neglect[29] and in order to avoid 'satellite litigation' under that Act the courts and ombudsmen will almost certainly require that the relevant eligibility criteria be given an expansive interpretation to ensure that those at risk are held to be eligible.

Maintaining financial affairs

4.26   Social services authorities have traditionally provided a range of advice and support to people needing help with their social security benefits and with managing their finances. Although this need has no specific mention in the eligibility criteria – it is clearly encompassed (at least in part) within outcome 'Maintaining a habitable home environment'. The statutory guidance on this outcome expressly refers to the circumstances where the adult may need says 'support to sustain their occupancy of the home and to maintain amenities, such as water, electricity and gas' (para 6.106).

4.27   Arguably the need to look after financial matters is also relevant to the ability to achieve other outcomes. For example, if the adult is unable to budget, then he or she may not be able to afford to buy the food necessary to maintain nutrition.

Managing medication

4.28   Again, this is not a prescribed outcome as such. However, it is not difficult to see how the ability to manage medication may be necessary to achieve one or more of the prescribed outcomes. For example, if epilepsy medication is not taken regularly it may be impossible for the person concerned to make use of their home safely or make use of facilities in the community. A difficulty in relation to this outcome concerns the division of responsibility for such support – between health and social services – and this is considered further at para 11.56.

---

27 Department of Health, *Response to the consultation on draft regulations and guidance for implementation of Part 1 of the Care Act 2014* Cm 8955, October 2014, p22.

28 Social Services and Well-being (Wales) Act 2014 s32(1)(b).

29 See in this respect *X, Y and Z v UK* Application no 32666/10, 5 July 2012; and *Đorđević v Croatia* Application no 41526/10, 24 July 2012.

Inability to achieve outcomes

4.29   In order to be eligible for care and support, the adult must be 'unable' to achieve the outcome. The eligibility regulations set out what is meant by this (reg 2(3)) namely:

(a) is unable to achieve it without assistance;[30]
(b) is able to achieve it without assistance but doing so causes the adult significant pain, distress or anxiety;
(c) is able to achieve it without assistance but doing so endangers or is likely to endanger the health or safety of the adult, or of others; or
(d) is able to achieve it without assistance but takes significantly longer than would normally be expected.

Fluctuating need

4.30   The question of ability or inability becomes a difficult one to answer when the level of the individual's needs fluctuate. In those circumstances, the eligibility regulations require the authority to take into account the adult's circumstances over a sufficient period to establish accurately the adult's level of need. What is sufficient is a judgment for the authority – it is such period 'as it considers necessary' (reg 2(4)). Statutory guidance on this question is provided at paras 6.58–6.59. The SCIE guidance stresses (among many factors) that this requires that assessments are:

> ... not simply a 'snapshot' of a person's care and support needs. Local authorities must consider the person's care and support needs over a suitable period of time to gain a complete picture of those needs.[31]

Significant impact on well-being

4.31   The adult must not only be unable to achieve the specified outcomes, but, to be eligible for care and support as a consequence, there must be (or likely to be) a *significant* impact on the adult's well-being (as defined in CA 2014 s1(2)). It is interesting that, in the two examples used in the statutory guidance to illustrate ineligibility (one for an adult at para 6.112 and one for a carer at para 6.129), the decision was made not on the basis that the individual did not demonstrate an inability to achieve the relevant number of outcomes, but because the authority concluded that the impact on well-being was not significant. In the pre-CA 2014 scheme there was no such additional hurdle. It is certainly arguable that the outcomes as specified in the new scheme appear to have lowered the initial hurdle when compared with the 'consequences' set out in the old *Prioritising need* criteria. However, the height of the final hurdle will be heavily dependent on how the test of 'significant impact' is applied, and that may well vary from authority to authority, or even from decision-maker to decision-maker.

4.32   The statutory guidance is surprisingly limited on the question of how 'significant impact' is to be interpreted, given the importance of this issue (see paras 6.108–6.110). First, it says that 'significant' must be taken to have its everyday meaning, but this takes the matter no further. Ultimately it will be a matter of judgment for the local authority, but it is a judgment

---

30   Which the statutory guidance advises includes where the adult needs prompting even though they can physically perform the task (para 6.103).
31   SCIE, *Fluctuating needs in assessment and eligibility for the Care Act 2014*, 2015.

that must be exercised lawfully. The authority must have regard to 'the importance of beginning with the assumption that the individual is best placed to judge the individual's well-being' (CA 2014 s1(3)[32] – see above at para 2.17). The statutory guidance reinforces that message (para 6.110):

> In making this judgement [whether the impact is significant], the local authority should look to understand the adult's needs in the context of what is important to him or her. Needs may affect different people differently, because what is important to the individual's well-being may not be the same in all cases. Circumstances which create a significant impact on the well-being of one individual may not have the same effect on another.

4.33   The judgment will therefore need to be founded on an adequate assessment of the impact on all aspects of well-being and include an assessment of the individual's perspective,[33] and an explanation in appropriate cases of why the impact is not considered 'significant'. This proposition is illustrated by a 2016 ombudsman's report[34] which concerned the reassessment of an adult with mental health difficulties who had been receiving a support package. The re-assessment found that it took her significantly longer than would generally be expected to achieve outcomes associated with work, accessing community services, maintaining hygiene, and maintaining a home environment due to her mental health conditions. Nevertheless (unlike the first assessment), it concluded that the difficulties did not significantly impact her well-being. In finding maladministration the ombudsman noted the absence of any explanation as to why her well-being was not significantly impacted by her difficulties in achieving the specified outcomes and this is maladministration. This omission was compounded by the failure to provide reasons as to why she was considered to be no longer eligible for support she had previously been assessed as needing.

4.34   The statutory guidance also states that the authority does not need to consider the impact of the inability to achieve each individual outcome, but should consider the cumulative effect overall (para 6.108). It is not, therefore, open to the local authority to say that a particular need is ineligible on the ground that it contributes to the inability to achieve an outcome which in itself does not have a significant impact. If the outcome is one of a number which overall have a significant impact, according to the statutory guidance, that is sufficient.

4.35   The SCIE guidance gives additional advice as to the meaning of significant impact,[35] suggesting that it could be:

- a consequence of a single effect;
- a consequence of a cumulative effect: this means that the individual may have needs across several of the eligibility outcomes, perhaps at a relatively low level, but as these needs affect the individual in various areas of their life, the overall impact on the individual is significant;

32 CA 2014 s1(3).
33 This is in any event required if the assessment is to be lawful – see CA 2014 s9(4)(a) and para 3.87 above.
34 Complaint no 15 001 422 against Milton Keynes Council, 20 September 2016.
35 SCIE, *Care Act 2014: assessment and eligibility: eligibility determination: what does significant impact mean?* – in relation to each of these three examples, the guidance gives illustrations of how these might be encountered in practice.

- a consequence of a domino effect: this means that currently the individual may have needs in relation to few eligibility outcomes, but it can be anticipated that in the near future other outcomes will be affected, causing a significant impact on the individual's well-being.

Evidencing significant impact

4.36 Evidence other than the individual's own account of impact may well be relevant. For example:

- A failure to manage incontinence is the second greatest cause for older people being institutionalised in the UK, and brings with it 'innumerable and well documented problems – not merely risks of infection and compromised skin viability but also issues of profound depression deriving from a sense of despair and shame'.[36]
- It is estimated that a third of older people in the UK are affected by loneliness.[37] The evidence suggests that for many people an inability to achieve develop and maintain personal relationships results in significant harm: the subjective feelings of loneliness and social isolation, for example, increases the risk of premature death by 26 per cent and 29 per cent respectively.[38]
- Depression is the most common mental health problem of later life, affecting 10–20 per cent of older people and up to 40 per cent of care home residents,[39] and it appears that an important factor concerns is the physical and social space within which they interact: a factor that becomes of increasing importance in advanced older age as the home environment becomes constricted.[40]
- Despite the many legislative interventions protecting the rights of disabled people over the last 20 years, their employment rates are still less than half those of non-disabled people.[41] The same discrepancy is also evident in relation to the numbers of disabled students in further and higher education – which in 2003 was five per cent, compared to ten per cent for the rest of the population.[42]

---

36 L Clements, *Elder law. Volume 1*, Jordans, 2011, pp47–52 at p50; and BAS Broome 'The impact of urinary incontinence on self-efficacy and quality of life' in *Health and Quality of Life Outcomes* (2003) 1 35.

37 Future Foundation, *The future of loneliness*, 2014, p10; and see also SCIE, *At a glance 60: Preventing loneliness and social isolation among older people*, 2012.

38 J Holt-Lunstad and others, 'Loneliness and social isolation as risk factors for mortality: a meta-analytic review' *Perspectives on Psychological Science* (March 2015) vol 10 no 2, 227–237.

39 National Institute for Mental Health in England, *Facts for champions*, Department of Health, 2005, p11.

40 M Godfrey, *Depression and older people*, Policy Press, 2004, p17; and see also M La Gory and K Fitzpatrick, 'The effects of environmental context on elderly depression' (1992) *Journal of Aging and Health* 4 459–479; and CPM Knipscheer and others, 'The effects of environmental context and personal resources on depressive symptomatology in older age' (2000) *Ageing and Society, 20*, 183–202.

41 S Riddell and others, *Disability, skills and employment: a review of recent statistics and literature on policy and initiatives*, University of Edinburgh, 2010.

42 Disability Rights Commission, *'Facts and figures' Disability Rights Commission educating for equality campaign*, 2003. The evidence suggests this discrepancy remains – see European Union, *Disability statistics – access to education and training*, Eurostat,

Disregard the input from carers

4.37   The eligibility criteria now put beyond any doubt that the eligibility determination must be made without consideration of whether the adult has a
carer, or what needs may be being met by a carer at that time. The question is whether the adult can achieve outcomes 'without assistance' (see
above at para 4.29). Even where needs are to be met by a willing and able
carer, they must be recorded as eligible needs.

4.38   The statutory guidance is absolutely clear on this issue. The contribution from a carer must not be taken into account until the care planning
stage (para 6.115):

> Authorities must only take consideration of whether the adult has a carer,
> or what needs may be met by a carer after the eligibility determination
> when a care and support plan is prepared.

The statutory guidance continues, explaining the reason for this approach
(para 6.115):

> This is to ensure that should there be a breakdown in the caring relation-
> ship, the needs are already identified as eligible, and therefore the local
> authority must take steps to meet them without a further reassessment.

The eligibility criteria for carers

4.39   The *form* of the criteria for carers is the same as the adult for whom care is
provided, but the *content* is different. Three conditions imposed by eligibility regulations reg 3(1) must be met:

1) The needs arise as a consequence of providing **necessary care** for an
   adult.
2) The effects of the carer's needs is that any of the circumstances in reg
   3(2) apply to the carer ie (a) the carer's physical or mental **health** is, or
   is at risk of, deteriorating; or (b) the carer is unable to achieve any of
   the prescribed **outcomes**.
3) As a consequence there is, or is likely to be, a significant impact on the
   carer's **well-being**.

'Necessary care'

4.40   The first eligibility condition for carers is that the carer's needs arise as
a consequence of providing 'necessary care' for an adult. This does not
mean that in order for a carer to be eligible for support, the adult for whom
care is provided must have eligible needs. The statutory guidance makes
it absolutely clear that carers can be eligible for support whether or not
the adult for whom they care has eligible needs (CA 2014 s20(7) and para
6.118). The adult's needs must be a distinct question, eg in those cases
where the adult has refused an assessment the local authority will not be
able to make an eligibility determination.

4.41   What, therefore, is meant by the phrase 'necessary care'? The statutory guidance takes what appears to be a fairly minimalist approach (para
6.119):

2015. There is potential for a deterioration in these rates given the withdrawal of
disabled students allowances in 2015.

If the carer is providing care and support for needs that the adult is capable of meeting themselves, the carer may not be providing necessary support.

On this basis it would appear that the intention is to give local authorities the scope to exclude care provided by (for example) the 'over-protective' carer. It is, however, possible for an adult to be unable to do something himself or herself but be ineligible on the ground that it does not have a significant impact on the adult's well-being. The point is that under the new scheme the carer could still be eligible for support.

4.42   It appears that some authorities are interpreting 'necessary' to mean care 'necessary to enable the adult to achieve one of the specified outcomes'. This must be mistaken, as on this approach it may not be 'necessary care' for a daughter to visit her elderly mother in a care home.[43] The daughter 'cares' and on any ordinary meaning of the word, this is 'necessary' even if keeping an adult 'safe' is not a specified outcome (see para 4.23 above). It must be necessary that visitors ask questions as to why their relative has a bruise; necessary that they observe the state of the placement; necessary that staff are aware that the resident has concerned relatives. There is additionally evidence that such visits promote emotional well-being – even if the resident has no conscious memory of the visitor.[44]

The effects of providing necessary care

4.43   The second condition in regulation 3(1) of the eligibility regulations for a carer to be eligible for support is that the carer's needs must be such that either:

(a) the carer's physical or mental health is, or is at risk of, deteriorating; *or*
(b) that the carer is unable to achieve any one (or more) of eight specified outcomes, namely:
    (i) carrying out any caring responsibilities the carer has for a child;
    (ii) providing care to other persons for whom the carer provides care;
    (iii) maintaining a habitable home environment in the carers home (whether or not this is also the home of the adult needing care);
    (iv) managing and maintaining nutrition;
    (v) developing and maintaining family or other personal relationships;
    (vi) engaging in work, training, education or volunteering;
    (vii) making use of necessary facilities or services in the local community, including recreational facilities or services; and
    (viii) engaging in recreational activities.

43 This would be the case even if the mother's dementia was so advanced that she no longer recognised or responded to her daughter, and the local authority made the contentious assertion that maintaining this particular personal relationship held no emotional benefits for the mother.

44 The evidence suggests that in the later stages of dementia that emotional memories stored is the amygdala are used to make sense of the world. In consequence it appears that although a person with dementia may not remember who someone is, he or she may derive a feeling of comfort and security from that person's visit – see GMM Jones and BML Miesen (eds), *Care-giving in dementia: research and application: Volume 3*, p57; and H Braak and E Braak, 'Evolution of neuronal changes in the course of Alzheimer's disease' *Journal of Neural Transmission Supplement* (1998); 53: 127–140.

4.44   The regulations and guidance mirror the approach adopted for adults in need (see para 4.17 above) – namely that the nature and scope of each of the specified outcomes are fleshed out by the statutory guidance (para 6.123). A key difference, however, is that the eligibility can be triggered if there is an actual or potential deterioration in health or an inability to achieve any *one* of the outcomes alone – whereas for adults in need, an inability to achieve 'two or more' of the specified outcomes is required. In the following section, the factors specified in reg 3(2) are in bold type.

The carer's physical or mental health is, or is at risk of, deteriorating

Many carers are likely to have little difficulty in establishing this need. Research suggests that over half of all carers have a caring related health condition,[45] and 2003 research[46] found that 43 per cent of carers had sought medical treatment for depression, stress or anxiety since becoming a carer. NHS England[47] cites research findings that 84 per cent of carers reported that caring had had a negative impact on their health and separate research that found a 23 per cent increased risk of stroke for spousal carers.

The Department of Health[48] refers to the strain of caring and the serious impact on mental well-being with 73 per cent of carers surveyed reporting increased anxiety; 82 per cent reporting increased stress since taking on their caring role; and half of carers surveyed stated they were affected by depression after taking on a caring role.

Or, the carer is unable to achieve any one or more of the following outcomes:

1) Carrying out any caring responsibilities the carer has for a child

Comments from the statutory guidance:

> Local authorities should consider any parenting or other caring responsibilities the carer has for a child in addition to their caring role for the adult. For example, the carer might be a grandparent with caring responsibilities for their grandchildren while the grandchildren's parents are at work.

It appears that there are about 2.4 million people in the UK sandwiched between providing support to an older adult with disabilities or chronic illnesses who have children to care for as well.[49] The statutory guidance provides an example of such a circumstance (para 11.38) concerning a mother who is caring for her dying father and for her young children. Although her father has a care package, her carer's assessment identifies that she is eligible for support due to her additional childcare responsibilities. The support plan that is developed for her consists of a carer's direct payment 'which she uses for her children to attend summer play schemes so that

---

45 Health and Social Care Information Centre, *Survey of carers in households 2009/10*, 2010; see also Carers UK, *Missed opportunities: the impact of new rights for carers*, June 2003.

46 Carers UK, *Missed opportunities: the impact of new rights for carers*, June 2003.

47 NHS England, *Commissioning for Carers: Principles and resources to support effective commissioning for adult and young carers*, 2014.

48 Department of Health (and others) *The Care Act and whole-family approaches*, 2015.

49 Carers UK, *Sandwich caring*, 2012.

she get some free time to meet with friends and socialise when the family member provides care to her father'.

2) Providing care to other persons for whom the carer provides care

Comments from the statutory guidance:

Local authorities should consider any additional caring responsibilities the carer may have for other adults. For example, a carer may also have caring responsibilities for a parent in addition to caring for the adult with care and support needs.

Caring for more than one person is increasingly common (as with the 'sandwich carers' above). The CA 2014 removes the requirement that a carer provide 'regular and substantial care', and with it the idea that a disabled person has a 'principal' carer. The cumulative effect of providing care for several people may have a significant impact on a carer's well-being – even though those for whom the care is provided may be individually ineligible (see para 4.40 above).

3) Maintaining a habitable home environment

Comments from the statutory guidance:

Local authorities should consider whether the condition of the carer's home is safe and an appropriate environment to live in and whether it presents a significant risk to the carer's well-being. A habitable home should be safe and have essential amenities such as water, electricity and gas.

This 'outcome' mirrors that for adults in need (see para 4.17 above). 2010 research found that due to financial difficulties, 23 per cent of parent carers were going without heating[50]. 2011 research found that 40 per cent of carers were in debt because of their caring roles (a figure that rose to 50 per cent for parent carers),[51] that a third were unable to afford their utility bills and that three-quarters had cut back on holidays, leisure activities, buying clothes and going out with friends and family.

4) Managing and maintaining nutrition

Comments from the statutory guidance:

Local authorities should consider whether the carer has the time to do essential shopping and to prepare meals for themselves and their family.

This 'outcome' mirrors that for adults in need (see para 4.17 above). 2010 research found that due to financial difficulties, 14 per cent of parent carers had gone without food[52] and Department of Health[53] guidance notes that 45 per cent of carers had reported that, as a result of caring, they found it hard to maintain a balanced diet.

5) Developing and maintaining family or other significant personal relationships

Comments from the statutory guidance:

Local authorities should consider whether the carer is in a position where their caring role prevents them from maintaining key relationships with

---

50 Contact a Family, *Counting the costs*, 2010.
51 Carers UK, *State of caring 2011* (involving 4,200 carers).
52 Contact a Family, *Counting the costs*, 2010.
53 Department of Health (and others), *The Care Act and whole-family approaches*, 2015.

family and friends or from developing new relationships where the carer does not already have other personal relationships.

This 'outcome' also mirrors that for adults in need (see para 4.17 above). 2014 research[54] found that almost 40 per cent of carers found it hard to maintain social networks because they did not have anyone to talk to about caring and that 57 per cent had lost touch with friends or family. The evidence suggests that the subjective feeling of loneliness and social isolation increases the risk of premature death by 26 per cent and 29 per cent respectively.[55]

6) Engaging in work, training, education or volunteering

Comments from the statutory guidance:

> Local authorities should consider whether the carer can continue in their job, and contribute to society, apply themselves in education, volunteer to support civil society or have the opportunity to get a job, if they are not in employment.

UK law imposes no obligation on adults to provide care for another adult: the liable family rule was abolished by NAA 1948 s1. CA 2014 s10(5) requires that assessments take into account the extent to which the carer is 'willing, and is likely to continue to be willing' to provide care and the statutory guidance notes that 'authorities 'should not assume that others are willing or able to take up caring roles' (para 2.48). This 'outcome' will therefore be of particular importance to the many cares who have had to give up work (or reduce their hours) or to forego the possibility of education, training and leisure activities. Research in 2007[56] found that, 54 per cent of carers had had to give up work to care, and 2014 research[57] concerning working carers found that nearly half had reduced their hours and nearly a third had refused a promotion or taken a less qualified job in order to manage their workload and caring responsibilities; that 2.3 million people had quit work to care and almost 3 million have reduced their working hours.

7) Making use of necessary facilities or services in the local community

Comments from the statutory guidance:

> Local authorities should consider whether the carer has an opportunity to make use of the local community's services and facilities and for example consider whether the carer has time to use recreational facilities such as gyms or swimming pools.

Department of Health guidance[58] refers to evidence that 58 per cent of carers said that they have reduced the amount of exercise they do since they started caring.

54   Carers UK, *State of caring survey 2014* (a survey of 5,000 carers).
55   J Holt-Lunstad and others, 'Loneliness and social isolation as risk factors for mortality a meta-analytic review' in *Perspectives on Psychological Science* March 2015 vol 10 no 2 227–237).
56   Carers UK, *Real change not short change*, 2007.
57   Carers UK, *State of caring survey 2014* (a survey of 5,000 carers).
58   Department of Health (and others), *The Care Act and whole-family approaches*, 2015.

8) Engaging in recreational activities

Comments from the statutory guidance:

> Local authorities should consider whether the carer has leisure time, which might for example be some free time to read or engage in a hobby.

2010 research concerning parent carers found that due to financial difficulties, 73 per cent went without leisure and days out.[59]

Unable to achieve

4.45 As with adults in need, 'unable' to achieve the outcome is given an expansive (but not identical) meaning:

- unable to achieve it without assistance;
- able to achieve it without assistance but doing so causes the carer significant pain, distress or anxiety; or
- able to achieve it without assistance but doing so endangers or is likely to endanger the health or safety of the carer, or of others.

Provision is also made for where carers' needs fluctuate which is in identical terms to that for the cared for adult (see para 4.30 above).[60]

Significant impact on carer's well-being

4.46 The statutory guidance on significant impact for the purpose of the carers' eligibility criteria is very similar to that applying to the adults' criteria (see para 4.31 above).[61] There is no mention of cumulative impact but there does not appear to be any good reason for using a different approach for carers.

The eligibility decision

A duty to make an eligibility decision

4.48 Once the assessment has established that either an adult has needs for care and support or a carer has needs for support, there is a statutory duty to determine whether any of the needs meet the relevant eligibility criteria (CA 2014 s13(1)). An unreasonable delay in making an eligibility decision will constitute maladministration and could amount to a breach of duty.[62]

Recording the eligibility decision

4.49 Whether or not the individual meets the eligibility criteria, the authority must provide a written record with reasons for the decision (CA 2014 s13(2)). This will be a very important document for those who are unhappy with an authority's conclusion. It may provide a satisfactory explanation

---

59 Contact a Family, *Counting the costs*, 2010.
60 Eligibility regulations reg 3(3).
61 Statutory guidance, paras 6.130–6.132.
62 In *R v Sutton LBC ex p Tucker* (1997–98) 1CCLR 251 the court held that a failure to make a service-provision decisions in respect of the claimant who had been found to be fit for discharge from hospital 2 years before constituted a breach of the duty to decide whether the claimants assessed needs called for the provision of community care services under National Health Service and Community Care Act 1990 s47(1)(b).

which may help avoid unnecessary disputes, but it may reveal errors in an authority's approach which would justify a challenge to the decision.

4.50   Authorities may be tempted to draft limited standard letters in response, but this in itself will carry a risk of challenge to the adequacy of the performance of this statutory duty. The statutory guidance says that 'the process should be transparent and understandable so that the individual is able to ... understand the basis on which decisions are reached' (para 6.36). The public law obligation to act fairly will inform the scope of this statutory requirement, requiring that the authority provide an explanation that is sufficient to enable the individual to challenge the decision if he or she wishes to do so.

Where the eligibility criteria are not met

4.51   Where the eligibility criteria are not met, the authority must, in addition to explaining its decision, provide written advice and information on prevention – what can be done to meet or reduce existing needs, and to prevent or delay the development of needs in the future (CA 2014 s13(5)). The duty applies to both adults and carers. Again, procedural economy may tempt authorities to send out a standard letter in such cases. This would not, however, satisfy the individual duty that exists – as the statutory guidance notes (para 10.29):

> This should be personalised and specific advice based on the person's needs assessment and not a generalised reference to prevention services or signpost to a general website.

Where the eligibility criteria are met

4.52   Where at least some of the assessed needs meet the eligibility criteria, the local authority must then take three steps (CA 2014 s13(4)):

1) consider what could be done to meet those needs that do;
2) ascertain whether the adult wants to have those needs met by the local authority; and
3) establish whether the adult is ordinarily resident in the local authority's area.

4.53   The purpose of the last two steps is clear. There is no point in moving to the care planning stage if it is unnecessary either because the individual does not want the authority to do so or the responsible authority is, in fact, a different local authority (see para 4.57 below). The second requirement will also ensure that a self-funder is made aware of his or her rights to have the local authority make the arrangements to meet his or her eligible needs (see para 4.60 below).

4.54   However, in the light of the duty to undertake full care and support planning, the first element appears to be superfluous. The statutory guidance has this to say (para 134):

> This does not replace or pre-empt the care and support planning process ... but is an early consideration of the potential support options, in order to determine whether some of those may be services for which the local authority may make a charge. Where that is the case, the local authority must carry out a financial assessment.

The duty to meet eligible needs

'Residence' and 'charging' conditions

4.55 Where an adult or carer has been assessed as having eligible needs, the authority will have a duty under CA 2014 s18 or s20 respectively to meet those needs as long as the individual meets the 'residence' and 'charging' conditions (see below). It is at this stage that any care provided by a carer is to taken into account. If all the cared-for person's needs are being met by a 'willing and able' carer, the duty does not arise (CA 2014 s18(7)).

4.56 CA 2014 s20 creates a clear and enforceable individual duty to meet the assessed needs of carers and is, the government states, 'the first ever legal entitlement to public support, putting them on the same footing as the people for whom they care'.[63]

The 'residence' condition

4.57 The duty to meet the eligible needs of an adult in need only arises if the adult concerned is either ordinarily resident in the authority's area or physically present but of no settled residence elsewhere (CA 2014 s18). The meaning of 'ordinary residence' is dealt with in chapter 6. If the adult is ordinarily resident elsewhere (even if physically present in the local authority's area) there will be no duty on that authority to meet needs (although there will be a power – see below at para 4.73).

4.58 The duty to meet a carer's eligible needs is not dependent on the carer's residence in the area, but on the residence of the adult for whom the carer provides care. Where the local authority is responsible for the adult, the same authority is also responsible for that adult's carer(s).[64] This provision has the potential to cause difficulties – for example, if a carer with eligible needs is providing care for two adults in different authority areas, this could give rise to an inter-authority dispute (particularly if neither of the adults have eligible needs for support – see para 4.40 below).

4.59 Until release from prison, the local authority for the area in which the prison is located will be responsible for meeting the needs of those imprisoned there (see para 15.145 below).

The 'charging' condition

4.60 This is a detailed and relatively complex condition but, in essence, its purpose is to exclude self-funders from the duty to meet eligible needs save in prescribed circumstances. Those circumstances are slightly different for the self-funding adult with care and support needs from those applicable to self-funding carers.

4.61 The first circumstance applies to both the adult and also the carer (where the carer's needs are met by provision of support to the carer).

---

63 Department of Health, *The Care Bill explained: including a response to consultation and pre-legislative scrutiny on the Draft Care and Support Bill* Cm 8627, The Stationery Office, 2013, para 73. The previous legislation (Carers and Disabled Children Act 2000) required authorities to consider *whether* to meet needs, but in the absence of eligibility criteria, a duty to make an eligibility determination or a duty to meet eligible needs, it was not uncommon for carers to find that their carer's assessment failed to translate into substantive support.

64 See para 6.84 below.

Where a self-funder requests the authority to meet his or her needs, then the duty applies irrespective of the fact that he or she is deemed by the charging scheme to have sufficient money to pay in full for his or her own care and support (CA 2014 s18(3) and s19(2)). In short, self-funders are entitled to have their needs met by the authority, although, if they do, the authority does have the power to charge an arrangement fee (CA 2014 s14(1)(b)).

4.62   The second circumstance applies only to adults with care and support needs, but will not become relevant until the 'cap on costs' provisions come into force. Since these have been delayed until at last 2020, this provision is not considered here.

4.63   The third scenario also only applies to adults in need. If a self-funder does not have sufficient mental capacity to make his or her own arrangements for care and support and there is no person authorised to do so under the Mental Capacity Act (MCA) 2005 or 'otherwise in a position to do so',[65] the authority will be under a duty to meet those needs (CA 2014 s18(4)).

4.64   Where the carer's needs are to be met by provision of care and support to the adult, it is that adult's financial circumstances that are relevant. If they are below the financial limits, the cared for person must agree to the care and support being provided to him or her (CA 2014 s20(4)). If he or she is a self-funder, he or she must request that, nonetheless, the authority makes provision (CA 2014 s20(5)).

A duty to meet which needs?

4.65   The answer is, in a sense, straightforward – the duty is to meet all eligible needs. The eligibility decision is based on whether the individual is unable to achieve certain outcomes (see above at para 4.17). The eligible needs are all those needs which are contributing to the inability to achieve outcomes which, cumulatively, are impacting on well-being to a significant extent. It is easy to see how an assessment may fail adequately to specify the needs that are causing the difficulties identified and, if that is the case, the care and support planning is also likely to prove to be inadequate.

4.66   The way that a need is defined can have very significant consequences, as demonstrated in the judgment of the Supreme Court in *R (McDonald) v Kensington and Chelsea RLBC*.[66] The appellant, who had limited mobility, was initially assessed as needing 'assistance to use the commode at night'. However, the respondent had been proposing to replace her night-time personal assistants with incontinence pads as a cheaper option and, following two care plan reviews, re-cast her needs in broader terms as 'assistance with toileting', thus arguing that the re-defined need could be met through the use of night-time incontinence pads. Lord Kerr, although troubled by the process, found it to be lawful:

---

65 Although this provision does not expressly require that the person in a position to make those arrangements consents to taking on that role, it is difficult to see how a local authority could either force them to do so or refuse to make arrangements for the mentally incapacitated person with eligible needs if they were unwilling.

66 [2011] UKSC 33, (2011) 14 CCLR 341.

On that basis, it can be said that the reviews in 2009 and 2010, although it was not their purpose, in fact involved a re-assessment of the appellant's needs and that they may now be regarded as the need to avoid having to go to the lavatory during the night. Viewed thus, the needs can be met by the provision of incontinence pads and suitable bedding. Not without misgivings, I have therefore concluded that it was open to the respondent to re-assess the appellant's needs, to re-categorise them as a need to avoid leaving bed during the night and to conclude that that need could be met by providing the appellant with the materials that would obviate the requirement to leave her bed (para 40).

This semantic debate cost the appellant her night-time care support. The dissenting opinion of Baroness Hale asserted that the decision was irrational in the *Wednesbury* sense on the basis that the need had not in fact changed and was about access not toileting per se:[67]

It seems to me that the need for help to get to the lavatory or commode is so different from the need for protection from uncontrollable bodily functions that it is irrational to confuse the two, and meet the one need in the way that is appropriate to the other. Of course, there may well be people who are persuaded that this is in fact a more convenient, comfortable and safer way of solving the problem; then it is no longer irrational to meet their need in this way (para 75).

4.67   However, the *McDonald* case pre-dated the CA 2014. The CA 2014 focuses on the ability to achieve a more clearly prescribed set of outcomes. One of those outcomes is 'Being able to make use of the adult's home safely' (see para 4.17 above). This includes accessing the bathroom (as the statutory guidance acknowledges). The local authority's response in the *McDonald* case left Ms McDonald unable to achieve the very outcome (accessing the toilet) that was having a significant impact on her dignity – an essential aspect of well-being. Her need (in order to be able to achieve this outcome) would be for some form of care and support so that she could mobilise in her home safely.

Discretion to meet urgent needs

4.68   An individual may have urgent needs for care and support and in such cases authorities may (irrespective of ordinary residence) meet those needs before a needs or financial assessment has been completed, or before an eligibility decision has been made (CA 2014 s19(3)). Authorities will be acting unlawfully if they operate blanket policies to always require a prior assessment or if social work staff fail to consider exercising the power in the belief that there is such a requirement. It is a discretion that must always be exercised by taking account of the individual's relevant circumstances. There is no equivalent provision for carers.

4.69   The power does not depend on a request being made. The duty is a proactive one. An authority must consider exercising the power in relevant cases when the appearance of urgent need comes to its attention (even

---

67 See also L Clements, 'Disability, dignity and the cri de coeur' in EHRLR [2011] 6 pp675–685; and R Gordon QC, *Counting the votes: a brief look at the McDonald case* (2011) 14 CCLR 337.

if it is clear that another body 'ought' to have intervened[68]). Staff having first contact with a case will need to be appropriately trained in identifying potential urgency early on.

4.70   The power existed under the previous legislative regime[69] and the associated case-law will continue to be relevant. In *R (Alloway) v Bromley LBC*,[70] for example, the applicant's urgent need for a care home placement had been delayed by the local authority's flawed assessment process. In his judgment, Crane J suggested that pending the outcome of a further reassessment, the authority could use its 'urgent' powers to provide a temporary placement in order to avoid the likely hardship that would result from further delay.

Discretion to meet the needs of the terminally ill

4.71   If someone who is terminally ill has been through the full assessment and eligibility decision-making process, the person is of course entitled to have his or her eligible care and support needs met under CA 2014 s18. However, it may well be inappropriate to subject someone in this situation to that process. There is express provision for meeting the person's needs without doing so, but the power is conferred by reference back to the provision for dealing with urgent needs in CA 2014 s19(3) (see above) (section 19(4)). One explanation for the making of an express and specific provision is that it is intended that the needs of those who are terminally ill are deemed to fulfil the requirement of appearance of urgency without more.

4.72   For the purposes of section 19(4) a person is terminally ill if he or she suffers 'from a progressive disease and the person's death in consequence of that disease can reasonably be expected within 6 months'.[71]

Discretion to meet the needs where the residence condition is not met

4.73   As noted above an authority is only under a duty to meet eligible care and support needs if the adult concerned is either ordinarily resident in the authority's area or physically present but of no settled residence elsewhere (CA 2014 s18). Where that person is ordinarily resident in another authority's area, there is no duty even if the person is physically present. Nevertheless, there is discretion to meet needs if, but for the residence issue, there would be a duty and the authority has notified the 'home' local authority of its intention to do so.

Discretion to meet ineligible needs

4.74   Authorities have the power to meet ineligible needs for care and support of those who meet the residence condition (CA 2014 s19(1)). There is a strong argument that, where the authority knows or should have been aware of a non-eligible need giving rise to a risk of significant harm (including

---

68 See *R (AM) v (1) Havering LBC and Tower Hamlets LBC* [2015] EWHC 1004 (Admin) considered further at para 6.10.
69 National Health Service and Community Care Act 1990 s47(5).
70 [2004] EWHC 2108 (Admin), (2005) 8 CCLR 61.
71 Welfare Reform Act 2012 s82(4).

abuse or neglect), this discretion will become an obligation by virtue of the authority's duty under Human Rights Act 1998 s6 to act in accordance with its obligation not to breach rights under the European Convention on Human Rights (ECHR) (see para 2.73 above). This provision could be used as the source of the authority's power to meet safeguarding-related needs that are not assessed as eligible needs under the eligibility criteria.

4.75 There is an equivalent power to meet the non-eligible needs of carers, but where this is done by providing care and support to the adult needing care, he or she must agree (CA 2014 s20(6).

Exception for people subject to immigration control

4.76 People subject to immigration control are excluded from entitlement to care and support. This continues the now longstanding exclusion of those falling within scope from entitlement to social welfare provision (CA 2014 s21).

4.77 This exclusion does not extend to carers, although it does prohibit the provision of care and support to an adult subject to immigration control even if that is provided to meet a carer's needs (CA 2014 s21(4)) – see para 16.24 below.

Eligible needs and resources

4.78 The principle established under the pre-CA 2014 regime that once a decision had been made that an individual had eligible needs, these had to be met irrespective of any limits on the council's financial resources,[72] continues to apply. The duties to meet the eligible needs imposed by CA 2014 ss18 and 20 are unqualified and enforceable as individual duties.

4.79 In this context, the statutory guidance notes that although a local authority's finances are relevant when it decides how to meet the eligible needs of an individual, they are not relevant to 'whether those needs are met' (para 10.27). It then adds that this does not mean that the local authority can 'set arbitrary upper limits on the costs it is willing to pay to meet needs through certain routes'.

Panels and the eligibility decision-making process

4.80 Authorities may seek to circumvent the rigours of the new regime through some kind of management control over the eligibility decision. For many years it has been not uncommon for social services authorities to use panels (commonly known as 'funding panels') at some point in the assessment, eligibility and care-planning process – these are considered further below see para 4.111. Where panels are used, it would appear that the information duty (see para 19.5 below) requires that the authority provide details as to their role and their constitution – ie what decisions they are making, why they are making these decisions and who the panel members are (for example, is there a member who has a financial/budgetary role).

---

72 See *R v Gloucestershire CC ex p Barry* [1997] AC 584, (1997-98) 1 CCLR 40 at 54F in relation to provision of services under Chronically Sick and Disabled Persons Act 1970 s2; *R v Wigan MBC ex p Tammadge* (1997–1998) 1 CCLR 581; *Prioritising needs* at para 1.24.

4.81   If a panel is being asked to determine the individual's eligible needs, it is impermissible for it to amend or, in effect, dis-apply, the eligibility criteria on financial grounds. The national eligibility criteria constitute a mandatory statutory scheme. But even if that pitfall is avoided, there is a real risk that panels will get into difficulties because of their disconnection from the individual concerned. Panels create a fault line between the data collection phase of the assessment process and the subsequent decision-making on eligibility (and care planning – see below) and they may well make decisions without having relevant information to hand.[73] It might even be too late – the eligibility decision may already have been made. *R v Wigan MBC ex p Tammadge*[74] is an example: objectively the individual officers had decided that the applicant had eligible needs. However, they were unable to progress this, since the authority's procedures stated that only a panel meeting was able to make a formal decision on resource allocation; a meeting at which the assessing social worker had little or no role. In quashing that decision, Forbes J held that Wigan's 'own professionally qualified staff and advisors' had concluded that there was a need and it was simply too late for this to be countermanded by the panel.

4.82   If part of a panel's role is to manage expenditure by deferring eligibility decisions, this is arguably unlawful. There is a statutory duty to determine whether needs meet the eligibility criteria (CA 2014 s13(1)). To delay making that decision on financial grounds for the purpose of delaying the triggering of the duty to meet those needs is, in effect, simply moving waiting lists for services – which have been criticised by both the courts and the ombudsman (see below at para 4.111) – to an earlier point in the process.

4.83   Panels might not only be tasked with making the decision whether an individual has eligible needs, but whether there is a duty to meet those needs. There is no duty to meet an adult's needs if a carer is doing so,[75] but, if assumptions are made about the carer's willingness to provide care, the resulting decision may well be vulnerable to challenge. This may be unintentional (albeit influenced by budgetary needs); for example, it could arise from a simple failure to recognise that a decision that day care is to be provided three days instead of five days a week is, in effect, based on an unwarranted assumption that a carer is willing to meet the individual's nutritional and personal hygiene needs on the other two days.

Meeting needs

Choice and control

4.84   Choice and control are key themes in the statutory guidance (see para 2.28 above). It would, however, be a mistake to view 'choice' as solely a matter of guidance (albeit statutory guidance). The statutory guidance fleshes out a statutory framework which confers rights on the individual to make

---

73 In *R (Goldsmith) v Wandsworth LBC* [2004] EWCA Civ 1170, (2004) 7 CCLR 472 a service provision decision under the pre-Care Act scheme was overturned in part because the panel had not even had the community care assessment before it – an assessment the Court of Appeal found impressive in its thoroughness.

74 (1997–98) 1 CCLR 581, QBD.

75 CA 2014 s18(7).

choices and to exert control over and above the right to a direct payment (see para 10.21). The starting point is CA 2014 s24, which sets out what the authority must do once the duty to meet needs has been triggered. The authority must not only prepare a written care and support plan for an adult and support plan for a carer (referred to generically in what follows as a 'care plan'), but also help the individual 'with deciding how to have their needs met', ie it is for the individual to make that decision.[76] The statutory guidance has this to say (para 10.48):

> It is important that people are allowed to be very flexible to choose innovative forms of care and support, from a diverse range of sources, including quality providers but also 'non-service' options such as Information and Communication Technologies (ICT) equipment, club membership and massage. Lists of allowable purchases should be avoided as the range of possibilities should be very wide and will go beyond what the local authority is able to list at any point in time.

4.85 Local authorities wishing to control the quality of what is purchased using public funds may draw up a list of quality accredited providers but this should be done 'to help people choose' (para 10.48). Such lists should not be used to constrain choice (para 10.48):

> Limited lists of 'prescribed providers' that are only offered to a person on a 'take it or leave it' basis do not fit with the Government's vision of personalised care and should be avoided.

4.86 On the face of it, there appears to be a tension between the right to choose conferred by section 24 and the more limited right in section 25(3), (4) and (5) which require a local authority to involve the individual in the preparation of their plan and take all reasonable steps to reach agreement about 'how the authority should meet the needs in question'. One way of resolving that tension would be to interpret section 24 as being limited to the decision whether arrangements to meet needs will be made by the local authority or by the individual themselves using direct payments or, for self-funders, using their own financial resources. Clearly, this would be (largely) a matter of choice for the individual. However, that analysis would overlook the requirements of the overarching duty to promote the individual's well-being, one aspect of which is 'control by the individual over day to day life (including over care and support, or support, provided to the individual and the way in which it is provided)' (CA 2014 s1(1)(d)). This requirement creates a presumption that the individual will be allowed to formulate his or her own care plan in the absence of cogent well-founded reasons to the contrary. This analysis is consistent with the statutory guidance (para 10.47):

> However, the person chooses to have their needs met, whether by direct payment, by the provision of local authority-arranged or directly provided care and support or third-party provision, or a mix of these, there should be no constraint on how needs are met as long as this is reasonable. The local authority has to satisfy itself that the decision is an appropriate and legal way to meet needs and should take steps to avoid the decision being made on the assumption that the views of the professional are more valid than

76 The term 'adult' is used in section 24 but arguably the context requires this to be read as including both adults with care and support needs and carers.

those of the person. Above all, the local authority should refrain from any action that could be seen to restrict choice and impeded flexibility.

4.87   Adults in need have a statutory right to choose accommodation (whether that is in a care home, or in a supported living or shared lives scheme) where this is to be provided to meet needs, subject to certain conditions being met.[77]

How to meet needs

4.88   There is no prescribed list of services that the authority can provide or commission for adults in need and carers. For adults in need, this has been presented as a radical departure from the pre-CA 2014 regime which was in part built on a set of statutorily defined services and where the purpose of the assessment process was to determine whether there was a need for one or more of those services (see chapter 7 below). In its place, CA 2014 s8(1) (under the heading 'How to meet needs') provides only examples of what may be provided:

- accommodation in a care home or in premises of some other type;
- care and support at home or in the community;
- counselling and other types of social work;
- goods and facilities;
- information, advice and advocacy.

4.89   The intention is to bring into play 'a greater variety of approaches' than the provision of services (statutory guidance, para 10.10):

> Meeting needs' is an important concept under the Act and moves away from the previous terminology of 'providing services' ... The concept of 'meeting needs' is intended to be broader than a duty to provide or arrange a particular service.

4.90   The statutory guidance also suggests that needs may be met through what is available 'universally', ie facilities that are open to anyone and not just those who have needs that meet the eligibility criteria. This might be a service provided by the authority as part of its prevention work, or could be something organised by a local community group or voluntary sector organisation (see statutory guidance para 10.13). Whatever the means used to meet needs, it must be adequate to the task and it must be recorded in the care plan and subject to review in the usual way (see below at para 8.324). It would not, for example, be sufficient to simply refer an individual (who had been assessed as eligible for support to 'maintain nutrition' and to 'develop personal relationships') to a local lunch club and take no further responsibility. Care and support to meet eligible needs must be identified, recorded and reviewed according to the rigours of the statutory regime. The reasons for this are clear. For example, the individual may be unable to cope with the level of social engagement necessary to attend the club without additional care and support such as a befriender to assist them.

---

77 CA 2014 s30 and the Care and Support and After-care (Choice of Accommodation) Regulations 2014 SI No 2670; see also below at para 8.241.

4.91 The care planning process must also take full account of the constraints that the charging provisions impose. The statutory charging scheme limits the amount that an individual can be required to contribute to the overall cost to the authority of meeting his or her needs. It would be inconsistent with that scheme if the authority were permitted to meet needs in such a way that the individual ended up paying more than the statutory limits on their contribution. This could arise, for example, if a voluntary 'sitting service' levied some kind of weekly fee to meet volunteers' and administration expenses and the total cost to the individual, taking into account any charge that they were assessed as having to pay for services arranged by the authority, might take their income below the minimum level protected by the charging regulations (see below at para 8.324). The fact that any such fee would be likely to fall to be taken into account as disability-related expenditure in a charging calculation might not fully address the problem. For example, if, without taking into account the fee, the individual would have had no charge to pay at all, then the fact that the individual was paying for using the community provision would be an additional cost.

Overlapping provision

4.92 The approach of the CA 2014 and the statutory guidance to the issue of 'overlapping provision' (ie where an individual may be entitled to some kind of benefit under other legislation which might meet some of their needs) is problematic. Although the Act deals expressly with potentially overlapping responsibilities with the NHS or housing authorities by limiting a social services authority's powers (see below at paras 12.12 and 14.12), it is silent on other areas of potential overlap.

4.93 The statutory guidance has this to say (para 10.24):

> Where there is a risk of overlapping entitlements (i.e. where two different organisations may be under a duty to provide a service in relation to the same needs), local authorities should take steps to support the individual to access the support to which they are entitled under other legislation.

The suggestion here is that the other entitlement – whatever it may be – will always be the first port of call. Arguably, this over-generalises the position. The relationship between two statutory schemes dealing with entitlement to welfare provision will be a matter of statutory interpretation and it is not obviously the case that the CA 2014 will always be the safety net of last resort. This issue arose under the pre-CA 2014 regime in relation to the provision of accommodation for disabled asylum-seekers. The House of Lords, after a careful analysis of the two statutory schemes, concluded that responsibility for provision fell to local social services authorities.[78]

4.94 The statutory guidance makes reference to two specific examples of potentially overlapping schemes (para 10.24). The first is disability-related benefits. However, requiring an individual to rely on his or her own income to fund the meeting of his or her own eligible needs where that would be inconsistent with the statutory charging scheme would, arguably, be unlawful. The second example is disabled facilities grants, which are

---

78 *Westminster City Council v NASS* [2002] UKHL 38, (2002) 5 CCLR 511 – and see also para 16.26 below.

provided, subject to means-testing, under the Housing Grants, Construction and Regeneration Act 1996 (see para 14.104 below). In the majority of cases it is unlikely that an individual will experience prejudice by being referred to the alternative provision (indeed there are many advantages to a scheme specifically dedicated to housing adaptations). However, it is certainly by no means evident that the relationship between the two is unproblematic.

The limits on how needs can be met

4.95   Where an authority is considering making the necessary care and support arrangements, it will be limited by the scope of its powers. Two such boundaries are set out in the CA 2014 itself: (1) the boundary with NHS responsibilities and (2) the boundary with housing responsibilities.

Limits on providing healthcare

4.96   The authority is not permitted to meet needs by arranging a service or facility that is required to be provided under the National Health Service Act (NHSA) 2006 unless it meets two conditions. First, it must be 'incidental or ancillary' to something else the authority is doing to meet needs; and second, it must be of a nature that the local authority could be expected to provide it (CA 2014 s22(1)).

4.97   A common mistake is to treat the determining issue as being whether the service in question is a healthcare service. That would be wrong. Social service authorities can (generally speaking) provide what might be classified as healthcare as long as these two conditions are met. The statutory exception to this general position is the provision of nursing care by a registered nurse. CA 2014 s22 prohibits this in all circumstances except where it is to be provided together with accommodation (such as in a nursing home), but only then if the local authority has the permission of the relevant clinical commissioning group (CCG).[79]

4.98   In the draft eligibility criteria regulations, the outcome relating to accessing community facilities was more expansive than the final version.[80] It included accessing 'medical services'. As a result of not inconsiderable criticism (that this represented an impermissible shift in the NHS/social services boundary), the reference to medical services was withdrawn. However, the statutory guidance on this outcome says that local authorities should consider 'needs for support when the adult is attending healthcare appointments'.[81] This owes much to pressure from organisations representing people who are deaf-blind. Escorts to health appointments for people with such impairments will often be vital, and arguably fall to be provided by the NHS provider as a reasonable adjustment pursuant to the Equality Act (EqA) 2010. However, a local social services authority is not necessarily prohibited by CA 2014 s22 from providing such care and support and if it is necessary to meet an eligible

---

79   The requirement for CCG permission is waived if the case is urgent, and the arrangement is only temporary – CA 2014 s22(4)(b). For discussion concerning the nature of the section 22 prohibition see para 12.12 below.
80   See para 4.15 above.
81   See para 6.107.

need (because appropriate adjustments to the NHS service have not been made) then the local authority will be subject to a duty to provide it. In some circumstances it will make much more sense for the escort to be a care worker who knows the adult and is able to help them provide relevant information to the clinician.

4.99   A 2016 local government ombudsman report[82] is illustrative for this purpose. It concerned an adult who needed support with every aspect of his personal care. This need also existed when he had hospital outpatient visits – which could take up to eight hours – during which he needed support in order to be able to eat, drink and go to the toilet. His care support was cut for a number of reasons, including the fact that 'transport to medical appointments and hospital is the NHS responsibility'. In finding maladministration, the ombudsman stated that the council:

> ... is correct in saying the cost of transport to medical appointments is the NHS' responsibility, but the Care Act Guidance says councils have to consider the needs for support when the adult is attending healthcare appointments and the Council's failure to consider this is fault.

4.100   The NHS/social services boundary is considered further at para 12.12 below.

The limit on the power to provide accommodation

4.101   CA 2014 s23(1) prohibits a local authority from meeting needs 'by doing anything which it or another local authority is required to do under' the Housing Act (HA) 1996 or under any other enactment specified in regulations.[83] This differs from the provision in the NAA 1948 s21(8) that it replaced. The latter prohibited the social services authority from doing anything that was authorised or required under the HA 1996. The statutory guidance makes a rather opaque reference to the change, saying that it is intended to 'clarify' the boundary (see para 15.51). However, arguably it goes further than this – social services may not be able to rely on the possibility that the individual may at some indefinite point in the future be rehoused into more suitable accommodation if accommodation is required to meet eligible needs immediately. In many such instances, the individual may be statutorily homeless and the housing authority under a duty to provide suitable alternative accommodation (see para 14.23 below). However, if not, arguably the duty to meet eligible needs under the CA 2014 will remain live and may require the social services authority to provide accommodation.

4.102   What the statutory guidance is clear about, is the importance of suitable housing to an individual's well-being and the need for there to be collaborative joint working between housing and social services (see paras 15.48–15.56). In such cases, public law requires that the social services authority endeavour to take decisive action – and as minimum, it would be expected to use its available powers – for example, those under CA 2014 s7 to try and ensure cooperation (see para 14.15).

---

82 Complaint no 15 015 000 against Barnsley Metropolitan Borough Council, 27 July 2016.
83 At the time of writing, no such regulations have been issued.

Ways of meeting needs

4.103   The CA 2014 sets out examples of (1) what an authority may provide to meet needs, and (2) the ways in which it can go about doing so (section 8(2)). The latter include the direct provision of a service by the authority, arrangements for some other person to do so or by making direct payments. The statutory guidance suggests that a local authority may also offer 'brokerage' ie assist the individual to make their own contractual arrangements (para 10.15):

> Brokering would involve the local authority supporting the individual to make a choice about the provider of their care, and to enter into a contract with that provider. The local authority would not need to hold a contract with that provider, but it would be required to assure itself that the chosen provider and terms of the contract were appropriate to meet the person's needs.

4.104   It appears clear from the context that this advice is not referring to the kind of assistance that might be offered to someone who had chosen to make their own arrangements with a direct payment. Given this, it is difficult to think of anyone other than a self-funder (who had asked the authority to meet his or her needs) to whom these arrangements might apply. That is indeed the conclusion reached in the statutory guidance (paras 10.16 and 10.18). In summary, brokerage (in the sense the term is used in the statutory guidance) seems to be an attempt to identify a mechanism by which self-funders might be able take advantage of the lower rates usually charged by providers to local authorities (by asking the authority to 'broker' the contract) while enabling them to retain the control which derives from being the contracting party.

Meeting needs and financial resources

4.105   Although an authority is not permitted to refuse to meet eligible needs on the ground of lack of money, it can take financial considerations into account when deciding how to meet needs. However, this is not an unconstrained discretion. The authority must act lawfully, in a general public law sense.

4.106   The statutory guidance puts it in the following terms (para 10.27):

> … the local authority should not set arbitrary upper limits on the costs it is willing to pay to meet needs through certain routes – doing so would not deliver an approach that is person-centred or compatible with public law principles. The authority may take decisions on a case-by-case basis which weigh up the total costs of different potential options for meeting needs and include the cost as a relevant factor in deciding between suitable alternative options for meeting needs. This does not mean choosing the cheapest option; but one which delivers the outcomes desired for the best value.

This would appear to require more than simply avoiding blanket policies by having an 'exceptional case' provision, eg a policy which says that the authority will not, save in exceptional circumstances, pay more for a package of home care services than it would spend on a residential care package for that person. Policies of this kind can often operate as presumptions against a particular type of provision subject to the right of the individual to put a case for why the presumption should be dis-applied in that individual's case. The statutory guidance seems to require the authority proactively to take an informed and individual best value decision based on costed care options. If this is right, it must have regard to its duty promote well-being and to have regard to the 'key principles' set out in CA 2014 s1(3) (see above at para 2.12). These include the 'least restrictive' principle: the need to ensure that any restriction on an individual's rights or freedom of action that is involved in the exercise of the function is kept to a minimum (section 1(3)(h)).

4.107   Public law principles also require that authorities apply the law correctly. For example, as suggested above, they cannot insist on meeting needs in a way that requires expenditure by the individual in excess of what the statutory charging scheme would require him or her to contribute (including by providing 'top ups' in inappropriate situations – see para 8.252).

4.108   Subject to these caveats, a council policy that refers to a particular costs figure as a 'guideline' rather than a fixed 'ceiling' will generally be lawful (unless the figure is entirely arbitrary). However, any such guideline must be the product of a rational and practical process that has taken into account all relevant factors – and is not an arbitrary figure dreamt up in the fog of a council meeting.[84] In a 1998 report[85] the local government ombudsman considered a council imposed financial ceiling on the level of domiciliary care provided, which reflected the average cost to the council for an older person in residential care. She found that in setting the limit the council had fettered its discretion since there was no evidence that it had ever exceeded the limit and that such a fees policy was unfair and unreasonably discriminated against older people (as opposed to other service users).

4.109   The requirement to 'get the law right' extends beyond the confines of the CA 2014 itself. Care planning may also engage rights under the ECHR and such rights may require authorities to set aside financial considerations [86] (see generally para 2.50 below).

The use of panels

4.110 On the use of panels, see also para 4.80 above.

4.111   In the last decade many authorities have inserted into the assessment, eligibility and care planning process formal mechanisms to impose centralised budgetary control in order to limit the cost of care packages or to defer expenditure and thereby ensure that the budget allocation lasts the financial year. These panels (variously described as 'allocation panels', 'funding panels' quality assurance panels,[87] 'purchasing panels' etc) are not the only rationing mechanism: the process may simply be that a senior manager has the power to veto, cut or delay an assessment/care plan produced by a social worker.

---

84 Complaint nos 90/A/2675, 2075, 1705, 1228 and 1172 against Essex County Council.
85 Complaint no 96/C/4315, 20 August 1998, (1999) 2 CCLR 128. A sum of £10,000 compensation was recommended by the ombudsman.
86 *McDonald v UK* [2014] ECHR 492, (2014) 17 CCLR 18.
87 Some authorities suggest their panels are quality control mechanisms – however, there can be difficulties in sustaining this argument, when relevant minutes are reviewed. Not unusually it can be shown that the panel process was developed as a response to a budgetary problem – rather than as a response to a concern about the quality of social workers' assessments.

4.112   The statutory guidance acknowledges concerns about the use of panels and cautions against inappropriate use which may cause unnecessary delays or inadequate decision-making (para 10.85):

> Due regard should be taken to the use of approval panels in both the timeliness and bureaucracy of the planning and sign-off process. In some cases, panels may be an appropriate governance mechanism to sign-off large or unique personal budget allocations and/or plans. Where used, panels should be appropriately skilled and trained, and local authorities should refrain from creating or using panels that seek to amend planning decisions, micro-manage the planning process or are in place purely for financial reasons. Local authorities should consider how to delegate responsibility to their staff to ensure sign-off takes place at the most appropriate level. In cases or circumstances where a panel is to be used, and where an expert assessor has been involved in the care and support journey, the same person or another person with similar expertise should be part of the panel to ensure decisions take into account complex or specialist issues.

4.113   The local government ombudsman has considered many complaints concerning panel decisions. A frequent scenario concerns disabled people with complex needs who require potentially expensive care packages. Their assessing social worker undertakes considerable research concerning available care and support providers and then recommends a particular care plan. The care plan is then considered by a panel and rejected – essentially the social worker being required to trim the assessment of need to fit the budget (to paraphrase Sedley J[88]) – even though no suitable alternative exists.

4.114   A 2005 ombudsman's report[89] is illustrative in this respect. It concerned the placement of a learning disabled adult in a series of inappropriate care homes. His social worker had undertaken a detailed assessment of needs and identified a suitable placement 'after a long, careful process over many months'. However, her plan was rejected by the council's Care Purchasing Panel, relying on advice from an acting manager who 'barely knew' the service user (he had observed him at most on three occasions in a day centre). The alternative care package proposed proved to be unsuitable and ultimately – once the ombudsman had become involved – a suitable placement was secured. In the ombudsman's opinion:

> Having correctly prepared a detailed assessment in accordance with the statutory guidance, it was wrong for the Council to dismiss all the information gathered in that process, and make a decision on the basis of [the acting manager's] assurance. The decision flew in the face of the assessment.

A 2013 complaint[90] concerned a need of 10.5 hours support for a disabled parent which was reduced by a 'resource panel' (see para 4.111 above) to six hours based on 'other cases'. The ombudsman found this to be maladministration as there was no evidence or no cogent reasons given for the reduction.

---

88 Sedley J referred to 'trimming the assessment of need to fit available provision' in *R v Islington LBC ex p Rixon* (1997–98) 1 CCLR 119 at 129B, QBD.

89 Complaint no 04/A/10159 against Southend on Sea BC, 1 September 2005.

90   Complaint no 12 012 268 against Thurrock Council, 10 October 2013.

4.115   A 2016 ombudsman report[91] concerned an assessor's identification of an adult having eligible needs for support three times a week with showering, washing her hair and dressing. The assessment was rejected by a panel. The report stated:

> I am not persuaded that this panel was purely looking at compliance with the Care Act and cost effectiveness. If this was its remit, it failed to do this adequately. It is possible Miss X's needs could be met in other ways but with proper care and support planning in consultation with Miss X. Not through a decision in direct contravention of the care manager's recommendations by a panel who was not involved in the assessment. I found the Council was at fault in the way it dealt with this 'funding application'.

Waiting lists and delay

4.116   The use of formal waiting lists for the purpose of delaying expenditure is arguably unlawful in the face of the clear statutory duties to meet eligible needs (and, given the real risk in many cases of exacerbation of need, their inconsistency with the prevention agenda). That was certainly the view taken by the Outer House of the Court of Session in the context of the individual duty to make arrangements for residential care in Scotland. In *R v South Lanarkshire Council ex p MacGregor* the applicant was one of 199 people in the council's area who (due to the local authority's limited resources) were on a waiting list for a place in a nursing home, of whom 106 were in hospitals.[92] The court held that the policy was unlawful, and that:

> ... once a local authority determines that an individual's needs call for a particular provision the local authority is obliged to make that provision. In particular having decided that an individual requires the provision of a permanent place in a nursing home ... a local authority could not ... refuse to make such a provision simply because it did not have the necessary resources.

4.117   The local government ombudsman has made similar findings on complaints made under the old statutory framework. For example, in 2001 the ombudsman upheld a complaint against Cambridgeshire that a resource-led policy that delayed the provision of residential care (once the person had been assessed as needing it) was maladministration,[93] and in a complaint against Essex[94] stated:

> The Council believes it does not have to provide a care service or funding for care immediately it has decided that it is necessary to provide the service to meet a person's assessed needs. It considers that it is acting correctly by having a waiting list on which the time a person may have to wait for resources to become available is indeterminate and depends to a significant extent on the needs and priority of other people on the waiting list and those who may come on to the list. That cannot, in my view, be correct.

---

91 Complaint no 15 017 591 against Brighton & Hove City Council, 30 August 2016 at para 20; and see also Complaint no 15 020 384 against London Borough of Bromley, 7 September 2016.
92 (2000) 4 CCLR 188 (CS(OH)).
93 Complaint no 99/B/04621 against Cambridgeshire CC, 29 January 2001.
94 Complaint no 00/B/00599 against Essex CC, 3 September 2001.

Physical resource shortages

4.118   In some cases the problem may be the difficulty in finding an appropriate means of meeting the assessed need, particularly if some kind of specialist resource is required. However, it will be rare that there is absolutely no alternative means of doing so. In *R v Islington LBC ex p Rixon* the local authority was found to be acting unlawfully because, having assessed the applicant as being in need of day centre provision, it had done nothing to put in place any alternative (such as providing home-based day care) when it found that the specialist facility that was required simply did not exist.[95] In the Northern Ireland case *LW: Re Judicial Review* the court held that where a particular respite care facility is unavailable, a reasonable authority will take action to identify alternative provision. [96] If, due to administrative inertia, this does not happen and the authority advances 'no convincing evidence of reasonable efforts' to discharge its continuing statutory duty, then whether 'viewed through the prism of an absolute (ie unqualified) duty of provision or a duty to be measured by the criterion of reasonableness' it will be held to be in breach of its statutory duty'.[97]

4.119   Even where there is no alternative, complete inaction is unlikely to be acceptable. In *R v Sutton LBC ex p Tucker* the local authority was found to have been acting unlawfully by reason of its failure to take steps to commission the required services.[98]

Care and support planning

The duty to prepare a care plan

4.120   The CA 2014 put 'care plans' on a statutory footing. Such documentary records had been considered essential (see para 4.126 below) but were not identified as such by statute. In consequence they have varied greatly. Authorities must now ensure that their care plans conform to the detailed requirements of the Act.

4.121   Where the duty to meet eligible needs has been triggered or the authority has decided to exercise its powers to meet non-eligible needs, a written care and support plan for the adult or a support plan for the carer must be prepared (CA 2014 s24) – both are referred to in the following section as a 'care plan'. A care plan carries a statutory definition in section 25(1) which, in effect, prescribes its content.[99]

4.122   First, the care plan must 'specify' (and the use of that term suggests a certain level of detail):

---

95   *R v Islington LBC ex p Rixon* (1997–98) 1 CCLR 119.
96   [2010] NIQB 62, 19 May 2010.
97   [2010] NIQB 62, 19 May 2010 at paras 48–49.
98   (1997–98) 1 CCLR 251.
99   There is provision for the making of regulations waiving some or all of the requirements CA 2014 s25(13). The statutory guidance makes reference to the Care and Support (Personal Budget Exclusion of Costs) Regulations 2014 which exclude the costs of intermediate and reablement services from the personal budget (see para 10.36).

1) all the needs identified in the assessment (including non-eligible needs);
2) which ones meet the eligibility criteria; and
3) how the local authority is going to meet them.

The care plan must also 'specify' to which of the following the provision of care and support 'could be' relevant:

- The impact on well-being.
- The outcomes the adult wishes to achieve and the contribution that the care and support could make to achieving those outcomes.

Although the statutory language is convoluted, in essence, this requires the authority to be clear about the impact of what it is proposing to do on well-being and the contribution it can make to the achievement of outcomes. In addition, for a carer, the care plan must also 'specify' the potential relevance of the support to the carer's ability and willingness to continue to provide care and any wish they have to work or participate in education, training or recreation.

4.123   In prescribing the content of the care plan the CA 2014 enacts, for the first time, a statutory requirement for a personal budget (CA 2014 s25(1)(e)). In summary, a personal budget is the amount of money that the local authority is proposing to spend on that individual's support (see para 10.3 below). Although personal budgets existed prior to the CA 2014, like 'care plans' they had no statutory basis.

4.124   If any direct payments are to be made in place of local authority arrangements, the plan must also 'specify' the needs that are to be met in this way, their amount and frequency (CA 2014 s25(2)).

4.125   Advice and information on prevention must also be included (CA 2014 s25(1)(f)).

4.126   All of the above is, of course, extremely important material. The importance of a care plan as an evidential document was expressly recognised, in the context of the old legislative scheme, in *R v Islington LBC ex p Rixon*.[100] Sedley J accepted the respondent's submission that 'nowhere in the legislation is a care plan, by that or any other name required' and that 'a care plan is nothing more than a clerical record of what has been decided and what is planned'. In his view, however, this state of affairs:

> ... far from marginalising the care plan, places it at the centre of any scrutiny of the local authority's due discharge of its functions. As paragraph 3.24 of the [1990] policy guidance indicates, a care plan is the means by which the local authority assembles the relevant information and applies it to the statutory ends, and hence affords good evidence to any inquirer of the due discharge of its statutory duties.

4.127   In *R (J) v Caerphilly CBC*[101] (a case under the Children Act 1989) it was held that care plans must 'set out the operational objectives with sufficient detail – including detail of the "how, who, what and when" – to enable the care plan itself to be used as a means of checking whether or not those objectives are being met'.

---

100 (1997–98) 1 CCLR 119 at 128, QBD.
101 [2005] EWHC 586 (Admin), (2005) 8 CCLR 255.

4.128   Although the core content of a care plan is now tightly prescribed by the CA 2014, nonetheless the plan should also be proportionate and personalised, and there is nothing in the legislation which requires a particular form or format to be used. The importance of having a document that works for the individual is stressed in the statutory guidance (para 10.45):

> There should be no restriction or limit on the type of information that the plan contains, as long as this is relevant to the person's needs or outcomes, It should also be possible for the individual to develop their plan in a format that makes sense to them, rather than this being dictated by the recording requirements of the local authority.

But proportionality 'does not equate to a light touch approach' (para 10.43):

> ... as in many cases a proportionate plan will require a more detailed and thorough examination of needs, how these will be met and how this connects with the outcomes that the adult wishes to achieve in day-to-day life.

4.129   The statutory guidance identifies fluctuating needs as a particular factor which indicates the need for comprehensive care planning. This is to be welcomed. The omission of contingency planning to deal with sudden changes in need has been a common problem. It is not something to be addressed 'when someone reaches crisis point' (para 10.44).

Combining care plans

4.130   Care plans can be combined with plans for others including plans provided under different legislative schemes as long as the consent condition is met – which is the same as for combining assessments (CA 2014 s25(11) and (12) – see para 3.102 above). There are three sets of circumstances where the issue is most likely to arise.

Adult in need and carer

4.131   The first circumstance is the combining of an adult in need and his or her carer's plans. This is likely to be particularly relevant where the carer's needs are to be met by the provision of services directly to the cared for person. This is encouraged in the statutory guidance (at para 10.40). However, the combination of plans does not override the statutory requirements on content, and the statutory guidance acknowledges the importance of not losing the individual aspects of each person's plan (para 10.78). It must still be possible to identify who has been assessed as having what need and what is being done to meet those needs. The importance of this separation is obvious in relation to the provision of respite/replacement care, which is often mistakenly conceptualised as a carer's service (see para 7.92 below). If viewed as such, it will be provided only to the extent necessary to meet the carer's needs. However, if correctly treated as a service for the cared for person, the duty to provide will turn on the carer's willingness (and not his or her ability) to provide care during the relevant period.

Local authority and NHS

4.132 The second circumstance in which combining care plans is likely to be an issue is where the adult is receiving care and support not just from the local authority but also from the NHS, for example those who are subject to the Care Programme Approach under the Mental Health Act 1983 (see para 15.42). While the statutory guidance encourages combined care planning in this situation (which is unsurprising in the light of the integration agenda and the introduction of personal health budgets to support that policy objective), again clarity is important. Local authorities need to ensure that they are not inadvertently arranging for the provision of services that they have no power to provide and adults need to take care that their rights under the CA 2014 are properly protected. The statutory duty to meet eligible needs in the CA 2014 is an individually enforceable duty, whereas the duty to provide certain NHS services[102] is more general in nature (see para 1.20 above).

4.133 Where there is to be a combined plan between two different organisations, the authority should work with its partner to establish which is to lead on monitoring, and the statutory guidance advises that a lead professional is named in the plan so that the individual knows who to contact (para 10.80).

Education, health and care plans

4.134 The third situation where care plan combination is likely to occur concerns education, health and care plans (EHC plans).[103] Such plans can continue until the young person is aged 25. The statutory guidance (chapter 16) deals with this potentially complex situation (which has all the hallmarks of a failure to dovetail these two statutory schemes) explaining that:

> 16.65 Where young people aged 18 or over continue to have EHC plans under the Children and Families Act 2014 and the make the move to adult care and support, the care and support aspect of the EHC plan will be provided under the Care Act. The statutory care and support and must form the basis of the 'care' element of the EHC plan ...

> 16.66 Under the Children and Families Act EHC plans must set out the care and support which is reasonably required by the learning difficulties and disabilities that result in the young person having SEN [special educational needs]. For people over 18 with a care and support plan, this will be those elements of their care and support which are directly related to their SEN. EHC plans may also include other care and support that is in the care and support plan, but the elements that are directly related to SEN should always be clearly marked out separately as they will be of particular relevance to the rest of the plan.

4.135 The issue is that the adults' care and support needs may be broader than the care needs that are related to their special educational needs. It is the latter that must be recorded in the EHC plan. The solution that the statutory guidance envisages is to incorporate the broader needs into the EHC

---

102 The duty to provide after-care services under Mental Health Act 1983 s117 is an individually enforceable duty.
103 Children and Families Act 2014 s37.

plan but record them in such a way that separates them from the SEN-related care needs.

The duty to involve

4.136   Participation is one of the 'key principles and standards' of the Act [104] and it is unsurprising, therefore, that section 25(3) and (4) establish a duty to involve the relevant individuals in the preparation of the plan.

4.137   For an adult's care plan, the requirement is to involve the adult and carer and any person at the adult's request, or, if he or she does not have sufficient mental capacity to make that request, any person who appears to be interested in the adult's welfare. There is a parallel requirement for carers (although without provision for incapacity). This duty is not subject to any consent requirement which will have information-sharing implications and the authority will need to take into account their obligations under the Data Protection Act 1998 (see para 19.39).

4.138   The statutory guidance recognises that involvement has potential advantages not only for the individual concerned, but also for the authority: it may reduce the risk of conflict and increase the chances that the resulting care package will be effective (para 10.54):

> The person, and their carers, will have the best understanding of how needs identified fit into the person's life as a whole and connect to their overall well-being ... They are well-placed to consider and identify which care and support options would best fit into their lifestyle and help them achieve the day to day outcomes they identified during the assessment process ... (para 10.49).

4.139   A *duty to involve* confers a *right* to be involved and not, of course, a *duty* to be involved. In this sense, involvement in care planning should be as person-centred as all other aspects of the process – the extent of the involvement is up to the individual concerned:

> The plan should be person-centred, with an emphasis on the individual having every reasonable opportunity to be involved in the planning to the extent that they choose and are able (para 10.33).

4.140   The reference to 'ability' to participate as a potential limiting factor does not mean that the authority need not take steps to support an individual to overcome difficulties. Not only does the statutory right to an independent advocate apply in care planning (see para 3.118 above), but, arguably, the duty to involve is itself an inherently proactive duty – as the statutory guidance states (para 10.33):

> This requires the local authority to ensure that information is available in a way that is meaningful to the person, and that they have support and time to consider their options.

Part and parcel of this proactive duty is taking 'all reasonable steps' to reach agreement on how the individual's needs are to be met (CA 2014 s25(5)). This must mean more than simply trying to persuade the individual to accept what is on offer. It would include listening to their ideas; considering seriously whether things can be done differently in a way that

---

104 See CA 2014 s1(3)(e) and statutory guidance, para 1.4.

is more acceptable to the person concerned; and giving reasons for the authority's standpoint.[105] If there is a dispute, 'people should not be left without support' while it is resolved (statutory guidance, para 10.86). People certainly should not be told that nothing at all can be provided unless and until the individual agrees to sign the plan.

4.141   Independent of the duty to involve is the discretion found in CA 2014 s25(7) to 'authorise' any person to prepare the care plan jointly with the authority. That discretion expressly contemplates the person whose plan is being prepared being the joint party. 'Involvement' as a concept includes the possibility of a plan's development being a joint enterprise.[106] So what does this add to the right to be involved? Section 25(7) arguably means that authority would be acting unlawfully if it sought to limit involvement to something short of a genuine partnership and requires it to make a decision on joint action based on the circumstances of the individual's case. It also opens up the possibility of joint working with others, including those who are not necessarily in a carer role. This is specifically referred to in the statutory guidance (para 10.58) and is likely to be of particular importance for those who do not have sufficient mental capacity to be able to take advantage of the opportunity to work jointly in this way, even with the support of an advocate. However, the power is not limited to cases of incapacity, nor does it require the individual's consent, although the statutory guidance suggests that authorities should start with the presumption that consent is required. A refusal of consent would be a relevant factor in the exercise of the discretion. Section 25(8) gives authorities a broad power to facilitate joint care planning by sharing information about the adult and carer.

4.142   Where there are concerns about the capacity of the individual in relation to care planning, then a 'social worker or other suitably qualified professional should carry out a capacity assessment in relation the specific decision to be made' (statutory guidance para 10.63). However, just because the individual may be proposing an unusual or risky solution does not mean that he or she lacks capacity to make decisions (para 10.62):

> The question to explore is whether it will meet the assessed needs and lead to the desired outcomes.

4.143   Where the individual lacks the requisite mental capacity, care planning must be undertaken on a best interests basis, although the incapacitated person has the same right to be involved to the maximum extent possible. A best interests approach does not mean, of course, that the authority is required to dispense with costs considerations, but to the extent that there are choices to be made, a best interests approach is required by the MCA 2005. That approach will require the least restrictive principle to be applied[107] which complements the parallel provision in the CA 2014

---

105 'In the event that the plan cannot be agreed with the person, or any other person involved, the local authority should state the reasons' – see statutory guidance, para 10.86.
106 Given the personalised nature of the concept and the mandatory requirement to try and reach agreement.
107 Before the act is done, or the decision is made, regard must be had to whether the purpose for which it is needed can be as effectively achieved in a way that is less restrictive of the person's rights and freedom of action (MCA 2005 s1).

s1(3)(h) which informs the development of the care planning options (see above at para 2.15). If the care plan is to involve a deprivation of liberty (DOL) that must be authorised either using the DOL procedures in MCA 2005 Sch 1A in the case of a placement in a care home or hospital, or by the Court of Protection in all other circumstances.[108] The statutory guidance issues a clear message to authorities that most potential deprivations of liberty may well be avoidable (para 10.69):

> Developing effective person-centered processes for planning in line with the guidance and the Act in general may in most cases avoid circumstances where a deprivation of liberty will arise.

The government may well have had in mind here the broader cost-effectiveness of reducing the Court of Protection's workload following the Supreme Court's *Cheshire West* judgment[109] – see para 13.89 below .

The right to a copy of the care plan

4.144   As with the right to a copy of an assessment (see para 3.136 above), the authority is under a duty to give a copy of the care plan to the individual who is the subject of the plan. If it is an adult's care and support plan, the duty extends to giving a copy to any carer or any other person if the adult requests it. There is a parallel duty in relation to a carer's support plan (to provide the adult concerned and any other person on the carer's request (CA 2014 s25(9) and (10)). The statutory provision does not deal expressly with the situation where the adult does not have sufficient mental capacity to make the request but, arguably, the failure proactively to make a best interests decision to offer a copy to a carer or other appropriate person would raise discrimination issues under the EqA 2010. This is not a minor administrative issue – the care plan is the main tool for assessing the effectiveness of implementation (see above at para 4.126).

Care plan reviews

The purpose of a review

4.145   A care plan review should be experienced primarily as an opportunity to check whether a care package is working as it should and to find a solution if it is not. Not uncommonly, however, the process creates an apprehension amongst carers and adults in need, as it is perceived as a process that provides authorities with an opportunity to make cuts. The statutory guidance acknowledges that this has been a problem and warns that reviews 'must not be used as mechanism to arbitrarily reduce the level of the person's personal budget' (para 13.4):

> Such behaviour would be unlawful under the Act as the personal budget must always be an amount appropriate to meet the person's needs. Any reduction to a personal budget should be the result of a change in need or circumstance (para 13.33).

---

108 See chapter 13 on mental capacity below.
109 *P (by his litigation friend the Official Solicitor) (Appellant) v Cheshire West and Chester Council and another* [2014] UKSC 19, (2014) 17 CCLR 5.

The duty to review

4.146 The obligation to keep a care plan under review is proactive and ongoing (CA 2014 s27(1)(a)). This is reflected in the statutory guidance which confirms that authorities should establish monitoring systems (para 13.11). The statutory guidance recommends building review dates into the care plan, in discussion with the individual concerned, but, arguably, this would not of itself discharge the duty to keep under general review (para 13.14). This is certainly consistent with the view taken in the statutory guidance (para 13.15). But what does this mean in practice? The statutory guidance is not particularly helpful here. An example might be circumstances where a local authority became aware that care workers from a particular care agency were not arriving on time. This might suggest a need to review the care plans of others using that particular agency to identify whether it was systemic problem.

4.147 The ombudsman[110] considers that a change in a care provider should trigger a review – even if the change involves over 1,000 people having their care transferred to a new provider.

4.148 An unplanned review might be triggered by a change of circumstances that comes to the local authority's attention, but, in addition, any person has the right to insist on a review as long as the request is reasonable (CA 2014 s27(1)(b)) and people should be to given information on how to make a request, what the process will involve and, very importantly, timescales (bearing in mind the emphasis on a prompt response in the statutory guidance), at the care planning stage (para 13.20). The use of the term 'any person' in the legislation is to ensure that a request can be made by anyone who might become aware of the need for review, for example, a care provider may be aware of an adult's deterioration. The statutory guidance suggests that it might be valuable if a local authority were to insert a 'duty to request a review' into its commissioning contracts (para 13.18). This would be of particular value where an adult is unable to make a review request themselves.

4.149 Although the right is not absolute (but dependent on the request being reasonable), 'in most cases the expectation is that a review should be performed' when requested (statutory guidance para 13.23). Nonetheless, given the nature of the right, it would be wise for a person requesting a review to give as much information as possible in support of that request so that the local authority has the full information to hand when making its decision. The example of a successful request in the statutory guidance is an email which 'provides details that the older person's condition is deteriorating and supplies evidence of recent visits to the GP' (para 13.24).

4.150 The statutory guidance offers some examples of factors which might suggest that refusal would be appropriate, some of which are not unproblematic. For example, it is suggested that if the request is in fact a complaint, the request might be refused. However, on the face of it, simply because a person frames the request in the form of a complaint does not mean that the request for a review is not reasonable. It would be troubling if authorities understood the statutory guidance as suggesting that,

110 Complaint no 15 006 613 against Sheffield City Council, 17 March 2016.

whenever this happens, they should refer the request into their complaints procedure without more. There is no reason why this step could not be taken in addition to a review.

4.151   If the review request is ultimately refused, the local authority should give reasons in an accessible format and explain how they can pursue the issue if they are unhappy with the decision (statutory guidance para 13.25).

Frequency of review

4.152   There is no prescribed review period, but as with the pre-CA 2014 regime,[111] the 'expectation' in the statutory guidance is that reviews will be at least annual.[112] The statutory guidance recommends an initial 'light touch' review of six to eight weeks after sign-off of the personal budget and plan, but otherwise frequency should be based on a personalised approach reflecting the circumstances of the case and taking into account the individual's own views (paras 13.14–13.15). Welcome advice in the statutory guidance is that reviews may need to be more frequent where an individual has few family and friends supporting him or her (para 13.18).

How a review should be carried out

4.153   The statutory guidance stresses that reviews should be person-centred, outcomes-focused, accessible, proportionate (para 13.2) and not be 'overly complex or bureaucratic' (para 13.12). The CA 2014 itself does not prescribe a review method, and the statutory guidance requires that the method chosen be agreed with the individual concerned where reasonably possible (para 13.17): this might include self-review, peer review and reviews conducted at a distance, as well as face-to-face reviews. The statutory guidance does not explore in detail when each might be appropriate, although suggests that self-review might be the method of choice where the individual has a stable, longstanding support package with fixed outcomes (para 13.16). However, even with self-review, it is the local authority's responsibility to ensure that it is conducted adequately and the statutory guidance notes that it would need local authority sign-off.

The content of a review

4.154   The CA 2014 s27 review duty is fleshed out in the statutory guidance (para 13.12), including the requirement that the following elements be communicated to the person before the review begins:

- Have the person's circumstances or needs changed?
- What is working in the plan; what is not working; and may need to change?
- Have the outcomes identified in the plan been achieved?

111 *Prioritising needs* at para 144 said that reviews should be carried out at least annually.
112 Para 13.32: notwithstanding this requirement in the year April 2015 to April 2016 less than half of all adults receiving long-term support had had a review: NHS Digital, *Community care statistics. Social services activity, England, 2015–16. Report on the social care activity of councils with adult social services responsibilities (CASSRs) in England between 1st April 2015 and 31st March 2016*, October 2016, p8.

- Does the person have new outcomes that he or she wants to meet?
- Could improvements be made to achieve better outcomes?
- Is the personal budget enabling needs to be met and the outcomes achieved?
- Is the current method of managing the individual's budget the best one? Eg should direct payments be considered?
- Is the personal budget still meeting the sufficiency test?
- Are there any changes in the individual's informal and community networks which might impact on the plan?
- Have there been any changes which might mean the person is at risk of abuse or neglect?
- Is the person, carer and/or independent satisfied with the plan?

4.155   The CA 2014 distinguishes between a reassessment and a review. A separate duty exists to carry out a re-assessment 'to the extent it thinks appropriate' where the local authority is satisfied that there has been a change in circumstances that affects a care plan (CA 2014 s27(4)). The distinction makes clear that an authority is not expected to carry out a full reassessment each time it undertakes a review of a care plan, although of course it might well be that it is the review which reveals the change of circumstances and thereby triggers the reassessment (para 13.4).

Revisions to a care plan

4.156   The power to revise a care plan arises irrespective of whether the local authority has carried out a prior review or reassessment. The statutory guidance acknowledges this but says:

> In many cases, the review and revision of the plan should be intrinsically linked; it should not be possible to decide whether to revise a care plan without a thorough review to ascertain if a revision is necessary, and in the best interests of the person ... (para 13.5).

Having said this, the statutory guidance goes on to suggest that where there have been only small or no changes in needs, it may be unnecessary to go through a full review and revision (para 13.6). Proportionality is the key. An example might be where a morning call by care workers is too late to ensure that the person concerned can be ready to get to a volunteer placement in time or where there have been small changes in needs which can be met within the existing personal budget.

4.157   However, as noted above, there is a duty to carry out an assessment (albeit to the extent that the local authority considers appropriate) where the local authority is satisfied that there has been a change in circumstances that affects a care plan (CA 2014 s27(4)). It seems clear that, in most cases where revision is needed, some form of reassessment will be required, and indeed this is acknowledged in paragraph 13.27 of the statutory guidance. However, it should be proportionate:

> ... The assessment process following a review should not start from the beginning of the process but pick up from what is already known about the person and should be proportionate ...

4.158   Where a care plan is to be changed, the authority must have regard to the same matters as in a full assessment, ie the impact on well-being, the outcomes the individual wishes to achieve and whether the provision of care and support could contribute to achieving those outcomes. In addition, as with the original assessment, for a carer, regard must also be had to whether the carer is willing and able to continue to provide care and whether he or she wishes to work or participate in education, training or recreation (CA 2014 s27(2)(a) and (3)(a)).

4.159   The duty to involve applies both in deciding whether to revise the plan and how (CA 2014 s27(2)(b) and (3)(b)). Independent advocacy rights also apply (see above at para 3.117). Where, having undertaken a reassessment, the local authority is proposing to change how it meets an individual's needs, and it is therefore intending to it is necessary to revise the care plan, it must take all reasonable steps to reach agreement with the individual concerned (CA 2014 s27(5)).

Support plan breakdowns

Breakdowns due to failure to meet needs

4.160   Where a support plan is not meeting a disabled person's needs, the authority is under a duty to address the problem – the urgency of the remedial action depending in part on the severity of the situation. Where complex support packages are involved, authorities may have difficulty in making rapid and effective changes to restore the position; nevertheless a failure to take prompt and, if necessary, urgent action in such cases may amount to maladministration.[113] Where a support package is breaking down, this may be explicable in terms of the authority failing to provide appropriate services to meet the disabled person's needs, or of having failed to build in a suitable contingency arrangement.[114] This may reflect the inadequacy of the assessment on which the service provision is based or a failure in service provision.

Breakdown due to service unavailability

4.161   Not infrequently, a support plan breakdown can occur because an existing service ceases to be available. This problem is illustrated by a 2002 local government ombudsman's report[115] concerning the care plan for a young adult with multiple and profound mental and physical disabilities. Her needs were assessed and provision made for her to have one weekend per month respite care in a residential unit, paid by the local authority, but provided by a charitable organisation. Several years later the family were notified that owing to funding problems the unit was closed at weekends, and the local authority, having no record of the assessment, asserted that respite at weekends was not needed. The ombudsman upheld the complaint, stating:

> The council says that because it was not responsible for the closure of [the respite facility] it cannot be held responsible for the withdrawal of [the complainant's] provision. I do not accept this. It is the council, not [the

---

113 See eg report on complaint no 04/C/12489 against Oldham MBC, 7 September 2006.
114 See eg para 4.129 above.
115 Complaint no 01/C/03521 against North Yorkshire CC, 19 August 2002.

charitable provider] which has statutory responsibility for providing for [the complainant's] needs. If [the respite facility] could not, for whatever reason, meet those needs, the council had a duty to find, in the locality, somewhere else where [the complainant] would feel equally settled and in which her parents would have confidence.

4.162 A further ombudsman's report[116] on the question of service delivery difficulties concerned a severely disabled man and his main carer, both aged over 90. He was assessed as needing help getting up and going to bed; the weekend and evening cover being provided by an agency. Because of recruitment problems, the agency gave notice to the council that it proposed to withdraw its service and the council was unable to find another agency willing to provide this service unless the council would pay travel costs to the staff, above the flat rate fee for the service, and the council refused as this was against its policy. In finding a fettering of discretion and maladministration the ombudsman commented:

> It cannot be easy to arrange for home care in the rural parts of the county's area, and even the best contractual agreements must fail from time to time. But it seems to me that when a service failure occurs, the council might well have to seize any realistic opportunity to make the service good. Here it had such an opportunity. Another home care contractor offered to provide the ... service but only if the council would pay its staff travel costs over and above the flat rate fee for providing home care. Doubtless there are many tussles between the council and its providers over such arrangements and I can understand why the council might have considered this a precedent and the thin end of the wedge, but what was that to Mr and Mrs Derwent? It seems to me that Mr Derwent's home care was entirely sacrificed to maintain the purity of the council's contractual arrangements ... This was a classic case of the council fettering its discretion, and was maladministration.

4.163 A service may cease to be available, because the local authority has taken a strategic decision not to continue to commission it (for example, a respite care centre[117]). It may well be unlawful to do so without consulting those affected. The local government ombudsman has found maladministration in such cases.[118]

Breakdowns in care packages due to service user behaviour

4.164 Many service users will have behavioural difficulties which are an inextricable part of their condition. Their care plan should therefore take into account these characteristics and in general it would be inappropriate to withdraw a service from such person because of his or her behaviour. Accordingly, the local government ombudsman has criticised a council for withdrawing respite care services from a young adult with severe learning disabilities because of a challenging outburst.[119] Although she accepted that 'sometimes brief withdrawal of provision is unavoidable in situations like this', she found that the prolonged exclusion was primarily the consequence of inadequate respite care provision services – and accordingly a

116 Complaint no 99/B/00799 against Essex CC, 29 March 2001.
117 See also para 4.161 above.
118 Complaint 11 017 875 against Suffolk CC, 11 October 2012.
119 Complaint no 03/C/16371 against Stockton-on-Tees BC, 18 January 2005.

failure to meet his assessed need. She recommended 'the council to adopt as a top priority the provision of a new local facility or facilities for [this client group]'.

4.165   Where, for example, a disabled person behaves offensively to home care assistants or refuses to comply with the reasonable requirements of a day centre etc, it might reach a point where the local authority cannot continue to provide a service and considers that it has discharged its duty. In deciding whether to withdraw the service, the applicant's mental health and its treatability may be relevant factors,[120] as indeed will be the authority's duties under EqA 2010 s15 (the 'less favourable treatment arising from disability' ground). The impact on carers in this situation is significant. The 2001 white paper, *Valuing people*, gave the following advice:[121]

> Excluding people with learning disabilities from services if they are found to be difficult to handle or present with challenging behaviour represents a major cause of stress for carers, who may be left unsupported to cope with their son or daughter at home. This practice is unacceptable and families must not be left to cope unaided. No service should be withdrawn on these grounds without identifying alternative options and putting a suitable alternative service in place where possible. Decisions to exclude a person with learning disabilities from a service should always be referred to the Learning Disability Partnership Board, which will be responsible for the provision of alternative services in such cases, provided the person meets the eligibility criteria.

Monitoring services

4.166   The local government ombudsman has made repeated criticism of local authority failures to monitor care services[122] – particularly those provided by independent agencies for whom they have private contracts. In a 2007 complaint against Liverpool City Council[123] she noted that although the one arm of the council had knowledge that the care agency was providing an unsatisfactory service, this did not stop the agency being paid by another arm of the council since the one had no input into the into the administration of the contract of the other. In her view, such a situation, placed 'the most vulnerable members of the community at serious risk' and was 'simply unacceptable and constitute[d] maladministration'.

4.167   Given the vulnerability of many such service users, the ombudsman has also stressed the need for councils to monitor carefully the quality of service provision and not simply to wait for complaints – noting (in a 2011) report:[124] 'I do not believe that the Council's reliance on any absence

---

120 See *Croydon LBC v Moody* (1999) 2 CCLR 92, CA.

121 Department of Health, *Valuing people: a new strategy for learning disability for the 21st century* Cm 5086, The Stationery Office 2001, para 5.7.

122 See eg complaint no 15 005 213 against Bradford MDC, 28 July 2016; complaint no 15 020 78 against Royal Borough of Kingston upon Thames 28 August 2016; complaint nos 05/C/18474 against Birmingham CC, 4 March; 2008; 05/C/06420 against Sheffield CC, 20 February 2007; 05/C/08592 against Liverpool CC, 17 January 2007; 03/C/17141 against Blackpool, 23 February 2006.

123 Complaint no 05/C/08592 against Liverpool CC, 17 January 2007, paras 30–31.

124 Complaint no 08 019 214 against Bromley LBC, 9 June 2011, para 43.

of complaint from the family during this time excuses this lack of proper attention to its statutory responsibilities.'

4.168   The Public Services Ombudsman for Wales has also expressed concerns in this area; a 2010 complaint, for example, criticising a council for failing to issue a contract default notice against a provider in a situation where the service it was providing was clearly substandard.[125]

Interim services

4.169   Unplanned reviews are most likely to be triggered by changes in circumstances and the change may be such that the individual needs an urgent adjustment to their care package in response. Although reviews should be carried out as quickly as possible, the local authority may need to consider putting in place an interim package to meet urgent needs while completing the review and revision process (statutory guidance, para 13.34).

Transition to the new scheme

4.170   The Act made no provision for the automatic transfer of existing users of adult social care to the new scheme on 1 April 2015. The Care Act 2014 (Transitional Provision) Order 2015[126] made provision for transition over a 12-month period.[127] The Order permitted 'support or services' already being provided, and charges already being made, to continue and, in such cases, to be subject to the original statutory provisions under which they were put in place. This transitional arrangement was authorised for a maximum of one year (until 31 March 2016).

4.171   The Order required each authority to review existing service users within that period (art 2) but if they failed to do so, on 1 April 2016 those service users were to be treated as being eligible under the new regime and as receiving their care and support/support under the CA 2014 until a review is completed (arts 3 and 4). However, if a local authority has continued to rely on that passporting provision, it risks being in breach of not only the duty to keep a care plan under review but various other requirements, for example, specifying a personal budget in that plan.

4.172   In relation to the transition process for carers, the statutory guidance advised that:

> ... local authorities should review existing local policies in light of the new national minimum eligibility threshold for carers. Where this indicates individuals or groups who may become eligible as a result, then a carer's assessment should be offered (para 23.13).

If a carer did not receive support to which they would have or might have been entitled had they been assessed at an earlier stage under the CA 2014 but they were not aware of this and their local authority had taken no proactive steps to identify carers in that position, a complaint of maladministration may well be justifiable based on this guidance.

125 Complaint no 200900324 against Powys CC, 1 October 2010, paras 115–116.

126 Care Act (Transitional Provision) Order 2015 SI No 995.

127 Care Act 2014 and Children and Families Act 2014 (Consequential Amendments) Order 2015.

CHAPTER 5

Hospital discharge

Introduction

5.1   This chapter begins by looking at the background to hospital discharges, turning then to a review of the current principal legal duties and guidance. It then explains the general discharge process, examines safe discharge, considers the issues involved in delayed discharge and finally discusses challenging a discharge decision.

Background

5.2   Patients have, in general,[1] no right to remain in a National Health Service (NHS) facility, and can be discharged against their wishes – provided that the NHS and social services authorities consider that it is safe (ie have satisfied themselves that it would not be negligent – by exposing the patient to an unnecessary or involuntary risk of harm).

5.3   For a number of reasons – but principally a significant rise in hospital admissions coupled with a decline in the number of NHS beds (see para 5.9 below) and concerns about hospital acquired infections – there is considerable pressure on hospitals to move patients from acute facilities as soon as it is safe to do so.

5.4   In the years immediately after the enactment of the Community Care (Delayed Discharges etc) Act 2003, there appeared to be a marked decline in the number of people in hospital recorded as subject to a 'delayed discharge'.[2] However, this trend has since gone into reverse. The average number of patients who were kept in hospital unnecessarily because social care was unavailable increased by 19 per cent between 2013/14 and 2014/15. In this period, 44 per cent more patients were waiting for health and care packages at home compared to the previous year, and 32.8 per cent more patients were waiting for a place in a nursing home.[3] Between June 2015 and June 2016, hospital discharge delays increased by a further 23 per cent.[4] It remains the case, however, that 'the majority of delayed discharge days are attributable to the NHS'[5] – at least 60 per cent in the year

---

1   Unless they are entitled to NHS continuing healthcare (NHS CC) support, detained under the Mental Health Act (MHA) 1983 or have been in NHS accommodation for a prolonged period – such that it might be deemed their 'home' for the purposes of European Convention on Human Rights (ECHR) Article 8.

2   The records indicate that these fell from 4,147 (of whom 3,025 were over 75) in the last quarter of 2002/03 to 2,175 (of whom 1,604 were over 75) in the last quarter of 2005/06. However, some of the success of the policy may be tempered with the knowledge that in the same quarters the number of people who were readmitted as an emergency within 28 days of discharge rose from 138,773 to 198,777 – a rise from 5.5 per cent to 7.1 per cent of all patients discharged: see *Report of the Chief Executive to the NHS*, June 2006.

3   Age UK, '2.4m bed days lost in 5 years from social care delays', news item on Age UK's website, 17 June 2015.

4   171,300 total delayed days in June 2016 compared to 139,500 in June 2015 – see NHS England, *Monthly delayed transfers of care data: statistical press notice*, 11 August 2016.

5   Statutory guidance, para 5.43.

to June 2016.[6] It is thought that delayed discharges cost the NHS around £900 million per year.[7]

5.5   It is clear that hospital discharge arrangements are not working well. A 2016 report from the King's Fund referred to 'NHS providers scrambling to get older people out of hospital before they deteriorate'.[8] It also noted that 'being discharged without proper support is an invitation to relapse, a worsening of their condition and re-admission'.[9] While it is currently harder to capture the precise financial cost of premature discharge, the National Audit Office estimated that in 2012/13 emergency re-admissions cost the NHS £2.4 billion.[10]

5.6   In 2016 the health services ombudsman published a special report concerning unsafe hospital discharges, prompted by the significant rise in complaints to her office on this issue: in 2015 it had investigated 221 such complaints, 'an increase of over a third in complaints in the previous year'.[11] The report noted that there was (p6):

> ... no shortage of clear guidance on what effective discharge planning should look like ... Yet our casework shows clear examples of trusts and local authorities failing to put it into practice.

Principal legal duties and guidance

Law

5.7   The law that regulates the hospital discharge responsibilities of the NHS and social services authorities is an amalgam of statute and tort:

- The patient is owed a duty of care (in the tort of negligence) by both the social services authority and the relevant NHS body.
- The NHS has a statutory responsibility to provide care under the National Health Service Act (NHSA) 2006.
- Social services have responsibilities under the Care Act (CA) 2014 (s74, Sch 3 and associated regulations[12]) to assess and, where eligible, to secure the necessary care and support. The CA 2014 repealed the Community Care (Delayed Discharges etc) Act 2003 (and its subordinate legislation[13]), albeit that it then re-enacted these provisions (with minor modification).

---

6   Statutory guidance, para 5.43.

7   Parliamentary and health service ombudsman, *A report of investigations into unsafe discharge from hospital*, 2016, p7.

8   R Humphries and others, *Social care for older people: home truths*, King's Fund, 2016, p72.

9   David Maguire, 'Premature discharge: is going home early really a Christmas gift?', The King's Fund Blog, 21 December 2015, www.kingsfund.org.uk/blog/2015/12/.

10   National Audit Office, *Emergency admissions to hospital: managing the demand*, 2013.

11   Parliamentary and Health Service Ombudsman, *A report of investigations into unsafe discharge from hospital*, 2016, p4.

12   Care and Support (Discharge of Hospital Patients) Regulations 2014 SI No 2823.

13   Care and Support (Discharge of Hospital Patients) Regulations 2014 SI No 2823 and the Delayed Discharges (Continuing Care) Directions 2009 – for detail of the relevant pre-CA 2014 law, see the 5th edition of this book at para 5.5 and following.

Guidance

5.8   As noted above there is 'no shortage' of guidance on the way the discharge process should operate. The principal documents cited in this chapter are:

- the statutory guidance to the CA 2014 (annex G) (Department of Health, *Care and support statutory guidance* to support implementation of Part 1 of the CA 2014 by local authorities, 2016 – referred to below as the 'statutory guidance'); and
- 2010 good practice guidance from the Department of Health (DH), *Ready to go? Planning the discharge and the transfer of patients from hospital and intermediate care* (the '2010 DH guidance'); and
- 2015 National Institute of Health and Care Excellence (NICE) guidance, *Transition between inpatient hospital settings and community or care home settings for adults with social care needs* (the '2015 NICE guidance').[14]

In 2015, NICE produced a 'quality standard' (QS136)[15] to accompany its 2015 guidance. Such standards have statutory force[16] and apply to both the NHS and social services.[17] The 2016 standard has six 'quality statements' against which health and social care bodies will be measured, these being (p15):

- (1) Adults with social care needs who are admitted to hospital have existing care plans shared with the admitting team.
- (2) Older people with complex needs have a comprehensive geriatric assessment started on admission to hospital.
- (3) Adults with social care needs who are in hospital have a named discharge co-ordinator.
- (4) Adults with social care needs are given a copy of their agreed discharge plan before leaving hospital.
- (5) Adults with social care needs have family or carers involved in discharge planning if they are providing support after discharge.

5.9   Other guidance includes NICE and good practice guidance in relation to people in mental health settings,[18] and good practice concerning people

---

14   NICE, *Transition between inpatient hospital settings and community or care home settings for adults with social care needs* NG 27, 2015 – see also A Winfield and W Burns, 'Let's all get home safely: a commentary on NICE and SCIE guidelines (NG27)' *Age and Ageing* (2016) 45 (6): 757–760.

15   NICE, *Transition between inpatient hospital settings and community or care home settings for adults with social care needs* Quality standard (QS136), December 2016.

16   Health and Social Care Act 2012 Part 8 s234.

17   They are designed (together with the 2015 NICE guidance) to be read in conjunction with the following documents (and their updated versions): Department of Health, *The adult social care outcomes framework 2015/16* (ASCOF), 2014; Department of Health, *NHS outcomes framework 2016–17*, 2016; and *Public health outcomes framework 2016–19* – a composite document, but see Department of Health, *Improving outcomes and supporting transparency*, 2016.

18   NICE, *Transition between inpatient mental health settings and community or care home settings* guideline NG53, 2016; and Care Services Improvement Partnership (CSIP), *A positive outlook – a good practice toolkit to improve discharge from inpatient mental health care*, 2007.

who are homeless[19] as well guidance on specific practices, for example the 'discharge to assess' process.[20] A Department of Health 2004 'toolkit' also exists for 'simple' discharge procedures'[21] – eg those where the patient returns to his or her home and does not require social services involvement (thought to make up at least 80 per cent of all discharges). The idea behind the 2004 guidance is to implement relatively simple procedures which it appears can have a dramatic impact on freeing up beds – including discharging patients earlier in the day before the peak demand for admissions (the build-up starts in general at 7am and reaches its peak at 12.30pm); having discharge procedures operating on the same basis seven days a week; and authorising less senior medical/nursing staff to implement the process.

The discharge process

Relationship between the NHS and social services

5.10   In most instances patients are keen to move on from a hospital ward. When a patient requires ongoing assistance either in the form of NHS services or social care, establishing whether it is (1) safe to discharge the patient and (2) assessing what services are needed following a hospital stay, are key to a smooth transition. In this respect the Health Select Committee's 2002 report on delayed discharges stated that the key objective was to ensure 'the right care in the right place at the right time'.[22] This objective is quoted in the 2010 DH guidance (p4) which stresses that 'discharge is a process and not an isolated event at the end of the patient's stay' (p6).

5.11   As noted above, the relationship between the NHS and social services in the discharge process is shaped by statute (namely the CA 2014), regulations and guidance.

5.12   The legal obligations that arise on hospital discharge are activated by the discharge of the patient from NHS care – not his or her transfer to another NHS facility. Patients do not have the right to choose the place at which they receive NHS care.[23] The decision that they are safe to be transferred to another NHS facility is therefore primarily that of the responsible consultant and the NHS team on the relevant ward. It follows that when discussing hospital discharge, the issue is not of internal transfer, but discharge from an NHS setting. A consultant's decision in conjunction with

19 Department for Communities and Local Government and Department of Health, *Hospital admission and discharge: people who are homeless or living in temporary or insecure accommodation*, 2006.

20 Department of Health, *Quick guide: discharge to assess*, 2016.

21 Department of Health, *Achieving timely 'simple' discharge from hospital: a toolkit for the multi-disciplinary team*, 2004.

22 House of Commons Health Committee, *Delayed discharges*, Third report of session 2001–2, HC 617–I, The Stationery Office, 2002, accessible at www.publications. parliament.uk/pa/cm200102/cmselect/cmhealth/617/617.pdf.

23 See, however, para 5.32 below.

the medical team that a patient is medically fit to be transferred is the 'sine qua non' – the key triggering event – in the discharge planning process.[24]

5.13   When such a decision has been made and the patient has (or may have) a need for social care support, a safe discharge cannot occur until the NHS and social services are satisfied that the patient is not only (1) ready for discharge; but also (2) safe to be discharged. In essence, this is therefore a twin key process. Once the system is activated, the discharge conveyor belt should only start to move when two keys have been turned – the first is primarily the responsibility of the NHS, and the second primarily the responsibility of social services. Once the two keys have been turned and the belt is in motion, then (if the process is regulated by the CA 2014) social services are generally unable to stop the system without incurring the possibility of reimbursing the NHS if they are the cause of any delay in the patient's discharge from hospital.

Patient and carer involvement

5.14   CA 2014 Sch 3 para 1(4) requires that before the NHS gives an 'assessment notice' (see para 5.34 below) the NHS must consult the patient and 'where it is feasible' any carer that the patient has. The notice is only issued where the NHS considers that 'it is not likely to be safe to discharge the patient unless arrangements for meeting the patient's needs for care and support are in place' (CA 2014 Sch 3 para 1(1)). On receiving such a notice, the local authority's duty to assess under CA 2014 s9 is triggered (see para 3.13 above) as well as the duty to assess any carer under section 10 (see para 3.16 above). Indeed, it appears that about 25 per cent of all requests for support for new clients aged 65 and over came through the hospital discharge process. [25] The statutory guidance explains this in the following terms (annex G para 17):

> On receiving an assessment notice, the local authority must carry out a need assessment of the patient and (where applicable) a carer's assessment so as to determine, in the first place, whether it considers that the patient and where applicable, carer has needs. If so, the local authority must then determine whether any of these identified needs meet the eligibility criteria and if so, then how it proposes to meet any (if at all) of those needs. The local authority must inform the NHS of the outcome of its assessment and decisions.

5.15   The statutory guidance states that it is 'fundamental that both the NHS body and the local authority involve the patient and, if appropriate, their carer about their current and ongoing care and support needs' (annex G para 54). The 2015 NICE guidance describes as an 'overarching principle' (para 1.1) that everyone receiving care is seen 'an equal partner who can make choices about their own care ... [and] treated with dignity and respect

---

24 The NHS/social services cannot (without invoking their powers under the MHA 1983) prevent patients from discharging themselves – provided they have sufficient mental capacity to make the decision (see chapter 13 below).

25 NHS Digital, *Community care statistics: social services activity, England, 2015–16*, October 2016, p6. This is a report on the social care activity of Councils with Adult Social Services Responsibilities (CASSRs) in England between 1 April 2015 and 31 March 2016.

throughout their transition'. It stresses the importance of involving 'families and carers in discussions about the care being given or proposed if the person gives their consent'. It states that (para 1.5.31):

> If the discharge plan involves support from family or carers, the hospital-based multidisciplinary team should take account of their:
> - willingness and ability to provide support
> - circumstances, needs and aspirations
> - relationship with the person
> - need for respite.

5.16 The 2010 DH guidance contains a chapter concerning the importance of 'involving patents and carers'. It requires that patients and carers are involved 'so that they can make informed decisions and choices that deliver a personalised care pathway and maximise their independence' and that practitioners must not assume a carer is 'able or willing to continue in a caring role' (p19.). It also requires that staff check the accuracy of information they are given from the patient about their relative's willingness and ability to care (pp12 and 29).

5.17 A 2015 Healthwatch report[26] found that one in ten trusts did not routinely notify relatives and carers that someone has been discharged, and that one in eight people did not feel they were able to cope in their own home after being discharged from hospital. A 2016 local government ombudsman complaint[27] concerned a failure to assess the main carer before an elderly person with dementia was discharged from hospital. In finding maladministration the ombudsman noted that the 'failure to complete a timely carer's assessment is not in line with section 10 of the Care Act 2014' and that it was important that the carer was present when the patient was assessed as she was the main carer.

Mental capacity

5.18 In relation to patients with limited mental capacity, the duties under the Mental Capacity Act (MCA) 2005 apply – as they do to any other assessment (see para 3.119 above). The 2015 NICE guidance[28] advises that if there is any 'doubt about the person's capacity to consent' the MCA 2005 principles must be followed. The 2010 DH guidance stresses the need for them to have appropriate support when making decisions concerning their discharge arrangements.[29] It further states that 'where the patient cannot represent themselves, the next of kin, carer, relative or an independent mental capacity advocate (IMCA) must be involved. Their role is to represent the patient's interests, and to challenge any decision that does not appear to be in the best interest of the patient' (p19).

---

26 Healthwatch England, *Safely home: what happens when people leave hospital and care settings?* 2015.

27 Complaint no 16 003 456 against Surrey CC, 8 Sept 2016 – and see also Complaint no 15 014 893 against Dorset CC, 1 September 2016.

28 At para 1.1.3; and see also the statutory guidance, annex G para 54.

29 2010 DH guidance, p11.

Advocacy

5.19   The CA 2014 s67 duty to provide independent advocacy (see para 3.117 above) applies to hospital discharge assessments as it does to other assessments under the CA 2014.[30] In such cases, the stipulation that the duty only arises if there is no other appropriate representative available (section 67(5)) does not apply, if there is (a) disagreement on a 'material issue' between the local authority and the person; and (b) the local authority and the person agree that advocacy support is in the person's best interests. If the person disagrees with a local authority decision that he or she is ready to be moved to another hospital, or that he or she should be discharged to a care home for an extended period,[31] then (subject to the best interests requirement) the duty arises. Given the many problems that arise on disputed hospital discharges (and the CA 2014 s1 assumption that the 'individual' is best placed to judge his or her well-being), the presumption must be that in such situations it would be in a person's best interests to have advocacy support.

Information/communication

5.20   In a number of investigations the health service ombudsman has been critical of trusts that have failed to communicate properly with (and provide adequate information to) patients and their carers.[32] The ombudsman has stressed that where the obligation to inform is a joint one (ie shared with the social services) this does not excuse a failure by the trust to provide the information (ie it cannot assume that social services will discharge its duty).[33] The ombudsman has also criticised as inadequate the provision of general brochures to patients and situations where staff provided patients with only limited advice on their possible options.[34]

5.21   The 2015 NICE guidance requires that (para 1.1.4):

> ... the person, their carers and all health and social care practitioners involved in someone's move between hospital and home are in regular contact with each other. This is to ensure the transition is coordinated and all arrangements are in place.

---

30   If it is 'is likely to' result in the NHS making funding the person in a hospital for a period of 28 days or more; or a care home for a period of eight weeks or more – Care and Support (Independent Advocacy Support) (No 2) Regulations 2014 reg 4(2)(a); and see also the revised statutory guidance, para 7.22.

31   Care and Support (Independent Advocacy Support) (No 2) Regulations 2014 reg 3.

32   Complaint nos E 1631/03–04 and E 2050/02–03, both in *Selected cases for October 2003 – March 2004* which contains five cases on the question of hospital discharge. More recently, the Welsh Ombudsman criticised the poor communication with the family regarding discharge (Case reference 200802248).

33   Fifth report for session 1995–96, *Investigations of complaints about long-term NHS care*, HMSO, Complaint E.685/94–95.

34   Fifth report for session 1995–96, *Investigations of complaints about long-term NHS care*, HMSO, Complaint E.672/94–95.

5.22 The 2010 DH guidance stresses the importance of effective communica-tion with patients[35] and requires that they be provided with written infor-mation on the discharge process, noting that:

> Considerate language, well-written literature, clearly designed diagrams, simple signposting and accessible media in any format all help to comple-ment and reinforce dialogue.[36]

Ward-based care/discharge co-ordination

5.23 Although the 2010 DH guidance stresses there should be a named lead discharge co-ordinator,[37] it adds a note of caution, that at ward level 'prac-titioners are becoming increasingly reliant on specialist discharge teams in cases where they should be able to manage the process themselves' and that in 'today's environment it is unrealistic to expect one person to be available each day to co-ordinate care'.[38] It suggests, therefore, that at ward level:

- one person has the lead for care planning each day;
- uninterrupted time is dedicated to discharge planning, ensuring that everyone is aware of his or her responsibilities in the process, and that there is a named person to hand over the role to;
- expected date of discharge should be set within 24–48 hours of admis-sion and discussed with the patient and the patient's family and reviewed daily with the patient;[39]
- a discharge checklist should be completed 24–48 hours before dis-charge to ensure that all actions essential to a smooth discharge have been completed.[40]

5.24 The 2015 NICE guidance reiterates the need for a discharge co-ordinator who is the 'central point of contact for health and social care practition-ers, the person and their family' and that a 'named replacement should always cover their absence' (para 1.5). It stresses, however, that in addition there is a need for hospital-based and community-based multi-disciplinary teams to co-ordinate the transfer of care process (para 1.3) – including therapists, social workers and other specialists. The importance of such key workers was highlighted in a 2011 joint ombudsmen's report[41] con-cerning a 'shocking' discharge of an adult with learning disabilities. The report noted that although the role of key worker was always important, in this case it was critical. Despite this, no one from health or social ser-vices represented his views or best interests and they collectively failed to

---

35 The guidance draws on the more extensive Welsh guidance *Passing the baton – a practical guide to effective discharge planning*, which devotes a complete chapter on communication (chapter 2).
36 2010 DH guidance, p30.
37 2010 DH guidance, p25.
38 2010 DH guidance, p15.
39 2010 DH guidance, pp16–18.
40 2010 DH guidance, p25.
41 A report by the health service ombudsman and the local government ombudsman about the care and support provided to a person with Down's syndrome, *Thirteenth report of the Health Service Commissioner for England Session 2010–12*, HC 1644, The Stationery Office, 2011.

involve his family sufficiently in planning his care and 'even more significantly, they failed to take appropriate steps to demonstrate that proper
consideration was given to [his] basic human rights (specifically to liberty
and to a family life) when decisions were being made'.

Safe discharge

5.25   Although both the 2015 NICE guidance and the 2010 DH guidance advise
that discharge planning should commence before or on admission, they
do not address the detail of what, in clinical terms, is necessary for there
to be a safe discharge. A 2003 Department of Health safe discharge protocol[42] is instructive for this purpose. It lists three key criteria for the making
of the discharge decision and emphasises that they 'are not separate or
sequential stages; all three should be addressed at the same time whenever possible':

1) a clinical decision has been made that the patient is ready for transfer;
2) a multi-disciplinary team decision has been made that the patient is
   ready for transfer; and
3) the patient is safe to discharge/transfer.

5.26   The protocol comments that:

> In some cases we are told the process consists almost entirely of the con-
> sultant deciding a patient is medically fit for discharge, followed by referral
> to social services. Hence the multi-disciplinary input to the decision mak-
> ing process is minimal and – in extreme cases – non-existent. In addition
> this does not fulfil the, now legal, requirement to begin planning for dis-
> charge as soon as possible during the hospital stay.

5.27   The safe discharge protocol goes on to analyse the critical questions in
relation to each of the three steps:

1) The clinical decision (ready to transfer/discharge)
   • Does the patient need to remain in an acute bed to receive intensive
     medical input from a consultant team?
   • Does the patient need intensive or specialist nursing, therapy or
     other clinical support only available in an acute setting, such as the
     administration of specialist drugs or intensive monitoring through
     the use of specialist equipment?
   • Has the patient's condition been monitored within an agreed
     period?
   • Is the patient's health likely to deteriorate significantly if moved
     elsewhere?
   • Has the patient recovered from the acute episode sufficiently to be
     able to return home or move to another setting?
   • Could the patient be managed at home by primary care or in a nurse
     or therapy led unit?

2) The multi-disciplinary team decision (ready to transfer/discharge)

---

42   Department of Health, *Definitions – medical stability and safe to transfer*, 2003 – as
a good practice guide this is still relevant and continues to be cited by the local
government ombudsman: see, for example, Complaint no 15 003 673 against Oxford
University Hospitals NHS Trust, 10 August 2015, para 11.

- Will the patient benefit from further acute treatment and/or rehabilitation?
- Can rehabilitation or recuperation be provided in an alternative setting, including the patient's own home and has the team come to a decision about where the patient should be managed?
- What are the risks of remaining in the acute bed?
- Has the patient (and have any carers) been involved in the assessment?

3) The objective decision (safe to transfer/discharge)
  - Does the multi-disciplinary team have a clear picture of the patient's living circumstances prior to this episode and know enough to be able to make a decision that the person is safe to discharge/transfer?
  - Can the assessment be continued/completed in another setting, including the person's own home?
  - What does the patient want and expect?
  - Has the carer been consulted and what are his or her views?
  - Has a similar level of need for this patient previously been met by primary and community care services?
  - Does everyone, including the patient and carer, understand the risk of transferring the patient?

5.28 Although the safe discharge protocol uses the word 'assessment' this does not appear to refer to a social care assessment but merely whether the patient and carer have been involved in the multi-disciplinary decision that he or she is safe to transfer.

Delayed discharge

Delayed discharge payments

5.29 The CA 2014 continues the legislative scheme[43] designed to penalise local authorities that fail to facilitate the speedy discharge of patients deemed 'ready to be discharged' from an acute hospital. The arrangements apply to local authorities who delay the discharge of adults who:

1) are safe to be discharged;
2) have been receiving acute medical care; and
3) are in need of social care services.

5.30 A lack of capacity in the social care system (for instance, the absence of any available care home places) does not exempt social services from their liability to make a payment. The provisions of the CA 2014 are designed to synchronise with the good practice guidance – thus the service of a notice under the CA 2014 should not be seen as an event that dominates or in any way undermines the operation of good discharge planning.

Acute medical care

5.31 The reimbursement rules only apply to patients receiving 'acute medical care'. The regulations provides that:

---

43 Introduced into England by the Community Care (Delayed Discharges etc) Act 2003 (which Act is repealed by the CA 2014).

'Acute care' means intensive medical treatment provided by or under the supervision of a consultant, that lasts for a limited period after which the person receiving the treatment no longer benefits from it.[44]

and that:

Care is not 'acute care if the patient has given an undertaking (or one has been given on the patient's behalf) to pay for it; nor is any of the following 'acute care'–

(a) care of an expectant or nursing mother;

(b) mental health care;[45]

(c) palliative care;

(d) a structured programme of care provided for a limited period to help a person maintain or regain the ability to live at home;

(e) care provided for recuperation or rehabilitation.[46]

NHS continuing healthcare

5.32   The 2012 National Framework for NHS continuing healthcare (NHS CC)[47] (considered further at para 12.39 below) stipulates that the NHS is required to consider whether patient's being discharged are eligible for NHS CC funding before approaching social services.[48] Although the Framework refers to the 2003 legislative scheme, this must remain the correct position as social services authorities are not permitted to provide care and support for an adult who is eligible for NHS CC funding (see para 12.13). It would also appear to be the case that if there is a disagreement between the NHS and social services over eligibility, then this would need to be referred to the 'dispute procedure' (see para 12.174) and would not be a case that fell to be considered under the delayed discharge arrangements.

5.33   The mere fact that a patient is eligible for NHS CC funding does not mean that the patient's hospital discharge should not be dealt with expeditiously. A 2010 ombudsman report[49] concerned a young man with Huntington's disease who was eligible to NHS CC funding. Although all involved agreed that it was in his best interests to live at home, his discharge was delayed (for almost three years) because no official took responsibility for identifying his domiciliary care needs.

---

44 Care and Support (Discharge of Hospital Patients) Regulations 2014 SI No 2823 reg 7(6).

45 Reg 7(8) provides that 'mental health care' means 'psychiatric services, or other services provided for the purpose of preventing, diagnosing or treating illness, the arrangements for which are the primary responsibility of a consultant psychiatrist'.

46 Reg 7(7).

47 Department of Health, *National framework for NHS continuing healthcare and NHS-funded nursing care.* November 2012 (revised) (DH 2012), para 62: a requirement imposed by National Health Service Commissioning Board and Clinical Commissioning Groups (Responsibilities and Standing Rules) Regulations 2012 SI No 2996 reg 21(1).

48 In addition, Care and Support (Discharge of Hospital Patients) Regulations 2014 SI No 2823 reg 4(b) provides for the withdrawal of an assessment notice if the NHS body considers that the patient needs NHS continuing healthcare.

49 Public Services Ombudsman for Wales decision ref 200802231, August 2010.

Delayed discharge process

5.34   CA 2014 s74, Sch 3 and the associated regulations[50] contain provisions designed to encourage social services to speed up the discharge of patients who no longer require acute care.[51] Schedule 3 enables a trust to serve on the relevant social services department an 'assessment' notice advising that a named patient is likely to be ready for discharge on a specified date. Within two days of receiving this notice the social services department must undertake an assessment of the patient's needs and an assessment of any person caring for the patient (reg 8).

5.35   As noted above, before issuing the assessment notice, the NHS body must 'consult the patient, and where it is feasible to do so, any carer that the patient has'[52] and the notice must state that this has been done and whether the patient/the patient's carer has objected to the giving of the assessment notice'.[53] As noted below, a refusal by the patient (or the carer, if the discharge is dependent upon the carer's involvement) has the effect of absolving the local authority from the liability to pay the discharge penalty.

5.36   The NHS may issue a 'discharge' notice giving at least one day's notice of the required discharge, and if after this the patient cannot be discharge for the 'reason alone'[54] that the local authority has not carried out the relevant assessments or put in place arrangements 'for meeting some or all' of the identified eligible needs, then it is liable to make a payment to the NHS (as at January 2017 of £155 or £130 per day, depending on whether it is a London Borough).

5.37   A major change with the CA 2014 regime is that reimbursement is no longer mandatory:[55] Schedule 3 para 4(1) merely states that in such cases 'the NHS body responsible ... may require the relevant authority to pay the specified amount'. In this context, the statutory guidance advises (para 15.41) that this possibility 'is intended to act as an incentive to improve joint working between the NHS and local government, but should not be seen in isolation' and at annex G para 39 'that NHS bodies should not use reimbursement as the first approach to address any local difficulties around delayed transfers of care' and that:

> While reimbursement remains available for use by the NHS body, they and local authorities are encouraged to use the provisions on the discharge of hospital patients (such as the issue of assessment and discharge notices) to seek to focus on effective joint working so as to improve the care of those people whose needs span both NHS and local authority care settings ...

5.38   Where, however, an authority has assessed and offered to put in place arrangements for meeting some or all of the patient's/carer's needs, then

---

50 Care and Support (Discharge of Hospital Patients) Regulations 2014 SI No 2823.
51 Maternity care, mental health care, palliative care, intermediate care and care provided for recuperation or rehabilitation are excluded from the definition of acute care.
52 CA 2014 Sch 3 para 1(4).
53 Care and Support (Discharge of Hospital Patients) Regulations 2014 SI No 2823 reg 3(f)(iii).
54 CA 2014 Sch 3 para 4(2).
55 As it was under Community Care (Delayed Discharges etc) Act 2003 s6(2).

a refusal by the patient or carer of such a package has the effect of absolving social services from its liability to pay the NHS for a delayed discharge
– because the delay is not solely attributable to a social services failure.[56]

5.39   As with the previous system, there appears to be no statutory provision
that enables a local authority to require the discharge notice to be withdrawn if the NHS has itself failed to do something crucial – eg to provide
social services with an occupational therapist or other relevant assessment
when serving the assessment notice. Not infrequently, the NHS staff will
simply forget to serve the notices on admission or at an early stage and
only realise the omission when the patient is ready for discharge – at
which point the two notices are served simultaneously. While two days
may be adequate for patients with straightforward after-care needs, this
may not be feasible for patients with complex after-care requirements.

5.40   The process as drafted is 'one-sided' and makes no allowance for NHS
omissions of this kind – even though (as the statutory guidance acknowledges) the majority of delayed discharge are attributable to NHS failures.
At the very least, the NHS assessment notice should be accompanied by a
checklist confirming that all the relevant papers (eg occupational therapist
assessments etc) are attached.[57]

The social services reimbursement liability

5.41   To be liable for reimbursement, it must be social services provision and
only social services provision which is not available.[58] If social services
do not have services in place by 11am of the day after the proposed discharge date, such that the discharge cannot take place, they are liable for a
charge[59] provided this is the sole reason for the delay. Liability ends when
the patient is discharged or the patient needs to remain in hospital for
other treatment or dies.[60]

Delays to discharge caused by moving into a care home

Guidance

5.42   The 2015 NICE guidance lists as a key principle, that health and social
services must ensure that 'people do not have to make decisions about
long-term residential or nursing care while they are in crisis' and that
'any pressure to make beds available does not result in unplanned and

---

56 As the delay does not result from the local authority's failure – that 'reason alone'
    – CA 2014 Sch 3 para 4(2).

57 Currently this is not required by Care and Support (Discharge of Hospital Patients)
    Regulations 2014 SI No 2823 reg 3.

58 CA 2014 Sch 3 para 4(2) provides that liability arises if 'the relevant authority
    has not put in place arrangements for meeting some or all of those of the needs
    under sections 18 to 20 that it proposes to meet in the case of the patient or (where
    applicable) a carer, and the patient has for that reason alone not been discharged by
    the end of the relevant day'.

59 Care and Support (Discharge of Hospital Patients) Regulations 2014 SI No 2823 reg
    9(4).

60 Care and Support (Discharge of Hospital Patients) Regulations 2014 SI No 2823 reg
    9(3).

unco-ordinated hospital discharges' (para 1.5). Earlier (2003) Department of Health guidance[61] stated that 'it is established good practice that where possible people should not move directly from a hospital to a care home for the first time, but should have a period of time to make personal arrangements and adjust'.[62] The 2010 DH guidance exhorts staff to:

> Always consider rehabilitation and enablement as the first options. Too many older people enter residential and nursing homes direct from acute care.[63]

Despite this advice, it remains not uncommon for patients to move permanently into care homes from an acute ward.[64]

5.43   Many patients considered to be inappropriately occupying NHS beds do so because they have been assessed as requiring a care home place, and either the home of their choice has no current vacancies or the patient does not wish to move into a care home. In this respect the 2003 guidance[65] advised:

> Although *patient choice* is considered extremely important, patients who have been assessed as not requiring NHS continuing in-patient care, do not have the right to occupy, indefinitely, an NHS bed (with the exception of a very small number of cases where a patient is being placed under Part 11 of the Mental Health Act 1983). They do, however, have the right to refuse to be discharged from NHS care into a care home. [Emphasis in original.]

5.44   Those who on discharge will be self-funders, are not generally the responsibility of social services[66] and so will not engage their reimbursement liability. It will, however, be for social services to organise interim arrangements for those patients who are their responsibility where their choices under the Choice of Accommodation provisions (see para 8.241 below) may delay their discharge, and a failure to do so, may trigger liability for reimbursement.

5.45   The 2003 discharge guidance dealt with this problem in the following terms:

> 97. ... [Local protocols] should make it clear that an acute bed is not an appropriate place to wait and the alternatives that will be offered. Where social services are responsible for providing services and a person's preferred home of choice is not immediately available, they should offer an interim package of care. All interim arrangements should be based solely on the patients assessed needs and sustain or improve their level of independence. If no alternative is provided which can meet the patient's needs, social services are liable for reimbursement.

61 Community Care (Delayed Discharges etc) Act 2003 Guidance for Implementation, September 2003, HSC 2003/009: LAC (2003)21.

62 Para 104.

63 2010 DH guidance, p20.

64 In a study investigating the implementation of the reimbursement scheme, the Commission for Social Care Inspection (CSCI) found that in some councils up to a third of older people needing council support on leaving hospital were moving into a care home. CSCI, *Leaving hospital – the price of delays*, October 2004.

65 Department of Health, *Discharge from hospital: pathway, process and practice*, 2003, para 2.2.

66 Unless unable to make their own arrangements and have no one else willing and able to assist them.

98. Social services should take all reasonable steps to gain a patient's agreement to a care package, that is to provide a care package which the patient can be reassured will meet the needs identified and agreed in the care plan
...

99. If the patient continues to unreasonably refuse the care package offered by social services they cannot stay in a hospital bed indefinitely and will need to make their own arrangements so that they can be discharged safely. If at a later date further contact is made with social services regarding the patient, the council should re-open the care planning process, if it is satisfied that the patient's needs remain such to justify the provision of services and there is no longer reason to think that the patient will persist in refusing such services unreasonably. Councils may wish to take their own legal advice in such circumstances.

100. Where appropriate alternative services, which take account of the patient's views, have been offered, and active encouragement given to the patient to transfer, but they unreasonably refuse to move to the alternative, social services will not be held responsible ...

5.46   Although the guidance stresses that patients have the right to refuse to move into a care home,[67] an NHS trust is able (in extreme situations) to evict those who have no need for NHS care. In *Barnet Primary Care Trust v X*[68] the patient had been in a hospital ward for a prolonged period and for the previous three years he had not had any medical reason to be there. Although services to meet his social care needs were available, he was not prepared to leave. Wilkie J held that the he was not entitled to remain on the trust's premises because he was not in need of any ongoing medical or nursing treatment. In his view, the evidence was overwhelming. Since alternative arrangements had been proposed, the court considered that eviction would not violate his European Convention on Human Rights Article 8 rights (right to respect for private and family life).

Where the preferred care home is full

5.47   A more frequent reason for delay is that the care home of choice is full, and the question arises as to what arrangements should then be made for the patient. The situation is generally of most concern to the statutory agencies, if the patient is in hospital awaiting discharge to such a home.

5.48   The statutory guidance (annex A para 13) advises that if the chosen accommodation is 'not immediately available' then it may be necessary to put in place:

... temporary arrangements – taking in to account the person's preferences and securing their agreement – and placing the person on the waiting list of their preferred choice of provider, for example. It should be remembered however that such arrangements can be unsettling for the person and should be avoided wherever possible.

It adds (annex A para 14):

In such cases, the local authority must ensure that in the interim adequate alternative services are provided and set out how long the interim

67   LAC 2004(20), para 2.5.13.
68   *Barnet Primary Care Trust v X* [2006] EWHC 787 (QB), (2006) 92 BMLR 17 and see also the similar fact case of *Sussex Community NHS Foundation Trust v Price* [2016] EWHC 3167.

arrangement may last for. In establishing any temporary arrangements, the local authority must provide the person with clear information in writing on the detail of the arrangements as part of their care and support plan. As a minimum this should include the likely duration of the arrangement, information on the operation of the waiting list for their preferred setting alongside any other information that may be relevant. If any interim arrangements exceed 12 weeks, the person may be reassessed to ensure that both the interim and the preferred option are still able to meet the person's needs and that remains their choice.

5.49   Earlier guidance addressed the question of hospital discharge delays due to this factor, stating:[69]

> Waiting for the preferred care home should not mean that the person's care needs are not met in the interim or that they wait in a setting unsuitable for their assessed needs, and this includes an acute hospital bed, until the most suitable or preferred accommodation becomes available ... councils should have contingency arrangements in place, that address the likelihood that an individual's preferred accommodation will not always be readily available. These arrangements should meet the needs of the individual and sustain or improve their level of independence. For some, the appropriate interim arrangement could be an enhanced care package at home.

Delayed discharge and ordinary residence

5.50   Difficult questions can arise concerning 'ordinary residence' since responsibility for the assessment process (and ultimately the reimbursement liability) depends upon the NHS body notifying the correct local authority – namely the one in which the patient is ordinarily resident (considered generally in chapter 6 below).[70]

5.51   The statutory guidance advises (annex G para 48) that:

> ... Where a local authority disputes the assertion that they are responsible for that individual based on ordinary residence, they must in the period of dispute still comply with the requirements of the Regulations[71] in terms of providing an assessment and any care and support provision which is identified as being needed to secure a safe transfer from one care setting to another.

5.52   The guidance continues (at para 49) that if the dispute cannot be resolved, the authorities must then seek a secretary of state's determination (see para 6.86 below).

Challenging a discharge decision

5.53   If a patient (or the patient's advocate or family) is dissatisfied with the assessment of the patient's needs or the proposed care package on offer

---

69 Department of Health, *Choice of accommodation guidance* LAC (2004) 20, para 2.5.9.

70 CA 2014 Sch 3 para 1(1) requires that the notice be served on '(a) the local authority in whose area the patient is ordinarily resident, or (b) if it appears to the body that the patient is of no settled residence, the local authority in whose area the hospital is situated'.

71 Care and Support (Discharge of Hospital Patients) Regulations 2014 SI No 2823 reg 12(1).

after the patient leaves hospital, then his or her remedy will generally be by complaint through the appropriate complaints procedure – or exceptionally a judicial review (see paras 20.76 and 20.139 below). The statutory guidance, 2015 NICE guidance and the 2010 DH guidance are all silent as to what happens in such cases.

CHAPTER 6

Ordinary residence

continued

Ordinary residence flowchart

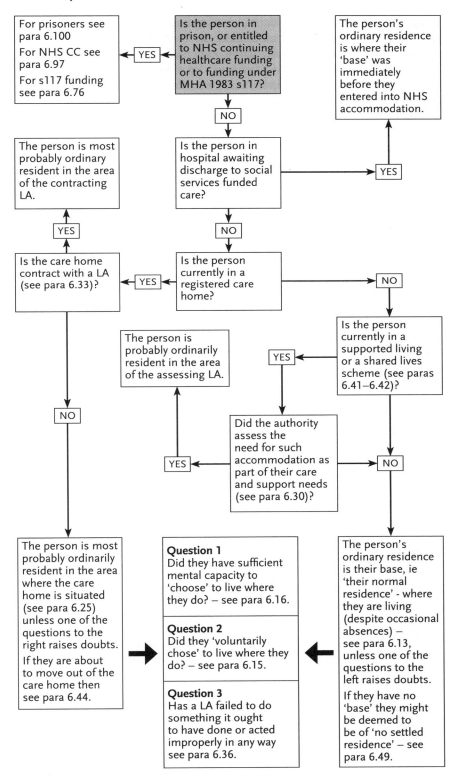

For prisoners see para 6.100

For NHS CC see para 6.97

For s117 funding see para 6.76

— YES ← Is the person in prison, or entitled to NHS continuing healthcare funding or to funding under MHA 1983 s117?

The person's ordinary residence is where their 'base' was immediately before they entered into NHS accommodation.

NO

Is the person in hospital awaiting discharge to social services funded care? → YES

The person is most probably ordinary resident in the area of the contracting LA.

YES

NO

Is the care home contract with a LA (see para 6.33)? ← YES ← Is the person currently in a registered care home? → NO

The person is probably ordinarily resident in the area of the assessing LA.

YES ← Is the person currently in a supported living or a shared lives scheme (see paras 6.41–6.42)?

YES ← Did the authority assess the need for such accommodation as part of their care and support needs (see para 6.30)? → NO

NO

The person is most probably ordinarily resident in the area where the care home is situated (see para 6.25) unless one of the questions to the right raises doubts.

If they are about to move out of the care home then see para 6.44.

Question 1
Did they have sufficient mental capacity to 'choose' to live where they do? – see para 6.16.

Question 2
Did they 'voluntarily chose' to live where they do? – see para 6.15.

Question 3
Has a LA failed to do something it ought to have done or acted improperly in any way see para 6.36.

The person's ordinary residence is their base, ie 'their normal residence' - where they are living (despite occasional absences) – see para 6.13, unless one of the questions to the left raises doubts.

If they have no 'base' they might be deemed to be of 'no settled residence' – see para 6.49.

Introduction

6.1   Responsibility for the provision of social care services rests with local bodies – most commonly local authorities, but occasionally National Health Service (NHS) clinical commissioning groups (CCGs). The responsible local authority is generally the one in which the person is 'ordinarily resident' – although different criteria determine which local NHS body is responsible, and these are considered separately below (see para 6.92).

6.2   This chapter considers the rules for determining 'ordinary residence'. The Care Act (CA) 2104 introduced specific measures to ensure that people who changed their ordinary residence have 'continuity of care' and these rules are considered separately at para 3.31 above.

Background

6.3   The baffling nature of the 'ordinary residence' provisions originate in the Poor Laws, which placed responsibility for the support of the poor on the parishes within which they were 'settled'.[1] There is considerable evidence to suggest that these parishes resorted to 'underhand means to get rid of paupers',[2] including clandestine exporting of the poor into neighbouring parishes.[3] Marshall comments that 'in some cases the law was so complex and obscure that both parishes might have good grounds for thinking themselves right'[4] – with the result that there was considerable litigation between the authorities.[5] Lord Denning in 1981 expressed his despair over such inter-authority disputes in the following terms: [6]

> ... this is a repeat performance of the disputes under the Poor Law 200 years ago. In those days each parish was responsible for the relief of those who were poor and unable to work. When a poor man moved from one parish to another, the question arose: which parish was responsible? The disputes, Blackstone tells us, 'created an infinity of expensive law-suits between contending neighbourhoods, concerning those settlements and removals'. Many of the cases that came before Lord Mansfield were settlement cases.

---

1   The responsibility can be traced to the Vagrancy Laws of Richard II (eg the Statute of Labourers 1351), although it was codified into the Act for the Relief of the Poor (1601) and (in relation to 'settlement') in the Act for the Better Relief of the Poor of this Kingdom 1662 – see L Charlesworth, *Welfare's forgotten past*, Routledge, 2011. Charlesworth describes the 1601 Act as the 'beating heart of welfare's twenty-first century behemoth' (p70).

2   ME Rose, *English Poor Law*, David and Charles, 1971, p191; and see also J Marlow, *The Tolpuddle martyrs*, Grafton Books, 1985, p30 where she refers to parishes smuggling their poor, one to another, to reduce the burden on the local rates. As recently as 2002, in a shocking case, a local authority not so much smuggled a young man with learning disabilities as dumped him and his suitcases on the local authority it considered should be funding him (Determination OR 1 2004).

3   Sir FM Eden, *The state of the poor. Volume 1 (1797)*, Frank Cass and Co, facsimile edition, 1966, p185.

4   D Marshall, *The English Poor Law in the eighteenth century*, Routledge, 1926, p169.

5   PA Fideler, *Social welfare in pre-industrial England*, Palgrave, 2006, p143.

6   *R v Ealing BC, ex p Slough BC* [1981] QB 801 at 808 cited by Holman J in *R (J & W) v Worcestershire CC* [2013] EWHC 3845 (Admin) at para 28.

History tends to repeat itself. If our present cases are anything to go by, we are in for another dose of the same medicine.

6.4 The litigation and 'secretary of state determinations'[7] since that time indicate that matters have not improved to any great extent. These determinations show that almost 70 years after the repeal of the Poor Laws it can still be said 'every parish is in a state of expensive war with the rest of the nation'.[8]

Ordinary residence – social services

6.5 The CA 2014 has, by its repeal of the many statutes dealing with the provision of community care support services, removed many of the complexities that bedevilled this branch of law prior to April 2015.[9] The CA 2014 broadly adopts the conception of 'ordinary residence' as defined in the National Assistance Act (NAA) 1948, but changes some of the 'deeming provisions' found in the NAA 1948. It is in relation to these 'deeming provisions' that material differences continue to exist between the ordinary residence rules under the CA 2014 and the Mental Health Act (MHA) 1983, and consideration of the rules relating to the MHA 1983 are dealt with separately at para 6.76 below.

Ordinary residence and the CA 2014

6.6 CA 2014 s39 places primary responsibility for the provision of its services on the authority in which the relevant person is 'ordinarily resident'.

6.7 The duty to provide care and support under the CA 2014 applies only to persons who are (among other things – see para 4.55 above) ordinarily resident in the local authority's area, whereas a power exists to provide services for most other persons.[10]

6.8 Although from an individual's perspective it will often be academic as to which authority has the responsibility for providing the individual's care and support services, this will not always be so – particularly where the person is suffering as a result of an inter-authority dispute as to which is responsible (considered at para 6.86 below). Two further problems can arise. The first concerns the administrative delay that may occur where a person's ordinary residence changes – the delay in the new authority undertaking an assessment and providing substitute services. The second arises where the new authority has a less generous approach to care and support provision than the former. In relation to these (often associated) problems, it has been said that they characterise the worst aspects 'of the

---

7 Selected 'Ordinary residence: anonymised determinations' are published by the Department of Health on the GOV.UK website – see para 6.88 below.

8 W Hay, *Remarks on the law relating to the poor with proposals for their better relief and employment*, 1951 cited in N Wikeley, *Child support law and policy*, Hart Publishing, 2006, p44.

9 For a detailed analysis of these rules see the 5th edition of this book, chapter 6.

10 CA 2014 s19(2); and see also *R v Berkshire CC ex p P* (1997–98) 1 CCLR 141, QBD.

Poor Law system of outdoor relief' not least the fact that entitlement to support is lost on crossing 'the parish (the local authority) boundary'.[11]

6.9 The CA 2014 (ss37–38) endeavours to streamline the process by which one local authority hands over to another its responsibility for a person's social care needs services[12] and this duty is considered separately at para 3.31 above. Welcome as the 'continuity of care' provisions are, it is nevertheless likely that individuals will continue to experience an interruption to their care packages when a change in their ordinary residence occurs. Where material harm results from the handover of responsibility from one authority to the other a formal complaint may be appropriate: that the authorities are failing to 'work together' contrary to the requirements of the statutory guidance[13] that authorities (para 20.50):

> ... must not allow their dispute to prevent, delay or adversely affect the meeting of the person's needs' and that they must 'ensure that the person is unaffected by the dispute and will continue to receive care for the needs that were identified by the first local authority.

6.10 The inter-authority duty to ensure that a person's needs are addressed extends to situations where there is little or no doubt over the person's ordinary residence. In *R (AM) v (1) Havering LBC and Tower Hamlets LBC*[14] Cobb J held that even though there was no ongoing duty on the authority (from which the person had moved) it was nonetheless 'an inexcusable failure of good social work practice to "wash its hands" of the family ...; continuity of social work involvement and practice best meets the obligations under statute and is indeed the most cost-efficient' (para 46).

6.11 The question of ordinary residence is also of importance when authority boundaries change. In *R (J and others) v Southend BC and Essex CC*[15] a number of service users had in effect become stranded when Southend became a unitary authority and ceased to be part of Essex County Council. Although initially some Essex service users continued to attend a day centre in the new unitary council area, when Southend BC decided to restrict its use to its residents, the court found no duty on Southend to assess an Essex resident prior to this decision – that responsibility lay with Essex.

Defining 'ordinary residence'

6.12 The CA 2014 does not define 'ordinary residence' and the statutory guidance makes clear that previous court judgments concerning the interpretation of this phrase remain relevant.

---

11 See eg the comments of Baroness Campbell of Surbiton, House of Lords, Hansard col GC641, 22 May 2008.
12 For example, an amendment tabled to the bill that became the Health and Social Care Act 2008 was withdrawn on the government undertaking to look again at this question – see comments of Baroness Thornton, House of Lords, Hansard col 161, 1 July 2008.
13 Department of Health, *Care and support statutory guidance* to support implementation of Part 1 of the CA 2014 by local authorities, 2016 ('the statutory guidance').
14 [2015] EWHC 1004 (Admin) para 46.
15 [2005] EWHC 3457 (Admin), (2007) 10 CCLR 428.

6.13   The key is in the word 'residence'. It will generally be the place where a person normally resides: where the person's normal residential address is to be found. The guidance (para 19.14) states that the phrase involves questions of fact and degree, and factors such as time, intention[16] and continuity (each of which may be given different weight according to the context) have to be taken into account.[17] The guidance then cites the 'leading case' of *R v Barnet LBC ex p Shah*[18] and Lord Scarman's judgment that:

> ... unless ... it can be shown that the statutory framework or the legal context in which the words are used requires a different meaning I unhesitatingly subscribe to the view that ordinarily resident refers to a man's abode in a particular place or country which he has adopted voluntarily and for settled purposes as part of the regular order of his life for the time being, whether of short or long duration.[19]

6.14   In *ex p Shah* Lord Scarman held that in determining a person's ordinary residence, the person's long-term future intentions or expectations were not relevant; the test was not what was a person's real home,[20] but whether a person could show a regular, habitual mode of life in a particular place, the continuity of which had persisted despite temporary absences.[21] A person's attitude is only relevant in two respects: (a) the residence must be voluntarily adopted, and (b) there must be a settled purpose in living in the particular residence.

Voluntarily adopted

6.15   The question of whether a residence has been 'adopted voluntarily' raises a number of issues, particularly where the individual was unable to make that choice – through lack of sufficient mental capacity or otherwise. In *R (Mani) v Lambeth LBC*[22] the applicant had had no choice over his residence, having been 'dispersed' there by the National Asylum Support Service (NASS) (see para 16.7 below). The court held that since he had been living there for six months, it was sufficiently voluntary. In doing so, the court relied on Lord Slynn's analysis in *Mohamed v Hammersmith & Fulham LBC*,[23] that:

16 In view of the comments of Lord Scarman in *R v Barnet LBC ex p Shah* [1983] 1 All ER 226, [1983] 2 AC 309, intention must be given a restrictive interpretation.

17 This advice is identical to that provided in relation to the NAA 1948 – see Department of Health, *Ordinary residence – guidance on the identification of the ordinary residence of people in need of community care services, England*, 2013, para 19.

18 House of Lords [1983] 2 AC 309 para 343: a case concerning the interpretation of 'ordinary residence' for the purposes of the Education Act 1962 (cited in the statutory guidance at para 19.14).

19 The last clause 'whether of short or long duration' is of importance and anecdotally it appears that local authorities in dispute are want, on occasions, to omit reference to this part of the judgment when it is not considered to be helpful.

20 House of Lords [1983] 2 AC 309 para 349.

21 House of Lords [1983] 2 AC 309 para 344.

22 [2002] EWHC 735 (Admin), (2002) 5 CCLR 486.

23 [2001] UKHL 57, [2002] 1 AC 547 para 18: a case concerning the meaning of 'normally resident' under Housing Act 1996 s199, which, however, the court held to have the same meaning as 'ordinarily resident'.

... so long as that place where he eats and sleeps is voluntarily accepted by him, the reason why he is there rather than somewhere else does not prevent that place from being his normal residence. He may not like it, he may prefer some other place, but that place is for the relevant time the place where he normally resides.

6.16   There will be cases where the individual lacks sufficient mental capacity to decide where to live (see chapter 13 below). The case-law on the ordinary residence implications in such situations has been conflicted, although the 2015 Supreme Court judgment in *R (Cornwall Council) v Secretary of State for Health*[24] has provided some clarification as to the general approach that should be taken.

6.17   The statutory guidance considers the judgment and advises that in cases of this kind, 'direct application of the test in *Shah* will not assist since it requires the voluntary adoption of a place' (para 19.26). Decisions in such cases will always be context specific, requiring a consideration of (para 19.32):

... all the facts, such as the place of the person's physical presence, their purpose for living there, the person's connection with the area, their duration of residence there and the person's views, wishes and feelings (insofar as these are ascertainable and relevant) to establish whether the purpose of the residence has a sufficient degree of continuity to be described as settled, whether of long or short duration.

6.18   The *Cornwall* judgment concerned a young man with physical and significant learning disabilities, who was born in Wiltshire and placed by Wiltshire in a foster placement in South Gloucestershire. His parents moved from Wiltshire to Cornwall and continued to be involved in decisions affecting his best interests. Although he had regular contact with them, he only stayed with them for brief periods. After he became 18 he was placed in care homes in Somerset.[25] The Supreme Court held that the placement in South Gloucestershire by Wiltshire did not change his ordinary residence and Wiltshire remained the responsible authority when he became 18.

6.19   The statutory guidance in its summary of the *Cornwall* judgment (at para 19.21) highlights the court's reference to the 'underlying purpose' of the ordinary residence regime (and the 'deeming provisions' – discussed below) was to ensure that 'an authority should not be able to export its responsibility for providing the necessary accommodation by exporting the person who is in need of it' (para 54 of the judgment).

6.20   The range of contexts that will exist in relation to adults lacking the requisite mental capacity to decide where to live will be considerable and these will significantly impact on the eventual ordinary residence determination. Two cases illustrate this point.

6.21   *R v Waltham Forest LBC ex p Vale*[26] concerned a 28-year-old applicant with profound learning disabilities such that she was totally dependent on her parents, albeit that she had from an early age been boarded in

---

24 [2015] UKSC 46, (2015) 18 CCLR 497.

25 The ordinary residence issue was complex for many reasons, not least that the rules under the Children Act 1989 are distinct from those of the adult legislation.

26 (1985) *Times* 25 February, QBD.

community homes. Importing principles from child care law,[27] the court determined that her ordinary residence was that of her parents, not because it was her real home, but because it was her 'base'. The Supreme Court in *Cornwall* considered this to be an unusual fact case and that the key question to ask in such cases was 'whether her period of actual residence with her parents was sufficiently "settled" to amount to ordinary residence' (para 47). *Vale* is probably best considered as a factual 'outlier' – the evidence suggested that the applicant had become 'severely disturbed due, it was thought, to her distance and detachment from her family'.

6.22   *R v Redbridge LBC ex p East Sussex CC*[28] which concerned two adult male twins with profound learning disabilities who were boarded at a school in East Sussex, but whose parents lived in Redbridge. Applying the principles enunciated in the *Vale* decision, the court held that the twins were at law ordinarily resident in Redbridge. Subsequently, however, the parents went to live in Nigeria. It was held that when this occurred, the twins ceased to have any settled residence and accordingly became the responsibility of East Sussex.

6.23   Although each case concerning adults without the requisite mental capacity will have to be judged on its specific factual context, there are probably two key presumptions. The first is that unless the person has particularly severe learning difficulties, the person should be regarded as capable of forming his or her own intention of where they wish to live.[29] The second (the 'public policy' ground) is that if a local authority has accepted responsibility for care managing the person's needs, then it should not be able to 'export its responsibility' to another authority simply by making an out-of-county placement. In most situations such action will be caught by the 'deeming provisions' (discussed below).

The 'deeming' provisions under Care Act 2014 s39

6.24   CA 2014 s39 contains two so-called 'deeming' provisions: situations where a person, although resident in one area, may be 'deemed' to be resident elsewhere for the purposes of the CA 2014. One such provision relates to persons in local authority arranged placements and the other to persons being discharged from NHS accommodation. The CA 2014 also contains provisions relating to the ordinary residence of people in prison or other approved premises – and this is considered separately at para 15.134 below.

The first 'deeming' provision: local authority arranged accommodation placements

6.25   The NAA 1948[30] contained a deeming provision in relation to residential accommodation placements made by a local authority: namely that

---

27 See eg *In re P (GE) (an infant)* [1965] Ch 568.
28 (1993) *Times* 3 January, [1993] COD 265, QBD.
29 This advice was given in Department of Health Circular LAC (93)7, para 12 (now revoked); and see also *R v Kent CC and Salisbury and Pierre* (2000) 3 CCLR 38, QBD.
30 NAA 1948 s24(5).

persons provided with such accommodation by a social services authority were, in effect, deemed to be ordinarily resident in the placing authority's area even if the accommodation is situated in the area of another authority. The CA 2014 continues this principle but expands its scope, and in so doing, adopts a form of wording that is best described as contorted.

6.26   CA 2014 s39(1) and (2) provides:

(1) Where an adult has needs for care and support which can be met only if the adult is living in accommodation of a type specified in regulations, and the adult is living in accommodation in England of a type so specified, the adult is to be treated for the purposes of this Part as ordinarily resident–

  (a) in the area in which the adult was ordinarily resident immediately before the adult began to live in accommodation of a type specified in the regulations, or

  (b) if the adult was of no settled residence immediately before the adult began to live in accommodation of a type so specified, in the area in which the adult was present at that time.

(2) Where, before beginning to live in his or her current accommodation, the adult was living in accommodation of a type so specified (whether or not of the same type as the current accommodation), the reference in subsection (1)(a) to when the adult began to live in accommodation of a type so specified is a reference to the beginning of the period during which the adult has been living in accommodation of one or more of the specified types for consecutive periods.

6.27   Although section 39 makes provision for regulations, these have only been issued in relation to the types of accommodation that are covered by this deeming rule[31] – ie care homes, supported living and shared lives schemes (considered below). This means that explanations as to the meaning of key (and potentially contentious) phrases such as 'which can be met only' are left to the guidance. The Care and Support (Ordinary Residence) (Specified Accommodation) Regulations 2014 SI No 2828 will be referred to in this chapter as the 'ordinary residence regulations'.

6.28   The intention behind subsections 39(1) and (2) is relatively clear, namely that where a local authority (LA) A assesses an individual and as a result decides to 'fund'[32] that person in accommodation of a specified kind in LA B, then nevertheless LA A is deemed to be the person's ordinary residence. This point has been confirmed by amendment[33] to the ordinary residence regulations reg 2(2), now specifying that the rule only applies 'if the care and support needs of the adult are being met under Part 1 of the Act while the adult lives in that type of accommodation'.

6.29   The statutory guidance explains that (para 19.50):

... the adult is treated as remaining ordinarily resident in the area where they were resident immediately before the local authority began to provide

---

31 Separate regulations – Care and Support (Disputes Between Local Authorities) Regulations 2014 SI No 2829 – have been issued relating to ordinary residence disputes (considered below).

32 As noted below (see para 6.33) in cases where the person is in effect a self-funder – the key question is likely to be whether the local authority enters into the contract with the provider.

33 Via the Care and Support (Miscellaneous Amendments) Regulations 2015 SI No 644 reg 4.

or arrange care and support in any type of specified accommodation. The consequence of this is that the local authority which first provided that care and support will remain responsible for meeting the person's eligible needs, and responsibility does not transfer to the authority in whose area the accommodation is physically located.

The guidance states that this presumption only applies where the local authority makes the necessary arrangements (ie with the accommodation provider) and that if the person moves into the accommodation (para 19.50):

> ... in a different area of their own volition, without the local authority making the arrangements, they would be likely to acquire ordinary residence in the area of the authority where the new accommodation is situated.

An amending order and regulations have been issued to address this issue.[34]

6.30   There is an additional condition that must be satisfied before the first deeming rule is triggered and this concerns the requirement that the person's support needs 'can be met only if' living in accommodation of the specified type. This is potentially problematical, given that a person's care needs may be capable of being met in many settings – for example, in the person's own home with a substantial care package or in a residential care home. The initial (2014) statutory guidance was considered insufficient to explain the scope of the 'can only be met' provision and an undertaking was given to clarify this question.[35] This is found at para 19.51 of the statutory guidance, which states:

> Need should be judged to be 'able to be met' or of a kind that 'can be met only' through a specified type of accommodation where the local authority has made this decision following an assessment and a care and support planning process involving the person ... Where the outcome of the care planning process is a decision to meet needs in one of the specified types of accommodation and it is the local authority's view it should be assumed that needs can only be met in that type of accommodation for the purposes of 'deeming' ordinary residence. This should be clearly recorded in the care and support plan. The local authority is not required to demonstrate that needs cannot be met by any other type of support. The local authority must have assessed those needs in order to make such a decision – the 'deeming' principle therefore does not apply to cases where a person arranges their own accommodation and the local authority does not meet their needs.

6.31   Welcome as this clarification is, it is lacks the status it would have if expressed in a regulation. It is also far from conclusive: the use of the phrase 'it should be assumed' appears to create a rebuttable presumption rather than a final determination. If this provision becomes contested, it is to be hoped that more extended guidance[36] will be issued in due course.

34 Care and Support (Miscellaneous Amendments) Regulations 2015 SI No 644 reg 4; and the Department of Health guidance note, *Update on final orders under the Care Act 2014* (at para 14(iv)) which accompanied the Care Act 2014 (Transitional Provision) Order 2015 SI No 995 advised that advised that 'the principle only applied when a person is living in a specified type of accommodation (such as a care home) before they begin to receive care and support from the local authority'.

35 HM Government, *Update on final orders under the Care Act 2014*, paras 22–23 (2014).

36 The statutory guidance does consider aspects of the deeming rule further at paras 19.51–19.59.

Status of past 'ordinary residence' decisions, determinations and guidance

6.32   The first deeming provision is, as noted, in principle the same as that which applied under the NAA 1948 and it appears that the clear policy intention is that the previous case-law should continue to be of relevance under the new scheme.[37] The 'determinations' made by the secretary of state (ie arising out of local authority disputes) will also continue to be of relevance.[38] In the following sections, secretary of state 'determinations' are cited by their departmental reference numbers – eg 'OR 5 2006'. Also of relevance must be guidance issued by the Department of Health (DH) in 2013: *Ordinary residence: guidance on the identification of the ordinary residence of people in need of community care services, England* (referred to in this chapter as the '2013 DH guidance'). Although it refers to the NAA 1948 and has been cancelled by the new regime,[39] the guidance must still be persuasive – particularly as it is much more extensive than the advice in the statutory guidance.

Did the local authority make the residential care arrangements?

6.33   The first deeming rule does not arise where a person makes their own arrangements to move into accommodation of the specified kind and this will be the general case even if the local authority assists with the move, provided it does not make the contract with the home:[40] Assistance with finding a placement but falling short of making a contract does not constitute making the arrangements: taking someone to the home does not, in itself, constitute making the placement.[41] However where the local authority is a contracting party, the rule applies even if the person is in

---

37 The Law Commission did undertake a review of the meaning of 'ordinary residence' – see Law Commission, *Adult social care*, Law Com No 326, HC 941, The Stationery Office, 2011, para 10.4. Neither the Joint Committee on the Draft Care and Support Bill nor the explanatory memorandum to the Care Bill contain comments to suggest that the scheme was to be materially different – see respectively *Draft Care and Support Bill* HL Paper 143 HC 822, The Stationery Office, 2013, paras 216–218; and the explanatory notes, paras 237–241. The publication by Cornerstone Barristers *Ordinary residence & the Care Act 2014*, February 2015 – endorsed by the Department of Health, the Association of Directors of Adult Social Services (ADASS) and the Local Government Association (LGA) – states that: 'Local authorities should apply the case law developed as to the meaning of ordinary residence under the National Assistance Act 1948' (para 25).

38 www.gov.uk/government/collections/ordinary-residence-pages/.

39 In annex I of the statutory guidance it is listed as 'To be cancelled'.

40 2013 DH guidance, paras 72, 81 and 82; see also determinations OR 3 1996, OR 5 2006, OR 4 2007 and OR 8 2007, OR 5 2010; and see also *Chief Adjudication Officer v Quinn and Gibbon* [1996] 1 WLR 1184, [1996] 4 All ER 72, (1997–98) 1 CCLR 529, HL Where Lord Slynn held: considered it essential that the accommodation must include a provision for payments to be made by a local authority (albeit that the specific provision being considered in the NAA 1948 (s26(2)) is not found in the CA 2014).

41 Determination OR 3 1996. It appears that this determination (although anonymised in its published form) is referred by local authorities as the '*Surrey and Hounslow* case'.

effect a 'self-funder' (see para 8.71) but has relied upon the local authority to make the placement and contract with the care home.[42]

6.34   In an unpublished determination, the secretary of state[43] found that a young man who lacked capacity and who had residential accommodation arranged for him remained the responsibility of that council after he moved to another authority in spite of an inheritance which meant he could afford to pay for his own care. Although he had a receiver to look after his finances, the council had not contacted her with a view to her making the contract with the home and there was no evidence that it expected her to do so. The invoices were sent to the council. The secretary of state found that the authority, by contacting the home in the new area, arranging a visit by the manager to see the young man and his subsequent immediate transfer, and the issuing of invoices to the council by the home, amounted to 'the characteristics of an arrangement for the provision of residential accommodation' under the NAA 1948.

6.35   Where a person is placed by a local authority in another area within the 12-week property disregard (see para 8.224 below), or has agreed to a deferred payment arrangement (see para 8.282 below), then that person is the responsibility of the placing authority. Where, however, the local authority contract comes to an end after the 12-week period and the resident specifically declines a deferred payment arrangement, then he or she ceases to be the placing authority's responsibility.[44] It follows that if the resident subsequently needs support (for example, because his or her capital falls below the maximum threshold) the resident would then need to approach the authority in whose area the care home is situated. However, those who have the benefit of a deferred payment arrangement are deemed to remain ordinarily resident in the area of the placing authority.[45]

Did the local authority fail to do something that was material?

6.36   In *R (Greenwich LBC) v Secretary of State for Health* Charles J considered that question of whether a local authority could avoid liability for care home fees, by failing to properly advise a resident – for example, by failing to offer a deferred payment arrangement. In his opinion, if 'arrangements should have been made but had not been made', then 'the deeming provision should be applied and interpreted on the basis that they had actually been put in place by the appropriate local authority'.[46]

6.37   The 2013 DH guidance picks up this point, by advising that where a local authority fails to make arrangements which it should have done, so the person was forced to make their own arrangements in another authority's

42   For instance, because they wish to make use of the deferred payment arrangements or because they lack capacity to make a contract with the home and there is no one else willing and able to do so on their behalf.

43   Determination dated 20 July 1999 (not published).

44   Unless of course the person does not have the capacity to enter into their own contract and there is no one willing and able to do so on the resident's behalf.

45   2013 DH guidance, paras 84–91.

46   [2006] EWHC 2576 (Admin), (2007) 10 CCLR 60, para 55.

area, then the person's ordinary residence would fall to be assessed at the date the person should have been provided with accommodation.[47]

Specified accommodation and ordinary residence

6.38   Under the NAA 1948, the first deeming provision only applied while individuals lived in registered residential care/nursing homes. This gave rise to a number of disputes when they moved into a non-residential care setting or, for example, the care home 'de-registered' (ie ceased to be a registered care home). These problems are likely to be less common under CA 2014 regime (as the rules have been amended) – but guidance relating to the pre-April 2015 situation can be found in the 2013 DH guidance and a number of secretary of state determinations.[48]

6.39   CA 2014 s39(1) provides for regulations which identify the types of accommodation that constitute 'specified accommodation' for the purposes of the first deeming rule. The ordinary residence regulations reg 2 specifies:

a) care home accommodation;
b) shared lives scheme accommodation; and
c) supported living accommodation.

Care home accommodation

6.40   The ordinary residence regulations (reg 3) define a care home as one defined in Care Standards Act 2000 s3 – ie an establishment that provides accommodation, together with nursing or personal care (see para 17.7). The first deeming rule under NAA 1948 also applied to this accommodation, so local authorities will be familiar with such arrangements.

Shared lives scheme accommodation

6.41   The ordinary residence regulations (reg 4) define 'shared lives scheme accommodation' as accommodation for an adult by a shared lives carer.[49] Shared lives (previously known as adult placement) is a care support arrangement that has historically focussed on supporting people with learning disabilities, but increasingly is used for the support of a much wider range of individuals 'in need'. Care and support under this arrangement is further considered at para 14.129 below.

Supported living

6.42   The ordinary residence regulations (reg 5(1)) define 'supported living accommodation' as:

(a) accommodation in premises which are specifically designed or adapted for occupation by adults with needs for care and support to enable them to live as independently as possible; and
(b) accommodation which is provided–

---

47 2013 DH guidance, paras 74 and 92.
48 2013 DH guidance, paras 92–101; and see determinations OR 3 2006, OR 6 2007, 7 2007, 9 2007, 10 2007, 14 2007, 3–2011: see Care Act 2014 (Transitional Provisions) Order 2015 SI No 995 Ord 6.
49 Regulation 4 then defines a 'shared lives carer'; a 'shared lives agreement'; and a 'shared lives scheme'.

(i) in premises which are intended for occupation by adults with needs for care and support (whether or not the premises are specifically designed or adapted for that purpose); and

(ii) in circumstances in which personal care is available if required.

6.43 Regulation 5(2) makes clear that the personal care does not have to be provided by the same person as who provides the accommodation.[50]

6.44 Given the increased variety of care provision models, the update to this deeming rule provides greater flexibility and certainty for local authorities, care providers and adults in need. As the statutory guidance explains, this not only covers situations where a care home decides to de-register and continue to provide care (as a supported living establishment) but ordinary residence should also be unaffected 'even if the person temporarily moves to another address whilst any changes to the property occur' (para 19.59).

6.45 The extension of the ordinary residence 'deeming rule' to shared lives schemes and supported living accommodation is also reflected in the Care and Support (Choice of Accommodation) Regulations (see para 8.243 below) which bring these schemes within the ambit of the choice of accommodation options available to individuals – where the local authority is proposing such a placement. The Department of Health (together with the Local Government Authority (LGA) and the Association of Directors of Adult Social Services Departments (ADASS)) has issued guidance concerning these new obligations.[51]

The second 'deeming' provision: people formerly in NHS care

6.46 Adults who are being provided with NHS accommodation are deemed to be ordinarily resident in the area in which they were ordinarily resident immediately before the accommodation was provided – CA 2014 s39(5)(a).[52] If they had no settled residence immediately before the accommodation was provided, then they will be deemed to be ordinarily resident in the area in which the adult was present at that time (CA 2014 s39(5)(b)).

6.47 The statutory guidance explains that the presumption that a person's ordinary residence is the local authority area where the person was living before he or she went into hospital 'applies regardless of the length of stay in the hospital' (para 19.61). The second deeming provision is not, however, restricted to hospital care. CA 2014 s39(6) defines 'NHS

---

50 This is, on its face, curious since if it was so provided, the accommodation would require to be registered under the 2000 Act.

51 Department of Health *Choice of accommodation* at www.local.gov.uk/ documents/10180/5756320/Guidance+on+choice+accommodation+AM.pdf/ d31f02f7-7e89-46b9-8bda-4c021047731c.

52 Replicating in large measure NAA 1948 s24(3) and (6); however, prior to 19 April 2010 the 'deeming provision' only applied if the person was in an NHS facility. NAA 1948 s24 was amended by Health and Social Care Act 2008 s148 to cover NHS continuing healthcare (NHS CC) funded by the NHS in care homes, and the 2013 DH guidance at para 115b clarified the transitional provisions for those in accommodation provided by the NHS prior to this amendment.

accommodation' as accommodation provided under the National Health Services Act (NHSA) 2006 (and the Scottish, Welsh and Northern Irish equivalents[53]). This means that if a person is provided with NHS Continuing Healthcare funding (see chapter 12) then if this comes to an end the responsible local authority will be the one in which the person was ordinarily resident when the person was accommodated by the NHS (ie when he or she entered the ambulance/the hospital ward or were declared eligible for NHS Continuing Healthcare funding).

6.48   The 2013 ordinary residence guidance[54] gave more detailed advice on the various scenarios that may arise in this context and advised that:

> ... where a CCG places a person in [accommodation funded by the NHS] it is good practice for it to inform the person's local authority of ordinary residence and, if the person is placed 'out of area', it is also good practice for the CCG to inform the local authority in which the care home is located (para 114).

No settled residence

6.49   The CA 2014 (as with the scheme under the NAA 1948) encompasses people who are without an ordinary residence – referred to as having 'no settled residence'. CA 2014 s39(1)(b) states that if the adult has of no settled residence then the general principle is that they are the responsibility of the local authority in whose area they are present. In this context, the statutory guidance (para 19.44) advises:

> Where doubts arise in respect of a person's ordinary residence, it is usually possible for local authorities to decide that the person has resided in one place long enough, or has sufficiently firm intentions in relation to that place, to have acquired an ordinary residence there. Therefore, it should only be in rare circumstances that local authorities conclude that someone is of no settled residence. For example, if a person has clearly and intentionally left their previous residence and moved to stay elsewhere on a temporary basis during which time their circumstances change, a local authority may conclude the person to be of no settled residence.

6.50   The lack of a 'settlement' under the Poor Law was a particular problem for individuals and parishes and the NAA 1948 retained provisions that perpetuated this distinction: local authorities only had a power (not a duty) to accommodate people in that situation.[55] The CA 2014 does away with this distinction – local authorities are under a duty to meet the eligible needs of adults in need and carers[56] even if they have no settled residence (provided they are present in the local authority's area).

53   Ie the National Health Service (Scotland) Act 1978, the National Health Service (Wales) Act 2006 and Health and Personal Social Services (Northern Ireland) Order 1972 Article 5(1) – and see also statutory guidance, para 19.62.

54   Department of Health, *Ordinary residence: guidance on the identification of the ordinary residence of people in need of community care services, England*, 2013, paras 112–115c (including examples). The guidance has been cancelled – but see para 1.56 above.

55   This was one of the reasons why courts considered it of importance to finding an ordinary residence for individuals, where possible – see *R (Greenwich LBC) v Secretary of State for Health* [2006] EWHC 2576, para 87, (2007) 10 CCLR 60.

56   CA 2014 s18(1)(a) and s20(1)(a) respectively; see also statutory guidance, para 19.45.

6.51   For people who leave accommodation and fail to find relatively secure alternative lodgings, the ordinary residence permutations can be complex – as an informative case example in the statutory guidance illustrates (para 19.46). In general, the position will often be less complex for people who arrive from abroad (which will include 'those people who are returning to England after a period of residing abroad and who have given up their previous home in this country'[57]) as they will generally be without settled residence in the UK. In relation to such returning nationals, further guidance is provided annex H of the statutory guidance. Annex H gives guidance on a number of additional issues, including cases of urgency (see below); where the individual is party to a deferred payments agreement (see para 8.282); where a person has been accommodated under the 12-week property disregard (see para 8.224); and where individuals have sufficient funds to pay for their own care and accommodation but for one reason or another, the local authority becomes involved in the identification and/or the securing of their accommodation.

Urgent need

6.52   The power of local authorities to provide support in urgent situations for individuals who are ordinarily resident in another authority is continued by the CA 2014: explicitly for adults in need (section 19(3) and implicitly for carers (section 20(6)).

6.53   Annex H of the statutory guidance provides guidance and scenarios of how this may arise in practice. Its analysis appears predicated on the idea that it is accommodation that is being provided – although the CA 2014 s18 power extends to all care and support needs. The obligation on the local authority 'of the moment' is expressed in the guidance as a strong one: it 'should exercise their power to meet the urgent needs' and in so doing it 'should inform the local authority where the person is ordinarily resident that it is doing so'.[58] It does not, however, require the consent of the responsible authority.[59] The guidance is coy on the question of reimbursement of the costs of the urgent action – noting merely that the 'authorities concerned may come to an agreement about sharing or transferring the costs'.[60] Objectively, the default position would appear to be that that these costs should be reimbursed.[61]

6.54   The situation of a person of no settled residence and in urgent need of residential accommodation was considered (in the context of the NAA 1948) in *R (S) v Lewisham LBC*[62] which held that when a person physically presents him/herself to a local authority as being in urgent need of

---

57 Statutory guidance, para 19.46.
58 Statutory guidance, annex H para 3.
59 Statutory guidance, annex H para 4.
60 Statutory guidance, annex H para 4.
61 Para 4 states 'For instance, the local authority of the moment, which is providing the accommodation, may recover some or all of the costs of the accommodation from the local authority where the person is ordinarily resident (and where the duty to meet needs would otherwise fall)'.
62 (2008) EWHC 1290 (Admin); and see 2013 DH guidance, para 50.

residential accommodation, whichever authority is approached is obliged to provide the accommodation (provided it is assessed as needed).

Prisoners

6.55   CA 2014 s76(1)–(3) makes it clear that the local authority responsible for providing care and support for prisoners[63] under the CA 2014 is the one in which the prison is situated. As noted below, the position may be different for some prisoners eligible for support under MHA 1983 s117.

6.56   There are no statutory 'deeming' rules for prisoners[64] but the statutory guidance advises that 'local authorities should start from a presumption that they remain ordinarily resident in the area in which they were ordinarily resident before the start of their sentence' (para 17.48). Since many prisoners may not wish to (or be able to) return to the area where they lived before their period in custody, the guidance indicates that this is a presumption that is easily rebutted, advising (para 17.50):

> In situations where an offender is likely to have needs for care and support services on release from prison or approved premises and their place of ordinary residence is unclear and/or they express an intention to settle in a new local authority area, the local authority to which they plan to move should take responsibility for carrying out the needs assessment.

6.57   This question is further considered at para 15.143 below.

Cross-border placements by local authorities

Overview

6.58   Cross-border placements have the potential to create considerable confusion – particularly where a person moves into independent living in Scotland having been previously placed in a care home in England by an English authority.[65] The general complexity stems from the mismatch between policy and legislation and the fact that the different residential and nursing care funding systems are devolved responsibilities. Put simply, the law in this context is a mess – and given the diverging policy agendas in the four nations, it is a mess that (absent concerted action) is likely to get worse. This is also a rare example of where the CA 2014 provides more restricted rights than under the previous legislation, as the 'choice of accommodation' rights under the NAA 1948 extended to Wales

---

63 Prisoners includes those in custody or custodial settings, approved premises and other bail accommodation, and can apply to people aged over 18 years in young offender institutions, secure children's homes and secure training centres (statutory guidance, para 17.3).

64 This was also the position under the NAA 1948, and the 2013 DH guidance (paras 107–111) provided very similar advice to that now located in the statutory guidance.

65 See OR 3 2010.

(and in theory Scotland),[66] whereas the CA 2014 regime restricts the right to England.[67]

6.59 CA 2014 Sch 1, regulations and chapter 21 of the statutory guidance explain how it is to be determined where an individual's ordinary residence is when they move from one of the UK's four 'territories' to another.

6.60 The statutory guidance stresses the importance of authorities being 'person centred' in the way they approach such moves (para 21.7) and suggests that there will, overall, be little 'financial disadvantage by making cross-border placements' and that 'all authorities are expected to co-operate fully and communicate properly' (para 21.8). In the succeeding paragraphs it then sets out a four stage process, namely:

1) care and support planning;
2) initial liaison between 'first' and 'second' authority;
3) arrangements for on-going management of placement;
4) confirmation of placement.

'Accommodation' placements from England to Wales, Scotland or Northern Ireland

6.61 CA 2014 Sch 1 para 1 provides that the first deeming rule applies where an English authority 'is meeting an adult's needs for care and support by arranging for the provision of accommodation in Wales,[68] Scotland[69] and Northern Ireland.[70] In such cases the individual is deemed to remain ordinarily resident in the English local authority area.

6.62 Where the placement is in nursing home accommodation, separate bilateral agreements exist in relation to the four 'administrations'[71] as to which bears the cost of NHS funded nursing care required for individuals. In relation to placements between England, Scotland and Northern Ireland the 'health service of the country of the first authority will be responsible for nursing costs'.[72] Accordingly, where an individual has been placed in Scotland or Northern Ireland by an English local authority, it will be the CCG that is liable for payment of the Registered Nursing Care Contribution (RNCC). Where the nursing home placement is between England and

---

66 See National Assistance Act 1948 (Choice of Accommodation) Directions 1992 direction 2 (as amended) and more generally see the 5th edition of this book, para 7.107 and following.

67 Care and Support and After-care (Choice of Accommodation) Regulations 2014 SI 2670 reg 2(1)(a) – see para 8.241 below.

68 CA 2014 Sch 1 para 12 defines this as accommodation of a type specified in regulations under Social Services and Well-being (Wales) Act 2014 s194.

69 CA 2014 Sch 1 para 12 defines as residential or other accommodation of a type which may be provided under Health and Personal Social Services (Northern Ireland) Order 1972 Article 15.

70 CA 2014 Sch 1 para 12 defines this as residential or other accommodation of a type which may be provided under Health and Personal Social Services (Northern Ireland) Order 1972 Article 15.

71 National Health Service Commissioning Board and Clinical Commissioning Groups (Responsibilities and Standing Rules) Regulations 2012 SI No 2996 reg 28(6A) and (6B); and see also the statutory guidance, para 21.48.

72 Statutory guidance, para 21.49.

Wales, it is the health service where the placement is made (ie where the person is to reside) that will be responsible for the RNCC costs.[73]

Placements from Wales, Scotland or Northern Ireland to England

6.63   CA 2014 Sch 1 para 2 contains a reciprocal provision – accordingly when, as a result of an assessment, a person is placed in accommodation in England[74] by a Welsh,[75] Scottish[76] or Northern Irish[77] authority the individual is deemed to remain ordinarily resident in the Welsh, Scottish or Northern Irish authority's area.

6.64   Where a Welsh local authority makes a placement in an English nursing home, then (as noted at para 6.62 above) it will be the relevant English CCG that will be responsible for the payment of the RNCC costs.[78]

Cross-border placements – general care planning principles

6.65   Statutory guidance paras 21.6–21.41 describe the choreography of cross-border placements where the placing authority (the 'first' authority) retains responsibility. This includes discussion with the individual and family/ friends; identification of a suitable placement; contact with the authority in whose area the accommodation is situated (the 'second' authority); liaison and ongoing care management of the placement. The guidance stresses the need for (at para 21.37):

> Any such arrangement should be detailed in writing – being clear as to what role the second authority is to play and for how long. Clarity should also be provided on the regularity of any reporting to the first authority and any payment involved for services provided by the second authority.

6.66   The statutory guidance gives a 'case study' example of an elderly person moving from England to Scotland (para 21.78). Everything goes smoothly in this hypothetical example – possibly because it avoids reference to the financial implications of such a move.

Ordinary residence and the deprivation of liberty safeguards

6.67   In general, the provisions in the MCA 2005 and the associated regulations mirror the ordinary residence provisions for the CA 2014 when deciding

---

73 Statutory guidance, para 21.50.
74 CA 2014 Sch 1 para 12 defines this as accommodation of a type specified in regulations under section 39 – ie the Care and Support (Ordinary Residence) (Specified Accommodation) Regulations 2014 SI 2828.
75 CA 2014 Sch 1 para 2 in discharge of its duty under Social Services and Well-being (Wales) Act 2014 s35.
76 CA 2014 Sch 1 para 2 in discharge of its duty under Social Work (Scotland) Act 1968 s12 or s13A; or Mental Health (Care and Treatment) (Scotland) Act 2003 s25.
77 CA 2014 Sch 1 para 2 in discharge of its duty under Health and Personal Social Services (Northern Ireland) Order 1972 Article 15.
78 Statutory guidance, para 21.50.

which authority should be the supervisory body in relation to a deprivation of liberty (DOL) application. Thus if a person is in a care home and is funding their own care (or has no settled residence) it will be the authority where the care home is situated that will be the authority of ordinary residence. Similarly, there are deeming provisions so if the person has been placed in a care home by another authority it will be the placing authority that will be the supervisory body.[79] The statutory guidance annex H (paras 51–63) provides detailed information on the various permutations of responsibility that can arise in such cases, including where the detained person is supported via NHS continuing healthcare funding.

6.68   Regulations specify that where there is a dispute about the ordinary residence of an individual, the local authority which receives the request for the standard authorisation must act as supervisory body until the question about the ordinary residence is determined. However, if another local authority agrees to act as supervisory body then that local authority will be the supervisory body until the question is determined. When the question has been determined then the local authority identified as the supervisory body will become the supervisory body.[80]

Ordinary residence and the Children Act 1989

6.69   Highly contested ordinary residence disputes are not confined to issues of social care: similar inter-authority wrangles concern such matters as the liability to maintain education, health and care (EHC) plans; the production of transition plans;[81] the duty to assess under the Children Act (CA) 1989;[82] and the funding of costs associated with special guardianship orders[83] – and in relation to which, an exasperated Hedley J was moved to hope that 'many citizens of this state will feel a touch of shame that things could work out as they appear to have done in this case'.[84]

6.70   As a matter of principle, children are presumed to have the ordinary residence of their parents.[85] The CA 1989, however, adopts a different test for determining responsibility for children in need. The duty under CA 1989 s17 (to safeguard and promote the welfare of children in need)[86] and the duty under CA 1989 s20 (to accommodate) are owed by social services authorities to children 'within their area'. However, financial responsibility for certain accommodation services provided under the Act[87] rests with

79 MCA 2005 Sch A1 para 183, apply the deeming provisions in NAA 1948 s24(5) and (6) of the for the purposes of the Deprivation of Liberty Safeguards; and see also statutory guidance, annex H para 54.

80 Mental Capacity (Deprivation of Liberty: Standard Authorisations, Assessments and Ordinary Residence) Regulations 2008 SI No 1858 reg 18.

81 In this respect, see, for instance, *R (L) v Waltham Forest LBC and Staffordshire CC* [2007] EWHC 2060 (Admin).

82 See, for example, *R (J & W) v Worcestershire CC* [2014] EWCA Civ 1518.

83 See, for example, *Suffolk CC v Nottinghamshire CC* (2012) [2012] EWCA Civ 1640.

84 Between Orkney Island Council and Cambridgeshire *O v L, I and Orkney Island Council* [2009] EWHC 3173 (Fam).

85 See eg *In re P (GE) (an infant)* [1965] Ch 568.

86 See para 15.191 below.

87 See CA 1989 ss20(2), 21(3) and 29(7), (9).

the local authority in whose area the child is 'ordinarily resident'. Thus a child may be ordinarily resident in local authority A but 'within the area' of local authority B. Accordingly provision is made in CA 1989 s20(2) for local authority A to take over the responsibilities of local authority B.

Within the area

6.71   A series of cases have considered the question of which authority is responsible for carrying out an assessment of children in need – and thus the true construction of the phrase 'within their area'. In *R (Stewart) v Wandsworth LBC, Hammersmith and Fulham LBC and Lambeth LBC*[88] the applicant applied to Hammersmith LBC for housing (under the homelessness provisions). Hammersmith accommodated her in a hostel in Lambeth and then determined that she was intentionally homeless and obtained a possession order against her. The applicant then requested that Hammersmith assess her children's needs under CA 1989 s17. Hammersmith refused on the basis that this was Lambeth's responsibility. Lambeth refused, as did Wandsworth LBC (the children's school being within their area). The court decided that 'within their area' was simply a question of physical presence (even though that might mean that more than one authority could be under the duty to assess). Accordingly it held that Lambeth and Wandsworth were responsible, but Hammersmith was not.

6.72   The decision was followed in a similar fact case, *R (M) v Barking and Dagenham LBC and Westminster LBC*[89] where the court agreed that the relevant test was physical presence. It noted that no formal guidance existed to deal with such jurisdictional problems and encouraged inter-authority co-operation in such cases:

> ... to avoid any impression that local authorities are able to pass responsibility for a child on to another authority ... To put it shortly, the needs should be met first and the redistribution of resources should, if necessary take place afterwards. It is also important, quite plainly, that the parents of children should not be able to cause inconvenience or extra expense by simply moving on to another local authority ...

Ordinary residence: the Children Act 1989/Care Act 2014 interface

6.73   The financial obligations imposed by the Children (Leaving Care) Act (C(LC)A) 2000 (particularly in the substituted sections 24A and 24B of the CA 1989) are the responsibility of the local authority that looked after the young person immediately before he or she left care.[90] This responsibility extends until the age of 21 (or beyond in the case of certain education and training costs). A 2006 protocol exists for inter-authority arrangements for care leavers outside of their responsible authority.[91]

---

88   [2001] EWHC 709 (Admin), (2001) 4 CCLR 446 and see also *R (Liverpool City Council) v Hillingdon LBC* [2008] EWHC 1702 (Admin).
89   [2002] EWHC 2663 (Admin), (2003) 6 CCLR 87.
90   See also statutory guidance, annex H para 40.
91   *National protocol: inter-authority arrangements for careleavers*, 2nd edition, revised July 2006.

6.74   The duties under the C(LC)A 2000 do not generally extend to the provision of accommodation, and there are times when the CA 1989 duties and the CA 2014 can run in tandem. The permutations on responsibility in such cases are numerous, and the statutory guidance provides advice on this issue.[92]

6.75   As noted above (para 6.16) in *R (Cornwall Council) v Secretary of State for Health*[93] (a case concerning an ordinary residence dispute of an adult who had, as a young person, been accommodated by a local authority) the Supreme Court considered that the 'underlying purpose' of the ordinary residence regime was to ensure that 'an authority should not be able to export its responsibility for providing the necessary accommodation by exporting the person who is in need of it'. It would appear that this case has extended the 'accommodation responsibilities' of placing local authorities[94] and the statutory guidance was updated to give guidance on the implications of this judgment (see para 6.17 above).

Ordinary residence and Mental Health Act 1983 s117

Overview

6.76   The duty to provide services under Mental Health Act (MHA) 1983 s117 is a joint health and social services responsibility.[95] MHA 1983 s117(3) stipulates that the responsible bodies in England are the CCG and the social services authority in which the person was ordinarily resident 'immediately before being detained'. Perplexingly, however, MHA 1983 s117(3)(c) then adds that 'in any other case' it is the CCG/local authority 'for the area in which the person concerned is resident[96] or to which he is sent on discharge by the hospital in which he was detained'.

6.77   It might appear, therefore, that MHA 1983 s117(3) gives a choice of responsible authorities – either the health/social services authorities in whose area the person was resident at the time of admission to hospital[97] or those to which he or she is sent on discharge. The basic principle is, however, that primary responsibility rests with the CCG/local authority

---

92 Annex H paras 41–45. It is of note that of the 56 published determinations, 13 are in relation to care leavers – an indication of the complexity of the legislation in this area. See ORs 1,3,4 and 6 2005, ORs 2 and 4 2006, ORs 2,3 and 5 2007, OR 5 2008, ORs 5 and 9 2009, and OR 6 2010.

93 [2015] UKSC 46, (2015) 18 CCLR 497 para 54 – and see also statutory guidance, para 19.17.

94 Lord Wilson in his dissenting judgment observed as such: 'I am not a legislator. Nor, with respect, are my colleagues' (para 66).

95 See para 15.63 for discussion about the nature of the support duty under MHA 1983 s117.

96 The use of the word 'resident' risks causing confusion until it is appreciated that it refers not only to local authorities but also to NHS bodies. The NHS 'responsible commissioner' rules (see para 6.92 below) uses 'usually resident'/'present' – rather than 'ordinarily resident'/'no settled residence' – and the process for the identification of these differs in England and Wales. It would seem that the CA 2014 resolves this difficulty by using the word 'resident' in section 117(3)(c).

97 A person does not cease to be resident in the area of an authority by reason only of his or her admission to hospital – *Fox v Stirk* [1970] 2 QB 463.

in which the person was resident at the time of *admission*. This was clarified by Scott Baker J in *R v Mental Health Review Tribunal ex p Hall*,[98] who observed that:

> Section 117 does not provide for multi social services department or health authority responsibility. The words 'or to whom he is sent on discharge from Tribunal' are included simply to cater for the situation where a patient does not have a current place of residence. The sub-section does not mean that a placing authority where the patient resides suddenly ceases to be 'the local social services authority' if on discharge the Applicant is sent to a different authority'.[99]

6.78   The identification of a person's ordinary residence under MHA 1983 s117 is a distinct process to that under the CA 2014. This stems from the fact that the first deeming rule under the CA 2014 is not replicated under the scheme of the MHA 1983 (see statutory guidance para 19.68). This incongruity (which existed with the NAA 1948) was highlighted in *R (Hertfordshire CC) v Hammersmith & Fulham LBC and JM*[100] – where the Court of Appeal held that although it was not clear why parliament had decided to take a different approach to ordinary residence under MHA 1983 s117, that is what it had done. The court agreed with the first instance decision[101] of Mitting J, that: (1) there was little or no difference in meaning between 'resident' and 'ordinarily resident' – they both connoted settled presence in a particular place other than under compulsion; and (2) that the first deeming rule (see para 6.25 above) had no application for MHA 1983 s117 purposes. On this basis, therefore, he held that responsibility for section 117 purposes lay with the local authority in which the person was 'resident'[102] in a care home at the time he or she was admitted to hospital under MHA 1983 s3 (albeit he had been funded by Hammersmith & Fulham because of the deeming provisions under the NAA 1948.)

6.79   *R (Sunderland City Council) v South Tyneside Council*[103] concerned an applicant, who while living in a registered residential college in Sunderland attempted suicide. She was taken to Sunderland Royal Hospital, then to the Queen Elizabeth Hospital in Gateshead, and then with her consent to a specialist short-term hospital for patients with a learning disability, in the South Tyneside area (although 'compulsion was never far from the horizon'). Her college placement was then terminated. In December 2009 she was detained under section 3. The Court of Appeal held that – for the purposes of MHA 1983 s117 – the *Shah* judgment (see para 6.13 above) was not helpful as an authority, preferring instead *Mohamed*

---

98 [1999] 3 All ER 132, (1999) 2 CCLR 361, QBD. Although the case went to the Court of Appeal – [2000] 1 WLR 1323, (1999) 2 CCLR 383 – the question of the responsible department was not argued in that court.

99 This is paraphrased at para 186 of the 2011 guidance.

100 [2011] EWCA Civ 77, (2011) 14 CCLR 224, and see also *R (Sunderland City Council) v South Tyneside Council* [2011] EWHC 2355 (Admin). See para 11.92 for the Law Commission's recommendations.

101 *R (M) v Hammersmith and Fulham LBC and others* (2010) 13 CCLR 217.

102 Ie *not* 'deemed' to be resident.

103 [2012] EWCA Civ 1232.

v Hammersmith & Fulham LBC.[104] In *Mohamed* Lord Slynn's held that this connoted a place where a person in fact resided and that so 'long as that place where he eats and sleeps is voluntarily accepted by him, the reason why he is there rather than somewhere else does not prevent that place from being his normal residence'. On this basis, once the college placement was terminated the applicant nowhere that could be considered as here residence other South Tyneside and so it was this authority that was responsible for her after-care.

6.80   The position is explained in para 19.65 of the statutory guidance in the following terms:

> Although any change in the patient's ordinary residence after discharge will affect the local authority responsible for their social care services, it will not affect the local authority responsible for commissioning the patient's section 117 after-care. Under section 117 of the 1983 Act ... if a person is ordinarily resident in local authority area (A) immediately before detention under the 1983 Act, and moves on discharge to local authority area (B) and moves again to local authority area (C), local authority (A) will remain responsible for providing or commissioning their after-care. However, if the patient, having become ordinarily resident after discharge in local authority area (B) or (C), is subsequently detained in hospital for treatment again, the local authority in whose area the person was ordinarily resident immediately before their subsequent admission (local authority (B) or (C)) will be responsible for their after-care when they are discharged from hospital.

Mental Health Act 1983 s117 and Care Act 2014 ordinary residence interface

6.81   Many individuals entitled to support under MHA 1983 s117 will also have CA 2014 support needs – ie support needs that are not related to the mental disorder which resulted in their detention for treatment.[105] Since the two Acts take a slightly different approach to ordinary residence, there is the risk the authority responsible for the support needs under the CA 2014 may be different to local authority responsible for the provision of care and support under MHA 1983 s117. This problem is addressed by the CA 2014 s39(4) which provides that an adult who is being provided with accommodation under MHA 1983 s117 is to be treated for the purposes of the CA 2014 'as ordinarily resident in the area of the local authority in England or the local authority in Wales on which the duty to provide the adult with services under that section is imposed'.[106] Although this provision only applies to accommodation, this would appear to all that is needed (due to the deeming rules relating to 'accommodation' under the CA 2014 not being replicated by the MHA 1983.

---

104 [2001] UKHL 57, [2002] 1 AC 547 at para 18, which concerned the meaning of 'normally resident' for the purposes of Housing Act 1996 s199.

105 MHA 1983 s117(6); and see para 15.65 below.

106 Ie the local authority in whose area the person was ordinarily resident immediately before being detained for treatment under the MHA 1983.

Mental Health Act 1983 s117 and restricted patients

6.82   In the pre-CA 2014 judgment of *R (Wiltshire) v Hertfordshire CC*[107] the Court of Appeal suggested that the ordinary residence rule under MHA 1983 s117 may be different for patients subject to a hospital order. As the court explained (para 15), where a patient is detained under MHA 1983 s3 'each admission to hospital involves a fresh decision, and generally the patient has been living in the community beforehand without restrictions'. However, where a person is (para 19):

> ... subject to a hospital order with restrictions, then conditionally discharged, then recalled to hospital, and then conditionally discharged for a second time, for the purposes of s117(3) of the Act he is still to be treated as 'resident in the area' of the same local authority as that in which he lived before the original hospital order was made.

6.83   In this context, the statutory guidance advises that where (para 17.6):

> ... prisoners have previously been detained under sections 47 and 48 of the Mental Health Act 1983 and transferred back to prison, their entitlement to section 117 after-care should be dealt with in the same way as it would be in the community ... Section 117(3), as amended by the Care Act 2014, will apply in determining which local authority is responsible for commissioning or providing the section 117 after-care.

Ordinary residence and the carers legislation

6.84   CA 2014 s20(1) stipulates that the local authority that is responsible for meeting a carer's eligible needs is the one in which the adult needing care 'is ordinarily resident in'.[108] The assumption therefore must be that the duty to undertake a carer's assessment is the responsibility of the local authority that is responsible for the person for whom the carer cares.[109] It is understood that ADASS is preparing a protocol on undertaking cross-border assessments to assist councils in making decisions about this.

6.85   The statutory guidance accepts that there will be situations where identifying the responsible authority may not be straightforward for example 'where the carer provides care for more than one person in different local authority areas' (para 19.7). It advises that in such cases the various authorities 'should consider how best to cooperate on and share the provision of support' (para 19.8) and then gives examples of how this may be achieved.[110]

---

107 [2014] EWCA Civ 712 19.
108 Or is present in its area but of no settled residence.
109 See also statutory guidance, para 19.6. The pre-CA 2014 guidance also advised that the disabled person's home authority was for the carer's assessment and the provision of any 'carer's services': Department of Health, *Practice guidance to the Carers and Disabled Children Act 2000*, paras 24–27.
110 The 2013 DH guidance advised in similar vein that 'where the carer is ordinarily resident in a different authority to the cared-for person, local authorities should work in partnership to ensure that carers' needs are properly assessed and met' (para 137).

Disputed ordinary residence

English social services authorities

6.86   Where two or more English social services authorities are in dispute over a person's ordinary residence (either in respect of their responsibilities under the CA 2014 or under MHA 1983 s117), CA 2014 s40 and 2014 regulations provide that the question is to be determined by the secretary of state. The relevant regulations are the Care and Support (Disputes Between Local Authorities) Regulations 2014 SI No 2829 (referred to in this chapter as the 'dispute regulations').

6.87   The statutory guidance (paras 19.76–19.90) describes the dispute procedures detailed in the regulations and includes the following salient matters (references below are to the statutory guidance and the dispute regulations):

- That it is 'critical that the person does not go without the care they need' during the dispute process and that the local authority (referred to as the 'lead' authority) 'that is meeting the needs ... on the date that the dispute arises, must continue to do so until the dispute is resolved' (para 19.78; reg 2).
- If no authority is currently meeting the person's needs, then the authority where the person is living or is physically present must accept responsibility until the dispute is resolved (reg 2(3)).
- The lead authority must keep the parties (and any carer) fully informed of dispute in question and of progress regarding any resolution (para 19.79; reg 3(6)).
- If despite all reasonable steps having been taken by the parties, the dispute cannot be resolved the lead authority must apply for a determination to the secretary of state within four months from the date when the dispute arose (para 19.80; reg 3).
- The provisional acceptance of responsibility by the lead authority will not influence any determination made by the secretary of state (para 19.80).
- The lead authority must provide the secretary of state with a statement of facts (which includes the information required by the regulations (para 19.80; reg 4).[111]
- If a determination finds another local authority to be the authority of ordinary residence, the lead local authority may recover costs from the authority which should have been providing the relevant care and support (para 19.86; reg 7).[112]

6.88   Determinations made by the secretary of state are published.[113]

---

111 For a cautionary note as to the consequences of failing to properly engage in a cross-border dispute, see *Neath And Port Talbot Council v Secretary of State for Health* [2013] EWHC 3341 (Admin) where HH J Jarman observed that 'it is very unfortunate in this case that so much money has been expended in litigation ... [when] much, if not all of this cost, could have been prevented if adequate care had been taken to supply documentation for the [Secretary of State's] determination' (at para 51).

112 And this can also arise if a local authority has mistakenly been funding a person (para 19.89).

113 Available at www.dh.gov.uk/en/Publicationsandstatistics/Publications/ PublicationsPolicyAndGuidance/DH_113627.

Cross-border dispute resolution

6.89   CA 2014 s39(8) and Sch 1 para 5 provide for regulations that detail the process for resolving cross-border ordinary disputes. In consequence, 2014 regulations – the Care and Support (Cross-border Placements and Business Failure: Temporary Duty) (Dispute Resolution) Regulations 2014 SI No 2843 – have been issued, supplemented by brief guidance.[114] They make clear that the responsible nation for determining such disputes is the one in which the individual is actually residing.[115]

6.90   As with domestic ordinary residence disputes, the regulations and guidance require that authorities co-operate and co-ordinate their actions, exchange relevant information and provide appropriate statements to the dispute determining body. Above all, the regulations provide that authorities 'must not allow the existence of the dispute to prevent, delay, interrupt or otherwise adversely affect the meeting of the needs of the adult'.[116] The CA 2014 makes provision for the recovery of payments made by an authority where it subsequently transpires that the individual is the responsibility of another authority.[117]

Disputed 'ordinary residence' and the Children Act 1989

6.91   Although, as noted above, there is no formal resolution process for inter-authority disputes as to whether or not a child is 'within their area', CA 1989 s30(2) provides a formal process for disputes concerning ordinary residence.[118] This mirrors the secretary of state process under CA 2014 s39 (above). Where there is a dispute as to responsibility between two councils, one or other must accept responsibility – or they both will be condemned, as was the case in *A v Leicester City Council*[119] where HHJ Farmer QC observed that:

> It is surely not beyond the wit of two local authorities with access to legal advice ... to devise plans and contingencies for such situations, which are said not to be uncommon and perhaps to share the cost of funding pending the resolution of such disputes as they arise. What is not lawful, in my judgment, is to defer the performance of the duty of good parenting under the Act to the resolution of what is essentially a resource led dispute.

114 Statutory guidance, paras 21.58–21.68.

115 Care and Support (Cross-border Placements and Business Failure: Temporary Duty) (Dispute Resolution) Regulations 2014 SI No 2843 reg 2.

116 Care and Support (Cross-border Placements and Business Failure: Temporary Duty) (Dispute Resolution) Regulations 2014 SI No 2843 reg 5.

117 CA 2014 Sch 1 para 6.

118 Children Act 1989 s30 (as amended by Children and Young Persons Act 2008 Sch 3 para 21) provides for a similar cross-border dispute process to that under the NAA Act 1948.

119 [2009] EWHC 2351 (Admin) para 51.

Establishing the responsible commissioner for NHS services

Overview

6.92 For the majority of individuals, the CCG that is responsible for their healthcare needs is the one to which their GP practice belongs (see para 11.13). For persons who are not registered with a GP practice, the responsible CCG is the one in whose geographic area the individual resides. This duty is expressed in NHSA 2006 s3(1A) in the following terms:

> For the purposes of this section, a clinical commissioning group has responsibility for–
> (a) persons who are provided with primary medical services by a member of the group, and
> (b) persons who usually reside in the group's area and are not provided with primary medical services by a member of any clinical commissioning group

6.93 Additionally, a CCG has responsibility for those in need of urgent and emergency care services who are in its area, as well as some patients eligible for NHS Continuing Care funding (see below).[120] NHS England has issued 2013 DH guidance[121] explaining how the responsible CCG is identified (referred to below as the '2013 DH guidance').

6.94 The 2013 DH guidance sets out the general rules (para 1)– namely that a CCG is responsible for:

- persons registered on the list of patients of a GP practice which is a member of the CCG (see para 11.13 below);
- persons who are not registered with a GP practice but who are 'usually resident' in the CCG's geographic area (see below).

Usually resident

6.95 Where a patient is not registered with a practice, annex B of the 2013 DH guidance advises on how their 'usual residence is to be determined. It states that 'usually resident' is not the same as 'ordinarily resident' (for the purposes of the CA 2014) and the 'main criterion … is the patient's perception of where they are resident in the UK'. In identifying what this is it advises as follows:

- Where the patient gives an address, he or she should be treated as usually resident at that address.
- Where the patient is reluctant to provide an address, it is sufficient that he or she is 'resident in a location (or postal district) within the CCG geographical area, without needing a precise address'.
- Where there is any uncertainty, the provider should ask the patient where he or she usually lives.

---

120 National Health Service Commissioning Board and Clinical Commissioning Groups (Responsibilities and Standing Rules) Regulations 2012 SI No 2996 reg 4 and Sch 1 para 3.
121 NHS England, *Who Pays? Determining responsibility for payments to providers*, August 2013.

- Holiday or second homes should not be considered as 'usual' residences.
- If patients consider themselves to be resident at an address, which is, for example, a hostel, then this should be accepted. If they are unable to give an address at which they consider themselves resident, but can give their most recent address, they should be treated as usually resident at that address.
- Another person (for example, a parent or carer) may give an address on a patient's behalf.
- Where a patient cannot, or chooses not to, give either a current or recent address, and an address cannot be established by other means, they should be treated as usually resident in the place where they are present.

6.96   The 2013 DH guidance (para 7) makes it clear that no treatments should be refused or delayed due to uncertainty as to which CCG is responsible for funding an individual's healthcare provision. In earlier (2007) guidance it was stated that ministers had specifically asked to be advised of those NHS bodies that had failed to reach local resolution of any disputes between themselves or with independent providers.[122]

Patients who receive fully funded NHS Continuing Healthcare

6.97   Different rules apply for people who receive NHS Continuing Healthcare (CC) funding (see chapter 12) or a jointly funded package with social services (see para 12.206) either in care homes or independent hospitals. In such cases, the general rule is that if the original CCG places the individual in another CCG's area, it remains responsible for the NHS contribution to the care, even where the person changes his or her GP practice (and associated CCG).[123] These arrangements do not apply to a situation where a person either independently chooses to move to a different part of the country or is placed there because of an arrangement made by a local authority only.[124]

6.98   Regulations[125] stipulate that the continuing obligation of the placing CCG only applies if the services required by the person in the care home/independent hospital include 'at least one planned service[126] (other than a service consisting only of NHS-funded nursing care) which is connected to

122 Department of Health, *Who pays? Establishing the responsible commissioner*, 2007, para 5.
123 2013 DH guidance, para 60 and the National Health Service Commissioning Board and Clinical Commissioning Groups (Responsibilities and Standing Rules) Regulations 2012 SI No 2996 reg 4 and Sch 1 para 3.
124 2013 DH guidance, para 60.
125 National Health Service Commissioning Board and Clinical Commissioning Groups (Responsibilities and Standing Rules) Regulations 2012 SI No 2996 reg 4 and Sch 1 para 3.
126 Earlier guidance – Department of Health, *Who pays? Establishing the responsible commissioner*, 2007, para 16 and annex C – gave as examples physiotherapy, occupational therapy, speech and language therapy, dietetics and podiatry.

the provision of such accommodation'. As the 2013 DH guidance explains (para 61), the continuing obligation of the placing CCG applies:

> ... regardless of whether nursing care by a registered nurse forms part of the care package, except in cases where the only planned service is NHS-funded nursing care provided in a nursing home. A need for care from a registered nurse would not be sufficient to trigger these commissioning rules.

People not ordinarily resident in the UK and overseas visitors

6.99 Although CCGs rely on usual residence to establish whether they are responsible for commissioning services, the test for whether the NHS should provide free services for those from abroad is based on whether the person has 'ordinary residence in the UK', and this question is analysed in the 2013 DH guidance at annex A para 5. Asylum-seekers who have made a formal application for refugee status are considered to be resident, and so the responsible CCG is based on their GP or where they are usually resident.[127]

Prisoners

6.100 NHS England (see para 11.10 below) is responsible for commissioning health services (excluding emergency care) for people in prisons, as well as young offender institutions.[128] CCGs are responsible for commissioning emergency care, including Accident and Emergency services, and ambulance services as well as out-of-hours primary medical services, for prisoners and detainees present in their geographical area.

Resolving disputes about who is the responsible commissioner

6.101 The 2013 DH guidance makes clear that 'NHS England expects that all disputes will be resolved locally' with CCGs (para 9):

> ... coming to pragmatic solutions where responsibility is not immediately obvious or where it may be shared. In cases that cannot be resolved at CCG level, Area Teams of NHS England should be consulted and should arbitrate where necessary.

6.102 The 2013 DH guidance (para 7) stresses that the 'safety and well-being of patients is paramount' and that there 'should be no gaps in responsibility – no treatment should be refused or delayed due to uncertainty

127 See 2013 DH guidance, para 11 and annex A: entitlement extends also to failed asylum seekers who are receiving section 4 or section 95 (IAA 1999) support from the Home Office (see para 16.7 below) and see *YA v Secretary of State for Health* [2009] EWCA Civ 225 which concerned earlier 2007 guidance: *Who pays? Establishing the responsible commissioner.*

128 National Health Service Commissioning Board and Clinical Commissioning Groups (Responsibilities and Standing Rules) Regulations 2012 SI No 2996 reg 10 – this responsibility also extends to some secure children's homes, immigration removal centres and training centres. See also the 2013 DH guidance at paras 94–97.

or ambiguity as to which CCG is responsible for funding an individual's healthcare provision'. Notwithstanding these fine words, the ombudsmen for Wales and England found maladministration in just such a case – where a patient with a serious and deteriorating condition had been forced to fund her own treatment while two health bodies squabbled over funding.[129]

6.103   The responsibility for patients who move across the borders of the UK nations, and disputes concerning such persons, is covered in paras 51–70 of the 2013 guidance.

---

129 Report by the Public Services Ombudsman for Wales and the Health Service Ombudsman for England of an investigation of a complaint about the Welsh Assembly Government (Health Commission Wales), Cardiff and Vale NHS Trust and Plymouth Teaching Primary Care Trust, Third Report Session 2008–2009 HC 858.

CHAPTER 7

Care and support services under the Care Act 2014

continued

Introduction

7.1 A primary purpose of a pre-Care Act (CA) 2014 community care/carers' assessment was to identify if the person had a need for 'services'. The community care statutes[1] contained exhaustive lists of services that could be provided, and the Carers and Disabled Children Act 2000 contained a generalised statement as to what a carer's 'service' might be.

7.2 The CA 2014 repealed these provisions (insofar as they applied to adults[2]) and in keeping with its 'outcomes'[3] rhetoric, endeavoured to avoid referring to the word 'service' when describing what may be provided to meet a person's needs. As the statutory guidance to the CA 2014[4] explains, the Act's new approach 'signifies a shift from existing duties on local authorities to provide particular services, to the concept of "meeting needs"' (para 1.9). One reason it gives for this approach is that 'everyone's needs are different and personal to them' (para 1.10). Although this is clearly true and important to acknowledge, it is also the case that all local authorities adopt generic responses to these needs – responses that in this chapter are referred to as 'services'.

7.3 This chapter considers such 'services': services that are provided as a result of an assessment.[5] These include general support such as social work, information and advocacy; care and support provided in people's own homes or in the community; and support that includes accommodation (for example in a care home or supported housing.

7.4 Chapter 10 considers a distinct form of response to need, namely the making of a direct payment; chapter 9 considers preventative and 'intermediate care' services; and services provided under Mental Health Act (MHA) 1983 s117 are considered at para 15.56 below.

Background

Background to the Care Act 2014

7.5 The CA 2014 reform of social care and support arrangements is more than mere rhetoric. The previous legal regime was contradictory, inconsistent and governed by 'a set of sometimes incomprehensible and frequently incompatible principles'.[6] Entitlement to support was based on whether a need related to residential or non-residential accommodation[7] and whether

---

1 Primarily Chronically Sick and Disabled Persons Act 1970 s2 and National Assistance Act (NAA) 1948 ss21 and 29.
2 As noted above (para 7.2), Chronically Sick and Disabled Persons Act (CSDPA) 1970 s2 was only repealed in so far as it applies to adults.
3 Outcomes aim to identify the person's 'aspirations, goals and priorities' – see also para 4.14 above.
4 Department of Health, *Care and support statutory guidance* to support implementation of Part 1 of the CA 2014 by local authorities, 2016 ('the statutory guidance').
5 Or less commonly, in cases of urgency, prior to an assessment – see para 4.68 above.
6 See the 5th edition of this book, para 9.9.
7 NAA 1948 s21 and s29 respectively.

the person was disabled[8] or frail elderly[9] or recovering from an illness[10] or 'mentally disordered'.[11] For each group, different service responses were available. The fine detail of the law, although of interest to solitary textbook writers and occasional barristers, was of complete irrelevance to adults in need, carers and to frontline workers. With the exception of the rights of certain people who have a 'mental disorder'[12] and people subject to immigration control[13] the CA 2014 swept away these unfathomable distinctions. Entitlement to care and support services/direct payments is now determined by a person's particular needs, rather than the person's categorisation.

7.6   In place of the exhaustive lists of services provided in the community care statutes, CA 2014 s8(1) provides an illustrative list of what may be 'provided' to an eligible adult in need or carer – namely:

(a) accommodation in a care home[14] or in premises of some other type;
(b) care and support at home or in the community;
(c) counselling, advocacy and other types of social work;
(d) goods and facilities;
(e) information and advice.

7.7   The list is much briefer than that provided under the pre-CA 2014 legal regime[15] and differs from that first proposed by the Law Commission.[16]

7.8   The absence of such things as 'adaptations', 'equipment', 'travel'; and 'holidays' (which were specifically cited in Chronically Sick and Disabled Persons Act (CSDPA) 1970 s2) was considered problematical by the joint committee that scrutinised the draft Care and Support Bill and in response to a question it asked the Department of Health, received confirmation that the Department considered that these services did fall within the ambit of the list.[17] The committee expressed the hope that the subsequent guidance would 'make clear that the list is not intended to limit the ways in which a local authority might meet any eligible needs or agreed outcomes, removing any possible ambiguity on that point' (para 170). Whether the statutory guidance satisfies this entreaty is a moot point, but para 10.12 states:

---

8   CSDPA 1970 s2.
9   Health Services and Public Health Act 1968 s45; Health and Social Services and Social Security Adjudications Act 1983 Sch 9.
10 National Health Service Act (NHSA) 2006 Sch 20 para 2.
11 MHA 1983 s117.
12 For whom entitlement to support under MHA 1983 s117 remains in addition to their rights under the CA 2014, see para 15.56.
13 See chapter 16 below.
14 CA 2014 s8(3) defines a 'care home' as having the meaning given by Care Standards Act 2000 s3.
15 For example, in Chronically Sick and Disabled Persons Act 1970 s2.
16 The Law Commission proposed that proposed that the wide ranging list of services that come within the definition of 'community care services' be replaced by a simple list – namely: (1) residential accommodation; (2) community and home-based services; (3) advice, social work, counselling and advocacy services; and (4) financial or any other assistance – see Law Commission, *Adult social care*, Law Com No 326, HC 941, 2011, Recommendation 28.
17 Joint Committee on the Draft Care and Support Bill, 'Draft Care and Support Bill' HL Paper 143 HC 822, The Stationery Office, 2013, paras 168–170.

Where the local authority provides or arranges for care and support, the type of support may itself take many forms. These may include more traditional 'service' options, such as care homes or homecare, but may also include other types of support such as assistive technology in the home or equipment/adaptations, and approaches to meeting needs should be inclusive of less intensive or service-focused options.

7.9   CA 2014 s8(2) slips out of the 'outcomes' mode and gives the following examples of the ways need may be met – namely:

(a) by arranging for a person other than it to provide a service;
(b) by itself providing a service;
(c) by making direct payments.

Care and support services are a means to an end. The 'end' is the promotion of the well-being of the adult in need or carer. CA 2014 s8 provides authorities with very wide powers to support almost any adult in need or carer. However, the duty only crystalises when the person (among other things) satisfies the eligibility criteria. The duty is then (under CA 2014 ss18 and 20) to provide care and support to meet those needs 'which meet the eligibility criteria'. Although this means that service responses will be tailored to the eligibility criteria, this is a process that must be managed thoughtfully. The outcomes listed in the regulations can relate to a cluster of multifaceted needs. It follows the 'service' responses that are required in any given situation may be multidimensional.

7.10   Local authorities are able to charge for the costs that they incur in providing such care and support under the CA 2014, and these powers are considered in chapter 8.

Domiciliary and community-based services – background

7.11   Policy papers concerning social care legislation since 1990 has made great use of phrases such as 'community care' and 'independent living'. What the research establishes is that these ambiguous aspirations have not resulted in significant additional resources being allocated for community-based health and social services. The numbers of district nursing staff have fallen, and expenditure on social care assistance has remained (at best) 'flat'. The 'community' has, however, absorbed the large numbers of people who in earlier times would have been institutionalised, as well as the significant increase in the elderly population (ie people over 80) – the 'community' in this sense being unpaid (largely family) carers. Fewer people get local authority funded community-based social care support today than in 1990, and as the 2016 King's Fund report[18] demonstrates, this decline is accelerating: in 2016 the numbers had declined by 30 per cent since 2009.

7.12   It appears likely that the fall in the quantity of domiciliary care support has been matched by a decline in its quality: in 2016 the local government ombudsman reported a 25 per cent rise in complaints about home care support services.[19]

---

18   R Humphries and others, *Social care for older people: Home truths*, King's Fund, 2016, p15.

19   Local government ombudsman, *Review of adult social care complaints 2015/16*, 2016.

The Care Act 2014 duties

7.13   As noted at para 7.95 below there is no prescribed list of services that a social services authority can provide or commission for adults in need and carers. CA 2014 s8(1) merely provides examples of what may be provided, and these include (in addition to accommodation – considered above):

- care and support at home or in the community;
- counselling and other types of social work;
- goods and facilities;
- information, advice and advocacy.

7.14   As already noted, although such things as 'adaptations', 'travel' and 'holidays' (which were specifically cited in CSDPA 1970 s2) are not named in CA 2014 s8, these services nevertheless fall within its ambit.[20] The intention behind this change was explained in para 10.10 of the statutory guidance – namely to move 'away from the previous terminology of "providing services"' as the 'concept of "meeting needs" is intended to be broader than a duty to provide or arrange a particular service'. The guidance nevertheless clarifies the scope of potential support services at para 10.12, stating that in addition to the 'more traditional "service" options, such as care homes or homecare' other support arrangements are included 'such as assistive technology in the home or equipment/adaptations'.

7.15   Although the CA 2014 seeks to redirect the aim of assessments away from 'services' and towards the achievement of well-being outcomes, in practice many commonly occurring problems relate to problems with specific 'services'. For this reason, the succeeding section considers the more common adult social care services provided to individuals and the relevant case-law, ombudsmen reports and good practice concerning these services. The eligible needs of many individuals are addressed through the making of a direct payment, and this form of support is considered separately at para 10.13 below.

7.16   Today local authorities provide fewer social care services themselves than in the past. The vast majority, although commissioned by the local authority, are actually provided by the independent sector. This arrangement does not, however, absolve the authority of its duties to ensure that the care is actually delivered. Its duty is to ensure that the assistance provided is 'adequate and effective' and to 'act reasonably'.[21] Thus, if the commissioned service is 'inadequate, inconsistent and subject to rapid fluctuation' such that 'a complaint of gravity and substance' arises, it will amount to breach of statutory duty.[22] It follows that it will be maladministration if there are inadequate mechanisms in place to monitor effectively

20 Joint Committee on the Draft Care and Support Bill, 'Draft Care and Support Bill', HL Paper 143 HC 822, The Stationery Office, 2013, paras 168–170.
21 *R (LW) v Belfast Health and SC Trust* [2010] NIQB 62, 19 May 2010 at para 38.
22 *R (LW) v Belfast Health and SC Trust* [2010] NIQB 62, 19 May 2010 at para 46, but see *R v Islington LBC ex p McMillan* (1997–98) 1 CCLR 7, QBD at 17 where the court considered the local authority had acted reasonably; that the service delivery failings were comparatively minor; and due to staff leave and staff sickness.

contracts with care agencies[23] and resolve promptly the problem of poor service these provide.[24]

Social work service, advice and support

7.17   CA 2014 s8(1) makes specific mention of the provision of social work support – which was a service directed to be provided under National Assistance Act (NAA) 1948 s29.[25] This duty is complemented by Local Authority Social Services Act (LASSA) 1970 s6(6), which obliges local authorities to provide 'adequate staff for assisting' the director of social services in the exercise of his or her functions.[26] It has generally been interpreted as including such services as welfare rights advice and counselling.[27] Such a service would complement the eligibility outcome of enabling the adult in need to maintain 'a habitable home environment'[28] in terms of providing welfare rights 'support to sustain their occupancy of the home and to maintain amenities, such as water, electricity and gas'.[29] Previous circular guidance[30] advised that the provision of advice and support would frequently necessitate offering advice and other help to the families of the disabled person; and that authorities should bear in mind the part that voluntary workers can play in delivering this service. Welfare rights advice has often been considered as a core local authority activity,[31] sometimes working in joint teams with the Department for Work and Pensions or other advice agencies.[32] The National Health Service (NHS) is also empowered to provide advice and assistance in relation to access to state benefits for its service users, under National Health Service Act (NHSA) 2006 s3(1)(e).[33]

---

23 Complaint no 05/C/06420 against Sheffield City Council, 20 February 2007.

24 See eg complaints no 05/C/08592 against Liverpool City Council, 17 January 2007; no 07/A/01436 against Hillingdon LBC, 18 September 2008; no 09 005 944 against Bristol City Council, 13 June 2011; and no 08 019 214 against Bromley LBC, 9 June 2011.

25 LAC (93)10, appendix 2 para 2(1)(a) – 'social work service and such advice and support as may be needed for people in their own homes or elsewhere'.

26 See para 1.5 above.

27 Complaint no 05/A/00880 against Essex CC, 16 January 2006.

28 Care and Support (Eligibility Criteria) Regulations 2015 SI No 313 reg 2(2)(f) – see para 4.17 above.

29 Statutory guidance, para 6.104f.

30 Department of Health and Social Security circular 13/74, para 11(ii) – cancelled by LAC (93)10.

31 Local authorities have a variety of powers to fund advice groups. Where a decision is taken to cease such support, it will need to comply with the principles of public law, including proper consultation and an equality impact assessment. In *R (Hajrula) v London Councils* [2011] EWHC 448 (Admin) para 69, Calvert-Smith J considered that, in relation to the public sector equality duty (see para 2.59 above) where a cut impacted on a vulnerable group the obligation to have 'due regard' to its impact was 'very high'.

32 See, for example, the trailblazer pilot sites established under the Disabled People's Right to Control (Pilot Scheme) (England) Regulations 2010 SI No 2862.

33 *R (Keating) v Cardiff Local Health Board* [2005] EWCA Civ 847, [2006] 1 WLR 159, (2005) 8 CCLR 504 – see para 11.16 below.

Information, advice and advocacy for adults in need and carers

7.18   CA 2014 s8(1) makes specific mention of the provision of information, advice and advocacy – and these services are considered separately at paras 3.9 and 19.2. The duty replicates the requirement in NAA 1948 s29 to make arrangements 'for informing [disabled] persons ... of the services available for them'.[34]

Day centres and other community recreational facilities

7.19   The reference in CA 2014 s8(1) to 'Care and support ... in the community' encompasses such facilities as 'Day Centres', 'workshops',[35] drop-in' clubs, recreational and other community-based activities. The duty to provide support of this kind was found in the directions accompanying NAA 1948 s29 which referred to the provision at 'centres or elsewhere, [of] facilities for occupational, social, cultural and recreational activities'[36] and in CSDPA 1970 s2(1)(c) which referred to the provision of 'lectures, games, outings or other recreational facilities outside' the home. Although support of this kind may address a number of the outcomes in the Care and Support (Eligibility Criteria) Regulations 2015 SI No 313 ('the eligibility regulations'), it will be particularly apt in relation to 'making use of necessary facilities or services in the local community including ... recreational facilities or services'.[37]

7.20   There has been a long-standing central government aim of reducing reliance on day centres and workshops.[38] Accordingly, in *R (J and others) v Southend BC and Essex CC*[39] (a case challenging the closure of a day centre) Newman J observed:

> It is plain that the underlying reason for the closure of the M Centre is to comply with Government policy and that policy itself is designed to foster the autonomy of the learning disabled, to ensure services are provided to them and that they are not set apart from the community. It is a situation in which the policy itself is driving towards what could be regarded as an aspect of private life which it is seen will be enhanced by these measures.

7.21   Desirable as it is to provide services that do not 'set apart from the community' people with learning disabilities, such an approach is not a universal

---

34 LAC (93)10, appendix 2 para 2(1)(2); and NAA 1948 s29(4)(g).
35 In the early post-war years many workshops were former poor-law workhouses which continued to be devoted to menial mechanical tasks. Almost all such workshops have now been closed with the current focus on enabling disabled people to access mainstream work using social security support – such as the Access to Work schemes - see Department for Work and Pensions (2011) *Getting in, staying in and getting on: disability employment support fit for the future,* a report by Liz Sayce Cm 8081.
36 LAC (93)10, appendix 2 para 2(1)(c).
37 Care and Support (Eligibility Criteria) Regulations 2015 SI No 313 regs 2(2)(i) and 3(2)(b)(vii); and see para 4.17 above.
38 Secretary of State for Health, *Valuing people: a new strategy for learning disability for the 21st century,* Cm 5086, March 2001, paras 4.7 and 7.21.
39 [2005] EWHC 3457 (Admin), (2007) 10 CCLR 407.

panacea. In *AH v Hertfordshire Partnership NHS Foundation Trust and others*[40] the Court of Protection noted that for the individual in question the local authority's proposal to move him out of a relatively segregated unit constituted the antithesis of person-centred planning or 'personalisation': that for him, community living did not hold benefits – and that 'facing up to these realities does not in any way diminish or demean [him], but values and respects him for who he is'. In the opinion of Jackson J (para 80):

> ... guideline policies cannot be treated as universal solutions, nor should initiatives designed to personalise care and promote choice be applied to the opposite effect ... These residents are not an anomaly simply because they are among the few remaining recipients of this style of social care. They might better be seen as a good example of the kind of personal planning that lies at the heart of the philosophy of care in the community.

7.22   In *R v Haringey LBC ex p Norton*[41] the council, when carrying out its assessment, only considered its obligation to provide 'personal care needs' rather than other needs such as social, recreational and leisure needs. The court held this to be unlawful; the assessment had to investigate all potential needs. This obligation will exist, regardless of where a person is living. Increasingly, it appears that local authorities are stipulating that if a resident in a care home has a need to take part in activities outside the care home, then these must be arranged and funded by the care home. At law, the duty to ensure that eligible needs for support in community settings rests with the local authority and not the care home. It follows that if these support needs are not being provided, the individual's redress lies through a complaint to the authority rather than the care home (as it would for any failure by a provide provider to meet an eligible need identified by a local authority).

7.23   Where a person's assessment identifies a need that could be met by services under CA 2014 s8 – for instance, in a community centre – that need must be met. If the appropriate centre is full, merely placing that person's name on the waiting list is likely to be an inadequate response (unless the wait is known to be reasonably short). This situation was considered by Sedley J in *R v Islington LBC ex p Rixon*[42] where he held:

> The duty owed to the applicant personally ... includes the provision of recreational facilities outside the home to an extent which Islington accepts is greater than the care plan provides for. But the local authority has, it appears, simply taken existing unavailability of further facilities as an insuperable obstacle to any further attempt to make provision. The lack of a day care centre has been treated, however reluctantly, as a complete answer to the question of provision for Jonathan's needs. As McCowan LJ explained in the *Gloucestershire* case, the [duty under the CSDPA 1970 – now the CA 2014] ... is needs-led and not resource-led. To say this is not to ignore the existing resources either in terms of regular voluntary care in the home or in budgetary terms. These, however, are balancing and not blocking factors.

For further consideration of waiting lists, see para 4.116 above.

40   [2011] EWHC 276 (COP), (2011) 14 CCLR 301.
41   (1997–98) 1 CCLR 168, QBD.
42   (1997–98) 1 CCLR 119 at 126D, QBD.

7.24   It follows that if a person's care arrangements are being met, satisfactorily, at a particular centre, then that centre cannot be closed without the council having undertaken a 'detailed analysis'[43] to satisfy itself that the needs can be met elsewhere. In most situations there is no set choreography that has to be followed between a proposal to close a centre and the care planning for those attending. Generally what occurs will be characterised (in the words of Stadlen J in *R (B) v Worcestershire CC*[44]) as:

> ... a multi-staged decision-making process [where] it is not possible at the first stage of the process or of closure to identify where the people will go, what their needs will be and whether those places will satisfy their needs.

7.25   Stadlen J accepted,[45] however, that in cases where service users have high level and very specific needs the care planning and the closure proposals may have to be linked – for example, if the authority was not sure that it could meet the disabled person's assessed needs at an alternative placement.

Practical assistance in the home (domiciliary services)

7.26   Means and Smith[46] chart the historical development of the home help service from its first statutory appearances in the Maternity and Child Welfare Act 1918, through the Public Health Act 1936 and its expansion during the World War II[47] (due in part to the mass discharge of frail and ill older people from hospital at that time) and the early involvement of the Women's Voluntary Service due to wartime labour shortages. The Beveridge reforms (discussed in the introduction to this book) created parallel duties to provide such support under the NHS legislation – eg NHSA 1946 s29[48] and under NAA 1948 s29. The NAA 1948 duty was reinforced by CSDPA 1970 s2(1)(a), which spoke of the provision of 'practical assistance' in the home. These various duties were repealed (insofar as they apply to adults) by the CA 2014.[49] The previous case-law is, however, of direct relevance since the CA 2014 s8(1) duty to provide (among other things) 'care and support at home or in the community' has been phrased to encompass and widen the previous provisions.[50] The phrase covers the provision of some home

---

43 See *R (B) v Worcestershire County Council* [2009] EWHC 2915 (Admin), (2010) 13 CCLR 13 at paras 76, 86 and 104.

44 [2009] EWHC 2915 (Admin), (2010) 13 CCLR 13 at para 85.

45 [2009] EWHC 2915 (Admin), (2010) 13 CCLR 13.

46 R Means and R Smith, *From Poor Law to community care*, Policy Press, 1998, pp81–92.

47 Defence (General Regulations) 1939 reg 68E; and Ministry of Heath Circular 179/44 'Domestic help'.

48 For 'households where such help is required owing to the presence of any person who is ill, lying-in, an expectant mother, mentally defective, aged or a child not over compulsory school age'. The duty reappeared in the subsequent NHS Acts, most recently as NHSA 2006 Sch 20 para 3, which was, however, repealed by Care Act 2014 and Children and Families Act 2014 (Consequential Amendments) Order 2015 SI No 914 Sch 1 para 83.

49 The Care Act 2014 and the Children and Families Act 2014 (Consequential Amendments) Order 2015 SI No 914.

50 Joint Committee on the Draft Care and Support Bill, 'Draft Care and Support Bill', HL Paper 143 HC 822, The Stationery Office, 2013, paras 168–170.

adaptations[51] and complements the powers under CA 2014 s8(1)(d) to provide 'facilities' (see para 4.31 below).

7.27   Although it is possible to divide domiciliary services into two broad categories – those primarily concerned with the maintenance of the home (eg, house cleaning, ironing, decorating etc) and those primarily concerned with the personal care of the disabled person (eg, help with getting out of and into bed, dressing, cooking, laundry, a sitting service etc) – it would be a mistake to suggest that the first category is of less importance than the second.[52] As noted above (para 4.17) two of the 'outcomes' in the eligibility regulations relate to the first category – ie (e) being able to make use of the adult's home safely; and (f) maintaining a habitable home environment – and four of the second – ie (a) managing and maintaining nutrition; (b) maintaining personal hygiene; (c) managing toilet needs; and (d) being appropriately clothed).[53]

7.28   Notwithstanding the identification of 'home maintenance' outcomes in the regulations and the CA 2014's presumption that the 'individual is best-placed to judge' his or her well-being (CA 2014 s1(3)(a) and see para 2.17 above), many social services departments are resistant to providing support of this nature. While it may follow that a need for personal care will generally be of higher priority (have a more 'significant' impact) than a need to live in a clean and safe environment, this will not always be the case.[54]

7.29   The local government ombudsman has held it to be maladministration for a council to have criteria that stipulate that no domestic assistance can be provided – unless accompanied by a need for personal care.[55] Previous (2000) guidance emphasised this point:[56]

> ... local authorities that have decided not to provide or commission certain services as community care services – such as shopping only, cleaning only, or other low-level services – should review their positions. Such services, if targeted purposively, can be of genuine assistance in sustaining the caring relationship, and be cost effective.

7.30   Potential service responses to needs identified by the eligibility regulations are very considerable, but will of course include traditional support such as

51 Home Adaptations Consortium, *Home adaptations for disabled people: a detailed guide to related legislation, guidance and good practice*, Care and Repair England, 2013, para 1.10.

52 Despite help with housework and other domestic tasks being highly valued and important 'proactive' support services, in practice social services do not consider these to be a priority – see eg T Ware and others, 'Commissioning care services for older people in England: the view from care managers, users and carers' (2003) *Ageing and Society* no 23, pp411–428; H Clark and others, *That bit of help: the high value of low level preventative services for older people*, Policy Press, 1998; J Francis and A Netten, 'Raising the quality of home care: a study of service users' views', (2004) *Social Policy and Administration*, no 38, pp290–305 (cited in C Glendinning and others, *Social Care Institute for Excellence (SCIE) adults' services knowledge review 13: outcomes-focused services for older people*, Policy Press, 2006, para 1.4.4.

53 Care and Support (Eligibility Criteria) Regulations 2015 SI No 313 reg 2(2).

54 See for instance, Complaint no 09 013 172 against Worcestershire CC, 6 July 2011.

55 Complaint no 01/C/17519 against Salford CC, 11 December 2003.

56 Department of Health, *Practitioners guide to carers' assessments under the Carers and Disabled Children Act 2000*, 2001, para 80.

that provided by care assistants, equipment, home adaptations, laundry,[57] house cleaning, shopping, cooking, the provision of meals, community activities etc.

7.31   Despite the value accorded to home help by disabled and elderly people, and their carers (and the demographic/deinstitutionalisation trends noted above), there has been a steady decline in the number of households receiving this support – falling from 528,500 in 1992 to 469,000 in 2014/15:[58] a proportion low by international standards.[59] All too often the home help that is provided, comes in inappropriately short, 'undignified and unsafe' timeslots (for example, 15 minutes)[60] provided by the independent sector.[61] In 2015, concerns about quality prompted the National Institute of Health and Social Care Excellence (NICE) to issue its first guidance concerning quality standards in the home care sector.[62]

7.32   Not only have some authorities adopted arbitrary and unlawful policies of not providing domestic assistance, many have also restricted their bathing support to cases where there is an identified medical need – essentially requiring the disabled person to produce a doctor's letter verifying that such a medical need exists. The local government ombudsman considers this to be maladministration – to suggest that bathing is not an essential activity. Some authorities have attempted to circumvent their duty to provide bathing assistance by suggesting that the 'service response' to a person's 'need to clean' might be a strip wash rather than a bath. In this respect, the ombudsman has held that the ability properly to manage bathing/washing with dignity is the entitlement of everybody[63] – and the eligibility regulations would now appear to close this off as an acceptable service response to such an identified need (see para 4.17 above).

7.33   In *R (T, D and B) v Haringey LBC*[64] the court held that the concept of 'practical assistance' within the meaning of CSDPA 1970 s2 could not cover the provision of services akin to medical treatment (in this case the replacement of oesophageal feeding tubes – see para 12.31 below) even where this service was not being undertaken by a qualified nurse.

7.34   The scope of CA 2014 s8(1) is less restrictive (in terms of permissible 'service' responses) than that under CSDPA 1970 s2, and would appear to enable the provision of equipment such as a personal computer, tablet, smartphone or similar system, as well as aids that facilitate community

---

57 Help with laundry was a support services that could be provided under CSDPA 1970 s2 as well as under NHSA 2006 Sch 20 para 3 (which was repealed by the CA 2014).

58 NHS Digital, *Community care statistics, social services activity, England – 2013–14*, 2014.

59 Commission for Social Care Inspection (CSCI), *Time to care? An overview of home care services for older people in England*, 2006, p4.

60 CSCI, *Time to care? An overview of home care services for older people in England*, 2006.

61 CSCI, *Time to care? An overview of home care services for older people in England*, 2006 – the proportion of home care purchased from independent sector increased from two per cent in 1992 to more than 73 per cent in 2005.

62 NICE, *Home care: delivering personal care and practical support to older people living in their own homes* NG 21, 2015.

63 Complaint nos 02/C/8679, 8681 and 10389 against Bolsover DC, 30 September 2003.

64 [2005] EWHC 2235 (Admin), (2006) 9 CCLR 58.

living such as a sound loop or audio-headphone for people with impaired hearing.[65]

7.35 Where home assistance is provided, it must suitable to meet the assessed needs – it must be 'fit for purpose' to meet the assessed needs. The statutory guidance advises that 'short home-care visits of 15 minutes or less are not appropriate for people who need support with intimate care needs, though such visits may be appropriate for checking someone has returned home safely from visiting a day centre, or whether medication has been taken' (para 4.101). NICE social care guidelines[66] require that local authorities ensure that home care workers have enough time to provide a good quality service, including having enough time to talk to the person and their carer, and to have sufficient travel time between appointments (para 1.4.1) and that home care visits shorter than half an hour should be made only if: the home care worker is known to the person, and the visit is part of a wider package of support, and it allows enough time to complete specific, time limited tasks or to check if someone is safe and well (para 1.4.2).

Work, educational, training and recreational support

7.36 The eligibility regulations give particular emphasis to adults in need and carers 'engaging in work, training, education or volunteering', as well as being enabled to use 'necessary facilities or services in the local community, including ... recreational facilities or services'.[67] The necessary CA 2014 s8(1) care and support responses to address these can be home or community based and would include both 'goods and services'.

7.37 The previous case-law on the provision of such support will also remain relevant, since similar (but less powerful) obligations existed under the NAA 1948,[68] the CSDPA 1970[69] and Carers (Equal Opportunities) Act (C(EO)A) 2004 s2. The duties under the NAA 1948 were largely directed at sheltered employment, and those under the CSDPA 1970 focussed on occupying the 'workless' – ie 'the provision of lectures, games outings or other recreational facilities outside' the home and the provision of a 'wireless, television, library or similar recreational facilities'. The C(EO)A 2004 created no duty to provide such support, merely a duty to consider during an assessment, the carer's work, education, training and leisure aspirations.

---

65 Equipment that would formerly have been provided under NAA 1948 s29 (LAC (93)10 appendix 2 para 2(1)(b)) namely 'facilities for social rehabilitation and adjustment to disability including assistance in overcoming limitations of mobility or communication'.

66 NICE, *Home care: delivering personal care and practical support to older people living in their own homes* NG21, 2015.

67 Care and Support (Eligibility Criteria) Regulations 2015 SI No 313 regs 2(2)(h), (i) and 3(2)(b)(vi), (vii).

68 At 'centres or elsewhere, [of] facilities for occupational, social, cultural and recreational activities' – see LAC (93)10 appendix 2 para 2(1)(c).

69 Sections 2(1)(b) and (c).

7.38   The CA 2014 is more directive in terms of the importance of work, educational, training and recreational support – both in the well-being principles (section 1(2)(e)) and the eligibility regulations.[70] It therefore opens the way for a new set of support arrangements. It also raises the expectations of adults in need, carers and disabled children/young carers in transition:[71] that for them, care and support arrangements will be made to facilitate these key outcomes.

7.39   The statutory guidance provides welcome advice concerning the sort of employment, educational and training support services that carers (including young carers in transition – see para 15.191) and disabled children in transition) can expect. It is, however, curiously laconic when it comes to explicit guidance on the equivalent support services that adults in need can expect. However, it must be that the carer/young adults' examples apply equally to all eligible individuals. Examples in the statutory guidance that focus on this group include (para 4.26) advice that young adults with learning disabilities will 'require new forms of care and support to live independently' and that these may include such things as 'employment support, training'. The guidance stresses that this will also be the case for carers – for example:

> ... some parent carers need extra support to juggle caring and paid work after their child leaves full time education. Loss of paid employment can have a significant impact on the carer's well-being and self-esteem as well as a significant impact on the family's financial circumstances. Similar issues can affect young carers ... support for a carer to manage an increased caring role (that allows them to stay in paid work if they wish to do so) can help families manage the transition and save money by avoiding unwanted out-of-county placements.

7.40   This advice is picked up in relation to all carers (statutory guidance, para 6.123) for whom local authorities must consider whether they 'can continue in their job, and contribute to society, apply themselves in education, volunteer to support civil society or have the opportunity to get a job, if they are not in employment'. Providing longer periods of replacement care is given as an example of one way of providing this support (para 11.39) 'to enable carers to have a longer break from caring responsibilities or to balance caring with education or paid employment'.

7.41   CSDPA 1970 s2(1)(c) placed a duty on local authorities to assist disabled adults[72] 'in taking advantage of educational facilities' available to them. Classically this would have been the disabled student who needed personal social care support while at college or university. The CA 2014 widens this obligation to include carers (including young carers) – and of course this duty applies to eligible individuals of any age. The example in the statutory guidance is, however, one that concerns a younger person, stating:

> The objective should be to ensure that there will be an appropriate package of care and support in place from the day the young person or carer starts

---

70 Care and Support (Eligibility Criteria) Regulations 2015 SI No 313 regs 2(2)(h), (i) and 3(2)(b)(vi), (vii).
71 See para 15.91 below; as well as statutory guidance, para 4.26.
72 And still does for disabled children.

at the institution. In many cases a young person or carer studying at university will have a dual location, for example coming home to stay with the parents during weekends or holidays. Where this is the case, local authorities must ensure their needs are met all year round (para 16.79).

7.42　In *R (M) v Birmingham City Council*[73] (a case under the CSDPA 1970) the court considered that the duty included personal care assistance at the educational facility, as well as escorted travel to and from it – and potentially it could include the provision of additional facilities at the institution. The relevant guidance at that time[74] stressed that the duty covered funding the personal care requirements of such students so as to enable them to pursue their studies (even if those studies are undertaken outside the local authority's area). The relevant part of the guidance stated:

> 9. Social services departments have been reminded of their duty ... to make arrangements for assisting a disabled person who is ordinarily resident in their area in taking advantage of educational facilities available to him/her, (even where provision is made outside that local authority's area), if they are satisfied that it is necessary in order to meet that person's needs. Such assistance might, in appropriate cases include the funding by the local authority of the personal care required to enable the student in question to pursue his/her studies. It is, of course, for the authority to decide, in each case, what the individual's needs are, and how they are to be met.

7.43　The scope of CA 2014 s8(1) is, as noted above, less restrictive (in terms of permissible 'service' responses) than that under CSDPA 1970 s2, and would appear to enable the provision of educational 'goods and facilities' such as a computers, iPads, tablets, smartphones, accessible IT software, a Wi-Fi service, 'talking books'[75] etc.[76] It is probably the case that the duty under the CA 2014 (as with the earlier duties) relates to facilitating access to work, education or training programmes – rather than the provision of the work, education or training itself,[77] although the CA 2014 fails to spell out the limits of its scope in these domains (unlike with healthcare or housing – see paras 12.12 and 14.12 below). As with the pre-CA 2014 regime, it is likely that inter-agency disputes will continue in relation to support services for which there is an overlapping NHS responsibility (for example, communication assistance via speech synthesisers, speech therapy, hearing and writing aids etc).

Travel and other assistance

7.44　Travel assistance is clearly a service that can be provided under CA 2014 s8 – in order to enable the adult in need or carer to make use of necessary

73　[2009] EWHC 688 (Admin), (2009) 12 CCLR 40.
74　LAC (93)12.
75　Complaint 11 017 875 against Suffolk County Council, 11 October 2012, para 6.
76　Ie including equipment that would formerly have been provided under NAA 1948 s29 (LAC (93)10 appendix 2 para 2(1)(b)) namely 'facilities for social rehabilitation and adjustment to disability including assistance in overcoming limitations of mobility or communication'.
77　Per Jowitt J, in *R v Further Education Funding Council and Bradford MBC ex p Parkinson* (1996) *Times* 31 October.

facilities or services in the local community. In relation to adults in need, the support can also extend to assisting the individual to make use of the transport itself (eg by way of an escort, or training etc).[78] In *Hurley v Secretary of State for Work and Pensions*[79] counsel for the secretary of state confirmed that the CA 2014 provided for 'stronger rights of and support for carers, which could include help with fares when travelling to the recipient of the care'.

7.45   The provision of transport under the CA 2014 continues the duty which was found in both the NAA 1948 (s29) and CSDPA 1970 (s2(1)(d)).

7.46   Where a local authority has assessed a person as eligible for care and support and one of the person's support needs is to make use of necessary facilities or services in the local community, the authority must ensure that this need is met. In the case of an adult in need, it cannot assume that a carer is willing or able to provide this and, as noted below, cannot assume that a person is able to fund this service himself or herself – for example, through the use of the person's mobility component of his or her disability living allowance (DLA) or personal independence payment (PIP). The care plan must therefore address this question, and a failure to provide for an appropriate and flexible arrangement will amount to maladministration.[80]

7.47   A 2016 ombudsman report[81] identified maladministration in a council's decision to reduce an adult's personal budget even though it accepted that his needs had not altered. The new budget had made no allowance of his transport to a day centre – which the council agreed to reinstate.

7.48   While social services authorities are empowered (but not obliged) to charge for such transport services (see chapter 8 below), in assessing a person's ability to pay, the person's mobility component (if received) must be ignored.[82] In this context, policy guidance issued by the Department of Health in 2012[83] would appear to be equally applicable to the CA 2014. It referred to evidence that 'some local authorities were taking the mobility component into account when considering what social services to be provide'. It then stated that the 'Department would like to make the position clear' that:

> ... local councils have a duty to assess the needs of any person for whom the authority may provide or arrange the provision of community care services and who may be in need of such services. They have a further duty to decide, having regard to the results of the assessment, what, if any, services they should provide to meet the individual's needs. This duty does not change because a particular individual is receiving the mobility component of Disability Living Allowance.

---

78 Care and Support (Eligibility Criteria) Regulations 2015 SI No 313 regs 2(2)(i) and 3(2)(b)(vii).

79 [2015] EWHC 3382 (Admin) at para 25 and see also para 6.

80 Complaint no 07C03887 against Bury MBC, 14 October 2009, paras 27 and 45.

81 Complaint no 16 000 679 against London Borough of Barking & Dagenham, 31 August 2016.

82 Social Security Contributions and Benefits Act 1992 s73(14).

83 Department of Health, *Charging for residential accommodation and non-residential care services* LAC(DH) (2012)03, 2012, paras 9–11.

7.49   The Welsh ombudsman has found maladministration where a local authority refused to provide transport to a day centre for a new service user because she was in receipt of the DLA mobility component. This did not apply to existing service users. Systematic maladministration was found on the basis there was an absence of any policy framework and no written guidelines on the eligibility of clients who could use local authority run transport.[84]

7.50   The application of any transport policy affecting disabled and older people engages the Equality Act (EA) 2010. It follows that all such polices must be considered from the perspective of the authority's public sector equality duty (section 149 – see para 2.59 above). Accordingly, a failure at a general level to consider this duty when making changes to such a policy will constitute maladministration,[85] as will such a failure on an individual level – for example, a failure by a council to provide appropriate home transport for a disabled child after attending an after-school club.[86] Regardless of any equality obligations, it will of course be maladministration to change a transport arrangement (eg changing the provider of this service) without discussing this with the service user.[87]

Home adaptations under the Care Act 2014

Adaptations

7.51   As noted above, the illustrative list of care and support 'services' that can be provided under CA 2014 s8 is much briefer than that provided under the pre-CA 2014 legal regime,[88] and the select committee sought (and received) confirmation from the government[89] that assistance with home 'adaptations' (among other services) fell within the ambit of the list. The statutory guidance advises that the range of services under the CA 2014 includes community equipment services and adaptations (para 2.9) and support such as assistive technology in the home or equipment/adaptations (para 10.12). Although the CA 2014 (section 23) limits a social services authority's power to provide basic housing (as this is an obligation under the Housing Act 1996 – see para 7.98 below), the guidance makes clear that this does not limit the power of the social services authority to provide housing related care and support such as housing adaptations (para 15.52), community equipment, telecare and aids (para 15.62).

7.52   Support with home adaptations and equipment is often vital to enable adults in need to live independently in the community. Commonly, this

---

84 Complaint no B2004/0180 against Newport City Council, 31 August 2006.
85 See the local government ombudsman report concerning complaints against seven councils commencing no 07B15825 against Havant Borough Council, 28 September 2009.
86 *Bedfordshire CC v D* [2009] EWCA Civ 6789.
87 Summary of a report issued under section 21 of the Public Services Ombudsman (Wales) Act 2005, Case Number: 200900664 (2010).
88 For example, in CSDPA 1970 s2.
89 Joint Committee on the Draft Care and Support Bill, 'Draft Care and Support Bill', HL Paper 143 HC 822, The Stationery Office, 2013, paras 168–170.

support can be provided by the housing authority by way of a disabled facilities grant (DFG) under the Housing Grants, Construction and Regeneration Act (HGCRA) 1996, and this process is considered separately at para 14.31 below. Not infrequently, the HCGRA 1996 may not address some or all of the individual's needs for adaptations and/or specialist equipment. This may be because the individual is ineligible for the grant or that the grant does not cover the work in question, or that the cost of the work exceeds the maximum mandatory grant. Disputes concerning local authority responsibilities for adaptations have attracted a disproportionately high number of complaints to the local government ombudsman – particularly the failure of social services authorities to be aware of their responsibilities (which now derive from the CA 2014).

7.53   The importance of adaptations is central to eligibility determinations – the eligibility regulations list as key outcomes (among others) 'being able to make use of the adult's home safely' and (for adults in need and carers) 'maintaining a habitable home environment' (regs 2(2)(e), (f) and 3(2)(b)(iii)). The statutory guidance (at para 6.107) gives examples of what these might mean – including consideration (in relation to (e)) of:

> ... the adult's ability to move around the home safely, which could for example include getting up steps, using kitchen facilities or accessing the bathroom. This should also include the immediate environment around the home such as access to the property, for example steps leading up to the home.

Interface with the disabled facilities grant obligation

7.54   Although the relationship between the duties under the HGCRA 1996 and CA 2014 is best characterised as one of overlapping and complementary responsibilities, in practice the existence of separate 'housing' and 'social care' duties has created a pretext for considerable administrative delay.[90]

7.55   In general, if social services identify an eligible need during a CA 2014 assessment that it considers should be addressed by an adaptation that could be covered by a DFG, then it would appear reasonable that the authority assist the disabled person to make an application to the housing authority for such a grant. All too often, however, the applicant will then be advised that before the DFG application can be made, an occupational therapist will have to undertake an assessment and that there is a lengthy waiting list. The problem of chronic delay in this context is well documented and, notwithstanding many critical reports from the local government ombudsman, persists.

7.56   When such delay occurs and the grant is being processed by a separate council (ie a district council), the appropriate response from the social services authority will be to assist the disabled person in resolving the problem – by actively intervening in the process if needs be. Such delay, however, does not of itself absolve the social services authority of its separate responsibility under the CA 2014: indeed it is maladministration for a council to fail to appreciate that it has a distinct duty to provide adap-

---

90 See paras 9.121 and 15.113 for a general analysis of the ombudsman's comments on such delay.

tations, separate from the obligation to process DFGs.[91] This point was emphasised in a pre-CA 2014 circular[92] which referred to the social services department as the 'lead body', and (as noted below) stated that its duty to act remained, regardless of the housing authority's actions.

7.57   Typically, home adaptations concern such matters as stair lifts, ground-floor extensions, doorway widening, ramps and wheelchair accessible showers. Unlike under HGCRA 1996 Part I (considered at para 14.31 below), the CA 2014 imposes no requirement that work be either 'appropriate' or 'reasonable and practicable'. All the CA 2014 requires is that the social services authority be satisfied that a duty arises under section 18.

7.58   This difference of approach was illustrated by the pre-CA 2014 guidance[93] which stressed that the introduction of DFGs did not change the responsibilities of social service's authorities (under what was then CSDPA 1970 s2). It noted, however, that their responsibility would 'in many instances, be effectively discharged on their behalf by the housing authority' by the making of a DFG. It then identified two specific situations where the underlying social services duty would be of particular relevance. The first being where the adaptations exceeded the scope of the HGCRA 1996, stating:

> 16. Such a responsibility might arise when for instance the [social services] authority considers there is need related to the individual's social needs that demands a greater level of provision than is required for the disability alone, and where the housing authority chooses not to exercise its discretionary powers. This may occur, for example, where the size of a bedroom for a disabled child is required to be greater than is necessary for sleeping, because it needs to fulfil the role of bed/sitting room to provide more independent social space.

7.59   The second situation arose where the individual asked the social services authority for financial assistance 'with that part of the costs of an adaptation which he is expected to finance himself in the light of the test of resources for the disabled facilities grant' noting that this might 'be as much as the total costs of the adaptation' (para 17). The guidance advised that in such cases there was a duty to assist.[94] It advised that in deciding how to provide support and 'in order to maintain consistency' the local authority should consider applying the same charging rules as for other social care support 'provided that they consider that the client is able to afford to repay this' – and should also consider alternatives, include loans,

---

91 Complaint no 05/C/13157 against Leeds City Council, 20 November 2007.
92 LAC (90)7 paras 14–15 which (insofar as it applied to social services authorities) remained in force until 2015 and would appear to be of continuing relevance: substituting references to the CSDPA 1970 with those to the CA 2014.
93 LAC (90)7 at paras 15–17 and also at para 58, for the full text of which see the 5th edition of this book, para 9.114. Similar advice was given in Department of the Environment circular guidance 17/96 paras 5–6; for the full text of which see the 5th edition of this book, para 9.115.
94 This advice was the subject of adverse comment by Richards J in *R (Spink) v Wandsworth LBC* [2004] EWHC 2314 (Admin) at para 59 in that he considered the duty did not necessarily crystalise if the disabled person had the resources to meet the identified. The judgment was upheld by the Court of Appeal – [2005] EWCA Civ 302, (2005) 8 CCLR 272.

with or without interest, possibly secured in either case by a charge on the property[95] or the placing of a charge on the property for a set period.

7.60   There is no reason to believe that the social services 'safety net' duty in relation to adaptations has been changed by the substitution of the CA 2014 for the previous duty under the CSDPA 1970.

7.61   Where a DFG is insufficient to cover the full cost of the necessary works, the social services authority can make up the shortfall by way of support under the CA 2014 and/or the housing authority can assist using its powers under the Regulatory Reform (Housing Assistance) (England and Wales) Order 2002 SI No 1860 (see para 14.92 below). In either situation, the relevant council can impose conditions on such a 'top-up' payment. In *R (BG) v Medway Council*[96] the High Court held that it was not unreasonable for a local authority in a case such as this to make the payment by way of a loan secured as a 20-year legal charge on the home which would not be repayable, unless the disabled person ceased to reside at the property during that period, and that any amount repayable would be subject to interest. In this case, the authority had agreed that in the event of repayment being required, it would have regard to the family's personal and financial circumstances and would not act unreasonably by insisting repayment immediately or on terms that would result in financial hardship.

7.62   The duty to provide adaptations under CA 2014 s18 will only crystalise when (among other things) there has been a financial assessment. Accordingly, case-law under the CSDPA 1970 concerning applicants who were not prepared to complete such an assessment would appear to be of no continuing relevance for disabled adults.[97]

Delay

7.63   As has been noted the local authority duties to assist with adaptations is all too frequently associated with unreasonable delay. In assessing whether this is unlawful or constitutes maladministration, it is necessary to consider separately the social services and the housing statutory obligations. In relation to the social services duty (now under the CA 2014), the principles relevant to the assessment and provision of services timetable apply – see para 3.58 above. The assessment will generally require specialist involvement and this may result in delay. The local government ombudsman has produced a number of reports on this issue.[98] A 1991[99] report for example dealt with a situation where the complainant had (among other things) waited nine months for an occupational therapist's (OT) assessment. In finding maladministration, the report noted:

95 Such a charge could presumably only be secured on the property with the owner's consent.
96 [2005] EWHC 1932 (Admin), (2005) 8 CCLR 448.
97 *R (Spink) v Wandsworth LBC* [2005] EWCA Civ 302, (2005) 8 CCLR 272, an unusual fact case, concerned CSDPA 1970 s2 which required that the authority be 'satisfied' that the support was 'necessary'; and see also *Freeman v Lockett* [2006] EWHC 102 (QB).
98 See para 20.87 below where the ombudsman's role is considered.
99 Complaint no 90/C/0336 against Redbridge LBC, 3 October 1991.

The Council say that they suffered from a shortage of OTs during 1989; while I recognise that this is a national problem, nevertheless the Council still retain their responsibility to assess their client's needs. If sufficient OTs are not available, they may need to find another way of assessing those needs.

7.64   The finding in this case does not, of course, mean that delays of less than nine months are acceptable: indeed the ombudsman has suggested that for even complex assessments, the time from an OT referral to the completion of his or her report would not exceed three months.[100] The finding means, however, that any council, knowing that the use of OTs for an assessment will cause a substantial delay, is guilty of maladministration when it opts to use OTs (ie, it is maladministration the moment such a procedure is adopted).

7.65   Unlike the CA 2014, the HGCRA 1996 s36 allows for the delayed payment of a DFG – up to a maximum of 12 months following the date of the application. The issue of delay in relation to DFGs is considered further at para 14.106 below.

7.66   In relation to the pre-CA 2014 regime, it was suggested that since the duty under the CSDPA 1970 only arose where the authority was satisfied its assistance was 'necessary', that the duty did not in general arise (if at all) until after a DFG application had been determined.[101] Although the CA 2014 does not use the same phrasing, it is important to appreciate why this was (and remains) an unattractive argument. Most obviously, this will be evident in cases of relative urgency. As noted above, the HGCRA 1996 permits a delay of the processing and the payment of a grant. In such a case, it would be unlawful for a social services authority to refuse to address a person's needs for an adaptation under the CA 2014 on the ground that it was possible that at some time in the future that a DFG might be awarded.

Equipment and additional facilities

Generally

7.67   As noted above (para 7.26) the CA 2014 replicates the duties in the previous statutory regime (and particularly CSDPA 1970 s2(1)(e)) in relation to the provision of community equipment and 'additional facilities' required by the individual. The need for these will generally relate to the outcomes listed in the eligibility regulations – for example, to enable the person to eat, drink, maintain personal hygiene, manage his or her toilet needs, dress, make use of his or her home safely and so on.

7.68   The statutory guidance refers to equipment/minor household adaptions in terms of preventative services (eg at para 6.25) and gives examples of the range of support, including 'assistive technology' (para 10.12), 'Information and Communication Technologies (ICT) equipment' (para 10.48) and 'telecare, aids and adaptations' (para 15.62). Not infrequently, support of this kind will include all manner of fittings and gadgets such

---

100 Complaint no 07/A/11108 against Surrey CC, 11 November 2008.
101 See *R (Fay) v Essex CC* [2004] EWHC 879 (Admin) at para 28.

as handrails, alarm systems, hoists, movable baths, adapted switches, handles, mobility scooter shelters and so on.

7.69 'Telecare' is largely predicated on the idea of technology for remote monitoring of the home such as pendant alarms, detectors for falls or movements or to confirm a bed is occupied etc. Although a number of authorities are investing significant sums in this technology, the research evidence questions its effectiveness.[102]

7.70 The importance of the provision of appropriate equipment in promoting the independence and quality of disabled peoples' lives attracted considerable attention about 15 years ago, but little specific guidance appears to have emerged since then. The emphasis was (and presumably remains) on the speedy provision of such equipment. This became a performance indicator under the pre-CA 2014 regime.[103] The *National service framework for older people*,[104] for instance, advised that (at para 2.48):

- services should take a preventive approach, recognising that effective equipment provision (including for people with moderate disabilities) is likely to:
  - help older people to maintain their independence and live at home
  - slow down deterioration in function and consequent loss of confidence and self-esteem
  - prevent accidents
  - prevent pressure sore damage
  - support and better protect the health of carers
- services should be timely and resolve the frequently long delays which inhibit older people's discharge from hospital, or their safety and confidence in coping at home.[105]

7.71 Two critical Audit Commission reports (2000 and 2002) on the state of public provision of equipment for disabled people[106] found that equipment services were in a parlous state; that users reported 'long delays for equipment of dubious quality'. The recommendation for a substantial overhaul of the service led to a government initiative to establish integrated 'community equipment services' where both NHS and social services equipment could be accessed at a single point. Each integrated community equipment service is required to meet the following criteria:[107]

- revenue funding from pooled health and social services contributions using Health Act 1999 flexibilities;

---

102 See Adam Steventon and others, 'Effect of telecare on use of health and social care services: findings from the Whole Systems Demonstrator cluster randomised trial' *Age and Ageing* (2013) 42(4), pp501–508 which suggests that telecare aids did not lead to significant reductions in service use.

103 Indicator AO/D54 (2006–07): the percentage of items of equipment and adaptations delivered within seven working days – see para 1.30 above.

104 See para 15.6 below.

105 This final point is given considerable emphasis in the now superseded NHS hospital discharge guidance: Department of Health, *Discharge from hospital: pathway, process and practice*, February 2003, appendix 5.3.1, pp71–72.

106 Audit Commission, *Fully equipped: the provision of equipment to older or disabled people by the NHS and social services in England and Wales*, 2000; and *Fully equipped 2002: assisting independence*, 2002; see also Department of Health, *Transforming community services. Demonstrating and measuring achievement: community indicators for quality improvement*, 2011.

107 *Community equipment services* HSC 2001/008; LAC (2001)13, para 8.

- a single operational manager for the service;[108]
- a board to advise the manager, whose members include representatives of stakeholder organisations;
- unified stock.

7.72   The guidance accompanying this initiative[109] defined 'community equipment' as follows:

> Community equipment is equipment for home nursing usually provided by the NHS, such as pressure relief mattresses and commodes, and equipment for daily living such as shower chairs and raised toilet seats, usually provided by local authorities. It also includes, but is not limited to:
> - Minor adaptations, such as grab rails, lever taps and improved domestic lighting.
> - Ancillary equipment for people with sensory impairments, such as liquid level indicators, hearing loops, assistive listening devices and flashing doorbells.
> - Communication aids for people with speech impairments.
> - Wheelchairs for short term loan, but not those for permanent wheelchair users, as these are prescribed and funded by different NHS services.[110]
> - Telecare equipment such as fall alarms, gas escape alarms and health state monitoring for people who are vulnerable.

7.73   The above guidance makes plain that the provision of some forms of equipment may be construed as joint social services/NHS responsibility. Similarly, some forms of equipment can be viewed as a joint social services/housing authority responsibility. An early community care circular[111] sought to clarify this question (at para 19):

> ... equipment which can be installed and removed with little or no structural modification to the dwelling should usually be considered the responsibility of the [social services] authority. However, items such as stair lifts and through-floor lifts, which are designed to facilitate access into or around the dwelling would, in the view of the Secretaries of State, be eligible for disabled facilities grant. With items such as electric hoists, it is suggested that any structural modification of the property – such as strengthened joists or modified lintels – could be grant aidable under the disabled facilities grant, but that the hoisting equipment itself should be the responsibility of the [social services] authority.

7.74   The CSDPA 1970 made specific reference to the provision of a telephone and any special equipment necessary to enable its use.[112] Clearly technology has moved on considerably in the intervening period, but the CA 2014 will continue, and widen, the scope for such support – for example, the installation of a telephone line as well as the provision of an appropriate handset, loud telephone bell (or a flashing visual or vibrating signal), amplifiers, inductive couplers for personal hearing aids, visual transmission machines such as minicoms, modems, broadband and so on.

---

108 Now NHSA 2006 s75/NHS(W)A 2006 s33.
109 LAC (2001)13, para 7.
110 See para 11.77 below concerning the provision of permanent wheelchairs.
111 LAC (90)7.
112 CSDPA 1970 s2(1)(h).

Minor adaptations under £1,000

7.75   Community equipment (aids and minor adaptations) are to be provided by social services authorities without charge. These are defined by the Care and Support (Charging and Assessment of Resources) Regulations 2014 SI No 2672 ('the charging regulations')[113] as:

> ... an aid, or a minor adaptation to property, for the purpose of assisting with nursing at home or aiding daily living and ... an adaptation is minor if the cost of making the adaptation is £1,000 or less.

It follows that there is no cost limit on the value of the equipment provided under this provision: the cost limit (of £1,000) only applies to minor adaptations.

7.76   This wording replicates provisions in the (now repealed) Community Care (Delayed Discharges etc) Act 2003.[114] In relation to this duty, 2013 guidance advised:

> 2.27 ... For adaptations the cost limit applies to the purchase and fitting of the adaptation. Social services authorities retain the discretion to charge for adaptations costing over £1,000 where those adaptations are made by the authority under its powers to provide community care services.

> 2.28 It should be noted that this regulation requires social services authorities to pay for minor adaptations costing up to £1,000 if they are for 'the purposes of assisting with nursing at home or aiding daily living'. The authority may not apply any test of resources but may apply local criteria regarding priority for assessment under 'Fair Access to Care Services' (FACS). Experience shows that the boundaries between community equipment/minor adaptations and adaptations generally are sometimes confused and in these situations, funding from the housing authority may be used to address a welfare authority responsibility.

7.77   Early guidance to the Community Care (Delayed Discharges etc) Act 2003 advised that 'all community equipment for older people (eg aids and minor adaptations) will be provided within seven days'.[115]

7.78   Many minor adaptations are relatively routine and straightforward and do not, therefore, require the input of an occupational therapist before being approved and provided. The College of Occupational Therapists has produced an excellent two-volume guide which identifies a range of minor adaptations for which there is a clear consensus that initial assessment by an OT is generally not required (such as grab and hand rails, threshold ramps and drop kerbs, kitchen and bathroom taps and handles).[116]

7.79   Concern has been expressed about social services authorities' responding inappropriately to requests for community equipment assistance. A

113 Reg 3(2)(a) and (3) pursuant to CA 2014 s14(5).

114 Community Care (Delayed Discharges etc) Act ss15 and 16; and Community Care (Delayed Discharges etc) Act (Qualifying Services) (England) Regulations 2003 SI No 1196 reg 3.

115 Department of Health, *Discharge from hospital: pathway, process and practice*, 2003, para 2.3 – now superseded by *Ready to go? Planning the discharge and the transfer of patients from hospital and intermediate care* (2010) which is silent on this question: see para 5.8 above.

116 College of Occupational Therapists, *Minor adaptations without delay: a practical guide and technical specifications for housing associations*, 2006.

2009 report[117] highlighted the primary responsibility of such authorities for the provision of this support and commented critically on the fact that in a number of cases social services had not conducted a proper assessment of need; had fettered their discretion by stating that they did not provide help with, for example, electrically operated adjustable beds or chairs; and had purported to discharge their statutory duties not by meeting the need but directing applicants to other agencies.

7.80   Evidence suggests that this practice continues, with some authorities no longer providing 'small items of equipment' in their stores, and instead signposting those in need, to where such items can be purchased. The legality of such approach will depend upon what is meant by a 'small item'; the procedure by which this policy decision was reached; and the extent to which it is applied as a 'blanket policy'. In principle, such policies would appear questionable given that the basic requirement is that such equipment 'be provided free of charge'[118] and the Department of Health 2010 policy guidance advises that 'councils should not assume that low-level needs will always be equated with low-level services or that complex or critical needs will always require complex, costly services in response'.[119] A brief 2015 statement by the Department of Health[120] has been issued to address these concerns. It advises that decisions concerning the provision of 'small equipment' will need to be taken on a case-by-case basis but that 'a blanket policy not to provide small equipment by way of prevention or meeting needs would be unlikely to be lawful and is not compatible with the aims of the Act'.

7.81   It will be maladministration for a housing authority to fail to refer an applicant to the social services where the applicant has a need for a minor adaptation of this nature.[121]

Holidays

7.82   As noted above (para 7.8) the CA 2014 duties include, in appropriate cases, the provision of a holiday for an adult in need and/or a carer. It would also appear that this could extend to the purchase of a caravan for such a purpose.[122]

---

117 Independent Review Service for the Social Fund, *The Social Fund Commissioner's annual report 2008/2009*, 2009, pp53–54.

118 Department for Communities and Local Government, *Delivering housing adaptations for disabled people: a good practice guide*, 2006, para 2.26.

119 Department of Health, *Prioritising need in the context of Putting People First: a whole system approach to eligibility for social care. Guidance on eligibility criteria for adult social care, England*, 2010, para 62.

120 Statement from Paul Moss, Social Care Policy and Legislation, Department of Health on community equipment, June 2015.

121 See in this respect Local government ombudsman, *Making a house a home: local authorities and disabled adaptations: focus report: learning lessons from complaints*, 2016, p11.

122 Association of Directors of Adult Social Services Departments (ADASS), *Personalisation and the law: implementing Putting People First in the current legal framework*, 2009, p15.

7.83   Both the NAA 1948[123] and the CSDPA 1970[124] specified holidays as a support service to be provided for disabled people. This focus owes much to the aspirations of the NAA 1948 and its aim of abolishing, not only the workhouse, but also the joyless oppressive Poor Law culture.[125] It has also been suggested that the reference to 'packages' of care that first appeared in 1990 community care reforms[126] derived from the development of the 'package holidays' that were then becoming popular.

7.84   Until comparatively recently, many local authorities owned holiday accommodation for people in need of social care support, and the provision of a holiday was not seen as an exotic arrangement. Despite the focus in the CA 2014 on well-being[127] (including recreation[128]), many local authorities would balk at the idea of including an annual holiday in the care and support plan for an adult in need or a carer – in much the same way that a Poor Law commissioner would have reacted to such a suggestion.[129]

7.85   It is, however, arguable that assessments under the CA 2014 should identify a need for an annual holiday – it is something recognised as a 'need' by a large majority of the population.[130] Such a need may be all the more important for disabled people to give them a break from the routine and exhaustion of living and caring for themselves. In *R (B) v Cornwall CC*[131] the court accepted that holiday expenses could be included as a disability-related expenditure for charging purposes and it would seem a reasonable presumption that, in appropriate cases, a care plan will have a holiday component. This was indeed the case for care home residents – when national minimum standards were first produced for such services,[132] standard 14, para 14.4 of which stated:

> Service users in long-term placements have as part of the basic contract price the option of a minimum seven-day annual holiday outside the home, which they help choose and plan.

123 NAA 1948 s29; LAC (90) 10, appendix 2 para 2(3)(a).

124 CSDPA 1970 s2(1)(f).

125 R Means and R Smith, 'From public assistance institutions to "sunshine hotels"' *Ageing and Society* (1983) 3(2) pp157–181.

126 Sir R Griffiths, *Community care: agenda for action. A report to the Secretary of State for Social Services*, HMSO, 1988; and Department of Health, *Caring for people* Cm 849, HMSO, 1989, para 3.4.1.

127 See, for example, S McCabe, T Joldersma and L Chunxiao, 'Understanding the benefits of social tourism: linking participation to subjective well-being and quality of life', *The International Journal of Tourism Research* (2010) 12(6), pp761–773.

128 CA 2014 s1(2)(e) and the Care and Support (Eligibility Criteria) Regulations 2015 SI No 313 regs 2(2)(i) and 3(2)(b)(vii).

129 Indeed Lord Browne-Wilkinson's comment that the CSDPA 1970 list of services was a 'strange list' is probably evidence that such perception was prevalent 20 years ago – see *R v East Sussex County Council, ex p Tandy* [1998] 2 WLR 884, [1998] AC 714 at 748.

130 The consumer price index (CPI) includes the cost of both overseas and domestic holidays.

131 *R (B) v Cornwall CC and Brendon Trust (interested party)* [2009] EWHC 491(Admin) upheld on appeal: [2010] EWCA Civ 55, (2010) 13 CCLR 117.

132 Department of Health, *Care homes for adults (18–65) and supplementary standards for care homes accommodating young people aged 16 and 17: national minimum standards care homes regulations*, 2003 – though such standards (in England) have now been withdrawn – see para 1.60 above, but see also para 17.31 below.

7.86   In *R v Ealing LBC ex p Leaman*[133] the council refused to consider a request made by the applicant for financial assistance in taking a privately arranged holiday – on the ground that it would only grant such assistance which it itself had arranged or sponsored. In quashing the council's decision Mann J held that this was, in effect, a classic fettering of its discretion (in this case under the CSDPA 1970).

7.87   Holidays can amount to a form of respite care for carers – where they have a need for a break and it is not possible or desirable for the disabled person not to be accompanied. In some cases, the authority will have to fund the full cost of the holiday under the CA 2014 (and not merely the additional costs attributable to the adult in need's impairment), where, for instance, the carer's attendance is necessary (ie as an escort) as was the case in *R v North Yorkshire CC ex p Hargreaves (No 2)*.[134]

Meals, food preparation and shopping

7.88   As noted above (para 7.8) the CA 2014 duties include the provision of meals as well as support with food preparation and, where appropriate, shopping (see para 4.17 above) for an adult in need and/or a carer. In general, a need for such support will result from the identification of the individual having an eligible need for assistance managing and maintaining nutrition.[135] The duty under the CA 2014 replaces equivalent obligations under the previous statutory regime.[136]

7.89   The origins of meals services (like home help services) owe much to the conditions created by the Second World War and the mass discharge of frail and ill older people from hospital. Means and Smith[137] describe the ad hoc development of services for older people by voluntary sector groups during this period with the Women's Royal Voluntary Service (WRVS – now the Royal Voluntary Service) emerging as the dominant player. The NAA 1948 continued this role,[138] as well as providing that a funding power (in relation to meals) should also be available to district councils.[139]

7.90   Between 2010 and 2014 there was a 63 per cent fall in the number of people receiving meals on wheels in England.[140] Between 2011 and 2015

133 (1984) *Times* 10 February, QBD.
134 (1997–98) 1 CCLR 331, QBD.
135 Care and Support (Eligibility Criteria) Regulations 2015 SI No 313 regs 2(2)(a) and 3(2)(b)(iv); and see para 4.17 above.
136 CSDPA 1970 s2(1)(g) and Health Service and Public Health Act 1968 s45.
137 R Means and R Smith, *From Poor Law to community care*, Policy Press, 1998, pp92–97.
138 NAA 1948 s31 by empowered local authorities to make contributions 'to any voluntary sector organisation whose activities consist in or include the provision of recreation or meals for old people'.
139 Under Health and Social Services and Social Security Adjudications Act (HASSASSA) 1983 Sch 9 Part II para 1 (now repealed). For an account of the genesis of the duty under the NAA 1948 s29, see the 5th edition of this book, para 9.138.
140 Rowena Mason, 'Meals on wheels for elderly in 63% decline under coalition', *Guardian*, 3 January 2015, concerning a freedom of information requests submitted by the then shadow care minister Liz Kendall: the figures being 296,000 in 2009/10 and 109,000 in 2014/15.

the number of hospital beds taken up by people with malnutrition rose by 61 per cent.[141]

7.91   There is a material difference between the provision of assistance to help an individual prepare a meal, and the provision of the meal itself. The manner in which the need is addressed should depend upon the assessed need, rather than (for example) the financial implication for the authority.[142] Supporting individuals in the preparation of their own meals (shopping, preparing and cooking) will be a service that is more likely to promote their ability to live independently than the mere provision of a cooked meal, and may also address user choice.

Carer support and replacement/respite care

Adults in need and carers

7.92   The CA 2014 distinguishes between adults in need and carers in the responses that a local authority should make to an eligibility determination. For adults in need, the response will generally take the form of 'care and support', whereas for cares it will be 'support' – the point being that carers are not in need of care. This means that when care services are provided as a result of a carer's assessment, these are in fact provided to the disabled person. Classically this has been referred to as 'respite care', although the CA 2014 statutory guidance uses the phrase 'replacement care'. In order for the carer to have a break from his or her caring role, the local authority provides a replacement service. Such a service may take the form of practical assistance in the home (for example, a sitting service), a community-based activity (for example, a day centre) or indeed a period in residential care accommodation. It follows that such care is (where it consists of a service delivered to the adult 'in need') a care and support arrangement for the adult in need, and not for the carer. A 2000 Department of Health note explained this well:[143]

> People who care may be assessed as needing a break from their caring role. This need will be clearly recorded on their own assessment documentation.
>
> The person they care for will then be assessed for the additional support that they will need to allow their usual carer to take a break. This need will be recorded on their assessment documentation. The additional service remains a community care service delivered to the cared for person, not a carer service under this Act.

141 Parliamentary Written Question 'Malnutrition 53159' Jonathan Ashworth (15 November 2016) Answer, Department of Health Nicola Blackwood (18 November 2016) the figures being 128,361 in 2010/11 and 184,528 2015/16.

142 Many councils impose a flat rate charge for meals (see para 8.324 below): a person on a low income may therefore be exempt from charging 'home help' but required to pay a not insignificant sum for their 'meals on wheels service'.

143 Department of Health, *Questions and Answers* – a note that accompanied the enactment of the 2000 Act; the Answer to Question 7 'Are short term breaks (respite care) a service for carers or cared for people?'

7.93 The CA 2014 envisages situations where a carer may be eligible for support, and it is felt appropriate that this be provided by way of care for the person for whom she or he cares – even if that person is not in fact eligible for support in his or her own right; this permutation is considered at para 4.75 above. Another example is provided in the statutory guidance (para 11.38) and it concerns Divya, who is caring for her dying father and for her young children. Her father has a care package in addition, but Divya's carer's assessment identifies her as eligible for support due to her additional child care responsibilities.[144] The support plan that is developed for her consists of a carers' direct payment 'which she uses for her children to attend summer play schemes so that she get some free time to meet with friends and socialise when the family member providers care to her father'.

Support provided directly to the carer

7.94 Although carers are generally supported by ensuring that the care and support package for the adult in need is appropriate and of high quality, the CA 2014 (as with the previous legislation[145]) provides for support services to be delivered directly to the carer. The statutory guidance gives examples of the type of support that are envisaged for carers (para 11.41):

> ... relaxation classes, training on stress management, gym or leisure centre membership, adult learning, development of new work skills or refreshing existing skills (so they might be able to stay in paid employment alongside caring or take up return to paid work), pursuit of hobbies such as the purchase of a garden shed, or purchase of laptop so they can stay in touch with family and friends.

Accommodation services

Background

7.95 Although NAA 1948 s1 abolished the Poor Law, it retained the distinction between indoor and outdoor relief.[146] The NAA 1948 intentions were, however, benign, in that it reversed the presumption in favour of indoor relief (ie a workhouse placement). Under NAA 1948 s21, publicly funded support in a care home was only available if the person's need for care and attention was 'not otherwise available' (ie if care in the community was impracticable). In this respect, it was probably the first example in the world of a statute that contained a presumption in favour of independent living. Unfortunately, to sustain the Poor Law's distinction between institutional and non-institutional care, the NAA 1948 relied upon provisions that severely taxed judicial intellect – in particular the requirement that for residential care a person had to have a 'need of care and attention' that

---

144 By virtue of the Care and Support (Eligibility Criteria) Regulations 2015 SI No 313 reg 3(2)(b)(i) – see para 4.17 above.

145 Principally under the Carers and Disabled Children Act 2000 s2.

146 Poor Law Amendment Act 1834 clause 52.

was 'not otherwise available'. The CA 2014 contains no special rules or presumptions of this nature.[147]

7.96   Despite the policy direction of governments for the last 45 years favouring non-residential social care arrangements, care homes remain a substantial element of the adult social care regime. Half of the adult social care workforce is employed in residential settings,[148] and the recent dramatic fall in the number of people receiving non-residential care support has not been mirrored by an equivalent reduction in residential placements.[149]

7.97   In 2015 there were 433,000 older or physically disabled people living in residential care settings (compared to 427,000 in 2014) of which 41 per cent were self-funding and 49 per cent local authority funded (albeit that 12 per cent of these residents were paying a top-up – see para 8.252) and ten per cent were funded by the NHS. Average weekly residential fees were £563, and for nursing homes these were £756 per resident.[150]

The nature of residential accommodation

Ordinary housing

7.98   The CA 2014 empowers local authorities to fund a wide range of residential and non-residential care and support arrangements. There are, however, limits. Authorities are unable to provide accommodation to meet a primary health care need (see para 12.44) or to meet a housing need for which a housing authority has a duty to meet under the Housing Act (HA) 1996.[151] The HA 1996 exclusion in the CA 2014 (s23(1)) is not a new development: NAA 1948 s21(8) was held to operate in the same way, although it did not make specific reference to HA 1996.[152]

7.99   The applicability of NAA 1948 s21(8) in relation to basic housing was considered in *R (Hughes) v Liverpool City Council*.[153] The case concerned a young man with severe mental and physical disabilities who lived with his mother in accommodation unsuitable to his needs. The property was incapable of being adapted and the local authority accepted that since 'the housing issues have remained unaddressed for a number of years ... it has now become a crisis situation'.[154] The applicant sought a judicial review, arguing that appropriate accommodation be provided under NAA 1948 s21, to which the local authority contended that NAA 1948 s21(8) excluded this possibility. Mitting J rejected this argument, holding that the homelessness legislation was 'not directed to cases in which a person has a requirement for specially adapted accommodation' and accordingly the prohibition in section 21(8) did not apply.

---

147 See para 2.40 above – although such a statement is found within the statutory guidance.
148 Skills for Care, *The state of the adult social care sector and workforce in England*, 2015.
149 R Humphries et al, *Social care for older people: home truths*, King's Fund, 2016, p25.
150 LaingBuisson, *Care of older people. UK market report. Twenty-seventh edition*, 2015.
151 CA 2014 s23(1).
152 See *R (Wahid) v Tower Hamlets LBC* [2002] EWCA Civ 287, (2002) 5 CCLR 239.
153 [2005] EWHC 428 (Admin), (2005) 8 CCLR 243 and see also *R (Mooney) v Southwark LBC* [2006] EWHC 1912, (2006) 9 CCLR 670 at paras 51–56.
154 [2005] EWHC 428 (Admin), (2005) 8 CCLR 243 at para 19.

7.100   While reservations have been expressed concerning the broad reasoning in the judgment,[155] the finding suggests a two-stage approach – an approach that would appear equally relevant under the CA 2014: (1) if the local authority secures suitably adapted accommodation for the disabled person through the use of its HA 1996 powers, then CA 2014 does not come into play (in relation to the provision of accommodation); (2) if, however, suitable accommodation is not so secured, then the CA 2014 duty is engaged.

7.101   The extent to which ordinary housing can be provided under the CA 2014 was considered in *R (GS) v Camden*[156] which concerned a homeless Swiss national who was wheelchair-dependent and had severe mental health problems. For the purposes of the proceedings it was agreed that she did not have the mental capacity to decide whether to return to Switzerland or consent to mental health treatment. She was provided with temporary accommodation, but it was argued that it was unsuitable for wheelchair access. The local authority undertook a CA 2014 assessment and decided that her sole need was for accommodation, which did not fall within the CA 2014 and which it concluded it had no power to provide. It was, however, argued by GS that 'care and support' was broad enough to include a need for simple accommodation.[157] This argument was rejected by the court, holding that a need for care and support under the CA 2014 'does not include a need for accommodation alone'.[158] In so finding, the court held that the case-law under the NAA 1948 continued to be or relevance. It noted that the NAA 1948 imposed a requirement that the person had a need for 'care and attention' whereas the CA 2014 stipulated a need for 'care and support', but then observed (para 29):

> Of course, 'need for care and support' is a different phrase and may mean something different to a 'need for care and assistance', but in my judgement, it does not include a need for accommodation alone ...

7.102   As noted at para 1.69 above, the court did, however, find that the authority was under a duty to provide GS with accommodation by exercising its power under Localism Act 2011 s1, as the seriousness of her physical disabilities and mental disorder were such that homelessness would breach her rights under Article 3 of the European Convention on Human Rights (prohibition of torture or inhuman or degrading treatment).

---

155 See eg (2005) 21 *Journal of Community Care Law* 6–8.

156 [2016] EWHC 1762 (Admin) and see also *R (SG) v Haringey LBC* [2015] EWHC 2579 (Admin), (2015) 18 CCLR 444 which was followed in *GS* (at January 2017 an appeal in *SG*). Both *GS* and *SG* have been the subject of criticism – see K Ashton and S Garlick 'Community care update' February 2016 *Legal Action* 30 and October 2016 *Legal Action* 36. The argument being that 'care and support' can include 'bare accommodation' under the CA 2014 provided that the statutory boundary between social services and housing authority responsibilities has not been crossed.

157 Not least because of the reference to 'accommodation in a care home or in premises of some other type' in CA 2014 s8(1)(a) and to the references in Care and Support (Eligibility Criteria) Regulations 2015 SI No 313 reg 2 to 'a habitable home environment' – see para 4.17 above.

158 Para 29 and see also paras 49–40.

Accommodation in care homes

7.103   The provision of accommodation under the CA 2014 almost invariably involves a placement in a registered care home. Although accommodation and care arrangements may involve supported living and shared lives placements (considered below paras 14.129 and 14.137), in such cases the cost of the actual accommodation is not covered by the CA 2014.

7.104   Where an assessed need is to be met in an independent care home, the authority's commissioners negotiate with the home provider in relation to the terms and conditions (including fees). Over the years in England there has been a plethora of Department of Health guidance on commissioning practice,[159] including regular exhortations for providers and commissioners to work in partnership and develop trust. *Guidance on fairer contracting* issued by the Care Services Improvement Partnership (CSIP)[160] acknowledges that in practice, relationships between providers and commissioners are not always mature and mutually sustaining, stating:

> In some instances the absence of close working relationship has led to providers cutting costs in unsustainable ways or by failing to adequately invest in their staff or by trying to be unrealistically price-attractive and competitive. Providers may also have been complicit in bad practice in order to keep prices down and maintain contracts in order to stay in business. Conversely, local authorities have felt that some providers have sought to increase margins without fully explaining the rationale behind this, or the size or purpose of their profit. This has raised suspicions among purchasers that public money has not been well spent.

Out of area accommodation

7.105   Not infrequently the accommodation offered by an authority in discharge of its CA 2014 duty is at some distance from the resident's family or home locality. There are many reasons why such an 'out of area' care home may be proposed by an authority. It may be because suitable accommodation to meet the person's needs is not available locally, especially in cases where the person needs specialised care. It may be, however, that accommodation at a price the local authority is prepared to pay is not available within a reasonable distance to enable visits from friends and family. Since individuals have a general right to choose their care home, under the 'choice of accommodation regulations' (see para 8.243 below – albeit that this may require a top-up payment), in some cases a placement will be out of area through the individual's choice.

---

159 Department of Health, *Building capacity and partnership in care*, 2001, and following on from this a Better Commissioning Learning Improvement Network was set up in 2004. This in turn, in 2010, became the National Market Development Forum resourced by the Putting People First Consortium and is formed of commissioners and providers from across the public, private and voluntary sectors. It has produced five briefing papers to help providers and purchasers to address the market development agenda in their area including one on Building Constructive Market Relations.

160 CSIP, *A guide to fairer contracting. Part 1*, 2005.

7.106   The law is silent on where individuals should be placed[161] other than that: (1) they should be given choice as to where they live; and (2) that if 'locality' is an assessed need, the care plan must ensure that this need is met (see para 4.65 above). Even where locality is not an expressly 'assessed need', it is arguable that there should be (at the very least) a presumption that placements will be in (or close to) the person's locality. Department of Health guidance (2003) on delayed discharges, for example, gave as an example of unreasonable practice a decision by a London council to move frail older people to care homes on the south coast unless the individuals in question wished to move there.[162]

Disputes about fee levels and contract issues

7.107   Since 1993 (when local authorities took over the major role in commissioning care in care homes) there have been tensions regarding the way local authorities use their negotiating power when fixing the fees they are prepared to pay. In 2010 the House of Commons Health Committee[163] noted that it is a 'common complaint of independent sector providers that they are underfunded by local authorities which relentlessly drive down contract values by capping prices below the cost of service provision and awarding contracts to the lowest bidder in a highly competitive market'.[164]

7.108   This obviously constrains providers' ability to provide a quality service'. The intervening years have not been marked by any change in this dynamic. In 2014 the National Audit Office considered that pressure by local authorities on fee rates was jeopardising financial sustainability of some providers[165] and the Association of Directors of Adult Social Services Departments (ADASS) accepted that local authorities did not always consider the profit margins of their suppliers, or the impact that reducing fees would have on their viability.[166] A 2015 Care Quality Commission (CQC) report expressed concern that the adult social care market was approaching a tipping point and that its analysis of the balance sheets of larger social care providers demonstrated that 'their profit margins were reducing – both due to pressures on fees that funders of care are able or willing to pay'.[167]

---

161 This is in contrast with housing legislation where Housing Act 1996 s208 obliges housing authorities (as far as possible) to provide accommodation in the district where the applicant resides – albeit that this is a limited right, see *R (Calgin) v Enfield LBC* [2005] EWHC 1716 (Admin), [2006] 1 All ER 112.

162 LAC (2003)21: HSC 2003/009, annex A.

163 House of Commons Health Committee, *Third Report of Session 2009–10, Social Care*, para 138.

164 The King's Fund estimates that average council fee rates have fallen by 6.2 per cent since 2011 – see R Humphries and others, *Social care for older people: home truths*, King's Fund, 2016, p23.

165 Report by the Comptroller and Auditor General, *Adult social care in England: overview*, HC 1102 Session 2013/14, National Audit Office, 2014, paras 2.11–2.13.

166 House of Commons Committee of Public Accounts, *Adult social care in England*, HC 518, The Stationery Office, 2014, p13 available at www.publications.parliament.uk/pa/cm201415/cmselect/cmpubacc/518/518.pdf.

167 CQC, *State of care*, 2015, pp7–8.

7.109   For a number of years, the courts proved resistant to care home proprietors' claims concerning the inadequate fees they receive from local authorities[168] – suggesting that these were not so much public law issues as 'fiercely contested private law' actions.[169] Thus in *R v Cumbria CC ex p Cumbria Professional Care Ltd*[170] it was held that the council's preference for its own in-house care services and its failure to enter into block contracts with private sector respite care providers was not unlawful; did not breach its obligations under the Public Service Contract Regulations 1993[171] or EEC Directive 92/50 article 1. In *R (Birmingham Care Consortium) v Birmingham City Council*[172] a challenge that home care fees were insufficiently high to enable residents to exercise a reasonable choice of accommodation[173] was likewise dismissed – so too was a generalised public law claim in *R v Coventry City Council ex p Coventry Heads of Independent Care Establishments and others.*[174] Likewise in *Amberley (UK) Ltd v West Sussex CC*[175] the right of a care home to unilaterally increase care home fees, in the face of local authority intransigence, was also rejected.

7.110   The courts' general position in such cases was summed up by Sullivan J in *R (S) v Birmingham City Council*[176] (when refusing leave to seek judicial review of the fees the authority had 'agreed') in the following terms:

> ... the court should be very wary indeed before intervening in what are essentially private law disputes between service providers and the defendant. I accept, of course, that it is possible that there might be a public law dimension, given the claimant's interest in the service provided by Mr Langston, but this court would intervene only where it was plain not simply that there was a commercial dispute but that the defendant's conduct was unreasonable in the Wednesbury sense.

7.111   More recently, however, public law challenges have fared better. *Forest Care Home Ltd and others v Pembrokeshire CC*[177] concerned the methodology used by the council in arriving at the figure the court was prepared to pay care home providers. The council, using an economic model, had determined the weekly fee per resident would be £390 for 2010/11, whereas the

---

168 In *Douce v Staffordshire CC* [2002] EWCA Civ 506, (2002) 5 CCLR 347 the court was prepared to consider 'arguable' that the authority's (then) regulatory functions under the Registered Homes Act 1984 could give rise to a duty of care to care home proprietors – but on the facts the claim (in tort) was rejected: see also *Yorkshire Care Developments Ltd v North Yorkshire CC* (2004) 6 August, Newcastle County Court, Lawtel.

169 In *R v Cumbria CC ex p Cumbria Professional Care Ltd* (2000) 3 CCLR 79 at 97K per Turner J and see also *Hampshire CC v Supportways Community Services Ltd* [2006] EWCA Civ 1035, (2006) 9 CCLR 484. In *R v Cumbria CC ex p Cumbria Professional Care Ltd* (2000) 3 CCLR 79 at 97K per Turner J and see also *Hampshire CC v Supportways Community Services Ltd* [2006] EWCA Civ 1035, (2006) 9 CCLR 484.

170 (2000) 3 CCLR 79.

171 SI No 3228.

172 [2002] EWHC 2188 (Admin), (2002) 5 CCLR 600.

173 Under what was then the NAA 1948 (Choice of Accommodation) Directions 1992.

174 (1997–98) 1 CCLR 379, QBD.

175 [2011] EWCA Civ 11, (2011) 14 CCLR 178.

176 [2007] EWHC 3330 (Admin).

177 *R (Forest Care Home Ltd and others) v Pembrokeshire CC and (1) the Welsh Ministers (2) Older People's Commissioner for Wales (Interested Parties)* [2010] EWHC 3514 (Admin), (2011) 14 CCLR 103.

claimants considered that they would not be financially viable and would be forced to close their homes unless the fee was about £480. The court held that the approach adopted by the council in relation to the assessment of the provider's capital costs was irrational; the council had failed: (1) to consider whether any local factors militated against the use of national benchmark staffing levels; (2) to consider the adverse impact on residents of a reduction in staffing levels; (3) to take into consideration local circumstances and the possible consequences for providers and residents; and (4) to give proper consideration to the effect on the provider and/or residents of inflation[178] and changes to other costs. In the court's opinion, although the council was entitled to take into account its own financial position when exercising its discretion in these matters, it was also bound to take into account and balance all other relevant factors, such as the quality of the service it provided and the need to maintain stability in the care services sector. The interests and rights of residents were of particular weight in that balance. In the judgment, Hickenbottom J quoted extensively from the then Welsh guidance regarding sustainability and the promotion of resident welfare and at para 143 held:

> However, when exercising its discretion in a manner which is adverse to an interested party – e.g. in this context, a provider or resident – the Council's own financial position is of course not necessarily determinative. It is bound to take into account and balance all relevant factors; and in particular it is bound to balance such matters as the quality of the service it provides and the need to maintain stability in the care services sector on the one hand, against the resources with which it has to provide that service on the other. The interests and rights of residents are of particular weight in that balance. The 2003 and now 2010 guidance makes them so, as does Article 8.

7.112   In *R (Members of the Committee of Care North East Northumberland) v Northumberland CC*[179] it was held that local authorities must have regard to legally relevant matters – including having due regard to the actual costs of care and undertaking a genuine consultation exercise. The authority was unable to demonstrate a rational basis for a number of multipliers/factors in its costs calculation (these had in the court's view been 'plucked out of the air') and its consultation had been inadequate – there had not been any genuine attempt to ascertain relevant information about actual costs, consider it and pass it on to decision-makers.

7.113   In similar vein, in *R (South Tyneside Care Home Owners Association and others) v South Tyneside Council*[180] it was held that in considering their 'usual rate' local authorities had to have regard to providers' return on equity or capital and this had to be done rationally and not on the basis of

---

178 In *Tameside and Glossop Acute Services NHS Trust v Thompstone* [2008] EWCA Civ 5 (consolidated proceedings) it was held that in certain situations the annual increases in care charges should be assessed, not according to the retail prices index (RPI) but by reference to the wage-related index, namely 'The Annual Survey of Hours and Earnings (ASHE) for the occupational group of care assistants and home carers, produced by the Office of National Statistics (ONS)'.

179 [2013] EWHC 234 (Admin), (2013) 16 CCLR 276.

180 [2013] EWHC 1827 (Admin).

arbitrary banding.[181] In addition it was held that the consultation process in fixing the usual rate required disclosure of the authority's background material essential to understand its methodology. In *R (South West Care Homes) v Devon CC*[182] the court made clear that the duty to 'have regard' in this context is more than a mere procedural formality holding that (para 43):

> Rights for people with disability, such as the right to choose where they live and to have support so as to prevent isolation or segregation from the community, are enshrined in the UN and European Conventions. The result of the exercise might affect those rights, and in my judgment should be carried out having regard to the specific provisions of section 149[183] in mind so as to have due regard to the need to eliminate discrimination and to advance equality of opportunity.

In its opinion, the risk of setting the usual rate too low was that accommodation opportunities to disabled and elderly people could be lost – and that 'even if most if not all homes identified in the Fee Structure Proposal report as at risk of closure would close in any event' this danger was of such seriousness that it called for 'proper consideration of mitigation measures or proper management of such closures in setting the fees' (para 53). In the court's opinion it was simply 'not good enough to say that the needs of individual residents had been or would be assessed if such a loss of accommodation resulted.

7.114   CA 2014 s5 places a duty on local authorities to promote an efficient and effective local market 'with a view to ensuring' that there is a variety of providers and high quality services to choose from. The select committee on the bill[184] considered that there had to be a mechanism that required local authorities to 'properly take into account the actual cost of care when setting the rates they are prepared to pay providers'. Such a mechanism is not to be found in the CA 2014 – but the statutory guidance is surprisingly direct on this question and likely to be cited frequently in cases challenging arbitrary local authority rates. It reminds local authorities that the way they commission services is 'a prime way to achieve effective market shaping' (para 4.4) as these have a 'significant influence on the market' (para 4.7). The effect of the guidance will, inevitable, make the provider market fee levels more transparent and this (together with the obligation to mitigate provider failure and have an overview of the market) is likely to 'exacerbate providers' concerns about the fee levels local authorities are willing to pay'[185] and may in consequence lead to further litigation in this field.

7.115   Where a resident is a party to a local authority agreement with a care home (a tripartite user agreement) then if the care home/local authority

---

181 See also *R (Torbay Quality Care Forum Ltd) v Torbay Council* [2014] EWHC 4321 (Admin) where it was held that the 'usual cost' calculations used by an authority was vulnerable to being struck down on *Wednesbury* grounds if it contained factors that 'no-one can explain as being necessary'.

182 [2012] EWHC 2967 (Admin) the local authority had set its 'usual cost' at a rate that – in effect – provided for a nil rate of return for the care home providers.

183 Equality Act 2010.

184 Joint Committee on the Draft Care and Support Bill, 'Draft Care and Support Bill' HL Paper 143 HC 822, The Stationery Office, 2013, para 113.

185 LGA and ADASS, *Joint consultation response Care Act: regulations and guidance*, August 2014, para 31.

element has an expiry date which has passed, the care home is not precluded from taking civil contract proceedings if it is dissatisfied with the new contract offered by the authority. Such a situation arose in *Abbeyfield Newcastle upon Tyne Society Ltd v Newcastle City Council*[186] where the authority refused to increase the care home fees. The court considered that there was an implied term that in the absence of agreement between the care home and the authority, that a reasonable price should be paid. In determining what this should be, it had regard to statutory and non-statutory guidance. In response to the local authority's a submission that the proceedings should have been taken by way of a judicial review – the court held that the case concerned a breach of contract and 'the mere fact that the party alleged to be in breach of contract is a public body plainly cannot, on its own, transform what would otherwise be a private law claim into a public law claim'.[187]

7.116 Given that some 49 per cent of care home places are commissioned or provided by local authorities (with a significantly higher percentage than this in some areas[188]) there is general concern that local authorities are, in relation to pricing, unreasonably exploiting their dominant position in the care home market. This concern resulted in 2003 in an informal super-complaint under the Enterprise Act 2000.[189] The Office of Fair Trading (OFT) agreed to investigate some of the areas of the complaint, most notably consumer information, contracts and redress. However, it declined to investigate local authority fee levels on the basis that care homes were not obliged to accept the rate local authorities were prepared to pay and this meant that public authorities were 'unlikely to persist in setting excessively low prices for care homes residents over the medium to long term, because care homes will refuse to accept older people at such rates'.[190] Such reasoning was always open to question – in that it failed to address a third possibility, namely that contract prices can be kept low and still satisfy local authority and private provider expenditure/profit objectives. This could be done by reducing the quality of care or by charging those funding their own care considerably more in order to remain viable. The last decade has demonstrated that this is exactly what has occurred.

7.117 If, as a result of a contractual dispute between a local authority and independent provider, notice to terminate the contract is to be given regarding a resident who lacks sufficient mental capacity to decide where he or she wishes to live, there is a requirement to convene a best interest meeting.[191] If in addition the resident is 'unbefriended' there will be a need for the local authority to appoint an independent mental capacity advocate (IMCA) (see para 13.81 below). It is indeed arguable that authorities should refer such

---

186 [2014] EWHC 2437 (Ch).

187 *R (Supportways Community Services Ltd) v Hampshire CC* [2006] EWCA Civ 1035, para 38.

188 LaingBuisson, *Care of older people. UK market report. Twenty-seventh edition,* 2015.

189 'Informal super-complaint on care home sector' *Which?* December 2003.

190 OFT, *Response to the supercomplaint on care homes made by the Consumers Association,* OFT 703, March 2004.

191 See eg in *R (W) v Croydon LBC* [2011] EWHC 696 (Admin) and *AH v Hertfordshire Partnership NHS Foundation Trust and Ealing PCT* [2011] EWHC 276 (COP), (2011) 14 CCLR 301 considered further at para 7.146 below.

a case to an IMCA at an earlier stage – namely when negotiations have become deadlocked: Mental Capacity Act 2005 ss35 and 39 require that an IMCA be engaged where the authority 'proposes to make arrangements' for a change in such a resident's residential accommodation.

Cost disputes and independent charitable providers

7.118   Charitable providers experience many of the same problems that other independent providers have when negotiating fee levels with local authorities. These problems can, however, lead to a conflict between their charitable aims and their need to be financially viable – a choice between accommodating an unreasonable council (and thereby using their charitable resources to subsidise a public body) or they abandon the disabled person (when there may be no viable or cheaper alternative care plan for the disabled person). As part of the negotiations, such a provider would not normally feel able to serve a contract termination notice, since the very issuing of such a notice could cause distress to the resident and the resident's family.[192] Unreasonable refusals (or delays) by a council to consider real costs increases born by such a provider may amount to maladministration.[193]

7.119   The view of the government is that charitable providers are entitled to full cost recovery and that statutory funders should accept this principle.[194] The Charity Commission has, however, expressed grave concern about the failure of statutory funders to implement full cost recovery contracts[195] – particularly in relation to contracts lasting more than three years where research suggests that full costs recovery is less likely to occur. In 2007 advice, the Charity Commission reinforced this view, stating:[196]

> In those circumstances where a public authority has an absolute legal duty to provide a service and no discretion over the level of service, there would have to be very clear justification in the interests of the charity for subsidising the service.

7.120   In 2010 the government published an updated 'Compact'[197] identifying (among other things) how it would comply with a set of principles in its

192 In complaint no 04/C/16195 against Birmingham City Council, 23 March 2006 the authority had advised a care provider in such a situation that she should simply abandon the service user if she was not prepared to accept the authority's payment rate – an attitude that the ombudsman considered 'extraordinary'.

193 Given the historic reluctance of the courts to become involved in such disputes the local government ombudsman would appear to provide the more appropriate remedy.

194 HM Treasury, *The role of the voluntary and community sector in service delivery: a cross cutting review*, 2002, paras 6.3 and 8.1.

195 Charity Commission, *Stand and deliver: the future for charities providing public services* RS15, 2007.

196 Charity Commission, *Charities and public service delivery: an introduction and overview* CC37, 2007, para 14.

197 Department for Work and Pensions, *Compact: the agreement between government and the voluntary/community sector*, 2010; and for a general discussion on the nature of the earlier (2009) Compact, see J Roberts, *Partners or instruments: can the Compact guard the independence and autonomy of voluntary organisations?* Voluntary Sector Working Papers, 8. Centre for Civil Society, London School of Economics and Political Science, 2007.

dealings with 'civil society organisations' (CSOs).[198] Earlier versions of the compact included commitments from local authorities – but the 2010 edition merely states (page 6) 'Local areas are encouraged to follow the principles in this document'. Key principles include commitments from the government to:

- respect and uphold the independence of CSOs to deliver their mission, including their right to campaign, regardless of any relationship, financial or otherwise, which may exist (para 1.1);
- ensure that CSOs are supported and resourced in a reasonable and fair manner where they are helping the government fulfil its aims (para 1.2);
- give early notice of forthcoming consultations, where possible, allowing enough time for CSOs to involve their service users, beneficiaries, members, volunteers and trustees in preparing responses; where it is appropriate, and enables meaningful engagement, conduct 12-week formal written consultations, with clear explanations and rationale for shorter time-frames or a more informal approach (para 2.4);
- commit to multi-year funding where appropriate and where it adds value for money; the funding term should reflect the time it will take to deliver the outcome; if multi-year funding is not considered to be the best way of delivering the objective, explain the reasons for the decision (para 3.4);
- ensure well-managed and transparent application and tendering processes, which are proportionate to the desired objectives and outcomes of programmes (para 3.5);
- assess the impact on beneficiaries, service users and volunteers before deciding to reduce or end funding; assess the need to re-allocate funds to another organisation serving the same group (para 4.2);
- give a minimum of three months' notice in writing when changing or ending a funding relationship or other support, apart from in exceptional circumstances, and provide a clear rationale for why the decision has been taken (para 4.4).

7.121   The status of the compact is uncertain, as is its applicability in any maladministration complaint.[199] As well as the national compact, many local authorities have a local compact which should reflect the national compact. In *R (Berry) v Cumbria CC*[200] it was described as 'more than a wish list but less than a contract'. Where a local authority decides to cut its grant funding to voluntary sector organisations, there is a general duty to consult[201] in addition to the specific obligations to undertake EA 2010 impact assessments.[202]

---

198 The introduction in the updated Compact indicates that this term include charities, social enterprises and voluntary and community groups.

199 It would seem that the Compact should be a bench-mark for administrative practice, although where the dispute is essentially of a private contractual nature, this factor might place it outside the Ombudsmen's remit – see R Low-Beer, *The future of the 3rd sector*, Public Law Project, 2009.

200 [2007] EWHC 3144 (Admin).

201 *R (Capenhurst) v Leicester City Council* [2004] EWHC 2124 (Admin), (2004) 7 CCLR 557.

202 See eg *R (Kaur and Shah) v Ealing LBC* [2008] EWHC 2062 (Admin) and *R (Hajrula and Hamza) v London Councils* [2011] EWHC 448 (Admin).

Individuals who contract directly with care homes (self-funders)

7.122   Currently about 40 per cent of care home residents in England contract directly for their residential care, and in the Home Counties this rises to over 50 per cent.[203] This may not be through choice, but because their resources make them ineligible for local authority support (see para 4.60). Such residents will self-evidently have a 'need for care and support' and in consequence the right to an assessment under CA 2014 s9 (see para 3.43) as well as the right to receive a range of information concerning how the system operates, the choices available to them and so on (see para 19.5 above).

7.123   The ombudsman has found maladministration where a local authority had failed properly to assess and advise a self-funder of the type of care that was needed. A place in a nursing home was found, although her care needs could have been met in a residential care home. As the resident had been self-funding this involved substantial excess payments being made.[204]

7.124   Lack of information to self-funders was the cause of maladministration in another ombudsman finding, where a relative was merely told that social services would contribute towards a resident's care if the private care insurance plan he proposed to purchase did not meet the full fees. The authority did not explain that this would only be up to a maximum rate. As the nursing home chosen was more expensive than the local authority 'maximum rate', the family were asked to make a top-up. Had they been advised of this at the outset, they might have chosen a different investment plan. The ombudsman considered that the information given was too general to be of use, and that the council should have been clear as to the approximate level of support that would have been available.[205]

7.125   It will not always be the case that a person prefers the local authority to be involved. A personal injury claimant is entitled to seek damages for future care and accommodation costs and therefore entitled to opt for self-funding in preference to reliance on local authority provision.[206]

7.126   Concern about the parlous position of those funding their own care has prompted several critical reports. In its 2008 report on the state of social care in England, the Commission for Social Care Inspection[207] described such residents as 'People lost to the system'.[208] A study for the report found people funding their own care to be disadvantaged and at risk

203 Laing and Buisson, *Care of elderly people. UK market survey 2009–10*, 2010. For England the figures are estimated to be 39.6 per cent in residential care homes and 47.6 per cent in nursing homes.

204 Complaint nos 00/C/03176 and 00/C/05525, against Nottingham CC and Nottingham City Council, 22 January 2002: the recommendation was for repayment of the excess fees amounting to almost £7,000 and in addition for £16,584 to cover the expenses of the attorney in dealing with the complaint.

205 Complaint no 05/B/12629 against Wiltshire CC, 30 April 2007.

206 *Peters (by her litigation friend Susan Mary Miles) v East Midlands Strategic Health Authority and others* [2009] EWCA Civ 145, (2009) 12 CCLR 299. See para 8.52 in relation to personal injury claims and charging.

207 Succeeded in 2009 by the CQC.

208 CSCI, *The state of social care in England 2006–07*, 2008.

of being fast tracked into residential care without an exploration of other options. Indeed none of the people questioned in the study funding their own arrangements had experienced a needs assessment prior to moving into a home. In spite of exhortations from successive governments[209] that councils should undertake assessments and provide guidance for all people who need care regardless of how it is to be funded, it is clear that this is not happening in many areas.[210] In a 2011 study the experience of those funding their own care was that:

> Almost nobody identified social services as a source of information and advice, and people who *did* have contact with the council had a negative experience that focused solely on their financial status rather than their need for care and support.[211]

7.127   Local authorities are not alone in failing to provide self-funders with appropriate support and information. A 2005 OFT report of its Market Study[212] made a number of recommendations regarding the need for better information and redress for residents as consumers.[213] The study found in a mystery shopping exercise that it was difficult to get fee information even with prompting, and 66 per cent of the 152 contracts scrutinised had more than one fee-related term that the OFT considered was potentially unfair, and six per cent had no fee-related terms. In a separate earlier exercise, the OFT had already scrutinised the contracts of ten of the larger providers and received undertakings that they would change their contracts to comply with the Unfair Terms in Consumer Contracts Regulations 1999.[214] The OFT also issued guidance to advisers and the public on what might constitute an unfair term in care homes.[215]

7.128   In 2006, in response to the OFT report, amended regulations were issued[216] to require the provision of information in the service user's guide (issued by a care home) about the fees payable[217] and the arrangements

---

209 See, for example, Department of Health, *Vision for adult social care: capable communities and active citizens,* 2010; LGA, ADASS and NHS, *Putting People First: a shared vision and commitment to the transformation of adult social care,* 2007; Think Local Act Personal: Next steps for transforming adult social care at www. thinklocalactpersonal.org.uk/Browse/ThinkLocalActPersonal/; and statutory guidance, para 6.13.

210 The Dilnot Commission noted that 'on the whole, our evidence strongly suggests people are bewildered by the system and do not know where to go or who to talk to for advice' – see Commission on Funding of Care and Support, *Fairer care funding: the report of the commission on funding of care and support,* July 2011, p16.

211 *Journeys without maps: the decisions and destinations of people who self fund – a qualitative study from Melanie Henwood Associates* (2010), in Putting People First, *People who pay for care – quantitative and qualitative analysis of self-funders in the social care market,* 2011, p49.

212 In response to a supercomplaint brought by *Which?* (see para 7.128).

213 OFT, *Care homes for older people: a market study* OFT780, 2005.

214 SI No 2083. Details about the homes can be found in a press release issued in March 2005 at webarchive.nationalarchives.gov.uk/20140402142426/http://www.oft.gov.uk/news/press/2005/51-05.

215 OFT, *Guidance on unfair terms in care home contracts* OFT 635, October 2003.

216 Care Standards Act 2000 (Establishments and Agencies) (Miscellaneous Amendments) Regulations 2006 SI No 1493.

217 In the case of nursing homes, the information about the total fees payable had to relate to the fee before any contribution from the NHS is taken into account.

for paying such fees; the arrangements for charging and paying for any additional services; and a statement of whether services, terms and conditions and fees vary according to the source of funding for a person's care. Although the evidence suggests that this obligation was routinely flouted,[218] it is of concern, given that care homes often charge those funding their own care considerably more than the fees negotiated by local authorities, that the duty to inform about the existence of such differential fee arrangements was repealed by the by Health and Social Care Act (HSCA) 2008.

Self-funders who have complaints

7.129   If a resident who is funding his or her own care has a complaint about the service provided by the care home, the resident can use the complaints procedure that all registered providers are required to have under the HSCA 2008. As a general rule, the CQC is not able to review the outcome of such a complaint, since they have no statutory duties or powers to investigate complaints. However, any self-funding resident who is dissatisfied with the outcome of his or her care home complaint can ask the local government ombudsman to investigate, as the ombudsman's powers have been amended to cover this function.[219]

NHS-funded care home placements

7.130   Although patients in NHS-funded care homes do not have a statutory right of choice; it is expected that before any placement there will be 'considerable consultation with the patient and his or her family and [hospitals should] take account of the patient's wishes'.[220] Additionally, it has been argued that the effect of principle 4 of the NHS Constitution (see para 11.27 below) that 'NHS services must reflect, and should be co-ordinated around and tailored to, the needs and preferences of patients, their families and their carers' means that CCGs should fund care home accommodation of choice unless they are able to provided good reasons to the contrary.[221]

7.131   The problem of patients having to move care home once they are funded by the NHS was mentioned in the health select committee report on continuing care. In its response, the government stated that:

> ... the risks (both physical and emotional) of moving that resident should be fully considered before the decision is made to move him/her. However, the Department cannot say that continuing care should always be provided in the care home where the individual is currently resident, since this would constrain the NHS's responsibility to provide appropriate care (the

---

218 A survey of 50 homes in March 2007 found that two in five packs sent by homes failed to mention fees, only two out of 43 packs received included the latest inspection report, and only eight homes sent an example of their contract – see 'Care essentials', *Which?* June 2007.

219 Local Government Act 1974 ss34A–34T.

220 Statement of the Minister for Health, John Bowis, to Health Committee, recorded at para 79 of *First report into long-term care*, HMSO, 1995.

221 See K Ashton and J Gould, 'Community care update', June 2009 *Legal Action* 11–16.

care home may not be able to provide the type of care needed) and manage its finances.[222]

7.132   The 2012 Framework guidance on NHS continuing healthcare[223] provides detailed advice concerning the limited situations in which eligible individuals are able to 'top-up' their residential care home fees as well as the approach to be taken where a self-funding resident in care home accommodation (whose fees are above the CCG's usual rate) becomes eligible for NHS funding. This guidance is considered at para 12.145 below.

Supported living and shared lives accommodation

7.133   Many individuals receiving CA 2014 care and support will be living in a 'supported living' or a 'shared lives' placement. Their care and support needs will be funded under the CA 2014, but not their housing costs. Individuals in supported living will, in general, have their housing costs covered by housing benefit. Individuals in shared lives schemes are in effect lodgers in the home of the shared lives carer who receives a payment from the placing authority – which covers (1) the care and support they provide; (2) the individual's day-to-day living expenses; and (3) a contribution towards the cost of accommodation.

7.134   Supported living and shared lives accommodation arrangements are considered further at paras 14.137 and 14.129 below. Individuals assessed as being in need of such support have a qualified right to choose their placements, and special provisions exist in the CA 2014 concerning the 'ordinary residence' rules for such placements: these questions are considered at paras 6.41 and 6.42 above.

Closure of care facilities

Care home closures

7.135   The closure of local authority care homes, in particular for older people, proved to be one of the more controversial effects of the community care reforms (considered in the introduction to this book). The period 1990–1995 saw a 25 per cent reduction in the number of local authority homes in England (amounting to almost 40,000 fewer residents). By March 2010 the figure had more than halved to 18,000[224] and it is to presumed that the current figure is significantly smaller. In some cases this fall was due to care homes being transferred to the independent sector rather than

222   *Response to the Health Select Committee Report on Continuing Care* Cm 6650, June 2005. As noted below (see para 12.137) NHS continuing healthcare can be funded in any setting (if deemed clinically suitable) and the Department of Health has confirmed that 'there is nothing within the regulatory framework, which would prevent a person in receipt of NHS continuing healthcare remaining within a Care Home (Personal Care)': Department of Health, *Joint Statement re: NHS continuing healthcare funding for end of life care within care homes*, 15 August 2008.

223   *National framework for NHS continuing healthcare and NHS-funded nursing care*, 2012: this framework is to be amended in 2017 – to update the references (to refer to the CA 2014 rather than the NAA 1948).

224   Department of Health, *Community care statistics: social services activity 2009–2010*, 2011.

closed. In other cases, due to reconfiguring services, some local authority homes have closed in order to concentrate resources on sheltered or extra care housing. The decline in the number of residents is not reflective of overall care home numbers: between 2010 and 2015 the number of older or physically disabled people living in residential care settings rose from 382,000[225] to 433,000.[226]

7.136   In relation to the closure of long-stay NHS accommodation, there is an obligation on health bodies to consult with patients and their representative bodies (including overview and scrutiny committees).[227] Registered social landlords are also subject to a duty to consult when contemplating the closure of a supported living scheme, as well as ensuring that suitable alternative accommodation is secured for tenants.[228]

7.137   Closures have not been confined to care homes in public ownership. The collapse in 2011 of the largest care home provider – Southern Cross, with over 750 homes and about 37,000 residents – resulted in specific provisions being introduced into the CA 2014 (fleshed out by three sets of regulations[229] and chapter 5 of the statutory guidance) requiring the regulators and local authorities to manage care markets and have contingency plans for provider failure and service interruptions. This book does not consider these provisions in detail, but in summary, they include 'market oversight' arrangements involving the CQC (among others)[230] and a temporary duty on social services to intervene if a particular provider 'fails'.[231] Since provider failure is likely to be due to macro economic conditions over which local authorities and the regulators have little or no control, it is questionable how effective these measures can be. The well-documented financial difficulties of the largest care home provider in 2016 (Four Seasons with 440 care homes with 18,500 residents) would suggest that the CA 2014 has not changed the care home market fundamentals. A 2016 CQC report expressed concern over care home providers withdrawing from the market, and pointed to the reduction in the number of English care homes (these fell from 18,068 in 2010 to 16,614 in 2016).[232]

225 Laing and Buisson, *Care of elderly people. Market survey 2010–2011.*
226 Laing and Buisson, *Care of older people. UK market report. Twenty-seventh edition,* 2015.
227 NHSA 2006 s242. See also Department of Health guidance, *Strengthening accountability involving patients and the public,* February 2003; *Overview and scrutiny of health – guidance,* July 2003; and *Real involvement,* October 2008. 'Healthwatch England' has a role in supporting public involvement in commissioning and provision decisions and scrutinising health and social care (Health and Social Care Act 2012 Part 5 ch 1).
228 Under the Housing Act 1985, landlords must consult secure tenants and take account of their views in 'matters of housing management' and the housing corporation (in its regulatory code) requires all registered landlords to meet similar requirements and offers good practice advice.
229 Care and Support (Market Oversight Information) Regulations 2014; Care and Support (Cross-border Placements) (Business Failure Duties) (Scotland) Regulations 2014; and Care and Support (Market Oversight Criteria) Regulations 2014.
230 CA 2014 ss53–57 – although doubts have been raised as to the capacity of the CQC to fulfil its monitoring role of the larger providers – see House of Commons Committee of Public Accounts, *Adult social care in England* HC 518, The Stationery Office, 2014, p8.
231 CA 2014 ss48–52.
232 CQC, *The state of health care and adult social care in England 2015/16,* p63.

Guidance on closure processes and transfers of patients

7.138   In 1998 the Department of Health issued health service guidance on the transfer of frail elderly patients to other long-stay settings.[233] Although primarily aimed at NHS bodies, the circular was copied to all directors of social services in England, and has formed the basis of many protocols developed by local authorities[234] (and referred to as the '1998 guidance' below). Since that time, a variety of good practice guidance has been issued concerning home closures.[235]

7.139   The 1998 guidance provides checklists of steps to be taken during the closure process and emphasises the importance of consultation at all stages. A key part of any strategy should be a 'project plan ... which is flexible enough to adapt to changing circumstances'. Authorities should set up a steering group to see the whole project through, with a project manager, a patient transfer co-ordinator, a key worker who works at the hospital and knows the patient and his or her needs and will liaise with the patient and relatives or carers as well as with staff in the receiving care setting. Contingency plans must be prepared for all aspects of the project and the vital importance of information sharing (both between all professionals, and with patients and carers) is stressed.

7.140   The 1998 guidance advises against winter and weekend transfers, and suggests that whenever possible groups of friends should be moved together. There should be a named staff member authorised to postpone or cancel the transfer of any individual should this become necessary – even if this means that the patient has to be moved within the hospital.

Challenging home closures

7.141   The courts have indicated that they consider home closure decisions to be an area where litigation should be avoided if at all possible. In *Cowl and*

233 Department of Health, *Transfer of frail elderly patients to other long stay settings* HSC 1998/048, 1998.

234 Many local authorities do, however, have protocols – see J Williams and A Netten, *Guidelines for the closure of care homes for older people: prevalence and content of local government protocols*, Personal Social Services Research Unit discussion paper 1861/2, 2003, available at www.pssru.ac.uk/pdf/dp1861_2.pdf.

235 See, for example, J Williams and A Netten, *Guidelines for the closure of care homes for older people: prevalence and content of local government protocols*, Personal Social Services Research Unit discussion paper 1861/2, 2003; ADASS, *Achieving closure: good practice in supporting older people during residential care*, 2011; SCIE, *Short-notice care home closures: a guide for local authority commissioners*, 2011; Department of Health, NHS and others, *Managing care home closures a good practice guide for local authorities, clinical commissioning groups, NHS England, CQC, providers and partners*, NHS England (05573), 2015; Department of Health and others, *Care and continuity: contingency planning for provider failure*, 2015; CQC, *New care home closures guidance for adult social care partners*, 2016 – and see also Welsh Assembly Government, *Statutory guidance on escalating concern with, and closures of, care homes providing services for adults*, 2009: the Welsh guidance is of persuasive value, is practical and has a valuable level of detail – requiring individual relocation plans and stressing the importance of comprehensive needs assessments of all residents (including self-funders).

others v Plymouth City Council[236] the Court of Appeal spoke of the heavy obligation on lawyers in such disputes to resort to litigation only it is really unavoidable, and in *R (Lloyd) v Barking and Dagenham LBC*[237] the Court of Appeal held that it was not an appropriate organ to prescribe the amount of consultation to be carried out with a resident's advisers. Courts are similarly reluctant to investigate the closure of community care facilities – see *R (Bishop) v Bromley LBC*[238] (a case concerning a day centre) where the court reaffirmed the Court of Appeal's view in *Coughlan* that it was only in exceptional circumstances that a comprehensive multi-disciplinary assessment would be required before a decision could be taken to close such a facility. Increasingly it appears that judicial review challenges to care home closures are being rejected at the permission stage (see, for instance, *R (Lindley) v Tameside MBC*[239] and *R (Grabham and others) v Northamptonshire CC*[240]).

7.142   The numerous challenges that have been mounted to local authority and NHS decisions to close care homes have raised many different public law arguments, which can be broadly categorised under the following five general headings: (1) promises for life; (2) failure to consult properly; (3) failure properly to assess existing residents; (4) failure to consider relevant matters; and (5) the Human Rights Act 1998.

Promises for life

7.143   Not infrequently, existing residents assert that they were given a promise – or at least formal or informal assurances – that on moving to the particular home, they would be able to remain there for the rest of their lives. Moving into a care home is a very major step for many people, and often taken at a time when they are frail and uncertain about the wisdom of giving up their independence. Such explicit or implicit assurances can be pivotal in the making of these crucial decisions.

7.144   *R v North and East Devon Health Authority ex p Coughlan*[241] concerned such a promise. The Court of Appeal took as its starting point that the health authority could break its promise 'if, and only if, an overriding public interest required it' (at para 52). Having considered the reasons advanced by the health authority (essentially budgetary), the court undertook an extensive review of the public law principles underlying the concept of legitimate expectation (see para 26.217) and considered that such expectations can fall into three broad categories:

1) where the public authority need only bear in mind its assurance when reaching a decision;

---

236 [2001] EWCA Civ 1935, [2002] 1 WLR 803, (2002) 5 CCLR 42 at 49B. Views reiterated by Maurice Kay J in *R (Dudley, Whitbread and others) v East Sussex CC* [2003] EWHC 1093 (Admin).
237 [2001] EWCA Civ 533, (2001) 4 CCLR 196 at 205G.
238 [2006] EWHC 2148 (Admin), (2006) 9 CCLR 635.
239 [2006] EWHC 2296 (Admin).
240 [2006] EWHC 3292 (Admin).
241 [2000] 2 WLR 622, (1999) 2 CCLR 285.

2) where the assurance was such as to require the authority to follow a particular procedural course in its decision-making process (for instance, consulting the relevant parties);

3) where the assurance was so specific that it gave rise to substantive rights – in which case the court must determine 'whether to frustrate the expectation is so unfair that to take a new and different course will amount to an abuse of power'.

The court considered that the *Coughlan* case fell into the third category, and after weighing up the competing questions it held:

89. We have no hesitation in concluding that the decision to move Miss Coughlan against her will and in breach of the Health Authority's own promise was in the circumstances unfair. It was unfair because it frustrated her legitimate expectation of having a home for life in Mardon House. There was no overriding public interest which justified it. In drawing the balance of conflicting interests the court will not only accept the policy change without demur but will pay the closest attention to the assessment made by the public body itself. Here, however, as we have already indicated, the Health Authority failed to weigh the conflicting interests correctly ...

7.145 What counts as overriding public interest justifying closure where 'home for life' promises have been made was the main issue in *CH and MH v Sutton and Merton PCT*.[242] A previous judicial review on the promise for life had been successful in 2000 (see para 7.156 below) but in 2004 it was proposed again that the hospital be closed as it was considered to be in the residents' 'best interests ... to re-provide services that enable residents to live in small groups in everyday settings'. Evidence from the assessments raised questions about whether a move would be in the best interests of a number of patients. The court found that the question as to whether there is an overriding public interest is one the court needs to resolve actively rather than measure from a distance, and patients were entitled to challenge whether the closure was in their best interests and the court must determine this for itself on the evidence.[243]

7.146 Although not concerned with a closure of a specific establishment, the issue of an individual's best interests in the context of the 'campus closure' policy (see paras 12.193 and 15.34 below) has been considered by the Court of Protection. The case concerned a proposal to move a resident from a rural residential care setting (in which he had been for many years) to a flat in an urban area. Notwithstanding that this new placement carried the label of 'independent living', the Court of Protection[244] considered that it was not in his best interests, holding that:

242 [2004] EWHC 2984 (Admin), (2005) 8 CCLR 5.

243 The difficulty in assessing whether or not closure of such facilities is in the best interests of the applicants who are seeking to stop the closure was brought into sharp relief in this case. The facility concerned was subsequently the subject of a report by the Healthcare Commission (*Investigation into the service for people with learning disabilities provided by Sutton and Merton Primary Care Trust*, January 2007) which was requested after a series of serious incidents including allegations of physical and sexual abuse.

244 *AH v Hertfordshire Partnership NHS Foundation Trust and Ealing Primary Care Trust* [2011] EWHC 276 (COP), (2011) 14 CCLR 301, para 80. At para 2 the court observed that: 'It is of importance that the NHS trust that is responsible for SRS has no plan to discontinue the service in the foreseeable future. Had the real issue been the

These residents are not an anomaly simply because they are among the few remaining recipients of this style of social care. They might better be seen as a good example of the kind of personal planning that lies at the heart of the philosophy of care in the community. Otherwise, an unintended consequence of national policy may be to sacrifice the interests of vulnerable and unusual people like AH.

7.147   The courts will in general only accept that a promise for life has been made when 'convincing' evidence is advanced by the applicant of a 'clear and unequivocal assurance'.[245] The assurance should, however, be viewed from the perspective of the resident – the test being 'what would the ordinary resident think that the [statement in question] was trying to convey'.[246]

Failure to consult properly

7.148   *R v Devon CC ex p Baker and Durham CC ex p Curtis and others*[247] concerned the proposed closure of residential homes in Devon and in Durham. The Court of Appeal held that (in respect of the procedure followed by Durham County Council) the decision to close a particular home was unlawful; the council had failed to consult the residents properly. The court approved the proposition that consultation contained four elements,[248] namely:

> First, that consultation must be at a time when proposals are still at a formative stage. Second, that the proposer must give sufficient reasons for any proposal to permit of intelligent consideration and response. Third, that adequate time must be given for consideration and response and, finally, fourth, that the product of consultation must be conscientiously taken into account in finalising any statutory proposals.

7.149   The consultation process must include a statement setting out the relevant context for the proposals under consideration – for instance, that some residents may have been promised a home for life. Although a failure to refer to such key topics may not vitiate the consultation process, it may render the decision-making process vulnerable to challenge on the basis of having omitted a relevant consideration.[249] Consultation will be held to be inadequate if the residents are not given the true reason for the closure, and for why one home was favoured to remain open rather than another.[250]

7.150   The court also approved the proposition that if a resident is to be transferred from one home to another (for whatever reason), he or she must be

continuation of the service rather than the interests of its individual occupants, the appropriate jurisdiction would have been judicial review and not the Court of Protection.'

245   *R (Phillips and Rowe) v Walsall MBC* [2001] EWHC 789 (Admin), (2001) 5 CCLR 383 at 387D; and see also *R (Lloyd) v Barking and Dagenham LBC* [2001] EWCA Civ 533, (2001) 4 CCLR 196.

246   *R (Bodimeade) v Camden LBC* [2001] EWHC 271 (Admin), (2001) 4 CCLR 246 at 255H.

247   [1995] 1 All ER 72 at 91, CA.

248   These elements were first propounded in *R v Brent LBC ex p Gunning* (1986) 84 LGR 168 and adopted by the Court of Appeal in *R v North and East Devon Health Authority ex p Coughlan* [2000] 2 WLR 622, (1999) 2 CCLR 285, CA at para 108.

249   *R v Merton, Sutton and Wandsworth Health Authority ex p Perry and others* (2000) 3 CCLR 378, QBD at para 112.

250   *R (Madden) v Bury MBC* [2002] EWHC 1882, (2002) 5 CCLR 622.

consulted over his or her removal from the existing home as well as over the home to which he or she is to be transferred.[251]

7.151   Provided the key stages of the consultation process are followed and the product of the consultation 'conscientiously taken into account',[252] the court will 'not strain to find technical defects which will make the obligations imposed on local authorities unworkable'.[253] The courts will also be slow to add additional obligations, for instance that a proposal could only be adopted (after consultation) if it enjoyed 'consensus or the agreement or consensus of the consultees'.[254] Whether or not there is a duty to 're-consult' if new issues emerge during the consultation process will depend upon the facts of a given case,[255] but in general there is 'no duty to consult further on [an] amended proposal which had itself emerged from the consultation process'.[256] Even if in the early stages, the consultation process is problematic, and the process of consultation 'challenging', such flaws may not, when viewed as part of the overall process, inevitably invalidate the consultation.[257] The consultation duty is further considered at para 20.200 below.

7.152   Another example of the court's reluctance to 'strain to find technical defects' concerns the extent to which local authorities are required to gather 'relevant information' in order to make the necessary determination.[258] The failure of an authority to obtain additional information formed the basis of *R (Karia) v Leicester City Council*,[259] a case concerning a decision to close the care home where the 101-year-old applicant had lived for 15 years. The court held that it would only be prepared to strike down such a decision on the basis that the authority should have obtained additional information if it could be established that 'no reasonable council possessed of that material held by the Council could suppose that the inquiries they had made were sufficient'.

Failure properly to assess existing residents

7.153   In *Coughlan* it was argued that prior to consulting on the closure of the resident's nursing facility there should have been a multi-disciplinary assessment of her individual needs and a risk assessment of the effects

---

251 [1995] 1 All ER 72 at 86: such a move would of course interfere with the residents rights under Article 8 in respect of their private life and their 'home'.

252 *R v North and East Devon Health Authority ex p Coughlan* [2000] 2 WLR 622, (1999) 2 CCLR 285, CA at para 108.

253 *R (Smith) v East Kent NHS Hospital Trust* [2002] EWHC 2640 (Admin), (2003) 6 CCLR 251 at para 276C.

254 [2002] EWHC 2640 (Admin), (2003) 6 CCLR 251 at 267C.

255 [2002] EWHC 2640 (Admin), (2003) 6 CCLR 251 at 271F.

256 *R v Islington LBC ex p East* [1996] ELR 74 at 88 cited with approval by Silber J in *Smith v East Kent NHS Hospital Trust* [2002] EWHC 2640 (Admin), (2002) 6 CCLR 251 at 266H.

257 *R (Grabham) v Northamptonshire CC* [2006] EWHC 3292 (Admin).

258 *Secretary of State for Education and Science v Tameside MBC* [1977] AC 1014 at 1065B.

259 [2014] EWHC 3105 (Admin) at para 102.

of moving her to new accommodation;[260] the argument being that if her needs were incapable of being met elsewhere then closure of the facility would not have been possible.

7.154   The health authority denied that such an obligation existed, arguing that under the relevant guidance[261] (see para 7.138 above) it was only after a closure decision that the detailed transfer procedures applied and that it was:

> ... impracticable and unrealistic in the vast majority of cases to carry out the assessments and to identify alternative placements prior to a closure decision, let alone prior to consultation on a proposed closure. Funds for the development of alternative facilities might only become available after the closure decision is taken; only then would the range of alternative available placements become clear; large closure programmes might take years to implement, in which case assessments and alternative facilities considered at the time of consultation or closure would change over time; and in practice the necessary co-operation of individual patients for effective assessments and alternative placements might be more difficult to obtain before rather than after a final decision has been taken on closure.[262]

7.155   On the facts of this particular case (and in view of its other findings against the health authority) the court considered that it was unnecessary to rule separately in the legality of the health authorities' actions in this regard.

7.156   However, *R v Merton, Sutton and Wandsworth Health Authority ex p Perry and others*[263] concerned a decision to close a long-stay hospital and provide alternative community-based replacement services for over a hundred long stay residents who had profound learning disabilities, and physical impairments such as lack of mobility, incontinence and eating problems. Some of the residents who challenged the closure decision had been at the facility for almost 30 years. They argued (among other things) that they had not had a full assessment of their needs prior to the consultation on closure, and the health authority responded by citing the Court of Appeal's judgment in *Coughlan* that a failure to undertake such an assessment did not necessarily render the process unlawful. Jackson J found in favour of the residents, stating:[264]

> It should be remembered that Miss Coughlan was not a person with learning disabilities. The government guidance which is applicable in the present case, but which was not applicable in Coughlan, is HSG(92)42. This circular states on page 2 as follows:
>
> > The large majority of people with learning disabilities not living with their families can be cared for in residential accommodation arranged through the relevant social services authority. There are, however, likely to be a small number of people with severe or profound learning disabilities and physical, sensory or psychiatric conditions who need long term residential care in a health setting. Where this seems to be the

---

260   *R v North and East Devon Health Authority ex p Coughlan* [2000] 2 WLR 622, (1999) 2 CCLR 285, CA at para 94: 'as required both by the guidance in both HSG(95)8 (paras 17–20) and HSC 1998/048 and also by the general obligation to take all relevant factors into account in making the closure decision'.

261   HSG 1998/048.

262   HSG 1998/048. para 98.

263   (2000) 3 CCLR 378, 31 July 2000, QBD.

264   (2000) 3 CCLR 378, 31 July 2000, QBD at [91]–[93].

case a multi-professional assessment and consultation with parents or carers are necessary to determine whether the services they need can only be provided by the NHS or whether other alternatives would be more appropriate and cost effective.

The residents of Orchard Hill, whose problems are far greater than those of the average person with learning disability, require a detailed assessment of the kind set out in HSG(92)42 before any decision can be taken about moving them out of NHS care.

7.157   In the absence of special factors, such as existed in the *Merton, Sutton and Wandsworth* proceedings, it would appear that as a general principle specialist assessments (such as specifically addressing the psychological and risk impacts of a relocation) are 'not necessary or appropriate when making decision on closure'.[265]

Failure to consider relevant matters

7.158   In *R (Dudley and others) v East Sussex CC*[266] the claimant argued that the authority had reached its closure decision without considering relevant guidance, including (1) a report prepared at the request of Plymouth City Council[267] following *Cowl and others v Plymouth City Council*[268] and (2) Department of Health guidance concerning *The transfer of frail older NHS patients to other long stay settings*, HSG 1998/048 (see para 7.138 above). In relation to the former, the court held that notwithstanding the eminence of the report's author, Plymouth did not have the authority to promulgate guidelines for the world at large and so the material was not something to which East Sussex had to have regard. In relation to HSG 1998/048, since it was specifically NHS guidance and not addressed to social services (although it had been copied to them) it was again not something to which the authority had to have regard. If, however, there was a best interests declaration that it would be a risk to move the person, this would be a relevant consideration that had to be addressed in relation to closure.

Human Rights Act 1998

7.159   Many local authority owned home closure cases have invoked the provisions of the HRA 1998. With the enactment of HSCA 2008 s145, independent sector care homes are also subject to the provisions of the HRA 1998.[269]

265 *R (Phillips and Rowe) v Walsall MBC* [2001] EWHC 789 (Admin), (2001) 5 CCLR 383 at 387J; see, however, *R (B) v Worcestershire CC* [2009] EWHC 2915 (Admin), (2010) 13 CCLR 13 – considered further at para 7.24 abovew.

266 [2003] EWHC 1093 (Admin).

267 *Report and findings of the extraordinary complaints panel – closure of Granby Way Residential Care Home for Older People, Plymouth – November 2002* (2002) 6 CCLR 393. See also D Latham, *Scrutiny inquiry into care homes, Gloucestershire County Council*, June 2003; and J Williams and A Netten, *Guidelines for the closure of care homes for older people: prevalence and content of local government protocols*, Personal Social Services Research Unit discussion paper 1861/2, 2003, available at www.pssru.ac.uk/pdf/dp1861_2.pdf.

268 [2001] EWCA Civ 1935, [2002] 1 WLR 803, (2002) 5 CCLR 42.

269 This is of course not restricted to matters such as home closures, but covers all aspects of care.

Article 2 (right to life)

7.160   The relocation of institutionalised older people to a new residence may have a dramatic effect on their mental health and life expectancy.[270] Although the research evidence is mixed,[271] adverse publicity concerning the deaths[272] of older people following such relocations add to the general concern about the consequences of home closures. Closure decisions engage the public authority's common law duty of care to the residents. Courts will be prepared to take action where there is 'any firm evidence' that the closure may shorten a resident's life.[273]

7.161   In *R (Dudley and others) v East Sussex CC*[274] a closure decision was challenged on human rights grounds (among others). Maurice Kay J accepted that Article 2 of the ECHR had been given 'an extended meaning', observing:

> As was said by the Strasbourg Court in *Osman v UK* [1998] 29 EHRR 245 at paragraph 115:
>
>> Article 2 of the Convention may also imply in certain well-defined circumstances a positive obligation on the authorities to take preventative operational measures to protect an individual whose life is at risk.

7.162   Although the risk in that case was of criminal acts, the principle is not so limited. However, the evidence does not point to a breach of Article 2 in this case. No particularised medical evidence has been filed showing that the life of any particular resident is seriously at risk. What the claimant needs to establish is that 'the authorities did not do all that could reasonably be expected of them to avoid a real and immediate risk to life of which they have or ought to have knowledge' – see *Osman*. The claimants have not established that in this case.

---

270   See eg (1994) *Times* 7 July, 'Elderly patients die within weeks of transfer'; JM Mallick and TW Whipple, 'Validity of the nursing diagnosis of relocation stress syndrome' (2000) 49(2) *Nursing Research* 97–100; JA Thorson and RE Davis, 'Relocation of the institutionalised aged' (2000) 56(1) *Journal of Clinical Psychology* 131–138; AA McKinney and V Melby, 'Relocation stress in critical care: a review of the literature' 2002 Mar 11(2) *Journal of Clinical Nursing* 149–157.

271   J Williams and A Netten, *Guidelines for the closure of care homes for older people: prevalence and content of local government protocols*, Personal Social Services Research Unit discussion paper 1861/2, 2003, available at www.pssru.ac.uk/pdf/dp1861_2.pdf. See also *R (Thomas) v Havering LBC*; *R (W) v Coventry City Council* (2008) EWHC 2300 (Admin) where HHJ Pelling QC, in refusing leave observed that whilst medical evidence established, at most, that in some studies geriatric relocation resulted in an increased mortality, in other studies it had not: that different people reacted in different ways, and a sensitively handled move was less likely to result in any increase in mortality – and see also *R (Turner) v Southampton CC* [2009] EWCA Civ 1290.

272   See for example, 'Care home woman "upset by move"', *BBC*, 10 June 2003, concerning the death of Violet Townsend; 'Woman, 102, dies after "eviction"', *BBC*, 8 July 2003, concerning the death of Winifred Humphrey; 'Pensioner dies after being evicted from care home with six hours notice', *Evening Standard*, 7 June 2007, concerning the death of Alice Elsworth; and Victoria Ward 'Pensioners who died after sudden care home closure are named', *Telegraph*, 25 January 2015.

273   *R (Watts) v Wolverhampton City Council* [2009] EWCA Civ 1168 at para 18.

274   [2003] EWHC 1093 (Admin) at paras 27–33.

Article 3 (prohibition of torture, and inhuman or degrading treatment or punishment)

7.163   Again in *R (Dudley and others) v East Sussex CC*[275] the court rejected the submissions concerning a violation of Article 3. In doing so, considerable reliance was placed on the fact that the residents had not been deliberately humiliated or debased by the local authority.[276] It is questionable whether European Court of Human Rights Article 3 case-law does in fact require such an intention or indeed outcome.[277]

Article 8 (right to respect for private and family life, home and correspondence)

7.164   The Court of Appeal in *ex p Coughlan*[278] considered the finding of the first instance judge that Miss Coughlan's rights under Article 8 of the ECHR had been violated, in the following terms:[279]

> Miss Coughlan views the possible loss of her accommodation in Mardon House as life-threatening. While this may be putting the reality too high, we can readily see why it seems so to her; and we accept, on what is effectively uncontested evidence, that an enforced move of this kind will be emotionally devastating and seriously anti-therapeutic.

> The judge was entitled to treat this as a case where the Health Authority's conduct was in breach of article 8 and was not justified by the provisions of article 8(2). Mardon House is, in the circumstances described, Miss Coughlan's home. It has been that since 1993. It was promised to be just that for the rest of her life. It is not suggested that it is not her home or that she has a home elsewhere or that she has done anything to justify depriving her of her home at Mardon House.

7.165   In *R (Madden) v Bury MBC*[280] Richards J held that in such cases Article 8 was engaged and in consequence there needed to be:

> ... a clear recognition of the interests at stake under article 8 and of the matters relied on by way of justification of an interference with those interests, with an appropriate balancing exercise to ensure that the principle of proportionality is observed. This can be done on a relatively generalised basis looking at the interests of residents as a whole and does not, in the absence of special circumstances, require an individualised balancing exercise by reference to an assessment of the needs of each individual resident. The detailed individual assessment can follow. It may well be that in a situation of this kind, the balancing exercise does not need to be elaborate, and that its outcome is reasonably predictable, especially given the existence of what are plainly substantial public interest considerations in favour of closure.

> The fact remains that the point needs to be addressed. There is no evidence in this case that is was addressed ... Thus there was a failure to consider article 8; a failure to reach a proper assessment that the admitted interference

275   [2003] EWHC 1093 (Admin) at 27–33.
276   Citing *R v North West Lancashire Health Authority ex p A* [2000] 1 WLR 977; *Tyrer v UK* [1978] 2 EHHR 1; *East African Asian v UK* [1973] 3 EHRR 76; the first *Greek* case (1969) 12 YB Eur Conv HR 1.
277   See, for example, *Pretty v UK* (2001) 35 EHRR 1 where the court referred to treatment that (among other things) 'arouses feelings of fear' or 'anguish' and see also *Price v UK* (2001) 34 EHRR 1285 and *Đorđević v Croatia* (2012) Application no 41526/10, 24 July 2012.
278   [2000] 2 WLR 622, (1999) 2 CCLR 285, CA.
279   [2000] 2 WLR 622, (1999) 2 CCLR 285, CA at 92–93.
280   [2002] EWHC 1882 (Admin), (2002) 5 CCLR 622 at 636–637.

with the rights of residents under article 8 was justified. In my judgment that amounts to a further and independent reason for upholding the decision to be unlawful.

7.166   In *R (Dudley and others) v East Sussex CC*,[281] however, Maurice Kay J was satisfied (on the facts of this case) that any interference with Article 8 could be justified,[282] stating:

> I am prepared to assume, without deciding, that Article 8 is engaged. That may be a generous assumption in a case which does not have the *Coughlan* element of a particular home for life, and when the Council will be finding alternative accommodation for the residents. The issue then becomes justification under Article 8(2). In my judgment, the Council has clearly established justification. It is relevant that the East Sussex area contains a higher proportion of residents aged 65-plus than any other local authority. It has also been 'zero' rated by the Audit Commission which restricts the level of finance available. That is not a matter for congratulation, but it highlights the circumstances in which the Council was carrying out its review of residential care homes. These are plainly relevant considerations as the Council seeks the most effective ways of fulfilling its various statutory responsibilities within existing financial constraints. It is hardly surprising that it was anxious not to lose the prospect of a £1 million grant from central government. The court is slow to interfere with decisions which 'involve a balance of competing claims on the public purse in the allocation of economic resources', see Neill LJ in *R v CICB ex p P* [1995] 1 WLR 845 at 857.

7.167   In *R (Goldsmith) v Wandsworth LBC*[283] the Court of Appeal noted:

> It is not in dispute that a change to a strange environment for a person of the Appellant's frailty could have serious if not fatal consequences. The proportionality of the response is, therefore, of the utmost importance. In my judgment it is not good enough for Wandsworth, after the institution of proceedings, to produce evidence that this was a factor in its mind when it made the decision (whenever that was). In my judgment, the court has to look at the decision at the time it was made and at the manner in which it was communicated to the person or persons affected by it.

---

281 [2003] EWHC 1093 (Admin) at [27]–[33].

282 See also *R (Lloyd) v Barking and Dagenham LBC* [2001] EWCA Civ 533, (2001) 4 CCLR 196, another disputed home closure case where the Court of Appeal upheld the first instance judge's finding that arguments under Article 8 added 'nothing to the case'.

283 [2004] EWCA Civ 1170, (2004) 7 CCLR 472.

CHAPTER 8

Charging

continued

Introduction

8.1   This chapter considers the charging provisions in respect of care and support provided to adults under the Care Act (CA) 2014 – both accommodation and non-accommodation (or 'domiciliary care') arrangements. Support for adults provided under the National Health Service (NHS) legislation (for example, those eligible for NHS continuing healthcare (CC) funding) is covered separately at chapter 12, as is support provided under Mental Health Act 1983 s117 – in this case at para 15.79. This text does not cover the charging provisions for services provided under Children Act 1989 Part III: this is covered in the companion volume *Disabled children: a legal handbook*.[1]

8.2   The major impetus to charge for domiciliary and community based social care services stemmed from the reforms of the early 1990s, in a political shift evidenced by the 1990 policy guidance,[2] which stated that the government expected that local authorities would 'institute arrangements so that users of services of all types pay what they can reasonably afford towards their costs'. This was then qualified by the assertion that the provision of services should 'not be related to the ability of the user or their families to meet the costs'.

8.3   Since these pivotal reforms, there has been an increasing disquiet about the system for charging with a series of inquiries and reviews.[3] Concerns about the charging system include the perverse incentives that have led to authorities too readily placing people in residential care, funded through sale of the sale of their former home; the general unfairness of some individuals facing vast care costs and the lack of 'insurability' of these risks; and the charging regimes acting as a disincentive for people to get the care they need until they reach a crisis (especially where they are not entitled to free care provision), leading to an earlier use of more expensive residential care.[4]

8.4   In 2015/16, the local government ombudsman (LGO) received 278 complaints and enquiries about charging for social care, with over 62 per cent being upheld after detailed investigation. The complaints 'showed that many people are not being given the right information, at the right time, about the cost of care'.[5] A 2015 LGO report[6] identified common themes in complaints about charging for residential care, including poor information and advice about charging and costs of going into a care home; delays in carrying out financial assessments; deprivation of assets; and inadequate notice of fee increases where care is privately arranged

---

1   S Broach, L Clements and J Read, *Disabled children: a legal handbook*, 2nd edn, Legal Action Group, 2016, para 3.155.
2   *Community care in the next decade and beyond: policy guidance*, 1990, para 3.31.
3   See, for example, S Sutherland *The Royal Commission on long term care with respect to old age: long term care – rights and responsibilities* Cm 4192-I, The Stationery Office, 1999; and D Wanless, *Securing good care for older people – taking a long-term view. Wanless social care review*, King's Fund, 2006.
4   Report of Joint Inquiry by the Primary Care and Public Health and Social Care All Party Parliamentary Groups, *Our health, our care, our say*, 2006, p33.
5   LGO, *Review of adult social care complaints 2015/16*, 2016.
6   LGO, *Adult social care: ASC matters*, 2015.

residential care.[7] There is no doubt that the law in this area is sometimes unclear or contradictory,[8] creating difficulties for the public, other professionals and local authorities.

8.5   In 2011 major proposals regarding the funding and paying of care were made by the Commission on Funding of Care and Support.[9] A key element of this proposal, the 'cap on costs', was incorporated into the CA 2014 (sections 15 and 16) but its implementation has been delayed (until at least 2020) and is therefore not covered in this book.

8.6   This chapter sets out the matters which are common to charging for a care in all settings. It is structured so that all the relevant information about a particular topic is, insofar as is possible, contained under one heading (eg the treatment of income). It includes developments in the law to the end of January 2017.

Charging arrangements prior to the introduction of the Care Act 2014

8.7   Prior to the introduction of the CA 2014, the duties on local authorities in England to provide and charge for accommodation in care homes were found in National Assistance Act (NAA) 1948 Part III.[10] These provisions were supplemented by the National Assistance (Assessment of Resources) Regulations 1992[11] and the statutory guidance *Charging for residential accommodation guidance* (CRAG).[12] In similar fashion, the discretionary powers of local authorities to charge for certain non-accommodation services derived from Health and Social Services and Social Security Adjudications Act (HASSASSAA) 1983 s17. Until 2001, no national policy guidance on non-accommodation charges existed, with the result that there were wide disparities in the charges levied by social services authorities. In 2001 the Department of Health published (now repealed[13]) statutory guidance *Fairer charging policies for home care and other non-residential social services*[14] (updated 2013), referred to in this chapter as 'Fairer Charging 2013'.[15]

---

7   This was swiftly followed by a further publication in September 2015 by the LGO, namely *Focus report: learning lessons from complaints. Counting the cost of care: the council's role in informing the public choices about care homes*. Although it considers cases which occurred before the introduction of the CA 2014, the report highlights issues which remain relevant under the CA 2014.

8   In *Crofton v NHS Litigation Authority* [2007] EWCA Civ 71, (2007) 10 CCLR 123, the CA commented 'We cannot conclude this judgment without expressing our dismay at the complexity and labyrinthine nature of the relevant legislation and guidance, as well as (in some respects) its obscurity' (para 111).

9   Commission on Funding of Care and Support, *Fairer care funding: the report of the commission on funding of care and support* (the 'Dilnot report'), 2011.

10 Under National Assistance Act 1948 ss21, 22 and 26.

11 SI No 2977, as amended and referred to as the 'AOR regulations 1992'.

12 Last published by the Department of Health in April 2014, now repealed.

13 For confirmation of previous legislation and guidance repealed as a result of the CA 2014, see the statutory guidance at annex I and also the Care Act 2014 and Children and Families Act 2014 (Consequential Amendments) Order 2015 SI No 914.

14 LAC (2001)32.

15 Department of Health, *Fairer charging policies for home care and other non-residential social services guidance for councils with social services responsibilities*, 2013.

Paying for care under the Care Act 2014

Background

8.8   The CA 2014 repealed the previous charging provisions. The Act outlines the basic structure of the new regime, the detail of which is fleshed out in regulations and the statutory guidance. As with the pre-CA 2014 charging regimes, the charging regulations have much in common with the Income Support (General) Regulations 1987 ('IS regulations 1987'). The relevant provisions considered in this chapter are set out below:

- CA 2014 ss14, 17, 30, 34–36, 69–70);
- Care and Support (Charging and Assessment of Resources) Regulations 2014 (cited as the 'charging and assessment regulations 2014');[16]
- Care and Support and After-care (Choice of Accommodation) Regulations 2014;[17]
- Care and Support (Deferred Payment) Regulations 2014;[18]
- Care and Support (Preventing Needs of Care and Support) Regulations 2014;[19]
- *Care and support statutory guidance* (chapters 8 and 9 and annexes A–F) (referred to in this chapter as 'the statutory guidance').[20]

8.9   The statutory guidance (para 8.1) states that the CA 2014 'provides a single legal framework for charging for care and support under s14 and s17'.[21] Unlike the pre-CA 2014 charging regime, local authorities have a discretion to charge for all types of care and support services. Where a local authority decides that it will impose a charge, the regulations operate to determine the maximum amount that can be charged (statutory guidance para 8.6). In assessing charges, authorities must follow the financial assessment process as set out the statutory guidance (Chapters 8 and 9 and Annexes A-F).

8.10   Notwithstanding the rhetoric of a 'single legal framework', the CA 2014 provides for different charging arrangements for persons requiring care home accommodation from those who need other forms of care and support.[22]

---

16 SI No 2672.
17 SI No 2670.
18 SI No 2671.
19 SI No 2673.
20 Department of Health, *Care and support statutory guidance* to support implementation of Part 1 of the CA 2014 by local authorities, 2016.
21 CA 2014 s14: power of local authority to charge and CA 2014 s17: assessment of financial resources.
22 Statutory guidance (para 8.5) states the reason for the different approaches is that the 'delivery model for care homes is relatively uniform across the country and it is therefore sensible to provide a single model for charging purposes. However, other models of care generally see a greater variety of approaches that we [the DH] wish to continue'.

The statutory guidance

8.11 The legal status of the statutory guidance is considered at para 1.44 above, but the expectation is that authorities must follow it, unless they can demonstrate sound legal reasons for not doing so. In respect of charging policy, the statutory guidance is significantly less comprehensive than the previous statutory guidance in this area (eg CRAG). This will inevitably reduce its operational effectiveness; specific examples of these problems are set out where relevant in this chapter.

8.12 Some of the problems inherent in the statutory guidance, as originally issued in October 2014, were addressed by the Department of Health with the publication in 2015 of its *Frequently asked questions – charging for care'* ('DH FAQ'), which still remain pertinent.[23] In addition, the Department of Health also issued *Update on final orders under the Care Act 2014* to provide clarification about aspects of the statutory guidance ('DH update'),[24] with the advice that the statutory guidance should not be read without cross-reference to both the DH FAQ and the DH update, otherwise errors would be inevitable. The Local Government Association (LGA) published a range of advice guides, toolkits, templates and letters for use by local authorities which focus on the CA 2014 charging regime. In March 2016, the statutory guidance was updated, with further revision in December 2016.

The provision of financial information and advice

8.13 CA 2014, s4(1) places a duty upon local authorities to establish and maintain a service for providing people in its area with information and advice relating to care and/or support for adults and carers. This universal information and advice[25] duty is considered further at para 19.5 above.

8.14 This section looks at the specific requirements for financial information and advice (including independent financial advice) in the context of paying for care, which is set out in the statutory guidance at paras 3.36–3.52. The statutory duty upon a local authority to provide financial advice, including the obligation to assist adults in accessing independent financial advice, derives from CA 2014 s4(3), as follows:

> In providing information and advice under this section, a local authority must in particular–
> (a) have regard to the importance of identifying adults in the authority's area who would be likely to benefit from financial advice on matters relevant to the meeting of needs for care and support, and
> (b) seek to ensure that what it provides is sufficient to enable adults–
>   (i) to identify matters that are or might be relevant to their personal financial position that could be affected by the system provided for by this Part,

---

23 Prepared by the Department of Health and the National Association of Financial Assessment Officers, published on the Local Government Association website.

24 Published on 17 March 2015 by the Department of Health, *Update on final orders under the Care Act 2014*, and available from the Local Government Association.

25 See the statutory guidance, para 3.23 for an explanation of what is included in this definition.

(ii) to make plans for meeting needs for care and support that might arise, and

(iii) to understand the different ways in which they may access independent financial advice on matters relevant to the meeting of needs for care and support.

8.15   A local authority must therefore ensure that a wide range of adults within the authority's area have access to 'financial information and advice'[26] as well as to 'independent financial advice'.[27] The statutory guidance also refers to 'regulated' financial advice ie provided by an organisation regulated by the Financial Conduct Authority (para 3.10). Once those adults within the authority's area who would be likely to benefit from financial advice have been identified (CA 2014 s4(3)(a)), the effect of section 4(3)(b) is to set out quality standards for the advice provision ie that it is 'sufficient' for the stated purposes.

8.16   CA 2014 s4(4) requires that information and advice provided by a local authority must be accessible and proportionate to the needs of those for whom it is being provided.[28] Any financial information and advice must be given in an accessible format and by a range of methods (eg face-to-face meetings; posters; community settings): the duty under the CA 2014 'will not be met by the use of digital channels alone' (para 3.29). The statutory guidance advises that local authorities are required to establish and maintain services about financial information and advice on matters relevant to care and support, some of which it should provide directly to people in its community (at para 3.38). However, it also cautions that, where it would not be appropriate for a local authority to provide it directly, it must ensure that people are helped to understand how to access independent financial advice.[29]

8.17   The statutory guidance sets out the following matters to be included in its financial information and advice service (paras 3.41):

- understanding care charges;
- ways to pay;
- cap on care costs, particularly early assessments (now delayed until 2020);
- money management;
- making informed financial decisions; facilitating access to independent financial information and advice; [30]and
- the cap on care costs, when preparing for its introduction in 2020.[31]

26 This includes a 'broad spectrum of services whose purpose is to help people plan, prepare and pay for their care costs' (statutory guidance, para 3.10).

27 This is defined as 'financial advice provided by a person who is independent of the local authority in question' (CA 2014 s4(5)).

28 This is considered in the statutory guidance, paras 3.27–3.35.

29 ADASS has expressed concern that the increased emphasis on the provision of independent financial advice may result in more people obtaining advice on how to reduce their contributions to their care fees (LGA and ADASS, *Joint consultation response Care Act: regulations and guidance*, 2014 at para 31.

30 The matters above are considered in the statutory guidance at paras 3.43–3.52.

31 For information about 'Preparing for funding reform' see the statutory guidance at para 23.41–23.62; it notes (at para 23.42) that '[t]he statutory guidance will be updated and re-published alongside the necessary regulations in April 2019, one year in advance of implementation, to set out how the capped cost system will impact

8.18   While some of the requirements were well established under the pre-CA 2014 regime (eg the local authority obligation to provide advice about social security benefits – para 3.45), some are new (eg the timing and context of any retirement decisions a person might be making and how this interacts with paying for their care and support – para 3.47). The duty to provide financial information and advice placed upon local authorities under the CA 2014 are in some ways onerous. For example, it is no longer sufficient for a local authority to provide generic information about paying for care – it has to be prepared 'to give information that would be particularly pertinent to a person's individual circumstances and facilitate access to an independent source of information or advice where relevant' (para 3.44).

8.19   To assist authorities with their enhanced obligations to provide financial information and advice, the Association of Directors of Adult Social Services Departments (ADASS), the Local Government Association (LGA) and the Department of Health have prepared *Practice guidance to support local authorities to facilitate access to independent financial information and advice under the Care Act 2014* (March 2015). As practice guidance, it is arguable that authorities should 'have regard' to it when determining how to implement their statutory duty to provide independent financial information and advice: a systematic failure to do so may be evidence of maladministration or sufficient to found a public law challenge.[32]

Charging schemes: the duty to consult

8.20   Under the pre-CA 2014 regime, as a matter of public law, consultation was required before any significant changes were made to a charging regime:[33] a point made in the Fairer Charging 2013 guidance.[34]

8.21   The CA 2014 does not provide for a specific statutory requirement to consult about charges. The advice to local authorities in respect of the need for consultation following the introduction of the CA 2014 is set out in the statutory guidance (at para 23.14):

> Local authorities should review the operation of their local charging framework, to ensure that this is consistent with the obligations set out by the Care Act and associated regulations, and the provisions set out in chapter 8. Where local authorities are satisfied that their approach to charging follows the detail required by the Act and regulations, they do not need to take further steps to review funding arrangements for individuals or to carry out new financial assessments, unless other circumstances have changed. Local authorities should consider the need to consult with their local population, but should not be expected to consult formally if their approach to charging has not changed as a result of the Act.

practically on the processes and requirements of the Act, and how the obligations of local authorities will change'.

32 Following the decision in *R v Islington LBC ex p Rixon* (1997–1998) 1 CCLR 119, 15 March 1996, QBD.

33 *R v Coventry City Council ex p Carton* (2001) 4 CCLR 41.

34 See para 11 (flat rate charges); para 19 (the level of the minimum income guarantee); para 31 (savings).

8.22   The statutory guidance makes various references to the need for authorities to exercise their discretion in respect of different aspects of charging for care and support,[35] which frequently provides for a concomitant need to consult. As a general principle, where a change in a local authority charging policy would result in an adverse impact on those persons receiving services, consultation will be required.[36] If an authority has decided not to change its charging policy in the belief that it is consistent with its post-CA 2014 obligations, but this proves to be mistaken, resulting in people having to pay more for their care and support, the authority would need to identify a strong reason for not undertaking a consultation exercise. Without such a reason, it would be vulnerable to challenge.

8.23   In the context of charging carers for carer's services, there is no explicit requirement to consult in the CA 2014. The statutory guidance makes it clear that local authorities 'should consider carefully the likely impact of any charges on carers' (statutory guidance, para 8.50), which may be a difficult task without proper consultation, given that carers are likely to experience a significant adverse impact if charges were to be introduced for the first time. In such a consultation, it would be prudent for the authority to consult not only with carers but with all persons who may be affected by such a change, particularly as the group for whom they care are 'protected groups' (eg disability and/or on the grounds of age) for the purposes of the Equality Act (EqA) 2010.[37]

8.24   The CA 2014 regime's changes to certain charging policies and the consequent need for consultation creates not insignificant administrative obligation for local authorities.[38] It is difficult to see how the obligation on each authority to devise a local charging policy for non-accommodation care settings will assist the charging principles of ensuring clarity and transparency or of reducing 'postcode' variations in charging policies throughout England.

8.25   Although determined before the introduction of the CA 2014, *KM v Northamptonshire CC*[39] remains a useful reminder to authorities of the need to ensure that charging policies follow the charging regulations and statutory guidance. The case involved charging for non-accommodation care services[40] and the court held that the council had failed to apply the

---

35   For example, see statutory guidance at para 8.7 in the context of charging for non-accommodation care: 'Therefore, local authorities should develop and maintain a policy setting out how they will charge people in settings other than care homes'; and, at para 8.48: 'Local authorities should also consider whether it is appropriate to set a maximum charge, for example these might be set as a maximum percentage of care home charges in a local area'.

36   For further consideration about the obligation upon local authorities to consult, see para 20.200 below.

37   For cases considering consultation under the EqA 2010, see, for example, *Bracking v Secretary of State for Work and Pensions* [2013] EWCA Civ 1345 and *R (Aspinall) v Secretary of State for Work and Pensions* [2014] EWHC 4134 (Admin). Adverse treatment of a carer may constitute unlawful associative discrimination contrary to EqA 2010 s13 – see *Coleman v Attridge* ECJ C-303/06 Judgment 17 July 2008.

38   See LGA and ADASS, *Joint consultation response Care Act: regulations and guidance*, August 2014 at p31.

39   [2015] EWHC 482 (Admin).

40   The dispute related to the treatment of the claimant's income in respect of the income support disability premium and enhanced disability premium – now by

statutory guidance or to make its policy sufficiently clear, with the result that it added about one third to the claimant's level of financial contribution (para 38). The case demonstrates the willingness of the courts to ensure that charging policies comply with national guidance.

8.26 Challenges to the legality of consultations concerning charging schemes, however, have their limits. In *R (Domb) v Hammersmith and Fulham LBC*,[41] the authority had decided to cut council tax by three per cent and, as a consequence, it sought to reintroduce charges for community care services. The Court of Appeal held that it was not unreasonable for the council to limit its consultation as to whether it should reintroduce charges or to raise eligibility criteria (once a decision had been made to cut council tax). However, Sedley LJ expressed his misgivings that the appeal had to be conducted on a debatable premise thus:[42]

> The object of this exercise was the sacrifice of free home care on the altar of a council tax reduction for which there was no legal requirement. The only real issue was how it was to be accomplished. As Rix LJ indicates, and as I respectfully agree, there is at the back of this a major question of public law: can a local authority, by tying its own fiscal hands for electoral ends, rely on the consequent budgetary deficit to modify its performance of its statutory duties? But it is not the issue before this court.

When must services be provided free of charge?

8.27 Care and support services (including care home accommodation) must be provided without charge[43] in the following circumstances:

1) where the service is being provided to the adult in need as part of a package of intermediate care and reablement support services, with the purpose of providing assistance to the adult to enable them to maintain or regain the ability needed to live in their own home[44] – and see para 9.13 below;

2) community equipment (aids and minor adaptations) to property for the purpose of assisting at home or aiding daily living. Aids must be provided free of charge where provided to meet or prevent/delay needs. A minor adaptation is one costing £1,000 or less[45] – and see para 7.75 above;

3) services provided under MHA 1983 s117[46] – and see para 15.79 below;

---

charging and assessment regulations 2014 reg 7 (calculation of the minimum income guarantee (MIG)).

41 [2009] EWCA Civ 941.

42 [2009] EWCA Civ 941 at para 80 – and see also para 2.62 above.

43 CA 2014 s14(6) and charging and assessment regulations 2014 reg 3 and see also the statutory guidance, para 8.14.

44 See para 7.75 above for discussion concerning intermediate care and reablement; CA 2014 s14(6), charging and assessment regulations 2014 reg 3 and the statutory guidance, para 8.14 states that the intermediate services provided under CA 2014 ss18, 19 and 20 are to be provided free of charge for up to six weeks, with the ability to extend this time period where there are clear preventive benefits.

45 CA 2014 s14(6) and charging and assessment regulations 2014 reg 3(3); and statutory guidance, para 8.14.

46 Statutory guidance, para 8.14.

4) where the adult in need is suffering from variant CJD;[47]
5) where a person's means have been assessed the same or lower than the prescribed amount within the guidance;[48]
6) assessment of needs and care planning may also not be charged for, since these processes do not constitute 'meeting needs'[49] – but see para 8.55 below;
7) any service or part of service which the NHS is under a duty to provide. This includes services provided under NHS CC (see chapter 12) and the NHS contribution to registered nursing care (see para 11.110 below);
8) any services which a local authority is under a duty to provide through other legislation may not be charged for under the CA 2014.

8.28   Where the services are provided by a local authority under 1 or 2 above, the costs of meeting those needs will not form part of the adult's personal budget (see statutory guidance paras 11.15 to 11.21).

Charging principles

8.29   The statutory guidance states that the 'overarching principle is that people should only be required to pay what they can afford' (para 8.2). In the same paragraph, the statutory guidance sets out the following principles, which apply to all care settings and which local authorities should take them into account when making decisions about charging, namely:

- ensure that people are not charged more than it is reasonably practicable for them to pay;
- be comprehensive, to reduce variation in the way people are assessed and charged;
- be clear and transparent, so people know what they will be charged;
- promote well-being, social inclusion, and support the vision of personalisation, independence, choice and control;
- support carers to look after their own health and well-being and to care effectively and safely;
- be person-focused, reflecting the variety of care and caring journeys and the variety of options available to meet their needs;
- apply the charging rules equally so those with similar needs or services are treated the same and minimise anomalies between different care settings;
- encourage and enable those who wish to stay in or take up employment, education or training or plan for the future costs of meeting their needs to do so; and
- be sustainable for local authorities in the long-term.

---

47 CA 2014 s14(6) and charging and assessment regulations 2014 reg 4; and statutory guidance, para 8.14.
48 See CA 2014 s14; charging and assessment regulations 2014 regs 7 and 12; and statutory guidance, para 8.7.
49 Statutory guidance, para 8.14.

8.30   These principles are repeated in the statutory guidance at para 8.45, in the context of non-accommodation charging with the additional 'principle' that a local authority can 'administer a charging policy for people who lack capacity or are losing capacity in a way that considers what capacity remains and their rights'. In practical terms, the issue of capacity is equally relevant for those people, with diminishing capacity, who are in need of care home accommodation. This principle therefore is of equal application to the provision of care home accommodation; the position of those persons who lack capacity is considered further below at para 8.344 below.

Reasonably practicable

8.31   The principle that 'people are not charged more than it is reasonably practicable for them to pay' is welcome, particularly as it now extends to those who receive care and support in a care home setting. However, for people receiving care in other settings, it represents a dilution of their legal protection since, prior to the introduction of the CA 2014, this prohibition was contained in statute[50] and so was only capable of being removed by parliament.[51]

8.32   Unlike the previous regime,[52] the CA 2014 contains no requirement that authorities have procedures for reducing or waiving the charge where it is not 'reasonably practicable' for the user to pay the full charge. Nevertheless, the need for such procedures is implicit in the requirement that authorities 'ensure' that people are not charged more than it is reasonably practicable for them to pay. Charges can be challenged though the normal complaints process – and this is considered at para 8.337 below.

8.33   In cases considered under the very similar pre-Care Act regime, the local government ombudsman has held it to be maladministration for an authority to adopt a charging policy which only permits exceptions if users provide 'proof of hardship'[53] since this is a materially more severe criterion than 'not reasonably practicable'. Likewise, in *R v Calderdale DC ex p Houghton*,[54] the local authority conceded that its procedures for assessing the reasonableness of its charges were unreasonably demanding: they required that applicants establish that their expenditure was so exceptional that it was not reasonable for the authority to charge the full amount. The ombudsman has further held that, where a claimant had produced evidence that her expenditure exceeds her income, the authority cannot insist on her paying the full charge without providing cogent reasons why it considers her able to pay the amount claimed.[55]

---

50 Health and Social Services and Social Security Adjudications Act 1983 s17.

51 The advice by the Select Committee that the prohibition be retained in statute (or at least in regulations) was rejected: Joint Committee on the Draft Care and Support Bill, *Draft Care and Support Bill*, HL Paper 143 HC 822, The Stationery Office, 2013, para 196. It now appears only in the statutory guidance, para 8.2.

52 Health and Social Services and Social Security Adjudications Act 1983 s17(3).

53 Complaint nos 99/C/02509 and 02624 against Gateshead, 28 February 2001.

54 Unreported; but see (1999) 2 CCLR 119.

55 Complaint nos 99/C/02509 and 02624 against Gateshead, 28 February 2001.

Who is to be charged?

8.34   The discretionary charging regime under the CA 2014 applies to adults[56] (as adults 'in need') and also to adult carers.[57] As well as charging for accommodation in a care home, the charging arrangements also cover any care and support setting, including the person's own home; extra care housing[58]; supported living accommodation or shared lives placements (statutory guidance para 8.39). The statutory guidance makes it clear that 'local authorities *must not* charge people for a financial assessment, a needs assessment or the preparation of the care and support plan'(at para 8.60, emphasis in the original).

Carers

8.35   Where a local authority decides to exercise its discretion to charge carers, it must do so in accordance with the non-residential charging rules.[59] The statutory guidance also expressly states that 'a local authority *must not* charge a carer for care and support provided directly to the person they care for under any circumstance'.[60]

8.36   Although adult carers are placed on the same footing as adults in need in terms of an authority's power to charge for support provided to carers (under CA 2014 s20), the statutory guidance appears ambivalent about local authorities doing so.[61] The statutory guidance states that charging carers would, in many cases, be a 'false economy'[62] and, further, that it is not envisaged that it would be 'efficient' for local authorities to systematically charge carers for meeting their eligible needs.[63] The rationale in the statutory guidance for the exercise of caution in charging carers is founded in the economic argument ie that 'carers voluntarily meet eligible needs that

---

56   'Adult' is defined as a person aged 18 years or older: CA 2014 s2(8).
57   See CA 2014 s10(3): 'Carer' means an adult who provides or intends to provide care for another adult (an 'adult needing care').
58   In LGO complaint no 11 022 479 against Walsall MBC, 12 March 2014, the council was criticised for not giving a man in his 60s, with complex multiple health problems, any option but to live in an extra care housing scheme and to pay care charges for a service he neither used nor wanted. As a remedy, the ombudsman required the council to waive all the man's personal care charges and 50 per cent of other charges, as well as requiring the council to review the current charging structure for the extra care scheme and also the information given to prospective tenants in advance of any move.
59   Statutory guidance, para 8.53.
60   Statutory guidance, para 8.49 (emphasis in the original), following CA 2014 s14(3); the principle also applies to charging for preventative services by virtue of Care and Support (Prevention of Care and Support Needs) Regulations 2014 SI 2673 reg 3(3).
61   Statutory guidance, paras 8.49–8.55.
62   Statutory guidance, para 8.50; the ADASS produced a short factsheet for local authorities to use when considering whether to put in place a policy to charge carers which sets out 'the evidence that charging would be a false economy' – see statutory guidance, para 8.51 which provides a link to the ADASS.
63   Statutory guidance, para 8.51.

the local authority would otherwise be required to meet'.[64] However, some local authorities are now imposing charges for carer support services.[65]

Preventative care

8.37   Local authorities are under a general duty[66] to provide preventative services which they 'consider' will, in broad terms, prevent, delay or reduce the needs of adults and carers for care and/or support in their area.[67] The charging and assessment regulations 2014 do not apply to charging for preventative services as these apply only to care and support provided under CA 2014 ss18–20. The statutory guidance advises local authorities that, when choosing to charge for any other preventative services,[68] 'it should consider how to balance the affordability and viability of the activity with the likely impact that charging may have on uptake' (para 2.75).

8.38   Where a local authority decides to charge for other preventative services, any charge must not reduce the person's income below the amount of the minimum income guaranteed amount.[69] The statutory guidance does not envisage that a full financial assessment will be necessary or proportionate. However, authorities will need to devise a method of assessment by which they can satisfy themselves that the person's income will not fall below that minimum income guaranteed amount and that any charges are affordable.[70] In any event, a local authority must not charge more than it costs to provide or arrange for the service, facility or resource.[71]

8.39   Where the preventative service provided as part of an intermediate care and reablement or in the form of community equipment must be provided free of charge. Intermediate care and reablement is usually provided for a period of six weeks (see para 9.19 below). It may be provided either as a (free of charge) preventative service under CA 2014 s2. However, the service may also be provided as part of a package of care and support to meet eligible needs, where it must not be charged for in the first six weeks, to ensure consistency (statutory guidance, para 2.61).

---

64 Statutory guidance, paras 8.50 and 8.51.
65 For example, see in relation to Redbridge LBC Douglas Patient, 'Carers charge would force vulnerable into poverty' in *Epping Forest Guardian*, 4 March 2015. It appears that Enfield LBC now charges carers for carers' services where the carer has capital in excess of the capital limit – see www.enfieldcarers.org/the-care-act-2014-carers-assessments-you/. In its 2015 report, *Charge on caring? Analysis of the use and impact of charges by councils providing support to unpaid carers*, the Carers Trust analysed data from 132 councils and found that eight councils (six per cent) were charging carers for the support that they offered them, with a further 23 councils considering charging in the next 12 months.
66 CA 2014 s2; and the Care and Support (Preventing Needs of Care and Support) Regulations 2014).
67 The topic is considered in this book at paras 9.2–9.12.
68 Charging for preventative services is to be found in the statutory guidance at paras 2.55–2.63.
69 Care and Support (Preventing Needs of Care and Support) Regulations 2014 reg 3(2); and see also para 8.234 for an explanation of 'minimum income guaranteed amount' (MIG).
70 Statutory guidance, para 2.59; see also para 8.324.
71 CA 2015 s2(5).

Prisoners

8.40   As noted below (see para 15.143) the provisions of the CA 2014 apply to those persons in custodial settings with needs for care and support. Prisoners are therefore entitled to an assessment of their needs for care and support with the provision of services to meet eligible needs.

8.41   In respect of paying for their care, prisoners will be subject to a financial assessment[72] to determine how much they should pay towards the cost of any care and support they receive, as a person would be in the community. While in prison, entitlement to social security benefits is restricted, and any earning in prison are to be disregarded in any financial assessment. However, the statutory guidance notes that any capital assets, savings and pension will need to be considered as part of any financial assessment, in accordance with the charging rules set out in the statutory guidance, chapter 8.[73] Local authorities with prisons within their area will therefore need to devise charging policies to include the financial assessment process for prisoners.

Financial assessments

Overview

8.42   Where a local authority has assessed a person's needs for care and/or support services (provided under CA 2014 ss18–20) and it has exercised its discretion (under CA 2014 s14) to charge for those services, it must carry out a financial assessment under CA 2014 s17.[74] In carrying out this assessment[75] the authority must assess:

a)   the level of the person's financial resources; and

b)   the amount (if any) the person would be likely to pay towards the cost of meeting the needs for care and/or support.[76]

The amount charged by a authority for the care and/or support service must not be more than the cost it incurs in meeting the assessed needs of the person.[77]

8.43   On completion of a financial assessment, the authority must give the person a written record of the assessment.[78] The record may be provided alongside the person's care and support plan or may be given separately (or via online means). It should provide an explanation of how the charge was calculated, the amount and frequency of the charge and, where there are fluctuations in the charge, the reasons for them. This information must be provided in a manner which the person can easily understand (see statutory guidance, para 8.16).

---

72   See statutory guidance, para 17.30.
73   Statutory guidance, para 8.10.
74   Charging and assessment regulations 2014 reg 9.
75   As described under CA 2014 s17(5).
76   CA 2014 s17(1)–(4).
77   Statutory guidance, para 8.15; CA 2014 s14(4).
78   CA 2014 s17(6).

8.44   The statutory guidance advises that, once a local authority had decided to meet a person's needs, it must then carry out a financial assessment if it wishes to charge the adult (para 6.12). The statutory guidance emphasises that (para 6.12):

> The financial assessment may in practice run parallel to the needs assessment, but it must never influence an assessment of needs. Local authorities must inform individuals that a financial assessment will determine whether or not they pay towards their care and support, but this must have no bearing on the assessment process itself.

This approach remains the same, regardless of the setting in which the care is to be delivered.

8.45   The approach – that the assessment of means 'may run in parallel to the needs assessment' – is a departure from the pre-CA 2014 guidance which placed the financial assessment process firmly after the assessment of need.[79] In practice, however, many authorities were capturing financial information at the same time as the needs assessments and challenges to this process were largely restricted to cases where the authority made a back dated claim (see also para 8.47 below).[80] The Fairer Charging 2013 guidance (para 98) emphasised that 'Charges should not be made for any period before an assessment of charges has been communicated to the user, although this may be unavoidable where the user has not co-operated with the assessment'.[81]

8.46   In 2013, the LGO found maladministration in relation to a council's home care charging policy that levied a standard provisional charge for period prior to the completion of the person's financial assessment and formal notification of the charge.[82]

8.47   The CA 2014 and the statutory guidance make no reference to this previous approach. However, the issue is addressed in the DH FAQ,[83] which advises that, as a general rule, an authority is able to levy charges from the date it starts to incur costs to meet a person's care and support needs. It also flags up the (rather obvious) expectation that the authority will work out how much the person is able to afford to pay before it collects any

---

79 See, for example, Department of Health, *Community care in the next decade and beyond: policy guidance*, HMSO, para 3.31; Department of Health, *Prioritising need in the context of Putting People First*, 2010, para 71: 'An assessment of the person's ability to pay for services should therefore only take place after they have been assessed as having eligible needs.'

80 See LGO decision complaint no 16-004-0614 against Kingston-upon-Thames RLBC, 20 September 2016, where the complainant refused to pay a debt of £10,003.28 (for her late mother's care home fees) after the authority took 18 months to send out an invoice for the sum due. The LGO found that the authority had been at fault for failing to issue the invoice, but did not find maladministration – the complainant had been properly advised of the charge when the care home placement was arranged.

81 This requirement did not apply to charging for care home accommodation under CRAG, which obliged authorities to ensure that residents were given a clear explanation (usually in writing) of how their assessed contribution had been calculated and why this figure may change, because of the changes in social security benefit payments following admission to the care home (CRAG, para 1.019).

82 Report on an investigation into complaint no 12 014 343 against Kent CC, 24 May 2013: the council had to refund the charges of £380 and pay £200 in compensation for bringing the complaint and refund all others who had been similarly charged under the policy.

83 See Q102 and Q201.

money from him or her. Authorities are, therefore, expected to complete a financial assessment as soon as possible so as to avoid people being faced with large, delayed bills and, if so, the person must be given a 'reasonable time' to pay any outstanding charges due.[84]

8.48   There are some circumstances where the local authority is to be treated (or 'deemed') as having carried out a full financial assessment where, for a variety of reasons, it may not have in fact done so.[85] These will include, for example, where an adult has either refused a financial assessment,[86] or has refused to co-operate with the financial assessment but the authority has nevertheless decided to meet some or all of the adult's care and/or support needs.[87] In such circumstances, the authority is deemed to have carried out a full financial assessment of the adult and it is entitled to decide that the adult's financial resources exceed the 'financial limit'[88] – the person is therefore to be charged the full cost of his or her care and support.

'Light touch' financial assessments

8.49   The CA 2014 introduces the concept of 'light-touch' financial assessments, to be carried out by the authority in the situations set out in the statutory guidance (at para 8.23). These are:

a) where the person has significant financial resources and does not wish to undergo a full financial assessment;

b) where the charge for the service is very modest, the person is clearly able to meet it and it would be disproportionate to carry out the full financial assessment; and

c) where a person is in receipt of benefits which demonstrate that they would not be able to contribute towards their care and support costs.

8.50   When undertaking a 'light touch' financial assessment, the authority must be satisfied on the basis of evidence provided by the person that they can afford, and will continue to be able to afford, any charges due' (statutory guidance, para 8.22). This approach stems from the overarching principle of the CA 2014 charging framework ie that 'people should only be required to pay what they can afford' (statutory guidance, para 8.2). Examples of the type of evidence which may be appropriate to satisfy the authority of the person's ability to afford the charges due are given at para 8.24 of the statutory guidance (eg 'savings worth clearly more than the upper capital limit'). The statutory guidance requires that authorities consider not just the evidence that the person is able to provide but also the level of the charge it proposes to make (para 8.26) – presumably on the basis that the

---

84   Where there has been culpable delay by a local authority in assessing care charges, resulting in the service user facing an unexpected and substantial claim for back charges, it may be maladministration if it seeks to recover of the entire amount: see LGO Report on complaint 11 022 473 against Kingston upon Thames RBL, 19 August 2014 at para 75.

85   Charging and assessment regulations 2014 reg 10(1)–(3).

86   Charging and assessment regulations 2014 reg 10(1)(a).

87   Charging and assessment regulations 2014 reg 10(1)(b).

88   For definition of 'financial limit', see CA 2014 s17(8)–(9): in general terms the maximum level of income, capital or combination of capital and income above which the authority would not be obliged to provide care and/or support.

higher the charge, the more evidence may be needed to satisfy the authority that the person is able to afford the charge.

8.51 The statutory guidance is silent on the evidence required where the person falls into the situation set out at para 8.23(c) ie that the person is in receipt of benefit which demonstrate that they would be unable to contribute towards their care and support costs. The 'benefit' example given in the statutory guidance is jobseekers' allowance (JSA), which is perhaps not as helpful as it could be, given that there are two distinct types of JSA.[89] It is evident that the authority will have to be alert to the precise type of social security benefits the person receives before determining, without a full financial assessment, that a person does not have the ability to contribute towards their care and support costs.

8.52 In practical terms, an authority will be required to carry out a 'mini' financial assessment in order to make a valid decision on the usual public law principles.[90] Any charging policies drawn up by local authorities will need to address the issue of what evidence will be required in cases where a light touch financial assessment is carried out. The authority must obtain the person's consent to carry out such an assessment and where it proposes to undertake one, it needs to be satisfied that the person not only consents[91] to this process, but also that they are willing (and will continue to be willing) to pay all the charges due. Where any of these conditions is not met, or where the person does not agree that the assessed charges calculated under the light touch assessment are affordable, the authority will be required to undertake a full financial assessment (statutory guidance, para 8.25).

8.53 Where the authority undertakes a light touch financial assessment, it must advise the person of the outcome.[92] The person must be informed that a light touch financial assessment has taken place and that there is a right to request a full financial assessment, if they so wish, with the authority ensuring that the person has access to sufficient information and advice, including the option of independent financial information and advice (statutory guidance, para 8.26).

8.54 Analysis of the light touch financial assessment process obliges the authority to (a) ensure that sufficient information is given to the person to

---

89 Where a person receives 'contribution based' JSA (payable for six months), Jobcentre Plus does not assess the claimant's assets (eg capital) as JSA is paid solely on the basis of the claimant's national insurance contribution record. Therefore, provided the person fulfils the eligibility conditions, contribution based JSA is payable to the claimant regardless of the amount of his or her capital assets. However, a claim for 'income based' JSA is means tested and is payable only where the claimant's capital assets are £16,000 or less. Therefore, authorities would be more able to be confident that a claimant in receipt of income based JSA is unlikely to exceed the relevant capital limit.

90 For a further discussion about 'public law' principles, see chapter 20.

91 Charging and assessment regulations 2014 regs10(2) and (3).

92 In accordance with CA 2014 s17(6) which requires an authority to give a written record of the financial assessment to the adult to whom it relates. Where an authority carries out a light touch financial assessment, it is treated as though it had carried out the full financial assessment under charging and assessment regulations 2014 reg 10. On that basis, the person whose charges are calculated following a light touch financial assessment is presumably deemed to be entitled to a written record of that assessment.

decide if it is right for him or her, and (b) to determine what information is required to prove that the person is over/under the relevant financial limits for capital and/or income. These requirements are illustrated by the decision of the Welsh ombudsman in a 2009 report.[93] The complainant, a daughter, had paid care home fees as a self-funder for her mother in the belief that the capital limit was exceeded by her mother's assets, which had been placed in income bonds. As the capital value of monies placed in income bonds should have been disregarded, her mother's care should have been funded by the local authority for a period more than three years. The ombudsman recommended that the authority repay the care costs for this period and observed that, in future, the council 'should provide sufficient information about the process to allow the client to make an informed decision as to whether disclosing full details of their financial affairs may be in their best interests'. Under the CA 2014 regime, such information forms part of the charging policy and must also comply with the authority's information and advice obligation under CA 2014 s4 (see para 8.13 above).

Arrangement fees

8.55   The provisions of the CA 2014[94] place local authorities under a duty to meet a person's eligible needs where their financial resources are above the financial limit, but the person requests the authority to meet their needs (other than in a care home) – see para 4.61 above. The original intention was that these provisions would also apply to self-funders who required care in care homes. However, at the time of the commencement of the CA 2014, this element had been delayed until April 2016 in order to allow the DH to undertake further work to explore the impact on the social care market of this provision, insofar as it related to care homes. In July 2015, it was announced that its introduction in respect of self-funders requiring care home accommodation would be again deferred to April 2020.[95]

8.56   Where the person requests[96] that the authority meets his or her eligible need for a care home placement, the local authority may choose to meet their needs but is not required to do so (a discretionary power). In other cases, where the eligible needs are to be met by care and support of some other type, the local authority must meet those eligible needs by making the necessary arrangements (statutory guidance, para 8.56) (a statutory duty). Where the person has resources above the financial limits, the local authority may charge the person for the full cost of their care and support.

93 Public Services Ombudsman for Wales, complaint no 2007/02004 against Powys County Council, 20 May 2009.

94 See CA 2014 s14(1)(b), 18(3), 20(3) and (5); statutory guidance, paras 8.56–8.64.

95 Letter Minister of State for Community and Social Care (Alistair Burt MP) to Local Government Association, 17 July 2015 on the grounds that extra time will enable the Department of Health to 'better understand the potential impact on the care market and the interaction with the cap on care costs system'.

96 Obviously, a person may only request it if the person knows that the provision exists: the statutory guidance (paras 8.57–8.58) sets out the obligations upon the authority to make people aware of it.

In such circumstances, the person remains responsible for paying for the cost of their care and support, but the local authority takes on the responsibility for meeting those needs (statutory guidance, para 8.63).

8.57 Where a self-funder requests[97] that the local authority meets their eligible needs, CA 2014 s14(1)(b) provides the authority with the discretionary power to charge an 'arrangement fee' for putting in place the arrangements to meet the person's care needs. However, where a local authority exercises its discretion to meet the needs of a person with resources above the financial limit who requires a care home placement, it must not charge an arrangement fee. The statutory guidance states that the arrangement fee may not be charged because it would support that person under its power (rather than its duty) to meet needs, and the ability to charge the arrangement fee applies only to circumstances when the authority is required to meet needs (para 8.59). This distinction, while it may be legally accurate, is arguably counter-intuitive: where an authority is under a duty to meet a person's care needs (for care at home), an arrangement fee may be incurred. However, where an authority exercises its discretion to arrange care in care home for a self-funder, no arrangement fee may be charged, even though the person would be receiving the benefit of the authority's skill and experience in arranging the placement. The fact that the authority would, in practical terms, have to carry out this work free of charge is therefore very little incentive for authorities to exercise its discretion to arrange care home placements.

8.58 The arrangement fee must cover only the costs that local authorities actually incur in arranging care, for example, 'the cost of negotiating and/or managing the contract with a provider and cover any administration costs incurred' (statutory guidance, para 8.59). It further notes that, while a local authority may charge a flat rate fee this must not exceed the actual costs incurred by the authority in arranging the person's care.[98] The statutory guidance reminds authorities to assure themselves that 'whilst the person remains responsible for paying for their own care, they have sufficient assets for the arrangements that it puts in place to remain both affordable and sustainable' (para 8.64). This suggests that the authority needs to make appropriate enquiries about the person's financial circumstances, if they have not already done so, possibly by means of a light touch assessment. It may be necessary for the authority to secure the person's agreement in writing to pay the costs of their care and support (statutory guidance, para 8.64).

97 The statutory guidance, para 8.56 states that such a request 'could be for a variety of reasons such as the person finding the system too difficult to navigate, or wishing to take advantage of the local authority's knowledge of the local market of care and support services'.
98 Statutory guidance, para 8.61.

The treatment of couples

8.59   The provisions of the CA 2014 reflect the previous position found in CRAG[99] and the Fairer Charging 2013 guidance,[100] which provided that councils should assess only the means (both income and capital) of the person who is subject to the financial assessment.[101] This approach applies in all care settings. It is wholly different approach from that taken in the assessment of social security benefits, including income support under the IS regulations 1987, which requires the joint income and assets of a couple to be included in the IS assessment.

Joint capital

8.60   Although the law is clear – that it is only the service user's means that can be taken into account for charging purposes – the assessment process in respect of couples may be complex. These difficulties were highlighted in the now repealed Fairer Charging 2013 guidance, as follows (para 68):

> Councils may wish to consider in individual cases whether a user's means may include resources not held in that person's name, but to which the user has a legal entitlement. The most likely instances of this kind will arise in relation to married or unmarried couples. In some circumstances, the user may have a legal right to a share in the value of an asset, for example a bank account, even if it is not in his or her name. In some circumstances, statutory provisions provide such a right. In other circumstances, what are known as 'equitable principles' may apply to give such a right, for example where there is an unwritten agreement between partners that they both own a property or an asset, even though the title is in only one of their names. If the council has some reason to believe that the user does have means other than those initially disclosed, a request may reasonably be made for the user to arrange for the partner to disclose his or relevant resources. If there is no such disclosure, the council may consider that it is not satisfied that the user has insufficient means to pay the charge for the service. It will be for the council to consider each case in the light of their own legal advice.

8.62   This guidance is not replicated in the statutory guidance, but its principles would appear to remain valid on general public law grounds.[102] Where it is believed by a local authority that a partner has assets also owned by the service user, which perhaps have not been declared in the financial assessment, the local authority would need to provide the evidence for its belief before seeking disclosure of the partner's assets. The service user may not, of course, be in a position to insist that the partner discloses his or her assets.

---

99   Following NAA 1948 Part II of the AOR regulations 1992: see CRAG sections 8 and 9.

100 HASSASSAA 1983 s17(3); Fairer Charging 2013 paras 66 and 69.

101 See CA 2014 s17; charging and assessment regulations 2014 reg 13 (treatment of income) and reg 18 (treatment of capital) refer to the income/capital of the 'adult', defined as 'the adult or, as the case may be, the carer in respect of whom the authority is carrying out the financial assessment' (charging and assessment regulations 2014 reg 2(1)).

102 See the statutory guidance, annex B paras 10–13, which considers legal and beneficial ownership of capital and also para 8.68 below

8.63   If the capital of a couple is in a joint account,[103] without any evidence that one partner owns an unequal share, the total value will be divided equally between the joint owners. For some couples it is advisable to split the account in order to avoid spending down more than necessary. For example, if a couple have £56,500 in a joint account, they would (at 2016/17 rates) need to spend down to £46,500 (ie spend £10,000) before the resident qualifies for help. If they split the account so they had £28,250 in each account, the resident will receive help after spending £5,000.

Joint income

8.64   The statutory guidance states that, where the person receives income as one of a couple (annex C para 5):

> … the starting presumption is that the cared-for person has an equal share of the income. A local authority should also consider the implications for the cared-for person's partner.

The statutory guidance is unhelpfully silent as to what those implications may be or how, once identified, they should be addressed. This matter is reviewed in the DH FAQ (at Q104), which advises that local authorities must consider the facts in each case when carrying out any financial assessment, with the starting assumption that each person holds an equal share and only the cared for person's share should be taken into account. It also notes that, where the cared for person is receiving care in a care home, the local authority should ensure that the partner living in the family home has enough money to live on, after the charges have been paid.

8.65   This situation is often most acute when the cared-for person requires residential care. A disregard of 50 per cent must be applied by the local authority where a person is in a care home and is paying half of the value of the person's occupational pension, personal pension or retirement annuity to his or her spouse or civil partner (statutory guidance, annex C para 20). It is noted that this does not apply to unmarried couples and so, where the cared-for person is in a care home, it may be appropriate for the authority to increase the personal expenses allowance (PEA).[104]

8.66   However, this disregard does not apply to situations where the only pension income is from state retirement pensions. It is possible that the presumption that the cared for person has an equal share of the income may leave the other partner, who usually remains at home, in financial difficulties, although the partner remaining at home may be eligible for means tested benefits in their own right.

8.67   In circumstances where taking into account the income of one of couple who needs care (regardless of the care setting) may result in financial hardship for the partner, it may be prudent for the partner to be willing to disclose his or her own financial situation. This approach would enable

---

103 Different rules apply in relation to jointly owned interests in land – see para 8.106 below.

104 See statutory guidance, annex C para 46(b); and for further consideration of the PEA, see below at para 8.299.

the authority to take into account all relevant factors when completing the financial assessment.[105]

The treatment of capital

8.68   The provisions relating to the treatment of capital are to be found in charging and assessment regulations 2014 Part 5 and Schedule 2, and also in the statutory guidance at annex B, which considers the treatment of capital in all care settings. It should be noted that the capital rules for charging for care under the CA 2014 differ in a number of respects from those used in calculating entitlement to income support and pension credit, particularly in the capital limits and the disregards.

8.69   'Capital' is not formally defined in annex B; it is noted that local authorities will need to 'consider the individual asset on its merits' (para 5). It provides a non-exhaustive list of capital, including buildings, land, savings, trust funds, premium bonds and shares (para 6). A system of disregards is in place and annex B makes it clear that a person's resources 'should only be treated as either capital or income, but not both' (para 7).

Capital limits

8.70   For the year 2016/17 the upper limit is £23,250 (above which fees have to be paid in full) and the lower limit is £14,250 (above which a 'tariff income is calculated, see para 8.72 below) (annex B para 24). The capital limits may be increased each year, although in England there has been no increase since 2010.

8.71   The statutory guidance states that, where a financial assessment demonstrates that a person's capital is above the (upper) capital limit, an authority is precluded from paying towards the cost of care only where a person is in a care home (para 8.7).[106] In all other care settings, local authorities have discretion as to whether or not to pay for care where the person's assets exceed the capital limits. It follows that authorities must develop and maintain a policy about how they will charge people whose care is provided in settings other than care homes (although they must not charge more than is permitted under the regulations and statutory guidance[107]). What is noteworthy is the clear need for local authorities to develop their own charging policies and with it, the need for consultation (discussed further at para 8.20 above).

---

105   Under the pre-CA 2014 regime, the National Association of Finance Officers issued its own advice which many local authorities appeared to follow, which suggested that couples should be given the option of a single or a joint assessment and could then choose the assessment most beneficial to them.

106   Note that this does not apply where there is a formal deferred payments agreement (see para 8.282) or where a person lacks capacity to arrange his or her care and no one else is able to do so on the person's behalf (for such a person the provisions of CA 2014 s18(4) place a duty on the authority to arrange their care and support – see also para 8.344).

107   See CA 2014 s14; Care and Support (Charging and Assessment of Resources) Regulations 2014 reg 12; and the statutory guidance, para 8.7.

8.72   The CA 2014 continued the previously established system of calculating tariff income.[108] The amount of capital between the upper and lower limits is taken into account by attributing a 'tariff income' of £1.00 per week for each £250 (or part of £250) above the lower limit. For example, where a resident in England has £18,100[109] capital, a tariff income of £16.00 per week is taken into account as income.[110] The advice in CRAG was that where tariff income was taken into account, any actual interest earned was not to be treated as income (to avoid double counting) (para 6.009). This advice is not precisely replicated in annex B although, at para 57(b), it states that income derived from a capital asset (eg building society interest or dividends) is be treated as capital.

How is capital valued?

8.73   When completing a financial assessment, the authority must establish the value of the asset in order to calculate the person's charge (if any) for care and support. Other than National Savings Certificates,[111] the value of the asset is usually the current market or surrender value of the capital asset, whichever is the higher. Where the capital asset has a current market value (eg stocks and shares or a property), it is assessed as being the price a 'willing buyer would pay to a willing seller'.[112]

8.74   Once the capital asset has been valued, a deduction of ten per cent will be applied if there are any expenses involved in selling the asset (eg legal fees in selling a property). The value of the capital asset will be calculated after deduction of any outstanding debts secured on the asset (eg a mortgage).[113] Once the asset is sold, the capital amount to be taken into account is the actual amount realised from the sale, less any actual expenses of the sale.[114]

8.75   The statutory guidance advises that, where the authority and the person agree that the value of the asset is more than the capital limit of £23,250, or less than the lower capital limit of £14,250, then it is not necessary to obtain a precise valuation (annex B para 16). However, where the value of the asset is disputed, a precise valuation by a professional valuer should be obtained (this is considered further in respect of property – see para 8.101).

---

108 Charging and assessment regulations 2014 reg 25 'Calculation of tariff income from capital'; and see also the statutory guidance, annex B para 27.

109 See annex B para 27 (the example of 'Nora' sets out the method of calculation).

110 Given the very low interest rates, this approach is punitive as it assumes an income on very modest capital which cannot be met by investing the money in any bank account or other savings product. To receive a weekly income of £4.00 per week on an investment of £1,000.00, it would be necessary to invest the money at a return in excess of 20 per cent.

111 The method of valuing National Savings Certificates is set out in the statutory guidance, annex B para 19.

112 Charging and assessment regulations 2014 reg 20; statutory guidance, annex B paras 14–15.

113 Charging and assessment regulations 2014 reg 20; statutory guidance, annex B para 14.

114 Statutory guidance, annex B para 17.

8.76   The treatment of capital which is not immediately realisable is considered in the statutory guidance at annex B para 23[115] and, where assets are held abroad, guidance is given in annex B paras 20–22.[116]

Capital disregards

8.77   The capital disregards[117] under the CA 2014 are very similar to those which existed under CRAG and Fairer Charging 2013 guidance. Some capital is taken into account in full and some is disregarded indefinitely or for a fixed period. Where the care is provided in a care home setting, the treatment of a former home is considered at para 8.233.

Capital disregarded indefinitely

8.78   Some assets must be disregarded indefinitely; these are set out in an extensive list in the statutory guidance, annex B para 33. The disregarded assets include the surrender value of a life insurance policy[118] or annuity; the value of any payment made from the social fund; payments 'in kind' from a charity; student loans; the value of funds held in trust or administered by a court which derive from a personal injury payment (see further paras 8.89); and payments from the Macfarlane, Eileen trusts, the Caxton Foundation, the MFET Ltd, the Skipton fund or the London Bombings charitable relief fund.

8.79   The statutory guidance also applies an indefinite capital disregard to '[p]ersonal possessions such as paintings or antiques, unless they were purchased with the intention of reducing capital in order to avoid care and support charges (Schedule 2, para 13)' (where the person has deliberately deprived himself or herself of capital by the purchase of such items – see para 8.144) (annex B para 33(e)).

Capital disregarded for 26 weeks or longer

8.80   This category of capital disregard applies in a range of circumstances. For example, business assets are disregarded where a self-employed person is unable to work because of ill-health but intends to take up the work again once they have recovered, as is money acquired for repairs to the resident's home and capital from the former home, if it is intended to

---

115 Eg where there are notice periods, it should be taken into account in the usual way at the time of the assessment and adjusted when the capital is realised or, where the person chooses not to realise the asset, it should be reassessed at intervals in the usual way.

116 Where the capital is held abroad, but may be transferred to the UK, it is assessed in the usual way. If transfer is not possible, evidence will be required for the reasons preventing the transfer and its value will need to be assessed, taking into account the value a willing buyer would pay in the UK for that particular asset.

117 Full details of the disregards are contained in charging and assessment regulations Part 5 and Sch 2; and see statutory guidance, annex B.

118 The statutory guidance makes no reference to how single premium investment bonds are to be treated in the financial assessment for care and support charging. The DH FAQ (Q103) advises that such bonds, which contain an element of life insurance, are currently disregarded in the financial assessment no matter how small the element of life insurance. Consideration is being given to how these bonds should be treated in future.

buy another property. The statutory guidance also provides the authority with the discretion to apply the disregard for a longer period where it considers it to be appropriate (eg where a person is taking legal steps to occupy the premises as their home but the legal process takes more than 26 weeks).[119]

Capital disregarded for 52 weeks

8.81 This category of disregarded capital includes arrears of, or any compensation due, arising from the non-payment of a range of social security benefits. As most benefits are paid for specific periods, arrears payments should be treated as income for that period, at the end of which any money left over should be treated as capital (and then disregarded under this provision).[120] An example of the operation of the 52-week disregard provision for payment of arrears of pension credit is given in the statutory guidance (annex B para 48 'Colin'), which gives a helpful example of the treatment of arrears payments where the person had not previously claimed a social security benefit to which he or she was entitled.

8.82 The statutory guidance states that the personal injury payments are to be disregarded for a period of 52 weeks (annex B para 48(c)). The provisions relating to monies paid as a result of a personal injury are considered at para 8.89.

Capital disregarded for two years

8.83 Payments from a trust established out of funds provided by the secretary of state made to relatives of CJD victims are to be disregarded.[121]

Trust funds

8.84 The statutory guidance states that trust funds are a capital asset (annex B para 6(h)). CRAG provided detailed advice and guidance to local authorities on the assessment of trust funds. Unfortunately, this information is not replicated in the statutory guidance. The information about trusts contained in section 10 of CRAG (paras 10.001–10.009) remains of relevance as it sets out a brief background to trust law. Trusts may arise in a number of ways, including under the terms of a will or a trust established by parents to ensure a regular income for a person who is unable to support himself by reason of illness or disability.[122] The treatment of the trust in the financial assessment depends in part on its type and there are separate provisions relating to the treatment of personal injury trusts, which are considered at (para 8.89).

---

119 Charging and assessment regulations 2014 Sch 2; statutory guidance, annex B para 47(a)–(g).
120 Statutory guidance, annex B para 48.
121 Statutory guidance, annex B para 49.
122 These are among the examples set out in CRAG, para 10.003.

Information to be obtained by the authority about the trust

8.85   CRAG (para 10.008) advised that certain information should be obtained by the authority in order to assess cases where a person has a trust fund from which s/he may benefit. In brief, it will be necessary to consider the trust deed itself to establish the type of trust (eg absolute, discretionary or a personal injury trust). Although not retained in the statutory guidance, the same information would appear to be required under the CA 2014 regime, not least to enable the local authority to make its decisions under general public law principles (see para 20.139 below).

Absolute trusts

8.86   Where the beneficiary of an absolute trust is not in actual possession of the capital to which he has an absolute entitlement, but the capital would become available to him upon application being made, the value of the trust fund should be treated as capital already belonging to him (see statutory guidance, annex B para 58) ie it is treated as actual, rather than notional, capital. The value of the capital asset in the trust fund would be calculated using the same principles as for the same type of capital asset (annex B paras 14–19).

8.87   Where the terms of an absolute trust direct that the beneficiary has an absolute right to receive an income from the capital, the payments are taken into account as income. The provisions of CRAG were explicit in that, where the income from the absolute trust fund was being received by the beneficiary, the capital would be disregarded (CRAG, para 10.016). This is not made expressly clear in the statutory guidance, other than the general statement that it is 'important that people are not charged twice on the same resources' (statutory guidance, annex B para 7). Therefore, it is arguable that for the period when the payments from an absolute trust are treated as income, the capital value of the fund is to be disregarded. Where the beneficiary has not applied for income to which he has an absolute entitlement under the terms of the trust, this would fall to be treated as notional income under the statutory guidance (annex C paras 34–37).

Discretionary trusts

8.88   The capital value of a discretionary trust is disregarded (statutory guidance, annex B para 58(a)). Any payment made from a discretionary trust is treated as a voluntary payment and should also be disregarded (statutory guidance, annex C paras 30–31)). Where payments from the discretionary trust are made with sufficient regularity to be an income, they are also disregarded (statutory guidance, annex C para 28(h)).

Personal injury trusts: capital

8.89   The statutory guidance states that when a personal injury payment is received by an adult, it must be disregarded as a capital asset for a maximum of 52 weeks from the date of receipt (annex B para 48(c)). The provision applies to all care settings. The idea behind the 52-week disregard is that it provides sufficient time for the recipient to determine how best to use the capital (eg perhaps to purchase a suitable property) and also to enable a personal injury trust to be established, if required.

8.90   However, the simplicity of the wording in the statutory guidance omits the important exception contained within the charging and assessment regulations 2014 ie that during the 52-week period, the disregard does not apply to the personal injury payment where the payment (or any part of the payment) has been specifically identified by a court to deal with the cost of providing care.[123] Any sum identified by the court as dealing with the cost of providing care is not to be disregarded during the 52-week period and it will be treated as part of the adult's capital under the usual capital provisions.

8.91   This exception was introduced in in 2008 and was clearly set out in CRAG (paras 10.026 and 10.027): '[w]here the capital consists of any payment made in consequence of personal injury and a court has specifically identified the payment as being to cover the cost of providing care, that capital is taken into account'. The omission of the exception is a clear example of the less comprehensive approach taken by the statutory guidance, unfortunately at the expense of transparency – annex B para 48(c) is misleading because of the omission.[124]

8.92   Once the personal injury trust is established, the value derived from the award is disregarded in any capital calculation (statutory guidance, annex B para 33(h)–(l)),[125] including the element of the personal injury payment which was specifically identified by a court to deal with the cost of providing care. The disregard for personal injury payments also extends to other types of personal injury funds, including the value of funds administered by a court which derive from a payment for personal injury to the person,[126] as well as the value of the right to receive any income under an annuity purchased with a personal injury award. It should be noted that arrangements arising out of personal injury awards constitute a specific exception to the deprivation rules (see para 8.89), permitting the awards to be placed in a trust for the benefit of the resident without being subject to the usual notional capital rules.

123 Charging and assessment regulations 2014 reg 18 and Sch 2 ('Capital to be disregarded') para 16, which refers to the disregard under IS regulations 1987 Sch 10 para 12A. Unhelpfully, it is necessary to consider the IS regulations 1987 to establish the precise terms of the disregard provision. This approach was first introduced in England by National Assistance (Sums for Personal Requirements and Assessment of Resources) Amendment (England) Regulations 2008 SI No 593 reg 6(a).

124 The only method of finding out about the exception (ie the treatment of the payment identified for the provision of the cost of care) is by reading the charging and assessment regulations 2014 and cross-referencing it with the IS regulations 1987, a task likely to prove to be an obstacle to both the public and local authority finance officers alike. Unfortunately, the statutory guidance fails to follow the approach taken in the CRAG, which helpfully makes reference in the body of the text to the relevant regulations in the AOR regulations 1992. The absence of the reference to the charging and assessment regulations 2014 makes it all the more difficult to be certain of finding the correct answer when seeking further information on a matter set out in the statutory guidance.

125 These provisions derive from charging and assessment regulations 2014 regs16 and 18; Sch 2 paras 14 and 15.

126 This includes funds held and administered by the Court of Protection: *R (ZYN) v Walsall MBC* [2014] EWHC 1918 (Admin), (2015) 18 CCLR 579.

8.93   There has been long-standing concern by local authorities that, apart from the limited provision to enable an authority to take into account the capital value of a personal injury payment identified to deal with the cost of providing care, no charges can be made for the local authority provision of care against personal injury awards.[127] The concern is that claimants may benefit from 'double recovery' and that insurers may gain by paying reduced damages where, for example, local authority residential care is to be provided: in effect, the public purse being used to subsidise the 'tortfeasor'. The pre-CA 2014 cases demonstrate the practical difficulties facing the courts in determining this issue and focused on whether payments for care costs should be included in a personal injury award if local authorities are not able to charge against them. The cases concerned the difficulty of predicting the future care needs of an individual, as well as the suitability of the care arrangements made by a local authority.[128]

8.94   In *Peters v East Midlands SHA, Halstead and Nottingham City Council*[129] the Court of Appeal approved a mechanism designed to limit the potential for 'double recovery' by a claimant. It held that where a person's affairs were being administered by the Court of Protection (ie via a deputy) the personal injury award could include an order prohibiting the claimant or the deputy from applying for publicly funded assistance without further order from the court. The Court of Protection has held that (notwithstanding the public policy argument to the contrary) the *Peters* provisions are not capable of being applied retrospectively.[130]

8.95   The CA 2014 does not address local authority concerns over social care funds being used to subsidise tortfeasors and there appears to be little political will to allow authorities to take account of personal injury awards unlike in other areas of state funded support (eg social security payments and NHS medical treatment).[131]

8.96   In the climate of limited financial resources, local authorities may be keen to take the view that a person with a significant personal injury award is able to fund their own care, without recourse to the local authority, usually on the grounds that it enables the local authority to use its limited

---

127   The issue was the subject of consultation in England in 2010 where the proposal was to allow local authorities to take into account any payment made for care, regardless of where the personal injury funds were held. No information was published about its outcome.

128   For a detailed discussion of the issue, see the 5th edn of this book at paras 8.53–8.59 where the case-law was reviewed, including *Sowden v Lodge; Crookdake v Drury* [2004] EWCA Civ 1370, [2005] 1 WLR 2129; the decision in the Court of Appeal in *Crofton v NHS Litigation Authority* [2007] EWCA Civ 71, [2007] 1 WLR 923, (2007) 10 CCLR 123.

129   *Peters v East Midlands SHA, Halstead and Nottingham CC* [2009] EWCA Civ 145, (2009) 12 CCLR 299.

130   See *In the matter of Mark Reeves* No 99328848, judgment 5 January 2010 available at www.7br.co.uk/uploads/court-of-protection-judgment-mark-reeves.pdf.

131   The provisions enabling the costs of NHS treatment for an injured person to be recovered in the event of a successful personal injury claim were introduced on 29 January 2007 by Part 3 of the Health and Social Care (Community Health and Standards) Act 2003. This follows provisions enabling repayment of social security benefits by the compensator (from 6 October 1997) and also the costs of NHS hospital charges following a successful personal injury claim after a road traffic accident, which commenced on 6 April 1997.

funds to pay for care for those who do not have other financial resources.[132] This is the position of St Helen's Metropolitan Council[133] where (as at January 2017) it is refusing to provide or fund home care services for Mr A on the basis he has a personal injury award of £2.85 million and so he has enough money to pay for his own care.[134] The council declined to accept the recommendations of the LGO, arguing that '[i]t would be grossly unfair to other residents of St Helens to be denied services because the Council had to meet the costs of Mr A's care when he had received damages to meet those needs'.[135]

8.97 Although case concerns the pre-CA 2014 charging provisions, it is noted that the provisions of the CA 2014 are very clear that the capital and income arising from a personal injury trust are to be disregarded as part of any financial assessment. In the case of *Crofton*, the Court of Appeal determined that the local authority, when assessing eligible needs, may not take into account resources which it must disregard at the financial assessment stage.[136] The decision by the LGO in the St Helens' case is therefore of immediate relevance to the CA 2014 charging regime. Having sought counsel's advice, the LGO is resolute that the council's approach is unlawful.[137]

Personal injury trusts: income

8.98 The statutory guidance – annex C (Treatment of Income) para 29(p), which applies to all care settings – states that any income from a personal injury trust, including those administered by a court, must be fully disregarded.[138]

---

132 See the case of *Re (Damien Tinsley (by his litigation friend and property and affairs deputy Hugh Jones) v Manchester City Council and South Manchester Clinical Commissioning Group* [2016] EWHC 2855 (Admin) where the court held that the council was not entitled to decline to provide services under MHA 1983 s117 where the applicant had a substantial personal injury award, which included an element for the future cost of care. This was determined on the basis that section 117 after-care services are to be provided free of charge as it is in effect treated as NHS provision, which is free at the point of need. Given on 10 November 2016 and so coincides with the LGO decision in the St Helens' case.

133 See LGO Report (ref no 14 009 949) 27 June 2016 and subsequent Report (ref no 14 009 949) 21 November 2016; it is noted that judgment in the *Tinsley* case was given on 10 November 2016 and so coincides with the LGO's second decision in the St Helens' case.

134 See LGO Report (ref 14.009 040) 27 June 2016 at para 34.

135 See LGO Report (ref 14.009 040) 27 June 2016 at para 40.

136 *Crofton (a patient suing by his father and litigation friend John Crofton) v National Health Service Litigation Authority* [2007] EWCA Civ 71 at para 65.

137 See LGO Report (ref no 14 009 949) 27 June 2016 (paras 20 and 51) and Report (ref no 14 009 949) 21 November 2016 (paras 21–24): in January 2017 it appeared that the matter was the subject of a judicial review proceedings instigated by Mr A.

138 The statutory guidance, annex C para 29(p) derives from the operation of charging and assessment regulations 2014 reg 15(1), which refers to the disregards set out in Schedule 1 Part 1. Schedule 1 para 15(1) and (3)(c)–(e) provides for the disregard of any relevant payment made, or due to be made, at regular intervals from capital assets deriving from personal injury trusts.

The treatment of property

8.99   Although the treatment of property under the CA 2014 is broadly the same as for other capital assets, particular issues arise in relation to such matters as establishing a beneficial interest and the valuation of jointly owned property – and these are considered in this section.

8.100   A further change is that the new legal regime fails to replicate the powers of local authorities to place a charge 'unilaterally' on land where a person has failed to pay his or her care charges or transferred his or her property to a third party.[139] .

8.101   Where the value of property is disputed, the statutory guidance makes it clear that authorities should try to obtain an independent valuation of the person's beneficial interest in the property within the 12-week disregard period (see para 8.224), where the person is in a care home.[140] This will enable to the local authority to calculate the correct charge for the person's care and enable a decision to be made about whether a deferred payment agreement (DPA) should be used (see para 8.282).[141]

Establishing beneficial interest

8.102   In the majority of cases, the ownership of property is easily established as the legal owners will also be the beneficial owners. However, as the statutory guidance notes, the ownership of the property is sometimes disputed on the grounds that, although not named as a legal owner, another person (usually another family member) will contend that they have a beneficial interest in the property (annex B para 10). Where it is contended that a property is jointly owned, or where the owner had undertaken to transfer a share to a third party (who had for example paid the mortgage), the Scottish Outer House, Court of Session held that such arguments must be investigated by the local authority – see *Cunningham v East Lothian Council*.[142] Where a beneficial interest is established, it will usually be the case that the legal owner holds the property 'in trust' for the beneficial owner.

8.103   This situation frequently arises in 'right to buy' cases where, although the property is in the name of the resident (who at the time the property was bought was the council tenant entitled to the statutory discount), other relatives have funded the purchase or paid the mortgage. In *Kelly v Hammersmith and Fulham LBC*[143] the resident had purchased her council house but her daughter had funded the entire purchase costs and mortgage repayments. The court nevertheless held that the local authority was entitled to maintain a caution on the property in the mother's name for outstanding residential home fees because the daughter was unable to

---

139 Under HASSASSA 1983 s21, s22 and s24 – see para 8.191 below.

140 Statutory guidance, annex B para 18. In a case determined under the CRAG provisions, the LGO held that local authorities should decide on the value of a resident's joint share in a property 'without hesitancy' and, further, this task must be undertaken openly, explaining the process being used and also ensuring that CRAG is being followed: Complaint no 10 014 187 against West Sussex CC, 23 May 2013.

141 Statutory guidance, annex B para 18.

142 [2011] ScotCS CSOH 185.

143 [2004] EWHC 435 (Admin), (2004) 7 CCLR 542.

adduce sufficient evidence to show that her mother had no beneficial interest in the property, in particular because of the £50,000 discount.

8.104   In *Brighton and Hove City Council v Audus*,[144] the court came to a different conclusion: namely that the purchasing relative had an overriding interest. In this case he had paid the purchase price on the understanding that he had ownership of the flat, but had postponed his rights to live in the property, and had met all the costs of the home whilst the elderly couple lived in the home rent free. In effect the purchasing relative was the legal owner, and therefore the local authority could not recoup the fees by way of a legal charge. In *Nottingham City Council v Beresford*[145] (a decision of the Adjudicator to the Land Registry) the house was purchased with a 60 per cent 'right to buy' discount and subject to an oral agreement: that the resident's children would pay all of the mortgage payments and maintain the property; that the property would be held on trust for the children in equal shares; and that the resident would live rent free for as long as she wished and was able to do so. When she moved into residential care the local authority sought to register a legal charge[146] as the property was in her sole name. On the evidence, the adjudicator was satisfied that a constructive trust existed in favour of the children.

8.105   A trust was also found to exist in *Campbell v Griffin*,[147] where a long term lodger, who had provided care over a number of years to an elderly couple prior to their moving into a care home, was held in consequence to have acquired an equitable interest in the property. Rather than providing him with the right to remain in the property, the court found entitlement to £35,000 from the proceeds of sale of the property.

Valuation of jointly owned property

8.106   Charging and assessment regulations 2014 reg 24 provides that, when valuing a jointly owned capital asset, the beneficial owner is to be treated as possessing an equal share of the whole beneficial interest of that capital asset, unless there is evidence that the adult owns more (or less) than an equal share. However, reg 24 specifies that this approach does not apply to the valuation of jointly owned interest in land but the regulations do not (curiously) make provision for the situation where the adult jointly owns a beneficial interest in land/property. This is in stark contrast to the pre-CA 2014 regime, where AOR regulations 1992 reg 27[148] and CRAG (chapter 7) provided comprehensive guidance about how to value jointly held property. The statutory guidance is, however, silent on how to value a person's

---

144 [2009] EWHC 340 (Ch).

145 [2011] EWLandRA 2010_0577, 30 March 2011 – see (2011) 74 *Journal of Community Care Law* 8.

146 The CA 2014 has removed a local authority's right to register a charge under Health and Social Services and Social Security Adjudications Act 1983 ss21, 22 and 24 – see also para 8.191 below.

147 [2001] EWCA Civ 990.

148 AOR regulations 1992 reg 27 provided that, where a resident owned a beneficial interest in a property with other co-owners, the resident's share was to be valued at an amount equal to the price which the resident's share would realise if it were sold to a willing buyer. However, reg 27 has no equivalent provision in the charging and assessment regulations 2014.

jointly owned interest in land, other than by treating it as any other capital asset.

8.107   The statutory guidance (annex B para 6) defines 'capital' as including land and buildings, the value of which is to be determined by its current market value ie the price a willing buyer would pay to a willing seller (annex B para 15). At annex B para 12, in the context of jointly owned capital, it states that where a capital asset is jointly owned, the total value should be divided equally between the joint owners and the person should be treated as owning an equal share, unless 'there is evidence that the person own[s] an unequal share'.

8.108   On that basis where, for example, it is established that a person has a 25 per cent beneficial interest (or share) in a house, that share should be valued at its current market value ie the price a willing buyer would pay to a willing seller. The 'current market value' is not assessed by taking the overall value of the whole house and dividing it by the number of beneficial owners, rather it is the price a willing buyer would pay to a willing seller for that person's particular share (beneficial interest).[149] This reflects the fact that, as a matter of land law, where a property is jointly owned, each person with a beneficial interest has the right to receive a proportionate share of the proceeds of sale. For this reason, it is the value of the person's interest in the property which is to be valued, not the value of the property itself.[150]

8.109   This approach reflects that previously set out in CRAG. However, despite the comprehensive nature of the guidance given in CRAG, anecdotal evidence suggested that some local authorities valued the person's interest in the property on the basis of a sale of the whole property on the open market, divided by the number of joint owners, rather than by the sale of the resident's share to a willing buyer. Unfortunately, given the absence of clear information in the statutory guidance on how to value jointly owned property, this confusion seems likely to continue. The omission seems incomprehensible and will not aid the stated principles under the CA 2014 regime ie that the approach should be 'clear and transparent, so people know what they will be charged'.[151]

8.110   In assessing the value of the resident's beneficial interest in the property, two factors have to be considered: first, the ability of the resident to reassign (or sell) their interest to someone else and, second, whether there is a market for that share ie there is a willing buyer.[152] It is unlikely that there is any legal impediment to prevent a joint beneficial owner of a share in a property selling it to a willing buyer, who may be either an existing co-owner or an external investor.

8.111   CRAG[153] previously advised that, where there was no willing buyer among the other beneficiaries, it was unlikely that any external investor would be willing to purchase the resident's beneficial interest unless the

---

149 This is the approach previously taken in CRAG and other means-tested benefits, including income support.

150 This is set out in CRAG, para 7.017 but must, as a matter of land law, apply to the CA 2014 charging regime.

151 Statutory guidance, chapter 8 para 8.2.

152 This follows CRAG, para 7.017.

153 CRAG, para 7.019.

financial advantages far outweighed the risks and limitations involved. Therefore, CRAG concluded that the 'value of the interest, even to a willing buyer, could in such circumstances effectively be nil'. However, this approach has been omitted from the statutory guidance. In the current climate of increasing house prices, it is less likely that a beneficial interest in a property would have 'nil' value, even where the other co-owners may be unable to purchase the resident's interest. The availability of external investors depends in part on the ease with which the asset may be realised at some point in the future, as well as the state of the property market in a particular area at any given time. These matters would need to fully explored as part of any independent valuation of the property carried out within the 12-week disregard period, based on the local property market and any evidence provided as part of the valuation process.

8.112   The ease with which the value of the asset (ie the share in the property) may be realised in the future is largely dependent on the circumstances in which the joint beneficial interest has arisen. For example, there is a difference between those situations where purpose of the joint purchase of the property is to provide a home for the joint beneficial owners (eg a parent purchasing a property with an adult child, both of whom live in the property) and those where the joint ownership arises because, for example, the property was inherited by some of the co-owners on the death of a relative. This is particularly the case where the property remains empty once the person moves into a care home.

8.113   Any beneficial owner of a jointly owned property (including an external investor) is able to apply to the court to seek an order for sale of the property.[154] In such cases, the court is required to have regard to a number of factors, including (under Trusts of Land and Appointment of Trustees Act 1996 s15(1)):

a) the intentions of the person or persons (if any) who created the trust,[155]

b) the purposes for which the property subject to the trust is held.

8.114   It follows that where the property was purchased to provide a home for the joint owners, it would seem unlikely that a sale could be forced.[156] In this context, in *Chief Adjudication Officer v Palfrey*[157] (a case concerning the valuation of a value of a property which is lived in by one of the joint owners and the other had moved into a care home) Hobhouse LJ in observed:

> Where the capital asset is a jointly owned dwelling house held for the purpose of accommodating the joint owners and that purpose is subsisting, there is nothing obscure or abstruse in the conclusion that the amount of capital which the applicant's joint possession of that dwelling house represents may fall, for the time being, to be quantified in a nominal amount.

154 Trusts of Land and Appointment of Trustees Act 1996 s14.

155 Where the beneficial interest in a property is jointly owned, the beneficial owners hold the property on trust for each other, hence the use of the word 'trust' in this context.

156 See *Bull v Bull* [1955] 1 QB 234 concerning a son claiming possession of property bought jointly with his mother and which was subsequently registered in his name only. The claim failed as his mother was in occupation of the home and thus the purpose of the acquisition subsisted.

157 [1995] 11 LS Gaz R 39, (1995) *Times* 17 February.

8.115   The position may, however, be otherwise, where the original purpose was not to provide a home for the joint owner – for example, where the joint ownership has arisen because children have inherited half of the property on the death of one parent and then the other parent moves into a care home. In such a situation Mummery LJ in *Wilkinson v CAO*[158] considered that *Palfrey* was not a relevant authority and that a sale could be enforced at market value.

8.116   Any valuation of a joint share of a property for charging purposes must take into account of all of the relevant factors[159] and should also provide proper reasons for its decision in such cases.[160]

The treatment of income

8.117   The charging and assessment regulations 2014 contain the procedure by which a resident's income – earned and unearned – is assessed for charging purposes; it is also addressed in chapter 8 and annex C of the statutory guidance. The provisions import many of the same rules used in the assessment of income under the IS regulations 1987.

8.118   Under the CA 2014 and the charging and assessment regulations 2014, income – defined as being net of any tax or national insurance contributions[161] – is taken into account, although some income may fall to be disregarded either in full or in part (statutory guidance, annex C para 7). The different types of income, together with the relevant rules, are set out below.

The treatment of earnings

8.119   Employed and self-employed earnings (irrespective of the type of the care setting) are fully disregarded (statutory guidance, annex C para 8).[162]

8.120   The definition of earnings, where the person is an employed earner, includes most payments other than payments in kind, expenses incurred as part of the person's employment duties and any occupational/personal pension (annex C para 9).[163]

158 [2000] EWCA Civ 88.

159 There is no information contained in CRAG or in the statutory guidance under the CA 2014 as to how local authorities should instruct an independent valuer but useful guidance is to be found in Department for Work and Pensions, *Decision maker's guide*, 2014, vol 5 chapter 29 paras 29642–29647.

160 See the decision in *R (Bhandari and another) v Croydon LBC*, QBD (Admin) (Blake J) 21 April 2016 (unreported); but see, for example, the article in *Local Government Lawyer*, 'Reasons challenges to charging and care home fees decisions' by Jonathan Auburn, 28 April 2016.

161 Statutory guidance, annex C para 6.

162 Para 8 quotes as its authority charging and assessment regulations 2014 reg 13. However, reg 13 relates to calculation of income, whereas reg 14 deals with earnings to be disregarded; it would therefore appear that the correct reference in para 8 should be reg 14, and not reg 13 as stated.

163 The definition of earnings as an 'employed earner' is that used in Housing Benefit Regulations 2006 reg 35 and, for self-employed earner, the definition follows that used in IS regulations 1987 reg 37 – charging and assessment regulations 2014 reg 14.

The treatment of benefits

Benefits taken into account

8.121   The statutory guidance advises that 'local authorities may take most of the benefits people receive into account' (annex C para 14). At annex C para 16 it provides a list of those benefits which must be taken fully into account when considering what a person is able to afford to pay from their income towards their care and support when they are in a care home. These include, for example, attendance allowance; the care component of disability living allowance (DLA); income support; jobseekers' allowance; state pension; pension credit; and carers allowance. In other care settings, the local authority may exercise its discretion as part of its charging policy, whether or not to take into account a particular benefit. In practical terms, this approach will create two different financial assessment processes, despite the assertion that the CA 2014 'provides a single legal framework for charging for care and support' (statutory guidance, para 8.1).

8.122   Where a person is going into a care home as a permanent resident, attendance allowance and disability living allowance (care component) are taken into account in full, although both these benefits would normally cease to be paid after four weeks where the resident is funded by the local authority. Where the resident is to repay the authority at a later date (eg they have a deferred payment agreement (DPA)), these benefits would continue to be paid as the resident is treated, for social security benefit purposes, as a 'self-funder'.

8.123   In a pre-CA 2014 case, *R v Coventry City Council ex p Carton*,[164] the local authority changed its non-residential care charging policy, removing the automatic disregard for the night component of higher rate DLA for service users receiving daytime care only. The court held that it was irrational, unlawful and unfair for the council to apply a charging policy which treated as income available for day care those sums of DLA paid in respect of night care. The court's approach was subsequently reflected in the Fairer Charging 2013 guidance (paras 32–48) which provided that, although disability living allowance (DLA) (care component) and attendance allowance could be taken into account, this was only in relation to services provided for the time of day for which the allowance is paid.

8.124   It is noted that the approach in *Carton* is not specifically referred to in the statutory guidance; the issue was addressed in the DH FAQ (Q203), published by the LGA. The response to the question refers to the statutory guidance (now at annex C paras 39 and 40) states that day or night care which is not being arranged by the local authority should be included as part of the person's disability related expenditure. Therefore, where a local authority includes as income payments of attendance allowance or DLA (care component), it must make an assessment of the person's disability related expenditure.[165] The authority must allow the person to keep

---

164 (2001) 4 CCLR 41, QBD.

165 As required by charging and assessment regulations 2014 reg 15 and Sch 1 Part 1 para 4, which make it clear that, where the local authority takes into account disability related benefits, it must disregard the person's DRE. It is considered below at para 8.325.

enough of his or her disability related benefits to meet any care needs (eg for night-time care) not being met by the authority.

8.125   However, this approach appears to fall short of the automatic disregard for night time payments applied in *Carton*. Where the person does not in fact pay for night time care, but receives high rate DLA care component as income[166], it is not entirely clear what sum, if any, is to be treated as disability related expenditure. Presumably, if there were an intention to provide for an automatic disregard for the income, following the *Carton* principle, this could have been made explicit in the statutory guidance, rather than by approach to the principles of disability related expenditure.[167]

8.126   A local authority would be able to exercise its discretion to include the approach in *Carton* as part of its non-residential charging policy, should it choose to do so. However, it is no longer set out in any statutory guidance and it is therefore a dilution of the protection previously afforded to those disabled people who require community care services. However, to include as income social security benefits which are paid for a time of the day for which community care services are not provided arguably remains open to challenge on general public law principles.[168] If it were 'irrational, unlawful and unfair' for the income to be taken into account prior to the CA 2014 – it is difficult to see how, in the absence of statutory authority to the contrary, it ceases to be was irrational, unlawful and unfair post CA 2014.

8.127   Recent case-law demonstrates the approach taken by the courts where a local authority had discretion as to whether or not DLA (care component) was to be taken into account as income when assessing discretionary housing payments (DHP). In *R (Hardy) v Sandwell MBC*,[169] the court accepted that taking into account DLA for discretionary benefit purposes discriminated against disabled people. The court held that the council was in breach of Article 14 of the European Convention on Human Rights (ECHR) and, further, it also had violated the public sector equality duty in EqA 2010 s149.[170] A similar approach may be successful where a local authority does not consider the principle set out in *Carton* when establishing its charging policy.

8.128   Where a social security benefit has been reduced because of a recovery by deduction from benefit (eg, to repay an earlier overpayment), the amount taken into account is the gross amount of the benefit before the reduction. Therefore, the person is to be treated as though he or she is receiving the full weekly amount. This will have the effect of making the

166 For those claimants aged 16–64 years, DLA is being replaced by personal independence payment (PIP), which is structured entirely differently from DLA in that there is no 'night time rate' for the care component. Its introduction on a national basis is still ongoing, but all new claimants are obliged to apply for PIP, rather than DLA.

167 The statutory guidance, annex C para 40(c)(i) advises that local authorities should include as part of the person's disability related expenditure 'day or night care not being arranged by the local authority'.

168 For further information about public law principles, see para 20.139.

169 [2015] EWHC 890 (Admin).

170 The courts took a similar approach in respect of DLA payments for a child in hospital: see *Cameron Mathieson v Secretary of State for Work and Pensions* [2015] UKSC 47.

income used to calculate the person's charges to be a greater sum than is actually being paid, meaning that the person is likely to be assessed as having a higher weekly charge to pay.[171] However, in such cases, a local authority would need to pay particular attention as to whether the resultant charge is 'reasonably practicable' for the person to pay (statutory guidance, para 8.2). Where, for example, the charge causes financial hardship, the local authority could use its discretion to reduce or waive the charge, in appropriate cases.

Benefits fully and partly disregarded

8.129 Some social security benefits and payments are fully disregarded, including the mobility components of DLA and the personal independence payment (PIP);[172] the Christmas bonus; winter fuel and social fund payments. [173] In addition, child benefit[174] and child tax credit must also be fully disregarded (a full list appears in the statutory guidance at annex C para 29).

8.130 The Welsh Ombudsman found maladministration where a new service user was told she could not use the transport to a day centre because she was in receipt of DLA mobility component, which did not apply to existing service users. She therefore had to use taxis and found this too expensive. Systematic maladministration was found on the basis there was an absence of any policy framework and no written guidelines on the eligibility of clients who could use local authority run transport.[175]

8.131 Pre-CA 2014 Department of Health policy guidance[176] (which would appear to remain of direct relevance) referred to evidence that 'some local authorities were taking the mobility component into account when considering what social services to be provide' and then stated that the 'Department would like to make the position clear' that:

> ... local councils have a duty to assess the needs of any person for whom the authority may provide or arrange the provision of community care services and who may be in need of such services. They have a further duty to decide, having regard to the results of the assessment, what, if any, services they should provide to meet the individual's needs. This duty does not change because a particular individual is receiving the mobility component of Disability Living Allowance.

171 Statutory guidance, annex C para 17, which replicates the provision of CRAG 2014 at para 8.007.

172 See statutory guidance, annex C paras 15(c) and (d), in accordance with Part 1 para 8 of the Care and Support (Charging and Assessment of Resources) Regulations 2014, following Social Security Contributions and Benefits Act 1992 s73(14), requiring DLA mobility component to be disregarded in any charging scheme.

173 Working tax credit must be disregarded where the care and support is arranged in any setting other than a care home (see annex C para 17).

174 Child benefit must be fully disregarded, except where the accommodation in which the adult and young person/child lives is arranged under the CA 2014 (annex C para 29(b)).

175 Complaint no B2004/0180 against Newport City Council, August 2006.

176 Department of Health, *Charging for residential accommodation and non-residential care services* LAC (DH) (2012) 03, paras 9–11.

8.132   Other social security benefits attract a partial disregard – for example, a £10 per week disregard is applied to certain war pensions (statutory guidance, annex C para 33(a)).

Savings credit disregard

8.133   The list of fully disregarded income also refers to a 'savings credit disregard' (at annex C para 29(r)). A 'savings disregard' was introduced for people aged 65 and over in 2003, which operates to disregard the amount of the 'savings credit' awarded within the pension credit scheme.[177]

8.134   Where a person receives his or her care and support other than a care home, the savings credit the adult receives should be fully disregarded (annex C para 30). Where the person receives his or her care in a care home, the provisions set out in annex C para 33(b) apply, which are based on both the person's weekly income and the amount of the savings credit.[178] The effect is to allow for a maximum 'savings disregard' of £5.75 for a single person and £8.60 for a couple.[179]

Annuity and pension income

8.135   For the purposes of assessing income, as noted above, any payments of state pension and pension credit must be fully taken into account where the person's care is to be provided in a care home (annex C para 16). Any income arising from an annuity is to be taken fully into account, although the capital is to be disregarded.[180]

8.136   However, where the annuity was purchased by means of a loan secured on the person's main or only home, known as a 'home income plan', a prescribed system of disregards exists in respect of the interest payments, subject to specific conditions (statutory guidance, paras 21–25). In broad terms, this operates to disregard from the income a sum equal to the interest payments on the loan.[181]

8.137   The statutory guidance anticipated the reforms to defined contribution pensions which came into effect in April 2015 (para 26). The aim of reforms is to increase flexibility in how people use their pension fund in later life (aged 55 years and over). In broad terms, the changes allow people to draw down the capital from pension fund, rather than being obliged to use it to purchase an annuity.

177 This is part of the pension credit scheme where people aged 65 and over, who have made provision for their old age through second pensions or similar savings, can benefit from weekly 'savings credit' ie an increase to the person's weekly pension credit income. Information about pension credit may be found at the Department of Work and Pensions, *A detailed guide to pension credit for advisers and others* PC10S.

178 The statutory guidance (at annex C paras 29, 30 and 33) which considers savings credit disregards, is written in a less than accessible style. For example, there appears to be a missing word in para 33 ('a savings disregard based on qualifying [?] is made to people ...'. It also does not use consistent terms and does not always make explicit the difference in treatment between care home and other care settings; these deficiencies had not been remedied in the revisions of the statutory guidance as at January 2017.

179 The rates set out in the statutory guidance, annex C remain the same as they were in 2011/2013.

180 See charging and assessment regulations 2014 reg 16(2); statutory guidance, para 19.

181 This is similar to the provisions under CRAG, paras 8.029–8.034.

8.138   The statutory guidance provides for rules to assess pension income for the purposes of charging, as follows:

- Where the person has removed their pension funds and placed them in another product or savings account, the usual rules for that product would apply (eg if in a savings account, the money would be treated as capital).
- Where a person chooses to draw a minimal income from his or her pension fund, the local authority should apply the 'notional income' rules to the amount of income available but undrawn (see para 8.171 below for the notional income rules).
- Where a person draws down income higher than the maximum available under an annuity product, the actual 'drawn' income received should be taken into account.

8.139   The statutory guidance gives examples of the inter-relationship between the rules in respect of pensions and its impact upon paying for care (annex C paras 35–37). In such cases, where the person reaches the pension credit qualifying age, the person is to be treated as though he or she has his or her pension income, even though the person may have not in fact been drawing it down (eg because the person has not purchased an annuity or arranged to draw down the equivalent maximum annuity income which would be available to him or her). The statutory guidance makes it clear that, as notional income is treated in the same way as actual income, any relevant disregards should continue to be applied to the notional income (annex C para 36).

8.140   These changes are complex and the government has set up an advice service to assist people in understanding their new pension options, with a brief reference to the potential consequences of the impact of their pension choices on how their care may be funded in the future.[182]

Other types of income

8.141   Income from insurance policies is usually taken into account. However, where the income derives from a mortgage protection policy, where the intention is to assist a person in the acquisition/repair of his or her only main home, the income from the policy must be disregarded. In order for the disregard to be applied, the income must be being used to make repayments due under the mortgage.[183]

8.142   Charitable and voluntary payments made on a regular basis must be fully disregarded. Where the payment is not made regularly, it is usually treated as a capital payment, rather than income. The statutory guidance makes it clear that charitable payments are not only those made by a recognised charity, but may also be made by individuals with charitable motives (annex C paras 31–32). It emphasises that the individual circumstances of the payment will have to be considered before making a decision as to whether a payment is to be disregarded.

---

182 See the website at www.pensionwise.gov.uk and also at www. pensionsadvisoryservice.org.uk for further information about pensions; for the impact on paying for care see: www.pensionwise.gov.uk/care-costs.

183 Statutory guidance, annex C paras 27–28.

8.143   Other income is also fully disregarded, including child support maintenance payments, payments in kind and any grants or loans paid for the purposes of education (see annex C paras 29–30).

Deprivation of capital and income

Generally

8.144   Charging and assessment regulations 2014 reg 22(1) provides that:

> The adult is to be treated as possessing capital of which the adult has deprived themselves for the purpose of decreasing the amount that they may be liable to pay towards the cost of meeting their needs for care and support, or their needs for support, except–
> (a) where that capital is derived from a payment made in consequence of any personal injury and is placed on trust for the benefit of the adult;
> (b) to the extent that the capital which the adult is treated as possessing is reduced in accordance with regulation 23 [the diminishing notional capital rule – see para 8.168]; or
> (c) any sum to which paragraph 44(1) or 45(a) of Schedule 10 to the Income Support Regulations[184] (disregard of compensation for personal injuries which is administered by the Court) refers.

8.145   Charging and assessment regulations 2014 reg 17(1) extends the concept of deprivation to include deprivation of income, as follows:

> The adult is to be treated as possessing income of which the adult has deprived themselves for the purpose of decreasing the amount they may be liable to pay towards the cost of meeting their needs for care and support, or their needs for support.

8.146   The wording of reg 22(1) mirrors that of AOR regulations 1992 reg 25(1); therefore, the legal test for deprivation of capital remains the same under the CA 2014 ie that an adult has deprived himself or herself of the capital for the purpose of decreasing the amount the person may be liable to pay towards his or her care costs. As the same wording is used in respect of deprivation of income in reg 17, the previous case-law determined under CRAG remains of relevance in determining whether the disposal of an asset or income is to be treated by the authority as deprivation within the financial assessment.

8.147   The deprivation of assets rule is not confined simply to those situations where a person may need residential care, but also applies to all care settings, including services provided to carers. The relevant guidance is now to be found in the statutory guidance, chapter 8 and annex E, which applies where a local authority carries out a financial assessment and identifying circumstances that suggest deprivation.[185]

8.148   The statutory guidance gives examples of potential deprivation of capital and/or income (annex E paras 9 and 13). These include making lump

---

184 The IS regulations 1987 provide for the disregard of capital where such sum derives from (a) an award of damages for a personal injury to that person; or (b) compensation for the death of one or both parents where the person concerned is under the age of 18.

185 Statutory guidance, annex E para 3.

sum payments as a gift, or transferring the ownership of property to some-one else, as well as placing assets in a trust which cannot be revoked or using assets to purchase an investment bond with life assurance. It would also include the conversion of an asset into one which would not be taken into account (see the example of 'Emma' and the painting in the statutory guidance, annex E para 10).

8.149   In respect of the deprivation of income (eg a person may give away or sell the right to an income from an occupational pension), the considera-tions are broadly the same as those for deprivation of capital. The authority must consider whether it is the person's income, as well as the purpose and timing of the disposal of the income (see statutory guidance, annex E paras 13–16).

8.150   The context in which local authorities have to make determinations about deprivation of assets is set out in the statutory guidance (annex E para 4):

> People should be treated with dignity and respect and be able to spend the money they have saved as they wish – it is their money after all. Whilst the Care Act 2014 represents an important step forward in redefining the part-nership between the state and the individual, it is important that people pay the contribution to their care costs that they are responsible for. This is key to the overall affordability of the care and support system. A local authority should therefore ensure that people are not rewarded for trying to avoid paying their assessed contribution.

8.151   This paragraph reveals the political and social-economic tensions inherent in this situation: the ability of individuals to save – and spend – their own money on the one hand and, at the same time, the requirement for those same individuals to pay the contribution to their care costs, rather than it be the responsibility of the state.

8.152   The local authority is required to consider the reasons for the disposal of the assets, the timing of the disposal, as well as whether the person had a reasonable expectation of needing to contribute towards the cost of the eligible care needs (annex E para 11).

Purpose of the disposal

8.153   Where an authority decides that an adult has deliberately deprived himself or herself of assets in order to avoid or reduce the care charge, it may treat the adult as still possessing the asset and charge him or her accordingly (statutory guidance, annex E paras 18 and 19). The wording of charging and assessment regulations 2014 regs 17 and 22 states that the adult must have deprived himself or herself of the asset for the purpose of decreas-ing the amount of their care charge. The meaning of these regulations is explored further in annex E (para 6), which emphasises the need for the person to have *intentionally* deprived or decreased his or her assets and/or income at a time when the person must have known that he or she needed care and support, so as to reduce the person's contribution towards his or her care costs. However, where the reduction in assets has been caused by repayment of a debt (even if not immediately due), this must not be considered to be deprivation (annex E para 7).

8.154   The statutory guidance cautions local authorities against assuming that a deprivation of assets will always be deliberate, stating that it should only be considered where the person ceases to possess assets that (a) would otherwise have been taken into account for the purposes of the financial assessment or (b) where the asset has been turned into one that is now disregarded (annex E para 10).

8.155   There may be many valid reasons why a person chooses to deprive himself or herself of his or her capital, and the authority must fully explore the circumstances before reaching a decision (annex E para 5). However, deprivation is likely to have occurred where avoiding the care and support charge was a 'significant motivation'.

Timing of the disposal

8.156   The length of time between disposal and the application of financial assessment is a relevant factor for the local authority to consider in respect of potential deprivation of both capital and income. There are two matters for consideration: (a) at the time of the disposal, could the person have a 'reasonable expectation of the need for care and support?' and (b) did the person have a 'reasonable expectation of needing to contribute to the cost of their eligible care needs?' (annex E para 11).

8.157   Annex E para 12 of the statutory guidance expresses the expectation of needing care and support as follows:

> For example, it would be unreasonable to decide that a person had disposed of an asset in order to reduce the level of charges for their care and support needs if at the time the disposal took place they were fit and healthy and could not have foreseen the need for care and support.

8.158   The leading judgment concerning a deprivation (under AOR regulations 1992 reg 25) is that of the Scottish Court of Session in *Yule v South Lanarkshire Council*.[186] It was held that a local authority was entitled to take account of the value of an elderly woman's home transferred to her daughter over 18 months before the woman entered residential care. The court held that there was no time limit on local authorities when deciding whether a person had deprived him/herself of assets for the purposes of avoiding residential care fees.

8.159   There is no further information contained within the statutory guidance of the implication of the second factor (ie the person having a reasonable expectation of the need to contribute to the cost of their eligible care needs (annex E para 11)). What knowledge would be sufficient for a person to be able to have a reasonable expectation? This issue was considered in *R (Beeson) v Dorset CC*[187], which concerned a challenge to a decision that the resident had deprived himself of his house for the purpose of decreasing his liability for residential care fees (again, a case under AOR regulations 1992 reg 25). Mr Beeson senior transferred his house to his son by deed of

---

186 (2001) 4 CCLR 383; as the wording of AOR regulations 1992 reg 25 is virtually identical to charging and assessment regulations 2014 regs 17 and 22, the reg 25 case-law on deprivation remains good authority for deprivation issues under the CA 2014.

187 [2001] EWHC 986 (Admin), (2002) 5 CCLR 5.

gift, his stated reason being that he wished to ensure his son had a home if he needed it following the breakdown of his marriage. He then continued to live in the house for two years before being assessed by the council as being in need of residential care. His wish had been to live at home as long as possible and to die there. He returned home after several spells in hospital and received home care. At the time of the transfer, social services had not mentioned the possibility of residential care being required, but the council took the view that residential care was an inevitability and that this was the motive in making the transfer and accordingly it treated the house as notional capital.

8.160   In the *Beeson* case, Richards J relied upon the following extract from the *Yule* judgment:[188]

> In determining the matter of notional capital, the local authority can only proceed upon the material which is available to them either from their own sources or upon that material as supplemented by material from the applicant and from such other sources as the local authority can reasonably be expected to apply to. We agree with counsel for the petitioner that in considering whether there is notional capital to be added to the actual capital of an applicant, the local authority must look to the information before them to determine whether a purpose to the effect specified in the regulations can be deduced. But in our opinion, this is not a matter of onus of proof. Rather, before the local authority can reach such a view, it must have material before it from which it can be reasonably inferred that the deprivation of capital took place deliberately and with a purpose of the nature specified. The local authority cannot look into the mind of the person making the disposition of capital or of others who may be concerned in the transaction. It can only look at the nature of the disposal within the context of the time at which and the circumstances in which that disposal took place.
>
> ... [W]e do not consider ... that it is necessary that the claimant should know of 'the' capital limit above which, in terms of the relevant regulations applicable at the time, the local authority is bound to refuse the application, if it is a reasonable inference, looking to the transaction in the whole surrounding circumstances relating to the applicant, that it must have been a purpose of the transaction to avoid having to pay any charges in the event of becoming a resident in residential accommodation provided by the local authority. In this respect we consider that the [AOR] 1992 Regulations have to be looked at in a different light to those concerned with provision for income related benefits, not least because the purpose of the individual may have formed possibly some time ahead of the prospect that he or she might require to enter such residential accommodation ...

8.161   The Court of Appeal[189] upheld the first instance decision of Richards J concerning the relevant test for disposals of assets, as stated in *Yule v South Lanarkshire*. Richards J held that the local authority had shown no evidence that Mr Beeson had transferred the property with the intention of reducing his potential liability for care home charges – indeed the evidence was the other way. The council's decision was therefore quashed and had to be reconsidered.

---

188 The extract from the *Yule* judgment is at (2001) 4 CCLR 383 at 395–396 and is cited in the *Beeson* judgment at [2001] EWHC 986 (Admin), (2002) 5 CCLR 5 at [9].
189 *R (Beeson) v Dorset CC* [2002] EWCA Civ 1812, (2003) 6 CCLR 5.

8.162   Given the obligations upon local authorities to provide financial information and advice to enable 'people to make well-informed choices about
how they pay of their care ... immediately or in the future'[190] it may be
less likely that people will be able to argue that they were uninformed
as to the possible costs of their future care. This is particularly the case
as the question of deprivation of capital and income now applies to all
care settings, rather than only at the time a person was seeking residential
accommodation.

Investigating deprivation

8.163   The statutory guidance makes it clear that it is up to the person to prove
that he or she no longer has the asset or income and, if the person is unable
to provide acceptable evidence of its disposal, the assessment proceeds as
if the person still had the asset or income (annex E paras 8 and 14). In the
vast majority of cases, the information required by the authority will be
available from the adult who disposed of the asset or, in cases where the
person lacks capacity, from others (eg family members, attorney, deputy
or social security appointee).[191]

8.164   The statutory guidance does not specify what enquiries a local authority
should make to determine whether or not a deprivation has occurred, nor
does it set out what information is needed. At annex E para 17, it notes that
a local authority may wish to conduct its own investigations into whether
deprivation of assets has occurred, rather than relying solely on the declaration of the person (or the person's representative). Such enquiries would
need to be made by the authority in accordance with the general principles
of disclosure, ECHR Article 8 and the requirements of the Data Protection
Act (DPA) 1998 (see chapter 19 below). Local authorities are reminded that
there is separate guidance under the Regulation of Investigatory Powers
Act 2000 which sets out the limits to local authority powers to carry out
investigations.[192]

8.165   Previous advice[193] was given to local authorities about what information
and enquiries were to be made, which remains of relevance. It advised as
follows:

>   Much information can be verified by reference to recent documentation
>   provided by the client such as bank statements and building society account
>   books. Authorities should also make use of information available to them
>   from other departments within the authority or District Councils to verify
>   client details, for example council tax benefit and housing records. They
>   should also, as appropriate and with the consent of the client, undertake
>   checks with other agencies such as the Social security office, banks and

190 CA 2014 s4; and see the statutory guidance, chapter 3 at para 3.36 (and see paras
3.36–3.43).

191 The statutory guidance, annex E para 8 provides a list of evidence of the disposal of
the asset, including a trust deed; deed of gift; proof of repayment of debts and also
receipts for expenditure.

192 See Home Office, *Protection of Freedoms Act 2012 – changes to provisions under the
Regulation of Investigatory Powers Act 2000 (RIPA). Home Office guidance to local
authorities in England and Wales on the judicial approval process for RIPA and the crime
threshold for directed surveillance*, October 2012.

193 See LAC (98)8, para 10.

private pension firms. Obviously it is not necessary for all information to be verified, and it is for authorities themselves to determine the extent and circumstances for verifying information.

8.166 It is also open to a local authority to seek disclosure of the legal advice given in connection with transactions alleged to have been made at an undervalue (eg a transfer of ownership of a property without consideration). An application to the court by a local authority for disclosure of the solicitor's file is likely to succeed where the evidence demonstrates that there was a prima facie case that there had been transactions at an undervalue, designed to prejudice the local authority's interests and put assets beyond its reach, for which no explanation had been advanced. Where the evidence supports a case of sharp practice or something underhand, a court is likely to order disclosure of the relevant documents which will not always be protected by considerations of legal privilege, as in the case of *Brent LBC v Estate of Owen Kane*.[194]

8.167 The Law Society practice note *Meeting the needs of vulnerable clients*[195] provides useful guidance about how solicitors should approach those who may lack capacity or who may be vulnerable to undue influence. It includes information about the role of carers and other third parties, as well as making gifts. The practice note reminds solicitors that the general rule is that a solicitor may act only on their client's instructions. Furthermore, without the appropriate formal authority (eg the appointment of an attorney or a deputy), no other person has the right to make decisions about the property, financial or legal affairs of a person without capacity. This practice note, together with an earlier Law Society practice note *Making gifts of assets*,[196] contains valuable advice of assistance to parties seeking to establish whether the disposal of property or other assets of a person without the requisite mental capacity has been carried out in a way which protects the person's interests (rather than those of others who may benefit from the transaction).

Diminishing notional capital

8.168 The statutory guidance reiterates the previous provisions of CRAG[197] so that, where a person has been assessed as having notional capital, its value must be reduced over time. This applies regardless of its source ie whether it is capital which would be available to the person if it were applied for, or is paid to a third party in respect of the person or where it arises out of a deprivation of capital.[198]

8.169 The rule is that the value of notional capital 'must be reduced weekly by the difference between the weekly rate the person is paying for their care and the weekly rate they would have paid if notional capital did not

---

194 [2014] EWHC 4564 (Ch) following the principle in *Barclays Bank plc v Eustice* [1995] 1 WLR 1238: the court held that the 'iniquity' principle was widely accepted *BBGP Managing General Partner Ltd v Babcock & Brown Global Partners* [2010] EWHC 2176 (Ch), [2011] Ch 296 and *JSC BTA Bank v Ablyazov* [2014] EWHC 2788 (Comm).

195 Law Society, *Meeting the needs of vulnerable clients*, 2015.

196 Law Society, *Making gifts of assets*, 2011.

197 CRAG, para 6.074.

198 Statutory guidance, annex B paras 28–31.

apply'.[199] The rule means that, over time, the person may nevertheless qualify for financial assistance from the authority in meeting the cost of his or her care and support, whether provided in the person's own home or in a care home.

8.170   The statutory guidance gives an example of the diminishing notional capital rule in the case of 'Hayley', as follows (annex B para 31):

> Hayley is receiving care and support in a care home. She is assessed as having notional capital of £20,000 plus actual capital of £6,000. This means her assets are above the upper capital limit and she needs to pay the full cost of her care and support at £400 per week. The notional capital should therefore be reduced by the difference between the sum Hayley is paying (£400) and would have paid without the notional capital (£100). If she did not have the notional capital it would not affect her ability to pay. This is as she has an income of £120.40 and a personal allowance of £24.40 per week and would therefore be assessed as being able to pay £100.

Notional income

8.171   In some circumstances, a person may be treated as having income that they do not actually have; this is known as 'notional income'.[200] This may be in circumstances where a person has not applied for income which would be payable to him or her (eg from an occupational or personal pension) or where the person has sought to deliberately deprive himself or herself of it for the purpose of reducing the amount the person is liable to pay for his or her care.

8.172   Where notional income is included in a financial assessment, it should be treated the same way as actual income.[201] Therefore, any income disregards should be applied in the usual way. Notional income should be calculated from the date it could be expected to be acquired if an application had been made. In doing so, a local authority should assume the application was made when it first became aware of the possibility and take account of any time limits which may limit the period of arrears.

The consequences of deprivation

8.173   Where deprivation has been found to have occurred, the local authority must decide whether or not to treat the person has still having the asset and charge them accordingly (ie as though the deprivation has not occurred and treating the asset as notional income or capital (annex E paras 18–19)).[202] Local authorities are reminded that they should therefore ensure that people are not rewarded for trying to avoid paying their

---

199 See charging and assessment regulations 2014 reg 23; and statutory guidance, annex B 'Treatment of capital' paras 28–31.

200 See charging and assessment regulations 2014 reg 17; and statutory guidance, annex C paras 34–37.

201 The statutory guidance, annex C para 36; and see also para 38, which provides for exemptions for certain types of income being treated as notional income, including working tax credit, income from trust funds and where occupational pensions are not being paid at the discretion of the trustees or managers of the pension scheme because of financial difficulties.

202 charging and assessment regulations 2014 regs 17 and 22.

assessed contribution.[203] At the same time, the local authority are also cautioned that the 'overall principle should be that when a person has tried to deprive themselves of assets, this should not affect the amount of local authority support they receive'.[204] This may mean that the authority would be obliged to fund out of its own resources more of the cost of a person's care than would have been the case, but for the proven deprivation of assets and/or income. This may occur, for example, where the person made a cash gift to a relative, which places the person below the capital limit in circumstances where the third party either refuses or is unable to return the cash to the person.

8.174   In this situation, the authority may decide to seek to recover the monies paid by it as a debt, recoverable from the person and/or the third party recipient of the asset, using powers under CA 2014 ss69 and 70 (see para 8.190 below).

8.175   Under the former CRAG provisions, local authorities often took a pragmatic approach to deliberate deprivations where the person was seeking a care home placement. Where a local authority had determined that a deliberate deprivation had occurred and that, in consequence, the resident had notional capital in excess of the upper capital limit, it would not arrange the accommodation at all on the basis that the person remained a 'self-funder' and that (to use the language of NAA 1948 s21) accommodation was 'otherwise available to them'. The provisions were subsequently amended, so that authority was not under an obligation to arrange care home accommodation to a person where their assets exceeded the capital limit.[205]

8.176   Deprivation of capital was considered in a 2015 ombudsman report;[206] the same approach could be taken by an authority under the CA 2014. The case involved an elderly lady who, in 2009 and when she was living in a care home, gifted the sum of £59,500 to her son from the proceeds of sale of her home. She was a self-funder. The authority decided to treat the gift as notional capital when the financial assessment was considered in October 2014, and made it clear to her son that it expected the elderly lady to continue to fund her care until such time as her resources reached the capital threshold. The ombudsman concurred with the council's view, stating that the 'Council is entitled to treat Mrs X as still possessing the money she gifted to her son in 2009 because she did so at a time when she

---

203 See statutory guidance, annex D para 4.
204 See statutory guidance, annex D para 5.
205 See *R v Sefton MBC ex p Help the Aged* (1997–1998) 1 CCLR 57, CA and NAA 1948 s21(2A). However, the policy guidance issued at the time recognised that there will be situations when the person's capital exceeds the statutory limit where the local authority cannot decide that care and attention is not otherwise available eg because of a lack of mental capacity (LAC (98) 19; WOC 27/98). See also the arguments set out in the cases of *Robertson v Fife Council* [2002] UKHL 35, (2002) 5 CCLR 543; *R (Beeson) v Dorset CC* [2001] EWHC 986 (Admin), (2002) 5 CCLR 5 at 22D; and *Ellis v Chief Adjudication Officer* [1998] FLR 184. For a detailed analysis, see the 5th edn of this book, at paras 8.95–8.100
206 LGO complaint no 14 021 012 against Brighton and Hove City Council, 23 April 2015.

was living in a care home, being clearly aware of the need for care services, and knowing she had to pay for her care fees'.[207]

8.177   It is arguable that the CRAG approach – that the authority is able to decline to arrange for the care home accommodation – may continue to apply in those situations where a person has deprived himself or herself of assets. Where the person retains mental capacity,[208] the authority is not under any obligation to arrange a care home placement (under CA 2014 s18(4)). However, if a person no longer has access to the amount assessed as notional capital (perhaps because the person to whom the funds have been transferred has spent them), the local authority may exercise its discretionary powers to meet the person's needs by arranging the accommodation as the person would not have any available funds to arrange and pay for the care themselves.[209] If it did so, the authority remains entitled to charge the person for the person's accommodation on the basis that the person has sufficient assets to pay for his or her own care (as actual and/or notional capital), with the usual options of recovery of any expenditure made by the authority for the person's care.[210]

Paying the financial contribution

8.178 The statutory guidance states that the overall cost of the personal budget 'must then be broken down into the amount the person must pay, following the financial assessment, and the remainder of the budget that the authority will pay' (statutory guidance, para 11.10).

8.179   Regardless of the care setting, where the person is required to pay towards the cost of his or her care, it should also be explained that this means that the person will be sent an invoice for the cost of that care by the local authority.[211] An agreement should be reached as to whom the invoices are to be sent (either to the person receiving the care or to the person's nominated agent).[212] The local authority should arrange to monitor that the person is maintaining payments of any financial contribution which the person is required to pay to the authority.

8.180   The action to be taken when a person fails to pay the required financial contribution, and the local authority seeks to recover the unpaid contributions as a debt, is set out in the statutory guidance, annex D, and is discussed at para 8.190.

---

207 There are a number of forthright LGO decisions on the issue of deprivation of capital: see Sheffield City Council (16 004 406) 17 October 2016; Durham CC (16 006 801) 11 October 2016; Norfolk CC (15 019 402) 10 October 2016.

208 Where the person requiring care no longer has mental capacity, see para 8.344 below.

209 The authority may exercise its powers under CA 2014 s19(1) where the authority is not obliged to meet needs under CA 2014 s18.

210 Under CA 2014 ss69 and 70; see also para 8.190.

211 Although not specifically referred to in chapter 3 'Information and advice' in the statutory guidance, it would be appropriate for a local authority to make this type of information available under this obligation – see, for example, statutory guidance, para 3.43.

212 See statutory guidance, annex D para 7, which relates to the recovery of care costs by the local authority, including both residential and non-residential care.

The consequences of non-payment

8.181 Prior to the introduction to the CA 2014, the ombudsman had held that it was maladministration to allow a person to terminate his or her care services due to an inability to pay for them, without advising the person that social services cannot withdraw services for non-payment.[213] The authority also could not take such action without first informing the service user of his or her right to challenge the charge.[214] The approach was decided on the basis that, where the community care service was provided by the authority in consequence of a statutory duty (eg under Chronically Sick and Disabled Persons Act (CSDPA) 1970 s2), the service could not as a matter of law be withdrawn merely because the service user was refusing to pay for it.

8.182 The previous policy guidance, Fairer Charging 2013, stated:

> Assessment of a person's need for care should not be confused with financial assessment of a person's ability to pay a charge. Once someone has been assessed as needing a service, that service should not be withdrawn because the user refuses to pay the charge. The council should continue to provide the service, while pursuing the debt, if necessary through the civil courts.[215]

8.183 Where services (both accommodation and non-accommodation) are being provided under the CA 2014 to meet an eligible need, this would be in consequence of a statutory duty. It appears that the ombudsman's decisions above would continue to apply following the introduction of the CA 2014. However, the statutory guidance itself is unhelpfully silent upon the subject of the continuation of a person's social care service in circumstances where the person refuses to pay for it. It makes reference only to disputes about charging being resolved by the social services complaint's procedure[216] or by recovery through the county court as a debt (see statutory guidance, annex D).

Charging for personal budgets and direct payments

8.184 In England, the policy intention underlying the charging provisions for direct payments and personal budgets (more generally considered at chapter 10) was that recipients were to be subject to the same regime as that which applied to other service users of non-accommodation services.[217]

---

213 Complaint no 99/C/1983 against Durham CC, 9 October 2000.
214 Complaint nos 02/C/14235, 02/C/15396, 02/C/15397 and 02/C/15503 against Derbyshire CC, 24 June 2004.
215 Fairer Charging 2013, para 99
216 See the statutory guidance, paras 8.68–8.70; and see chapter 20 below.
217 Fairer Charging 2013, para 90 stated: 'Councils should refer to *Fairer Contributions Guidance 2010, Calculating an Individual's Contribution to their Personal Budget,* when assessing how much users may be asked to contribute towards their Direct Payments and/or Personal Budgets. *Fairer Contributions* guidance sits alongside and should be read in conjunction with *Fairer Charging* guidance, as both use the same process for calculating an individual's contribution.'

8.185   The CA 2014 'places personal budgets into law for the first time, making them the norm for people with care and support needs'.[218] Furthermore, the statutory guidance makes it clear (at para 11.10) that:

> The personal budget must always be an amount sufficient to meet the person's care and support needs, and must include the cost to the local authority of meeting the person's needs which the local authority is under a duty to meet, or has exercised its power to do so. This overall cost must then be broken down into the amount the person must pay, following the financial assessment, and the remainder of the budget that the authority will pay.

8.186   The Care and Support (Personal Budget Exclusion of Costs) Regulations 2014[219] set out the limited circumstances in which local authority charges may not be included in the personal budget, namely that the provision of intermediate care and reablement services must be excluded from the personal budget.[220]

8.187   Where a local authority charges an 'arrangement fee' (for arranging the care and support of a person whose resources are above the financial limit – see para 8.55 above), it does not form part of the person's 'personal budget' as it does not relate directly to meeting the person's eligible needs (see statutory guidance, paras 8.56–8.64). Local authorities are advised that consideration should be given to how best to set out this information to the person (where necessary, in an appropriately accessible format) and the arrangement fee may be presented alongside the personal budget to help the person understand the total charges to be paid and how those costs are allocated (statutory guidance, para 11.13).

8.188   The same principles are applied where the person, or a third party on their behalf, pays an additional payment (or 'top-up') to be able to secure the care and support of their choice, where this would cost more than the local authority is prepared to fund. The top-up does not form part of the personal budget, which must reflect the costs to the local authority of meeting the person's needs. Again, local authorities should consider how best to present the information to the person, so that the amount of the charges paid is clear and the link to the personal budget is understood (statutory guidance, para 11.14).

8.189   The provision of direct payments is included (CA 2014 s8(2)(c)) as a method of meeting a person's eligible needs (under CA 2014 ss18–20); they are considered in more detail in chapter 10. Where a person is in receipt of a direct payment and, following the financial assessment, has to pay a contribution towards his or her care and support, it is for the local authority to determine whether the direct payments are paid on a gross or net basis. Such a decision should be made by the authority in consultation with the appropriate stakeholders. However, the statutory guidance provides a steer to local authorities that a 'net direct payment' ie one which is allocated to the person after deduction of the relevant charges is 'generally seen as the easiest and most efficient way to administer direct payments'.[221]

218 See CA 2014 s26; and statutory guidance, para 11.2.
219 2014 SI No 2840.
220 See statutory guidance, para 11.16.
221 See statutory guidance, para 12.20 and annex J 'Glossary'.

Recovery of debts

Generally

8.190 The statutory guidance describes the introduction of the CA 2014 as introducing a 'modern legal framework for the recovery of any debts that may have accrued as a result of a local authority meeting a person's eligible care and support needs'.[222] In general terms, the Act extends the powers of local authorities – most notable are CA 2014 ss69[223] and 70,[224] to include all monies owed to an authority by a person who has received any type of care and support from a local authority, not just care home accommodation as was previously the case.

8.191 The ability of a local authority to place a charge on a person's property,[225] where a person had failed to pay their care home charges or transferred their property to a third party, has been removed. The stated reason for the change in approach being that the new powers under section 69 provide 'equal protection to both the local authority and the person'.[226] The argument being that the previous powers to local authorities were 'unilateral' ie they did not give the person (from whom the debt was being recovered) the power to seek alternative means of payment.[227] This material change has caused authorities concern that (1) that they will be unable to recover outstanding fees when someone dies or sells their property; and (2) that this may result in 'more older people being involved in complicated and potentially distressing court cases'.[228]

8.192 The changes introduced by the CA 2014 enable a local authority to take an ordinary debt action in the county court for a judgment against the debtor to recover the outstanding debt.[229] In these circumstances, the debt will be for the costs of care (eg unpaid care home fees or charges for care at home) which remain unpaid by, or unrecovered from, the person receiving the care and support.

8.193 Where a person has been offered a deferred payment agreement (DPA), and it has been refused, the authority may decide to pursue the costs of residential care by means of an action for debt recovery in the

---

222 Statutory guidance, annex D para 1.
223 CA 2014 s69 provides for the recovery of charges; it states: 'Any sum due to a local authority under this Part is recoverable by the authority as a debt due to it'.
224 CA 2014 s70 provides for the power to recover charge from a third party where a person has transferred assets to them in order to avoid charges for care and support.
225 HASSASSAA 1983 s22.
226 Statutory guidance, annex D para 1.
227 Statutory guidance, annex D para 2. The imposition of a section 22 charge may also be challenged by the property owner by means of the dispute process of the Land Registry and/or the Land Tribunal.
228 LGA and ADASS, *Joint consultation response Care Act: regulations and guidance*, August 2014 at para 30.
229 The LGA has published a *Debt implementation toolkit*, provided by the Department of Health and the and National Association of Financial Assessment Officers (NAFAO), available at www.local.gov.uk/care-support-reform/-/journal_content/56/10180/6522471/ARTICLE.

county court.[230] In all other circumstances, a local authority may not take an action for debt recovery against a person with a DPA.[231]

8.194   The immediate consequence of the revised approach to debt recovery is that all types of unpaid financial contributions are treated in the same way and it equalises the recovery of debts procedures: for those who own their home and those who do not and for those who need care and support in a care home and those who need care in their own homes. In applying their debt recovery powers,[232] the statutory guidance cautions authorities to be aware that they are not dealing with the general population as much of this debt is 'likely to be from a move into care homes of very frail people in the 80s and 90s, many with dementia'.[233]

8.195   The advantage of the county court process is that the case will be considered by a judge with greater expertise in determining realistic debt repayment arrangements. Where a local authority seeks to enforce charges through a county court action, the court is permitted to review the reasonableness of the original charging decision and the reasons given for its refusal to waive the charges.[234] If the reasons for not waiving the charges are irrational at public law, the county court is entitled to refuse the application.[235]

8.196   The position of those persons who lack mental capacity is considered in this chapter at para 8.344. There is inevitably a risk of conflict of interests when a local authority acts as the person's deputy, which is acknowledged in the statutory guidance (annex D para 20). However, the court process itself, as well as the supervisory role of the Office of the Public Guardian and the likely need to involve the Official Solicitor, would provide additional safeguards to those without capacity against whom debt recovery action is taken by the authority.

Time limit for recovery of debts

8.197   For debts accrued from April 2015 onwards, the time limit for recovery of debts under CA 2014 s69 is within six years of the date on which the sum became due, regardless of whether the debt accrued relates to unpaid charges for care home accommodation or for domiciliary care charges.[236]

230   See CA 2014 s69(2) and statutory guidance, annex D para 3.
231   See also statutory guidance, annex D paras 22–26 for further information about the recovery of debt and the use of DPAs.
232   Statutory guidance, annex D para 4 cites the example of local authorities recovering debts such as 'rent arrears' which is perhaps an unhelpful example, given that failure to pay rent is a grounds for possession of the property, rather simply a claim for a money judgment through the standard debt procedures in the county court, as is introduced by CA 2014 s69.
233   Statutory guidance, annex D para 5; see also para 4 for further guidance to local authorities about how to structure and organise social services debt recovery work within local authorities, making clear the need for this function to be adequately resourced with clear lines of responsibility for making decisions on taking cases forward.
234   *Wandsworth LBC v Winder* [1985] UKHL 2, [1985] 1 AC 461.
235   As did HHJ Hawkesworth QC in *City of Bradford MDC v Matthews* (2002) BD No 108518, 9 October 2002.
236   See statutory guidance, annex D para 11 as to how to calculate when the debt becomes due.

8.198 Where the debt accrued before the commencement of the CA 2014, the time limit would appear to remain three years after the debt became due where the debt to be recovered is for non-payment of care home fees.[237] Where the debt relates to non-payment of non-accommodation charges for services under NAA 1948 s29 and CSDPA 1970 s2, the recovery of the charge falls to be made under HASSASSAA 1983 s17 which is six years from date of breach.[238]

Principles underpinning the approach to debt recovery

8.199 The statutory guidance notes that the 'recovery of debts from those who are receiving care and support is a sensitive issue given the potentially vulnerable nature of the client group and local authority's ultimate responsibility to meet needs'.[239] The tension between the inherent vulnerability of the client group and the responsibilities upon local authorities to meet the social care needs of the population as a whole, at a time of austerity[240] is self-evident. In order to minimise the consequences of these sensitive situations, the statutory guidance sets out the principles underpinning local authorities' approach to debt recovery, as follows:

- Possible debts must be discussed with the person or their representative;
- The local authority must act reasonably;
- Arrangements for debt repayments should be agreed between the relevant parties;
- Repayments must be affordable; and
- Court action should only be considered after all other reasonable avenues have been exhausted'.[241]

8.200 The principles are a hybrid of public law principles,[242] combined with the steps which any claimant authority must take prior to the issue of a debt action in the county court, in accordance with the relevant court rules.[243] The advantage for both the authority and the person is that, where properly followed by the local authority, these principles and processes will to

---

237 By virtue of CA 2014 s69(3)(b), the former time limit of three years under NAA 1948 s56 continues to apply for those cases: see also statutory guidance, annex D para 11; however, there is an argument that the time limit for recovery of care home fees through the civil courts has always been six years and that the three year time limit applies only where the authority sought recovery as a summary debt in the magistrates' court (see Magistrates' Court Act 1980 ss58 and 150). For further analysis, see J Auburn, 'Care Act conundrum: Did parliament legislate in error to mistakenly confer an amnesty on care home fees?' in Community Care Blog 11KBW, 5 February 2016.

238 As a civil debt, the time limit would be six years from date of breach by virtue of Limitation Act 1980 s5.

239 Annex D para 6.

240 For further information about the funding of social care, see the report by the LGA, *Adult social care funding: 2016 state of the nation report*, 2016.

241 Annex D paras 6–10.

242 Ie that the authority must act 'reasonably at all times', in accordance with human rights legislation and the well-being principles set out in the CA 2014 (see statutory guidance, annex D para 8).

243 See the statutory guidance, annex D paras 12–16 'Options to recover debt'; and the *Practice direction – Pre-action conduct* issued by the Ministry of Justice.

some degree at least ensure that the rights and responsibilities of all parties are protected.

8.201   Certainly, it is to be hoped that the focus on information and transparency within the CA 2014 will prevent all parties falling into the tangle which developed in the complex case of *Aster Healthcare Ltd v Batool Shafi*.[244] The resident, an elderly man, was placed in an independent care home under NAA 1948 s21 by the local authority, Brent LBC, as he lacked the mental capacity to make his own care arrangements. There was a lack of clarity by all parties about who was responsible for paying the care home fees; it subsequently transpired that the resident had assets in excess of the capital limit. Brent LBC declined to pay the care home fees on the basis that the resident was a self-funder but the care home fees remained unpaid for a period of approximately two years until the death of the resident. The care home brought a claim again the resident's estate for the recovery of care home fees; the care home did not pursue a claim against the council. The High Court held that, by virtue of the provisions of the NAA 1948, there was no direct financial relationship between a resident and a care home provider where the local authority makes the arrangements to place a person with sufficient funds in an independent care home. The court noted that, even where all parties entered into an agreement for the resident to pay the care home charges direct to the provider, the primary legal obligation to pay the fees rests with the local authority. In the event of any default, the local authority must pay the care home provider and then recover the monies from the resident. Given the virtually identical approach to the authority's responsibility for the payment of care home fees (see statutory guidance, annex A paras 28–30), it seems likely that the same outcome would be reached if the case were brought under the CA 2014, rather than the NAA 1948 as local authorities would be in a similar position where a person lacked capacity by virtue of CA 2014 s18(4).

8.202   Any decision made by a local authority to take proceedings for debt recovery against a person in such circumstances is a discretionary one and it should therefore be an action last resort, when all other efforts have failed.[245] The emphasis in the statutory guidance, annex D (see para 12) is on authorities considering the full range of options available to recover the monies, including: effective social work skills, negotiation, use of advocacy, mediation, arbitration and assisting families (or others as appropriate) to become the person's attorney or deputy or the authority itself being the person's deputy.

8.203   When exercising its discretionary powers, the statutory guidance (annex D, para 9) makes it clear that the authority should consider whether, before pursuing any course of action, it is appropriate to recover the debt. It may therefore decide not to so or, as an alternative, recover only part of the debt. The reasons given (annex D para 9) are that it may not be economically viable to do so or, for example, where the person or the person's representative could not reasonably have been aware that the asset

244 (2014) EWHC 77 (QB).
245 See annex D paras 9 and 10, the latter requires that the local authority 'should also consider how different approaches might impact on a person's well-being, in line with a local authority's general duty to promote a person's well-being'.

in question needed to be included in the financial assessment. However, the duty upon the local authority to provide information and advice under CA 2014 s4 (see para 8.13 above) arguably makes it less likely that a person will be uninformed about charging matters,[246] as has been the case in the past. In these circumstances, there may be a perception by local authorities that it is less likely that such errors by a person (or the person's representatives) are 'reasonably' made.

Misrepresentation and failure to disclose

8.204 The wording of CA 2014 s69(4) provides that 'where a person misrepresents or fails to disclose (whether fraudulently or otherwise) to a local authority any material fact in connection with the provisions of this Part', the authority may recover from the person any expenditure (or unrecovered sum) which it incurred, or did not recover, as a result of the person's misrepresentation or failure to disclose. The wording of CA 2014 s69 broadly mirrors the provision of Social Security Administration Act 1992 s71 (as amended), which provides for the recovery of overpaid social security benefits, usually by means of weekly deductions from a person's ongoing social security benefit payments. There is no similar provision within the CA 2014, nor the regulations, to allow for a formal system of recovery from a person's ongoing community care payments. However, such sums would be recoverable as a debt by the authority in the county court, by virtue of CA 2014 s69(1).

8.205 The common feature between the recovery of social security benefit overpayments and the provisions of CA 2014 s69(4) is the concept that the misrepresentation or failure to disclose by the person need not be deliberate or in any way fraudulent. For example, the person may not have provided accurate information at the time of the financial assessment as he or she had a mistaken, but genuine, belief that the asset did not have to be disclosed. Alternatively, a person's representative subsequently became aware that there were other assets which may have only come to light after the financial assessment process had been completed. When innocent errors are identified, the local authority is entitled to treat such sums as 'due to the authority from the person' (CA 2014 s69(4)) and may choose to seek recovery from the person of the expenditure it had – albeit incorrectly – incurred as a result of the earlier, innocent misrepresentation or failure to disclose. While this may not be objectionable, there are concerns that the provisions may be used by authorities to recover monies from persons in situations which are perhaps not desirable, particularly given the often very vulnerable client group.

8.206 The risk of local authorities acting inappropriately and seeking to recover monies in circumstances where it may not be reasonable to do so is increased because, rather curiously, no reference is made to s69(4) is anywhere in the statutory guidance. There is a worrying absence of

246 Indeed, it is possible that the opposite may result – as ADASS has expressed it, there is a concern that the increased emphasis on the provision of independent financial advice may result in more people obtaining advice on how to reduce their contributions to their care fees (LGA and ADASS, *Joint consultation response Care Act: regulations and guidance*, 2014 at para 31).

guidance to local authorities about the circumstances in which it may be 'reasonable' – or not – for the monies to be recovered from the person. The omission is inexplicable, given what is in practical terms the importation into community care law of a highly complex social security provisions for the recovery of welfare benefits (and now 'overpaid' community care monies).[247]

The issue of court proceedings

8.207   The process of issuing a claim for recovery of a debt, and its subsequent enforcement, is set out in the statutory guidance, annex D paras 27–51. The Court of Appeal has held that in any enforcement proceedings the respondent is, as a general principle, entitled to plead a public law breach by the local authority as one of its grounds for resisting a claim (for instance a failure to follow CRAG or other guidance etc). [248] Although this case pre-dates the CA 2014 provisions, it remains relevant to recovery of a debt under CA 2014 ss69 and 70. Certainly, as the statutory guidance makes explicit, the conduct of the local authority will be a relevant consideration by the court in determining which party is liable for the costs of any proceedings, which are awarded on a discretionary basis.[249]

Recovering charges from a third party

8.208   Where an asset has been transferred to a third party, the provisions of CA 2014 s70 operate to make the third party liable to pay towards the costs of the person's care. The conditions are that:

1) the person's needs have been, or are being, met by the local authority under CA 2014 ss18–20;
2) the adult has transferred an asset to a third party with the 'intention of avoiding charges for having the adult's needs met'; and
3) the transfer was either at an undervalue or without any consideration.[250]

8.209   The provisions of CA 2014 s70 are similar to the those under HASSASSAA 1983 s21(1), which enabled the local authority to take enforcement proceedings against a third party recipient. However, there are two important differences in the CA 2014 regime. First, the provisions of CA 2014 s70 apply to all types of care settings, so the issue of deprivation of assets by means of a transfer to a third party no longer applies only in care home settings.

247 The recovery of overpayments of social security benefits is beyond the scope of this book; further information on this complex area of law may be found in *Welfare benefits and tax credits handbook 2016/17*, 18th edn, published by CPAG (ISBN 978-1-910715-07-9).
248 *Derbyshire CC v Akrill* [2005] EWCA Civ 308, (2005) 8 CCLR 173; see also *Rhondda Cynon Taff CBC v Watkins* [2003] EWCA Civ 129, [2003] 1 WLR 1864.
249 See annex D para 12: 'Whilst it is at the discretion of the Court to award costs, if no effort has been made to reach an agreement first a judge may hold this against the local authority when considering making an order for payment of the costs in the case.' The authority may add to the 'sum due' its costs in recovering the debt by virtue of CA 2014 s69(5).
250 CA 2014 s70(1)(a)–(c).

Second, CA 2014 s70 does not provide for a time limit of six months, so therefore a local authority may rely on a transfer made at any time providing it was done with the intention of avoiding care charges (for further information as to how intention is established, see para 8.213). The time limit for the issue of proceedings under CA 2014 s70 would be the six-year limitation period set out in CA 2014 s69, although the statutory guidance cautions that proceedings must only be taken when all other avenues have been exhausted.[251].

8.210   Where the conditions in CA 2014 s70 are satisfied, the third party is liable to pay to the local authority the difference between what it would have charged the person receiving the care and what it did in fact charge. The third party is not liable to pay more than the benefit which they received from the transfer and, where the transfer was to one or more parties, the sum payable by each party is calculated on a proportionate basis of their share of the asset.[252]

Proceedings to set aside the transfer of the asset

8.211   The statutory guidance advises that local authorities may consider other options in the recovery of debts, including Insolvency Act (IA) 1986 s423 relating to transactions defrauding creditors (annex D para 49). The court is empowered to make any order it sees fit, including setting aside such transfers or making other orders to protect the interests of those who are the victims of the transaction. This provision goes beyond requiring the third party recipient of the asset to pay towards the person's care, as under CA 2014 s70, and may instead operate to reverse the transfer, so that the person who transferred the asset has it restored to them. This outcome would have the effect that the person making the transfer once again owns the asset and has actual, rather than notional, capital for the purposes of any financial assessment by the authority. Alternatively, the court could order that the third party pays the full value of the asset to the person who transferred to them.

8.212   The first condition for a successful application to the court under IA 1986 s423 is that the person must have entered into a transaction where there was no consideration (eg a gift) or where the third party paid less that the actual value of the asset. The powers available to the court under section 423 are without time limit and are exercisable without the need for bankruptcy proceedings[253] or even for the individual in question to be insolvent.

8.213   The second condition considers the intention or purpose of the person making the transfer. Under IA 1986 s423(3), the court must satisfy itself that the person who entered into the transfer did so with the purpose of putting assets beyond the reach of another (ie a local authority) who is making, or who may at some time make, a claim against him or her. Alternatively, the court may satisfy itself that the purpose of the person

---

251 See statutory guidance, annex E 'Deprivation of assets' at para 23.
252 CA 2014 s70(2)–(4); and statutory guidance, annex E 'Deprivation of assets' at paras 21–23.
253 See generally *Midland Bank v Wyatt* [1995] 1 FLR 697.

making the transfer of the asset was to otherwise prejudice the interests of such a person (ie a local authority) in relation to the claim which is being, or may be, made. There is no need for the authority making the claim to prove the person's dishonesty, beyond an intention to prejudice creditors: it is a question of proof of the intention or purpose of the transaction.[254] The intention to prejudice creditors need not be the only purpose of the person making the transaction;[255] it is sufficient if the intention was a real or substantial purpose rather than being the dominant purpose.[256]

8.214   The breadth of IA 1986 s423 has been explained thus:

> While the burden of proof remains on the applicant, establishing the necessary purpose should be less difficult to achieve than proving intent to defraud under the previous law ... The inclusion of persons who 'may at some time claim' against the debtor envisages potential future creditors who, individually unknown to the debtor at the time of the transaction, become victims of a risky business enterprise against the consequences of failure of which the debtor seeks to protect himself at the outset. In extending the purposes of present or future claimants, the ambit of the section is made very wide ...[257]

8.215   Where the resident has transferred the capital asset using a firm or business which specifically markets schemes designed to avoid the value of the asset being taken into account for residential fee purposes, this may, perversely, be used as evidence to establish the purpose behind the transaction.[258]

8.216   In *Derbyshire CC v Akrill*[259] the local authority's claim included a claim under IA 1986 s423 for an order that the house be retransferred to the deceased's estate. In this case the deceased had completed various transactions, including a gift and leaseback of the house in which he had been living, and a declaration of solvency while in hospital following several strokes a few weeks before moving into a care home. Although the case was remitted back to the county court to resolve, it was held that IA 1986 s423 could be used to set aside a gift of property in such situations, where the purpose was to put property beyond the reach of the authority.

8.217   The Law Society, in its practice note *Making gifts of assets*,[260] observes that:

> Although some local authorities have threatened to use insolvency proceedings, few have actually done so, perhaps because of lack of expertise, cost or the prospect of bad publicity. However, with increasing pressures on local authority resources to provide community care services, the incidence of this may rise in the future.

---

254 *Midland Bank v Wyatt* [1995] 1 FLR 697 and *NatWest v Jones* [2001] 1 BCLC 98; affirmed [2002] 1 BCLC 55.

255 See *Choan v Saggar* [1992] BCC 306.

256 See *IRC v Hashmi* [2002] 2 BCLC 489.

257 Berry and others, *Personal insolvency*, Butterworths, 1993: an analysis largely vindicated by the subsequent case-law – see eg *Hill v Spread Trustee Co Ltd* [2006] EWCA Civ 542, [2007] 1 WLR 2404 and *Curtis v Pulbrook* [2011] EWHC 167 (Ch).

258 See *Barclays Bank v Eustice* [1995] 1 WLR 1238, CA.

259 *Derbyshire CC v Akrill* [2005] EWCA Civ 308, (2005) 8 CCLR 173.

260 Law Society, *Making gifts of assets*, 2011.

8.218 Given the recovery powers provided to local authorities under the CA 2014, in particular the removal of the six-month time limit, it is uncertain whether claims under IA 1986 s423 will increase in the immediate future. However, with the ever-increasing pressure on resources, it is possible that such applications will become more attractive to local authorities, particularly where such action forms part of a properly considered and consulted debt recovery policy.

Services not directly provided by the social services authority

NHS services

8.219 The principles of charging for social care services become more complex in the case of jointly supplied services, such as those provided by a jointly funded NHS/social services arrangement.

8.220 Prior to the introduction of the CA 2014, the following paragraphs (not replicated in the CA 2014 statutory guidance) were contained in the policy guidance contained in Fairer Charging 2013, which advised:

XVI. Use of Powers to transfer funds

91. Local councils and health authorities may jointly commission social care services under section 28A of the NHS Act 1977.[261] The details of any charges should be devised with advice from the local council's own lawyers. The council may recover from users up to the full cost of the social care service, even though the NHS may have met some or all of the cost of the social care service. Local councils must, however, bear in mind that section 17 of the HASSASSA Act 1983 is not a provision designed to enable them to raise general revenue. If a council purchases social care and a health authority purchases health care services from the same provider, then charges to users may only be made for the social care element. Any services for which the NHS has underlying responsibility are automatically free at the point of use,[262] in whatever setting they are provided and whichever agencies provide or commission the service in practice.

XVII. Health Act 2006 Partnerships

92. The National Health Service Act 2006 (which replaced the partnership provisions in the National Health Service Act 1999) did not alter the local authority powers to charge in the event of a partnership arrangement. In agreeing partnership arrangements, agencies will have to consider how best to manage charging (where local councils charge for services) and how to clarify the difference between charged-for and non-charged for services. There is no intention to increase or expand charging arrangements through the Partnership Arrangements. In entering into an arrangement, the partners will need to agree on the approach to be taken on charging.

93. Partners will need to bear in mind that, where charging is retained, the arrangements will need to be carefully explained to users of services, to avoid any misunderstanding that NHS services are being charged for, especially when an NHS Trust is providing a service, part of which is being

261 Now NHSA 2006 s256.
262 Other than services for which specific charging powers exist, such as NHS prescription charges.

charged for. It will be critical that charging arrangements are properly explained at the outset of the assessment process ... The existing charging review or appeals mechanisms should be made clear to the user.

8.221   The effect of the integration obligations under CA 2014 s3 (see para 11.134 below) will mean that local authorities are likely to increase the number of partnership arrangements, under National Health Service Act (NHSA) 2006 s75 in respect of their 'health related functions':[263] arrangements that are not superseded by the power to delegate functions under CA 2014 s79 (see para 1.26).

8.222   The above paragraphs from Fairer Charging 2013 are still relevant to the extent that they set out the parameters of a charging regime imposed where a package of care is provided jointly by the local authority and by the NHS. The principles may be summarised as follows and would need to form part of a local authority's charging policy:

1) Any part of the care package provided by the NHS must be provided free at the point of use.

2) The user may be charged for the full cost of the social care element of the service, subject to the usual financial assessment principles.

3) Local authorities are not permitted to raise revenue from such charges ie the charge cannot be more than the actual cost to the authority of that service.

4) The services which are being charged for, and those which are provided free of charge under the NHS, must be explained clearly to service users at the outset.

5) The mechanism for reviewing or appealing charges must also be made clear to the service-user.

Charging for care and support in a care home

Property disregards

8.223   There are a number of circumstances in which the value of the person's 'main or only'[264] home must be disregarded. These are considered below and operate only where the person receiving care has been assessed as needing a place in a care home. The value of a person's home is disregarded where the person continues to reside in his or her own home when receiving care and support provided by the local authority.[265]

12-week property disregard

8.224   Where the adult is a permanent resident in a care home, the value of the person's main or only home (ie the one which he or she would normally occupy) is disregarded for a period of 12 weeks beginning with the day on which the adult first moves into accommodation in a care home.[266] The

---

263 NHS Bodies and Local Authorities Partnership Arrangement Regulations 2000 SI No 617.

264 Statutory guidance, annex B para 34.

265 Statutory guidance, annex B para 34(a).

266 Charging and assessment regulations 2014 Sch 2 para 2.

statutory guidance states that a 'key aim' of the charging framework is 'to prevent people being forced to sell their home at a time of crisis', with the 12-week disregard being used to 'create space' for people to make decisions as to how to meet their contribution towards the cost of their eligible care needs (annex A para 45).

8.225 Under the NAA 1948 regime, residents living permanently in a care home as self-funders, who approached the local authority for funding after being there for more than 12 weeks (usually because their funds were about fall below the capital limit), were entitled to the 12-week disregard at the time the resident applied to the authority for financial assistance with his or her care home fees. CRAG was amended[267] to confirm that[268] the 12-week disregard applied irrespective of whether the resident was already in a care home as a self-funder before being provided with accommodation under the NAA 1948.

8.226 The application of the 12-week disregard, where a person ceases to be a self-funder, is not addressed in either the charging and assessment regulations 2014 or the statutory guidance. The wording of the charging and assessment regulations 2014 (that the person's home is disregarded from the day on which the adult *first* moves into the care home accommodation), together with the intended purpose behind the 12-week disregard being to avoid the sale of the home at a time of crisis, indicates that the obligation upon local authorities to apply an automatic 12-week disregard where the person ceases to be a self-funder no longer exists under the CA 2014 regime.[269] This change of approach is, presumably, because a self-funder whose capital is about to fall below the relevant capital limit is a foreseeable event, which can be planned for in advance.

8.227 The statutory guidance, however, does make provision for a mandatory 12-week disregard period in circumstances where unexpected events would require the need to 'create space' to enable the resident to sort out their financial situation (annex B para 45(b)). This applies where a property disregard (ie disregarded other than under the 12-week disregard provisions[270]) unexpectedly ends, for example, because the 'qualifying relative' (see para 8.231 below) occupying the property has died or moved into a care home.[271]

8.228 In addition, a local authority has general discretion to apply a 12-week disregard of the value of the adult's main or only home where there is a sudden and unexpected change in the person's financial circumstances (statutory guidance, annex B para 46[272]). Each case is to be decided by the authority on its merits. The statutory guidance (annex B para 46) sets out situations where the authority may properly apply these disregard: the key factor is the 'unexpected' nature of the change.

---

267 Following the Department of Health circular LAC (DH) (2009) 3, para 19.
268 CRAG, para 7.006.
269 See charging and assessment regulations 2014 Sch 2 para 2; and also DH FAQ, Q305.
270 See para 8.224.
271 Charging and assessment regulations 2014 Sch 2 para 4(3).
272 Charging and assessment regulations 2014 Sch 2 para 3.

8.229   The 12-week disregard may also be applied by a local authority where the property was occupied in whole or in part by a 'qualifying relative' as their main or only home and, because of an unexpected change of circumstances, the relative no longer occupies the property.[273] This situation is not specifically referred to in the statutory guidance but, in accordance with the common theme, the unexpected nature of the event justifies the discretionary imposition of the 12-week disregard ie to enable the person in the care home to plan how to fund his or her care costs in the future.

Mandatory property disregard

8.230   Where the resident no longer occupies the property, but it is occupied as the main or only home by a 'qualifying relative' of the adult in the care home, a mandatory disregard applies where the qualifying relative has continuously occupied the property as his/her main or only home since before the adult was first provided with accommodation in a care home under the CA 2014 (statutory guidance Annex B para 34(c)).[274]

8.231   In this context, the 'qualifying relative' is defined as:

- the person's partner, former partner or civil partner, except where they are estranged;[275]
- a lone parent who is the person's estranged or divorced partner; or
- a relative[276] of the person or member of their family[277]) who:
    - is aged 60[278] or over, or
    - is aged under 18, or
    - is incapacitated.[279]

---

273 Charging and assessment regulations 2014 Sch 2 para 4(4).

274 Charging and assessment regulations 2014 Sch 2 para 4(1)(b).

275 'Partner' is defined in the charging and assessment regulations 2014 by reference to the IS regulations 1987 (as amended) (Sch 1 para 2); it includes couples who are married, in a civil partnership or who are living together as though married/in a civil partnership.

276 'Relative' is specified as including: parents, parents-in-law, sons, sons-in-law, daughters, daughters-in-law, step-parents, step-sons, step-daughters, brothers, sisters, grandparents, grandchildren, uncles, aunts, nephews, nieces and the spouse, civil partner or unmarried partner of any except the last five (statutory guidance, annex B para 35). The relevant point here is that this is an 'inclusive' definition rather than an exclusive one.

277 This phrase 'member of the person's family' is defined in the statutory guidance at annex B para 36 as 'someone who is living with the qualifying relative as part of an unmarried couple, married to or in a civil partnership'.

278 The age at which the disregard applies is currently not being increased in line with the qualifying age for pensions. This was explained in LAC (DH) 2010(2) as 'raising the relatives property disregard from 60 to 65 would result in properties, that would have been disregarded under the current AOR regulations [the pre-CA 2014 regulations], being taken into account and, possibly, having to be sold to pay for residential care, forcing the relative to move' (para 12). This is not addressed in the statutory guidance, but presumably the same rationale applies.

279 The meaning of 'incapacitated' is not defined by the regulations, but the statutory guidance, annex B para 37 advises that it includes a person receiving (or whose incapacity is sufficient to that required to qualify for) one of the following: 'incapacity benefit, severe disablement allowance, disability living allowance, personal independence payment, armed forces attendance allowance, attendance allowance, constant attendance allowance, or an analogous benefit'. Again this is an inclusive

8.232 Where the relative meets the qualifying conditions, ie aged 60 years or over or is incapacitated and has occupied the property as their main or only home since before the resident entered into the care home, the mandatory disregard must be applied (annex B para 41). In cases where the relative is occupying the property as his or her main or only home at the time the resident moved into a care home and later reaches the age of 60, or becomes incapacitated, the mandatory disregard should apply from the date the relative reaches 60 or becomes incapacitated.

Meaning of 'occupy'

8.233 The meaning of the word 'occupy', in the context of the property disregard, is not defined (annex B para 38). In most cases, the statutory guidance notes that it will be 'obvious' whether or not the property is occupied by a qualifying relative as their main or only home. Where, for whatever reason, the situation is not clear, the local authority should undertake a factual enquiry weighing up all the relevant factors to reach a decision. It is noted that an emotional attachment to the property is not of itself sufficient for the disregard to apply (annex B para 38).

8.234 The main examples of cases where it is perhaps less evident that the relative is in fact occupying the property are those where the relative is not always present in the property (eg working away from home or in prison). There are straightforward examples given in the statutory guidance (annex B para 39). In order to assist the local authority in deciding, on a case by case basis, whether or not a relative is in fact occupying the property as their main or only home, the statutory guidance (annex B para 40) suggests some factors for the authority's consideration, including:

- Does the relative currently occupy another property?
- If the relative has somewhere else to live does he or she own or rent the property (ie how secure/permanent is it)?
- If the relative is not physically present, is there evidence of a firm intention to return to or live in the property?
- Where does the relative pay council tax?
- Where is the relative registered to vote?
- Where is the relative registered with a doctor?
- Are the relative's belongings located in the property?
- Is there evidence that the relative has a physical connection with the property?

8.235 This emphasis in the CA 2014 approach to the property disregard reflects – and makes overt – the decision of the Court of Appeal in *Worcestershire CC v Walford*.[280] The court held that the time for consideration of whether a person 'occupied' the property was to be determined at the date on which the person entered into residential care.

---

rather than an exclusive definition; medical or other evidence may be needed before a decision is reach where the relevant benefit is not actually in payment.
280 [2015] EWCA Civ 22.

Discretionary property disregard

8.236 Where a person's circumstances do not justify the application of the mandatory disregard as set out above, the local authority has a discretion as to whether or not the property may be disregarded, whilst at the same time recognising that the authority must balance its discretion and ensure that 'a person's assets are not maintained at public expense' (statutory guidance, annex B para 42). The example of when it may be appropriate for a local authority to apply the disregard is where the property is the only residence of someone (not a qualifying relative) who has given up his or her own home to care for the person who now requires care home accommodation or who is perhaps the elderly companion of the person (see the example of 'Jayne' in the statutory guidance, annex B para 42).

8.237 Unlike CRAG, the statutory guidance addresses the situation where a relative, who would normally qualify for a mandatory disregard, moves into the property as his or her home after the resident has moved into a care home (annex B para 43). In such situations, local authorities have a discretionary power to disregard the value of a property. It must consider the individual circumstances of each case, including factors such as the timing and purpose of the move, while recognising that the purpose of the disregard is to 'safeguard certain categories of people from the risk of homelessness' (annex B para 43). If, for example, the principle reason for relative's move into the property is to ensure that he or she has somewhere to live as his or her main or only home, the authority may apply its discretion and disregard the property. However, the statutory guidance cautions local authorities against applying the discretionary disregard if the purpose of the move is, for example, to protect the family's inheritance (annex B para 44).

8.238 Given the fact that the person's move may be motivated by the desire to prevent the property being included in the assets of the person requiring a care home placement, this situation is likely to be approached with some caution by authorities, who may view such action as a potential deprivation of assets. The statutory guidance provides for a list of factors that should be considered when dealing with such a situation.[281] It is noted that, in such cases, it is often the actions of the residents' family who are under scrutiny by the authority, some of whom may be attorneys or deputies, particularly in those cases where the resident lacks capacity. This situation may, in some circumstances, raise safeguarding concerns about the management of the resident's finances (see para 8.344 below about persons without capacity). The statutory guidance provides examples ('Fred' and 'Hilda') of when it may be appropriate to apply the discretionary disregard after the resident has moved into a care home.[282]

281 Statutory guidance, annex B para 44 gives a list of factors to consider, including 'Was the relative occupying another property as their main or only home at the time of the previous financial assessment?' and 'Would [a] failure to disregard the property result in the result in the eligible relative becoming homeless'.

282 As with many of the examples given in the statutory guidance, the evident and simple worthiness of the situations in the examples make them of limited use, particularly to local authorities who are required to reach public law decisions on situations of far greater factual complexity and less obvious merit than the examples found in the statutory guidance.

Property owned but rented to tenants

8.239   The pre-CA 2014 guidance provided[283] that where a resident owned property, the value of which took the resident's total capital above the upper capital limit, and the property was rented to tenants, the resident was to be assessed as being able to pay the standard charge for the accommodation (because of the level of capital). In such a situation, the local authority was able to deem the resident to be a 'self-funder' or require that he/she paid the rental income (along with any other income) to it in order to reduce the accruing debt. In cases where no deferred payment arrangement had been agreed, authorities were able to place a legal charge on the property and wait until the tenant died before enforcing payment of the accrued debt against the estate. However, given that authorities are no longer able to place a charge on a property outside of the new DPA scheme (see para 8.191 above), this option is not available under the CA 2014 regime, as the local authority has no method of obtaining security for any care home fees paid by the authority.

8.240   The DPA scheme provides for a resident to rent out their home while in residential care, advising that authorities should allow the resident to retain a percentage of any rental income. It also advises that authorities may want to consider whether to offer other incentives to individuals to encourage rental of properties, with such incentives – presumably – forming part of any charging policy formulated by the authority. There is nothing to prevent the resident from using some or all of the rental income to pay towards their care home fees, as this would reduce the amount of the charge accruing under the DPA.[284]

Choice of accommodation and top-up payments

Introduction

8.241   The NAA 1948 (Choice of Accommodation) Directions 1992 (the '1992 directions')[285] constituted one of the few examples of genuine choice for individuals in relation to their community care services. In general, a person's wishes and preferences were to be taken into account, although not necessarily satisfied. However, when they were engaged, the directions gave service users a legal right to choose the setting of their residential care.[286]

8.242   The provisions contained in the 1992 directions are broadly replicated in the Care and Support and After-care (Choice of Accommodation)

---

283 See CRAG, para 7.023.

284 See statutory guidance, para 9.46 and case study (Lucille and Buster).

285 The directions were accompanied by guidance LAC (2004) 20, referred to as 'Choice of Accommodation (England) Guidance 2004'.

286 This did not extend to the right to choose to remain at home. However, the ombudsman has stated in Complaint No 07/A/01436 against Hillingdon LBC, 18 September 2008, that a council had no right to disregard the client's wishes to remain at home and promoting independent living should not be lightly disregarded.

Regulations 2014[287] ('choice of accommodation regulations 2014') which enable a person to have the right to choose the particular provider or location for their care, subject to certain conditions. Further guidance is contained in the statutory guidance at annex A 'Choice of accommodation and additional payments', and the Department of Health (together with the LGA and ADASS) has issued guidance concerning these new obligations.[288]

Choice of accommodation

8.243   An important extension of the principle of 'choice of accommodation' is that it applies to accommodation of a 'specified type' and includes not only care home accommodation but also shared lives scheme accommodation[289] and supported living accommodation.[290] Furthermore, the choice of preferred accommodation must not be limited to those settings or individual providers with whom the local authority already contracts[291] or where the accommodation is within the authority's own geographical boundary.[292] The choice is between different settings of the same type of accommodation so, for example, a person may not choose to move into a shared lives placement where their assessed need is for care home accommodation (annex A para 9).

8.244   Those persons who qualify for after-care under MHA 1983 s117 are now able to express a preference for a particular type of accommodation[293] and they broadly have the same rights as to choice of accommodation as those who receive care and support under the CA 2014.[294] The main difference is that after-care is provided free of charge and the care programme approach (CPA) is used to identify what type of accommodation would be suitable to meet needs (see para 15.42 below for further analysis).

8.245   Where a person chooses to be placed in a setting outside the authority's area, the authority must still arrange for the person's preferred care and, in doing so, should 'have regard to the cost of care in that area when setting a person's personal budget' (annex B para 7). Furthermore, the authority 'must have regard to the actual cost of good quality care in deciding the personal budget to ensure that the amount is one that reflects local market conditions' (annex B para 11). Although it is not expressly stated, the combined effect of these provisions is that the authority should set the personal budget at a level which would enable the person to move to his or

---

287 SI No 2670.
288 Department of Health, ADASS and LGA, *Choice of accommodation* (undated).
289 Choice of accommodation regulations 2014 reg 7.
290 Choice of accommodation regulations 2014 reg 8.
291 Annex A para 19 advises that local authorities should ensure that contractual conditions are broadly the same as those negotiated with any other provider and that strict or unreasonable conditions should not be used as a means to avoid or deter the arrangement.
292 Statutory guidance, annex A para 6.
293 By virtue of regulations made under MHA 1983 s117A; see para 15.82 below.
294 See statutory guidance, annex A paras 44–50.

her preferred accommodation, provided the fees charged reflected the fair cost of care.[295]

8.246   The provisions of choice of accommodation apply at all stages of the care process. This includes those persons who are entering care for the first time; those who have already been placed by a local authority (and who wish to move); and those who were previously self-funding, but whose diminishing resources mean that they are on the verge of needing local authority support (annex A para 3).

8.247   Where a local authority is going to meet a person's needs by providing or arranging for accommodation of a specified type in England,[296] and the conditions set out in choice of accommodation regulations 2014 reg 3 are satisfied, the local authority must provide or arrange for provision of the person's preferred accommodation.[297] The conditions are:

1) the care and support plan for the adult specifies that the adult's needs are going to be met by the provision of accommodation of a specified type;
2) the preferred accommodation is of the same type as that specified in the adult's care and support plan;
3) the preferred accommodation is suitable[298] to the person's assessed needs;
4) the preferred accommodation is available;
5) where the preferred accommodation is not provided by the local authority, the provider of the accommodation agrees to provide the accommodation to the adult on the local authority's terms.

8.248   The preferred accommodation must not cost the local authority more than the amount specified in the adult's personal budget for that type of accommodation.[299] However, local authorities should take into account cases or circumstances where the 'cost to the authority' may have to be adjusted to ensure that a person's needs are met, with a concomitant increase to the personal budget where necessary. Local authorities are reminded that they should not 'set arbitrary amount or ceilings for particular types of accommodation that do not reflect a fair cost of care' and 'must have regard to

---

295 The statutory guidance (at annex A) is weaker than the Choice of Accommodation Guidance (England) 2004 (para 2.4), which made it explicit that any higher cost of placing a person outside the authority's geographical area must be paid for by the authority.

296 Choice of accommodation regulations 2014 reg 2. The regulations envisage persons moving out of the local authority's area to another local authority area in England. The statutory guidance, annex A para 7 reminds local authorities of the need to consider the guidance on ordinary residence, considered in the statutory guidance at Chapter 19. The implications for ordinary residence and the position with cross-border placements (eg a move from England to Wales, Scotland or Northern Ireland) are considered at para 6.58 above.

297 As required by choice of accommodation regulations 2014 reg 2.

298 In *R (S) v Leicester City Council* [2004] EWHC 533 (Admin), (2004) 7 CCLR 254. it was held that the Choice of Accommodation Directions did not require a service user to live in the most suitable accommodation available. So long as the service user's preferred accommodation was suitable to meet his or her needs, it should not matter that another residential placement would provide a better range of services which on the face of it appears to be applicable under the choice of accommodation regulations 2014.

299 Statutory guidance, annex A para 5.

the actual cost of good quality care in deciding the personal budget to ensure that the amount is one that reflects local market conditions' (annex A para 11).

8.249   The statutory guidance emphasises that there 'must be a genuine choice across the appropriate provision' (annex A para 6). The local authority '*must* ensure that at least one option is available that is affordable within a person's personal budget and should ensure that there is more than one' (annex A para 12, emphasis in the original). The ombudsman, in a 2015 Focus Report,[300] observed that offering at least one choice ensures 'that people have a genuine choice over their placement' (p2). It appears, therefore, that the offer of one placement within the personal budget would satisfy the requirement. However, this would be a narrower interpretation of the word 'choice' than the everyday use of the word would suggest: there would be only one offer for a person to 'choose'.

8.250   A person must not be asked to pay a 'top-up' (see below) towards the cost of his or her accommodation because of market inadequacies or commissioning failures. In the situation where the person has not expressed a preference, and no suitable accommodation exists within the level of the personal budget, the local authority must arrange care in a more expensive setting and increase the personal budget to ensure that the person's needs are met.[301] The duty is, as the local government ombudsman has stated, to 'offer families the option of a nursing or care home placement which does not need a top-up fee'.[302]

8.251   The statutory guidance (annex A paras 51–52) reminds local authorities of the obligation under CA 2014 s4 to establish and maintain a service for providing people in its area with information and advice in relation to care and support, as well as providing principles for local authorities to follow when applying the choice of accommodation provisions (annex A para 2). Any failure by a local authority to comply with these requirements in respect of the choice of accommodation provisions and/or the circumstances in which top-up fees may properly be charged is likely to be a factor which may be used against the authority in the event of any challenge, via the complaints process, the ombudsman[303] or by means of judicial review. Such matters would also be relevant to any consideration by a court in the event of debt recovery by the authority in respect of unpaid top-up fees.

The use of top-ups

8.252   If the cost to the local authority of providing or arranging the preferred accommodation is greater than the amount specified in the adult's personal

---

300 *Focus report: learning lessons from complaints. Counting the cost of care: the council's role in informing public choices about care homes,* 2015, discussed further below at para 8.275.

301 Statutory guidance, annex A para 12.

302 Report concerning a complaint no. 14 014 177 against Solihull MBC, 11 January 2016.

303 See the LGO decision in Essex CC 13 010 872 as an example of a case where the council failed to provide the information and support to find a suitable care home placement for the complainant's elderly mother; the authority voluntarily repaid the top-up fees of £14,118 to settle the complaint.

budget, the adult may be provided with his or her preferred accommodation only in circumstances where a top-up[304] payment may be made.[305] It is emphasised that the top-up provisions apply only where a person has chosen a more expensive care setting. It does not apply where the person is placed in a more expensive care setting because the authority has been unable to make arrangements within the personal budget; such a situation would require an increase in the amount of the personal budget and not a top-up payment (annex A paras 20–21). The amount of the top-up is the difference between the amount in the adult's personal budget and the actual cost of the preferred provider. Local authorities are cautioned that they should not 'automatically default to the cheapest rate or to any other arbitrary figure' when setting the amount of the personal budget (annex A para 26).

8.253   Where a person's preferred accommodation is more expensive than the accommodation proposed by the authority, the authority may be required to support the person in the preferred accommodation.[306] The condition is that the payer of the top-up is able and willing to pay it for the duration of the period when the authority expects to meet the adult's needs by the provision of the preferred accommodation.[307] The 'payer' of the top-up must usually be a third party (ie not the adult receiving care). However, where the adult is subject to the 12-week property disregard, or where they have entered into a DPA, the adult is able to fund the top-up himself or herself.[308]

8.254   The previous guidance advised local authorities that persons making top-up payments needed to demonstrate that they were be able to meet the payment for the duration of the arrangements.[309] This point is not overtly expressed in the statutory guidance but the use of the wording 'able and willing' in the regulations[310] implies that authorities are obliged to make sufficient enquiries to satisfy themselves that the arrangement is sustainable and, if not, to decline to enter into it. In a pre-CA 2014 case, *R (Daniel) v Leeds City Council*,[311] Richards J held (when refusing permission for a judicial review) that a local authority was entitled to refuse to enter into a such an arrangement because it had doubts as to whether the third party would, in fact, pay the top-ups.[312]

8.255   The statutory guidance acknowledges that decisions about choosing preferred accommodation are often made at a 'time of crisis' and it emphasises the need for good information and advice, including financial information.[313] The need to make a decision at such a time is perhaps

---

304 The phrase 'top-up' and 'additional costs' are used interchangeably in the statutory guidance; this book uses the term 'top-up'.

305 Choice of accommodation regulations 2014 reg 3(2) and reg 5.

306 Choice of accommodation regulations 2014 reg 3(2) and reg 5.

307 Choice of accommodation regulations 2014 reg 5(1)(a).

308 Choice of accommodation regulations 2014 reg 5(5)(a) and (b); and statutory guidance, annex A para 39. For information about the 12-week disregard and deferred payments, see paras 8.224 above and 8.282 below.

309 LAC (2004), para 3.5.4; NAFWC 46/2004, para 4.9.

310 Choice of accommodation regulations 2014 reg 5(1)(a).

311 [2004] EWHC 562 (Admin).

312 (2004) 12 *Community Care Law* 8.

313 Statutory guidance, annex A paras 22 and 24.

more common for people going into a care home setting. A fair criticism of the statutory guidance is that it overlooks the fact that, post-CA 2014, the concept of choice of accommodation applies to care settings other than care homes. While from a practical perspective, it appears that the need to pay top-ups is more likely to occur in the care home setting, the need for top-ups in other care settings should not be overlooked.

8.256   Where the need for a top-up payment has been identified and agreed, there must be a written agreement which, at a minimum, sets out the following information:[314]

1) the additional amount to be paid;
2) the amount specified for the accommodation in the person's personal budget;
3) the frequency of the payments;
4) to whom the payments are to be made;
5) provisions for reviewing the agreement;
6) a statement on the consequences of ceasing to make payments;
7) a statement on the effect of any increases in charges that a provider may make;
8) a statement on the effect of any changes in the financial circumstances of the person paying the 'top-up'.

8.257   The statutory guidance provides further advice about aspects of the content of the written agreement and the need to provide clear information as part of any top-up arrangement.[315] The obvious risk for any top-up arrangement is that it will break down should the payer be unable to sustain the required level of payments. The written agreement must make clear the consequences of a breakdown of the top-up payments, which are that the person may need to be moved to alternative accommodation which would be suitable to meet his or her needs within the personal budget.[316] The written agreement must also set out the responsibilities of the payer to inform the authority in the event of a change in his or her circumstances which prevented the top-ups being paid and, further, how it would respond to that change of circumstances. In the event that there is any outstanding debt as a result of the non-payment, the authority may seek to recover it.[317]

8.258   Where there is a failure of the top-up payments, the person may not be moved from the preferred accommodation without the authority undertaking a needs assessment before considering that course of action. The assessment must also include (among other things, see chapter 3 above) consideration of a requirement for an assessment of their health needs and have regard to the person's well-being.[318] If the needs assessment demonstrated that it would be detrimental to the person's well-being to move

---

314 The content of a top-up agreement is set out in choice of accommodation regulations 2014 reg 5 and also in the statutory guidance, annex A paras 22–25.
315 Statutory guidance, annex A paras 26–38.
316 Statutory guidance, annex A para 33.
317 Statutory guidance, annex A para 38.
318 Statutory guidance, annex A para 33.

elsewhere, this could be a reason for the authority to review the level of the personal budget to include the full cost of the existing accommodation.[319]

Where the preferred care home is full

8.259 Local authorities are reminded in the statutory guidance that they 'have specific duties to shape and facilitate the market of care and support services locally, ensuring sufficient supply' (annex A para 13). However, not infrequently the preferred accommodation will be full; the question arises as to what arrangements should then be made for the person's care. The situation is generally of most concern to the statutory agencies where, for example, the patient is in hospital awaiting discharge[320] and the usual response is for the authority to make alternative arrangements on an interim basis. However, the statutory guidance cautions against interim arrangements, noting that they can be 'unsettling for the person and should be avoided wherever possible' (annex A para 13).

8.260 The approach to be taken by local authorities when providing 'Interim Accommodation' is as follows:

> A person should not have to wait for their assessed needs to be met but sometimes this may be unavoidable, particularly when a person has chosen a particular setting that is not immediately available. The local authority may, with the person's agreement, arrange an interim placement and put the person on the waiting list of their preferred choice of provider, setting out the arrangements in writing, including the likely duration. If any interim arrangements exceed 12 weeks, the person may be reassessed to ensure that both the interim and the preferred option are still able to meet the person's needs and preferences. A person can decide to remain in the interim setting if this is available and if they fully understand any financial implications.[321]

8.261 The pre-CA 2014 guidance on choice of accommodation made it clear that, if the temporary accommodation were more expensive than the authority would normally pay, councils should make up the cost difference.[322] This specific detail is absent from the statutory guidance but, on the basis that the person's care needs may not be met without the provision of the interim accommodation, the personal budget should reflect the full cost of the interim arrangement. Therefore, any requirement by the authority for payment of a top-up fee in such circumstances would be inappropriate

---

319 This approach reflects the LGO decision in complaint no 12 004 137 against Worcestershire CC in January 2014. It concerned a frail elderly person with vascular dementia, who was doubly incontinent. His NHS continuing healthcare funding was withdrawn. The local authority assessment agreed that his current nursing home met his needs and that a move would be detrimental to his health. Nevertheless the authority advised the family that he would have to move, as the care home rate was more than its 'usual rate' for nursing home care. The ombudsman found that the council had (1) failed to consider if a move should take place in the circumstances; (2) not carried out an assessment as to the suitability of the proposed new placement and (3) failed to give correct advice to the family about the position surrounding the payment of the top-up fees.

320 For further information on this issue, see chapter 5.

321 See Department of Health, ADASS and the LGA, *Supporting implementation of the Care Act: choice of accommodation* (undated) at p2.

322 LAC (2004) 20 at paras 2.5.10 and 2.5.11.

and arguably unlawful.[323] If a person later chooses to remain in the interim accommodation, even if a place at the preferred accommodation becomes available, the person must be advised so that the financial consequences, including any potential to pay a top-up fee, are understood and accepted before any final arrangements are made.

8.262   Any top-up agreement must be reviewed at least annually, and the authority must set out in writing the review arrangements, what may trigger a review and when any party can request a review (annex A paras 31–32).

Price increases

8.263   An area of difficulty in respect of top-up fees is that of any increase in costs, for example caused by provider increasing their prices beyond the amount which the authority has agreed to pay in the personal budget. The statutory guidance details the steps authorities should take in such cases, at annex A paras 34–37. The authority must set out in writing its approach to how any increase in costs may be shared, advising that there is no guarantee that any increase in costs will automatically be shared evenly, should the provider's costs rise more quickly than the amount of any increase in the personal budget. It also advises that authorities may wish to negotiate further price increases with the provider at the time of entering into the contract which would help clarify the position and also ensure that any top-up remains affordable.

8.264   However, the scenario may arise where the authority declines to fund any price increase and there is no one able or willing to fund a top-up fee. In such cases, the person will not have chosen to move into more expensive accommodation but rather the preferred accommodation has become more expensive than the local authority is prepared to fund within the personal budget. The guidance is silent on what should then happen, and it remains uncertain at this stage how such agreements will be framed. However, as a general principle, the person should not be moved without there being a proper assessment of his or her health and social care needs,[324] including any risks associated with any proposed moved and including an assessment of the suitability of any proposed new placement. Where the person has lived in the accommodation for a long period, and to move would cause severe distress or harm to health, then the assessment would most probably conclude that there is an 'assessed need' to remain. In such a scenario, there could be no requirement to pay a 'top up' since the placement would be the only one that could meet the person's needs (and top-ups are only payable when an alternative and cheaper placement exists).

---

323 This approach reflects the position in the LGO report where a family were incorrectly charged a top-up of £200 per week after the council was unable to provide her with a place in a care home which accepted the authority's standard rate. The LGO recommended that the authority should refund all the top-up fees paid by the family, as well as pay the sum of £500 for the distress caused: complaint no complaint no 11 021 923 against Southampton Council, 1 October 2012.

324 See statutory guidance, annex A paras 25 and 33.

Responsibility for costs and to whom top-up payments are made

8.265 Authorities in England were reminded in 2009 that:[325]

> ... when making arrangements for residential care for an individual under the 1948 Act, a council is responsible for the full cost of that accommodation. Therefore, where a council places someone in more expensive accommodation, it must contract to pay the accommodation's fees in full. The resident's or third party's contribution will be treated as part of the resident's income for charging purposes and the council will be able to recover it in that way.

8.266 Even where, by agreement, the third party makes their payment direct to the home, the council is still liable for the full cost of the accommodation.[326]

8.267 This approach is broadly retained in the statutory guidance (annex A paras 28–30) which makes it clear that, when entering into a contract to provide care in a setting which is more expensive than the amount identified in the personal budget, the authority remains responsible for the total cost of the placement. Where the arrangement to pay the top-up breaks down, the authority remains obliged to pay the full fees until either it recovers the third party costs or makes alternative arrangements to meet the person's care needs. It is also emphasised that local authorities should maintain an overview of all top-up agreements and should deter arrangements where the person pays it directly to the provider, as it is the authority's responsibility to step in if a top-up arrangement were to fail (annex A para 25).[327]

Payment arrangements for top-ups

8.268 The authority has three options to secure the funds needed to meet the total cost of care, including the top-up element, as follows:[328]

1) where the third party is paying it directly to the person with care needs, the authority may treat it as part of the person's income and include it in the financial assessment;
2) where the person, the third party and the provider all agree, the 'top-up' payment may be made direct to the provider, although this option should be deterred as it makes it more difficult for the local authority to keep an overview of the contract; or
3) the person making the top-up payment can pay it directly to the local authority, who then pays the full amount to the provider.

---

325 Department of Health, *Charges for residential accommodation – Crag Amendment No 28* LAC (DH) 2009(3), para 24.
326 Department of Health, *Charges for residential accommodation – Crag Amendment No 28* LAC (DH) 2009(3), para 25.
327 This is the approach taken by the High Court in *Aster Healthcare Ltd v Shafi* [2014] EWHC 77 (QB) and discussed in para 8.201 above.
328 This does not apply where there is a deferred payment agreement, as the top-up is simply added to the amount owed (statutory guidance, annex A para 29).

8.269   In the *Forest Care Home* litigation,[329] one aspect concerned the legality of the care home seeking top-up payments. The care home contracts specifically required local authority agreement to any funding arrangement that arose out of a resident exercising choice over the use of any service. In the court's opinion, this precluded any such payment without the council's approval and that (para 151):

> The claimants appeared intent on breaching their contracts with the Council by soliciting contributions from third parties without the Council's consent. In the circumstances, the Council were entitled to prevent such a breach of contract in the manner of the modest steps that they took.

8.270   The modest steps taken by the council was to send its own letters to the next of kin and others responsible for residents asking them to contact the council if such a request was made.

Choices that cannot be met and refusal of arrangements

8.271   In the majority of cases,[330] a person has the right to refuse to enter a care setting, whether on a permanent or interim basis. Local authorities are reminded that they should do everything they can to meet a person's choices (annex A paras 17 and 18), but acknowledges that there will be some occasions where the choice cannot be met.[331] Where a local authority is unable to meet the person's choice, it must set out in writing the reasons why it has been unable to meet that choice and should offer suitable alternatives, together with information about the authority's complaints procedure as well as any arrangements to review the decision.

8.272   Where a person 'unreasonably refuses' the arrangements, the authority is entitled, as a step of last resort, to consider that it has fulfilled its statutory duty and inform the person in writing[332] of the need for them to make their own arrangements (annex A para18). Before doing so, the authority should consider the risks posed by such an approach, both for the person and for the authority itself. However, the guidance is unhelpfully silent as to what is meant by 'unreasonably refuses' and it seems inevitable that this approach will be a source of conflict, perhaps more so where the authority has made only limited offers of accommodation.

Difficulties with choice of accommodation and top-up payments

8.273   Despite the pre-CA 2014 guidance clearly explaining the responsibilities of local authorities in relation to enabling genuine choice, there have been longstanding concerns about widespread disregard by councils of the directions and guidance. For example, a 2005 Office of Fair Trading

---

329 R *(Forest Care Home Limited and others) v Pembrokeshire CC and others* [2010] EWHC 3514 (Admin), (2011) 14 CCLR 103.

330 The exception would be where the person is placed under guardianship (MHA 1983 s7).

331 The example given is when the preferred accommodation is full, which unhelpfully overlooks the possibility that a vacancy will arise at some point in the future.

332 See choice of accommodation regulations 2014 reg 9.

(OFT) *Market study* report[333] found that between 30 and 35 per cent of local authority residents were relying on top-ups, and that 40 per cent of the authorities surveyed suspected that more top-ups were being paid than they knew about.[334]

8.274   A July 2013 report into top-up fees[335] estimated that 56,000 families in England were then paying a top-up[336](ie 28 per cent of local authority funded residents) with the majority of care homes expecting an increase in third party top-ups as consequence of the low rates paid by local authorities for care home places.[337] Its findings, set out below, are a concern, not least because the pre-CA 2014 guidance was unambiguous on this issue:

- Most councils are failing properly to record, monitor and regulate the number and level of top-up fees paid in their area. Many top-up fee contracts are in fact negotiated without the knowledge of the council, so no one knows the true extent of top-up fee payments in England, nor are councils fully aware of the extent of their financial liability.
- Since many top-up fee contracts are negotiated without the involvement of councils, they are in no position to fulfil their legal responsibility to ensure that relatives are 'able and willing' to pay them.
- There is a clear belief from care homes that the incidence of top-up fees is increasing because the rates that councils pay for care home places are simply too low.
- There are large variations between councils – and even within councils – in their approach to top-up fees, with some minimising their use and yet others regarding them as normal and routine.[338]

8.275   In 2015, the LGO published a *Focus report*,[339] which identified common mistakes made by authorities in respect of care home top-up fees. Although the complaints related to the period prior to the introduction of the CA 2014, the report noted that the principles remain the same, despite the different legal context. The report used examples to illustrate council's shortcomings in the process and it highlighted as 'common issues' the following:

- **The lack of, or the wrong, information:** The ombudsman found that councils did not give people the information they needed to make an informed choice. Sometimes, this led to a person selecting a care home which they might otherwise have not chosen. The ombudsman advised that councils should give people 'written information about choosing

---

333 Office of Fair Trading, *Care homes for older people: a market study*, OFT 780, 2005.

334 A further study of ten councils in 2007 by the Commission for Social Care Inspection, *A fair contract with older people?* found 5 to 75 per cent of homes councils dealt with charged a top-up.

335 A Passingham and others, *Care home top-up fees: the secret subsidy*, Independent Age, July 2013 (the 'Passingham Report').

336 Laing & Buisson, *Care of elderly people UK market survey 2012/2013*, p20.

337 Passingham Report p20.

338 Think Local Act Personal Partnership (TLAPP), *Older people who pay for care: final report*, 2012 found 'a wide variation in the proportion of people in care homes with third party top-ups: from one per cent in Hartlepool to 21 per cent in Bradford'.

339 *Focus Report: learning lessons from complaints Counting the cost of care: the council's role in informing public choices about care homes*, published in September 2015 and available at www.lgo.org.uk.

a care home before they start looking for one, explaining the financial implications of moving to a care home and including information about top-ups and deferred payment agreements'.

- **Lack of choice:** This included a lack of choice or that the only choices available were the ones which cost more than the funding provided by the council. The remedy put forward by the ombudsman was that councils must communicate all the options so that the person had a 'proper choice' and reminding councils that, if there was no affordable accommodation available, they were under a duty to offer the person the place without requiring a top-up.

- **Councils abdicating responsibility for top-ups:** This related to the practice of some councils failing to contract with care homes to pay the full chargeable rate. The care home then had to collect the financial contribution and any top-up payment, leaving the placements vulnerable if payments were not made. The ombudsman also described as 'wrong' the routine practice of some councils leaving care homes to enter into top-up arrangements with residents or third parties.

- **Care providers charging top-ups 'behind the council's back':** These charges were made by the providers despite having agreed with the council to accept the placement at an affordable rate. The ombudsman's view is that councils were responsible for such failings because the care provider was acting as agent of the council when it entered into an agreement to care for someone.[340] The correct approach was that the council should refund any top-ups paid by the payer and seek their own redress from the provider.

- **Introducing top-ups:** These payments may be introduced because the care home had increased its fees without the council making the same increase or, alternatively, the council reduced the amount it was paying for the care home, even though the provider had not in fact reduced its fees. The payer was then asked to pay a top-up fee to cover the difference without there being any agreement. The ombudsman's view is that councils cannot ask someone to pay a top-up unless an assessment of needs showed the resident could be moved and that an affordable, alternative placement had been offered.[341]

- **Assessing finances before assessing needs:** The ombudsman's view was that it was 'wrong' to calculate a person's personal budget before the person's social care needs had been assessed. This might arise when a person, who was previously a self-funder, applied to the council for assistance with fees, as his or her assets have diminished.

340 This reflects the LGO decision in complaint no 12 010 181 against Merton LBC, 3 September 2013, where the ombudsman found the care provider's actions, in charging a top-up without the knowledge of the council, were deemed to be on behalf of the authority.

341 See the LGO decision in complaint no 12 019 862 against Tameside MBC, 24 September 2014, where an 80-year-old woman with dementia had been provided with care home accommodation by the local authority, without any top-up fee being required. As a result of commissioning changes, it decided to delist the care home and wrote to her, advising that either a top-up was paid or 'alternative accommodation would have to be found'. The ombudsman found maladministration and criticised the council for failing to assess the impact of any move to a different care home before writing to her in those terms.

8.276　It is evident from the above findings that these problems have been present within the care system for over a decade. Given the clarity contained in the pre-CA 2014 directions and guidance, it is difficult to see how this is likely to change in the near future; it arguably will require a cultural shift in attitudes of not only local authorities but also providers. It is to be hoped that the information and advice obligations under CA 2014 s4 will assist those who receive care, and their families, to be able to make more informed decisions and choices in the future.

Challenging top-up payments

8.277　The need for a third party top-up payment may be challenged[342] through the authority's complaints procedure. One route for challenge is via the assessment and the setting of the level of the personal budget,[343] both of which require consideration of the person's particular circumstances. Where the assessment establishes that the person's care needs may only be met in more expensive setting than originally allowed in the personal budget, the personal budget should be increased accordingly rather than the use of a top-up arrangement.[344]

8.278　A further ground for challenge arises where the authority has imposed an arbitrary costs ceiling, which the statutory guidance[345] specifically prohibits: 'the local authority should not set arbitrary amounts or ceilings for particular types of accommodation that do not reflect a fair cost of care' and authorities are reminded of the need to consider the guidance on market shaping and commissioning (statutory guidance, chapter 4) and on personal budgets (statutory guidance, chapter 11). The authority must be able to demonstrate that there is accommodation available (in all care settings) at prices which would be funded by personal budgets; any failure to do so would be open to challenge for setting arbitrary ceilings.

8.279　Given the pressure on council budgets,[346] it seems likely that such challenges will arise, with third parties being asked to pay, or increase, a top-up in circumstances where this is not appropriate or lawful. There is a clear imbalance in the negotiating power of the parties to a top-up agreement, as the vast majority of top-up agreements will usually be made on the authority's standard terms. This raises the possibility of being able to use other legal approaches as a means of challenge, such as consumer legislation which has already been used in different contexts. For example, the Court of Appeal[347] has held that the Unfair Terms in Consumer Contracts Regulations 1999[348] (the 'UTCC' regulations 1999) apply to

342　See also the matters highlighted by the LGO in the Focus report, see para 8.275 above.
343　For further discussion on setting personal budgets, see chapter 10 of this book; see also statutory guidance, annex A paras 11 and 12.
344　Statutory guidance, annex A para 12.
345　Statutory guidance, annex A para 11.
346　The Institute of Fiscal Studies reported that councils' net spending on social care per capita was cut by 16.7 per cent between 2009/10 and 2014/15, quoted in the LGO *Focus Report: learning lessons from complaints. Counting the cost of care: the council's role in informing public choices about care homes*, 2015.
347　*Newham LBC v Khatun, Zeb, Iqbal and the Office of Fair Trading* [2004] EWCA Civ 55.
348　1999 SI No 2083.

contracts relating to land, ie tenancy agreements. In 2005 the OFT issued guidance[349] on this question, stating:

> ... the Directive[350] and the Regulations apply to public authorities such as a local council (even where the landlord has a duty to supply housing); and that, when acting in a business capacity (eg: as a landlord), a council is a 'seller or supplier' and tenants are 'consumers' within the meaning of the Regulations and the Directive.

8.280   On the face of it, therefore, there appears to be the possibility of being able to apply the UCCT regulations 1999 to local authority top-up agreements, although a definitive answer is outside the scope of this book. Certainly, the statutory guidance advises that the UCCT regulations 1999 are applicable to the creation of DPAs (statutory guidance, para 9.83) so it is open to argument that they should be applied to third party agreements.

8.281   The UCCT regulations 1999 apply a test of 'fairness' to most standard terms; any terms deemed to be 'unfair' by the courts are not binding on the parties. The OFT Guidance 2005 also observes (at para 2.5) that the 'requirement of 'good faith' embodies a general principle of fair and open dealing[351] and, further, that it also:

> ... requires a supplier not to take advantage of consumers' weaker bargaining position, or lack of experience, in deciding what their rights and obligations shall be. Contracts should be drawn up in a way that respects consumers' legitimate interests.

Even if the UCCT regulations 1999 are not applicable to top-up agreements, their principles are closely aligned with the public law concepts of 'fairness' and 'reasonableness,' potentially providing another approach to any challenge to terms in top-up agreements which are perceived as taking advantage of the payer's weaker bargaining position.

Charges to enable the sale of property to be deferred

8.282   Health and Social Care Act (HSCA) 2001 ss53–55 introduced a discretionary 'deferred payments' scheme which enabled a resident to enter into an agreement with the local authority whereby the value of their main home was 'disregarded'. The authority then paid the resident's care home fees, placing a legal charge on the property to recover the payments from the sale of the property, normally after the resident's death. The scheme was implemented, by means of regulations and guidance.

8.283   CA 2014 ss34–36, together with the provisions of chapter 9 of the statutory guidance, establish a 'universal deferred payment scheme' ('the DP scheme'). The intention behind the DP scheme is set out in the statutory guidance at para 9.3, as follows:

---

349 OFT, *Guidance on unfair terms in tenancy agreements* OFT356, 2005, para 1.5.

350 All suppliers using standard contract terms with consumers must comply with the 1999 regulations, which implement EU Directive 93/13/EEC on unfair terms in consumer contracts.

351 Cited in the OFT guidance 2005 as per Lord Bingham of Cornhill in *Director General of Fair Trading v First National Bank plc* [2001] UKHL 52, [2002] 1 All ER 97, HL.

The establishment of the universal deferred payment scheme will mean that people should not be forced to sell their home in their lifetime to pay for their care. By entering into a DPA, a person can 'defer' or delay paying the costs of their care and support until a later date. Deferring payment can help people to delay the need to sell their home, and provides peace of mind during a time that can be challenging (or even a crisis point) for them and their loved ones as they make the transition into care.

8.284 Local authorities are required to offer a DPA where the person meets certain eligibility criteria for the DP scheme; they are also encouraged to offer the DP scheme more widely to anyone who may benefit but who does not fully meet the criteria. It may also be used by those persons who wish to defer payment of care costs until such time as they choose to sell their property, rather like a bridging loan (see statutory guidance, paras 9.5 and 9.6).[352] The statutory guidance makes it clear that, whilst the DP scheme may provide greater flexibility in how care costs are met, those care costs are not written off but rather that their payment is simply delayed (para 9.4). A deferred payment is effectively a consensually-accruing debt to the local authority, where it becomes the lender and the person who has a DPA is the borrower.

8.285 The DP scheme places greater obligations upon both the authority and the recipients of the DPA than the pre-CA 2014 arrangements; the following paragraphs summarise the main points (the case study of 'Lucille' in chapter 9 of the statutory guidance is a helpful example in explaining the scheme).

8.286 In contrast to the previous DPA scheme, the CA 2014 DP scheme is intended to be run on a cost-neutral basis, with authorities being able to recoup the costs associated with deferring fees by charging interest[353] and administrative fees, which must be paid by in full by the individual (statutory guidance, para 9.65). Local authorities may apply interest to the amount deferred by the DPA, as well as to any deferred administrative fees, which will be calculated on a compound interest basis and can continue to accrue once the equity limit has been passed. Any administrative fees charged by the authority may not exceed the actual costs incurred by the authority in the provision of the DPA.[354]

8.287 An authority must offer a DPA to a person where: (a) their needs are to be met by the provision of care in a care home; (b) their assets, excluding the value of the person's home, are less than (or equal to) the capital limit

---

352 For example, the DP scheme may be particularly valuable where a resident is appealing a refusal of NHS continuing healthcare funding: this was previously specifically referred to in CRAG, requiring that 'Local Authorities should liaise with PCT's to provide appropriate information to patients, and make every effort to ensure that residents who are appealing against refusal of CHC funding are made aware of the scheme' (CRAG, para 7.025).

353 Authorities may not charge more than the national maximum interest rate, which will change every six months (on 1 January and 1 June) to track the market gilts rate specified in the most recently published report by the Office of Budget Responsibility (statutory guidance, para 9.67).

354 See statutory guidance, paras 9.65–9.73; it advises that fees and charges should be publicly available and also that it 'good practice' for local authorities to separate charges into a fixed set-up fee for deferred payment agreements and other reasonable onetime fees incurred during the course of the agreement.

in force (ie in savings and other non-housing assets); and (c) their home is not disregarded.[355] The statutory guidance, paras 9.19–9.31 sets out in detail the obligations placed upon local authorities to provide information about DPAs before entering into any such arrangement. As well as providing 'easy to read information about how the scheme works' which may be in the form of a standardised information sheet, local authorities are also reminded of the need to ensure that they comply with the requirements of the EqA 2010 and the Mental Capacity Act 2005.

8.288   Authorities do, however, retain discretion to refuse to enter into a DPA (even when the eligibility criteria are satisfied) in order to provide themselves with a reasonable safeguard against default or non-repayment. Such situations may be, for example, where the authority is unable to secure a first charge on the person's property or where the person refuses to agree to the terms and conditions contained in the DPA (eg to insure and maintain the property). However, the statutory guidance also makes it clear that, where possible, the authority may choose to exercise its discretion and, in any event, enter into the DPA but only in circumstances where it may be reassured that the care costs will be able to be repaid in the future (statutory guidance, paras 9.10–9.13).

8.289   The circumstances in which an authority may refuse to defer any more care charges are set out at statutory guidance, paras 9.16–9.18. The main one is where the amount of care charges already deferred under the DPA has reached the 'equity limit'; in such a situation, the authority must cease to defer further care charges, although interest and administrative charges may continue to accrue (statutory guidance, para 9.41).

8.290   The calculation of the equity limit is set out in the statutory guidance, paras 9.36–9.41; it is noted that in most cases, the asset will be the person's property. The process to be followed by the authority is that it must obtain a valuation of the person's property (see statutory guidance, para 9.37), from which must be deducted an allowance of ten per cent of the value of the property, with a further deduction for the lower capital limit (£14,250 in 2015/16) and also the amount of any encumbrance secured upon it. The resulting figure then forms the equity limit. This limit provides protection for both local authorities and individuals by ensuring that there is a small 'cushion' to protect, for example, against property price fluctuations, while at the same time ensuring that those persons who have reached the equity limit are able to receive local authority funded care without the need to sell their home (statutory guidance, para 9.38). Once the amount of the care costs paid by the authority is about to reach or has reached 70 per cent of the equity limit, the authority should review the DPA with the person so as to establish whether, among other things, the DPA remains appropriate (statutory guidance, para 9.39)

8.291   While the full costs of a person's care may be deferred under a DPA, in reality the amount to be deferred depends not only on the equity limit available but also on other factors, such as the amount which the person may pay each week towards their care; the payment of top-ups as well

355 See statutory guidance, paras 9.7–9.9: the DP scheme also provides authorities with a discretionary power to enter into a DPA where a person's care and support is being provided in supported living accommodation, rather than a care home (para 9.9).

as the total amount of care costs which a person may need to fund. The authority must satisfy itself as to the sustainability of the arrangement being secured by the DPA (statutory guidance, paras 9.32–9.35).

8.292   The authority may require a person to pay a contribution from the person's ongoing income towards his or her care costs. However, the person must be allowed to keep a weekly sum, known as a disposable income allowance (DIA), which is set at a maximum amount of £144 per week. The person may choose not to keep all of his or her DIA (although it is emphasised in the statutory guidance that this must be the person's own choice and something which the authority cannot compel the person to do (para 9.44)) or the person may make payments towards his or her care from other resources (eg savings). Such steps would result in less of the person's care costs being deferred under the DPA, and thereby reduce the amount ultimately repayable to the authority.

8.293   A person's likely future care costs are another factor in a local authority determining whether it will agree to enter into a DPA. In broad terms, both the person and the authority should have a rough idea of these costs as a result of the care planning process and, in particular, it also retains discretion as to whether or not to agree to a top-up, on the basis of affordability, sustainability and available equity (statutory guidance, paras 9.48 and 9.49). Further matters for consideration by both the person and the authority in determining sustainability of a proposed DPA are set out in the statutory guidance, paras 9.50–9.57.[356] In brief, the range of factors to consider are the length of time the DPA is likely to last (eg is it intended to last only until the property is sold); the amount of any contributions being paid by the person from the person's savings; what happens when the person may not be able to afford the top-up payments; and whether the person's care needs are likely to increase in the future.

8.294   The statutory guidance (paras 9.58–9.64) sets out what would be 'adequate security' for an authority to enter into a DPA, in the first instance, a first legal mortgage charge over the property. For most people, the main asset to use as adequate security is their home, upon which the authority will seek to place a first legal mortgage charge, although the statutory guidance provides for other suggestions (see para 9.62).

8.295   Where the property is jointly owned, or where a person has a beneficial interest but is not a legal owner, the local authority must seek the other owners' consent (and agreement) to a charge being placed on the property. The other owners will need to be signatories to the charge agreement, and will also need to agree not to object to the sale of the property for the purpose of repaying the debt due to the local authority. Where such an agreement may not be reached, the authority has full discretion not to agree to enter into a DPA.

8.296   The authority is advised to revalue the security when the amount secured under the DPA reaches 50 per cent of the value of the security, at which point the authority may also need to review the person's 'equity limit' and the amount which may therefore be deferred under the DPA. After this revaluation, the authority should monitor and revalue the security from

356 A series of DPA resources including a Department of Health 'sustainability toolkit' can be accessed at the 'Deferred Payments Agreements' section of the LGA website.

time to time, to establish if there are any substantial changes in value which, once again may, have an impact on the amount of the equity limit and/or the amount of the care costs which may be deferred under the DPA.

8.297   Once it has been determined by both the authority and the individual that a DPA is the appropriate way forward, a formal agreement is required. The statutory guidance sets out (at paras 9.74–9.84), comprehensive information on the content of local authority DPA agreements. It also reminds local authorities that DPAs will be subject to the UTTC regulations 1999, so the terms will have to be written in plain, intelligible English and will not be binding if they are unfair to the borrowers.[357] Both local authorities and the individual with the DPA have ongoing obligations while the DPA remains in force; these are helpfully set out in the statutory guidance at paras 9.85–9.94.

8.298   Matters relating to the termination of the DPA are set out in the statutory guidance at paras 9.95–9.105. Where the DPA is terminated because the person has died, the local authority is advised that it should not approach the executors about the repayment of the DPA for two weeks after the person's death. Interest continues to accrue until the DPA is repaid in full and, 90 days after the death of the person, the whole sum falls due to be repaid to the authority. Where the authority believes that the monies are not likely to be repaid under the DPA, the authority may start to take proceedings to recover the monies under the DPA (see para 8.190 above).

Personal expenses allowance

Generally

8.299   Where a person's care and support needs are met by a placement in a care home, the effect of the charging regime is that the resident is required to pay all of his or her assessed income, less a minimum amount (known as the personal expenses allowance (PEA)), towards the charge for the person's care home accommodation. This was the approach set out in NAA 1948 s22 and CRAG, and it is replicated in CA 2014 s14(7), charging and assessment regulations 2014 reg 6, in the statutory guidance (para 8.35 and at annex C paras 43-46).

8.300   The PEA is the minimum amount of a person's own income which must be left after the charges have been deducted (statutory guidance, annex C para 44). In 2016/17 the amount of the PEA set out in the Care and Support (Assessment of Resources) Regulations 2014 SI No 2672

357 The statutory guidance (paras 9.81-9.83) states that local authorities will have to ensure that they do not contravene the Consumer Protection from Unfair Trading Regulations 2008 and, further, that they will need to consider whether the DPAs which they enter into are regulated credit agreements to which the Consumer Credit Act (CCA) 1974 and Financial Services and Markets Act (FSMA) 2000 apply. Other than the vague assertion that it 'is likely that most DPAs will fall within such an exemption' (from the CCA 1974), the statutory guidance is silent on whether it applies and how a local authority, or a member of the public, is to reach a proper conclusion. Such lack of clarity is unfortunate and unhelpful on a subject that is of universal application.

reg 6 was £24.90 and it is increased by means of uprating regulations, notified to local authorities by means of a local authority circular (statutory guidance, annex C para 43).

8.301 The statutory guidance (annex C para 45) states that the 'purpose of the PEA is to ensure that a person has money to spend as they wish'. This echoes the CRAG advice that the PEA should not be spent on aspects of board, lodgings and care which had been assessed as necessary to meet individuals' needs by the council and the NHS. The CRAG additionally made it clear that neither councils nor care home providers had the 'authority to require residents to spend their PEA in particular ways, and pressure of any kind to the contrary is extremely poor practice'.[358] The equivalent point is to be found in the statutory guidance (annex C para 45) where it advises that any pressure from a local authority or provider to spend their PEA for their contracted/assessed care and support needs 'is not permitted'. This clear prohibition is to be welcomed but, in other areas to do with guidance about the PEA, the statutory guidance lacks the comprehensive nature of the CRAG provisions, particularly in terms of explaining how and when the local authority may exercise its discretion to increase the sum allowed for the PEA.

Discretion to allow different amounts of personal expense allowance

8.302 The pre-CA 2014 regime for the administration of PEA gave a local authority the power to exercise its discretion to allow in 'special circumstances' for the resident to have a PEA which was higher than the prescribed sum. This was a result of the operation of the statutory discretion which operated under NAA 1948 s22(4)[359] and implemented by CRAG.

8.303 The 2014 version of CRAG made it clear that residents were not precluded from buying extra services which were genuinely additional to those assessed as necessary by the council or NHS.[360] Whilst this approach may sometimes have had its own inherent difficulties (eg how to define 'genuinely additional'), CRAG reminded local authorities their discretionary power to increase a resident's PEA in special circumstances if, for example, the purchase of the extra services or activities, 'although not specifically included in their care plan, can nevertheless contribute significantly to optimum independence and well-being'.[361]

8.304 The CRAG gave various examples (at para 5.008) of 'special circumstances' where it may be appropriate for an authority to allow a resident to retain a higher amount of PEA, in accordance with the authority's exercise of its discretionary power set out in NAA 1948 s22(4). These CRAG examples are broadly replicated in the statutory guidance (annexe C para 46), with

358 CRAG, para 5.005.
359 NAA 1948 s22(4) stated that the sum (ie the PEA) may be prescribed by the minister, or such other sum as in special circumstances the authority may consider appropriate.
360 CRAG, para 5.006.
361 CRAG, para 5.006, although it may be argued that such activities or services should have been included in any care plan which is based on an assessment of risk to independence or well-being.

the advice to local authorities that there may be 'some circumstances where it would not be appropriate for the local authority to leave a person only with the personal expenses allowance after charges' – and the following examples are given:

- Where a person has a dependent child, the local authority should consider the needs of the child in determining how much income a person should be left with after charges (this applies whether the child is living with the person or not).
- Where a person is paying half of his or her occupational or personal pension or retirement annuity to a spouse or civil partner who is not living in the same care home, the local authority must disregard this money. This disregard does not automatically apply to unmarried couples, although the local authority may wish to exercise its discretion in individual cases.[362]
- Where a person is temporarily in a care home and is a member of a couple (whether married or unmarried), the local authority should disregard any income support or pension credit awarded to pay for home commitments[363] and should consider the needs of the person at home in setting the PEA. It should also consider disregarding other costs related to the maintenance of the couple's home.
- Where a person's property has been disregarded the local authority should consider whether the PEA is sufficient to enable the person to meet any resultant costs. For example, allowances should be made for fixed payments (like mortgages, rent and council tax), building insurance, utility costs (gas, electricity and water, including basic heating during the winter) and reasonable property maintenance costs.
- Where a person has moved to local authority support and has a DPA in place, the local authority should ensure the person retains sufficient resources to maintain and insure the property in line with the DIA.

8.305   It is a fair criticism of CRAG that the wording (at para 5.008) could have made it clearer that these examples of 'special circumstances' were just that: illustrative examples and not an exhaustive list for local authorities to follow. This shortcoming is also unfortunately evident in annexe C para 46.

8.306   Where a resident is experiencing hardship or the resident's well-being is otherwise adversely affected, a request by way of a review may be made to the authority for an increase in the PEA. The need to increase the PEA may be particularly relevant to those residents who are planning to move into more independent living settings and for whom the basic PEA is restricting their ability to acquire independent living skills. However, it would apply to all residents for whom their lack of income under the

---

362 Arguably, this operates as a disregard for the resident's income, rather than an increase to the PEA, although the latter approach may be appropriate in cases where the couple are unmarried and the authority exercises its discretion by treating the payment of the pension as an increase to the resident's PEA.

363 The phrase 'any Income Support or Pension Credit awarded to pay for home commitments' is ambiguous, as neither benefit has a specified component for 'home commitments'. For example, income support is calculated by a system of 'personal allowances' and additional sums, known as 'premiums', to help people specific situations eg they are sick or disabled.

PEA means that they are unable to live as independent a life as possible (eg being unable to take part in community activities or attend family gatherings etc) or, indeed, for any other reason. The local authority must consider any such request in accordance with its obligation to promote well-being.[364] Where it declines to increase the PEA, it should be prepared to provide the reasons for its decision and the overarching 'well-being' concept may make it more difficult for an authority to refuse a reasonable request to increase the PEA.

Short term and temporary residents

8.307 'Short term' residents are defined in the charging and assessment regulations 2014 as 'a person who is provided with accommodation in a care home ... for a period not exceeding 8 weeks', and the definition of a 'temporary resident' remains as under pre-CA 2014 regime, namely a resident whose stay is unlikely to exceed 52 weeks or, in exceptional circumstances, is unlikely to substantially exceed that period. It must be intended that the person's stay in the care home is for a limited period of time and there is a plan to return home.[365]

8.308   In the case of a short-term resident in a care home (eg for respite stays of up to eight weeks), the local authority has discretion whether to charge at all and/or to assess and charge as if the person were having needs met other than by the provision of accommodation in a care home.[366] It is therefore open to each authority to determine the approach it wishes to take, as part of its own charging policy.[367] However, where an authority chooses to charge for short term care, it must take into account the charging principles, as set out in the statutory guidance (at para 8.2). Such policies are able to be more generous that the minimum set out in the regulations and guidance.[368] Where temporary residents are to be charged by a local authority, the statutory guidance in annex F must be followed when carrying out the resident's financial assessment.[369]

8.309   Where a person moves into a care home, with the intention that it will be a permanent stay, but subsequently it becomes clear that the stay is a temporary one, the local authority should treat the person as temporary from the date of initial admission for the purposes of charging. However, a stay that was initially intended to be temporary but which then becomes permanent should only be assessed as such for charging purposes from

---

364 CA 2014 s1; and for a discussion of 'well-being', see para 2.3 above.
365 See charging and assessment regulations 2014 reg 2(1) and statutory guidance, annex F at para 4.
366 See charging and assessment regulations 2014 reg 8 and the statutory guidance at para 8.34 and annex F para 8.
367 Where the care home placement is being provided to the resident as part of a package of intermediate care and reablement support services with the purpose of providing assistance to enable the resident to regain the ability needed to live in their own home, the service should be provided free of charge (see para 8.27 above).
368 See DH FAQ, Q301.
369 See statutory guidance, annex F para 9.

the date that the change in status is agreed with the resident (or the resident's representative) and the care plan is amended.[370]

Capital: temporary residents

8.310   Other that the person's own home, the treatment of capital is the same as for permanent residents (see statutory guidance, annex B). Where the care home placement is intended to be temporary, the person's 'main or only' home must be disregarded where the person:[371]

1) intends to return to that property as their main or only home and it remains available to them; or

2) has taken steps to dispose of the home in order to acquire one that is more suitable and intends to return to that property.

Income: temporary residents

8.311   The statutory guidance makes it clear that both income and earnings should be treated in the same way as for permanent residents (see annex C on income). However, in the financial assessment for temporary residents, further disregards may be applied to the resident's income for the 'housing-related costs' of their only or main home, for example, mortgage repayments, rent or ground rent, council tax or service charges.[372] The intention behind this disregard is to enable the resident to maintain his or her home during the resident's temporary stay, so that it is in a fit condition for the resident's return. The statutory guidance emphasises that the extent of the disregard is not limited solely to these items.[373]

8.312   The statutory guidance provides that the authority should also disregard any other payment the person receives in order to meet the cost of the person's housing and/or to support independent living. This may include, for example, payments to provide warden support, emergency alarms or the meeting of cleaning costs where the person (or someone in the household) is unable to do it himself or herself.[374]

8.313   Although the statutory guidance makes clear that financial assessments must be based on the individual resources of the temporary resident, it cautions that regard should be had to any partner or spouse remaining at home to ensure he or she is left with a basic level of income support or pension credit to which the partner or spouse may be entitled in his or her own right.[375] There are specific rules for income support and income-related employment support allowance, where one member of a couple enters a care home for a temporary period, which should be taken into account in considering what the temporary resident can afford to pay.[376] It

370 See statutory guidance, annex F paras 6 and 7.
371 See charging and assessment regulations 2014 Sch 2 para 1(b) and 2(b); and statutory guidance, annex F para 10.
372 See charging and assessment regulations 2014 Sch 1 para 2; and statutory guidance, annex F para 12
373 See statutory guidance, annex F para 12.
374 See statutory guidance, annex F para 17.
375 See statutory guidance, annex F para 3.
376 See statutory guidance, annex F para 15.

is arguable that any charging policy for temporary residents, which operated to leave the spouse/partner at home with an income below the basic IS/income-based ESA, would be challengeable on public law grounds ie that it is unreasonable to expect the spouse/partner to live on a level of income which is below the amount the state had already determined was the minimum amount needed to meet basic needs.

8.314 A move into a care home as a temporary resident will have implications for the person's ongoing entitlement to certain social security benefits, including disability living allowance (care component); attendance allowance, the severe disability premium and the enhanced disability premiums for income support. Local authorities will need to provide such information and advice to prospective temporary residents as part of their information and advice obligations (see the statutory guidance, chapter 3).

Paying the financial contribution in a care home

8.315 The pre-CA 2014 provisions enabled residents, placed by local authorities in independent sector homes, to pay the assessed charge[377] direct to the home with the authority paying the remainder.[378] This provision was introduced in 1993 as an administrative convenience, when benefits were paid by order book. Given the changes in the social security system, including the withdrawal of order books, the purpose behind the provision has become obsolete.

8.316 The payment of the assessed charge directly to the care home was not without its difficulties. Local authorities would sometimes fail to make clear that there was no obligation to make payments directly to the care home or that they retained contractual and legal liability to the care provider for the full cost of the care.[379]

8.317 Unfortunately, the statutory guidance is unhelpfully silent about the approach to take by those whose financial contribution is paid towards their care home charges. It provides that (para 8.33):

> Where a local authority is meeting needs by arranging a care home, it is responsible for contracting with the provider. It is also responsible for paying the full amount, including where a 'top-up' fee is being paid.

On the face of it, this intimates that the authority will pay the full fee to the care home, including the top-up element, and the resident will pay to the authority the financial contribution towards their care as part of the personal budget arrangements. However, the method of payment of the financial contribution by the resident is not specifically addressed in

---

377 Under CRAG, the amount a person was required to pay towards his or her care in a care home was known as the 'assessed charge'; this term is not used in the statutory guidance. For clarity, the phrase 'financial contribution' is used in this chapter to mean the amount a person has to pay towards their care and support, regardless of the care setting.

378 NAA 1948 s26(3A): where the resident, the authority and the organisation or person managing the home *all* agreed, the resident had the choice of paying the assessed charge direct to the home with the authority paying the remainder, with the authority remain responsible for the full fee.

379 Complaint No 08 019 214 against the Bromley LBC, 9 June 2011.

the statutory guidance and there is a lack of clarity around the distinction between the 'financial contribution' and 'top-ups'.

8.318   In the DH FAQ (Q401), in respect of top-up fees, the Department of Health confirmed that it is open to the local authority, the person and the care provider jointly to agree that, instead of paying the top-up payment to the local authority, the individual or the third party will pay it direct to the care provider with the authority paying the difference. Authorities are reminded that all parties need to agree to the arrangement and the authority must contract with the provider so that it remains responsible for the full cost of care and support should the individual or the third party fail to pay the top-up payment to the provider. The payment of top-up fees is considered further at para 8.252 above.

8.319   It is therefore arguably open to a local authority to devise a policy where the resident has the option of paying his or her financial contribution directly to the care home provider, subject to the usual consultation process. It would, however, require careful monitoring by authorities to ensure that significant debts do not accrue without any action being taken. Any local policy about payments of financial contributions cannot alter the substantive legal position, otherwise the authority would be acting outside of its legal powers. In the event of any default by the resident, the full cost of the care home placement would have to be met by the local authority, who would then have to recover the unpaid financial contribution from the resident following the usual debt recovery process (see statutory guidance, annex D).

8.320   Where the local authority has the contract directly with the care home and is paying the gross fee, the amount of the financial contribution is not a relevant matter for the care home. The existence of any financial contribution, or of the amount to be paid by the resident, should not be included in the authority's contract with the care home. Any disclosure of such financial information to the care home would of course engage the authority's duty of confidentiality (see chapter 19 below).

Capital reducing towards the capital limit

8.321   Pre-CA 2014 guidance advised that authorities could be liable to reimburse self-funding residents for any payments they made after the authority was aware that the residents' capital was approaching the capital limit, where there had been undue delay in taking over responsibility for these fees.[380]

8.322   Although the statutory guidance fails to address this question, the public law obligation would appear to be straightforward. Where an authority has reasonable notice that a person's capital is about to fall below the upper capital limit, then any failure to take prompt action to assume responsibility is likely to constitute maladministration.

---

380 See LAC (2000)11 and LAC (2001)25 (para 25).

Charging for non-accommodation services

Introduction

8.323 Under the pre-CA 2014 regime, wide variations existed in the charges people faced for non-accommodation social care services. 2004 research[381] concerning local authority charges found that the charge for a person needing ten hours of care and two sessions at day care varied from £nil in one authority to £103 per week in another. The 'postcode' lottery over such charges persisted despite Department of Health policy guidance on fairer charging[382] issued in 2001 (and updated in 2003 and again in 2013), referred to in this chapter as 'Fairer Charging 2013'. This has now been superseded by the provisions of the CA 2014, the charging and assessment regulations 2014 and the statutory guidance.

The charging regime

8.324 The main principles relating to non-accommodation charges are summarised as follows:

1) The value of the property which the adult occupies as his or her main or only home must be excluded from the financial assessment for care at home (statutory guidance, para 8.43).

2) After charging, the adult must be left a sum of at least[383] the minimum income guarantee (MIG) after charges have been deducted. The MIG is calculated as a sum equivalent to basic level of income support plus a buffer 25 per cent.[384] Its purpose it to 'promote independence and social inclusion and ensure that [the adult has] sufficient funds to meet basic needs such as purchasing food, utility costs or insurance' (statutory guidance, annex C para 49).

3) charging and assessment regulations 2014 reg 7 sets out the specific amounts to be used in the assessment ie the relevant income support amounts plus the 25 per cent buffer. This has the benefit of providing clarity as to what is included within the definition of 'basic level of income support' and thereby the amount of the MIG.[385] It also provides for the MIG to include the relevant amount for income support premiums (eg disability premium) in circumstances where the local

---

381 P Thompson and D Mathew, *Fair enough?*, Age Concern England, 2004.

382 *Fairer charging policies for home care and other non-residential social services* LAC (2001)32.

383 See statutory guidance, annex C para 48: the 25 per cent buffer set out in the regulations 'is only a minimum and local authorities have discretion to set a higher level if they wish'.

384 Statutory guidance para 8.42; and the charging and assessment regulations 2014.

385 The MIG is based on social security benefits which vary significantly according to age (eg the standard MIG for a couple over 18 years is £71.05 per week, significantly less than the couple rate for those of pension credit age, which is £141.55). This difference was an issue in the previous system under Fairer Charging 2013 as it leads to large variations in the amount of income younger disabled people and older people are able to keep. A few authorities try to avoid this potential age discrimination by exercising its discretion to use the more generous pension credit rates for younger people.

authority considers the person would be entitled to that premium, if they were in receipt of income support.[386]

4) The person's income to be assessed for the purposes of applying the MIG is the amount after the deduction from that income of the person's housing costs such as rent and council tax, net of any welfare benefits (eg housing benefit) paid to support those costs, as well as after the any allowance for disability related expenditure (see further below at para 8.325).[387]

5) However, the amount of the MIG may be reduced in specified circumstances. Where an adult receives from the local authority 'non-care related support' (eg services or activities such as meals on wheels, shopping or transport services or recreational activities), the costs incurred by the local authority in providing that non-care related support are deducted from the MIG.[388] The statutory guidance is silent on how this operates in practice, and also as to the extent of the definition of 'non-care related support'.[389] The phrase 'an amount equal to the cost the local authority incurs in providing that non-care related support for the adult concerned' (charging and assessment regulations 2014 reg 7(8) and (9)) is unhelpful: for example, is it the actual cost incurred to the authority or the amount paid by the person for the non-care related support service eg meals on wheels? This is an example where the brevity of the statutory guidance is at the expense of clarity for all those who are required to use it. The charges broadly appear to be 'flat-rate charges' which, under the pre-CA 2014 charging regime, were acceptable only in limited circumstances (for instance, where they were a substitute for ordinary living costs – such as for meals on wheels or meals at a day centre).[390] However, the statutory guidance is silent upon the use of flat-rate charges,[391] although they will undoubtedly continue to be part of many local authorities' non-accommodation charging policies, subject to the obligation to consult. Taking a logical approach, if the amount of the MIG is to be reduced by the cost incurred by the authority in providing the non-care support service, the sum charged for that service should be deducted from the person's assessed income before the MIG is applied. This approach would be in accordance with the principle that a person is not charged more than it is reasonable practicable for them to pay and also in accordance with its obligation (see item (6) below) to consider how to protect a person's income. However, unfortunately, these issues have not been considered by the revisions to the statutory guidance (as at the time of writing, January 2017) – it seems inevitable that this will lead to confusion, potential hardship and challenge in the future.

---

386 Charging and assessment regulations 2014 reg 7(5), (6) and (7).
387 Statutory guidance, annex C para 49.
388 Charging and assessment regulations 2014 reg 7(1), (8) and (9).
389 The phrase used in charging and assessment regulations 2014 reg 7(8) and (9) – 'non-care related support' – does not appear anywhere in the statutory guidance.
390 In the Fairer Charging 2013 guidance, para 84a made it clear that 'flat-rate charges are acceptable only in limited circumstances eg where they are a substitute for ordinary living costs such as meals on wheels at home or meals in a day centre'.
391 The phrase 'flat-rate charge' does not appear in the statutory guidance.

6) Local authorities should consult people with care and support needs when deciding how to exercise their discretion when determining how to assess non-accommodation care charges and, in doing so, they should consider how to protect a person's income.[392] The statutory guidance states that the 'government considers that it is inconsistent with promoting independent living to assume, without further consideration, that all of a person's income above the minimum income guarantee (MIG) is available to be taken in charges' (para 8.46). Furthermore, the statutory guidance advises local authorities to consider whether it is appropriate to set a maximum percentage of disposable income (over and above the MIG) which may be taken into account in charges (para 8.47).[393]

7) Local authorities are also advised to consider the need to set a maximum charge, which it suggests may be set as a percentage of care home charges in its local area to encourage people to remain in their own homes (statutory guidance, para 8.48).

8) The CA 2014 reflects the approach contained in Fairer Charging 2013 where local authorities could exercise discretion as to whether or not they would include disability benefits as income in the financial assessment (eg DLA (care component)). The statutory guidance advises that authorities should 'allow the person to keep enough benefit to pay for necessary disability-related expenditure to meet any needs which are not being met by the local authority' (annex C para 39).

Disability related expenditure

8.325 The statutory guidance is clear that, where local authorities take into account disability related benefits in the financial assessment, the person should be allowed to keep enough of their benefit to pay for 'necessary' disability related expenditure (DRE) to meet any needs not being met by the authority (annex C para 39). A lengthy list of what may be appropriately included as DRE is contained in the statutory guidance (annex C para 40), but it is not intended to be an exhaustive list.[394] For example, it includes such items as the costs of any privately arranged care services required, including respite care;[395] the additional costs of special dietary needs due to illness or disability; above average heating costs and special clothing or footwear. Local authorities are advised that the adult's care plan may be a good starting point for consideration what is necessary DRE, advising of the need to take an flexible approach and also cautioning that it should not be limited to what is necessary for care and support (eg it should

392 Statutory guidance, para 8.46.
393 This approach, ie of having a MIG which is greater than the statutory minimum, would arguably address at least in part the matters set out in para 5 above ie by allowing the person to have sufficient funds to pay for the additional costs of non-care related support.
394 This list replicates the DRE guidance contained in Fairer Charging 2013 at para 51.
395 See statutory guidance Annex C para 40(b), although it is less evident why such services would not form part of an adult's assessed need to be met by the local authority.

include above average heating costs) (statutory guidance, annex C para 41). The pre-CA 2014 system of determining DRE had a similarly wide degree of discretion for local authorities in determining what expenditure they would – or would not – take into account.[396] Previous studies[397] have noted wide variations by authorities in assessing DRE. It is regrettable that the approach set out in the statutory guidance is unlikely to ensure greater consistency across the country, as each local authority will set its own policy.

8.326 In *R (B) v Cornwall CC*[398] the claimant's initial means test assessment concluded that there should be no charge because of the high level of disability expenditure. A paper review by the council then determined that some items of expenditure should not have been classed as disability related and that other items should not have been included due to the lack of sufficient supporting evidence – such that a charge was payable of £68.50 per week. The court held the authority had acted unlawfully in failing to consult with the claimant and his family;[399] that there was evidence in the care plan to justify the level of expenditure; that the authority had failed to offer the family opportunity to provide the necessary evidence; and that the authority had been over rigid in its application of its guidance. The court further considered that holiday expenses could be included as a disability related expenditure – including the consequent extra expenses of carers required.

Capital expenditure and equipment repairs

8.327 In general, it is not unlawful for a local authority to adopt a policy that the purchase of a capital item (for instance an electrical reclining bed) should be spread out over the life of the item – ie if the item costs £1,800 and the local authority considers it to have a life of ten years, then this would equate to a weekly disability related expenditure of £3.46.[400] Such items would arguably fall within the definition of DRE in the statutory guidance (annex C para 40(vii)), which provides for the costs of any specialist items needed to meet the person's disability needs 'occasioned by age, medical condition or disability'. Where it may be possible for the cost of repairs to be established in advance of the repair being required (eg because of a maintenance contract), this may also be an appropriate cost to be included

---

396 In a pre-CA 2014, the LGO criticised a local authority for failing to provide written reasons for rejecting claimed disability related expenditure to enable a person to decide whether or not to appeal. Furthermore, the LGO also found that the council must not only taken into account the full range of DRE but also look at the associated costs to the carers and the family's wider circumstances – see Complaint no 09 006 887 and 09 011 195 Northamptonshire CC,16 November 2011 (paras 94 and 97).

397 In one of the case studies in P Thompson and D Mathew, *Fair enough?*, Age Concern England, 2004, the amount allowed by local authorities for a list of disability related expenditure ranged from £4.09–£70.38.

398 *R (B) v Cornwall CC and Brendon Trust* (interested party) [2009] EWHC 491 (Admin), (2009) 12 CCLR 681 upheld on appeal [2010] EWCA Civ 55, (2010) 13 CCLR 117.

399 As required by the Community Care Assessment Directions 2004. Although the directions have been repealed, it is arguable that a public law obligation to consult remains and the outcome would be little different under the CA 2014 regime.

400 Following the guidance given in Fairer Charging 2013 at para 53, which is not replicated in the statutory guidance.

in the DRE calculation; each case would have to be determined on its merits.

Housing costs

8.328   The Fairer Charging 2013 policy guidance was silent on the position of housing costs (commonly referred to as 'board and lodgings') where service users are living with their families: this remains the case with the statutory guidance. Most often, this situation arises where disabled adults live with their parents or older people with adult children. There is no duty on families to provide support in such cases – the 'liable family' rule (which required families to support disabled adult members) was abolished by NAA 1948 s1.

8.329   The issue of how a local authority should treat 'board and lodgings' was addressed by the High Court in *R (C) v North Tyneside Council*.[401] The parents of a 20-year-old daughter with learning disabilities claimed that, when assessing her charge for her community care services, a sum should be deducted from her income (ie so as to reduce the amount on which the charge could be levied) to take into account her board and lodgings, which they had calculated at £25 and £40 per week respectively.[402]

8.330   In that case, Hickinbottom J rejected the claimant's argument that, at the very least, a sum equivalent to the standard non-dependent deductions for housing and council tax benefit should be disregarded for charging purposes.[403] His decision in respect of this point was based on the fact that that 'the service user's basic level [employment and support allowance (ESA)] (for which allowance is already made) includes a sufficient element for board and lodging, such that it is reasonable to expect them to make any contribution to their relatives out of that income'. Therefore, a social services authority is entitled to assume that no specific allowance or disregard need be made in relation to housing costs for community care service users who live with parents, other close relatives or other informal carers, where the user has no legal obligation to a third party to pay mortgage, rent or council tax.[404]

8.331   However, the claimant ultimately succeeded, on the basis that the judge held that the council's policy with regard to service users who lived

---

401 [2012] EWHC 2222 (Admin); the case made reference to the wording of the 5th edition of this book (2011) at paras 10.36–10.37 (see para 28 of the judgment).

402 During the course of the case, counsel for the claimant conceded that the 'parents or other informal carers could not simply charge what they liked for lodging, and the Council were not bound to allow the whole of the £40 proposed for "lodgings" by C's parents' (para 34).

403 Hickinbottom J determined that an authority cannot be unreasonable in expecting a person in the same position as the claimant to make 'an exactly similar contribution' to their housing costs from their ESA income, based on the non-dependent deduction for housing benefit (£11.45) and for council tax (£3.45).

404 [2012] EWHC 2222 (Admin) at para 46 – where the service-user does have a legal obligation to contribute towards costs such as a mortgage etc, it would be reasonable for an authority to disregard or make an allowance for their payment. In addition, the judge indicated that there may be some cases where the person's 'exceptional circumstances' may require the authority to consider an additional allowance or disregard, eg if the user, by virtue of his or her disability, has additional housing needs (para 47).

with their parents or other informal carers to be legally flawed. The council's policy allowed in the financial assessment a sum equal to the non-dependent deduction for housing benefit towards the claimant's housing costs, but the exercise of the discretion applied only in cases where the parents/close relative with whom the disabled person lived was on housing benefit (the claimant's parents were not). It distinguished between users who lived with carers who were on housing benefit and those who lived with carers who are not. As there was no reason for such a distinction, the judge held the policy to be legally irrational:[405] there was no inevitability that a person on housing benefit was poorer than one who was not on housing benefit and, further, the approach in any event focussed on the means of a third party and not the service user. The financial assessment must take into account the income and expenditure of the service-user, not those of third parties, which was contrary to the statutory guidance then in force; the position remains the same under the CA 2014 provisions.[406]

8.332   These issues will need to be addressed by local authorities when designing their post-CA 2014 charging policies. However, in the light of the *Tyneside* judgment (see paras 35–36), it seems inevitable that local authorities may decide not to allow any additional sums for board and lodgings as this is included in the ESA rate (ie the current non-dependent deductions for housing benefit and council tax benefit) and it would be reasonable to expect a disabled person to pay this amount towards his or her board and lodgings. However, what is clear from the judgment is that, where the disabled person has a specific liability for their housing costs, local authorities must be prepared to exercise its discretion to make an appropriate allowance. It is not acceptable for local authorities, in determining whether or not to make any additional allowance housing costs, to do so in accordance with the financial status of the disabled person's family. Furthermore, local authorities must make its decisions on public law principles: any policy must therefore be sufficiently flexible to allow authorities to take appropriate decisions about housing costs where the person's circumstances justify doing so.

Costs of transport to services

8.333   As noted above (see para 8.129) the mobility component of DLA must be ignored when assessing a person's income for charging purposes, and the fact that a person is receiving this benefit is not a relevant consideration when determining whether a particular need exits or the eligibility of such a need.

8.334   Charging and assessment regulations 2014 reg 7(8) states that, where a local authority provides non-care related support, the cost to the authority of providing that service is deducted from the adult's MIG. Regulation 7(9) defines 'non-care related support' as including transport services.[407]

---

405 [2012] EWHC 2222 (Admin) at para 48.
406 [2012] EWHC 2222 (Admin) at para 44.
407 Care and Support (Assessment of Resources) Regulations 2014 SI No 2672 reg 7(9) also includes services such as the provision of meals on wheels, shopping and recreational activities in the definition of 'non-care related support'.

This in effect represents a 'charge' to the adult, at least in the sense that the approach operates as a reduction in the amount of the guaranteed income ie the amount below which a person will not be obliged to use their income to pay for the service. This may apply, for example, where a person uses local authority funded transport to attend a luncheon club, which is itself provided by a charitable or community group. There would be no reduction in the person's MIG for the attendance at the luncheon club (as the service may not properly be described as being 'provided' by the local authority) but the amount of the transport costs operates to reduce the amount of the adult's assessed MIG.

8.335   In terms of the DRE, the only reference to transport costs in the statutory guidance (at annex C para 40(xii)) replicates the advice contained in the Fairer Charging 2013 (para 51 iii):

> ... other transport costs necessitated by illness or disability, including costs of transport to day centres, over and above the mobility component of DLA or PIP, if in payment and available for these costs. In some cases, it may be reasonable for a council not to take account of claimed transport costs – if, for example, a suitable, cheaper form of transport, eg council-provided transport to day centres is available, but has not been used.

8.336   Therefore, transport costs may be assessed as DRE, provided they are in excess of the amount which would normally covered by the mobility component of DLA or PIP. Where an authority decides to charge for transport (eg a flat rate charge for transport to day services), it must take care to ensure that the adult's income is not left below the level of the MIG and it should consider including the transport charges as part of the person's DRE. A failure by a local authority to include such charges as part of the person's DRE may be challenged on the grounds that the person is being asked for more than it is 'reasonably practicable' for them to pay (statutory guidance, para 8.2; and see para 8.29 above).

Challenging the assessed charge

8.337   Where a service user wishes to challenge a charge in any care setting, about any aspect of the financial assessment or how a local authority has chosen to charge, the usual procedure will be to pursue the matter through the local authority's complaints procedures (see para 20.7 below).[408] Although many authorities have ad hoc informal appeals processes, these do not override the ability to use the complaints process.

8.338   The statutory guidance (at para 8.70) makes this point explicit, stating that where the authority has established a special panel or fast track review process to deal with financial assessment/charging issues, it should remind the person that they are still able to access the social services statutory complaint's procedure. The ombudsman has in the past been critical of the lack of clear references to a right of appeal in decision letters sent to

---

408 Statutory guidance, paras 8.68–8.70; the complaints process is found under the Local Authority Social Services and NHS Complaints (England) Regulations 2009.

users;[409] the statutory guidance (at para 8.68) now makes it mandatory that local authorities must make clear what its complaints procedure is and provide information and advice on how to lodge a complaint.[410]

8.339   In a wide ranging 2011 report, the LGO[411] identified a significant number of defects of a local authority's home care charging arrangements. The matters identified by the LGO remain relevant to the post-CA 2014 provisions as general points of principle for other charging policies:

- the council departed materially from the Fairer Charging guidance on the basis that it believed that its policy was simpler and provided 'certainty': the ombudsman held that certainty is not a substitute for 'fairness' (para 90);
- the council adopting a banded approach to charges, without these procedures being comprehensible to service users so as to enable them to make 'an informed decision about whether to request a full assessment' (para 92);
- the council's materials had the effect of discouraging 'people from seeking a full financial assessment' (ie by suggesting that 'in most cases the banded charge will be the lower cost') (para 93);
- paper-based only assessments were criticised by the ombudsman in circumstances where it was evident that the person's letters indicated to the council that he would have found it difficult to manage the assessment process by letter, particularly as the authority's own guidance made reference to the importance of 'personal help and advice' during the financial assessment, including 'face to face contact is important' (para 95).

8.340   The LGO has emphasised that service users should be given clear information as to the criteria for having charges reduced or waived, and of their right to a hearing before an appeal panel if their initial challenge was unsuccessful. He has also stressed the need for panel decisions to be as consistent as possible and that clear reasons for their decisions should be given so that appellants can then decide whether or not to pursue the matter further.[412] At any hearing, the panel will need to bear in mind that an authority's power to reduce or waive charges is not limited to a consideration of the service user's financial means. As the authority has an overall discretion whether or not to levy any charges, it must retain discretion to waive or reduce charges on any ground.

8.341   In the past, the LGO has specifically criticised the lack of proper advocacy assistance to appellants during the appeals process.[413] Although the CA 2014 places a duty upon local authorities to provide advocacy services

---

409 Complaint nos 02/C/14235, 02/C/15396, 02/C/15397 and 02/C/15503 against Derbyshire CC, 24 June 2004.

410 Although the paragraph is silent as to the nature of the complaint's procedure (ie social services statutory complaint's procedure or its own internal procedure), in order to comply with para 8.68, an authority would have to advise of the availability of both procedures where a specific charging appeals' procedure exists.

411 Complaint nos 09 006 887 and 09 011 195, 16 November 2011.

412 Complaint nos 90/A/2675, 90/A/2075, 90/A/1705, 90/A/1228 and 90/A/1172 against Essex CC (1990).

413 Complaint nos 98/C/0911, 98/C/1166, 98/C/1975, 98/C/1977 and 98/C/1978 against Stockton-on Tees BC, 29 July 1999.

to persons in certain circumstances (see para 3.117 above), the provision of advocacy to assist in the means assessment process is not specifically included.

8.342 However, although the authority may not for the time being be under a statutory duty to provide support and/or advocacy services during the financial assessment and/or appeal process, it will still need to be mindful of the need to assist in the provision of appropriate support to those persons who will have difficulties in coping with these processes. Where the need arises out of circumstances which are also protected characteristics under the EqA 2010,[414] authorities must ensure that their policies and procedures comply with its requirements and be prepared to make reasonable adjustments, where necessary. The demands of public law will also require that authorities recognise individual difficulties, such as language or literacy problems, and be prepared to provide appropriate advocacy assistance or other suitable support.[415]

8.343 The problems identified above can be summarised as a breach of the parliamentary and health services ombudsman's principles of good administration.[416] To this extent, they remain as valuable guiding principles for local authorities.

Charging and those who lack mental capacity

8.344 An overview of the mental capacity law is provided at chapter 13 below.

8.345 The statutory guidance reminds authorities that (at para 14.55):

> People must be assumed to have capacity to make their own decisions and be given all practicable help before anyone treats them as not being able to make their own decisions. Where an adult is found to lack capacity to make a decision then any action taken, or any decision made for, or on their behalf, must be made in their best interests.

8.346 The needs of those who lack capacity should be considered by local authorities at the earliest stage, when devising their charging policies so as to consider what capacity remains and their rights (statutory guidance, para 8.45). More specifically, the statutory guidance (para 8.9) notes that:

> where a person lacks capacity, they may still be assessed as being able to contribute towards the cost of their care. However, a local authority must put in place policies regarding how they communicate, how they carry out financial assessments and how they collect any debts that take into consideration the capacity of the person as well as any illness or condition. Local authorities are expected to use their social work skills both to communicate with people and also to design a system that works with, and for, very vulnerable people.

---

414 The protected characteristics are: age, disability, gender reassignment, race, religion or belief, sex, sexual orientation, marriage and civil partnership, and pregnancy and maternity.

415 See the LGO decision in Northamptonshire CC, Complaint nos 09 006 887 and 09 011 195, 16 November 2011.

416 Parliamentary and Health Services Ombudsman, *Principles of good administration*, 2009 – see para 20.132 below.

8.347   Where a person lacks mental capacity[417] to give consent to a financial assessment, the authority must find out whether there is anyone with the authority to act on the person's behalf, such as an appointee for social security benefits or an attorney appointed under an enduring/lasting power of attorney or a deputy appointed by the Court of Protection. If not, then it would be usual for family members (or perhaps someone else close to the person) to make an application to the Court of Protection for a property and affairs deputyship. Where there is no one, or where the relative is perhaps not engaging with the authority or has indicated their unwillingness to be the deputy, the local authority may apply for deputyship or it may ask for a panel deputy to be appointed. While the application is being processed, the person without capacity should not be required to undergo a financial assessment or sign forms he or she no longer understands.[418]

8.348   Additional guidance about deferred payments and those who lack capacity (or who may do so in the future) is set out in the statutory guidance (paras 9.24 and 9.25). Further guidance is provided to local authorities about debt recovery and those who lack capacity, in particular the need to consider any conflict of interest where a local authority applies for a property and financial affairs deputyship where a person owes money to the local authority (statutory guidance, annex D paras 17–21). A preferable option may be for the authority to request that a panel deputy is appointed to act for the person without capacity, rather than for the local authority to take on the role (statutory guidance, annex D para 20).

8.349   Given the nature of the financial assessment, local authority finance staff are often in the frontline of highlighting possible financial abuse, either by a deputy/attorney or by a family member who has involvement in the financial arrangements of the person without capacity, as well as others who may be vulnerable. The statutory guidance focuses on all types of financial abuse from a safeguarding perspective and provides a helpful context (at paras 14.24–14.32).

8.350   The statutory guidance highlights the ability of the Office of the Public Guardian to investigate the actions of a deputy or attorney and, if necessary, make an application to the Court of Protection to consider whether or not action should be taken against them (para 14.61). Unfortunately, cases where local authorities become aware of potential financial abuse by family members are not uncommon. A perhaps extreme example of which is found in the case of *Re SF (The Public Guardian)*,[419] where the son, who was the attorney for his elderly mother, was described by Senior Judge Lush as a 'callous and calculating attorney'. The judge described as 'repugnant' the son's action in charging his elderly mother £400 per day

---

417 The phrase 'lack capacity' is used here as a shorthand to include those whose capacity to make decisions about the financial aspects of their care is compromised so that either they lack it altogether, or it is otherwise diminished or is fluctuating.

418 Statutory guidance, paras 8.18 and 8.19. Note that where the person's assessed need is for a care home bed, and the person lacks capacity to make those arrangements, the authority is obliged to provide the placement regardless of their financial situation (CA 2014 s18(1) and 18(4)).

419 [2015] EWCOP 68; see also the *Public Guardian v DA, YS and ES* [2015] EWCOP 41 and *Re AH the Public Guardian v CH* [2016] EWCOP 9, where the court found that the son and deputy for an elderly lady in a care home had 'failed to treat her with any semblance of dignity, empathy or respect'.

for acting as her attorney. In ordering the son's removal as his mother's attorney, the judge noted that the appointment of a panel deputy for her would place her at the centre of the decision-making process, 'rather than view the preservation and enhancement of [the son's] inheritance as the paramount consideration'.

CHAPTER 9

Preventative services, intermediate care and reablement

Introduction

9.1   The Care Act (CA) 2014 places a general duty on social services authorities to provide a range of preventative services for adults in need and carers. The CA 2014 also repealed and then restated local authority/NHS obligations in relation to the provision of intermediate care and reablement. This chapter considers these duties in turn.

Preventative services

Background

9.2   The CA 2014 places a general duty on social services authorities to provide a range of preventative services for adults in need and carers. The CA 2014 repealed not dissimilar obligations under the previous legal regime – most notably under the National Assistance Act (NAA) 1948[1] and the National Health Service Act (NHSA) 2006.[2]

9.3   The joint committee[3] that scrutinised the draft care and support bill doubted that the overall level of funding for preventative support would enable the government to achieve its stated goal of 'shifting the emphasis from crisis intervention to prevention and early intervention'. This concern appears to have been well founded. In July 2014 the Public Accounts Committee referred to the severe problems local authorities faced in relation to adult social care funding and noted that the Department of Health accepted that it did 'not know whether some preventative services and lower level interventions are making a difference'.[4] In the same year an influential report[5] expressed scepticism about investing in preventative services given the scale of the budget reductions that councils were experiencing. An Association of Directors of Adult Social Services (ADASS) *Budget survey 2015*[6] noted that spending on preventative services fell between 2014 and 2105 by six per cent, and its *Budget survey 2016*[7] found that spending on preventative services had fallen by a further four per cent.

9.4   Given the serious financial problems of most local authorities and the lack of any significant 'new' money to accompany the CA 2014, it is difficult to see how (in the short-term) this duty can be made to be more than

---

1 NAA 1948 s29(1) and LAC (93)10 appendix 2 para 2(1)(a) – services 'whether at centres or elsewhere, facilities for social rehabilitation and adjustment to disability including assistance in overcoming limitations of mobility or communication'.

2 NHSA 2006 Sch 20 para 2 – 'services for the prevention of illness, and the care and after-care of sufferers' and LAC (93)10 appendix 3.

3 Joint Committee on the Draft Care and Support Bill, *Draft Care and Support Bill*, HL Paper 143 HC 822, The Stationery Office, 2013, para 15.

4 House of Commons Committee of Public Accounts, *Adult social care in England* HC 518, The Stationery Office, 2014, p7.

5 Association of Directors of Adult Social Services (ADASS) and the Local Government Association (LGA), *Joint response to the Care Act regulations and guidance consultation*, August 2014, para 21; and see also LGA, *Under pressure: how councils are planning for future cut*, 2014.

6 ADASS, *Budget survey 2015*.

7 ADASS, *Budget survey 2016*.

cosmetic. To invest in preventative services without new money would require a local authority to disinvest in an existing area. In many authorities this would require (in essence) disinvestment from crisis services. In 2016 a King's Fund survey of care services reported that 'across all our case study sites, interviewees spoke about a 'gradual erosion' of preventive services as a result of the difficult process local authorities had undertaken to reduce budgets'.[8]

9.5   The problem appears to be much the same with the NHS. In 2015 the Public Accounts Committee identified a need for radical change that involved the better use of community and primary care services – but noted that this reconfiguration would require significant upfront investment.[9]

The general duty: CA 2014 s2

9.6   CA 2014 s2(1) requires that every local authority provides a range of preventative services that it considers will:

(a) contribute towards preventing or delaying the development by adults in its area of needs for care and support;
(b) contribute towards preventing or delaying the development by carers in its area of needs for support;
(c) reduce the needs for care and support of adults in its area;
(d) reduce the needs for support of carers in its area.

9.7   The statutory guidance to the CA 2014[10] describes 'prevention' as 'critical to the vision in the Care Act' and states that it will 'be vital that the care and support system intervenes early to support individuals ... and prevents need or delays deterioration wherever possible' (para 2.1). In discharging their duty to promote well-being, section 1(3)(c) requires that authorities' have regard to the 'the importance of preventing or delaying the development of needs for care and support or needs for support and the importance of reducing needs of either kind that already exist'.

9.8   While it is reasonably straightforward to conceptualise generic 'preventative' public health interventions (eg gritting footpaths in icy weather, or mass vaccination programs) it is less obvious how this can be done in relation to social care: less obvious how one can distinguish between such generic 'preventative' interventions and person centred specific individual interventions. Apart from broad 'information/signposting' services and support inherent within a vibrant community, it appears that almost all preventative services described in the statutory guidance and the Social Care Institute of Excellence (SCIE) guidance[11] are either 'public health' interventions or low-level specific social care services provided to individuals.

8 R Humphries and others, *Social care for older people: home truths*, King's Fund, 2016, p59.
9 House of Commons Committee of Public Accounts, *Financial sustainability of NHS bodies* Thirty-fifth Report of Session 2014–15 HC 736, The Stationery Office, 2015.
10 Department of Health, *Care and support statutory guidance* to support implementation of Part 1 of the CA 2014 by local authorities, 2016 ('the statutory guidance').
11 SCIE has a 'Prevention Library' resource that 'aims to help inform commissioners and service providers to find information and examples of emerging research and practice in the provision of prevention services across England'.

9.9   The statutory guidance[12] accepts that there is no single definition for what constitutes 'preventative activity', but suggests that this can be broken down into three general approaches – primary, secondary and tertiary prevention:

- **Primary prevention** is aimed at individuals who have no current particular health or care needs, and would include activities such as exercise classes and befriending schemes to address loneliness (para 2.6).
- **Secondary prevention** consists of early intervention schemes aimed at individuals who have an increased risk of developing needs – for example, helping someone with a learning disability to manage his or her money, or extra support to help a family carer cope with a challenging care situation (para 2.7). It would also include a 'fall prevention' clinic, adaptions to housing to improve accessibility or provide greater assistance, handyman services, short-term provision of wheelchairs or telecare services (para 2.8).
- **Tertiary prevention** is described as minimising the effect of disability or deterioration for people with established or complex health conditions; supporting people to regain skills; and manage or reduce need where possible (para 2.9).

9.10   A potential problem with the promotion of preventative services is that their existence could be used as an argument to restrict access to personalised support programmes: that individuals would have to establish that these services had been tried (and had failed) before formal support is available. Although the 2014 legislative regime could be interpreted in this way, such an approach would upend the principle of personalised/person-centred care support (for example, the right to a direct payment) and run counter to the well-being principle that individuals should have control over (among other things) the care and support they receive (CA 2014 s1(2)(d)). If parliament had intended such an interpretation, it would have expressed this in clear terms in the eligibility criteria regulations[13] (see para 4.6 above). It seems that the Welsh Assembly did intend such an interpretation, and this is reasonably clear in its equivalent regulations.[14] These require that it be established that a need for care and support 'can and can only' be met by personalised services. The English legislation is not drafted in this way.

9.11   The statutory guidance gives young carers as an example of where specific preventative services are required – that where a local authority becomes aware that a child is carrying out a caring role 'it should consider how supporting the adult with needs for care and support can prevent the young carer from under taking excessive or inappropriate care and support responsibilities' (para 2.50).

---

12 See generally, paras 2.4–2.5.
13 Care and Support (Eligibility Criteria) Regulations 2015 SI No 313.
14 For a discussion of this danger, see L Clements 'Welsh social care law risks taking us back 20 years by providing bare minimum', *Community Care* 2014; and see also Amy Clifton 'The future of social care' in *Assembly Research Service Key issues for the Fifth Assembly*, 2016, p42 and see also Stephen Boyce 'Carers' Week 2016' in *In Brief*, National Assembly for Wales Research Service, 2016.

9.12   Although authorities are not empowered to charge for intermediate care and reablement services (see para 8.27 below) they have the power to charge for preventative services. Where local authorities are considering making a charge for such support, the statutory guidance advises that they balance the 'affordability and viability ... with the likely impact of charging on the uptake' – and that this be considered individually as well as at a general policy level (paras 2.55–2.57 – and see also para 8.37 above).

Intermediate care and 'reablement'

Background

9.13   In 2000 the government announced that it would be investing £900 million between 2001 and 2004 into 'new intermediate care and related services to promote independence and improve the quality of care for older people'.[15] The initial programme was not underpinned by legislation, but was shaped by statutory guidance[16] that sought to build on health and social services' legislative joint working obligations – with the aim of improving rehabilitation services as well as services that helped avoid unnecessary hospital admissions.

9.14   In 2003, regulations[17] were issued to require that intermediate care services should be provided without charge and the detail of the obligation was set out in non-statutory 'best practice' guidance (the '2009 DH guidance').[18] This was augmented by charging-specific guidance[19] issued as a result of concerns that some authorities were improperly making charges for this service. Although the 2003 regulations have been repealed and replaced by CA 2014 regulations,[20] the 2009 DH guidance appears to remain the principal guidance.[21]

9.15   The intermediate care initiative is aimed at freeing up acute hospital beds and promoting the independence of all adults in need, although it has a particular focus on older people. It provides intensive short-term support services to prevent unnecessary admissions and facilitate earlier

---

15 Department of Health, *NHS plan: the plan for investment and reform*, Cm 4818–1, 2000, para 7.4.

16 LAC (2001)1/HSC 2001/01 issued under LASSA 1970 s7: now superseded by the 2009 DH guidance.

17 Community Care (Delayed Discharges etc) Act (Qualifying Services) (England) Regulations 2003 SI No 1196.

18 Department of Health, *Intermediate care – halfway home: updated guidance for the NHS and local authorities*, 2009.

19 LAC (DH) 2010 (6).

20 Care and Support (Charging and Assessment of Resources) Regulations 2014 SI No 2672 reg 3(3).

21 At the time of writing (January 2017) the National Institute of Health and Care Excellence (NICE) is consulting on the publication of an 'Intermediate care – including reablement' guideline – which is expected to be published in July 2017. The consultation document NICE, *Intermediate care including reablement: in development* [GID-SCWAVE0709] states that the guideline has been commissioned by the Department of Health and refers to the 2009 DH guidance as 'existing guidance'.

discharge, either back home or via 'step-down' community hospital/care home facilities.[22] The 'effectiveness of reablement' has been adopted as a key service to be supported by the Better Care Fund initiative (see para 11.134 above).[23]

9.16   It appears that the majority of people using intermediate care are older people, with over half being over 85 years of age[24] and that while the programme has clear benefits for many patients, it is questionable whether short-term intermediate care is effective in meeting the needs of older people with more severe cognitive problems or of those who are suffering from depression.[25]

9.17   A 2002 Nuffield Foundation Research Report suggested that this failure can be attributed to inadequate assessment, skills shortages, cash limits, inadequate home support and the timescale of six weeks being inappropriate for many people with mental health needs. It appears that because of this skills (or 'attitude') deficit, many people with dementia are deteriorating, through inappropriate care in acute settings such that they are not being enabled to maximise their coping skills.

9.18   An authoritative 2015 report[26] noted that people who had had access intermediate care generally expressed high levels of satisfaction with the service. However, it raised concerns about the limited range of support available from most local intermediate care services – particularly the lack of assistance with domestic tasks and with goals to improve social contact, and it states:

> Is intermediate care making a difference at a whole system level? There is no direct audit data that relates to this fundamental issue but the likely answer is 'no'. This is because the capacity of intermediate care remains stubbornly stuck, and almost certainly stuck at a level below the threshold for whole system impact (page 4).

Definition

9.19   Care and Support (Charging and Assessment of Resources) Regulations 2014 reg 3(3)[27] define 'intermediate care and reablement support services' as:

> ... care and support, or support provided to an adult by the local authority under section 18, 19 or 20 of the Act which–
> (a) consists of a programme of care and support, or support;

22 The Department of Health produced a model contract for use when contracting with independent sector care homes for intermediate care – see Department of Health, *A guide to contracting for intermediate care services*, 2001.

23 Department of Health, *2016/17 Better care fund policy framework*, 2016.

24 Institute of Health Sciences and Public Health Research, *An evaluation of intermediate care for older people final report*, University of Leeds, 2005.

25 Institute of Health Sciences and Public Health Research, *An evaluation of intermediate care for older people final report*, University of Leeds, 2005.

26 NHS Benchmarking Network, *National audit of intermediate care: summary report 2015. Assessing progress in services for older people aimed at maximising independence and reducing use of hospitals*, 2015: the report suggested that the level of spend on intermediate care was consistent with about a half of the capacity required to meet demand; and that since 2013 the capacity in health-based intermediate care had remained static while capacity in reablement services had reduced.

27 SI No 2672.

(b) is for a specified period of time ('the specified period'); and

(c) has as its purpose the provision of assistance to an adult to enable the adult to maintain or regain the ability needed to live independently in their own home.

9.20 Regulation 3(2)(b) specifies that intermediate care and reablement support services must be provided without charge 'for the first 6 weeks of the specified period or, if the specified period is less than 6 weeks, for that period'.

9.21 Although the provision of intermediate care services will often satisfy a patient's needs for rehabilitation and recuperation, this will not always be the case. Given the time-limited nature of the service, it will frequently be only a first stage of a programme – for which the 'reablement team' may have full responsibility.[28] In this respect the statutory guidance states that (para 2.62):

> ... neither intermediate care nor reablement should have a strict time limit, since the period of time for which the support is provided should depend on the needs and outcomes of the individual. In some cases, for instance a period of rehabilitation for a visually impaired person (a specific form of reablement), may be expected to last longer than 6 weeks. Whilst the local authority does have the power to charge for this where it is provided beyond 6 weeks, local authorities should consider continuing to provide it free of charge beyond 6 weeks in view of the clear preventative benefits to the individual and, in many cases, the reduced risk of hospital admissions.

9.22 The statutory guidance then adds that local authorities should consider 'the potential impact and consequences of ending the provision of preventative services' when deciding whether or not to charge for the additional period – noting that 'poorly considered exit strategies can negate the positive outcomes of preventative services, facilities or resources, and ongoing low-level care and support can have significant impact on preventing, reducing and delaying need' (para 2.63).

9.23 The statutory guidance makes clear that the duty to provide free intermediate care or reablement support applies to 'all adults, irrespective of whether they have eligible needs for ongoing care and support'. It notes that 'such types of support will usually be provided as a preventative measure under section 2 of the Act' before stating that it 'may also be provided as part of a package of care and support to meet eligible needs' (para 2.61).

9.24 The statutory guidance (para 2.12) notes that there is a 'tendency for the terms "reablement", "rehabilitation" and "intermediate care" to be used interchangeably' and then adopts a fourfold categorisation of intermediate care as:

- crisis response – services providing short-term care (up to 48 hours);
- home-based intermediate care – services provided to people in their own homes by a team with different specialities but mainly health professionals such as nurses and therapists;
- bed-based intermediate care – services delivered away from home, for example, in a community hospital;

---

28 See in this respect, comments in para 11.65 below.

- reablement – services to help people live independently which are provided in the person's own home by a team of mainly care and support professionals.

9.25   In relation to this list, the statutory guidance states that three of the categories 'have historically been clinician-led and provided by health staff, with reablement being provided by local authorities' (para 11.18). It refers to the *National audit of intermediate care* report[29] that identified the role played by 'health professionals such as nurses and therapists' in such teams (para 11.17). It follows that although intermediate care and reablement services may be defined in the regulations (para 9.14 above) as care and/or support provided 'under section 18, 19 or 20 of the [CA 2014]' – this is only part of the picture. Not infrequently a local intermediate care service will deliver a significant component of NHSA 2006 care and support services: services that must also, of course, be provided without charge.

9.26   The statutory guidance describes 'rehabilitation' as a service that may constitute intermediate care in part (ie initially) or entirely and defines it as a service (para 2.13):

> ... designed to help a person regain or re-learn some capabilities where these capabilities have been lost due to illness or disease. Rehabilitation services can include provisions that help people attain independence and remain or return to their home and participate in their community, for example independent living skills and mobility training for people with visual impairment.

9.27   Developing the definition in the regulations (above) the statutory guidance (para 2.14) emphasises that intermediate care is most commonly provided to 'people after they have left hospital or when they are at risk of being sent to hospital' and that 'they provide a link between places such as hospitals and people's homes, and between different areas of the health and care and support system – community services, hospitals, GPs and care and support'.

9.28   The 2009 DH guidance stresses that the services should not be limited to older people: that it should be available to adults of all ages including young people managing transition to adulthood, people with dementia, flexibility over the length of the time limited period, integration with mainstream health and social care, timely access to specialist support, and governance and quality. In particular, it suggests that intermediate care could also form part of a pathway for end-of-life care if there were specific goals for the individual and carer(s) that could be addressed in a time limited period. It gives as an example 'enabling someone to move back home, establishing a suitable environment and routine, setting up a care package and helping carers to develop the skills they might need'.[30]

9.29   The 2009 DH guidance stresses the importance of considering those who might be facing admission to residential care – that the aim of intermediate care is to ensure that they:

---

29 NHS Benchmarking Network, *National audit of intermediate care: summary report 2015. Assessing progress in services for older people aimed at maximising independence and reducing use of hospitals*, 2015.

30 2009 DH guidance, p5.

... should be given the opportunity to benefit from rehabilitation and recuperation and their needs to be assessed in a setting other than an acute ward [see also para 5.9]. People in this position should not be transferred directly to long-term residential care from an acute hospital ward unless there are exceptional circumstances.

The exceptional circumstances might include those who have already completed a period of specialist rehabilitation; those judged to have had sufficient previous attempts at being supported at home and those for whom a period in residential intermediate care followed by another move is judged likely to be distressing.[31]

Service models

9.30   For planning purposes, intermediate care can be categorised into various service models, which are identified in 2009 DH guidance as:

- rapid response teams to prevent avoidable admission to hospital for patients referred from GPs, A&E or other sources, with short-term care and support in their own home;
- acute care at home from specialist teams, including some treatment such as administration of intravenous antibiotics;
- residential rehabilitation in a setting such as a residential care home or community hospital, for people who do not need 24-hour consultant-led medical care but need a short period of therapy and rehabilitation, ranging from one to about six weeks;
- supported discharge in a patient's own home, with nursing and/or therapeutic support, and home care support and community equipment where necessary, to allow rehabilitation and recovery at home; the arrangements may work well in specialist accommodation such as extra care housing;
- day rehabilitation for a limited period in a day hospital or day centre, possibly in conjunction with other forms of intermediate care support.

9.31   The 2009 DH guidance also reminds authorities that sheltered or extra care housing can be part of intermediate care, and that telecare, rapid care and repair services also enable people to move back home.

Charging

9.32   As noted at para 8.27 above, the 2014 regulations require that intermediate care be provided free for any period up to and including six weeks. While this appears clear, it is dependant on the service being so described by the authorities. The potential exists, therefore, for it not to be free purely because the service does not bear this label. It also appears that on occasions the intermediate care team is unable (due to resource constraints) to take on new work, such that patients may be referred elsewhere. In such cases, the mere fact that the service is not being provided by the intermediate care team should not be used as a reason for charges to be levied. This view is given weight by the functional approach taken by the 2009 DH guidance (see para 9.28 above).

31 2009 DH guidance, p4.

Personal budgets and direct payments

continued

Introduction

10.1   The Care Act (CA) 2014 places a duty on local authorities to provide adults with a personal budget, and an obligation on social services authorities to provide direct payments.

10.2   Personal budgets are entirely notional: they are a sum theoretically allocated by the local authority to cover a person's care costs. A local authority can, as part of this abstract exercise, allocate all or part of the budget to be spent on care services which it is providing. This not a 'purchase' in the conventional sense of the word: no money changes hands, no money is moved across a spreadsheet, no contract is concluded – it is simply a hypothetical transaction. Direct payments, on the other hand, are not 'notional' (or at least they should not be – see para 10.92 below) – such a payment requires cash to leave the council's coffers and go into an account in the recipient's name (or a nominated account on the recipient's behalf). This chapter will consider personal budgets and direct payments in turn.

Personal budgets

Background

10.3   CA 2014 s25(1)(e) places a duty on local authorities to include in all care and/or support plans a 'personal budget for the adult concerned'.

10.4   Personal budgets are an ideological construct – the basis of which is that commodification is a good thing and that providing more than 1.3 million people[1] with details of how much their care package costs is a cost-effective exercise that improves the quality of their care.[2] It is not something that is done for NHS patients, and the evidence as to its effectiveness is far from promising.[3]

10.5   The statutory guidance to the CA 2014[4] describes a personal budget as (para 11.3):

> ... the mechanism that, in conjunction with the care and support plan, or support plan, enables the person, and their advocate if they have one, to exercise greater choice and take control over how their care and support needs are met.

The guidance emphasises that it is 'vital' that people are clear how their budget is calculated – that the process is 'transparent' and 'robust so that people have confidence that the personal budget allocation is correct and therefore sufficient to meet their care and support needs' (para 11.4). The

---

1   A significant proportion of whom have limited mental capacity, inadequate advocacy support, limited experience of making social care choices, and not infrequently encounter the system when in crisis.

2   For details of the policy origins of personal budgets, see L Clements, 'Individual budgets and irrational exuberance' in (2009) 11 CCLR 413–430.

3   See, for example, Richard Titmuss, *The gift relationship*, George Allen & Unwin, 1970.

4   Department of Health, *Care and support statutory guidance* to support implementation of Part 1 of the CA 2014 by local authorities, 2016 ('the statutory guidance').

evidence suggests that the process can be transparent or accurate but not both – and in practice it is often neither.[5]

10.6   Personal budgets would appear to be a detached legal appendage, serving little purpose in terms of improving user choice. They have been described as 'a cog spinning inside a machine with which it does not engage'.[6] Since local authorities are required to cost individual care packages, it is difficult to see how providing an 'indicative amount' at the start of the process is a cost-saving exercise for local authorities – and it is troubling that this assertion has been accepted without question by the courts. In *R (KM) v Cambridgeshire CC*[7] it is stated that ascertaining the reasonable cost of services to meet an identified 'would be unacceptably laborious and expensive' (para 24). The court neither questions why this cost has to be ascertained in every case,[8] nor why, if the package has subsequently to be costed with some precision,[9] this first stage does not in fact represent an additional cost to the authority.

Calculating a personal budget

10.7   CA 2014 s26 states that the amount of an adult's personal budget is 'the cost to the local authority of meeting those of the adult's needs which it is required or decides to meet'. The Joint Committee that scrutinised the care and support bill expressed concern that this phrasing was different to the pre-CA 2014 requirement (in relation to direct payments) – that the amount be that which the 'the authority estimate to be equivalent to the reasonable cost of securing the provision of the service concerned': it considered that the word 'reasonable' was important and should be included in the Act.[10] In response the government stated that the wording meant that the amount had to be 'sufficient to meet' the adult's needs. The committee was not reassured by this response.[11] The statutory guidance goes some way to allay these concerns, stating that (para 11.10):

> The personal budget must always be an amount sufficient to meet the person's care and support needs, and must include the cost to the local authority of meeting the person's needs which the local authority is under a duty to meet, or has exercised its power to do so. This overall cost must then be broken down into the amount the person must pay, following the financial assessment, and the remainder of the budget that the authority will pay.

---

5 See, for example, C Slasberg, P Beresford and P Schofield, 'The increasing evidence of how self-directed support is failing to deliver personal budgets and personalisation' in *Research, Policy and Planning* (2013) 30(2), 91-105 and L Series and L Clements, 'Putting the cart before the horse: resource allocation systems and community care' in *Journal of Social Welfare and Family Law* (2013) 35 (2), pp207–226.

6 L Series and L Clements, 'Putting the cart before the horse: resource allocation systems and community care' in *Journal of Social Welfare and Family Law* (2013) 35 (2), pp207–226.

7 [2012] UKSC 23.

8 At the time of the case, personal budgets were not a legal requirement.

9 A point accepted at para 28 of the judgment.

10 Joint Committee on the Draft Care and Support Bill, *Draft Care and Support Bill*, Stationery Office, HL Paper 143 HC 822, 2013, para 208.

11 Joint Committee on the Draft Care and Support Bill, *Draft Care and Support Bill*, Stationery Office, HL Paper 143 HC 822, 2013, para 208.

10.8 The expectation is therefore that the personal budget will change as the care and support planning process progresses. At the start of the process, it will be an 'indicative amount' shared with the person and anybody else involved, with the 'final amount of the personal budget confirmed through this process' (para 11.7). In *R (KM) v Cambridgeshire CC*[12] this requirement is expressed in the following terms:

> What is crucial is that, once the starting-point (or indicative sum) has finally been identified, the requisite services in the particular case should be costed in a reasonable degree of detail so that a judgement can be made whether the indicative sum is too high, too low or about right (para 28).

This means there is (at law) no need for an authority to use a resource allocation system (RAS) to generate a figure at the commencement of the process – an authority might have, for example, a simple set of 'bands'. As noted above, research suggests that most RAS generate incorrect figures and have serious defects – not least their complexity and the rigidity with which some local authorities then apply them. In this context the statutory guidance advises that 'complex RAS models of allocation may not work for all client groups' (para 11.23) and that 'regardless of the process used, the most important principles in setting the personal budget are transparency, timeliness and sufficiency' (para 11.24).

10.9 A 2015 ombudsman report[13] has confirmed the legal position – namely that the hourly rates on which personal budgets and direct payments are assessed must not be arbitrary and that the calculations must be shared with adults in need or carers.

Carers' personal budgets

10.10 The CA 2014 s25(1)(e) duty to include a personal budget in all care/support plans applies with equal force to carers.

10.11 The statutory guidance considers the possible complexities[14] that may arise when it is unclear as to whether a particular service is for a carer or for the 'adult' –advising that local authorities (para 11.38):

> ... should consider how to align personal budgets where they are meeting the needs of both the carer and the adult needing care concurrently. Where an adult has eligible needs for care and support, and has a personal budget and care and support plan in their own right, and the carer's needs can be met, in part or in full, by the provision of care and support to that person needing care, then this kind of provision should be incorporated into the plan and personal budget of the person with care needs, as well as being detailed in a care and support plan for the carer.

10.12 As noted above, there will be situations where a carer may be assessed as eligible for support when the person for whom he or she cares may be

---

12 [2012] UKSC 23.
13 Complaint no 13 006 400 against Cornwall Council, 26 February 2015.
14 See generally, C Glendinning, W Mitchell and J Brooks, *Carers and personalisation. Discussion paper for the Department of Health*, Working Paper No DH 2576, School for Social Care Research (SSCR) Research Findings, Social Policy Research Unit, 2013.

ineligible.[15] The statutory guidance addresses some of the implications of this situation, explaining that where the carer is eligible for support but the adult being cared is not – and accordingly 'does not have their own personal budget or care plan' (para 11.42) – the carer could, for example, request a direct payment, and use that to commission his or her own replacement care from an agency (para 11.44). It then states (para 11.45):

> If such a type of replacement care is charged for ... then it would be the adult needing care that would pay, not the carer, because they are the direct recipient of the service.

Direct payments

Background

10.13   Direct payments involve local authorities (and sometimes the NHS – see para 10.97 below) transferring money to an individual (or someone on the individual's behalf) to enable the individual to make arrangements himself of herself to meet some or all of the individual's eligible care and/or support needs.

10.14   Prior to 1997 such an arrangement was not possible. Although the principal social care statutes provided social services with flexibility as to how they discharged their obligations, the statutes almost invariably prohibited the payment of cash directly to the service user.[16] The inability of service users to make their own care arrangements was frequently seen as disabling and disempowering.[17] In addition, research suggested that the making of direct payments could result in much improved user satisfaction, and indeed cost-savings to local authorities.[18] Kestenbaum, for instance, drew attention to the high value placed by service users on choice and control and that in general this could not be provided by local authorities:

> It is not simply a matter of resource levels, though these are significant. As important are the qualities that any large-scale service providing organisation would find hard to deliver: choice of care assistant, flexibility, consistency, control of times and tasks, etc.[19]

---

15 CA 2014 s20(7) – a local authority may meet some or all of a carer's needs for support in a way which involves the provision of care and support to the adult needing care, even if the authority would not be required to meet the adult's needs for care and support under CA 2014 s18.

16 See eg National Assistance Act (NAA) 1948 s29(6)(a) and National Health Service Act (NHSA) 2006 Sch 20 para 2(4)/National Health Service (Wales) Act (NHS(W)A) 2006 Sch 15 para 2(4). Although Children Act (CA) 1989 s17(6) (prior to its amendment by the Carers and Disabled Children Act (CDCA) 2000) permitted the payment of cash, this was only in 'in exceptional circumstances' (section 17(6)) and has now been amended by Children and Young Persons Act 2008 s24 to omit the words 'in exceptional circumstances'.

17 See eg J Morris, *Independent lives: community care and disabled people,* Macmillan, 1993.

18 See eg K Kestenbaum, *Independent living: a review,* Joseph Rowntree Foundation, 1996.

19 K Kestenbaum, *Independent living: a review,* Joseph Rowntree Foundation, 1996, p77.

10.15 As a consequence of this pressure for reform, a number of direct payment options were developed. Initially these consisted of 'indirect' or 'third party schemes' whereby the local authority paid the cash to an intermediary who then brokered the care arrangements that the service-user required. 1988 saw the development of the first 'Independent Living Fund' which specifically allowed for direct payments to a restricted group of disabled people from a fund set up by the Department of Social Security rather than via local authorities. In 1996 the provisions of the Community Care (Direct Payments) Act (CC(DP)A) 1996 brought the possibility of direct payments by social services to many adult disabled people.[20] The CC(DP)A 1996 was augmented by the Carers and Disabled Children Act 2000 which extended[21] direct payments to certain carers and parents of disabled children.[22]

10.16 Notwithstanding the perceived benefits of the direct payments scheme, local authorities incur not inconsiderable costs in providing support for direct payment service-users and in the training of staff. A 2006 Audit Commission study suggested that these costs generally outweighed potential savings in transferring administrative responsibilities to direct payment recipients,[23] although 2009 research has suggested that such payments may be cost-neutral, but that the 'opportunity costs savings' are appreciable.[24]

10.17 The Department of Health has put considerable pressure on councils to increase the number of individuals receiving such support. Initially the target numbers were expressed as 'crucial performance indicators'[25] before being subsumed into targets set for the implementation of the personalisation programme.[26]

10.18 There has been a linear increase in number of people receiving direct payments – rising from 24,000 users in 2004/05 to 107,000 in 2009/10 to 153,000 in 2013/14 (14.5 per cent of all people who received community based services in that year).[27] Spending on direct payments amounted to £1.4 billion or eight per cent of total spending in 2013/14 – a 103 per cent increase in real terms from 2008/09.[28] The data suggests a wide variation

20 Although older people had to wait until 2000 before they could be make use of direct payments.
21 By amendment to the CA 1989 – inserting section 17A.
22 The direct payment provisions in both Acts were consolidated by Health and Social Care Act 2001 ss57–58 and are now found in CA 2014 ss31–33.
23 Audit Commission, *Choosing well*, 2006.
24 T Stainton, S Boyce and C Phillips, 'Independence pays: a cost and resource analysis of direct payments in two local authorities', *Disability and Society*, Vol 24, No 2, March 2009, pp161–172.
25 In England the number of direct payment arrangements in any particular authority were (until 2007) included as a Key Performance Indicator.
26 Department of Health, *Putting People First: a shared vision and commitment to the transformation of adult social care*, 2007; and see also Department of Health, *A vision for adult social care: capable communities and active citizens*, 2010 which proposed that by April 2013 all authorities would provide personal budgets, preferably as direct payments, to everyone eligible (at para 4.9): for further detail see the 5th edition of this book, para 3.7.
27 NHS Digital, *Community care statistics, social services activity, England – 2013–14, final release*, 2014.
28 Health and Social Care Information Centre (HSCIC), *Personal social services: expenditure and unit costs, England – 2013–14, final release*, 9 December 2014.

in the types of people seeking these payments: in 2010 although 9.5 per cent of adults aged 18–64 receiving community-based or carers services received direct payments; for those aged 65 and over the figure was only 3.6 per cent.[29]

Direct payments and the Care Act 2014

10.19   The obligation on social services authorities to provide direct payments is found in CA 2014 ss31–33. The legislative scheme under the CA 2014 is very similar to the one it replaced, such that previous case-law and ombudsman decisions will continue to be of direct relevance. The detail of the CA 2014 regime is spelled out in regulations[30] – the Care and Support (Direct Payments) Regulations 2014 (referred to in the succeeding section as the 'DP regulations'). The statutory guidance provides further detail as to how local authorities are expected to operate the scheme (chapter 12). It is, however, significantly less detailed than the 2009 Department of Health guidance[31] it replaces (18 pages compared to 106 pages). Given this disparity, and the strong similarities of both schemes, reference is made below to the '2009 DH guidance' where this is considered appropriate.

10.20   The CA 2014, in effect, creates two parallel and closely linked direct payment systems: one for adults who have the capacity to request such a payment (section 31); and the other for adults who lack the requisite capacity (section 32). As would be expected, the legislative scheme provides for greater checks and balances for adults in the latter category. Parents of disabled children also have a similar entitlement to require their child's eligible needs (and their needs as carers) to be met by way of a direct payment.[32]

Adults with the capacity to request a direct payment

10.21   CA 2014 s31(2) places a duty on local authorities to make direct payments to adults/carers who have the capacity to request a direct payment, in the following circumstances:

1) the local authority has decided[33] that the person is eligible for care and/ or support or has decided to exercise its discretion to meet the person's needs;[34]

2) the adult requests a direct payment for some or all of his or her needs (which can be paid to the adult or a person he or she nominates);

---

29   Care Quality Commission (CQC), *The state of healthcare and adult social care in England: key themes and quality of services in 2009*, HC 343, 2010, p30.

30   SI No 2871, issued pursuant to CA 2014 s33.

31   Department of Health, *Guidance on direct payments for community care, services for carers and children's services England*, 2009.

32   Children Act 1989 s17A and for details of this legislative scheme see S Broach, L Clements and J Read, *Disabled children: a legal handbook*, 2nd edn, Legal Action Group, 2016, para 3.98.

33   Under CA 2014 s18 or s20(1) (the duty); or s19(1) or (2) or 20(6) (the power).

34   CA 2014 s31(1)(a) expresses this in somewhat tangential terms by reference to the adult having a personal budget that specifies an amount which must be used to meet pay for the costs of meeting their needs.

3) the adult has capacity to make the request (and where there is a nominated person, that person agrees to receive the payments);
4) the adult is not a proscribed person (effectively someone with an addiction problem who is subject to certain court orders);
5) the authority is satisfied that the adult or the nominated person is capable of managing direct payment alone or with assistance to which the person has access;
6) the authority is satisfied that making direct payments to the adult or nominated person is an appropriate way to meet the needs in question.

Adults without the capacity to request a direct payment

10.22 CA 2014 s32(2) places a duty on local authorities to make direct payments for adults who lack the requisite capacity to request a direct payment, in the following circumstances:

1) the local authority has decided[35] that the person is eligible for care and/or support or has decided to exercise its discretion to meet the person's needs;[36]
2) an authorised person requests that the local authority makes a direct payment to him or her for some or all of the adult's needs;
3) the adult is not a proscribed person (effectively someone with an addiction problem who is subject to certain court orders);
4) the authority is satisfied that the authorised person will act in the adult's best interests in relation to the direct payments ;
5) the authority is satisfied that the authorised person is capable of managing direct payment alone or with assistance to which he or she has access.

Authorised person

10.23 Where an adult lacks the requisite mental capacity, a direct payment is dependent upon there being a person willing and able to fulfil the role of an 'authorised person'. CA 2014 s32(4)[37] provides that in such cases, a person is 'authorised' if one of the following applies:

a) **The person is authorised under the Mental Capacity Act (MCA) 2005.** The person is authorised under the MCA 2005 'to make decisions about the adult's needs for care and support' (CA 2014 s32(4)(a)). Such a person would either be: (a) a Court of Protection appointed 'deputy' whose powers include the making of personal welfare decisions for the adult; or (b) a Personal Welfare Lasting Power of Attorney (see para 13.140 below).

b) **Another person authorised under the MCA 2005 consents.** Where a person exists who fulfils the requirements of (a) above but does not

---

35 Under CA 2014 s18 or s20(1) (the duty); or s19(1) or (2) or s20(6) (the power).
36 CA 2014 s32(1)(a) expresses this in somewhat tangential terms by reference to the adult having a personal budget that specifies an amount which must be used to meet pay for the costs of meeting their needs.
37 Replicating in large measure the provisions of Health and Social Care Act (HSCA) 2001 ss57(1A)–57(5C) inserted by HSCA 2008 s146.

agree to act as the authorised person, then section 32(4)(b) provides that he or she can agree with the local authority that someone else act in this capacity.

c) **There is no one authorised under the MCA 2005.** No one fulfils the requirements of (a) or (b) above – in which case the authorised person will be someone who the local authority considers to be a suitable person for direct payments purposes (CA 2014 s32(4)(c)).

The obligation to make direct payments

10.24   Individuals are not assessed for direct payments. The direct payment scheme is integral to the assessment and care planning process, and such payments are not available unless and until the appropriate assessment has been undertaken. However, once a local authority has decided that care and/or support is required, then (unless one of the above exemptions apply) it can be required to provide direct payments in lieu of services – the relevant legislation being phrased in mandatory terms. It follows that it is unlawful for a local authority to have a policy of refusing direct payments for certain services (eg for respite care or services it can provide 'in house'[38] or via a block contracted service[39]) or of requiring reasons to be given by a potential recipient of direct payments as to why he or she wishes this facility.[40]

10.25   The statutory guidance advises that 'authorities must consider requests for direct payments made at any time, and have clear and swift processes in place to respond to the requests' (para 12.10). Although it suggests that it may sometimes be convenient to consider the request 'at the same time as a review of the care plan', it makes clear that this will not always be the case. It will generally be maladministration to delay providing direct payments until a review has been undertaken.[41]

People to whom direct payments cannot be made

10.26   Prisoners are not entitled to direct payments (CA 2014 s76(5)) and the DP regulations list other service users who are prohibited from receiving direct payments.[42] The list includes persons who are subject to certain court orders or controls arising out of their drug and/or alcohol dependencies (eg being subject to a drug rehabilitation or alcohol treatment requirement).

---

38   Complaint no 08 005 202 against Kent CC, 18 May 2009.
39   Complaint no 06/A/08746 against Ealing LBC, 7 May 2008.
40   Public Service Ombudsman (Wales) Complaint no B2004/0707/S/370 against Swansea City Council, 22 February 2007, para 75.
41   Complaint 15 011 661 against Hammersmith & Fulham LBC, 21 July 2016, para 22.
42   Care and Support (Direct Payments) Regulations 2014 SI No 2871 Sch 1.

People for whom a discretion exists for direct payments

10.27 The CA 2014[43] provides for regulations to restrict the right of certain adults to direct payments, such that local authorities would have a *power* rather than a *duty* to make payments to them. Although such a situation existed under the pre-CA 2014 regime,[44] the DP regulations are silent on this question. Presumably this is because the CA 2014 already provides authorities with the necessary powers, checks and safeguards – most obviously, the requirement that the authority be 'satisfied' that the making of the payment is 'an appropriate way to meet the needs in question' (sections 31(7) and 32(9)).

Consent

10.28 CA 2014 s31(1)(b) requires direct payments to be made only where the proposed recipient requests such an arrangement. This brings with it the notion of 'informed consent' and the question of sufficient mental capacity (considered below), as well as the important principle that an individual can refuse to have such a payment. The statutory guidance is clear that adults are 'free to choose how their needs are met' (whether by direct payment or otherwise) (para 12.3); they 'must not be forced to take a direct payment against their will' (para 12.5); and that they can 'decide at any time that they no longer wish to continue receiving direct payments' (para 12.69).

10.29 It appears that some councils are putting disabled and older people under considerable pressure to agree to a direct payment – either as a mechanism to avoid commissioning difficult care packages, or as a way of hitting their central government targets. Essentially service-users are told that the only way their care needs can be met is if they accept a direct payment and make the arrangement themselves. In such a situation, direct payments become disabling rather than enabling, placing a further and unwelcome burden on the service-user. Such an approach not only constitutes maladministration, but it also calls into question whether the requisite 'consent' is genuine and freely given. As the statutory guidance states, 'local authorities must not ... allow people to be placed in a situation where the direct payment is the only way to receive personalised care and support' (para 12.9).

10.30 In *P (MP) v Hackney LBC*[45] (a case under the pre-CA 2014 legal regime) Andrew Nicol QC did not find it necessary to decide whether there was a requirement for a service-user to give reasons for refusing a direct payment. However, since the legislation is clear – that payments cannot be made without a request and the CA 2014 creates a specifically enforceable

---

43 CA 2014 ss31(5)(b) and 32(6)(b).

44 Community Care, Services for Carers and Children's Services (Direct Payments) (England) Regulations 2009 SI No 1887 Sch 2 provided only a discretion to make direct payments for adults subject to specified controls under MHA 1983 – eg under section 8, as a result of a guardianship order or under 17B as a result of community treatment order – or persons on section 17 leave.

45 [2007] EWHC 1365 (Admin) para 39.

duty to provide services – it must follow that there is no need for a potential recipient of direct payments to give any reason for refusal.

Mental capacity and direct payments

10.31   The law concerning mental capacity (as it impacts on social care law) is considered in chapter 13 below.

Use of the direct payment

10.32   Whether or not a person has sufficient mental capacity to consent to a direct payment will depend in part on the use to which the direct payment is put. A person may have sufficient mental capacity to manage certain direct payments but not others. For instance, a direct payment to pay for meals might require very little capacity, whereas a direct payment used to employ a care assistant would generally require significantly more capacity – since employment responsibilities bring with them a number of significant legal responsibilities (eg PAYE, the drafting of the employment contract, the overseeing of the care assistant's training needs etc). Although such a person might have assistance in managing these arrangements, ultimately if the arrangement broke down it would be his or her name on the unfair dismissal complaint. It is difficult to see how it could be argued that a person could have capacity to enter into a contract of employment but lack capacity to be a party in any consequent employment proceedings.

10.33   In *South Lanarkshire Council v Smith and others*[46] the Scottish employment appeal tribunal heard a complaint concerning unfair dismissal by a care assistant ostensibly employed by two service-users, one of whom had significant learning disabilities. The employment arrangements were put in train by the local authority and a brokerage intermediary – but the contract of employment specified the two service-users as the employer. The care assistant named the local authority as one of her employers, and the appeal tribunal agreed. It was, however, at pains to emphasise that this was an unusual case. Lord Johnstone in his judgment noted that 'we would not for a moment seek to suggest that disabled persons cannot be an employer, particularly over someone caring for them'.

Guidance on capacity

10.34   The statutory guidance advises against the use of blanket assumptions that whole groups of people will or will not be capable of managing direct payments – that assessments 'must always be made on a case-by-case basis, in relation to the specific decision to be made' (para 12.12).

10.35   The 2009 DH guidance advised that many people with impaired mental capacity are able to receive payments, particularly if they have access to help and support'.[47] It continued:[48]

---

46   19 January 2000, unreported (transcript available).
47   2009 DH guidance, para 69.
48   2009 DH guidance, para 71.

If a council is concerned that a person who wishes to receive direct payments may not be able to manage the payments, the council should ensure that it takes into account and subsequently records all relevant factors before making a decision not to make direct payments. These decisions may need to involve professional staff who are trained to assess capability and help people make decisions, and who should consider:

- the person's understanding of direct payments, including the actions required on their part;
- whether the person understands the implications of taking or not taking on direct payments;
- what help is available to the person;
- what kind of support the person might need to achieve their identified outcomes; and
- what arrangements the person would make to obtain this support.

In this context, the 2009 DH guidance provided further helpful advice[49] on issues such as the use of a nominee to manage day-to-day finances and the development of a trust to take on employment responsibilities.

10.36   Where the adult in need has an episodic condition that could result in fluctuating levels of mental capacity, the statutory guidance advises that this should be addressed in the adult's care plan (para 12.13). The 2014 DP regulations make provision for payments to continue where an adult's loss of requisite capacity is expected to be temporary; and there is someone capable of managing the payment who is willing to do this during the interim period (reg 8).

10.37   Where a local authority proposes to make a direct payment in relation to an adult who lacks the requisite mental capacity, the DP regulations[50] require that the authority:

- undertakes a best interests determination for the purposes of MCA 2005 s4 (see para 13.31 below); and
- obtains an enhanced criminal records certificate[51] (unless the payment is to a family member or friend caring for the adult).

A direct payment can only be made to an authorised person in such situations if, having undertaken these formalities, the authority is satisfied that it is an appropriate way to meet the needs in question (CA 2014 s32(9)).

The provision of assistance in managing the direct payment

10.38   CA 2014 s31(6) specifies that direct payments can only be made to the adult or nominated person if the person is capable of managing direct payments himself or herself, or 'with whatever help the authority thinks [the person] will be able to access'.

10.39   It is not only people with limited mental capacity that are likely to benefit from assistance in the managing of a direct payment, and the statutory guidance advises that authorities should have 'signposting' arrangements directing potential direct payment recipients 'to local organisations (such as user-led organisations and micro-enterprises) and the local authority's

---

49 2009 DH guidance, para 73–77.
50 Care and Support (Direct Payments) Regulations 2014 SI 2871, reg 5(2).
51 Under Police Act 1997 s113B.

own internal support, who offer support to direct payment holders, and information on local providers' (para 12.7).

10.40   In this respect, however, the guidance is materially weaker than that provided under the pre-CA 2014 regime. Given that in making a direct payment the local authority is – in essence – transferring substantial risk to the recipient, and given that many recipients may be unfamiliar with these risks, there must be a fiduciary duty on the authority to do more than simply act as a 'signpost'. This point was acknowledged in the 2009 DH guidance,[52] which stressed the importance of councils providing support – particularly from user-led organisations/local centres for independent living since (as the guidance stated) the 'experience of existing recipients of direct payments is that they find it easier to seek advice from someone who is independent of their local council.' The 2009 DH guidance provided an illustrative list of the practical support that could be provided to direct payment recipients:[53]

- a list of local provider agencies or available personal assistants;
- support and advice in setting up and maintaining a direct payment scheme, including financial management;
- help for people to draft advertisements, job descriptions and contracts;
- help in explaining the safeguards needed in the employment of people to work with children or adults;
- rooms for interviews and assistance with interviewing;
- an address for responses to advertisements;
- support and advice about the legal responsibilities of being an employer;
- support and advice about being a good manager of staff;
- support and advice about issues of religion and ethnicity;
- information about income tax and National Insurance;
- a payroll service;
- advice on health and safety issues, including moving and handling;
- regular training, for example on assertiveness or budgeting skills;
- some emergency cover support;
- signposting to other services such as welfare benefits and advocacy; and
- advice about user-controlled trusts.

10.41   Many councils provide 'brokerage services' of this kind by funding an independent living support scheme or an independent company. By emphasising the importance of such support, the 2009 DH guidance put councils on notice that without them, direct payment recipients are likely to experience particular difficulties. Given the existence of a fiduciary duty or duty of care and the foreseeability of difficulties, it may follow that councils who fail to provide adequate support services become vulnerable to a complaint of maladministration, where, for instance, a direct payment recipient incurs liability (eg due to a payroll or unfair dismissal problem)

---

52 2009 DH guidance, paras 33–37.
53 2009 DH guidance, para 37.

which might have been avoided if general assistance of this nature had been available.

The assessed need will be met by the direct payment

10.42   The CA 2014 stipulates that authorities can only make a direct payment to the adult or nominated person if satisfied that it is 'an appropriate way to meet the needs in question' (sections 31(7) and 32(9)).

10.43   Given the importance attached to individuals having control over their care and/or support, and the assumption that they are best-placed to judge their well-being,[54] it would appear to follow that there must be a presumption (most probably a 'strong' presumption) that: (1) adults will be able to satisfy their assessed needs if they receive a direct payment; and (2) that if a local authority is of a contrary view, it will be obliged to provide cogent reasons for its opinion. The statutory guidance refers to the need for authorities to provide 'reasons' as well as advice on how to appeal a refusal decision (para 12.7).

Excluded service providers

10.44   Recipients of a direct payment are subject to few restrictions as to who they engage in delivering their services. They are, for instance, exempted from the key requirements of the Safeguarding Vulnerable Groups Act 2006, section 6(5) of which excludes from the definition of 'a regulated activity provider' private arrangements made by individuals.[55]

Care services

10.45   The DP regulations, however, restrict the ability of the recipients of direct payments to use the monies to purchase care services from their close relatives or partners (reg 3(3)). They provide that direct payments *cannot* (subject to the proviso listed below) be used to purchase services from:

1) the direct payment recipient's spouse or civil partner;
2) anyone who lives with the direct payment recipient 'as if their spouse or civil partner' (ie in a common law relationship);
3) anyone living in the same household as the direct payment recipient who is also the recipient's:
   a) parent or parent-in-law (or such person's spouse, or civil partner or common law partner);
   b) son or daughter (or such person's spouse, civil partner or common law partner);
   c) son-in-law or daughter-in-law (or such person's spouse, civil partner or common law partner);

54 CA 2014 s1(2)(d) and (3)(a), respectively – as well as the policy underpinning the 2001 reforms which was to make mandatory the previous discretionary entitlements to direct payments.

55 Regulatory power exists for the government to require local authorities to 'inform direct payment recipients of their right to receive information under the new Vetting and Barring Scheme' – Safeguarding Vulnerable Groups Act 2006 s30(8); and see also statutory guidance, para 12.50.

d) stepson or stepdaughter (or such person's spouse, civil partner or common law partner);

e) brother or sister (or such person's spouse, civil partner or common law partner);

f) aunt or uncle (or such person's spouse, civil partner or common law partner); or

g) grandparent (or such person's spouse, civil partner or common law partner).

The DP regulations provide, however, that a direct payment recipient can purchase services (or have management support) from someone on the above list if the authority 'considers it is necessary to do so' (reg 3(2)). This discretion was also found in the pre-CA 2014 regime,[56] save only that it has now been extended to cover payments in relation to management support (considered below).

10.46   It follows that there is no legal restriction on individuals using their direct payment to pay close relatives unless they live in the same household, in which case the restriction can be displaced where it is deemed necessary.

10.47   The statutory guidance provides little detail as to when it might be considered 'necessary' to use a direct payment to pay someone on the above list – in the section 'paying family members' it merely states (para 12.35):

> The direct payment is designed to be used flexibly and innovatively and there should be no unreasonable restriction placed on the use of the payment, as long as it is being used to meet eligible care and support needs.

10.48   Although the regulations create a presumption against using direct payments to pay certain family members, it would appear to be a low threshold presumption. If there is evidence that paying a family member to provide the care and support would be a better arrangement for promoting the 'well-being' of the direct payment recipient, then the onus shifts to the local authority to provide evidence to demonstrate that it is not necessary. This would presumably require it to establish that an alternative, available mechanism exists that would meet the individual's eligible need equally well. In practice it appears that some authorities have policies that only permit payments to same-household family members in 'exceptional' circumstances – and this must be incorrect.[57]

10.49   Two local government ombudsman reports provide valuable guidance on the approach that should be taken in such cases.

• A 2015 complaint[58] concerned an adult who sustained serious spinal injuries at university and requested he be allowed to employ his mother as his personal assistant using direct payments. She was a single mother who had given up work to care for him. In refusing, the council

---

56 Paying relatives is not a novel development: Elizabethan Poor Laws parish officers 'commonly' paid 'needy close relatives to care for the mentally or physically sick, disabled, and aged poor' – see P Thane, *Old age in English history*, OUP, 2000, p109.

57 'Exceptional' puts the presumptive bar significantly higher than 'necessary' – see, by analogy, *R (Ross) v West Sussex PCT* [2008] EWHC 2252 (Admin), (2008) 11 CCLR 787 and *R (M) (Claimant) v Independent Appeal Panel of Haringey* [2009] EWHC 2427 (Admin) at para 27.

58 Complaint No 14 005 078 against Cheshire East, 22 July 2015.

applied a test of 'exceptional circumstances', which the ombudsman held was incorrect– the test was (and remains) 'whether employing a family member is "necessary"'. The ombudsman held that any assessment as to whether it was 'necessary' to employ the adult's mother, had to include consideration of how his care needs would otherwise be met – and there was no evidence that the council had looked at this question.

- A 2013 complaint[59] concerned a disabled young person.[60] She was blind, deaf and required constant supervision to meet all her needs. Due to the need to keep the number of people involved in her care to a minimum – to reduce her stress – the direct payments were being used to pay her father to provide the care. The authority decided that it would no longer allow the father to be paid with the direct payments. In finding maladministration, the ombudsman noted that the authority accepted that the father was best placed to provide the care (particularly given her communication difficulties) but had given no rational reason for requiring the direct payments to be used for an alternative carer.

10.50 Relatives who are employed under a direct payment arrangement may cease to be entitled to an assessment and services under the carers' legislation,[61] since these rights only relate to carers who do not provide the care in question 'under or by virtue of a contract' (CA 2014 s10(3)). If, however, the relative provides additional (and substantial) care over and above that to which the payment relates, the entitlement to an assessment/services would remain.[62]

Family members fulfilling an administrative and management role

10.51 The DP regulations also enable authorities to pay partners or close relatives living in the same household for administrative and management support they provide if this is considered 'necessary' (reg 3(2)(b)). The statutory guidance explains that (para 12.37):

> ... the management and administration of a large payment, along with organising care and support can be a complex and time consuming task. This allows family members performing this task to be paid a proportion of the direct payment, similar to what many direct payment holders pay to third party support organisations, as long as the local authority allows this.

10.52 Although the payment is not intended to be income replacement, the guidance advises that anyone 'requesting this option should be informed of tax and employment implications, any impacts upon other benefits and given (or signposted to) information and advice to help them decide'

---

59 Complaint no 12 015 328 against Calderdale Council, 20 November 2013.
60 For which the same rule applies as for adults – Community Care, Services for Carers and Children's Services (Direct Payments) (England) Regulations 2009 SI No 1887 reg 11.
61 Carers may also cease to be entitled to social security in the form of the carers allowance.
62 See CA 2014 s10(1) and the statutory guidance at para 6.17.

(para 12.38). It also explains that the amount of the payment should be agreed with all parties and recorded in the care plan.[63]

10.53   Research evidence suggests that the additional responsibilities involved in administering direct payments cause carers high levels of stress, exacerbated by the relative lack of social services support.[64]

Excluded services

Residential care

10.54   Direct payments cannot – in general (see para 10.57 below) – be used to purchase prolonged periods of residential care. Regulation 6 of the DP Regulations caps the amount of residential accommodation that can be funded by direct payments to a maximum of four consecutive weeks in any period of 12 months – the important word being 'consecutive'. The statutory guidance gives an example to illustrate the rule (para 12.43), although it was more clearly expressed in the 2009 DH guidance (for which the same restrictions applied):

> 103. For example, someone might have one week of residential care every six weeks. Because each week in residential care is more than four weeks apart, they are not added together. The cumulative total is only one week and the four-week limit is never reached. Another person might have three weeks in residential care, two weeks at home and then another week in residential care. The two episodes of residential care are less than four weeks apart and so they are added together making four weeks in total. The person cannot use their direct payments to purchase any more residential care within a 12-month period.

10.55   A person living full-time in a residential care home is able to receive direct payments in relation to non-residential care services – for instance, to take part in day-time activities or 'to try out independent living arrangements before making a commitment to moving out of their care home'.[65] If a resident has an eligible need for non-residential activities, it would be unlawful for a council to insist on rolling this need up into the care home fee – since there is, as noted above, a right to have a direct payment to meet these needs.

10.56   In *R (M) v Suffolk CC*[66] Charles J held that the above restriction did not mean that a person in residential care could not receive direct payments. The case concerned a 17-year-old with learning disabilities at a special school. He considered that anyone in such care had three categories of expense, namely (a) education, (b) social care and practical care and (c) basic residence, and that the prohibitory regulation did not in principle preclude direct payments to cover that portion of the overall fees that related to social care and practical care (at para 23). This is a slightly

---

63   Statutory guidance, paras 12.39–12.40 which also states that the amount of the payments, their frequency and the activities that are covered should be recorded in the care and support plan.

64   J Woolham, N Steils, G Daly and K Ritters, 'The impact of personal budgets on unpaid carers of older people' in *Journal of Social Work*, 17 June 2016.

65   Statutory guidance, para 12.46.

66   [2006] EWHC 2366 (Admin).

surprising conclusion, and possibly one that should be limited to the particular facts of the case.

10.57   The Law Commission in its 2011 report on adult social care law reform recommended that direct payments should be extended to cover residential accommodation,[67] and the CA 2014 was expected to implement this proposal.[68] It is difficult to understand why this recommendation was made since the practical difficulties that such a change would cause would appear to outweigh any benefits (for the local authority and for the resident).[69] A pilot study involving a number of authorities identified the problems and relative lack of demand for such an arrangement,[70] and in January 2016 the government announced that implementation would be postponed until 2020.[71] The DP regulations (reg 6 and Sch 2), however, authorise those authorities who were piloting the programme to continue making such payments if they so choose.[72]

Local authority in-house services

10.58   Although previous legislation has not explicitly proscribed the use of direct payments to purchase local authority provided services, 2001 guidance[73] stated that they could not be so used. It explained that the restriction existed because, legally, local authorities were not permitted to sell their services. The validity of this argument was questioned,[74] and in Wales the

67 Law Commission in its report *Adult social care*, Law Com No 326 HC941, Recommendation 35.

68 Such payments are not prohibited in Wales – the Care and Support (Direct Payments) (Wales) Regulations 2015 SI No 1815 (W.260) do not prohibit such payments and see the Social Services and Well-being (Wales) Act 2014 Part 11 Code of Practice (Miscellaneous and General) p33.

69 These include the problem of establishing a person's ordinary residence where the person enters the home using direct payments; the difficulty in controlling care home fee rates in such cases (many care homes have two rates: a higher rate for self-funders who contract directly with the home and a lower rate for residents for whom the local authority contracts); and the risk that residents using their direct payment may be more vulnerable to demands by providers that they 'top-up' local authority payments.

70 L Williams and others, 'Will direct payments make adult residential care more personalized? Views and experiences of social care staff in the direct payments in residential care trailblazers' in *Social Policy & Administration* (2016) DOI: 10.1111/spol.12276.

71 In late January 2016 the government announced that it had decided to postpone the 'national rollout of direct payments in residential care' until 2020 – see Department of Health, *Direct payments in residential care*, 19 February 2016.

72 These are listed in DP regulations Sch 2 – and see also S Ettelt and others, *Direct payments in residential care trailblazer programme evaluation: preliminary report*, Policy Innovation Research Unit (PIRU), Department of Health Services Research & Policy, London School of Hygiene & Tropical Medicine, PIRU Publication 2014-7, 2014. The authorities being:Bristol City Council; Cornwall Council; Dorset County Council; Gateshead Council; Hertfordshire County Council; Hull City Council; Lincolnshire County Council; London Borough of Enfield; London Borough of Havering; London Borough of Redbridge; Manchester City Council; Milton Keynes Council; Norfolk County Council; North Lincolnshire Council; Nottinghamshire County Council; Staffordshire County Council; Stockport Council; and Surrey County Council.

73 Department of Health, LAC (2000)1 para 32.

74 See the 5th edition of this book, para 12.51, where it was suggested that Local Government Act 2000 s2 might provide such a power – notwithstanding the restrictions imposed by section 3(2) of that Act/Localism Act 2011 s3(2). The

legislation is explicit in permitting direct payments be used to purchase care and support from (among others) 'the authority which made the payment'.[75]

10.59   The joint committee that scrutinised the care and support bill recommended the lifting of the 'ban on direct payments being used to pay for local authority direct services'[76] but this was rejected by the government in its response.[77] However, in the event, the CA 2014 contains no prohibition on the use of direct payments for this purpose, and the statutory guidance explains that payments are permitted under the new regime – albeit prefacing its comments with the statement 'as a general rule, direct payments should not be used to pay for local authority-provided services from the "home" local authority' (para 12.55).

10.60   The statutory guidance gives three examples of where such an arrangement would be reasonable:

- 'where a person who is using direct payments wants to make a one-off purchase from the local authority such as a place in day care. In these cases, the local authority should take into account the wishes of the person requiring care and support when making a decision' (para 12.56);
- where a person 'decides to use a local authority run day service on an infrequent basis and requests to pay for it with his direct payment so that he retains flexibility about when he attends. The local authority service is able to agree to this request and has systems already in place to take payments as self-funders often use the service' (para 12.56); and
- where a person decides to use 'their direct payment to purchase care and support from a different local authority. For example, a person may live close to authority boundaries and another local authority could provide a particular service that their 'home' authority does not provide' (para 12.57).

The amount of the direct payment

10.61   Unlike the previous legislation,[78] the CA 2014 (and indeed the regulations) is silent as to how much a direct payment should be.

10.62   The statutory guidance explains that the calculation is done by reference to the person's personal budget and must therefore be 'an amount which is sufficient to meet the needs the local authority has a duty or power

restrictions limit the power to charge to cases where the service is not provided under a statutory duty. Although a direct payment is generally paid as a result of a statutory duty, the local authority would appear to have a discretion as to whether it sells its services to such a person.

75 Social Services and Well-being (Wales) Act 2014 s53(9).
76 Joint Committee on the Draft Care and Support Bill, *Draft Care and Support Bill*, HL Paper 143 HC 822, The Stationery Office, 2013, para 211.
77 Secretary of State for Health, *The Care Bill explained including a response to consultation and pre-legislative scrutiny on the Draft Care and Support Bill* Cm 8627, The Stationery Office, May 2013, para 88.
78 Health and Social Care Act 20101 s57(4) required that direct payments be calculated on the basis of the 'reasonable cost of securing the provision of the service concerned'.

to meet' (para 12.25).[79] The guidance stresses the need for authorities to explain clearly how the budget is calculated, and that 'the method used is robust so that people have confidence that the personal budget allocation is correct and therefore sufficient to meet their care and support needs' (para 11.4). Individuals must have this relevant information:

> ... at a stage which enables them to effectively engage in care and support planning, and that they can have confidence that the amount includes all relevant costs that will be sufficient to meet their identified needs in the way set out in the plan (para 11.24).

10.63　The intention, therefore, is that direct payments are to be calculated in the same way as before – namely to produce a sum that is the 'reasonable cost of securing the provision of the service concerned'.[80] The calculation process which produces the final sum must be transparent, and be one in which the individual has confidence: it must be rational and show how that sum has been reached, and sufficiently demonstrate that the direct payment will meet the individual's needs.[81]

10.64　As with social care provision generally, there is no limit on the maximum or minimum amount of a direct payment, either in the amount of care that can be purchased using one, or the value of the payment itself.[82] In this context, the ombudsman has been critical of authorities that seek to impose indirect limits on the amount of a direct payment: a 2015 report, for example, rejected a council's argument that the working time directive imposed a limit on the hours that could be worked by a family carer.[83]

10.65　Local authorities are permitted to make gross or net payments. As a footnote to para 12.26 of the statutory guidance explains:

> Gross payments are for the full direct payment amount, and the local authority then recovers any applicable charges from the person. A net direct payment is allocated after any appropriate charges have been subtracted, and is generally seen as the easiest and most efficient way to administer direct payments.

10.66　In some cases the calculation of the appropriate amount of a direct payment may be complex. Advice on how this should be done was given in specialist 2007 guidelines produced by the Chartered Institute of Public Finance and Accountancy (CIPFA) for local authorities;[84] and in the 2009 DH guidance, which (for example) advised as follows:

> In estimating the reasonable cost of securing the support required, councils should include associated costs that are necessarily incurred in securing

---

79　Secretary of State for Health, *The Care Bill explained including a response to consultation and pre-legislative scrutiny on the Draft Care and Support Bill* Cm 8627, The Stationery Office, May 2013, para 88.

80　Health and Social Care Act 20101 s57(4) and as the government stated '[section] 26 ... makes clear that the personal budget is the cost to the local authority of meeting the needs it is required or has decided to meet' – see Secretary of State for Health, *The Care Bill explained including a response to consultation and pre-legislative scrutiny on the Draft Care and Support Bill* Cm 8627, The Stationery Office, May 2013, para 89.

81　*R (KM) v Cambridgeshire CC* [2011] EWCA Civ 682, (2011) 14 CCLR 83 at [26].

82　See 2009 DH guidance at para 111.

83　Complaint No 14 005 078 against Cheshire East, 22 July 2015, para 94.

84　Chartered Institute of Public Finance and Accountancy (CIPFA), *Direct payments and individual budgets: managing the finances*, 2007.

provision, without which the service could not be provided or could not law-fully be provided. The particular costs involved will vary depending on the way in which the service is secured, but such costs might include recruit-ment costs, National Insurance, statutory holiday pay, sick pay, maternity pay, employers' liability insurance, public liability insurance and VAT.[85] Some councils have found it helpful to include a one-off start-up fund with-in the direct payments to meet these costs as well as other forms of support that might be required, such as brokerage, payroll services and Criminal Records Bureau checks on employees (para 11).

10.67   The Personal Social Services Research Unit (PSSRU) has expressed con-cern about the process by which direct payment rates are calculated. This normally results in the authority deducting their direct and indirect over-heads such that average direct payment rates 'are almost universally lower than the costs of contracted home care, the main service for which direct payments substitutes'. In the PSSRU's opinion, by setting rates at a level below market value for any form of care other than that of recruiting a personal assistant, the opportunities of direct payments are likely to be reduced.[86] Conversely, however, a 2006 Audit Commission study suggests that in order for direct payment schemes to be cost-neutral (ie no more expensive than the local authority providing or commissioning the serv-ice), councils should reduce the value of payments below the sum they paid for comparable levels of care.[87]

10.68   Most local authorities have standard rates for the more common ser-vices for which a direct payment is required, for instance an hourly rate for day care. Occasionally there are alternative rates, depending upon whether the service-user employs a care assistant directly or uses an agency, with the agency rate being higher. Such an arrangement would of course address some of the concerns raised by the PSSRU above. It would also enable service users to have direct payments who did not wish to employ a care assistant but preferred to purchase agency services. Provided such an arrangement was no more expensive than the cost that the authority would bear if it was responsible for the service provision arrangements, it would appear that a service user could insist on such an option.

10.69   The ombudsman has held that where an authorised person, admin-istering a direct payment on behalf of a person who lacks the requisite capacity to request a direct payment (under CA 2014 s32) does not wish to employ a personal assistant, then the direct payment should be sufficient to enable an agency to be paid to provide the necessary care.[88]

10.70   The rate proposed by the authority may be insufficient to cover the cost of the services required, for instance because no suitable care assistant or agency can be identified that is prepared to provide the service at that rate.

85   To this would be added contributions under the workplace pension scheme – see Disability Rights UK, *Individual employers and workplace pension schemes for personal assistants*, Disability Rights UK Factsheet F61, March 2016.

86   V Davey, *Direct payment rates in England*, PSSRU, 2006.

87   Audit Commission, *Choosing well: analysing the costs and benefits of choice in local public services*, 2006.

88   Complaint no 13 006 400 against Cornwall Council, 26 February 2015.

In such cases, the service user can challenge the rate through the complaints process. In this respect CIPFA 1998 guidance[89] advised:

> 87. There may be cases where an individual thinks that the total value of the direct payment should be greater than the local authority proposes, and/or that his or her contribution or the amount they are asked to pay by way of reimbursement should be less than the council proposes. Where these cases cannot be resolved through discussion, local authorities should advise the individual that he or she can pursue the matter through the authority's complaints procedure.

> 88. A local authority should give individuals as much notice as possible of the value of a direct payment, and the contribution or repayment they will be expected to make to the cost of their care package. This should be done before the payment begins, or its level is changed, to provide the opportunity for any dispute over the level to be resolved before the payment begins or the change takes effect. If that is not possible, whilst any complaint is being considered, individuals may choose either to manage on the amount of direct payments being offered or refuse to accept the direct payments. If a person does not agree to a direct payment, the authority remains responsible for providing or arranging the provision of the services they are assessed as needing.

Frequency of payments

10.71 Local authorities must agree with the service user the frequency of payments – ensuring that the service user is in a position to pay for services when payment is due. The guidance advises that it may also be necessary to 'set up procedures for making additional payments in emergencies, for example, if needs change or regular payments go astray' and should ensure that recipients clearly understand these arrangements.[90] The 2009 DH guidance advised that payments can be made such that the recipient accumulates a reserve, namely (para 123):

> The flexibility inherent in direct payments means that individuals can adjust the amount they use from week to week and 'bank' any spare money to use as and when extra needs arise (this might be particularly helpful for people with long-term and fluctuating conditions). As long as overall the payments are being used to achieve the outcomes agreed in the care plan, the actual pattern of support does not need to be predetermined.

10.72 Most direct payment recipients have traditionally had a 'float' in their bank account equivalent to about a month's payments. Collectively this represents a very considerable sum – and one which, if repaid, could significantly ease many local authority cash flow difficulties. It is for this reason (among others) that local authorities are attracted to payment card arrangements (see para 10.92 below). In general it may not be unreasonable for a local authority to have a condition allowing it to claw back payments after eight weeks if they have not been used. Such a policy must, however, admit exceptions – eg for people with fluctuating conditions that

---

89 CIPFA, *Community Care (Direct Payments) Act 1996: accounting and financial management guidelines*, 1998.
90 2009 DH guidance at para 122.

need them to accumulate more than eight weeks' payments in good times to cover more significant draw-down in times of crisis.

Direct payments and social security

10.73   The relevant social security regulations require 'any payment' made under the direct payments legislation to be disregarded for benefits purposes.[91] This does not, however, apply to carers who are paid using these payments – since the disregard does not apply to 'earnings'.[92] In such cases, a carer could, however, still benefit from the means-tested benefits earnings disregard (though modest).

The obligations upon the recipient of direct payments

10.74   The recipient of the direct payment must ensure that it is spent on services to meet the assessed need (CA 2014 s33(3)). In relation to the monitoring and auditing of the payments, the statutory guidance advises that (para 12.4):

> For direct payments to have the maximum impact, the processes involved in administering and monitoring the payment should incorporate the minimal elements to allow the local authority to fulfil its statutory responsibilities. These processes must not restrict choice or stifle innovation by requiring that the adult's needs are met by a particular provider, and must not place undue burdens on people to provide information to the local authority.

In the same vein, at para 12.24 the statutory guidance states:

> Local authorities should not design systems that place a disproportionate reporting burden upon the individual. The reporting system should not clash with the policy intention of direct payments to encourage greater autonomy, flexibility and innovation. For example, people should not be requested to duplicate information or have onerous monitoring requirements placed upon them. Monitoring should be proportionate to the needs to be met and the care package. Thus local authorities should have regard to lowering monitoring requirements for people that have been managing direct payments without issues for a long period.

10.75   Recipients are generally required to open a single bank account into which only direct payment money (and other money related to personal assistance) is paid. In certain situations it may be necessary for the account to be in a nominee's name if the service user has problems opening an account (because of, for instance, a bad credit rating) – although a local authority cannot insist on such an intermediary arrangement.[93] CIPFA guidance draws attention to the use of payment cards in such cases – which it suggests have many additional benefits.[94] A 2006 exchange of letters

91 Income Support (General) Regulations 1987 SI No 1967 Sch 9 para 58; Jobseekers Allowance Regulations 1996 SI No 207 Sch 7 para 56; Housing Benefit Regulations 2006 SI No 213 Sch 5 para 57.
92 See *Casewell v Secretary of State for Work and Pensions* [2008] EWCA Civ 524.
93 *H and L v A city council* [2011] EWCA Civ 403, (2011) 14 CCLR 381, paras 86–87.
94 CIPFA, *Self directed support: direct payments. A guide for local authority finance managers*, 2009.

between the Department of Health and the British Bankers' Association has endeavoured to clarify (and resolve) some common banking problems encountered by service users, such as difficulties in proving their identity and being unable through disability to sign cheques.[95]

10.76 Direct payment users are legally responsible for the services they purchase with the monies they receive from social services. It follows that in respect of any problem they encounter with the service they purchase, they cannot make complaint to social services, although they can seek the authority's assistance. In this context the 2009 DH guidance advised:

> 237. Councils should make people aware that they should plan for the unexpected and discuss with each person what arrangements they will make for emergencies, to ensure that the person receives the care they need when the usual arrangements break down (e.g. through the sickness of one of the person's personal assistants). The council will need to be prepared to respond in these circumstances just as it would with any other person using a service. It may decide to step in and arrange services where this is necessary to meet its responsibilities. The council could also explore other ways of providing assistance to enable the person to continue to manage their own care using direct payments, particularly if the difficulty is temporary or unforeseen.

> 238. Councils may also wish to make people aware that, in planning for the unexpected, they might consider giving someone a lasting power of attorney to manage their affairs relating to personal welfare, in the event that they lose capacity and are unable to do so themselves. This person, for example a close relative or friend already involved in the provision of their care, could then continue to manage the direct payments to purchase services on their behalf.

Reviewing direct payments

10.77 The DP regulations detail the review requirements for recipients of direct payments, specifying that the first review should take place 'at least once within the first six months of the direct payment being made and at intervals not exceeding 12 months thereafter' (reg 7).

10.78 The statutory guidance explains that such reviews are 'intended to be light-touch to ensure that the person is comfortable with using the direct payment' (para 12.62) and that ideally they should be combined with general care and support plan reviews. It advises that reviewing officers should be 'appropriately trained' to review direct payments (para 12.62). At para 12.66 it is stated:

> The outcome of the review should be written down, and a copy given to all parties. Where there are issues that require resolving, the resolution method should be agreed with all parties involved, as far as is reasonably practicable. Where appropriate, local authorities should advise people of their rights to access the local authority complaints procedure.

95 Letter, Secretary of State for Health to Ian Mullen, 26 October 2006; and letter, British Bankers' Association to the Secretary of State for Health, 10 November 2006.

Repayment and discontinuance

10.79 CA 2014 s33(5) provides authorities with the power to seek repayment of a direct payment if satisfied that it has not been used to secure the provision of the service to which it relates (or that the person has not met any condition that the council has properly imposed – under section 33(2)).

10.80 The statutory guidance advises that 'payments should only be terminated as a last resort' and that 'authorities should take all reasonable steps to address any situations without the termination of the payment' (para 12.67). Where a decision is taken to cease making payments, authorities 'must ensure there is no gap in the provision of care support' and there should be a revision of the care and support plan, or support plan, to ensure that the plan is appropriate to meet the needs in question' (para 12.68). The statutory guidance is silent on the question of when a repayment should be sought, but the 2009 DH guidance (paras 245–247) advised that:

> ... Councils should bear in mind that repayment should be aimed at recovering money that has been diverted from the purpose for which it was intended or that has simply not been spent at all, or where services have been obtained from someone who is ineligible to provide them. It should not be used to penalise honest mistakes, nor should repayment be sought where the individual has been the victim of fraud.

> Councils are able to seek repayment where a suitable person has been responsible for managing direct payments on behalf of someone lacking capacity if they are satisfied that:
> • the suitable person has not used the direct payments to secure the services for which they were intended; or
> • the suitable person has not met a condition properly imposed by the council.

> In such situations, councils should seek repayment from the suitable person, not the person lacking capacity for whose care and support the direct payments were made. Before commencing the making of direct payments to a suitable person, therefore, councils should inform the suitable person from the outset of their responsibilities for ensuring appropriate use of the money.

> A council should be satisfied, before it begins to make payments, that the potential recipient of that payment understands all of the conditions that they will be required to meet. The council should also discuss with potential recipients of direct payments the circumstances in which it might wish to consider seeking repayment. Councils may wish to take into account hardship considerations in deciding whether to seek repayments. Councils should also bear in mind that there might be legitimate reasons for unspent funds. There may be outstanding legal liabilities necessitating a direct payment recipient to build up an apparent surplus (for example to pay their employees' quarterly PAYE, or to pay outstanding bills from a care agency).

10.81 CA 2014 s33(4) requires payments to cease if any of the specified 'conditions' in sections 31 or 32, apply. The statutory guidance considers the various permutations that may occur if a person for whom a direct payment is being made ceases to have, or acquires, the requisite capacity. Accordingly:

- Where someone receiving direct payments loses the capacity to consent, the payments should cease and the authority should: (a) consider making payments to an authorised person instead; and (b) in the interim make alternative arrangements to ensure continuity of support (para 12.76).
- If the authority believes the loss of capacity is temporary, it may continue to make payments (on a 'strictly temporary and closely monitored' basis) if there is someone else who is willing to manage payments on the person's behalf (para 12.77).
- Where direct payments are being paid to an authorised person and the adult for whom the payment is made regains capacity 'on a long-term or permanent basis', the payments should not be terminated to the authorised person before beginning to make direct payments to the adult or arranging services for them (para 12.79).

10.82 Where a local authority does decide to terminate a direct payment due to 'very serious concerns' over the use of the funds, then there is no obligation that it maintain the same funding as before – provided the court is satisfied that the level of services that had been previously assessed as required had been maintained.[96]

Payments during hospital stays

10.83 The statutory guidance advises that where a direct payment recipient is admitted to hospital, there is no requirement that the direct payment be suspended, and that (para 12.52):

> ... consideration should be given to how the direct payment may be used in hospital to meet non-health needs or to ensure employment arrangements are maintained. Suspending or even terminating the payment could result in the person having to break the employment contract with a trusted personal assistant, causing distress and a lack of continuity of care when discharged from hospital.

10.84 Where it is the nominated or authorised person managing the direct payment admitted to hospital, the statutory guidance advises that the authority (para 12.54):

> ... must conduct an urgent review to ensure that the person continues to receive care and support to meet their needs. This may be through a temporary nominated/ authorised person, or through short-term authority arranged care and support.

---

96 See *TG and AH v North Somerset DC*, unreported, 1 July 2011. The payments had been made under a third party arrangement (see para 10.104 below) to the disabled person's trustees. The court accepted that there it was arguable that the revised care plan may have failed to meet all the assessed needs, but considered this failure to be 'de minimis'.

Equipment and adaptations

10.85   Direct payments can be used to purchase equipment or pay for adaptations of fixtures/fittings assessed as being required by the disabled person.[97] They cannot, however, be used to pay for services or equipment for which the authority is not responsible, for example services that the NHS provides. Although the statutory guidance is silent on this question, the 2009 DH guidance advised that direct payments were not a substitute for a disabled facilities grant (see para 14.31) for major property adaptations (para 108).

10.86   Local authorities may be reluctant to make direct payments for the purchase of equipment, even though equipment is exempt from charging (see para 8.27) because of a concern that it might thereby cease to be available for 're-use'. Many authorities recycle the majority of their equipment, recovering and redeploying it when no longer required by a particular service user. The 2009 DH guidance made clear that direct payments may not conflict with this practice, stating:

> 109. When making direct payments, councils will need to satisfy themselves that the person's eligible needs will be met by their own arrangements. In the case of direct payments for the purchase of items of equipment, councils will wish to ensure that the direct payment recipient is adequately supported by specialist expertise. This is particularly true in the case of major items, when advice may be needed to ensure that the equipment purchased is safe and appropriate.

> 110. Where a council makes a direct payment for equipment, it needs to clarify with the individual at the outset where ownership lies as well as who has responsibility for ongoing care and maintenance (just as it should where it arranges for the provision of equipment itself). A council will need to consider what conditions, if any, should be attached to the direct payment when it is used to purchase equipment, for example concerning what will happen to the equipment if it is no longer required by the individual. Equipment can also be purchased as part of making a package cost-effective, for example supplying pagers or mobile phones to personal assistants.

Contractual and employment issues

10.87   It appears that local authority direct payments budgets are largely expended on significant packages of care, involving ten or more hours of personal care each week.[98] The assumption appears to be that many, if not most, of these will involve the disabled person employing one or more care support workers.

10.88   The statutory guidance (paras 12.24–12.33 and 12.48–12.51) contains advice on various administration and employment issues, including:

---

97 One-off payments for equipment appear to be relatively common – see V Davey and others, *Direct payments: a national survey of direct payments policy and practice*, PSSRU, London School of Economics and Political Science, 2007, p52.

98 One-off payments for equipment appear to be relatively common – see V Davey and others, *Direct payments: a national survey of direct payments policy and practice*, PSSRU, London School of Economics and Political Science, 2007, chapter 5.

- The need to consider (and if relevant, to include in the direct payment or as a one-off payment) costs such as recruitment costs, employers' national insurance contributions etc (para 12.27).
- Contingency arrangements that would come into play in the event of the personal assistant being absent, for example due to sickness, maternity or holiday (para 12.28).
- Plans for redundancy payments due to circumstances such as moving home, a change in care and support needs, or the result of the death of the direct payment holder, or care recipient (para 12.29): the guidance states that 'as with other costs the personal budget must be a sufficient amount to meet the person's needs, including the provision of any redundancy costs' (para 12.32).
- Ensuring that direct payment recipients are supported and given information in regards to having the correct insurance cover in place (para 12.33).
- That where the recipient is considering becoming an employer, the authority should ensure that they are given appropriate information and advice that explains the difference between a regulated and unregulated provider to help the person make a fully informed decision on how best to meet their needs (para 12.50).
- That authorities should provide recipients, who wish to directly employ their own personal assistant with appropriate levels of ongoing support[99] (para 12.51).

10.89 The general position at law – that the funding local authority will not be responsible for the service secured by a recipient of a direct payment – also applies when the payment is used to employ a care assistant. The employee's well-being and employment rights are the responsibility of his or her employer, not the funding council. In this context, a number of commentators have suggested that such personal assistants may be at a significant disadvantage – for example, that their rates of pay are generally lower than that of other home care workers; that they lack training and external support; and in general have no pension provision or awareness of their right to sickness pay.[100] Other research has suggested that direct payment assistants are more likely to have concerns about what they consider to be aspects of 'emotional blackmail'[101] connected with their work, including a feeling that they are being required to undertake tasks they feel inappropriate.[102]

---

99 The guidance refers to the 'Skills for care information hub' with links to 'Being an employer' and 'Employing personal assistants'.

100 J Leece, 'Direct payments and the experience of personal assistants', *Community Care*, November 2008, issue 27, pp32–33; and see also J Leece, 'Paying the piper and calling the tune: power and the direct payment relationship', (2008) *British Journal of Social Work* 1–19.

101 C Ungerson, 'Whose empowerment and independence? A cross-national perspective on "cash for care" schemes' (2004) *Ageing and Society*, 24(2) pp189–212.

102 C Glendinning, S Halliwell, S Jacobs, K Rummery and J Tyrer, *Buying independence: using direct payments to integrate health and social services*, Policy Press, 2000.

Local authority imposed conditions

Permitted conditions

10.90 CA 2014 s33(2)(b) permits local authorities to impose conditions when making direct payments, and the scope of these are delineated in the DP regulations (reg 4(2)). This permits conditions that require:

a) that the needs may not be met by a particular person (see para 10.45 above); and

b) the provision of information by the adult or authorised person to the authority.

Regulation 4(3), however, stipulates that the conditions may not require that the needs of the adult to be met by any particular person; or that the authority make unreasonable requests for information[103] – which should be limited to ensuring that the payments are being used in an appropriate way and incompliance with the relevant conditions.

10.91 From the direct payment recipient's perspective, however, there is sometimes a perception that the local authority is seeking to impose inappropriate conditions on the way the recipient discharges his or her role as employer. *H and L v A City Council*[104] concerned a council's attempt to impose a condition that the payment went into a managed account over which the local authority retained control, rather than directly to the disabled person. In finding such an arrangement to be unlawful, Munby LJ held that the legal right to impose a condition could not be used 'to destroy the very essence of the right'. In so doing, he cited with approval the 2009 DH guidance (para 92) that:

> Councils may set reasonable conditions on the direct payments, but need to bear in mind when doing so that the aim of direct payments is to give people more choice and control over their support and how it is delivered. For example, individual choice and control would not be delivered were a condition to be set that someone who receives direct payments might only use certain providers. Conditions should be proportionate and no more extensive, in terms or number, than is reasonably necessary. Councils should also avoid setting up disproportionately intensive monitoring procedures. Financial payments should not begin until the recipient has agreed to any conditions that the council considers are necessary in connection with the direct payments. In order to avoid delays for people requiring support, councils should take all reasonable steps to resolve issues about conditions in a timely manner.

Pre-payment cards

10.92 As noted above, *H and L v A City Council*[105] concerned the validity of conditions on the use of direct payments under the previous, but similar, legal regime, and the court held that the relevant regulations did not permit the local authority to insist on a managed account.

---

103 For example, asking for it in a format that is not reasonably practicable for the adult or authorised person to provide.

104 [2011] EWCA Civ 403, (2011) 14 CCLR 381, paras 86–87.

105 [2011] EWCA Civ 403.

10.93   It appears, however, that a number of authorities are insisting that all CA 2014 direct payments be paid by way of a pre-paid or pre-payment card. Such schemes hold out considerable advantages for local authorities – particularly in terms of cash flow, since they obviate the need for each adult to have a 'cash float' in his or her account. They also simplify the monitoring of individual accounts. Although such arrangements are permitted, the statutory guidance is at pains to stress that they 'should not be provided as the only option to take a direct payment' and that 'the offer of a 'traditional' direct payment paid into a bank account should always be available if this is what the person requests and this is appropriate to meet needs' (para 12.58). The guidance continues (para 12.59):

> It is also important that where a pre-paid card system is used, the person is still free to exercise choice and control. For example, there should not be blanket restrictions on cash withdrawals from pre-paid cards which could limit choice and control. The card must not be linked solely to an online market-place that only contains selected providers in which to choose from. Local authorities should therefore give consideration to how they develop card systems that encourage flexibility and innovation, and consider consulting care and support user groups on any proposed changes to direct payment processes.

Manual handling

10.94   An area where some local authorities have sought to impose significant conditions concerns the way that the disabled person's manual handling needs should be undertaken. In relation to this matter the 2009 DH guidance gave the following advice:

> **Health and Safety**
>
> 132. ... As a general principle, councils should avoid laying down health and safety policies for individual direct payment recipients. Individuals should accept that they have a responsibility for their own health and safety, including the assessment and management of risk. They should be encouraged to develop strategies on lifting and handling and other tasks, both in the home and outside it where lifting equipment, for example, may not be available.
>
> 133. ... councils will wish to take appropriate steps to satisfy themselves that recipients and potential recipients are aware of the health and safety issues that affect them as individuals, anyone they employ, and anyone else affected by the manner in which their support is delivered.
>
> 134. ... councils should give the recipients and potential recipients the results of any risk assessments that were carried out as part of the initial assessment or support plan. This allows the individual to share the assessment with the care agency or the employee who provides the service. They can therefore take reasonable steps to minimise the risks to the health and safety of any staff they employ. (The recipient or potential recipient has a common law duty of care towards the person they employ.)

10.95   The 2009 DH guidance sought to tread the delicate line between ensuring that recipients of a direct payment were made aware of their legal responsibilities as an employer and yet not letting this information dampen their enthusiasm for taking on such a role – advising that this information should not be given 'in such a way as to put off the recipient, for example by overstressing the extent and complexity of these responsibilities, but neither should the council fail to make recipients aware of what is involved' (para 140). The 2009 DH guidance further advised:

> 138. Individuals should be made aware of their legal responsibilities in terms of providing written details of the main terms of the employment contract within two months of commencement of the employment. The essential terms that must be provided include, for example:
> - the date on which employment commenced;
> - hours of work;
> - particulars of remuneration (which must meet the national minimum wage);
> - place of work;
> - job title;
> - whether the job is fixed-term or permanent;
> - statutory entitlement to sick pay and annual leave;
> - pension scheme provision (where appropriate); and
> - notice requirements.
>
> Any changes to the terms must also be notified in the same way.
>
> 139. If support services are provided, councils may wish to include a payroll service, which will take responsibility for administering wages, tax and National Insurance for the direct payment recipient. A written contract between the employer and the employee will help ensure that the parties have the same understanding about the terms of employment and statutory disciplinary and grievance procedures.

Transition into adulthood

10.96   Direct payments can be paid to the parents of a disabled child until the young person becomes 18. At that age, the payment must either pass to the young adult or cease or be paid to an authorised person. Children Act 1989 s17A(2) provides, however, for direct payments to be paid to disabled young people at the age of 16. Chapter 16 of the statutory guidance gives advice on the transition process, and the relevant law and policy is considered in the Legal Action Group volume *Disabled children: a legal handbook*.[106]

NHS and direct payments

10.97   In *R (Harrison) v Secretary of State for Health*,[107] relying heavily on statutory construction, the High Court held that there was no power in the NHS Acts 2006 (as originally enacted) to make direct payments to patients (notwithstanding that there was nothing in the Acts to say they could not be made).[108]

---

106 S Broach, L Clements and J Read, 2nd edition, 2016.
107 [2009] EWHC 574 (Admin), (2009) 12 CCLR 335.
108 An appeal in this case became academic and was withdrawn when the day before it was listed for hearing the Health Act (Commencement No 1) Order 2010 brought the material provisions of the Health Act 2009 into force. At the same time separate proceedings (*R (Garnham) v Secretary of State for Health and Islington PCT* (No C1/2009/0802) concerning the powers of health bodies to make indirect payments by transferring funds to social services via NHSA 2006 s256 (NHSWA 2006 s194 (see para 11.130 below)) were adjourned. For analysis of this complex question, see

10.98   The absence of such a power caused problems for a number of service users, and mechanisms for overcoming them include the use of Independent User Trusts (IUTs) and the use of the powers in the NHS Acts 2006 which enable health bodies to make funding transfers to local authorities.[109] The enactment of the Health Act 2009 has, however, largely addressed these historic problems by providing clinical commissioning group (CCGs) with the power/duty to make such payments.

NHS Act 2006 s12A direct payments

10.99   NHS Act 2006 s12A[110] enables health bodies in England to provide personal budgets and pay direct payments to patients along similar lines to those paid by social services. Initially, health bodies had a *power* to make such provision, but since October 2014 this has become a *duty*[111] in relation to adults or children eligible for NHS continuing healthcare.[112] The budget can take the form of a direct payment or a CCG/broker-managed personal budget – in much the same way (and subject to very similar rules) as for a social services personal budget. Detailed (2014) guidance concerning the scheme has been published by NHS England (the '2014 NHS guidance').[113]

10.100   The guidance noted that the government was committed to ensuring that 'from 2015 personal health budgets, including direct payments for healthcare, should be an option for people who could benefit from one'[114] – ie including 'people who use NHS services outside of NHS Continuing Healthcare'.[115] Certain forms of 'healthcare' are excluded from this entitlement – including services provided by GPs, screening, surgical procedures as well as urgent or emergency treatment services.[116]

10.101   NHS England has developed a toolkit to assist CCGs in developing procedures to ensure that such budgets are available in their areas.[117] The adoption of the right to a personal health budget follows a series of pilot programmes – which found that the cost-savings to the NHS arose in general from 'high-value personal budgets' (ie over £1,000).

10.102   Where an adult is eligible for a joint package of NHS/CA 2014 funded care (see para 12.206 below) then the statutory guidance advises that 'the local authority and the NHS should consider agreeing that the direct

L Clements and P Bowen 'NHS continuing care and independent living' (2007) 10 CCLR 343 at 350.

109   See paras 10.108 and 11.130 respectively.

110   Inserted by Health Act 2009 s11.

111   National Health Service Commissioning Board and Clinical Commissioning Groups (Responsibilities and Standing Rules) Regulations 2012 SI No 2996 (as amended) reg 32B.

112   National Health Service Commissioning Board and Clinical Commissioning Groups (Responsibilities and Standing Rules) Regulations 2012 SI No 2996 reg 32A(1).

113   NHS England, *Guidance on direct payments for healthcare: understanding the regulations*, 2014.

114   Department of Health, *NHS mandate*, 2012.

115   2014 NHS guidance, para 19.

116   2014 NHS guidance, para 3.2.

117   NHS England, *Personal health budgets toolkit*, 2012.

payments be combined and that the monitoring is performed solely by one organisation, reporting to the other as appropriate' (para 12.34).

Direct payments and Mental Health Act 1983 s117

10.103   Mental Health Act (MHA) 1983 s117(2C) stipulates that the DP regulations[118] apply with necessary modifications to people eligible for section 117 support (discussed generally at para 15.56 below). In relation to direct payments under the CA 2014, these modifications are detailed in the DP regulations. Regulation 11 stipulates (in effect) that scheme applies to support under section 117 as it does to support under the CA 2014, and accordingly when considering the legal position under section 117, in the regulations the phrase 'after-care services to the adult to discharge the duty under section 117' should be substituted for the phrase 'the care needs of the adult'.

Independent user trusts and third party payments

Social services IUTs

10.104   Prior to the implementation of the direct payments reforms (via the CC(DP)A 1996) social services departments were (with few exceptions) subject to a specific prohibition against making payments of cash to disabled people, in lieu of services.[119] They were, however, permitted by NAA 1948 s30 to pay third parties (such as independent home care service providers) that had undertaken to deliver the assessed services. A number of authorities accordingly developed 'third party' schemes whereby they made payments to an intermediary (typically a trust fund or brokerage scheme) which then worked closely with the disabled person in the purchasing of his or her care. Such schemes gave the disabled person effective control over the purchasing of care services, and also provided assistance with the administrative obligations inherent in any employment situation (recruitment and appointment of carers, employment contracts, grievance procedures, PAYE, etc).

10.105   Although the CA 2014 has materially relaxed the restrictions on direct payments, there remain a few instances whereby third party schemes may still be of value. A failure to consider the use of an IUT may in certain situations constitute maladministration.[120]

10.106   With the passing of the CC(DP)A 1996, questions were raised as to whether third party schemes continued to be lawful (despite government assurances[121]). This question was settled in *R (A and B) v East Sussex CC*

---

118 As well as the direct payment regulations under NHSA 2006 s12A(4).

119 See eg NAA 1948 s29(6)(a), NHSA 2006 Sch 20 para 2(2)(a) and NHS(W)A 2006 Sch 15 para 2(2)(a).

120 Report by the Public Services Ombudsman for Wales on an Investigation into a Complaint no 200801373 against Powys County Council, 7 July 2010.

121 Asked to confirm that the 'new possibilities created by the' CC(D)PA 1996 would not affect the status of existing third party schemes, the minister, John Bowis, stated that 'schemes that are in place now should not be affected. We are not seeking to undermine such schemes': HC Debates, col 380, 6 March 1996.

(No 1)[122] where the High Court concluded that such trusts were compatible with the legal requirements of NAA 1948 s29. Had this not been the case, he expressed himself satisfied that the scheme would have been lawful in any event by virtue of both Local Government Act 1972 s111 and Local Government Act 2000 s2.

10.107   The Care Quality Commission (CQC) has advised that in general trusts of this nature – if set up solely for the support of a specified disabled user (or siblings) – will not require to be registered as a domiciliary care agency.[123]

NHS IUTs

10.108   As noted below (para 12.214) in *Gunter v SW Staffordshire PCT*[124] Collins J held that there was nothing in principle in the NHS Acts 2006 to preclude a health body from making direct payments to an IUT which would then arrange for the healthcare needs of the profoundly disabled 21-year-old applicant, stating:

> 26. It seems to me that Parliament has deliberately given very wide powers to Primary Care Trusts to enable them to do what in any given circumstances seem to them to achieve the necessary provision of services. I have no doubt that this could involve the use of a voluntary organisation such as an IUT as the supplier. There seems to me to be no difference in principle between an IUT set up specially for a small number of persons or an individual and a nursing or other agency so far as the defendants are concerned. It would obviously be necessary for a member of the defendants to be a trustee so as to ensure that money was properly and prudently spent.

10.109   It is arguable that Collins J's comments concerning the governance arrangements are an 'aside' in the sense that these were not central to the proceedings and not (it appears) the subject of specific argument. With respect, while the trustees in such a scheme would need to ensure financial accountability, proper co-ordination and sound clinical governance, there would appear to be no overarching legal imperative that (for example) a health body member would need to be a trustee in every such scheme.

Taxation and IUTs

10.110   Trust and taxation law is a complex area, and outside the scope of this text. Many trusts are subject to taxation disadvantages compared to most individuals – for example, the trust rates of income tax can be equivalent to the highest rates of income tax paid by individuals; trusts may not benefit from the annual personal allowance enjoyed by most individuals, etc. When considering the development of a trust, expert advice should be sought, especially where a trust might hold any significant assets and/or receive non-direct payment income. The pitfalls of not taking such advice were highlighted in *Pitt v Holt*[125] where a discretionary trust had been

---

122 [2002] EWHC 2771 (Admin), (2003) 6 CCLR 177.
123 See CQC guidance on 'Direct payment support schemes' (2011).
124 [2005] EWHC 1894 (Admin), (2006) 9 CCLR 12.
125 [2011] EWCA Civ 197.

created which gave rise to a very large unanticipated and largely avoidable tax liability. As the Court of Appeal noted, it 'would have been easy to create the settlement in a way which did not have these tax consequences'.

10.111   Subject to the above caveat, what follows should be taken as a general guide designed to identify some of the key issues – but in every case, independent advice should be obtained, not least because this is an area of law that is particularly subject to change.

10.112   In some cases IUTs may be able to avoid some of the adverse aspects of the trust taxation regime since direct payment income from a local authority or the NHS should not normally be deemed taxable income, so the only taxable income of the trust normally will be on any interest earned on sums deposited in the trust's bank or building society account. Likewise, capital gains tax may not be a problem if the trust is not acquiring and disposing of chargeable assets.

10.113   It appears that IUTs may also be able to benefit from specific rules on trusts created to safeguard certain 'vulnerable persons', including 'disabled persons'.[126] Guidance on these trusts can be obtained from the HM Revenue and Customs (HMRC) website.[127] To take advantage of these rules, the trust must be a qualifying one and the trustees will need to make a vulnerable person election. Under the rules, the income tax liability of the trustees can be reduced to the same amount that would have been paid by the beneficiary had the income been earned by the beneficiary rather than by the trust. In other words the beneficiary's own annual allowance can be used (to the extent that it is not used on other income that the beneficiary receives) and the beneficiary's own income tax rates can apply. For capital gains tax purposes, if the trustees do actually dispose of a chargeable asset, the beneficiary's annual exemption can be used instead of the smaller trustees' annual exemption.

10.114   A vulnerable person election does not have the same impact for inheritance tax purposes, although it appears likely that the beneficiary of the trust will be regarded as having a right to the income of the trust (and thus, for inheritance tax purposes, an 'interest in possession'). This would mean that if the beneficiary died whilst the trust was still in existence, the value of the trust property might be aggregated with the value of his or her estate when calculating whether inheritance tax is payable.

---

126 Finance Act 2005 Part 2 chapter 4 s38.
127 HMRC, *Trusts and taxes* at www.hmrc.gov.uk/trusts/types/vulnerable.htm.

NHS general responsibilities for services

continued

11.124   Budget sharing arrangements

Section 75 partnerships arrangements • Better Care Fund arrangements • Dowry payments and post dowry arrangements • Section 64 agreements

Introduction

11.1   At no time since the formation of the National Health Service (NHS) in 1948 has there been a clear separation between its responsibilities for healthcare and those of the local authorities for social care services. As we note at para 1.10 above, the creation of the NHS did not initially wrest responsibility for health services from local authorities, and the present division of responsibilities between social services and the NHS has developed largely as a consequence of subsequent legislation.

11.2   Until 1990, successive governments sought, by simultaneous amendment[1] of the community care and NHS legislation, to transfer most health functions from local authorities to specific NHS bodies. During this period, however, perceptions as to what was a 'health function' changed. In consequence, the NHS tended to concentrate on the provision of acute healthcare and sought to shed its responsibilities for the long-term healthcare needs of individuals.

11.3   During the 1980s, responsibility for people who would formerly have been resident in a long stay mental hospital or geriatric ward was in large measure transferred to the social security budget, leading to a substantial increase in the number of private residential and nursing homes. Accordingly, the legislative changes of the last 30 years have been dominated by the tripartite tension between the NHS, DHSS and local authorities. The National Health Service and Community Care Act (NHSCCA) 1990 radically altered the respective responsibilities of the Department of Health and Social Security (as the Department for Work and Pensions was then called) and local authorities, but left virtually unchanged the interface between the NHS and local authorities. In contrast, however, the most recent reforms of the NHS have sought to redraw the relationship between the NHS and local authorities.

11.4   This chapter concentrates on the non-acute services for which the NHS is responsible: it does not cover the NHS responsibilities for hospital provision for acute care, nor the ever-changing structure of the NHS, which is outlined briefly at para 1.10 above.

11.5   This chapter first considers the legislation, and then the general services which the NHS provides in the community and to care homes; it then covers the specific duties on health bodies to meet the registered nursing needs of nursing home residents. Chapter 12 then turns to the vexed question of when the NHS is responsible for the full cost of a patient's health and social care needs under what is termed NHS 'continuing healthcare' funding – it is the chapter that takes us to the heart of the health and social care divide.

---

1   The National Health Service Act (NHSA) 1946 and the National Assistance Act (NAA) 1948 came into force on the same day; as did the Health Services and Public Health Act 1968 and the Local Authority Social Services Act (LASSA) 1970; as did the Local Government Act 1972 and the NHS Reorganisation Act 1973.

The National Health Service Acts 2006

Background

11.6 The NHS in England and Wales was created by the enactment of the National Health Service Act (NHSA) 1946, which came into effect on 5 July 1948. The NHSA 1946 was replaced by the NHSA 1977, which consolidated the changes that had occurred in the intervening years. In 2006 a further codification occurred with the repeal of the NHSA 1977 and its replacement by two principal Acts: the NHSA 2006 and the NHS (Wales) Act (NHS(W)A) 2006. A third Act, the NHS (Consequential Provisions) Act (NHS(CP)A) 2006, addressed technical drafting requirements that attended the codification.

11.7 The decision to have two principal Acts is an expression of the extent to which devolution has created a distinct legal regime for the health service in Wales. However, it is a mistake to consider the NHSA 2006 as an English statute. Although it was possible in most places to 'split' the provisions of the NSHA 1977 into two separate statutes, in drafting terms this was not feasible in relation to certain cross-cutting obligations. Accordingly, by default these common provisions appear in the NHSA 2006 together with the 1977 provisions which were not devolved to the Welsh Government.[2] By way of example, the duty on NHS bodies to co-operate with local authorities (being a duty that could require co-operation between an English local authority and a Welsh NHS body) is not found in the NHS(W)A 2006. Instead it is found in NHSA 2006 s82 which, when read with NHS(W)A 2006 ss28(6) and 275(1), makes it clear that the duty encompasses local health boards (LHBs) and Welsh NHS trusts.

The core health service obligation

11.8 The general NHS duty is to be found in NHSA 2006 s1, which provides:

(1) The secretary of state must continue the promotion in England of a comprehensive health service designed to secure improvement–
   (a) in the physical and mental health of the people of England, and
   (b) in the prevention, diagnosis and treatment of illness.[3]
(2) For that purpose, the Secretary of State must exercise the functions conferred by this Act so as to secure that services are provided in accordance with this Act.
(3) The Secretary of State retains ministerial responsibility to Parliament for the provision of the health service in England.
(4) The services provided as part of the health service in England must be free of charge except in so far as the making and recovery of charges is expressly provided for by or under any enactment, whenever passed.

The duty on the secretary of state is not only to promote a 'comprehensive' health service, but to do so in a way that secures (NHSA 2006 s1A):

---

2 Government of Wales Act 1998 and the National Assembly for Wales (Transfer of Functions) Order 1999 SI No 672.
3 NHSA 2006 s275(1) defines 'illness' as including 'any mental disorder of the mind and any injury or disability requiring medical or dental treatment or nursing'.

... continuous improvement in the quality of services provided to individuals for or in connection with–
(a) the prevention, diagnosis or treatment of illness, or
(b) the protection or improvement of public health.

11.9   The distinction in section 1A between general 'illness' related services and 'public health' is entrenched in section 2B, which places responsibility for public health services on social services authorities. In the context of social care, the public health services of most relevance relate to people affected by substance misuse – these are considered separately at para 15.88 below.

11.10   NHSA 2006 s1H[4] makes the NHS 'Commissioning Board' (now known as 'NHS England') responsible (concurrently with the secretary of state) for discharging the Act's 'prevention, diagnosis or treatment of illness' responsibilities. The secretary of state retains the power to issue a direction to NHS England where a significant failure in the discharge of its functions occurs.[5]

11.11   The hiving off of public health functions to local authorities (by the Health and Social Care Act (HSCA) 2012) did not mean that the NHS was unable to provide prevention services – such as treatments for HIV on a preventative basis (ie prescribing an anti-retroviral drug for those at high risk of contracting HIV). In *R (National Aids Trust) v NHS Commissioning Board and others*[6] it was held that although NHSA 2006 s1H(2) limits NHS England's responsibility for 'public health functions', this does not mean that it is unable to commission preventative health services (such as anti-retroviral drug treatment for use those at high risk of contracting HIV). The court considered that NHS England has such preventative functions.[7]

Clinical commissioning groups

11.12   At the local level, NHSA 2006 s1I[8] devolves the discharge of the 'prevention, diagnosis or treatment of illness' responsibilities to clinical commissioning groups (CCGs) – of which there were (in January 2017) 209. CCGs are overseen by NHS England, which has the power to issue directions to a CCG if satisfied that there is a failure (or risk of failure) in the discharge any of its functions.[9]

11.13   CCGs (which replaced primary care trusts (PCTs) on 1 April 2013) are independent bodies responsible for the planning and commissioning of healthcare services for their local area. Their membership comprises the local general practitioner (GP) practices, and they have an elected governing body which is made up of GPs, clinicians and lay members. CCGs

---

4   Inserted by Health and Social Care Act (HSCA) 2012 s9.
5   NHSA 2006 s13Z2.
6   [2016] EWCA Civ 1100.
7   In particular NHSA 2006 s13E; National Health Service Commissioning Board and Clinical Commissioning Groups (Responsibilities and Standing Rules) Regulations 2012 SI No 2996 Sch 4; and in relation to anti-retroviral drugs para 17 in particular.
8   Inserted by the HSCA 2012 s10.
9   NHSA 2006 s14Z21.

often chose to receive financial and contracting support from commissioning support units (CSUs) on questions such as finance, human resources, data management or contracting.

11.14   Health and well-being boards (HWBs) are seen as one of the key mechanisms for promoting joint-working between CCGs and local authorities (particularly in relation to the public health responsibilities assumed by local authorities; see para 15.96 below). HWBs derive from HSCA 2012 s194. They have limited powers and are constituted as a local authority committee. Their role is to promote greater integration and partnership between local CCGs, public health and local government. Together with local CCGs, HWBs have a statutory duty[10] to produce a joint strategic needs assessment and a joint health and well-being strategy for their local population. Together with local Healthwatch[11] groups, the theory is that they address the local democratic deficit within the NHS.

11.15   Although NHSA 2006 s1(3) makes clear that the secretary of state retains ministerial responsibility for the provision of the health service, section 3(1) sets out those general services which a CCG must ensure are provided 'to such extent as it considers necessary to meet the reasonable requirements of the persons for whom it has responsibility'. The list comprises:

(a) hospital accommodation,

(b) other accommodation for the purpose of any service provided under this Act,

(c) medical, dental, ophthalmic, nursing and ambulance services,

(d) such other services or facilities for the care of pregnant women, women who are breastfeeding and young children as the group considers are appropriate as part of the health service,

(e) such other services or facilities for the prevention of illness, the care of persons suffering from illness and the after-care of persons who have suffered from illness as the group considers are appropriate as part of the health service,

(f) such other services or facilities as are required for the diagnosis and treatment of illness.

11.16   The courts have been reluctant to interfere with the decisions of local NHS bodies (including CCGs) concerning the discharge of their obligations under NHSA 2006 s3 unless they are 'uninformed', 'made in blind faith'[12] or in breach a fundamental human right.[13] However, in *R (Keating) v Cardiff Local Health Board*[14] the Court of Appeal held that the word 'facilities' in section 3(1)(e) included not only the accommodation, plant and other means by which health services were provided, but also the personnel who actually provided the services. Accordingly, the NHS body had acted unlawfully (by misconstruing the law) concerning its power to fund

10   Local Government and Public Involvement in Health Act 2007 s116A.

11   Health and Social Care Act (HSCA) 2008 Sch 1 para 6(1A).

12   *R (JF) v NHS Sheffield CCG* [2014] EWHC 1345 (Admin) para 52; and see also *R (Whapples) v Birmingham CrossCity CCG* [2014] EWHC 2647 (Admin), (2014) 17 CCLR 308.

13   *Rabone v Pennine Care NHS Foundation Trust* [2012] UKSC 2, (2012) 15 CCLR 13.

14   [2005] EWCA Civ 847, [2006] 1 WLR 159, (2005) 8 CCLR 504.

a project providing a service of advice and assistance in relation to access to state benefits for those with mental health problems.

NHS trusts

11.17   The responsibility for the actual provision of services under the NHS Acts 2006 is, in general terms, delegated to NHS trusts. Trusts are semi-autonomous bodies set up to assume responsibility for the ownership and management of hospitals or other establishments or facilities. NHS trusts do not receive funding in the way that CCGs do, but rather through obtaining contracts for their services from CCGs.[15]

11.18   NHSA 2006 s8 empowers the secretary of state to issue directions to NHS trusts. There is no provision in the NHSA 2006 concerning the power to issue general guidance akin to that in Care Act 2014 s78, although NHSA 2006 s13R(4) requires NHS England to issue guidance 'as it considers appropriate' and to which CCGs must 'have regard' (NHS 2006 s13R(6)).[16]

The duty to promote a 'comprehensive' health service

11.19   In contrast to the detailed legislative duties laid upon social services authorities, the NHS's statutory duties under NHSA 2006 ss1 and 3 are general and indeterminate: 'target duties' in the language of public law (see para 1.16 above). Accordingly, the courts have been reluctant to disturb NHS administrative decisions where these general public law duties are involved. In *R v Cambridge Health Authority ex p B*[17] the decision in question concerned 'the life of a young patient'. At first instance Laws J criticised the authority's justification for its decision not to fund any further chemotherapy treatment for the child as consisting 'only of grave and well-rounded generalities', stating that:

> ... where the question is whether the life of a 10-year-old child might be saved, however slim a chance, the responsible authority ... must do more than toll the bell of tight resources ... they must explain the priorities that have led them to decline to fund the treatment.

The Court of Appeal felt unable to sustain this line, holding instead:

> Difficult and agonising judgements have to be made as to how a limited budget is best allocated to the maximum advantage of the maximum number of patients. That is not a judgement which the court can make ... It is not something that a health authority ... can be fairly criticised for not advancing before the court ...

> It would be totally unrealistic to require the authority to come to court with its accounts and seek to demonstrate that if this treatment were provided for B then there would be a patient, C, who would have to go without

---

15 NHS contracts are dealt with in NHSA 2006 s9. Such contracts are not legally enforceable but are subject to arbitration by the secretary of state.

16 In practice, courts have given considerable weight to guidance issued by the Secretary of State and NHS England – see, for example, *R (Whapples) v Birmingham CrossCity CCG* [2014] EWHC 2647 (Admin), (2014) 17 CCLR 308.

17 [1995] 1 WLR 898, CA.

treatment. No major authority could run its financial affairs in a way which would permit such a demonstration.

11.20   The *ex p B* decision should not be seen as an abrogation by the court of its duty to scrutinise 'anxiously' questions which engage fundamental human rights (see para 2.64 above). In the case, the court heard evidence of the lengths to which the health authority had gone to weigh up the likelihood of the treatment being successful, the adverse effects of the treatment and had consulted with the family. The court accepted that it was a bona fide decision taken on an individual basis and supported by respected professional opinion. In such cases, where the key consideration is expertise that the court does not possess, even with the enactment of the Human Rights Act (HRA) 1998,[18] the court will inevitably hesitate to substitute its opinions. The situation will, however, be otherwise where the issue concerns questions of law or logic, or where an NHS body is seeking to provide a service that does not properly meet the person's needs – or subjects the person to inappropriate institutionalisation.[19]

11.21   Health bodies must, therefore, comply with the law, respect fundamental human rights and ensure that their decisions are reached in accordance with established public law principles. They must not, for instance: ignore circular guidance;[20] violate European Union law;[21] operate an irrational[22] or a perverse policy;[23] fetter their discretion to fund the treatment;[24] fail to consult before reaching certain decisions; or refuse funding due to the patient's financial circumstances.[25]

11.22   NHSA 2006 ss1 and 3, the 'core NHS provisions', were subjected to considerable scrutiny by the Court of Appeal in *R v North and East Devon Health Authority ex p Coughlan*.[26] There the court noted (at para 22) that:

> Section 1(1) does not place a duty on the secretary of state to provide a comprehensive health service. His duty is 'to continue to promote' such a service. In addition the services which he is required to provide have to be provided 'in accordance with this Act.'[27]

and (at para 23):

18   In *R (Watts) v Bedford PCT* [2003] EWHC 2228 (Admin), (2003) 6 CCLR 566 Munby J reviewed the domestic and Strasbourg jurisprudence concerning the public law obligations to provide healthcare services. He concluded that notwithstanding the enactment of the Human Rights Act 1998, section 1 remained a 'target' duty (see para 1.16 above); see also *R (Watts) v Bedford PCT* [2004] EWCA Civ 166, (2004) 77 BMLR 26.

19   See eg *Gunter v South Western Staffordshire PCT* [2005] EWHC 1894 (Admin), (2006) 9 CCLR 121 at [19]–[20].

20   *R v North Derbyshire Health Authority ex p Fisher* (1997–98) 1 CCLR 150, QBD.

21   *R (Watts) v Bedford PCT* [2004] EWCA Civ 166, (2004) 77 BMLR 26.

22   *R (Rogers) v Swindon NHS PCT* [2006] EWCA Civ 392, [2006] 1 WLR 2649, (2006) 9 CCLR 451 – but see also *R (Condliff) v North Staffordshire PCT* [2011] EWCA Civ 910.

23   *R (Ross) v West Sussex Primary Care Trust* [2008] EWHC 2252 (Admin), (2008) 11 CCLR 787.

24   *R v North West Lancashire Health Authority ex p A* [2000] 1 WLR 977, (1999) 2 CCLR 419, CA.

25   *R (Booker) v NHS Oldham and Directline Insurance plc* [2010] EWHC 2593 (Admin), (2011) 14 CCLR 315.

26   [2000] 2 WLR 622, (1999) 2 CCLR 285, CA. The case concerned the NHSA 1977 but the context of sections 1 and 3 in that Act and in the NHS 2006 Acts is identical.

27   (1999) 2 CCLR 285, CA at para 22.

... the secretary of state's section 3 duty is subject to two different qualifica-tions. First of all there is the initial qualification that his obligation is lim-ited to providing the services identified to the extent that he considers that they are *necessary* to meet *all reasonable requirements* ...[28]

and:

24. The first qualification placed on the duty contained in section 3 makes it clear that there is scope for the secretary of state to exercise a degree of judgment as to the circumstances in which he will provide the services, including nursing services referred to in the section. He does not automatic-ally have to meet *all* nursing requirements ...

25. When exercising his judgment he has to bear in mind the comprehen-sive service which he is under a duty to promote as set out in section 1. However, as long as he pays due regard to that duty, the fact that the service will not be comprehensive does not mean that he is necessarily contraven-ing either section 1 or section 3. The truth is that, while he has the duty to continue to promote a comprehensive free health service and he must never, in making a decision under section 3, disregard that duty, a compre-hensive health service may never, for human, financial and other resource reasons, be achievable ...

26. In exercising his judgment the secretary of state is entitled to take into account the resources available to him and the demands on those resources. In *R v Secretary of State for Social Services and Others ex p Hincks* [1980] 1 BMLR 93 the Court of Appeal held that section 3(1) of the Health Act does not impose an absolute duty to provide the specified services. The secretary of state is entitled to have regard to the resources made available to him under current government economic policy.

11.23   Where a health body decides to fund a care package in such a way that it has an adverse impact on a right under the European Convention on Human Rights (ECHR), that decision will not be immune from court or ombudsman scrutiny. In *Gunter v South Western Staffordshire PCT*[29] the applicant wished to remain in her own home rather than be placed in an institutional setting by the health body (which accepted continuing care responsibility for her). Collins J considered this to be a 'very import-ant' consideration which had to 'be given due weight in deciding on her future' since to remove her from her home would 'interfere with her right to respect for her family life'.

11.24   In respect of the health body's argument that it would be less expensive to provide the care in an institutional setting, the judge observed:

I do not regard evidence of what benefits could accrue from the expenditure of sums which could be saved in providing a less costly package for Rachel as helpful. It is obvious that Health Authorities never have enough money to provide the level of services which would be ideal, but that cannot mean that someone such as Rachel should receive care which does not properly meet her needs.

In his opinion:

The interference with family life is obvious and so must be justified as pro-portionate. Cost is a factor which can properly be taken into account. But the evidence of the improvement in Rachel's condition, the obvious quality

---

28 (1999) 2 CCLR 285, CA at para 23.
29 [2005] EWHC 1894 (Admin), (2006) 9 CCLR 121.

of life within her family environment and her expressed views that she does not want to move are all important factors which suggest that to remove her from her home will require clear justification.

NHS Constitution

11.25   NHSA 2006 s1B2 obliges the secretary of state, when performing his or her NHS functions,[30] to have regard to the NHS Constitution. NHSA 2006 ss13C and 14P require NHS England and CCGs, when exercising any of their functions, to do so in a way that promotes 'the NHS Constitution' as well as promoting awareness of it among 'patients, staff and members of the public'.

11.26   The preamble to the NHS Constitution (2015)[31] states:

This Constitution establishes the principles and values of the NHS in England. It sets out rights to which patients, public and staff are entitled, and pledges which the NHS is committed to achieve, together with responsibilities, which the public, patients and staff owe to one another to ensure that the NHS operates fairly and effectively. The Secretary of State for Health, all NHS bodies, private and voluntary sector providers supplying NHS services, and local authorities in the exercise of their public health functions are required by law to take account of this Constitution in their decisions and actions.

11.27   The Constitution is built around seven key principles, which in summary comprise:

1. **The NHS provides a comprehensive service, available to all.** It is available to all irrespective of gender, race, disability, age, sexual orientation, religion, belief, gender reassignment, pregnancy and maternity or marital or civil partnership status. The service is designed to improve, prevent, diagnose and treat both physical and mental health problems with equal regard. It has a duty to each and every individual that it serves and must respect their human rights ...

2. **Access to NHS services is based on clinical need, not an individual's ability to pay** ...

3. **The NHS aspires to the highest standards of excellence and professionalism.** It provides high quality care that is safe, effective and focused on patient experience ...

4. **The patient will be at the heart of everything the NHS does.** ... NHS services must reflect, and should be coordinated around and tailored to, the needs and preferences of patients, their families and their carers ... Patients, with their families and carers, where appropriate, will be involved in and consulted on all decisions about their care and treatment...

5. **The NHS works across organisational boundaries.** It works in partnership with other organisations in the interest of patients, local communities and the wider population ... The NHS is committed to working jointly with other local authority services, other public sector organisations and a wide range of private and voluntary sector organisations to provide and deliver improvements in health and well-being.

30 Defined in Health Act 2009 s2(3) as 'any function under an enactment which is a function concerned with, or connected to, the provision, commissioning or regulation of NHS'.

31 Department of Health, *The NHS Constitution*, 2010.

6. **The NHS is committed to providing best value for taxpayers' money.** It is committed to providing the most effective, fair and sustainable use of finite resources …

7. **The NHS is accountable to the public, communities and patients that it serves.** … The system of responsibility and accountability for taking decisions in the NHS should be transparent and clear to the public, patients and staff …

11.28 Accompanying the Constitution is a substantial handbook 'designed to give NHS staff and patients all the information they need about the NHS Constitution for England'.[32]

11.29 In *R (Booker) v NHS Oldham and Directline Insurance plc*,[33] a health body's decision to refuse funding for a patient was scrutinised by reference to (among other things) the Constitution, and in finding the practice to be unlawful, the court placed considerable reliance on principle 2 (that access to NHS services is based on clinical need, not an individual's ability to pay).

11.30 The health services ombudsman has signalled that she intends to use the Constitution as a benchmark in her investigations (together with the 'Ombudsman's principles' – see para 20.132 below). In a 2011 report[34] reference is made to the need for the Constitution's principles to be seen in their wider contexts, embracing as they do 'the principles of human rights – fairness, respect, equality, dignity and autonomy'. The report's concluded that the 'NHS must close the gap between the promise of care and compassion outlined in its Constitution': that 'every member of staff, no matter what their job, has a role to play in making the commitments of the Constitution a felt reality for patients' (p10).

11.31 It has been argued[35] that the mandatory nature of the statutory obligation to 'have regard to' may well be interpreted by the courts as requiring NHS bodies to act in line with the Constitution, unless they have articulated good reasons for not doing so.

Choice

11.32 The Constitution's emphasis on 'choice' has attracted considerable analysis.[36] Although the seven underpinning principles do not mention this word (talking instead of reflecting individual 'needs and preferences', and of people being 'involved in and consulted on' relevant decisions), a heading 'Informed choice' asserts the individual right: (1) to choose a GP practice; (2) to express a preference for using a particular doctor within that

32 Department of Health, *The handbook to the NHS Constitution*, 2015.

33 [2010] EWHC 2593 (Admin), (2011) 14 CCLR 315 at [27].

34 Health Service Commissioner, *Care and compassion? Report of the health service ombudsman on ten investigations into NHS care of older people. Fourth report of the Health Service Commissioner for England. Session 2010–2011* HC 778, 2011, p9.

35 K Ashton and J Gould, 'Community care law update', June 2009 *Legal Action* 11–16.

36 See eg K Ashton and J Gould, 'Community care law update', June 2009 *Legal Action* 11–16; D Wolfe and R Logan, 'Public law and the provision of healthcare', (2009) *Judicial Review*, 14(2), pp210–223; and S Farg and A Chapman, 'Who cares wins?', (2010) NLJ, 160(7417), pp671–672.

GP practice; and (3) to make choices about the services commissioned by NHS bodies and to information to support these choices.

11.33   To bolster these 'rights', in 2009 the Department of Health issued directions[37] and best practice guidance on the 'right to choice',[38] which have now been superseded by 2012 regulations.[39] The regulations place a qualified duty on NHS bodies to ensure that patients requiring an elective referral[40] are able to choose any clinically appropriate health service provider with whom any relevant body has a commissioning contract for their first outpatient appointment (reg 39). The regulations (reg 42) also oblige health bodies to publicise the availability of the right to makes such choices.

11.34   2016 guidance issued by the Department of Health[41] describes briefly the choices open to most patients including, for example: choice over their GP; where their first appointment as an outpatient is; who carries out a specialist test; which services are provided in the community; to have a personal health budget. All these choices are, however, circumscribed. Ashton and Garlick[42] argue that the 2016 guidance departs impermissibly from the underlying statutory frameworks. They give the example of the guidance suggesting that CCGs are free to decide who can request a personal health budget (other than those who are eligible for NHS continuing healthcare (NHS CC) funding). They note, however, that the relevant regulations[43] confer on the CCG a discretion to refuse a direct payment. It follows, therefore, that: (1) this discretion has to be exercised in relation to each individual case; (2) everyone has the right to request such a payment; and (3) if the payment is refused, there is a right to have reasons for that decision.

11.35   Ashton and Gould[44] have argued that one aspect of the emerging 'right' to make choices about the services commissioned by NHS bodies will be to create a general expectation that such bodies will fund care home placements of choice unless they provide good reasons for not doing so (and see para 12.147 below on choice and NHS CC).

The medical/social divide

11.36   The conflict between health and social care is not a new one. Distinguishing between what is a social need and what is a medical need is an intractable problem. In general it is only of practical importance to social care

---

37 Department of Health, *Primary care trusts (choice of secondary care provider) directions*, 2009.

38 Department of Health, *Implementation of the right to choice and information set out in the NHS Constitution*, 2009.

39 National Health Service Commissioning Board and Clinical Commissioning Groups (Responsibilities and Standing Rules) Regulations 2012 SI No 2996 Part 8.

40 Defined in reg 38 as a referral by a 'general medical practitioner, dental practitioner or optometrist to a health service provider'.

41 Department of Health, *The NHS choice framework: what choices are available to me in the NHS?* 2016.

42 K Ashton and S Garlick, 'Community Care: update' October 2016 *Legal Action* 33–37.

43 National Health Service (Direct Payments) Regulations 2013 SI 1617 – see para 10.99 above.

44 See note 42 above.

service users because a service provided by the NHS is generally free at the point of need, whereas a service provided by the social services department is generally subject to a means-tested charge. Help with bathing is therefore free if provided in a person's home by the district nurse (or other NHS employee), whereas if provided by a social services care assistant it may be subject to a charge. The argument is repeated in a hundred different ways, with such items and services as walking sticks, hoists, commodes, speech therapy, chiropody, medication prompting and toenail cutting.

11.37 Exhortations to organisations, professionals and other service providers to work together more closely and effectively, litter the policy landscape – yet the reality is all too often a jumble of services factionalised by professional culture, organisational boundaries and by tiers of governance.[45] Lymberry,[46] for example, has pointed to the differences of power and culture between health and social services authorities as being a key factor in this continuing failure, together with the 'inherently competitive nature of professions jostling for territory in the same areas of activity'. He like many researchers in this field concludes that 'these issues cannot be resolved unless they are properly understood; a rhetorical appeal to the unmitigated benefits of 'partnership' alone will not produce more effective joint working'.

The duty to co-operate

11.38 There are a number of statutory duties on local authorities and health bodies to work together constructively. These fall into three broad categories, namely:

1) the obligation to co-operate at the **strategic level**, ie in the preparation of plans for the improvement of the health of the general population (see para 11.14 above);

2) the obligation to co-operate on a **general day-to-day level** requiring co-operation in the delivery of services to individuals who are disabled, elderly or ill (these are considered below);

3) the obligation to co-operate **under the Mental Health Act (MHA) 1983** (which is considered at para 15.70 below).

Statutory duties to co-operate under the NHS Act 2006

11.39 NHSA 2006 s72 places a duty on all NHS bodies to co-operate with each other in exercising their functions, and section 82 provides that:

45 A Webb, 'Co-ordination: A problem in public sector management', (1991) 19(4) *Policy and Politics* 229–241; quoted in R Means and R Smith, *Community care*, Macmillan, 1994. There has been considerable criticism of successive governments' concentration upon creating administrative joint planning structures, on creating coterminosity, and other organisational devices to promote joint working. The research evidence suggested, however, that 'where mutual trust has existed between senior officers from health and local authorities, the relationship has appeared to be far more important than joint planning machinery', R Davidson and S Hunter, *Community care in practice*, Batsford, 1994; see also L Clements and P Smith, *A 'Snapshot' survey of social services' responses to the continuing care needs of older people in Wales*, 1999.

46 M Lymbery, 'United we stand? Partnership working in health and social care and the role of social work in services for older people', (2006) 36(7) *British Journal of Social Work* 1119.

In exercising their respective functions NHS bodies (on the one hand) and local authorities (on the other) must co-operate with one another in order to secure and advance the health and welfare of the people of England and Wales.

11.40   The section 82 duty (as with the section 72 duty) is a cross-border obligation extending to all English and Welsh health bodies and local authorities. This extensive obligation derives from an amendment made by Health Act (HA) 1999 s27. The notes of guidance to the HA 1999 explained that the purpose of the amendment was to extend the duty of partnership in order to:

> ... secure and advance the health and welfare of the people of England and Wales, to cover Primary Care Trusts and NHS trusts as well as Health Authorities and Special Health Authorities. This recognises the need to work in partnership in commissioning and delivering care, as well as at the strategic planning level. Welfare is used in its wide general sense and is designed to cover functions relating to social services, education, housing and the environment.

11.41   The NHSA 2006 s72 duty requires, as noted above, NHS bodies to co-operate with each other and (like the section 82 duty) is augmented by principle 5 of the NHS Constitution (considered at para 11.25 above). Accordingly, if two or more health bodies are in a funding dispute, it will generally be maladministration[47] if they fail to agree on one of them funding the patient on an interim basis until the matter had been resolved and in all the circumstances to take a flexible approach to the needs of patients. A 2007 Welsh ombudsman's report[48] concerned such a case. The complainant required a specialist profiling bed and a specialised seating system, but there was a dispute between two trusts as to which should fund this equipment. The ombudsman, in finding maladministration, considered that the relevant LHB should have taken responsibility as an interim measure, pending the resolution of the dispute between the various NHS bodies.[49]

11.42   Where a community care service user suffers as a result of an inter-agency dispute, it is generally appropriate for complaints to be made against each authority primarily on the basis that they have failed to 'work together' in violation of their specific statutory obligations. The local government ombudsman has repeatedly criticised authorities for failing to provide services whilst they squabbled over their respective obligations. A 1996 ombudsman complaint, for example, concerned the failure of a health authority and social services department to co-operate. Although the ombudsman considered that the health authority's involvement had been 'reluctant, if not unhelpful', she nevertheless found the social services

---

47 *Report by the Public Services Ombudsman for Wales and the Health Service Ombudsman for England of an investigation of a complaint about the Welsh Assembly Government (Health Commission Wales), Cardiff and Vale NHS Trust and Plymouth Teaching Primary Care Trust*, Third Report, Session 2008–2009, HC 858.

48 Public Services Ombudsman for Wales Complaint against Bro Morgannwg NHS Trust, Cardiff and Vale NHS Trust, Vale of Glamorgan Council and Vale of Glamorgan Local Health Board case ref 200501955, 200600591 and 20070064, 28 November 2007 – see pp28 and 30.

49 See para 6.92 above for details about establishing the responsible commissioner.

authority guilty of maladministration. In her opinion, having accepted that a need existed, social services should have 'grasped the nettle' and secured the provision, before entering into protracted negotiations with the NHS on liability for the care costs.[50]

Statutory duty to co-operate under the Care Act 2014

11.43   The Care Act (CA) 2014 s6 places a general 'two-way' duty on local authorities and their relevant partners to co-operate in relation to the exercise of their respective functions relating to adults with needs for care and support and carers. 'Relevant partners' include NHS England as well as the CCGs and NHS trusts within the local authority area. In addition, section 6(2) requires local authorities to co-operate in relation to such matters with 'such other persons as it considers appropriate' and section 6(3)(b) gives as an example GPs, NHS dentists, opticians and pharmacists. Chapter 15 of the statutory guidance to the CA 2014[51] provides general advice on the expectations of local authorities and 'relevant partner' organisations.

11.44   CA 2014 s7 enables social services authorities to request the co-operation of a 'relevant partner' or another local authority (and vice versa) in relation to the exercise of its functions for an individual in need or a carer (including a parent carer and a young carer). The partner must comply with the request unless (section 7(3)) the partner or authority considers that doing so would be 'incompatible' with its duties, or would 'have an adverse effect on the exercise of its functions' – and in such a case the body must provide 'reasons'. See appendix B below for a precedent section 7 letter.

11.45   Although the CA 2014 s7 duty only applies between different authorities, it is almost certain that the courts will interpret it as requiring the same degree of co-operation between departments in a unitary authority.[52] Section 7 provides a substantial new power for local authorities – for example, to require a CCG to take positive action to address the needs of a carer (see para 12.202 below) or in relation to a delayed assessment (for example, for community equipment) or an NHS continuing care decision.

11.46   Under the pre-CA 2014 legislation, a duty was placed on local authorities to refer to the local health body any healthcare need they identified, when undertaking social care assessment.[53] The select committee that scrutinised the care and support bill expressed concern that this provision had not been transposed into the CA 2014.[54] The committee did, however, note the view of the Department of Health that the provisions of what are now sections 6 and 7 of the Act 'will ensure that [local authorities] work with partners such as the NHS' (see also para 3.116 above).

---

50 Complaint no 96/C/3868 against Calderdale MBC, 24 November 1998, para 30.
51 Department of Health, *Care and support statutory guidance* to support implementation of Part 1 of the CA 2014 by local authorities, 2016 ('the statutory guidance').
52 See *M and A v Islington LBC* [2016] EWHC 332 (Admin), (2016) 19 CCLR 122 para 15 where this conclusion was reached in relation to Children Act 1989 s27, on which CA 2014 s7 is based (see for example, *R v Northavon DC ex p Smith* 1994 3 WLR 403, HL).
53 NHSCCA 1990 s47(3).
54 Joint Committee on the Draft Care and Support Bill, *Draft Care and Support Bill*, HL Paper 143 HC 822, The Stationery Office, 2013, paras 175–176.

Additional specific duties to co-operate

11.47   A similar, but more extensive, duty to co-operate exists in relation to patients detained under MHA 1983 s3 or one of the criminal provisions of that Act. The after-care duty, under MHA 1983 s117, is considered at para 15.56 below.

11.48   Certain patients who are being discharged from hospital care are the subject of the specific hospital discharge provisions in CA 2014 s74 and Sch 3, and for them a duty to co-operate between the NHS and social services arises although the obligations are largely one way – on the social services to facilitate a discharge. The duty is considered at para 5.34 above.

General duties to provide NHS services in the community and to care homes

11.49   The NHS general duty to promote a comprehensive health service requires a range of services in the community and elsewhere. All people within the UK have a right to these services – regardless of where they are living. These services include access to primary care (such as that provided by GPs and dentists) as well as the full range of services such as physiotherapy, occupational therapy, chiropody, district nursing, community nursing and general ophthalmic services etc.

11.50   2012 guidance[55] gives examples of the range of health services which CCGs are expected to arrange and fund, stating that the list 'includes, but is not limited to':

- primary healthcare;
- assessment involving doctors and registered nurses;
- rehabilitation/reablement and recovery (where this forms part of an overall package of NHS care, as distinct from intermediate care);
- respite healthcare;
- community health services;
- specialist support for healthcare needs; and
- palliative care and end of life healthcare.

Earlier 2001 guidance[56] lists, in addition to the above, equipment and specialist transport as NHS responsibilities – these are considered further below (see paras 11.95 and 11.105 below).

General practitioner services

Primary medical services and general medical services contracts

11.51   NHSA 2006 Part 4 empowers NHS England to arrange with medical practitioners to provide 'primary medical services' and to enter into a 'general

---

55   Department of Health, *National framework for NHS continuing healthcare and NHS-funded nursing care*, 2012, para 115.

56   Department of Health guidance LAC (2001)18, *Continuing care: NHS and local councils' responsibilities*, para 16: specialist transport is also listed in the equivalent Welsh Guidance, namely NHS Wales, *Continuing NHS healthcare. Implementation in Wales*, 2014, para 4.61.

medical services' (GMS) contract to this end. As with hospital services, it is not the CCG itself which provides the service; instead, it enters into separate statutory arrangements with independent practitioners for the provision of those services. GPs are not, therefore, employees of the CCG, but independent professionals who undertake to provide general medical services in accordance with a GMS contract,[57] the terms of which are prescribed by regulations – currently the National Health Service (General Medical Services Contracts) Regulations 2015.[58]

11.52 Longstanding concern exists as to the general performance of GPs in fulfilling their social care obligations: primarily, the responsibility of ensuring that people in need of community care services are provided with the necessary assistance to obtain them.[59] Regulation 17(5)(b) of the GMS regulations requires that GPs refer (as appropriate) patients 'for other services under the [NHSA 2006]'. As noted elsewhere in this text (see, for example, para 15.95) the NHSA 2006 places substantial duties on social services authorities.[60] It follows that GPs are contractually obliged to make appropriate referrals to social services where it appears that a patient may be entitled to such services. In those cases where the patient lacks the necessary mental capacity or is otherwise unlikely to respond to such advice or referral, there will frequently be an equivalent duty owed to the patient's carer.

11.53 Disquiet also exists about the difficulty that some care home residents experience in accessing GP services[61] and the failure of GPs to make appropriate referrals for NHS continuing care assessments. Although residents of care homes are entitled to be registered with a GP on the same basis as anyone else[62] it appears that many care homes have to pay a retainer[63] to obtain such support. Guidance concerning the rights of care home residents to GP care has been issued by the Social Care Institute of Excellence (SCIE).[64] Although there appears to be no specific guidance that requires GPs to advise patients of their right to seek NHS continuing care

---

57 At the time of writing (January 2017) the GP contract is: NHS England Standard General Medical Services Contract 2015/16.

58 SI No 1862 – as amended by the National Health Service (General Medical Services Contracts and Personal Medical Services Agreements) (Amendment) Regulations 2015 SI No 196.

59 See eg EL (96)8 para 11.

60 This is particularly so in relation to the NHS's public health functions (for example, under NHSA 2006 s2B, Part 3 and Sch 1) although the previous obligations to provide care and support under section 254(1) were repealed by CA 2014 and Children and Families Act 2014 (Consequential Amendments) Order 2015 SI No 914 Sch 1 para 82(2).

61 C Glendinning and others, 'A survey of access to medical services in nursing and residential homes in England' (2002) 52 *British Journal of General Practice* 545.

62 Department of Health, *NHS-funded nursing care practice guide* (revised), 2013, para 43. See also British Medical Association (BMA), *GP practices: primary care in institutions and residential homes*, 2016.

63 In 2004 the House of Commons Health Committee called for the abolition of such retainer fees – see House of Commons Health Committee, *Elder abuse*, Second Report of Session 2003–04 vol 1, HC 111-I, The Stationery Office 2004, p52.

64 SCIE, *GP services for older people: a guide for care home managers*, SCIE Guide 52, December 2013.

funding, CCGs (of which GP practices must be a member[65]) are obliged to ensure that an appropriate assessment is carried out in all cases where it appears there may be a need for continuing care services (see para 12.52 below). GPs should therefore be aware of the eligibility criteria for NHS CC and make the appropriate referrals if when visiting patients they consider they meet that criteria.

GPs' obligation to prescribe drugs and appliances

11.54   The obligation on GPs to provide general medical services for their patients brings with it a need to prescribe. This requirement is addressed by the GMS regulations[66] which provide (subject to certain exceptions) that GPs 'must order any drugs, medicines or appliances which are needed for the treatment of any patient who is receiving treatment under the contract' by issuing a prescription.

11.55   The responsibility for prescribing and the administration of prescription medicines, brings with it the question of whether the whole process is an NHS function, and if so whether charges can be levied by social services, when what it is arguably fulfilling an agency role in this process.

11.56   The administration of prescription medication stems from an NHS professional's decision that the patient needs to take that medication. From this decision flows the concomitant obligation on the NHS to ensure that the drugs are correctly administered (eg as to the frequency, quantity, and circumstances etc); that records of when the drugs are taken are maintained (if the patient is unable to do this); that contra indications or adverse reactions to the medication are closely monitored; and that the regime kept under appropriate review.[67] All of these 'control' functions would appear to be the responsibility of the NHS – even though there may be no need for every aspect to be undertaken by an NHS employee (provided that appropriate training, guidance and back-up support is available). If this is so, the lawfulness of a social services authority levying charges to a patient for its role in this process, is open to question. It is arguable that the authority (which must be incurring substantial expense in fulfilling this role) should instead be seeking payment from the health body, for discharging this health function on its behalf (eg under NHSA 2006 s256 – see para 11.128 below).

11.57   As noted above, the requirement in the GMS regulations includes the prescribing of 'appliances';[68] ie medical aids, dressings, pads etc as well as basic equipment to help overcome the effects of disability. In relation to

---

65   National Health Service (General Medical Services Contracts) Regulations 2015 SI No 1862 reg 21.

66   National Health Service (General Medical Services Contracts) Regulations 2015 SI No 1862 reg 56.

67   It appears to be not uncommon for care assistants to pick up errors on Medication Administration Records (MAR charts) requiring liaison with the pharmacy to clarify and correct the error and to ensure that the correct chart and medication is provided (sometimes urgently) to the service user.

68   'Appliance' is defined in National Health Service (General Medical Services Contracts) Regulations 2015 SI No 1862 reg 3 as an appliance included in an approved list under NHSA 2006 s126 – which in turn refers to items listed in the National Health Service (Pharmaceutical and Local Pharmaceutical Services) Regulations 2013 SI No 349.

disability equipment there is frequently an overlap of responsibility with the local social services department's community care duties. It is therefore common practice for health and social services to arrange joint equipment stores which can be accessed by both social services and the relevant NHS trust (see para 7.72).

11.58 The appliances which a GP can prescribe are detailed in a list known as the drug tariff[69] at Part IX of the National Health Service (General Medical Services Contracts) Regulations 2015.[70] The lists enable GPs to provide a range of general items. Where more specialist equipment is needed, this may be obtained via a hospital consultant (see below).

11.59 The appliance list in the drug tariff includes such items as:

- stoma (Part IXC) and some incontinence care equipment (Part IXB) (see also para 11.87 below where CCG responsibility for incontinence supplies is considered);
- elastic hosiery, dressings, bandages, trusses etc (Part IXA);
- respiratory equipment (including oxygen cylinders and oxygen concentrators);[71]
- chiropody appliances (Part IXA). GPs can refer patients to NHS chiropodists and consultants for more specialist equipment. CCGS must also ensure that adequate chiropody services are available to residents placed by social services in care home accommodation (see para 11.91 below).

GPs' obligation to provide statements of fitness for work

11.60 GPs have an important role in providing certificates for a variety of purposes, including establishing whether the patient is fit for work. Accordingly, GMS regulations reg 22 provides that GPs are required to issue free of charge to their patients (or their personal representatives) any medical certificate which is reasonably required for certain specified purposes, these being set out in column 1 of Schedule 2 to the GMS regulations.

Rehabilitation and recovery services

11.61 Guidance stresses the importance of the NHS's role the provision of aftercare services where they help promote independent living.[72] Rehabilitation is defined as:

> A programme of therapy and re-enablement designed to maximise independence and minimise the effects of disability.[73]

11.62 Although the NHS's role in promoting rehabilitation is frequently linked with reablement and 'intermediate care' (discussed in more detail in

---

69 A copy of the Electronic Drug Tariff compiled by the NHS Business Services Authority NHS Prescription Services can be viewed at www.nhsbsa.nhs.uk/ PrescriptionServices/4940.aspx.

70 SI No 1862.

71 Part X – services now subcontracted to regional suppliers.

72 See, for instance, Department of Health, *Transforming rehabilitation services: best practice guidance*, 2009.

73 Department of Health, *National framework for NHS continuing healthcare and NHS-funded nursing care*, 2012, p122.

chapter 9) the NHS has core obligations to provide such support independent of its specific intermediate care functions.[74] This important point is given emphasis in the 2012 framework NHS CC guidance.[75] At para 64 it advises that NHS CC assessments 'should always consider whether there is further potential for rehabilitation and for independence to be regained'. It then explains at para 115 that independent of NHS-funded nursing care (see para 11.110 below) 'additional health services may also be funded by the NHS, if these are identified and agreed as part of an assessment and care plan' and that these may be 'distinct from intermediate care'. Paragraph 13.5, which refers to the desirability of NHS CC assessments being undertaken after a person's discharge from hospital, notes that this may entail NHS-funded services being provided in the interim – including 'rehabilitation, if that could make a difference to the potential further recovery of the individual in the following few months' either as 'intermediate care' or 'an interim package of support in an individual's own home or in a care home'.

National service framework for long-term conditions

11.63   The 'National service framework (NSF) for long-term conditions'[76] placed considerable emphasis on the importance of appropriate rehabilitation support. Although the ten-year NSF programme has now reached an end, the standards it set are still relevant benchmarks of service provision and best practice against which the performance of health bodies should be assessed. Paragraph 16 explained what is meant by a long-term condition, namely one that is primarily neurological in origin[77] and 'results from disease of, injury or damage to the body's nervous system (ie the brain, spinal cord and/or their peripheral nerve connections) which will affect the individual and their family in one way or another for the rest of their life'. The NSF 'broadly categorised' such conditions as follows (para 17):

- **Sudden onset conditions**, for example acquired brain injury or spinal cord injury, followed by a partial recovery. (Note: stroke for all ages is covered in the 'NSF for older people').
- **Intermittent and unpredictable conditions**, for example epilepsy, certain types of headache or early multiple sclerosis, where relapses and remissions lead to marked variation in the care needed.
- **Progressive conditions**, for example motor neurone disease, Parkinson's disease or later stages of multiple sclerosis, where progressive deterioration in neurological function leads to increasing dependence on help and care from others. For some conditions (eg motor neurone

---

74 A brief review of some of the past guidance on the NHS duty to provide this support (historically referred to as 'convalescence') is provided in the 5th edition of this book at paras 13.57–13.59.

75 Department of Health, *National framework for NHS continuing healthcare and NHS-funded nursing care*, 2012 – see para 12.39 below.

76 Department of Health, March 2005.

77 Para 4 states, however, that although this NSF focuses on people with neurological conditions, much of the guidance it offers can apply to anyone living with a long-term condition.

disease) deterioration can be rapid. (Note: dementia for all ages is covered in the 'NSF for Older People').

- **Stable neurological conditions, but with changing needs due to development or ageing**, for example postpolio syndrome or cerebral palsy in adults.

11.64 At the heart of the NSF were 11 quality requirements which were to be fully implemented by 2015, three of which (standards 4, 5 and 6) specifically related to rehabilitation support, namely:

4. Early and specialist rehabilitation;
5. Community rehabilitation and support;
6. Vocational rehabilitation.

Intermediate care

11.65 The intermediate care initiative is aimed at freeing up acute hospital beds and promoting the independence of older people. It is a time limited service, normally for no more than six weeks, and is considered further at chapter 9. Although the provision of intermediate care services will often satisfy a patient's needs for rehabilitation and recuperation, this will not always be the case. Given the time limited nature of the service, it will frequently be only a first stage of a programme. If at the end of a period a patient has not fully recovered, it may be that he or she can no longer receive rehabilitation support from the intermediate care team. This does not mean that NHS responsibility for rehabilitation has come to an end – merely that the specialised input of the intermediate care team is no longer appropriate. A similar situation arises in some areas where the intermediate team is unable to provide a full service to all patients due to excessive demand. Again, in such cases, the duty remains with the NHS, notwithstanding that the intermediate care team is unable to field it.

Respite services

11.66 In *R (T, D and B) v Haringey LBC*[78] the High Court held that the provision of respite care was capable of being a core NHS responsibility. The 2012 'National framework for NHS Continuing healthcare'[79] includes respite healthcare within the 'range of services that the NHS is expected to arrange and fund'.

11.67 The superseded 1995 guidance[80] was more expansive on the nature of respite healthcare, requiring that health bodies arranged and funded 'an adequate level of such care' and gave three examples of the type of patient who ought to be able to access NHS funded respite services, namely:

- people who have complex or intense healthcare needs and will require specialist medical or nursing supervision or assessment during a period of respite care;

---

78 [2005] EWHC 2235 (Admin), (2006) 9 CCLR 58.

79 Department of Health, *National framework for NHS continuing healthcare and NHS-funded nursing care*, 2012, para 115.

80 *NHS responsibilities for meeting continuing healthcare needs* LAC (95)5: HSG (95)8 (WOC 16/95 and WHC (95)7 in Wales).

- people who during a period of respite care require or could benefit from active rehabilitation; and
- people who are receiving a package of palliative care in their own homes but where they or their carer need a period of respite care.

The above reference to 'active rehabilitation' is directed towards the needs of people whose condition is chronic rather than acute. By providing such persons with regular periods of respite care where they also receive such services as intensive physiotherapy, speech and occupational therapy, the NHS can prolong their ability to live independently in the community and reduce the pressure on their carers.

11.68   Follow-up guidance in 1996[81] advised that NHS eligibility criteria would be too restrictive if confined to the above three examples, suggesting that the criteria should cover other contingencies, such as 'where carers have been providing a level of healthcare which is not reasonably available in a residential setting'. It is likely that all such respite care provided by the NHS should be fully funded and so free at the point of use.

11.69   The NSF for long-term conditions[82] addressed respite care in the context of it being a shared obligation of the NHS and social services and highlighted the importance of 'appropriate respite care at home or in specialised settings', noting that 'respite care is a key factor in enabling care to be provided at home over a long period'.

Palliative healthcare

11.70   The provision of palliative care is also considered at para 12.150 below (in the context of NHS's continuing healthcare responsibilities).

11.71   Palliative healthcare has been defined as:

> ... an approach that improves the quality of life of patients and their families facing the problem associated with life-threatening illness, through the prevention and relief of suffering by means of early identification and impeccable assessment and treatment of pain and other problems, physical, psychosocial and spiritual.[83]

11.72   Palliative care should be distinguished from end of life care, which the Department of Health defines as:[84]

> Care that helps all those with advanced, progressive, incurable illness to live as well as possible until they die. It enables the supportive and palliative care needs of both patient and family to be identified and met throughout the last phase of life and into bereavement. It includes management of pain and other symptoms, and provision of psychological, social, spiritual and practical support.

81 EL (96)8 para 16.
82 Department of Health, March 2005, p47 para 6.
83 World Health Organisation definition (2016) at www.who.int/cancer/palliative/definition/en/.
84 Department of Health, *End of life care strategy – promoting high quality care for all adults at the end of life*, 2008, para 3.6.

11.73　1995 guidance[85] required health authorities to fund palliative health care in a range of settings, including as an inpatient, in a care homes and patients own homes. Concern about the inadequate level of support led the Department of Health remind health bodies that eligibility criteria which applied time limits for palliative care would be inappropriate: that such care should be provided by the NHS purely on the basis of clinical need.[86]

11.74　This concern led in 2004 to a critical report from the House of Commons select committee[87] which characterised the system for providing palliative care for terminally ill patients as unfair, 'abhorrent' and leading to 'unseemly arguments about who should pay for different elements of a care package [which could result in] inexcusable delays and poor practice that is anything but patient-centred'.

11.75　One result of this disquiet was the publication in 2008 of the government's End of Life Care Strategy[88] which committed significant resources[89] and required health bodies to improve coordination of their palliative care services; provide round the clock home care services; improve ambulance transport services for people near the end of life; provide additional specialist palliative care outreach services to provide advice and care for non-cancer patients; to increase input into care homes and community hospitals; and to improve education and training of existing staff in care homes, hospitals and the community.

11.76　In 2015 an independent review commissioned by the secretary of state for health was published concerning the reform of the support and funding regime of patients with palliative needs.[90] The report recommended (among other things) that everyone in need of end of life care be offered 'choices in their care focused on what is important to them'. The NHS has additional responsibilities for patients entering a terminal phase of their illness and these are considered at paras 12.59 and 12.150 below.

Specialist support for healthcare needs

Wheelchairs

11.77　It is estimated that there are 1.2 million wheelchair users in England and that two-thirds of them are regular users[91] and almost 70 per cent of whom

85　*NHS responsibilities for meeting continuing healthcare needs*, LAC (95)5: HSG (95)8, p15 (WOC 16/95 and WHC (95)7 in Wales) building on earlier English guidance – see eg EL (93)14 annex C paras 10–14 and HSG (92)50.

86　EL (96)8, para 16.

87　House of Commons Health Committee Fourth Report of Session 2003–04, *Palliative care, Volume 1*, HC 454-I.

88　Department of Health, *End of life care strategy – promoting high quality care for all adults at the end of life*, 2008.

89　Department of Health, *End of life care strategy – promoting high quality care for all adults at the end of life*, 2008, para 28.

90　The Choice in End of Life Care Programme Board, *What's important to me. A review of choice in end of life care*, 2015. The report built on an earlier 2011 review, *Palliative care funding review. Funding the right care and support for everyone creating a fair and transparent funding system. The Final Report of the Palliative Care Funding Review*, 2011.

91　NHS England, *Improving wheelchair services*, 2016.

are over 60.[92] There are additionally many more people needing the use of a wheelchair for a time limited period.[93]

11.78   There is little doubt that the service provided by the NHS has for many years been far from satisfactory, not least due to 'inequitable variations in prescribing, management structures, staffing, criteria, funding, costs and levels of services' and the lack of any national minimum standards.[94] Over the last 30 years, a steady stream of critical reports concerning the inadequacies of the NHS wheelchair services have emerged[95] and the evidence suggests that the service continues to leave much to be desired. In 2010, for example, the minister accepted that it was 'quite common for people to wait months for a wheelchair, and not uncommon for them to wait years for a powered wheelchair' and that '57% of wheelchair budgets currently go on back-office costs'.[96] In 2016, NHS England acknowledged that:[97]

- many wheelchair users face delays in getting their chair – 70 per cent waiting more than three months, 30 per cent face a delay of more than six months with 15 per cent waiting more than 12 months;
- up to half of all people who use a wheelchair develop a pressure ulcer at some point during their life caused, in part, by ill-fitting or ill-equipped chairs;[98]
- a powerful economic case existed for providing suitable wheelchairs without delay.[99]

11.79   In an attempt to redress this problem, NHS England has supported the development by the Wheelchair Leadership Alliance of a 'National Wheelchair Charter'.[100]

---

92 Department of Health, *Local innovations in wheelchair and seating services: best practice guidance*, 2010.

93 Department of Health/ Care Services Improvement Partnership, *Out and about: wheelchairs as part of a whole-systems approach to independence*, 2006, p5.

94 See *National standards for wheelchair services: final consultation draft document*, 2003..

95 See, for example, I McColl, *Review of artificial limb and appliance centre services*, Department of Health and Social Security, 1986; *National prosthetic and wheelchair services report 1993–1996* (the Holderness report), College of Occupational Therapists; Audit Commission, *Fully equipped: the provision of equipment to older or disabled people by the NHS and social services in England and Wales*, 2000; Audit Commission, *Fully equipped 2002: assisting independence*, 2002; Department of Health, *Evaluation of the powered wheelchair and voucher system 2000*, 2002; emPower, *NHS wheelchair and seating services mapping project: final report*, Limbless Association, 2004; Prime Minister's Strategy Unit,
    Improving the life chances of disabled people, 2005; N Sharma with J Morrison, *Don't push me around! Disabled children's experiences of wheelchair services in the UK*, 2006; and Muscular Dystrophy Campaign *Get Moving – the case for effective wheelchair services*, 2010.

96 HC Hansard, 28 Jun 2010: col 693: The Minister of State, Department of Health (Mr Paul Burstow).

97 NHS England, *Improving wheelchair services*, 2016.

98 Noting that the cost of treating the worst cases of a pressure ulcer can be as much as 16 total hip replacements.

99 Noting that for every 182 wheelchair users not able to work, the benefits bill can increase by up to £1m, whereas the positive economic contribution made when in work can be up to £4.7m.

100 Wheelchair Leadership Alliance, *The Wheelchair Charter*, 2015.

11.80   Delay in the provision of a wheelchair may amount to maladministration particularly where it results in prolonged use of inadequate equipment or potential harm to carers.[101]

11.81   Wheelchairs are seen as a facility or service provided by the NHS under NHSA 2006 s3.[102] NHSA 2006 Sch 1 para 9 empowers CCGs to provide wheelchairs and other vehicles for 'persons for whom the group has responsibility and who appear to it to have a physical impairment which has a substantial and long-term adverse effect on their ability to carry out normal day-to-day activities'. Paragraph 10 deals with such questions as the adaptation of vehicles to address the needs of disabled people, their maintenance and repair, insurance, and the provision of 'a structure in which the vehicle may be kept'.

11.82   Wheelchair services are generally commissioned by CCGs.[103] They are the subject of brief Department of Health guidance issued in 1996[104] (when electrically powered indoor/outdoor wheelchairs (EPIOCs) and vouchers became available for severely disabled people through the NHS) and 2004 good practice guidance.[105] Individuals can also obtain a powered wheelchair (or a scooter) through the Motability Scheme by surrendering their high rate mobility component of disability living allowance (DLA).

11.83   Wheelchairs may be obtained from NHS trusts for temporary use on discharge from hospital,[106] and residential care homes are expected to provide wheelchairs for occasional use[107] – but for regular use they should access the same wheelchair services as disabled people living independently.[108] It appears that not infrequently the provision of wheelchairs for nursing home residents is unsatisfactory.[109] In such situations, where a resident is disadvantaged, the difference in treatment could be challenged

101 See eg NHS Ombudsman, *Listening and learning: a review of complaint handling by the NHS in England 2009/10*, 2011, p28 where the recommendation was for a compensation payment by the PCT of £5,000.

102 Department of Health/ Care Services Improvement Partnership, *Out and about: wheelchairs as part of a whole-systems approach to independence*, 2006, p30.

103 Wheelchair services are capable of being delegated to social services as part of an NHSA 2006 s75 agreement – see para 11.130 and this appears to have occurred in a number of cases.

104 Department of Health, *Powered indoor/outdoor wheelchairs for severely disabled people* HSG (96)34, 1996 and Department of Health, *The wheelchair voucher scheme* HSG(96)53, 1996.

105 Department of Health, *Improving services for wheelchair users and carers: good practice guide*, 2004.

106 It appears that in practice many trusts fail to provide wheelchairs in such situations, relying on separate PCT commissioning (eg, from the local Red Cross) or via a joint equipment store (see para 7.73 above).

107 Department of Health, *Discharge from hospital: pathway, process and practice*, 2003, para 5.3.1 – although this guidance has now been superseded by Department of Health, *Ready to go? Planning the discharge and the transfer of patients from hospital and intermediate care*, 2010, which does not mention wheelchairs.

108 Department of Health, *Community equipment services*, HSC 2001/008: LAC (2001)13, 2001, which at para 7 makes clear that although community equipment services may provide wheelchairs for short-term loan, the service is not for permanent wheelchair users, 'as these are prescribed and funded by different NHS services'.

109 The misunderstanding may have arisen due to a flawed interpretation of former Department of Health guidance (*Discharge from hospital: pathway, process and practice*, 2003, para 5.3.1) which stated that nursing homes should provide 'some standard items of equipment for anyone needing them and for the safety of staff'.

as unjustified discrimination in relation to goods and services: when the difference stems from the location of the care, rather than individual need.[110]

11.84   The assessment of need for, and the provision of, wheelchairs (and wheelchair cushions etc) is in practice undertaken by local NHS wheelchair services in England.[111] The assessment is undertaken by a specialist, usually an occupational therapist, physiotherapist or consultant who will then identify the most suitable wheelchair. If the disabled person has difficulty using a manual wheelchair, the CCG can supply an electric model, including one for outdoor use if appropriate. The NHS additionally operates a 'wheelchair voucher scheme' that gives users the option of purchasing from an independent supplier or from the wheelchair service. In either case, the user can top-up the voucher cost (which covers only the cost of a 'standard' wheelchair to meet the user's needs – ie not an EPIOC) to enable a more expensive model to be acquired. However, if the chair is purchased from an independent supplier, it is owned by the user who is responsible for its maintenance and repair, whereas if the 'wheelchair services' option is chosen, the CCG retains ownership but is also responsible for its maintenance.

11.85   Since 1996 funding has been available for the provision of EPIOCs, although targeted on 'more severely disabled users (including children) who could benefit from them to enjoy enhanced levels of independent mobility inside and outside their home'.[112] The general criteria (1996) for such wheelchairs being that the severely disabled person is:[113]

- unable to propel a manual chair outdoors;
- able to benefit from the chair through increased mobility leading to improved quality of life;
- able to handle the chair safely.

Research has, however, suggested that these criteria exclude significant numbers of potential beneficiaries.[114]

11.86   Research from 2012 has identified a wide range of health problems experienced by carers as a result of pushing manual wheelchairs and the inadequacy of carers' assessments when wheelchairs are being allocated.[115]

---

110 In this respect, see also Department of Health, *Guidance on free nursing care in nursing homes* HSC 2001/17: LAC (2001)26, 2001, p8 para 9 which states that PCTs should ensure that care home residents should have access to the full range of specialist NHS support that is available in other care settings including 'aids to mobility'.

111 An (internet) accessible Directory of Wheelchair Services is maintained by the National Wheelchair Managers Forum.

112 As a general rule, once an individual receives an EPIOC, the manual wheelchair should also be retained as a back-up.

113 Department of Health, *Powered indoor/outdoor wheelchairs for severely disabled people,* HSG (96)34, 1996.

114 Department of Health, *The evaluation of the powered wheelchair and voucher scheme initiatives,* York Health Economics Consortium, 2000.

115 J Roberts and others, 'The needs of carers who push Wheelchairs' in *The Journal of Integrated Care* Vol 20 No 1, 2012, pp. 23–34.

Continence services

11.87   Continence services, despite their significant cost,[116] frequently appear to be of poor quality. A 2006 report[117] expressed concern over the reduced availability of specialist nurses, the continued inadequate assessment of incontinence and the over emphasis on the use of pads rather than less expensive preventative measures which gave greater dignity to users.[118] A 2010 report commissioned by the Department of Health's Healthcare Quality Improvement Partnership[119] concluded that (p6):

> The great majority of continence services are poorly integrated across acute, medical, surgical, primary, care home and community settings, resulting in disjointed care for patients and carers.

11.88   The way continence services are presently commissioned means that:

- those providing the care are not included in the process of commissioning;
- many services are not set up to provide joined-up care across health-care boundaries;
- most lack a designated lead whose responsibility it is to organise, develop and improve the delivery of continence care to patients;
- users almost never contribute to service planning or evaluation.

11.89   Since April 2004, continence supplies in England should be provided free of charge by CCGs in all settings.[120] Department of Health 2001 guidance[121] stated that health bodies were 'responsible for arranging ... the provision of nursing advice, eg continence advice and stoma care' and that it was their responsibility to provide 'continence pads and equipment and nursing aids'. The 2013 NHS funded nursing care practice guidance[122] advises:

> 48. Residents of care homes, including those providing nursing care, should have access to professional advice about the promotion of continence. See Good Practice in Continence Services.[123]

---

116   The annual cost of these services to the NHS in 2004 was estimated to be in the region of £743 million per year: DA Turner, C Shaw, CW McGrowther and others, 'The cost of clinically significant urinary storage symptoms for community dwelling adults in the UK' (2004) 93(9) *BJU International* 1246–1252. A National Institute for Health and Clinical Excellence guide *Faecal continence service for the management of faecal incontinence in adults*, 2008 made the important point, that it was not only the cost that was of concern – that the failure of the current service represents a 'missed opportunity to assess, treat and reduce the numbers of incontinent people' (pp4–5).

117   Royal College of Physicians, *National audit of continence care for older people*, 2006.

118   Assistance managing toilet needs is an eligible need under the Care and Support (Eligibility Criteria) Regulations 2015 SI No 313 reg 2 – see para 4.17 above.

119   Royal College of Physicians, *National audit of continence care combined organisational and clinical report*, 2010; and see also The All Party Parliamentary Group For Continence Care 'Report Cost-effective Commissioning For Continence Care', 2011.

120   Prior to 2001 in England people in nursing homes were not provided with incontinence supplies by the NHS.

121   LAC (2001)18, paras 23 and 29.

122   Department of Health, *NHS-funded nursing care practice guide* (revised), 2013, paras 50–51.

123   Citing the Department of Health, *Good practice in continence services* PL CNO (2000)2, 2000 and the accompanying 45-page guidance of the same title.

49. As well as prevention and advice services, the continence service should also include the provision of continence products, subject to a full assessment of an individual's needs. Continence products or payments should be made available by the NHS to care homes for residents who are also receiving NHS-funded nursing care, if required.

Detailed practice guidance has additionally been issued in England concerning the organisation and range of continence services that should be made available.[124]

11.90   The nature and quantity of continence supplies made available will depend upon an individual assessment of need in every case. The evidence suggests[125] that despite the need for continence pads to be available on the basis of clinical need, that the majority of health bodies operate a fixed policy which stipulates a maximum number that can be provided over a specified period. A 2010 report[126] found that contrary to the stated policy of most health bodies (that provision of continence products was based on clinical need), 66 per cent of them imposed a limit on provision. Such policies are contrary to the guidance, fetter the authorities' discretion and, where individual hardship results, constitute maladministration.

Physiotherapy, speech therapy and chiropody

11.91   The NHS is responsible for the provision of such services as physiotherapy, speech and language therapy and chiropody[127] for all people in need of such services, regardless of whether they are living independently or in a care home. To this list, 2001 Department of Health guidance[128] added occupational therapy, dietetics and podiatry; and 2013 guidance[129] lists podiatry, physiotherapy, occupational therapy, speech and language therapy services, tissue viability nursing and palliative care services.[130]

11.92   Cutbacks to chiropody services have been widespread over recent years. In many areas toenail cutting services have been withdrawn, and increasingly chiropody services are only available to people with specific conditions such as diabetes.

11.93   As a result of many people in care homes having to pay for chiropody services, guidance has reminded local authorities that residents should

124 Department of Health, *Good practice in continence services* PL CNO (2000)2, 2000.
125 Royal College of Physicians, *National audit of continence care for older people*, 2006, which found that almost 75 per cent of PCTs had maximum number of pads policy.
126 Royal College of Physicians, *National audit of continence care combined organisational and clinical report*, 2010, p33, table 40.
127 LAC (92)24, para 2 and see also Department of Health, *NHS responsibilities for meeting continuing health care needs* LAC (95)5, 1993.
128 LAC (2001)18, paras 23 and 29. This is now superseded by the 2012 National Framework (see para 12.40 below) which does not mention these services, absent an announcement to the contrary it is inconceivable that the policy intention (or indeed legal obligation) that the NHS provide this range of services, does not remain.
129 See also Department of Health, *GP consortia: what allied health professionals (AHPs) can do for you*, 2011, where such practitioners are referred to as 'allied health professionals', which it states includes additionally dietitians, occupational therapists, orthoptists, orthotists, prosthetists, paramedics, diagnostic radiographers, therapeutic radiographers, art therapists, dramatherapists and music therapists.
130 Department of Health, *NHS-funded nursing care practice guide* (revised), 2013, para 42.

not be expected to use their personal expenses allowance for items that have been assessed as necessary to meet their needs by the council or the NHS. Guidance from 2013 reminded authorities that the care plans of residents must fully reflect their chiropody needs.[131]

Transport

11.94 A 2006 Department of Health white paper[132] committed the government to extending eligibility for two NHS transport schemes, namely:

- the patient transport service (PTS), which had traditionally provided only for transport to and from hospital. The commitment was to extend this to cover transport for health services which were delivered in a community setting; and
- the healthcare travel costs scheme (HTCS) for patients on low incomes.

Patient transport service

11.95 Guidance on the revised PTS scheme was issued in 2007,[133] including updated performance standards for emergency and urgent ambulances. In relation to non-emergency transport services, the decision as to a patient's eligibility is determined 'either by a healthcare professional or by non-clinically qualified staff who are both clinically supervised and/or working within locally agreed protocols or guidelines, and employed by the NHS or working under contract for the NHS' (para 10). Eligible patients are those (para 8):

- where the medical condition of the patient is such that the patient requires the skills or support of PTS staff on/after the journey and/or where it would be detrimental to the patient's condition or recovery if the patient were to travel by other means;
- where the patient's medical condition impacts on his or her mobility to such an extent that the patient would be unable to access healthcare and/or it would be detrimental to the patient's condition or recovery to travel by other means;
- recognised as a parent or guardian where children are being conveyed.

11.96 The scheme also provides for the transport of a patient's escort or carer where (para 9):

> ... their particular skills and/or support are needed e.g. this might be appropriate for those accompanying a person with a physical or mental incapacity, vulnerable adults or to act as a translator.

---

131 Department of Health, *Charging for residential care guide 2013*, para 5.007 – this advice is, however, not, repeated in the statutory guidance to the CA 2014.

132 Department of Health, *Our health, our care, our say: a new direction for community services*, white paper: Cm 6737, 2006, paras 6.67–6.68.

133 Department of Health, *Eligibility criteria for patient transport services: best practice guidance*, 2007.

Healthcare travel costs scheme

11.97   Guidance on the revised HTCS scheme was issued in 2010.[134] The scheme is underpinned by regulations[135] and applies to all health bodies (ie CCGs, NHS trusts and NHS foundation trusts). It provides for patients on low incomes or receiving specific qualifying benefits to be reimbursed in full or in part for the costs incurred on some journeys that are made in order to receive certain NHS services. The eligible 'NHS travel expenses' are defined in the regulations,[136] which the guidance explains are travel expenses that a person necessarily incurs:

1) in attending any place in the UK for the provision of any services under the National Health Service Act 2006 ('the 2006 Act') (except primary medical, primary ophthalmic or primary dental services) which are provided pursuant to a referral by a doctor, ophthalmist or dentist (and which are not provided at the same visit and on the same premises as the primary medical services which lead to a referral for such services), or

2) in travelling to a port in Great Britain for the purpose of travelling abroad in order to receive services provided pursuant to arrangements made under the provisions of the 2006 Act.

11.98   The guidance explains the effect of the eligibility criteria which are to be applied, namely that (p11):

1) The patient must be:
   a) in receipt of one of the qualifying benefits or allowances specified in the 2003 Regulations (or in certain cases be a member of the same family as a person receiving a qualifying benefit or allowance), or
   b) be named on a NHS Low Income Scheme certificate HC2 or HC3 (or in certain cases be a member of the same family as a person named on a NHS Low Income Scheme certificate).

2) The journey undertaken must be made to receive services under the National Health Service Act 2006, which are not primary medical or primary dental care services, for which the patient has been referred by a doctor or dentist ;

3) Where a doctor or dentist has provided the primary medical or primary dental services which lead to the referral for non-primary care services, those services must be provided on a different visit or involve an additional journey to the premises where the primary medical or primary dental services which lead to that referral were provided.

11.99   The permitted travel costs are calculated on the basis of the cheapest form of transport appropriate to the patient and should be 'reasonable', taking into account that patient's personal circumstances. The guidance goes into considerable detail as to the factors that should be taken into account in determining what is reasonable and the application of the means-testing criteria.

---

134   Department of Health, *Healthcare travel costs scheme: instructions and guidance for the NHS*, 2010.

135   National Health Service (Travel Expenses and Remission of Charges) Regulations 2003 SI No 2382 as extensively amended.

136   Reg 3 of the amended 2003 Regulations.

NHS specialist or intensive services for people in care homes

11.100 It is a basic tenet of the NHS that all medical and nursing services are provided free at the point of need. While this principle is curtailed insofar as it applies to the needs of residents in nursing homes not funded by the NHS, the limitation only applies to the non-registered nursing[137] needs of such residents.

11.101 The respective responsibilities of the NHS and social services authorities in this area have been the subject of successive guidance. LAC (92)24 advised (at para 2):

> Local authority contracts for independent sector residential care should not include provision of any service which it is the responsibility of the NHS to provide. It will continue to be the responsibility of the NHS to provide where necessary community health services to residents of LA and independent residential care homes on the same basis as to people in their own homes. These services include the provision of district nursing and other specialist nursing services (eg, incontinence advice) as well as the provision, where necessary, of incontinence and nursing aids, physiotherapy, speech and language therapy and chiropody. Where such services are provided they must be free of charge to people in independent sector homes as well as to residents of local authority Part III homes.

11.102 Guidance from 1995[138] clarified this distinction in the following terms:

> Some people who will be appropriately placed by social services in nursing homes, as their permanent home, may still require some regular access to specialist medical, nursing or other community health services. This will also apply to people who have arranged and are funding their own care. This may include occasional continuing specialist medical advice or treatment, specialist palliative care, specialist nursing care such as incontinence advice, stoma care or diabetic advice or community health services such as physiotherapy, speech therapy and language therapy and chiropody. It should also include specialist medical or nursing equipment (for instance specialist feeding equipment) not available on prescription and normally only available through hospitals ...

> Assessment procedures and arrangements for purchasing care should take account of such needs and details should be identified in individual care plans. In such cases the NHS can either provide such services directly or contract with the home to provide the additional services required. Such additional services should be free at the point of delivery.

11.103 LAC (92)24 defined what was meant by 'specialist nursing' as:

> ... primarily continence advice and stoma care, but also other specialist nursing such as diabetic liaison and other community health services (primarily physiotherapy, speech and language therapy and chiropody.

---

137 The NHS is responsible for all nursing care provided by a registered nurse, or nursing care planned, supervised and/or delegated by a registered nurse (even if actually undertaken by a non-registered nurse) – see para 11.110 below.

138 Department of Health, *NHS responsibilities for meeting continuing health care needs* LAC (95)5, 1995.

11.104   In relation to English NHS services for care home residents, the range of general health services described in 2012 National framework for NHS CC[139] should also be made available.

Specialist medical equipment in care homes

11.105   The joint responsibilities of social services and the NHS for the community equipment services is considered at para 7.72 above. However, the issue of 'specialist medical and nursing' equipment can cause problems. In general, however, a care home providing nursing only has to provide the general equipment which is a prerequisite for its registration.[140] Thus if a patient is in need of equipment which is not part of the basic registration requirement, it may be argued that this is therefore 'specialist' in the sense that it ought to be funded by the NHS.[141] The health service ombudsman has, for instance, investigated a complaint[142] concerning an elderly nursing home resident who had to be fed by means of a gastric tube. Although the liquid feed was supplied on prescription, she was required to pay for the tubes through which the feed was delivered (at £25 per week). The health authority accepted that this was incorrect and refunded the cost of the tubes.

11.106   The 2012 National framework for NHS continuing healthcare[143] advises (at para 172) that where a care home resident requires equipment to meet their care needs, 'there are several routes by which this may be provided':

    a) If the individual is, or will be, supported in a care-home setting, the care home may be required to provide certain equipment as part of regulatory standards or as part of its contract with the CCG. Further details of the regulatory standards can be found on the Care Quality Commission's website at www.cqc.org.uk.

    b) In accordance with the principles set out in paragraphs 113–117, individuals who are entitled to NHS continuing healthcare have an entitlement – on the same basis as other patients – to joint equipment services. CCGs should ensure that the availability to those in receipt of

---

139 Department of Health, *National framework for NHS continuing healthcare and NHS-funded nursing care*, 2012, para 115.

140 Health and Social Care Act 2008 (Regulated Activities) Regulations 2014 SI No 2936 reg 12(2)(f) require that where regulated providers provide equipment they must ensure that there 'are sufficient quantities of these to ensure the safety of service users and to meet their needs'. Regulation 2 states that 'equipment' includes a medical device; and that a 'medical device' has the same meaning as in the Medical Devices Regulations 2002 SI No 618 as amended.

141 Department of Health, *Discharge from hospital: pathway, process and practice guidance*, 2003, para 5.3.1 (which has now been superseded (see para 5.8 above)) states that 'care homes providing nursing care are expected to have, as part of the facilities they provide, some standard items of equipment for anyone needing them and for the safety of staff. These should include hoists, wheelchairs for occasional use, bath and shower seats and fixed items such as grab rails. All other items of equipment to meet the needs of an individual should be, or should have been, provided to them on the same basis as if they were living in a private house, applying the same eligibility criteria'.

142 *Selected investigations April–September 1996*, Case no E.985/94, p61.

143 Department of Health, *National framework for NHS continuing healthcare and NHS-funded nursing care*, 2012, para 115; see also Department of Health, *NHS-funded nursing care practice guide* (revised), 2013, para 47.

NHS continuing healthcare is taken into account in the planning, commissioning and funding arrangements for these services.

c) Some individuals will require bespoke equipment (or other non-bespoke equipment that is not available through routes (a) and (b) above) to meet specific assessed needs identified in their NHS continuing healthcare care plan. CCGs should make appropriate arrangements to meet these needs. CCGs should ensure that there is clarity about which of the above arrangements is applicable in each individual case.

11.107 Guidance has been issued concerning the provision of such equipment through joint community equipment stores[144] (see para 7.73). Department of Health circular HSC 2001/17: LAC (2001)26[145] additionally made the following comments concerning specialist equipment:

> 8. For the majority of care home residents, much of the equipment necessary for their care will be available in the care home. Equipment is also available on prescription from a GP or a prescribing nurse. Details are contained in the Drug Tariff. This covers a range of appliances, including stoma and incontinence appliances, as well as the domiciliary oxygen therapy service.
>
> 9. Care home residents should have access to the full range of specialist NHS support that is available in other care settings and to people receiving care at home. In addition to equipment that is provided or secured by the care home in accordance with the minimum standards, the NHS should also consider whether there is a need to provide residents with access to dietary advice, as well as to the full range of available community equipment services, including pressure redistributing equipment, aids to mobility, and communication aids, etc that are available in other settings. Specialist equipment needs for individual use should be specified in the assessment and subsequent care plan, together with the arrangements for getting the equipment in place, and any after-care that may be necessary. Residents should have access to other NHS services, such as the wheelchair service, and staff working for the NHS should be responsible for assessing them.

11.108 LAC 2003 (7): HSC 2003/006[146] states (para 30):

> Where the NHS has determined that the individual requires a particular piece of equipment, it should ensure either that the care home provides it; or provide it on a temporary basis until the care home is able to provide it; or provide it to the individual as long as they need it. It would be unreasonable to expect care homes to provide items of equipment, that by the nature of the design size and weight requirements, need to be specially tailored to meet the individual's needs and would not be capable of being used by other care home residents.

---

144 Department of Health, *Community equipment services* HSC 2001/008: LAC (2001)13, 2001.

145 Department of Health, *Guidance on free nursing care in nursing homes*, 2001. Although this guidance has been discontinued as a result of the new free nursing care guidance (see para 11.110 below), its advice in this respect would appear to remain valid, not least because it is cited frequently in the (extant) guidance, Department of Health, *Community equipment and care homes: integrating community equipment services*, 2004.

146 Department of Health, *Good practice in continence services*, April 2000.

11.109   One approach to the difficulty in distinguishing between standard items, that should be provided by the care home, and items to be funded by the health bodies was suggested in 2004 non-statutory guidance:[147]

> If a significant number of people use a particular item of equipment in a particular care home it is more likely to be for the care home to provide. If it is for a single user as part of a specific agreed care plan, then it is more likely for health or social services to be the provider even though some of these items may not always be called 'specialist'.

NHS payments for registered nursing care in nursing homes

11.110   In 1999 the Royal Commission on long-term care published its report *With respect to old age*[148] recommending that personal care and nursing services should be provided free of charge to all persons assessed as being in need of these services (regardless of whether they were living in the community, a care home or a hospital). The government in England felt unable to accept the full recommendations and opted instead only to extend (free at the point of need) funding to cover the registered nursing care costs of residents in nursing homes.[149]

11.111   The policy proposal was brought into effect in England and Wales via Health and Social Care Act (HSCA) 2001 s49 which made it unlawful for a local authority to provide nursing 'by a registered nurse'. This prohibition is now found in the CA 2014 s22(3) which states:

> A local authority may not meet needs under sections 18 to 20 by providing or arranging for the provision of nursing care by a registered nurse.[150]

11.112   CA 2014 s22(8) then provides that:

> A reference to the provision of nursing care by a registered nurse is a reference to the provision by a registered nurse of a service involving–
> (a) the provision of care, or
> (b) the planning, supervision or delegation of the provision of care,
> other than a service which, having regard to its nature and the circumstances in which it is provided, does not need to be provided by a registered nurse.

11.113   Section 22 does not, however, prohibit local authority placements in nursing homes provided CCG consent to the placement has been obtained

---

147   Department of Health, *Community equipment and care homes: integrating community equipment services*, 2004. It states that it does not create new guidance, nor resolve contradictions that may occur from the application or interpretation of existing or future government guidance, nor does it necessarily represent the views of the Department of Health.

148   Royal Commission on Long-Term Care, *With respect to old age: long-term care – rights and responsibilities*, Cm 4192, 1999.

149   Announced in Department of Health, *The NHS Plan*, July 2000, para 15.181 and enacted as HSCA 2001 s49.

150   In *Forge Care Homes Ltd v Cardiff & Vale University Health Board* [2016] EWCA Civ 26 the Court of Appeal reviewed the background and interpretation of HSCA 2001 s49 and held, in effect, that it did not prevent a registered nurse carrying out non-NHS functions– ie that not 'everything she does on duty is to be treated as a service which "need[s] to be provided by a registered nurse"' – Laws LJ at para 31.

(unless it is urgent and temporary).[151] Such placements are governed by regulations (the 'CCG regulations' in the following sections)[152] and in any event the 'registered nursing care element' must be funded by the CCG (considered below).

Registered nursing contribution

11.114 Practice guidance from 2013 concerning the process of assessing and reviewing eligibility for the NHS-funded nursing care has been published by the Department of Health.[153] Whenever an individual enters a nursing home, or is in need of such a placement,[154] the responsible CCG must undertake an assessment[155] to decide if he or she is eligible for NHS CC funding.[156] If the assessment identifies that the person is in need for nursing care but ineligible for NHS CC funding, then the CCG must 'pay to a registered person for the relevant premises' (reg 28(6)) a flat rate payment in respect of the individual's nursing care until such time as the person ceases to be eligible. Regulations 6A–6C deal with the situation where the local authority has arranged accommodation for the individual in Northern Ireland or Scotland.

11.115 The flat rate payment for NHS funded nursing care was introduced in 2007[157] and prior to this a banded system operated. Those individuals under the previous system who had been assessed as eligible for the 'high band'[158] have preserved entitlement to this more generous rate[159] (CCG regulations reg 30), unless there is a material change in their

---

151 CA 2014 s22(4) and National Health Service Commissioning Board and Clinical Commissioning Groups (Responsibilities and Standing Rules) Regulations 2012 SI No 2996 reg 30.

152 National Health Service Commissioning Board and Clinical Commissioning Groups (Responsibilities and Standing Rules) Regulations 2012 SI No 2996.

153 Department of Health, *NHS-funded nursing care practice guide* (revised), July 2013.

154 National Health Service Commissioning Board and Clinical Commissioning Groups (Responsibilities and Standing Rules) Regulations 2012 SI No 2996 reg 20 refers to 'relevant premises' which it defines as premises where a 'regulated activity' is carried out – namely the provision of residential accommodation, together with personal or nursing care, specified in Health and Social Care Act 2008 (Regulated Activities) Regulations 2014 Sch 1 para 2.

155 National Health Service Commissioning Board and Clinical Commissioning Groups (Responsibilities and Standing Rules) Regulations 2012 SI No 2996 reg 28.

156 The assessment being required by National Health Service Commissioning Board and Clinical Commissioning Groups (Responsibilities and Standing Rules) Regulations 2012 SI No 2996 reg 21.

157 As a result of the judgment in *R (Grogan) v Bexley NHS Care Trust and others* [2006] EWHC 44 (Admin), (2006) 9 CCLR 188, para 61. For a background to this case and its impact see the 5th edition of this book, para 13.114.

158 The assessment process was referred to as a 'RNCC determination' and this is defined in the National Health Service Commissioning Board and Clinical Commissioning Groups (Responsibilities and Standing Rules) Regulations 2012 SI No 2996 as 'a determination as to the Registered Nursing Contribution to Care taken in respect of a person in accordance with the National Health Service (Nursing Care in Residential Accommodation) (England) Directions 2001'. Problematically, the 2001 Directions are no longer available (ie no longer on the Department of Health website or otherwise).

159 See National Health Service (Nursing Care in Residential Accommodation) (England) Directions 2007, Direction 4, paras (2) and (3).

circumstances. In January 2017 the 'flat rate' NHS funded nursing care contribution amounted to £156.25 per week, and those individuals with preserved entitlement to the higher rate receive £215.04 per week.

11.116 Patients in all care settings also have the right to a full range of primary, community, secondary and other health services,[160] including continence care supplies (see para 11.87 above) and provision of such products or payments must be in addition to the payment for NHS-funded nursing care.[161]

NHS funded nursing care and its interface with continuing care

11.117 It could be argued that with the advent of the NHS funded nursing care contribution, continuing healthcare responsibilities came to an end, since the arrangement provides a reasonably clear demarcation between the respective responsibilities of the NHS and social services. This is not the case. The payment was introduced to encourage NHS bodies to maximise patient rehabilitation, as the explanatory note to HSCA 2001 s49 made clear – to 'strengthen the incentives for the NHS to ensure effective rehabilitation after acute illness or injury'.

11.118 Earlier (now superseded) 2001 English guidance[162] was explicit about the distinction between such payments and continuing care:

> Nothing in this guidance changes the duties of [health bodies] to arrange and fully fund services for people whose primary needs are for healthcare rather than for accommodation and personal care.

11.119 As noted above, the CCG regulations (and the 2012 continuing healthcare guidance para 14) also stipulate that eligibility for NHS CC must be determined before consideration is given to an individual's potential entitlement to NHS-funded nursing care.

Payments during absences

11.120 The 2013 practice guidance[163] adopts a pragmatic approach to payments while a resident is temporarily in hospital. It suggests that in order to secure a place in the home, 'CCGs should consider' paying a retainer equivalent to the value of the payment for NHS-funded nursing care. It points out that custom and practice has been for local authorities to agree to pay the full fee for a set period of time (usually six weeks).

Responsible commissioner

11.121 The CCG responsible for making the NHS-funded nursing care payments for nursing home residents is based on the 'responsible commissioner' rules – considered at para 6.92 above. In general this is the responsibility

---

160 See Department of Health, *NHS-funded nursing care practice guide* (revised), 2013, paras 39–49.

161 See Department of Health, *NHS-funded nursing care practice guide* (revised), 2013, para 49.

162 Department of Health, *Guidance on free nursing care in nursing homes*, HSC (2001)17: LAC (2001)26, appendix 6.

163 Department of Health, *NHS-funded nursing care practice guide* (revised), 2013, paras 65–68.

of the CCG that funds the GP practice with whom the resident is registered. This question (including the cross-border protocols that have been developed to deal with the differing amounts paid by England and Wales) is considered further at para 6.103 above.

Reviews of the payment of NHS-funded nursing care

11.122 The 2013 guidance requires that NHS-funded nursing care payments should be reviewed within three months of the initial eligibility decision and annually thereafter (or more often should the resident's circumstances warrant it).[164]

11.123 If a person is dissatisfied with the outcome of a decision relating to his or her eligibility for NHS-funded nursing care, then the person is entitled to seek a review of that decision, and if the person remains dissatisfied his or her remedy is through the NHS complaints procedure (see para 20.7 below).[165]

Budget sharing arrangements

11.124 The gap between the political rhetoric urging joint working and the organisational imperatives of the health bodies and councils, has been noted above (see para 11.36). Lymbery, citing Means and Smith's[166] view that the 'Berlin wall' that exists between the two services is in large measure a creation of successive governments, argues that 'to imply that organizations or professions are responsible for this is disingenuous at best or duplicitous at worst'.[167]

11.125 Since the creation of the health service, attempts have been made to span this organisational divide by amending the successive NHS Acts to provide legal mechanisms that can be used, if and when there is a common desire to collaborate. CA 2014 s3 adds a further provision to this statutory mix – with a general obligation on local authorities to exercise their functions under the CA 2104 with a view to 'ensuring integration' with health provision.

11.126 These provisions inevitably come with complex governance requirements,[168] which derive from the macro distinction (in budgetary terms) between the two organisations: the 'free at the point of need' NHS and the 'means-tested' social care service. Accountability is an additional material

164 Department of Health, *NHS-funded nursing care practice guide* (revised), 2013, paras 50 and 55.

165 Department of Health, *NHS-funded nursing care practice guide* (revised), 2013, para 57.

166 R Means and R Smith, *From Poor Law to community care,* 2nd edn, Policy Press, 1998; and R Means, H Morbey and R Smith, *From community care to market care?* Policy Press, 2002.

167 M Lymbery 'United we stand? Partnership working in health and social care and the role of social work in services for older people' *British Journal of Social Work* (2006) 36 1120.

168 See eg Audit Commission, *Clarifying joint financing arrangements: a briefing paper for health bodies and local authorities,* 2008; and Audit Commission, *Working better together? Managing local strategic partnerships,* 2009.

distinction: unlike local health bodies, local authorities rely on local taxes (council tax) for which their elected politicians are answerable.

11.127   Historically the ability of the NHS and social services authorities to pool budgets, or transfer resources from one to another was severely curtailed. In consequence it was argued that innovation had been stifled and 'cost shunting' between authorities encouraged.[169] In response to these concerns, HA 1999 ss29–31, enabled health bodies and social services to enter into a wide range of 'partnership arrangements'. These provisions are now to be found in NHSA 2006 ss75–76 and 256–257.

11.128   NHSA 2006 ss256–257 enable NHS England and CCGs to make payments to local authorities and voluntary organisations in respect of any local authority function that is health-related; and section 76 provides a reciprocal power for local authorities to make payments to NHS England and CCGs in relation to 'prescribed functions'. 'Prescribed functions' have been defined widely in regulations,[170] excluding only such matters as 'surgery, radiotherapy, termination of pregnancies, endoscopy, [certain] laser treatments and other invasive treatments'.[171]

11.129   In relation to people with learning disabilities in English long-stay NHS accommodation, a major structural transfer of this kind has occurred as a result of a 2007 Department of Health initiative – the *Valuing people now: from progress to transformation* – and this is considered further at para 15.34 below.

Section 75 partnerships arrangements

11.130   NHSA 2006 s75 allows NHS bodies and local authorities to pool their resources, delegate functions and transfer resources from one party to another and enable a single provider to provide both health and local authority services. Such arrangements derive from provisions in Health Act (HA) 2009 s31 and were therefore formerly referred to as 'section 31 agreements'. Section 75, in effect, permits:

- **Pooled fund arrangements:** Where authorities pool resources so that they will effectively 'lose their health and local authority identity', allowing staff from either agency to develop packages of care suited to particular individuals irrespective of whether health or local authority money is used.
- **Delegation of functions – lead commissioning:** Where CCGs and local authorities delegate functions to one another (including the secondment or transfer of staff). In the case of health and social care, this enables one of the partner bodies to commission all mental health or learning disability services locally.
- **Delegation of functions – integrated provision:** This consists of the provision of health and local authority services from a single managed

169 Department of Health, *Partnership in action*, discussion paper, September 1998.
170 NHS Bodies and Local Authorities (Partnership Arrangements, Care Trusts, Public Health and Local Healthwatch) Regulations 2012 SI 3094 to include services under the NHS Acts 2006 ss3, 3A and 3B as well as functions under MHA 1983 s117.
171 NHS Bodies and Local Authorities (Partnership Arrangements, Care Trusts, Public Health and Local Healthwatch) Regulations 2012 SI 3094 reg 13.

provider. The arrangement can be used in conjunction with lead commissioning and pooled fund arrangements.

11.131   It appears that the most common pooled budget arrangements involve local authorities taking the lead role as commissioners of learning disability services and health bodies taking the lead role as commissioners of mental health services.

11.132   As with the budget sharing regulations above, most NHS functions can be the subject of partnership arrangements (with the same exceptions – see para 11.124 above). Likewise, a wide range of social services functions can be the subject of partnership arrangements – including charging for care and support under the CA 2014.[172] NHSA 2006 s75(5) provides that any partnership arrangements made under section 75 will not affect the liability of the NHS body or the local authority for the exercise of its functions. Liability remains, therefore, with the body primarily responsible for the discharge of the function (ie the body with this responsibility prior to the partnership arrangement). Guidance on these arrangements was issued in England in 2000.[173] Current guidance focuses on the potential for section 75 arrangements to advance the government's objectives with the 'Better Care Fund' (see below).

11.133   As noted above (para 1.25), local authorities are able to delegate almost all of their functions under CA 2014. Historically such function sharing/devolving was effected by section 75 agreements – and these may continue to predominate. Many existing section 75 agreements will refer to pre-CA 2014 legislation, and authorities may need to update these to ensure they make (where necessary) specific references to the CA 2014.

Better Care Fund arrangements

11.134   CA 2014 s3 places a duty on local authorities to promote integration with health provision where it would:

a)   promote the well-being of adults with needs and carers in its area; or

b)   contribute to the prevention of the development of needs in adults/carers; or

c)   improve the quality of care for adults/carers provided.

11.135   A component of this new duty includes the establishment of the 'Better Care Fund'.[174] The underpinning legal mechanisms for this fund are complex – essentially CA 2014 s121 amended NHSA 2006 s223B to enable the

172   NHS Bodies and Local Authorities Partnership Arrangements Regulations 2000 SI No 617 as amended. Significant amendments were made in 2016, via the NHS Bodies and Local Authorities Partnership Arrangements (Amendment) Regulations 2015 SI No 1940 which included, among other things, the removal of CCGs duty to consult persons who appear to be affected by such arrangements.

173   Department of Health, *Implementation of Health Act partnership arrangements* HSC 2000/010/LAC (2000)9, 2000 accompanied by guidance on 'The Health Act section 31 Partnership Arrangements'.

174   For technical detail about the fund, see NHS England, *Better Care Fund planning*, 2016; and Department of Health, *Better Care Fund: how it will work in 2016 to 2017*; and for general requirements for NHS/social services transfers see National Health Service (Conditions Relating to Payments in connection with property by NHS Bodies to Local Authorities and other bodies) Directions 2016.

secretary of state to attach strings to payments made to the NHS England – including that the relevant NHS body have a pooled fund with its local authority(ies) aimed primarily at easing pressure on NHS acute beds – eg to facilitate hospital discharges/prevent unnecessary admissions; promote integrated packages of care etc.

11.136   Since its inception doubts have been expressed about the true level of 'new' resources that the government has provided the fund and about its strategic viability. In 2014 the Public Accounts Committee expressed concern about government departments' understanding of the pressures on the adult social care system and that the impact on this of the Better Care Fund.[175] The committee's report confirmed doubts as to whether the NHS was able to make the anticipated transfers to social services and the general scepticism about the success of such 'integrations'.[176] Further criticism concerning the quality planning for the Better Care Fund followed in November 2014 from the National Audit Office,[177] and in 2015 the Public Accounts Committee noted that the government was only confident that proposed savings it would produce would be £55 million rather than the £1 billion assumed and that 'planning for the Fund was deeply flawed'.[178] Local authority perception of the fund appears to be 'predominantly negative': that at the local level plans were being 'dictated' by CCGs 'without much space for collaboration'[179] and generally it appears that the integration proposals have made 'little progress'.[180]

11.137   There are a number of legal mechanisms by which that the integration process can be advanced – including through the development of agreements under the NHSA 2006 s75.[181] 'Section 75 agreements' are relatively common in relation to mental health services, and to a lesser degree in relation to other health and social care functions. Authorities will need to check existing agreements – to update specific references to pre-CA 2014 provisions in the delegation sections.

11.138   In 2016 the Department of Health announced that for the financial year 2016/17,[182] the Better Care Fund will be a minimum of £3.9 billion. Locally agreed plans must be signed off by NHS England and must meet four key conditions:

175 House of Commons Committee of Public Accounts, *Adult social care in England* HC 518, The Stationery Office, 2014, p6.

176 See, for example, A Cameron, R Lart, L Bostock and C Coombe, *Factors that promote and hinder joint and integrated working between health and social care services*, SCIE Research Briefing 41, 2012; and B Hudson 'Joint commissioning: organisational revolution or misplaced enthusiasm?' (1995) 23 *Policy & Politics* p233.

177 Department of Health, Department for Communities and Local Government and NHS England, *Planning for the Better Care Fund*, HC 781 Session 2014–15 11, National Audit Office, 2014.

178 Public Accounts Committee Chair's comments: *Planning for the Better Care Fund report*, 26 February 2015.

179 R Humphries and others. *Social care for older people: home truths*, King's Fund, 2016, p69.

180 David Williams, 'Little progress by "integration pioneers"', *Health Service Journal*, 6 May 2016.

181 See para 11.130 above; and generally the statutory guidance, chapter 15.

182 Department of Health, *2016/17 Better Care Fund policy framework*, January 2016.

1) the project funding is made from pooled funds via a NHS Act 2006 s75 agreement;
2) the agreement must be approved by the Health and Wellbeing Boards and signed-off by the relevant local authority and CCG(s);
3) a proportion of the Better Care Fund allocation must be spent on NHS 'commissioned out of hospital services, which may include a wide range of services including social care';
4) there is a 'clear, focused action plan for managing delayed transfers of care including locally agreed targets'.[183]

Dowry payments and post dowry arrangements

11.139   Prior to the HA 1999 amendments, budget transfers were only permitted one way – from NHS bodies to local authorities, housing associations and certain other bodies in respect of personal social services, education for disabled people and housing. Detailed guidance[184] and directions[185] were issued in relation to these payments. These provisions permitted various schemes, including an arrangement known as 'dowry' payments.

11.140   Dowry payments were used to facilitate the transfer of patients from long-stay hospitals into the community. They involved a lump-sum payment or annual payment to a local authority taking over the patient's care; the amount of the lump-sum or annual payment and the length of time for which annual payments were to be made being negotiated by the respective authorities. In this context HSG (95)45 advised:[186]

> ... in respect of people being discharged from long stay institutions, the NHS is responsible for negotiating arrangements with local authorities, including any appropriate transfer of resources which assist the local authority meeting the community care needs of such people and of their successors who may otherwise have entered the institution.

11.141   The relevance of such arrangements (or more precisely the lack of these) was spelled out in 1992 guidance[187] which stated that:

> Where residential care arrangements in the community for a person who was formerly a patient in a long-stay hospital appear to be breaking down ... then the LA ... should take the lead in seeing that the appropriate

---

183   See also The Better Care Fund, *Delayed transfers of care signposting resource*, March 2016.

184   LAC (92)17, HSG (92)43 and HSG (95)45.

185   Directions under NHSA 1977 s28A being contained as annex C to HSG (92)43.

186   Department of Health, *Arrangements between health authorities and NHS Trusts and private and voluntary sector organisations for the provision of community care Services* HSG (95)45, 1995, annex, para 4.1. The circular was cancelled by the Department of Health, *Continuing care: NHS and local councils' responsibilities* HSC 2001/015: LAC (2001)18, 2001, annex A which was, however, silent on this question. The 2001 circular has now been superseded by Department of Health, *National framework for NHS continuing healthcare and NHS-funded nursing care*, 2012 which places considerable emphasis on the importance of neither the CCG nor local authority unilaterally withdrawing from a funding arrangement.

187   LAC (92)17: HSG (92)43, annex A para 10. This circular was 'superseded' by Department of Health, *Commencement of sections 29 and 30 of the Health Act*, 1999 HSC 2000/011: LAC 2000/10, 2000, which although silent on this specific issue, is framed in terms of local authority/health body agreements on funding and funding transfers.

arrangements are secured ... Where no agreement has been made between the DHA responsible for the hospital care before discharge and the LA about respective responsibilities, the HA should assist the LA ... and if the resecuring or reprovisioning of care leads the LA to incur additional expenditure, the HA will be expected to use its powers under s28A to assist the LA to fund the care.

11.142   Where there has been a dowry agreement, then it appears that this will be subsumed into the receiving local authority's finances. It appears that if an individual to whom the dowry relates then moves to a new authority, the funding will not follow that individual (or be relevant to any subsequent ordinary residence dispute – see chapter 6) even if the individual is named on the memorandum of the grant relating to the dowry.

11.143   Despite the emphasis on a joint agreement between health and social care bodies for any funding transfer (collective or individual) this is not always found in practice.[188] In the past decades, health bodies have often transferred responsibility for individuals or groups of individuals to third parties: for example, to independent supported living schemes or by the misuse of arrangements under Health Services and Public Health Act (HSPHA) 1968 s64 (see below). The health bodies gained financially from such transactions, by essentially transferring the cost of supporting the individual to another public budget (eg the housing benefit and/or supporting peoples' budgets). With the demise or curtailment of these funding streams, the care arrangements for some of these individuals are breaking down: individuals for whom no funding agreement has been secured from social services. In such cases, there remains considerable weight to the above advice (not least from a public accounting perspective) – namely that 'if the resecuring or reprovisioning of care leads the [local authority] to incur additional expenditure' the health body would be expected to use its powers under what is now NHSA 2006 ss256–257.

11.144   It would appear that there has been a consistent government view on this question. The first NHS CC guidance in 1995[189] advised that where 'either health or local authorities are proposing a significant change in the pattern of services which will impact on the resources of the other agencies for providing care, they must seek the agreement of the other agency.' The current 2012 guidance states that 'neither the NHS nor an [local authority] should unilaterally withdraw from funding of an existing package ... [and that if] agreement between the [local authority] and NHS cannot be reached on the proposed change ... current funding and care management responsibilities should remain in place until the dispute has been resolved'.[190]

---

188 In some cases, it appears that although agreements have been reached concerning a patient or a cohort of patients, these have not been evidenced in writing (or the written agreement has expired). In such cases, significant problems can result when there is a change in the status quo – eg if there is an increase in the service costs or of the needs of a particular individual.

189 *NHS responsibilities for meeting continuing healthcare needs* LAC (95)5: HSG (95)8.

190 Department of Health, *The national framework for NHS continuing healthcare and NHS funded nursing care*, 2012, para 143.

Section 64 agreements[191]

11.145   Although NHSA 2006 ss256–257 are the appropriate statutory provisions by which a health body transfers to a social services authority its responsibility for patients who are capable of being supported through the community care regime, it appears that in the past, a number of health bodies (ie authorities and PCTs) inappropriately sought to use their powers under HSPHA 1968 s64. This improper use was highlighted by the Department of Health in a 2003 report.[192]

11.146   HSPHA 1968 s64 gave the secretary of state powers to make grants to voluntary and community sector organisations. These could be made nationally (from the 'general scheme'), although most frequently they were made locally, for which the use of section 64 had been delegated to CCGs. There was no requirement to report on the use made of section 64, and, as the Department of Health report made clear, it did not hold any information about the grants that had been awarded.

11.147   The 2003 report described how PCTs (and indeed the Department of Health) had been using section 64 inappropriately. Instead of making grants under this provision, they entered into service level agreements with voluntary and community sector organisations. As the report stated (para 10), the 'distinction between a grant and a contract for the provision of a service is clear'. The report also explained that the appropriate mechanism for a health body to enter into a contract for services, is to use its powers under what is now NHSA 2006 s12 or to transfer the money to social services via what is now NHSA 2006 ss256–257. The importance of the latter arrangement is that, in order to do so, the health body would have had to have obtained social services' agreement to it discharging the (hitherto) NHS function. In the absence of such an agreement, the function remains with the NHS – if, for example, the voluntary/community sector organisation withdraws from the contract. This has occurred on a number of occasions – where, for example, the scheme became uneconomic.

191   Under Health Services and Public Health Services Act 1968 s64. For details of the section 64 grant replacement scheme, see Department of Health, *Third sector investment programme innovation excellence and service development fund 2010–11*, 2009.

192   Department of Health, *Report of a review group established to examine the use of the power to make grants under section 64 of the Health Services and Public Health Act 1968*, 2003.

NHS continuing healthcare responsibilities

continued

Introduction

12.1 This chapter considers the responsibilities of the National Health Service (NHS) for social care support under the National Health Service Acts 2006. Although local authorities have primary responsibility for the provision of social care, some individuals with significant healthcare needs may move across the interface – from the means-tested social services system to the 'free at the point of need' NHS system. In most cases, this is an interface between two statutes: the social care Act – the Care Act (CA) 2014, and the health Act – the National Health Service Act (NHSA) 2006. In some cases, however, the Mental Health Act (MHA) 1983 constitutes an additional (and complicating) role, and this is considered separately at para 12.194 below.

12.2 This chapter considers the legal position in England as at January 2017.

Historical and legal context of the health and social care divide

12.3 The debate over NHS continuing healthcare (NHS CC) responsibilities is not new. Means, Morbey and Smith[1] chart the organisational tensions that have existed over the health/social care divide since the formation of the NHS in 1948. They conclude that these have been characterised by a failure of the NHS to invest in community health services or to transfer significant resources to social services. They describe how the conflict has generally been expressed in debates over what is healthcare and what is social care. Guidance issued in 1957[2] on the relative responsibilities of local authorities and the NHS shows how far the demarcation line has shifted since that time[3] – a point emphasised by commentators who have suggested that health bodies had not merely been effective at shifting their responsibilities to social services[4] but that they had 'reneged on their responsibilities for funding continuing care and shunted costs on to councils'.[5]

12.4 Although in practice the demarcation of the health/social care boundary has changed considerably over the years since 1948, legally there has been no material diminution in the scope of the NHS CC responsibilities since that time. The material changes have been in terms of demography,

---

1 R Means, H Morbey and R Smith, *From community care to market care?* Policy Press, 2002, p85.

2 The 'Boucher report', cited in R Means, H Morbey and R Smith, *From community care to market care?* Policy Press, 2002, p78.

3 Suggesting eg that the NHS should provide care for 'the chronic bedfast who may need little or no medical treatment, but who do require prolonged nursing care over months or years'.

4 See eg, J Lewis, 'Older people and the health-social care boundary in the UK: Half a century of hidden policy conflict' (2001) *Social Policy and Administration* 35(4) pp343–59.

5 The Parliamentary Under-Secretary of State for Health Ivan Lewis, quoted in *Community Care* 22–28 February 2007 p8, see also Hansard, HC 23 October 2007: col 23WH.

policy and funding arrangements. In relation to the latter two factors, the most significant concerned the availability in 1979 of supplementary benefit payments (later income support) to cover the cost of private nursing home accommodation. This situation led to the closure of many NHS continuing care wards, with the patients being transferred to privately run nursing homes funded by the social security budget. The strain on this budget resulted in targeted action against NHS bodies deemed to be inappropriately exploiting the situation (most notably in *White v CAO*[6]) and ultimately in the wholesale reform of the social care system.

12.5   On 1 April 1993, social services authorities became the 'gate keepers' for such community placements. This led to a general, but incorrect, assumption that the NHS no longer had the same responsibility for funding long-term care. The fact that social services authorities were (for the first time) empowered to make payments towards the cost of independent nursing home placements also encouraged the view that the NHS was no longer an agency responsible for making similar payments. In fact, the responsibility for the care of persons in need of nursing home accommodation is an overlapping one between the two services.

12.6   The 1980s were characterised by a rapid closure of long-term NHS beds[7] and an increase in individuals' inheritable wealth.[8] By the early 1990s, many individuals found that when they became chronically ill and needed care outside their own home, they had to pay for this in a nursing home – whereas previously such people had received it free in a long-stay NHS bed. They and their carers accordingly paid substantial sums for their nursing needs (not infrequently having to sell their former family home[9]) in situations where previously the care would have been provided without charge by the NHS.

12.7   It is this aspect that came prominently to the fore with the publication by the Health Service Commissioner of a critical report into a hospital

6   *White v Chief Adjudication Officer* (Social Security Decision R(S) 8/85; (1993) *Times*, August 2) where the court held that patients transferred to a nursing home under a contract with the NHS body, remained the responsibility of the NHS as they were deemed to be in a 'hospital or similar institution'; and see also the Tribunal of Commissioners Decision R(DLA) 2/06, CDLA/3161/2003 27 July 2005 where the tribunal, in finding against the NHS body, criticised it for believing that it was 'legitimate to make every effort to minimise its proper liabilities under the 1977 Act by seeking to transfer them to a budget of another limb of Government through a wholly artificial scheme'.

7   Between 1983 and 1993 there was a 30 per cent (17,000) reduction in the number of long-term geriatric and psychogeriatric NHS beds (T Harding and others, *Options for long-term care*, HMSO, 1996, p8) and between 1988 and 2001 a loss of 50,600 such beds; see House of Commons Health Committee, *Delayed discharges: Third Report of Session 2001–02 Volume 1*, HC 617-I, 2002, p35.

8   Due in significant measure to the dramatic rise in house prices during that period, as well as the extension of home ownership to former council tenants.

9   It is generally considered that about 40,000 homes are sold each year to pay for care home fees – see M Henwood, *Self-funding of long-term care and potential for injustice*, background paper prepared for BBC Panorama, 2006 – although research commissioned by NFU Mutual in 2013 is reported as finding that a million homes had been sold in the previous five years to fund care costs – see J Bingham, 'Elderly care crisis claims a million family homes', *Telegraph*, 3 September 2013.

discharge by the Leeds Health Authority in 1994.[10] The report concerned a 55-year-old man who had had a stroke which rendered him with little or no physical or mental capacity (details of his condition are contained at para 12.217). The patient was discharged from a long-stay hospital placement to a nursing home where he had to pay for his care. A complaint concerning the payment was upheld by the ombudsman, who found that 'the failure to make available long-term care within the NHS for this patient was unreasonable and constitutes a failure in the service provided by the Health Authority' (para 22). The ombudsman considered the case to be 'clear cut', and it was conceded by the National Association of Health Authorities and Trusts that health bodies had 'been bailing out of long-term care and discharging people to private nursing homes ... [made possible] by social security picking up the bill for those poor enough, although others have had to meet the full fees'.[11]

12.8   The ombudsman was so concerned about the situation disclosed by the complaint that he took the exceptional step of having his report separately published. In response, the government undertook to issue guidance, indicating:

> If in the light of the guidance, some health authorities are found to have reduced their capacity to secure continuing care too far – as clearly happened in the case dealt with by the Health Service Commissioner – then they will have to take action to close the gap.[12]

12.9   The evidence suggests that successive governments have failed to take effective action 'to close the gap'. While there has been an increase in the numbers of people in England receiving NHS CC funding (see para below 12.41 below) this has to be set against the numbers of NHS beds that have been lost from the system during the same period[13] and the growing dependency of the population (including for example the greater number of 'old old' people). This failure has not only placed substantial cost burdens on social services authorities and their family carers but it has created significant challenges for many individuals, for whom in former times a 'free' long-stay NHS bed would have been provided. For such people who require a care home placement and who have savings above the social care maximum threshold (see para 8.70 above), the position is stark: during the period 2014/15 the average weekly nursing home fee amounted to £790 per week[14] – and in some areas, particularly London and the Home Counties, fees were considerably higher.

---

10 Health Service Commissioner Second Report for Session 1993–94; Case no E62/93–94.

11 N Timmins, 'NHS faces financial time bomb over care; Long-term nursing 'must be provided', The *Independent* 3 February 1994.

12 Virginia Bottomley, Secretary of State for Health, 4 November 1994.

13 Between 1988 and 2014 the number overnight' NHS beds available in England fell by 50 per cent from almost 300,000 to less than 150,000 – see Nuffield Trust, *Average daily number of overnight beds available and occupied in England*, 2015. Between 2007 (when the new framework in England was introduced) and April 2016 there was a loss of about 30,000 NHS overnight beds in England (from 160,000 to 130,000) – see NHS England, *Bed availability and occupancy data – overnight*, KH03 records (available and occupied beds open overnight that are consultant led).

14 'Care home fees', *Which? Elderly care*, 2016.

The statutory context

12.10   In order to understand the interface between the NHS's responsibilities for continuing healthcare funding and the social services responsibility for providing social care support, it is necessary to understand the relationship between the two principal statutes that regulate this boundary – the CA 2014 and the NHSA 2006.[15]

12.11   The NHSA 2006 is the principal statute governing the health service in England and the general scheme of this Act is considered in chapter 11 above. The responsibility for securing the provision of NHS services rests with the secretary of state in England, although this has in large measure been delegated to clinical commissioning groups (CCGs) (see para 11.12 above).

12.12   The key NHS CC provision is not, however, found in the NSHA 2006, but in the CA 2014. CA 2014 s22 places a limit on the support that can be provided by social services authorities under the Act – prohibiting support that is required to be provided under the NHSA 2006 unless:

(a) doing so would be merely incidental or ancillary to doing something else to meet needs under those sections, and

(b) the service or facility in question would be of a nature that the local authority could be expected to provide

The wording of section 22 is designed to replicate as precisely as possible provisions in the repealed National Assistance Act (NAA) 1948, and the wording of the Court of Appeal in the leading case of *R v North and East Devon health authority ex p Coughlan*[16] (considered below). As the minister responsible for the implementation of the CA 2014 stated:[17]

> The provisions in section 22 are not intended to change the current boundary – let me place that clearly on the record – and we do not believe that they will have that result. The limits on the responsibility by reference, as now, to what should be provided by the NHS remain the same'.

12.13   The CA 2014 imposes what is referred to as a 'limit to social care': a point at which an individual's health care needs are such that it ceases to be lawful for social services to provide support for him or her under the CA 2014. In general[18] the consequence is that all their health and social care needs fall to be provided under the NHSA 2006.

12.14   The statutory scheme is underpinned by regulations[19] and by high level 'Framework guidance',[20] both of which repeat the wording found in CA

---

15 Although as noted above, in some cases the MHA 1983 constitutes an additional (and complicating) role and this is considered separately at para 12.194 below.

16 *R v North and East Devon Health Authority ex p Coughlan* [2000] 2 WLR 622, [2000] 3 All ER 850.

17 Public Act Committee Report, 16 January 2014, pp205–208.

18 The most common exception would be where some of those needs are required to be met under MHA 1983 s117 – see para 12.194 below.

19 National Health Service Commissioning Board and Clinical Commissioning Groups (Responsibilities and Standing Rules) Regulations 2012 SI No 2996.

20 National Framework for NHS Continuing Healthcare and NHS-funded Nursing Care, 2012: this framework is to be amended in 2017 – to update the references to refer to the CA 2014 rather than the NAA 1948.

2014 s22.[21] In addition, in 2014 a best practice guidance was published jointly by the Association of Directors of Adult Social Services Departments (ADASS) and NHS England.[22]

The *Coughlan* judgment

12.15 In 1999 the Court of Appeal delivered its judgment in *R v North and East Devon Health Authority ex p Coughlan*.[23] It reinforced the finding of the Health Service Commissioner in the Leeds health authority complaint (para 12.7 above) that entitlement to NHS CC support arose, not merely when a patient's healthcare needs were complex, but also when they were substantial – the so called 'quality/quantity' criteria.

12.16 Pamela Coughlan was seriously injured in a road traffic accident in 1971. The court described her health care needs in the following terms (para 3):

> She is tetraplegic; doubly incontinent; requiring regular catheterisation; partially paralysed in the respiratory tract, with consequent difficulty in breathing; and subject not only to the attendant problems of immobility but to recurrent headaches caused by an associated neurological condition.

12.17 The health body responsible for her care wanted to close the specialist facility in which she lived – arguing that in order to be eligible for NHS CC funding, a need for 'specialist nursing' had to be established and that Pamela Coughlan only had a need for 'general nursing'. At the time of the hearing, the relevant guidance[24] emphasised the need for such 'specialist' support.

12.18 Pamela Coughlan challenged this decision, and her application was resisted by the Department of Health. The department affirmed its belief in the 'special/general' nursing divide (para 32) and argued that the relevant test concerned the identification of a primary health need (para 31). Neither of these interpretative approaches were adopted by the court. It considered that the 'special/general' divide was at best 'idiosyncratic' (para 41) and that the primary health need test did not in itself determine the question. The court's concern was the failure of the departmental guidance to acknowledge the shifting nature of NHS provision: the fact that long-stay beds were being closed and healthcare was being provided in settings other than hospitals. As the court noted, there was a failure to acknowledge the fact that:

> 41. ... a case does not qualify for in-patient treatment in a hospital does not mean that the person concerned should not be a NHS responsibility. The importance of there being clear statements as to this arise because of the increased emphasis being placed on care in the community. This could result in it being assumed that, because patients who would previously have been treated as in-patients in hospital no longer qualify for such

21 Reg 21(7) and paras 34–35 respectively.
22 Association of Directors of Adult Social Services (ADASS) and NHS England NHS, *Continuing healthcare: guide for health and social care practitioners. Ensuring a consistent person-centred assessment*, September 2014.
23 [2000] 2 WLR 622, (1999) 2 CCLR 285, CA.
24 Department of Health, LAC (95)5: HSG (95)8, *NHS responsibilities for meeting continuing health care needs*.

treatment, they are automatically disqualified from receiving care on the NHS. This is not what is permitted.

42. ... the resident at a nursing home does not require in-patient treatment in a hospital does not mean that his or her care should not be the responsibility of the NHS.

12.19   Having set out its concerns about the government's approach, the court opted for an altogether different test, namely the 'quantity/quality' test, which sets the limits on what social services can provide. It held that social services could only lawfully fund low-level nursing care – low in terms of its quality and its quantity. The court expressed this as follows (at para 30):

(d) There can be no precise legal line drawn between those nursing services which are and those which are not capable of being treated as included in such a package of care services.

(e) The distinction between those services which can and cannot be so provided is one of degree which in a borderline case will depend on a careful appraisal of the facts of the individual case. However, as a very general indication as to where the line is to be drawn, it can be said that if the nursing services are:

- merely incidental or ancillary to the provision of the accommodation which a local authority is under a duty to provide to the category of persons to whom section 21 refers; and
- of a nature which it can be expected that an authority whose primary responsibility is to provide social services can be expected to provide, then they can be provided under section 21.

It will be appreciated that the first part of the test is focusing on the overall quantity of the services and the second part on the quality of the services provided.

12.20   The court emphasised that the setting of a person's care was not determinative of eligibility for continuing healthcare funding. In its view, 'where the primary need is a health need, then the responsibility is that of the NHS, even when the individual has been placed in a home by a local authority' (para 31) and 'the fact that a case does not qualify for in-patient treatment in a hospital does not mean that the person concerned should not be a NHS responsibility' (para 41).

12.21   In relation to the specific eligibility criteria of North and East Devon Health Authority, the court stated (para 48):

However, the eligibility criteria cannot place a responsibility on the local authority which goes beyond the terms of section 21. This is what these criteria do. Cases where the healthcare element goes far beyond what the section permits were being placed upon the local authority as a result of the rigorous limits placed on what services can be considered to be NHS care services. That this is the position is confirmed by the result of the assessment of Miss Coughlan and her fellow occupants. Their disabilities are of a scale which are beyond the scope of local authority services.

12.22   It is perhaps in this respect that the *Coughlan* case is most remarkable. Pamela Coughlan has a C-5/6 neurologically-complete spinal cord injury. As a consequence, she is doubly incontinent, requires regular catheterisation and has partial paralysis in the respiratory tract (although she is able to breathe without artificial support – details of her condition are at para 12.129 below). However, in many respects her nursing needs are comparatively modest (when compared with many residents of nursing homes) – she is able to move her upper body (including her arms); she leads a relatively autonomous life, being able to study, campaign and to use her electric wheelchair. Nevertheless, when applying the court's 'quality/quantity' formulation, it concluded that her needs were 'wholly different category' to that which a social services authority could fund (para 118).

Nursing

12.23 The court in *Coughlan* does not use the verb 'to nurse' to mean 'something done by a nurse'. The *Oxford English Dictionary* definition of the verb is extensive, and of the nine principal meanings it identifies and the 21 variations, it uses the noun 'nurse' only twice – in the context of a 'wet-nurse' and 'to perform the duties of a sick nurse'.

12.24 As noted, in the last 30 years the NHS has deinstitutionalised the care of ill people – ie moving all but the most acutely ill people into the community and frequently back into their own homes. This is of course something to be welcomed: the problem is that this trend has not been accompanied by a corresponding transfer of NHS personnel into community settings.[25] Accordingly, very many 'carers' are doing tasks which in previous times would have been done in hospital: changing catheter bags, peg feeding, stoma care, administering intravenous medication, manual stool evacuations and so on. These tasks are 'nursing' in the OED sense – it matters not who is doing them. This interpretation is endorsed by the 2012 framework (para 56) and by the 2010 hospital discharge guidance that many 'carers are becoming expert in managing long-term chronic conditions and often provide care that is equivalent to that provided by a registered nurse'.[26] In the 2003 ombudsman's *Pointon* report she rejected an NHS body's policy of defining (for the purpose of NHS CC funding) 'nursing tasks' as those which had to be done a qualified nurse (para 35).

Key post-*Coughlan* developments

Guidance

12.25 There is little doubt that the reaction of the Department of Health to the *Coughlan* judgment was less than satisfactory.[27] It took two years to issue revised NHS CC guidance:[28] guidance that was heavily criticised by the

---

25 The number of qualified district nurses fell by 23 per cent between 1996 and 2006 (Queen's Nursing Institute, *Position statement*, 2010) – a trend that appears to be continuing, with a 47 per cent fall in numbers in England between 2003 and 2013 (see J Ball, J Philippou, G Pike and J Sethi, *Survey of district and community nurses in 2013. Report to the Royal College of Nursing*, Kings College, 2014) – and with the risk of extinction by the end of 2025 (see D Campbell, 'District nurses are facing "extinction"', *Guardian*, 17 June 2014).

26 Department of Health, *Ready to go? Planning the discharge and the transfer of patients from hospital and intermediate care*, 2010, p13.

27 For a detailed review of the relevant guidance and directions issued between 2001 and 2007 see the 5th edition of this book, paras 14.25–14.44.

28 HSC 2001/015: LAC (2001)18.

Health Service Commissioner[29] and the High Court.[30] The 2001 guidance could be viewed as an attempt to blunt the impact of the *Coughlan* judgment – to use guidance in effect to frustrate the law.[31] While the department redeemed its position with the publication of generally excellent guidance in 2007, the absence of sound guidance between 1999 and 2007 has left a legacy of what could be described as 'an entrenched culture of ineligibility': a perception by both health and social services professionals that eligibility for NHS CC is almost unattainable.[32]

Reports and judgments

12.26   During the post-*Coughlan* period (and prior to the introduction of the 2007 Framework) a series of important standard setting reports and judgments emerged from the Health Service Commissioner and the High Court, which are reviewed below (and summarised in paras 12.217–12.235 below).

Pointon and the health service ombudsman's report[33]

12.27   In 2004 the ombudsman published an individual report relating to the home care provided to Malcolm Pointon, who had been diagnosed with dementia. The care was provided by his wife with the aid of two full-time carers working alternate weeks (funded by social services direct payments with contributions from Mr and Mrs Pointon). Mrs Pointon asked the local NHS body if it would fund respite care every fifth week, in order to provide her with a break. This was refused on the ground that this was social care and not eligible for NHS CC funding.

12.28   The ombudsman's report identifies a particular problem with the approach taken by the local health body to the NHS CC eligibility assessment – namely the interpretation of what amounts to 'nursing care' (see para 12.23 above). The report notes that the health body did not consider that Mrs Pointon was providing nursing care – as 'it took many years to gain nursing qualifications and skills and that these could not be self taught'; and that 'care given could not be highly professional, as it was not provided by a qualified nurse' (p25). The mistake here is to equate

29 Health Service Ombudsman's Second Report for Session 2002–03, *NHS funding for long-term care*, HC 399, 2003, para 38.

30 *R (Grogan) v Bexley NHS Care Trust and others* [2006] EWHC 44 (Admin), (2006) 9 CCLR 188 – see para 12.36 below.

31 An approach that has a reasonable pedigree – see, for example, *R v Secretary of State for Health ex p Pfizer Ltd* (1999) 2 CCLR 270, QBD.

32 See, for example, the All Party Parliamentary Group on Parkinson's (APPGP), *Failing to care: NHS continuing care in England*, 2013, p16. There appear to be no recent published statistics concerning the number of challenges to NHS CC decisions or their outcomes. Research in 2011 suggested that appeals against adverse decisions rose by nine per cent between 2009/10 to 2010/11 and that during this period the proportion of successful completed challenges rose from 33 per cent to 40 per cent – see M Samuel, 'PCTs facing more appeals against continuing care decisions' in *Community Care* 25 October 2011. In a letter dated 10 June 2013 to the APPGP NHS Continuing Care Inquiry, the Health Service Commissioner indicated that she had about 500 NHS CC complaints each year, of which about 200 were considered in detail and about a quarter of these referred back to the NHS organisation to take further action; see also APPGP, *Failing to care: NHS continuing care in England*, 2013.

33 Case no E.22/02/02–03 Funding for long-term care (the *Pointon* case).

'nursing' with something done exclusively by 'qualified' nurses – and as the ombudsman noted in her report: 'Mrs Pointon was giving highly personalised care with a high level of skill ... nursing care equal if not superior to that that Mr Pointon would receive in a dementia ward' (para 46).

12.29   The ombudsman held that the fact that Mr Pointon was receiving nursing care from his wife, did not mean he could not qualify for NHS CC; that the health bodies had failed to take into account his severe psychological problems and the special skills it takes to nurse someone with dementia; that the assessment tools used by the NHS were skewed in favour of physical and acute care; and that the fact that Mr Pointon needed care at home – rather than in a nursing care home – was not material to the question of continuing healthcare responsibility.

12.30   The *Pointon* report is of considerable importance, not only because it helps clarify what is meant by 'nursing care' – but also as it provides a clear example of entitlement to continuing healthcare funding where: (1) the nature of the healthcare need was not for acute medical support but for nursing of a quality that could manage his psychologically challenging behaviour; and (2) the need arose from someone living in the community and not a residential care setting.

R (T, D and B) v Haringey LBC

12.31   *R (T, D and B) v Haringey LBC*[34] concerned a three-year-old child who had a congenital obstruction to her airways including a narrowing of her larynx that required a tracheostomy (a tube in the throat) which needed regular suctioning and was replaced each week by a nurse. In a number of respects this case highlights the healthcare changes that have characterised the NHS in recent decades. Although the insertion and management of a tracheostomy is a complex healthcare intervention, it is no longer necessary for people with this condition to be cared for in a hospital setting. As the judgment notes, it is 'quite common now for children who have tracheostomies to be discharged from hospital and cared for at home' (para 5) and that the 'Great Ormond Street Hospital provides training for parents in how to manage those requirements at home; the Claimant mother has been trained fully in those areas' (para 7).

12.32   The case concerned the mother's need for respite care in the form of a night sitting service, as the tracheostomy needed suctioning about three times a night. It was agreed that this could be covered by an assistant who was suitably trained (but did not need to be a registered nurse) and could wake the mother if an emergency arose (para 34). The child's mother argued that the respite care could be provided by the local authority: that in effect the child's nursing needs did not mean she was above the limits of social care. It was argued that the limitation on social care in the NAA 1948 did not apply to children since the NAA 1948 only applied to adults: that there was no provision in the Children Act (CA) 1989 equivalent to NAA 1948 s21(8) (now CA 2014 s22).

12.33   The argument failed. In the opinion of Ouseley J the *Coughlan* criteria applied with equal force to children, regardless of the fact that the relevant

34   [2005] EWHC 2235 (Admin), (2006) 9 CCLR 58.

social services care regime was regulated by the CA 1989 and not the NAA 1948. In his opinion (para 61):

> ... the provisions of the Children Act are not to be regarded in general as reducing or replacing the important public obligations ... [in the NHS Act]. I do not see that the impact there of section 21(8) of the NAA 1948 means that the principles enunciated were peculiar to that Act.

Ouseley J considered that the decisive factors were the 'scale and type of nursing care' and the purpose of the care – in this case it was 'designed to deal with the continuing medical consequences of an operation, which if not met will give rise to urgent or immediate medical needs'.

12.35   The court additionally addressed a central dilemma of the case, namely the different public law entitlements provided by the social care statutes and the NHS Acts: the former creating specifically enforceable duties and the latter 'target duties'.[35] The judge accepted that in principle there could be an entitlement gap – essentially that a person could cease to be eligible for social care support because his or her need fell above the limits of what social care could provide (ie the NAA 1948 s21(8) cut-off) but have needs below that which the Department of Health had specified as necessary to qualify for NHS continuing care support, ie the 'primary health need' requirement.

R (Grogan) v Bexley NHS Care Trust

12.36   The question of the 'gap' in entitlement identified in the *Haringey* judgment was addressed directly in *R (Grogan) v Bexley NHS Care Trust and others*.[36] In essence, Charles J held that the NAA 1948 s21(8) 'limits of social care' test was the crucial determinant. The reason for this conclusion was straightforward. The 'limits of social care' test is statutory in origin (ie NAA 1948 s21(8) – now CA 2014 s22(1)) and had been authoritatively interpreted by the Court of Appeal in *Coughlan*. On the other hand, the 'primary health need' test is a policy construct developed by the secretary of state. While it is the secretary of state's entitlement under the NHS Acts to propound such a policy, she could not (by guidance) undermine the statutory regime. Since the secretary of state had made unequivocal statements that there must be no gap in entitlement, then in Charles J's opinion the only way of resolving this dilemma (short of statutory amendment) was for the NHS to drop the policy 'bar' to the height set by the Court of Appeal in *Coughlan* when defining the limits of social care support.

12.37   Developing this point, the ombudsman has held that once a person has been held to be eligible for NHS CC, an individual duty crystallises of the same nature as the duty on social services under the CA 2014.[37]

12.38   The *Grogan* judgment additionally addressed the incongruity between the continuing healthcare criteria and the registered nursing care contribution (RNCC) criteria (see para 11.110 above). Charles J rejected the

---

35 See para 1.16 above. The case was heard prior to the enactment of the Children and Families Act 2014 and the legal position today might be materially different – by virtue of section 42(3) of that Act – see S Broach, L Clements and J Read, *Disabled children and the law*, 2nd edn, Legal Action Group, 2016, para 5.45.

36 [2006] EWHC 44 (Admin), (2006) 9 CCLR 188.

37 Public Services Ombudsman for Wales Report no 201101810 concerning Cardiff and Vale University Health Board, 24 April 2013, para 44.

health body's argument that eligibility for a RNCC was a relevant factor in determining whether a person qualified for NHS CC. A RNCC could only be considered after a NHS CC decision had been made: all nursing care (including that which might trigger a RNCC) had to be below the quality/quantity threshold before eligibility of such a contribution could be considered (para 66).

The national framework

Background

12.39   In June 2007 a new *National framework for NHS continuing healthcare and NHS funded nursing care in England* was issued by the Department of Health, accompanied other associated publications, including a *Decision support tool* (DST), a *Checklist* and a *Fast track pathway tool* designed to provide a fair and effective way of establishing individual entitlement to continuing health care. With the publication of these documents, the 2001 guidance[38] was cancelled.

12.40   In July 2009 minor revisions to the all four documents occurred.[39] In 2012, to coincide with the abolition of primary care trusts (PCTs) in England, a revised national framework,[40] DST, checklist and fast track pathway tool were issued. In large measure, these documents merely substitute for 'PCT' – 'CCG'. In 2016, a very slightly revised DST[41] was issued. The 2012 guidance and 2016 DST are referred to below, unless the context indicates otherwise.

12.41   Since its introduction in England in 2007, the framework appears to have resulted in a significant increase in the numbers of people qualifying for NHS CC – from 27,822 at the end of September 2007 to 59,377 in March 2016 (although the numbers have fallen by over five per cent since 2014).[42] It is, however, by no means certain that the increase is attributable to the introduction of the framework or indeed to the landmark 1999

---

38   HSC 2001/015: LAC (2001)18.
39   All are accessible on the Department of Health website at www.dh.gov.uk
   – however, controversially the revision created a more challenging breathing domain
   – downgrading breathing requiring the use of CPAP (continuous positive airway
   pressure ventilator) (see para 12.110 below) from a high to a moderate.
40   Department of Health, *National framework for NHs continuing healthcare and NHS-funded nursing care* (revised), November 2012.
41   The Department of Health has provided no public explanation as to the amendments in this document, but it appears the only changes are bureaucratic, ie in terms of the information collected – for example, p17 added a question on the form to be completed asking 'Was this DST completed whilst the individual was in an acute hospital?' At the time of writing (September 2016) the National Health Service Commissioning Board and Clinical Commissioning Groups (Responsibilities and Standing Rules) Regulations 2012 SI No 2996 (reg 21(5)) still referred to the 2012 DST.
42   Health and Social Care Information Centre, *NHS continuing healthcare activity statistics for England, Quarter 4 2015–16 Report, Experimental Statistics*, 2016.

Coughlan judgment[43] (when it appears that only 18,000[44] individuals were in receipt of NHS CC funding). What must be appreciated is that the last 30 years have seen an unprecedented retrenchment by the NHS: withdrawing from many forms of long-term care (through the closure of long-stay mental hospitals, 'mental handicap' hospitals and long-stay geriatric wards).[45] This withdrawal, combined with the significant and ongoing increase in the numbers of older people (ie over 80), is more probably the main 'driver' of this increase.

Status of the framework

12.42   NHSA 2006 s2 empowers the secretary of state to do anything 'whatsoever which is calculated to facilitate, or is conducive or incidental to, the discharge' of the duties under the Act. The courts have accepted that the framework is to be interpreted on this basis – and that in discharging their functions, health bodies are obliged to take it into account[46] – and that if they fail to consider or misconstrue or misapply it, they will be susceptible to legal challenge.[47]

12.43   Regulations have been issued which underpin the new regime[48] and require that in carrying out their duties CCGs and the NHS Commissioning Board (now renamed 'NHS England') must 'have regard' to the national framework (reg 21(12)).

The framework definition of NHS continuing healthcare

12.44   The 2012 framework states that (para 13):

> '**NHS continuing healthcare**' means a package of ongoing care that is arranged and funded solely by the NHS where the individual has been found to have a 'primary health need' as set out in this guidance. Such care is provided to an individual aged 18 or over, to meet needs that have arisen as a result of disability, accident or illness. The actual services provided as part of the package should be seen in the wider context of best practice and service development for each client group. Eligibility for NHS continuing healthcare places no limits on the settings in which the package of support can be offered or on the type of service delivery.

---

43 *R v North and East Devon Health Authority ex p Coughlan* [2000] 2 WLR 622, (1999) 2 CCLR 285, CA.

44 Laing & Buisson, *Market survey*, 2000.

45 By way of example, between 1988 and 2014 the number of hospital admissions doubled but overnight the number of NHS beds available in England fell from almost 300,000 to less than 150,000 – see Nuffield Trust, *Average daily number of overnight beds available and occupied in England*, 2015: in December 2016 the number had fallen to 130,404 – see National Health Executive (NHE), 'Fall in number of hospital beds contributing to patient deaths', news item on NHE website, 14 December 2016).

46 In *R (Whapples) v Birmingham CrossCity CCG* [2015] EWCA Civ 435 para 25.

47 *R v North Derbyshire Health Authority ex p Fisher* (1997) 38 BMLR 76 per Dyson J at p89.

48 National Health Service Commissioning Board and Clinical Commissioning Groups (Responsibilities and Standing Rules) Regulations 2012 SI No 2996 Part 6 creating the new 'Standing rules: NHS continuing healthcare and NHS funded nursing care'.

The legal and policy framework and the health/social care divide

The 'primary health need' v 'limits of social care' assessments

12.45　The framework states that the secretary of state has developed the concept of 'primary health need' to assist in deciding what treatment and health services it is appropriate for the NHS to provide 'and to distinguish between those and the services [local authorities] may provide' (para 33). In applying the test, health bodies must avoid adopting a simple quantitative approach – ie merely asking whether health needs are more significant than personal care or accommodation needs.[49]

12.46　As noted above, the primary health need test was not adopted by the Court of Appeal in *Coughlan*, where it referred to this approach on only one occasion (para 31), noting that the 'Secretary of State accepts that, where the primary need is a health need, then the responsibility is that of the NHS, even when the individual has been placed in a home by a local authority'. The court held that the correct approach was to apply a quantity/quality test (see para 12.19 above).

12.47　The framework guidance resolves the differences between these two approaches by stating (in terms) that a 'primary health need' arises where a person has exceeded the limits of the social care responsibility.[50] This acceptance is important and is contained at para 34, which provides:

> There should be no gap in the provision of care. People should not find themselves in a situation where neither the NHS nor the relevant [local authority] (subject to the person meeting the relevant means test and having needs that fall within their eligibility criteria for adult social care[51]) will fund care, either separately or together. Therefore, the 'primary health need' test should be applied, so that a decision of ineligibility for NHS continuing healthcare is only possible where, taken as a whole, the nursing or other health services required by the individual:
> a) are no more than incidental or ancillary to the provision of accommodation which [local authority] social services are, or would be but for a person's means, under a duty to provide; and
> b) are not of a nature beyond which [a local authority] whose primary responsibility it is to provide social services could be expected to provide.

12.48　The framework guidance retains reference to the terms 'nature, intensity, complexity and unpredictability' which first appeared in the 1995 guidance. Although these indicators have been criticised as unnecessarily complicating the assessment process,[52] the guidance attempts to link them

49　*R (Green) v South West Strategic Health Authority and others* [2008] EWHC 2576, 28 October 2008.

50　An approach also adopted in Department of Health, *NHS continuing healthcare practice guidance*, 2010, at para 4.1.

51　The guidance then refers by footnote stating 'See *Prioritising need in the context of Putting People First: A whole system approach to eligibility for social care. Guidance on Eligibility Criteria for Adult Social Care, England 2010*'.

52　See eg Law Society, *National framework for NHS continuing healthcare and NHS-funded nursing care in England: Comments by the Law Society of England and Wales*, 2006, where they were described as 'elusive, overlapping and likely to confuse'. In *R (Grogan) v Bexley NHS Care Trust and others* [2006] EWHC 44 (Admin), (2006) 9

to the *Coughlan* quantity/quality criteria, with the following explanations (para 35):

> **Nature**: This describes the particular characteristics of an individual's needs (which can include physical, mental health or psychological needs) and the type of those needs. This also describes the overall effect of those needs on the individual, including the type ('quality') of interventions required to manage them.

> **Intensity**: This relates both to the extent ('quantity') and severity ('degree') of the needs and to the support required to meet them, including the need for sustained/ongoing care ('continuity').

> **Complexity**: This is concerned with how the needs present and interact to increase the skill required to monitor the symptoms, treat the condition(s) and/or manage the care. This may arise with a single condition, or it could include the presence of multiple conditions or the interaction between two or more conditions. It may also include situations where an individual's response to their own condition has an impact on their overall needs, such as where a physical health need results in the individual developing a mental health need.

> **Unpredictability**:[53] This describes the degree to which needs fluctuate and thereby create challenges in managing them. It also relates to the level of risk to the person's health if adequate and timely care is not provided. Someone with an unpredictable healthcare need is likely to have either a fluctuating, unstable or rapidly deteriorating condition.

12.49 The DST is considered below, but crucial to its correct application is the way in which its user notes are interpreted, particularly the following:

> 31. In all cases, the overall need, the interactions between needs in different care domains, and the evidence from risk assessments should be taken into account in deciding whether a recommendation of eligibility for NHS continuing healthcare should be made. It is not possible to equate a number of incidences of one level with a number of incidences of another level, as in, for example 'two moderates equals one high'. The judgement whether someone has a primary health need must be based on what the evidence indicates about the nature and/or complexity and/or intensity and/or unpredictability of the individual's needs.

12.50 The DST (having described the four descriptors – nature, intensity, complexity and unpredictability – in the above terms) states that each of the characteristics 'may, in combination or alone, demonstrate a primary health need, because of the quality and/or quantity of care required to meet the individual's needs' (p47).

12.51 The details of Pamela Coughlan's condition are well documented and were analysed in detail by the Court of Appeal. It concluded that her needs were well outside what social services could provide – of a 'wholly different category'.[54] It is of concern, therefore, that the DST does not clearly

CCLR 188 para 91 Charles J adverted to the nebulous nature of these factors – absent clear explanation as to what they meant: potentially leaving the decision-maker to 'drift on a sea of factors without guidance as to the test or tests he should apply'.

53 '[B]eing predictably unpredictable' should never be used as a reason for *not* giving NHS CC – Department of Health, *A national framework for NHS continuing healthcare and NHS-funded nursing care in England: Response to consultation*, 2007, p13.

54 *R v North and East Devon Health Authority ex p Coughlan* [2000] 2 WLR 622, (1999) 2 CCLR 285 at [118].

establish that she would qualify for NHS CC funding – indeed, unless substantial weight is given to the above advice, it would appear likely that she would not satisfy the requirements of the DST.[55]

Assessment – regulations and 2012 framework

12.52　The regulations[56] accompanying the 2012 framework require CCGs to take reasonable steps to ensure that an assessment is carried out where it appears to it that there may be a need of NHS CC services – or that an individual who is receiving such support may no longer be eligible for such care; to inform the person of the decision; and to make a record of that decision and how to apply for a review if dissatisfied (reg 21).

12.53　The 2012 regulations are to be read in conjunction with the Care and Support (Discharge of Hospital Patients) Regulations 2014[57] (considered at para 5.7 above). These require (among other things) that prior to an assessment notice being issued, the NHS body must have considered the patient's eligibility for NHS CC (reg 3) and that the patient is not eligible.[58]

12.54　The 2012 framework contains detailed guidance on the assessment process, amplifying the requirements of the 2012 regulations. It provides updated guidance on:

- the fast track pathway tool;
- the checklist to help practitioners identify who will need a full assessment; and
- the DST.

Key extracts from the 2012 framework

12.55　The 2012 framework guidance makes a number of important statements about the way the full NHS CC assessment should be carried out:

Central role of patient and carers
- The process of assessment and decision-making should be person-centred. This means placing the individual, their perception of their support needs, and their preferred models of support at the heart of the assessment and care-planning process ... (para 42).
- Assessments of eligibility for NHS continuing healthcare and NHS-funded nursing care should be organised so that the individual being

55　This was a problem with the 2001 guidance identified by the House of Commons Health Select Committee in their report *NHS continuing care* HC 399-I, The Stationery Office 2005, para 103p – and arguably persist with the current DST – see, for example, L Clements, 'Social care law lecture series – NHS continuing health care & law', 2015 at www.youtube.com/watch?v=HrpFLLwGqhs&feature=youtu.be.

56　National Health Service Commissioning Board and Clinical Commissioning Groups (Responsibilities and Standing Rules) Regulations 2012 SI No 2996: these are in similar terms to the previous NHS Continuing Healthcare (Responsibilities) Directions 2009 (issued on 29 September 2009).

57　SI No 2823. The 2012 regulations were issued before the commencement of the CA 2014 and repealed the Delayed Discharges (Continuing Care) Directions 2009.

58　Regulation 4. The framework guidance at para PG13.3 nevertheless remains correct that 'delayed discharges' procedures ... are not triggered until the NHS trust or NHS foundation trust are satisfied that the relevant individual is not entitled to NHS continuing healthcare'.

assessed and their representative understand the process, and receive advice and information that will maximise their ability to participate in informed decision-making about their future care ... (para 44).

Setting

* NHS continuing healthcare may be provided in any setting (including, but not limited to, a care home, hospice or the person's own home). Eligibility for NHS continuing healthcare is, therefore, not determined or influenced either by the setting where the care is provided or by the characteristics of the person who delivers the care ... (para 56).

Well managed need

* The decision making rationale should not marginalise a need because it is successfully managed: well managed needs are still needs. Only where the successful management of a healthcare need has permanently reduced or removed an ongoing need, such that the active management of this need is reduced or no longer required, will this have a bearing on NHS continuing healthcare eligibility.[59]

Reasons for determining eligibility' (para 58)

The reasons given for a decision on eligibility should not be based on:

* person's diagnosis;
* the setting of care;
* the ability of the care provider to manage care;
* the use (or not) of NHS employed staff to provide care;
* the need for/presence of 'specialist staff ' in care delivery;
* the fact that the need is well managed;
* the existence of other NHS-funded care;
* or any other input-related (rather than needs-related) rationale.

Rehabilitation

* Anyone who carries out an assessment of eligibility for NHS continuing healthcare should always consider whether there is further potential for rehabilitation and for independence to be regained ... (para 64).

Location

* The risks and benefits to the individual of a change of location or support (including funding) should be considered carefully before any move or change is confirmed ... (para 144).

Timing of the assessment

* ... that assessment of eligibility that takes place in an acute hospital may not always reflect an individual's capacity to maximise their potential ... In order to address this issue and ensure that unnecessary stays on acute wards are avoided, there should be consideration of whether the provision of further NHS-funded services is appropriate. This might include therapy and/or rehabilitation, if that could make a difference to the potential of the individual in the following few months. It might also include intermediate care or an interim package of support in an individual's own home or in a care home. In such situations, assessment of eligibility for NHS continuing healthcare should usually be deferred until an accurate assessment of future needs can be made. The interim services (or appropriate alternative interim services if needs change) should continue in place until the determination of eligibility for NHS continuing healthcare has taken place. There must be no gap in the provision of appropriate support to meet the individual's needs (paras 64–65).

---

59 Para 56; and see also PG 11.

Unilateral withdrawal

- Neither the NHS nor an LA should unilaterally withdraw from an existing funding arrangement without a joint reassessment of the individual, and without first consulting one another and the individual about the proposed change of arrangement ... (para 143).

Timescales

12.56 The framework specifies the timescale for NHS CC assessments (para 95):

> The time ... between the Checklist ... being received by the CCG and the funding decision being made should, in most cases, not exceed 28 days. In acute services, it may be appropriate for the process to take significantly less than 28 days if an individual is otherwise ready for discharge ...

12.57 Annex F of the 2012 framework creates a presumption that where the CCG has unjustifiably taken longer than 28 days to reach a decision on eligibility it should (para 9):

> ... refund directly to the individual or the LA, the costs of the services from day 29 of the period that starts on the date of receipt of a completed Checklist (or where no Checklist is used, other notification of potential eligibility for NHS CC) and ends on the date that the decision was made ...

12.58 The guidance advises, however, that the duty to make a refund does not apply if the CCG can demonstrate that the delay is 'due to circumstances beyond [its] control', for example (para 9):

 i) evidence (such as assessments or care records) essential for reaching a decision on eligibility have been requested from a third party and there has been delay in receiving these records from them;
 ii) the individual or their representatives have been asked for specific information or evidence or for participation in the process and there has been a delay in receiving a response from them;
 iii) there has been a delay in convening a multidisciplinary team due to the lack of availability of a non-CCG practitioner whose attendance is key to determining eligibility and it is not practicable for them to give their input by alternative means such as written communication or by telephone.

Fast track pathway tool

12.59 The 2012 framework explains that the fast track pathway tool exists for people 'with a rapidly deteriorating condition, which may be entering a terminal phase and who require fast tracking for immediate provision of NHS CC' (para 97). This might be where the person wishes to return home to die or to allow appropriate end of life support to be arranged. In such cases, the rate of deterioration would bring the patient within the 'primary health needs'.

12.60 The fast track pathway authorisation is a clinician led process and, once authorised, cannot be questioned or countermanded by the health body bureaucracy.[60] The relevant regulations[61] explain that the use of the

---

60 National Health Service Commissioning Board and Clinical Commissioning Groups (Responsibilities and Standing Rules) Regulations 2012 SI No 2996 reg 21(9) and (10).
61 National Health Service Commissioning Board and Clinical Commissioning Groups (Responsibilities and Standing Rules) Regulations 2012 SI No 2996 reg 21.

checklist/the requirement to follow the DST process does not apply where an appropriate clinician decides that (reg 21(8)):

    (a) an individual has a primary health need arising from a rapidly deteriorating condition; and

    (b) the condition may be entering a terminal phase, and that clinician has completed the Fast Track Pathway Tool stating reasons for the decision.

12.61 An appropriate clinician is defined as a person who is (reg 21(13)):

    (a) responsible for the diagnosis, treatment or care of the person under the 2006 Act in respect of whom the Fast Track Pathway Tool is being completed, and

    (b) a registered nurse or a registered medical practitioner.

12.62 The 2012 framework advises that 'the clinician should have an appropriate level of knowledge or experience of the type of health needs, so that they are able to comment reasonably on whether the individual has a rapidly deteriorating condition that may be entering a terminal phase' (para 97). It also confirms that an appropriate clinician may be someone 'employed in voluntary and independent sector organisations that have a specialist role in end of life needs (for example, hospices), provided they are offering services pursuant to the [NHSA 2006]' (para 98). In all other cases, where someone considers that a fast track tool should be used the framework advises that they contact the appropriate clinician to ask that its use be considered (para 98).

12.63 Justification for the use of the tool can be supported with a prognosis, but 'strict time limits that base eligibility on some specified expected length of life remaining should not be imposed'.[62] In this context, the 2012 framework notes (para 100):

> Where a recommendation is made for an urgent package of care via the fast-track process, this should be accepted and actioned immediately by the CCG. It is not appropriate for individuals to experience delay in the delivery of their care package while concerns over the use of the Fast Track Tool are resolved. CCGs should carefully monitor use of the tool and raise any specific concerns with clinicians, teams and organisations. Such concerns should be treated as a separate matter from the task of arranging for service provision in the individual case.

12.64 Concern has been expressed about health bodies seeking to move residents in ordinary care homes (following an assessment of eligibility for NHS CC funding) into nursing homes – for example, where the 'fast track pathway' tool has identified the person as entering the final phase of their lives. In response to this concern, the Department of Health has issued guidance stating that 'there is nothing within the regulatory framework, which would prevent a person in receipt of NHS continuing healthcare remaining within a Care Home (Personal Care)'.[63]

12.65 Once a person has been identified through the fast track process as eligible for NHS CC, the person should be dealt with in the same way as others who are eligible. It follows that the funding should not be stopped

---

62 Framework guidance para 99.
63 Department of Health, *Joint Statement re: NHS Continuing Healthcare Funding for End of Life Care within Care Homes*, 15 August 2008.

without the eligibility being reviewed (which would include completion of a DST etc).[64] Where a local authority disputes such a decision, then the requirement against 'unilateral withdrawal' would also apply (see para 12.55 below).

The checklist

12.66 The 2012 regulations[65] stipulate that if a health body 'wishes to use an initial screening process to decide whether to undertake an assessment of a person's eligibility for NHS CC', then it must use the 2012 checklist[66] for this purpose (reg 21(4)). The checklist is not, however, appropriate where it is proposed to use the fast track pathway tool (see para 12.59 above).

12.67 In practice, it appears that all English CCGs use the checklist. When used, there is a requirement to record the use of the checklist and to inform in writing the person who is being assessed (or someone 'lawfully acting on that person's behalf') of the decision whether to carry out an assessment of that person's eligibility for NHS CC (reg 21(4)).

12.68 The checklist is a relatively brief document – essentially a simplified version of the DST. It 'could' be completed by either a health professional (ie a nurse, doctor, other qualified healthcare professional) or a social care professional – who should, however, be familiar with the guidance concerning its use, as well as the framework and DST guidance.[67] The checklist replicates the 11 domains of the DST, but divides these into only three broad bands: A, B and C. The DST domains in which there is a priority band are marked as A*. Assessors are required to state which band the patient falls into and to identify (but not supply) the evidence that supports this assessment (and where the evidence can be accessed).[68] The evidence could be an observation made by an individual so there is no requirement that the evidence be in written form. Guidance on this question is provided by the framework which includes the following statement (para PG 23):

> The Checklist is intended to be relatively quick and straightforward to complete. In the spirit of this, it is not necessary to submit detailed evidence along with the completed Checklist. However, the Checklist asks practitioners to record references to evidence that they have used to support the statements selected in each domain. This could, for example, be by indicating that specific evidence for a given domain was contained within the inpatient nursing notes on a stated date.

12.69 The checklist advises that if the person scores (para 21):

- one A*; or
- two As; or

---

64 See 2012 framework para 101.
65 National Health Service Commissioning Board and Clinical Commissioning Groups (Responsibilities and Standing Rules) Regulations 2012 SI No 2996 reg 21.
66 Department of Health, *The NHS continuing healthcare checklist*, 28 November 2012. As noted above, in 2016 a (very slightly) revised DST was published, but at the time of writing (January 2017) the 2012 regulations (reg 21(5)) still refer to the 2012 DST.
67 2012 framework guidance, para 73: the framework gives no definition of 'professional' but the context would suggest that its use would not be restricted to those who were formal members of a 'professional body'.
68 Checklist, para 19.

- five Bs, or
- one A and four Bs;

then this should trigger a full assessment for NHS CC (ie the use of the DST). Although the 2012 framework guidance states that the checklist threshold 'has intentionally been set low, in order to ensure that all those who require a full consideration of their needs have this opportunity' it then notes that 'there may also be circumstances where a full assessment for NHS continuing healthcare is appropriate even though the individual does not apparently meet the indicated threshold' (para 72). Since it is quite possible that Pamela Coughlan might only be given a score of one A and three Bs, this is of course essential advice.

12.70   Written reasons must be given for checklist decisions, and individuals and their representatives must be informed and advised that if they disagree with the decision not to proceed to a full assessment for NHS continuing healthcare, they may ask the CCG to reconsider it.[69] If, however, the decision is reaffirmed, the individual or the individual's representative will need to resort to the NHS complaints process.[70]

12.71   The framework cautions against the use of the checklist in an acute hospital setting 'until the individual's needs on discharge are clear' (para 68). In line with the increasing use of the 'discharge to assess' process (see para 5.9 above), the guidance advises that patients who appear to be eligible for a full DST assessment can nevertheless be discharged without a checklist on the basis that the CCG retains responsibility for their funding until a full assessment of eligibility take place 'in the most appropriate setting – whether another NHS institution, the individual's home or some other care setting'.[71] Delays in assessments of this kind are often explained in terms of waiting for the patient to 'optimise'. While this is eminently sensible advice in such cases as the above, it appears that it is being applied in other contexts: where it is being used to delay the assessment of individuals who are in the community (and not being funded by the CCG) on the basis that their condition is not yet 'stable'. This would appear to be contrary to the mandatory requirements of the 2012 regulations that CCGs assess eligibility for NHS CC 'where it appears that ... there may be a need for such care' (reg 21(2)). The inappropriate use of the 'optimise' criteria is an example of a troubling trend that appears to be emerging concerning the use of checklist. In some CCG areas the procedure is (in effect) becoming little different to the DST process with the forms being subjected to a level of scrutiny and bureaucratic delay that would appear to undermine their ultimate purpose – namely to create a simple and effective way of weeding out hopeless cases, ie cases where there is no prospect of the individual being eligible for NHS CC or jointly funded NHS and social services care.

12.72   There is no automatic right to challenge an adverse checklist decision, but the framework advises that individuals 'may ask the CCG to reconsider its decision and agree to a full assessment of eligibility' (para 145). This should be given 'due consideration' and result in a 'clear and

---

69 Framework, para 148.
70 Framework, para 76.
71 Framework, para 74 and see also framework para PG 13.

written response' which must also explain that the remedy if dissatisfied is a complaint through the standard NHS complaints procedure (para 20.7 below).

The decision support tool

Overview

12.73 The 2012 regulations[72] mandate the use of the DST in NHS CC determinations (unless the person is the subject of a fast track decision).[73] Regulation 21(5) and (6) provides that:

> (5) When carrying out an assessment of eligibility for NHS Continuing Healthcare, a relevant body[74] must ensure that–
>   (a) a multi-disciplinary team–
>   (i) undertakes an assessment of needs, or has undertaken an assessment of needs, that is an accurate reflection of that person's needs at the date of the assessment of eligibility for NHS Continuing Healthcare, and
>   (ii) uses that assessment of needs to complete the Decision Support Tool for NHS Continuing Healthcare issued by the Secretary of State and dated 28th November 2012;[75] and
>   (b) the relevant body makes a decision as to whether that person has a primary health need in accordance with paragraph (7), using the completed Decision Support Tool to inform that decision.
> (6) If a relevant body decides that a person has a primary health need in accordance with paragraph (5)(b), it must also decide that that person is eligible for NHS Continuing Healthcare.

12.74 High level guidance on the use of the DST is provided in the 2012 framework, and the DST (now dated 2016)[76] itself contains practice guidance as to how it should be applied.

12.75 There are severe limitations in using standardised assessment tools of this nature to assess patient entitlement. Such tools tend to require micromeasurement of various factors, which are then combined to produce a determination or presumption for or against qualification. Such tools, while they have their uses, are clearly open to considerable criticism. Most obviously, they cannot say where the line between NHS and social services responsibility lies.

12.76 Additionally, standardised assessment tools seek to render empirical, a process that has been legally (not scientifically) determined and may depend upon highly subjective factors (eg patient perceptions of pain – see para 12.112 below). The choice of the individual factors to be measured and the range of scores available for these factors is also a subjective process.

---

72 National Health Service Commissioning Board and Clinical Commissioning Groups (Responsibilities and Standing Rules) Regulations 2012 SI No 2996.
73 Reg 21(8).
74 Defined by reg 2 as a CCG or NHS England.
75 The Department of Health published a very slightly amended DST in 2106 (at p17 a question was added as to whether the individual was in an acute hospital when the form was completed). At the time of writing (January 2017) the National Health Service Commissioning Board and Clinical Commissioning Groups (Responsibilities and Standing Rules) Regulations 2012 SI 2996 (reg 21(5)) still refer to the 2012 DST.
76 Department of Health, *The NHS continuing healthcare checklist* (2016).

The ombudsman's report on the *Pointon*[77] complaint was, for instance, critical of the criteria adopted by the relevant health body as they were 'skewed in favour of physical and acute care' and did not take into account the patient's significant psychological problems. Criticism has also been levelled at the use of tools, on the ground that they could inhibit communication with patients and their carers – and thereby sideline crucial user information from the decision-making process.[78]

12.77   The DST has been the subject of criticism – particularly that if used 'legalistically' it could rule Pamela Coughlan ineligible for NHS CC.[79] The Department of Health and Welsh Government (which mandates the use of an identical DST) have sought to emphasise the limitations of the tool. The relevant Welsh Government guidance[80] acknowledges that the DST 'is not without its critics and that no tool will be perfect' and stresses that the DST 'must be used in context. It cannot and should not replace professional judgement'. In similar vein, the 2016 DST states (p6) that it is 'not an assessment in itself' and (para 6):

> Although the tool supports the process of determining eligibility, and ensures consistent and comprehensive consideration of an individual's needs, it cannot directly determine eligibility. Professional judgement will be necessary in all cases to ensure that the individual's overall level of need is correctly determined and the appropriate decision made.

12.78   The implementation materials accompanying the 2007 DST[81] emphasised that it was 'not a substitute for professional judgement'[82] and that it was not 'A decision MAKING tool' (capitals in the original). It follows that the tool should not be used mechanistically: it is merely a way of recording the relevant information, of 'bringing together and applying evidence in a single practical format to facilitate consistent evidence-based decision making' on NHS continuing healthcare eligibility.[83] It is a 'tool' and like many such tools, requires skilled use. It has been designed to ensure that decisions on entitlement to NHS continuing healthcare are consistent with the *Coughlan* judgment: indeed, if this were otherwise, it would be unlawful.

12.79   The DST comprises 12 care domains (one of which is blank), all of which must be completed by the multi-disciplinary team: there is space in each domain for the reasons why a particular level – 'no need'; 'low'; 'moderate'; 'high', 'severe'; or 'priority' – is appropriate. The following diagram

77 Case no E.22/02/02–03 Funding for Long-Term Care (the *Pointon* case).
78 See eg G Huby and others, 'Planning older people's discharge from acute hospital care: linking risk management and patient participation in decision-making' (2004) 6(2) *Health, Risk and Society* 115–132 who found that standardised assessment tools inhibited communication because they did not afford older people the opportunity to put any results into context for staff – cited in Social Care Institute for Excellence (SCIE), *Using qualitative research in systematic reviews: older people's views of hospital discharge*, February 2006, p36.
79 See, for example, the All Party Parliamentary Group on Parkinson, *Failing to care: NHS continuing care in England*, 2013, p21; and see also para 12.25 above.
80 Welsh Government, *Decision support tool for continuing NHS healthcare*, June 2014, p3.
81 Department of Health, Resource pack: PowerPoint Introduction Module 1: slide 19, 2007.
82 Welsh framework guidance, para K15.
83 DST, para 2; and Welsh framework guidance, para 2.

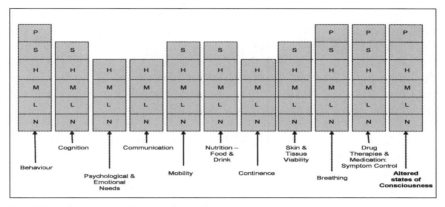

Decision support tool: care domains

summarises the domains, from which it can be seen that not all have a 'priority' or 'severe' category.

12.80 Notwithstanding the reservations expressed by the framework about using the DST mechanistically and the limited role that the DST plays in the decision 'making' process, the DST states that a 'clear recommendation of eligibility' for NHS CC would be expected if the individual scores (para 31):

- A level of priority needs in any one of the four domains that carry this level.
- A total of two or more incidences of identified severe needs across all care domains.

12.81 Given the extreme nature of the severe and priority descriptions, this must be a statement of the self-evident. However, of concern is the statement that then follows (also at para 31), namely that:

... where there is:
- one domain recorded as severe, together with needs in a number of other domains, or
- a number of domains with high and/or moderate needs,

This may also, depending on the combination of needs, indicate a primary health need and therefore careful consideration needs to be given to the eligibility decision and clear reasons recorded if the decision is that the person does not have a primary health need.

12.82 The practical impact of the unfortunate phrasing of paragraph 31 has been to create in the minds of many practitioners the inappropriate presumption of ineligibility if an individual has not been scored as having a 'priority or two severes'. It is not improbable that the application of the present DST to Pamela Coughlan's needs (in 1999) would result in a score of one high; two moderates and three lows. The court did not regard her eligibility for NHS CC as 'borderline', but of a 'wholly different category'.

12.83 As the analysis below suggests, the level of nursing need required to score a 'severe' means that this band is (in the context of paragraph 31) unrealistically high. No doubt this was done by those drafting the document out of fear of 'opening the flood gates', but this error bears a strong resemblance to that identified by Charles J in *R (Grogan) v Bexley NHS*

Care Trust and others[84] concerning the 2003 registered nursing care bands: namely that the top band (which logic demanded should be below the limit set by *Coughlan*) had been placed well above it.[85] It is arguable that the same criticism arises with the DST: that the severe band is well above the limit set by *Coughlan* – particularly (as Charles J noted) the decision of the Court of Appeal that the care she needed was well outside the limits of what could be lawfully provided by a local authority.

12.84   Examples of the unrealistically high requirements for a 'severe' score are outlined below – but include the fact that (for example): (1) a person cannot 'take food and drink by mouth, intervention inappropriate or impossible'; and (2) has open wounds/pressure ulcers that are 'not responding to treatment' or wounds/pressure ulcers that include 'necrosis extending to underlying bone'. In either case, it is stretching credibility to suggest that prima facie entitlement to NHS CC funding does not arise where a person whose condition is destined to result in their death by starvation/dehydration or which consists of such severe wounds that their bone is actually visible. Equally difficult to understand is the suggestion that, in relation to breathing difficulties, an appropriate indicator for when a person has traversed the CA 2014 s22(1) line, is where he or she is incapable of breathing 'independently' and 'requires invasive mechanical ventilation'. To suggest that 'being on a ventilator' is a useful indicator is problematic. The inclusion of such stark healthcare conditions in a scale designed to tease out the subtleties of the health/social care divide, does not illuminate: it casts a long shadow and makes more opaque the already difficult task faced by those who have to make this judgment call. Such descriptors (wrongly) reinforce the impression that NHS CC funding is only available to those whose conditions are of an exceptional order of gravity.

Individual involvement

12.85   A key element in the decision making process is the full involvement of the individual and/or the individual's representatives. The framework[86] gives detailed advice on this question, stressing that the 'whole process of determining eligibility and planning and delivering services for NHS continuing healthcare should be "person-centred"' (PG 4 para 4.1) – noting that in practice this has not always been the case. As a minimum, a person-centred approach must (among other things) ensure that the individual and/or the individual's representative are fully involved and directly involved in the decision-making, and that full account is taken of the individual's 'individual's own views and wishes' (PG para 4.3). The framework also addresses the importance of ensuring that any communication needs are addressed.

---

84   [2006] EWHC 44 (Admin), (2006) 9 CCLR 188 para 61 (see para 12.36 above).
85   In order to be eligible for the higher payment of RNCC, the individual had to have: high needs for registered nursing care with complex needs that require frequent mechanical, technical and/or therapeutic interventions; need frequent intervention and re-assessment by a registered nurse throughout a 24 hour period; and their physical/mental health state will be unstable and/or unpredictable.
86   PG 4 at pp53–55.

Advocacy support during the NHS CC process

12.86 The 2012 framework stresses the importance of individuals being supported by an advocate – even if they do not fall under the provisions of the Mental Capacity Act 2005 (paras 52–53).[87] CCGs are required to:

> ... ensure that individuals are made aware of local advocacy and other services that may be able to offer advice and support, and should also consider whether any strategic action is needed to ensure that adequate advocacy services are available to support those who are eligible or potentially eligible for NHS continuing healthcare. In addition, any person may choose to have a family member or other person (who should operate independently of [local authorities] and CCGs) to act as an advocate on their behalf.

12.87 The CA 2014 obligation to provide independent advocacy (section 67) applies to assessments determining eligibility for NHS CC funding[88] as it does to CA 2014 assessments.[89] In such cases, the stipulation that the duty only arises if there is no other appropriate representative available (section 67(5)) does not apply if there is: (a) disagreement on a 'material issue' between the local authority and the person; and (b) the local authority and that person agree that advocacy support is in the person's best interests. If the local authority and the NHS consider that the person is not eligible for NHS CC funding, then (subject to the best interest requirement) the duty arises. If, however, the local authority disagrees with the NHS over eligibility, then the local authority would be obliged to trigger its inter-authority dispute process.[90] In either case, given the complexity of the NHS CC process, the presumption must be that it would be in a person's best interests to have advocacy support.

12.88 Even for those who do not come within the parameters of this right, 2015 Social Care Institute for Excellence (SCIE) guidance[91] advises (p8):

> Historically this arrangement has often been difficult for people who use services, their carers and friends to understand and be involved in. Local authorities and clinical commissioning groups will therefore want to consider the benefits of providing access to independent advice or independent advocacy for those who do not have substantial difficulty and/or those who have an appropriate person to support their involvement.

Multi-disciplinary team decision making

12.89 The 2012 regulations (reg 21(5)) require that the DST must be completed by a multi-disciplinary team (MDT), which is defined in reg 21(13) as:

87 Including where a right might exist to an independent mental capacity advocate (IMCA).
88 If it is 'is likely to' result in the NHS funding the person in a hospital for a period of 28 days or more; or a care home for a period of eight weeks or more – Care and Support (Independent Advocacy Support) (No 2) Regulations 2014 SI No 2889 reg 4(2)(a).
89 See the revised statutory guidance, para 7.22.
90 National Health Service Commissioning Board and Clinical Commissioning Groups (Responsibilities and Standing Rules) Regulations 2012 SI 2996 reg 22.
91 SCIE, *Commissioning independent advocacy: independent advocacy under the Care Act 2014*, 2015.

(a) two professionals who are from different healthcare professions, or

(b) one professional who is from a healthcare profession and one person who is responsible for assessing persons for community care services under section 47 of the National Health Service and Community Care Act 1990.[92]

12.90   The 2012 framework explains that in practice the default position for MDT composition should be a health and social care professional – 'who are knowledgeable about the individual's health and social care needs' (PG 30). It stresses the importance of multi-disciplinary discussions which 'should normally involve a face-to-face MDT meeting' (PG 31.2) with the individual and/or the individual's representative 'fully involved in the process and be given every opportunity to contribute to the MDT discussion' (PG 30.3); and that the meeting should take place 'as near to the individual's location as possible so that they are enabled to be actively involved in the process' (PG 32.1).

12.91   The ombudsmen have been critical of the substance and process of MDT's decision making. In a 2010 report the ombudsman,[93] for example, expressed concern about:

• the lack of clarity as to the professional qualifications of the two people who constituted the MDT;

• the fact that the MDT only had two people (the adviser was of the opinion that these two people would not constitute a MDT);

• the lack of a MDT truly representative of the patient's healthcare needs;

• the fact that the decision on a patient's eligibility for NHS CC was discussed with the family before the MDT experts had scrutinized the assessments and reports (and that 'families are involved in the multi-disciplinary team in a meaningful way in reaching decisions about eligibility for Continuing Healthcare'[94]);

• the lack of an up-to-date nursing assessment at the time the decision was taken;

• a failure to take into consideration a request by the social work assessor that a nursing assessment and a psychiatric report were required;

• a failure to keep recorded minutes of key meetings and how decisions were reached.

12.92   The ombudsman has separately suggested that it is desirable for the MDT to physically meet together at one time in one place.[95]

---

92 At the time of writing (September 2016) the regulations had yet to be amended to refer to the CA 2014.

93 Report no 200802583 concerning the former Carmarthenshire Local Health Board, 17 September 2010, para 68.

94 Report no 200802454 concerning the former Gwynedd Local Health Board, 22 February 2010, para 66 and 80.

95 See report no 200801759 concerning the former Carmarthenshire Local Health Board, 20 September 2010, para 65 and see also report no 200802454 concerning the former Gwynedd Local Health Board, 22 February 2010.

The decision support tool domains

12.93   While a detailed analysis of the 12 individual DST domains is beyond the scope of this book, brief comment is made on each below, particularly in relation to those cases considered by the courts and the ombudsman.

Behaviour domain

12.94   This domain contains a 'priority' band – a finding for which would (if the DST is used mechanistically) create the expectation of eligibility for NHS CC.

12.95   In interpreting this provision (as with all DST descriptors) it is necessary to bear in mind the framework advice (para 56), that 'well managed needs are still needs'. It follows that the person being assessed need not be exhibiting the requisite 'challenging behaviour', but merely that this would resurface if the care regime were removed. It is also important that any interpretation of the descriptor be consistent with the ombudsman's findings in the *Pointon*[96] complaint. In that case she concluded that Mr Pointon was eligible for NHS continuing healthcare funding on the basis of his challenging behaviour – which was managed in the family home by his wife and a rota of care assistants. Mr Pointon suffered from the advanced stage of dementia characterised by mood changes and behavioural disturbance, although by the time of the decision the NHS ombudsman noted that the severe behavioural problems, which had characterised his illness (during the earlier stage of dementia), had diminished.

12.96   Alexander Slavin's behaviour (in *Secretary of State for Work and Pensions v Slavin*[97]) necessitated that he be continuously supervised by at least one, and sometimes two, care staff who had to be ready to intervene in order to attempt to prevent him causing damage to property or injury to himself or others. This was sufficient to make him eligible for NHS CC even though he lived in a residential care home (not a nursing home) and the staff, although trained to meet his needs, did not have any medical or nursing qualifications.

Cognition domain

12.97   The cognition domain does not contain a 'priority' band, only a 'severe'.

12.98   A key issue here is the risks the individual may run as a result of their impaired ability to make decisions and choices. In 2009 the DST was amended to make it clear that the cognitive impairment did not have to be associated only with 'short-term memory issues' and that the risks could be greater than 'harm' – ie extending to 'neglect or health deterioration'.

Psychological and emotional needs domain

12.99   The omission of a 'mental health' domain in the DST is perhaps curious, and lends weight to the suggestion that (as the ombudsman observed in the *Pointon* complaint (para 12.27 above)) that there is a tendency for such descriptors to favour physical and acute care over care that addresses psychological and mental health needs. The 2010 Welsh DST had such a

96 Case no E.22/02/02–03 Funding for Long-Term Care – see para 12.27 above.
97 [2011] EWCA Civ 1515.

domain which contained a 'severe' category, described in the following terms:

> Significant changes in mental health which manifests in extremely chal-lenging unstable, unpredictable and repetitive behaviour over 24 hours on a prolonged basis. Requires the continual intervention of specialist health-care professionals over and above what can be provided by core NHS serv-ices. High risk of suicide.

12.100   There will be many individuals who have a health condition that is graver than the current 'high' descriptor in this domain (ie for whom 'a severe impact on the individual's health and/or well-being' does not adequately describe the depth of the health impact). This could be because their men-tal illness is utterly debilitating, or their extreme obsessional compulsive disorder manifests itself on such a rigid way that any deviation can result in catastrophic consequences. In such cases this would need to be record-ed in this domain and also on the 12th (blank) box – namely that the mere fact that this has been recorded as a 'high' in no way does justice to the severity of the healthcare impact on the individual in question.

Communication domain

12.101   Although this domain also has a maximum score of 'high', there will be situations where this fails to reflect the gravity of the problem. For example, if an inability to communicate is associated with significant or severe unexplained medical problems. These might, for example, be due to the patient experiencing extreme pain which he or she cannot communicate,[98] or being prone to unexplained and extreme behavioural outbursts.[99] Such a combination would again need to be recorded in this domain and also on the 12th (blank) box – namely that the mere fact that this it had been recorded as a 'high' in no way does justice to the severity of the healthcare impact on the individual in question.

Mobility domain

12.102   This domain contains a 'severe' but not a 'priority' band. Pamela Cough-lan has control of her arms but impaired hand function and could be described as being 'completely unable to weight bear but able to assist or cooperate with transfers'. This could result in a score of 'moderate' in this domain. However, as noted above, the current DST might score her as having only one 'high' but nevertheless at law her eligibility for NHS CC is beyond question and serves therefore as a paradigm example of why the DST should not be used mechanistically as a decision 'making' tool.

Nutrition, food and drink domain

12.103   The nutrition domain does not contain a 'priority' band, only a 'severe'.

12.104   In a number of respects the descriptors in this domain sit uneasily with the court and ombudsman NHS CC findings. In 2003 the ombudsman

---

98 See, for example, EG Carr and JS Owen-DeSchryver, 'Physical illness, pain and problem behaviour in minimally verbal people with developmental disabilities', *Journal of Autism and Developmental Disorders*, (2007) 37, 413–424.

99 See, for example, L Taylor, C Oliver and G Murphy, 'The chronicity of self-injurious behaviour: A long-term follow-up of a total population study', *Journal of Applied Research in Intellectual Disabilities*, (2011) 24, 105–117.

reported on a complaint concerning the refusal of NHS CC funding for a patient who had had several strokes, as a result of which she had no speech or comprehension and was unable to swallow and required feeding by a PEG tube (a percutaneous endoscopic gastronomy (PEG) tube is passed into a patient's stomach through the abdominal wall).[100] Although there was no evidence that the PEG was causing particular problems, the ombudsman concluded that no health body could 'reasonably conclude that her need for nursing care was merely incidental or ancillary to the provision of accommodation or of a nature one could expect Social Services to provide'. Notwithstanding this finding, the DST only accords as 'moderate' a non-problematic PEG – and even if there are problems (requiring skilled assessment and review) this is only scored as a 'high'.[101] The evidence suggests that although the use of PEGs has increased significantly, they remain dangerous health interventions – and particularly so for some categories of patient (for example, those with dementia).[102]

12.105   The fact that the 'severe' category is only available to those who are destined to die of starvation[103] verges on the incomprehensible – and is an example of the overshadowing effect of including extreme health conditions in the domains (see para 12.84 above).

12.106   A 2012 ombudsman report[104] illustrates the potential interactions between the nutrition domain and other DST domains. It concerned a patient who was able to swallow but had cognitive problems in recognising food, leading to food pooling in her mouth and a risk of choking. Although ultimately the health body accepted that the patient was eligible for NHS CC funding, the ombudsman was concerned that it had focused on the patient's ability to swallow rather than looking at her care needs 'holistically' – at the 'totality' of her needs. The impact of the cognitive problems meant that 'she needed to be assisted and monitored when eating, and affected her diet and her ability to maintain adequate weight and hydration' (para 30). The ombudsman was also unimpressed by the health body's reasoning: its initial ineligibility decision was based on its assessment that the patient's 'needs [were] currently being met' – which

100 Complaint concerning the Wigan and Bolton Health Authority and Bolton Hospitals NHS Trust Case no E.420/00–01 in the Health Service Ombudsman's Second Report for Session 2002–03 NHS funding for long term care, HC 399, 2003 – see para 12.220.

101 See, however, the framework PG 59 which provides an example of a person who has had a stroke but lives at home and can manage to walk to his local shop, is continent, can dress/care for himself and has no behavioural or cognitive problems – but has a PEG feed. The suggestion being that he would be eligible for a jointly funded care package.

102 See, for example, DS Sanders and others 'Survival analysis in percutaneous endoscopic gastrostomy feeding: a worse outcome in patients with dementia', *The American Journal of Gastroenterology* (2000) 95, 1472–1475 where the research indicated that for all patients requiring gastrostomy feeding there was a high initial mortality (28 per cent at 30 days) and that for patients with dementia the prognosis was worse (54 per cent having died at 1 month and 90 per cent at one year).

103 The severe band describes patients who are unable to take food and drink by mouth, and either require ongoing skilled professional intervention or monitoring of artificial means of meeting nutritional requirements, eg IV fluids, or such intervention is inappropriate or impossible.

104 Report no 2010001820 and 2010002050 concerning Aneurin Bevan HB and Caerphilly CBC, 21 June 2012, para 30.

the ombudsman observed was not the test: that the 'eligibility test relates solely to the level of someone's needs, not whether those needs are being met or not' (para 29).

Continence domain

12.107 The continence domain only provides for a 'high' band scoring for those with the most complex continence care needs: interventions that may be needed on a daily basis to prevent life-threatening situations. It must be debatable whether a person with continence needs that are 'problematic, requiring skilled non-routine intervention including "manual evacuations"[105] as well as frequent re-catheterisation and bladder wash outs' is receiving nursing that is of a nature one would expect social services to provide and/or which is merely incidental to social care.[106]

12.108   As with other domains, there will be cases where the interactions between this and other DST domains creates situations that take the nursing care needs above the limits of social care. Most commonly this would be where those with complex continence care needs are additionally at risk of pressure ulcers or other skin and tissue complications (even if these are being 'well-managed' – see para 12.55 above).

Skin (including tissue viability) domain

12.109 Reference has been made above (para 12.84) to the problematical nature of the banding for this domain: that someone who has open wounds/pressure ulcers that are 'not responding to treatment' or wounds/pressure ulcers that include 'necrosis extending to underlying bone' would only be scored as 'severe' and (if the DST was applied mechanistically) not presumed to be eligible for NHS CC funding. On the face of it, it is hard to see how the nursing care needs of such a person could be described as 'of a nature one would expect social services to provide and/or merely incidental to social care'.[107]

Breathing domain

12.110 As noted above (para 12.84) the scoring of the breathing domain is problematic. It serves as a further example of the overshadowing effect of including extreme health conditions in the descriptors: essentially requiring that the patient be on a ventilator.

---

105 Although the DST uses this phrase the current appropriate terminology would be 'intimate digital bowel care procedures'.

106 See generally A Emmanuel and others, *Long-term cost-effectiveness of transanal irrigation in patients with neurogenic bowel dysfunction* (2016) PLOS ONE 11(8): http://dx.doi.org/10.1371/journal.pone.0159394. Objectively these would be better described as 'delegated healthcare tasks' if performed other than by a registered nurse (in care packages it is not uncommon for this component of the care to be delivered by a district nurse).

107 Category IV: Full thickness tissue loss of this kind, even with appropriate treatment, may require surgical intervention deep debridement or possibly amputation. It carries serious risk of infection and, especially among older people – see, for example, H Courtney and others, 'Pressure ulcers: a patient safety issue' in R Hughes (ed) *Patient safety and quality: an evidence-based handbook for nurses*, Rockville, 2008.

12.111   The 'severe' band requires 'difficulty in breathing, even through a tracheotomy, which requires suction to maintain airway or demonstrates severe breathing difficulties at rest, in spite of medical therapy'. In *R (T, D and B) v Haringey LBC*[108] (para 12.31 above) the High Court considered that such a need equated with a primary health need – and that to suggest otherwise would be 'to provide an impermissibly wide interpretation, creating obligations on a social services authority which are far too broad'. On that authority, it would seem to follow that this descriptor should appear in the 'priority' rather than the 'severe' band of the DST.

Drug therapies domain

12.112   Although the domain contains a 'priority', it requires some very fine (arguably impossible) differences to be identified by the assessors – for example, to distinguish between a person's untreatable 'severe recurrent or constant pain' and their 'unremitting and overwhelming pain': the former being accorded a 'severe' scoring and the latter a 'priority'. Since there is no independent way of measuring pain,[109] it is difficult to see how such an exercise can be objectively accomplished and, in any event, it is difficult to understand how a person whose condition consists of living with untreatable 'severe recurrent or constant pain' should not be considered, prima facie, to have a primary healthcare need.

Altered states of consciousness domain

12.113   The reference to people in comas in the altered states of consciousness (ASC) domain (in the 'priority' band) is a further example of the overshadowing effect (para 12.84 above). The domain also includes 'ASC that occur on most days, do not respond to preventative treatment, and result in a severe risk of harm' – and this could of course include (for example) people subject to brittle diabetes or constant epileptic fits.

'Other significant care needs'

12.114   The blank (12th) box is of importance, since it is in this box that the factors (and combinations of factors) not properly recognised in, or outside the scope of, the other 11 domains should be described. For instance, in persons with spinal cord injury, a risk of and/or history of autonomic dysreflexia and/or impaired temperature regulation (poikilothermia). It is in this box that reference should also be made to the factors and cases that have been used by the courts and the ombudsmen as of relevance. Above all, it is in this box that issues of professional judgment taking into account all such factors should be detailed.

108 [2005] EWHC 2235 (Admin), (2006) 9 CCLR 58.
109 See eg Social Security Commissioner's Decision no CDLA 902 2004, 18 June 2004 which at para 15 found that 'medical professionals who are expert in pain do not recognise a direct link between clinical findings and pain [accordingly authorities state that] ... there is no direct causal link between disease or injury and pain, the only direct evidence of pain can come from the claimant'.

Recommendation

12.115   The DST then requires the MDT to provide their recommendation, which 'should include consideration of' the nature, intensity, complexity and unpredictability of the person's needs. As noted above (para 12.19 above), the law actually requires that the decision makers focus on the quality/quantity criteria, and it would appear essential therefore that the recommendation is articulated in these terms: as the DST guidance states, these factors should be (p15):

> ... taken into account in deciding whether a recommendation of eligibility for NHS continuing healthcare should be made ... [e]ach of these characteristics may, in combination or alone, demonstrate a primary health need, because of the quality and/or quantity of care required to meet the individual's needs.

12.116   The recommendation should also consider the 'interactions between needs in different care domains' (p15) and these will presumably have been highlighted in the individual domains and box 12. Not infrequently (as discussed in the above analysis of the domains) these may prove to be pivotal. A 2014 ombudsman's report[110] illustrates this point. The patient had Parkinson's disease and her symptoms included night time wakefulness, noisiness, restlessness, increased lethargy and increased physical rigidity. Over the period of review, these symptoms increased. Although individually these were minor in nature, the ombudsman considered that they should have been properly recorded by the NHS body. Cumulatively they were significant and the NHS body had failed to consider 'how a need in one domain might intensify or complicate needs in another'.

The funding decision

12.117   The MDT's recommendation requires approval by the relevant CCG. The framework guidance recognises that many CCGs use panels,[111] but cautions against their use as a gate keeping function or as a financial monitor. The framework guidance states (para 91):

> ... a panel should not fulfil a gate-keeping function, and nor should it be used as a financial monitor. Only in exceptional circumstances, and for clearly articulated reasons, should the multidisciplinary team's recommendation not be followed. A decision not to accept the recommendation should never be made by one person acting unilaterally.

In similar vein, it stresses the need for CCGs 'to ensure an appropriate separation between the coordinator role and those responsible for making a final decision on eligibility for NHS continuing healthcare' (para PG 26.3).

---

110   Investigation by the Public Services Ombudsman for Wales of a complaint against Powys Teaching Health Board and the Welsh Government No 201303895/201304550, 10 September 2014.

111   There is no requirement for CCGs to use a panel as part of their decision-making processes – see framework, para PG 39.1.

12.118   There appears to be ongoing concerns that in this context, CCG decision making is financially led (rather than 'needs led'[112]): with the panel/CCG either disputing, delaying or overturning MDT recommendations. In consequence department of health gave the following explanation as to what it meant by 'exceptional':

> ... it means exactly what it says on the tin, there must be something truly exceptional. If more than 1% of MDT recommendations are not being followed then something is wrong: exceptional circumstances means that there is something 'truly unusual'.[113]

12.119 The framework guidance makes the additional point that (para 93):

> ... because the final eligibility decision should be independent of budgetary constraints, finance officers should not be part of a decision-making panel.

12.120 The ombudsman has considered a number of complaints concerning unreasonable panel processes. A 2009 report[114] concerned a patient who sustained a severe traumatic brain injury, and when ready for discharge an application for NHS CC was made. The NHS CC panel delayed making a decision on the pretext of seeking additional assessments and evidence. The ombudsman considered this to be 'perverse' and suggested and that the panel 'appeared to be trying to avoid making a decision'. A 2015 report concluded that a 15-week delay by a panel in approving a trial 'at home' placement of a person eligible for NHS CC funding also amounted to maladministration.[115]

12.121   A number of the ombudsman's investigations have suggested that MDT members, panels and key NHS decision makers have misunderstood the relevant legal requirements. A 2010 report, for example,[116] found systemic failure in the panel's application of NHS CC criteria and recommended (among other things) that: (1) relevant staff 'are made fully aware of the role and responsibilities of the MDT'; and (2) 'all Chairs of its Independent Continuing Care Review Panels receive adequate training to assist them to effectively carry out their roles'.

Reviews and reassessments

12.122 The 2012 framework advises that where as a result of an NHS CC eligibility decision a CCG is commissioning, funding or providing any part of the care, that a review should take place within the first three months 'in order to reassess care needs and eligibility for NHS continuing healthcare,

---

112 House of Commons Health Select Committee in their report, *NHS continuing care* HC 399-I, The Stationery Office, 2005, para 146 – and see also the All Party Parliamentary Group on Parkinson, *Failing to care: NHS continuing care in England*, 2013, p19.
113 Department of Health Stakeholders meeting, 1 July 2010.
114 Public Services Ombudsman for Wales Report on a Complaint against Carmarthenshire Local Health Board 15 December 2009 No. 200800779.
115 Complaint No 201404540 and 201409309 against Pembrokeshire CC and Hywel Dda University Health Board 18 November 2015.
116 Report no 200802583 concerning the former Carmarthenshire Local Health Board, 17 September 2010, para 84–85.

and to ensure that those needs are being met' and then annually thereafter (para 139).

12.123   Eligibility for NHS CC can only be removed by a review through the use of the full MDT-led DST process and never unilaterally (framework para 143) – and this applies also to people who have been 'fast-tracked' (framework para 110). Any proposed change must be put in writing to the individual, and if agreement between the local authority and NHS cannot be reached on the proposed change, the local disputes procedure should be invoked (framework para 143 – and see para 12.174 below).

12.124   A 2013 report drew attention to concerns expressed by a number of organisations that patients with progressive or 'non-improving conditions' (for example, spinal cord injuries) were either having their eligibility for NHS CC removed on reassessment or their care support 'dramatically reduced after reassessments without there being any evidence of beneficial clinical improvement'.[117] The report highlighted the illogicality of such decisions and the importance of NHS bodies appreciating the 2012 framework guidance concerning 'well managed needs' (see para 12.55 above).

12.125   Where a decision is made that a person no longer qualifies for NHS CC, the ombudsman requires this be explained with clarity and supported by evidence. Accordingly, a 2010 report[118] was critical of a nursing assessor's conclusion that a resident's 'aggressive and disruptive behaviour' appeared to have stopped following a review of her medication (the suggestion being that this behaviour may have been due to a side effect of the medication). He accepted his adviser's finding that in order to make this suggestion the assessor:

> ... needed to explain in detail why she felt this was probable by recording in more detail the presentation of Mrs C's arthritis, dementia and Parkinson's disease, the drugs she was taking, any interactions and any relevant side effects. The Adviser was of the opinion that to state that the changes in Mrs C's behaviour and the reduction in falls could be related to the stopping of medication without any evidence was inadequate.

Care planning for NHS CC

12.126   The 2012 framework requires that CCGs 'should identify and arrange all services required to meet the needs of all individuals who qualify for NHS Continuing Healthcare and for the healthcare element of a joint care package' (executive summary para 9) and distinguishes between those qualifying for NHS CC (for whom the CCG is responsible for 'all services'), and those for whom there is a joint NHS/social services responsibility (for whom the CCG is responsible for only the 'healthcare element'). The same distinction is made in the guidance, which states (para 108):

> Where an individual is eligible for NHS continuing healthcare, the CCG is responsible for care planning, commissioning services and for case management. It is the responsibility of the CCG to plan strategically, specify outcomes and procure services, to manage demand and provider performance

117 All Party Parliamentary Group on Parkinson, *Failing to care: NHS continuing care in England*, 2013, p22.

118 Report no 200802583 concerning the former Carmarthenshire Local Health Board, 17 September 2010, para 64.

for all services that are required to meet the needs of all individuals who qualify for NHS continuing healthcare, and for the healthcare part of a joint care package. The services commissioned must include ongoing case management for all those entitled to NHS continuing healthcare, as well as for the NHS elements of joint packages, including review and/or reassessment of the individual's needs.

12.127 In addition to the assumption of responsibility by the NHS for the social care needs of a patient in such cases, the ombudsman has identified[119] a further obligation: namely, that the NHS is obliged to meet the person's *full* health care needs (in the particular case, this included a substantial package of speech, language, occupational and physiotherapy).

12.128 The 2012 framework stresses the need for CCGs to commission services 'using models that maximise personalisation and individual control and that reflect the individual's preferences'[120] and to ensure that 'commissioning and procurement arrangements' are person-centred and avoid unnecessary changes of provider (para 170). The guidance applies to all commissioning, including for those in receipt of a joint package (para 171). Where a CCG lacks sufficient expertise in this respect, they have the option of subcontracting the commissioning and support role to the social services authority.

12.129 The ombudsman has considered a number of complaints concerning commissioning/care support failings by NHS bodies. These include:

- making changes to services without adequate notice and without ensuring the new system was fair and accessible – in this case, failing to give notice about changes to the system for providing catheter bags;[121]
- refusing to continue a funding arrangement with a care home agreed by another health body (there had been a change in responsible commissioner) until it had itself assessed the person as eligible.[122]

12.130 Although the CCG is not bound by the views of the local authority[123] as to what services the individual needs, their contribution to the assessment will be important in identifying the individual's needs and the options for meeting them (para 167). CCGs will be under the same public law duty as social services to provide a care plan for any person it accepts as eligible for CC funding – since this is the means by which it 'assembles the relevant

119 Public Services Ombudsman for Wales Report on a Complaint against Carmarthenshire Local Health Board No 200800779, 15 December 2009.

120 See in particular paras 108–111, 166–171 and PG4.

121 Parliamentary and Health Service Ombudsman, 'Listening and learning: The Ombudsman's review of complaint handling by the NHS in England 2011-12' HC 695, The Stationery Office, 2012, p19.

122 Parliamentary and Health Service Ombudsman, 'Listening and learning: The Ombudsman's review of complaint handling by the NHS in England 2011-12' HC 695, The Stationery Office, 2012, p20.

123 Provided the NHS has regard to the local authority assessment it is the NHS that decides on which of the person's health and social care needs are eligible for support 'within the limits of public law reasonableness': *R (S) v Dudley PCT* [2009] EWHC 1780 (Admin). Public law would require that it's decision making is rational and that it is able to explain any significant differences between its assessment and that of the local authority – see, for example, *R v Birmingham CC ex p Killigrew* (2000) 3 CCLR 109, *R v Lambeth LBC ex p K* (2000) 3 CCLR 141 and *R (Goldsmith) v Wandsworth LBC* [2004] EWCA Civ 1170, (2004) 7 CCLR 472 – considered at para 7.167 above.

information and applies it to the statutory ends, and hence affords good evidence to any inquirer of the due discharge of its statutory duties'.[124]

12.131   In the context of care planning, the framework guidance stresses that:

169 CCGs should commission services using models that maximise person-alisation and individual control and that reflect the individual's preferences, as far as possible. It is particularly important that this approach should be taken when an individual who was previously in receipt of an LA direct payment begins to receive NHS continuing healthcare; otherwise they may experience a loss of the control they had previously exercised over their care.

170 CCGs and LAs should operate person-centred commissioning and pro-curement arrangements, so that unnecessary changes of provider or of care package do not take place purely because the responsible commissioner has changed from a CCG to an LA (or vice versa).

12.132   It follows that although there is the potential for a 'gap' to arise when a person transits from social services to NHS CC responsibility, it is the responsibility of the NHS body to ensure that care planning continuity remains despite the transfer of commissioning and funding responsibility. The NHS body must have full regard to the local authority social care assessment, and in an unusual situation where it disagreed with the assessed needs – should provide cogent reasons for its disagreement.

12.133   The above cited framework guidance is particularly important, given that there is evidence that the health bodies can be more rigid in the care arrangements that they are prepared to put in place for those who become eligible for NHS CC funding. In this context, the ombudsman, in a 2010 report,[125] noted that:

... this is one of a number of reports that I have issued which has high-lighted the difficulties which can be caused when the responsibility for someone's care transfers from social services to the NHS. Care provided by the NHS has traditionally been less flexible and allows patients and their carers less control than care provided and funded by social services and the [Independent Living Fund].

12.134   The 2012 framework provides guidance on those situations where the CCG considers that an individual's care support preferences are more expensive than alternatives (para PG83). The advice stresses (among other things): (a) that any cost comparison has to be on the basis of the genuine costs of alternative models and should take into account human rights considerations; (b) that where the person wants to be supported in his or her own home, the actual costs of doing this should be identified on the basis of the individual's assessed needs and agreed desired outcomes; and (c) that cost has to be balanced against other factors in the individual case,

---

124 *R v Islington LBC ex p Rixon* (1997–98) 1 CCLR 119, 128D.

125 Public Services Ombudsman for Wales report concerning the former Cardiff Local Health Board and the former Cardiff and Vale NHS Trust Nos 200802231 and 200802232, 6 August 2010 at para 171. The case concerned a young man with Huntington's disease who remained in hospital for almost three years even though all involved in his care agreed that it was in his best interests to live at home: the problem was that no single NHS official took responsibility for managing the care needs.

such as an individual's desire to continue to live in a family environment (and in this respect, the guidance refers to the *Gunter* judgment[126]).

NHS CC care packages in care homes

12.135 It is likely that the majority of NHS CC care packages will be funded in nursing homes. In such cases the CCG will be subject to the same care planning principles as apply to social services, including being clear with the care home about the outcomes desired and the need to deliver care in a person centred manner.

12.136   Concern has been expressed about 'blanket' statements made by health bodies that if a person in a residential care home is held to be eligible for NHS CC funding then the person will have to move into a nursing home – for example, where the 'fast track pathway' tool has identified the person as entering the final phase of his or her life. In response to this concern, the Department of Health has issued guidance stating that 'there is nothing within the regulatory framework, which would prevent a person in receipt of NHS continuing healthcare remaining within a Care Home (Personal Care)'.[127]

NHS CC in community settings

12.137 In *Coughlan* the court held that 'the fact that the resident at a nursing home does not require in-patient treatment in a hospital does not mean that his or her care should not be the responsibility of the NHS' (para 42). The 2012 framework reiterates this by emphasising that NHS CC may be provided in any setting (including a person's own home) and that eligibility is 'not determined or influenced either by the setting where the care is provided or by the characteristics of the person who delivers the care' (para 56).

12.138   In practice, however, the 'setting' in which the care is delivered can be an issue. A 2003 ombudsman's report[128] was critical of an NHS body whose CC statement had the effect of requiring 'on-site medical provision' (ie hospital based) in order to qualify for full NHS funding. The ombudsman's report in the *Pointon*[129] complaint also expressed concern about a health body's requirement that funding was only available if it was no longer possible for the person to be nursed at home. A 2015 ombudsman report[130] concerned (among other things) a 15-week delay by a health

126 *Gunter (Rachel) v SW Staffordshire Primary Care Trust* [2005] EWHC 1894 (Admin), (2006) 9 CCLR 121. See also para 13.21.
127 Department of Health, *Joint statement re: NHS continuing healthcare funding for end of life care within care homes*, 2008.
128 Berkshire Health Authority Case no E.814/00-01; Second Report for Session 2002–03, *NHS funding for long-term care*, HC 399, 2003.
129 Case no E.22/02/02–03 Funding for Long-Term Care (the *Pointon* case) p23 – and see also para 12.27 above.
130 Complaint No 201404540 and 201409309 against Pembrokeshire CC and Hywel Dda University Health Board, 18 November 2015.

body to implement a recommendation that a NHS CC funded care home resident should have a trial period at home. The report criticised (a) the fact that it took three weeks for the decision to be signed off by the care co-ordinator; (b) the fact that it took a further month for the case to be presented to the panel; (c) the fact that it took the panel making two separate requests for additional information; (d) that although on each occasion the information was provided promptly, the application was not considered again until the following monthly panel meeting; (e) and that as a consequence, agreement to provide funding for the trial period took 15 weeks, and this amounted to maladministration.

Costs

Cost ceilings

12.139 An increasing number of CCGs appear to be imposing 'cost ceilings' for the funding that they are prepared to make for those eligible for NHS CC. Although CCGs cannot have fixed ceilings on such costs, there is nothing unlawful in a public body having a guideline figure above which it would require the assessor to consider certain options (for example, the placing of the person in a care home or other institutional setting[131]). A CCG must, however, in every case, consider the specific facts of an individual's needs: ie it must not operate a blanket policy of not funding above a specific level – and it must in all cases, meet the individual's needs. If there are two care plans that could meet these needs, then it can opt for the cheaper one, but only if it meets the person's eligible needs. In so choosing it must have particular regard to factors such as European Convention on Human Rights Article 8 (right to private and family life) and the UN Convention on the Rights of Persons with Disabilities Article 19 (right to independent living) (see para 2.40).[132] It has also been argued that health bodies must ensure that any costs restriction complies with the NHS National Tariff Payment System, which requires, among other things, that the amount of funding must be in the best interests of patients and not compromise service quality.[133]

Accommodation and home equipment

12.140 The framework reminds CCGs of their responsibilities and powers to meet the care related housing costs of patients entitled to NHS continuing healthcare (para PG 79.4).[134] In *R (Whapples) v Birmingham Crosscity*

---

131 *R (D) v Worcestershire CC* [2013] EWHC 2490 (Admin).

132 In this respect see the submission made by the Spinal Injuries Association, *Response to the Mid-Essex NHS continuing healthcare consultation*, 4 July 2015 proposing a limit on funding linked to the estimated cost of residential care at www.disabilityrightsuk.org/sites/default/files/pdf/SpinalInjuriesAssociationresponse.pdf.

133 See briefing paper by David Collins solicitors, *Can we expect to see a fair rate for CHC?* 2014, which refers to the NHS England/Monitor, *2014/15 National Tariff Payment System*.

134 Namely the general responsibility under NHSA 2006 s3(e), the power to make payments to housing bodies, etc under NHSA 2006 ss256 and 257, the general

CCG,[135] however, the Court of Appeal held that where a patient was eligible for NHS CC funding, the CCG responsibility did not extend to cover paying for ordinary housing costs – that:

> Read as a whole, the National Framework does not, in circumstances where a patient is receiving NHS continuing healthcare in his own home, generally contemplate that the NHS will be responsible for defraying the costs of that accommodation (para 32).

12.141   In this case the court referred to the practice guidance (PG) in Part 2 of the 2012 framework with approval – citing para 85.1:

> Where someone is assessed as eligible for NHS continuing healthcare but chooses to live in their own home in order to enjoy a greater level of independence, the expectation in the Framework is that the CCG would remain financially responsible for all health and personal care services and associated social care services to support assessed health and social care needs and identified outcomes for that person, e.g. equipment provision (see PG 79), routine and incontinence laundry, daily domestic tasks such as food preparation, shopping, washing up, bed-making, support to access community facilities, etc. (including additional support needs for the individual whilst the carer has a break). However, people who choose to live in their own home may have additional community care needs which it may be appropriate for the LA to address subject to their local eligibility threshold and charging policy, e.g. assistance with property adaptation (see PG 79), support with essential parenting activities, support to access other community facilities, carer support services that may include additional general domestic support, or indeed any appropriate service that is specifically required to enable the carer to maintain his/her caring responsibilities (bearing in mind PG 89 below[136]).

12.142   PG 79 (cited in the above extract) refers to the need for care planning to 'consider the need for equipment to assist with activities of daily living and the provision of healthcare, personal care, social care support and wider housing adaptation needs' (79.1) and (citing para 172 of the framework) to the importance of joint equipment services (see para 7.73 above). It also notes, however, that some:

> ... individuals will require bespoke equipment (and/or specialist or other non-bespoke equipment that is not available through joint equipment services) to meet specific assessed needs identified in their NHS continuing healthcare care plan. CCGs should make appropriate arrangements to meet these needs.

12.143   PG 79.3 of the framework refers to the availability of disabled facilities grants (DFGs) for larger adaptations, and this is considered at para 14.125

---

power to make payments to local authorities, and the wider partnership agreements under NHSA 2006 s75.

135   [2015] EWCA Civ 435, (2014) 17 CCLR 308.

136   PG 89 advises that in such cases 'where the involvement of a family member/friend is an integral part of the care plan' then (among other things) 'the CCG may need to provide additional support to care for the individual whilst the carer(s) has a break from his/her caring responsibilities and will need to assure carers of the availability of this support when required. This could take the form of the cared-for person receiving additional services in their own home or spending a period of time away from home (eg a care home)'.

below. It also notes that CCGs (as with local authorities) have 'discretionary powers to provide additional support where appropriate'.

12.144   In *R (MH) v NHS (Sheffield CCG)*[137] a decision by a CCG not to fund a profoundly disabled person's travel costs to a day centre was struck down as irrational. The CCG accepted that his attendance at the day centre was a crucial element of his care plan and that he was unable to access public transport safely.

Top-ups

12.145   A contentious issue in relation to care packages in care homes arises when an individual wants to move into (or is currently living in) a home that is more expensive than the CCG considers necessary to meet his or her needs. There is no specific right to choose an NHS-funded home in the same way as there is for local authority residents to 'top-up' within the Choice of Accommodation Regulations (see para 8.252 above).

12.146   This issue was raised in *R (S) v Dudley PCT*[138] where the health body wanted the applicant to move to a cheaper facility within the same site as the home he had chosen. The court did not find it unlawful to top-up hotel type costs, noting that (paras 21 and 22):

> ... it has always been the case within the National Health Service that those who wish to enjoy what are known in National Health Service jargon as 'hotel-type services', may do so at their own cost. Thus, ever since the foundation of the National Health Service there have been available within National Health Service hospitals enhanced facilities, such as individual rooms, available to patient who are willing to pay for such facilities, but the principle has always been, and remains, subject to exceptions recently canvassed in relation to drugs administered to those with life-threatening illnesses, that healthcare services are provided free.
>
> By reference to what is on any view a fairly fine line, the defendant is thus able to provide free continuing healthcare while at the same time accepting that additional contributions can be made for facilities that may meet non-healthcare needs.

12.147   As noted above, however (para 11.32), the NHS Constitution provides individuals with a right to make choices about the services commissioned by NHS bodies. The department of health has previously noted that although patients in NHS-funded care homes do not have a statutory right of choice, it is expected that before any placement there will be 'considerable consultation with the patient and his or her family and [health bodies should] take account of the patient's wishes'.[139]

12.148   The 2012 framework confirms that 'topping up' is not permissible under NHS legislation and provides guidance on this question (para PG 99) including that:

---

137 [2015] EWHC 4243 (Admin), (2016) 19 CCLR 592: an extempore oral judgement the text of which sadly misquotes passages from the framework guidance – see, for example, para 32 of the judgment.

138 [2009] EWHC 1780 (Admin).

139 Statement of the Minister for Health, John Bowis, to Health Committee, recorded *First Report into Long-Term Care*, HMSO, 1995, para 79.

- the funding provided by CCGs should be sufficient to meet the needs identified in the care plan and that it is 'appropriate to the individual's needs and have the confidence of the person receiving the services' (para 99.1);
- unless it is possible to separately identify and deliver the NHS-funded elements of the service, it will not usually be permissible for individuals to pay for higher-cost services and/or accommodation (as distinct from purchasing additional services) (para 99.2);[140]
- CCGs should consider the case for paying a higher than usual cost in various situations including on an interim basis[141] or where 'the need is for identified clinical reasons (for example, an individual with challenging behaviour wishes to have a larger room because it is identified that the behaviour is linked to feeling confined, or an individual considers that they would benefit from a care provider with specialist skills rather than a generic care provider) (para 99.2);
- where a person already resident in care home accommodation (whose fees are above the CCG's usual rate) becomes eligible for NHS CC funding, the CCG should consider 'whether there are reasons why they should meet the full cost ... such as that the frailty, mental health needs or other relevant needs of the individual mean that a move to other accommodation could involve significant risk to their health and well being' (para 99.4);
- where an individual in an existing out of area placement becomes entitled to NHS CC and where the cost of this placement is above the CCG's usual rate – for which the advice is similar to the above (para 99.5).

12.149 The framework advises that all such cases should be dealt with 'sensitivity and in close liaison with the individuals affected and, where appropriate, their families' and where the CCG decides that it will not fund the higher cost 'advocacy support should be provided where this is appropriate' (para 99.6).

Palliative care and end of life care

12.150 The NHS's duty to provide palliative care exists regardless of the individual's eligibility for NHS CC,[142] and this general duty is considered at para 11.70 above.

140 The requirement that the private services be 'separate'; would appear to rule out an individual paying a top up for a larger room in a care home. The Welsh Framework guidance gives examples of what might be possible eg where an individual who is assessed as requiring one NHS physiotherapy session a week but wishes to purchase an additional session privately or where an individual purchases an additional visit each day from the care provider (Welsh Government, *Continuing NHS healthcare. the national framework for implementation in Wales*, June 2014, para 4.31).

141 Eg until a decision is made on whether to fund this or until arrangements made for an alternative placement (para 99.7).

142 There is most probably a civil and political human right to palliative healthcare (like accident and emergency care): see, for example, D Lohman, R Schleifer and J Amon, 'Access to pain treatment as a human right', BMC Medicine 2010, 8:8 doi:10.1186/1741-7015-8-8 at www.biomedcentral.com/1741-7015/8/8 and *Washington v Glucksberg* (1997) 521 US 702.

12.151   The fast track pathway tool (see para 12.59 above) is designed to ensure that disputes and delay are avoided concerning the care of people in need of palliative and end of life care. In this context, the framework guidance advises that 'strict time limits that base eligibility on some specified expected length of life remaining should not be imposed' and that where the tool has being applied for someone expected to die in the very near future, the CCG should 'continue to take responsibility for the care package until the end of life' (paras 99 and 103).

12.152   Concern has been has expressed about the patchy nature of health bodies' accepting responsibility for patients who require palliative care, and whose prognosis is that they are likely to die in the near future.[143] In response[144] the government in 2004 outlined plans as to how it proposed to make the option of dying at home a reality including requiring health bodies to accept responsibility for 'unscheduled care' (ie 24-hour care and support at home). One aspect of this commitment has been reflected in strengthened advice (now found in the 2012 framework) concerning such care. For example, the guidance stresses the importance of taking into account likely (rather than present) deterioration in a condition (para 38). It then provides four examples, including:

- If an individual has a rapidly deteriorating condition that may be entering a terminal phase, he or she may need NHS continuing healthcare funding to enable his or her needs to be met urgently (eg to allow the individual to go home to die or appropriate end of life support to be put in place). This would be a primary health need because of the rate of deterioration. In all cases where an individual has such needs, consideration should be given to use of the fast track pathway tool (as set out in paras 97–107 of the guidance).
- Even when an individual does not satisfy the criteria for use of the Fast Track Pathway Tool, one or more of the characteristics listed in para 35 of the guidance may well apply to those people approaching the end of their lives, and eligibility should always be considered.

12.153   The 2102 framework requires that in end of life cases 'particular account' should be taken of person-centred commissioning and procurement arrangements (para 106), including that:

> 169. CCGs should commission services using models that maximise personalisation and individual control and that reflect the individual's preferences, as far as possible. It is particularly important that this approach should be taken when an individual who was previously in receipt of [a local authority] direct payment begins to receive NHS continuing healthcare; otherwise they may experience a loss of the control they had previously exercised over their care.

> 170. CCGs and [local authorities] should operate person-centred commissioning and procurement arrangements, so that unnecessary changes of provider or of care package do not take place purely because the responsible commissioner has changed from a CCG to [a local authority] (or vice versa).

143 See, for example, House of Commons Health Committee Fourth Report of Session 2003–04 on Palliative Care, Volume 1, HC 454-I, accessible at www.publications. parliament.uk/pa/cm200304/cmselect/cmhealth/454/454.pdf.

144 Secretary of State for Health, *Government response to House of Commons Health Committee Report on Palliative Care: Fourth Report of Session 2003–04*, Cm 6327, 2004.

Dispute resolution

12.154 The procedure by which individuals can seek a review of an NHS continuing health care decision is found in the 2012 regulations,[145] with the detail fleshed out in the 2012 framework. In the following section, paragraph references are to the framework.

12.155 The regulations and the framework[146] require that CCGs inform individuals (or persons acting on their behalf) about eligibility decisions and in all cases to provide 'clear reasons' for the decision. The notification must explain the procedure and the timescales should the individual or someone acting on their behalf wish to seek a review. The standard process (which does not apply to checklist refusals – see para 12.72 above) is: (1) the 'local resolution procedure (unless the Board decides that requiring the person to do so would cause undue delay)';[147] followed, if necessary, by (2) reference to NHS England for an independent review of the decision.

The individual dispute procedures

12.156 The 2012 regulations provide for a two-stage NHS-led process for individuals who wish to challenge NHS CC decisions.[148]

Stage 1 dispute process: CCG review

12.157 The procedure for the stage 1 review is for each CCG to determine, subject to the requirement to have regard to the framework (reg 21(12)). The procedures they adopt must include timescales, which should be 'publicly available, and a copy should be sent to anybody who requests a review of a decision' (para 151). All requests for review must be dealt with 'promptly' (para 149).

12.158 The framework makes clear that parties involved should be able to view and comment on the evidence[149] and it identifies a number of 'key principles' for both stages of the review process (para 153):

- gathering and scrutiny of all available and appropriate evidence, whether written or oral (the guidance provides an illustrative list of what might be included);
- compilation of a robust and accurate identification of the care needs;
- audit of attempts to gather any records said not to be available;
- involvement of the individual or their representative as far as possible;
- a full record of deliberations of the review panel, made available to all parties;

---

145 National Health Service Commissioning Board and Clinical Commissioning Groups (Responsibilities and Standing Rules) Regulations 2012 SI No 2996 Part 6 creating the new 'Standing rules: NHS continuing healthcare and NHS funded nursing care'.

146 Reg 21(10) and paras 144–145 respectively.

147 The 2012 regulations, reg 23(3)(b).

148 There is in addition the possibility of seeking a judicial review (see para 20.139 below) and at the conclusion of the NHS process, complaint is also possible to the ombudsman (see para 20.127 below).

149 Para 154 – as well as advising on the process where restrictions are placed on sharing of evidence with the parties.

- clear and evidenced written conclusions on the process followed by the NHS body and also on the individual's eligibility for NHS CC, together with appropriate recommendations on actions to be taken. This should include the appropriate rationale related to the guidance.

12.159 The review process can prove to be highly problematic – not infrequently with an individual having concurrent appeals (as each review decision has to be appealed separately) – and in consequence the process taking months if not years. Concern has also been voiced in relation to the competencies of the review members – in the sense that the guidance fails to emphasise the need that they have sufficient expertise/understanding of the individual's particular healthcare condition.

Stage 2 dispute process: Independent Review Panel review

12.160 Regulation 23 provides that where a person, or someone 'lawfully' acting on their behalf, is dissatisfied with the outcome of the first stage resolution process (or NHS England is satisfied that requiring the person to use the process 'would cause undue delay'), then they may apply in writing to NHS England for a review of that decision. The 2012 framework advises that even when cases are before the Independent Review Panel (IRP) process 'CCGs should continue to seek to informally resolve the matter' and that NHS England can ask CCGs to attempt further local resolution prior to the IRP hearing' (PG 73 p96).

12.161   The regulations requires that NHS England appoints sufficient panel chairs[150] to ensure that an IRP can be held anywhere in England and to establish a list of suitable CCG/social services members for each CCG/ social services authority. These individuals are then appointed on an ad hoc basis when an IRP is required – in each case comprising a chair, a CCG and a social services member. The CCG member must not be from the CCG whose decision is being challenged and the social services member must not be from an area in which the CCG is situated.

12.162   The detail of the IRP process is provided in annex e of the framework. IRP parties can be represented ('by family, advocates, advice services or others in a similar role') although the framework states that it is 'not necessary for any party to be legally represented' (para 155). The IRP is advisory, however the regulations specify that its recommendations should be accepted by NHS England (and subsequently by the CCG) in all but exceptional circumstances.[151]

12.163   If the original decision is upheld and the individual remains dissatisfied, there is the option of asking the NHS ombudsman to investigate the complaint (see para 20.127 below).

Support pending a decision, disputes and refunds guidance

12.164 The 2012 framework allows 28 days for the CCGs to make a decision from the time of receipt of the checklist (para 95), adding that if there are 'valid

---

150 Regs 24–27 concern the formalities of the appointment of members/chairs, their disqualification etc.

151 Reg 23(8) and see also para 156 and annex E para 29.

and unavoidable reasons for the process taking longer, timescales should be clearly communicated to the person and (where appropriate) their carers and/or representatives' (para 96).

12.165 The 2012 framework explains the responsibilities for providing services/financial refunds in three situations – namely when (annex F para 1):

1) support is required pending an NHS CC decision (except if a hospital discharge is concerned);[152] or
2) the NHS 'has unjustifiably taken longer than 28 days to reach a decision'; or
3) the individual has succeeded in their dispute and the NHS CC eligibility decision has been revised.

Support pending a decision

(1) Support pending the NHS decision

12.166 In relation to these situations the guidance (annex F) advises:

- Any package already existing should continue, unless there is urgent need for adjustment.
- If services are provided by a local authority, but some health services are needed in the interim which are not within the power for a local authority to provide, the CCG should consider its responsibilities to provide them prior to a decision being made on NHS CC.
- If the individual is not getting local authority or CCG support, then if he or she is in need of social care support, the local authority should assess (and if necessary provide services urgently in advance of an assessment). If the local authority identifies health needs, the CCG should consider its responsibilities pending a decision. The local authority and CCG should jointly agree actions to be taken until the outcome of the decision making process is known. No individual should be left without appropriate support.

(2) Unjustifiable delay

12.167 Where a CCG has unjustifiably taken longer than 28 days to reach a decision on eligibility for NHS CC:

- and the delay was not outside of the CCG's control, the individual or local authority should be refunded from the 29th day;
- the local authority should be refunded the gross amount[153] and then pay back the individual any contributions they made. In the case of a person who has funded his or her own care, the CCG should make an ex gratia payment.

(3) The individual has succeeded in having the NHS CC decision revised

12.168 Where, as a result of an individual disputing an NHS CC eligibility decision, a CCG has revised its decision:

---

152 The relevant duties in such cases are addressed in paras 62–67 of the 2012 framework.
153 Using the powers under NHSA 2006 s 256 – see para 11.127 above.

- the decision remains in effect until the CCG revises its decision;
- if the local authority has funded in the interim the CCG should refund gross to the local authority which should refund any contributions made by the individual;
- if the individual has funded themselves in the interim an ex gratia payment should be considered. [154]

Disputes

12.169 Where an individual disputes a CCG decision on whether to provide redress to them, or disputes the amount of redress payable, this should be considered by the CCG through the NHS complaints process (see para 20.7 below).

Calculating the amount of redress

12.170 There have been a number of disputes concerning how the amount of redress to individuals should be calculated. The framework makes reference to Treasury guidance[155] on this general point – which is primarily concerned about ensuring the person is put in the position they would have been, had the failure not occurred (and in this respect chiming with the guidance given by the ombudsman concerning compensation – see para 20.59).

12.171   In 2007 the ombudsman[156] found that there was maladministration in the department of health's decision making and communication of its approach to recompense for those wrongly denied continuing care funding. The department had advised the NHS to make payments based on the principle of restitution for only those monies paid out in care fees. This approach discouraged health bodies from considering full redress, including, for example, for financial loss due to the premature sale of a property or inconvenience and distress that individuals had suffered in making unnecessary difficult decisions about how to fund care. As a result of the 2007 report, the Department of Health issued revised guidance which, among other things: reminded health bodies that they were empowered to make ex gratia payments; advised them how to calculate interest payments for redress; and reminded them about the powers of local authorities regarding deferred payment agreements.[157]

12.172   The court has also scrutinised the question of interest and found that the it should be 'tailor made to each case'.[158] It agreed that no account should be taken of payments made to the claimant by third parties (such

154 The 2012 framework annex F para 14 refers to at HM Treasury Managing Public Money (2013) for which the relevant paragraph in the updated (2015) document is A4.14.4: it advises that when a public sector organisation has caused injustice or hardship because of maladministration or service failure, it should consider among other things – providing a remedy so that, as far as reasonably possible, it restores the wronged party to the position it would have been in had things been done correctly.

155 Ibid.

156 Parliamentary Ombudsman and the Health Service Ombudsman, *Retrospective continuing care funding and redress* HC 386, The Stationery Office, 2007.

157 Department of Health, *NHS continuing healthcare; continuing care redress*, 2007.

158 *R v Kemp and Denbighshire Health Board* [2006] EWHC 1339 (Admin).

as the benefits paid by the department for work and pensions) in deciding the rate of interest payable. The court changed its provisional decision that the applicant should receive interest at the retail price index rate and ordered that he should receive interest at the (higher) court rate.

Impact on social security benefits

12.173   The Department for Work and Pensions and the Department of Health issued guidance in 2004[159] concerning the impact on social security benefits of a decision that a person is eligible for NHS CC support. For people who live in their own homes, benefits are not affected by NHS CC payments. Those living in nursing homes[160] (but not other placements[161]) will generally be treated as hospital inpatients for benefits purposes. This will be from the date the CCG made a formal entitlement decision. Any payments made to refund patients for the period during which they were wrongly charged for their care do not retrospectively turn these claimants into hospital inpatients for that period (ie provided the resident notifies the Department for Work and Pensions of the funding, there should be no overpayment).

Where the CCG or local authority are in disagreement

12.174   The 2012 regulations require that CCGs must, so far 'as is reasonably practicable', consult and co-operate with the relevant social services authority before making a decision about person's eligibility for NHS CC (reg 22). Where, however, a dispute arises between these two bodies about entitlement – or continuing entitlement to NHS CC or their respective contributions to a joint package – they must agree a dispute resolution procedure 'and resolve the disagreement in accordance with that procedure'.[162] Regulation 22 accordingly puts to an end any continuing misunderstanding about the *St Helen's* judgment.[163]

159   The Department for Work and Pensions guidance was a Decision Makers Guide memo 08/04 but it no longer appears on the website.

160   *White v Chief Adjudication Officer* (1993) WL 963025.

161   *Secretary of State for Work and Pensions v Slavin* [2011] EWCA Civ 1515.

162   Reiterated in the 2012 framework at para 159. See also Joint Investigation by the Parliamentary and Health Service Ombudsman and the Local Government Ombudsman JW-199678/14 006 021 concerning Sheffield Health and Social Care NHS Foundation Trust and Sheffield City Council, March 2015 – which found a failure to work together/to communicate effectively and that the lack of any rational explanation for deciding that a person was not eligible (where she had been eligible prior to her condition deteriorating) to be 'perverse' (para 53).

163   It appears that in a number of local authority/CCG protocols, inappropriately refer to the decision in *R (St Helen's BC) v Manchester PCT and another* [2008] EWCA Civ 921. The decision ceased to be relevant in 2009 (when the directions at the heart of the dispute were replaced by the NHS Continuing Healthcare (Responsibilities) Directions 2009 and now by the 2012 regulations). In its judgment the Court of Appeal stated (para 37) that the judgment did not necessarily have any bearing on the scheme created by the National Framework (which did not apply when the dispute arose).

12.175   The 2012 framework states (para 159):

> Disputes should not delay the provision of the care package, and the proto-col should make clear how funding will be provided pending resolution of the dispute. Where disputes relate to LAs and CCGs in different geographi-cal areas, the disputes resolution process of the responsible CCG should normally be used in order to ensure resolution in a robust and timely manner. This should include agreement on how funding will be provided during the dispute, and arrangements for reimbursement to the agencies involved once the dispute is resolved.

12.176   Throughout the framework guidance, the underpinning requirement con-cerning local authority/NHS joint working is that any differences between the two authorities should not adversely impact on the patient: that the patient's care pathway/transfer of care should not be affected by any such dispute. Decisions on patient discharge from hospital or patient transfer to other settings should be based upon health and social care needs – and not 'who pays'. As the guidance states (para 143):

> Neither the NHS nor [a local authority] should unilaterally withdraw from an existing funding arrangement without a joint reassessment of the indi-vidual, and without first consulting one another and the individual about the proposed change of arrangement. It is essential that alternative funding arrangements are agreed and put into effect before any withdrawal of exist-ing funding, in order to ensure continuity of care. Any proposed change should be put in writing to the individual by the organisation that is propos-ing to make such a change. If agreement between the [local authority] and NHS cannot be reached on the proposed change, the local disputes proce-dure should be invoked, and current funding and care management respon-sibilities should remain in place until the dispute has been resolved.

12.177   In a 2009 ombudsman report, strong criticism was made of a health body that decided without liaison with social services that an individual with a serious acquired brain injury was no longer entitled to NHS CC (which he had been receiving for four years). The health body stopped funding his placement, such that the local authority felt obliged to step in and con-tinue paying the care fees. In finding maladministration, the ombudsman considered that the health body was simply 'attempting to unload its own financial obligations onto the Council'.[164]

12.178   The framework provides guidance on local dispute procedure proto-cols (annex G). It includes a requirement that local authorities and CCGs should agree:

- arrangements for care/support and funding (including 'without preju-dice' funding) while the decision-making process is carried out, not-ing that if someone is being discharged from hospital then the CCG retains funding responsibility whilst the DST is being completed and the eligibility decision is being made;
- on what counts as a disagreement and what counts as a formal dispute – some protocols include disagreements/disputes at checklist and DST stage, as well as at panel decision making stage;

---

164 Public Services Ombudsman for Wales complaint no 2008/00349 against Anglesey LHB 4 September 2009 (at para 97) where recommended compensation amounted to £114,000.

- different levels of dispute resolution – the aim is usually to resolve disputes at practitioner level, but most procedures have the option of escalating the dispute through appropriate levels to senior management level where necessary. Some dispute resolution processes include referring the case to a second panel to check the original decision; in some cases there are agreements to refer to a panel in another area. It is important that dispute resolution processes have a clear end or final resolution point;[165]
- what types of dispute are covered – protocols should deal with disputes over NHS continuing healthcare eligibility, joint funding arrangements and refunds;
- what paperwork/information is needed at each stage;
- timescales at each stage of the process;
- arrangements to ensure individuals get the care/support they need whilst disputes are being resolved, bearing in mind the principle of 'no unilateral withdrawal of funding';
- what happens over interim or 'without prejudice' funding – including over any backdating arrangements for reimbursing costs and how charging the service user will be handled in a variety of possible situations.

Individuals who refuse to be assessed for NHS CC

12.179 Although an award of NHS CC is generally welcome (especially for individuals who have to pay for their social care support needs), some individuals would prefer to remain funded by social services and refuse to co-operate with the NHS CC assessment process. Where they have sufficient mental capacity to make such a decision, then generally CCGs will not persevere with the assessment.

12.180 If a social services authority believes a person to have a primary healthcare need above the limits imposed by CA 2014 s22, then it may be unlawful for that authority to continue to fund that person. The 2012 framework guidance puts the position as follows (para 47):

> If an individual does not consent to assessment of eligibility to NHS continuing healthcare, the potential effect this will have on the ability of the NHS and the [local authority] to provide appropriate services should be carefully explained to them.

12.181 What would need explaining is that by declining an assessment the local authority may decide that it is no longer legal for it to continue the funding: that the refusal by the individual cannot place any additional legal responsibility on the local authority.

12.182 The 2012 framework stresses the importance of exploring the reasons for the refusal and dealing with any concerns that the individual may have

---

165 PG 71 of the 2012 framework refers to the importance of having 'levels of escalation' for disputes – including 'a level by which the matter has to be finally resolved' and gives the example of 'the matter being referred jointly to another to another CCG and LA, and agreeing to accept their recommendation'.

about the CCGs ability to personalise care/support etc (PG 6). Ultimately, however, it states (para 6.4):

> If [a local authority] decides that the refusal to consent to an assessment for NHS continuing healthcare means that [local authority] services can no longer be provided, they should give reasonable notice and clear reasons to the person concerned and give them the opportunity to request a review of the decision or to take it through the complaints process.

Patients covered by NHS CC guidance

Children

12.183 The framework guidance applies only to adults who have care needs that have arisen 'as a result of disability, accident or illness' (para 13). It follows that the guidance does not cover children, although it does address the obligations owed to young people 'in transition' into adulthood (paras 124–138). In January 2016 a new *Framework for children's NHS continuing care* was published in England, together with a revised *Decision support tool* and *Children and young people's continuing care pre-assessment checklist*.[166] The Department of Health explained that the changes were to:

- simplify the language and streamline the guidance;
- clarify how the domains should be interpreted;
- provide advice on how the continuing care process fits into education, health and care plan assessments for children with special educational needs and disability, and multi-agency assessments.

12.184 This book does not cover the healthcare needs of children: these are analysed in the companion volume *Disabled children: a legal handbook* at chapter 5.[167]

Learning disability services and NHS CC

12.185 NHS Act 2006 s275(1) defines 'illness' as including any disorder or disability of the mind and any injury or disability requiring medical or dental treatment or nursing. 'Mental disorder' is the same term used in MHA 1983 s1 and would be given the same interpretation[168] – namely, as any disorder or disability of the mind. A learning disability is therefore an illness for the purposes of NHS law and people with this condition are therefore 'ill' and as much the responsibility of CCGs as local authorities.

12.186 There is some evidence that health bodies have treated people with learning disabilities less favourably in relation to NHS CC decisions than those with other illnesses. The 2012 framework, however, makes clear that its guidance applies 'irrespective of ... client group/diagnosis' (para PG 38.1) and that the 'question is not whether learning disability is a health

166 Accessible at www.gov.uk/government/publications/children-and-young-peoples-continuing-care-national-framework.
167 S Broach, L Clements and J Read, *Disabled children: a legal handbook*, 2nd edn, Legal Action Group, 2016.
168 *Secretary of State for Work and Pensions v Slavin* [2011] EWCA Civ 1515.

need, but rather whether the individual concerned, whatever client group he or she may come from, has a 'primary health need' (para 38.5).

12.187   *Secretary of State for Work and Pensions v Slavin*[169] concerned a 30-year-old resident in receipt of NHS CC funding, who lived in a residential care home (not a nursing home). He had a diagnosis of severe learning disability and Fragile X Syndrome (autistic traits). He had challenging behaviour that meant that he needed to be continuously supervised by at least one, and sometimes two, care staff, who had to be ready to intervene in order to attempt to prevent him causing damage to property or injury to himself or others. The staff were trained to meet the needs of residents, but did not have any medical or nursing qualifications. Although the case concerned the question of eligibility for social security benefits, the Court of Appeal held that his learning disability meant that he fell within the definition of 'illness' in NHSA 2006 s275(1) that 'his healthcare needs qualify him for an NHS-funded residential placement at a care home where he is provided with the specialist care he requires by reason of his illness' (para 52).

12.188   Challenging behaviour arising out of other conditions (such as Alzheimer's disease) can of course give rise to a determination of eligibility for NHS CC – as was the case in the *Pointon* decision (see para 12.27 above).

12.189   The ombudsman has drawn attention to the need for health bodies to take into account a person's learning disabilities in order to satisfy their obligations under the Equality Act 2010. The case concerned a failure to consider if the person's disability might explain why he had missed hospital appointments and had become 'very agitated'. The ombudsman considered that in such cases it was particularly important that staff listen to the people who know the patient best – is the social care team and person's family.[170]

12.190   Circular guidance HSG (92)43 and LAC (92)17 has referred to the historically anomalous position of people with learning difficulties – essentially that although their needs are primarily social, historically the NHS has provided for people with learning difficulties and therefore the NHS has received the funding for the CC needs of such people. Thus the 1992 guidance states that:

> ... it is well recognised that many people (ie people with learning difficulties) traditionally cared for in long-stay hospitals are predominantly in need of social care, and should be cared for in the community. In order to support in the community ex long-stay patients and people who might in earlier times have been cared for in long-stay hospitals, health finance may be spent on social services rather than on health services.

12.191 Until the large-scale closure of the large NHS hospitals specifically catering for people with learning disabilities, one-fifth of people with severe or profound learning disabilities received their care services from the NHS.[171] The 1992 guidance advocates, therefore, not only that the NHS

---

169 [2011] EWCA Civ 1515.

170 Parliamentary and Health Service Ombudsman, 'Listening and learning: The Ombudsman's review of complaint handling by the NHS in England 2011-12' HC 695, The Stationery Office, 2012, pp22–23.

171 LAC (92)15.

transfer monies to social services for the present support of such persons (and their successors[172]) but also that it should develop new and innovative services to meet the social (as opposed to health) needs of such persons.

12.192   People with learning disabilities will qualify directly for NHS CC funding on the general ground that as a consequence of the nature, complexity, intensity or unpredictability of their healthcare needs, the care they require is neither incidental or ancillary to the provision of social services nor of a nature such that an authority whose primary responsibility is to provide social services can be expected to provide it – ie the *Coughlan* criteria. In this respect, particular regard should also be given to the comments of the Health Service Ombudsman in the *Pointon* complaint[173] that health bodies must take into account a person's psychological problems and the special skills it takes to care for such people.

12.193   The 2012 framework guidance advises there may be other circumstances when the NHS is expected to take responsibility for a person's long-term care (para 112)– and gives the example of people with learning disabilities where there is 'an existing agreement to fund ongoing care' (eg a dowry under what used to be NHSA 1977 s28A, now NHSA 2006 s256 – see para 11.127 above):

> ... for individuals following the closure of long-stay hospitals or campuses. These responsibilities arise independently of a CCG's responsibility to provide NHS continuing healthcare, and there should be no assumption that these responsibilities equate to eligibility for NHS continuing healthcare or vice versa. Such agreements vary in terms of the commitments they make to fund needs that subsequently arise. Where additional needs do arise, it will be important for the CCG to first check whether there is clarity in such agreements on whether or not they cover responsibilities to meet such needs. If the additional needs fall outside the agreement, CCGs must consider their responsibilities to meet them, in terms both of the CCG's general responsibilities and potential eligibility for NHS continuing healthcare.

Mental health services and NHS CC

Care Act 2014 and Mental Health Act 1983

12.194 The complex interface between NHS and social services funding responsibilities that characterise the NHS CC boundary, derive from the limitations imposed by CA 2014 s22. Healthcare cannot be provided under the CA 2014 unless it satisfies the so-called quality/quantity test (see para 12.19 above). However, if a patient is eligible for support under MHA 1983 s117, then the support provided under the MHA 1983 will not, on the face of it, be subject to the limitation in the CA 2014. It is nevertheless arguable that there is an implicit limitation on that which can be funded by social services under the MHA 1983 – on the basis of the judgment in *R (T, D and B) v Haringey LBC*.[174] As noted above, although the CA 1989 (like the MHA 1983) lacks any express limitation on what social services can provide in terms of healthcare, Ouseley J considered that such a limitation

---

172 HSG (92)43: LAC (92)17.
173 Case no E.22/02/02-03 Funding for Long Term Care (the *Pointon* case).
174 [2005] EWHC 2235 (Admin), (2006) 9 CCLR 58.

did indeed exist for the CA 1989 (and by implication the MHA 1983): in essence that these provisions should not be regarded as *reducing* or replacing the important public obligations in the NHS/social services boundary and that the limitation in CA 2014 s22 should not be regarded as peculiar to that Act.

12.195　The joint nature of the duty under MHA 1983 s117 has created tensions, since it is arguable that a patient could fall within the entitlement criteria for both regimes. Although this may be immaterial to the individual (as in either case the care is free at the point of need), the question is of considerable budgetary relevance to local authorities and local health bodies since MHA 1983 s117 services are a joint responsibility.

12.196　The 2012 framework guidance considers the interface between these two duties. However, it fails to provide detail concerning the division of the inter-authority funding responsibilities, stating merely that because MHA 1983 s117 services are free and constitute a free standing duty 'it is not appropriate to assess eligibility for [CC] if all the services in question are to be provided as after-care under section 117' (para 121). It goes on to state (para 122):

> However, a person in receipt of after-care services under section 117 may also have ongoing care/support needs that are not related to their mental disorder and that may, therefore, not fall within the scope of section 117. Also a person may be receiving services under section 117 and then develop separate physical health needs (e.g. through a stroke) which may then trigger the need to consider NHS continuing healthcare only in relation to these separate needs, bearing in mind that NHS continuing healthcare should not be used to meet section 117 needs. Where an individual in receipt of section 117 services develops physical care needs resulting in a rapidly deteriorating condition which may be entering a terminal phase, consideration should be given to the use of the Fast Track Pathway Tool.

12.197　If social services' duties are potentially more extensive under MHA 1983 s117 than under the CA 2014, it could lead to surprising outcomes – for example, had Mr Pointon (after being awarded NHS CC) been detained under MHA 1983 s3 and then discharged, he would most probably have ceased to be entitled to NHS CC – and accordingly some potential funding responsibility could have returned to the local authority.

12.198　In such cases, it is clearly of importance that the health and social services bodies have a protocol as to how they determine their respective contributions to such packages – and the 2012 framework mandates this, requiring that CCGs and local authorities should have in place local policies detailing their respective responsibilities, including funding arrangements (para 119).

12.199　PG 64 of the 2012 framework is more expansive on the nature of such a protocol. It should detail: how health and social services bodies will carry out their MHA 1983 s117 responsibilities; which services fall under section 117; and which authority should fund them. It advises that CCGs should have separate budgets for funding section 117 support (ie distinct from NHS CC) and then suggests that there are:

> ... a variety of different models and tools as a basis for working out how section 117 funding costs should be apportioned. However, where this results

in a CCG fully funding a section 117 package this does not constitute NHS continuing healthcare.

What is 'joint' responsibility?

12.200   The 2012 framework identifies the joint nature of the responsibility that local authorities and the NHS have for MHA 1983 s117 support services (para 120) and it appears that some health bodies have sought to argue that this limits their liability to 50 per cent of any section 117 package. This would seem to be misguided. The *Shorter Oxford English Dictionary* provides four definitions of 'joint' – none of which suggest that it can be conceptualised in terms of a 50:50 split. Most apt is the reference to 'a joint burden' – and with this the idea of an 'undivided whole': of each party having 100 per cent of the responsibility. There have been various suggestions as to how agreements can demarcate the respectiveresponsibilities in practice. For example:

- The 2012 framework notes: '[Local authorities] and CCGs may use a variety of different models and tools as a basis for working out how section 117 funding costs should be apportioned. However, where this results in a CCG fully funding a section 117 package this does not constitute NHS continuing healthcare' (para PG 64.2).
- A 2007 ADASS and Local Government Association (LGA) report[175] noted that 'some [local authorities] consider funding on a case-by-case basis, others use the local NHS Continuing Healthcare criteria as an indicator and others look for an equitable 50:50 share of costs'.

The nature of any written agreement

12.201   It appears that until 2015 few local authorities and health bodies had in place a written agreement that apportioned their financial responsibilities for MHA 1983 s117 support. Where this position exists, the agreement will be ascertained by past custom and practice. Not infrequently this appears to have been that those eligible for section 117 support were taken through the NHS CC process. This was not to decide if they were eligible for NHS CC support, but to answer the question: 'But for this person being eligible for section 117 support, how would he or she have been funded?' If the answer was that the person would have been eligible for NHS CC funding – then the CCG would accept 100 per cent funding responsibility. The funding responsibilities would have been adjusted pro rata for other answers – eg 'not eligible but eligible for a shared health and social care package' or 'only eligible for a social care package'. Such an approach would appear to be closest to the requirements of the law – if (as appears probable) the 'limits of social care' principle identified in *Coughlan* is one that is not peculiar to the CA 2014.[176]

---

175 Association of Directors of Adult Social Services (ADASS) and the Local Government Association (LAG), *Commentary and Advice for Local Authorities on The National Framework for NHS Continuing Healthcare and NHS-funded Nursing Care*, 2007 at para 6a.

176 *R (T, D and B) v Haringey LBC* per Ouseley J [2005] EWHC 2235 (Admin), (2006) 9 CCLR 58, para 61.

Carers

12.202 Where a person is eligible for NHS CC, local authorities retain responsibility for undertaking assessments of their carers and for providing support to the carers where required. If, however, the necessary support involves the provision of 'respite/short break/replacement care' to the adult in need, then this will be the responsibility of the NHS (as illustrated in the *Pointon* and *Haringey* decisions – paras 12.27 and 12.31 above). Not infrequently, CCGs appear resistant to providing such support or inflexible in the way they respond. In such cases, it may be necessary for the local authority to use its power under CA 2014 s7 to request that the CCG provides the necessary care (see para 11.43 above).

12.203   The 2012 framework contains additional guidance concerning NHS responsibilities to carers in the following terms (at PG 89):

> 89.1 When a CCG decides to support a home-based package where the involvement of a family member/friend is an integral part of the care plan then the CCG should give consideration to meeting any training needs that the carer may have to carry out this role. In particular, the CCG may need to provide additional support to care for the individual whilst the carer(s) has a break from his/her caring responsibilities and will need to assure carers of the availability of this support when required. This could take the form of the cared-for person receiving additional services in their own home or spending a period of time away from home (e.g. a care home). Consideration should also be given to referral for a separate carer's assessment by the relevant [local authority].

Services for rare and very rare conditions

12.204 National Health Service Commissioning Board and Clinical Commissioning Groups (Responsibilities and Standing Rules) Regulations 2012 SI No 2996 reg 11 and Sch 4 provide a list of what are described as 'services for rare and very rare conditions' that CCGs must arrange services for. Itemised are 144 separate conditions, and the list can be of use if there is a dispute over a particular condition (eg severe obsessive compulsive disorders; specialist morbid obesity services; specialist rehabilitation services for patients; spinal cord injury services etc).

Deprivation of liberty

12.205 The framework guidance advises that 'the fact that a person who lacks capacity needs to be deprived of his or her liberty in these circumstances does not affect the consideration of whether that person is eligible for NHS continuing healthcare' (para 123).

Joint NHS and social services funding

Cost sharing

12.206 One of the ways that the NHS and social services are able to provide support for individuals with healthcare needs that appear to fall in the gap between the upper limit of social services responsibility and below those for which the NHS is prepared to accept NHS CC responsibility (if such cases exist) is for them to share the costs. This was suggested by the Court of Appeal in *Coughlan*,[177] although it indicated that if the parties could not agree on their respective contributions, then the NHS would have to fund the whole package:

> ... the position can be remedied by the Health Service taking responsibility for the whole cost. Either a proper division needs to be drawn (we are not saying that it has to be exact) or the Health Service has to take the whole responsibility. The local authority cannot meet the costs of services which are not its responsibility because of the terms of section 21 (8) of the [NAA 1948] [now CA 2014 s22].

12.207   In *Grogan*, although Charles J accepted that shared funding was an option, he observed (at para 78):

> But, I note that in *Coughlan* at paragraphs 43 to 46 the Court of Appeal envisages the possibility of nursing (and in my view other care) being shared between the local authority and the NHS. In the *Coughlan* case difficulties in setting a coherent division were referred to (paragraph 44) and the answer of the Court of Appeal was that if a proper division was not drawn the NHS would have to take the whole responsibility.

12.208   Where a joint package of care is agreed, this can be delivered either by the CCG and local authority: (a) each delivering direct services to the individual; or (b) individually or jointly commissioning care/services to support the care package, or (c) using their powers to transfer funds to whichever body agrees to be the lead commissioner.[178] The framework provides an example of a joint package (para PG 59). It involves a person who has had a stroke, and has returned to his home. He can manage to walk to his local shop, is continent, can dress himself and care for himself and has no behavioural or cognitive problems – but has a PEG feed.

12.209   It has been suggested that jointly funded packages should be more common – for example, advice in 2007 by the ADASS and the LGA[179] expressed the view that:

> Any individual who 'crosses' the Checklist threshold but is ultimately deemed not to be eligible for NHS Continuing Healthcare is still likely to have their care jointly funded/provided by the [local authority] and PCT.

The 2007 advice also stated:

> In a care home setting, ADASS and LGA expect that for a some people the NHS element of any joint funding may need to go beyond what used to be called the Registered Nursing Care Contribution (RNCC) but is to become the flat rate 'NHS-funded Nursing Care payment'. Joint funding by the NHS should not be limited to situations where the individual is in a 'nursing home' setting.[180]

---

177   *R v North and East Devon Health Authority ex p Coughlan* [2000] 2 WLR 622; [2000] 3 All ER 850 at para 45.

178   Framework para PG 58.3 and see para 11.124 above for the mechanisms by which funding can be transferred between the local authority and NHS.

179   ADASS and LGA, *Commentary and advice for local authorities on the national framework for NHS continuing healthcare and NHS-funded nursing care*, 2007 p5.

180   In this respect see also Department of Health, *NHS-funded nursing care practice guide* (revised), July 2013, para 44.

12.210   The statutory guidance to the CA 2014 requires that where a person 'has both health and care and support needs, local authorities and the NHS should work together effectively to deliver a high quality, coordinated assessment'.[181]

12.211   Where there is a dispute concerning the respective contributions to a joint package it will be maladministration if the respective NHS and local authority bodies do not have a process for resolving this speedily and without causing delay or injustice to the individual.[182]

Joint funding matrix tools

12.212   A number of CCGs and local authorities are developing tools (sometimes referred to as 'joint funding matrix' tools) to determine how to apportion their funding contributions where a person is held to be a joint responsibility. While these tools may lead to a reduction of inter-agency conflict, they are not without their dangers. Most obviously that fewer people will be identified as eligible for fully funded NHS CC with the consequence that they bear partial financial liability for their care package. Additionally, these tools risk removing professional judgment and crudely equating bands in the DST to percentages. Some tools have significant similarities to the bands criticised in the *Grogan* judgment –apportioning a joint package to someone who should (on the *Coughlan* criteria) objectively be eligible for full funding (see para 12.36 above).

12.213   It appears that in other areas, local authorities and CCGs have locked themselves into joint funding agreements that can be overly rigid – for example, that the CCG contribution will never exceed 49 per cent. Agreements of this kind risk challenge – not only on their flawed understanding of the concept of 'joint' (see para 12.200 above) but also because of their potentially adverse impact on individuals (eg those paying significant social care charges). In such cases, they would appear to constitute an unlawful fetter on the NHS duty to provide an appropriate contribution and risk challenge on the further ground that they may not have been subject to appropriate public consultation before adoption. Such inter-authority agreements will invariable contain a 'review date' and presumably this should afford an opportunity for reflection by both bodies (if not before).

---

181   Department of Health, *Care and support statutory guidance* to support implementation of Part 1 of the CA 2014 by local authorities, 2016 ('the statutory guidance'), para 6.80 and following.

182   Joint Investigation by the Parliamentary and Health Service Ombudsman and the Local Government Ombudsman JW-199678/14 006 021 concerning Sheffield Health and Social Care NHS Foundation Trust and Sheffield City Council: March 2015 – which found a failure to work together/to communicate effectively and that the lack of any rational explanation for deciding that a person was not eligible (where she had been eligible prior to her condition deteriorating) to be 'perverse' (para 53).

Direct payments, personal budgets and the NHS

12.214   Although the courts have previously held that the NHSA 2006 did not permit direct payments to be made in relation to NHS responsibilities,[183] in *Gunter v SW Staffordshire PCT*[184] it was accepted that there was nothing in principle in the Act to preclude a health body making direct payments to an independent user trust (IUT) which would then arrange for the patient's health care needs – see (see para 10.104 above).

12.215   The previous prohibition on the NHS making of direct payments has been removed by statutory amendment.[185] The NHS Act 2006 s12A(1) now provides that CCGs may provide direct payments in relation to any of their functions (including under the MHA 1983 s117[186]) more particularly detailed in regulations (issued under section 12B).[187] In October 2014 the CCG power to provide a personal budget became a duty[188] in relation to adults or children eligible for NHS CC.[189] The budget can take the form of a direct payment or a CCG or broker managed personal budget. Detailed (2014) guidance concerning the scheme has been published by NHS England.[190] The conditions and exclusions in relation to the making of such direct payments are very similar to those that apply in relation to social services direct payments (see para 10.44 above).

12.216   The guidance drew attention to the government's policy intention of widening the scope of personal health budgets/direct payments[191] for healthcare needs outside of NHS CC. Certain forms of 'healthcare' are excluded from this entitlement – including services provided by GPs, screening, surgical procedures as well as urgent or emergency treatment services.[192]

---

183   *R (Harrison) v Secretary of State for Health and others* [2009] EWHC 574 (Admin).

184   [2005] EWHC 1894 (Admin) 26/08/05.

185   Health Act 2009 s11.

186   Section 12A(4). Section 12(1) also enables local authorities to provide direct payments in relation to their public health functions – subject to regulations under section 12B.

187   National Health Service (Direct Payments) Regulations 2013 SI No 1617 as amended by National Health Service (Direct Payments) (Amendment) Regulations 2013 SI No 2354.

188   National Health Service Commissioning Board and Clinical Commissioning Groups (Responsibilities and Standing Rules) Regulations 2012 SI No 2996 (as amended) reg 32B.

189   Reg 32A(1).

190   NHS England, *Guidance on direct payments for healthcare: understanding the regulations*, 2014: NHS England has also published a toolkit to assist CCGs in developing procedures to ensure that such budgets are available in their areas NHS England, *Personal health budgets toolkit*, 2012.

191   Department of Health, *NHS Mandate*, 2012.

192   2014 guidance at 3.2.

Resume of patients involved in continuing care disputes

Leeds Ombudsman Report Case no E.62/93–94, January 1994

12.217   The report states (para 22):

> A man suffered a brain haemorrhage and was admitted to a neuro-surgical ward ... He received surgery but did not fully recover. He was incontinent, unable to walk, communicate or feed himself. He also had a kidney tumour, cataracts and occasional epileptic fits, for which he received drug treatment. After 20 months in hospital he was in a stable condition but still required full time nursing care. His condition had reached the stage where active treatment was no longer required but he was still in need of substantial nursing care, which could not be provided at home and which would continue to be needed for the rest of his life.

12.218   The importance of this assessment was emphasised in NHS guidance EL (96)8, which criticised continuing care statements which placed an 'over-reliance on the needs of a patient for specialist medical supervision in determining eligibility for continuing in-patient care' and specifically referred to the fact that this was not considered by the ombudsman in the Leeds case as an acceptable basis for withdrawing NHS support (at para 16).

R v North and East Devon Health Authority ex p Coughlan[193]

12.219   The judgment states (para 3):

> Miss Coughlan was grievously injured in a road traffic accident in 1971. She is tetraplegic; doubly incontinent; requiring regular catheterisation; partially paralysed in the respiratory tract, with consequent difficulty in breathing; and subject not only to the attendant problems of immobility but to recurrent headaches caused by an associated neurological condition.

Wigan and Bolton Health Authority and Bolton Hospitals NHS Trust Case no E.420/00–01[194]

12.220   The report states (para 1, p24):

> Mrs N had suffered several strokes, as a result of which she had no speech or comprehension and was unable to swallow, requiring feeding by PEG tube (a tube which allows feeding directly into the stomach). Mrs N was being treated as an in-patient in the Trust's stroke unit and was discharged to a nursing home.

12.221   The Health Services Commissioner concluded (para 30, p32):

> I cannot see that any authority could reasonably conclude that her need for nursing care was merely incidental or ancillary to the provision of accommodation or of a nature one could expect Social Services to provide (paragraph 15). It seems clear to me that she, like Miss Coughlan, needed services of a wholly different kind.

(In essence the ombudsman had found the decision *Wednesbury* unreasonable.)

---

193   [2000] 2 WLR 622, (1999) 2 CCLR 285, CA.

194   From the Health Service Ombudsman's Second Report for Session 2002–03 *NHS funding for long-term care*, HC 399, 2003.

Dorset Health Authority and Dorset HealthCare NHS Trust Case no E.208/99–00[195]

12.222   Mr X suffered from Alzheimer's disease and was admitted to a nursing home (p11 para 1), allegedly receiving services very similar to Miss Coughlan's (p20 para 23).

12.223   The Health Services Commissioner concluded (at para 26, p21):

> I ... recommend that the ... Authority should, with colleague organisations, determine whether there were any patients (including Mr X senior) who were wrongly refused funding for continuing care, and make the necessary arrangements for reimbursing the costs they incurred unnecessarily ... Mr X senior suffered a degenerative condition, so he was more likely to be eligible for funding as time went by.

Berkshire Health Authority Case no E.814/00–01[196]

12.224   Mrs Z was a 90-year-old admitted to a hospital suffering with vascular dementia (para 1, p35) and in need of 'all help with daily living, except feeding' and resistant to help and needing supervision if she was to take the medication she needed (para 12, p38).

12.225   The Health Services Commissioner concluded (at para 39, p46):

> It is certainly very possible (but not entirely certain) that, if appropriate criteria had been applied, Mrs Z would have qualified for fully funded care.

Birmingham Health Authority Case no E.1626/01–02[197]

12.226   Mrs R was a 90-year-old admitted to hospital following a severe stroke, which had left her immobile, incontinent, and confused (and unlikely that her condition would change) (para 1, p49).

12.227   The Health Services Commissioner concluded (at para 23, p54):

> Had Mrs R been assessed against criteria which were in line with the then guidance and the Coughlan judgment, she might (though it is not possible to be certain) have been deemed eligible for NHS funding for her nursing home care.

Complaint against the former Shropshire Health Authority Case no E.5/02–03[198]

12.228   Mrs F has Alzheimer's Disease and in June 2000 was assessed by a consultant psychiatrist as needing specialist elderly mentally ill (EMI) care. A nursing assessment in November 2000 noted that she required full assistance with all her personal tasks including washing, dressing, feeding and toiletting. She was also doubly incontinent, was dependent upon others for her safety, and could only mobilise with assistance.

12.229   The ombudsman was advised by her independent clinical assessor that Mrs F required significant nursing care and it was debatable whether that could properly be regarded as merely incidental or ancillary to the accommodation which Mrs F also needed. The ombudsman upheld the complaint.

---

195 *NHS funding for long-term care*, HC 399, 2003.
196 *NHS funding for long-term care*, HC 399, 2003.
197 *NHS funding for long-term care*, HC 399, 2003.
198 Health Service Ombudsman's Fifth Report for the Session 2002–03, HC 787, 2003.

Complaint against the former Shropshire Health Authority Case no E.2119/01[199]

12.230 Mr C suffered a severe stroke and the clinical assessment found that he was unable to manage any aspect of personal care independently. The notes recorded that he had an in-dwelling urinary catheter, occasional faecal incontinence (largely avoided by regular toiletting by hoist transfer to commode/toilet); that he required to be fed soft pureed diet with thickened oral fluids; that he had a PEG gastrostomy tube in place, used to administer additional fluids overnight if necessary; that a hoist was used for all transfers; that all pressure areas remained intact with repositioning two hourly; that communication was by eye contact and head movement; that he could not speak.

12.231 The ombudsman's specialist assessor concluded that from the information provided, Mr C's needs were primarily health needs.

Complaint against Cambridgeshire Health Authority and PCT (the *Pointon* case)[200]

12.232 Mr P is severely disabled with dementia and unable to look after himself. His wife cared for him at home. She took a break one week in five but had to pay more than £400 for the substitute care assistant, because the NHS would not pay, because Mrs P was not a qualified nurse (and could not therefore be offering nursing care).

12.233 It was held that the fact that Mr P was receiving (what was in effect) nursing care from his wife, did not mean he could not qualify for continuing healthcare; that the health bodies had failed to take into account his severe psychological problems and the special skills it takes to nurse someone with dementia; that the assessment tools used by the NHS were skewed in favour of physical and acute care; the fact that Mr P needed care at home – rather than in a nursing care home – was not material to the question of continuing healthcare responsibility.

R (T, D and B) v Haringey LBC[201]

12.234 This concerned a patient who required – among other things – a tracheostomy (a tube in the throat). The tube needed suctioning regularly and replacing about once a week. If the tube was not suctioned the patient could die within minutes. Patients in this condition could be cared for at home if their carers are trained to make the daily routines and cope with the emergencies that may arise.

12.235 The judge held that care of this type could not be provided by local authorities – that it was an NHS responsibility. In his opinion the decisive factors were the 'scale and type of nursing care' and the purpose of the care – in this case it was:

> ... designed to deal with the continuing medical consequences of an operation, which if not met would give rise to urgent or immediate medical needs. The advice on management is provided by a hospital: the training is provided by the medically qualified.

199 Health Service Ombudsman's Fifth Report for the Session 2002–03, HC 787, 2003.
200 Case no E.22/02/02–03 Funding for Long-Term Care (the *Pointon* case).
201 [2005] EWHC 2235 (Admin), (2006) 9 CCLR 58.

CHAPTER 13

Mental capacity

continued

Challenging an authorisation in the Court of Protection – section 21A •
Independent mental capacity advocates within the deprivation of liberty
safeguards framework • Law reform and DOLS

Introduction

13.1   Over recent years, the law relating to mental capacity – the ability of adults[1] with mental impairment to make decisions about their personal welfare and their property – has become central to the social care arrangements of those who may lack capacity to take important decisions, in particular about their needs for care and support. As a result, an understanding of the principles of the Mental Capacity Act (MCA) 2005 is necessary for all of those whose responsibility it is to plan and provide services to meet care needs. This increased prominence of mental capacity law has a number of causes:

- Notwithstanding serious concerns (referred to below) about how the MCA 2005 is implemented, the principles and underlying structure of mental capacity law have gradually gained traction. Local authorities and clinical commissioning groups (CCGs) have progressively developed practices which are 'MCA compliant'.

- The expanding workload of the Court of Protection, particularly in personal welfare cases of acute difficulty (for example, decisions about sterilisation, or caesarean sections for those who lack capacity to decide on those issues), and the Court of Protection's increasing willingness to have its proceedings publicised have raised the profile of the jurisdiction among the public at large.

- As the personalisation agenda has gathered momentum, it has become necessary to define how the wishes and values of those without the capacity to participate in the assessment and planning processes – in the language of the Care Act (CA) 2014 the identification and meeting of desired 'outcomes' – can be realised.

- An increasing percentage of adult social care expenditure relates to the needs of adults lacking capacity to make decisions about care and support arrangements.[2] The policy drive towards independent living in the community involves authorities in funding care and support packages (for example, in cases of adults who present with severe challenging behaviour) with high staff ratios and annual funding which can exceed £250,000 for an individual package.

- Of those aged 65 and over, who account for more than half of adult services expenditure, significant numbers are likely to lack capacity to participate in the assessment and planning of their care, often as a result of dementia.

- Following the Supreme Court's judgment in *P v Cheshire West and Chester Council and P and Q v Surrey County Council*[3] (the '*Cheshire West*' judgment in this chapter) a much higher proportion of those who lack capacity to make decisions about their care arrangements will require approval of the Court of Protection, or an 'authorisation' through the

---

1   This chapter concerns those 16 and over who may, or do, lack capacity to take specific decisions.

2   In particular, the majority of higher value packages funded by local authorities relate to learning disabled adults under 65 – see National Audit Office, *Adult social care in England* HC 1102, 2014, figure 13.

3   [2014] UKSC 19, (2014) 17 CCLR 5.

deprivation of liberty safeguards (DOLS) procedures. Either process requires involvement of family and carers in the processes of the MCA 2005.

13.2   Community care legislation and guidance prior to the CA 2014 made scant reference to the ways in which processes of assessment and care planning should be adjusted to take into account the needs of people with impaired capacity to take decisions about their own care, in particular to participate in the assessment of needs, and the planning and arrangement of care to meet needs.[4]

13.3   In contrast, the CA 2014, its regulations and its statutory guidance[5] are prescriptive and detailed: the Act making specific provision for adults who lack capacity to participate in the assessment and care planning processes (section 9(5)(c)), support planning (section 25(3)(c)) and reviews (section 27(2)(b)). CA 2014 s11(2) provides that where an adult refuses an assessment but is assessed as lacking capacity to refuse the local authority, must nonetheless carry out an assessment if satisfied that doing so is in the adult's best interests.

13.4   Additionally, whereas the pre-CA 2014 guidance[6] instructed councils to consider 'the use of Independent Mental Capacity Advocates ... to ensure that as far as possible people are supported to be involved in the decision-making process' the CA 2014 (ss67–68) imposes a duty on local authorities (providing certain conditions are met) to arrange for an independent advocate to 'to represent and support the individual for the purpose of facilitating the individual's involvement' in a variety of assessment, care planning and safeguarding contexts (see para 13.81 below for further discussion on independent advocates).

13.5   In this chapter 'P' is used to mean a person who has been found to lack capacity to make a specific decision at the time it needs to be made.

The Mental Capacity Act 2005 – overview

13.6   The law relating to mental capacity is governed by the MCA 2005. The Act applies principally[7] to persons 16 and over, who are habitually resident

---

4   The Pre-CA 2014 guidance (Department of Health, *Prioritising need in the context of Putting People First: a whole system approach to eligibility for social care*, 2010) dealt with the subject only briefly – noting that 'adults who lack capacity may find it harder to communicate their needs and aspirations' and that councils 'pay particular attention' to the statutory principles in the MCA 2005 Act (para 89).

5   Department of Health, *Care and support statutory guidance* to support implementation of Part 1 of the CA 2014 by local authorities, 2016 ('the statutory guidance').

6   Department of Health, *Prioritising need in the context of Putting People First: a whole system approach to eligibility for social care*, 2010, para 22.

7   The court's powers under section 16 may be exercised in relation to the property and affairs of a person under 16 where the disabilities causing the lack of capacity to manage property and affairs will continue into adulthood.

in England and Wales.[8] Although the Act creates and provides jurisdiction for the Court of Protection, its much wider purpose is to set out the underpinning principles which apply in determining whether a person has capacity to make a specific decision, and where that capacity is lacking, in making decisions, or acting, in that person's best interests. These principles apply to every situation where decision makers – whether informal carers, care providers, local authorities, or ultimately the Court of Protection itself – need to determine capacity, or make decisions on someone's behalf.[9]

13.7   The MCA 2005 is supported by a code of practice.[10] MCA 2005 s42(4) places a duty to 'have regard to' the code on any person who is 'acting in relation to a person who lacks capacity' in one or more of the following ways:

a) as the donee of a lasting power of attorney;
b) as a deputy appointed by the court;
c) as a person carrying out approved research (under MCA 2005 ss30–34);
d) as an independent mental capacity advocate (IMCA);
e) in the exercise of functions under MCA 2005 Sch A1 (DOLS);
f) as a relevant person's representative under MCA 2005 Sch A1 Part 10;
g) in a professional capacity;
h) for remuneration.

13.8   As the code comments, the last two categories cover a wide range of roles, including social and health care staff, support staff, the police and anyone 'contracted to provide a service to people who lack capacity to consent to that service', which will encompass lawyers and advocates as well as for example commissioned taxi drivers and escorts. While there is no statutory duty to comply with the code, it is statutory guidance and, as with all such guidance (for example, that issued under CA 2014 s78 – see para 1.39 above) those who do not follow it 'will be expected to give good reasons why they have departed from it'.[11].

13.9   The code goes on to explain:

> However, the Act applies more generally to everyone who looks after, or cares for, someone who lacks capacity to make particular decisions for themselves. This includes family carers or other carers. Although these carers are not legally required to have regard to the Code of Practice, the guidance given in the Code will help them to understand the Act and apply it. They should follow the guidance in the Code as far as they are aware of it.

---

8 Schedule 3 dealing with the international protection of adults empowers the Court of Protection to take a 'protective measure' which is 'temporary and limited in its effect to England and Wales' in relation to those who are not habitually resident, but are actually present, in England and Wales.

9 See *G v E and others* [2010] EWHC 2042 (COP) where the court emphasised the obvious reality that 'the vast majority of decisions concerning incapacitated adults are taken informally and collaboratively'.

10 Department for Constitutional Affairs, *Mental Capacity Act code of practice*, TSO, 2007.

11 Introduction to the code of practice; see also *R v Islington LBC ex p Rixon* (1997–98) 1 CCLR 119.

Capacity

Meaning

13.10   MCA 2005 s2 makes clear that the capacity to make a particular decision is 'matter' specific – as the code explains:

> Whenever the term 'a person who lacks capacity' is used, it means a person who lacks capacity to make a particular decision or take a particular action for themselves at the time the decision or action needs to be taken.

13.11   Capacity is therefore both issue specific and time specific: a person with a fluctuating condition may have capacity to take a certain decision at a certain time of day, or during a period of remission from illness, but not at other times.[12] A person may at any particular time have capacity to take decisions about one issue, for example with whom to have contact, but not another issue, for example, management of their income. Furthermore, in certain areas of decision making, capacity should not be considered in broad brackets such as 'medical treatment': a person may have capacity to manage treatment for a physical health condition, but not for a mental health condition (for example, because of lack of acceptance of the latter). The extent to which some other areas of decision making are divisible into separate areas of capacity is unclear (and may indeed vary according to individual facts). Is a decision about consumption of alcohol a separate area of capacity, or part of making decisions about social care arrangements? Can a person retain capacity to manage small amounts of money, but lack capacity to manage larger amounts, or are decisions about property and affairs a single area of capacity?

13.12   An individual's insight into his or her difficulties in understanding, retaining or using information, which causes the individual to ask for assistance, is certainly a key consideration. The greater the individual's appreciation that he or she has a problem on which he or she needs advice, the more likely it is that the individual will be deemed to have the necessary capacity: all of us need help in understanding certain information.[13]

13.13   The five principles underpinning the operation of the MCA 2005, set out in section 1, are:

> (2) A person must be assumed to have capacity unless it is established that he lacks capacity.
>
> (3) A person is not to be treated as unable to make a decision unless all practicable steps to help him to do so have been taken without success.

---

12   There is, however, a point at which it is necessary to be 'pragmatic'. In *IM v LM (Capacity to consent to sexual relations)* [2014] EWCA Civ it was argued that it was not possible to make a general order that a person had capacity to consent to a sexual relationship – since in every case the assessment would have to be 'act-specific' and 'situation-specific'. The court considered it 'totally unworkable' to have to look at every particular situation and on 'a pragmatic basis, if for no other reason, capacity to consent to future sexual relations can only be assessed on a general and non-specific basis' (para 77).

13   As Boreham J noted in *White v Fell* (12 November 1987, unreported, cited in *Masterman-Lister v Jewell* [2002] EWCA Civ 1889), 'few people have the capacity to manage all their affairs unaided': the crucial requirement for 'capacity' was that the individual had the insight and understanding that they had a problem (on which they might need advice).

(4) A person is not to be treated as unable to make a decision merely because he makes an unwise decision.

(5) An act done, or decision made, under this Act for or on behalf of a person who lacks capacity must be done, or made, in his best interests.

(6) Before the act is done, or the decision is made, regard must be had to whether the purpose for which it is needed can be as effectively achieved in a way that is less restrictive of the person's rights and freedom of action.

13.14 The first three principles concern the assessment of whether a person has capacity to take a particular decision; the last two principles underpin the approach which must be taken by those making decisions on behalf of a person who is determined to lack that capacity.

13.15 The code explains that the aim of the statutory principles in the MCA 2005 is both to protect people who lack capacity, and to 'help them take part, as much as possible, in decisions that affect them ... to assist and support people who lack capacity to make particular decisions, not to restrict or control their lives'.[14]

Assessment of capacity

13.16 Determination of capacity is fundamental. It is only where lack of capacity is established that the MCA 2005 permits others (whether informal carers, local authorities, or the Court of Protection) to make a decision on behalf of another adult.[15]

13.17 Before turning to the first three principles of the Act, it is necessary to consider the constituents of lack of capacity, set out in MCA 2005 ss2 and 3.

Lack of capacity

The diagnostic and functional tests

13.17 MCA 2005 s3(1) provides that a person is 'unable to make a decision' if at the material time the person is: (a) unable to understand the information relevant to the decision; (b) unable to retain that information; (c) unable to use or weigh that information as part of the process of making the decision; or (d) unable to communicate the decision. The 'information relevant to the decision'[16] includes information about 'the reasonably foreseeable consequences of (a) deciding one way or the other, or (b) failing to make a decision'. The requirement to establish an inability to take a decision is often referred to as 'the functional test'.

13.18 MCA 2005 s2(1) provides that a lack of capacity means that 'at the material time he is unable to make a decision for himself in relation to the

---

14 Para 2.1.

15 Although not permitted by the MCA 2005, the High Court can, when exercising its 'inherent jurisdiction' make a limited range of decisions in order to protect vulnerable adults who have capacity but may in practice be unable to exercise it. See para 18.89.

16 As to what the 'relevant information' is, see discussion concerning *CC v KK and STCC* (2012) [2012] EWHC 2136 (COP) at para 13.67 below.

matter because of an impairment[17] of, or a disturbance in the functioning of, the mind or brain'. It does not matter whether the impairment or disturbance is permanent or temporary. This requirement to identify an impairment in or disturbance of the functioning of the brain or mind is often referred to as 'the diagnostic test'.

13.19   Both the diagnostic and the functional tests must be fulfilled. The fact that a person may have a diagnosis of mental disorder – for example, learning disability, schizophrenia, or dementia – is not sufficient in itself to establish a lack of capacity. Such conditions are types of impairment of, or disturbance in, the functioning of the mind or brain, but it must also be shown under section 2(1) that there is an inability to make a decision 'because of' the identified impairment or disturbance.

Understanding, retaining and using the relevant information

13.20   The 'relevant information' will frequently be the consequences of making or not making the decision. When assessing a person's ability to understand, retain and use relevant information, the information must be presented in a way that is appropriate to a person's needs and circumstances, using the most effective form of communication for that person (MCA 2005 s3(2)). The nature and quantity of information, and so the ability to understand the consequences of making (or not making) a decision, will vary according to what the decision is, and the particular characteristics of the person concerned. For example, a decision, about where to live is likely to involve consideration of a range of factors, short- and long-term, including an understanding of one's care and support needs, the ability of others to offer support, access to facilities etc. The relevant information will be complex in most cases. Other decisions, for example, what to eat, may usually involve simple information, but in particular cases – say for a person with Type 1 diabetes or serious allergies – the reasonably foreseeable consequences of not being able to understand the information may be very serious.

13.21   The inability to retain information for more than a short period is not of itself sufficient to establish lack of capacity (MCA 2005 s3(3)). The requirement is for information to be retained sufficiently long to allow the decision to be made.

13.22   In practice, the most crucial element of the ability to take decisions is often the ability to 'use or weigh' the relevant information for example in the case of individuals affected by mental illness. *A Local Authority v E*[18] concerned a woman with a long history of acute anorexia, for whom death was imminent. There were two options for treatment: the first – as she wished – that she remain in a community hospital receiving palliative care until she died of starvation; the second that she was transferred to an intensive care unit where she would receive artificial nutrition under restraint

17 The MCA does not define 'impairment', however section 2(1) has been described as setting a 'diagnostic threshold'. The association of 'impairment' with 'diagnosis' can in practice mean that individuals who may be assessed as unable to take certain decisions as a result of (for example) intellectual difficulties falling just outside the Learning Disability IQ range, are regarded as not having an 'impairment' for the purposes of section 2(1).

18 [2012] EWHC 1639 (COP).

and/or sedation, and thereafter intensive and long-term therapy. E was an intelligent woman who had no difficulty in understanding and retaining the information relevant to the decision, however the court found that she lacked capacity to take a decision about her treatment because she was unable to weigh the information:

> ... the compulsion to prevent calories entering her system has become the card that trumps all others. The need not to gain weight overpowers all other thoughts.[19]

13.23   The fourth strand of inability to make a decision is the inability to communicate a decision, arising from such conditions as 'locked-in syndrome', where an individual is assessed to be aware and cognitively able, but is unable to communicate at all, even by eye movement. It may also arise if an authority encounters a person who has just had a stroke or who has severe communication difficulties, and despite all efforts is unable to understand what they are saying, and for whom an emergency decision has to be made.

Principles of the Mental Capacity Act 2005

The presumption of capacity

13.24   The first principle in MCA 2005 s1 is the presumption of capacity. It is not for a person to prove that he or she has capacity. The fact that a person may have a particular diagnosis, or that the person is detained in a psychiatric hospital under the Mental Health Act (MHA) 1983, does not rebut the presumption. There must be evidence sufficient to establish on balance of probabilities (more likely than not), that the person does not have the relevant capacity. However, the presumption of capacity should not lead to failures to act on evidence that challenges the presumption. A joint local government ombudsman and parliamentary and health service ombudsman report (2014)[20] concerned a 58-year-old man with paranoid schizophrenia, whose family complained to the local authority about his poor self-care and inadequate diet. The ombudsmen found that the trust's failure to carry out a proper capacity assessment of his ability to make decisions about managing food and looking after himself was a service failure. There was sufficient evidence to challenge the presumption of capacity, as occupational therapy reports had recorded that he was underweight and that there was no food in his flat. As a result, said the local government ombudsman, 'the presumption that [he] had the mental capacity to make his own decisions resulted in him being malnourished'.

Enabling capacity

13.25   The second principle in MCA 2005 s1, that a 'person is not to be treated as unable to make a decision unless all practicable steps to help him to do so have been taken without success' goes to the heart of what the House

---

19   [2012] EWHC 1639 (COP) para 49.
20   Complaint no 11010604/JW111510 against South Essex Partnership Trust and Bedford BC, May 2014.

of Lords select committee[21] referred to as the 'enabling ethos' of the MCA 2005. The principle chimes with the UN Convention on the Rights of Persons with Disabilities (CRPD), Article 12(3) of which requires that states 'take appropriate measures to provide access by persons with disabilities to the support they may require in exercising their legal capacity'.

13.26   Practical steps may include using different methods of communication,[22] or assessing capacity at particular times, or in particular environments. An assessment may involve communication by the person concerned with an individual with whom he or she feels secure, or over a series of meetings in order to build up a relationship between the person concerned and those helping him or her to make a decision. What is 'practicable' is likely to depend on the gravity and complexity of the decision, as well as its urgency. It may involve providing significant education or therapeutic support in relation to the issues engaged by the particular decision[23]. The code sets out guidance on how capacity should be assessed, and the circumstances in which professional assessment is necessary or advisable (chapter 4).

13.27   A common complaint in the social care context is that assessments are carried out by individuals without sufficient expertise, or time. This applies particularly to those with fluctuating or complex conditions – for example, acquired brain injury, autism or dementia. Such practice, if replicated in the context of capacity assessments, may fall short of taking 'all practicable steps'.[24]

13.28   Where formal assessments of capacity are required, they should also be carried out promptly. In *City of Sunderland v MM*[25] a declaration was made that the failure over a period of ten months to carry out an assessment of a person's capacity to make decisions about contact with her partner, resulting in a significant delay in the issue of Court of Protection proceedings (and so in contact being re-established) amounted to a breach of the local authority's positive obligation under European Convention on Human Rights (ECHR) Article 8 to secure her private and family life, and that of her partner.[26]

Unwise decisions

13.29 The third principle in MCA 2005 s1 is that a person is not to be treated as unable to make a decision merely because he or she makes an unwise

21 House of Lords Select Committee on the Mental Capacity Act 2005, *Report: Mental Capacity Act 2005: post-legislative scrutiny*, Report of Session 2013–14 HL Paper 139, The Stationery Office, 2014.

22 For an example of this, see *LBX v K and others* [2013] EWHC 3230 (Fam) where the use of tangible aids such as drawings were said to have the potential to help P in making a decision.

23 See, for a good example, *Re DE* [2013] EWHC 2562 (Fam), in which an intensive programme of education was provided to a learning disabled man who, as a result, gained the capacity to consent to sexual relations.

24 In relation to CA 2014 assessments, see Care and Support (Assessment) Regulations 2014 SI No 2827 reg 5(2) (considered at para 3.108 above).

25 [2009] COPLR Con Vol 881.

26 In this case the Official Solicitor as litigation friend to MM did not support the application, which was made by her partner, but the court's decision meant that her Article 8 rights in addition to his own were breached.

decision. The principle is related to the understanding of foreseeable consequences referred to in MCA 2005 s3(4), but is also fundamental to the balance to be struck between protection and autonomy. A person who understands the consequences of his decision, but decides to make a choice which most people would regard as unwise, should not as a result be treated as lacking capacity.

Information relevant to the decision

13.30   Lack of capacity involves (save in those cases where only an inability to communicate a decision prevents capacity) inability to understand, retain or use 'information relevant to the decision'. The Court of Protection has developed substantial case-law which describes the types of information relevant to particular classes of decision, and (as noted above) frequently this will include the consequences of making or not making the decision in question. Although a review of the Court of Protection case-law on this issue is beyond the scope of this text, the discussion at para 13.51 concerning the interface with 'needs assessment' is of particular relevance.

Best interests

13.31   The fourth principle in MCA 2005 s1 provides that once a lack of capacity to take a specific decision has been established, a decision maker must act, or make the decision, in P's 'best interests'. MCA 2005 s4 sets out the approach which decision makers should take to deciding best interests, but does not attempt a definition of what 'best interests' means. Best interests decisions must not be made purely on the basis of a person's diagnosis, age, appearance or behaviour, although each of those factors may be relevant. Decisions (or even the necessity of taking a decision at the particular time) must take into account the possibility that P may regain capacity on that issue. P must be allowed and encouraged to participate in any act done, or decision made for him or her. MCA 2005 ss4(6) and (7) make crucial requirements of any decision maker:

> (6) He must consider, so far as is reasonably ascertainable–
>> (a) the person's past and present wishes and feelings (and, in particular, any relevant written statement made by him when he had capacity),
>> (b) the beliefs and values that would be likely to influence his decision if he had capacity, and
>> (c) the other factors that he would be likely to consider if he were able to do so.
> (7) He must take into account, if it is practicable and appropriate to consult them, the views of–
>> (a) anyone named by the person as someone to be consulted on the matter in question or on matters of that kind,
>> (b) anyone engaged in caring for the person or interested in his welfare,
>> (c) any donee of a lasting power of attorney granted by the person, and
>> (d) any deputy appointed for the person by the court,
> as to what would be in the person's best interests and, in particular, as to the matters mentioned in subsection (6).

13.32   It will be seen that there are both subjective (what P would have done, or wished) and objective (what others judge to be in P's best interests) elements contained within MCA 2005 s4, which does not, however, contain a hierarchy of considerations. Accepting this dual approach to best interests, the courts have brought varying emphases to the concept of 'best interests'. In *W v M, S and a PCT*[27] a case which concerned a decision whether or not to withdraw artificial nutrition and hydration from a minimally conscious person, the judge in declining the family's request to authorise withdrawal, said (para 81):

> ... best interests is not a test of 'substituted judgment' (what the person would have wanted), but rather it requires a determination to be made by applying an objective test as to what would be in the person's best interests.

13.33   In *Aintree University Hospitals NHS Foundation Trust v James*[28] the family of a man with severe health problems who had lost capacity to make decisions about treatment opposed the application of the NHS trust for authority not to provide specific treatments in defined clinical circumstances. In the Supreme Court Lady Hale said:

> 24 ... This is, as the Explanatory Notes to the Bill made clear, still a 'best interests' rather than a 'substituted judgement' test, but one which accepts that the preferences of the person concerned are an important component in deciding where his best interests lie.
>
> 26. ... Beyond this emphasis on the need to see the patient as an individual, with his own values, likes and dislikes, and consider his interests in a holistic way, the Act gives no further guidance
>
> 45. ... The purpose of the best interests test is to consider matters from the patient's point of view. That is not to say that his wishes must prevail, any more than those of a fully capable patient must prevail. We cannot always have what we want. Nor will it always be possible to ascertain what an incapable patient's wishes are ... In this case, the highest it could be put was ... that 'It was likely that Mr James would want treatment up to the point where it became hopeless'. But insofar as it is possible to ascertain the patient's wishes and feelings, his beliefs and values or the things which were important to him, it is those which should be taken into account because they are a component in making the choice which is right for him as an individual human being.[29]

13.34   Subsequent Court of Protection judgments on issues of this nature have reflected the Supreme Court's lead, particularly in circumstances where it is not possible for P to express wishes or feelings, and he or she has not made an advance decision or appointed a welfare deputy.

13.35   In *Lindsey Briggs and Paul Briggs v The Walton Centre NHS Foundation Trust*[30] the court had to determine whether it was in P's best interests, as his family urged, that clinically assisted nutrition and hydration (CANH) should be withdrawn from a police officer who had suffered severe brain injuries in a road traffic accident and was in a minimally conscious state. The result of withdrawing the treatment would be to bring about his death.

27   [2011] EWHC 2443 (Fam).
28   [2013] UKSC 67, (2013) 16 CCLR 554.
29   See also *St George's Healthcare NHS Trust v P & Q* [2015] EWCOP 42 and *Re G (TJ)* [2010] EWHC (COP).
30   [2016] EWCOP 53.

The court emphasised that the enabling provisions in the MCA 2005 relating to advance decisions and powers of attorney recognise 'that the right to self-determination can dictate future decisions or steps to be taken in the future'. Noting the requirement in MCA 2005 s4(6) on decision makers – in this case the Court of Protection itself – to take reasonable steps to ascertain the wishes, beliefs, values and other factors which would influence the decision which P would make, if he had capacity to do so, the court accepted the strong and consistent evidence of P's family that he would not have wished to continue receiving CANH. The court identified that the 'weighing exercise' was between the strong presumption in favour of preserving life, and 'the great weight to be attached to what Mr Briggs as an individual would have decided himself if he had the capacity and so was able to'. While recording that 'a conclusion on what P would have done is not determinative of the MCA best interests case', the judge's nevertheless held (paras 129–130):

> I have concluded that as I am sure that if Mr Briggs had been sitting in my chair and heard all the evidence and argument he would, in exercise of his right of self-determination, not have consented to further CANH treatment, that his best interests are best promoted by the court not giving that consent on his behalf.

> This means that the court is doing on behalf of Mr Briggs what he would have wanted and done for himself in what he thought was his own best interests if he was able to do so.

13.36 The Court of Protection has also held that in reaching a best interests decision, the present wishes and views of a person who lacks capacity to take the decision in question are not to be given less weight by virtue simply of their lack of capacity. In *Wye Valley NHS Trust v Mr B*[31] the trust submitted that the views expressed by P that he did not wish to undergo amputation of his leg (adjudged by the trust to be in P's best interests) were in principle entitled to less weight than those of a person with capacity. The court, in refusing the application, disagreed, noting (at para 11):

> As the Act and the European Convention make clear, a conclusion that a person lacks decision-making capacity is not an 'off-switch' for his rights and freedoms. To state the obvious, the wishes and feelings, beliefs and values of people with a mental disability are as important to them as they are to anyone else, and may even be more important. It would therefore be wrong in principle to apply any automatic discount to their point of view.[32]

13.37 The increased willingness of the Court of Protection to attach greater weight to P's present wishes and feelings and to what P, if he had capacity, would have done, may anticipate law reform. In its interim statement[33] on reform to the law on deprivation of liberty, the Law Commission proposed 'giving greater priority to the person's wishes and feelings when a best interests decision is being made', presumably by amendment to MCA 2005 s4.

---

31 [2015] EWCOP 60.

32 For a careful analysis of best interests placing P's values, wishes and feelings at the centre of best interests determination, see *also M v Mrs N and others* [2015] EWCOP 59.

33 See para 13.131 below.

13.38   In disputed personal welfare cases in the Court of Protection, it is common practice to instruct experts (typically independent social workers) who are being asked to express an opinion about P's best interests to draw up a 'balance sheet'[34] listing the advantages and disadvantages of each available option. Such an approach has been commended by the Court of Protection as one which should apply generally to best interests decision making,[35] although '[i]f a balance sheet is used it should be a route to judgment and not a substitution for the judgment itself'.[36]

13.39   The code provides useful guidance on the process of determining best interests (chapter 5).

Least restrictive option

13.40   The fifth and final principle under MCA 2005 s1 is often referred to as the 'least restrictive option' principle. It is the duty to decide or act proportionately. The phrasing of MCA 2005 s1(6) is precise: before a best interests decision is made, or act done, 'regard must be had' to whether the purpose sought can be achieved in a way that is 'less restrictive of the person's rights and freedom of action'. The principle is ultimately subsumed in the best interests principle. An egregious example of failure to consider the principle occurred in *Essex CC v RF (deprivation of liberty and damage)*[37] where the local authority purported to justify the removal from home of a 91-year-old man on the basis (in part) that he was at risk of financial abuse, a risk that could have been addressed proportionately by the appointment of a property and affairs deputy.

Protection and risk

13.41   In the context of decisions about residence, and care and support arrangements, the balance to be struck between the protective and the enabling functions of the MCA 2005 has been an issue of debate. The House of Lords select committee[38] identified 'the prevailing cultures of paternalism (in health) and risk-aversion (in social care)', and a number of Court of Protection cases have emphasised that risk is a necessary part of quality of life. In *Re M (best interests: deprivation of liberty)*[39] the court was asked to decide whether to uphold a DOLS authorisation which permitted the local authority to place a pensioner, who lacked capacity to take decisions in relation to management of her insulin dependent diabetes, in a residential

---

34 See *Re A (medical treatment: male sterilisation)* [2000] 1 FLR 549.

35 *AH v Hertfordshire Partnership NHS Foundation Trust and Ealing PCT* [2011] EWHC 276 (COP), (2011) 14 CCLR 301, where a failure on the part of health and social care professionals to adopt a balance sheet approach was criticised.

36 *Re F (a child) (international relocation cases)* [2015] EWCA Civ 882 at para 52.

37 [2015] EWCOP 1.

38 House of Lords Select Committee on the Mental Capacity Act 2005, *Report: Mental Capacity Act 2005: post-legislative scrutiny*, Report of Session 2013–14 HL Paper 139, The Stationery Office, 2014.

39 [2013] EWHC 3456 (COP).

care setting, against her strongly expressed wishes to return to her home where she would receive a 'standard care package' with twice daily district nurse visits. Declining to uphold the authorisation the judge explained:

> 38. In the end, if M remains confined in a home she is entitled to ask 'What for?' The only answer that could be provided at the moment is 'To keep you alive as long as possible.' In my view that is not a sufficient answer. The right to life and the state's obligation to protect it is not absolute and the court must surely have regard to the person's own assessment of her quality of life. In M's case there is little to be said for a solution that attempts, without any guarantee of success, to preserve for her a daily life without meaning or happiness and which she, with some justification, regards as insupportable.

13.42   A similar point had been made in *Re MM (an adult)*[40] where Munby J observed:

> The fact is that all life involves risk, and the young, the elderly and the vulnerable, are exposed to additional risks and to risks they are less well equipped than others to cope with. Physical health and safety can sometimes be bought at too high a price in happiness and emotional welfare. The emphasis must be on sensible risk appraisal, not striving to avoid all risk, whatever the price, but instead seeking a proper balance and being willing to tolerate manageable or acceptable risks as the price appropriately to be paid in order to achieve some other good – in particular to achieve the vital good of the elderly or vulnerable person's happiness. What good is it making someone safer if it merely makes them miserable?

Proscribed decisions

13.43   The Court of Protection is called upon to resolve best interests issues in complex, urgent and grave circumstances. However, there are some areas of decision making, set out in MCA 2005 s27, where the court cannot make declarations or orders consenting on P's behalf. These are marriage, civil partnership (or divorce/dissolution), sexual relations, adoption decisions or consent under the Human Fertilisation and Embryology Acts.[41] Subject to these limitations, the court's powers are considerable – extending, for example, to authorising restraint and forced sterilisation,[42] injunctive relief against third parties with committal for breach,[43] and specifying very detailed processes to authorise strip searches and monitoring of correspondence.[44]

---

40 [2009] 1 FLR 443.
41 Human Fertilisation and Embryology Act 1990 and the Human Fertilisation and Embryology Act 2008.
42 *A local authority v E* [2012] EWHC 1639 COP.
43 *Stoke City Council v Maddocks* [2012] EWCOP B31.
44 *J Council v GU and others* [2012] EWHC 3531 (COP).

Acts in connection with care and treatment

13.44   As noted above, the great majority of best interests decisions are made by carers, family, support workers and social and healthcare professionals as part of day-to-day and routine care. MCA 2005 s5 provides that (save for liability arising from negligence) nobody will be liable for an act done 'in connection with the care and treatment' of P providing that before doing the act they have taken reasonable steps to establish whether P lacks capacity in relation to the matter in question, and that they reasonably believe both that P does lack the requisite capacity and that the act done is in P's best interests. Section 5 will not, however, protect a person whose act is in contravention of a valid advance decision (of which she or he is aware).

13.45   MCA 2005 s6 provides that if the act involves restraint, the decision maker will not be protected unless, additionally, he believes that the act is necessary to prevent harm to P, and that the act is proportionate to the likelihood and seriousness of that harm. 'Restraint' is widely defined and can involve verbal threats, mechanical devices like cot sides, confining P to a room, or use of medication. In *Commissioner of Police for the Metropolis v ZH*[45] the Court of Appeal upheld an award of substantial damages against the police who had forcibly removed a young man with severe autism and learning disabilities from a swimming pool (where he was standing in the water) and subsequently restrained him in a caged police vehicle for about 45 minutes. The court decided that the police were unable to rely on the defences in MCA 2005 ss5 and 6 because they had failed to consult P's care workers (who were present), or therefore to gain any understanding of the nature of his disabilities, or what less restrictive (and so proportionate) steps might have been taken.

13.46   The scope of actions to which the section 5 defence – a statutory version of the common law doctrine of 'necessity' – applies is unclear. The code explains that what is referred to are tasks which (chapter 6):

> ... involve the personal care, healthcare or treatment of people who lack the capacity to consent to them. The aim is to give legal backing for acts that need to be carried out in the best interests of [P].

The Code provides examples of personal care and healthcare tasks which would be covered. A decision to prohibit P's contact with a specific person is unlikely to be covered by MCA 2005 s5. Given that court-appointed deputies are prohibited from making such a decision, it is unlikely that it could be taken informally. It is less clear whether other decisions about contact, for example to arrange it at set times, or in particular settings, would fall within the ambit of section 5.

13.47   A particular issue relevant to the application of MCA 2005 ss5 and 6 is the administration of covert medication, which is often a feature of care arrangements where P lacks capacity to take decisions about medical treatment, and is not compliant with medication. Recent case-law[46] has emphasised the administration of covert medication represents a serious

---

45   [2013] EWCA Civ 69.
46   See *AG v BMBC and another* [2016] EWCOP 37 – a district judge decision and so not binding, but containing valuable guidance on this issue for care providers and responsible statutory bodies.

interference with P's Article 8 rights (right to respect for one's private and family life and home) and can engage Article 5 (right to liberty and security) if its effect is to apply chemical restraint to P because of the sedative effect of the medication. A care provider or public authority administering covert medication to P will not be able to rely on sections 5 and 6 if the decision to administer covert medication has not been approved, and regularly reviewed, in best interests decision making processes which comply with MCA 2005 s4.

Payment for necessary goods and services

13.48　MCA 2005 s7 clarifies the obligation, existing at common law and under Sales of Goods and Services legislation,[47] to pay a reasonable price for the provision of necessary goods or services to a person who lacks capacity to enter into a contract for them. Payment is due from the person who lacks capacity. 'Necessary' is defined in MCA 2005 s7(2) and elaborated upon in the code (para 6.58).

Entering into tenancies

13.49　In *Wychavon District Council v EM (HB)*[48] it was held that where P lacked capacity to enter into a tenancy (because of inability to understand, retain or use the relevant information) an order of the Court of Protection could permit someone to sign a tenancy for P and further that a contract for a tenancy might be covered by MCA 2005 s7.

13.50　　The practical difficulty may be that P will not be able to enter into occupation of rented supported living accommodation until such time as a tenancy agreement has been signed. A property and affairs deputy or lasting powers of attorney (LPA) attorney will have authority to sign a tenancy agreement on P's behalf. If there is no such person, application may be made to the court to make an order in relation to the tenancy issue alone. The Court of Protection has issued a guidance note[49] on this question, confirming that it will accept a consolidated application dealing with a number of tenants, but proof of lack of capacity in relation to entering into a tenancy must be provided for each individual.

Capacity, best interests and care assessments

13.51　A local authority (or in the case of an NHS continuing healthcare patient, a CCG) which is under a duty to meet needs is entitled to take into account the comparative costs of different ways of meeting needs (see para 4.105). Although CA 2014 s25(5) requires authorities to 'take all reasonable steps

---

47　Sale of Goods Act 1979 s3(2).
48　[2012] UKUT 12 (AAC).
49　Court of Protection, *Applications to the Court of Protection in relation to tenancy agreements. Court of Protection guidance on tenancy agreements,* updated February 2012.

to reach agreement with the adult or carer for whom the plan is being prepared about how the authority should meet the needs in question', ultimately the duty on the authority (under section 26) is to provide a personal budget which represents 'the cost to the local authority of meeting the adult's needs'. Local authorities are not necessarily required to provide the individual's 'preferred services', or the 'best' service: the requirement is that they provide suitable support to meet the eligible need – and that insofar as is possible they do so in a cost effective way that accords with a person's wishes.

13.52   Decisions made by local authorities about the services they will fund, or arrange, for people who lack capacity to make decisions about their own care needs, may appear to comprise both best interests decisions made on behalf of the incapacitated person, and decisions made by the authority in order to fulfil its public law duties to meet the needs of an adult with needs. In the absence of a personal welfare attorney, or deputy, with appropriate authority, a local authority will therefore fulfil a number of roles: it will be responsible for assessing the needs of the adult, and deciding how to meet adequately the adult's eligible needs (having regard to its duty to promote the adult's well-being under the CA 2014), but it is also likely to be the 'decision maker' responsible for reaching best interests decisions for the adult, for example deciding the type of accommodation or care arrangements that are in the adult's best interests. Questions of both law and practice arise as to how the role of decision maker as to the adult's best interests can be reconciled with the separate duty to the individual under the CA 2014.

13.53   One, increasingly common, scenario arises where an adult with high care needs, who lacks capacity to make decisions about residence, wishes to remain in his or her own or family home (or the adult's family or carers consider that it is best for him or her to do so), but the responsible local authority refuses to fund the services which are necessary to support the adult at home, and decides instead to fund a residential care placement, at a lower cost.

13.54   The questions of law which arise in such circumstances demand analysis of whether the local authority is making a best interests decision on the part of the adult – that only a residential care placement can properly meet their needs – or a public law decision that whilst the adult's needs might be met either at home, or in residential care, the local authority is only prepared to fund the costs of residential care. That analysis will determine what avenues of challenge are available to the adult (or the adult's carers on the adult's behalf).

13.55   In practice it may be difficult to discover the nature of the decision. A local authority may embark on a best interests decision making process about the adult's social care arrangements without having first established the extent of the personal budget which is available to meet the adult's eligible needs. It may argue that it cannot decide what the adult's eligible needs are, or how to meet them, until it has ascertained[50] what decision about their care arrangements is in their best interests. The best interests

50 Taking into account – among other things – the adult's past and current wishes, their beliefs and values – MCA 2005 s4(6).

decision is thus elided with the process of identifying eligible needs and how to meet them.

13.56   This relationship between best interests decision making (a 'private' law issue) and the public law duties of statutory bodies responsible for meeting community care needs has been examined in the case of *ACCG v MN* first by the High Court,[51] and subsequently the Court of Appeal.[52] The parents of the adult with needs (who lacked capacity to take decisions about care and contact arrangements, and who lived in residential accommodation), wanted the CCG responsible for meeting his needs, to make arrangements for them to have supervised contact with their son at their own home, rather than at the residential placement. Such arrangements would have involved significantly greater expense, and the CCG declined to offer them as an available option. The parents sought to persuade the Court of Protection that it should make a declaration that contact at their home was in their son's best interests, with a view to forcing the CCG to fund such an arrangement.

13.57   King J, with whom the Court of Appeal agreed, refused to make such a declaration. Her starting point was Lady Hale's statement in *Aintree University Hospitals NHS Foundation Trust v James*[53] that the MCA 2005 is:

> ... concerned with enabling the court to do for the patient what he could do for himself if of full capacity, but it goes no further. On an application under this Act, therefore, the court has no greater powers than the patient would have if he were of full capacity.

King J further referred to the danger of:

> ... blurring of the distinction as between the Court of Protection's statutory duties in a private law context, (namely to consider the best interests of an incapacitated adult), with public law challenges in relation to the willingness, unwillingness, reasonableness or rationality of the services a public authority is willing or able to provide.

Judicial review was the correct remedy to challenge unreasonable or irrational decisions made by public authorities. In King J's opinion, apart from:

> ...circumstances where there was 'a credible argument that a provider, in failing to agree to fund a package of care, has in doing so, breached or might breach the human rights of one or more of the parties to the proceedings', (see below) the court could choose only between the available options in the same way as a person could if of full capacity.

13.58   The court's analysis therefore assumes that a statutory authority will have crystallised the available options, ie those capable of meeting the eligible needs of the adult, and that where the adult lacks capacity the (subsequent) task of the best interests decision maker, and so ultimately of the Court of Protection in the event of dispute, is to make a choice from those available options.

---

51 [2013] EWHC 3859 (COP).

52 [2015] EWCA Civ 411. An appeal to the Supreme Court, *N v ACCG* [2017] UKSC 22, was dismissed on 22 March 2017.

53 [2013] UKSC 67.

13.59   The Court of Appeal approved King J's description of the Court of Protection's role:

> There will undoubtedly be cases where courts wish to explore with providers the possibility of funding being made available for packages of care which may, for example, have been identified by independent social workers. In my judgment, such discussions and judicial encouragement for flexibility and negotiation in respect of a care package are actively to be encouraged. Such negotiations are however a far cry from the court embarking on a 'best interests' trial with a view to determining whether or not an option which has been said by care provider (in the exercise of their statutory duties) not to be available, is nevertheless in the patient's best interest [57].

13.60 It appears that, therefore, local authorities can legally propound a care and support plan for an individual even though the plan diverges materially from what might be in that person's 'best interests' (as defined by MCA 2005 s4). In so finding, the Court of Appeal approved the judgment in *R (Chatting) v (1) Viridian Housing (2) Wandsworth LBC*[54] which concerned a challenge to the reconfiguration by a charity to the care arrangements of residents. Miss Chatting was a 92-year-old resident who lacked capacity to take decisions in relation to care. An independent social worker had concluded that the proposed change of care arrangements gave rise to 'practical difficulties which have the potential to run contrary to Miss Chatting's best interests', and had expressed concern at the apparent absence of any formal best interests decision making process. Miss Chatting sought a declaration (among other things) that her local authority had acted unlawfully in failing to take into account her best interests as required by the MCA 2005. She relied on a passage in 2010 statutory guidance[55] which said of the five principles of the MCA 2005 (see para 13.13 above): 'Councils are expected to follow these principles carefully during assessment and supporting planning'.

13.61   The court rejected the application, holding that the decision to reconfigure care arrangements was not a decision taken 'for or on behalf of' Miss Chatting, and so not one to which the best interests principle at MCA 2005 s1(5) applied. It held:

> Plainly [the Council] would have erred in law if they had regarded Miss Chatting's best interests as an irrelevance, because they would have been in breach of section 21(2) of the 1948 Act[56] to have regard for her welfare. But the fact that Miss Chatting is mentally incapacitated does not import the test of 'what is in her best interests?' as the yardstick by which all care decisions are made.

13.62 Pressure on budgets is likely to lead to more local authority decisions to confine 'available options' to those they consider are affordable, for example to offer only the cost of residential care in circumstances where an incapacitated adult wishes, or the adult's family believes that it is the adult's

---

54 [2012] EWHC 3595 (Admin), [2013] COPLR 108, para 99,

55 Department of Health, *Prioritising need in the context of Putting People First: a whole system approach to eligibility for social care*, 2010.

56 National Assistance Act 1948 s21(2) (now repealed) imposed a duty on a local authority, when making arrangements to provide residential accommodation for persons in need of care and accommodation, to 'have regard to the welfare of all persons for whom accommodation is provided.'

best interests, to remain in his or her own or the family home. In *Milton Keynes Council and RR*[57] both the Official Solicitor on behalf of RR, an 81-year-old woman with a diagnosis of vascular dementia, and RR's son, consented to final declarations that it was in RR's best interests to reside at the care home where she had been placed by the local authority, the son making it clear that he had 'little choice other than give his consent as no more suitable residential option was available for RR'. The council had decided not to fund a package of care for RR in the community and had commented: 'It is felt that the Care Home is the appropriate placement for RR's needs'.

13.63   Faced with the refusal of a statutory body to fund the option preferred by the incapacitated adult, or their family, the initial analysis will be whether the adult's eligible needs will in fact be met by the personal budget or services proposed to meet them. For example the adult's psychological and emotional well-being (which in the case of those lacking capacity to decide on residence and care arrangements may easily be overlooked or undervalued) may mean that their personal budget should include not just the cost of 'standard' residential or nursing care, but also the cost of additional one to one care in the home or community. Further, as the CA 2014 statutory guidance[58] states:

> ... the concept of 'independent living' is a core part of the well-being principle. Section 1 of the Care Act includes matters such as individual's control of their day-to-day life, suitability of living accommodation, contribution to society – and crucially, requires local authorities to consider each person's views, wishes, feelings and beliefs.

13.64   Where the 'available options' advanced by the local authority are contrary to the incapacitated adult's wishes (or opposed by the adult's family or carers) the Court of Protection may, aside from 'judicial encouragement' to statutory bodies to think again, at least ensure that all available options are properly described to enable them to be evaluated. The Court of Appeal in *MN v ACCG*[59] confirmed that:

> ... the court has the power to direct the local authority to file evidence or to prepare and file a further plan, including, if the court directs, a description of the services that are available and practicable for each placement option being considered by the court. The local authority is obliged to do so even though the plan's contents may not or do not reflect its formal position, for it is not for the local authority (or indeed any other party) to decide whether it is going to restrict or limit the evidence that it presents ... [37].

13.65   The freedom of local authorities to propound care and support plans that diverge materially from what might be in that person's 'best interests', is not without limits. A person's 'best interests' are material considerations in the care planning process and the greater the plan diverges from these interests (and the greater the interference with fundamental rights – such as ECHR Article 8) the greater will be the court's scrutiny of the plan.

---

57 [2014] EWCOP B19.

58 Paragraph 1.18 see para 2.40 above.

59 [2015] EWCA Civ 411. An appeal to the Supreme Court, *N v ACCG* [2017] UKSC 22, was dismissed on 22 March 2017.

Ultimately, as noted below, a care plan that bears little or no relationship to the best interests assessment will be liable to be a struck down.[60]

Capacity and 'information relevant to the decision'

13.66   More fundamentally, 'the services that are available and practicable for each placement option' will be relevant both to assessment of capacity and to determination of best interests.

13.67   As noted above, assessment of capacity requires, under MCA 2005 s3, evaluation of P's ability to understand, retain and use 'information relevant to the decision'. In circumstances where P's capacity to make decisions about residence is in issue, P must be presented with the relevant information about all the potentially available options: if P's capacity to make a decision to stay in P's own home with a limited care package, rather than move to residential care, is being assessed, part of the relevant information is the extent of that limited care package. This was the situation in *CC v KK and STCC*[61] which concerned an elderly woman with dementia who wished to return from residential care to her bungalow. Rejecting the assessment of the local authority that KK lacked capacity to make decisions about residence, the judge noted 'the real danger that in assessing KK's capacity professionals and the court may consciously or subconsciously attach excessive weight to their own views of how her physical safety may be best protected and insufficient weight to her own views of how her emotional needs may best be met' (para 67). He continued

> ... in assessing capacity it is inappropriate to start with a 'blank canvas'. The person under evaluation must be presented with detailed options so that their capacity to weigh up those options can be fairly assessed ... In order to understand the likely consequences of returning home KK should be given full details of the care package that would or might be available.

13.68   Should the adult lack the relevant capacity, it is then the decision maker who must be able to, and must, evaluate the available options. In *R (Khana) v Southwark LBC*[62] it was held that where an authority's option of residential care had been rejected by the adult (who lacked the relevant capacity and acted by the Official Solicitor as litigation friend) the local authority could not 'treat themselves as discharged from any further duty to provide community services'. In some circumstances there might exist the option of care (for example, at home) with formal support limited to the value of the personal budget but supplemented by whatever P or a third party may be able to contribute by purchasing additional care, and by informal care, which in turn may be supported by services to meet the carer's eligible needs under the CA 2014. That is the alternative option which the decision maker (including the Court of Protection) must have the opportunity of considering, alongside the option of residential care, in order to make a best interests decision.

60 See, for example, *AH v Hertfordshire NHS Foundation Trust & Ealing PCT* [2011] EWHC 276 (COP), (2011) 14 CCLR 301 – considered at para 13.80 below.
61 [2012] EWHC 2136 (COP).
62 [2001] EWCA Civ 999, (2001) 4 CCLR 267 at 51.

13.69   In *A local authority v X*[63] the Court of Protection was faced with a dispute about P's capacity to make a decision to return to his own home, in the context of the local authority declining to make available the funding (said to be around £468,000pa) which was assessed as necessary to meet his needs in that setting, but instead assessing him as requiring a personal budget of £156,000 which it said was the cost of meeting his needs in his specialist residential placement. The court questioned the purpose of embarking on a protracted and expensive hearing to determine whether P had the relevant capacity, noting that P:

> ... can fairly ask through the Official Solicitor what minimum and lesser level of care the local authority would be willing to fund if he does have capacity to decide to return home and does, in fact, choose to return home. I do not know what answer the local authority will give; but one possibility is that they will say that they cannot fund any care on that basis, for the situation would be so unsafe for him that they would not be willing to participate in it.

This passage is an 'aside', but suggests that having assessed the viability of the adult using the personal budget to fund part of the home care package assessed as necessary to meet his needs an authority (in fulfilment of its duties under the CA 2014) would be permitted not to deliver the personal budget if it considered that the overall result would be unsafe, or would not meet the adult's needs. In *Khana*[64] it was suggested that:

> Mrs Khana's refusal of the offer of residential home accommodation – the only course that would meet her assessed needs – [would be] unreasonable in the sense intended by Potter L.J., when he was considering in *ex p Kujtim*[65] what would discharge a local authority from any further duty for so long as such refusal was maintained.

13.70   Those whose views contribute to a best interests decision, because they have a right under MCA 2005 s4(7) to have their views taken into account, must also be provided with information about 'the services that are available and practicable for each placement option'. *R (W) v Croydon LBC*[66] was a judicial review case in which the court quashed the local authority's decision to move a young adult, who lacked capacity to decide on residence, from his residential placement to independent supported living. The local authority had failed to alert W's parents to its view that the residential placement was unsuitable, and so deprived them of the opportunity, during the community care assessment process, of responding and presenting their views.

ECHR Article 8 considerations

13.71   The facts in *MN* (see para 13.56 above) did not give rise to any realistic argument that the only option(s) being made available by the statutory body would result in a (disproportionate) breach of P's Article 8 rights (right to respect for one's private and family life, home and correspondence).

---

63 [2016] EWCOP 44.
64 At para 57.
65 *R v Kensington and Chelsea RLBC ex p Kujtim* (1999) 2 CCLR 340, CA.
66 [2011] EWHC 696 (Admin).

However, the decision of a statutory body not to fund care of an adult in his or her own, or family's, home, but only in residential care, fundamentally engages the adult's Article 8 rights. Both the High Court and the Court of Appeal agreed that there may be 'exceptional' cases where the only option(s) put forward arguably breached P's human rights. King J said:

> [71] ... If a human rights issue is properly raised and pleaded and appears to the court on the pleadings to have some credibility, the court may choose exceptionally to conduct a best interests analysis which includes a consideration of hypothetical options. This would be ordered so as to determine whether the assertion that there is a breach of a party's Article 8 ECHR rights, consequent upon the provider failing to provide funding for their preferred option, has been made out.

> [72] I should be absolutely clear that it does not follow that in every case where a provider has declined to fund a package, or limited the available options, that there should thereafter routinely be an assessment of whether such an option would be in the best interests of the patient in order to ascertain whether there has been a breach of Art 8 rights. Far from it.

13.72   In *A local authority v X*,[67] however – a case raising fundamental ECHR Article 8 considerations – the Court of Protection did not suggest that P had any remedy within the Court of Protection but rather that any challenge to the option put forward by the local authority would be through judicial review proceedings.

13.73   A decision of a statutory body which has the effect of the adult who lacks capacity to take decisions about residence, no longer being supported in his or her home, will in most cases also mean that the adult is deprived of his or her liberty for the purposes of ECHR Article 5 (right to liberty and security). Accordingly, the Court of Protection – whether on an application for a welfare order under MCA 2005 s16, or on application under MCA 2005 s21A (on behalf of P who objects to his or her care home or hospital placement, challenging an authorisation under MCA 2005 Sch A1) – will in any event have to consider whether to authorise P's deprivation of liberty, which will require consideration of whether the option put forward by the local authority is in P's best interests, applying the 'least restrictive option' principle.[68] It would appear to follow that in all such circumstances, the Court of Protection may be required to consider the hypothetical alternative options.

13.74   The application of the judgment in *Re MN* to care arrangements comprising a deprivation of liberty was considered in *North Yorkshire CC v MAG and another*[69] which concerned a 35-year-old man with severe mental and physical disabilities who lived in a one-bedroom flat supported by care arrangements which it was agreed amounted to a deprivation of liberty. He lacked capacity to consent to the care arrangements which were put in place by the CCG. It was accepted by the CCG that the accommodation was unsuitable for his physical needs, but in the absence of any

67 [2016] EWCOP 44.
68 The test for the best interests requirement being met for the purposes of an authorisation under Schedule A1 is whether the detention of the resident is 'a proportionate response to – (a) the likelihood of the relevant person suffering harm, and (b)the seriousness of that harm' (para 16(5)).
69 [2016] EWCOP 5, (2016) 19 CCLR 169.

immediately available alternative the authority applied to the Court of Protection to authorise his deprivation of liberty there. At first instance, a District Judge refused to authorise the deprivation of liberty, finding that the local authority had culpably delayed in finding suitable alternative accommodation. Distinguishing *MN* she made a direction requiring the local authority to 'take the steps necessary to ensure that there is no breach'.

13.75   The appeal of the local authority and the CCG was allowed. The court held that the District Judge had failed to determine whether it was in MAG's best interests to live at the property, noting that although he was deprived of his liberty at the placement, there was no alternative available which offered a lesser degree of restriction, and therefore that it must have been in MAG's best interests to remain there (and indeed no party had argued before the District Judge that it was not).

13.76   A second question was: 'Whether the accommodation provided to MAG was so unsuitable as to be unlawfully so provided, breaching MAG's rights under the ECHR (notably Article 5)'. The judge held:

> ... deprivation of liberty of a person who lacks capacity in his own home, under a care plan delivered by qualified care providers, is most unlikely to breach his Article 5 rights; indeed, the MCA 2005 specifically provides statutory authorisation to deprive someone of their liberty in this way.

13.77   The judge held that the District Judge had been wrong to distinguish *MN*, which applied to all welfare determinations in the Court of Protection including those involving a deprivation of liberty; the effect of her refusal to authorise the deprivation of liberty was (and was intended to) require the local authority urgently to locate and provide alternative accommodation. This was to exert impermissible pressure. He reiterated that the Court of Protection was confined to choosing between available options.

13.78   MAG occupied a flat under a tenancy agreement and sought, through the mechanism of the Court of Protection (which was required to authorise his care arrangements as a deprivation of liberty), to force the local authority to provide alternative accommodation. It is not clear to what extent the court's reasoning in relation to Article 5, and *MN*, would apply to the more common scenario of P wanting to remain in his or her own home in circumstances where the responsible local authority (or CCG) refuses to provide a personal budget sufficient to support P there, but offers only the budget adequate (on the statutory authority's analysis) to meet P's needs in a care home. While such a decision is highly likely to produce a deprivation of liberty, and so require authority of the Court of Protection, the predominant issue faced by the court when told that an authority is not making any other option (ie any increased personal budget) available is arguably the breach of P's Article 8 right to respect for his private life, rather than whether placement in a care home is likely to breach his Article 5 rights.[70]

13.79   Decisions by local authorities to remove adults who lack capacity to decide on residence from their family home, or from specialist residential

---

70 The appeal judgment has been the subject of significant criticism – not least the fact that it was not MAG (who lacked capacity to litigate) who chose the Court of Protection rather than the Administrative Court – see B Clough, *Choosing the 'lesser of two evils' – the empty vessel of best interests?* Small Places, 15 October 2016.

units, to independent supported living arrangements (typically at a lower cost to adult social services departments) may also engage both MCA 2005 best interests decisions and public law community care duties. In particular, local authorities and NHS bodies have argued that the emphasis in pre-CA 2014 guidance, and now in the CA 2014 itself, on the individual having control over his or her day-to-day life, strongly favours living arrangements which are as independent as possible.

13.80   In *Northamptonshire Healthcare NHS Foundation Trust v ML*[71] the Court of Protection decided that it was in the best interests of a 25-year-old man with severe autism to move from his parental home, where he attended a National Autistic Society day centre, to a specialist hospital, the judge holding that 'I would be failing to respect [ML's] personal integrity and autonomy if I did not afford him this chance'. However, the danger of local authorities in making best interests decisions which prioritise autonomy above other elements of well-being is highlighted by *AH v Hertfordshire NHS Foundation Trust and Ealing PCT*,[72] a case in which the Court of Protection considered the best interests decision of the NHS trust to move AH, a 48-year-old man with learning disabilities and autism, from the semi-rural care home where he had lived for ten years to independent supported living. Peter Jackson J, noting that 'it has not been possible to identify a single dependable benefit arising from the proposed move', concluded:

> This case illustrates the obvious point that guideline policies cannot be treated as universal solutions, nor should initiatives designed to personalise care and promote choice be applied to the opposite effect. The very existence of [the residential unit AH had occupied], after most of the institutional population had been resettled in the community, is perhaps the exception that proves this rule. These residents are not an anomaly simply because they are among the few remaining recipients of this style of social care. They might better be seen as a good example of the kind of personal planning that lies at the heart of the philosophy of care in the community. Otherwise, an unintended consequence of national policy may be to sacrifice the interests of vulnerable and unusual people like Alan.

Independent mental capacity advocates in best interests decision making

13.81   MCA 2005 ss35-41 (supplemented by the code chapter 10) provide for the instruction of an IMCA to 'represent and support' P in certain circumstances. IMCAs should play an important role under the MCA 2005 in ensuring that where a serious best interests decision is to be made, P's wishes, feelings and values are taken into account under MCA 2005 s4(6), when there is no person whom it is appropriate to consult about P's best interests.

13.82   IMCAs have specific statutory functions, which are separate from, but may overlap with, the role of advocates in other contexts. In particular, CA 2014 ss67–68 and accompanying regulations (see para 3.117 above) impose a duty on local authorities – in the context of assessments, care

71   [2014] EWCOP 2.
72   [2011] EWHC 276 (COP), (2011) 14 CCLR 301.

planning and where the individual is the subject of safeguarding enquiries – to ensure that independent advocacy support is available for adults who experience 'substantial difficulty' in understanding, retaining or using information relevant to those processes, or in communicating their views, wishes or feelings.

13.83   Regulations[73] contain detailed provisions about the functions of IMCAs. The functions of an IMCA include:

- providing support to P in the decision making process;
- obtaining and evaluating relevant information (which may include in treatment cases, a medical report);
- ascertaining P's wishes, beliefs and values; and
- ascertaining what the alternative courses of action are.

13.84   IMCAs need not be instructed[74] where there is an attorney appointed under an LPA to take the best interests decision; a deputy with power to make the decision; or a person nominated by P as a person to be consulted about the issue.

13.85   Where one of the following decisions needs to be taken and there is no one whom it would be appropriate to consult about what is in the best interests of a person lacking the requisite capacity (excluding those engaged in his or her professional care or treatment), then an IMCA must – save where arrangements must be made as a matter of urgency – be instructed:

a) Where it is proposed that the person undergoes 'serious medical treatment', to which the person cannot consent. What is 'serious medical treatment' is defined in regulations[75] and more usefully amplified in a practice direction[76] and the code.[77] It excludes compulsory treatment for mental disorder to detained patients under MHA 1983 Parts 4 and 4A (MCA 2005 s37).

b) Where the NHS proposes to arrange (or change) accommodation in a hospital (save for compulsory detention in hospital under MHA 1983) for 28 days or longer (MCA 2005 s38).

c) Where a local authority proposes to arrange (or change) residential accommodation under CA 2014 s18 or MHA 1983 s117 for eight weeks or longer, and there is no appropriate person to consult (MCA 2005 s39).

---

73   Mental Capacity Act 2005 (Independent Mental Capacity Advocate) (General) Regulations 2006 SI No 1832; Mental Capacity Act 2005 (Independent Mental Capacity Advocate) (Expansion of Role) Regulations 2006 SI No 2883.

74   MCA 2005 s40. This provision is problematic in the context of the DOLS provisions where the deputy or attorney may be an RPR who is not fulfilling their duty to support P in challenging a DOLS authorisation, but no IMCA can be instructed under MCA 2005 s39D.

75   Mental Capacity Act 2005 (Independent Mental Capacity Advocates) (General) Regulations 2006 SI No 1832 (as amended) reg 4.

76   Practice direction E – Applications relating to serious medical treatment (PD9E).

77   Para 10.45 of the code states that it is impossible to set out all types of procedures that may amount to 'serious medical treatment', but by way of illustration suggests – chemotherapy, ECT, sterilization, major surgery (such as open-heart surgery or brain/neuro-surgery), major amputations, treatments which will result in permanent loss of hearing or sight, the withholding or stopping artificial nutrition and hydration, and termination of pregnancy.

13.86   Additionally, the regulations[78] provide that IMCAs may be instructed in the context of reviews of residential care and adult safeguarding. In the latter context, an IMCA may be instructed even if the local authority is satisfied that there is someone whom it is appropriate to consult.

13.87   In all of these contexts (save adult safeguarding) where an IMCA must or may be instructed the MCA 2005 appears to preclude instruction where there is a person 'whom it is appropriate to consult'. The code says that: 'If a family disagrees with a decision maker's proposed action, this is not grounds for concluding that there is nobody whose views are relevant to the decision' (para 10.79).

13.88   The 2014 House of Lords select committee[79] (see para 13.121 below) recommended that the discretionary role of IMCAs should be increased to allow the 'wider and earlier use' of the services; that they be made more professional; and that a form of self-referral to the service be introduced. In its response, the government said that it had decided 'to build on the new duties to provide advocacy in the Care Act 2014, linking these to the existing duties to provide advocacy under the MCA'. Although the CA 2014 regulations[80] apply only to advocates exercising functions under the CA 2014, the statutory guidance to the CA 2014 states that the same individual should wherever possible fulfil both CA 2014 advocate and IMCA functions (para 7.65). In this respect, therefore, it would appear that the aim of increasing the professionalisation of the IMCA service will (to an extent) have been achieved by the regulations.

Deprivation of liberty

Introduction

13.89   Following the Supreme Court's 2014 judgment in the *Cheshire West* case (see para 13.1 above)[81] it appears that most adults[82] lacking capacity to make decisions about their residence and care arrangements who live in residential care, shared lives arrangements and supported living arrangements, and who have 24-hour care, will be deemed to be deprived of their liberty for the purposes of ECHR Article 5 (right to liberty and security), as may some adults who continue to live with their families.

13.90   The distinction between a 'deprivation' of liberty and a 'restriction' on liberty is crucial: a deprivation falls under ECHR Article 5; a restriction

---

78 Mental Capacity Act 2005 (Independent Mental Capacity Advocate) (Expansion of Role) Regulations 2006 SI No 2883.

79 House of Lords Select Committee on the Mental Capacity Act 2005, HL Paper 139, The Stationery Office, 2014.

80 Care and Support (Independent Advocacy Support) (No 2) Regulations 2014 – see para 3.117 above.

81 *P (by his litigation friend, the Official Solicitor) v Cheshire West and Chester Council and another and P and Q (by their litigation friend the Official Solicitor) v Surrey CC* [2014] UKSC 19, (2014) 17 CCLR 5.

82 The MCA 2005's welfare jurisdiction applies to those 16 and over. Consideration of the law relating to the capacity of people under 16 to make decisions is outside the scope of this book – but for an analysis see S Broach, L Clements and J Read, *Disabled children: a legal handbook*, 2nd edn, Legal Action Group, 2016, chapter 7.

that is a lesser degree of interference with the individual, does not, and so does not merit the safeguards under Article 5.

13.91 A deprivation of liberty must be authorised by a 'procedure prescribed by law' (Article 5(1)) and those deprived of liberty must have the means of taking proceedings 'by which the lawfulness of [their] detention shall be decided speedily by a court and [their] release ordered if the detention is not lawful' (Article 5(4)).

What is a deprivation of liberty?

13.92 Over recent years the Court of Protection has wrestled with what should be the threshold for deprivation of (as opposed to the restriction on) liberty, however the elements are clear. First, there must be a subjective element – ie the inability to consent to the deprivation. Second, the person must be objectively deprived of his or her liberty. Third, the deprivation must be imputable to the state.

13.93 Imputability to the state goes beyond direct state (local authority or NHS) involvement in funding or arranging care. In *Staffordshire CC v SRK and others*[83] the Court of Protection held that where P was subject to privately funded and provided care arrangements, amounting to an objective deprivation of liberty, there was a duty on the civil court awarding damages, the Court of Protection itself, and on those involved in privately funding or arranging P's care – for example, P's property and affairs deputy, trustees or attorney – to notify the local authority with safeguarding duties towards P of the arrangements. That knowledge on the part of the authority would trigger its obligation to investigate P's arrangements so as to comply with its positive obligations under Article 5 to prevent arbitrary deprivation of liberty. P's deprivation of liberty would therefore become the indirect responsibility of the state, requiring an application to the Court of Protection for authority.[84] The decision was upheld in the Court of Appeal.[85]

13.94 It is, however, the second element –the point at which a 'restriction' becomes 'deprivation' – which has proved most difficult to define.

13.95 In *HL v UK*[86] (considered further below) the European Court of Human Rights held that:

.... the starting point must be the specific situation of the individual concerned and account must be taken of a whole range of factors arising in a particular case such as the type, duration, effects and manner of implementation of the measure in question. The distinction between a deprivation of, and restriction upon, liberty is merely one of degree or intensity and not one of nature or substance.

13.96 In the *Cheshire West* case Lady Hale identified as the 'acid test' for deprivation of liberty that P is both under continuous (or 'constant') supervision and control, and not free to leave his or her residence. P's compliance

---

83 [2016] EWCOP 27.

84 The position for self-funding care home residents is similar: the application by a care home to the supervisory body for a Schedule A1 authorisation makes the state indirectly responsible for any deprivation of liberty.

85 [2016] EWCA Civ 1317.

86 (2004) 40 EHRR 761, ECtHR.

with the arrangements, their purpose, or their relative normality are all irrelevant.

13.97   Questions remain about the threshold for deprivation of liberty.[87] What is meant by 'continuous' or 'free to leave'?[88] It is also unclear in what circumstances restrictions on an adult living in his or her own or a family home with a care package (which may include assistive technology such as alarms, GPS etc) funded or arranged by a local authority, should be regarded as amounting to a deprivation of liberty.[89]

13.98   Nevertheless the 'acid test' identified by Lady Hale had the effect of exponentially increasing the numbers of people in respect of whom care homes have made applications to local authorities for DOLS authorisations under MCA 2005 Sch A1.[90]

13.99   Concern that there would inevitably be a similar increase in the numbers of applications made by local authorities to the Court of Protection in respect of people who are in supported living, or their own home, resulted in two judgments – *Re X (deprivation of liberty)*[91] and *Re X (deprivation of liberty) (No 2)*[92] – addressing the practical and procedural implications of the anticipated increase in applications to the Court of Protection for DOL authority. In these judgments, the president of the Court of Protection set out the mechanism for a streamlined procedure for application to the Court of Protection (the '*Re X* procedure') which was to involve applications being considered on the papers by judges of the social entitlement chamber, a branch of the tribunals service the principal function of which is in deciding appeals against decisions of the Department for Work and Pensions relating to social security benefit entitlements.[93]

13.100   The *Re X* judgments were designed to deal with the overwhelming majority of cases where there was no substantive dispute about the lack

---

87 The Law Society has produced *Identifying a deprivation of liberty: a practical guide*, 2015.

88 In *PJ v A local health board and others* [2015] UKUT 480 (AAC) Charles J expressed the view that it was inappropriate to take a narrow view of the elements of the 'acid test'; that temporary freedom to come and go is best analysed as an aspect of supervision and control, and that 'free to leave' means freedom to effect a permanent change of residence.

89 Three of the seven judges dissented in the cases of *P and Q v Surrey CC*, asserting that it was unrealistic to describe 'people living happily in a domestic setting as deprived of their liberty'. In *W City Council v Mrs L* [2015] EWCOP 20 Bodey J in a 'finely balanced decision' found a 93-year-old woman with Alzheimer's living at home not to be deprived of her liberty. He would also have found the arrangement not to be imputable to the state, referring to a 'shared arrangement set up by agreement with a caring and pro-active family ... the responsibility of the State is ... diluted by the strong role which the family has played and continues to play'.

90 During the year 2013/2014 a total of 13,700 DOLS applications were made and in 2014/2015 (beginning the month after the judgment of the Supreme Court was given) this rose to 137,540 – a ten-fold increase: Health and Social Care Information Centre, *Mental Capacity Act (2005) deprivation of liberty safeguards (England) annual report, 2014–15*, September 2015.

91 [2014] EWCOP 25, (2014) 17 CCLR 297.

92 [2014] EWCOP 37, (2014) 17 CCLR 464.

93 The allocation of this branch of the judiciary to the *Re X* procedure, rather than those who sit on the First-tier Tribunal (Mental Health), who already had familiarity with the principles of the MCA 2005, appears to have been dictated solely by the fact that the number of social security appeals had fallen, leaving judges in that chamber with insufficient work.

of capacity of P, and where the arrangements comprising the deprivation of liberty were in P's best interests. The *Re X* procedure envisaged that in such cases it would not be necessary for P to be made party to the proceedings. The judgments identified a number of 'triggers' which would make individual cases unsuitable for the streamlined procedure. These included evidence of disagreement by P or others interested in his or her welfare that P lacks capacity, or that the care arrangements are in P's best interests.

13.101   Following the judgments, a new practice direction was issued[94] and substantial amendments were made to the Court of Protection Rules,[95] which came into force on 1 July 2015. Most importantly, a new rule 3A requires the court to consider whether P's participation can be secured, and P's interests protected, in a way other than being a party to proceedings – for example, by the appointment of a 'representative' or an 'accredited legal representative' (although no accreditation scheme is yet in operation).

13.102   On appeal[96] from the *Re X* judgments, the principal argument was that proceedings to authorise deprivation of P's liberty, in which P was not a party, would breach P's ECHR rights. The Court of Appeal decided that it had no jurisdiction to decide on the lawfulness of the *Re X* procedure, as the *Re X* judgments had not been decisions (relating to one or more Ps) of the Court of Protection against which an appeal could be brought, but rather hypothetical and advisory judgments about the law; however, all three judges made it clear that had they been required to do so, they would have decided that P should be a party to any proceedings concerning P's deprivation of liberty.

13.103   Notwithstanding the Court of Appeal's comments, a subsequent judgment of Charles J in *Re NRA*[97] has put the streamlined procedure envisaged by *Re X* into effect, albeit with procedural refinements. The judge held that family members (or friends) who had been devoted to caring for P over many years were generally to be trusted to advocate for P's best interests and should be appointed rule 3A representatives;[98] in such circumstances P should not be joined as a party to proceedings. The court envisaged that where no trusted family member was available, rather than make P a party, the Court of Protection should itself inquire into whether the care arrangements comprising a deprivation of liberty were in P's best interests.

13.104   The position of those without any trusted family member or friend to act as a rule 3A representative was considered again by the same judge in *Re JM*.[99] The judge was highly critical of the failure of the secretary of state to provide funding for professional rule 3A representatives, an approach which he said 'prioritises budgetary considerations over responsibilities to vulnerable people who the Supreme Court has held are being deprived

---

94 Available at: www.judiciary.gov.uk/wp-content/uploads/2014/05/PRACTICE-DIRECTION-10AA-consolidated-FINAL.pdf.

95 Court of Protection (Amendment) Rules 2015 SI No 548.

96 [2015] EWCA Civ 599.

97 [2015] EWCOP 59, (2015) 18 CCLR 392.

98 In *Re VE* [2016] EWCOP 16 Charles J produced a helpful guidance note for prospective rule 3A representatives.

99 [2016] EWCOP 15.

of their liberty'. He joined both the secretary of state and the minister of justice as parties, and stayed the proceedings to allow the parties to identify a practicable alternative procedure to allow a rule 3A representative to be appointed. He ordered that the same course should be taken in all similar cases, acknowledging that this would inevitably create a backlog of stayed cases. The judge suggested a range of possible solutions, including the secretary of state entering into contracts with advocates to act as rule 3A representatives; providing funding to local authorities to enable them to make such arrangements; changing (ie increasing) legal aid funding; providing further resources to the Official Solicitor; or setting up an accredited legal representative scheme. An alternative, the judge said, was to take the issue of deprivation of liberty back to the Supreme Court to invite them to reconsider the decision in *Cheshire West.*

13.105   The government has neither appealed nor responded to the judgment, although steps have been taken to create a panel of accredited legal representatives. As of January 2017 large numbers of similar cases remained stayed.

Deprivation of liberty safeguards in the Mental Capacity Act 2005

Introduction

13.106 The landmark case of *HL v UK*[100] (commonly referred to as the 'Bournewood judgment') concerned a 48-year-old man with autism and learning disability. He was unable to speak, was frequently agitated and had a history of self-harming behaviour. For over 30 years he lived in Bournewood hospital before being placed with carers in 1994. In 1997 he became disturbed at his day centre and was admitted informally to Bournewood Hospital as he was assessed not to meet the criteria for MHA 1983 admission. A decision was taken by treating clinicians that his contact with his carers should be restricted. When the careers asked for HL's discharge, this was refused. The consultant psychiatrist made clear that were HL to attempt to leave the hospital, he would be detained under the MHA 1983. The European Court of Human Rights noted that health professionals exercised 'complete and effective control over his care and movements' and concluded that he was deprived of his liberty for the purposes of ECHR Article 5(1). The Strasbourg court found that there had been a violation of Article 5(1) because HL's deprivation of liberty had not been 'in accordance with a procedure prescribed by law', and of Article 5(4) because HL had no means of applying quickly to a court to challenge the lawfulness of his deprivation of liberty.

13.107   As a result of the Bournewood judgment, the MCA 2005 was amended.[101] Under section 16(2)(a) the Court of Protection had power to make a welfare order which deprives someone of their liberty (a power that can apply to P in any setting, but is most often used to authorise deprivations of liberty where P is in a supported living environment). The amendments

---

100 (2004) 40 EHRR 761, ECtHR.
101 Through the Mental Health Act 2007.

provided (section 4A(5)), that where P is in a care home or hospital setting, a deprivation of liberty may also be authorised under MCA 2005 Sch A1, that is under the deprivation of liberty safeguards (DOLS) framework.

13.108 Neither power may be exercised where a person becomes 'ineligible', applying the confusingly named Schedule 1A, which defines classes of people who are ineligible to be deprived of their liberty under the MCA 2005, as a result of the interrelationship between the MCA 2005 and the MHA 1983.[102]

Deprivation of liberty safeguards – the framework

13.109 The overly complex DOLS provisions set out in MCA 2005 Sch A1 are briefly summarised below. Schedule A1 is supported by a separate code of practice.[103]

13.110 Schedule A1 provides for authorisations for deprivation of liberty. Urgent authorisations may be self-granted by a care home or hospital (a 'managing authority') for up to seven days (and may be extended for up to a further seven days by a supervisory body, on request).

13.111 Standard authorisations may be granted by the supervisory body (in all cases the local authority) for up to one year, after which a further application will be needed. A standard authorisation must be requested by the managing authority where it appears that P is, or will within 28 days, be accommodated in a care home or hospital in circumstances amounting to a deprivation of liberty. The duty of the supervisory body is to carry out an assessment of whether P meets the six qualifying requirements:

1) P is over 18.
2) P has a mental disorder.
3) P lacks capacity to decide that he should be accommodated in the relevant care home or hospital.
4) It is in P's best interests to be subject to a deprivation of liberty, which is necessary and proportionate.
5) P is not ineligible by virtue of MCA 2005 Sch 1A.
6) The no refusals requirement, ie that there is no relevant valid advance decision, or valid conflicting decision of an attorney under a lasting power of attorney, or of a deputy.

13.112 If the requirements are met, the local authority must grant a standard authorisation. MCA 2005 Sch A1 para 53 permits the local authority to attach conditions to a standard authorisation, having regard to any recommendations made by the best interests assessor. The DOLS code of practice (4.74) suggests that conditions should 'directly relate to the issue of deprivation of liberty', for example 'recommendations around contact

---

102 Illustrated by the judgment of Charles J in *AM v South London and the Maudsley NHS Foundation Trust and the Secretary of State for Health* [2013] UKUT 365 (AAC). See also chapter 13 to the MHA 1983 code of practice, TSO, 2015 available at www.gov.uk/government/publications/code-of-practice-mental-health-act-1983.The application of Schedule 1A to Schedule A1 has proved complex and problematic, for example in circumstances where patients detained under the MHA 1983 require authority for a 'residual' deprivation of liberty under the MCA – see eg *A local health board v AB* [2015] EWCOP 31.

103 Ministry of Justice, *Deprivation of liberty safeguards code of practice*, TSO, 2008.

issues'. It is unclear how far this could go: it would be surprising if a condition prohibiting contact between P and a named individual could be attached to a DOLS authorisation given that a personal welfare deputy is expressly prohibited from making such a decision.[104]

Relevant person's representatives

13.113   MCA 2005 Sch A1 para 139 provides that the supervisory body must appoint a relevant person's representative (RPR) as soon as possible after a standard authorisation is granted. Detailed regulations[105] govern the appointment of the RPR. The functions of the RPR are to stay in contact with P and to represent and support P in matters related to Schedule A1. In *AJ v A Local Authority*[106] the common situation arose of the RPR being a relative (and in that instance also the attorney) of P, who did not support P's wish to challenge the authorisation. The court found that the supervisory body should not have allowed the appointment of the RPR given his evident unwillingness to support P in challenging the authorisation: his appointment defeated the ability of P to challenge the lawfulness of his authorisation, as required by ECHR Article 5(4).

Challenging an authorisation in the Court of Protection – section 21A

13.114   P, his or her RPR or the managing authority have the right to request a review of a standard authorisation under MCA 2005 Sch A1 Part 8, or to apply to the Court of Protection under MCA 2005 s21A to vary or terminate either an urgent or standard authorisation.[107] Special administrative arrangements exist within the Court of Protection to enable section 21A applications to be dealt with on an urgent basis.

13.115   It is the right to apply to the Court of Protection under MCA 2005 s21A, which has the potential to satisfy the requirement in ECHR Article 5(4) of speedy access to a court to challenge the lawfulness of the authorisation.

Independent mental capacity advocates within the deprivation of liberty safeguards framework

13.116   Following the introduction of the DOLS regime, the MCA 2005 was amended to provide for the instruction of IMCAs where P becomes subject to a DOLS authorisation. The role of IMCAs in the DOLS process is described in the DOLS code of practice (para 3.22 onwards).

13.117   Briefly summarised:

- An IMCA must be instructed by the local authority where an urgent authorisation is made, or a standard authorisation requested, and there

---

104   MCA 2005 s20(2)(a).

105   In England: Mental Capacity (Deprivation of Liberty: Appointment of Relevant Person's Representative) Regulations 2008 SI No 1315; in Wales: Mental Capacity (Deprivation of Liberty: Appointment of Relevant Person's Representative) (Wales) Regulations 2009 SI No 266.

106   [2015] EWCOP 5.

107   In *Re D and others* [2016] EWCOP 49 the court provided detailed guidance to RPRs (and to an extent MCA 2005 s39 IMCAs on how they should decide whether to bring an application to the Court of Protection under MCA 2005 s21A).

is no person whom it is appropriate to consult about P's best interests (MCA 2005 s39A). The role of a section 39A IMCA is to support P through the DOLS assessment process.

- An IMCA must be instructed where an authorisation is in place, the appointment of an RPR ceases, and there is no person whom it is appropriate to consult about P's best interests (MCA 2005 s39C). In these circumstances the IMCA's role is to fulfil the functions of an RPR.
- An IMCA must be instructed (MCA 2005 s39D) where P is subject to an authorisation, there is an unpaid RPR, and:
  - either P or the RPR asks the local authority to instruct an advocate; or
  - the local authority have reason to believe that without an advocate P and the RPR would be unable to exercise their rights to a request a part 8 review of the authorisation, or to apply to court under MCA 2005 s21A; or
  - P and the RPR have each failed to exercise, or are each unlikely to exercise, those rights.

13.118　The role of the MCA 2005 s39D IMCA is crucial in protecting the rights of P where P's RPR (possibly a family member) is unwilling or unable to exercise rights to challenge a DOLS authorisation. The role of the section 39D IMCA is:

- to help P and the RPR understand the effect, purpose and duration of the authorisation, any conditions to which it is subject, the reasons why P was found on assessment to meet the qualifying requirements, what their rights are to challenge it, and how to exercise those rights;
- to 'take such steps as are practicable' to help P or the RPR to exercise the right to a review or to apply to the court under MCA 2005 s21A;
- on a review, to make submissions to the local authority or an assessor carrying out the review.

13.119　The IMCA's duties cease to apply in most circumstances if a paid 'professional' RPR is appointed. However, an IMCA must still be instructed where either P or the RPR requests their instruction, or where the local authority considers it necessary to help ensure that P's rights under the DOLS procedures are protected (see DOLS Code 7.37).

13.120　　In *AJ v A local authority*[108] Baker J was critical of a local authority which delayed in appointing a MCA 2005 s39D IMCA for an elderly woman who did not wish to remain in a care home where she was placed subject to a standard authorisation, and then failed to ensure that the IMCA was acting so as to ensure that her right to apply to the Court of Protection under MCA 2005 s21A (ie to challenge the authorisation) was exercised.

108 [2015] EWCOP 5.

Law reform and DOLS

13.121   A 2014 House of Lords select committee[109] report concerning DOLS found them to be 'poorly drafted, overly complex ... not well understood ... poorly implemented' and:

> ... far from being used to protect individuals and their rights, they are sometimes used to oppress individuals, and to force upon them decisions made by others without reference to the wishes and feelings of the person concerned.

13.122   The committee's call for the wholesale replacement of the DOLS provisions and the practical implications of the *Cheshire West* judgment resulted in the government asking the Law Commission to come up with proposals for a 'new legislative framework' in this field.[110]

13.123   Similar concerns to those expressed by the select committee were raised by the Care Quality Commission (CQC) in 2015.[111] These included a systemic failure to notify the CQC of applications for standard authorisations, wide regional variations in numbers of applications[112] and a failure to appoint an IMCA in appropriate cases which it 'deplored'.

13.124   It is clear that there are structural problems in the DOLS framework, particularly P's access, which call into question its compliance with ECHR Article 5(4). European case-law (usefully summarised at para 35 of Baker J's judgment in *AJ v A local authority*[113]) has identified that Article 5(4) requires 'special procedural safeguards' to ensure that those who lack mental capacity to exercise their rights have practical and effective access to a court.

13.125   In *MH v UK*,[114] for example, the European Court of Human Rights held that the absence of special procedural safeguards to facilitate access to a tribunal for patients detained under MHA 1983 s2 who lack the capacity to make an application themselves, violated Article 5(4).

13.126   European case-law[115] has also established that Article 5(4) may not be complied with where access to a court is dependent on the exercise of discretion by a third party, rather than an automatic entitlement.

13.127   Against that background, there are a number of ways in which the DOLS framework would appear to fall short of the practical and effective access to the MCA 2005 s21A jurisdiction which Article 5(4) requires. The failings include:

---

109   House of Lords Select Committee on the Mental Capacity Act 2005, HL Paper 139, The Stationery Office, 2014.

110   HM Government, *Valuing every voice, respecting every right: making the case for the Mental Capacity Act: the government's response to the House of Lords Select Committee report on the Mental Capacity Act 2005* Cm 8884, HMSO, 2014; HM Government, *Valuing every voice, respecting every right: making the case for the Mental Capacity Act: the government's response to the House of Lords Select Committee report on the Mental Capacity Act 2005* Cm 8884, HMSO, 2014.

111   CQC, *Monitoring the use of the Mental Capacity Act deprivation of liberty safeguards in 2013/14*, CQC-267-500-WL-012015, 2015.

112   A problem also identified by the Department of Health – see its *Independent Mental Capacity Advocacy service: sixth annual report*, 2014.

113   [2015] EWCOP 5.

114   [2013] ECHR 1008.

115   *Shtukatarov v Russia* (2008) 54 EHRR 962.

- the unrealistic expectation that unpaid RPRs (most of whom are likely to be family members or carers, who may have arranged or supported the residential care placement) will exercise a discretion to support P in challenging the authorisation;
- the lack of clarity as to when a supervisory body is required to appoint a MCA 2005 s39D IMCA;
- the fact that many local authorities (as supervisory bodies) are failing to refer to MCA 2005 s39D IMCAs;
- the evidence that many MCA 2005 s39D IMCAs find the process of challenging an authorisation 'lengthy and dauntingly complex'.[116]

13.128 Unsurprisingly, such a dysfunctional process has led to (well publicised) examples of cases where serious violations of P's Article 5 and Article 8 rights have been found to have occurred, often in the context of poorly conducted Safeguarding enquiries: for example:

- *Hillingdon LBC v Neary*[117] concerned a young man who was admitted to respite care at the request of his father in December 2009. From January to December 2010, against his own family's wishes, Mr Neary was kept there by the local authority, which granted from April 2010 onwards a series of standard authorisations. The court was highly critical of the authority's failures within a short timescale to refer the issue to the Court of Protection, appoint an IMCA or effectively scrutinise the best interests assessments under the DOLS process. The court said that the function of DOLS is to regulate the care and treatment of P who is in a placement which involves a deprivation of liberty, and is 'not to be used by a local authority as a means of getting its own way on the question of whether it is in the person's best interests to be in the place at all' (para 33).[118] The court found Mr Neary's rights under ECHR Articles 5 and 8 had been breached (the authority subsequently paid £35,000 in damages).
- In *Somerset v MK*,[119] MK, a young woman with severe learning disabilities and autism who had been placed in a residential respite placement to enable the family to have a holiday, was considered by the council (on the basis of what the judge found to be inadequate evidence) to have sustained non-accidental injuries. Following a safeguarding meeting in June 2013, MK was not permitted to return to her home. She remained in what the judge found to be an inappropriate placement for six months, during which she was prescribed anti-psychotic medication without consultation with the family. It was not until 12 December 2013 (by which time MK had been transferred to an assessment and treatment unit) that the local authority granted a standard authorisation (an urgent authorisation having been granted on 28 November 2013). During this entire period, MK's contact with her younger siblings was not facilitated and contact with members of her family who were not under suspicion of inflicting injuries on her was supervised.

116 CQC, *Monitoring the use of the Mental Capacity Act deprivation of liberty safeguards in 2013/14*, CQC-267-500-WL-012015, 2015, p28.
117 [2011] EWHC 1377 COP.
118 See also *C v Blackburn with Darwen BC* [2011] EWHC 3321 (COP).
119 [2014] EWCOP B25.

There was no consultation by the local authority in relation to these restrictions. There was a failure to appoint an IMCA for many months. Summing up the litany of local authority failures, the judge noted the 'many depressing similarities' to the *Neary* case.

- *Essex CC v RF (deprivation of liberty and damage)*[120] concerned a 91-year-old retired civil servant with dementia and physical health problems, who had lived in his own home for about 50 years. Following safeguarding concerns about financial exploitation and self-neglect, he was visited by a social worker and told that he had to accompany her. He complied, but was said to be reluctant and very distressed. He was placed in a locked dementia unit where he remained for 13 months until he returned home. A capacity assessment failed even to record his views about leaving his home. No application for a DOLS authorisation, or application to the Court of Protection was made. The local authority was ordered to pay £60,000 in compensation and RF's costs.

13.129 In 2014 the Law Commission was asked to carry out a review of the DOLS provisions. It published a consultation in July 2015.[121] Following wide consultation in May 2016 the Commission published its final report and draft bill on 13 March 2017.[122] The final report emphasises the need to strike 'a proportionate balance between responding efficiently to the volume of cases requiring authorisation since *Cheshire West* and giving proper safeguards to people whose objections are too easily over-ruled under the current law'.

13.130   The focus of the proposed reforms is on replacing the DOLS process, but the Commission goes further in particular by proposing a number of amendments and additions to MCA 2005:

- MCA 2005 s4(6) would be amended to require all decision makers to 'ascertain, so far as is reasonably practicable' P's wishes and feelings and, in making the best interests determination, to 'give particular weight to any wishes or feelings ascertained'.
- Professionals providing care and treatment for P would be prevented from relying on the 'general defence' in MCA 2005 s5 in relation to a specified list of 'relevant decisions', unless they had prepared a written record of the decision-making process recording defined information for example in relation to assessment of capacity, the steps taken to ascertain P's wishes and compliance with the statutory obligations in relation to provision of an advocate. 'Relevant decisions' would include a decision to restrict P's contact with named individuals, a decision to provide serious medical treatment, a decision to administer treatment in a covert manner and a decision to administer treatment which D knows, or reasonably suspects, to be against P's wishes.
- A new section 63A would empower the appropriate authorities to establish, through regulations, supported decision-making schemes, ie to support persons in making decisions about their personal welfare and/ or property and affairs, an approach consistent with Article 12 CRPD.

---

120 [2015] EWCOP 1.
121 Law Commission, *Mental capacity and deprivation of liberty: a consultation paper*, Consultation Paper No 222, 2015.
122 www.lawcom.gov.uk/wp-content/uploads/2017/03/lc372_mental_capacity.pdf.

- The draft bill proposes to put on a statutory footing the concept of an advanced consent to a deprivation of liberty. The Commission proposes that there are a number of circumstances in which such a consent would not remain valid, including if P did anything clearly inconsistent with the advance consent.

13.131 The Commission proposes a new scheme of 'Liberty Protection Safeguards' (LPS) to replace DOLS. LPS would cover deprivations of liberty in all settings, removing the need to apply to the Court of Protection for authorisation where there is a deprivation of liberty in for example independent supported living. Responsibility for authorising deprivation of liberty would lie with the local authority or the NHS body for deprivations of liberty in hospital or relating to NHS CC patients. Where arrangements amounting to a deprivation of liberty were put in place privately, ie by someone other than a local authority or an NHS body, application for an authorisation would need to be made to the local authority.

13.132 The LPS would apply to individuals 16 or over (the current DOLS provisions only apply to those 18 or over). Authorisations would provide approval relating to residence (potentially more than one to cover for example respite or planned hospital admissions), care arrangements and transport between venues, but would not apply to admissions for assessment or treatment of mental disorder. For an LPS authorisation to be granted the arrangements must not conflict with the decision of the donee of an LPA or of a court appointed deputy. Before an LPS authorisation could be granted consultation with relevant people must have been carried out (the proposals are similar to the provisions of MCA 2005 s4(7), with the additional obligation to consult whose with parental responsibility for 16- to 17-year-olds, and where appropriate local authorities looking after them).

13.133 In all cases the responsible body would have to arrange for three assessments to be carried out: an assessment to confirm that P lacks capacity to consent to the care or treatment arrangements which would give rise to a deprivation liberty; a medical assessment, and replacing the 'best interests' assessment in the DOLS scheme, an assessment that the arrangements are 'necessary and proportionate' having regard to either the likelihood of harm to P if the arrangements were not in place and the seriousness of that harm, or the likelihood of harm to other individuals if the arrangements were not in place and the seriousness of that harm. In general if the three assessments confirm these requirements the responsible body would put in place an internal 'on the papers' review by someone with 'operational independence' and subject thereto, authorise the deprivation of liberty. However if P is opposed to the proposed arrangements or where the proposed arrangements, are mainly for the protection of others, the independent reviewer would be under a duty to refer the case to an Approved Mental Capacity Professional whose role would be to check by that the conditions are met.

13.134 It is unclear when parliamentary time may be made available, although the fact the proposals are predicted to save costs may incentivise early legislation. Once enacted the new legislation will require substantial tranches of regulations to be passed and the Commission proposes that a new MCA

Code of Practice is produced. It therefore seems unlikely that the current DOLS system will be replaced before 2019.

Court of Protection

13.135 The Court of Protection derives its power from MCA 2005 Part 2 and is based at the Royal Courts of Justice in London, but also operates at regional courts in England and Wales. Decisions of the Court of Protection may be made by district, circuit or High Court judges depending upon the complexity and stage of the case. The court has jurisdiction to decide issues relating to whether an individual does or does not have capacity to take a particular decision, and if capacity is lacking, to make decisions in that person's best interests (including in relation to the exercise of the functions of deputies and attorneys appointed under LPA and (pre-MCA 2005) enduring powers of attorney). If a person is found to have capacity to make a specific decision, the Court of Protection has no jurisdiction to make an order on their behalf.[123] The great majority of the court's work is concerned with property and affairs issues, but it also deals with personal welfare issues to the extent that these are 'complex and serious issues'.[124] Subject to the presumption of capacity being rebutted, the Court of Protection may make a range of declarations and orders under MCA 2005 ss15 and 16 regulating all aspects of P's finances, and most aspects of health and welfare including where P lives, what care is in P's best interests, with whom P should have contact, what medical treatment should be administered, and by whom. As noted above, MCA 2005 s27 prohibits the court from making certain decisions relating to family relationships.

13.136 Where the Court of Protection is deciding issues relating to P's health and welfare, it had been invariable practice that P was made party to the proceedings, and thus required a litigation friend. Following the judgment in *Re NRA*[125] (see para 13.103 above) and the amendments to the Court of Protection Rules, it is now clear that in uncontested reviews of P's deprivation of liberty in a community setting this is no longer necessary.

13.137 It is likely to remain the case that in disputed health and welfare cases before the Court of Protection P will be made a party, and will act through a litigation friend. A range of people – including carers, family and friends, or advocates – may act as litigation friend,[126] providing that they do not have a conflict of interest with P. As a last resort, the Official Solicitor[127]

---

123 However, where a person with capacity is unable to exercise it for reasons associated with their status as a 'vulnerable adult' the High Court's inherent jurisdiction may be invoked (see para 18.89 below).

124 See *G v E and others* [2010] EWHC 2042 COP (COP).

125 [2015] EWCOP 59, (2015) 18 CCLR 392 (see para 13.103 above).

126 For comprehensive guidance designed for non-professional litigation friends, see A Ruck Keene *Acting as a litigation friend in the Court of Protection: guidance note*, University of Manchester, 2014.

127 The Official Solicitor (OS) is a public officer who represents the interests of persons under a disability of age or mental capacity in legal proceedings. In practice caseworkers at the OS's office instruct private solicitors experienced in Court of Protection work to represent P.

will act as litigation friend, but only if funding for his legal costs is secured (whether privately or through the legal aid system).

Legal aid in the Court of Protection

13.138 Public funding from the Legal Aid Agency is available for representation in Court of Protection proceedings subject to meeting merits and financial eligibility tests, however a MCA 2005 s21A application brought by P or P's RPR is not subject to any financial assessment. It has been held[128] that the scope of section 21A (and thus the availability of non-means tested public funding for P) is wider than the issue of physical liberty, extending to the conditions of that detention, and so to issues of care and treatment, extending even to a decision about withdrawal of artificial nutrition and hydration. It may be regarded as anomalous that there should be non-means-tested legal aid for those challenging a deprivation of liberty under MCA 2005 Sch 1A by making an application under MCA 2005 s21A, but that those objecting to their deprivation of liberty in a community setting must apply for means-tested legal aid for which they are frequently ineligible given the low capital limits.

Office of the Public Guardian

13.139 The function of the Office of the Public Guardian (OPG), an executive agency of the Ministry of Justice, is to supervise deputies appointed by the court and to oversee and record LPAs. The OPG may refer cases to the Court of Protection so that it may exercise its jurisdiction in relation to deputyships and powers of attorney.

Lasting powers of attorney

13.140 MCA 2005 ss9–14 deal with LPAs. Guidance is given at chapter 7 of the code of practice. A LPA involves a person with capacity to do so (the donor) giving authority to one or more people (an attorney) to take decisions on his or her behalf, including an authority to do so after the donor has lost the relevant capacity. The donor may specify which particular decisions he or she wishes the attorney to take decisions about. To be valid, a LPA must comply with formalities set out in the MCA 2005. In carrying out their functions, an attorney must act within the parameters of the LPA and in accordance with the section 1 principles, which include acting in the donor's best interests. Under MCA 2005 ss22–23 the Court of Protection has power[129] to determine any issues relating to the validity or operation of LPAs.

---

128 *Briggs v Briggs* [2016] EWCOP 48.
129 The court may, where appropriate, revoke a LPA where the donee is acting in a way which contravenes P's authority or is not in P's best interests, as happened for example in *Re DP sub nom Public Guardian v JM* (2014).

13.141   LPAs come in two forms:

1) Property and affairs – this type of LPA cannot be used until it has been registered with the OPG.
2) Personal welfare – which allows a donor to nominate others to make decisions about his or her medical treatment and care once the donor has lost capacity to make those decisions himself or herself. However, attorneys cannot consent to or refuse treatment for a mental disorder for a person detained under the MHA 1983, and any power to consent to or refuse life-sustaining treatment must be expressly authorised in an LPA.

13.142   The OPG has an online system to assist in the writing and registration of LPAs.[130]

13.143   A health and welfare attorney will in most cases be a person 'interested in the adult's welfare' for the purposes of CA 2014 ss9(5)(c) and 25(3)(c) and therefore a local authority assessing needs, or preparing a care and support plan under the CA 2014 will be under a duty to involve the attorney.

13.144   The courts have held that a person may have the mental capacity to appoint someone to be his or her financial attorney – even though the person lacks the necessary mental capacity to manage his or her affairs, as there is no logical reason why a person who understands that something needs to be done, but who lacks the requisite understanding to do it personally, should not confer on another the power to do what needs to be done.[131] Accordingly, a person with (for example) learning disabilities or dementia may have insufficient mental capacity to manage his or her financial affairs, but have sufficient capacity to delegate this function to an attorney. In *Re K (enduring powers of attorney)*[132] the judge considered that although a person appointing a property and affairs attorney had to understand 'the nature and effect of the power' this did not mean that they had to be 'able to pass an examination on the provisions of the Act'. Essentially, the understanding (in most cases) will be that:

1) the attorney will be able to assume complete authority over the donor's affairs;
2) the attorney will in general be able to do anything with the donor's property which the donor could have done;
3) the authority will continue so long as the donor is mentally incapable;
4) the power will be irrevocable without confirmation by the court.

Advance decisions

13.145   MCA 2005 ss24–26 give statutory effect to advance decisions – ie decisions made by an adult with capacity to refuse specified treatments in the event that the adult loses capacity to make decisions about treatment.

---

130 See www.gov.uk/government/publications/make-a-lasting-power-of-attorney.
131 *Re K (Enduring Powers of Attorney)* [1988] Ch 310.
132 *Re K (Enduring Powers of Attorney)* [1988] Ch 310.

13.146 Such advance decisions need not be in writing, unless they include a decision to refuse 'life-sustaining' treatment, in which case there must be a document containing a clear statement that the decision is intended to apply even if the treatment in question is necessary to sustain life, and the document must be signed[133] and witnessed. What is 'life-sustaining' treatment will vary according to the circumstances – for example, antibiotics may be life-sustaining to treat very severe infections, but may not be in other contexts. According to the code, an advance decision cannot refuse 'basic or essential care', which is necessary to keep a person comfortable (para 9.28). This includes 'the offer of food and water by mouth', but an advance decision can refuse artificial nutrition and hydration. No matter how serious the consequences, a valid and applicable advance decision is to be respected as if it was the decision of a person with capacity. Advance decisions, unless subsequently withdrawn or overridden by a power of attorney, are therefore binding on healthcare professionals, who may commit an assault if they treat in contravention of the advance decision.[134]

13.147 It is good practice to set out all advance decisions in writing. Chapter 9 of the code gives practical guidance.

13.148 An advance decision may be withdrawn at any time if the person concerned has capacity to do so, and is treated as superseded by a subsequent LPA which gives authority to make decisions about the same treatment to which the advance decision relates. Other limited circumstances in which an advance decision will not be treated as valid are set out in MCA 2005 s25, including that 'there are reasonable grounds for believing that circumstances exist which P did not anticipate at the time of the advance decision and which would have affected his position had he anticipated them' (MCA 2005 s25(4)(c)), and that an advance decision is not valid if P 'has done anything ... clearly inconsistent with the advance decision remaining his fixed decision' (section 25(2)(c)). The precise scope of this provision is unclear. It may include a sustained expression of wishes contrary to those set out in the advance decision, even at a time when P has lost the relevant capacity,[135] although it was commented in *Briggs v The Walton Centre NHS Foundation Trust*[136] that an interpretation of section 25(2)(c) that 'sets a low threshold to rendering an advance decision invalid or inapplicable would run counter to the enabling intention' of the statutory provisions relating to powers of attorney and advance decisions (see para 13.140 above).

133 The code, para 9.24 sets out the formalities for an advance decision to refuse life-sustaining treatment, and provides for circumstances in which the person making the advance decision is unable to write. The difficulties which may arise if formalities are not strictly adhered to is illustrated by *X (PCT) v XB and YB* [2012] EWHC 1390 (Fam).

134 In *Nottinghamshire Healthcare NHS Trust v RC* [2014] EWCOP 1317 the judge found that P (a Jehovah's Witness who was self-harming) had capacity to refuse blood transfusions, but also that P had made a valid advance decision to refuse blood transfusions which would bind clinicians in the event that P were to lack capacity, and therefore that to impose a blood transfusion would be a 'denial of a most basic freedom'.

135 See *Re QQ* [2016] EWCOP 22.

136 [2016] EWCOP 53 para 22.

13.149   Advance decisions to refuse certain treatments should be distinguished from advance requests for particular treatment (or advance requests relating to any other personal welfare issues, for example contact or residence arrangements) which are not binding, but must be considered in coming to a view about P's best interests under MCA 2005 s4(6).[137]

Deputies

13.150   MCA 2005 ss19–20 empower the Court of Protection to appoint a deputy to take decisions on behalf of P in circumstances where P has not made an applicable LPA, and lacks capacity to make the decisions in question. As with LPAs, there are two types of deputyship:

1) **Property and affairs** – which authorises a deputy to take decisions (as described in the order appointing the deputy) about P's finances. A property and affairs deputy will be necessary if P has assets or income beyond state benefits[138] and does not have an attorney, as otherwise no one will have authority to deal with P's finances. Consequently such applications are very common.

2) **Personal welfare** – which authorises a deputy to take decisions (as described in the order, appointing the deputy) about P's health and welfare. However, a personal welfare deputy never has power to prohibit a named person from having contact with P, or to direct who should give healthcare to P, or to refuse life-sustaining treatment: these issues will always need to be referred to the Court of Protection. Appointments of health and welfare deputies are uncommon[139] because MCA 2005 s16(4) states as a principle that 'a decision by the court is to be preferred to the appointment of a deputy to make a decision' and that if a deputy is appointed their powers should be 'as limited in scope and duration' as possible. The code sets out specific circumstances in which appointment of a health and welfare deputy may be appropriate (para 8.38).

13.151   A health and welfare deputy will usually be a person 'interested in the adult's welfare' for the purposes of CA 2014 ss9(5)(c) and 25(3)(c), and therefore a local authority assessing needs, or preparing a care and support plan under the CA 2014, will be under a duty to involve the deputy. The deputy may also be a person 'authorised under the MCA 2005 to make decisions about the adult's needs for care and support', and so under CA 2014 s32 be entitled both to request direct payments to meet P's assessed needs, and to receive the payments from the local authority.

---

137 For information and precedents concerning advance decisions, see, for example, Compassion in Dying at www.compassionindying.org.uk.

138 If P's only income is state benefits an individual may be appointed as 'appointee'.

139 In 2013 there were only 205 appointments of personal welfare deputies in contrast to 14,209 property and affairs deputyships.

Appointees

13.152 Social Security (Claims and Payments) Regulations 1987 SI No 1968 reg 33 permits the secretary of state (in practice the Department for Work and Pensions (DWP)) to make (and revoke) the appointment of an appointee where the person entitled to social security benefits is 'unable for the time being to act'. The appointee may be an individual or an organisation, such as a local authority. Guidance to DWP staff[140] issued in 2012 explains that the requirement is that the person must be 'incapable of managing their own affairs' and that this will usually arise because they are 'mentally incapable'. Grounds for revocation of an appointment are set out in the guidance, and include that the person concerned is capable of managing their benefits themselves. If the person entitled to benefits maintains that he or she is capable of managing his or her own benefits, DWP staff are advised to send a letter to the appointee asking if the appointee agrees, and advising that a visit will be made to the person entitled to discuss the issue.

13.153   Concerns have been expressed that the lack of an appeal process breaches the ECHR Article 6(1) (right to a fair trial) rights of the person concerned, a point which was tacitly acknowledged by the government which entered a reservation to the UN Convention on the Rights of Persons with Disabilities Article 12.4 (safeguards for substituted decision making) on the basis that the DWP was 'working to establish a proportionate system of review to address this issue'.

140 DWP, *Agents, appointees, attorneys and deputies guide*, 2012.

Housing and social care

continued

Introduction

14.1 Appropriate housing has been described as 'the basic requirement – the foundation – of community care'.[1] As the Audit Commission has noted,[2] 'appropriate housing' is not just a question of bricks and mortar:

> ... it is not simply the provision of a roof over people's heads that makes housing's contribution so important, it is the personal support to help vulnerable people cope with everyday living – for example, negotiating the complexities of rent payments or resolving problems with water, gas and electricity suppliers – that makes the difference between life in the community and institutionalisation.[3]

14.2 This chapter is concerned with the general obligations on housing authorities in relation to matters that impinge upon social care support services – including those that may arise in eviction proceedings; in relation to the provision of disabled facilities grants (DFGs); and accommodation for homeless people who have community care needs. It additionally considers discrete questions of services provided under the 'supporting living' and the 'shared lives' regimes which are aimed at helping people have more choice in their accommodation arrangements. It does not, however, attempt to set out all the duties owed to adults in need and carers under the Housing Act (HA) 1996 and related legislation. Not only would this be impossible given the limited space, but also a number of other excellent handbooks can provide this information.[4]

Responsibilities of housing authorities

14.3 Housing authorities, in meeting their responsibilities under Housing Act (HA) 1985 s8 (to consider housing conditions and provision in their area), are required, by Chronically Sick and Disabled Persons Act (CSDPA) 1970 s3, to have specific regard to the special needs of chronically sick and disabled persons. In this respect, 2006 good practice guidance[5] issued to housing authorities stresses the importance of aspiring 'for the social inclusion of all their citizens' and the general need 'to design in access and accept a corporate responsibility for countering disabling environments'.

---

1 P Arnold and others, *Community care: the housing dimension*, Joseph Rowntree Foundation, 1993; see also P Arnold and D Page, *Housing and community care*, University of Humberside, 1992.

2 Audit Commission, *Home alone: the housing aspects of community care*, 1998, para 7.

3 A survey of directors of adult services revealed that over half of those responding had taken on responsibility for housing services, and suggests that the importance of housing in the well-being of a community is now being recognised more clearly (*Community care*, 4 April 2007).

4 See, for example, D Astin, *Housing law handbook*, 3rd edn, Legal Action Group, 2015; and A Arden QC, E Orme and T Vanhegan, *Homelessness and allocations*, 10th edn, Legal Action Group, 2017.

5 *Delivering housing adaptations for disabled people: a good practice guide*, June 2006, issued by the Department for Communities and Local Government (DCLG) in conjunction with the Department for Education and Skills and the Department of Health.

The promotion of independent living is clearly as much a goal for housing authorities as it is for social services authorities.

14.4   Housing authorities must, in the framing of their allocation schemes (which determine who is to have priority for housing) give reasonable preference to people who need to move on medical or welfare grounds, including grounds relating to a disability.[6] In *R (Ireneschild) v Lambeth LBC*[7] the High Court considered the relationship between a housing needs assessment undertaken by the housing department (to ascertain the applicant's priority for rehousing) and a social care assessment (assessing the person's need for accommodation).[8] In the court's opinion, the two assessments had 'entirely different' focuses. The fact that the housing assessment indicated an urgent need for rehousing did not mean that social care accommodation had to be provided. However, the housing needs assessment was a material (and possibly a 'compelling') consideration to be taken into account in the social care assessment.

Eviction

14.5   The social care needs of disabled, elderly and ill people will not infrequently come to the notice of the courts by way of possession proceedings founded upon their failure to pay rent or their behaviour. In such cases, the courts have power to adjourn to enable an urgent assessment of needs to be carried out. Such an assessment will inevitably involve the social services department liaising with the housing authority under Care Act (CA) 2014 ss6 and 7 (see para 11.43 above).[9]

14.6   The courts have wide powers to adjourn possession proceedings in secure and assured tenancy cases;[10] however, in assured shorthold cases judges will generally need to rely on the power they have to adjourn under the Civil Procedure Rules (CPR) 3.1 and 3.2 in furtherance of the overriding objective in CPR 1.1 to enable the court to deal with the case 'justly'. In *Manchester City Council v Pinnock*[11] the Supreme court accepted that in all possession proceedings there was scope for the courts to consider the proportionality of such action, for the purposes of European Convention on Human Rights (ECHR) Article 8 (right to respect for one's private and family life, one's home and one's correspondence), and that (para 64):

> ... proportionality is more likely to be a relevant issue 'in respect of occupants who are vulnerable as a result of mental illness, physical or learning disability, poor health or frailty', and that 'the issue may also require the

---

6 HA 1996 s167(2)(d).

7 [2006] EWHC 2354 (Admin), (2006) 9 CCLR 686: this finding was approved by the Court of Appeal.

8 Under the under National Assistance Act (NAA) 1948 s21 – now CA 2014 s9.

9 The ombudsman has held it to be maladministration if a council's housing department receives a homelessness application from someone with clear social care needs but fails to make an immediate referral to their social services department – see complaint against Cardiff County Council Public Services Ombudsman for Wales, Case no 2009/00981, 15 March 2011.

10 HA 1985 s85 and HA 1988 s9.

11 [2010] UKSC 45, [2011] 1 All ER 285.

local authority to explain why they are not securing alternative accommodation in such cases'.

14.7 *Barber v Croydon LBC*[12] concerned a decision by the council to seek possession proceedings against a person with learning disabilities and a personality disorder who, in an isolated incident, swore, kicked and spat at a caretaker. The Court of Appeal held that this was a decision that no local authority could reasonably have taken, not least because it had failed to consult the specialist agencies, consider alternatives and pay proper regard to an expert report that the behaviour was a manifestation of the tenant's mental disorder. The local government ombudsman has come to similar conclusions in possession proceedings involving disabled people.[13]

14.8 A decision to commence possession proceedings will engage the public sector equality duty[14] ((see para 2.59 above) and any question as to the tenant's mental capacity to litigate must be resolved before the possession proceedings hearing takes place.[15]

14.9 Section 15 of the Equality Act (EqA) 2010 makes it discriminatory if the discriminator:

- treats the person unfavourably because of something arising 'in consequence of' his or her disability; and
- cannot show that the treatment is 'a proportionate means of achieving a legitimate aim'.

14.10 It follows that if action is being taken as a result of a tenant's actions (or inactions) and these can reasonably be said to arise in consequence of the tenant's disability (which is known to the person taking the action), then the onus will be on the landlord to show that the action is 'a proportionate means of achieving a legitimate aim'. In doing this it will generally be necessary to show that the person taking the action: (1) has adopted as flexible a policy as is reasonable in the situation; (2) has attempted to help the tenant modify his or her behaviour, or the consequences of that behaviour; and (3) that the action is the least discriminatory way of achieving the legitimate aim.

14.11 Where a person is evicted because of his or her disability related conduct, the social services authority will have a duty to that person under the social care legislation. However, in *R v Kensington and Chelsea RLBC ex p Kujtim*[16] the Court of Appeal held that the duty to provide accommodation[17] can be treated as discharged if the applicant 'either unreasonably refuses to accept the accommodation provided or if, following its provision, by his

---

12 [2010] EWCA Civ 51, [2010] HLR 26; see also *Carmarthenshire CC v Lewis* [2010] EWCA Civ 1567.

13 See eg complaint no 05/C/04684 against Kirklees MC, 28 February 2007 where a failure to make proper enquiries before taking legal action was held to constitute maladministration and Complaint no 03/A/14278 against Southend-on-Sea BC, 27 June 2005 where the authority instituted possession proceedings based on arrears that had arisen due to the authority's failure to take into account the claimant's mental illness when processing his housing benefit claims.

14 *Barnsley MBC v Norton* [2011] EWCA Civ 834.

15 *Carmarthenshire CC v Lewis* [2010] EWCA Civ 1567.

16 [1999] 4 All ER 161, (1999) 2 CCLR 340, CA at 354I.

17 Under the NAA 1948 s21 – now CA 2014 s18.

conduct he manifests a persistent and unequivocal refusal to observe the reasonable requirements of the local authority in relation to the occupation of such accommodation' (see para 3.55 above).

Housing and social services interface

14.12   CA 2014 s23(1) defines the boundary between social services responsibilities and those under the HA 1996[18] – it provides:

> (1) A local authority may not meet needs under sections 18 to 20 by doing anything which it or another local authority is required to do under–
> (a) the Housing Act 1996, or
> (b) any other enactment specified in regulations.

14.13   The extent to which section 23(1) limits the power of social services to provide 'bare accommodation' (for example a simple tenancy) is further considered at para 7.98 above.

Collaboration and joint working

14.14   Although the functions under the two Acts are distinct, suitable accommodation is a fundamental necessity for adults in need and carers, and suitable care and support will often be essential to ensuring the continued occupation of the accommodation. As the revised statutory guidance[19] to the CA 2014 makes clear:

> 15.51 ... Where housing forms part of the solution to meeting a person's needs for care and support, or preventing needs for care and support, then a local authority may include this in the care or support plan even though the housing element itself is provided under housing legislation. Any care or support needed to supplement housing is covered by this Act.
> ...
> 15.53 Housing plays a critical role in enabling people to live independently and in helping carers to support others more effectively. Poor or inappropriate housing can put the health and well-being of people at risk, where as a suitable home can reduce the needs for care and support and contribute to preventing or delaying the development of such needs. Housing services should be used to help promote an individual's well-being, in which people in need of care and support and carers can build a full and active life. Suitability of living accommodation is one of the matters local authorities must take into account as part of their duty to promote an individual's well-being.

14.15   Housing and social services authorities are under a variety of statutory duties to co-operate in the social care planning and assessment processes, however an explicit duty under the pre-CA 2014 regime[20] has not been replicated in the new regime. As noted above (para 11.46), this omission troubled the select committee that scrutinised the Care and Support Bill,

---

18   In similar terms to the limits of NHS responsibilities defined in section 22 – see para 12.12 above).

19   Department of Health, *Care and support statutory guidance* to support implementation of Part 1 of the CA 2014 by local authorities, 2016 ('the statutory guidance').

20   NHS and Community Care Act 1990 s47(3).

although it noted that the CA 2014 s6 and s7 duties on local authorities to co-operate had the potential to address this problem (see para 11.43 for a discussion about these duties).

14.16 The revised statutory guidance stresses that the duty of co-operation is not only inter-authority, it is also inter-departmental (para 15.3) and that:

> 15.23 ... Local authorities must make arrangements to ensure co-operation between its officers responsible for adult care and support, housing, public health and children's services, and should also consider how such arrangements may also be applied to other relevant local authority responsibilities, such as education, planning and transport ...

> 15.24 ... [I]t is important that local authority officers responsible for housing work in co-operation with adult care and support, given that housing and suitability of living accommodation play a significant role in supporting a person to meet their needs and can help to delay that person's deterioration ...

14.17 The guidance stresses the 'crucial'[21] importance of considering the suitability of accommodation during the care assessment and planning process of adults and carers (para 15.50).

14.18 A duty on housing authorities to co-operate with social services is also found in HA 1996 s213(1) which requires social services to co-operate to the extent that 'is reasonable in the circumstances' where its assistance is sought by a housing authority in relation to the discharge of its duties under the HA 1996.

14.19 The local government ombudsman has held it to be maladministration if a council's housing department receives a homelessness application from someone with clear social care needs (in this case a young woman with schizophrenia) but fails to make an immediate referral to their social services department.[22]

14.20 Homelessness Act 2002 s3 requires all housing authorities to have a homelessness strategy that seeks to prevent homelessness, to secure that sufficient accommodation is available for people in their district who are or may become homeless, and that there is satisfactory provision of support for people who are or are at risk of homelessness. The social services authority must assist with the development of these strategies, and the English 2006 *Homelessness code of guidance for local authorities*[23] (the 'homelessness guidance') stresses the need for housing authorities to:

> 8. ... ensure that all organisations, within all sectors, whose work can help to prevent homelessness and/or meet the needs of homeless people in their district are involved in the strategy. This will need to include not just housing providers (such as housing associations and private landlords) but also other statutory bodies such as social services, the probation service, the health service and the wide range of organisations in the private and voluntary sectors whose work helps prevent homelessness or meet the needs of people who have experienced homelessness.

---

21 At para 15.53 this is expressed as a 'critical role in enabling people to live independently and in helping carers to support others more effectively'.

22 Complaint against Cardiff County Council Public Services Ombudsman for Wales, Case no 2009/00981, 15 March 2011.

23 DCLG, *Homelessness code of guidance for local authorities*, July 2006.

9. Housing authorities will also need to give careful consideration to the scope for joint working between social services and the many other key players in the district who are working to meet the needs of people who are homeless or have experienced homelessness.

14.21   The homelessness guidance gives examples of the collaborative working envisaged, for instance (para 5.6):

- establishment of a multi-agency forum for key practitioners and providers to share knowledge, information, ideas and complementary practices;
- clear links between the homelessness strategy and other key strategies such as supporting people, and the National Health Service (NHS) local delivery plan;
- protocols for the referral of clients between services and sharing information between services – for example, a joint protocol between hospital-based social workers and housing officers to address the housing needs of patients to be discharged from hospital;
- joint consideration of the needs of homeless people by housing and social services authorities under Children Act 1989 Part 7 and community care legislation;
- establishment of formal links with other services – for example, with those provided by voluntary and community sector organisations.

14.22   The homelessness guidance specifically refers to local authorities' general powers of competence (now located in Localism Act 2011 s1[24] (see para 1.65 above)) suggesting that these provide substantial opportunity for 'cross-boundary partnership working with other authorities and partners, such as the health and social services sectors' (para 5.14). In relation to healthcare, this will be of particular relevance in the context of hospital discharge, for which specific guidance in England, has as its 'over arching aim' to 'ensure that no one is discharged from hospital to the streets or inappropriate accommodation'.[25]

Housing homeless persons overlap

14.23   The obligation to house homeless persons originated as National Assistance Act (NAA) 1948 s21(1)(b), being a power to provide temporary accommodation for persons who were homeless in circumstances that could not have been foreseen. The power was repealed by the Housing (Homeless Persons) Act 1977, although the NAA 1948 retained a relic duty to provide residential accommodation for persons 'in urgent need'.[26] The CA 2014 contains no such provision.

14.24   Disabled, elderly or ill people may, however, come within the scope of the homelessness provisions of HA 1996 Part VII since it provides that:

24   The homelessness guidance refers to Local Government Act 2000 s2 – this was repealed in England and replaced by the wider powers under the Localism Act 2011 in February 2012.

25   DCLG and Department of Health, *Hospital admission and discharge: people who are homeless or living in temporary or insecure accommodation*, 2006.

26   NAA 1948 s21(1)(a).

1) a person is homeless for the purposes of the HA 1996 if he or she has no accommodation which 'it would be reasonable for' him or her to occupy[27] (HA 1996 s175(3)); and

2) a person is considered in priority need if he or she 'is vulnerable as a result of old age, mental illness or handicap or physical disability or other special reason, or with whom such a person resides or might reasonably be expected to reside' (HA 1996 s189(1)(c)).[28]

14.25 Once a person is found to be homeless for the purposes of the HA 1996 (and to be in priority need and not intentionally homeless) the housing authority is under a duty to secure that suitable accommodation[29] is available for their occupation (section 193), and (by virtue of section 176) and 'any other person who normally resides with him as a member of his family, or any other person who might reasonably be expected to reside with him'.

14.26 *Boreh v Ealing LBC*[30] concerned a homeless (wheelchair using) applicant who was also entitled to the full housing duty under HA 1996. The council offered her accommodation, which although not suitable, could (the council asserted) be adapted. The court held that this might be an acceptable discharge of the duty, provided the necessary adaptations were clearly stated in the offer and subject to 'assurances that the applicant could fairly regard as certain, binding and enforceable' (para 27). The proposals did not, however, explain how the applicant could access the property, since the front door was inaccessible (although it might have been possible for her to access via a side alleyway and rear patio doors). In the court's view, access through a front door is generally an essential requirement for a property to be suitable – stating that 'a proper regard for Mrs Boreh's comings and goings in the ordinary course of her occupation of the house required that she should be able to access it via the front door' (para 37).

14.27 Homelessness Act 2002 s1(2) requires social services authorities to assist housing authorities in the formulation of their homelessness strategies. This obligation is explained in the 2006 homelessness guidance as follows:

> 1.6. In non-unitary districts, where the social services authority and the housing authority are different authorities, section 1(2) of the 2002 Act

---

27 HA 1996 s175(3); which section 176 qualifies by stipulating that accommodation shall be treated as available for a person's occupation only if it is available for occupation by him or her together with any other person who normally resides with him or her as a member of the family, or any other person who might reasonably be expected to reside with him or her – see eg *Sharif v Camden LBC* [2011] EWCA Civ 463.

28 As a cautionary note, see *Ortiz v City of Westminster* (1995) 27 HLR 364, CA.

29 A person may have to remain in less than perfect accommodation for a short period, but in the opinion of the House of Lords 'one cannot overlook the fact that Parliament has imposed on [councils] clear duties to the homeless, including those occupying unsuitable accommodation': see *Birmingham City Council v Ali* [2009] UKHL 36, [2009] 4 All ER 161, [2009] 1 WLR 1506.

30 [2008] EWCA Civ 1176. See also Public Services Ombudsman for Wales Complaint No 201001198 against Carmarthenshire CC, 22 December 2011 where a it was held to be maladministration to allocate a property to a disabled person that the local authority should have known was unsuitable and then to take no interim action to address the inadequacy pending rehousing.

requires the social services authority to give the housing authority such assistance as may be reasonably required in carrying out a homelessness review and formulating and publishing a homelessness strategy. **Since a number of people who are homeless or at risk of homelessness will require social services support, it is unlikely that it would be possible for a housing authority to formulate an effective homelessness strategy without assistance from the social services authority. It will be necessary therefore in all cases for housing authorities to seek assistance from the social services authority.**[31] In unitary authorities the authority will need to ensure that the social services department assists the housing department in carrying out a homelessness review and formulating and publishing a homelessness strategy.

14.28   The homelessness guidance advises that the critical test of vulnerability for applicant is (para 10.13):[32]

... whether, when homeless, the applicant would be less able to fend for him/herself than an ordinary homeless person so that he or she would suffer injury or detriment, in circumstances where a less vulnerable person would be able to cope without harmful effects.

14.29   The homelessness guidance then provides advice in relation to the specific classes of people deemed to be 'vulnerable'[33] and in so doing stresses the importance of 'close co-operation between housing authorities, social services authorities and mental health agencies' (including undertaking, where appropriate, joint assessments). The guidance highlights the need to consider information from all relevant sources, for example from medical professionals and current providers of care and support: of keeping 'an open mind' and avoiding 'blanket policies that assume that particular groups of applicants will, or will not, be vulnerable'.

14.30   When a person in priority need becomes homeless (including in circumstances where the homelessness duty arises because there is currently no accommodation available which it would be reasonable for him or her[34]) the local housing authority's duty to provide accommodation both pending enquiries[35] and following acceptance of what is often referred to as a full housing duty[36] is a duty to provide suitable accommodation.[37]

Disabled facilities grants

14.31   DFGs are grants paid towards the cost of building works which are necessary in order to meet the needs of a disabled occupant. The housing authority is responsible for the administration and payment of the grant,

---

31   Emphasis as in the original code.
32   See also *R v Camden LBC ex p Pereira* (1998) 31 HLR 317 and *Osmani v Camden LBC* [2004] EWCA Civ 1706, [2005] HLR 22.
33   English 2006 homelessness code, paras 10.15–10.32.
34   Together with others who normally reside (or might reasonably be expected to reside) with them – see para 14.24 above.
35   Housing Act 1996 s188.
36   Housing Act 1996 s193.
37   Housing Act 1996 s206; see also the Homelessness (Suitability of Accommodation) Orders 2003 SI No 3326; and 2012 SI No 2601; and the homelessness guidance, in particular at para 17.5.

although the original application may be instigated (and referred to it) by a social services authority as part of the social care needs assessment process. Grants are subject to a means test for disabled adults (see para 14.104 below).

14.32 Since their inception, core funding for DFGs has come from the central government, although local authorities have made additional contributions. Both funding streams were significantly reduced after 2010,[38] but since 2015 this trend has been reversed. Funding now derives from the better care fund[39] (see para 11.134 above) and it appears that DFG allocations to this fund increased by almost 80 per cent in 2016/17 (to £394m) and it the intention is that the funding will, by 2019/20, amount to £500m.[40]

14.33 In England, about 40,500 DFG awards were made in 2014/15[41] and during this period the average grant was slightly in excess of £7,000 with almost 60 per cent being under £5,000 (and only five per cent were above the maximum of £30,000).[42]

14.34 Guidance in 2006 recognised that the obligation to facilitate adaptations for disabled people extended beyond the mere detail of the specific statutory regime, since the underlying purpose was 'to modify disabling environments in order to restore or enable independent living, privacy, confidence and dignity for individuals and their families'.[43] While the precise extent of the 'right to independent living' is uncertain (see para 2.40 above), it is undoubtedly the case that a gross failure by a public authority to discharge its responsibilities in this respect will engage ECHR Article 8.

14.35 *R (Bernard) v Enfield LBC*[44] concerned a disabled applicant and her family, who through the local authority's failure to assess her social care needs properly, and then to provide the necessary adaptations, was forced to live in 'deplorable conditions' for over 20 months. The court considered that the council's failure to act on its assessments had the effect of condemning the applicant and her family to live in conditions which made it virtually impossible for them to have any meaningful private or family life and accordingly found a violation of ECHR Article 8.

14.36 The local government ombudsman has taken a similar line with delayed DFGs, concluding a 2008 report with the following finding:

> I have considered whether her rights under Article 8 ... were engaged and I conclude they were, given the common goal was for Joanna to live at home,

---

38 L Cheshire, *The long wait for a home*, 2015; and S Mackintosh and P Leather, *The disabled facilities grant*, Foundations, 2016, p6.

39 See Department of Health, *Better Care Fund: how it will work in 2015 to 2016. Policy Framework*, 2014, para 3.5; and, generally, Care & Repair England, *Disabled facilities grant funding via Better Care Funds – an opportunity to improve outcomes*, 2015.

40 S Mackintosh and P Leather, *The disabled facilities grant*, Foundations, 2016, para 3.14; and HM Treasury, *Spending review and autumn statement 2015* Cmd 9162, 2015, para 1.109.

41 S Mackintosh and P Leather, *The disabled facilities grant*, Foundations, 2016, para 5.2.

42 S Mackintosh and P Leather, *The disabled facilities grant*, Foundations, 2016, para 6.14 and p6

43 *Delivering housing adaptations for disabled people: a good practice guide*, June 2006, jointly issued by the DCLG, Department for Education and Skills and the Department of Health, at para 1.6.

44 [2002] EWHC 2282 (Admin), (2002) 5 CCLR 577.

and enjoy the benefits of family life. The greater a person's disability, the greater is the need to give proper and timely consideration to that person's basic rights and, what concerns me most, the values and principles underlying those rights – such as dignity, equality, fairness and respect.

If the Council had properly considered Joanna's case, with her human rights clearly in mind, she would not have been denied the full enjoyment of her home and family life in the way described in this report. A proper consideration of human rights issues and values would have led to an improvement in Joanna's and her mother's lives.[45]

14.37   The failure of local authorities comply with their statutory duties in relation to the processing and award of DFGs are well documented. A 2015 research report[46] found that a third had failed to approve DFGs within the statutory period (six months) and that about 4,000 people every year wait longer than they should for a decision – including about 2,500 who wait over a year for funding – and that almost half of councils had examples people waiting more than two years for payment.

14.38   Evidence of systemic failing in the processing and award of DFGs and the related works, can be found from the disproportionate number of local government ombudsman reports published concerning this subject. Reports that have not pulled punches – for example, describing council behaviour as 'appalling'; 'impenetrable, insensitive and disrespectful';[47] constituting 'institutionalised indifference'; 'breathtaking insensitivity';[48] and which 'beggars belief'.[49] Reports which frequently conclude with recommendations that thousands of pounds be paid in compensation as well as, for example, the commissioning of a report as to 'capacity of senior managers in the relevant services to provide leadership' and to respond to 'front line concerns about service failures and pressures'.[50]

14.39   The local government ombudsman has additionally stressed the importance of councils ensuring that their local policies concerning the award of DFGs have been subjected to a full impact review under (what is now) EqA 2010 s149 (see para 2.59 above).[51]

Statutory regime and guidance

Statutory regime

14.40   The relevant statutory provision regulating the availability of DFGs is Housing Grants, Construction and Regeneration Act (HGCRA) 1996 Part I, section 23 of which provides:

Disabled facilities grants: purposes for which grant must or may be given.
23(1)   The purposes for which an application for a grant must be approved, subject to the provisions of this Chapter, are the following–

---

45   Complaint no 07/A/11108 against Surrey CC, 11 November 2008, paras 48–49.
46   L Cheshire, *The long wait for a home*, 2015.
47   Complaint no 07 C 05809 against Kirklees, 26 June 2008 paras 47 and 50.
48   Complaint no 07C03887 against Bury MBC, 14 October 2009 paras 40 and 43.
49   Complaint no 07/B/07665 against Luton BC, 10 September 2008 para 37.
50   Complaint no 07C03887 against Bury MBC, 14 October 2009 paras 49.
51   Confidential Report of which a résumé appears in the Digest of Cases 2008/09 Section F, Housing, at p2.

(a) facilitating access by the disabled occupant to and from–
  (i) the dwelling, qualifying houseboat or caravan, or
  (ii) the building in which the dwelling or, as the case may be, flat is situated;
(b) making–
  (i) the dwelling, qualifying houseboat or caravan, or
  (ii) the building,
  safe for the disabled occupant and other persons residing with him;
(c) facilitating access by the disabled occupant to a room used or usable as the principal family room;
(d) facilitating access by the disabled occupant to, or providing for the disabled occupant, a room used or usable for sleeping;
(e) facilitating access by the disabled occupant to, or providing for the disabled occupant, a room in which there is a lavatory, or facilitating the use by the disabled occupant of such a facility;
(f) facilitating access by the disabled occupant to, or providing for the disabled occupant, a room in which there is a bath or shower (or both), or facilitating the use by the disabled occupant of such a facility;
(g) facilitating access by the disabled occupant to, or providing for the disabled occupant, a room in which there is a washhand basin, or facilitating the use by the disabled occupant of such a facility;
(h) facilitating the preparation and cooking of food by the disabled occupant;
(i) improving any heating system in the dwelling, qualifying houseboat or caravan to meet the needs of the disabled occupant or, if there is no existing heating system there or any such system is unsuitable for use by the disabled occupant, providing a heating system suitable to meet his needs;
(j) facilitating the use by the disabled occupant of a source of power, light or heat by altering the position of one or more means of access to or control of that source or by providing additional means of control;
(k) facilitating access and movement by the disabled occupant around the dwelling, qualifying houseboat or caravan in order to enable him to care for a person who is normally resident there and is in need of such care;
(l) such other purposes as may be specified by order of the secretary of state.
  ...
(3) If in the opinion of the local housing authority the relevant works are more or less extensive than is necessary to achieve any of the purposes set out in subsection (1), they may, with the consent of the applicant, treat the application as varied so that the relevant works are limited to or, as the case may be, include such works as seem to the authority to be necessary for that purpose.

14.41 The provisions of the HGCRA 1996 are fleshed out by regulations, principally the Housing Renewal Grants Regulations 1996[52] and separate regulations dealing with such matters as the maximum amount of the grant,[53] the prescribed forms to be used for the application process.

---

52 These are updated regularly – see eg the Housing Renewal Grants (Amendment) (England) Regulations 2014 SI No 1829.
53 See eg the Disabled Facilities Grants (Maximum Amounts and Additional Purposes) (England) Order 2008 SI No 1189.

14.42   The secretary of state's powers under HGCRA 1996 s23(1)(l) to extend the purposes for which an application for a grant must be approved, have been exercised to include:

1) facilitating access to and from a garden[54] by a disabled occupant; or
2) making access to a garden safe for a disabled occupant.[55]

14.43   DFGs are only available where a disabled person has been assessed as needing the relevant adaptations. It follows that there is a clear overlap with the responsibilities owed by social services authorities to disabled people who are assessed as needing assistance with adaptations under the CA 2014 (see para 7.51 above). Since the duty under the CA 2014 only arises where the authority is satisfied that the adult has an eligible need for such support it has been argued that this duty does not in general arise (if at all) until after a DRG application has been determined.[56]

Guidance

14.44   In 2013 good practice guidance in relation to the award of DFGs was published by the Home Adaptations Consortium (HAC): *Home adaptations for disabled people: a detailed guide to related legislation, guidance and good practice.*[57] The consortium's membership comprises a broad spectrum of national non-governmental organisations – albeit that the guidance states that it is 'supported by' the Department of Health and the Department for Communities and Local Government (DCLG):[58] This guidance supersedes[59] 2006 DCLG departmental guidance.[60] In the following section these are referred to as the '2013 HAC guidance' and the '2006 DCLG guidance' respectively.

14.45   Valuable as the guidance is, there is a need for authoritative and up-to-date departmental guidance. The 2013 HAC guidance refers to the pre-CA 2014 law but lacks the 'timescale' detail in the 2006 DCLG guidance – which itself failed to deliver on commitments made by the government. Given the increase in central government funding for DFGs, the research evidence on their cost effectiveness,[61] their importance in relation to facilitating hospital discharges and the abundant evidence that the system is

---

54 Disabled Facilities Grants (Maximum Amounts and Additional Purposes) (England) Order 2008 SI No 1189, Article 3.

55 Disabled Facilities Grants (Maximum Amounts and Additional Purposes) (England) Order 2008 SI No 1189, Article 3.

56 See *R (Fay) v Essex CC* [2004] EWHC 879 (Admin) at [28].

57 Published by Care & Repair England, 2013.

58 2013 HAC guidance, para 1.15.

59 The 2006 DCLG guidance is shown as 'withdrawn on 5 February 2015' on the Government website although it is cited in the 2013 HAC guidance, has been much cited by the local government ombudsman and would appear to be of continuing relevance (see para 1.56 above).

60 DCLG, *Delivering housing adaptations for disabled people: a good practice guide*, June 2006. Paragraph 1.14 explains that it replaces the previous guidance contained in annex I of Department of Environment circular 17/96 annex I and states that it should be read in conjunction with Office of Deputy Prime Minister circular 05/2003 (and, in particular, chapter 4 of that Circular) which is primarily concerned with the impact of the RRO – see para 14.92 below.

61 See Leeds University, *The cost effectiveness of disabled facilities adaptations*, Cerebra, 2017.

not working properly, it is troubling that departmental guidance of this nature has not been issued.

Eligibility

Disability

14.46 The grant is only payable in respect of disabled occupants. The definition of a 'disabled person' for this purpose is provided in HGCRA 1996 s100(1) – namely a person:

a) whose sight, hearing or speech is substantially impaired; or
b) who has a mental disorder or impairment of any kind; or
c) who is physically substantially disabled by illness, injury, impairment present since birth, or otherwise.

In addition, HGCRA 1996 s100(2) also includes adults whose names are on the social services authority's CA 2014 sight impaired register[62] or their discretionary register under CA 2014 s77(3) (see para 15.169).

Main residence

14.47 HGCRA 1996 ss21(2)(b) and 22(2)(b) provide that DFGs are only available to disabled people who live (or intend to live) in the accommodation as their only or main residence.

14.48 A DFG is available regardless of tenure: they are 'tenure neutral'[63] – ie for owner-occupiers, tenants and licensees.[64]

Tenants

14.49 All disabled owner-occupiers, tenants (council, housing association[65] and private[66]) and licensees[67] are eligible to apply for disabled facilities grants as are landlords on behalf of disabled tenants. The 2013 HAC guidance advises (para 5.21):

> Access to adaptations should not depend upon tenure. A local authority may decide that it will fund adaptations in its own properties by an alternative route to DFGs. Likewise some housing associations provide funding and carry out adaptations to assist their tenants. However, this should not result in a worse service to their social tenants than that received by applicants who live in other tenures, or vice versa. This applies to the level of

---

62 CA 2014 s77(1) and (3).
63 W Wilson, *Disabled facilities grants (England)* SN/SP/3011, House of Commons Library, 2013, p3.
64 See HGCRA 1996 s19(5) re licensees.
65 A failure by a council to appreciate that housing association tenants are able to apply for a DFG, will constitute maladministration – see complaint no 09 001 059 against Lewes DC, 6 April 2010.
66 It appears that only about seven per cent of grants go to tenants in the private rented sector – see S Mackintosh and P Leather, *The disabled facilities grant*, Foundations, 2016, p5.
67 HGCRA 1996 s19(5) extends eligibility for a DFG to a range of licensees, eg secure or introductory tenants who are licensees, agricultural workers, and service employees such as publicans.

support received, the type of adaptation provided and the time taken to provide a service.

Accordingly any material difference in treatment of council and non-council tenants may constitute maladministration.[68]

14.50   In certain cases councils may have an agreement with a housing provider that it will be responsible for facilitating the necessary adaptations (eg where former council housing stock has been passed to a registered social landlord). However, this agreement cannot 'trump' the statutory duty:[69] a point made clear in the 2013 HAC guidance (para 5.22):

> It is for the local authority to decide whether they will apply a test of resources to those whose adaptations are funded by means other than DFG. In achieving equity it may be regarded as good practice that all recipients of assistance from public funds should be assessed in a comparable fashion. This however does not alter the mandatory entitlement of tenants of social landlords to a DFG in the same way that private landlord might apply for an adaptation from the main DFG programme for their tenant ...

14.51   The local government ombudsman has found maladministration in such a case,[70] where a disabled person was advised by his landlord (with whom the council had an adaptations protocol) that the necessary adaptations would be delayed by at least two years. Instead of the council intervening and securing the necessary works, it failed to take any action, seeking to rely rigidly on the protocol.

14.52   The local government ombudsman has highlighted a problem with the DFG scheme in that it only applies to existing tenancies (HGCRA 1996 s24(2)).[71] Accordingly, where it is proposed that a disabled person move to a new tenancy and that tenancy be adapted prior to the move, in order to obtain the grant it will be necessary to take on the new tenancy. During this period the applicant will bear the cost of two tenancies. It follows that there is a need for such works to be done as quickly as possible and without any unnecessary delays.[72]

14.53   Where the tenant is the applicant for the DFG, the consent of the landlord of the property will be required. The 2013 HAC guidance advises that the authority should make every effort to secure this approval 'and in appropriate circumstances authorities should be prepared to assure the landlord that if requested they will "make good" when a tenant no longer requires the adaptation' (para 7.66), and at para 7.67 it states:

> Experience in recent years has shown that some housing associations and local authority landlords are withholding their approval on the basis that the dwelling is "inappropriate" for adaptation, even when there is no physical reason why the property cannot be adapted. Tenants have been asked to move to alternative property where the DFG applicant is judged by the landlord to be under-occupying the dwelling or where the landlord has decided

---

68   See the report and further report on complaint no 99/B/00012 against North Warwickshire DC, 15 May 2000 and 30 November 2000 respectively.

69   2006 DCLG guidance para 29.

70   Complaint no 10 008 979 against Liverpool City Council, 4 April 2011.

71   In *R v Bradford MDC ex p Pickering* (2001) 33 HLR 38, Munby J held that a purchaser under an (uncompleted) rental purchase agreement had a sufficient 'owner's interest' for the purposes the grant.

72   Complaint no 00/C/19154 against Birmingham, 19 March 2002.

they do not allow adaptations in certain types of property, i.e. level access showers in accommodation above ground floor level. In such circumstances landlords should be reminded that they *'may not unreasonably withhold their consent'* to the adaptation being undertaken.

14.54 EqA 2010 Part 4 places significant obligations on landlords in such situations – not least the section 36 duty to make reasonable adjustments (including to 'common parts') – which is fleshed out in EqA 2010 Sch 4.

Caravans, mobile homes and houseboats

14.55 The DFG scheme was extended in 2003[73] to persons living in mobile homes and houseboats. However, only mobile home owners living in a 'qualifying park home' were covered, ie people on a protected site within the meaning of the Mobile Homes Act 1983. As a result of representations made concerning the discriminatory effect of this measure (Gypsies living on local authority sites did not come within the scope of the provision) the scheme has been amended cover such situations.[74]

14.56 HGCRA 1996 s19(1)(c) now provides that DFGs are available where 'the applicant is an occupier (alone or jointly with others) of a qualifying houseboat or a caravan and, in the case of a caravan, that at the time the application was made the caravan was stationed on land within the authority's area.

Five years' occupancy requirement

14.57 Grants are payable subject to a requirement that the disabled person lives (or intends to live) in the accommodation as their only or main residence throughout the grant condition period 'or for such shorter period as his health and other relevant circumstances permit'.[75] HGCRA 1996 s44(3)(a) provides that 'the "grant condition period" means the period of five years, or such other period as the secretary of state may by order specify or as may be imposed by the local housing authority with the consent of the secretary of state, beginning with the certified date' and section 44(3)(b) states that 'the "certified date" means the date certified by the local housing authority as the date on which the execution of the eligible works is completed to its satisfaction'.

14.58 In relation to this question, the 2013 HAC guidance advises as follows (para 7.70):

> Where it appears to the person carrying out the assessment, or the person evaluating the application for grant, that the applicant may not continue to occupy the adapted property for a period of five years or more they should consider the circumstances. If the reason for suspecting this is a prognosis of a deteriorating condition or possible imminent death of the applicant, this should not be a reason for withholding or delaying grant approval. This is the case whether or not the prognosis is known to the disabled. The critical issue in this case is the intention.

---

73 By virtue of an amendment to HCGRA 1996 s23 via RRO art 2.
74 HA 2004 s224 substituted references to 'park homes' in the 1996 Act with the term 'caravans' and likewise the references to 'pitch' with references to 'land'.
75 HCGRA 1996 ss21(2)(b), 22A(2)(b) and 22(2)(b).

14.59   In this context, 2013 HAC guidance at para 7.34 is also of relevance:

> Services should seek sensitively to provide for the progress of the illness which may be difficult to predict. A relatively limited period in which a particular adaptation is appropriate should not be regarded as a sufficient reason for delaying or withholding its provision.

14.60   However, para 35 of annex C to the 2013 HAC guidance qualifies this advice, stating that 'where an applicant's prognosis implies that degeneration in the short term will occur, then this should be taken into account when considering the eligible works'.

Maximum grant

14.61   The maximum mandatory grant is currently £30,000 in England,[76] although authorities are empowered to make higher awards. Special rules apply for minor adaptations under £1,000 (see para 14.63 below). In England the government in 2007 undertook to keep the maximum grant figure under review 'with the aim of increasing it to £50,000 in stages'.[77]

14.62   Where an adaptation is assessed as costing more than the grant maximum, various options exist to cover the excess, including the housing authority providing additional sums by exercising its discretionary powers (see para 14.92 below) and/or the social services authority paying for the excess. A council's failure to inform an applicant that costs exceeding the maximum amount are discretionary (although see para 7.56 above) may constitute maladministration, as will be a fixed policy of not funding above the maximum sum.[78]

Adaptations under £1,000

14.63   Community equipment costing less than £1,000, aids and minor adaptations are required to be provided by social services authorities without charge.[79] This support is considered further at para 7.75 above.

Role of the housing authority

Administration of the grant

14.64   The housing authority is responsible for the administration of the DFG, through all stages from initial enquiry (or referral by the social services authority) to post-completion approval. This requirement stems from HGCRA 1996 s24(3):

> (3) A local housing authority shall not approve an application for a grant unless they are satisfied—

---

76 Disabled Facilities Grants (Maximum Amounts and Additional Purposes) (England) Order 2008 SI No 1189 order 2.

77 DCLG, *Disabled facilities grant programme: the government's proposals to improve programme delivery*, 2007, para 31a.

78 Complaint no 07/B/07346 against Walsall MBC, 17 June 2008 paras 23–24.

79 Care and Support (Charging and Assessment of Resources) Regulations 2014 SI No 2672 reg 3(2)(a) and reg 3(3) pursuant to CA 2014 s14(5).

(a) that the relevant works are necessary and appropriate to meet the needs of the disabled occupant, and

(b) that it is reasonable and practicable to carry out the relevant works having regard to the age and condition of–
  (i) the dwelling, qualifying houseboat or caravan, or
  (ii) the building.

In considering the matters mentioned in paragraph (a) a local housing authority which is not itself a social services authority shall consult the social services authority.

14.65 Although the HGCRA 1996 specifically requires housing authorities to consult with social services authorities over whether the proposed works are 'necessary and appropriate', it is nevertheless for housing authorities to decide in any particular case whether or not to approve a grant: they are not bound to follow the social services authority's advice.[80] Provided the housing authority has considered all the facts and has acted rationally, the court is unlikely to interfere with that decision.[81] Where, however, a dispute arises between the occupational therapist's view and that of the grants officer about what work is 'necessary and appropriate', it will be maladministration for the authority not to have a means of resolving this conflict.[82]

Reasonable and practicable

14.66 HGCRA 1996 s24(3)(b) charges the housing authority with the duty of deciding whether it is 'reasonable and practicable' to carry out the proposed adaptation works. In making its assessment, a housing authority is specifically required to have regard to the age and condition of the dwelling or building. In determining whether the work is reasonable and practicable, the guidance refers to other relevant considerations, including the architectural and structural characteristics of the property, conservation considerations, the practicalities of carrying out work on properties with difficult or limited access (such as steep flights of steps or narrow doorways, etc) and the impact on other occupants of the proposed works.[83]

More suitable alternative accommodation

14.67 On occasions a housing authority may have misgivings about approving a DFG on the basis that it would be more cost-effective if the disabled person moved to different accommodation. It is unclear as to whether the existence of such an alternative would constitute lawful reasons for refusing a grant – if the proposed adaptations were in every other respect 'reasonable and practicable' and 'necessary and appropriate'. Much would no doubt turn on the context of the individual case and the extent to which 'what is

80 2013 HAC guidance, annex C para 39.
81 *R (L) v Leeds City Council* [2010] EWHC 3324 (Admin).
82 Complaint no 05/C/13157 against Leeds City Council, 20 November 2007.
83 That is, if the works would lead to substantial disruption to other tenants (eg the noise of an air-compressor, in *R v Kirklees MBC ex p Daykin* (1997–98) 1 CCLR 512, QBD or alternatively be of indirect benefit to neighbours as in *R v Kirklees MBC ex p Good* (1997–98) 1 CCLR 506, QBD. 2013 HAC guidance, annex C para 40.

reasonable' would encompass a consideration of other alternatives which might appear 'more reasonable'.[84]

14.68   The 2013 HAC guidance advises that (para 8.13):

> ... where major adaptations are required and it is difficult to provide a cost-effective solution in a service user's existing home, particularly in the context of the 'reasonable and practicable' judgements, then the possibility of moving elsewhere should be considered. This could be either into a local authority or housing association dwelling, or a more suitable dwelling in the private sector. If the service user is willing to consider this option, they may need considerable help and support through the re-housing process.

14.69   Assistance in such cases could be provided by the use of the authority's powers under the Regulatory Reform Order (RRO) 2002[85] (for example, helping with the removal expenses,[86] purchase and adaptation of a new property either within or outside the authority's area) or under Localism Act 2011 s1 (see para 1.65 above).

Necessary and appropriate

14.70   In deciding whether the proposed works are 'necessary and appropriate' to meet the needs of the disabled occupant, HGCRA 1996 s24 requires housing authorities, which are not themselves social services authorities, to consult the relevant social services authority on the adaptation needs of disabled people.[87]

14.71   The consideration of what 'meets' the assessed needs of a disabled person may include consideration of any alternative way of meeting the need. Thus in *R v Kirklees MBC ex p Daykin*[88] the disabled person was assessed as needing to be able to get into and out of his council flat. Collins J held that it was reasonable for the authority to decide that this need could either be met by the provision of a stair lift, or by re-housing, and for it to take into account the respective costs of both options, in deciding which was to be preferred.

14.72   In *R (B) v Calderdale MBC*[89] the Court of Appeal considered the interplay between HGCRA 1996 s23 and s24(3), commenting as follows:

> 28. ...What ... the local authority has ... failed to do ... [is] to separate the s24(3) question from the s23(1) question, and to answer it in the light of the fact that the claimant has established his grant-eligibility in principle under [section 23(1)]. The council must now decide whether it is satisfied

---

84   See in this respect Local Government Ombudsman, *Making a house a home: local authorities and disabled adaptations: focus report: learning lessons from complaints*, 2016 at p10 concerning a local authority's failure to assist a family with adaptations to their tenancy where the family were reluctant to move to new accommodation.

85   Regulatory Reform (Housing Assistance) (England and Wales) Order 2002 SI No 1860 Article 3.

86   S Mackintosh and P Leather, *The disabled facilities grant*, Foundations, 2016, para 2.40.

87   See in this respect Local Government Ombudsman, *Making a house a home: local authorities and disabled adaptations: focus report: learning lessons from complaints*, 2016 at p6 which concerns a finding of maladministration where the housing authority failed to consult with social services over a change in a person's circumstances (which justified a new DFG application).

88   (1997–98) 1 CCLR 512, QBD a case concerning Chronically Sick and Disabled Persons Act 1970 s2.

89   [2004] EWCA Civ 134, [2004] 1 WLR 2017.

that a loft conversion is necessary and appropriate to meet D's particular needs, which include the need not to harm his brother. This is a matter for the council's considered judgment. Unless it is so satisfied it cannot pay the grant.

29. One has no wish to be critical of non-lawyers who have to apply this difficult and sensitive legislation not in the calm of a courtroom but in the course of a pressured day's work in the office. But one straightforward guideline is that s23(1) and s24(3) should be applied sequentially. A lot of the difficulty in the present case arose from decision-makers running the two together. S23(1) is a gateway provision. S24(3) is a control for those applications which get through the gateway. In a suitable case, no doubt, it may be legitimate to decide that, even assuming that the application passes the s23(1) threshold, the work cannot be regarded as necessary or as appropriate. But that too is sequential reasoning. What is not permissible is to decide the s23(1) issue by reference to the s24(3) criteria.

14.73 The fact that the statutory duty to consult only exists where the housing authority is not itself a social services authority, does not mean that a similar level of co-operation is not required in unitary authorities. The local government ombudsman has found maladministration where, although the housing and social services sections were within the same directorate, their actions were characterised by 'inadequate communication, a lack of co-ordination, inattention and inactivity'.[90]

14.74 When undertaking its assessment, the social services authority will generally rely on an assessment by an occupational therapist. Such assessments should, as a general rule, look at all the relevant needs of the disabled person and it may constitute maladministration (particularly in complex cases) if they merely confine themselves to matters that can be funded by a DFG.[91]

Grant-eligible works

Mandatory grants

14.75 HGCRA 1996 s23(1) details the purposes for which mandatory grants may be awarded – principally to facilitate access and provision. As detailed above, these are primarily for the purpose of:

- facilitating a disabled person's access to:
  - the dwelling (including a qualifying houseboat and caravan);
  - a room usable as the principal family room, or for sleeping in;
  - a WC, bath, shower, etc (or the provision of a room for these facilities);
- facilitating the preparation of food by the disabled person;
- improving/providing a heating system to meet the disabled person's needs;
- facilitating the disabled person's use of a source of power;
- facilitating access and movement around the home to enable the disabled person to care for someone dependent upon him or her;

---

90 Complaint no 07C03887 against Bury MBC, 14 October 2009, para 38.
91 Complaint no 07/A/11108 against Surrey CC, 11 November 2008.

- making the dwelling safe for the disabled person and others residing with him or her;
- facilitating the disabled person's access to and from a garden; or
- making access to a garden safe for the disabled person.

14.76   In practice it appears that almost 80 per cent of DFGs are provided to fund level floor showers, stairlifts, WCs and ramps.[92]

14.77   The duty is not a 'resource' dependent duty (see para 1.16 above); thus in *R v Birmingham CC ex p Taj Mohammed*[93] Dyson J held that housing authorities were not entitled to take resources into account when deciding whether or not to approve a DFG. It follows that it will be maladministration for the responsible authority not to allocate sufficient funds to 'meet the demand for DFGs'.[94]

14.78   Works eligible for grant support will generally be within a dwelling but may in certain situations be elsewhere, for instance, in the common parts of a building containing flats[95] or in relation to accessing the garden.[96]

14.79   Such works can be conveniently grouped as follows.

Making the dwelling safe

14.80   HGCRA 1996 s23(1)(b) allows a grant to be given for adaptations to make a property safe for the disabled person and other persons residing with him or her. The 2013 HAC guidance[97] explains that works under this heading may include 'adaptations designed to minimise the risk of danger where a disabled person has behavioural problems', as well as such things as enhanced alarm systems for those with hearing difficulties, adaptations in connection with the use of cooking facilities, specialised lighting, toughened glass, guards around fires or radiators, cladding of exposed surfaces and corners to prevent self-injury and so on.

14.81   In *R (B) v Calderdale MBC*[98] Sedley LJ considered that a grant to make a dwelling safe (under HGCRA 1996 s23(1)(b)) required that (para 24):

> ... the proposed works must be such as to minimise the material risk, that is to say to reduce it so far as is reasonably practicable, assuming that it cannot be eliminated.

Facilitating access and provision

14.82   Annex C para 17 of the 2013 HAC guidance explains that this includes works which remove or help overcome any obstacles which prevent the disabled person from moving freely into and around the dwelling and enjoying the use of the dwelling and the facilities or amenities within it. In particular, this includes works which enable the disabled person to pre-

92 S Mackintosh and P Leather, *The disabled facilities grant*, Foundations, 2016, p6.
93 (1997–98) 1 CCLR 441, QBD.
94 Complaint no 07/C/01269 against Lincoln CC and 07/C/09724 against West Lindsey DC, 14 October 2009 para 34.
95 HGCRA 1996 s23(1)(a)(ii); and see also 2013 HAC guidance, annex C para 36.
96 Disabled Facilities Grants (Maximum Amounts and Additional Purposes) (England) Order 2008 SI No 1189 Article 3.
97 Annex C paras 19–12.
98 [2004] EWCA Civ 134, [2004] 1 WLR 2017.

pare and cook food as well as facilitating access to and from the dwelling (and garden) and to the following:

- the principal family room;
- a room used for sleeping (or providing such a room);
- a room in which there is a lavatory, a bath or shower and a washbasin (or providing such a room).

Room usable for sleeping

14.83 The 2013 HAC guidance[99] advises that the building of a new room 'usable for sleeping' should only be grant funded if the housing authority is satisfied that the adaptation of an existing room (or access to that room) is not a suitable option.[100] It states, however, that where the disabled person shares a bedroom, grant funding may be given to provide a room of sufficient size 'so that the normal sleeping arrangements can be maintained'.

Bathroom

14.84 The 2013 HAC guidance[101] explains that the HGCRA 1996 separates the provision of a lavatory and washing, bathing and showering facilities, in order to clarify that a grant support is available to ensure that the disabled person has access to each of these facilities (as well as facilitating their use). The local government ombudsman considers that DFG grants officers should not expect disabled persons and their families to give up a family room in order to make way for a ground floor shower/toilet[102] and has stressed the fundamental importance of disabled people being able properly to manage bathing/washing with dignity[103] – see para 2.20 above.

14.85 A 2016 ombudsman's report[104] concerned an adult who was unable to manage getting in or out of her bath. The occupational therapist decided that there was no need for a level access shower as she was able to maintain her hygiene by strip washing at the sink. In finding maladministration, the ombudsman referred to the specific duty under HGCRA 1996 s23(1) to facilitate 'access by the disabled occupant to [among other things]... a bath or shower (or both)'.

Facilitating preparation and cooking of food

14.86 Eligible works under this heading include the rearrangement or enlargement of a kitchen to ease manoeuvrability of a wheelchair, and specially modified or designed storage units, gas, electricity and plumbing installations to enable the disabled person to use these facilities independently.

---

99 Annex C para 23.
100 However – as noted below – the local government ombudsman considers that DFG grants officers should not expect disabled persons and their families to give up a family room in order to make way for such provision – see Complaint no 05/C/13157 against Leeds City Council, 20 November 2007.
101 Annex C para 24.
102 Complaint no 05/C/13157 against Leeds City Council, 20 November 2007.
103 Complaint nos 02/C/8679, 02/C/8681 and 02/C/10389 against Bolsover DC, 30 September 2003.
104 Complaint no 15 015 721 against Birmingham City Council, 7 September 2016.

The 2013 HAC guidance[105] advises, however, that a full adaptation of a kitchen would not generally be appropriate where most of the cooking and preparation is done by another household member.

Heating, lighting and power

14.87   The guidance[106] advises that although grant support may be made in order to provide (or improve, or replace) a heating system, this should only extend to rooms normally used by the disabled person and central heating should only be funded 'where the well-being and mobility of the disabled person would be otherwise adversely affected'. Works in relation to lighting and power may include the relocation of power points and the provision of suitably adapted controls.

Safe access to a garden

14.88   As noted above, in 2008 the scope of the mandatory grants regime was extended to cover:[107]

- facilitating the disabled person's access to and from a garden; or
- making access to a garden safe for the disabled person.

14.89   Article 3(3) of the relevant order in each case defines a garden as (among other things) including a balcony, a yard, outhouse or land adjacent to a mooring.

Dependent residents

14.90   Grant support is available to cover work which improves a disabled person's access and movement around a dwelling in order to care for another person who normally resides there (HGCRA 1996 s23(1)(k)). The 2013 HAC guidance[108] makes it clear that the dependent being cared for need not be a disabled person and need not be a relation, and could 'include adaptations to a part of the dwelling to which the disabled person would not normally need access but which is used by a person to whom they are providing care and it is therefore reasonable for such works to be carried out.'

Sensory impaired disabled people

14.91   Mandatory grants are available to meet the adaptation needs of disabled people whose needs 'are less obvious such as those with sight or hearing impairment'.[109] The guidance gives the following example:

> ... partially sighted people may require an enhanced form of lighting of a particular kind in the dwelling to enable them to carry out everyday tasks and activities in the home. Such works may be required to facilitate access into and around the home and for such purposes as the preparation and cooking of food, to improve the ability to use sources of power or to provide greater safety of the disabled occupant. Works for these purposes qualify for

---

105 Annex C paras 27–28.
106 Annex C paras 29–30.
107 Disabled Facilities Grants (Maximum Amounts and Additional Purposes) (England) Order 2008 SI No 1189 Article 3.
108 Annex C para 33.
109 Annex C para 34.

mandatory grant under section 23(1). Where safety is an issue, the works could qualify under subsection (1)(b).

Discretionary grants

14.92 Prior to July 2003, the HGCRA 1996 provided for discretionary grants (under section 23(2)) to be made in certain situations. Although this provision has been repealed, it has been replaced with a wide ranging power under article 3 of the RRO 2002 which enables housing authorities to give discretionary assistance, in any form, for adaptations or other housing purposes. The financial assistance can also be provided indirectly to the disabled person through a third party and may be paid in addition, or as an alternative, to the grant, and there is no restriction on the amount of assistance that may be given. Guidance on the RRO 2002 was issued by the Office of Deputy Prime Minister as circular 05/2003.[110]

14.93 The 2013 HAC guidance[111] gives examples of the type of assistance that can be provided under the RRO 2002 powers:

- to provide small-scale adaptations to either fulfil needs not covered by mandatory DFGs or, by avoiding the procedural complexities of mandatory DFGs, to deliver a much quicker remedy for urgent adaptations;
- to provide top-up assistance to mandatory DFG where the local authority takes the view that the amount of assistance available under DFG is insufficient to meet the needs of the disabled person and their family; and
- to assist with the acquisition of other accommodation (whether within or outside the authority's area) where the authority is satisfied that this will benefit the occupant at least as much as improving or adapting his existing accommodation.

14.94 The 2006 DCLG guidance advised that the RRO 2002 powers could additionally be used where an authority considers that the statutory means test is 'biting particularly harshly in a particular case' (para 6.18). Assistance provided under the RRO 2002 may be in any form deemed appropriate by the authority – for instance, as an outright grant or as a loan or by way of an equity release.[112]

14.95 The existence of this discretionary power, allied with the public sector equality duty, may, in appropriate situations, be such as to create a substantial obligation on a council to facilitate necessary works – or at the very least, to provide cogent reasons why this is not possible.[113]

Ineligibility for grant and the social services overlap

14.96 Cases arise where the social services authority assesses a need for an adaptation, but the housing authority refuses or is unable to approve the grant. This may occur because the works in question do not come under the mandatory scheme, or because the housing authority does not consider

---

110 Office of Deputy Prime Minister circular 05/2003 *Housing renewal.*
111 Para 2.24.
112 2013 HAC guidance at para 2.22.
113 Complaint no 07 C 05809 against Kirklees MBC, 26 June 2008 at para 50.

the proposed works to be reasonable or practicable, or because the applicant fails the means test. In addition, it may be that the proposed works will cost significantly more than the maximum grant.

14.97   In such situations, the failure of the DFG application does not absolve the social services authority of its duty to meet an assessed need under CA 2014 s18. As noted above (para 7.56), the services that can be provided under the CA 2014 are as extensive as those that could be provided under the previous legislation. Although 'adaptations' and 'additional facilities designed to secure ... greater safety, comfort or convenience' were specifically mentioned in CSDPA 1970 s2(1)(e), these are encompassed within the care and support arrangements that can/must be provided under CA 2014 s8.[114] In this respect, the revised statutory guidance to the CA 2014 states:[115]

> Where the local authority provides or arranges for care and support, the type of support may itself take many forms. These may include more traditional 'service' options, such as care homes or homecare, but may also include other types of support such as assistive technology in the home or equipment/adaptations ...

14.98   The interlinking role of social services support for adaptations/fixtures and fittings is well established, particularly by filling gaps or topping up shortfalls[116] in the statutory DFG scheme – for example, by 'providing loan finance to a disabled person to enable them to purchase these facilities, or by providing a grant to cover or contribute to the costs of provision'.[117]

14.99   It is maladministration for a social services authority to fail to appreciate that it has such a duty to provide adaptations – separate from the obligation to process DFGs.[118] The social services authority obligation under the CA 2014 in relation to adaptations and other facilities is considered at para 7.51 above.

14.100   In *R (BG) v Medway Council*[119] the High Court held that it was not unreasonable for an authority to impose conditions on a grant that it made under its social services functions (in this case under CSDPA 1970 s2) to cover the shortfall in the monies awarded under a DFG. The 'top-up' loan in question was to be secured by way of a 20-year legal charge on the home – which would not be repayable, unless the disabled person ceased

---

114 Joint Committee on the Draft Care and Support Bill, *Draft Care and Support Bill*, HL Paper 143 HC 822, The Stationery Office, 2013, paras 168–170.

115 At para 10.12 – and see as para 15.52 where it is made clear that social services authorities role includes the provision of 'services such as housing adaptations' and the annex J definition of 'care and support' expressly includes 'the provision of aids and adaptations'.

116 As para 8.5 of the 2013 HAC guidance notes, 'social services funding streams have also been used to increase the overall resource to fund an adaptation in many cases'. It appears that such top up funding from social services 'has become increasingly hard to obtain' and Mackintosh and others stress the need for guidance clarifying the responsibilities of the social care authority 'as this seems to be inconsistent across the country' – see S Mackintosh and P Leather, *The disabled facilities grant*, Foundations, 2016, para 5.20.

117 2013 HAC guidance, para 2.8.

118 Complaint no 05/C/13157 against Leeds City Council, 20 November 2007; and see also complaint no 10 008 979 against Liverpool City Council, 4 April 2011.

119 [2005] EWHC 1932 (Admin), (2005) 8 CCLR 448.

to reside at the property during the 20-year period, and any amount repayable would be subject to interest. The authority, however, undertook that in the event of repayment being required it would have regard to the family's personal and financial circumstances and would not act unreasonably by insisting on repayment immediately or on terms that would result in financial hardship.

Fixtures and fittings

14.101 While DFGs are available to cover (among other things) adaptations to the fabric of a building, questions do arise as to whether items such as specialist equipment come within the scheme. The 2013 HAC guidance is largely silent upon this question. It notes that some equipment (such as stair-lifts) will contribute to the access/making safe objectives of the DFG scheme, 'other equipment, particularly in the context of assistive technology and monitoring equipment may form part of a wider package of care contributed to by health and social care services' (para 2.14). Earlier (1996) guidance[120] gave more practical and useful advice how the line should be drawn – namely:

> 7.6.1 ... help with equipment which can be easily installed and removed with little or no modification to the dwelling, is normally the responsibility of the social services authority ... with larger adaptations requiring structural modification of a dwelling normally coming within the scope of a disabled facilities grant. However, it is for housing authorities and social services authorities between them to decide how the particular adaptation needs of a disabled person should be funded. In taking such decisions authorities should not forget that the needs of the disabled occupant are paramount within the framework of what can be offered.
>
> 7.6.2 Close cooperation between the respective authorities is vital to ensure that those requiring help in paying for works for essential adaptations to meet their special needs, are given the most efficient and effective support.

14.102 Additional advice in the 1996 guidance stated (at annex I):

> 7. It is for housing authorities and social services authorities between them to decide how particular adaptations should be funded either [social services functions] or through a DFG.
>
> 8. However, since DFGs were introduced in 1990 under the Local Government and Housing Act 1989, it has been common practice that equipment which can be installed and removed fairly easily with little or no structural modification of the dwelling is normally the responsibility of the social services authority.
>
> 9. For larger items such as stairlifts and through floor lifts which require such structural works to the property, help is normally provided by housing authorities through DFG. However, some routine installations may not involve structural work. To ensure that such adaptations are progressed quickly, the respective authorities should jointly agree a standard line on the installation of lifts which will apply unless there are exceptional circumstances. Authorities will wish to include arrangements for routine servicing, maintenance, removal and possible re-use.

120 Department of the Environment guidance circular 17/96 – now revoked.

Equipment service costs

14.103   The 2013 HAC guidance advises that where items of equipment have been installed (such as stair and through-floor lifts, ceiling hoists etc) which will need 'regular servicing and provision made for repair in cases of failure' then it is (para 10.1):

> ... good practice for these arrangements, covering the likely service life of the equipment, to be secured by the local authority at the time of installation. The cost of securing services by way of extended guarantee or service contract, when met by a single payment on commissioning, needs to be included in the calculation of any grant payable.

Means testing of disabled facilities grants

14.104   HGCRA 1996 s30 provides that eligibility for a DFG is subject to a means test. Only the financial circumstances of the disabled occupant,[121] his or her spouse or civil partner[122] or co-habiting partner are assessed and not other members of the household. If the DFG is required in order to enable a spouse or civil partner to return to his or her home and that person's absence is likely to exceed 52 weeks, his or her financial circumstances alone may be relevant.[123] Applications for a disabled person under the age of 19 no longer require a means test.

14.105   The details of the means test are determined by regulations[124] and are relatively complex, although in many instances the calculation adopts housing benefit principles – thus the value of a person's savings is determined in the same way as for housing benefit and a tariff income is applied to any capital in excess of £6,000 (there is no upper capital limit).

Timescales, delay and grant deferment

14.106   HGCRA 1996 s34 requires housing authorities to approve or refuse a grant application as soon as reasonably practicable, and in any event not later than six months after the date of application. By section 36 the actual payment of the grant may be delayed until a date not more than 12 months following the date of the application.

14.107   Section 36 provides the only statutory flexibility local authorities have in the managing of the cost implications of the grant: a grant, as noted above, payable as a consequence of a non-resource dependent duty.[125] Notwithstanding the mandatory nature of this obligation, evidence suggests that some local authorities adopt extra-statutory impediments to frustrate the

---

121   The disabled occupant may or may not be the applicant.

122   It is at least arguable that estranged spouses living in the premises may not, however, be members of the same 'household' – see *R (Fay) v Essex CC* [2004] EWHC 879 (Admin) at [15].

123   Housing Renewal Grant Regulations 1996 SI No 2890 reg 9(2)(b) and see also local government ombudsman complaint no 05/B/06334 against Stafford BC, 20 July 2006.

124   Housing renewal grants regulations which are subject to annual amendment in England.

125   *R v Birmingham CC ex p Taj Mohammed* (1997–98) 1 CCLR 441, QBD – (see para 14.77 above).

expeditious processing of grant applications. These include: not making the application form available until social services have provided specific supporting evidence; waiting lists for applications and approvals; advising applicants that the DFG budget for the year has been spent and so to defer making applications until the following year, etc. Since the statutory clock only starts ticking once a completed application has been submitted to the housing authority, a not uncommon tactic appears to be to delay the pre-application assessment process, by creating inappropriate administrative hurdles[126] and by delaying the preliminary assessments (for instance, by claiming a shortage of assessors).[127]

14.108   The HGCRA 1996 sets out a statutory timetable triggered by the application. It follows that it would be a breach of public law and maladministration for local authorities to have policies or practices of these kinds. This point is endorsed by 2013 HAC guidance which stresses that the 6- and 12-month periods are the 'maximum times allowed for these processes rather than the norm'; that a delay of 12 months would be 'exceptional'; and that 'such delays are contrary to the intention of the DFG programme' (para 11.10).[128] In relation to processes designed to delay the making of an application, it states (annex C para 11):

> The legislation makes it quite clear that an individual is entitled to complete and lodge a formal application on their own behalf or with the assistance of a third party. Some local authorities prefer to complete applications on the disabled person's behalf or with the assistance of a HIA [Home Improvement Agency]. However any applicant that wishes to complete their own application should be assisted to do so. This should include the provision of application forms, owners/tenants certificates and all relevant information. Local authorities should not in any way attempt to create obstacles to such a process. Once a formal application has been validly made, authorities are under a duty to consider it. An authority could be open to challenge if they were to refuse to entertain a valid application, or to comply with any reasonable request by a potential applicant to be furnished with the necessary application forms.

126 See eg complaint no 02/C/04897 against Morpeth BC and Northumberland CC, 27 November 2003 where the ombudsman criticised a process which required an applicant to queue twice – once for the social services input and then again for the housing authority determination.

127 Local authorities have previously claimed that a shortage of occupational therapists (OTs) has rendered it impossible for them to undertake timely assessments. In complaint no 90/C/0336, 3 October 1991 the local government ombudsman, in holding that a wait of nine months for an OT assessment amounted to maladministration, observed that if insufficient OTs were available, authorities should find other way of assessing the needs. This advice is reinforced by the 2013 HAC guidance which refers (at para 7.8) to the use of 'other staff' to carry out assessments for minor adaptations and at para 7.14 noes that the HGCRA 1996 'makes no reference to assessment of need for an adaptation' and it refers to advice from the Department for Communities and Local Government 'that an occupational therapy [(OT)] assessment is not a legislative requirement' and that OT assessments should 'not be used in every case'. See also *R (Fay) v Essex CC* [2004] EWHC 879 (Admin) at [28].

128 In 2007 the local government ombudsman found maladministration where a local authority delayed by four months a financial assessment – see complaint no 05/C/13157 against Leeds City Council, 20 November 2007.

Table 14.1: DFG timescales

Stage		Urgent (working days)	Non-urgent (working days)
1	Initial enquiry at first point of contact to occupational therapist recommendation provided to adaptation service (landlord, HIA or grant provider)	51	20
2	Occupational therapist recommendation to approval of scheme (grant approval or issue of works contract/order)	30	50
3	Approval of scheme to completion of works	20	80
Total	Total time taken (ie sum of above three stages)	552	150

1   See in this respect Local Government Ombudsman, *Making a house a home: local authorities and disabled adaptations: focus report: learning lessons from complaints*, 2016 at p5 which stressed the need, in urgent cases, for occupational therapy reports confirming the need for adaptations to be completed within five working days of receiving a referral.
2   See, for example, the local government ombudsman report on a Complaint against Cornwall Council no 15 019 763, 4 July 2016 where maladministration was found when an urgent need for adaptions took 22 months.

14.109   The 2006 DCLG and 2013 HAC guidance provide target timescales for the completion of the various stages of the DFG process and the local government ombudsman has placed considerable reliance in these[129] – for example, that for a grant of £5,000, there should be a maximum target time of 52 weeks from the initial enquiry about services to completion of adaptations work; and that even in complex assessments, the time from referral to the completion of an occupational therapist's report should not exceed three months.[130]

14.110   The target timescales in the 2013 HAC guidance are less detailed than those in the 2006 DCLG guidance, but are valuable nevertheless. Local authorities should provide 95 per cent of adaptations within the timescales detailed above (in Table 14.1).

14.111   The expectation is therefore that all adaptions will be completed within 30 weeks of the initial enquiry (ie not the completion of the application) and urgent adaptations should be completed within 11 weeks of the initial enquiry. Given the statutory 'maximum' of 52 weeks and the increased funding for DFGs these would appear to be not unreasonable.

129   Complaint no 07/A/11108 against Surrey CC, 11 November 2008, para 10; and see eg Complaint no 06/C/16349 against Sheffield City Council, 26 June 2008 para 46; See eg Complaint no 07/C/01269 against Lincoln CC and 07/C/09724 against West Lindsey DC, 14 October 2009; Complaint no 07C03887 against Bury MBC, 14 October 2009; Complaint no 15 019 763 against Cornwall Council, 4 July 2016; Complaint no 16 001 198 against Barking & Dagenham LBC, 1 July 2016; and Local Government Ombudsman, *Making a house a home: local authorities and disabled adaptations: focus report: learning lessons from complaints*, 2016 at p4.
130   Complaint no 07/A/11108 against Surrey CC, 11 November 2008.

14.112   While the courts have not as yet been called upon to consider the legality of the widespread use by local authorities of rationing mechanisms,[131] this may be due to cases of this nature being settled at an early stage by local authorities. In *Qazi v Waltham Forest LBC*[132] Richards J dismissed a private law claim which alleged that the authority had deliberately delayed the processing of grant applications and failed to explain clearly the status of applications – namely that they were not 'pending applications' (to which the mandatory timescales in the Act applied) but merely 'enquiries'. While the judgment addressed the specific private law issues in the case, the judge observed that 'it is plainly arguable that the scheme operated by the defendant was unlawful' and that:

> Notwithstanding the difficulties that the 1989 Act[133] created for local authorities, with their limited resources, I confess to a degree of surprise that systems of this kind received approval in principle, as I am told, from the Local Government Commissioner. Had an application been made at the time to challenge the system by way of judicial review, there must be a good chance that it would have been successful or at the very least that leave would have been granted.

14.113 Where hardship is being caused by the delayed processing of a grant, social services authorities should be pressed to facilitate the works via their underpinning duties under CA 2014 (see above) and, if it be the case, requiring that the works be completed urgently and without the delay occasioned by a full social care assessment (see para 3.63 above).

14.114   Where the maladministration (for example, delay in implementing adaptations or in failing to honour promises to take action) is attributable to a social housing provider and not a local authority, then it may be possible to complain to the housing ombudsman service.[134] The housing ombudsman is able to undertake investigations and to make compensation recommendations in much the same way as the local government ombudsman.[135]

Assistance and support for the applicant

14.115 A DFG grant can cover not only the building works but also other charges necessarily incurred in undertaking the grant-aided works, including costs such as architects' and surveyors' fees and charges for planning

---

131 Research suggests that a third of local authorities routinely breach the legal timescales affecting over 4,000 people every year – see L Cheshire, *The long wait for a home*, 2015.

132 (1999) 32 HLR. 689, a case based upon an allegation of misfeasance in public office and negligent misstatement.

133 The case concerned the Local Government and Housing Act 1989 under which DFGs were payable at the time. The material parts of the Act are now found in the 1996 Act.

134 Housing Ombudsman Service Housing Ombudsman Service, Exchange Tower, Harbour Exchange Square, London, E14 9GE

135 See eg complaint reference 200901278 – Adaptations, Repairs, 30 July 2010 – a complaint that involved delayed adaptations and where the ombudsman awarded compensation for the social landlord's failure to communicate, lack of co-ordination and the lack of timeliness in completing the work.

permission or building regulations approvals.[136] As a consequence, the housing authority is responsible for supporting the applicant through the process, including ensuring that plans and the completed the works are fit for purpose. As the 2013 HAC guidance advises (para 1.9):

> Quality and choice should be the shared and corporate goals of all partners in the delivery of an adaptations service. A corporate responsibility, binding on all partners, will ensure that the adaptation is delivered sensitively, is fit for the purpose identified by the end user and within a specified time-frame.

14.116 It follows that authorities must intervene to challenge undue delays in obtaining building regulation approval or clarifying the need for planning permission.[137] A number of ombudsman reports have also concerned the failure of councils to ensure that the adaptations were suitable and the building work of a sufficient quality[138]

Priority cases and interim arrangements

Priority cases

14.117 The 2013 HAC guidance accepts that in processing DFG applications authorities will prioritise some applications over others (para 4.10) – but requires that individuals are made aware that a prioritisation scheme operates.[139] It advises that although most such schemes depend upon an assessment of medical risk these should be 'broadened to reflect the social model of disability' (para 7.8) and that particular attention need be paid to people with deteriorating conditions where the response 'should be as fast as possible' with consideration being given 'to expedited procedures and interim solutions where some measure of delay is inevitable' (para 7.33).

14.118 The need for expedition is often particularly acute in relation to people being discharged from hospital. The 2013 HAC guidance stresses that 'patients who need an adaptation to enable them to return to their home safely should not be discharged without either the necessary adaptation or appropriate interim arrangements already in place' (para 7.36). Its assertion that it 'is not acceptable that the disabled person and carers should be left for a period of weeks or months without such interim help'[140] has been forcefully endorsed by the local government ombudsman.[141]

---

136 Housing Renewal Grants (Services and Charges) Order 1996 SI No 2889; and 2013 HAC guidance, para 37.

137 Complaint no 12 021 104 against Sandwell MBC, 30 January 2014.

138 See, for example, the case described in the Local Government Ombudsman, *Making a house a home: local authorities and disabled adaptations: focus report: learning lessons from complaints*, 2016, p8.

139 The Local Government Ombudsman has found maladministration where a local authority failed to provide clear information to applicants concerning the way its priority system for the processing of DFG applications operated – see Complaints no 97/B/0524, 0827–8, 1146 and 1760 against Bristol CC 1998.

140 2013 HAC guidance, para 7.57; 2006 DCLG guidance, para 5.40.

141 Complaint no 06/C/16349 against Sheffield City Council, 26 June 2008. In this case the delay was such that the disabled person and his family put in place the adaptations, before the grant was finalised: the ombudsman noted that the council had reimbursed this expenditure (over £14,000) and paid £2,000 compensation for

14.119   The guidance advises that the measurement of the target time for the completion of assessment should begin at the point at which a priority is assigned and that this must be done within two working days of the receipt of an enquiry or referral (paras 7.9–7.10) and that the applicant must be advised and given an explanation of (among other things) the likely timescale for the completion of the assessment (para 7.13).

14.120   Any social welfare system of this nature must endeavour to prioritise those whose needs are most urgent while ensuring that all potential applicants are dealt with expeditiously and in accordance with the law. Inevitably there is potential for conflict, since a clear prioritisation process is only one part of a fair and legal scheme. A poorly resourced system might have an admirable prioritisation process – but in practice might only progress the applications of those in most urgent need. Although the local government ombudsman has long accepted (and indeed advocated for) local authority DFG prioritisation procedures,[142] this approach was questioned by the High Court (as noted above – see para 14.112) in *Qazi v Waltham Forest LBC*.[143]

14.121   The local government ombudsman's concern about chronic delay and the importance of having reasonable time targets for the completion of works, is evidenced in a 2002 report in which it was stated that she did 'not accept that lack of resources is an acceptable reason for excessive delays in helping people whose need have been clearly assessed and accepted' and that she 'would generally regard any delay beyond six months as unjustified'.[144] Likewise, in a 2006 report[145] the ombudsman stated:

> It seems to me that eight months is an unreasonable length of time for a disabled person to have to wait for a request for adaptations to be properly assessed; and then to wait a further six months for the relatively minor adaptations recommended to be carried out … In my view, a process taking 14 months should have taken no longer than six months to complete.

Interim arrangements

14.122 In many, if not most, cases there will be a delay between the identification of a need for adaptations and the completion of the works. Local authorities have an obligation, not only to process the DFG application with expedition, but also to ameliorate – to the extent that they are able – the hardship experienced by the disabled person (and all others affected) by any delay and by the works, if they are extensive and if they severely disrupt ordinary living arrangements. In this respect the 2013 HAC guidance advises that (para 7.57):

'the indignity, inconvenience and distress that he experienced and his time and trouble in pursuing his complaint'.

142 See eg complaint no 04/C/12312 against West Lancashire DC, 9 June 2005, complaint no 02/C/04897 against Morpeth BC and Northumberland CC, 27 November 2003; and complaint no 04/C/12312 against West Lancashire DC, 9 June 2005.

143 (1999) 32 HLR 689, a case based upon an allegation of misfeasance in public office and negligent misstatement.

144 Complaint nos 02/C/8679, 02/C/8681 and 02/C/10389 against Bolsover DC, 30 September 2003.

145 Complaint no 05/B/00246 against Croydon LBC, 24 July 2006 para 37.

It is not acceptable that the disabled person and carers should be left for a period of weeks or months without such interim help when the timescale for the provision of an adaptation is foreseen to be lengthy. In addition to the problems an absence of interim measures may cause for the disabled person and for carers, it may result in additional costs for health and social care authorities.

14.123   In relation to the disruption caused by building works the advice is as follows:

7.60 ... where the period of significant disruption is expected to be only a few days then the disabled person may be able to stay with friends or family, or take a holiday. The social services and the housing authority should consider meeting all or part of the costs arising from such arrangements.

7.61 Where more prolonged disruption is unavoidable then a temporary move to alternative accommodation should be considered. A housing association or the local authority housing service may have an appropriate home available. Arranging such a temporary move is a complex and difficult business in which practical and financial support should be available where the disabled person requests it ...

14.124   The local government has considered complaints where councils have failed to make suitable interim arrangements. In a 2009 report, a delay in processing a DFG meant that the family were without suitable bathing assistance. A proposal that the bathing take place on an interim basis at a nearby day centre was turned down by the panel (see para 18.86) – a decision found to be maladministration by the ombudsman. A 2008 report came to a similar finding where the disabled person had to spend an extended period in a residential placement – the costs of which the ombudsman recommended be reimbursed to the disabled person.[146]

NHS powers

14.125   The NHS has power to fund adaptations, and brief guidance concerning the use of this power is provided in the 2012 National Framework for NHS Continuing Healthcare (see para 12.143 above).[147] This includes encouragement that partner bodies 'work together locally on integrated adaptations services' and that 'CCGs should consider having clear arrangements with partners setting out how the adaptation needs of those entitled to NHS continuing healthcare should be met, including referral processes and funding responsibilities'.[148] The framework draws attention to the possibility of such adaptations being provided through the use of a DFG although if this is not possible, then the NHS will be responsible for the necessary support. As it notes, where individuals:

---

146 Complaint no 07/B/07346 against Walsall MBC, 17 June 2008 paras 25 and 28.
147 Department of Health, *National framework for NHS continuing healthcare and nhs-funded nursing care (revised)*, 2012 – see PG Guidance (Part 2) and in particular PG 79 and 85–89. Although this framework applies to adults, the guidance on the principles is relevant to children.
148 2012 National framework for NHS continuing healthcare, para PG 79.3. This guidance was cited with approval in *R (Whapples) v Birmingham CrossCity Clinical Commissioning Group* [2015] EWCA Civ 435, (2015) 18 CCLR 300 para 32.

... require bespoke equipment (and/or specialist or other non-bespoke equipment that is not available through joint equipment services) to meet specific assessed needs identified in their NHS continuing healthcare care plan. CCGs should make appropriate arrangements to meet these needs.[149]

14.126 NHS bodies have extensive statutory powers to transfer monies to social services (discussed at para 11.124 above) and the 2006 DCLG guidance advised[150] that these can be used to facilitate housing adaptation, particularly if in so doing it 'releases beds by expediting discharge'. It cautions, however, that patients 'should not be discharged without either an adaptation in place or appropriate interim arrangements already in place'. The NHS has, of course, the power to fund or jointly fund adaptations where the need is health related – for example, a disabled person with severe cellulitis who requires frequent washing for hygiene purpose or an immobile patient who requires a ceiling track rail in his home before being discharged from hospital.

14.127 The local government ombudsman found maladministration in a case where a profoundly disabled woman whose care package was funded by the NHS under continuing healthcare, was confined to bed in one room of her house for two years longer than necessary. The ombudsman criticised the council's failure recognise its legal duties to the woman, its failure to have any direct social work contact with the family for 15 months, and its handling of her DFG application.[151]

14.128 As noted above (para 7.73) health/social services have the power to provide integrated community equipment services for 'community equipment and minor adaptations for home nursing, daily living and communication – including such things as commodes, shower chairs, raised toilet seats, grab rails, lever taps, improved lighting, and telecare equipment such as fall alarms'.[152]

Shared lives accommodation/adult placement schemes

Overview

14.129 Shared lives (previously known as adult placement) is a care support arrangement that has historically focussed on supporting adults[153] with learning disabilities but increasingly is used for the support of a much wider range of individuals 'in need'.

---

149 2012 National framework for NHS continuing healthcare, para PG 79.2.

150 2006 DCLG guidance, para 5.26. The 2013 HAC guidance makes mention of the use if pooled budgets in this context at para 8.11.

151 Complaint No 05/C/13157 Leeds City Council, 20 November 2007.

152 See also S Mackintosh and P Leather, *The disabled facilities grant*, Foundations, 2016, para 2.20; and Department of Health, *Guide to integrating community equipment services*, 2001.

153 CA 1989 s23CZA enables local authorities to extend the foster care placements of care leavers beyond the age of 18 – and see also CA 1989 Sch 2 paras 19B and 19BA.

14.130   As at 2015, there were over 150 shared lives schemes in the UK with over 8,000 shared lives carers.[154] It is the scheme that is registered and regulated in England by the Care Quality Commission (CQC).[155] Schemes are most typically local authority led. The dramatic growth in shared lives schemes (14 per cent in 2015)[156] is almost certainly due to the significant cost savings they deliver,[157] although there is also evidence concerning its potential materially to improve individual well-being.[158]

14.131   The purpose of shared lives schemes is to enable the person to live as independently and to have as normal a life in the community as is possible. Placements may be long term or as a transitional arrangement. The individual shares family and community life with the shared lives carer. About half of shared lives arrangements involve the disabled person living with his or her shared lives carer, and half visit their shared lives carer for day support or overnight breaks.[159]

14.132   Shared lives carers are generally paid on the basis of the individual's degree of need (for which different 'bands' exist). The payments are capable of being tax exempt[160] if part of a formal scheme or if the council creates a one-off 'virtual shared lives' arrangement.[161]

Shared lives, choice of accommodation and ordinary residence

14.133   As with supported living placements (see paras 14.137 below), where a local authority has determined that a person has a need that it proposes to meet by way of a shared lives arrangement, the individual has the right to 'express a preference' for a particular accommodation (CA 2014 s30(1)) – considered further at para 8.241 above) and the local authority is required to provide or arrange that accommodation – even if it is in another local authority area. If the cost of the placement is more than the authority considers necessary, then it can require a 'top-up' payment from a third party to cover the additional cost.[162] Where a local authority funds a shared lives package in the area of another local authority, the disabled person is 'deemed' to be ordinarily resident in the funding authority's area

---

154 See generally information at Shared Lives Plus, *What is shared lives?*, 2015.

155 Health and Social Care Act 2008 (Regulated Activities) Regulations 2014 SI No 2936.

156 Shared Lives Plus, *What is shared lives?*, 2015.

157 See, for example, Shared Lives Plus, *A shared life is a healthy life how the shared lives model of care can improve health outcomes and support the NHS*, 2015; and Institute for Research and Innovation in Social Service, *Money matters: case study one: shared lives*, 2011.

158 See, for example, Shared Lives Plus, *A shared life is a healthy life how the shared lives model of care can improve health outcomes and support the NHS*, 2015.

159 Shared Lives Plus, *What is shared lives?*, 2015.

160 For details on this process see HMRC, *HS236 Qualifying care relief: foster carers, adult placement carers, kinship carers and staying put carers*, 2016.

161 See complaint no 15 005 526 against the Isle of Wight Council, 10 March 2016.

162 Care and Support and After-care (Choice of Accommodation) Regulations 2014 SI No 2670.

(ie its continuing responsibility) even though in fact he or she is resident elsewhere.[163]

14.134 For the purposes of the ordinary residence[164] and choice of accommodation provisions,[165] 'shared lives scheme accommodation' means:[166]

> ... accommodation which is provided for an adult by a shared lives carer, and for this purpose–
>
> 'shared lives carer' means an individual who, under the terms of a shared lives agreement, provides, or intends to provide, personal care for adults together with, where necessary, accommodation in the individual's home;
>
> 'shared lives agreement' means an agreement entered into between a person carrying on a shared lives scheme and an individual for the provision, by that individual, of personal care to an adult together with, where necessary, accommodation in the individual's home; and
>
> 'shared lives scheme' means a scheme carried on (whether or not for profit) by a local authority or other person for the purposes of–
> (a) recruiting and training shared lives carers;
> (b) making arrangements for the placing of adults with shared lives carers; and
> (c) supporting and monitoring placements.

14.135 The ordinary residence and choice of accommodation provisions as they relate to 'shared lives schemes' are considered further at paras 6.41 and 8.243 respectively.

Charging

14.136 Disabled people in an adult placement can be charged for their accommodation in the normal way – and apply for housing benefit to help with such costs.[167] Their care support services are subject to the standard charging rules applying to all non-domiciliary care services – these are considered at chapter 8 above.

Supported housing/supported living

Overview

14.137 'Supported living' is a generic term which has come to describe arrangements whereby an elderly, ill or disabled person has the benefit of a package of care and support together with accommodation – for which the person

---

163 Care and Support (Ordinary Residence) (Specified Accommodation) Regulations 2014 SI No 2828; and see para 6.41 for further discussion on this point.

164 Care and Support (Ordinary Residence) (Specified Accommodation) Regulations 2014 SI No 2828 reg 4.

165 Care and Support and After-care (Choice of Accommodation) Regulations 2014 SI No 2670 reg 7.

166 The definition mirrors that in Health and Social Care Act 2008 (Regulated Activities) Regulations 2014 SI 2936 reg 2.

167 Almost invariably, such schemes will not, however, qualify as exempt accommodation for housing benefit purposes – see Upper Tribunal decision [2009] UKUT 12 (AAC).

will ordinarily have a tenancy.[168] Such an arrangement separates the delivery of care (at an organisational level) from the provision of accommodation: the effect of this is that it is not deemed to be a registered care home and therefore exempt from registration under the relevant legislation.[169] The care provider will, however, generally be required to be registered with the CQC. A consequence of not being a registered care home is that those living in such schemes are entitled to claim housing benefit[170] – and crucially, housing benefit at higher rates than for non-disabled people.[171] Such schemes require, however, that the housing body provides care, support or supervision for the tenant.[172]

14.138   The development of such arrangements in the 1990s owed much to the philosophy of the independent living/deinstitutionalisation movement: enabling disabled people to live ordinary lives in the community with the same choices as others. The best supported living schemes can achieve this and help their tenants realise their UN Convention on the Rights of Persons with Disabilities Article 19 right to independent living. However, this is not true of all such schemes and much has also been written about the problems they have encountered.[173]

14.139   As with many of the 'personalisation' initiatives in social care, their enthusiastic adoption by providers and commissioners has frequently

168 For discussion concerning situations where a person is not considered to have sufficient mental capacity to enter into a tenancy agreement – see para 13.49 above.

169 Care Standards Act 2000 s3(2) requires establishments to be registered if they provide accommodation 'together with nursing or personal care'; and in England in general the provision of residential accommodation, 'together with nursing or personal care' is a regulated activity under Health and Health and Social Care Act 2008 (Regulated Activities) Regulations 2014 SI No 2936 Sch 1 para 2(1) – see para 17.6 below.

170 And retain their disability living allowance (DLA) personal independence payment (PIP) care component – unlike in residential care – although these benefits can be taken into account for care charging purposes.

171 Most supported living schemes access higher rates of housing benefit as they are 'exempt accommodation – ie exempt from the general cap on housing benefit by virtue of the maximum 'local reference' rent – Housing Benefit and Council Tax Benefit (Consequential Provisions) Regulations 2006 SI No 217 Sch 3 para 4(10) – ie accommodation provided by a non-metropolitan county council in England; a housing association (as defined in Housing Associations Act 1985 s1(1)); a registered charity (as defined in Charities Act 2006 Part 1), or voluntary organisation (as defined in Housing Benefit Regulations 2006 SI No 213 reg 2(1)); see also Commissioner's decisions CH/423/2006, CH/3811/2006 and CH/779/2007 – the 'Turnbull' decision.

172 For example, the provision of an alarm; help ensuring rent is paid; liaising with all relevant agencies, both statutory and voluntary, on the tenant's behalf; assisting people to claim housing benefit and other welfare benefits; helping to keep people safe by monitoring visitors, including contractors and professionals, and by carrying out health and safety and risk assessments of property.

173 Mansell highlights the failure, not of the concept, but of 'management and leadership' noting that all too often the problem has been 'wrong buildings, in the wrong places, with the wrong furnishings, staffed by people with the wrong training, managed according to the wrong rules, with the wrong policies, the wrong leadership and the wrong purposes' – see J Mansell, 'The "implementation gap" in supported accommodation for people with intellectual disabilities', foreword to Clement and Bigby, *Group homes for people with intellectual disabilities: encouraging inclusion and participation*, Jessica Kingsley, 2009. See also R McConkey 'End of the beginning for supported accommodation?' in *The Lancet Psychiatry* online, 19 October 2016.

been attributable to other policy objectives. For providers they have the twin benefits of being 'lucrative'[174] and less regulated and for local authorities the benefits can be measured in terms of government targets and local finances. A department of health performance indicator places emphasis on councils spending that less than 40 per cent of their overall adult social care budget on 'residential care'[175] and the social security system places a greater burden on local finances for placements in care home accommodation than it does for those living 'independently'. In practice, authorities can improve local finances[176] and their 'performance ratings' simply by changing the status of someone's accommodation – for instance, by encouraging the home to 'deregister'.

14.140　Such a change may result in no greater independence for the service user and in certain situations it may result in less security and indeed an inferior support package. It follows that local authority activity to promote 'supported living' packages is not necessarily synonymous with the promotion of independent living. Indeed, not infrequently, a person may have little or no practical choice over their placement in a supported living scheme. Where a disabled person requires a substantial package of care, there are risks with supported living arrangements (unless there is a clear agreement to the contrary with the local authority) which include the risk that the care provider can be changed at short notice and the risk that the person(s) providing the necessary care may have insufficient understanding/expertise to provide the necessary care and support.

14.141　Where a local authority decides to cease providing support for a disabled person in a supported living (or similar placement) it will need (in addition to its usual obligations that arise when changes are made to a care package – see para 4.172 above) to have regard to the person's rights under ECHR Article 8 (respect for one's 'home').[177]

14.142　Key elements of 'supported living' arrangements include:

1) **Non-residential care:** The service user does not live in a residential care home ie is not funded under CA 2014 s8(1). It follows that the local authority social services support provided under the arrangement will be delivered as a domiciliary care package – most probably under CA 2014 s24 (see para 4.84 above).

2) **Tenancy rights:** Most commonly the adult in need is granted an assured tenancy of the property they occupy in order to attract housing benefit for the rental component. On occasions there may be questions as to whether the person has sufficient mental capacity to enter into a tenancy[178] and this question is considered further at para 13.49 below. The

---

174 P Kinsella, *Supported living: a new paradigm*, National Development Team, 1993.

175 Department of Health, *Use of resources in adult social care – a guide for local authorities*, 2009, p6.

176 Research suggests that significant savings can be made by moving people with learning disabilities into supported living – see Local Government Association, *Learning disability services efficiency project interim position report*, 2015.

177 *R (Clarke) v Sutton LBC* [2015] EWHC 1081 para 29 and see para 2.85 above.

178 It appears that if the landlord is aware of the incapacity (to enter into a tenancy) at the time the tenancy is entered into, this has the effect of creating a valid (but voidable) contract – voidable by the tenant – and so housing benefit is payable for such an arrangement. See decision of Social Security Commissioner Mesher,

courts and the CQC have made it clear that the mere fact that a person has a tenancy agreement does not in itself mean that it is not a residential care home for registration purposes.[179]

3) **Mixed funding streams:** A wider range of funding streams may be attracted by such an arrangement, than is the case with a residential care placement. Most obviously this includes housing benefit, but additionally tenants may become eligible for social security and disability related benefits – for example, they are entitled to apply for the care component of disability living allowance (DLA)/personal independence payments (PIP). In appropriate cases, funding can also be available via NHS Act 2006 ss256–257 in cases where the NHS and social services agree to a joint funding arrangement (see para 11.127 above).

14.143 In many cases, the mix of benefits and grants that are attracted by supported living arrangements have the advantage of increasing an individual's income and decreasing the social services authority financial liability for the individual's care. There are, however, dangers, since some of the funding streams are insecure – as has proved to be the case with the loss of the previous 'supporting people' programme and closure of the independent living fund[180] – and even those that may endure, may see changes to their qualifying criteria.

Supported living, choice of accommodation and ordinary residence

14.144 Where a local authority has determined that a person has a need that it proposes to meet by way of a supported living arrangement, the individual has the right to 'express a preference' for a particular placement[181] and the local authority is required to provide or arrange that accommodation – even if it is in another local authority's area. If the cost of the placement is more than the authority considers necessary, then it can require a 'top-up' payment from a third party to cover the additional cost.[182] Where a local authority funds a supported living package in the area of another authority, the disabled person is 'deemed' to be ordinarily resident in the funding authority's area (ie its continuing responsibility) even though in

CH/2121/2006, 13 November 2006 analysed in *Social Care Law Today*, Issue 47, May 2007.

179 CQC *Supported Living Schemes: regulated activities for which the provider may need to register* (2011) pp7–8.

180 For details of these two funding streams see the 5th edition of this book at para 15.119 and para 12.95 respectively.

181 CA 2014 s30(1); and see para 8.243 above.

182 Care and Support and After-care (Choice of Accommodation) Regulations 2014 SI No 2670. Although this is clearly the policy intention underpinning the regulations, it has been argued that the revised statutory guidance to the CA 2014 enables people to choose more expensive accommodation out of county: annex A para 7 requires a local authority to arrange a person's preferred care in a different authority's area and do so by reference to 'the cost of care in that area'. see B Schwer, *Your questions answered on choice and top-ups under the Care Act*, Community Care, 29 September 2016.

fact the person is resident elsewhere if the accommodation meets the criteria set down in regulations.[183]

14.145   For the purposes of the ordinary residence[184] and choice of accommodation provisions,[185] 'supported living accommodation' means:

(1) (a) accommodation in premises which are specifically designed or adapted for occupation by adults with needs for care and support to enable them to live as independently as possible; and

(b) accommodation which is provided–

(i)   in premises which are intended for occupation by adults with needs for care and support (whether or not the premises are specifically designed or adapted for that purpose), and

(ii) in circumstances in which personal care is available if required.

(2) The accommodation referred to in paragraph (1)(a) does not include adapted premises where the adult had occupied those premises as their home before the adaptations were made.

(3) For the purposes of paragraph (1)(b)(ii) personal care may be provided by a person other than the person who provides the accommodation.

14.146 The ordinary residence and choice of accommodation provisions as they relate to 'supported living schemes' are considered further at paras 6.42 and 8.243 respectively.

Extra care housing

14.147 Extra care housing is a term applied to specialised housing for older people who have varying care needs. Although such housing schemes can take various forms, their key features are that residents live in their own self-contained flats; that these are designed to be accessible; that there is support available, including an emergency alarm and a warden and generally a care and support team; and there are communal facilities such as a restaurant, activity rooms, a laundry etc.

14.148   The charging rules for extra care housing have been considered by the local government ombudsman. In a 2014 report[186] she considered it important that residents were offered genuine choice about their placements and if they were not receiving community care support services, then this had to be factored into their charges. The complaint concerned a resident that had been placed in such a setting – even though the placement was a 'poor fit' in terms of his needs. He was charged the standard rate, even though he was paying for his personal care independently. The ombudsman cited the main source of guidance on this question for extra care housing schemes,[187] which specifies that (at para 7):

183 Care and Support (Ordinary Residence) (Specified Accommodation) Regulations 2014 SI No 2828.

184 Care and Support (Ordinary Residence) (Specified Accommodation) Regulations 2014 SI No 2828 reg 5.

185 Care and Support and After-care (Choice of Accommodation) Regulations 2014 SI No 2670 reg 8.

186 Complaint no 11 022 479 against Walsall MBC, 12 March 2014; and see also Complaint no 15 005 212 against Cumbria CC, 8 August 2016.

187 Housing Learning and Improvement Network (LIN) Factsheet 19, *Charging for care and support in extra care housing*, 2007, p5.

1) all residents will generally be responsible for their housing costs and for service and support charges with assistance from benefits where applicable (section 4 of the guidance);
2) service and support charges should generally be shared equally among residents of the scheme regardless of the use individuals make of the services;
3) care charges 'will more often apply only to those using care services';
4) residents with assessed care needs may pay a flat rate, an hourly rate for the care they receive, or be charged a 'banding rate';
5) in schemes where all residents have to have a minimum care requirement to be eligible for admission the flat rate may also include a basic number of care hours'.

CHAPTER 15

Group-specific care and support duties

continued

15.1 In previous editions of this book, separate chapters have been devoted to people whose needs have arisen for different reasons: age, learning disability, mental illness, substance misuse and so on. The reason for this approach arose from the fact that the legislation dealt with these groups differently.

15.2 Previous editions were critical of this legislative approach – contradictory, inconsistent and governed by 'a set of sometimes incomprehensible and frequently incompatible principles'.[1] The categories were functionally inappropriate, since need generally arises from multiple factors and they were artificial since people are individuals with continuums of identify and need – not simply 'old' or 'learning disabled', for example.

15.3 The Care Act (CA) 2014 repealed most of the Acts that created these distinctions, and in so doing removed the need for separate chapters for these categories of need. Nevertheless, there remain a number of provisions (in policy and in legislation) that are of specific relevance to people whose needs have arisen for different reasons or, in the case of prisoners, whose needs exist in different setting. These provisions are considered in this chapter, namely needs in relation to:

- older people;
- people with learning disabilities and/or autism;
- mental health service users;
- drug and alcohol misusers;
- prisoners;
- people with sensory impairments;
- disabled parents;
- young carers; and
- disabled children and carers in transition.

Older people

Background

15.4 The proportion of people aged 65 and over is growing – from 17 per cent in 2010 to an estimated 23 per cent by 2035. However, the fastest growth is in the number of people aged 85 and over. By 2035 the number of people in this age range is projected to be 2.5 times larger than in 2010, reaching 3.6 million and accounting for five per cent of the total population.[2]

15.5 In 2014/15, 42 per cent of social services' budgets was spent on people over the age of 65 (£5.12 billion after user charges and other income is taken into account).[3] In the same year, about 40 per cent of the National Health Service (NHS) budget was spent on older people (over £46 billion).[4] Social services spending on older people is therefore, as Humphries

---

1 See the 5th edition of this book, para 9.9.
2 Office of National Statistics, *Ageing*, 2011.
3 R Humphries and others, *Social care for older people: home truths*, King's Fund and Nuffield Trust, 2016, p12.
4 R Humphries and others, *Social care for older people: home truths*, King's Fund and Nuffield Trust, 2016, citing D Robineau, 'Ageing Britain: two-fifths of NHS budget is spent on over-65s', *Guardian*, 1 February 2016.

notes, relatively modest given that total public expenditure amounts to £755 billion (ie less than 0.7 per cent). Despite the steady increase in the number of older people, local authority spending on older people fell by nine per cent in real terms between 2009/10 and 2014/15.[5]

Policy framework

15.6   In response to the social and healthcare challenges posed by an ageing population, in 2001 the government published a *National service framework for older people* (NSF).[6] The NSF sets out eight key standards, providing in each case guidance on the local action required to ensure these are implemented – with detailed timescales and 'milestones to ensure progress, with performance measures to support performance improvement'. The eight standards are as follows:

Standard 1: Rooting out age discrimination. NHS services will be provided, regardless of age, on the basis of clinical need alone. Social care services will not use age in their eligibility criteria or policies, to restrict access to available services.

Standard 2: Person-centred care. NHS and social care services treat older people as individuals and enable them to make choices about their own care. This is achieved through the single assessment process, integrated commissioning arrangements and integrated provision of services, including community equipment and continence services.

Standard 3: Intermediate care. Older people will have access to a new range of intermediate care services at home or in designated care settings, to promote their independence by providing enhanced services from the NHS and councils to prevent unnecessary hospital admission and effective rehabilitation services to enable early discharge from hospital and to prevent premature or unnecessary admission to long-term residential care.

Standard 4: General hospital care. Older people's care in hospital is delivered through appropriate specialist care and by hospital staff who have the right set of skills to meet their needs.

Standard 5: Stroke. The NHS will take action to prevent strokes, working in partnership with other agencies where appropriate. People who are thought to have had a stroke have access to diagnostic services, are treated appropriately by a specialist stroke service, and subsequently, with their carers, participate in a multidisciplinary programme of secondary prevention and rehabilitation.

Standard 6: Falls. The NHS, working in partnership with councils, takes action to prevent falls and reduce resultant fractures or other injuries in their populations of older people. Older people who have fallen receive effective treatment and, with their carers, receive advice on prevention through a specialised falls service.

Standard 7: Mental health in older people. Older people who have mental health problems have access to integrated mental health services, provided by the NHS and councils to ensure effective diagnosis, treatment and support, for them and for their carers.

---

5 R Humphries and others, *Social care for older people: home truths*, King's Fund and Nuffield Trust, 2016, p12.
6 Department of Health, *National service framework for older people*, 2001.

Standard 8: The promotion of health and active life in older age. The health and well-being of older people is promoted through a co-ordinated pro-gramme of action led by the NHS with support from councils.

15.7　Despite the policy aim in the first standard – of rooting out age discrimina-tion and ensuring that age is not an element in 'eligibility criteria or poli-cies' – the reality is that many authorities have policies that disadvantage older people.[7] For example, many councils have limits (general or rigid) on the amount of domiciliary care that an older person is entitled to before a care home placement would be expected (limits that are not imposed for younger disabled people). Such policies may additionally amount to unlawful discrimination under the Equality Act (EqA) 2010: the Act con-tains no specific health or social care exceptions. A difference in treatment will only be lawful if it is a 'proportionate means of achieving a legitimate aim' (section 13(2)). In this context the Equality and Human Rights Com-mission (EHRC) give the following example:[8]

> A local authority develops a contract specification to commission a day cen-tre service primarily targeted at people aged 75 and over. Evidence suggests people in this age group are more likely to benefit from the centre because of social isolation and physical or mental health conditions. Ensuring that appropriate services are available for this age group would be a legitimate aim.

Care Act 2014 and older people

15.8　The CA 2014 repealed the previous legislation that made specific provi-sion for the social care needs of older people[9] and the statutory guidance[10] replaces the previous 'older people specific' assessment guidance.[11] Older people with care and support needs should now be assessed in the same way as all other adults in need, and the eligibility criteria are age and impairment neutral.

Learning disability and autism: policy and services

Background

15.9　Many attempts have been made to define 'learning disability' (see below), although not infrequently statistical studies adopt the relatively crude

---

7　See eg I Carruthers and J Ormondroyd, *Achieving age equality in health and social care*, Secretary of State for Health, 2009, para 5.27.

8　Equality and Human Rights Commission, *Technical guidance on age discrimination in services, public functions and associations*, 2016, para 3.19.

9　Health Services and Public Health Act 1968 s45; National Assistance Act 1948 s21; and Social Services and Social Security Adjudications Act 1983 Sch 9 – for detail of these provision as they applied to older people, see the 5th edition of this book, chapter 19.

10　Department of Health, *Care and support statutory guidance* to support implementation of Part 1 of the CA 2014 by local authorities, 2016 ('the statutory guidance').

11　In particular, HSC 2002/001: LAC (2002)1, *Guidance on the single assessment process for older people*, January 2002.

measure of IQ: typically that someone with an IQ below 70 is deemed to have a learning disability.

15.10   Estimates as to the number of adults in England with a learning disability vary, but in 2015 Public Health England put the figure at 930,400 (equivalent to 2.16 per cent of the English adult population).[12]

15.11   The number of working age adults with learning disabilities supported by English local authorities fell between 2013/14 and 2014/15 from 141,980 to 124,000.[13]

15.12   In 2013/14, the total gross expenditure by local authorities for social care for working age adults with learning disabilities was £5.38 billion, and the net figure (after deducting client contributions and other transfers) amounted to £4.6 billion. Of this, over 50 per cent was spent on long-term care in residential and nursing homes.[14]

15.13   Whereas the average life expectancy of a person with learning disabilities was estimated to be less than 20 years in 1930,[15] today the median age at death for someone with learning disabilities is 65 for men and 63 for women. This is 13 years younger than the national figure for men in the general population, and 20 years younger than that for women.[16]

15.14   It is estimated that there are about 700,000 people on the autism spectrum in the UK[17] of which about 50 per cent have an associated learning disability.[18]

Policy background

15.15   The specific needs of people with learning disabilities are such that historically they have been the focus of a number of policy initiatives. In 2001 the Department of Health published a white paper *Valuing people: a new strategy for learning disability for the 21st century*,[19] which undertook to ensure that four key principles would underpin all new proposals: 'Rights, Independence, Choice and Inclusion'. Although *Valuing people* is no longer a current policy document (it is not referred to in the statutory guidance, for example) it remains an important document in terms of 'good practice' (see para 1.56 above).

15.16   In large measure the white paper sought to ensure that existing schemes were sensitive to the needs of people with learning disabilities. It committed the government to take measures to increase the potential for people with learning disabilities to benefit from direct payments, and to improve their access to advocacy services. It proposed the development

---

12 Public Health England, *People with learning disabilities in England 2015*, 2016, p14.

13 Public Health England, *People with learning disabilities in England 2015*, 2016, p49.

14 Public Health England, *People with learning disabilities in England 2015*, 2016, p60.

15 *Mental capital and well-being: making the most of ourselves in the 21st century. Foresight mental capital and well-being project. Final Project report*, The Government Office for Science, 2008.

16 Public Health England, *People with learning disabilities in England 2015*, 2016, p15.

17 T Brugha and others, *Estimating the prevalence of autism spectrum conditions in adults*, Health and Social Care information Centre, 2012.

18 E Fombonne and others, 'Epidemiology of pervasive developmental disorders' in D Amaral and others (eds), *Autism spectrum disorders*, OUP, 2011, p99.

19 Cm 5086, March 2001.

within each local authority area of Learning Disability Partnership Boards, whose responsibility it would be to implement the adult aspects of the programme. Policy guidance followed in 2001[20] outlining the composition and responsibilities of these boards, and in 2008 this was fleshed out by more detailed practice guidance on implementation.[21]

15.17   In 2008 the Joint Committee on Human Rights[22] expressed its concern that the *Valuing people* programme appeared to have had limited 'impact in Government departments other than the Department of Health or the wider public sector' and that implementation by local authorities and individual service providers had 'patchy'. In response, in 2010 the Department of Health published a three-year strategy *Valuing people now*,[23] following which it commissioned what has become a highly influential report by Professor Mansell (the 'Mansell report'[24]) concerning the support needs of adults with profound intellectual and multiple disabilities. Subsequently, in 2010 the Department of Health published its 'delivery plan' for such services.[25]

15.18   Objectively, however, the *Valuing people* initiative has been 'left to wither on the vine'.[26] The specialist team within the Department of Health has been disbanded, and the central website no longer exists. The clear impression is that the government now considers this to be an issue to be dealt with at a local level and by Learning Disability Partnership Boards. This view is largely confirmed by the content of the 2015 policy document *Transforming care for people with learning disabilities – next steps*.[27]

Winterbourne View

15.19   The disengagement by central government was jolted by the Winterbourne View scandal in May 2011, where an undercover investigation by the BBC's Panorama programme revealed criminal abuse by staff of patients at Winterbourne View Hospital near Bristol. A flurry of Department of Health policy initiatives followed, with a 2012 Concordat[28] making

20 Department of Health, *Valuing people: a new strategy for learning disability for the 21st century: implementation guidance*, HSC 2001/016: LAC(2001)23, 2001 (statutory guidance for the purposes of Local Authority Social Services Act 1970 s7) (see para 1.39 above).

21 See Department of Health, *Planning with people towards person centred approaches – guidance for partnership boards*, 2001; and Department of Health, *Health action planning and health facilitation for people with learning disabilities: good practice guidance*, 2008, p36.

22 Joint Committee on Human Rights, *A life like any other? Human rights of adults with learning disabilities*, HL 40-I/HC 73-I, 2008, para 104.

23 See eg Department of Health, *Valuing people now: a new three-year strategy for people with learning disabilities*, 2009.

24 J Mansell, *Raising our sights: services for adults with profound intellectual and multiple disabilities*, Department of Health, 2010.

25 Department of Health, *Valuing people now: the delivery plan 2010–2011 'making it happen for everyone'*, 2010

26 Rescare, *Valuing people & valuing people now*, 2015.

27 Department of Health, Health Education England, NHS England, ADASS, CQC and the LGA, *Transforming care for people with learning disabilities – next steps*, 2015.

28 Department of Health, *Winterbourne View review: concordat: a programme of action*, 2012.

the commitment that everyone who was inappropriately placed in hospital would be moved to a community-based setting by 1 June 2014. This commitment failed – indeed more people were admitted inappropriately after this than discharged. A subsequent 2014 review[29] expressed concern that the (p15):

> ... intense focus on ... people currently in inpatient settings ... must not be at the expense of catering for the larger number at risk of admission. Failure to do better for them will result in failure to reduce inpatient numbers overall.

The reported added (para 1.2):

> People with learning disabilities and/or autism and their families have an array of rights in law or Government policy - through human rights law, the Equalities Act, the NHS constitution, the Mental Health Act, the Care Act, the Mental Capacity Act, the UN Convention on the Rights of Persons with Disabilities, and so on ... [but] the lived experience of people with learning disabilities and/or autism and their families is too often very different. Too often they feel powerless, their rights unclear, misunderstood.

15.20   It will be the responsibility of health and social services bodies to meet the care and support needs of people who are resettled into community-based placements under their standard statutory duties – ie (as the case may be) the CA 2014 (see para 4.55 above), Mental Health Act (MHA) 1983 s117 (see para 15.56 below) or under the National Health Service Act (NHSA) 2006 by way of NHS continuing healthcare funding (NHS CC) (see para 12.44 above).

Definition and IQ

15.21   *Valuing people* did not attempt an exhaustive definition of what constitutes a learning disability, but it stated that it includes the presence of (para 1.5):

> A significantly reduced ability to understand new or complex information, to learn new skills (impaired intelligence), with a reduced ability to cope independently (impaired social functioning) which started before adulthood, with a lasting effect on development.

15.22   The report cautioned against overreliance on IQ scores (at para 1.6). Not infrequently, however, local authorities do define learning disability in such terms – typically having a score of less than 70. There has been substantial criticism of such an approach,[30] and reliance on this fact alone could not be considered a rational way of approaching the social care assessment duty. Although the Department of Health's definition includes many people with (among other conditions) autism, as noted above, only about 50 per cent of people with autism have an associated learning disability.

---

29 Transforming Care and Commissioning Steering Group, chaired by Sir Stephen Bubb, *Winterbourne View – time for change: transforming the commissioning of services for people with learning disabilities and/or autism*, 2014.

30 There is an extensive literature on this question, but see eg D Francis and others, 'Defining learning and language disabilities' (1996) 27 *Language, Speech, and Hearing Services in Schools* 132–143; and L Siegel 'IQ is irrelevant to the definition of learning disabilities' (1989) 22(8) *The Journal of Learning Disabilities* 469–478, 486.

Care Act 2014 and learning disability

15.23 All eligible adults 'in need' are entitled to the full range of social care services under the CA 2014 and the NHSA 2006. The Care and Support (Eligibility Criteria) Regulations 2015 SI No 313 ('eligibility criteria regulations 2015') refer to the need arising from (or relating to) 'a physical or mental impairment or illness'.[31] It follows that people who have a learning disability of any description come within this definition.

15.24 Since the CA 2014 is impairment neutral, local authorities will have to address the eligible needs of all adults. If an authority decides to have a specialist learning disability team and its terms of reference exclude a person with (for example 'high functioning autism), that may not be unreasonable. The authority must, however, be able to point the individual to a responsible specialist who was authority to address the individual's eligible CA 2014 needs.[32] A 2015 local government ombudsman report[33] concerned a local authority that refused to accept responsibility for people with Asperger Syndrome, signposting them instead to an NHS trust. As the ombudsman noted, the local authority 'appears to assume this absolves it of all responsibility to them. This is incorrect. The Council cannot delegate its duty' in this way.

15.25 Any discussion of the rights of people with learning disabilities to social care intersects with two fundamental and cross-cutting legal themes. First, the Mental Capacity Act (MCA) 2005 and the importance of early consideration of the requirements of this Act when undertaking any assessment or care planning exercise; the requirements of the MCA 2005 are considered at chapter 13. Second, the impact of the EqA 2010. Although detailed consideration of this Act are outside the scope of this book (but see para 2.46 above), the importance of considering the obligations it creates should always be borne in mind. The local government ombudsman made this point in a 2012 report, stating that:

> A failure to take into account a person's learning disabilities will breach the legal obligation under disability discrimination law. In particular – not realising that this might account for the reasons why a person missed hospital appointments, or why a person became 'very agitated' – and such cases make it particularly important that staff listen to the people who know the patient best – is the social care team and person's family. [34]

Autism Act 2009

15.26 The Autism Act (AA) 2009 originated as a private member's bill, promoted by Cheryl Gillan MP. It requires the secretary of state to publish an 'autism strategy' for meeting the needs of adults in England with autistic spectrum

---

31 Eligibility criteria regulations 2015 reg 2(1)(a) – see para 4.11 above.
32 A failure of a local authority to address the needs of such a person may also raise questions under the EqA 2010 – see eg *Dunham v Ashford Windows* [2005] IRLR 608, EAT.
33 Complaint no 13 019 566 against Somerset CC, 30 September 2015, para 37.
34 Parliamentary and Health Service Ombudsman, *Listening and learning: the ombudsman's review of complaint handling by the NHS in England 2011–12*, HC 695, The Stationery Office, 2012, pp22–23.

conditions by improving the provision of relevant services to such adults by local authorities, NHS bodies and NHS foundation trusts.

15.27   The first strategy was published in 2010[35] and lists actions necessary to improve health, social care and other public services for people with autism (including action to improve employment and staff training). It emphasises (among other things) the need for staff training; clear procedures and 'pathways' to enable speedy diagnosis; and the fact that people with autism have a right to a social care assessments even if they have average or above average IQ. Further guidance followed in 2010[36] concerning the adjustments that the strategy required to existing programmes and practices (ie increasing awareness and understanding of autism among frontline professionals and improving access to the services and work) without creating a new architecture of specific obligations.

15.28   Section 2 of the Act requires guidance to be issued to health and social care bodies (see para 1.64 above) which the Act specifies (section 2(5)) 'must in particular include' guidance about:

(a) the provision of relevant services for the purpose of diagnosing autistic spectrum conditions in adults;
(b) the identification of adults with such conditions;
(c) the assessment of the needs of adults with such conditions for relevant services;
(d) planning in relation to the provision of relevant services to persons with autistic spectrum conditions as they move from being children to adults;
(e) other planning in relation to the provision of relevant services to adults with autistic spectrum conditions;
(f) the training of staff who provide relevant services to adults with such conditions;
(g) local arrangements for leadership in relation to the provision of relevant services to adults with such conditions.

15.29   Guidance in compliance with section 2 was issued in 2010[37] focusing on key areas where it was thought that health and social care bodies could practically change the way they support adults with autism – namely by: (1) increasing understanding of autism amongst staff; (2) strengthening diagnosis and assessment of needs; (3) improving transition support for young people with autism; and (4) ensuring adults with autism are included within local service planning.

15.30   In April 2014 the guidance was updated by *Think autism*,[38] and in 2015 by revised statutory guidance: *Statutory guidance for local authorities and NHS organisations to support implementation of the adult autism strategy.*[39]

35 Department of Health, *Fulfilling and rewarding lives – an adult autism strategy for England*, 2010.
36 Department of Health, *Towards 'fulfilling and rewarding lives': the first year delivery plan for adults with autism in England*, 2010.
37 Department of Health, *Implementing 'fulfilling and rewarding lives': statutory guidance for local authorities and NHS organisations to support implementation of the autism strategy*, 2010.
38 Department of Health, *Think Autism. Fulfilling and rewarding lives, the strategy for adults with autism in England: an update*, 2014.
39 Department of Health, *Statutory guidance for local authorities and NHS organisations to support implementation of the adult autism strategy*, 2015.

The autism guidance is issued under section 2 of Act (see paras 1.64 and 15.29) and explains (para 8) that the term 'autism' is used as an as an umbrella term for all autistic spectrum conditions, including Asperger Syndrome, adding that:

> Many people with autism also have related hidden impairments such as attention deficit hyperactivity disorder, dyspraxia, dyslexia, dyscalculia and language impairments as well as associated mental health conditions and linked impairments that may not be obvious to other people.

15.31 The 2015 autism guidance places particular focus on seven issues, namely:

(1) Training of staff who provide services to adults with autism
The 2015 autism guidance notes that this requirement is reinforced by the Care and Support (Assessment) Regulations 2014 SI No 2827 that require authorities 'to ensure that a person undertaking an assessment of an adult's care and support needs has suitable skills, knowledge and competence in the assessment they are undertaking, and is appropriately trained' (see in this context para 15.28 above) (para 1.3).

The statutory guidance to the CA 2014 emphasises the importance of appropriately trained and competent assessors who undergo regular, up-to-date training on an ongoing basis with 'skills and knowledge to carry out an assessment of needs that relate to a specific condition or circumstances requiring expert insight – for example, when assessing an individual who has autism, learning disabilities, mental health needs or dementia' (para 6.86). It also stresses the need for specialists or interpreters to support communication difficulties by people with 'Autistic Spectrum Disorder or Profound and Multiple Learning Disabilities' (para 6.23 and see also para 6.39).

(2) Identification and diagnosis of autism in adults, leading to assessment of needs for relevant services
The 2015 autism guidance notes the importance of diagnosis, especially for 'adults who did not have their condition or sensory issues recognised as children' (para 2.1). It states that although local authorities have (para 2.2):

> ... lead commissioning for care and support services for people with autism, [clinical commissioning groups (CCGs)] are expected to take the lead responsibility for commissioning of diagnostic services to identify people with autism, and work with local authorities to provide post-diagnostic support for people with autism.

The guidance adds that each local authority must have 'an easily accessible autism diagnostic service', although it is not 'expected that a specialist diagnostic team will be located in all areas' (para 2.6).

(3) Planning in relation to the provision of services for people with autism as they move from being children to adults
See para 15.195 below.

(4) Local planning and leadership in relation to the provision of services for adults with autism

The 2015 autism guidance requires that local authorities and NHS bodies (para 4.1):

> ... develop commissioning plans for services for adults with autism and review them annually. Local authorities should also allocate responsibility to a named joint commissioner/senior manager to lead commissioning of care and support services for adults with autism.

It adds that 'Health and Wellbeing Boards have a crucial role to play in overseeing implementation of the Adult Autism Strategy' (para 4.6).

(5) Preventative support and safeguarding in line with the CA 2014

See para 9.2 above.

(6) Reasonable adjustments and equality

(7) Supporting people with complex needs, whose behaviour may challenge or who may lack capacity

The 2015 autism guidance requires that:

> People with autism should be assessed, treated and cared for in the community wherever possible, and when they need to go into inpatient care it should be for the minimum time necessary and in a facility close to their home. Having complex needs does not mean people should go into long-term inpatient, residential care or assessment and treatment centres inappropriately or indefinitely.

Service reconfigurations

15.32   The 2001 *Valuing people* white paper sought to address the severe social exclusion experienced by many people with learning disabilities by endeavouring (among other things) to bring about service reconfigurations including (para 4.19) a requirement that local bodies make 'significant progress' in relation to the reduction in the use of large day centres. In the government's opinion (at para 1.18) some of these offered little more than 'warehousing'. Authorities were to replace these services with flexible and individual support (para 7.25).

15.33   Since the turn of the century there has been a large-scale closure of day centres, and not infrequently users and carers have questioned whether the replacement provision has proved to be an 'improvement'. Challenges to such closures have resulted in limited litigation (see, for example, para 7.135 above). As a general rule, the courts have required, not only evidence that the authority has addressed the community care impact on individual users of the closure, but also (where they lack the necessary mental capacity to choose their care support) that a best interests assessment has been undertaken (see para 13.31 above). A 2011 judgment[40] illustrates the importance of such an assessment, since it ensures that an individual's well-being is not sacrificed on the twin alters of dogma and budgetary advantage – or as the court expressed it: 'guideline policies cannot be

---

40   *AH v Hertfordshire Partnership NHS Foundation Trust and Ealing PCT* [2011] EWHC 276 (COP), (2011) 14 CCLR 301 para 80 – and see also para 13.80 above.

treated as universal solutions, nor should initiatives designed to personal-ise care and promote choice be applied to the opposite effect'.

NHS learning disability funding transfer

15.34 In 2007 the government announced its intention[41] to transfer funding for all learning disability social care services from the NHS to local govern-ment. The transfer proved to be a complex and contentious operation,[42] and follow-up guidance in 2009[43] addressed a number of difficult issues. These included: (1) the so-called 'campus closure' programme, namely that all NHS facilities/campuses accommodating people with learning disabilities were to be closed[44] by the end of 2010 with their running costs being transferred in advance of the closure to the relevant local authority; and (2) attempts by some health bodies to reduce their funding transfer to councils by deciding that some residents in fact qualified for NHS con-tinuing healthcare funding and then proposing to deduct the cost of those residents from the amount for transfer; the guidance advised that this was unacceptable.

Mental health: policy and services

Background

15.35 Mental ill health in the UK is the largest single cause of disability and represents up to 23 per cent of the total burden of ill health.[45] At least one in four people will experience a mental health problem at some point in their life,[46] and at any one time approximately one in six people of working age have a mental health problem (most often anxiety or depression) and over a lifetime about one in 50 people will have schizophrenia or a bipolar affective disorder.[47]

15.36 There is little doubt that mental health support services are under severe pressure.[48] In 2015 the Care Quality Commission (CQC)[49] concluded that the service provided was, overall, 'unsafe and inherently unfair'. Over the last decade there has been a steady increase in the use of compulsory

---

41 Department of Health, *Valuing people now: from progress to transformation*, 2007, para 1.4.3.

42 See eg V Pitt, 'Progress report on *Valuing people now*', *Community Care*, 15 January 2010.

43 Department of Health, Letter 17 December 2009 to PCT/LA LD Commissioners: *Transfer of commissioning and funding of social care for adults with learning disabilities from the NHS to local government*, 2009.

44 A commitment made by the government in Department of Health, *Our health, our care, our say: a new direction for community services* Cm 6737, 2006, para 4.90.

45 Department of Health, *No health without mental health: a cross-government mental health outcomes strategy for people of all ages*, 2011, p10.

46 Department of Health, *No health without mental health: a cross-government mental health outcomes strategy for people of all ages*, 2011, p8.

47 Perala and others, 'Lifetime prevalence of psychotic and bipolar I disorders in a general population' in *Archives of General Psychiatry* (2007) 64:19–28.

48 See generally King's Fund, *Mental health under pressure*, 2015.

49 CQC, *Right here, right now – help, care and support during a mental health crisis*, 2015.

detentions under the MHA 1983, with an almost ten per cent increase between 2014 and 2015.[50] Although the increase is attributable to a variety of reasons, it appears that (perversely) the shortage of suitable beds is a significant factor: that unless a patient is sectioned they are unlikely to get a bed.[51]

15.37   People who have a mental disorder of any description are entitled to the full range of social care services under the CA 2014 and the NHSA 2006. Some, however, are entitled in addition to distinct care and support services under MHA 1983 s117 (considered at para 15.56 below).

National service framework for mental health

15.38   There have been many national policy initiatives to improve the care and support provided for people with mental health difficulties in the last two decades. In 1999 the government published a *National service framework for mental health*[52] (NSF). The NSF was reviewed and its scope widened in 2004,[53] and in 2011 the coalition government published a new mental health strategy.[54]

15.39   The 1999 mental health NSF set out seven key standards together with detailed guidance on the local action required to ensure these were implemented. The standards concerned: (1) mental health promotion; (2) and (3) primary care and access to services; (4) and (5) effective services for people with severe mental illness; (6) caring about carers; and (7) preventing suicide.

15.40   The 2011 strategy listed six 'outcomes', namely that: (1) more people will have good mental health; (2) more people with mental health problems will recover and (3) will have good physical health; (4) more people will have a positive experience of care and support; and (5) fewer people will suffer avoidable harm and (6) experience stigma and discrimination.

15.41   A 2015 review[55] of these various mental health transformation initiatives concluded that they had failed to deliver on many of their targets, not least because the necessary funding and workforce requirements were underestimated. A separate 2015 review[56] noted that these policy initiatives represented 'a leap in the dark, with little formal evaluation to indicate impact on the quality of or access to care'.

50 Health and Social Care Information Centre, *Inpatients formerly detained in hospitals under the Mental Health Act 1983: annual statistics, 2014/15.*

51 Royal College of Psychiatrists, *Trainee psychiatrist survey reveals mental health beds crisis*, 2014, cited in King's Fund, *Mental health under pressure*, 2015.

52 Department of Health, *A national service framework for mental health: modern standards and service model*, 1999.

53 Department of Health, *A National Service Framework for Mental Health – five years on*, 2004.

54 Department of Health, *No health without mental health: a cross-government mental health outcomes strategy for people of all ages*, 2011 – which superseded Department of Health, *New horizons: a shared vision for mental health*, 2009.

55 King's Fund case study 2: *The national service framework for mental health in England*, 2015.

56 See generally King's Fund, *Mental health under pressure*, 2015, p17.

The care programme approach

Background

15.42 The care programme approach (CPA) was introduced by a joint health/ social services circular.[57] Health authorities were given lead responsibility for implementing the policy, although there was an obligation on health and social services authorities to reach formal and detailed inter-agency agreements to ensure its full implementation.[58] The Department of Health has consistently stressed the importance it attaches to the CPA, which has been subject to revisions[59] culminating with the current 2008 guidance (the 'CPA guidance').[60] In many respects the CPA can be viewed as a specialised social care assessment – and the relationship between these two processes is considered below.

15.43 The 2008 CPA guidance applies to persons who are entitled to support from secondary mental health services and 'who have complex characteristics'. There is no specific intervention under the MHA 1983, that triggers entitlement although anyone subject to a Community Treatment or Guardianship Order (under MHA 1983 s17A and s7 respectively) will be subject to the 2008 CPA regime unless for 'reasons ... clearly documented in care records' it is not considered appropriate.[61]

15.44 People in contact with secondary mental health services will be subject to the 2008 CPA if one or more of the following factors are considered to be relevant to their situation:[62]

- severe mental disorder (including personality disorder) with high degree of clinical complexity;
- current or potential risk(s), including:
  - suicide, self-harm, harm to others (including history of offending);
  - relapse history requiring urgent response;
  - self-neglect/non concordance with treatment plan;
  - vulnerable adult; adult/child protection, eg:
    - exploitation, eg financial/sexual;
    - financial difficulties related to mental illness;
    - disinhibition;
    - physical/emotional abuse;
    - cognitive impairment;
    - child protection issues;
- current or significant history of severe distress/instability or disengagement;

---

57 HC (90)23: LASSL (90)11.

58 Department of Health, *Social services departments and the care programme approach: an SSI inspection report*, 1995, para 4.3.11.

59 See Department of Health, *Guidance on the discharge of mentally disordered people and their continuing care in the community*, HSG (94)27: LASSL (94)4, 1994; Department of Health, *Audit pack for monitoring the care programme approach*, (1996; and Department of Health, *Effective care co-ordination in mental health services: modernising the care programme approach – a policy booklet*, 1999.

60 Department of Health, *Refocusing the care programme approach: policy and positive practice guidance*, 2008.

61 2008 CPA guidance, pp14–15.

62 2008 CPA guidance, table 2.

- presence of non-physical co-morbidity, eg, substance/alcohol/prescription drugs misuse, learning disability;
- multiple service provision from different agencies, including: housing, physical care, employment, criminal justice, voluntary agencies;
- currently/recently detained under MHA 1983 or referred to crisis/ home treatment team;
- significant reliance on carer(s) or has own significant caring responsibilities;
- experiencing disadvantage or difficulty as a result of:
  - parenting responsibilities;
  - physical health problems/disability;
  - unsettled accommodation/housing issues;
  - employment issues when mentally ill;
  - significant impairment of function due to mental illness;
  - ethnicity issues (eg, immigration status; race/cultural issues; language difficulties; religious practices); sexuality issues; or gender issues.

15.45 Notwithstanding the above list of individuals qualifying for CPA, the evidence suggested that some key groups were not 'being identified consistently and that services are sometimes failing to provide the support they need'.[63] Accordingly, the 2008 CPA guidance creates a presumption that the following categories of person (in contact with secondary mental health services) will qualify for the CPA 'unless a thorough assessment of need and risks shows otherwise' – those:[64]

- who have parenting responsibilities;
- who have significant caring responsibilities;
- with a dual diagnosis (substance misuse);
- with a history of violence or self-harm;
- who are in unsettled accommodation.

15.46 Chapter 34 of the MHA 1983 code of practice (2015),[65] provides additional detail on CPA assessment and care planning requirements, including who should be involved in this process – stressing for example that 'professionals with specialist expertise should also be involved in care planning for people with autistic spectrum disorders or learning disabilities' (para 34.21).

15.47 The 2015 code states that care planning under the CPA 'is likely to involve consideration of' (para 34.19):

- continuing mental healthcare, whether in the community or on an outpatient basis;
- the psychological needs of the patient and, where appropriate, of their carers;
- physical healthcare;
- daytime activities or employment;
- appropriate accommodation;

63 2008 CPA guidance, p14.
64 2008 CPA guidance, p14.
65 Department of Health, *Mental Health Act 1983: code of practice*, The Stationery Office, 2015.

- identified risks and safety issues;
- any specific needs arising from, eg co-existing physical disability, sensory impairment, learning disability or autistic spectrum disorder;
- any specific needs arising from drug, alcohol or substance misuse (if relevant);
- any parenting or caring needs;
- social, cultural or spiritual needs;
- counselling and personal support;
- assistance in welfare rights and managing finances;
- involvement of authorities and agencies in a different area, if the patient is not going to live locally;
- the involvement of other agencies, eg the probation service or voluntary organisations (if relevant);
- for a restricted patient, the conditions which the Secretary of State for Justice or the first-tier tribunal has – or is likely to – impose on their conditional discharge; and
- contingency plans (should the patient's mental health deteriorate) and crisis contact details.

15.48　In relation to the content of the resulting CPA care plan, the 2015 code advises that it should include (para 34.3):

- a treatment plan which details medical, nursing, psychological and other therapeutic support for the purpose of meeting individual needs promoting recovery and/or preventing deterioration;
- details regarding any prescribed medications;
- details of any actions to address physical health problems or reduce the likelihood of health inequalities;
- details of how the person will be supported to achieve his or her personal goals;
- support provided in relation to social needs such as housing, occupation, finances etc;
- support provided to carers;
- actions to be taken in the event of a deterioration of a person's presentation; and
- guidance on actions to be taken in the event of a crisis.

15.49　It will constitute maladministration not to have a detailed MHA 1983 s117 after-care plan that details all the individual's identified after-care needs on discharge from hospital and how they will be met: this is especially important in relation to accommodation – so as to be clear what the responsibilities are in this respect. [66]

Review

15.50　At every formal CPA review, consideration must be given as to whether the support provided as part of the CPA intervention is still needed. However, the 2008 CPA guidance cautions against withdrawing support prematurely and distinguishes between CPA support and other services (eg

---

66　Joint Report: Local Government and Health Service Ombudsmen: Complaint no 11 020 010 against Plymouth Council and NHS Plymouth PCT, May 2014 at para 64.

social care support services – see para 15.54 below). CPA support can only be withdrawn after a formal review which satisfies the requirements of the guidance – including the production of a care plan detailing who is to take over day to day responsibility and which contains 'a clear statement about the action to take, and who to contact, in the event of relapse or change with a potential negative impact on that person's mental well-being'.[67]

15.51   The ombudsman has held it to be maladministration not to have six-monthly reviews – which should be thorough and not perfunctory. [68]

CPA and social care/section 117 assessments

15.52   The relationship between the administrative obligation on joint NHS/ social services teams to prepare CPA assessments and the social services duties to assess the social care support needs of people with mental health difficulties (considered at para 15.55 below) has on occasions been misunderstood.

15.53   In a number of respects the CPA can be considered to be a formalised social care assessment and care planning process. However, in some respects it is distinct – for example, it is often undertaken by an NHS employee and is largely directed at providing care coordination – via an expert key worker or 'care co-ordinator'.[69] Those subject to the CPA have a right to a level of support which goes beyond the core entitlement of any social care service user, notably a right to:

- a comprehensive multi-disciplinary, multi-agency assessment covering the full range of needs;
- a comprehensive formal written care plan, including a risk and safety/ contingency/crisis plan;
- ongoing review, formal multi-disciplinary, multi-agency review at least once a year but generally more frequently; and
- increased advocacy support.

15.54   Once a person is no longer in need of the level of intensive support provided by the CPA, the person may still require ongoing support from health and social services. As the 2008 CPA guidance states (p15):

> ... it is important that service users and their carers are reassured that when the support provided by .... CPA is no longer needed that this will not remove their entitlement to receive any services for which they continue to be eligible and need, either from the NHS, local council, or other services.

15.55   The interplay between the obligations under the CPA and the social care legislation was considered in *R (HP and KP) v Islington LBC*.[70] The case concerned a patient being cared for by his family at home. He was assessed by the psychiatric services as suffering from a form of depression

---

67   2008 CPA guidance p15.
68   Joint Report: Local Government and Health Service Ombudsmen: Complaint no 11 020 010 against Plymouth Council and NHS Plymouth PCT, May 2014 at para 33.
69   Page 36 of the 2008 CPA guidance describes who can be the care co-ordinator, and states that it 'should usually be taken by the person who is best placed to oversee care management and resource allocation and can be of any discipline depending on capability and capacity'.
70   [2004] EWHC 7 (Admin), (2005) 82 BMLR 113.

and at risk of severe neglect and 'vulnerable to deterioration in his mental state particularly if he stops taking his medication'. He was, however, considered not to have a 'severe and enduring mental illness' and was therefore deemed ineligible for CPA support. In view of this finding the local authority determined that he was not eligible for 'community care provision'. In quashing this decision, Munby J held that the authority had misunderstood the relationship between the CPA and the duty to assess for social care needs. The fact that the patient lacked a severe and enduring mental illness ... was not determinative of whether he nonetheless had a need for generic health or social services community care'.[71]

Services under Mental Health Act 1983 s117

15.56   Most care and support provided by local authorities for people with a mental health difficulty is delivered under the CA 2014. Support under the Act is available to all adults in need, and the Care and Support (Eligibility Criteria) Regulations 2015 SI No 313 ('eligibility criteria regulations 2015') refer to the need arising from (or relating to) 'a physical or mental impairment or illness'.[72]

15.57   Only a small minority of people who receive community care services are entitled to their services under MHA 1983 s117. The full text of the section (including sections 117A and 117B) is provided at appendix A below. The section places a joint responsibility on the NHS and social services to provide 'after-care' services for persons who are in hospital as a result of being detained/transferred/admitted under MHA 1983 s3,[73] s37,[74] s45A,[75] s47[76] or s48[77] – 'and then cease to be detained and (whether or not immediately after so ceasing) leave hospital'.

The assessment duty under section 117

15.58   Under the pre-CA 2014 statutory regime section 117 services were defined as 'community care services'[78] and National Health Service and Community Care Act (NHSCCA) 1990 placed a duty on local authorities to assess those who might be in need of community care services.

---

71 [2004] EWHC 7 (Admin), (2005) 82 BMLR 113 at [37].

72 Reg 2(1)(a); see para 4.11 above.

73 Where a patient is admitted for treatment (as opposed to being admitted under MHA 1983 s2 for assessment).

74 Where a patient is detained by a criminal court after being convicted of a serious criminal offence and the court being satisfied (among other things) that at the time of conviction the offender was suffering from a mental disorder.

75 An order (subject to certain provisos) made by a Crown Court when sentencing a person who has a mental disorder which makes it appropriate that he or she be detained in a specified hospital.

76 Persons serving a sentence of imprisonment for whom the secretary of state is satisfied (among other things) that they are suffering from a mental disorder and should in consequences be removed and detained in a hospital.

77 As for NHSCCA 1990 s47 above, save only it applies to persons who, although detained, are not serving a sentence of imprisonment (eg, they are on remand pending trial, are civil prisoners or being detained under the Immigration Act 1971).

78 NHSCCA 1990 s46(3).

15.59   The CA 2014 contains no equivalent provision. It follows that the duty
to assess an adult in need under the 2014 Act only relates to the needs that
can be satisfied by the 2014 Act. It would appear that it was only during the
implementation of the 2014 reforms that it was appreciated that the repeal
of the NHSCCA 1990 would remove the statutory duty to assess individuals for their needs under MHA 1983 s117. In consequence, NHSCCA 1990
s47 has been amended (but not repealed). Materially it now provides:

> (1) Subject to subsections (5) and (6) below, where it appears to a local
>   authority that any person for whom they may provide or arrange for the
>   provision of services under section 117 of the Mental Health Act 1983
>   may be in need of any such services, the authority–
>   (a) shall carry out an assessment of his needs for those services; and
>   (b) having regard to the results of that assessment, shall then decide
>   whether his needs call for the provision by them of any such
>   services.
>   ...
> (3) If at any time during the assessment of the needs of any person under
>   subsection (1)(a) above, it appears to a local authority–
>   (za) that there may be a need for the provision to that person, pursu-
>   ant to arrangements made under the National Health Service Act
>   2006 by such clinical commissioning group as may be determined
>   in accordance with regulations, of any services[79]
>   ...
>   (b) that there may be a need for the provision to him of any services
>   which fall within the functions of a local housing authority (within
>   the meaning of the Housing Act 1985) which is not the local author-
>   ity carrying out the assessment,
>   the local authority shall notify that clinical commissioning group, ... or
>   local housing authority and invite them to assist, to such extent as is
>   reasonable in the circumstances, in the making of the assessment; and,
>   in making their decision as to the provision of the services needed for
>   the person in question, the local authority shall take into account any
>   services which are likely to be made available for him by that clinical
>   commissioning group ... or local housing authority.
>   ...
> (5) Nothing in this section shall prevent a local authority from temporarily
>   providing or arranging for the provision of services mentioned in sub-
>   section (1) for any person without carrying out a prior assessment of his
>   needs in accordance with the preceding provisions of this section if, in
>   the opinion of the authority, the condition of that person is such that he
>   requires those services as a matter of urgency.
> (6) If, by virtue of subsection (5) above, services have been provided tempor-
>   arily for any person as a matter of urgency, then, as soon as practicable
>   thereafter, an assessment of his needs shall be made in accordance with
>   the preceding provisions of this section.

15.60   It follows that the assessment of a person's needs for care and support
under MHA 1983 s117 is not subject to the CA 2014 eligibility criteria
regulations 2015,[80] and indeed the assessment and care planning process

---

79 Including public health services for which the secretary of state is responsible under
    NHSA 2006 s7A and see also the National Health Service Commissioning Board and
    Clinical Commissioning Groups (Responsibilities and Standing Rules) Regulations
    2012 SI No 2996 Part 4 (Mental health after-care services).
80 See para 4.6 above.

is independent of the statutory guidance insofar as it describes the CA 2014 requirements. While the statutory guidance advises (annex A para 45) that section 117 care planning should be undertaken in accordance with the 'guidance on the Care Programme Approach', the process must also comply with the guidance in chapter 33 of the MHA code of practice (2015),[81] discussed below.

15.61 Although the duty to provide care and support services under MHA 1983 s117 only arises when the person is discharged from hospital, there must be an obligation on health and social services to undertake assessments when it is reasonably clear that the person is likely to be discharged within the not distant future. In a 2006 local government ombudsman report it was held that a failure to undertake an expeditious social care assessment which resulted in the delay in discharging a compulsorily detained patient constituted maladministration.[82]

15.62 This importance of timely assessments is reinforced by the following extracts from the MHA code of practice:

> 33.10 Although the duty to provide after-care begins when the patient leaves hospital, the planning of after-care needs to start as soon as the patient is admitted to hospital. CCGs and local authorities should take reasonable steps, in consultation with the care programme approach care co-ordinator and other members of the multidisciplinary team to identify appropriate after-care services for patients in good time for their eventual discharge from hospital or prison.
>
> 33.11 When considering relevant patients' cases, the Tribunal and hospital managers will expect to be provided with information from the professionals concerned on what after-care arrangements might be made if they were to be discharged. Some discussion of after-care arrangements involving local authorities, other relevant agencies and families or carers (where appropriate) should take place in advance of the Tribunal hearing

The nature of the section 117 duty

15.63 The duty to provide after care services under MHA 1983 s117 crystallises when the person 'ceases to be detained'. The nature of the duty under section 117, and the meaning of the phrase 'ceases to be detained', have been considered in a number of diverse fact cases, including by the Court of Appeal in *R (K) v Camden and Islington Health Authority*[83] and the House of Lords in *R (IH) v Secretary of State for the Home Department and others*.[84] From these decisions, it appears that the section 117 duty:

1) only arises on the patient's discharge from hospital, although the NHS body has the power to take preparatory steps prior to discharge.[85]

---

81 Department of Health, *Mental Health Act 1983: code of practice*, The Stationery Office, 2015.

82 Complaint no 04/B/01280 against York City Council, 31 January 2006 – see also *R (K) v Camden and Islington Health Authority* [2001] EWCA Civ 240, (2001) 4 CCLR 170 at [20].

83 [2001] EWCA Civ 240, (2001) 4 CCLR 170.

84 [2003] UKHL 59, (2004) 7 CCLR 147.

85 *R (K) v Camden and Islington Health Authority* [2001] EWCA Civ 240, (2001) 4 CCLR 170 at [20].

In *R (B) v Camden LBC and others*[86] Stanley Burnton J held that no express duty to take steps to secure after-care services arose until the health/social services authorities were informed of the discharge of a detainee;

2) insofar as it relates to the provision of ordinary social care services, there is a specific duty (see para 1.16 above) to ensure that these services are made available;[87]

3) insofar as it relates to the provision of personal/professional services (most notably by the NHS in the form of securing a psychiatrist prepared to accept responsibility for the patient on discharge into the community), the duty is merely to 'use its best endeavours to procure' the services it deems necessary (or those specified by a mental health review tribunal).[88]

15.64   MHA 1983 s117 services are also available to patients on MHA 1983 s17 leave.[89] Section 17 provides that a 'responsible clinician' may authorise leave of absence to patients detained under Part II of the Act (ie under non-criminal detention). This entitlement arises because section 117 services are available to persons who are detained under (amongst others) section 3 and then 'cease to be detained and (whether or not immediately after so ceasing) leave hospital'. A person can therefore be entitled to section 117 services even though still formally detained under section 3, since the crucial question is whether or not he or she is physically detained in a hospital rather than legally 'liable to be detained' under MHA 1983 s3.

Services

15.65   CA 2014 s75(5) amended the MHA 1983 by inserting section 117(6), which provides that 'after-care services' for the purposes of MHA 1983 s117 means:

> ... services which have both of the following purposes–
> (a) meeting a need arising from or related to the person's mental disorder; and
> (b) reducing the risk of a deterioration of the person's mental condition (and, accordingly, reducing the risk of the person requiring admission to a hospital again for treatment for mental disorder).

15.66   Prior to this amendment, although 'after-care' was not defined by the MHA 1983, the courts had held that section 117 support services were restricted to those necessary to meet a need arising from a person's mental

---

86   [2005] EWHC 1366 (Admin), (2005) 8 CCLR 422 at [66]–[67].

87   *R v Ealing District Health Authority ex p Fox* [1993] 1 WLR 373, QBD.

88   *R (IH) v Secretary of State for the Home Department and others* [2003] UKHL 59, (2004) 7 CCLR 147 at para 29; and see also in this regard *R (K) v Camden and Islington Health Authority* [2001] EWCA Civ 240, (2001) 4 CCLR 170.

89   See Department of Health, *Mental Health Act 1983: code of practice* The Stationery Office, 2015, para 27.26; and *R v Richmond LBC and others ex p Watson and others* (1999) 2 CCLR 402, QBD.

disorder.[90] In *Clunis v Camden and Islington Health Authority*,[91] Beldam LJ considered that these:

> ... would normally include social work, support in helping the ex-patient with problems of employment, accommodation[92] or family relationships, the provision of domiciliary services and the use of day centre and residential facilities.

15.67 In *R (Mwanza) v Greenwich LBC and Bromley LBC*[93] Hickinbottom J was not prepared to rule that the provision of 'bare accommodation' (ie a tenancy and nothing else) could not be provided under section 117 – but in his view this would only be possible very exceptionally. However, the court in *R (Afework) v Camden LBC*[94] was of the view that in no circumstances could a 'mere roof over the head' be provided under section 117. In the court's opinion this was simply a question of statutory construction – that 'after-care':

> ... is a single compound noun with two components viz 'after-care' and 'services'. The hyphenated linking of the word 'after' with 'care' within the first component shows that the services in question must be consequential to the detention in hospital.

15.68 In reaching this conclusion, the court was 'fortified' by the finding in *R (Gary Baisden) v Leicester City Council*[95] where it was held that there was only a duty under section 117 to provide 'accommodation plus' – ie 'specialised accommodation with elements of support'.

15.69 The MHA code of practice (2015) advises support needs could include (para 34.19):

- the psychological needs of the patient and, where appropriate, of the patient's carers;
- physical healthcare;
- daytime activities or employment;
- appropriate accommodation;
- identified risks and safety issues;
- any specific needs arising from, eg co-existing physical disability, sensory impairment, learning disability or autistic spectrum disorder;
- any specific needs arising from drug, alcohol or substance misuse (if relevant);
- any parenting or caring needs.

A joint health/social services duty

15.70 In *R v Mental Health Review Tribunal ex p Hall*[96] the Divisional Court held that the duty to provide after-care services under MHA 1983 s117(2) was

90 See, for example, *R (Mwanza) v Greenwich LBC and Bromley LBC* [2010] EWHC 1462 (Admin), (2010) 13 CCLR 454, paras 66 and 79.
91 [1998] 1 WLR 902, (1997–98) 1 CCLR 215 at 225G, CA.
92 See in this context *R (B) v Lambeth* [2006] EWHC 2362 (Admin), (2007) 10 CCLR 84.
93 [2010] EWHC 1462 (Admin) at para 77, and see also a joint report, by Local Government Ombudsman and the Health Service Commissioner concerning Wiltshire Council No 09 005 439, 30 October 2012 where a similar finding occurred.
94 [2013] EWHC 1637 (Admin).
95 [2011] EWHC 3219 (Admin) para 33.
96 [2000] 1 WLR 1323, (1999) 2 CCLR 383, DC.

jointly shared by the health and social services authority in which the patient was resident at the time he or she was detained. It is therefore up to individual health bodies and social services authorities to decide among themselves how they will discharge these joint responsibilities. Although the Department of Health has advised health and social services authorities to develop local policies clarifying their respective responsibilities,[97] it appears that in practice this is something that has been neglected.

15.71   Many patients entitled to section 117 services have healthcare needs which could also qualify them for NHS continuing healthcare funding, and the interface between these responsibilities is considered at para 12.194 above.

The duration of the duty

15.72   The services provided under MHA 1983 s117 must continue to be supplied until the authorities are satisfied that the former patient is no longer in need of them. In this context, the MHA code of practice (2015) states:

> 33.20 The duty to provide after-care services exists until both the CCG and the local authority are satisfied that the patient no longer requires them. The circumstances in which it is appropriate to end section 117 after-care will vary from person to person and according to the nature of the services being provided. The most clearcut circumstance in which after-care would end is where the person's mental health improved to a point where they no longer needed services to meet needs arising from or related to their mental disorder. If these services included, for example, care in a specialist residential setting, the arrangements for their move to more appropriate accommodation would need to be in place before support under section 117 is finally withdrawn. Fully involving the patient and (if indicated) their carer and/or advocate in the decision-making process will play an important part in the successful ending of after-care.
>
> 33.21 After-care services under section 117 should not be withdrawn solely on the grounds that:
> - the patient has been discharged from the care of specialist mental health services
> - an arbitrary period has passed since the care was first provided
> - the patient is deprived of their liberty under the MCA
> - the patient has returned to hospital informally or under section 2, or
> - the patient is no longer on a CTO or section 17 leave.

15.73   In *R v Richmond LBC and others ex p Watson and others*[98] (a case concerning the lawfulness of charging for services under MHA 1983 s117 – see para 15.79 below), Sullivan J held that after-care provision under section 117 does not have to continue indefinitely, although it must continue until such time as the health body and the local authority are satisfied that the individual is no longer in need of such services.

15.74   In his judgment he considered the extent of a local authority's duties under section 117 towards a person who had been provided with residential accommodation under the social care legislation and then became mentally unwell and was detained under MHA 1983 s3. He was subsequently

---

97   Department of Health, *After-care under the Mental Health Act 1983: section 117 after-care services* HSC 2000/003: LAC (2000)3, 2003.

98   (1999) 2 CCLR 402, QBD.

discharged from hospital to his former accommodation as part of his after-care package. The question being was this now provided under the social care legislation (as it had been before he was sectioned) or was it now provided under section 117? Sullivan J held that it was provided under section 117. He however noted that:

> There may be cases where, in due course there will be no more need for after care services for the person's mental condition' but he or she will still need social services provision for other needs, for example, physical disability. Such cases will have to be examined individually on their facts ... In a case ... where the illness is dementia, it is difficult to see how such a situation could arise.

15.75 The question of the lawfulness of the discharge of MHA 1983 s117 responsibilities was central to the case of *R (Mwanza) v Greenwich LBC and Bromley LBC*.[99] The applicant had been detained under section 3 in September 2000 and was discharged from section and from hospital in January 2001. A brief care plan was prepared by the community mental health team (CMHT) and in the following six months home visits and out-patients appointments ensued. His condition fluctuated, but by July 2001 the view was that his condition had much improved; and in November, due to his failure to engage with the CMHT, his GP was advised that he was to be discharged from the CMHT's allocated cases. The file was then closed and he made no further contact with the CMHT until mid-2009 when, for reasons connected with his immigration status (see para 16.43 below) he argued that his entitlement to section 117 support subsisted.

15.76 In the court's opinion, the 2001 decision by the CMHT to discharge its section 117 responsibilities was a lawful decision, based upon a proper conclusion that he was no longer in need of such after-care services. Effectively, the court considered that if the responsible local authority and NHS body decide that a person is no longer in need of after-care services and no longer receiving such services, then provided the decision is made at a properly constituted meeting the court will not look too closely at the merits of the decision (ie limiting its remit to administrative law review). In the proceedings it was argued that *R v Richmond LBC ex p Watson*[100] was authority for the proposition that a person could not be discharged from section 117 lawfully without a prior social care assessment being undertaken. The court sidestepped this argument on the basis of the evidential difficulties in establishing exactly what had occurred, due to the delay in this case (ie between 2001 and the launch of the judicial proceedings). The local government ombudsman has, however, held that as a general rule such an assessment is mandatory: that any decision that a person no longer needs after-care should only be taken following a multi-disciplinary meeting of those involved in a person's care and who understand his or her needs and a formal reassessment of need. The ombudsman requires

99 [2010] EWHC 1462 (Admin).
100 (1999) 2 CCLR 402, QBD.

that the correct procedures are followed and that there is adequate documentation to evidence this fact.[101]

15.77   The local government ombudsman has considered a significant number of complaints concerning the inappropriate termination of a funding arrangement under section 117.[102] In a 2007 report, for example, it was held it to be maladministration to discharge a person from section 117 after-care merely because she had 'settled' in a residential care home – where if that home were withdrawn, the resident would be at risk of admission to hospital.[103] In this respect the MHA code of practice (2015) cautions against the discharge of section 117 support even where the after-care arrangements have proved to be successful and the 'the patient is now well-settled in the community' since he or she 'may still continue to need after-care services, eg to prevent a relapse or further deterioration in their condition' (para 33.23).

District or area of residence

15.78   MHA 1983 s117(3) provides that services under that section are the responsibility of the social services/health body for the area in which 'the person concerned is resident or to which he is sent on discharge by the hospital in which he was detained'. The question of ordinary residence under section 117 is considered further at para 6.76 above.

Charging for section 117 services

15.79   In *R v Manchester City Council ex p Stennett and others*[104] the House of Lords held that it was unlawful for local authorities to charge for services under MHA 1983 s117. Although the judgment confirmed the consistent view of the Department of Health,[105] many local authorities had hitherto been charging for such services and accordingly a substantial number of claims were then made for reimbursement – many of which came to the notice of the local government ombudsman. This resulted in a special report which advised on the extent to which authorities should undertake retrospective reviews of individuals who may have been charged inappropriately as well as the calculation of the sums due in restitution.[106]

---

101 Complaint no 06/B/07542 against Poole BC 5 September 2007 – but see also the joint report, by Local Government Ombudsman and the Health Service Commissioner concerning Wiltshire Council No 09 005 439, 30 October 2012.

102 See, for example, complaint against Clwyd (1997–98) 1 CCLR 546; and see also Report no 98/B/0341 from the English local government ombudsman against Wiltshire where a similar finding was made coupled with a recommendation that the cases of other people who might have had to pay for services inappropriately also be reviewed.

103 Complaint no 06/B/16774 against Bath and North East Somerset Council, 12 December 2007.

104 [2002] UKHL 34, [2002] 3 WLR 584, (2002) 5 CCLR 500.

105 See eg *After-care under the Mental Health Act 1983: section 117 after-care services*, LAC (2000)3.

106 Local Government Ombudsmen, *Special report: advice and guidance on the funding of after-care under section 117 of the Mental Health Act 1983*, LGO 604 (07/03), 2003 – considered in greater detail in the 5th edition of this book at para 20.45.

15.80   Local authorities are not permitted to charge even where the individual has received personal injuries compensation to cover this element of his or her care needs[107] unless in the compensation proceedings it was argued that the care needs arose for a non-mental health reason.[108]

Direct payments and section 117

15.81   MHA 1983 s117(2C) provides that direct payments made under CA 2104 ss31–33 or NHSA 2006 s12A(4) (and the regulations under each of these provisions) apply to people eligible to section 117 after-care support. The duty to make direct payments under the CA 2014 are considered at para 10.103 above, and the duty under the NHSA 2006 at para 12.214 above.

Choice of accommodation and section 117

15.82   Although the pre-CA 2014 statutory regime did not explicitly provide for individuals subject to section 117 after-care to exercise 'choice of accommodation' rights, the ombudsman had expressed the view that such a right probably existed.[109]

15.83   The Law Commission in its final report recommended[110] that the new legislation should contain regulation making powers to enable the right of choice of accommodation and the making of additional payments to extend to residents accommodated under section 117. This recommendation was implemented by the CA 2014. CA 2014 s75(6) amends the MHA 1983 by inserting a new section (section 117A) which provides for regulations to enable individuals eligible for section 117 after-care to 'express a preference for particular accommodation'. As the statutory guidance explains (annex A para 45) the regulations[111] provide for broadly the same rights as those who receive care and support under the CA 2014. The rights are however subject to the same conditions as under the CA 2014 (considered at para 8.241 above) namely that:[112]

a) the person must be aged 18 or over;
b) the accommodation which the local authority is providing or arranging must be of a specified type;
c) the preferred accommodation must be of the same type that the local authority has decided to provide or arrange;
d) the preferred accommodation must be suitable to meet the person's needs;
e) the preferred accommodation must be available;

107 *Tinsley v Manchester City Council* [2016] EWHC 2855 (Admin): this decision was subject to an appeal in January 2017.
108 *R (Afework) v Camden LBC* [2013] EWHC 1637 (Admin).
109 Complaint no 04/B/01280 against York City Council, 31 January 2006; and see also *North Dorset NHS PCT v Coombs* [2013] EWCA Civ 471.
110 Law Commission, *Adult social care*, Law Com No 326, HC 941, 2011, Recommendation 61.
111 Care and Support and After-care (Choice of Accommodation) Regulations 2014 SI No 2670.
112 Care and Support and After-care (Choice of Accommodation) Regulations 2014 SI No 2670 reg 4; and see also the statutory guidance, annex A para 45.

f) where the preferred accommodation is not provided by the local authority, the provider of the accommodation must agree to provide the accommodation to the person on the local authority's terms; and

g) where the cost to the local authority of providing or arranging for the provision of the preferred accommodation is greater than the amount that the local authority would expect to be the usual cost of providing or arranging for the provision of accommodation of that kind, the additional cost conditions in para 15.84 below must also be met.[113]

Top-up payments and section 117

15.84   Although the pre-CA 2014 statutory regime did not explicitly exclude the possibility of individuals subject to section 117 after-care topping up the cost of their accommodation, the courts had indicated that this was permissible in certain situations.[114] This has now been put beyond doubt by regulations[115] that provide for individuals to make top-up payments where the cost of the person's preferred accommodation is above the amount deemed reasonable by the local authority/NHS to meet the person's section 117 after-care needs.[116] In this situation the regulations differ slightly from those applying to CA 2014 top-ups, since the additional payment can be made not only by a third party but also by the person themselves. Such payments are subject to the same conditions as specified by the CA 2014 (considered in chapter 10 above).

NHS continuing healthcare and s117

15.85   The interface between the 'joint' responsibilities of local authorities and CCGs for the funding of packages of care under MHA 1983 s117 and the responsibilities of CCGs to fund the care needs of people eligible for NHS continuing healthcare funding is considered at para 12.194 above.

Prisoners and section 117

15.86   The statutory guidance advises that (para 17.6):

> ... where prisoners have previously been detained under MHA 1983 ss 47 and 48 and transferred back to prison, their entitlement to section 117 after-care should be dealt with in the same way as it would be in the community, apart from any provisions which are disapplied in custodial settings, such as direct payments and choice of accommodation, which are set out in more detail below.

---

113 See para 15.84 below.

114 See *North Dorset NHS PCT v Coombs* [2013] EWCA Civ 471 where the Court of Appeal held that neither the MHA 1983 nor the NHSA 2006 excluded the possibility of detained patients or their families paying for, or contributing to, the cost of their treatment or care – albeit that the choice of appropriate placement or treatment would remain to be made by the detaining authority or the patient's responsible clinician.

115 The right of Care and Support and After-care (Choice of Accommodation) Regulations 2014 SI No 2670 reg 4(3); and see also the statutory guidance, annex A paras 48–49.

116 It is of course important to establish that the price offered to the care home reflects in full the assessed needs of the particular person, rather than the general price the local authority/NHS are prepared to pay for people with mental health problems.

15.87 The social care rights of prisoners are considered further at para 15.136 below.

Drug and alcohol misuse

Background

15.88 This section considers the social care responsibilities for people who misuse drugs and alcohol. In the UK in 2010 it was estimated that over 3 million adults use an illicit drug each year.[117] The figure appears to be increasing, although there has been a significant fall in the number of heroin and crack cocaine users.[118] It is estimated that of the 1.6 million people in the UK with 'alcohol dependence', about a third of these face challenges similar to those dependent on drugs and need support to help them recover.

15.89 The social and economic costs associated with drug misuse are thought to be in the region of £15.4 billion a year, and the equivalent costs for alcohol in the region of £18–25 billion a year[119] (of which the cost to the NHS alone is estimated at £2.7 billion a year).[120]

15.90 In 2014/15 it is estimated that there were 1.1 million alcohol-related hospital admissions and 6,831 deaths.[121] This compares to slightly over 2,000 deaths from drug misuse registered in same period.[122]

Drug and alcohol misuse policy framework

15.91 In 1998 the government published a strategy paper *Tackling drugs to build a better Britain*[123] in order to co-ordinate its 'combating misuse' policies. The policy was revised in 2002 and in 2006 when the aim was to target those considered to have a serious drug problem and who were not in treatment.

15.92 The numbers in treatment have increased substantially from 125,000 people in 2003/04[124] to over 190,000 people in 2011.[125] In 2015/16[126] there

---

117 Home Office, *Drug strategy 2010: reducing demand, restricting supply, building recovery: supporting people to live a drug free life*, 2010, pp5–7.

118 From 320,000 in 2010 to 294,000 in 2014 – Home Office, *Drug strategy 2010: 'a balanced approach' third annual review*, 2015; and see also in England and Wales in 2013/14, Health and Social Care Information Centre, *Statistics on drug misuse in England 2014*, 2014.

119 It is argued that this is a significant under-estimate – see Institute of Alcohol Studies, *Economic impacts of alcohol*, 2016.

120 Home Office, *Drug strategy 2010*, 2010, pp5–7.

121 These represented an increase of four per cent on 2013 and 13 per cent on 2004 – Health and Social Care Information Centre, *Statistics on alcohol ,*2016.

122 Public Health England, *Trends in drug misuse deaths in England, 1999 to 2014*, 2016.

123 Department of Health, *Tackling drugs to build a better Britain: the government's ten-year strategy for tackling drugs misuse*, Cm 3945, The Stationery Office, 1998.

124 Department of Health and Home Office, *Models of care for treatment of adult drug misusers*, 2006, para 2.3.

125 National Treatment Agency for Substance Misuse, 'Facts & figures' at www.nta.nhs.uk/facts.aspx.

126 Public Health England, *Drug and alcohol treatment stats for 2015/16*.

were 288,843 adults in contact with drug and alcohol services, of which 138,081 had started their treatment during the year. People with a dependency on opiates made up the largest proportion (52 per cent, 149,807) and those seeking treatment for alcohol made up the second largest group (144,908). The most recent English strategy (2010) retains the commitment to providing treatment, but additionally aims by 2014 'to break the cycle of dependence on drugs and alcohol' by (1) reducing demand; (2) restricting supply; and (3) building recovery in communities. [127]

15.93   The service provision strategy in England was co-ordinated via the National Treatment Agency for Substance Misuse (NTA), a special health authority created in 2001[128] to improve the availability, capacity and effectiveness of treatment for drug misuse. In 2013 NTA was absorbed into Public Health England, although much of the relevant policy and practice guidance was issued by NAT prior to that date. Public Health England distributes funding to local drug partnerships, generally in the form of drug and alcohol action teams (referred to as DAATs) comprising representatives of the local agencies involved in tackling the misuse of drugs, including CCGs, the local authority, police and probation. It is the responsibility of DAATs to provide misusers with access to advice and information, needle exchanges, and counselling.

15.94   A number of similar alcohol misuse policy initiatives have occurred in parallel with these programmes, including the 2004 *Alcohol harm reduction strategy for England*[129] and the 2006 Department of Health guidance *Models of care for alcohol misusers* (hereafter referred to as the *Models of care (alcohol misuse)*).[130] These are considered further below.

Statutory regime

15.95   Local authority responsibilities for drug and alcohol services derive from two principal functions: the NHSA 2006 and the CA 2014.

NHSA 2006

15.96   Under NHS Act 2006 s2B[131] local authorities in England assumed the public health promotion duties (although these still rest with the secretary of state – though now delegated to Public Health England). Local authorities receive a ring-fenced public health grant and in addition to the Better Care Fund (see para 11.134 above) monies available for public health priorities.

15.97   In 2014/15 the NHSA 2006 public health grant (paid to local authorities) amounted to £2.79 billion.[132] This is, however, being progressively

---

127 See also Home Office, *Drug strategy 2010: 'a balanced approach'. Third annual review*, 2015.

128 National Treatment Agency (Establishment and Constitution) Order 2001 SI No 713.

129 Cabinet Office, *Alcohol harm reduction strategy for England*, 2004.

130 Department of Health, National Treatment Agency for Substance Misuse, *Models of care for alcohol misusers*, 2006.

131 By amendment Health and Social Care Act 2012 s12.

132 Department of Health, *Public health ring-fenced grant conditions – 2014/15*, LAC (DH) (2013)3.

reduced, such that by 2020 the government estimates that there will have been 'a reduction in cash terms of 9.6 per cent',[133] although the Health Select Committee consider this to be almost 15 per cent,[134] describing it as a 'false economy, creating avoidable additional costs in the future'.

15.98   The public health responsibilities of local authorities cover a wide range of areas (identified in NHSA 2006 s73B[135]) but in terms of expenditure, substance misuse services are the largest item.[136] Local authorities have a number of targets/measures in their use of these funds including:[137]

> 2.15 Number of drug users that left drug treatment successfully (free of drug(s) of dependence) who do not then re-present to treatment again within six months as a proportion of the total number in treatment
>
> 2.16 People entering prison with substance dependence issues who are previously not known to community treatment
>
> ...
>
> 2.18 Alcohol-related admissions to hospital

15.99   It follows from the above analysis that the NHSA 2016 s2B public health function is the main funding route for the assessment and provision of (non-acute) care support services for people who misuse drug and alcohol. Even though this is an NHSA 2006 statutory function, it is one discharged by local authorities. This in turn means that the assessment and eligibility criteria for this support is not determined by the CA 2014 – but provisions under the NHSA 2006. A further consideration is that the prohibition in CA 2014 s22 (considered at para 12.12 above) applies: that a local authority may not in general meet eligible CA 2014 needs if these are required to be provided under the NHSA 2006. NHSA 2006 s2B(1) creates a duty to (among other things) to provide:

> (b) providing services or facilities designed to promote healthy living (whether by helping individuals to address behaviour that is detrimental to health or in any other way);
>
> (c) providing services or facilities for the prevention, diagnosis or treatment of illness;[138]
>
> (d) providing financial incentives to encourage individuals to adopt healthier lifestyles;

---

133   Department of Health, *Public health ring-fenced grant 2016/17 and 2017/18* LAC (DH) (2016)1 p1. The total grant has increased, but this is because responsibility for the public health of children aged 0–5 has been included (ie a transferred responsibility) amounting to about £800 million per annum – see D Buck, *Local government public health budgets: a time for turning?*, King's Fund, 2016.

134   An estimated real terms reduction from £3.47 billion in 2015/16 to £3 billion in 2020/21 – see House of Commons Health Select Committee, *Impact of the spending review on health and social care* HC 139, House of Commons, 2016, para 93.

135   See also NHS Bodies and Local Authorities (Partnership Arrangements, Care Trusts, Public Health and Local Healthwatch) Regulations 2012 SI No 3094 Part 3.

136   See S Heath, *Local authorities' public health responsibilities (England)*, Briefing Paper SN06844, House of Commons Library, 2014, p13.

137   Department of Health, *Improving outcomes and supporting transparency part 2: summary technical specifications of public health indicators*, January 2012.

138   Although it is not without controversy, addiction is commonly interpreted as an illness/disease – see, for example, the American National Institute on Drug Abuse which defines it as a 'a chronic relapsing brain disease' and as noted below (para 15.115) the CA 2014 treats it as an illness.

Assessment procedures under the NHS Act 2006

15.100   It appears that the principal public health guidance relating to drug mis-use strategies remains the 2006 *Models of care (drug misuse)*.[139] This advises that the relevant professionals adopt three broad levels of assessment, each of which incorporates a risk assessment that addresses (at para 4.5):

- risk of suicide or self-harm;
- risks associated with substance use (such as overdose);
- risk of harm to others (including harm to treatment staff, harm to children and domestic violence);
- risk of harm from others (including domestic violence);
- risk of self-neglect.

15.101   The three levels of assessment are:

1) **Screening assessment** (at para 4.1). These are brief assessments that seek to establish whether there is a drug and alcohol problem, what other related problems exist, and whether there is an immediate risk for the client. The assessment will identify whether there is a need to refer on to drug treatment services and the urgency of the referral.

2) **Triage**[140] **assessment** (at para 4.2). These are usually undertaken when the misuser makes contact with the specialist drug treatment services. The assessment seeks to determine the seriousness and urgency of the problems, the most appropriate treatment and the person's motivation to engage in treatment, current risk factors and the urgency of need to access treatment. The assessment will generally include 'an initial care plan' (para 4.3).

3) **Comprehensive assessment** (at para 4.4). These are targeted at drug misusers with 'more complex needs and those who will require struc-tured drug treatment interventions'. Comprehensive assessments will be an ongoing process rather than a single event and may have input from various professionals, such as doctors (for prescribing expertise) and psychologists.

15.102   The *Models of care (alcohol misuse)*[141] guidance adopts the same terminol-ogy and requires the same three broad levels of assessment, which (with the necessary changes) require the same content and level of analysis.

The provision and commissioning of services

15.103   Although the statutory responsibility for the provision of non-acute care services for drug and alcohol misusers rests with the social services authorities, in practice the assessment and service provision functions are discharged by DAATs.

---

139 Department of Health and Home Office, *Models of care for treatment of adult drug misusers*, 2006, augmented by National Institute of Health and Care Excellence (NICE) Clinical guideline [CG51], *Drug misuse in over 16s: psychosocial interventions*, 2007.

140 A process for sorting people based on their need for, or likely benefit from, treatment (from the French 'trier' – to sort).

141 Department of Health National Treatment Agency for Substance Misuse, *Models of care for alcohol misusers*, 2006, para 2.3 onwards.

15.104   Every DAAT should have access to a range of services to cater for the assessed needs of misusers. These services are detailed in *Models of care (drug misuse)*.[142] Although the precise nature of the guidance is unclear, its predecessor guidance stated that it was to have a 'similar status to a national service framework'.[143] The guidance anticipates that a person may receive a number of different forms of treatment at the same time (for example, someone may be receiving counselling as well as medication) or a sequence of treatments (for example, as a hospital inpatient for a detoxification programme, followed by a residential rehabilitation service).

15.105   *Models of care (drug misuse)* provides general advice on the care planning process, outlining the format and contents of care plans (at chapter 5). More detailed guidance on the care process has also been issued.[144] *Models of care (drug misuse)* envisages care plans as being not merely descriptive of the care package that is to be provided, but also an 'agreement on a plan of action between the client and service provider' (para 5.3.2). Care plans should be 'brief and readily understood by all parties involved' and explicitly identify the roles of specific individuals and services in the delivery of the care plan. Considerable emphasis is placed on the need to sustain and retain the service user during the early phases of treatment and for there to be a key worker in this context (paras 5.3.3–5.3.4).

15.106   Care plans should address four key domains, in order to identify goals by which progress can be measured. The domains are:

1) drug and alcohol misuse;
2) health (physical and psychological);
3) offending;
4) social functioning (including housing, employment and relationships).

15.107   *Models of care (drug misuse)* requires that DAATs ensure that users have access to four 'tiers' of service. The 2006 guidance requires 'far greater emphasis' to be given to reducing drug-related harm (para 3.2.1) and seeks to expand the commissioning of tier 4 services (specialist residential services) which it considers to be 'crucial' and to have been (in comparative terms) neglected. A 2007 report[145] makes the same point:

> One major weakness in the existing array of treatment options is in the provision of services involving residential care. Residential rehabilitation has been found to be generally more effective than treatment in the community where 'effective' is taken to mean enabling people to become drug-free[146] ... In recent years, as the treatment system has developed, the residential rehabilitation sector has been neglected in favour of maintenance prescribing and other services at the Tier 3 level, delivered in the community. At

---

142 Department of Health and Home Office, *Models of care for treatment of adult drug misusers*, 2006.

143 Department of Health, *Models of care for treatment of adult drug misusers; Framework for developing local systems of effective drug misuse treatment in England*, 2002, para 2.1.

144 National Treatment Agency for Substance Misuse, *Care planning practice guide*, 2006.

145 Royal Society for the Encouragement of Arts, Manufactures and Commerce, *Drugs facing facts*, 2007, pp199–200.

146 M Gossop, 'Developments in the treatment of drug problems', 2004; in P Bean and T Nemitz (eds), *Drug treatment: what works?*, Routledge, 2004.

present it can accommodate no more than 5 per cent of all the people in drugs treatment.

and

> Moreover, even if there were a system in place for making referrals to residential rehabilitation, as often as not the funding is not there to pay for them. Drug rehabilitation has tended to come, like other forms of residential care, out of the community care budgets of local authorities' social services departments and it therefore competes with all the other demands on these overstretched budgets.

15.108   *Models of care (drug misuse)* advises that in commissioning care packages, greater emphasis should be given to 'effective and well-co-ordinated' drug-related after-care provision and that Supporting People funding should be considered in tandem with other funding streams (para 3.7).

15.109   *Models of care (drug misuse)* describes the four tiers of intervention that must be commissioned and provided locally (p20 onwards). It recommends that these be in a range of settings and that local systems should 'allow for some flexibility in how interventions are provided, with the crucial factors being the patterns of local need and whether a service provider is competent to provide a particular drug treatment intervention' (para 3.8). The four tiers are summarised as follows:

Tier 1: Drug-related information and advice, screening and referral to specialised drug treatment services

This level of support will usually be provided in general healthcare settings (where the main focus is not drug treatment, eg liver units, antenatal wards, Accident and Emergency and pharmacies), as well in social services, education or criminal justice settings. As a minimum, commissioners must ensure that the following services are available:

- drug treatment screening and assessment;
- referral to specialised drug treatment;
- drug advice and information;
- partnership or 'shared care' working with specialised drug treatment services to provide specific drug treatment interventions for drug misusers.

Tier 2: Assessment, referral to structured drug treatment, brief psychosocial interventions, harm reduction interventions (including needle exchange) and after-care

This level of support will generally be provided by specialised drug treatment services or in hospital – however they may be provided in outreach services, primary care settings, pharmacies, criminal justice settings and so on.

As a minimum, commissioners must ensure that the following services are available:

- triage assessment and referral for structured drug treatment;
- drug interventions;
- interventions to reduce harm and risk due to blood-borne viruses including dedicated needle exchanges;
- interventions to minimise the risk of overdose and diversion of prescribed drugs;

- brief psychosocial interventions for drug and alcohol misuse;
- brief interventions for specific target groups including high-risk and other priority groups;
- drug-related support for clients seeking abstinence;
- drug-related after-care support for those who have left care-planned structured treatment;
- liaison and support for generic providers of tier 1 interventions;
- outreach services to engage clients into treatment and to re-engage people who have dropped out of treatment;
- a range of the above interventions for drug-misusing offenders.

Tier 3: Community-based specialised drug assessment and co-ordinated care planned treatment and drug specialist liaison.

This level of support will generally be provided by the same range of providers as Tier 2 interventions above.

As a minimum, commissioners must ensure that the following services are available:

- comprehensive drug misuse assessment;
- care planning, co-ordination and review for all in structured treatment, often with regular keyworking sessions as standard practice;
- community care assessment and case management for drug misusers;
- harm reduction activities as integral to care-planned treatment;
- a range of prescribing interventions[147] as part of a package of care including: prescribing for stabilisation and oral opioid maintenance prescribing; community based detoxification; injectable maintenance prescribing, and a range of prescribing interventions to prevent relapse and ameliorate drug and alcohol-related conditions;
- a range of structured evidence-based psychosocial interventions to assist individuals to make changes in drug and alcohol using behaviour;
- structured day programmes and care-planned day care;
- liaison services for acute medical and psychiatric health services (eg pregnancy, mental health and hepatitis services);
- liaison services for social care services (eg social services (child protection and community care teams), housing, homelessness);
- a range of the above interventions for drug-misusing offenders.

Tier 4: Specialised drug treatment (including inpatient drug detoxification and stabilisation) 'care planned and care coordinated to ensure continuity of care and after-care'

This level of support will generally be provided in specialist settings such as residential substance misuse units or wards, specialist inpatient detoxification beds or specialist addiction units attached to residential rehabilitation units, step programmes, residential rehabilitation or halfway houses which may be located away from their area of residence and drug misusing networks.

---

147 In compliance with Department of Health, *Drug misuse and dependence – UK guidelines on clinical management*, 2007, known as 'the clinical guidelines'.

As a minimum, commissioners must ensure that the following services are available:

- inpatient specialist drug and alcohol assessment, stabilisation, and detoxification/assisted withdrawal services;
- a range of drug and alcohol residential rehabilitation units to suit the needs of different service users;
- a range of drug halfway houses or supportive accommodation for drug misusers;
- residential drug and alcohol crisis intervention units (in larger urban areas);
- inpatient detoxification/assisted withdrawal provision, directly attached to residential rehabilitation units for suitable individuals;
- provision for special groups for which a need is identified (eg for drug-using pregnant women, drug users with liver problems, drug users with severe and enduring mental illness);
- a range of the above interventions for drug-misusing offenders.

15.110   *Models of care (alcohol misuse)*[148] adopts a similar four-tiered service provision response requirement, which are, in brief:

- **Tier 1. The provision of alcohol-related information and advice; screening; simple brief interventions; and referral.** At this stage the intervention is aimed at **identifying** hazardous, harmful and dependent drinkers; providing information on sensible drinking; simple brief interventions to reduce alcohol-related harm; and referral of those with alcohol dependence or harm for more intensive interventions.
- **Tier 2. Open access, non-care-planned, alcohol-specific interventions.** At this stage interventions include the provision of open access facilities and outreach services that provide alcohol-specific advice, information and support; extended brief interventions to help alcohol misusers reduce alcohol-related harm; and assessment and referral of those with more serious alcohol-related problems for care-planned treatment.
- **Tier 3. Community-based, structured, care-planned alcohol treatment.** At this stage interventions include providing community-based specialised alcohol misuse assessments, and alcohol treatment that is care co-ordinated and care-planned.
- **Tier 4.** Specialist inpatient treatment and residential rehabilitation: at this stage interventions include the provision of residential, specialised alcohol treatment services which are care-planned and co-ordinated to ensure continuity of care and after-care.

Service user failure

15.111   Drug and alcohol services can be expensive, and early social services guidance stated, 'there is a comparatively rapid turnover' of such service users in residential accommodation due in part to the relatively high 'failure rate' experienced by people trying to rid themselves of an addiction.[149] The NTA endorsed this advice – that relapses are to be expected and planned

---

148 Department of Health, National Treatment Agency for Substance Misuse, *Models of care for alcohol misusers*, 2006, pp20–23.
149 (LAC (93)2 para 11 – see para 15.119 below.

for, stating that 'it takes time for users to overcome addiction or manage it so they can lead normal lives ... relapse is an ever-present risk'.[150]

15.112   The importance of this factor was also stressed in 1997 *Purchasing effective treatment and care for drug misusers*[151] which stated (at para 1.7):

> Drug misusers suffer relapses, and may need several periods of treatment before they achieve the ultimate aim of 'abstinence'. 'Instant' cures are relatively rare, partly because drug misuse is closely associated with many other problems. These include unemployment, family break up, homelessness and crime. Tackling drug misuse effectively may therefore involve a range of interventions by several agencies, for people at different stages of their drug misusing careers. If these are not properly co-ordinated resources will be wasted.

15.113   *Models of care (drug misuse)* refers to US evidence that suggests that (at para 3.9.1):

> ... an average time in treatment for someone with a heroin or crack dependence problem is five to seven years, with some heroin users requiring indefinite maintenance on substitute opioids. Evidence also tells us that service users gain cumulative benefit from a series of treatment episodes. However, the biggest improvements in client outcomes are likely to be made in the first six years of treatment.

15.114   In a similar vein, *Models of care (alcohol misuse)*[152] advises that alcohol dependence is recognised to be a commonly recurring condition, and that individuals:

> ... may require a number of episodes of treatment before they reach their goals, which in relation to their drinking behaviour are likely to be either lower-risk drinking or abstinence. Some more 'entrenched' or recurrent alcohol misusers with severe dependence, and who may have other problems, may not reach their drinking goals or other goals in a particular episode of care. Treatment interventions may, in some cases, need to be carried out over extended periods, or individuals may benefit from multiple treatment episodes.

Care Act 2014

15.115   Prior to the enactment of the CA 2014, local authorities had specific community care responsibilities for drug and alcohol misusers.[153] These obligations have been repealed.[154] The CA 2014 duties, however, apply to (among others) all adults in need, and the eligibility criteria regulations 2015 require that their need arises from, or is related to 'a physical or

---

150 National Treatment Agency, *Drug treatment in England: the road to recovery*, 2012.

151 Department of Health, *Purchasing effective treatment and care for drug misusers guidance on commissioning better services for people with drug related problems*, Health Promotion Division, Drugs Services Team, 1997.

152 Department of Health, National Treatment Agency for Substance Misuse, *Models of care for alcohol misusers*, 2006, para 2.5.

153 National Assistance Act (NAA) 1948 s21 and LAC (93)10 appendix 1 para 2(6) and NHSA 2006 Sch 20 – for discussion of the scope of this obligation see the 5th edition of this book, para 22.34 and 22.37.

154 CA 2014 and Children and Families Act 2014 (Consequential Amendments) Order 2015 SI No 914 Sch 1 para 83.

mental impairment or illness'.[155] The statutory guidance in explaining what this requirement encompasses states (para 6.104):

> ... Local authorities must consider at this stage if the adult has a condition as a result of either physical, mental, sensory, learning or cognitive disabilities or illnesses, substance misuse[156] or brain injury. The authority should base their judgment on the assessment of the adult and a formal diagnosis of the condition should not be required.

15.116 It follows that social services owe the same duty under the CA 2014 to all adults in need, whether their need results from 'physical, mental, sensory, learning or cognitive disabilities or illnesses, substance misuse or brain injury'.

15.117 Any substance misuser in touch with a local authority substance misuse team should also be assessed under CA 2014 s9 and any carer they have should be assessed under section 10. Where, as is common, the local authority has delegated its substance misuse public health function (for example, to a DAAT – see para 15.93 above) public law would require that the delegation agreement contain an explicit protocol as to how the CA 2014 responsibilities are to be addressed. Presumably this would be by way of further delegation of these functions (under CA 2014 s79 – see para 1.25 above) or by requiring the DAT to refer all substance misusers and their cares to the local authority adult services department.

15.118 Although, as noted above, all adults in need have the same rights under the CA 2014 whether their need results from 'physical, mental, sensory, learning or cognitive disabilities or illnesses, substance misuse or brain injury' – this message is well concealed. The statutory guidance makes no mention of 'addiction'; has just two substantive mentions of 'drug'/ 'alcohol'; and 'substance misuse' is mentioned on only four occasions. By way of contrast, the term 'deafblind' is mentioned 27 times.

15.119 The virtual invisibility of drug and alcohol misusers is not new. The only specific Department of Health guidance for this group under the previous community care regime was issued in 1993 – *Alcohol and drug services within community care*. Although this would appear to have been withdrawn, it makes a number of enduring 'good practice' points of enduring relevance.[157] These include:

> 13. People with serious and urgent alcohol and/or drug problems are likely to need a rapid response because of crises and to capture fluctuating motivation. Serious deterioration which may carry social, legal and care implications may ensue if there is delay before assessment or if assessment procedures are prolonged.
>
> ...
>
> **Adapting assessment to the special needs of alcohol and drug misusers**
> 15. LAs will need to ensure that their assessment systems take full account of the different ways in which alcohol and drug misusers present for services, their different characteristics and their particular needs:

---

155 Reg 2(1)(a); see para 4.6 above.
156 As noted above (footnote 139) addiction is commonly interpreted as an illness/ disease – see, for example, the American National Institute on Drug Abuse which defines it as a 'a chronic relapsing brain disease'.
157 For the status of withdrawn guidance, see para 1.56 above.

- standard LA assessment procedures and documentation should include consideration of substance misuse.
- LA staff will need to be able to identify the indications of substance misuse so that specialist agencies can be involved where appropriate.

...

Probation service
25. Some alcohol and/or drug misusing clients of the Probation Service will continue to seek access to residential and non-residential care, and LAs should liaise with probation services to ensure that these needs can be considered within the community care arrangements. Attention should be given to establishing joint assessment or common assessment procedures, such as those LAs have developed with other client groups.

15.120   In this respect, the strategy paper, *Tackling drugs to build a better Britain*[158] also highlighted the crucial role of inter-disciplinary working (particularly between health, social services, housing, education and employment services). The interlinking role of the Probation Service in relation to prisoners is considered further at para 15.143 below.

Dual diagnosis

15.121   Between a third to a half of people with severe mental health problems have substance misuse related problems.[159] In order to avoid such persons being 'shuttled between services, with a corresponding loss of continuity of care', attempts have been made to ensure that specialist mental health services and specialist substance abuse services co-operate closely.

15.122   In 2002 the Department of Health published a 'good practice guide'[160] which has been augmented by 2006 guidance[161] concerning the assessment and clinical management of such patients who are in psychiatric inpatient or day care settings. The National Institute for Health and Care Excellence (NICE) has issued two clinical guidelines concerning coexisting severe mental illness and substance misuse – one for managing the challenges posed in healthcare settings[162] and one relating to community health and social care services.[163]

15.123   The 2002 guidance seeks to better integrate working between the specialist agencies – rather than create a separate organisation for 'dual diagnosis' users. In relation to the policy that should inform specialist units working in these fields, it summarises the key points of its advice thus:

- Mainstream mental health services have a responsibility to address the needs of people with a dual diagnosis.

---

158 Cm 3945, 1998, p23.
159 Department of Health, *Mental health policy implementation guide dual diagnosis good practice guide*, 2002, para 1.3.1.
160 Department of Health, *Mental health policy implementation guide dual diagnosis good practice guide*, 2002.
161 Department of Health, *Dual diagnosis in mental health inpatient and day hospital settings. Guidance on the assessment and management of patients in mental health inpatient and day hospital settings who have mental ill-health and substance use problems*, 2006.
162 NICE, Clinical guideline [CG120], *Coexisting severe mental illness (psychosis) and substance misuse: assessment and management in healthcare settings*, NG 120, 2011.
163 NICE, Clinical guideline [CG58], *Coexisting severe mental illness and substance misuse: community health and social care services*, NG 58, 2016.

- Where they exist, specialist teams of dual diagnosis workers should provide support to mainstream mental health services.
- All staff in assertive outreach must be trained and equipped to work with dual diagnosis.
- Adequate numbers of staff in crisis resolution and early intervention teams, community mental health teams (CMHTs) and inpatient settings must also be so trained.
- They must be able to link up with each other and with specialist advice and support, including from drug and alcohol agencies.
- All local health and social care economies must map need including for those in prison.
- Project teams must be set up and must agree a local plan to meet need which must contain an agreed local focused definition, care pathways/ care coordination protocols and clinical governance guidelines.
- All clients must be on the care programme approach (CPA) and must have a full risk assessment regardless of their location within services.

15.124   The 2016 NICE guidance is extensive, and in many respects complements and fleshes out the 2002 guidance. It advises, for example:

1.2.1 Ensure secondary care mental health services:
- Do not exclude people with severe mental illness because of their substance misuse.
- Do not exclude people from physical health, social care, housing or other support services because of their coexisting severe mental illness and substance misuse.
- Adopt a person-centred approach to reduce stigma and address any inequity to access to services people may face ...
- Undertake a comprehensive assessment of the person's mental health and substance misuse needs ...

1.2.4 Involve the person (and their family or carers if the person wants them involved) in developing and reviewing the care plan (as needed) to ensure it is tailored to meet their needs ...

1.2.5 Ensure the care plan:
- Is based on a discussion with the person about how their abilities (such as the extent to which they can take part in the activities of daily living) can help them to engage with services and recover.
- Takes into account the person's past experiences (such as their coping strategies to deal with crises).
- Lists how the person will be supported to meet their identified needs and goals. This includes listing any carers they have identified to help them, and the type of support the carer can provide ...
- Takes into account the concerns of the person's family or carers.
- Recognises and, if possible, reconciles any goals the person may have decided for themselves if they differ from those identified by their service provider.
- Is optimistic about the prospects of recovery.
- Is reviewed at every contact.

...

1.5.12 Ensure practitioners have the resilience and tolerance to help people with coexisting severe mental illness and substance misuse through a relapse or crisis, so they are not discharged before they are fully equipped to cope or excluded from services ...

Carers and substance misuse

15.125 It is estimated that about 1.5 million people are 'significantly affected' by a relative's drug use[164] and who subsequently assume caring roles – and whose caring saves the state £747 million each year – care that would otherwise have to be provided by the health and social care sector.[165]

15.126 In 2003 it was estimated that there may be as many as 350,000 children affected by parental drug use in the UK,[166] and in 2009 it was estimated that at least 120,000 children were living with a parent then engaged in treatment.[167] Inevitably many of these children will assume caring roles,[168] and these will therefore be young carers who have significantly enhanced rights under the post-2014 legislative regime (see para 15.178 below).

15.127 Carers of drug and alcohol users have the same rights to a needs-assessment and access to support as any other carer under the CA 2014. The evidence suggests that such carers experience substantial stress and health problems, as well as an impact on their employment, social lives, relationships and finances.[169]

15.128 Just as it appears that the social care guidance largely ignores the needs of substance misusers (see para 15.118 above), this is also true in relation to their carers[170] – for example, the 2006 NTA care planning practice guide[171] only mentions carers twice. One of these mentions brings into stark contrast the NHS approach and that of the CA 2014. Whereas under the CA 2014 carer involvement in the user's assessment and care planning process is mandatory,[172] the 2006 guidance states (p14):

> Care plans should be developed in a way that empowers clients to take control over their health. In appropriate circumstances and with the client's consent, carers, family and significant others should be included as partners in the care planning process.

15.129 Carers are less invisible when the guidance relates to adults who have a dual diagnosis. The 2016 NICE guidance, for example, advises that all care plans list any carers the substance misusers has identified to help them

---

164 UK Drug Policy Commission, *Supporting the supporters: families of drug misusers*, 2009 cited in Adfam, *The Care Bill: what does this mean for carers of drug and alcohol users?*, 2014.

165 A Copello and L Templeton, *The forgotten carers: support for adult family members affected by a relative's drug problems*, UK Drug Policy Commission, 2012.

166 Advisory Council on the Misuse of Drugs, *Hidden harm: responding to the needs of children or problem drug users*, 2003.

167 National Treatment Agency for Substance Misuse, *Moves to provide greater protection for children living with drug addicts*, 2009.

168 A point highlighted by A Copello and L Templeton, *The forgotten carers: support for adult family members affected by a relative's drug problems*, UK Drug Policy Commission, 2012.

169 A Copello and L Templeton, *The forgotten carers: support for adult family members affected by a relative's drug problems*, UK Drug Policy Commission, 2012.

170 A Copello and L Templeton, *The forgotten carers: support for adult family members affected by a relative's drug problems*, UK Drug Policy Commission, 2012; and see, for example, UK Drug Policy Commission, *The forgotten carers: support for adult family members affected by a relative's drug problems*, 2012 and J Manthorpe, J Moriarty and M Cornes 'Supportive practice with carers of people with substance misuse problems' in *Social Work in Action*, 27(1), 2015, pp51–65.

171 National Treatment Agency for Substance Misuse, *Care planning practice guide*, 2006.

172 See Care Act 2014 s9(5)(b).

and take account of the concerns of the person's family or carers (para 1.2.5). It also advises care plans are copied/shared 'with the person's family or carers (if the person agrees)' (para 1.2.6). Further guidance includes:

> 1.2.7 Ensure carers (including young carers) who are providing support are aware they are entitled to, and are offered, an assessment of their own needs. If the carer wishes, make a referral to their local authority for a carer's assessment[173] (in line with the Care Act 2014). When undertaking an assessment, consider:
> * carers have needs in their own right
> * the effect that caring has on their mental health
> * carers may be unaware of, or excluded from, any plans or decisions being taken by the person
> * any assumptions the person with coexisting severe mental illness and substance misuse has made about the support and check that they agree the level of support their carer will provide.
>
> 1.2.8 Based on the carer's assessment:
> * Advise the carer that they may be entitled to their own support. For example, using a personal budget to buy care or to have a break from their caring responsibilities.
> * Give information and advice on how to access services in the community, for example respite or recreational activities or other support to improve their well-being.

15.130   The statutory guidance gives young carers as an example of where specific preventative services are required – that where a local authority becomes aware that a child is carrying out a caring role 'it should consider how supporting the adult with needs for care and support can prevent the young carer from under taking excessive or inappropriate care and support responsibilities' (para 2.50). As noted above, it appears that about 120,000 children are living with a parent actually engaged in a drug treatment programme.[174]

15.131   The statutory guidance envisages substance misuse services (particularly in prisons) as an area where delegation may be appropriate and advises that in such cases 'local authorities should consider retaining the functions relating to requirements for continuity of care between settings and must retain the functions in relation to charging and safeguarding' (para 17.43).

15.132   As noted at para 10.26 above, the Care and Support (Direct Payments) Regulations 2014 SI No 2871 prohibit the making of direct payments to persons who are subject to certain court orders or controls arising out of their drug and/or alcohol dependencies (eg being subject to a drug rehabilitation or alcohol treatment requirement).[175]

The responsibilities of NHS bodies under the NHSA 2006

15.133   The effects of alcohol/drug misuse can be life-threatening and frequently require specialist medical and nursing interventions (for example, funding periods in specialist detoxification units). CCGs have clear responsibilities

---

173 In this respect see para 3.15 above.
174 National Treatment Agency for Substance Misuse, *Moves to provide greater protection for children living with drug addicts*, 2009.
175 Reg 2 and Sch 1.

in this field, although in relation to such matters as rehabilitation and recovery, it is an overlapping responsibility with social services authorities.[176]

15.134   NHS purchasing guidelines identify a number of specific health services that ought to be available for drug misusers. These include hospital drug detoxification[177] (known medically as 'assisted withdrawal'), which usually involves an inpatient stay of about 28 days. In addition to medication to help clear their bodies of drugs, in-patient treatment can also include stabilisation on substitute medication, emergency medical care for drug users in crisis, and in some cases treatment for stimulant users.[178]

15.135   The above guidance has now been augmented by NICE 'co-morbidity' guidance ie concerning the management of coexisting severe mental illness and substance misuse –in healthcare settings.[179]

Prisoners

Background

15.136 In 2016 the prison and probation ombudsman[180] observed that 'mental ill-health is one of the most prevalent and challenging issues in prisons and is closely associated with the depressingly high rates of suicide and self-harm in custody'. His report considered the deaths of 557 prisoners in custody between 2012 and 2014.

15.137   There are about 3,500 prisoners aged over 60 – and older prisoners are the fastest growing segment of the prisoner population:[181] there are nearly three times as many older prisoners as 15 years ago.[182] It appears that over 80 per cent of older prisoners have a serious illness or disability.[183]

---

176 LAC (93) 2 para 7 confirmed that: 'the new community care arrangements do not affect health authorities' responsibilities for funding the healthcare element of any alcohol and drug service. LAs will need to consider and draw up agreements with health authorities covering arrangements for funding treatment and rehabilitation services for people with alcohol and/or drug problems.'

177 Department of Health, *Drug misuse and dependence: UK guidelines on clinical management*, 2007, known as 'the clinical guidelines'.

178 National Treatment Agency for Substance Misuse, *Healthcare professionals and partners: building recovery; treatment options* (undated).

179 NICE, Clinical guideline [CG120], *Coexisting severe mental illness (psychosis) and substance misuse: assessment and management in healthcare settings*, 2011.

180 Prison and Probation Ombudsman, *Prisoner mental health*, 2016.

181 Association of Directors of Adult Social Services Departments (ADASS), *The Care Act and prisoners – implications for local authorities*, 2015; and see also R Epstein, 'Zimmer frames and hearing aids: growing old in prison', *Criminal Law & Justice Weekly*, Vol 180 No33 2016; L Caroline, et al 'Older prisoners and the Care Act 2014: an examination of policy, practice and models of social care delivery', *Prison Service Journal*, (2016) Issue 224, pp35–41; and A Hayes and others 'The health and social needs of older male prisoners', *International Journal of Geriatric Psychiatry*, (2012) 27: 11 (1155–1162).

182 N Cornish, K Edgar, A Hewson and S Ware, *Social care or systematic neglect? Older people on release from prison*, Prison Reform Trust and Restore Support Network, 2016. People aged 50 and over currently make up 14 per cent of the prison population – Ministry of Justice, *Offender management statistics, prison population 2015*, Ministry of Justice, 2015.

183 A Moll, *Mental health foundation losing track of time: dementia and the ageing prison population*, Mental Health Foundation, 2013.

15.138　　In addition to the high addiction rates among prisoners, it is estimated that 72 per cent of male and 70 per cent of female sentenced prisoners suffer from two or more diagnosable mental health disorders.[184] Seven per cent of male and 14 per cent of female sentenced prisoners have a psychotic disorder[185] and 20–30 per cent of offenders have learning difficulties or learning disabilities that interfere with their ability to cope within the criminal justice system.[186]

15.139　　A 2009 government-led review of mental health and learning disabilities within the criminal justice system concluded that:

> ...there are now more people with mental health problems in prison than ever before. While public protection remains the priority ...custody can exacerbate mental ill health, heighten vulnerability and increase the risk of self-harm and suicide.[187]

15.140　The Law Commission's research underpinning its 2010 consultation paper[188] endorsed these poor prisoner well-being statistics. It noted that (compared to the general population) 'prisoners experience poorer physical and mental health; higher levels of learning difficulties; and poorer social skills'.[189] It referred to the practice within some prisons of prisoners 'providing care for disabled prisoners (sometimes paid care), such as assistance with getting dressed, cell cleaning and personal hygiene'.[190] It however noted that there were 'few examples of adult social care services being provided for prisoners' and suggested that one reason for this could be the 'lack of clarity in the law'.

15.141　　Although the Law Commission considered that the social care legal obligations towards individuals (disabled people or carers) were not affected by the fact of imprisonment, it considered that there was a requirement for clarity in relation to this responsibility (not least which local authority would be responsible). In its opinion if this was provided 'it would not create onerous demands on local authorities'.

15.142　　In its final report (2011), the Law Commission[191] noted that no one had disputed that prisoners were entitled to the same social care support

184　Prison Reform Trust, *Care not custody*, 2011, p10; and see also C Cunniffe and others, *Research summary 4/12 estimating the prevalence of disability amongst prisoners: results from the surveying prisoner crime reduction (SPCR) survey*, Ministry of Justice, 2012.

185　14 and 23 times the level in the general population – see Singleton and others, *Psychiatric morbidity among prisoners in England and Wales*, Office for National Statistics, 1998.

186　N Loucks, *No one knows: offenders with learning difficulties and learning disabilities*, Prison Reform Trust, 2007.

187　K Bradley, *Lord Bradley's review of people with mental health problems or learning disabilities in the criminal justice system*, 2009.

188　Law Commission, *Adult social care*, Consultation Paper 192, 2010, paras 11.39–11.42.

189　Citing A Bridgwood and G Malbon, *Survey of the physical health of prisoners 1994*, 1995; T Marshall and others, *Health care in prisons: a health care needs assessment*, 2000; P Mottram, HMP Liverpool, Styal and Hindley, *Study Report*, 2007; and C Smith 'Assessing health needs in women's prisons' (1998) 118 *Prison Service Journal* 22.

190　Citing HM Inspectorate of Prisons, *'No problems – old and quiet': older prisoners in England and Wales: a thematic review*, 2004, para 1.63.

191　Law Commission in its report *Adult social care*, Law Com No 326 HC941, para 11.134.

from local authorities as non-prisoners. In its opinion, therefore, if it was decided that 'prisoners should not be excluded from adult social care, then the legal framework must facilitate this policy, for example through the ordinary residence rules and eligibility framework'. This advice was heeded by parliament.

Care Act 2014 and prisoners

15.143   CA 2014 s76 provides welcome clarification as to local responsibilities for prisoners who have care and support needs, and provides that the responsible local authority for 'ordinary residence' purposes is the one in which the prison is located (section 76(1)).[192] The law relating to 'ordinary residence' is considered further at chapter 6 above. The statutory guidance, however, makes the important point that the 'ordinary provisions' are used by analogy, since prisoners cannot in fact be 'said to be ordinarily resident there because the concept of ordinary residence relies on the person voluntarily living there and those in custody have not chosen to live there' (para 17.42)

15.144   58 local authorities in England have prisons within their boundaries and several of these have more than one. A central government grant is paid to these authorities[193] to cover the additional costs arising from this legal clarification. A 2015 ADASSS report[194] noted that the response of authorities would vary depending upon the size and nature of their prison populations (whether long stay or high turnover remand) and considered that the:

> ... actual numbers of prisoners requiring support is likely to be limited'. It suggested that authorities might choose to 'explore the feasibility of developing an integrated health and social care service with the specialist Health and Justice NHS England Commissioners for their area ... [as] health provision is not the responsibility of CCGs and is not always provided by local NHS provider organisations.[195]

It appears that several authorities have created a social work team or designated a social worker to have specialist responsibility for the prison population.

15.145   On release a prisoner is presumed to be ordinarily resident in the area that he or she was resident immediately before the start of his or her sentence (para 17.48).[196] This is a presumption that appears to be easily rebutted, as the statutory guidance notes (para 17.50):

> In situations where an offender is likely to have needs for care and support services on release from prison or approved premises and their place of ordinary residence is unclear and/or they express an intention to settle in

---

192 See National Offender Management Service, *Adult Social Care*, 2016.

193 £10.45m for 2016/17 – see Department of Health, LASSL (DH)(2016), *Adult personal social services: specific revenue funding and grant allocations for 2016/17*, 2016.

194 ADASS, *The Care Act and prisoners – implications for local authorities*, 2015.

195 See the National Health Service Commissioning Board and Clinical Commissioning Groups (Responsibilities and Standing Rules) Regulations 2012 SI No 2996 reg 10.

196 Para 17.48 advises that the deeming provisions in CA 2014 s39 do not apply to people who are leaving prison.

a new local authority area, the local authority to which they plan to move should take responsibility for carrying out the needs assessment.

15.146   Problems will inevitably occur with local authorities reluctant to accept responsibility for prisoners – especially if they are 'expressing an intention' to settle in a local authority area in which they were not resident immediately before the start of their sentence. Not infrequently it may indeed be a term of the prisoner's licence that the prisoner does not return to his or her former area of residence.

15.147   The above suggestion (in the statutory guidance) that in such cases the 'receiving' authority should undertake the assessment is unrealistic. What will presumably happen is that the prison probation and social work team will undertake the preliminary assessment and only when the proposed care and support plan has reached a relatively advanced stage – will the 'receiving' authority then be required to complete the process. Key factors in this process will be the wishes of the prisoner and the willingness of a probation team to accept offender management responsibility for him or her. The statutory guidance advises (para 17.51; and see also para 17.48):

> Given the difficulties associated with determining some offenders' ordinary residence on release, prisons or approved premises, the probation provider (NPS or CRC) and the local authority providing care and support should initiate joint planning for release in advance. Early involvement of all agencies, particularly providers of probation services, should ensure that the resettlement plan is sustainable in the local authority area where the individual will reside. Prisons and probation services should support assessment and care and support planning for those offenders who will require care and support services on their release from prison.

The duty to assess

15.148   The CA 2014 starts from the principle that all 'adults in custody, as well as offenders and defendants in the community, should expect the same level of care and support as the rest of the population' (statutory guidance, para 17.9). The Act, however, excludes four specific rights and these are considered at para 15.161 below.

15.149   Local authorities must therefore carry out an assessment, when made aware that a prisoner may have care and support needs. The 'standards and approach to assessment and determination of need' are the same as for non-prisoners (statutory guidance, para 17.17).

15.150   The duty to assess is on the 'appearance of need' (see para 3.19 above) and this knowledge will generally result, not from direct contact with a local authority officer but from a referral. In this respect the statutory guidance anticipates these coming from 'managers of custodial settings or the prison's health providers' but notes that prisoners have the right to self-refer and that 'local authorities should work with the managers of the custodial setting to consider how to facilitate and respond to self-referrals' (para 17.20).

15.151   It will of course be for a local authority to determine whether there is sufficient information in a referral to establish an 'appearance of need'. Although this is a 'low threshold' decision (see para 3.19 above), it is a decision that rests with the authority, and a 2015 survey of local authority responses suggests that this is one being done with some rigour, stating:[197]

> A referral does not automatically lead to a full care and support assessment being undertaken as they are screened first to see if the presenting issue is one that is appropriate for a social care response. As a consequence an average of 74% of the referrals led to a care and support assessment being undertaken.

15.152 Once a referral has been accepted, assessments should be undertaken as for any other adult in need and the 'threshold for the provision of care and support does not change in custodial settings' (statutory guidance, para 17.23). The guidance also highlights the importance, where appropriate and possible, of involving 'family members directly in assessment or care planning' as well as asking the prisoner 'whether they would like to involve others in their assessment or care planning' (para 17.27).

15.153 If it is held that the individual does not meet the eligibility criteria, then, as with all other adults, the individual must be given written information about (para 17.22):

- what can be done to meet or reduce needs and what services are available; and
- what can be done to prevent or delay the development of needs for care and support in the future.

Care planning

15.154 Where a prisoner has an eligible need, then the duty to meet this arises as with any other adult and the local authority must prepare a care and support plan and involve the individual to decide how to have their needs met (statutory guidance, para 17.32). Care plans must contain all the usual elements (see para 4.120 above) including a personal budget (para 17.33). The well-being principle (see para 2.3 above) applies in the same way, which requires (for example) that 'every effort should be made to put people in control of their care and for them to be actively involved and influential throughout the planning process' (para 17.33). Care and support plans will be subject to the same review processes as all other plans (para 17.37)

15.155 Although the need may be addressed by the prison authorities (in practice it appears that this includes care and support being provided by other prisoners), local authorities are also able to 'commission or arrange for others to provide care and support services, or delegate the function to another party' (statutory guidance, para 17.36). In such cases the care assistants will presumably require the necessary security clearances.

15.156 The care and support is subject to the same charging provisions as for other adults, and this is considered at para 8.40 above.

---

197 ADASS, *A report on the findings of the ADASS survey of social care activity in prisons and approved premises – Quarter 1 2015/16*, September 2015, p4.

Equipment and adaptations

15.157 If the assessment identifies an eligible need equipment or adaptations then, as the statutory guidance notes, 'the custodial regime may limit the range of care options available' (para 17.35). The guidance continues:

> Where this relates to fixtures and fittings (for example, a grab rail or a ramp), it will usually be for the prison to deliver this. But for specialised and moveable items such as beds and hoists, then it may be the local authority that is responsible. Aids for individuals, as defined in the Care and Support (Preventing Needs for Care and Support) Regulations 2014, are the responsibility of the local authority, whilst more significant adaptations would the responsibility of the custodial establishment.

Carers

15.158 The statutory guidance states that (para 17.29):

> It is not the intention of the Care Act that any prisoner, resident of approved premises or staff in prisons or approved premises should take on the role of carer as defined by the Act and should therefore not in general be entitled to a carer's assessment.

15.159 This of course avoids the key question, since it is 'likely that there are a large number of unrecognised informal carers in prison in England'.[198] Given the prevalence of impairment and illness in prisons, it is self-evident that very many prisoners will be providing care sufficient to qualify them as carers for the purposes of the CA 2014 (see para 3.7 above) such that they are entitled to a carers assessment. The above reference in the statutory guidance is inadequate and suggests that this question was considered by the Department of Health as simply too difficult to think about (para 17.29). Legally, however, the local authority has a duty to respond to referrals from carers in exactly the same way as it has to adults in need.

Independent advocacy and prisoners

15.160 The statutory guidance notes that (para 17.68):

> Adults in custody are entitled to the support of an independent advocate during needs assessments and care and support planning and reviews of plans if they would have significant difficulty in being involved in the process. It is the local authority's duty to arrange an independent advocate, as they would for an individual in the community.

15.161 CA 2014 rights that do not apply to (or are modified for) prisoners are as follows:

- **Choice of accommodation:** CA 2014 s76(4) excludes prisoners from the choice of accommodation rights of adults in need (see para 8.241) 'except for the purpose of making provision with respect to accommodation for the adult' on release from prison (including temporary release) or on their ceasing to reside in approved premises. The statutory guidance in this respect advises:

---

198 JD Tabreham, *Prisoners' experience of healthcare in England*, University of Lincoln, 2014, p285.

17.26 The right to a choice of accommodation does not apply to those in a custodial setting except when an individual is preparing for release or resettlement in the community. Release into an approved premises amounts to moving from one custodial setting to another.

- **Direct payments:** CA 2014 s76(5) provides that the right to a direct payment (see para 10.26) does not apply to adults who, having been convicted of an offence, are detained in prison, or residing in approved premises.
- **Safeguarding:** CA 2014 s76(7) provides that the safeguarding provisions in CA 2014 ss42-47 do not apply to prisoners. Although the duty to safeguard prisoners is the responsibility of the prison authorities,[199] the statutory guidance stresses the need for local authority and care provider staff to understand 'what to do where they have a concern about abuse and neglect of an adult in custody' (para 17.61). The guidance also suggests that local authorities 'should consider inviting prison and probation staff to be members of Safeguarding Adult Boards' as these 'can act as a forum for members to exchange advice and expertise to assist prison and probation staff in ensuring that all people in custodial settings are safeguarded' (para 17.62).
- **Continuity of care:** CA 2014 s76(6) modifies the continuity of care provisions in the CA 2014 ss37–38 (see para 3.31 above). The detail of this is explained in the statutory guidance (paras 17.41–17.47), but in essence the intention is that local authorities should follow 'a similar process' to that specified in sections 37–38 for all prisoners who have eligible needs who are moved to 'another custodial setting or where they are being released from prison and are moving back in to the community' (para 17.41). However, as the guidance explains, the actual mechanics of the process will differ on occasions not least because the available options may be limited by virtue of the nature of the offence (para 17.43).

People with sensory impairments

Background

15.162 Prior to the enactment of the CA 2014, local authorities had specific community care responsibilities for people who had certain sensory impairments.[200] These obligations have been repealed.[201] The CA 2014 duties, however, apply to (among others) all adults in need and the eligibility criteria regulations 2015 clearly encompass people with sensory impairments,

---

199 See in this respect National Offender Management Service, *Adult safeguarding in prison* PSI 16/2015 (re-issued December 2016) which contains (among other things) guidance for prison governors on engaging with local adult safeguarding boards.

200 The duty under National Assistance Act 1948 s29(1) (and LAC (93)10 appendix 2 para 2(1)) applied to (among others) people who were 'blind, deaf or dumb ... ': see the 5th edition of this book, paras 9.29–9.38.

201 Care Act 2014 and Children and Families Act 2014 (Consequential Amendments) Order 2015 SI No 914 Sch 1 para 83.

referring as they do to needs that arise from or are related to 'a physical or mental impairment or illness'.[202]

15.163   It follows that references to 'adults in need' in this book will include people with sensory impairments. This brief section, therefore, covers aspects of the legislation and guidance that are of specific relevance to people with sensory impairments.

15.164   With the exception of people who are both deaf and blind (whose needs the statutory guidance refers to on 27 occasions[203]) the needs of people with sensory impairments receive little attention: for example the statutory guidance only makes three references to the needs of people who are deaf (but not also blind). This is not a new problem. Longstanding concerns exist in relation to the assessment, care and support arrangements for people who are deaf.[204] These concerns exist in equal measure in relation to the failure of some health and social services authorities to assess properly the needs of people with visual impairments, such that they 'slip into ill-health and premature dependency'.[205] Various initiatives have been launched to address these problems including the production by the Association of Directors of Social Services in 2002 of national standards for services for people with visual impairment[206] – which included that 'the waiting time for an assessment should be closely monitored to ensure that it is not more than four weeks from the date of referral'.[207]

15.165   The personalisation programme has arguably exacerbated this problem, given that the rehabilitation workers who specialised in this field were predominantly employed by local authorities and it is unclear how their services are now being delivered in a 'spot purchasing system' of crude personal budgets: many of the supports they provided (and in some authorities still provide) involved the provision of low cost but important

---

202 Reg 2(1)(a); see para 4.11 above.
203 The greater reference to the needs of people who are deafblind in official guidance does not necessarily result in increased support – in 2013 it was estimated that at most only ten per cent of deafblind children were being identified by social services – see K Fitch, 'New legislation for children with disabilities will not reverse widespread failure', *Community Care*, 30 December 2013.
204 See, for example, Department of Health, *A service on the edge: inspection of services for deaf and hard of hearing people. Social services inspectorate report*, The Stationery Office, 1997; and A Young and others, 'A profile of 15 social work services with deaf and hard of hearing people in England' in *Research Policy and Planning* (2004) vol 22 no 1.
205 Royal National Institute of Blind People (RNIB), *Facing FACS: applying the eligibility criteria in 'Fair access to care services' to adults with sight problems*, 2005; and see, for example, local government ombudsman's concerns expressed in complaint no 02/C/03831 against Stockport MBC, 28 August 2003 about delays in the assessment of people who have suffered sight loss and about inadequate referral arrangements between the NHS and social services.
206 ADASS, *Progress in sight: national standards of social care for visually impaired adults*, October 2002 now largely superseded by RNIB, *Good practice in sight*, 2008 (a collaborative publication with ADASS and Department of Health endorsement; see also RNIB, *10 principles of good practice in vision rehabilitation*, 2016.
207 ADASS, *Progress in sight: national standards of social care for visually impaired adults*, October 2002 para 11.2 – the four-week period being the limit recommended by the Social Services Inspectorate in its report, *A sharper focus: inspection of services for adults who are visually impaired or blind*, Department of Health, 1998.

items[208] which substantially enhance independence and reduced risk – and no less problematic is the simple commodification of their support and training roles.[209]

15.166   The social care statistics are also a cause for concern: between 2005 and 2013, there was a 43 per cent decline in the number of blind and partially sighted people in England community care services (from 55,875 people to 31,740).[210]

Statutory guidance

15.167   References in the CA 2014 statutory guidance to the specific needs of people with sensory impairments include the following:

Information:
- Paragraph 3.30 highlights the need for authorities to ensure that their information and advice service has due regard to the needs of (among others) people with sensory impairments, 'such as visual impairment, deafblind and hearing impaired'. Clearly this will also be an obligation under EqA 2010 s20 (the duty to make reasonable adjustments).
- This obligation is reiterated at para 6.22 in relation to the duty to provide (as early as possible) information about the assessment process – and for this to be in an accessible format.

Assessment and care planning:
- Paragraph 6.39 stresses the importance of ensuring that people with severe communication needs are provided, where appropriate, with a specialist interpreter to help them to communicate and engage in the assessment.
- Paragraph 6.87 notes that in such cases the assessor may also require the support of an expert to help them carry out the assessment.
- Paragraphs 6.91–6.97 are devoted to the specific assessment and care planning needs of people who are deafblind. Paragraph 6.91 states that people are regarded as deafblind 'if their combined sight and hearing impairment causes difficulties with communication, access to information and mobility. This includes people with a progressive sight and hearing loss'. [211] The guidance in paras 6.91–6.97 is in addition to the requirement in the assessment regulations[212] (that the assessor have

---

208 Eg tactile/high visibility markers to aid access to appliance settings; electronic reading aids and access technology; liquid level indicators; white canes or support sticks; talking clocks/watches to enable access and orientation etc.

209 Eg in developing daily living, mobility, orientation and independence skills; training in using specialist equipment, in developing communication skills (eg Braille, moon etc); advising on low vision strategies etc.

210 A Kaye and P Connolly, *Facing blindness alone*, RNIB, September 2013.

211 Para 6.91 cites '*Think dual sensory*, Department of Health, 1995' as the source of this definition. This document is no longer accessible, although a 1997 document Department of Health, *Think dual sensory: good practice guidelines for older people with dual sensory loss*, 1997 has, at para 1.2.1, a slightly different definition stating that 'dual sensory loss' refers to: 'people whose combined sight and hearing losses cause difficulties with communication, access to information, and mobility. It may also be called deafblindness'.

212 Care and Support (Assessment) Regulations 2014 SI No 2827 reg 6(1).

training and expertise in relation to their needs) and to pre-CA 2014 guidance relating to their needs, which remains in force.[213] The specific section in the statutory guidance includes the following advice:

- the duty to ensure that an expert is involved in the assessment of adults who are deafblind (para 6.91);
- the duty to consider a specialist assessment even if each sensory impairment appears relatively mild and that the assessor or team undertaking the assessment must have training of at least QCF or OCN level 3 where the person has higher or more complex needs (para 6.92);
- the importance of considering the need for an interpreter even where the assessor has had specialist training (para 6.96).

Registers of sight-impaired adults and other disabled people

15.168   The obligation on local authorities to compile registers derives from the 16th century requirement that parishes maintain registers of their 'impotent poor'.[214] The National Assistance Act (NAA) 1948[215] obliged social services authorities to maintain a register of disabled adults ordinarily resident in their area.[216] The maintenance of a register was seen by many authorities as an administrative chore of little practical value, and the Law Commission in its 2011 report[217] found that as a general rule registers failed to be effective as a strategic planning tool and (other than for blind and partially sighted people) were of little value in proving eligibility for services.[218] Accordingly it recommended that (other than for blind and partially sighted people) the duty to establish and maintain registers should be downgraded to a 'power'.[219]

15.169   The CA 2014 reflects this recommendation. Section 77(1) creates a duty on social services authorities 'to establish and maintain a register of sight-impaired and severely sight-impaired adults' who are ordinarily resident in their area. Section 77(3) empowers authorities to have a similar register for any other category of adults they consider appropriate (including disabled people).[220]

15.170   The need for a register of sight-impaired adults derives from the fact that a variety of other provisions refer to adults who are registered as sight-impaired and severely sight-impaired. This includes Income Tax Act 2007

---

213   Department of Health, *Social care for deafblind children and adults*, LAC (DH) (2009) 6; and Department of Health, *Think dual sensory: good practice guidelines for older people with dual sensory loss*, 1997 – see para 3.113 above.

214   Poor Law Act 1572 s16 'and shall make a register book of the names and surnames of such ... aged poor impotent and decayed persons'.

215   NAA 1948 s29(4)(g) and LAC (93)10 appendix 2 para 2(2): this duty was supplemented by Chronically Sick and Disabled Persons Act 1970 s1, which required local authorities to 'inform themselves' of the number of persons in their area to whom NAA 1948 s29 applied.

216   See chapter 6 for the definition of 'ordinary residence'.

217   Law Commission (2011), *Adult social care*, Law Com No 326 HC941, para 12.15.

218   Law Commission (2011), *Adult social care*, Law Com No 326 HC941, para 13.7.

219   Law Commission (2011), *Adult social care*, Law Com No 326 HC941, Recommendation 73.

220   CA 2014 s77(4).

s38(2) which provides for a blind person's personal income tax allowance – if registered as 'a severely sight-impaired adult in a register kept under section 77(1) of the Care Act 2014'. People who are registered are also eligible for a reduction in their television licence fee and car parking concessions, such as under the Blue Badge Scheme.

15.171   CA 2014 s77(2) provides for regulations which define 'sight-impaired' and 'severely sight-impaired'. These have been issued[221] and specify that a person is to be treated as being sight-impaired or severely sight-impaired if they have been certified as such by a consultant ophthalmologist. The certification procedure is initiated by a hospital eye clinic completing the relevant form – a certificate of vision impairment (CVI).

Disabled parents

15.172 The needs of disabled parents have not infrequently been poorly addressed by social services authorities. Disabled parents have often found themselves caught in a funding dispute between adult and children's services.

15.173   As a matter of good practice, the division of responsibilities is straightforward. A key role for all parents is to care for their children. If, as a result of a disability, this is impaired, then they will need help to fulfil this role. Accordingly if (for instance) as a result of an impairment a parent is unable to get his or her child to school, this is a parental need, not a need of the child under the Children Act (CA) 1989. Unfortunately, in this context disabled parents may encounter two major impediments. They may face doubts about their parenting ability, rather than receiving the additional support they need; and they may experience significant problems of poor co-ordination between adult and children services.[222] A 2009 report[223] referred to a gap between services through which disabled parents fell, and found this was exacerbated by the administrative separation of children and adult social care services as a result of the Children Act 2004 (which separated adult and children services).

15.174   In 2007, specific guidance was issued by the Department of Health[224] to address this problem, and this was followed by a Social Care Institute of Excellence (SCIE) resource guide.[225]

15.175   The CA 2014 has replaced the good practice guidance obligations towards disabled parents with a regulatory duty. Eligibility criteria regulations 2015 reg 2(2)(j) specifies as a key outcome 'carrying out any caring responsibilities the adult has for a child'. For consideration of the implications of this provision, see para 4.17 above.

221 Care and Support (Sight-impaired and Severely Sight-impaired Adults) Regulations 2014 SI No 2854 reg 2.

222 R Olsen and H Tyers, *Think parent: disabled adults as parents*, National Family and Parenting Institute, 2004.

223 Commission for Social Care Inspection (CSCI), *Supporting disabled parents: a family or fragmented approach?*, 2009.

224 Department of Health, *Good practice guidance on working with parents with a learning disability*, 2007.

225 J Morris and M Wates, *Supporting disabled parents and parents with additional support needs*, adult services resource guide 9, SCIE, 2007.

15.176   Research suggests that there is a 'clustering of childhood and adult disability within households'[226] with a 2010 study reporting that almost half of disabled children, compared with about a fifth of non-disabled children, live with a parent who also is disabled.[227] Parents of disabled children have additional rights (as carers)[228] to an assessment and support. Consideration of this right is outside of the scope of this text but is dealt with in detail in the sister volume to this book, S Broach, L Clements and J Read, *Disabled children: a legal handbook*, 2nd edn, Legal Action Group, 2016, chapter 8; and see also L Clements, *Carers and their rights*, 6th edn, Carers UK, 2016, chapter 11.

15.177   The Human Rights Act (HRA) 1998 additionally places a positive obligation on states to provide support for parents in such situations and this is considered further at para 2.94 above.

Young carers

15.178   Previous editions of this book have contained a separate, and extensive, chapter devoted to the needs of carers. The reason for this approach was primarily because separate legislation[229] dealt with the rights of carers to that which addressed the needs of disabled, elderly and ill people.

15.179   A key aim of the CA 2014 was to provide adult carers with the same rights to assessment and support as the adult's that they care for. Accordingly, throughout this book the rights of carers and adults in need have been considered in parallel – and as a consequence there is no need for a separate 'carers' chapter.

15.180   There is, however, one category of carer whose needs are not addressed by the CA 2014 and which deserves specific mention: young carers (ie carers who are under the age of 18). This is of particular importance since it appears that 66 per cent of young carers care for their parents and, accordingly, are most likely to come to the notice of the adult social services department. As noted above (para 15.126), it is also estimated that about 120,000 children are living with a parent actually engaged in a drug treatment programme, and many of these also 'young carers'. Research suggests that 80 per cent of young carers receive no support.[230]

15.181   The 2014 reforms included co-ordinated amendments to the CA 1989 by the Children and Families Act (CFA) 2014. CFA 2014 s96 amended the CA 1989[231] to address the needs of (among others) young carers.

---

226 S Broach, L Clements and J Read, *Disabled children: a legal handbook*, 2nd edn, Legal Action Group, 2016, para 1.30.

227 C Blackburn, N Spencer and J Read, 'Prevalence of childhood disability and the characteristics and circumstances of disabled children in the UK: secondary analysis of the Family Resources Survey', (2010) *BMC Pediatrics* 10, p21.

228 Principally under CA 1989 s17ZA.

229 Carers (Recognition and Services) Act 1995; the Carers and Disabled Children Act 2000; and the Carers (Equal Opportunities) Act 2004.

230 Children's Commissioner for England, *The support provided to young carers in England*, 2016.

231 By inserting a new section 17ZA.

15.182 Prior to the enactment of the CA 2014 and the CFA 2014, 'young carer' was not a term that appeared in any legislation. For a local authority to have an obligation to a young carer (ie someone aged under 18 who provided care on an unpaid basis for another person), he or she had to be labelled a 'child in need' – for the purposes of CA 1989 s17. This is no longer the case, as both Acts address the needs of 'young carers' directly.

15.183 As a result of the amendments, the CA 1989[232] defines a young carer as 'a person under 18 who provides or intends to provide care for another person', but it excludes those who provide this care either as part of their paid employment of as part of formal 'voluntary work'.[233] The same definition is provided by the CA 2014.[234] 'Care' in this context includes emotional as well as 'practical support'.[235]

15.184 The amendments create detailed obligations (fleshed out in regulations) including a duty to assess a 'on the appearance of need' (ie without a 'request' having to be made – CA 1989 s17ZA(1)) and a strategic duty on local authorities to take reasonable steps to identify the extent to which there are young carers within their area who have needs for support (section 17ZA(12)).

15.185 Young Carers (Needs Assessments) (England) Regulations 2015[236] ('young carers assessment regulations 2015') reg 2 requires that local authorities undertake 'young carer's needs assessments' in a manner 'which is appropriate and proportionate to the needs and circumstances of the young carer' and that in doing so they must have particular regard to:

(a) the young carer's age, understanding and family circumstances;
(b) the wishes, feelings and preferences of the young carer;
(c) any differences of opinion between the young carer, the young carer's parents and the person cared for, with respect to the care which the young carer provides (or intends to provide); and
(d) the outcomes the young carer seeks from the assessment.

15.186 As with assessments under the CA 2014, authorities are required to provide relevant parties[237] with information 'about the manner and form of the assessment' to enable their effective participation.

15.187 Regulation 3 of the young carers assessment regulations 2015 requires that those undertaking the assessment must have sufficient knowledge and skill (having regard, among other things, to the young carer's age, sex and understanding), and be appropriately trained. Where necessary, the authority is required to consult third parties with 'expertise and knowledge in relation to the young carer' and consider any other relevant assessments that have been carried out.

15.188 Regulation 4 details what must be determined by the assessment – including:

---

232 Section17ZA(3) inserted by Children and Families Act 2014 s96.
233 CA 1989 s17ZB(3).
234 CA 2014 s63(6).
235 CA 1989 s17ZB(5) and CA 2014 s63(9).
236 Young Carers (Needs Assessments) (England) Regulations 2015 SI No 527.
237 Regulation 2(4) specifies that these are (a) the young carer; (b) the person cared for; (c) the young carer's parents; and (d) any other person whom the young carer or a parent of the young carer requests should participate in the assessment.

(a) the amount, nature and type of care which the young carer provides/intends to provide;

(b) the extent to which this care is (or will be) relied upon by the family, including the wider family, to maintain the well-being of the person cared for;

(c) whether the care which the young carer provides (or intends to provide) impacts on the young carer's well-being, education and development;

(d) whether any of the tasks which the young carer is performing (or intends to perform) when providing care are excessive or inappropriate for the young carer to perform having regard to all the circumstances, and in particular the carer's age, sex, wishes and feelings;

(e) whether any of the young carer's needs for support could be prevented by providing services to–
    (i) the person cared for, or
    (ii) another member of the young carer's family;

(f) what the young carer's needs for support would be likely to be if the carer were relieved of part or all of the tasks the young carer performs (or intends to perform) when providing care;

(g) whether any other assessment of the needs for support of the young carer or the person cared for has been carried out;

(h) whether the young carer is a child in need;

(i) any actions to be taken as a result of the assessment; and

(j) the arrangements for a future review.

15.189 Once an assessment identifies a young carer as providing 'excessive or inappropriate' care, the local authority should address this by adjusting the care and support provided to the person cared for by the young carer – the aim being to stop the young carer providing this care.

15.190   For a further detail concerning the rights of young carers, see L Clements, *Carers and their rights*, 6th edn, Carers UK, 2016, chapter 10.

Disabled children and carers in transition

15.191 The scope of this edition of this book is limited to adults in need and their carers. The needs of disabled children and their carers are considered in the sister volume to this book, S Broach, L Clements and J Read, *Disabled children: a legal handbook*, 2nd edn, Legal Action Group, 2016. At chapter 10 the *Handbook* addresses the detailed provisions that relate to disabled young people when they are approaching adulthood. It also considers the provisions that relate to: (1) their carers at this stage (whose support needs will also transfer from being met under the CA 1989 to the CA 2014); and (2) the support needs of young carers in transition as their support needs will also transfer from being the responsibility of the CA 1989 to the CA 2014. The following section provides a brief overview of the law – but reference should be made to the *Handbook* chapter 10 for a more detailed account of the relevant law and policy.

Background

15.192 CA 2014 s66 creates a complex set of provisions,[238] the effect of which is (in essence) that the assessments of disabled children/young carers that take place before the young people become 18, will either continue to apply when they become 18 (until reviewed)[239] or if the local authority decides not to treat the assessments as a continuing obligation – then it must reassess.

15.193 The CA 2014 contains the detail of the legal obligations of authorities for supporting carers and disabled children whose care and support needs will transfer to the adult social services. The Act has a formulaic approach to the duty – essentially that if it appears to an authority that: (1) it is 'likely' that a disabled child and/or the child's carer/a young carer will have care and support needs after transition; and (2) it will be of 'significant benefit' to be assessed – then the authority must assess or give reasons if it refuses to assess.

15.194 The statutory guidance provides considerable detail on the way authorities should approach their duties in relation to disabled children; the parents of disabled children; and young carers (chapter 16).

Disabled children in transition

15.195 The provisions in the CA 2014 (sections 58–59) relating to disabled children (as well as those concerning carers 'in transition' to adulthood) are overly complicated – as the Act contains considerable detail on the issue of consent/capacity to consent and what must be included in the assessment.[240] Put simply, however, the general formula (above) applies – namely: a local authority must undertake a needs assessment of a disabled child if it considers that the child is likely to have needs for care and support after becoming 18 and that the assessment would be of 'significant benefit' to the child. Such an assessment is referred to as a 'child's needs assessment'. If a local authority decides not to undertake such an assessment, it must give reasons for its refusal. The statutory guidance is, however, helpful in advising that 'control' not only encompasses the idea of moving from one area to another – but also 'from children's services to the adult system without fear of suddenly losing care and support' (para 1.25).

15.196 The right to a CA 2014 transition assessment is triggered when the local authority considers that it would be of significant benefit for the young carer/disabled child or the parent carer of a disabled child and that the young person or carer is 'likely to have needs' – neither of which terms are defined in the legislation.

15.197 The statutory guidance advises that a young person or carer is 'likely to have needs' if he or she has 'any likely appearance of any need for care and support as an adult' (para 16.9):

---

238 These are delivered by inserting in the CA 1989 new sections (s17ZB and s17ZC) and also by amending the Chronically Sick and Disabled Persons Act 1970 by adding a new s2A.

239 Ie be treated as a 'needs assessment under s60 Care Act 2014'.

240 Important as these issues are – it is a level of detail one would have expected to find in the regulations rather than the primary statute.

... not just those needs that will be deemed eligible under the adult statute. It is highly likely that young people and carers who are in receipt of
children's services would be 'likely to have needs' in this context, and local
authorities should therefore carry out a transition assessment for those
who are receiving children's services as they approach adulthood, so that
they have information about what to expect when they become an adult.

15.198   The statutory guidance explains that it will generally be of 'significant benefit' to assess 'at the point when their needs for care and support as an
adult can be predicted reasonably confidently, but will also depend on a
range of other factors' (para 16.6). In relation to young people with special
educational needs (SEN) who have an education, health and care (EHC)
plan, the statutory guidance is unequivocal in stating that the transition
assessment process should begin from year 9[241] (para 16.11), adding that
even 'for those without EHC plans, early conversations with local authorities about preparation for adulthood are beneficial' (para 16.12).

15.199   The statutory guidance gives further guidance as to the point at which
the young persons' needs for care and support (as an adult) can be predicted reasonably confidently, stating (para 16.7):

Transition assessments should take place at the right time for the young
person or carer and at a point when the local authority can be reasonably
confident about what the young person's or carer's needs for care or support will look like after the young person in question turns 18. There is no
set age when young people reach this point; every young person and their
family are different, and as such, transition assessments should take place
when it is most appropriate for them.

15.200   The statutory guidance states that the question of whether or not an
assessment would be of 'significant benefit' is 'not related to the level of
a young person or carer's needs, but rather to the timing of the transition
assessment' (para 16.10). It then provides an illustrative list of factors that
should be considered when trying to establish the right time to assess
– namely:

- the stage they have reached at school and any upcoming exams
- whether the young person or carer wishes to enter further/higher education or training
- whether the young person or carer wishes to get a job when they become
a young adult
- whether the young person is planning to move out of their parental
home into their own accommodation
- whether the young person will have care leaver status when they become
18
- whether the carer of a young person wishes to remain in or return to
employment when the young person leaves full time education
- the time it may take to carry out an assessment
- the time it may take to plan and put in place the adult care and support
- any relevant family circumstances
- any planned medical treatment

15.201   In relation to the timing of a transition assessment, an informative case
study is provided in the statutory guidance that concerns a 15-year-old who
attends an education funded residential school and also receives a funding

241 Department of Health, *SEN code of practice preparing for adulthood*, 2014, para 88.11.

package from social services (para 16.15). Her parents request a transition assessment on her 16th birthday. After a discussion with the family, the local authority realises that when the young person leaves school at 19 'it will not be appropriate for her to live with her parents and she will require substantial supported living support and a college placement'. The authority then appreciates that this will necessitate 'a lengthy transition in order to get used to new staff, a new environment and a new educational setting' not least because the 'college has also indicated that that they will need up to a year to plan for her start'. On this basis the local authority concludes that it would be of 'significant benefit' for the transition assessment to take place.

Parent carers in transition

15.202　In very similar terms (to the rights of a disabled child to a transition assessment), CA 2014 ss 60–62 place obligations on local authorities to assess the disabled child's adult carers (referred to as a 'child's carer) during this transition process. In simple terms[242] the Act provides that a local authority must undertake a needs assessment of the carer of a disabled child if it considers that the carer is likely to have needs for support after the child becomes 18 and that the assessment would be of significant benefit to the carer. Such an assessment is referred to as a 'child's carer's assessment'. If a local authority decides not to undertake such an assessment it must give reasons for its refusal. See discussion above (paras 15.198 and 15.197) as to how 'significant benefit' and 'likely to have needs' should be construed.

15.203　　A child's carer is defined as 'an adult (including one who is a parent of the child) who provides or intends to provide care for the child' (CA 2014 s61(7)) but is not paid to provide the care or a formal volunteer (section 61(8)).

Young carers in transition

15.204　CA 2014 ss63–64 concern young carers 'in transition'. The Act (in simple terms[243]) requires a local authority to undertake a needs assessment of a young carer if it considers that he or she is likely to have needs for support after becoming 18 and that the assessment would be of significant benefit to him or her. Such an assessment is referred to as a 'young carer's assessment'. If a local authority decides not to undertake such an assessment it must give reasons for its refusal. See the discussion above (paras 15.198 and 15.197) as to how 'significant benefit' and 'likely to have needs' should be construed.

15.205　　A young carer is defined as 'a person under 18 who provides or intends to provide care for an adult' (CA 2014 s63(6)) but is not paid to provide the care or a formal volunteer (section 63(7)).

---

242 The Act, again, contains overly complicated provisions on the issue of consent/capacity to consent and what must be included in the assessment.

243 The Act, again, contains overly complicated provisions on the issue of consent/capacity to consent and what must be included in the assessment.

Disabled young people/young carers not receiving children's services

15.206   The statutory guidance highlights the importance of local authorities being proactive in relation to transition assessments – particularly in relation to disabled young people and young carers who are not already receiving children's services. An approach suggested by the guidance is that authorities should consider how to 'establish mechanisms in partnership with local educational institutions, health services and other agencies' (para 16.20) and gives as examples of those who might be targeted, including (para 16.18):

- young people (for example, with autism) whose needs have been largely met by their educational institution, but who once they leave, will require their needs to be met in some other way;
- young people and young carers receiving children and adolescent mental health services (CAMHS) may also require care and support as adults even if they did not receive children's services from the local authority.

15.207   Transition planning should consider, not only the sustaining of the care and support needs of disabled young people and carers – but also 'how carers', young carers' and other family members' needs might change' – the example in the statutory guidance being (para 16.21):

> ... some carers of disabled children are able to remain in employment with minimal support while the child has been in school. However, once the young person leaves education, it may be the case that the carer's needs for support increase, and additional support and planning is required from the local authority to allow the carer to stay in employment.

15.208   In this context, the statutory guidance requires social services to be aware of the SEN code of practice[244] relating to the transition arrangements for disabled young people and the importance of them gaining access to full-time programmes (para 16.22). It notes, however, that such an option may not be suitable or available for all young people and advises that in addition the authority should consider 'other provision and support ... such as volunteering, community participation or training'.

---

244   Department of Health, *SEN code of practice*, 2014, chapter 8.

Asylum-seekers and other overseas nationals

continued

Introduction

16.1 This chapter deals with the community care support available to asylum-seekers and to other overseas nationals in the UK who, for whatever reason, are unable to access social welfare assistance (public housing support and welfare benefits). Constant legislative change over the course of the last two decades[1] and the consequent case-law has made the subject exceedingly complex and on occasions brought the higher courts to the point of exasperation. In order, therefore, to make the subject comprehensible, it is necessary to commence with a review of the relevant history and of the key definitions.

Definitions

16.2 In loose terms, an 'asylum-seeker' is someone who has applied for asylum in the UK and whose application remains pending (either before the secretary of state or at appeal). The statutory definition, however, is set out in Immigration and Asylum Act (IAA) 1999 s94(1), which defines an 'asylum-seeker' as:

> ... a person who is not under 18 and has made a claim for asylum which has been recorded by the Secretary of State but which has not been determined.

16.3 Section 94 also clarifies the meaning of a 'claim for asylum', namely:

> ... a claim that it would be contrary to the United Kingdom's obligations under the Refugee Convention, or under Article 3 of the Human Rights Convention, for the claimant to be removed from, or required to leave, the United Kingdom.

16.4 Asylum-seekers within this definition are, in general, entitled to accommodation and financial support while in the UK. The key question which this chapter considers in relation to this group is the circumstances when they are entitled to local authority support under community care provisions, and when they are entitled to support from the Home Office under IAA 1999. This question is important because where accommodation is provided by the Home Office, it is offered on a strictly no-choice basis, normally outside London and the South East, and in very basic accommodation. Thus the ability of asylum-seekers with community care needs to secure accommodation and support from the local authority under the Care Act (CA) 2014 can be critical to their ability to remain in their local area with their existing support networks. Moreover, the standard of accommodation provided by the Home Office is such that the delivery of social care within that accommodation can be problematic.[2]

---

1 At the time of writing (January 2017), further changes to be made by the Immigration Act (IA) 2016 are pending. These are expected to be brought into force in mid-2017 but because much of the detail is to be included in regulations which have yet to be published in draft, this chapter does not seek to address those prospective amendments. A summary of the changes is provided at the end of the chapter.

2 See the concerns expressed by the Law Commission in *Adult social care* Law Com No 326 HC941, 2011, para 6.26.

16.5   As will be seen, for the purposes of community care provision, there are essentially two groups: (1) asylum-seekers and people who were, but are no longer, asylum-seekers within the definition above ('former asylum-seekers'); and (2) other overseas nationals, including:

- migrant children – both unaccompanied children and children who are present in the UK with their families (see para 16.64 below);
- European Economic Area (EEA) nationals and others with a right to reside under European Union (EU) law (see para 16.76 below); and
- victims of domestic violence (see para 16.91 below) and others subject to a 'no recourse to public funds' condition.

Asylum-seekers

Historical background[3]

16.6   Until 6 February 1996, asylum-seekers were entitled to means tested benefits and housing through the homeless provisions.[4] However, from that date applicants who applied for asylum 'in country' rather than 'at port' (ie those who claimed after they had entered the UK rather than on their arrival) were excluded from social welfare benefits and homelessness assistance. This change was brought about by virtue of Asylum and Immigration Act (AIA) 1996 ss9 and 11. Subsequently IAA 1999 s115 extended the disentitlement of benefits from late-claiming asylum-seekers to almost all those subject to immigration control.

16.7   The IAA 1999 envisaged that the majority of asylum-seekers would become the responsibility of a new designated body, namely the National Asylum Support Service (NASS[5]). However, persons who had made a claim for asylum on arrival ('at port') in the UK on or before the introduction of the IAA 1999[6] continued to be entitled to means tested benefits.[7] These people (known as the '2000 transitional protected' cases) retained their

---

3 For a detailed and authoritative description of the history of community care for persons from abroad, see the speech of Baroness Hale in *R (M) v Slough BC* [2008] UKHL 52, [2008] 1 WLR 1808, at [7]–[29].

4 Housing Act 1996 Part VII.

5 In March 2007 asylum cases were transferred to a new regime known as 'new asylum model' or NAM. NAM was designed to be a more efficient and streamlined approach to processing and deciding asylum claims. In addition to changes to the asylum process, NASS as an organisation ceased to exist and decisions on eligibility for asylum support were made by NAM case owners for asylum-seekers who initially sought asylum in or after March 2007, and by the Case Resolution Directorate (CRD) for 'legacy' cases ie those who claimed asylum before that date. In the previous edition we referred to support provided by the Home Office as UK Border Agency (UKBA) support, but in April 2013 the UKBA was abolished and immigration functions brought back within the Home Office. Asylum cases are now dealt with by UK Visas and Immigration (UKVI), and support decisions are made by designated support teams within UKVI. Reference will therefore be made in this chapter to support under IAA 1999 (whether under section 4, 95 or 98) as 'UKVI support'.

6 Which came into force on 2 October 2000.

7 Social Security (Immigration and Asylum) Consequential Amendment Regulations 2000 SI No 636 reg 12(4).

entitlement to benefits until the first negative decision on their asylum claim[8] (after which time they fell to be supported by NASS).

16.8   As a consequence of the 1996 removal of benefit entitlement from in-country asylum applicants, a number of asylum-seekers became destitute and sought assistance under National Assistance Act (NAA) 1948 s21(1)(a) on the basis that they came within the 'any other circumstance' category (now replaced by the CA 2014 – see para 16.24 below) and were thus entitled to residential accommodation from the local authority. In *R v Hammersmith LBC ex p M*[9] their claims succeeded, albeit that the Court of Appeal stressed that section 21 was not a 'safety net' provision 'on which anyone who is short of money and/or short of accommodation can rely'.[10]

16.9   The *Hammersmith* judgment caused not inconsiderable financial problems for a number of local authorities. A 1998 government white paper described the position thus:[11]

> The Court of Appeal judgment ... meant that, without warning or preparation, local authority social services departments were presented with a burden which is quite inappropriate, which has become increasingly intolerable and which is unsustainable in the long term, especially in London, where the pressure on accommodation and disruption to other services has been particularly acute.

16.10   The *Hammersmith* judgment has come to be seen as a landmark decision, since when many aspects of asylum and immigration law have become inextricably intertwined with community care law. As the case-law has developed, parliament has responded with new Acts and regulations such that the system is today complex to a degree bordering on the Kafkaesque, and so lacking in any obvious logic that it has prompted judicial exasperation – as occurred, for example, in *R (AW and others) v Croydon LBC*,[12] where Laws LJ observed:

> In the course of this judgment we have used the term 'paper chase', and have done so advisedly. This important area of the law governs the use of scarce public resources in a difficult and sensitive field. We have already referred ... to the pressing and uneven burden borne by some local authorities. One part of the overall scheme has had to be litigated in the House of Lords. Now this part, closely related, has had to be litigated in this court. No doubt there are great pressures on the legislators. But the distribution of responsibility which is at the core of this case could surely have been provided much more clearly and simply.[13]

16.11   This chapter treads a difficult line. It seeks to focus on the rights to community care support of people who are non-UK nationals and either seeking

---

8   Social Security (Immigration and Asylum) Consequential Amendment Regulations 2000 SI No 636 regs 2 and 12.

9   This being a consolidated appeal, comprising *R v Hammersmith LBC ex p M; R v Lambeth LBC ex p P and X and R v Westminster City Council ex p A* (1997–98) 1 CCLR 85, QBD.

10   (1997–98) 1 CCLR 85 at 94K.

11   Home Office, *Fairer, faster and firmer – a modern approach to immigration and asylum*, Cm 4018, 1998, para 8.14, cited by Lord Hoffmann in *Westminster CC v NASS* [2002] UKHL 38, [2002] 1 WLR 2956, (2002) 5 CCLR 511 at 519C.

12   [2007] EWCA Civ 266 at [55], (2007) *Times* 11 May.

13   Judgment at [55].

asylum or unlawfully in the UK or for some other reason have restricted rights to such services. It is difficult, however, to focus on this question without straying occasionally into the more general area of immigration law. Of necessity, however, we have had to limit these incursions severely, and a reader wishing to understand these issues in further detail should refer to a specialist text on the subject.[14]

Asylum support under the IAA 1999

16.12   Following the *Hammersmith* judgment, the government announced its intention to amend the NAA 1948[15] to:

> ... make clear that social services departments should not carry the burden of looking after healthy and able bodied asylum-seekers. This role will fall to the new national support machinery.

16.13   The vehicle for this change was IAA 1999 Part VI, which inserted section 21(1A) into the NAA 1948 to exclude support for 'able bodied' asylum-seekers. Support for such persons is now provided for by the Home Office UK Visas and Immigration directorate (UKVI).[16] On first applying for asylum support, asylum-seekers who appear to be 'destitute'[17] are entitled to 'initial' or 'emergency' accommodation provided under IAA 1999 s98 until a decision is reached on the person's claim for 'full asylum support' under IAA 1999 s95. Full UKVI support can include accommodation and financial support but, unlike community care services, accommodation under section 95 is almost always provided away from London and the South East (in accordance with the government's policy to disperse those reliant on this support away from these areas). An applicant for section 95 support who has access to available accommodation but not the means to meet his or her other essential living needs, can apply for subsistence only support.

Destitution

16.14   Destitution is a key concept in the determination of entitlement to asylum support[18] and is defined in IAA 1999 s95(3) as follows:

---

14   See eg S Willman and S Knafler QC, *Support for asylum-seekers and other migrants: a guide to legal and welfare rights*, 3rd edn, Legal Action Group, 2009; or G Clayton, *Textbook on immigration and asylum law*, 6th edn, OUP, 2014.

15   Home Office, *Fairer, faster and firmer – a modern approach to immigration and asylum*, Cm 4018, 1998, para 8.23.

16   See note 5 above. Community care services under the Health Services and Public Health Act 1968 and the NHS Acts 2006 were also excluded and equivalent provision is now made by CA 2014, s21 in respect of care and support provided under CA 2014 Part 1 to adults in need.

17   There is some irony in the reappearance of the word 'destitute' into the NAA 1948, since its drafters considered that the omission of any reference to the notion of destitution was one of its greatest achievements– see comments of Mrs Braddock MP, *Hansard* HC Debates 24 November 1947 on the National Assistance Bill, para 1631.

18   This definition applies to both section 95 support and to section 4 support (see further para 16.54 below).

For the purposes of this section, a person is destitute if–
(a) he does not have adequate accommodation or any means of obtaining it (whether or not his other essential living needs are met), or
(b) he has adequate accommodation or the means of obtaining it, but cannot meet his other essential living needs.

16.15 The Asylum Support Regulations 2000[19] set out what UKVI caseworkers must consider when assessing whether an applicant is destitute. The whole family's circumstances must be considered in assessing whether any individual member is destitute (regs 6 and 12), and when assessing an applicant's resources account must be taken of any other support which the person might reasonably be expected to have during the prescribed period (reg 6(4)). For the purposes of an initial application for support, the prescribed period is 14 days' essential living needs. Where other support is 'available', UKVI support can be denied: a point of importance in situations where an asylum-seeker might be seeking social care support.[20]

Late claims and Nationality, Immigration and Asylum Act 2002 s55

16.16 In order to qualify for UKVI support, asylum-seekers are expected to show that they claimed asylum 'as soon as reasonably practicable' after their arrival in the UK. Failure to do so can result in support being refused (Nationality, Immigration and Asylum Act (NIAA) 2002 s55(1)).[21] Applicants cannot be excluded under section 55 if they have dependent children under the age of 18 (section 55(5)(b) and (c)) or if to do so would result in a breach of their human rights (section 55(5)(a)).

The human rights exemption

16.17 In *R (Limbuela) v Secretary of State for the Home Department*[22] the House of Lords sought to identify the point at which deprivation becomes so grave that the state is obliged to intervene and provide support. The Lords held that an asylum-seeker would be at risk of suffering degrading treatment (contrary to Article 3 of the European Convention on Human Rights (ECHR)) if he, with 'no alternative sources of support, unable to support himself, is, by the deliberate action of the state, denied shelter, food or the most basic necessities of life'.[23] The state therefore had a duty to provide support when:[24]

> ... it appears on a fair and objective assessment of all relevant facts and circumstances that an individual applicant faces an imminent prospect of serious suffering caused or materially aggravated by denial of shelter, food

19 SI No 704 as amended. This contains the detailed rules concerning UKVI support. In addition, the UKVI has produced asylum support instructions, which set out the internal guidance that UKVI caseworkers should follow when making support decisions; these are available on the GOV.UK website at: www.gov.uk/government/collections/asylum-support-asylum-instructions.
20 See para 16.21 below.
21 Local authorities are also prohibited from providing support to asylum-seekers excluded under NIAA 2002 s55 under their general well-being powers in Local Government Act (LGA) 2000 s2 or Localism Act (LA) 2011 s1.
22 [2005] UKHL 66, [2005] 3 WLR 1014, (2006) 9 CCLR 30.
23 [2005] UKHL 66, [2005] 3 WLR 1014, (2006) 9 CCLR 30 at [7].
24 [2005] UKHL 66, [2005] 3 WLR 1014, (2006) 9 CCLR 30 at [8].

or the most basic necessities of life. Many factors may affect that judgment, including age, gender, mental and physical health and condition, any facilities or sources of support available to the applicant, the weather and time of year and the period for which the applicant has already suffered or is likely to continue to suffer privation.

16.18   While it was not possible to 'formulate any simple test applicable in all cases' the court considered that the potential breach of Article 3 would require that a person be supported if the person was:

> ... obliged to sleep in the street, save perhaps for a short and foreseeably finite period, or was seriously hungry, or unable to satisfy the most basic requirements of hygiene.

16.19   Baroness Hale in her judgment did come close to providing a simple test – essentially arguing that 'cashlessness + rooflessness = inhuman and degrading treatment' (para 78).[25]

16.20   In *MSS v Belgium and Greece*,[26] the Grand Chamber of the European Court of Human Rights affirmed that while Article 3 did not impose a general obligation to house the homeless, given the particular vulnerability of asylum-seekers and the positive obligations to provide material reception conditions imposed by EU law,[27] a failure to provide any accommodation or support at all to asylum-seekers could violate the prohibition on inhuman and degrading treatment in Article 3.[28]

16.21   The current position is, therefore, that on receiving a NIAA 2002 s55 'refusal of support decision' an asylum-seeker must show that he or she or a dependant is facing an imminent prospect of serious suffering caused, or materially aggravated, by denial of shelter, food or the most basic necessities of life, and that a failure to support will result in a breach of their rights under Article 3. They must be able to point to evidence that they have sought charitable support and that this is either not available or has been exhausted.

16.22   In practice, since the decision in *Limbuela*, UKVI will normally only apply NIAA 2002 s55 to those who are seeking subsistence only support, ie those who have accommodation available to them but are unable to meet their other essential living needs, the rationale for this being that such cases are less likely to be able to demonstrate the necessary level of suffering because they will have a roof over their heads and access to sanitary facilities, and be able to obtain food and other essential items from

---

25   See in this regard the commentary in A Mackenzie, 'Case analysis: *R v Secretary of State for the Home Department ex p Adam, Limbuela and Tesema*' [2006] EHRLR 67–73.

26   Application no 30696/09, judgment of 21 January 2011.

27   Specifically, Directive 2003/9 on minimum standards for the reception of asylum-seekers.

28   Paras 249–264. The court upheld the applicant's claim that conditions in Greece did breach Article 3, observing that: 'the Greek authorities have not had due regard to the applicant's vulnerability as an asylum seeker and must be held responsible, because of their inaction, for the situation in which he has found himself for several months, living in the street, with no resources or access to sanitary facilities, and without any means of providing for his essential needs. The Court ... considers that such living conditions, combined with the prolonged uncertainty in which he has remained and the total lack of any prospects of his situation improving, have attained the level of severity required to fall within the scope of Article 3 of the Convention' (para 263).

charities.[29] It is also UKVI policy that support will not be denied to a pregnant woman, or a household including a pregnant woman, under NIAA 2002 s55 because such women are particularly vulnerable.[30] Applicants should not be refused under section 55 unless they have been interviewed about their circumstances.[31] There have been serious delays in the making of section 55 decisions in such cases, leaving applicants with no form of support for weeks or months, although steps have been taken recently to address these issues.

16.23   An understanding of the *MSS* and *Limbuela* jurisprudence is essential to an assessment of whether support is necessary to prevent a breach of a person's human rights, which is also the critical question in relation to people excluded from social care services under NIAA 2002 s54 and Sch 3 (discussed at para 16.42 below). It requires a consideration of whether such persons may be expected to leave the country in order to avoid a breach of their ECHR rights (in the case of current asylum-seekers, this is unlikely to be a possibility, but it is more relevant in the case of former asylum-seekers and other migrants), as well as whether their circumstances in the UK are such that they are likely to be exposed to inhuman or degrading treatment. That consideration requires attention to be paid to the individual characteristics of the person concerned, and the threshold will more readily be crossed in the case of a child, or of a person suffering from mental or physical illness or disability.[32]

Eligibility of asylum-seekers for social care services

Prior to the implementation of the Care Act 2014

16.24   At the same time as introducing the national system of asylum support under IAA 1999 Part VI, in order to achieve the aim of excluding able-bodied asylum-seekers from section 21 support, amendments were made to the community care legislation[33] (including NAA 1948 s21) by IAA 1999 s116, which inserted into NAA 1948 s21 a new subsection (1A), excluding those subject to immigration control (including asylum-seekers) from section 21, unless their needs were not solely attributable to destitution.[34]

16.25   The 1999 amendment to NAA 1948 s21 did not achieve its objective of relieving social services authorities from the bulk of their obligations to

---

29 See UKVI Section 55 guidance v12, 1 June 2015 ('section 55 guidance'), section 3.9, available at www.gov.uk/government/uploads/system/uploads/attachment_data/file/431346/Section_55_v12.pdf.

30 Section 55 guidance, section 3.10.1.

31 Section 55 guidance, Part 1 'Introduction' and section 3.1.

32 The section 55 guidance acknowledges that even where accommodation is available, those with particular vulnerabilities such as old age or physical or mental ill health may be more likely to show that the denial of support would breach their rights under the European Convention on Human Rights: see section 3.10.

33 See also para 16.12 above.

34 IAA 1999 s117 inserted a similar exclusion into Health Services and Public Health Act (HSPHA) 1968 s45.

asylum-seekers.[35] As Lord Hoffmann noted in *Westminster CC v NASS*[36] (hereafter the '2002 *Westminster*' case):

> 29. What may have escaped notice in the aftermath of *ex p M*[37] was that the 1996 Act had brought into the scope of section 21 of the 1948 Act two distinct classes of asylum seekers who would not have been entitled to Part III accommodation if the 1996 Act had not excluded them from the normal social security system. The first class were the able bodied asylum seekers who qualified solely because, being destitute, they were already or were likely to become in need of care and attention. This was the class highlighted in *ex p M*. I shall call them 'the able bodied destitute', who came within section 21 solely because they were destitute. The second class were asylum seekers who had some infirmity which required the local social services to provide them with care and attention, but who would not ordinarily have needed to be provided with accommodation under section 21 because it was available in other ways, for example, under the homelessness legislation. They would not have come within the section 21 duty because they would not have satisfied the third condition which I have quoted from the judgment of Hale LJ in *Wahid's* case[38] ...

16.26   The problem highlighted by Lord Hoffmann was that use of the word 'solely' in amended NAA 1948 s21(1A) had the effect of only excluding the 'able bodied' destitute. The second class (which he referred to as the 'infirm destitute') were able to claim assistance from social services authorities under NAA 1948 s21, not 'solely' because of their destitution, but additionally because of their infirmity. And since they had access to such assistance they were excluded from the IAA 1999 scheme by virtue of Asylum Support Regulations 2000 reg 6(4)(b)[39] which requires the UKVI, in deciding whether an asylum-seeker is destitute, to take into account any other support which was, or could reasonably be expected to be, available to the asylum-seeker. Lord Hoffmann accordingly held:

> The present case has been argued throughout on the footing that [the applicant] has a need for care and attention which has not arisen solely because she is destitute but also (and largely) because she is ill. It is also common ground that she has no access to any accommodation in which she can receive care and attention other than by virtue of section 21 or under Part VI of the 1999 Act. The first question for your Lordships is whether in those circumstances she comes prima facie within section 21(1)(a) and, if so, the second is whether she is excluded by section 21(1A). In my opinion, the answers to these questions are yes and no respectively. The third question

35   The close connection between this amendment and asylum policy was recognised by the Law Commission in its consultation and report on adult social care, in which, despite concerns expressed by many consultees about the negative impact of the 'destitution plus' test on asylum-seekers' health, it made no recommendation about reform of this test, recognising it was a matter of asylum policy rather than legal reform (Report no 326, 10 May 2011, paras 11.34, 11.37).

36   [2002] UKHL 38, [2002] 1 WLR 2956, (2002) 5 CCLR 511 at 519E.

37   This being a consolidated appeal, comprising *R v Hammersmith LBC ex p M; R v Lambeth LBC ex p P and X and R v Westminster City Council ex p A* (1997–98) 1 CCLR 85, QBD.

38   Namely that 'the care and attention which is needed must not be available otherwise than by the provision of accommodation under section 21': *R (Wahid) v Tower Hamlets LBC* [2002] EWCA Civ 287, (2002) 5 CCLR 239 at 247H – see para 7.98 above.

39   SI No 704.

is whether the existence of a duty under section 21 excludes [the applicant] from consideration for asylum support. Again, in agreement with the Court of Appeal, I think that the answer is yes.[40]

16.27 In the 2002 *Westminster* case, regard was had to two earlier consolidated appeals, *R v Wandsworth LBC ex p O* and *R v Leicester CC ex p Bhikha*[41] in which the local authorities argued that the insertion of subsection (1A) into NAA 1948 s21 made the claimants ineligible under that section. In the leading judgment, Simon Brown LJ (as he then was)[42] adopted the applicants' construction of section 21, namely:

... that if an applicant's need for care and attention is to any material extent made more acute by some circumstance other than the mere lack of accommodation and funds, then, despite being subject to immigration control, he qualifies for assistance.[43]

In this respect, Simon Brown LJ observed that:

The word 'solely' in the new section is a strong one and its purpose there seems to me evident. Assistance under the Act of 1948 is, it need hardly be emphasised, the last refuge for the destitute. If there are to be immigrant beggars on our streets, then let them at least not be old, ill or disabled.

16.28 In *R (M) v Slough BC*,[44] he[45] said:

If, however, that state of need has been accelerated by some pre-existing disability or infirmity – not of itself sufficient to give rise to a need for care and attention but such as to cause a faster deterioration to that state and perhaps to make the need once it arises that much more acute – then for my part, consistently with the views I expressed in the earlier cases, I would not regard such a person as excluded under section 21(1A).[46]

16.29 It follows that an applicant, in order to cross the CA 2014 s21(1) threshold, must establish that he or she is a person whose need for care and support does not arise solely because of destitution or its physical, or anticipated physical, effects. This requirement is commonly referred to as the 'destitution plus' test.

16.30 The *ex p O* and *ex p Bhikha* decisions were followed in *R (Mani) v Lambeth LBC*.[47] The question in *Mani* was whether a local authority has a

---

40 [2002] UKHL 38, [2002] 1 WLR 2956, (2002) 5 CCLR 511 at [49].
41 [2000] 1 WLR 2539, (2000) 3 CCLR 237, CA.
42 [2000] 1 WLR 2539, (2000) 3 CCLR 237 at 2548D–2549B.
43 In the light of *R (L) v Westminster City Council* [2013] UKSC 27, the words 'he qualifies for assistance' must be read as meaning 'he is not excluded by section 21(1A)', and it is still necessary for the individual to meet the other criteria for support under NAA 1948 s21(1)(a), including that his need for care and attention is 'accommodation-related': see at [47].
44 [2008] 1 WLR 1808.
45 By this stage, sitting in the House of Lords as Lord Brown.
46 At 1822F; Baroness Hale, who had also been party to the decision in *ex p O* in the Court of Appeal, commented that the Court of Appeal had not appreciated that the effect of the Asylum Support Regulations 2000 was that any asylum-seeker who was eligible for section 21 accommodation would not be eligible for UKVI support; she said the court had 'assumed that the new national asylum support scheme would provide for destitute asylum seekers even if they were especially vulnerable, if the care and attention they needed could be provided for them in the accommodation provided by the new scheme' (at 1817F).
47 [2002] EWHC 735 (Admin), (2002) 5 CCLR 486.

duty to provide residential accommodation for a destitute asylum-seeker who suffers a disability which, of itself, gives rise to a need for care and attention which falls short of calling for the provision of residential accommodation. The decision in *Mani* was overruled on this point in *R (L) v Westminster City Council*[48] on the grounds that in order to qualify for support under NAA 1948 s21(1)(a), there must be a need for care and attention which is 'accommodation-related'. However, the Supreme Court upheld the conclusion on the facts in *Mani*,[49] and its decision does not undermine the correctness of the *ex p O* line of authority in relation to what kind of care need passes the 'destitution plus' test.

16.31   This line of case-law, culminating in the 2002 *Westminster* case, established that where an asylum-seeker does satisfy the destitution plus test, the responsibility for financially supporting and accommodating that person lies with the local authority, rather than with UKVI. As Lord Carnwath explained in *R (L) v Westminster City Council*:[50]

> ... the national scheme is designed to be a scheme of 'last resort'. The regulations require the Secretary of State, in deciding whether an asylum seeker is destitute, to take into account any other support available to the asylum seeker, including support available under section 21 of the 1948 Act ... Conversely, the local authority, in answering the questions raised by that provision, must disregard the support which might hypothetically be available under the national scheme ...[51]

16.32   An important consequence of this under the statutory scheme prior to the implementation of the CA 2014 was that where an asylum-seeker fell within section 21(1)(a) and was not excluded by section 21(1A) the fact that his community care needs were not 'such as necessarily to call for the provision of residential accommodation' did not mean that the local authority was entitled to meet those needs by way of services under NAA 1948 s29 and Chronically Sick and Disabled Persons Act 1970 s2(1).[52]

Position under the Care Act 2014

16.33   The exclusion is now contained in CA 2014 s21, which provides:

> (1) A local authority may not meet the needs for care and support of an adult [subject to immigration control, including asylum seekers] and whose needs for care and support have arisen solely–
> (a) because the adult is destitute, or
> (b) because of the physical effects, or anticipated physical effects, of being destitute.
> ...
> (4) The reference in subsection (1) to meeting an adult's needs for care and support includes a reference to providing care and support to the adult in order to meet a carer's needs for support.

---

48 [2013] UKSC 27 at [47].
49 [2013] UKSC 27 at [48].
50 [2013] UKSC 27.
51 Paragraph 9.
52 *R (Z) v Hillingdon LBC* [2009] EWCA Civ 1529 at [18].

Section 21(5) prohibits the performance by a local authority of its duty under CA 2014 s2(1)[53] in relation to an adult subject to immigration control whose needs arise solely from destitution.

There are important differences, explored elsewhere in this text,[54] between local authorities' duties and powers to meet adults' needs for care and support under CA 2014, and their duty under NAA 1948 s21(1)(a) to provide residential accommodation for a person in need of care and attention which is not otherwise available. The construction of section 21(1A) in the cases has undoubtedly been influenced by the context of the NAA 1948 in which it was located. The discussion of those cases below is retained because CA 2014 s21 is obviously intended to replicate the wording of the earlier provisions so that it is undoubtedly persuasive.[55] However, it must be read with those differences in mind; in particular it should be remembered that:

- CA 2014 s21 excludes adults subject to immigration control who are not 'destitute plus' (see para 16.30 below) from eligibility for *all* services provided under CA 2014 to meet their needs for care and support, as well as their carers' needs for support, and not merely from the provision of residential accommodation.
- By virtue of regulation 2 of the Care and Support (Eligibility Criteria) Regulations 2015 SI No 313 (the 'eligibility regulations'), the duty to meet needs under CA 2014 s18 only arises for needs which (among other conditions) 'arise from or are related to a physical or mental impairment or illness' and not solely from age or other circumstances rendering a person more vulnerable. One consequence of this narrower eligibility criterion is that, as the no recourse to public funds (NRPF) network[56] has observed, the effect of the section 21 exclusion is likely in practice to be much more limited.[57]
- As has been pointed out by the NRPF network, there is no specific test for eligibility for accommodation as a service to meet an adult's needs, and no statutory requirement that before accommodation can be provided the local authority must be satisfied that the care and attention is not available to the individual otherwise than through the provision of accommodation.[58]

53 See para 9.6 above.
54 See para 7.95 above.
55 In *R (SG) v Haringey LBC* [2015] EWHC 2579 (Admin), (2015) 18 CCLR 444, the Deputy Judge said at [29] that CA 2014 s21 'replicates the effect of NAA 1948 s21(1A). See further the discussion at para 16.34 below.
56 The No Recourse to Public Funds (NRPF) Network is a network of over 2,800 organisations focusing on the statutory response to people with care needs who have no recourse to public funds. It provides information and guidance, training, and carries out research and policy work on these issues.
57 NRPF Network, *Practice guidance for local authorities (England): assessing and supporting adults who have no recourse to public funds (NRPF)*, April 2016, section 3.7.
58 NRPF Network, *Response to the Department of Health consultation on the Care Act 2014*, August 2014.

16.34   In *R (SG) v Haringey LBC*,[59] the deputy judge held that CA 2014 s21 replicated NAA 1948 s21(1A) and applied the guidance in *R (M) v Slough*[60] and
R (L) v Westminster City Council[61] in determining whether the local authority had been entitled to refuse to provide accommodation to an asylum-
seeker with care needs under the CA 2014.[62] Since the AS Regs 2000
have not been amended, it is clear that UKVI is entitled to take account
of the potential availability of support under the CA 2014 when assessing
whether an asylum-seeker is destitute, and the rationale for treating support under the IAA 1999 as 'residual' has not altered. Provided that an
asylum-seeker's needs for care and support arise from something more
than mere destitution, local authorities are under the same duty to meet
eligible needs as they are for any other adults.

CA 2014 s8 makes clear that the services provided to meet eligible
needs can include accommodation, and the statutory guidance[63] to the
CA 2014 emphasises the importance of suitable living accommodation
in meeting care and support needs, promoting well-being and in meeting
local authorities' duties to prevent care and support needs arising under
CA 2014 s2. [64] Although the statutory guidance emphasises that accommodation needs may be met by other agencies (such as local housing
authorities), there is no basis to consider that there should be any departure from the principle established in the cases on NAA 1948 s21 that local
authorities must ignore the possibility of UKVI support when considering
whether to provide accommodation under the CA 2014. The local authority conceded this point in *R (SG) v Haringey LBC and Secretary of State for
the Home Department*.[65]

The statutory guidance is entirely silent on the relationship between
asylum support and the provision of accommodation to meet needs under
the CA 2014. The NRPF network's practice guidance published in April
2016 suggests that (1) following *R (SG) v Haringey LBC*, local authorities
must not take account of the potential availability of UKVI support when
deciding what services it is under a *duty* to provide to meet assessed eligible
needs under CA 2014 s18; but (2) that 'when it comes to the local authority
exercising the power under section 19 of the Care Act, then it seems likely
that the local authority can take into account the availability of asylum support'.[66] The correctness of this distinction has yet to be tested in court.

59 [2015] EWHC 2579 (Admin). See the discussion of the judge's approach to the
power/duty to provide accommodation under the CA 2014 in this case at para 3.135.
The claimant has been granted permission to appeal to the Court of Appeal with the
appeal expected to be heard in 2017.

60 [2008] UKHL 52.

61 [2013] UKSC 27.

62 See [47]–[53] in particular. His decision on this point was followed by Mr Peter
Marquand (sitting as a Deputy High Court Judge) in *R (GS (by her litigation friend
the Official Solicitor)) v Camden LBC* [2016] EWHC 1762 (Admin), who rejected the
argument that *SG* was wrongly decided: see [25]–[29].

63 Department of Health, *Care and support statutory guidance* to support implementation
of Part 1 of the CA 2014 by local authorities, 2016 ('the statutory guidance').

64 Paragraphs 15.48–15.68 in particular.

65 [2015] EWHC 2579 (Admin), (2015) 18 CCLR 444 at [12].

66 NRPF Network, *Practice guidance for local authorities (England): assessing and
supporting adults who have no recourse to public funds (NRPF)*, April 2016, section 7.

16.35   Another difference between the CA 2014 regime and the previous regime is that CA 2014 s21 prohibits the provision of *any* services to meet needs which arise solely from destitution or from the anticipated physical effects of destitution, whereas previously, it was only the provision of accommodation and related services under NAA 1948 s21(1)(a) and Health Services and Public Health Act (HSPHA) 1968 s45 that were caught by the 'destitution plus' test. However, given that the eligibility criteria under the eligibility regulations limit the duty to meet needs to needs which 'arise from or are related to a physical or mental impairment or illness',[67] this is unlikely to have much practical effect.

16.36   In order to qualify for the provision of accommodation and other services to meet assessed needs under the CA 2014, asylum-seekers must therefore satisfy the following criteria:

1) That they are not excluded from support by virtue of NIAA 2002 Sch 3 (see para 16.42 below). For most asylum-seekers this is straightforward as they are not excluded from community care provisions under Schedule 3.[68]

2) That they have an eligible need for care and support which requires the provision of accommodation-related services, following *R (SG) v Haringey LBC*[69] and *R (L) v Westminster City Council.*[70]

3) That they pass the 'destitution plus' test under CA 2014 s21. As outlined above, the predecessor to this proviso in NAA 1948 s21(1A) has been interpreted[71] to mean that their need for care and attention is to any material extent made more acute by some factor other than destitution or the effects or anticipated physical effects of destitution.

4) In deciding whether the local authority should provide accommodation which is required to meet assessed eligible care and support needs, the potential availability of UKVI support is to be disregarded because, by virtue of AS Regs 2000 reg 6(4) a person who is entitled to accommodation under the CA 2014 is not entitled to asylum support because he or she is not destitute.[72]

16.37   Since the 2002 *Westminster* case the courts have been asked to consider what illness or level of infirmity would satisfy the 'destitution plus' test. Accordingly, in *R (M) v Slough BC*[73] the Court of Appeal held that an HIV-positive asylum-seeker had to be accommodated by the authority: that he satisfied the 'destitution plus' test even though he was not suffering symptoms and his condition was stable. However, that decision was reversed in the House of Lords, which held that the 'need for care and attention'

---

67 Reg 2(1)(a).
68 The only exception being EEA nationals or persons who already have refugee status in another EEA state.
69 [2015] EWHC 2579 (Admin).
70 [2013] UKSC 27.
71 Consolidated appeals as *R v Wandsworth LBC ex p O* and *R v Leicester City Council ex p Bhikha* [2000] 1 WLR 2539, (2000) 3 CCLR 237.
72 *Westminster City Council v NASS* [2002] UKHL 38, [2002] 1 WLR 2956, (2002) 5 CCLR 511; but note the discussion at para 16.59 below of the position of families where some but not all members of the family would qualify for community care provision under NAA 1948 s21.
73 [2006] EWCA Civ 655, (2006) 9 CCLR 438.

in NAA 1948 s21(1)(a), while not limited to a need for nursing or personal care, required that a person needed 'looking after', and that a person whose only needs were for medication (which was provided by the NHS), a refrigerator in which to store it and regular appointments with a doctor could not be said to need 'looking after'.[74] The fact that M's condition might deteriorate in the future did not mean that he presently had a need for care and attention.[75] Accordingly, the House of Lords did not find it necessary (or indeed possible) to consider whether M's need for care and attention arose 'solely' from his destitution.

16.38   'Destitution plus' status may also arise through mental health difficulties.[76] In *R (PB) v Haringey LBC*[77] the court considered that if the applicant's depression arose from factors other than just destitution,[78] it could not be said that destitution and its physical effects are the sole cause. In *R (Pajaziti) v Lewisham LBC*,[79] the claimants' mental health problems made their need for 'shelter and warmth' more acute, and accordingly it did not arise *solely* from their destitution.[80]

16.39   UKVI's asylum support instruction on asylum-seekers with care needs[81] advises that in 'clear and urgent cases',[82] immigration officers or UKVI screening officers should refer asylum applicants with care needs directly to the local authority; in all other cases, applicants should first be dispersed and any community care assessments (CCAs) carried out in the dispersal area.[83] The policy suggests that where a CCA has been commenced in emergency accommodation or an induction centre but not completed, the assumption should be that the asylum-seeker will be dispersed and a new CCA commenced by the new local authority. UKVI will

---

74 *R (M) v Slough BC* [2008] UKHL 52, [2008] 1 WLR 1808; see para 16.28 above.

75 Baroness Hale at [35]–[36]; Lord Neuberger at [55] and [65].

76 Where entitlement to Mental Health Act (MHA) 1983 s117 support exists, there is no prohibition in the provision of such community care support.

77 [2006] EWHC 2255 (Admin), (2007) 10 CCLR 99 at [49]–[50].

78 PB's anxieties were largely attributable to her fragile mental health and her concern about her children who were subject to care proceedings.

79 [2007] EWCA Civ 1351.

80 Although as noted above, it is doubtful whether the authority's concession that a need for 'shelter and warmth' was a need for 'care and attention' within section 21(1)(a) would be made following *R (M) v Slough BC*.

81 UKVI, *Asylum seekers with care needs*, September 2014. This instruction replaced Policy Bulletin 82 with effect from September 2014. It is available at www.gov. uk/government/uploads/system/uploads/attachment_data/file/356217/Asylum_ Seekers_with_care_needs.pdf.

82 Defined as cases where an asylum-seeker has 'a clear care need and an urgent need for services', such as 'where the person has an illness giving rise to obvious care needs, or is severely disabled and has no accommodation available to them' (para 2.1) and 'where it is immediately apparent that the person is severely disabled or needs care due to an illness' (chapter 9).

83 Para 2.1 and chapter 9. This guidance applies to single adults only; see para 21.60 below for the policy in relation to families with children. In relation to families with adult dependents but no children, the policy expresses an expectation that the local authority will support close relatives as well as the person with care needs, although they are not under a duty to do so, and indicates that otherwise UKVI will 'liaise with the local authority to consider whether it is appropriate and possible to identify a location where he/she can be provided with accommodation within close proximity to the dependant with the care need' (chapter 6).

not therefore ordinarily accept the fact that there is a CCA in progress as a 'reasonable excuse' for failing to travel to the dispersal accommodation.[84]

Exclusions and exemptions

Exclusions from social care services under the Nationality, Immigration and Asylum Act 2002

16.40 Before considering the position of former asylum-seekers and other migrants, it is necessary to refer to the provisions of the NIAA 2002 which exclude certain categories of migrant from community care services. The NIAA 2002 was a response, in part, to the perceived failure of the IAA 1999 to deter sufficient numbers of unlawful immigrants and asylum-seekers from entering the UK. In addition, it sought to deal with what the government termed 'entitlement shopping' – namely 'individuals who move to the UK for the sole or main purpose of accessing residential accommodation and other services in preference to similar services in the EEA[85] country of origin'.[86]

16.41 The NIAA 2002 does not change the law concerning social services responsibilities to asylum-seekers (whose claims have not been determined), although (as discussed above) section 55 did materially change the obligations of the UKVI to asylum-seekers who failed to make their asylum claim 'as soon as reasonably practicable' after their arrival in the UK.[87] It did, however, significantly alter the position in respect of former asylum-seekers and a number of other categories of migrant.

16.42 NIAA 2002 s54 and Sch 3 prohibit local authorities from providing community care services in general (including all services provided under CA 2014 Part 1), services under Children Act (CA) 1989 s17 (except for minors) and services under Local Government Act (LGA) 2000 s2 and Localism Act (LA) 2011 s1 for:

- individuals with refugee status in other EEA countries;
- citizens of other EEA countries;
- former asylum-seekers who have not co-operated with removal directions;[88] and
- individuals who are unlawfully in the UK and who are not asylum-seekers.[89]

---

84 Para 3.1.
85 European Economic Area – this consists of the EU countries together with Iceland, Liechtenstein, Norway and Switzerland.
86 Department of Health, *Section 54 of the Nationality, Immigration and Asylum Act 2002 and community care and other social services for adults from the EEA living in the UK: note of clarification*, 2003, para 4, available at www.dh.gov.uk/prod_consum_dh/idcplg?IdcService=GET_FILE&dID=4171&Rendition=Web
87 NIAA 2002 s55.
88 Note that where there are dependent children who were supported with the main applicant before his or her application for asylum was refused, the asylum-seeker continues to be eligible for section 95 support while he or she remains in UK, and will only be covered by Schedule 3 if the secretary of state certifies that the main applicant has failed to take reasonable steps to leave the UK.
89 The exclusions also apply to people who are dependents of the above, unless they are British citizens or children.

16.43   As noted above, these exclusions do not apply to *current* asylum-seekers (save where they are EEA nationals or have refugee status in another EEA state), and nor do they exclude entitlement to care under Mental Health Act (MHA) 1983 s117.

16.44   Paragraph 1 of Schedule 3 was amended when CA 2014 was brought into force to apply to the whole of CA 2014 Part 1. However, the exclusions only prevent the provision of 'support and assistance' under the social care provisions to which they apply. They do not, therefore, prevent local authorities from exercising functions that do not amount to the provision of 'support and assistance'. In an email to the NRPF network on 29 July 2015, the Home Office and Department of Health reportedly set out their position that the correct interpretation is that:

- Schedule 3 prevents excluded groups from receiving 'support or assistance' under the CA 2014.
- Local authorities may undertake needs assessments for adults requiring care and support (under section 9) and carers (under section 10).
- Local authorities may meet urgent needs for care and support whilst undertaking the relevant assessments (section 19(3)).
- There is no prohibition on a local authority undertaking its general duties with regards to providing information and advice (section 4) or prevention (section 2).[90]

The rights-based exemption

16.45   As with NIAA 2002 s55 (para 16.16 above), there is a human rights exemption, ie the prohibition does not apply where support is necessary to prevent a breach of a person's ECHR rights and also an exception where the provision of support is necessary to prevent a breach of a person's EU Treaty rights.

16.46   As noted above, the jurisprudence on the human rights exemption to NIAA 2002 s55 will be relevant to the equivalent exemption under Schedule 3. However, in section 55 cases it will be assumed that applicants cannot avoid being exposed to inhuman and degrading treatment by leaving the UK because by definition they will have an extant (first) asylum claim. Social care support may, however, also be necessary to avoid a breach of individuals' ECHR rights either (a) pending their departure from the UK if they are taking reasonable steps to leave or (b) where it would be unreasonable to expect the person to leave the UK in order to avoid being exposed to the degrading treatment which is likely to follow from any extended period of destitution and street homelessness, following *Limbuela*[91] and *MSS v Belgium and Greece*.[92] The additional issue that arises in respect of exclusion from social care services under Schedule 3 is thus whether it is possible or reasonable to expect the applicant to immediately leave the UK,

90   See the NRPF Network, *Practice guidance for local authorities (England): assessing and supporting adults who have no recourse to public funds (NRPF)*, April 2016, section 2.3, pp14–15.
91   [2005] UKHL 66, [2005] 3 WLR 1014, (2006) 9 CCLR 30.
92   ECtHR, Application no 30696/09, judgment 21 January 2011. See para 16.20 above.

and the extent to which the local authority should investigate that issue for itself.

16.47　　In the case of former asylum-seekers who have made a 'fresh asylum claim' (ie further representations to UKVI that their removal would breach the UN Refugee Convention or ECHR Article 3), then support should be regarded as necessary to prevent a breach of their Convention rights pending consideration of that claim by UKVI. The local authority should not attempt to assess the fresh asylum claim for itself, although it may refuse to provide community care services if the representations were merely repetitious or manifestly unfounded.[93]

16.48　　Although some earlier cases had adopted a more conservative approach where a claim to remain in the UK was founded on ECHR Article 8[94] grounds,[95] the correct approach is now set out in the decision of the Court of Appeal in *R (Clue) v Birmingham City Council*,[96] which was concerned with the availability of accommodation and services under CA 1989 s17 to an overstayer and her children who would otherwise have been on the street. Dyson LJ held that the local authority had to consider a series of questions:

1) First, it must consider whether the person concerned is excluded from support by NIAA 2002 Sch 3, save to the extent that it is necessary to prevent a breach of his ECHR rights.[97]

2) Next, it must consider whether the person has available to him or her any other source of accommodation and support, so that withholding assistance would not in any event result in a breach of ECHR rights.[98]

3) Third, and only if the answer to the second question is that the person would otherwise be destitute, it must consider whether there is 'an impediment' to the person returning to his or her country of origin.[99] If the impediment is 'practical in nature', such as an inability to pay for flights, the local authority might legitimately arrange transport: *R (Grant) v Lambeth LBC.*[100]

4) If, however, there is a 'legal impediment' to return, in the form of a claim that return would itself breach ECHR rights, the local authority must first consider whether the person has made an application to UKVI for leave to remain which 'expressly or implicitly raises grounds under the

---

93　*R (AW) v Croydon* [2005] EWHC 2950 (Admin); this part of the judgment of Lloyd Jones J was not appealed to the Court of Appeal.

94　Article 8 protects the right to respect for private and family life, and has been interpreted as entitling a person to resist removal from the UK where that would result in a substantial interference with the person's family life with one or more persons with a right to remain in the UK, or where the person has established a 'private' life through a long period of residence, particularly if the person came to the UK as a child.

95　See *R (Grant) v Lambeth LBC* [2004] EWCA Civ 1711, [2005] 1 WLR 1781 and *R (Kimani) v Lambeth LBC* [2003] EWCA Civ 1150, [2004] 1 WLR 272 – both of which were distinguished and not overruled by *Clue*.

96　[2010] EWCA Civ 460, [2011] 1 WLR 99, (2010) 13 CCLR 276.

97　Judgment at [54].

98　Judgment at [54]–[55].

99　Judgment at [55].

100　[2005] 1 WLR 1781; *Clue* at [56].

Convention'.[101] If so, and if support is otherwise necessary to prevent a breach of ECHR rights, the local authority may only refuse to provide support if the application is 'not "obviously hopeless or abusive"' which would include applications which are 'merely a repetition of an application which has already been rejected'.[102] It may not have regard to its financial resources.[103] It is the responsibility of the UKVI to decide applications for leave to remain in the UK and local authorities are not permitted to usurp that responsibility by making it impossible for the person concerned to remain in the UK.[104] UKVI accepted it should prioritise consideration of applications for leave to remain from families who were being supported by local authorities.[105]

5) If no application has in fact been made to the UKVI, or none is pending, then the local authority must consider for itself whether the applicant's circumstances engage the ECHR and, in an Article 8 case, is 'entitled to have regard to the calls of others on its budget in deciding whether an interference with a person's Article 8 rights would be justified and proportionate within the meaning of Article 8.2'.[106]

16.49   This approach was applied to a claim under NAA 1948 s21 in *R (Mwanza) v Greenwich LBC and Bromley LBC*,[107] Hickinbottom J considered it to be 'well-settled' law that where an immigration application was outstanding, 'claims for section 21 support should only be dismissed if such an immigration claim is manifestly unfounded or not "obviously hopeless or abusive"'.[108] In the case before him, he held that the claimant had not established that he had any pending application for leave to remain and that any potential ECHR Article 8 claim (none having in fact been advanced) was 'unarguable', so that the local authority was prohibited by section 54 and Schedule 3 from providing support to the claimant and his family.

16.50   In a case in which there is no practical or legal impediment to the applicant returning to his or her country of origin to avoid a breach of the applicant's ECHR rights, support will not be 'necessary to prevent a breach of a person's rights'. In *R (Kimani) v Lambeth LBC*,[109] the Court of Appeal rejected Ms Kimani's case that as she would not return to her own country, Kenya, the refusal of the local authority to provide accommodation and support for her and her ten-year-old son would inevitably lead to breaches of their rights under ECHR Articles 3 and 8 (because of the likelihood that if she was homeless, her son would be taken into care). The Court of Appeal held that any interference in their rights would not be the

---

101 Judgment at [53] and [60].
102 Judgment at [66].
103 Judgment at [72].
104 Judgment at [63]–[66].
105 Judgment at [84].
106 Judgment at [73].
107 [2010] EWHC 1462 (Admin).
108 Para [47].
109 [2003] EWCA Civ 1150, [2004] 1 WLR 272.

result of the refusal of support, but rather of her unreasonable refusal to leave the UK.[110]

16.51   In *R (KA) v Essex CC*,[111] the claimant had made an application for leave to remain on Article 8 grounds which had been refused by the Home Office. As she was an overstayer, the refusal did not in itself trigger a right of appeal under NIAA 2002 s82. A right of appeal would arise only when the Home Office made a decision under IAA 1999 s10 to remove her from the UK. The High Court held that the local authority might be obliged in such circumstances to provide KA and her children with support under CA 1989 s17 in order to enable them to remain in the UK so as to protect her procedural rights under ECHR Article 8 to exercise her right of appeal as and when it arose. Essex appealed to the Court of Appeal but its appeal was dismissed as academic[112] as KA had in the meantime acquired a right of appeal, and the Home Office had published guidance which stated that an appealable removal decision should be issued on request in such cases, where a person was being supported by the local authority under CA 1989 s17 or NAA 1948 s21.[113] Changes made to immigration appeal rights by the Immigration Act (IA) 2014 mean that (since April 2015) a decision to refuse a human rights claim (including an Article 8 claim) now ordinarily carries a right of appeal without the need for a decision to remove. However, further changes introduced by Immigration Act (IA) 2016 s63 from 1 December 2016 mean that in many cases, this right of appeal will only be exercisable *after* the appellant leaves, or is removed from, the UK.[114] These developments will have significant implications for the eligibility for social care of individuals whose Article 8 claims have been refused.

Withholding and Withdrawal of Support (Travel Assistance and Temporary Accommodation) Regulations 2002

16.52   As well as the rights-based exemptions, NIAA 2002 Sch 3 paras 8–10 and the Withholding and Withdrawal of Support (Travel Assistance and Temporary Accommodation Regulations 2002[115] create very limited powers for local authorities to:

- make travel arrangements for people who are excluded because they are EEA nationals or EEA refugees, to enable them to leave the UK;[116]

---

110 Note that in *Clue*, the court distinguished *Kimani* on the grounds that Ms Kimani's appeal against the refusal of an EEA residence card could be pursued from Kenya, whereas Ms Clue's application for leave to remain on Article 8 grounds would in all probability be treated as having lapsed if she left the UK.

111 [2013] EWHC 43 (Admin).

112 [2013] EWCA Civ 1261.

113 UKVI guidance, *Requests for removal decisions*, October 2014, available at www.gov.uk/government/uploads/system/uploads/attachment_data/file/364512/Requests_for_Removal_Decisions_v6.0_EXT.pdf.

114 If the claim is 'certified' under NIAA 2002 s94B. The power to certify has existed for cases involving deportation on grounds of criminality since July 2014.

115 SI No 3078.

116 Sch 3 para 8.

- provide accommodation for such people pending their departure from the UK;[117]
- provide accommodation for people who are excluded because they are in breach of immigration law, but who have not failed to comply with removal directions.[118]

Accommodation can only be provided in either case if the person has a dependent child.[119]

16.53   Local authorities are required to comply with guidance issued by the Secretary of State for the Home Department[120] in providing support and making travel arrangements under these provisions. In *R (M) v Islington LBC*,[121] the Court of Appeal considered the impact of that guidance[122] in a case involving a mother who was ineligible for CA 1989 services because she was unlawfully present in the UK, having stayed beyond the expiry of her visa. The guidance stated that it would be 'preferable' for accommodation to be provided only for ten days in such a case. The Court of Appeal held that the local authority was entitled – and indeed, on the facts of the case, bound – to provide accommodation for longer than ten days in circumstances where the UKVI had not yet issued directions for M's removal from the UK. It was unreasonable to withdraw accommodation because M had not been removed from the UK after ten days, when that was a matter entirely outside the control of both M and the local authority.

Former asylum-seekers

Immigration and Asylum Act 1999 s4 support

16.54   Asylum-seekers whose applications for asylum have been refused and finally determined (ie appeal rights exhausted) are expected to leave the UK. However, there are some former asylum-seekers who are destitute and unable to leave the UK immediately due to circumstances beyond their control. In such cases, they can be provided with support under IAA 1999 s4(2) ('section 4 support').[123] Section 4 support (previously commonly known as 'hard case support') was intended as a limited and temporary form of support for people who are expected to leave the UK within a short period of time. Many former asylum-seekers, however, find themselves supported under section 4 for indefinite periods.

16.55   In order to obtain support, the applicant must show that he or she is destitute. The definition of destitution for IAA 1999 s4 purposes is the same as in IAA 1999 s95(3) (see para 16.14 above). It can be particularly difficult to demonstrate destitution to the satisfaction of UKVI if a former

---

117 Sch 3 para 9.
118 Sch 3 para 10.
119 Sch 3 paras 9(2) and 10(2).
120 Reg 4(4).
121 [2004] EWCA Civ 235.
122 The guidance at that time being Home Office, *Guidance to assist authorities to determine whether to make travel arrangements/grant temporary short-term accommodation*, 2002.
123 As amended by NIAA 2002 s49.

asylum-seeker has been without UKVI support for any significant period, and a very detailed account will be required of how the applicant has maintained himself or herself and any dependents in that period, and why he or she cannot continue to do so.[124]

16.56   Former asylum-seekers requesting support under section 4 must also meet the eligibility criteria in the relevant regulations.[125] Broadly speaking, these limit support to situations where it would not be reasonable to expect the former asylum-seeker to immediately leave the UK. They include cases where the person is taking reasonable steps to leave the UK but cannot do so immediately, such as where travel documentation needs to be obtained,[126] where there is a medical impediment to travel,[127] and a catch-all provision allowing support to be provided where there would otherwise be a breach of the person's ECHR rights.[128] This latter provision most commonly arises where the former asylum-seeker has made a fresh claim for asylum which is still under consideration by UKVI, but in light of *Limbuela*,[129] it would cover any situation where it would be unreasonable to expect the applicant to leave the UK to avoid the breach of his or her Article 3 rights which would arise if he or she were left destitute and street homeless for any significant period.

16.57   Section 4 support is circumscribed by the statutory term 'facilities for the accommodation of a person'. What can be provided under section 4 must be linked to the accommodation being provided. There is thus no provision within the relevant regulations for support to be provided as cash,[130] and it is ordinarily provided by way of accommodation and a

---

124 For a critique of the application of this test by UKVI to applications under IAA 1999 s4 – see Asylum Support Appeals Project (ASAP), *No credibility. UKBA decision making and section 4 support. Why 80% of destitution refusals are overturned on appeal*, 2011; and ASAP, *UKBA decision making audit: one year on still 'no credibility'*, 2013.

125 Immigration and Asylum (Provision of Accommodation to Failed Asylum Seekers) Regulations 2005 SI No 930 reg 3.

126 Reg 3(2)(a); current UKVI policy severely limits the time for which support will ordinarily be provided in these cases, notwithstanding that it can in some cases take months or years to obtain travel documentation.

127 Reg 3(2)(b); note that this is very limited in its application and will only apply where a person is physically *unable* to travel. It also applies to pregnant women in the late stages of pregnancy and those with newborn children – UKVI policy is currently not to normally grant support until six weeks before the estimated date of delivery (EDD) and to withdraw it once the baby is six weeks old. However, the First-Tier Tribunal (Asylum Support) has upheld appeals on grounds of pregnancy earlier than six weeks before the EDD.

128 Reg 3(2)(e). The other two classes are where the secretary of state has declared that there is no viable route of return to a given country (reg 3(2)(c)) – in practice, extremely unlikely – and where the applicant has been granted permission to apply for judicial review (reg 3(2)(d)). In *R (NS) Somalia v First Tier Tribunal (Social Entitlement Chamber)* [2009] EWHC 3819 (Admin), the Administrative Court held that a person who was claiming judicial review but did not yet have permission was likely to qualify for support under reg 3(2)(e) and the First-tier Tribunal will often allow an appeal under reg 3(2)(e) where an individual is in the process of applying for legal aid to bring judicial review proceedings, or has sent a pre-action protocol letter and is awaiting a response.

129 [2005] UKHL 66, [2005] 3 WLR 1014, (2006) 9 CCLR 30; see para 16.17 above.

130 Immigration and Asylum (Provision of Accommodation to Failed Asylum Seekers) Regulations 2005 SI No 930.

payment card pre-loaded each week.[131] This inevitably causes problems, in particular in terms of clothing, telephone calls and travel.[132]

16.58   Immigration, Asylum and Nationality Act 2006 s43 alleviated the situation somewhat by amending IAA 1999 s4 to allow the Secretary of State for the Home Department to make regulations allowing for the provision of facilities and services. These are the Immigration and Asylum (Provision of Services or Facilities) Regulations 2007,[133] and they allow for additional support to be provided to pay for travel for necessary healthcare treatment or to register a birth,[134] birth certificates,[135] telephone calls and correspondence for limited purposes,[136] additional support for pregnant women and young children[137] and other exceptional specific needs.[138] It is of course possible, in the case of a former asylum-seeker with a child, for a request to be made to the local authority for an assessment and services under CA 1989 s17 (see paras 16.69 and 16.88 below)[139] for items that section 4 cannot provide.

16.59   One of the most problematic issues which the limitation of IAA 1999 s4 support to 'facilities for accommodation' creates is that, given the impermissibility of providing support to meet essential living needs without also providing accommodation, families where some family members are not eligible for section 4 support (for example, because they are British or otherwise have permission to reside in the UK) may not be accommodated together. In *R (MK and others) v Secretary of State for the Home Department*,[140] the Court of Appeal affirmed that the Secretary of State for the Home Department was not entitled under section 4 to provide subsistence support without also taking some responsibility for the provision of accommodation, and was accordingly entitled to have a general policy of only providing support under target contracts: section 4 is not a provision aimed at alleviating destitution, but at providing accommodation to those who are unable to leave the UK. However, the Court of Appeal did not rule out that Article 8 might, in some circumstances, require the provision of accommodation for a family together.

---

131 The weekly rate of support is £35.39 per person. For single adults, any amount over £5 cannot be carried over to the following week. As at 8 March 2015, the shops in which the payment card could be used included Tesco, Asda, Boots, Sainsbury's, the Co-operative, Mothercare, Iceland and Morrisons, as well as British Red Cross and Salvation Army charity shops; see www.gov.uk/government/uploads/system/uploads/attachment_data/file/406786/Azure_Card_Carrier_2015.pdf.

132 See *R (AW (Kenya)) v Secretary of State for the Home Department* [2006] EWHC 3147 (Admin).

133 SI No 3627.

134 SI No 3627 reg3.

135 SI No 3627 reg 4.

136 SI No 3627 reg 5.

137 SI No 3627 regs 6–8.

138 SI No 3627 reg 9.

139 NIAA 2002 Sch 3 does not prevent services being provided to a child.

140 [2011] EWCA Civ 671.

Social care provision

16.60 As with asylum-seekers, former asylum-seekers who satisfy the 'destitution plus' test are likely to be the responsibility of local authority social services departments under CA 2014 s18, subject to NIAA 2002 Sch 3.[141] In *R (AW) v Croydon LBC*[142] the Court of Appeal held that vulnerable former asylum-seekers whose human rights call for accommodation are to have that accommodation provided by local authorities, and not by UKVI.[143] Laws LJ observed that there was 'nothing to show that the legislature intended to distribute responsibility for the support of failed asylum-seekers between central and local government in a radically different manner from the arrangements which ... were made in relation to asylum seekers'.[144] For social care purposes, the law divides former asylum-seekers into two distinct categories.

16.61 The first category comprises those asylum-seekers who claimed asylum as soon as they arrived in the UK ('at port'). They will normally have been granted temporary admission to enter the UK which means they are in the UK lawfully.[145] As they are lawfully present, they remain entitled to local authority support until such time as formal steps to remove them from the UK are not complied with. If a former asylum-seeker fails to comply with removal directions (by which in this context we mean directions given to a carrier such as a ship or aeroplane) at any time, they are excluded from social care services by virtue of NIAA 2002 Sch 3.[146]

16.62 The second category comprises former asylum-seekers who did not claim at port and who are therefore in the UK in breach of immigration law. They are excluded by NIAA 2002 Sch 3 and can only receive social care assistance if and to the extent that support is necessary to avoid a breach of their ECHR rights. In consequence, former asylum-seekers who claimed asylum 'at port' ordinarily remain eligible for CA 2014 support even after their claim for asylum has been refused, whereas those who did not claim 'at port' cease to be eligible for CA 2014 support once their claims for asylum have been finally determined, unless support is required to prevent a breach of their ECHR rights.[147]

---

141 This was the position under NAA 1948 s21 and given the similarity of the statutory wording in CA 2014, s21 and the absence of any amendment to the AS Regs 2000, there is no reason to think it will be any different under the CA 2014.

142 [2007] EWCA Civ 266, [2007] 1 WLR 3168, (2007) 10 CCLR 225.

143 Since the definition of 'destitution' for IAA 1999 s4 purposes is the same as that under IAA 1999 s95, which, as discussed above, requires the UKVI to take account of any other support which is, or might reasonably be expected to be, available. A person who is entitled to community care is thus unlikely to be destitute.

144 [2007] EWCA Civ 266, [2007] 1 WLR 3168, (2007) 10 CCLR 225 at [54].

145 NIAA 2002 s11 and British Nationality Act (BNA) 1981 s50A(6).

146 Subject to the human rights exemption discussed below.

147 At the time of writing, the case-law still is based on NAA 1948 s21 rather than the CA 2014, but since this depends on the interpretation of NIAA 2002 Sch 3 it seems unlikely that the position will be any different. For an example of a case where the provision of section 21 accommodation was held not to be necessary to prevent a breach of the claimant's human rights because he could return to his own country, his appeal against removal on Article 3 grounds having been dismissed by the Asylum and Immigration Tribunal, see *R (N) v Coventry City Council* [2008] EWHC 2786 (Admin). Note that in that case the local authority had offered to 'assist

16.63   In *R (GS) v Camden LBC*,[148] the deputy judge held that a Swiss woman who lacked the capacity to decide whether to return to Switzerland was not eligible for accommodation under CA 2014 because her needs were not such as to require the provision of accommodation-related services. However, he concluded that the local authority had the power to provide GS with accommodation using its general well-being power in LA 2011 s1 and nothing in the CA 2014 constituted a 'post-commencement restriction' on that power.[149] In the light of the medical evidence 'that the claimant is vulnerable and social stressors around accommodation and finances exacerbate her mental condition, including suicidal ideation', and taking account of all the circumstances, he held that there would be a violation of ECHR Article 3 if GS were to become homeless.[150] In the circumstances, the local authority was under a duty to exercise its LA 2011 s1 power to provide the claimant with accommodation.[151]

Duties owed to children[152]

Children of asylum-seekers

16.64   As noted above, IAA 1999 s95 empowers the secretary of state (through UKVI) to provide support for adult asylum-seekers who are destitute or likely to become destitute. However, by IAA 1999 s122, there is a duty on UKVI to support destitute asylum-seekers with dependent children, and, in particular, under section 122(3), to make available 'adequate accommodation for the child'. In *R (A) v NASS and Waltham Forest LBC*[153] the court held that the accommodation of asylum seeking families with disabled children was the sole responsibility of NASS (now UKVI), although in discharging this duty it could seek assistance from a local authority under IAA 1999 s100 (and in such cases the authority must assist so far as is 'reasonable in the circumstances').

16.65   UKVI's policy is to refer families with children with a clear care need to the local authority for an assessment to be carried out and any necessary services to be provided in addition to UKVI support.[154] The policy also makes clear that accommodation provided by UKVI to a family which includes a child with care needs must be 'adequate' for the needs of that

the claimant in directing him to free air services to his country of origin and to accommodate him to a period of 14 days ... whilst arrangements are made' (at [51]).

148 [2016] EWHC 1762 (Admin).

149 At [51]–[62].

150 At [75].

151 At [76] and [78].

152 For a more detailed consideration of the entitlement of migrant children and their families to services under CA 1989 Part III, see I Wise QC, S Broach, J Burton, C Gallagher, A Pickup, B Silverstone and A Suterwalla, *Children in need: local authority support for children and families*, 2nd edition, Legal Action Group, 2013, chapter 6.

153 [2003] EWCA Civ 1473, [2004] 1 WLR 752, (2003) 6 CCLR 538 – see also *R (O) v Haringey LBC* [2003] EWHC 2798 (Admin) where it was held that UKVI had responsibility even where there were disabled adult family members.

154 UKVI, *Asylum support instruction: Asylum seekers with care needs*, September 2014, Chapter 4: Families whose children have a care need.

child, and that the duty to ensure the accommodation is adequate is a continuing one.[155] However, in assessing whether accommodation is adequate, UKVI is entitled to take account of the length of time for which the family is likely to be in the accommodation (the assumption being that it will be short-term given the aim of resolving asylum claims quickly), and of the availability of accommodation in different areas. The fact that a dependent child has a care need will not normally be regarded as a reason not to disperse a family providing those needs can be met in the dispersal area.[156]

16.66   In *R (Refugee Action) v Secretary of State for the Home Department*,[157] the court considered the division of responsibility between local authorities and UKVI in the case of such families. It concluded that UKVI had a duty to ensure that the accommodation provided to the family was adequate to meet the needs of any disabled children. UKVI also has a duty to meet any 'essential living needs' of the family, including any additional or specific needs arising out of the children's disabilities. However, under IAA 1999 s122(4), it is entitled to take account of other support which may reasonably be expected to be available to meet those needs, including support from local authorities *other* than support under CA 1989 s17 which is intended to meet essential living needs (because the effect of IAA 1999 s122(5) is to exclude that support). So, for example, UKVI is entitled to take account of services which might be provided to such children under other provisions of the CA 1989 such as section 18, or services which are not 'essential living needs' which are provided under CA 1989 s17(10), including pursuant to the duty under the Chronically Sick and Disabled Persons Act (CSDPA) 1970 s2(4).[158]

16.67   In *R (O) v Haringey LBC and Secretary of State for the Home Department*[159] the facts were reversed in that it was the mother who was disabled, not the children. In that case, the Court of Appeal held that the local authority owed the mother a duty under NAA 1948 s21, but this did not extend to accommodating her children, for whom NASS was responsible under IAA 1999 s122(5).[160] On a practical level, the court suggested that the local authority should accommodate the whole family, with NASS making a financial contribution to cover the cost of accommodating the children.[161] This suggestion is reflected in UKVI's policy guidance, which states that UKVI will contribute 'the full subsistence rate for a child of that age and a contribution towards accommodation costs', but not any additional costs which arise from the adult's care needs.[162]

---

155 UKVI, *Asylum support instruction: Asylum seekers with care needs*, September 2014, Chapter 4: Families whose children have a care need.

156 UKVI, *Asylum support instruction: Asylum seekers with care needs*, September 2014, Chapter 4: Families whose children have a care need.

157 [2014] EWHC 1033 (Admin).

158 Judgment at [79]–[80].

159 [2004] EWCA Civ 535, (2004) 7 CCLR 310.

160 They are to be treated as 'destitute' by virtue of Asylum Support Regulations 2000 regs 6 and 12 even though living with their mother.

161 These authorities are reflected in the guidance in UKVI, *Asylum support instruction: Asylum seekers with care needs*, September 2014,

162 UKVI, *Asylum support instruction: Asylum seekers with care needs*, September 2014, Chapter 6: Families with an adult who has a care need (dependent children in household).

Children of former asylum-seekers

16.68   IAA 1999 s122 only applies to asylum-seekers. The case of former asylum-seekers is materially different, since there is no free-standing obligation or power enabling UKVI to accommodate or fund the child of a former asylum-seeker. However, where the family included a dependent child under the age of 18 before the asylum claim was finally determined, they do not cease to be 'asylum-seekers' for support purposes until the child turns 18 or both the parent and child leave the UK.[163]

16.69   Where the local authority is supporting an adult former asylum-seeker under NAA 1948 s21 it also falls to the local authority to support the children under CA 1989 s17. This is because a person who has ceased to be an asylum-seeker is not entitled to be considered for support under IAA 1999 s95 and therefore the provisions under IAA 1999 s122 do not apply. The power to accommodate dependents of a former asylum-seeker is found in IAA 1999 s4(2) and only exists where there is a power to accommodate the adult former asylum-seeker. Unlike with asylum-seekers, the local social services authority in this situation is not precluded from providing support under CA 1989 s17 (subject to the provisions of NIAA 2002 s54 and Sch 3).

16.70   In *R (VC) v Newcastle City Council*,[164] the Divisional Court considered a case in which a local authority had purported to terminate accommodation and support provided under CA 1989 s17 on the grounds that the family was eligible for IAA 1999 s4 support (see para 16.54 above). Munby LJ held that section 4 support was a 'residual' power and it was not open to the local authority to terminate support solely on that ground, and without having carried out any reassessment of needs. He further held that, where the local authority is approached by a family who may be eligible for section 4 support, if it assessed that any child in the family was in fact 'in need', it could not refuse to provide services under CA 1989 s17 'unless it can be shown, first, that the Secretary of State is actually able and willing (or if not willing can be compelled) to provide section 4 support, and, second, that section 4 support will suffice to meet the child's assessed needs'.[165] The Divisional Court left open the question of whether the Home Office was entitled to refuse to provide section 4 support, if approached first, on the ground that CA 1989 s17 support would be available to the family.

Unaccompanied asylum-seeking children

16.71   The UKVI defines an unaccompanied asylum seeking child as:

> ... a person who: a) is under 18 years of age when the asylum application is submitted; b) is applying for asylum in their own right; and c) is separated from both parents and is not being cared for by an adult who in law or by custom has responsibility to do so.[166]

---

163 IAA 1999 s94(5).
164 [2011] EWHC 2673 (Admin), (2012) 15 CCLR 194.
165 Para 91.
166 Immigration Rules HC395, as amended, para 352ZD.

16.72 CA 1989 s 20(1) provides that the local authority shall:

> ... provide accommodation for a child in need who requires it as a result of there being no-one with parental responsibility for him; being lost or abandoned or the person caring for him has been prevented (whether or not permanently and for whatever reason) from providing him with suitable accommodation or care.

16.73 The duty of the local authority under CA 1989 s20 applies in relation to a child in need 'within their area'. The duty of accommodating and supporting unaccompanied asylum seeking children therefore falls to the local authority within whose area the child is residing or has just arrived. However, under an 'interim national transfer protocol', introduced in July 2016,[167] local authorities can enter into voluntary arrangements to transfer unaccompanied asylum seeking[168] children (UASC) to other local authorities. The protocol is triggered where the proportion of UASC in the local authority area reaches 0.07 per cent of all children in the area.[169] Once triggered, there is an expectation that children will be transferred to another local authority.[170] However, the decision whether to request a transfer rests with the individual local authority and requires consideration of what is in the child's best interests and all other relevant considerations.[171] The purpose is stated to be to achieve a more equitable distribution of UASC across the UK, and once a transfer request has been made, a central administration team within UKVI will decide which region the child will be transferred to. Once transferred under the protocol, the child becomes the responsibility of the host authority, and is treated as if he or she had always been looked after by the receiving authority, rather than by the transferring authority.[172]

16.74 If the local authority disputes the claimed age of the applicant, it has the power to conduct a detailed age assessment.[173] Following the judgment of

---

167 To give effect to the power to enter into arrangements for the transfer of responsibility for 'relevant children' under IA 2016 s69. The *Interim national transfer protocol for unaccompanied asylum seeking children 2016–17*, version 0.8, July 2016, is available at www.gov.uk/government/uploads/system/uploads/attachment_data/file/534258/Interim_National_UASC_transfer_protocol.pdf.

168 The power in IA 2016, s69 applies to 'relevant children', namely (a) unaccompanied asylum seeking children, (b) unaccompanied children who require leave to enter or remain but do not have it in specified circumstances and (c) other specified unaccompanied children who do have leave to enter or remain: section 69(9). Regulations are required in order to specify the circumstances in which the power will apply to children within (b) and (c) and have not been laid at the time of writing. The protocol makes clear that it only applies to unaccompanied asylum seeking children at this stage.

169 This threshold is stated to have been reached through consultation with the Association of Directors of Children's Services, the Local Government Association, the Home Office and the Department for Education, and will be reviewed in April 2017 and annually thereafter.

170 *Interim national transfer protocol for unaccompanied asylum seeking children 2016–17*, Version 0.8, July 2016.

171 *Interim national transfer protocol for unaccompanied asylum seeking children 2016–17*, Version 0.8, July 2016.

172 IA 2016 s69(3).

173 *B v Merton LBC* [2003] EWHC 1689 (Admin), [2003] 4 All ER 280, (2003) 6 CCLR 457.

the Supreme Court in *R (A) v Croydon LBC*,[174] if there is any dispute about the age of the applicant following the local authority's assessment, the matter will be determined as a question of precedent fact by the court on an application for judicial review. In *R (FZ) v Croydon LBC*,[175] the Court of Appeal indicated that all such judicial review claims should be transferred to the Upper Tribunal (Immigration and Asylum Chamber) under Senior Courts Act 1981 s31A(3).[176]

16.75   Just as in the case of any other person leaving care, when a UASC turns 18, the local authority may owe them obligations as a former relevant child if they have accrued sufficient 'looked after' time. If the young person has been granted leave to remain, his or her position is likely to be identical to that of any other young person.[177] As for those who are still asylum-seekers or are former asylum-seekers, in *R (SO) v Barking and Dagenham LBC*,[178] the Court of Appeal held that in deciding whether to provide accommodation to a care leaver who is a former relevant child under CA 1989 s23C(4)(c), the local authority is not entitled to take account of the availability of UKVI support. Thus responsibility for the accommodation and subsistence of former relevant children remains with the local authority.[179]

EEA nationals

Generally

16.76   The EEA consists of 31 countries, made up of the EU states together with Norway, Iceland and Liechtenstein.[180]

16.77   Under the Treaty of Rome 1959 (and subsequent treaties and legislation) citizens of these states enjoy various rights of free movement within the territory of the EEA. These rights are set out in various European directives and regulations.[181]

---

174 [2009] UKSC 8, [2009] 1 WLR 2557.

175 [2011] EWCA Civ 59, (2011) 14 CCLR 289, [2011] HLR 22.

176 Inserted by Tribunals, Courts and Enforcement Act 2007 s19. For a more detailed discussion of the age assessment process and challenges to it following *R (A) v Croydon*, see I Wise QC, S Broach, J Burton, C Gallagher, A Pickup, B Silverstone and A Suterwalla, *Children in need: local authority support for children and families*, 2nd edition, Legal Action Group, 2013, chapter 3.

177 Provided that the grant of leave to remain is still current, it will ordinarily carry no restriction on recourse to public funds. If it has expired but an application for further leave to remain was made before expiry, and that application or any appeal is still pending, Immigration Act 1971 s3C means that leave is statutorily extended with the same conditions.

178 [2010] EWCA Civ 1101, (2010) 13 CCLR 591, [2011] HLR 4.

179 This judgment changes the position as set out in the previous edition of this work and reflected in the UKVI, *Asylum support instruction: Transition at age 18*, December 2014, which suggests that in the case of asylum-seekers, such young people will remain in local authority accommodation, but that the costs of their accommodation and subsistence will be met by UKVI.

180 The full list of EEA states is Austria, Belgium, Croatia, Denmark, Finland, France, Germany, Greece, Holland, Ireland, Italy, Luxembourg, Portugal, Spain, Sweden, the UK, Norway, Iceland, Liechtenstein, Cyprus, Malta, Czech Republic, Estonia, Hungary, Latvia, Lithuania, Poland, Slovakia, Slovenia, Bulgaria and Romania.

181 Of which the most important are EC/1612/68 and EC/2004/38.

16.78   Free movement benefits not only citizens of the member states but also certain of their family members (whatever the nationality of the family member), and confers rights of residence and various associated rights and entitlements (eg to social assistance and benefits entitlements). These rights vary, however, according to the nationality and economic status of the citizen in question. The most extensive rights are enjoyed by nationals of the 18 states who were members of the EEA prior to 1 May 2004 (the so-called 'pre-enlargement' states) as well as nationals of Cyprus and Malta.[182] With the EU enlargement since 2004, more limited rights have been enjoyed by nationals of the new member states for a transitional period. In the case of nationals of eight of the countries that joined the EU on 1 May 2004 (the so-called 'A8' countries[183]), the restrictions applied until 30 April 2011,[184] and in the case of Romanian and Bulgarian nationals (so-called 'A2' nationals), the restrictions applied until 31 December 2013. Concerns about the likely effect of lifting of the restrictions on Romanian and Bulgarian nationals have contributed to further restrictions on all EEA nationals' access to social assistance during periods of unemployment.

16.79   Restrictions continue to apply to nationals of Croatia, which joined the EU on 1 July 2013, and will continue to apply at least until 30 June 2018, with the possibility of extension for a further two years. The restrictions affect access to the labour market for Croatian nationals and have consequential limitations on their access to social assistance (welfare benefits and housing assistance). The restrictions applied to Croatian nationals are similar to those which previously applied to A2 nationals, which were far more extensive than for A8 nationals.

EEA nationals other than Croatian nationals[185]

16.80   The key concept in EEA law for the purposes of this text is that of the 'qualified person' as defined in the Immigration (European Economic Area) Regulations 2006.[186] An EEA national (other than a Croatian national) is qualified if he or she is:

---

182 Rights of free movement also apply to citizens of Switzerland.

183 Czech Republic, Estonia, Hungary, Latvia, Lithuania, Poland, Slovakia and Slovenia.

184 Accession (Immigration and Worker Registration) (Revocation, Savings and Consequential Provisions) Regulations 2011 SI No 544.

185 As noted above, A8 nationals had more restricted rights prior to 1 May 2011; their position prior to that date is not considered further here and readers are referred to earlier editions of this work, or to S Willman and S Knafler QC, *Support for asylum-seekers and other migrants: a guide to legal and welfare rights*, 3rd edn, Legal Action Group, 2009, chapter 2; the situation of A2 nationals prior to 1 January 2014 was similar to that of Croatian nationals now; see further below.

186 SI No 1003. With effect from 1 February 2017, the 2006 regulations will be revoked and replaced by the Immigration (European Economic Area) Regulations 2016 SI No 1052. These are intended mainly to consolidate and clarify the existing law, in particular by reflecting judgments from the Court of Justice of the EU (CJEU) and to 'clarify the basis on which restrictive measures may be taken to restrict the free movement rights of people who pose a threat to the UK by setting out a non-exhaustive list of the "fundamental interests of society"': see the explanatory memorandum, paras 2.1–2.4.

- a worker;[187]
- a work seeker;
- a self-employed person or a service provider;
- a student;
- economically self-sufficient.

16.81   A qualified EEA national has an entitlement to reside in the UK 'without the requirement for leave to remain under the Immigration Act 1971 for as long as he remains a qualified person'.[188] Such persons are said to enjoy 'full free movement rights' and have unrestricted access to the UK labour market.

16.82   Qualified EEA nationals are not excluded from social welfare assistance (housing and welfare benefits) under IAA 1999 s115 and thus should not normally need to access social care provisions. However, EEA nationals who are not qualified have no access to social assistance provisions (with the exception of contributory benefits). The consequence is that on facing destitution, these EEA nationals frequently turn to the local social services authority for assistance. However, EEA nationals are excluded from most community care provision under NIAA 2002 s54 and Sch 3.[189]

16.83   As previously noted, the prohibition in NIAA 2002 s54 against social services providing care services does not apply where a failure to provide assistance would constitute a breach of the person's ECHR rights. This applies equally where failure to provide services would breach a person's rights under an EU treaty. The Department of Health considers that the EU exception will mean that:

> EEA nationals who work or have worked in the UK, their families, self-employed and former self-employed EEA nationals, and students should be provided with social care services by councils if they are eligible for such care in order to protect their freedom of movement. They are entitled on the same basis as UK nationals.[190]

Croatian nationals

16.84   Croatian nationals are subject to the Worker Authorisation Scheme which came into effect on 1 July 2013. The restrictions imposed on Croatian nationals under this scheme are similar to those imposed on A2 nationals between 2007 and 2013, and are more extensive than those which were imposed on A8 nationals under the Worker Registration Scheme prior to 1 May 2011.

---

187 This definition includes workers temporarily unfit for work through illness or accident or pregnancy and childbirth.

188 *Barnet LBC v Ismail and Abdi* [2006] EWCA Civ 383, [2006] 1 WLR 2771 clarified that an EEA national who is not a qualified person does not have a right to reside and is subject to immigration control. However, note that certain persons have a right to reside as a matter of EU law even though they are not qualified persons within the terms of the regulations.

189 Indeed this was, as noted above (para 16.40), one of the objects of the legislation.

190 Department of Health, *Section 54 of the Nationality, Immigration and Asylum Act 2002 and community care and other social services for adults from the EEA living in the UK: note of clarification*, 2003, para 13.

16.85   In general, Croatian workers are required to obtain work authorisation from the Home Office before taking up employment.[191] Croatian nationals are entitled to 'in-work benefits' during their 12-month period of authorised work, and acquire full movement rights after 12 months' lawful employment. Note, however, that these restrictions only apply to 'workers' and not to self-employed persons, students or those who are self-sufficient.

16.86   Croatian job seekers do not have a right to reside. They are thus excluded from most benefits, and like other EEA nationals, they are also excluded from community care services by NIAA 2002 Sch 3, but will not be able to rely on their EU law rights to non-discrimination because they do not have a right to reside in the UK.

'Zambrano' carers and those with leave to remain as parents

16.87   In *Ruiz Zambrano v Office national de l'emploi*,[192] the European Court of Justice decided that the third-country national carers of an EU national child had a right to reside in their child's state of nationality in order to care for their child, if the child would otherwise have to leave the EU. This decision created a new class of third country national (ie non-British, non-EU nationals) with a potential right to reside in the UK as a matter of EU law. So-called '*Zambrano* carers' can now apply for a residence card evidencing their entitlement to remain in the UK under 2006 EEA regulations reg 15A(4A).[193] This has given many overstayers a route to regularising their status in the UK, but in November 2012 amendments were made to benefits regulations which excluded *Zambrano* carers from access to means-tested benefits,[194] tax credits and homelessness assistance or allocations of housing.[195] A challenge to the compatibility of these exclusions with EU law was rejected by the Court of Appeal in *Sanneh and others v Secretary of State for Work and Pensions and others*,[196] in which Arden LJ, giving the lead judgment, expressed her conclusions as follows:

> I conclude that Zambrano carers who are in need and unable to work are not entitled to the same level of payments of social assistance as is required by EU law to be paid to EU citizens lawfully here. The UK must pay them such amount as will enable them to support themselves in order to be the carer for the EU citizen child within the EU, but, subject to that, may determine to pay social assistance to them on some different basis.[197]

---

191 The details of the scheme are involved and beyond the scope of this text.

192 Case C-34/09, 8 March 2011, [2012] QB 265.

193 Replaced by reg 16(4) in the 2016 regulations.

194 Income support, income-based jobseekers' allowance, income-related employment and support allowance, state pension credit, housing benefit, council tax benefit, child benefit and child tax credit.

195 The amendments were made by the Social Security (Habitual Residence) (Amendment) Regulations 2012 SI No 2587; Allocation of Housing and Homelessness (Eligibility) (England) (Amendment) Regulations 2012 SI No 2588; and Child Benefit and Child Tax Credit (Miscellaneous Amendments) Regulations 2012 SI No 2612.

196 [2015] EWCA Civ 49.

197 Para 2.

16.88   A critical step in the reasoning was that in practice *Zambrano* carers and their children could be – and were being – supported by local authorities under CA 1989 s17 so that their exclusion from benefits was not leaving them destitute or forcing them to leave the UK, and their children were able to enjoy the substance of their rights as EU citizens. As Elias LJ, agreeing with Arden LJ, expressed it:

> ... section 17 of the Children Act provides a back-stop provision which is designed to save the carer and child from homelessness and destitution, and we are not in a position to say that it fails in that objective. In my judgment, that suffices to meet the State's Zambrano obligation; there is no duty to provide fuller benefits.[198]

16.89   The Court of Appeal also noted the ability of *Zambrano* carers to apply for leave to remain under Appendix FM of the Immigration Rules, introduced in July 2012. Under these provisions, detailed consideration of which is outside the scope of this text, a parent who is the primary carer of a British citizen child is normally eligible for a grant of limited leave to remain. Although such leave is normally subject to a condition of no recourse to public funds, the Immigration Rules allow that restriction not to be imposed where the applicant is destitute, there are 'particularly compelling reasons relating to the welfare of a child on account of the child's parent's very low income', or there are other exceptional circumstances.[199] It has been UKVI policy to accept that where a local authority is providing support under CA 1989 s17, the family are destitute but the current version of the policy[200] requires UKVI to carry out its own evaluation of whether the family are genuinely destitute.[201]

16.90   These developments have placed a significant additional burden on local authorities by increasing the numbers of families who are not excluded from the provision of services under CA 1989 s17 by NIAA 2002 Sch 3 (because they are lawfully resident), but who are excluded from access to the means tested benefits and housing assistance which would otherwise enable them to avoid destitution. For many of these families, their caring responsibilities (which are the reason for which they are granted a right to reside or leave to remain in the UK) mean that it is difficult for them to earn enough to make ends meet, and it has been left to local authorities to fill in the gaps.

Domestic violence

16.91   A difficult situation can arise in relation to foreign spouses of British or settled persons where the foreign spouse has suffered domestic violence and as a consequence needs social services support and accommodation. More commonly than not, the foreign spouse is the wife and she has fled

198   Para 171.
199   Para GEN.1.11A of appendix FM and para 276A02 of the Immigration Rules.
200   Published in August 2015.
201   Home Office, *Immigration directorate instruction: family migration: appendix FM section 1.0b. Family Life (as a Partner or Parent) and Private Life: 10-Year Routes,* August 2015, para 13.3.

before being granted indefinite leave to remain[202] or after her spousal visa has expired.[203]

16.92   Provided the foreign national spouse is in the UK on a spouse visa, she will have express permission to work but there will ordinarily be a prohibition on recourse to public funds. When the violence causes the spouse to flee, she may turn to the local authority social services department for assistance. Frequently there are children, meaning that the wife's ability to work is impaired (not least that she will not be able to claim tax credits for her childcare costs) or she may have been prevented from learning sufficient English to be able to communicate effectively enough to work.

16.93   A spouse in the UK on a visa is not precluded from support under social care provisions by NIAA 2002 Sch 3. Unfortunately, many women who have experienced domestic violence have also had their husbands refuse to put in an extension application, such that they are then in the UK unlawfully, having overstayed. 'Overstayers' are precluded from social care provisions by NIAA 2002 Sch 3 unless support is required to prevent a breach of their ECHR rights.

16.94   Where there are children who are dependent on the foreign spouse, she may turn to the local authority for support under CA 1989 s17. Children are not excluded from support by NIAA 2002 Sch 3, regardless of their immigration status, and the local authority will have a duty to assess their needs under CA 1989 s17 and a power to provide services. Local authorities are able to accommodate the parent together with the children under CA 1989 s17(6), but in practical terms unless there is some legitimate impediment to the parent and children leaving the UK together (such as, for example, that the children still have regular contact with their other parent), local authorities will often offer to accommodate the children only under CA 1989 s20. In *R (G) v Barnet LBC*,[204] the House of Lords held that local authorities were in general entitled to have a policy of not accommodating families together under section 17, but instead offering to accommodate the children if necessary under section 20, subject to assessment of the individual child's needs and ECHR Article 8 considerations.[205] There is thus in practice little distinction between the position of overstayers, who must show that support is necessary to prevent a breach of their ECHR rights, and those with leave to remain, where the local authority has a wide discretion whether to provide support to the parents, likely be amenable to

---

202 A grant of indefinite leave to remain attracts full recourse to public funds.

203 Prior to July 2012, ordinarily, the spouse of a British citizen or a person with indefinite leave to remain in the UK will be granted an initial probationary period of two years' leave to remain; if the marriage is subsisting at the end of that period and the spouse can be maintained and accommodated without recourse to public funds, indefinite leave to remain will ordinarily be granted. Changes in the Immigration Rules in July 2012 meant that spouses now normally have to complete either a five- or ten-year qualifying period with limited leave to remain (depending on the 'route' through which they qualified for leave to remain in the UK), subject to a condition of no recourse to public funds, before they can qualify for indefinite leave to remain.

204 [2003] UKHL 57, (2003) 6 CCLR 500.

205 For more detailed consideration of this decision, its relationship with *Clue* and the power or duty of local authorities to provide accommodation under section 17(6) to families of children in need, see I Wise QC, S Broach, J Burton, C Gallagher, A Pickup, B Silverstone and A Suterwalla, *Children in need: local authority support for children and families*, 2nd edition, Legal Action Group, 2013, paras 6.31–6.40.

challenge in practice only where the refusal of support would breach the authority's obligations under Human Rights Act (HRA) 1998 s6.

16.95   Where there are no children it is less likely that the foreign spouse will be able to access social care services, as domestic violence itself does not satisfy the 'destitution plus' test for services under the CA 2014. The destitution is said to result from the domestic violence, but the domestic violence is not a need for care and attention over and above destitution. In such a situation, in *R (Khan) v Oxfordshire CC*[206] it was decided that domestic violence was the cause of destitution only and the need for care and attention arose solely from the destitution. However, the court considered that in some circumstances, in addition to causing destitution, domestic violence could make the need for care and attention more acute. When faced with such a case, careful consideration should be given to establish whether there are any additional circumstances which create an eligible need for care and support. Examples might include physical or mental injury caused by the domestic violence, or where the domestic violence exacerbates existing physical or mental health problems.

16.96   In 2009, the Home Office established and funded a pilot project with Eaves Housing to provide accommodation and subsistence for women whose marriages had broken down during their initial two-year probationary period of their spousal visa, along with any dependent children.[207] The pilot project ran until April 2012, when it was abolished and replaced with the 'Destitution Domestic Violence Concession', under which victims of domestic violence who were last granted leave as the spouse or partner of a British citizen or settled person[208] can apply for a short period of leave (normally three months) with access to public funds while they prepare to make an application for indefinite leave to remain under the Home Office's domestic violence rule.[209]

Immigration Act 2016

16.97   As indicated at the outset, the IA 2016 will, when it enters into force, make significant changes to the framework for support of asylum-seekers and other migrants, particularly families and care leavers. Much of the detail will be contained in regulations, which have not been published in draft at the time of writing (December 2016). The below is a brief summary of the key changes as they relate to the provisions discussed in this chapter:

206 [2004] EWCA Civ 309, (2004) 7 CCLR 215: see also para 1.67 above.

207 The programme is known as the Sojourner Project.

208 The concession does not apply to those granted leave as the spouse or partner of a person with limited leave to remain, including refugees, even if that person has subsequently become settled: *R (T) v Secretary of State for the Home Department* [2016] EWCA Civ 801.

209 The form to apply for access to benefits can be downloaded from the gov.uk website at www.gov.uk/government/publications/application-for-benefits-for-visa-holder-domestic-violence.

- Asylum-seeker families with dependent children who become appeal rights exhausted will no longer be eligible for IAA 1999 s95 support (following a 'grace period').[210]
- IAA 1999 s4 will be repealed.[211] It will be replaced by more limited provision under which:
  - asylum-seekers with further submissions or judicial reviews pending will be eligible for s95 support;[212]
  - a new form of support under IAA s95A will be provided for former asylum-seekers who face a genuine obstacle[213] to leaving the UK.[214]
- All non-asylum-seekers who require leave to enter or remain in the UK but do not have it will be excluded from social care support under NIAA 2002 Sch 3 new para 7B.[215] For those who are not eligible for IAA 1999 s95A support, two new forms of accommodation and subsistence support will be available under NIAA 2002 Sch 3:[216]
  - for those with dependent children who have a pending application for leave to remain or in-country appeal; or who have not failed to co-operate with arrangements to leave; or where it is necessary to safeguard and promote the welfare of a dependent child;[217]
  - care leavers who have a pending application for leave to remain or in country appeal; or where a 'specified person' is satisfied the support is necessary.[218]
- The rights-based exemption in NIAA 2002 Sch 3 para 3 does not apply to the provision of support or assistance which could be provided under these new provisions, or, in the case of care leavers, under IAA 1999 s95A.[219] Families and care leavers will only be able to receive accommodation and subsistence support under the new arrangements.
- Those who are not eligible for these new forms of support will continue to be able to rely on the rights-based exemption to access social care where necessary to prevent a breach of their ECHR or EU rights. Similarly, families with children will be entitled to other services (ie apart from accommodation and subsistence) under CA 1989 s17, to the extent necessary to prevent a breach of their rights.

---

210 IA 2016 Sch 11 para 7 repealing IAA 1999 s94(5).
211 IA 2016 Sch 11 para 1.
212 IA 2016 Sch 11 para 3.
213 The meaning of 'genuine obstacle' will be prescribed in regulations.
214 IA 2016 Sch 11 para 9.
215 The main difference from the current situation being that former asylum-seekers who claimed asylum at port will now be excluded.
216 Under amendments made by IA 2016 Sch 12 para 10.
217 NIAA 2002 Sch 3 new para 10A.
218 NIAA 2002 Sch 3 new para 10B.
219 NIAA 2002 Sch 3 new paras 3A and 3B, inserted by IA 2016 Sch 12 para 6.

CHAPTER 17

Inspection and registration of adult care services

continued

Introduction

17.1 This chapter looks at the obligation on care service providers in England to register their activities, and the corresponding inspection powers of the regulatory authority. It explains the requirement to register; which services are registrable; regulatory requirements (including the fundamental standards); the authority's obligations to service users; and finally, regulatory action, including the authority's powers of entry and inspection, how funding authorities should respond to regulatory action, enforcement policies and reviews and performance assessments.

The requirement to register with the Care Quality Commission

17.2 A provider of a care service in England must be registered because it is a criminal offence to carry on an unregistered registrable service. The registration authority is the Care Quality Commission (CQC),[1] which was established by Health and Social Care Act (HSCA) 2008 s1.

17.3 Whether or not the regulated activity is intended to be profit making is irrelevant (HSCA 2008 s97(5)). Hence, where a local authority itself carries on a regulated activity it must be registered in respect of it.

Who can rely on the regulatory requirements for adult social care?

17.4 Service users (the term used by the legislation) and those authorised to act for them are entitled to rely on the regulatory requirements to effect a change in the service provided by a registered provider. Additionally, where care is purchased by a local authority, it should satisfy itself that a service is being provided in compliance with regulatory requirements. That follows from the requirement in Care Act (CA) 2014 s1 that local authorities, in exercising their functions under that Act, must promote an individual's well-being. Well-being is not promoted by commissioning a service that is not compliant with regulatory requirements.

17.5 The CQC stress that their function is not to 'settle individual complaints'. Their website states 'our role as the regulator means that we do not settle individual complaints ourselves'.[2] However, this cannot remove or dilute the CQC's obligations, as the regulator, to consider and investigate matters drawn to its attention about the quality of care services whether styled as a complaint, 'tip-off' or 'experience'.[3]

---

1 The CQC replaced the Healthcare Commission (officially the Commission for Healthcare Audit and Inspection), the Commission for Social Care Inspection and the Mental Health Act Commission.
2 See www.cqc.org.uk/content/how-we-involve-you.
3 The CQC website has a 'share your experiences' online form: www.cqc.org.uk/content/how-we-involve-you.

Registrable services

Regulated activity

17.6   Departing from the sector-specific approach taken by previous care stand-ards legislation, under the HSCA 2008 registration is required in respect of 'regulated activity'. So there is no longer, for example, a set of care homes regulations for England.

17.7   'Regulated activity' is defined by regulations, rather than on the face of the HSCA 2008. These are the Health and Social Care Act 2008 (Regulated Activities) Regulations 2014[4] ('HSCA regulations 2014'). Schedule 1 to the HSCA regulations 2014 describes a number of types of regulated activity. The focus in this chapter is on those of most interest to the social care sector.

17.8   Schedule 2 to the HSCA regulations 2014 specifies certain general exceptions to the definitions of regulated activity, including:

a) a non-commercial activity carried on in the course of a family or per-sonal relationship which includes:
    i)   a relationship between two persons who live in the same household and treat each other as though they were members of the same fam-ily; and
    ii) a relationship between or among friends;
b) any activity regulated by the Office for Standards in Education, Child-ren's Services and Skills (OFSTED) under the Care Standards Act 2000, for example a children's home.

Provision of personal care

17.9   The provision of personal care is a regulated activity if:

a) provided for persons who, by reason of old age, illness or disability, are unable to provide it for themselves; and
b) provided 'in a place where those persons are living at the time the care is provided'.[5]

17.10   However, the HSCA Regulations 2014 specify, in Schedule 1, that the fol-lowing are not the provision of personal care:

a) the supply to service provider of carers by an employment agency or business;
b) the introduction of carers to an individual where the supplier has no ongoing role in directing or controlling the service provided by the carer;
c) the provision of services by a carer employed by an individual, without the involvement of an employment agency or business, where the carer works wholly under the direction and control of the individual or a related third party such as an individual with power of attorney giving lawful authority to make arrangements for the individual in need of

4 2014 SI No 2936.
5 HSCA Regulations 2008 Sch 1.

care. For this reason, a carer employed by an individual, using direct payments, should not normally be required to register with the CQC.

17.11 'Personal care' is also defined by the HSCA regulations 2014. Two types of activity amount to personal care:

a) physical assistance but only where given to a person in connection with various intimate activities, namely: eating or drinking; toileting; washing or bathing; dressing; oral care; or care of skin hair and nails;

b) prompting (together with supervision) in relation to any of the above intimate activities but only if the person being cared for is unable to make a decision about performing an activity without prompting and supervision.

17.12 These definitions catch services which previously triggered the requirement to register in respect of a domiciliary care agency. However, they go further and are likely to include certain non-physical support services (those involving the prompting and supervision described in (b) above).

Accommodation

17.13 The provision of residential accommodation together with nursing or personal care is a regulated activity.[6] However, the following are excepted:

a) accommodation provided by a shared lives carer under the terms of a shared lives agreement;

b) accommodation provided in a school or 16–19 academy;

c) accommodation provided in a further education institution where the number of persons to whom nursing or personal care and accommodation are provided is not more than one-tenth of the number of students to whom both education and accommodation are provided.

Accommodation for persons who require treatment for substance misuse

17.14 The provision of residential accommodation for a person together with treatment for drug or alcohol misuse, where the person is required to accept such treatment, is a regulated activity.[7]

Treatment of mental disorder

17.15 The provision of treatment for a disease, disorder or injury by or under the supervision of a social worker, or a team which includes a social worker, is a regulated activity where the treatment is for a mental disorder.[8]

6 HSCA regulations 2014 Sch 1 para 2.
7 HSCA regulations 2014 Sch 1 para 3.
8 HSCA regulations 2014 Sch 1 para 4.

Assessment or medical treatment for persons detained under the Mental Health Act 1983

17.16   The assessment of, or medical treatment for, a mental disorder affecting a person in a hospital is a regulated activity where that person is detained in that hospital under the Mental Health Act (MHA) 1983.

Nursing care

17.17   The provision of nursing care, including nursing care provided in a person's own home is a regulated activity if it is not provided as part of any other regulated activity.[9]

Regulatory requirements

Regulations and guidance

17.18   Regulatory requirements are contained in the HSCA regulations 2014. Enacting a wide range of regulatory reforms – in particular through the introduction of 'fundamental standards', fitness requirements for directors and a duty of candour – the HSCA regulations 2014 were in part a response to the failures identified by the inquiries into the conduct of Mid Staffordshire NHS Foundation Trust[10] and Winterbourne View Hospital.[11]

17.19   The HSCA regulations 2014 are generic which, for the most part, apply to all forms of regulated activity. Despite their stated purpose as a clear baseline for acceptable service provision (according to the explanatory memorandum to the 2014 regulations), the requirements are often expressed in general terms and, as a result, their application is dependent on the judgement of the CQC. However, the risk of arbitrary or inconsistent interpretation is reduced by the requirement, under HSCA 2008 s23, for the CQC to issue guidance about compliance with the regulatory requirements. The CQC must take into account such guidance in making regulatory decisions as must the First-Tier Tribunal on any appeal against a CQC decision (HSCA 2008 s25). The CQC guidance is described below, alongside the regulatory requirements to which it relates.

17.20   The most recent CQC's guidance, *Regulations for service providers and managers*, was issued in 2015 ('the CQC guidance'). In addition the CQC has also issued various explanatory 'provider handbooks', including:

   a) *Community adult social care services: Provider handbook*, 2016;
   b) *Residential adult social care services: Provider handbook*, 2016;
   c) *Specialist mental health services: Provider handbook*, 2015; and
   d) *Specialist substance misuse services: Provider handbook*, 2015.

---

9   HSCA regulations2014 Sch 13 para 1.
10   Following poor care and high mortality rates among patients at the Stafford Hospital, Stafford, in the late 2000s.
11   Following an undercover investigation by the BBC's Panorama programme revealed criminal abuse by staff of patients at Winterbourne View Hospital near Bristol (2011).

Fitness requirements: individuals and partnerships

17.21   Where a service provider is an individual, or carried on by a partnership, the HSCA regulations 2014 impose fitness requirements on the individual, members of the partnership and the partnership itself. Where the provider is a corporate body, by contrast, fitness-type requirements are imposed on the body's key decision-makers.

17.22   Regulation 4(2) prohibits an individual or partnership from carrying on a regulated activity unless the individual or partnership 'is fit to do so'.

17.23   An individual service provider is not 'fit' unless:

a)   the individual 'is of good character', the assessment of which must include criminal convictions and any erasure, removal or striking off a register of health care or social work professionals; CQC guidance on good character (for all regulatory purposes) says its assessment should take into account honesty, trustworthiness, reliability and respectfulness; and

b)   the individual 'is able by reason of their health, after reasonable adjustments are made, of properly performing tasks which are ... intrinsic to the carrying on of the regulated activity'; and

c)   the CQC is able to be supplied with specified information about the individual; the information is set out in HSCA regulations 2014 Sch 3 and includes relevant criminal records and safeguarding checks, evidence of conduct in previous relevant employment, satisfactory verification of the reason why any previous employment with vulnerable adults ended and a full employment history to include 'a satisfactory written explanation of any gaps in employment'; and

d)   the individual 'has the necessary qualifications, competence, skills and experience to carry on the regulated activity'; the CQC guidance says individuals should have appropriate knowledge of the regulatory scheme and relevant best practice and guidance.

17.24   A partnership service provider is not 'fit' unless

a)   each of the partners 'is of good character' (taking into account the same matters as must be taken into account for individual service providers); and

b)   each of the partners 'is able by reason of their health, after reasonable adjustments are made, of properly performing tasks which are ... intrinsic to their role in the carrying on of the regulated activity'; and

c)   the CQC is able to be supplied with the information, in relation to the partners, specified in HSCA regulations 2014 Sch 3; and

d)   the partnership has 'through the combination of the qualifications, competence, skills and experience of the partners ... the necessary qualifications, skills and experience to carry on the regulated activity'.

Fitness requirements: corporate bodies

17.25   Where a service provider is a body, other than a partnership, HSCA regulations 2014 reg 5 prohibits the body from appointing a director, or a person to perform similar functions to a director unless:

a) the individual is of 'good character', the assessment of which must include criminal convictions and any erasure, removal or striking off a register of health care or social work professionals; and

b) the individual 'has the qualifications, competence, skills and experience which are necessary for the relevant office or position or the work for which they are employed'; and

c) the individual 'is able by reason of their health, after reasonable adjustments are made, of properly performing tasks which are intrinsic to the office or position for which they are appointed or to the work for which they are employed', and

d) the individual 'has not been responsible for, been privy to, contributed to or facilitated any serious misconduct or mismanagement (whether unlawful or not) in the course of carrying on a regulated activity'; and

e) none of the grounds of unfitness specified in HSCA regulations 2014 Sch 4 Part 1 apply to the individual, for example the person is not included in the children's or adults' barred list maintained by the Disclosure and Barring Service.

17.26   The CQC guidance states, in the case of a local authority provider, these requirements do not apply to elected members because 'they are accountable through a different route'.

17.27   If an individual no longer meets the above requirements, HSCA regulations 2014 reg 5(6) requires the service provider to ensure that the office or position in question is held by an individual who meets such requirements. Further, where the individual is a social worker, the service provider must inform the regulatory body for social workers.

17.28   HSCA regulations 2014 reg 6 requires the provider body to inform the CQC of a 'nominated individual' who is employed as a director, manager or secretary of the body and is responsible for supervising the management of the carrying on of the regulated activity. The body must 'take all reasonable steps to ensure that the nominated individual':

a) is of good character, to include an assessment of convictions and adverse professional regulatory decisions (see above); and

b) has 'the necessary qualifications, competence, skills and experience to properly supervise the management of the carrying on of the regulated activity'; and

c) is 'able by reason of their health, after reasonable adjustments are made, of properly doing so'; and

d) is able to supply to the body the information specified in Schedule 3 to the regulations.

17.29   Any assessment of character must include the matters listed in HSCA regulations 2014 Sch 4 Part 2.

Registered manager

17.30   Where a service provider is required to have a registered manager by a condition of registration, HSCA regulations 2014 reg 7 requires the individual to be fit. An individual is not fit to manage a regulated activity unless:

a) 'of good character'; and

b) 'has the necessary qualifications, competence, skills and experience to manage the carrying on of the regulated activity'; and

c) the individual is 'able by reason of ... health, after reasonable adjustments are made, of [managing the regulated activity]'; and

d) the individual is able to supply to the CQC the information specified in HSCA regulations 2014 Sch 3.

The fundamental standards

17.31   The regulatory requirements set out in HSCA regulations 2014 regs 9–20A are referred to by the regulations as the 'fundamental standards':

- person-centred care;
- dignity and respect;
- need for consent;
- safe care and treatment;
- safeguarding service users from abuse and improper treatment;
- meeting nutritional and hydration needs;
- premises and equipment;
- receiving and acting on complaints;
- good governance;
- staffing;
- fit and proper persons employed;
- duty of candour.

Each of these standards is explained below, with reference to both the regulations and the CQC guidance.

Person-centred care

17.32   HSCA regulations 2014 reg 9, headed 'person-centred care', requires the care and treatment of service users to be appropriate, meet their needs, and, subject to reg 11 (need for consent) reflect their preferences. The CQC guidance says its purpose is to 'make sure that people using a service have care or treatment that is personalised specifically for them'.

17.33   Examples of what must be done to comply with the person-centred care requirements are contained in reg 9(3)(a)–(i), namely:

a) 'carrying out, collaboratively with the relevant person, an assessment of the needs and preferences for care and treatment of the service user' (CQC guidance: the person should be involved 'as much or as little as they wish to be'; assessment should include 'emotional, social, cultural, religious and spiritual needs'; commonly encountered specific issues should be taken into account such as 'diseases or conditions such as continence support needs and dementia in older people, and diabetes in certain ethnic groups'; assessments should be reviewed regularly, including 'when they transfer between services, use respite care or are re-admitted or discharged'; where a multi-disciplinary team is involved, assessment should draw on information from other professionals involved in care and treatment);

b) 'designing care or treatment with a view to achieving service users' preferences and ensuring their needs are met' (CQC guidance: 'There may be times when a person's needs and preferences can't be met. In these instances, providers must explain the impact of this to them and explore alternatives so that the person can make informed decisions'; 'A clear care and/or treatment plan, including agreed goals, must be developed and made available' to all involved in providing the care'; 'Where relevant, the plan should include ways in which the person can maintain their independence'; 'Plans should include an agreed review date'; 'use nationally recognised evidence-based guidance when designing, delivering and reviewing care'; staff must be kept up to date on changes to 'a person's needs and preferences'));

c) 'enabling and supporting relevant persons to understand the care or treatment choices available to the service user and to discuss, with a competent health care professional or other competent person, the balance of risks and benefits involved in any particular course of treatment' (CQC guidance: 'discuss care and treatment choices with the person and/or person lawfully acting on their behalf'; 'provide support to make sure the person understands all the risks and benefits associated with those choices and enable them to make informed decisions'; the person 'must be able to discuss care and treatment choices continually and have support to make any changes to those choices'; provide information about risks and benefits of any changes in a way the person can understand);

d) 'enabling and supporting relevant persons to make, or participate in making, decisions relating to the service user's care or treatment to the maximum extent possible' (CQC guidance: the support provided should include 'physical, psychological or emotional support, or support to get information in an accessible format or to understand the content'; actively encourage involvement in decision-making; record all assessments, care and treatment plans and decisions made);

e) 'providing opportunities for relevant persons to manage the service user's care or treatment' (CQC guidance: provide opportunities for people to 'manage as much of their care and treatment as they wish and are able to'; 'Manage' may mean 'being actively involved, overseeing or making decisions ... depending on how much they need or want to be involved. This may include managing their medicines, managing or supporting their personal care including eating and drinking, or using appropriate equipment and technology');

f) 'involving relevant persons in decisions relating to the way in which the regulated activity is carried on in so far as it relates to the service user's care or treatment' (CQC guidance: actively seek views about how care and treatment meets a person's needs; providers 'must be able to demonstrate that they took action in response to any feedback');

g) 'providing relevant persons with the information they would reasonably need for the purposes of sub-paragraphs (c) to (f)' (CQC guidance: information to be provided in the most suitable way for the individual and in a way they can understand; relevant information includes; all relevant options and the associated risks and benefits; any costs/fees/tariffs);

h) 'making reasonable adjustments to enable the service user to receive their care or treatment';

i) 'where meeting a service user's nutritional and hydration needs, having regard to the service user's well-being' (CQC guidance: provide a reasonably practical choice of food and drink; assess each person's nutritional and hydration needs).

17.34   For the purposes of this regulation, the 'relevant person' is either the service user or, if he or she is aged under 16 and not competent to make a decision in relation to a matter, a person lawfully acting on the person's behalf.

17.35   For service users aged 16 or over who lack capacity in relation to a matter to which regulation 9 applies, the person-centred care requirements are subject to any duty placed on the registered person or body by the Mental Capacity Act (MCA) 2005.

Dignity and respect

17.36   HSCA regulations 2014 reg 10(1) requires service users to be 'treated with dignity and respect'. The CQC guidance states that this includes:

- all communication must be respectful which includes 'using or facilitating the most suitable means of communication and respecting a person's right to engage or not to engage in communication';
- 'Staff must respect people's personal preferences, lifestyle and care choices';
- 'When providing intimate or personal care, provider must make every reasonable effort to make sure that they respect people's preferences about who delivers their care and treatment, such as requesting staff of a specified gender';
- 'People using the service should be addressed in the way they prefer'.

17.37   Regulation 10(2)(a)–(c) specifies that treating service users with dignity and respect specifically includes:

a) 'ensuring the privacy of the service user' (CQC guidance: maintain privacy at all times including when a person is asleep, unconscious or lacks capacity; make all reasonable efforts to ensure discussions about care, treatment and support cannot be overheard; ensure privacy when treatment is delivered; support people to wash, bath, use the toilet and hold private conversations in privacy; identify and record a person's privacy needs and expectations; 'People's relationships with their visitors, carer, friends, family or relevant other persons should be respected and privacy maintained as far as reasonably practicable during visits'; people 'should not have to share sleeping accommodation with others of the opposite sex, and should have access to segregated bathroom and toilet facilities without passing through opposite-sex areas'; 'Where appropriate, such as in mental health units, women should have access to women-only day spaces'; surveillance must only be used in the best interests of service users and in accordance with separate CQC guidance on surveillance[12]);

12 CQC, *Using surveillance: information for providers of health and social care on using surveillance to monitor services*, December 2014 (updated with new regulations in June 2015).

b) 'supporting the autonomy, independence and involvement in the community of the service user' (CQC guidance: support people to maintain
   autonomy and independence, respecting their expressed wishes to act
   independently 'but also identify and mitigate risks in order to support
   their continued independence as safely as possible'; support people
   to maintain relationships that are important to them; support people
   'to be involved in their community as much or as little as they wish';
   'actively work with people who wish to maintain their involvement in
   their local community as soon as they begin to use a service; ensure
   'people are not left unnecessarily isolated');

c) 'having due regard to any relevant protected characteristics (as defined
   in section 149(7) of the Equality Act 2010) of the service user' (CQC
   guidance: the protected characteristics are age, disability, gender, gender reassignment, pregnancy and maternity status, race, religion or
   belief and sexual orientation).

Obtaining consent

17.38   HSCA regulations 2014 reg 11(1) provides: 'Care and treatment of service
users must only be provided with the consent of the relevant person'. However, if a service user is 16 or over and unable to give such consent because
he or she lacks capacity to do so, the registered person must instead act in
accordance with the MCA 2005 (reg 11(3)). The CQC guidance provides
that staff who obtain the consent must be familiar with the principles and
codes of conduct associated with the MCA 2005.

17.39   The CQC guidance on obtaining consent states that, generally:

> Consent is an important aspect of providing care and treatment, but in
> some cases, acting strictly in accordance with consent will mean that some
> of the other regulations cannot be met. For example, this might apply with
> regard to nutrition and person-centred care. However, providers must not
> provide unsafe or inappropriate care just because someone has consented
> to care or treatment that would be unsafe.

17.40   The CQC guidance on obtaining consent further provides:

- In asking for consent, providers must provide information about proposed care and treatment in ways that people can understand, including information about 'the risks, complications and any alternatives'.
  The staff member giving the information should be able to 'answer any
  questions about it to help the person consent to it'.
- Discussions about consent must be appropriate to a person's communication needs, for example by using different formats or languages and
  involving a speech and language therapist or independent advocate.
- '[C]onsent may be implied and include non-verbal communication
  such as sign language or by someone rolling up their sleeve to have
  their blood pressure taken or offering their hand when asked if they
  would like help to move.'
- 'Consent must be treated as a process that continues throughout the
  duration of care and treatment, recognising that it may be withheld
  and/or withdrawn at any time.'
- 'Consent procedures must make sure that people are not pressured
  into giving consent and, where possible, plans must be made well in

advance to allow time to respond to people's questions and provide adequate information.'

- 'Policies and procedures for obtaining consent to care and treatment must reflect current legislation and guidance, and staff must follow them at all times.'

17.41 By HSCA regulations 2014 reg 22(1)(a), non-compliance by a registered person with regulation 11 amounts to an offence (as well as a potential ground for regulatory action).

Safe care and treatment

17.42 HSCA regulations 2014 reg 12(1) requires care and treatment to be 'provided in a safe way for service users'. Regulation 12(2)(a)–(i) provides that this includes:

a) 'assessing the risks to the health and safety of service users of receiving the care or treatment' (CQC guidance: risk assessments 'must be completed and reviewed regularly by people with the qualifications, skills, competence and experience to do so'; risk assessments should include plans for managing risks; risk assessing is required at all stages of the care journey, including admission, discharge and transfer between services);

b) 'doing all that is reasonably practicable to mitigate any such risks' (CQC guidance: follow good practice guidance and adopt control measures to keep risks 'as low as is reasonably possible'; review measures to address changing practice; include health and safety concerns in care and treatment plans/pathways, including 'allergies, contraindications and other limitations'; co-ordinate medication reviews with care and treatment assessments and plans; 'comply with relevant Patient Safety Alerts, recalls and rapid response reports issued from the Medicines and Healthcare products Regulatory Agency (MHRA) and through the Central Alerting System (CAS)'; report safety incidents internally and to relevant external authorities; incidents, including those with only the potential for causing harm, are 'thoroughly investigated by competent staff' and monitored to ensure remedial action taken, further occurrences prevented and improvements made; staff should receive information about safety incidents 'to promote learning'; investigation outcomes must be shared with the person concerned and, where relevant, families, carers and advocates; policies and procedures must be in place for raising concerns about care and treatment; 'Medicines must be administered accurately, in accordance with any prescriber instructions'; 'When it is agreed to be in a person's best interests, the arrangements for giving medicines covertly must be in accordance with the Mental Capacity Act 2005');

c) 'ensuring that persons providing care or treatment to service users have the qualifications, competence, skills and experience to do so safely' (CQC guidance: 'Staff must only work within the scope of their qualifications, competence, skills and experience' and should 'seek help when they feel they are being asked to do something that they are not prepared or trained for'; staff should be appropriately supervised when learning new skills; only relevant regulated professionals with the appropriate qualifications must plan and prescribe care and treatment, including medicines; delivery of care and treatment must only be done by relevant regulated professionals or suitably skilled and competent staff);

d) 'ensuring that the premises used by the service provider are safe to use for their intended purpose and are used in a safe way'; and

e) 'ensuring that the equipment used by the service provider for providing care or treatment to a service user is safe for such use and is used in a safe way' (CQC guidance (regarding regs 12(2)(d) and (e) together): providers should be aware they retain legal responsibility to meet regulatory requirements 'when they delegate responsibility through contracts or legal agreements to a third party, independent suppliers, professionals, supply chains or contractors'; the contracting mechanism must ensure compliance with regulatory requirements; providers should have 'up to date induction and training plans for the safe operation of premises and equipment, including incident reporting and emergency and contingency planning'; financial planning should include the capital and revenue costs of maintaining safety; staff using the equipment have the training, competency and skills needed);

f) 'where equipment or medicines are supplied by the service provider, ensuring that there are sufficient quantities of these to ensure the safety of service users and to meet their needs' (CQC guidance: medicines must be available in the necessary quantities at all times to prevent the risks associated with medicines not being administered as prescribed, including when people manage their own medicines; equipment and medical devices should be kept in full working order and 'available when needed and within a reasonable time without posing a risk'; 'The equipment, medicines and/or medical devices that are necessary to meet people's needs should be available when they are transferred between services or providers');

g) 'the proper and safe management of medicines' (CQC guidance: relevant staff must be suitably trained and competent to prescribe and administer medication; medication policies and procedures should address supply and ordering, storage, dispensing and preparation, administration, disposal and recording);

h) 'assessing the risk of, and preventing, detecting and controlling the spread of, infections, including those that are health care associated' (CQC guidance: reminds providers they should follow the Department of Health's code of practice about the prevention and control of healthcare associated infections;[13] risk assessments 'should consider the link between infection prevention and control, antimicrobial stewardship, how medicines are managed and cleanliness');

i) 'where responsibility for the care and treatment of service users is shared with, or transferred to, other persons, working with such other persons, service users and other appropriate persons to ensure that

13 Available at www.gov.uk/government/publications/the-health-and-social-care-act-2008-code-of-practice-on-the-prevention-and-control-of-infections-and-related-guidance.

timely care planning takes place to ensure the health, safety and welfare of the service users' (CQC guidance: when care is shared with other providers or where there are integrated services, there 'should be appropriate arrangements to share relevant information promptly and in line with current legislation and guidance, and to plan and deliver care in partnership'; when more than one provider is responsible for a person's safety ' the responsibility for providing safe care rests with the principal care provider at the time it is given'; carry out risk assessments when people move between services or providers; 'Decisions about a move between services or providers relating to people who may lack mental capacity to make that decision for themselves must be made in accordance with the Mental Capacity Act 2005'; put in place plans for managing major incidents and emergency situations).

17.43   As well as a potential ground for regulatory action, a failure to comply with regulation 12 is an offence if the failure results in avoidable harm to a service user, the exposure of a service user to a significant risk of such harm or, in the case of theft or misuse of money or property, results in loss to a service user (regulation 22(2)).

Safeguarding

17.44   HSCA regulations 2014 reg 13(1) requires service users to be 'protected from abuse' (which includes neglect) 'and improper treatment' in accordance with the other provisions of regulation 13. The CQC guidance says: 'To meet the requirements of this regulation, providers must have a zero tolerance approach to abuse, unlawful discrimination and restraint'.

17.45   Regulation 13(2)–(5) imposes the following requirements:

2) 'Systems and processes must be established and operated effectively to prevent abuse of service users' (CQC guidance: staff induction must include safeguarding training which should be repeated at appropriate intervals; 'staff must be aware of their individual responsibilities to prevent, identify and report abuse'; information about safeguarding procedures should be accessible to service users, other interested persons and staff.; 'providers should work in partnership with other relevant bodies to contribute to individual risk assessments, developing plans for ... safeguarding adults at risk; 'providers and their staff must understand and work within the requirements of the Mental Capacity Act 2005');

3) 'Systems and processes must be established and operated effectively to investigate, immediately upon becoming aware of, any allegation or evidence of such abuse' (CQC guidance: 'providers must take action as soon as they are alerted to suspected, alleged or actual abuse, or the risk of abuse' in line with any procedures agreed by local Safeguarding Adults Boards; providers and staff must understand local safeguarding policy and procedures, including timescales for action and local arrangements for investigation; staff should have support from line management when considering how to respond to concerns of abuse; providers must keep staff up to date about changes to national and local safeguarding arrangements; providers must respond without delay to

the findings of any investigations; service users who allege or experience abuse 'must receive the support they need'; where allegations of abuse are substantiated, providers must take action, including taking steps to ensure the abuse is not repeated; 'when required to, providers must participate in serious case reviews');

4) 'Care or treatment for service users must not be provided in a way that–'

a) 'includes discrimination against a service user on grounds of any protected characteristic (as defined in section 4 of the Equality Act 2010) of the service user' (CQC guidance: providers should have systems for dealing with allegations and acts of discrimination to include a description of the required actions and timescales; providers must support service users who allege or experience discrimination and must not victimise those who complain; 'When allegations of discrimination are substantiated, providers must take corrective action and make changes to prevent it happening again');

b) 'includes acts intended to control or restrain a service user that are not necessary to prevent, or not a proportionate response to, a risk of harm posed to the service user or another individual if the service user was not subject to control or restraint' (CQC guidance: staff induction must include training to ensure 'any control, restraint or restrictive practices are only used when absolutely necessary, in line with current national guidance and good practice, and as a last resort'; training should be updated at appropriate intervals; when restraint is used, it must be only used when absolutely necessary, be proportionate to the risk of harm and the seriousness of that harm to the person using the service or another person and takes account of the person's needs assessment and their capacity to consent to such treatment; 'Providers and staff should regularly monitor and review the approach to, and use of, restraint and restrictive practices'; 'Where a person lacks mental capacity to consent to the arrangements for their care or treatment, including depriving them of their liberty, providers must follow a best interest process in accordance with the Mental Capacity Act 2005, including the use of the Mental Capacity Act 2005 Deprivation of Liberty Safeguards, where appropriate');

c) 'is degrading for the service user, or'

d) 'significantly disregards the needs of the service user for care or treatment' (CQC guidance (regarding reg(4)(c) and (d) together): non-exhaustive examples of acts contrary to this requirement: not providing continence help and aids so that people can attend to their continence needs; leaving people in soiled sheets for long periods; leaving people on the toilet for long periods without the means to call for help; leaving people naked or partially or inappropriately covered; making people carry out demeaning tasks or social activities; ridiculing people; providers should consult and consider the views of people using their service when defining the meaning of 'degrading');

(5) 'A service user must not be deprived of their liberty for the purpose of receiving care or treatment without lawful authority' (CQC guidance: 'enough time is allocated to allow staff to provide care and treatment in accordance with the person's assessed needs and preferences'; 'When a person lacks the mental capacity to consent to care and treatment, a best interests process must be followed in accordance with the Mental Capacity Act 2005. Other forms of authority such as advance decisions must also be taken into account'; 'Staff should raise any concerns with the provider about their ability to provide planned care' and 'the provider should respond appropriately and without delay'; hospitals and care homes must comply with the deprivation of liberty safeguards scheme and 'other types of services must ensure that any deprivation of the liberty of a person who lacks mental capacity is authorised by the Court of Protection').

17.46 As well as a potential ground for regulatory action, a failure to comply with the above requirements is an offence if the failure results in avoidable harm to a service user, the exposure of a service user to a significant risk of such harm or, in the case of theft or misuse of money or property, results in loss to a service user (reg 22(2)).

Nutritional and hydration needs

17.47 HSCA regulations 2014 reg 14 requires that the 'nutritional and hydration needs of service users must be met' in certain cases, for example where accommodation is provided or meeting such needs is part of an individual's care arrangements.

17.48 In relation to nutritional and hydration needs, the CQC guidance says:

- 'Providers should have a food and drink strategy that addresses the nutritional needs of people using the service.'
- 'Providers must meet people's nutrition or hydration needs wherever an overnight stay is provided as part of the regulated activity.'
- 'Providers must follow people's consent wishes if they refuse nutrition and hydration unless a best interests decision has been made under the Mental Capacity Act 2005. Other forms of authority such as advance decisions should also be taken into account.'
- 'Nutrition and hydration assessments must be carried out by people with the required skills and knowledge.' The assessment should include dietary intolerances, allergies, medication contraindications, the level of associated support needed for example timing of meals and provision of appropriate and sufficient quantities of food and drink.
- 'Nutrition and hydration needs should be regularly reviewed.'
- 'A variety of nutritious, appetising food should be available to meet people's needs and be served at an appropriate temperature. When the person lacks capacity, they must have prompts, encouragement and help to eat as appropriate.'
- where a person needs a specific diet, this must be provided and '[n]utritional and hydration intake should be monitored and recorded to prevent unnecessary dehydration, weight loss or weight gain. Action must be taken without delay to address any concerns.'

- 'Staff must follow the most up-to-date nutrition and hydration assessment for each person and take appropriate action if people are not eating and drinking in line with their assessed needs'. They must also know how to determine whether specialist nutritional advice is required and how to obtain it.
- 'Water must be available and accessible to people at all times. Other drinks should be made available periodically throughout the day and night and people should be encouraged and supported to drink.'
- arrangements should be made for meals to be served at a different time if a person is absent or asleep when meals are served. 'Snacks or other food should be available between meals for those who prefer to eat "little and often".'

17.49　As well as a potential ground for regulatory action, a failure to comply with regulation 14 is an offence if the failure results in avoidable harm to a service user, or the exposure of a service user to a significant risk of such harm (regulation 22(2)).

Premises and equipment

17.50　HSCA regulations 2014 reg 15 requires all 'premises and equipment used by the service provider' to be clean, secure, suitable for their purpose, properly used, properly maintained, appropriately located for their purpose and maintained to appropriate standards of hygiene.

17.51　The CQC guidance includes the following provisions about the requirements for premises and equipment:

- Providers should operate a cleaning schedule appropriate to the care and treatment being delivered from the premises or by the equipment, and monitor cleanliness levels.
- 'Security arrangements must make sure that people are safe while receiving care, including: Protecting personal safety, which includes restrictive protection ... [which] includes the use of window restrictors or locks on doors, which are used in a way that protects' a service user, 'when lawful and necessary', but without restricting the liberty of other people using the service.
- If any surveillance is used, this must be done in the best interests of service users 'while remaining mindful of ... responsibilities for the safety of ... staff'.
- Premises must be suitable, including their layout, 'and be big enough to accommodate the potential number of people using the service at any one time'.
- Adequate support facilities must be provided including sufficient toilets and bathrooms, adequate storage space, seating and waiting space.
- People should be able to easily enter and exit premises and independently find their way around, and if they can't, 'providers must make reasonable adjustments in accordance with the Equality Act 2010'.
- 'Reasonable adjustments must be made when providing equipment to meet the needs of people with disabilities, in line with requirements of the Equality Act 2010'.
- The provider's statement of purpose and operational policies and procedures should specify how the premises and equipment will be used.

Any change of use of premises and/or equipment should be informed by a risk assessment.

- Regular health and safety risk assessments for the premises (including grounds) and equipment should be conducted assessment findings must be acted on without delay if improvements are required.
- 'Providers must have operational policies and procedures and maintenance budgets to maintain their equipment, buildings and mechanical engineering and electrical systems so that they are sound, operationally safe and exhibiting only minor deterioration'.
- 'All equipment must be used, stored and maintained in line with manufacturers' instructions. It should only be used for its intended purpose and by the person for whom is it provided'. Staff must be trained to use equipment appropriately;
- In planning the location of premises, providers must take into account the anticipated needs of service users and 'ensure easy access to other relevant facilities and the local community'.
- 'Equipment must be ... available when needed, or obtained in a reasonable time so as not to pose a risk to the person using the service. Equipment includes chairs, beds, clinical equipment, and moving and handling equipment'.
- 'Multiple use equipment and devices must be cleaned or decontaminated between use. Single use and single person devices must not be re-used or shared'.

Complaints

17.52   HSCA regulations 2014 reg 16(1) requires a service provider to investigate any complaint received and, if a failure is identified, to take 'necessary and proportionate' rectifying action. The CQC includes the following provision about regulation 16(1):

- All staff must know how to respond when they receive a complaint; complainants must not be discriminated against or victimised.
- 'Unless they are anonymous, all complaints should be acknowledged whether they are written or verbal'.
- 'Appropriate action must be taken without delay to respond to any failures identified by a complaint or the investigation of a complaint'.
- 'Information must be available to a complainant about how to take action if they are not satisfied with how the provider manages and/or responds to their complaint' including internal procedures and 'when complaints should/will be escalated to other appropriate bodies'.
- Providers should co-operate with 'any independent review or process' when a complaint has been escalated.

17.53   Regulation 16(2) requires a provider to 'establish and operate' accessible complaints procedures, to include complaints made by service users and other persons. These must deal with the 'identifying, receiving, recording, handling and responding to' complaints. The CQC guidance includes the following provision about the regulation 16(2) requirement:

- 'When complainants do not wish to identify themselves, the provider must still follow its complaints process as far as possible'.

- Complaints systems should include:
  - undertaking a review to establish the level of investigation and immediate action required, including referral to appropriate external authorities for investigation such as local authority safeguarding teams;
  - responding to complaints without delay.
- 'Providers should monitor complaints over time, looking for trends and areas of risk that may be addressed'.
- 'Consent and confidentiality must not be compromised during the complaints process unless there are professional or statutory obligations that make this necessary, such as safeguarding'.
- Complainants must be kept informed of the status of their complaint and its investigation.
- 'Providers must maintain a record of all complaints, outcomes and actions taken in response to complaints. Where no action is taken, the reasons for this should be recorded.'

17.54   If the CQC requests, a service provider must provide a summary of complaints made and how they have been responded to. The time limit for providing the information is 28 days from the date the provider receives the CQC's request (regulation 16(3)). A failure to comply is a criminal offence, as well as a potential ground for regulatory action (regulation 22(1)).

Good governance

17.55   HSCA regulations 2014 reg 17, headed 'good governance', requires a provider to establish and operate effective systems or processes to ensure compliance with the fundamental standards. CQC guidance states: 'The system must include scrutiny and overall responsibility at board level or equivalent.'

17.56   Regulation 17(2)(a)–(f) requires these systems or processes to enable the registered person to:

a) 'assess, monitor and improve the quality and safety of the services provided in the carrying on of the regulated activity (including the quality of the experience of service users in receiving those services)' (CQC guidance: regular audits must be carried out; 'systems and processes should be continually reviewed to make sure they remain fit for purpose'; providers should actively seek the views of a wide range of stakeholders about their experience of, and the quality of care and treatment delivered by the service; providers must analyse and respond to information gathered, and seek professional advice as needed; progress must be monitored against plans to improve quality and safety; 'Subject to statutory consent and applicable confidentiality requirements, providers must share relevant information, such as information about incidents or risks, with other relevant individuals or bodies. These bodies include safeguarding boards, coroners, and regulators');

b) 'assess, monitor and mitigate the risks relating to the health, safety and welfare of service users and others who may be at risk which arise from the carrying on of the regulated activity' (CQC guidance: adequate systems and processes for assessing these matters are in place; steps must be taken to reduce identified risks; 'Risks to the health, safety and/or welfare of people who use services must be escalated within the organisation or to a relevant external body as appropriate');

c) 'maintain securely an accurate, complete and contemporaneous record in respect of each service user, including a record of the care and treatment provided to the service user and of decisions taken in relation to the care and treatment provided' (CQC guidance: records must be 'complete, legible, indelible, accurate and up to date, with no undue delays in adding and filing information' and 'include an accurate record of all decisions taken in relation to care and treatment ... this includes consent records and advance decisions to refuse treatment'; records must be accessible in order to deliver safe and appropriate care and treatment; records must be 'kept secure at all times and only accessed, amended, or securely destroyed by authorised people'; 'Decisions made on behalf of a person who lacks capacity must be recorded and provide evidence that these have been taken in line with the requirements of the Mental Capacity Act 2005');

d) 'maintain securely such other records as are necessary to be kept in relation to– (i) persons employed in the carrying on of the regulated activity, and (ii) the management of the regulated activity' (CQC guidance: employment and management records 'must be created, amended, stored and destroyed in accordance with current legislation and guidance'; management records must include 'anything relevant to the planning and delivery of care and treatment');

e) 'seek and act on feedback from [service users] and other persons on the services provided in the carrying on of the regulated activity, for the purposes of continually evaluating and improving such services' (CQC guidance: encourage feedback, formal and informal, from a wide range of interested persons and bodies about the quality of care; 'All feedback should be listened to, recorded and responded to as appropriate' and used to improve quality and safety of services; 'Improvements should be made without delay once they are identified, and the provider should have systems in place to communicate how feedback has led to improvements');

f) 'evaluate and improve their practice in respect of the processing of the information referred to in sub-paragraphs (a) to (e)' (CQC guidance: 'providers must ensure that their audit and governance systems remain effective').

17.57 Regulation 17(3) requires a registered person, on request, to send to the CQC a written report on compliance with the requirements in regulation 17(2)(a) and (b) (see para 17.56 above), and any plans that the registered person has for improving the standard of the services provided. A failure to comply is a criminal offence, as well as a potential ground for regulatory action (regulation 22(1)).

Staffing

17.58 HSCA regulations 2014 reg 18(1) requires a provider to have 'sufficient numbers of suitably qualified, competent, skilled and experienced persons' in order to comply with the fundamental standards. In relation to this requirement, the CQC guidance says;

- 'Providers should have a systematic approach to determine the number of staff and range of skills required'.
- 'Staffing levels and skill mix must be reviewed continuously and adapted to respond to the changing needs and circumstances of people using the service'.
- 'There should be procedures to follow in an emergency that make sure sufficient and suitable people are deployed to cover both the emergency and the routine work of the service'.

17.59   Regulation 18(2)(a)–(c) requires a provider's employees to:

a) 'receive such appropriate support, training, professional development, supervision and appraisal as is necessary to enable them to carry out the duties they are employed to perform' (CQC guidance: induction programmes must be in place and 'providers that employ healthcare assistants and social care support workers should follow the Care Certificate standards'; training and developments needs must be regularly reviewed and staff supported to undertake training, learning and development; 'staff must be supervised until they can demonstrate required/acceptable levels of competence'; 'Staff should receive appropriate ongoing or periodic supervision'; training should be monitored and action taken quickly when training requirements are not being met; staff should receive regular appraisals; 'Health, social and other care professionals must have access to clinical or professional supervision as required');

b) 'be enabled where appropriate to obtain further qualifications appropriate to the work they perform'; and

c) 'where such persons are health care professionals, social workers or other professionals registered with a health care or social care regulator, be enabled to provide evidence to the regulator in question demonstrating, where it is possible to do so, that they continue to meet the professional standards which are a condition of their ability to practise or a requirement of their role' (CQC guidance: providers must ensure staff are able to meet the requirements of any relevant professional regulator throughout their employment; 'Staff should be supported to join Accredited Voluntary Registers if they wish'; 'Providers must not act in a way that prevents, limits or would result in staff not meeting requirements required by professional regulators').

Fit and proper persons employed

17.60   HSCA regulations 2014 reg 19(1)(a)–(c) requires persons 'employed for the purposes of carrying on a regulated activity' to:

a) 'be of good character' (CQC guidance: 'When assessing whether an applicant is of good character, providers must have robust processes and make every effort to gather all available information to confirm that the person is of good character'; 'we would expect to see that the processes followed take account of honesty, trust, reliability and respect'; 'If a provider discovers information that suggests a person is not of good character after they have been employed, they must take appropriate and timely action to meet this regulation');

b) 'have the qualifications, competence, skills and experience which are necessary for the work to be performed by them' (CQC guidance: where a qualification is required for a role, providers check that employees hold the appropriate qualification; providers must have appropriate processes for assessing and checking that people have the competence, skills and experience required to undertake the role; 'Providers should have systems in place to assess the competence of employees before they work unsupervised in a role');

c) 'be able by reason of their health, after reasonable adjustments are made, of properly performing tasks which are intrinsic to the work for which they are employed'.

17.61　However, these requirements do not apply to a director of a provider or a person performing similar functions to a director. In such cases, the requirements of regulation 5 apply instead (regulation 19(6)).

17.62　If an employee no longer meets the criteria in paragraph 19(1), the registered person must take necessary and proportionate action to ensure the relevant requirement is complied with. If the employee is a healthcare professional, social worker or other professional registered with a healthcare or social care regulator, the provider must inform the regulator (regulation 19(5)). In this respect, the CQC guidance says: fitness must be regularly reviewed; providers should respond without delay to concerns about fitness but the response should be fair to the person and follow correct procedures; and 'where a person's fitness to carry out their role is being investigated, appropriate interim measures must be taken to minimise any risk to people using the service'.

17.63　Providers must inform others as appropriate about concerns or findings relating to a person's fitness and must support any related enquiries and investigations that others have carried out. They may inform bodies such as professional regulators, police, and safeguarding authorities about concerns.

17.64　Where an employee's work, or the title the employee uses (for example, 'social worker') requires him or her to be registered with a relevant professional body, regulation 19(3) requires a provider to ensure that the employee is so registered.

17.65　Regulation 19(2) requires a provider to have recruitment procedures to ensure that employees meet the above requirements. Regulation 19(3) requires the information specified in Schedule 3, to be available in relation to employees.

The duty of candour

17.66　HSCA Regulations 2014 reg 20, headed 'duty of candour', originally applied only to health service bodies but was made a general requirement to be complied with by all service providers, as a result of amendments made to the 2014 regulations, with effect from 1 April 2015.[14]

17.67　The duty of candour under reg 20(1)–(3) requires a service provider to:

14　HSCA 2008 (Regulated Activities) (Amendment) Regulations 2015 SI No 64.

1) act in an open and transparent way with service users in relation to their care and treatment (CQC guidance: providers must promote a culture that encourages candour, openness and honesty at all levels, reflected at board level or equivalent; 'Providers should take action to tackle bullying and harassment in relation to duty of candour'; 'In cases where a provider is made aware that something untoward has happened, they should treat the allegation seriously, immediately consider whether this is a notifiable safety incident and take appropriate action');

2) as soon as reasonably practicable after becoming aware that a notifiable safety incident has occurred, notify the relevant service user, or a lawful representative if the service user has died or is aged 16 or over and lacks capacity in relation to the matter, and provide the person with 'reasonable support'. This notification must be given in person, provide the relevant facts, explain what further enquiries are appropriate, include an apology and be recorded in writing (the record must be securely kept). By regulation 22(1), a failure to notify is an offence, as well as a potential ground for regulatory action;

3) the in-person notification must be followed by a written notification to include the results of any further enquiries carried out.

17.68   The notification requirements do not apply if a service user cannot be contacted in person or declines to speak to the representative of the provider, although a written record must be kept of attempts to contact or to speak to the relevant person (regulation 20(5)).

17.69   'Apology' is defined by regulation 20(7) as 'an expression of sorrow or regret in respect of a notifiable safety incident'. The CQC guidance says 'in making a decision about who is most appropriate to provide the notification and/or apology, the provider should consider seniority, relationship to the person using the service, and experience and expertise in the type of notifiable incident that has occurred'.

17.70   Where a provider is not a health service body, a 'notifiable safety incident' is defined by regulation 20(9). The lengthy definition reads:

> any unintended or unexpected incident that occurred in respect of a service user during the provision of a regulated activity that, in the reasonable opinion of a health care professional–
> (a) appears to have resulted in–
>   (i) the death of the service user, where the death relates directly to the incident rather than to the natural course of the service user's illness or underlying condition,
>   (ii) an impairment of the sensory, motor or intellectual functions of the service user which has lasted, or is likely to last, for a continuous period of at least 28 days,
>   (iii) changes to the structure of the service user's body,
>   (iv) the service user experiencing prolonged pain or prolonged psychological harm [for a continuous period of at least 28 days], or
>   (v) the shortening of the life expectancy of the service user; or
> (b) requires treatment by a health care professional in order to prevent–
>   (i) the death of the service user, or
>   (ii) any injury to the service user which, if left untreated, would lead to one or more of the outcomes mentioned in sub-paragraph (a).

Requirement to display performance assessments

17.71 Introduced in April 2015, HSCA regulations 2014 reg 20A applies where a service provider has received a rating of its performance by the CQC following an assessment of performance under section 46(1) of the HSCA 2008. Regulation 20A(2), (3) and (5) requires the provider:

- to display on its website(s) a link to that part of the CQC website containing the most recent assessment, and the CQC's most recent performance rating;
- to display at each of its premises the most recent CQC performance rating (either the overall performance rating or a rating relating to the specific premises);
- to display at the service provider's principal place of business at least one sign showing the most recent CQC performance rating(s).

17.72 A failure to comply with regulation 20A is an offence, as well as a potential ground for regulatory action (regulation 22(1)).

The CQC's obligations towards users of care services

17.73 The CQC was established with a clear service user focus. HSCA 2008 s3(1) provides that the 'main objective' of CQC 'in performing its functions is to protect and promote the health, safety and welfare of people who use health and social care services'. Section 3(2) also requires the CQC to perform its functions 'for the general purpose of encouraging' certain matters, including 'the provision of health and social care services in a way that focuses on the needs and experiences of people who use those services'.

17.74 HSCA 2008 s4(1) requires the CQC, in performing its functions, to have regard to certain matters, including:

- views expressed by or on behalf of members of the public about health and social care services;
- experiences of people who use health and social care services and their families and friends;
- the need to protect and promote the rights of people who use health and social care services.

17.75 HSCA 2008 s5 requires the CQC to publish a statement on user involvement. Its contents must include a description of how the CQC proposes to:

- promote awareness among service users and carers of its functions;
- promote and engage in discussion with service users and carers about the provision of health and social care services and about the way in which the Commission exercises its functions;
- ensure that proper regard is had to the views expressed by service users and carers; and
- arrange for any of its functions to be exercised by, or with the assistance of, service users and carers.

17.76 At the time of writing (February 2017), the CQC's most recent public engagement plan was *Our strategy for engaging the public in CQC's work in 2015–2016*, 2015.

The legal requirement to register

17.77   HSCA 2008 s10(1) provides that 'any person who carries on a regulated activity without being registered ... in respect of the carrying on of that activity is guilty of an offence'. The maximum penalty for commission of the offence is 12 months' imprisonment and/or a fine (section 10(4)).

17.78   In order for an application for registration to be granted, the CQC must be satisfied that the requirements of the regulatory requirements will be met (see above), as well as the requirements of any other enactment which appears to the CQC to be relevant, for example the Data Protection Act 1998 or health and safety legislation (HSCA 2008 s12(2)). Registration may be subject to conditions (section 12(3)) and failure to comply with a condition is an offence (section 33).

17.79   The application process is structured in such a way as to provide the applicant with the opportunity to make representations against a proposed negative decision (including the imposition of unagreed conditions of registration). CQC must issue a notice of proposal (section 26), following which the applicant has the right to make written representations (section 27). There is a right of appeal to the First-tier Tribunal (Health, Education and Social Care Chamber) and an onward right of appeal to the Upper Tribunal on a point of law. Similar rights of appeal exist against CQC enforcement activity decisions. Permission is required for an appeal to the Upper Tribunal which can be granted by either the First-tier Tribunal or the Upper Tribunal. Very few appeals come before the Upper Tribunal and, as a result, there is little binding case law about the operating of the current regulatory scheme.

17.80   The manager of a regulated activity is not, in all cases, also required to be registered. This is another departure from the earlier registration scheme. In certain cases, regulations require a service provider's registration to be subject to a registered manager condition. For example, a corporate body provider, apart from a health service body, must have a registered manager (Care Quality Commission (Registration) Regulations 2009 SI No 3112 reg 5). In other cases, the CQC may impose a registered manager condition.

Regulatory action

Cancellation of registration

17.81   The ultimate regulatory sanction is cancellation of registration. If a service provider's registration is cancelled yet the service remains operational, the offence of carrying on an unregistered regulated activity under HSCA 2008 s10(1) will be committed. The grounds for cancellation are set out in HSCA 2008 s17(1) and include that the regulated activity is being, or has at any time been, carried on otherwise than in accordance with the regulatory requirements or a condition of registration.

Regulatory decision-making

17.82   The HSCA 2008 requires a structured approach to regulatory decision-making, designed to give the registered person an opportunity to make representations against proposed regulatory action, including a proposal to cancel registration and impose an additional condition of registration (HSCA 2008 s26). The CQC must issue a notice of proposal (section 26), following which the applicant has the right to make written representations (section 27). The registered person has a right of appeal against the final decision to the First-tier Tribunal (Health, Education and Social Care Chamber).

17.83   Normally, the CQC's decision does not take effect until the 28-day period for appealing expires and, if an appeal is made, the appeal is determined or abandoned (HSCA 2008 s28(6)). However, section 30(1) contains an urgent procedure for cancellation under which the CQC may apply to a justice of the peace for a cancellation order on the ground that 'unless the order is made, there will be a serious risk to a person's life, health or well-being'. Section 30(2) permits such an application to be made without notice having been given to the registered person. Section 31 also allows the CQC to take urgent action to alter conditions of registration (including imposing new conditions of registration) or suspend registration. A section 31 notice takes effect from the time when it is given.

CQC powers of entry and inspection

17.84   CQC inspectors have powers of entry and inspection in connection with their enforcement powers, as well as their review/investigation powers (HSCA 2008 s62). The powers do not permit CQC to require entry to a private dwelling (section 62(4)). CQC inspectors have associated powers to inspect and take copies of documents or records, and interview staff including officers and staff of local authorities (section 63(2)). A CQC inspector is only permitted to carry out an examination in private of a person receiving care if the inspector is a registered doctor or nurse (section 63(3)).

17.85   The HSCA 2008 makes it a criminal offence for any person knowingly or recklessly to disclose any confidential information obtained by the CQC and which identifies a living individual (section 76). There are various defences in section 77, including that disclosure was necessary for the purpose of protecting the welfare of the individual.

17.86   The CQC itself has powers to require production of documents or records (section 64) and to require a person to provide it with an explanation of a relevant matter.[15]

Reports

17.87   After each inspection carried out for registration purposes, the CQC must prepare and publish a report (HSCA 2008 s61).

---

15 Care Quality Commission (Registration) Regulations 2009 SI No 3112 reg 10.

How funding authorities should respond to regulatory action

17.88   Local authorities ought to become aware of regulatory action in respect of services they have purchased due to the CQC's legal obligations to give notice of regulatory action under HSCA 2008 s30. Once on notice, the local authority will need to consider whether its obligations under the Care Act 2014 require it to take steps to secure an individual's welfare.

Enforcement policies

17.89   The HSCA 2008 gives the QCC power to take less drastic regulatory action than cancellation of registration or imposition of additional conditions of registration:

- under section 29, the CQC may issue a warning notice specifying a regulatory breach and, if it is of a continuing nature, setting out what the registrant needs to do to become compliant. Warning notices cannot be appealed to the First-tier Tribunal;
- many contraventions of the Act, and regulations, amount to criminal offences. The CQC has the power to prosecute alleged regulatory offences (section 90). Section 91 sets out when officers or members of a local authority are concurrently liable for a criminal offence committed by the authority;
- under section 86, the CQC may give a person a penalty notice where it is satisfied the person has committed a fixed penalty offence. These offences are specified in Schedule 5 to the HSCA regulations 2014 (eg most offences under the HSCA regulations 2014, carrying on unregistered regulated activity and failing to comply with a condition of registration). If the notice is duly paid within 28 days, the person cannot be prosecuted for the offence. The amount of the penalty varies according to the transgression, as set out in Schedule 5 to the HSCA regulations 2014. For example, the penalty for carrying on an unregistered regulated activity is £4,000 but a failure to display a performance assessment attracts a penalty of only £100.

17.90   The CQC's enforcement policy is available on its website as *CQC enforcement policy*, 2015.

Reviews and performance assessments

17.91   As well as its responsibilities as regulator of individual services, the CQC is also responsible for monitoring the performance of local authority functions connected to care services and the care services sector more generally. Under HSCA 2008 s46, the CQC has functions of conducting reviews of regulated activity and assessing the performance of service providers.

17.92   HSCA 2008 s48(1) permits the CQC to carry out 'special reviews and investigations' and also permits the secretary of state to require a special review or investigation to be carried out. However, the CQC may not if its own volition carry out a special review or investigation of 'the exercise of the functions of English local authorities in arranging for the provision of adult social services'; the secretary of state's approval is required. The CQC must publish a report of a special review or investigation. This may then give rise to a duty to report matters of concern to the secretary of state.

17.93   A section 46 review, or section 48 investigation, may lead the CQC to consider that a local authority is failing to discharge any of its adult social services functions to an acceptable standard. If so, the CQC:

a) must inform the secretary of state and recommend any special measures which it considers the secretary of state should take (section 50(2)); unless

b) the CQC, considers the failure is 'not substantial', in which case the CQC may instead give the local authority a notice specifying the failure, what needs to be done to remedy it and within what timescale (section 50(4). The CQC must inform the secretary of state if it gives such a notice.

17.94   The CQC also has the function under section 54 of carrying out economy, efficiency and effectiveness studies into, for example, the provision of adult social services (although a study into the making of arrangements by a local authority for provision of adult social service requires the secretary of state's approval to be carried out). The CQC may also carry out or promote studies for improving the management of an English local authority in its provision of adult social services and for enabling it to prepare reports as to the impact of statutory provisions or government guidance or directions.

CHAPTER 18

Safeguarding: an overview

continued

Introduction

18.1   Safeguarding rests in turbulent waters: in the ideological cross currents of the two key forces that shape social care – paternalism and autonomy; neither of which are very pleasant in their extremes.

18.2   Much criticism has been made of the law, deriving as it does 'from a complex mishmash of legislation, guidance and ad hoc court interventions'.[1] This is as true today as it was under the pre-Care Act (CA) 2014 legal regime, but it is perhaps a little unfair. Notwithstanding the need for better laws and better guidance, ultimately this will always be a complex contested field. This is because the black and white lettering of the law will seldom resolve difficult cases. These will depend upon experienced professionals having open discussions with adults at risk; having time to consider the material facts; being unconstrained by excessive caseloads and a risk averse bureaucratic culture that puts adherence to budget compliance and time-limited imperatives above all other considerations.[2]

18.3   The theory and practice of 'adult safeguarding' is a fascinating, much researched and much debated subject.[3] A detailed review of the relevant law and practice lies outside the scope of this book, and what follows is a brief review of the key legal provisions that cover this field.

Background

Statistics

18.4   It is unclear whether the enactment of the CA 2014 has had a significant impact on the number of safeguarding referrals received by local authorities. Prior to its implementation there had been a steady rise in referrals – for example, between 2011 and 2013 referrals rose by 13 per cent (of which 43 per cent were substantiated). The rise was attributed to either/both an increased awareness of abuse and/or 'overstretched resources and pressure within the system'.[4]

---

1   Cobb J in *The Mental Health Trust v DD* [2015] EWCOP 4 at para 23.
2   See for example, L Butler and J Manthorpe, 'Putting people at the centre: facilitating Making Safeguarding Personal approaches in the context of the Care Act 2014' in *The Journal of Adult Protection* (2016) Vol 18, Issue 4 pp204–213.
3   J Herring, *Vulnerable adults and the law*, OUP, 2016 represents an excellent point of departure for studies in this field; and see also A Brammer, *Safeguarding adults*, Palgrave Macmillan, 2014.
4   House of Commons Committee of Public Accounts, *Adult social care in England*, HC 518, The Stationery Office, 2014, p8.

18.5   In the immediate aftermath of the implementation of the CA 2014 there were suggestions that there had been a dramatic (50 per cent) increase in referrals,[5] however official figures suggest that was not the case.[6]

18.6   In 2015/16 there were 102,970 individuals with safeguarding enquiries under CA 2014 procedures. Neglect and acts of omission were the most common type of risk involved (accounting for 34 per cent of risks), followed by physical abuse (26 per cent). The location of risk was most frequently the home of the adult at risk (43 per cent of enquiries) or in a care home (36 per cent). On average, there were 239 individuals per 100,000 population for whom CA 2014 s42 enquiries were instigated. The rate of enquiries increased with age: for adults aged 75–84 the rate was more than three times the average, and for those 85 and over the increase was tenfold (ie 2,297 per 100,000 adults).[7]

Legislative background

18.7   Attempts to reform adult safeguarding law in England have been controversial and ultimately politically unpalatable: unpalatable because positive action by the state can be construed as 'paternalistic' and because a coherent system would come at a cost.

18.8   In 1995 the Law Commission published a draft bill which provided for the 'Public law protection for vulnerable people at risk',[8] but this part of the bill made no further progress in England.[9] When confronted by a serious example of an adult for whom the law provided no protection, the courts in 2000 developed a procedure of 'declaratory relief' in an effort to fill the statutory void – as Sedley LJ expressed it 'to speak where Parliament, although the more appropriate forum, was silent'[10] (see para 18.93 below for further discussion of this procedure).

18.9   The Law Commission in its 2011 report on *Adult social care* law reform[11] was altogether more circumspect than it had been in 1995. Although its chapter on safeguarding is the second longest in the report, it ultimately proposed little in the way of reform. In this respect it was no doubt being pragmatic, noting at para 9.52:

---

5   A McNicoll and R Carter, 'Care Act triggers surge in safeguarding cases' *Community Care*, 16 March 2016 which cited evidence (Department of Health, Association of Directors of Adult Social Services Departments (ADASS) and Local Government Association (LGA), *Care Act implementation: results of local authority stocktake*, 2015) which stated that there had been '100,000 safeguarding enquiries in the first 6 months of 15/16'.

6   NHS Digital, *Safeguarding adults, annual report, England 2015–16, experimental statistics*, Figure 1.3a p9) 2014/15 and 2015/16 there was no significant increase in 'safeguarding concerns' – ie 'where a council is notified about a risk of abuse, which instigates an investigation under the local safeguarding procedures' (p6).

7   NHS Digital, *Safeguarding adults, annual report, England 2015–16, experimental statistics*, .

8   Law Commission, *Mental incapacity*, Law Com No 231, HMSO, 1995, Part IX.

9   The draft bill led to the enactment of the Mental Capacity Act (MCA) 2005 but Part IX was discarded, however many of its proposals are evident in the Adult Support and Protection (Scotland) Act 2007.

10   *Re F (adult: court's jurisdiction)* [2000] 3 WLR 1740, (2000) 3 CCLR 210, CA.

11   Law Commission, *Adult social care*, Law Com No 326, HC 941, May 2011.

... the distinctions we have made between law reform and politics are difficult judgements to make and we might not have got them right. Part of our consultation, therefore, was to determine whether we had drawn the correct line between law reform and politics in areas such as safeguarding.

18.10 The CA 2014 provides local authorities with very little, in terms of substance, to enhance their pre-existing safeguarding powers. The CA 2014 contains no power of entry to interview an adult thought to be at risk of abuse[12] and no power to remove a person found to be in this position.[13] As a leading commentator observed, the content is 'minimal' defining only 'the infrastructure ... that must exist'.[14] The safeguarding chapter in the draft statutory guidance was considered unsatisfactory by many and lacking 'legal literacy'[15] and sadly this criticism has also been levelled against the 'disappointing' revised version.[16]

Well-being and safeguarding

18.11 As noted above (para 2.3) CA 2014 s1(1) creates a general duty to promote well-being and in this context, section 1(2)(c) specifically identifies the 'protection from abuse and neglect'. The Law Commission[17] in 2011, in recommending that there be such a duty,[18] noted arguments that (para 4.12):

> ... safeguarding and adult protection are connected but essentially different; with one relating to the prevention of abuse and the other relating to intervention once abuse has occurred, and consequently there would be merit in including a safeguarding principle.

18.12 The section 1 duty to protect from abuse and neglect is a well-being obligation that cannot be taken in isolation as the statutory guidance[19] to the CA 2014 makes clear (at para 14.7):

> ... safeguarding ... is about people and organisations working together to prevent and stop both the risks and experience of abuse or neglect, while at the same time making sure that the adult's well-being is promoted including, where appropriate, having regard to their views, wishes, feelings and beliefs in deciding on any action. This must recognise that adults sometimes have complex interpersonal relationships and may be ambivalent, unclear or unrealistic about their personal circumstances.

---

12 Such a power exits in Social Services and Well-being (Wales) Act 2014 s127 and Adult Support and Protection (Scotland) Act 2007 s7. For an account of the attempts to amend the Care Bill to include a right of access to interview people suspected of being abused, see J Manthorpe and others, 'Parliamentary arguments on powers of access – the Care Bill debates' in *The Journal of Adult Protection*, (2016) Vol 18 I: 6.

13 Such a power exits in Adult Support and Protection (Scotland) Act 2007 ss11 and 14.

14 G Fitzgerald, 'It is not enough to simply reflect the wording of the legislation' in *Community Care*, 31 March 2016.

15 L Series, *Care Act 2014: consultation on draft guidance & regulations*, Small Places, 2014.

16 G Fitzgerald, 'It is not enough to simply reflect the wording of the legislation' in *Community Care*, 31 March 2016.

17 Law Commission, *Adult social care*, Law Com No 326 HC 941, May 2011.

18 Law Commission, *Adult social care*, Law Com No 326 HC 941, May 2011, Recommendation 5 which proposed a duty to 'safeguard adults wherever practicable from abuse and neglect'.

19 Department of Health, *Care and support statutory guidance* to support implementation of Part 1 of the CA 2014 by local authorities, 2016 ('the statutory guidance').

The safeguarding duties

18.13   The CA 2014 places on a statutory footing some of the safeguarding obligations that were previously only located in guidance (principally the Department of Health's *No secrets* guidance of 2000[20]) – for example, the duty to
make enquiries and to decide what action should to be taken. The reforms
have led to the repeal of *No secrets,* and its replacement is to be found in
chapter 14 of the statutory guidance to the CA 2014.

The duty to make enquiries

18.14   CA 2014 s42(1) creates a statutory duty to make enquiries, namely:

> 42(1) This section applies where a local authority has reasonable cause to sus-
> pect that an adult in its area (whether or not ordinarily resident there)–
>   (a) has needs for care and support (whether or not the authority is meet-
>   ing any of those needs),
>   (b) is experiencing, or is at risk of, abuse or neglect, and
>   (c) as a result of those needs is unable to protect himself or herself
>   against the abuse or neglect or the risk of it.

18.15   It has been argued[21] that a literal interpretation of section 42(1) would
mean that the safeguarding duty does not arise in relation to a person
who, although having no care and support needs, is a victim of financial abuse/undue influence and unable to protect themselves. Likewise it
would appear that that there is no general duty to make enquires where a
person has been the victim of historic abuse (possibly by a local authority
care worker) but the abuser has been suspended.

Terminology

General

18.16   Concern about the lack of clarity over safeguarding terms has been long
standing. A 2008 paper published by the Commission for Social Care
Inspection (CSCI)[22] noted that there was 'no shared understanding of
what "safeguarding adults" means', and the absence of generally accepted
definitions for the terms 'safeguarding', 'abuse', 'harm' and 'vulnerable' contributed to 'the lack of clarity about roles and responsibilities in
responding to situations where adults need assistance to stay safe'.

---

20   Department of Health and the Home Office, *No Secrets: guidance on developing and
    implementing multi-agency policies and procedures to protect vulnerable adults from abuse,*
    2000.
21   Examples taken from G Fitzgerald, 'It is not enough to simply reflect the wording of
    the legislation' in *Community Care,* 31 March 2016.
22   CSCI, *Safeguarding adults: a study of the effectiveness of arrangements to safeguard adults
    from abuse,* 2008.

Vulnerable adult

18.17 The term 'vulnerable adult'[23] (used in the 2000 guidance *No secrets*[24]) was considered unhelpful because it located 'the cause of the abuse within the victim, rather than in placing the responsibility with the actions or omissions of others'.[25] It 'can also suggest that vulnerability is an inherent characteristic of a person and does not recognise that it might be the context, the setting or the place which makes a person vulnerable'. Although the Law Commission proposed that this term should be replaced by 'adults at risk',[26] the CA 2014 (as noted above) opts for a compound set of criteria, at its core is the existence of an adult who 'is experiencing, or is at risk of, abuse or neglect'.

Abuse and neglect

18.18 The CA 2014 does not explain what is meant by 'abuse' and 'neglect' – save to specify that it includes financial abuse, which is broadly defined in section 42(3) as including:

(a) having money or other property stolen,
(b) being defrauded,
(c) being put under pressure in relation to money or other property, and
(d) having money or other property misused.

18.19 The statutory guidance, however, provides an expansive explanation, cautioning authorities against limiting 'their view of what constitutes abuse or neglect' (para 14.17). The following brief extracts give an indication of the breadth of what local authorities are required to regard as abuse/neglect:

- physical abuse;
- domestic violence – including psychological and emotional abuse;
- sexual abuse – including 'inappropriate looking or touching';
- psychological abuse – including 'deprivation of contact, blaming, controlling, cyber bullying, isolation';
- financial or material abuse (as above);
- modern slavery;
- discriminatory abuse – including forms of 'harassment, slurs or similar treatment; because of race, gender and gender identity, age, disability, sexual orientation or religion';
- organisational abuse – including 'neglect and poor care practice within an institution or specific care setting such as a hospital or care home' ranging from 'one off incidents to on-going ill-treatment' and 'neglect

---

23 In relation to the extensive literature on vulnerability see, for example, M Fineman, '"Elderly" as vulnerable: Rethinking the nature of individual and societal responsibility' in *Elder Law Journal* (2012) 20(1): 71–122; and L Series 'Relationships, autonomy and legal capacity: Mental capacity and support paradigms' in *International Journal of Law and Psychiatry* (2015) 40: 80–91.

24 Department of Health and the Home Office, *No Secrets: guidance on developing and implementing multi-agency policies and procedures to protect vulnerable adults from abuse*, 2000.

25 Association of Directors of Social Services, *Safeguarding adults*, 2005.

26 The term used in the Adult Support and Protection (Scotland) Act 2007: see the discussion on the definition of 'vulnerable adult' in Law Commission, *Adult social care – scoping report*, 2008, paras 4.280–4.293.

or poor professional practice as a result of the structure, policies, processes and practices within an organisation';

- neglect and acts of omission – including 'ignoring medical, emotional or physical care needs, failure to provide access to appropriate health, care and support or educational services, the withholding of the necessities of life, such as medication, adequate nutrition and heating';
- self-neglect – including a wide range of behaviour neglecting to care for one's personal hygiene, health or surroundings and includes behaviour such as hoarding.

Self-neglect[27]

18.20   In addition to the above reference to self-neglect, the statutory guidance states (para 14.17):

> This covers a wide range of behaviour neglecting to care for one's personal hygiene, health or surroundings and includes behaviour such as hoarding. It should be noted that self-neglect may not prompt a section 42 enquiry. An assessment should be made on a case by case basis. A decision on whether a response is required under safeguarding will depend on the adult's ability to protect themselves by controlling their own behaviour. There may come a point when they are no longer able to do this, without external support.

18.21   Concern has been expressed about the failure of the statutory guidance to distinguish between self-neglect that is 'a chosen lifestyle' and that which is 'caused through external factors, such as a loss of income or the death of a relative'.[28]

18.22   While there is difficult line to tread in responding to self-neglect referrals, in cases where significant harm is resulting it will be maladministration for an authority to fail to investigate: to fail to appreciate that there is a 'balance to be struck between an individual's autonomy and dignity'.[29] Where there is sufficient information to challenge the presumption of capacity, it will be also maladministration for a local authority/NHS body to fail to undertake the necessary capacity assessments.[30]

Local authority safeguarding enquiries

18.23   Where the triggering criteria exist for the purposes of CA 2014 s42(1) – ie the individual has needs for care and support; is at risk of abuse or neglect; and unable to protect himself or herself – then a duty to investigate crystallises under section 42(2) to:

---

27 See S Braye and others, *Self-neglect policy and practice: building an evidence base for adult social care*, Social Care Institute for Excellence (SCIE) Report 69, 2015; and M Day and others, 'Self-neglect: ethical considerations' in *Annual Review of Nursing Research*, Vol 34, No 1, 2016, pp89–107(19).

28 See, for example, G Fitzgerald, 'It is not enough to simply reflect the wording of the legislation' in *Community Care*, 31 March 2016.

29 Health Service Ombudsman and the Local Government Ombudsman, *Report about the care and support provided to a vulnerable person living independently in the community*, 4 July 2011, HC 1355, The Stationery Office, 2011, para 115.

30 Complaint No 11010604/JW 111510 against South Essex Partnership Trust and Bedford BC, 22 May 2014 (a case concerning a disabled person living in the community who was significantly malnourished and with poor dental care).

... make (or cause to be made) whatever enquiries it thinks necessary to enable it to decide whether any action should be taken ...

18.24 The nature of the resulting enquiry can, as the statutory guidance explains, 'range from a conversation with the adult ... through to a much more formal multi-agency plan or course of action' (para 14.77). The purpose of the enquiry is 'to decide whether or not the local authority or another organisation, or person, should do something to help and protect the adult' (para 14.78).

18.25 The statutory guidance contains considerable detail on the investigation process once it has been agreed that an enquiry is necessary – together with a series of lists detailing the aims and principles of safeguarding (summarised below). What is, however, evident from the abundant local government ombudsman reports concerning failures in relation to this function – is that safeguarding is about the 'doing the basics' properly: ensuring that the adult is involved to the maximum extent possible; getting evidence; acting fairly and using measured language; keeping records and keeping people informed; exercising professional judgement; taking timely and proportionate decisions; keeping control of the process so that if new evidence arises or the balance of evidence changes then the process is reconsidered; and avoiding delay.

18.26 Ombudsman concerns about local authority failures in relation to safeguarding issues frequently include:[31]

- a failure to refer an enquiry to the adult protection coordinator in a timely manner and to hold meetings in accordance the council's policy;
- a failure to ensure relevant parties are invited to the meetings[32] and to keep complainants adequately informed about the process/progress;
- delay/insufficient urgency being given to the investigation;
- a lack of clarity as to which procedures are being followed;
- a failure to adhere to relevant policy documents and the timescales in these documents (especially initially – ie ensuring a prompt medical or other investigation is undertaken; the police informed etc);
- a lack of a clear investigation strategy;
- lengthy delay between meetings and a failure to follow up meeting decisions with expedition;
- poor record keeping and delay in writing up minutes of meetings;[33]
- a failure to take swift action when problems arise – especially if these are not entirely unforeseeable;

---

31 See, for example, Public Services Ombudsman for Wales: Investigation Report concerning the Vale of Glamorgan Council Case: 201202374, 4 June 2013; complaint no 11 001 206 against Essex CC, 15 May 2013; and complaint no 12 004 137 against Worcestershire CC, January 2014.

32 Social services cannot assume that parties to a safeguarding investigation will be briefed by third parties (eg the police – even if a prosecution being considered) and so must ensure it in regular contact to update – see complaint no 15 000 600 against Ealing LBC, 19 July 2016; and see also Public Service Ombudsman for Wales Report concerning Cardiff Council no 201002439, 2012 where there was a failure to consider inviting the wife of the vulnerable adult to the safeguarding meeting.

33 In complaint no 14 001 973 against Lancashire CC, 12 September 2016 the ombudsman was critical of the delay in writing up minutes – 'The minutes should have been written up immediately and certainly before the senior practitioner went on leave'.

- failure to have regard to external information – eg reports by the Care Quality Commission (CQC) (the independent regulator of health and social care in England) and the council's own Care Quality Services Team;
- a lack of consistency in the terminology used (ie failing to reflect the terminology used in the relevant policy documents);
- a failure to be clear about the source of evidence and avoiding unsubstantiated hearsay and inflammatory statements;[34]
- a failure to take follow-up action after a police investigation has concluded;[35]
- a failure to record properly the reasons for a decision to close a safeguarding investigation and for reasons to be detailed and evidence based.

18.27   The statutory guidance states that the aims of adult safeguarding are to (para 14.11):

- prevent harm and reduce the risk of abuse or neglect to adults with care and support needs
- stop abuse or neglect wherever possible
- safeguard adults in a way that supports them in making choices and having control about how they want to live
- promote an approach that concentrates on improving life for the adults concerned
- raise public awareness so that communities as a whole, alongside professionals, play their part in preventing, identifying and responding to abuse and neglect
- provide information and support in accessible ways to help people understand the different types of abuse, how to stay safe and what to do to raise a concern about the safety or well-being of an adult
- address what has caused the abuse or neglect

18.28   It then explains that in order to achieve these aims, it is necessary to (para 14.12):

- ensure that everyone, both individuals and organisations, are clear about their roles and responsibilities
- create strong multi-agency partnerships that provide timely and effective prevention of and responses to abuse or neglect
- support the development of a positive learning environment across these partnerships and at all levels within them to help break down cultures that are risk-averse and seek to scapegoat or blame practitioners
- enable access to mainstream community resources such as accessible leisure facilities, safe town centres and community groups that can reduce the social and physical isolation which in itself may increase the risk of abuse or neglect

---

34 The ombudsman was particularly critical of a local authority report that used phrases such as 'it is reported that'; 'I have been informed that' without providing any supporting documentary evidence and the use of 'inflammatory language' such as referring to a 'smokescreen of irrelevant information' – see complaint no 15 017 811 against Lancashire CC, 2 September 2016.

35 See, for example, Complaint no 11 001 206 against Essex CC, 15 May 2013; Complaint no 12 004 137 against Worcestershire CC, January 2014.

- clarify how responses to safeguarding concerns deriving from the poor quality and inadequacy of service provision, including patient safety in the health sector, should be responded to

18.29 Fearful of an insufficiency of lists, the statutory guidance then states that there are six key principles that 'underpin all adult safeguarding work', namely:

1) empowerment;
2) prevention;
3) proportionality;
4) protection;
5) partnership; and
6) accountability,

each of which is accompanied by a brief explanation (para 14.13).

Action following an enquiry

18.30 A range of possible responses may follow an enquiry (see statutory guidance, paras 14.104–14.105). If, however, the local authority decides that it must itself take further action, then it is under a duty to do so, and in general this will include the preparation of a 'protection plan' (para 14.106), which should set out (para 14.111):

- what steps are to be taken to assure their safety in future
- the provision of any support, treatment or therapy including on-going advocacy
- any modifications needed in the way services are provided (for example, same gender care or placement; appointment of an OPG deputy)
- how best to support the adult through any action they take to seek justice or redress;
- any on-going risk management strategy as appropriate
- any action to be taken in relation to the person or organisation that has caused the concern

18.31 The statutory guidance contains further detail about the nature of the action that may be taken against those identified as responsible for the abuse or neglect (see paras 14.112–14.119) including guidance concerning action against those who hold (or held) a position of trust (paras 14.120–14.132).

Safeguarding as a route to eligibility

18.32 As noted in chapter 4 above, although the eligibility regulations[36] made pursuant to the CA 2014 fail to identify an inability on the part of the person to 'keep safe' as an eligible need in itself, it is likely that the positive obligations on local authorities under the Human Rights Act (HRA) 1998 will address this failure – reference should be made to paras 4.23 and 2.73 for further discussion of this question.

---

36 Care and Support (Eligibility Criteria) Regulations 2015 SI No 313.

Powers of access

18.33 As noted above (para 18.10) the CA 2014 contains no power of entry to interview an adult thought to be at risk of abuse, and no power to remove a person found to be in this position. During the debate on the Care Bill, the minister[37] argued that there was no need for such additional powers referring to the existing power to apply to the High Court to use its inherent jurisdiction (see para 18.89 below) and evidence from the Association of Chief Police Officers (ACPO), that:

> … the police already have sufficient powers of entry to protect people from harm. Powers of entry are provided to us under both common law and PACE and I am satisfied that these would afford us access to premises where vulnerable individuals are considered to be at risk.

18.34 In this respect the Social Care Institute for Excellence (SCIE) has issued guidance[38] in which it provides an overview of the powers which may be relevant to adult safeguarding situations – including under the Mental Capacity Act (MCA) 2005, the Mental Health Act (MHA) 1983 and the Police and Criminal Evidence Act (PACE) 1984 (together with the common law including the inherent jurisdiction of the High Court (see para 18.89 below) and common law powers of the police to prevent or deal with a breach of the peace.

18.35 District councils and unitary authorities' environmental health departments have a variety of powers under the Public Health Acts (PHAs) that are available in limited circumstances. PHA 1936 s83 authorises councils to give notice to owners or occupiers of premises that are 'in such a filthy or unwholesome condition as to be prejudicial to health' and a power of entry is provided by section 287. Where the owner or occupier fails to take remedial action, the local authority can give notice to require vacation of the premises during the work that they undertake or commission (PHA 1961 s36).

18.36 A little-used power of environmental health departments under National Assistance Act (NAA) 1948 s47 was repealed by the CA 2014[39] (the power to remove to a care home placement people 'suffering from grave, chronic disease or, being aged, infirm or physically incapacitated, is living in unsanitary conditions').[40]

The duty to protect property: Care Act 2014 s47

18.37 NAA 1948 s48 placed a duty on local authorities to prevent the loss or damage of a person's property when admitted to hospital or provided with accommodation under the NAA 1948, if there was danger of loss or damage and there were no other suitable arrangements that could be made.

37 Minister of State, Department of Health (Norman Lamb) House of Commons Public Bill Committee 4 February 2014 Hansard 609–610.

38 SCIE, *Gaining access to an adult suspected to be at risk of neglect or abuse: a guide for social workers and their managers in England*, 2014.

39 CA 2014 s46.

40 For a review of section 47 see the Law Commission in its report *Adult social care*, Law Com No 326, HC 941, May 2011, paras 9.60–9.96.

The Law Commission recommended that this be retained in any reformed legal regime.[41]

18.38   The section 48 duty has been repealed but re-enacted in similar terms as CA 2014 s47. Section 47(1) sets out the key conditions for the duty to arise, namely that a local authority is providing the person with accommodation under CA 2014 s18 or s19 (see paras 4.55 and 4.74 above) and/or they are admitted to hospital and:

> it appears to the authority that there is a danger of loss or damage to their movable property in the authority's area because–
> (i) the adult is unable (whether permanently or temporarily) to protect or deal with the property, and
> (ii) no suitable arrangements have been or are being made.

18.39   In such a situation, CA 2014 s47(2) places a duty on the authority to take reasonable steps to prevent or mitigate the loss or damage. Section 47(3) provides the authority with a power of entry to protect the property. For this to apply, section 47(4) requires that the authority has obtained the adult's consent, or if they lack the necessary capacity, it either: (a) has the consent of 'a person authorised under the Mental Capacity Act 2005' (see paras 13.140 and 13.150), or (b) if there is no such person, then it 'is satisfied that exercising the power would be in the adult's best interests'.

18.40   Section 47(6) makes it a criminal offence for a person who, without reasonable excuse, obstructs the lawful use of this power.

18.41   Local authorities are empowered to recover their reasonable expenses in relation to the action they take under section 47.

18.42   The statutory guidance gives advice on the section 47 duty (at paras 10.88–10.94). It notes that this includes arranging for the care of pets where 'someone who is having their care and support needs provided away from home in a care home or hospital, and who has not been able to make other arrangements' (para 10.89).

Safeguarding Adults Boards

18.43   CA 2014 s43(1) places a duty on every social services authority to establish a Safeguarding Adults Board (SAB). Since these already existed in practice,[42] the reform made little difference in terms of substance. The objective of SABs is to help and protect adults in their areas experiencing, or at risk of, abuse or neglect (section 43(2)), and in order to achieve this they may do anything which appears 'necessary or desirable' (section 43(4)), although this must include 'co-ordinating and ensuring the effectiveness' of each of the SABs members' actions (section 42(3)).

18.44   Further details concerning the membership, functions and funding of SABs are contained in Schedule 2 to the 2014 Act and section 43(6)

---

41 Law Commission, *Adult social care*, Law Com No 326, HC 941, May 2011, Recommendation 43.

42 The *No Secrets* (2000) guidance (see above) had advised authorities to create multi-agency management committees (para 3.4). See also Department of Health, *Safeguarding adults, report on the consultation on the review of 'No Secrets'*, 2009; and the Law Commission, *Adult social care*, Law Com No 326, HC 941, May 2011, para 9.104.

provides for local authorities to combine their SABs with neighbouring authorities.

18.45   CA 2014 Sch 2 para 1(1) specifies that the members of an SAB are:

(a) the local authority which established it,

(b) a clinical commissioning group the whole or part of whose area is in the local authority's area,

(c) the chief officer of police for a police area the whole or part of which is in the local authority's area, and

(d) such persons, or persons of such description, as may be specified in regulations.

18.46   The statutory guidance gives examples of who might in addition be invited 'to some meetings depending on the specific focus or to participate in its work more generally (para 14.146). The examples it gives are

- ambulance and fire services
- representatives of providers of health and social care services, including independent providers
- Department for Work and Pensions
- representatives of housing providers, housing support providers, probation and prison services
- general practitioners
- representatives of further education colleges
- members of user, advocacy and carer groups
- local healthwatch
- Care Quality Commission
- representatives of children's safeguarding boards
- trading standards

18.47   The statutory guidance fleshes out in considerable the detail of the role of SABs and how they should operate in practice (see paras 14.133–14.161). It explains that Schedule 2 provides for each SAB to have three core duties, namely (para 14.136):

- it must publish a strategic plan for each financial year that sets how it will meet its main objective and what the members will do to achieve this. The plan must be developed with local community involvement, and the SAB must consult the local Healthwatch organisation. The plan should be evidence based and make use of all available evidence and intelligence from partners to form and develop its plan
- it must publish an annual report detailing what the SAB has done during the year to achieve its main objective and implement its strategic plan, and what each member has done to implement the strategy as well as detailing the findings of any safeguarding adults reviews and subsequent action
- it must conduct any safeguarding adults review in accordance with Section 44 of the Act.

Safeguarding adults reviews

18.48   CA 2014 s44(1) places a duty on SABs to hold a formal 'safeguarding adult review' (SAR) in specific situations, namely when, in relation to an adult in their area with needs for care and support (whether or not the local authority has been meeting any of those needs):

- there is reasonable cause for concern about how the SAB, members of it or other persons with relevant functions worked together to safeguard the adult; and
- either:
  - the adult has died, and the SAB knows or suspects that the death resulted from abuse or neglect; or
  - the adult is still alive, and the SAB knows or suspects that the adult has experienced serious abuse or neglect.

18.49   Section 44(4) creates a power for there to be a SAR in any other case involving an adult in the SAB's area with needs for care and support (whether or not the local authority has been meeting any of those needs).

18.50   A detailed consideration of SARs lies outside the scope of this book. For further information, reference should be made to the statutory guidance (paras 14.162–14.186) which advises on (among other things) the way SARs must be conducted, the records that must be kept, the need for appropriate confidentiality protocols and how SAR findings should be disseminated.[43]

Disclosure and Barring Service

18.51   The Safeguarding Vulnerable Groups Act (SVGA) 2006 was to have introduced an extensive 'vetting and barring' scheme for those wishing to work with children and/or vulnerable adults (whether paid or unpaid): protecting them by stopping those who pose a known risk from working with them. This scheme was in response to the Bichard Inquiry report,[44] which found a range of flaws with the then existing arrangements for recruiting and vetting individuals wishing to work with these two groups.

18.52   The SVGA 2006 was, however, the subject of major amendment by the Protection of Freedoms Act (PFA) 2012, which resulted in the creation of the Disclosure and Barring Service (DBS).[45] In addition to the DBS's role in holding details of people barred from working with children or vulnerable adults, it fulfils the role formerly discharged by the Criminal Records Bureau.

18.53   The PFA 2012 repealed the previous definition of 'vulnerable adult', such that any adult receiving certain forms of personal care is now considered 'vulnerable' at the time the care is provided. As the Department of Health has explained in relation to this amendment, it:[46]

---

43 See also J Manthorpe and S Martineau 'Engaging with the new system of safeguarding adults reviews concerning care homes for older people' in *British Journal of Social Work* (2016) bcw102.

44 M Bichard, *The Bichard Inquiry Report*, HC 653, 2004, established to enquire into child protection procedures following the conviction of Ian Huntley for the murders of Jessica Chapman and Holly Wells.

45 PFA 2012 s87.

46 Department of Health, *Regulated activity (adults). The definition of 'regulated activity' (adults) as defined by the Safeguarding Vulnerable Groups Act 2006 from 10th September 2012*, 2011, p5.

... no longer label adults as 'vulnerable' because of the setting in which the activity is received, nor because of the personal characteristics or circumstances of the adult receiving the activities.

This means, for example, anyone providing personal care to an adult is in [a] regulated activity irrespective of whether that occurs in, say, a hospital, a care home, a day care centre, a prison or in sheltered housing.

18.54   The definition of a regulated activity is set out in SVGA 2006 Sch 4 Part 2 and although there are exceptions (particularly relating activities by friends and family) this includes most forms of: personal care; social work; assistance with general household matters; assistance in the conduct of a person's own affairs; conveying; and transporting.

18.55   It is unlawful for a barred person to engage (or seek to engage) in a regulated activity (SVGA 2006 s7) and for a person to permit a barred person to engage in a regulated activity (SVGA 2006 s9); and there is a duty on a 'regulated activity provider' to ensure that a person they are considering engaging in an regulated activity is not a barred person (SVGA 2006 s11). This is generally done by checking directly with the DBS. SVGA 2006 s35 places a duty on regulated activity providers to refer individuals to the DBS if (statutory guidance, para 14.75):

... someone is removed by being either dismissed or redeployed to a non-regulated activity, from their role providing regulated activity following a safeguarding incident, or a person leaves their role (resignation, retirement) to avoid a disciplinary hearing following a safeguarding incident and the employer/volunteer organisation feels they would have dismissed the person based on the information they hold ...

18.56   The statutory guidance reminds local authorities of this duty and notes that 'if an agency or personnel supplier has provided the person, then the legal duty sits with that agency. In circumstances where these actions are not undertaken then the local authority can make such a referral' (para 14.75).

Regulating the provision of health and social care

18.57   The regulation of health and social care providers is considered at chapter 17 of this book. The regulatory scheme[47] contains a series of 'fundamental standards', which include 'safeguarding'.[48] This requires (among many other things) that service users are protected from abuse (which includes neglect) and improper treatment in accordance with the other provisions of the regulatory scheme.[49] The CQC 2015 guidance *Regulations for service providers and managers* states that to meet the requirements of this obligation, providers must have 'a zero tolerance approach to abuse, unlawful discrimination and restraint'.

47 Health and Social Care Act 2008 (Regulated Activities) Regulations 2014 SI No 2939.
48 Health and Social Care Act 2008 (Regulated Activities) Regulations 2014 SI No 2939 reg 13(1).
49 Health and Social Care Act 2008 (Regulated Activities) Regulations 2014 SI No 2939 reg 13(1).

18.58 The regulatory regime also imposes a 'duty of candour' on all service providers, and this too is considered at para 17.66 above.

Adult protection and the CQC

18.59 The CQC has a significant role in relation to the safeguarding of adults. However, the lack of a clear investigatory remit in cases where abuse against individuals is suspected may leave residents in care homes and other settings, such as private psychiatric hospitals, vulnerable to abuse.

18.60 Although the CQC regards safeguarding to be a 'priority area', and health and social care providers are required to inform it of any allegations of abuse,[50] the CQC's 2013 safeguarding protocol describes a supervisory, rather than a lead role, in the area of adult protection; and makes clear that the CQC's function is primarily, as a regulator, to ensure that commissioners and providers of care have adequate systems in place to safeguard vulnerable adults.[51] The CQC, in its 2015 statement on its roles and responsibilities for safeguarding children and adults, describes this role as including 'if necessary, referring safeguarding alerts to the local authority – who have the local legal responsibility for safeguarding – and the police, where appropriate, to make sure action is taken to keep children and adults safe'.[52] It further notes that it does not have a 'formal role on Safeguarding Adults Boards' but that it works 'closely with them, sharing information and intelligence where appropriate to help them identify risks to children and adults'.[53]

18.61 Where concerns about safeguarding suggest that there has been a breach of regulations or that the person registered to provide health or social care is not fit to do so, the CQC will consider what action it can take. The CQC powers are far-reaching, ranging from the provision of advice and guidance to providers where there are minor concerns about compliance, to cancelling the registration and/or issuing criminal prosecutions against registered providers in cases where there are failures to comply with legal requirements or other serious concerns. However, these powers focus on regulating the health and social care providers rather than responding to concerns about incidents of abuse against individual service users.

18.62 The CQC has powers to carry out reviews and investigations into the provision of health or social care. It has a wide discretion about the circumstances which will lead to an investigation. In relation to enforcement action, the CQC in its 2015 enforcement policy[54] explains:

- The starting point for considering the use of all enforcement powers is to assess the harm or the risk of harm to people using a service.

50 Outcome 20 Notification of other incidents, Prompt 20N, in CQC, *Guidance on compliance: essential standards of quality and safety*, 2010.

51 CQC, *Our safeguarding protocol. The Care Quality Commission's responsibility and commitment to safeguarding*, 2013, para 5.1.

52 CQC, *Statement on CQC's roles and responsibilities for safeguarding children and adults*, 2015, p4. The document states that it is to be updated in '2016/17'.

53 CQC, *Statement on CQC's roles and responsibilities for safeguarding children and adults*, 2015, p4.

54 CQC, *Enforcement policy*, 2015, pp7–8.

- We will not tolerate breaches that add up to inadequate care, whether they give rise to a risk of harm or not. Where there are failures in care that do not improve, we will be prepared to use our enforcement powers.
- We will have regard to the interests of people using care services and others affected by any failure in care as part of considering how to use our enforcement powers.

18.63   The CQC announced that it was undertaking such a review following a 2011 BBC Panorama programme on the abuses that took place in a private hospital for people with learning disabilities, Winterbourne View.[55] The CQC acknowledged that it had failed to respond adequately to the concerns raised by former employee of the private hospital. However, it noted that as a safeguarding meeting had been set up, 'CQC took the view that the concerns were being examined'.[56] This raises a particular and serious concern with existing safeguarding procedures within health and care system, namely the need to ensure that prompt action is taken by a responsible authority. A similar failing was identified in a local government ombudsman's report upholding a complaint against Bristol City Council about the poor quality of care provided to an elderly woman with dementia. The council's delay in taking action to address the serious concerns with the care home identified by the CQC on two consecutive visits was considered to be maladministration.[57]

18.64   The statutory guidance stresses the need for there to be 'a clear understanding between partners at a local level when other agencies such as the local authority, CQC or CCG need to be notified or involved and what role they have' (para 14.72).[58]

Mental Capacity Act 2005

18.65   Although the MCA 2005 does not include specific powers to protect vulnerable adults from abuse,[59] it has a significant role in relation to safeguarding. The statutory guidance to the CA 2014 makes this point when stressing the importance of those involved in safeguarding of understanding and always working in line with the MCA 2005 (para 14.56), noting that (para 14.58):

> The requirement to apply the MCA in adult safeguarding enquiries challenges many professionals and requires utmost care, particularly where it appears an adult has capacity for making specific decisions that nevertheless places them at risk of being abused or neglected.

55 See para 15.19 above.
56 CQC's statement on Panorama's investigation, 31 May 2011.
57 Report on an investigation into complaint no 09 005 944 against Bristol City Council, 13 June 2011.
58 The guidance also refers to a 'a high level guide on these roles and responsibilities' jointly published by CQC, ADASS, NHS England and others, *Safeguarding adults. Roles and responsibilities in health and care services*, 2014.
59 Despite the Law Commission's recommendations: see chapter 9: Public Protection for Vulnerable People at Risk, in The Law Commission *Mental Incapacity*, Law Com 231, 1995.

18.66 The MCA 2005 also contains a number of provisions that are of importance in relation to aspects of adult safeguarding, including:

- the powers of the Office of the Public Guardian to investigate cases of abuse;
- the power to appoint deputies (which could include local authorities) to take social welfare decisions in addition to financial decisions to ensure that the incapacitated person is adequately protected (see para 13.150 above); and
- the criminal offence of ill-treating or wilfully neglecting people lacking capacity (see para 18.120 below).[60]

18.67 The CQC also highlights the importance of the deprivation of liberty safeguards (DOLS) under the MCA 2005 (see para 17.45 above) which apply to care homes and hospitals, noting that the CQC has a monitoring role in relation to the operation of these safeguards.[61]

Guardianship

18.68 MHA 1983 s7 provides for the circumstances in which a person can be made subject to guardianship.[62] The purpose of guardianship is 'to enable patients to receive care outside hospital where it cannot be provided without the use of compulsory powers'.[63] It can be applied where the guardian's powers 'and the structure imposed by guardianship, may assist relatives, friends and professionals to help a mentally disordered person manage in the community'.[64] Under MHA 1983 s8 the guardian has three specific powers:

1) to require the patient to reside at a place specified;
2) to require the patient to attend at specified places and times for medical treatment, occupation, education or training; and
3) to require access to the patient to be given.

18.69 Individuals may only be received into guardianship if they are aged 16 or over, have a 'mental disorder', the mental disorder is 'of a nature or degree' which warrants their reception into guardianship and that this is necessary in the interests their welfare, or for the protection of other persons (MHA 1983 s7(2)). It follows that mental incapacity is not a necessary prerequisite for the use of guardianship.

18.70 The term 'mental disorder' has a broad definition (MHA 1983 s1), namely: 'any disorder or disability of the mind'. However, in relation to persons with learning disabilities, guardianship can only be applied if their

---

60 See also the discussion of MCA 2005 – Department of Health, *Safeguarding adults. Report on the consultation on the review of 'No Secrets'*, 2009, paras 2.24–2.27.

61 CQC, *Our safeguarding protocol. The Care Quality Commission's responsibility and commitment to safeguarding*, 2013, para 4.4.

62 For further information on guardianship, see Department of Health, *Mental Health Act 1983: code of practice*, The Stationery Office, 2015, chapter 26; and *Reference guide to the Mental Health Act 1983*, chapter 28.

63 Department of Health, *Mental Health Act 1983: code of practice*, The Stationery Office, 2015, para 30.2.

64 Department of Health, *Reference guide to the Mental Health Act 1983*, 2015, para 28.3.

learning disability is 'associated with abnormally aggressive or seriously irresponsible conduct' (see MHA 1983 s1(2A) and (2B)).[65] Noting that this limitation on the application of guardianship 'removes a significant potential framework for the protection of adults with learning difficulties', the Law Commission in 2011 recommended that the government review the current application of guardianship to people with learning disabilities. Removing this qualification would:

> ... enable professionals in an adult safeguarding situation to set conditions to protect the person – such as to allow professionals access to visit the person who is subject to guardianship and specifying where the person should live.[66]

18.71   In *Lewis v Gibson and MH*[67] it was held that there is no requirement that a local authority seek 'declaratory relief' (see para 18.89 below) in preference to a guardianship order. However, when seeking to displace a nearest relative as a component of a guardianship application, it was essential (for the purposes of Articles 6 and 8 of the European Convention on Human Rights (ECHR)) that the patient be served and his or her capacity to act ascertained.

Whistleblowing

18.72   The Public Interest Disclosure Act 1998 should, in theory, give workers who raise concerns about abuse and malpractice – 'whistleblowers' – protection from dismissal and victimisation. Covering all areas of employment, it can be of particular use where care workers are concerned about abusive practices experienced by service users within their organisation.

18.73   However, concerns about the lack of protection for whistleblowers continue. A 2011 report found that many workers in the care sector who had raised concerns reported that these were 'initially ignored, mishandled or denied by organisations' and the majority of whistleblowers are unaware of their organisation's whistleblowing policy.[68] A 2009 survey of NHS hospital doctors showed that while many doctors raised concerns about patient care, of those that reported their concerns, nearly half were not told what had happened as a result of doing so. Reasons for not reporting concerns included fear for career prospects, and a lack of confidence in the outcomes of such processes.[69] A 2009 report by Health Committee of the House of Commons quoted the results of the Royal College of Nursing's survey of its members, that:

---

65 See also *Re F (Mental Health Act: guardianship)* [2000] 1 FLR 192, (1999) 2 CCLR 445, CA.

66 Law Commission, *Adult social care*, Law Com No 328, HC 941, 2011, para 9.141; and see also Recommendation 46.

67 [2005] EWCA Civ 587, (2005) 8 CCLR 399.

68 *Speaking up for vulnerable adults: what the whistleblowers say*, a report from Public Concern at Work, the whistleblowing advice line, April 2011 – see also Complaint no 1999/200600720 against Carmarthenshire CC, 16 September 2009, para 357.

69 *British Medical Association [BMA] survey: speaking up for patients, final report*, Health Policy and Economic Research Unit, May 2009.

99% of registered nurses understood their professional responsibility to report worries about patient safety but fears about personal reprisals meant that only 43% would be confident to report concerns without thinking twice.[70]

The Committee noted that the information it had received indicated 'that the NHS remains largely unsupportive of whistleblowing'.[71]

18.74 The publication in 2013 of the report into serious failings at the Mid Staffordshire NHS Foundation Trust[72] led to a further report by Sir Robert Francis concerning the failure of Trust to respond to whistleblowers.[73] In welcoming the commissioning of this report, the Health Select Committee[74] referred to the 'treatment of whistleblowers [as] a stain on the reputation of the NHS'. In response to the report, the secretary of state promised action,[75] and this has included a commitment in the *Handbook to the NHS Constitution*[76] to protect staff 'from detriment in employment and the right not to be unfairly dismissed for 'whistleblowing' or reporting wrongdoing in workplace' and changes to the *NHS Constitution* (see para 11.25 above) which:[77]

... encourage and support all staff in raising concerns at the earliest reasonable opportunity about safety, malpractice or wrongdoing at work, responding to and, where necessary, investigating the concerns raised and acting consistently with the Employment Rights Act 1996.

The role of the Office of the Public Guardian

18.75 The Public Guardian (supported by the Office of the Public Guardian (OPG)) is a creature of the MCA 2005[78] and is responsible for the administration of the registers of lasting powers of attorney (LPAs), enduring powers of attorney (EPAs) and court appointed deputies (see para 13.139 above). The Public Guardian is, however, only responsible for supervising deputies and accordingly, will normally only investigate attorneys if representations have been made about the way they are carrying out their duties.[79]

---

70 House of Commons Health Committee, *Patient safety*, Sixth Report of Session 2008–09 Vol 1, 18 June 2009, HC 151–11, paras 281–284. And see also *The Shipman Inquiry*, Fifth Report chapter 11, 2004; and *Safeguarding patients. the government's response to the recommendations of the Shipman Inquiry's Fifth Report*, Cm 7015, 2007, para 5.33.

71 Para 295.

72 R Francis, *The Mid Staffordshire NHS Foundation Trust public inquiry chaired by Robert Francis QC*, HC 947, The Stationery Office, 2013.

73 R Francis, *Freedom to speak up – a review of whistleblowing in the NHS*, 2015.

74 House of Commons Health Select Committee, *Freedom to speak up*, HC 350, The Stationery Office, 2015, para 113.

75 Department of Health, *Learning not blaming*, Cm 9113, 2015.

76 Department of Health, *Handbook to the NHS Constitution*, 2015, p113 – see also para 11.28 above.

77 NHS England, *NHS Constitution*, 2015, section 4a.

78 MCA 2005 s57. See also Lasting Powers of Attorney and Public Guardian Regulations 2007 SI No 1253.

79 MCA 2005 s58; and see also the Department for Constitutional Affairs, *Mental Capacity Act 2005: code of practice*, The Stationery Office, 2007, paras 14.12–14.14.

18.76   The Public Guardian can send 'Court of Protection Visitors'[80] to visit people who may lack capacity and those who have formal powers to act on their behalf (ie attorneys and deputies). The code of practice to the MCA 2005 comments that these Visitors 'have an important part to play in investigating possible abuse' but in addition they can 'check on the general well-being of the person who lacks capacity, and they can give support to attorneys and deputies who need help to carry out their duties'.[81] The code states that attorneys and deputies must 'co-operate with the visitors and provide them with all relevant information'; if they fail to do so, 'the court can cancel their appointment, where it thinks that they have not acted in the person's best interests'.[82]

18.77   The Public Guardian has no direct powers of enforcement or sanction. Furthermore, the code of practice states that the OPG will not always be the most appropriate organisation to investigate all complaints and that it would 'usually refer concerns about personal welfare LPAs or personal welfare deputies to the relevant agency', which in some cases might be the police.[83] However, the OPG has since issued its own safeguarding vulnerable adults policy which outlines a range of ways in which the OPG may be involved. This includes undertaking investigations into the actions of individuals acting on behalf of a person who lacks capacity, such as a deputy or registered attorney (LPA or EPA). It can also make applications to the Court of Protection for the suspension, discharge or replacement of a deputy or to cancel registration and revoke an EPA/LPA.[84]

18.78   A 2016 report from the OPG[85] shows that in the year 2015/16 it received a total of 2,681 new safeguarding referrals (an increase of over 25 per cent from the previous year). It investigated 876 cases, (an increase of 15 per cent) of which 151 cases resulted in an application to the Court of Protection. In addition 'Court of Protection Visitors' completed 9,829 visits during the year.

The role of independent mental capacity advocates

18.79   The MCA 2005 established the independent mental capacity advocate (IMCA) service. The role and scope of the IMCA service is considered at para 13.81 above. NHS bodies and local authorities are required to make arrangements for individuals to receive help from an IMCA if they lack capacity to make certain decisions (relating to serious medical treatment

---

80 There a two types of visitors: general and special – the Special Visitors are doctors with relevant expertise.

81 Department for Constitutional Affairs, *Mental Capacity Act 2005: code of practice*, The Stationery Office, 2007, para 14.11.

82 Department for Constitutional Affairs, *Mental Capacity Act 2005: code of practice*, The Stationery Office, 2007, para 14.10.

83 Department for Constitutional Affairs, *Mental Capacity Act 2005: code of practice*, The Stationery Office, 2007, paras 14.19–14.21.

84 Policy paper SD8: *Office of the Public Guardian Safeguarding Policy*, December 2015. See also OPG's *Office of the Public Guardian and Local Authorities: Working together to safeguard vulnerable adults*, 2008.

85 OPG, *Annual report & accounts 2015/16*, HC 308, HMSO, 2016, p15–17.

or changes of accommodation) and no relative or friend is able to assist them (considered further at para 13.87 above).[86]

18.80   Regulations also provide that, if such representation will be of benefit to the person, IMCAs may be appointed to represent individuals who lack capacity where an NHS body or local authority is contemplating taking adult protection measures.[87] Such appointments can be made, whether or not family, friends or others are involved.[88] Accompanying guidance to these regulations suggests that local authorities and NHS bodies should draw up a policy statement outlining who would most benefit from receiving support from an IMCA, and that this should be made widely available.[89] The guidance reminds councils and NHS bodies that if a person meets the qualifying criteria it would be unlawful for them not to consider exercising their power to instruct an IMCA.[90]

18.81   The SCIE has issued a practice guide for IMCAs involved in safeguarding adults' proceedings. This points out that local authorities and NHS bodies that instruct an IMCA for adults at risk are legally required to have regard to any representations made by the IMCA when making decisions concerning protective measures, and that IMCAs can make representations on any matter they feel is relevant to decisions concerning protective measures, including concerns about the investigation process or the involvement of the police.[91]

18.82   IMCAs must also be made available to individuals subject to the deprivation of liberty safeguards (DOLS).[92] If they or their representative (not being a paid representative) request such assistance, this must be provided. In addition, if the supervisory body considers that an IMCA is needed to enable the person subject to DOLS to exercise their rights, it must instruct an IMCA[93] (see para 13.116 above).

Misuse of adult protection procedures

Heavy-handed response to allegations

18.83   While some consultees to the Law Commission's review on adult social care argued that the law was inadequate in this area and that local

---

86   MCA 2005 ss35–41. Note that the Health and Social Care Bill, published in January 2011, seeks to amend the MCA 2005 so that local authorities are directly responsible for arrangements for IMCAs.

87   Mental Capacity Act 2005 (Independent Mental Capacity Advocate) (Expansion of Role) Regulations 2006 SI No 2883 regs 3 and 4.

88   See Department for Constitutional Affairs, *Mental Capacity Act 2005: code of practice*, The Stationery Office, 2007, para 10.66.

89   Department of Health, *Adult protection care reviews and IMCAs*, 2007.

90   Department of Health, *Adult protection care reviews and IMCAs*, 2007, para 10.

91   SCIE Guide 32: *Practice guidance on the involvement of Independent Mental Capacity Advocates (IMCAs) in safeguarding adults*, 2009: www.scie.org.uk/publications/guides/guide32/imcarole.asp.

92   For further information about DOLS, see para 13.106 above.

93   See MCA 2005 s39D and also *Hillingdon LBC v Steven Neary and others* [2011] EWHC 1377 (COP) in which the court highlighted the important role of the IMCA in such cases (para 194).

authorities needed to have emergency powers to protect individuals from being abused or neglected,[94] others took a different view, reporting:

> ... that local authorities are already heavy handed and too eager to intervene without proper legal authority to remove service users arbitrarily from domestic settings.[95]

18.84   A similar note of caution was made in *A local authority v A*. Munby LJ commented that while social workers needed to be alert to issues of concern and 'must act quickly and decisively' where these arise, they 'must guard against being seen as prying or snooping on the families who they are there to help and support':

> Nothing is more destructive of the 'working together' relationship which in this kind of context, as in others, is so vitally important than a perception by family carers that the local authority is being heavy-handed or worse.[96]

18.85   Concerns about the misuse of adult protection measures have also been highlighted by the local government ombudsman. For example, the ombudsman found that the decision by a council to initiate adult protection procedures in relation to a disabled young man, during a time when there were ongoing problems with various aspects of his care plan, amounted to maladministration. In addition to upholding the family's complaint that they had not received appropriate services from the council, the ombudsman stated:

> Quite apart from any procedural shortcomings, it beggars belief that the referral was made at all, and this was compounded by the fact that the family was informed far too late. I have no doubt that the family found the referral extremely hurtful, not least because it perceived itself as providing care for Shahid in the absence of any significant care provision by the Council. The adult protection referral and the delay in telling the family of it were maladministration by the Council, which caused the family distress and outrage when they found out.[97]

18.86   Similarly, the ombudsman admonished a social services panel for describing the action of a mother of two severely disabled children – who, due to the 'totally inappropriate accommodation where they could not be adequately bathed', had no option but to hose her sons down in the back garden – as being 'abusive'. Noting that the mother's parenting skills and her commitment to care for her sons had never been in question, the ombudsman considered that such comments were of 'breathtaking insensitivity', and it was maladministration for the panel to then fail to secure any immediate alternative.[98]

18.87   A 2012 investigation which 'shocked' the ombudsman concerned a council that commenced an adult protection investigation with no supporting evidence, then tried to defend its failure to treat the injured party

---

94   Law Commission, *Adult social care*, Law Com No 326, HC 941, May 2011. Some argued that such a review was necessary in the light of Article 16 CRPD (Freedom from exploitation, violence and abuse).

95   Paras 9.54–9.55.

96   [2010] EWHC 978 (Fam), (2010) 13 CCLR 404 at [98].

97   Complaint no 07/B/07665 against Luton BC, 10 September 2008, para 37.

98   Complaint no 07C03887 against Bury MBC, 14 October 2009, para 43.

fairly and then waged a correspondence 'war of attrition'.[99] A 2014 report concerned delay in telling a suspected abuser that an investigation had found no evidence to support the allegations – which caused distress and for her 'to feel like a criminal'.[100]

Failure to respond adequately to allegations

18.88 Another area of concern is the failure to respond adequately to allegations of abuse. The Public Services Ombudsman for Wales[101] detailed a catalogue of failures in the way that complaints about the abuse by staff of a day centre of a woman with learning disabilities was handled. The ombudsman concluded that this amounted to 'many instances of serious maladministration and service failure'. There was 'overwhelming evidence of pervasive management failure within the Learning Disabilities service at the time, characterised by a failure of leadership, a lack of accountability and, crucially, the failure to create and sustain a culture which valued the rights of service users and protect them against abuse.[102] This maladministration and service failure had caused considerable distress to the member of staff who had reported the abuse as well as other staff obliged to work in such an environment. It was particularly unjust for the users of the service who had been left at risk by the failure of the social services department.

Declaratory relief and the role of the High Court

Background

18.89 Since the enactment of the HRA 1998, the higher courts have dynamically developed a number of latent common law doctrines and mechanisms in an effort to provide legal protection for vulnerable adults.

18.90 The MCA 2005 preserves the right of concerned parties to apply to the court for a declaration of 'best interests' – known as 'declaratory relief' (MCA 2005 s15). Such applications are made to the Court of Protection, which has the full powers of the High Court to make declarations on financial or welfare matters affecting people who lack capacity to make decisions. It also enables a concerned party to apply to be appointed an incapacitated person's 'deputy', and it can remove deputies and attorneys who are acting inappropriately (MCA 2005 ss16–20).

18.91 While the Court of Protection established under MCA 2005 has assumed the 'declaratory relief' jurisdiction developed by the High Court since 2000, its jurisdiction is limited to cases concerning people who lack mental capacity as defined under MCA 2005 (or cases in which the court

---

99 Complaint no. 07C13163 against Birmingham City Council, 8 October 2012, paras 69–74.

100 Joint NHS and Local Government Ombudsman Report on complaint no 12 004 807 and 12 013 660 against Essex CC, Suffolk CC, North Essex Partnership NHS Foundation Trust and Norfolk and Suffolk NHS Foundation Trust, 15 January 2014.

101 Complaint no 1999/200600720 against Carmarthenshire CC, 16 September 2009.

102 Paras 356–358.

is asked to determine whether the person lacks mental capacity). The Court of Appeal has also confirmed that, 'where it is necessary, lawful and proportionate', the High Court's 'inherent jurisdiction' has survived the introduction of MCA 2005. This means that the court can 'exercise its inherent jurisdiction in relation to mentally handicapped adults along-side, as appropriate, the Mental Capacity Act 2005', so long as this is not 'deployed so as to undermine the will of Parliament'.[103]

18.92   However, over the last two decades the High Court (Family Division) had also developed its jurisdiction in relation to people who, although considered to have mental capacity, are otherwise vulnerable and in need of protection. With the introduction of MCA 2005 it was unclear as to whether the inherent jurisdiction could continue to be invoked in such cases. This question has now been resolved, and is considered further at para 18.100 below.

The development of declaratory relief

18.93   The High Court's declaratory relief procedure for vulnerable adults first found full expression in *Re F (adult: court's jurisdiction)*.[104] The case concerned a young adult who lacked sufficient mental capacity to make informed decisions as to where she should live or who posed a risk to her safety. As a minor she had been neglected and exposed to abuse while in the care of her parents, and had accordingly been made a ward of court and placed in specialist accommodation. The wardship came to an end on her 18th birthday, and the local authority feared that without some form of fresh court order her mother would seek her return home where she would be at risk of further abuse. As Dame Butler-Sloss observed:

> There is an obvious gap in the framework of care for mentally incapacitated adults. If the court cannot act … this vulnerable young woman would be left at serious risk.[105]

18.94   To fill this gap, the court's solution was for it to 'grow' and 'shape'[106] the common law principle of 'necessity'. In the court's judgment, therefore, where a serious justiciable issue arose as to the best interests of an adult without the mental capacity to make the relevant decision, then the High Court was able to grant declarations (in the exercise of its inherent juris-diction) as to what would be in that person's best interests.[107]

18.95   The courts have in subsequent judgments developed the principles established by *Re F* and, in so doing, have clarified the scope and avail-ability of the declaratory jurisdiction.[108] This is an area in which the law

---

103 Lord Justice Wall endorsing the findings of Roderic Wood J, para 55 *City of Westminster v IC (by his friend the Official Solicitor)* and *KC and NN* [2008] EWCA Civ 198, [2008] 2 FLR 267.

104 [2000] 3 WLR 1740, (2000) 3 CCLR 210, QBD.

105 [2000] 3 WLR 1740, (2000) 3 CCLR 210, QBD at 219.

106 [2000] 3 WLR 1740, (2000) 3 CCLR 210, QBD per Sedley LJ at 227B.

107 [2000] 3 WLR 1740, (2000) 3 CCLR 210, QBD at 218C–E.

108 Proceedings should be commenced in the High Court under CPR Part 8 – *M v B, A and S* [2005] EWHC 1681 (Fam), [2006] 1 FLR 117.

continues to develop, particularly in the light of the HRA 1998.[109] The key issues are summarised below.

Requirement to seek the authority of the courts

18.96 The courts have emphasised that in some circumstances local authorities will be under a duty to take action to intervene in relation to the care of vulnerable adults, see, for example, *Re Z (local authority: duty)*[110] and *X and another v Hounslow LBC*.[111] However, save for cases where the MHA 1983 applies, 'if a local authority seeks to control an incapacitated or vulnerable adult it must enlist the assistance of either the Court of Protection or the High Court.'[112]

The existence of mental incapacity or other barriers to decision making

18.97 Much of the early case-law suggested that the court could only deploy its declaratory relief jurisdiction once it was established that the person in question was incapable (by reason of mental incapacity) of making the relevant decision – see, for instance, *Newham LBC v BS and S.*[113] However, in *A local authority v MA, NA and SA*,[114] Munby J held that incapacity was not essential. In his view the court could exercise its inherent jurisdiction:

> ... in relation to a vulnerable adult who, even if not incapacitated by mental disorder or mental illness, is, or is reasonably believed to be, either (i) under constraint or (ii) subject to coercion or undue influence or (iii) for some other reason deprived of the capacity to make the relevant decision, or disabled from making a free choice, or incapacitated or disabled from giving or expressing a real and genuine consent.[115]

18.98 In coming to this conclusion Munby J cited an extensive case law,[116] including *Re G (an adult) (mental capacity: court's jurisdiction)*[117] where the court held that G lacked capacity because of her 'father's ability to overbear [her] decision-making' ability. As a consequence, G was placed by the court under a protective regime, which limited the father's access to her – and as a result she recovered her capacity to make decisions. The problem was that if the court's power ceased when she recovered capacity, then she would fall under her father's power again – and so be caught in a rotating door. As Bennett J stated:

> If the restrictions were lifted ... it is probable that the situation would revert to what it was prior to March 2004. G's mental health would deteriorate to

---

109 As predicted by Munby J, as he then was, in *In re S (adult patient) (inherent jurisdiction: family life)* [2002] EWHC 2278 (Fam), [2003] 1 FLR 292 at [52].
110 [2004] EWHC 2817 (Fam), [2005] 1 FLR 740 at [19].
111 [2008] EWHC 1168 (QB)
112 *A v A local authority* [2010] EWHC 978 (COP) at [68].
113 [2003] EWHC 1909 (Fam), (2004) 7 CCLR 132.
114 [2005] EWHC 2942 (Fam), [2006] 1 FLR 867 at [55].
115 In many respects this development follows the Law Commission's 1995 proposals in their original Mental Incapacity Bill which suggested (at clause 36) that the adult protection powers could be used where the person was (among other things) 'unable to protect himself against significant harm or serious exploitation'.
116 [2005] EWHC 2942 (Fam), [2006] 1 FLR 867 at [59]–[60].
117 [2004] EWHC 2222 (Fam).

such an extent that she would again become incapacitated to take decisions about the matters referred to. Such a reversion would be disastrous for G.

18.99   In the circumstances the court held that incapacity was not an essential requirement for it to exercise its inherent jurisdiction.

18.100   These cases were decided prior to the introduction of MCA 2005. The question as to whether MCA 2005 and its accompanying code of practice had ousted the High Court's jurisdiction in relation to vulnerable adults was addressed in *DL v A local authority and others*.[118] In this case the local authority wished to intervene to safeguard elderly parents from the threatening and abusive behaviour of their son, who lived with them. For the purposes of the proceedings it was accepted that the parents were mentally capable of making relevant decisions. Having given extensive consideration to relevant case-law, in addition to reviewing the impact of the HRA 1998 and MCA 2005, McFarlane LJ concluded that the inherent jurisdiction remained available for use in cases which fell outside the MCA 2005. In doing so he considered that (para 63):

> There is, in my view, a sound and strong public policy justification for this to be so. The existence of 'elder abuse', as described by Professor Williams, is sadly all too easy to contemplate. Indeed the use of the term 'elder' in that label may inadvertently limit it to a particular age group whereas, as the cases demonstrate, the will of a vulnerable adult of any age may, in certain circumstances, be overborne. Where the facts justify it, such individuals require and deserve the protection of the authorities and the law so that they may regain the very autonomy that the appellant rightly prizes.

18.101   The inherent jurisdiction can only be invoked for purposes that fall outside the scope of the MCA 2005. In *LBL v RYJ and VJ*.[119] Macur J had 'no doubt' that it could be used to 'supplement the protection afforded' by the MCA 2005 but that this is only 'for those who, whilst "capacitous" for the purposes of the Act, are "incapacitated" by external forces – whatever they may be – outside their control from reaching a decision' in order to 'facilitate the process of unencumbered decision-making'. In so holding, she specifically rejected the contention that 'the inherent jurisdiction of the court may be used in the case of a capacitous adult to impose a decision upon him/her whether as to welfare or finance'.[120]

18.102   In *XCC v AA*[121] it was confirmed that the jurisdiction is also available in cases involving adults who lack the requisite capacity but for one reason or another fall outside the available remedies provided for in MCA 2005.

A serious justiciable issue

18.103   A 'serious justiciable issue' which requires resolution must exist. The courts have not sought to define precisely what is meant by this phrase, but have made clear that this will cover a broad range of issues – any genuine question as to what the best interests of a patient require or justify – extending 'to all that conduces to the incompetent adult's welfare and

---

118 [2012] EWCA Civ 253, (2012) 15 CCLR 267.
119 [2010] EWHC 2665 (COP).
120 [2010] EWHC 2665 (COP) at [62].
121 [2012] EWHC 2183 (COP), (2012) 15 CCLR 447.

happiness, including companionship and his domestic and social environment'.[122] It will exist when the facts 'demonstrate a situation in which the doctrine of necessity might arise' (ie a matter that requires a resolution in the best interests of an adult who lacks mental capacity to decide for himself or herself).[123] It is not the same as the threshold test for care proceedings under Children Act (CA) 1989 s31, so there is no requirement to establish risk of significant harm before intervening.[124]

What is the question that needs to be determined?

18.104 In *Newham LBC v BS and S*[125] a question arose as to whether the 'significant issue' that had to be determined was (a) if abuse had occurred; or (b) where the incapacitated person should live. The local authority applied for a declaration, basing its application on evidence that the disabled person's father drank excessively and had assaulted her. The court rejected this evidence, but nevertheless considered that an order should be made. In this respect Wall J considered that while there 'must be good reason for local authority intervention' and that there may be a need for the court to resolve disputed issues of fact: 'if their resolution is necessary to the decision as to what is in S's best interests. Findings of fact against [the father] ... would plainly reflect upon his capacity properly to care for S.' He held:

> But it does not follow, in my judgment, that the proceedings must be dismissed simply because the factual basis upon which the local authority instituted them turns out to be mistaken, or because it cannot be established on the balance of probabilities. What matters (assuming always that mental incapacity is made out) is which outcome will be in S's best interests. There will plainly be cases which are very fact specific. There will be others in which the principal concern is the future, and the relative suitability of the plans which each party can put forward for both the short and the long term care of the mentally incapable adult. The instant case, in my judgment, is one of the cases in the latter category.

Best interests and the 'balance sheet' assessment

18.105 The meaning of 'best interests' is considered at para 13.31 above. When exercising their declaratory powers, the courts have generally required a 'balance sheet' to be drawn up listing the potential benefits and 'disbenefits' that may flow from an intervention. This approach was identified by the Court of Appeal in *Re A (medical treatment: male sterilisation)*,[126] in the following terms:

> The ... judge ... should draw up a balance sheet. The first entry should be of any factor or factors of actual benefit ... Then on the other sheet the judge should write any counter-balancing disbenefits to the applicant ... Then the judge should enter on each sheet the potential gains and losses in each

---

122 See *A v A health authority and another In re J (a child) R (S) v Secretary of State for the Home Department* at [39]–[43].

123 *Re F (adult: court's jurisdiction)* [2000] 3 WLR 1740, (2000) 3 CCLR 210, QBD, per Butler Sloss LJ.

124 *Re S (adult patient) (inherent jurisdiction: family life)* [2002] EWHC 2278 (Fam), [2003] 1 FLR 292, per Munby J at para 45.

125 [2003] EWHC 1909 (Fam), (2004) 7 CCLR 132.

126 [2000] 1 FLR 549 at 560F–H.

instance making some estimate of the extent of the possibility that the gain or loss might accrue. At the end of that exercise the judge should be better placed to strike a balance between the sum of the certain and possible gains against the sum of the certain and possible losses. Obviously only if the account is in relatively significant credit will the judge conclude that the application is likely to advance the best interests of the claimant.

18.106 In the *Newham LBC* proceedings Wall J considered that the benefits of the daughter remaining with her father included his love for, and strong sense of duty towards, her and the fact that he had adequately provided for her in the recent past. The benefits of her moving to an independent residential care placement included the fact that her father (due to his age and poor health) would progressively find it difficult to care for her; that she could have contact with her siblings (who were not prepared to visit her at her father's house); and that the proposed care home would provide her with an opportunity for social contact with people of her own age group. In addition the court considered that the professional evidence was 'crucial': the social and health professionals were of the opinion that the care home placement was the better option. In the judge's opinion, therefore, the balance sheet came down firmly in favour of the care home placement.

18.107   The need for decision makers to 'balance the pros and cons of all relevant factors' is highlighted in the MCA code of practice (para 5.62) and is accordingly adopted by the Court of Protection.[127] The code also notes that the decision maker will need to find a way of balancing the differing concerns and opinions of relatives and carers (para 5.64), adding that the decision-maker has the ultimate responsibility for working out the person's best interests. In *A local authority v C and others*,[128] the court stated:

> In practical terms best practice both in proceedings before the Court of Protection and generally is to apply a structured approach to the decision to be made. The decision maker draws up a notional balance sheet of welfare factors describing the benefits and detriments of the available courses of action having encouraged the person concerned to participate in the process and having ascertained wishes and feelings, beliefs and values and other considerations particular to the person including consulting with relevant third parties.

The proportionality of interventions

18.108 The 'benefits/disbenefits' assessment process will almost always relate to an issue of fundamental relevance to a disabled person's private and family life and their home – and thus require an examination of the proportionality of the proposed action from the perspective of Article 8 of the ECHR. In this context, it would appear that there are certain presumptions – for instance, that the state interference will be the least restrictive and presumably that there should be no 'order' unless strictly necessary.[129] However, the courts have been reluctant to adopt such an approach in declaratory relief proceeding. For example, they have taken the view that

127 See eg, *Re P (adult patient: consent to medical treatment)* [2008] EWHC 1403 at [22].
128 [2011] EWHC 1539 (Admin) at para 59.
129 In this context, see the approach to a not dissimilar balancing exercise taken by Munby J in *R (A and B) v East Sussex CC (No 2)* [2003] EWHC 167 (Admin), (2003) 6 CCLR 194 at 226–232.

there is no presumption that mentally incapacitated adults will be better off if they live with a family rather than in an institution. Nevertheless, they have emphasised that the burden will be on the state (eg on a local authority) to establish, if it sought to do so, that it was the more appropriate person to look after the mentally incapacitated adult than his or her own family.[130]

18.109 The central importance of the ECHR, and in particular Article 8, to decisions on where individuals who lack capacity should live, was emphasised in *Hillingdon LBC v Steven Neary and others*,[131] which concerned the local authority's decision to detain a young disabled man in a residential unit, despite the objections of his father (and main carer):

> Decisions about incapacitated people must always be determined by their best interests, but the starting point is their right to respect for their family life where it exists. The burden is always on the State to show that an incapacitated person's welfare cannot be sustained by living with and being looked after by his or her family, with or without outside support.

18.110 For a number of significant reasons, the court found that the local authority had breached the young man's rights under Article 8, the first being that the local authority had not considered the positive obligation to respect the right to family life and the requirement that in order to justify removing a children or vulnerable adults from their families 'can only be on the basis that the State is going to provide a better quality of care than that which they have hitherto been receiving'.[132] The court found:

> Nowhere in their very full records of Steven's year in care is there any mention of the supposition that he should be at home, other things being equal, or the disadvantages to him of living away from his family, still less an attempt to weigh those disadvantages against the supposed advantages of care elsewhere. No acknowledgement ever appears of the unique bond between Steven and his father, or of the priceless importance to a dependent person of the personal element in care by a parent rather than a stranger, however, committed. No attempt was made at the outset to carry out a genuinely balanced best interests assessment, nor was one attempted subsequently.[133]

Ex parte applications

18.111 Ex parte applications to the court may, in appropriate cases, be made without other parties being notified – for instance, in situations of urgency. In *B BC v S and S*[134] a nursing home was no longer willing or able to cope with an elderly resident, but his wife was known to be implacably opposed to a temporary placement in hospital and the local authority had reached (in the court's opinion) the reasonable view that she would have tried to 'preempt a decision of the court by seeking to remove her husband from the nursing home'. However, the court expressed concern that practitioners

---

130 *Re S (adult patient) (inherent jurisdiction: family life)*, [2002] EWHC 2278 (Fam), [2003] 1 FLR 292. See also *A local authority v E* [2008] 1 FCR 389 at 412.
131 [2011] EWHC 1377 (COP).
132 Quoting from Munby LJ in *SA*.
133 [2011] EWHC 1377 (COP) at [154].
134 [2006] EWHC 2584 (Fam), (2006) 9 CCLR 596.

were making without notice applications that were not necessary or appropriate, nor properly supported by appropriate evidence.[135] This concern was echoed by Munby LJ in *A local authority v A*:

> Too often, in my experience, local authorities seeking the assistance of the court in removing an incapacitated or vulnerable adult from their home against their wishes or against the wishes of the relatives or friends caring for them, apply ex parte (without notice) and, I have to say, too often such orders have been made by the court without any prior warning to those affected and in circumstances where such seeming heavy-handedness is not easy to justify and can too often turn out to be completely counterproductive ...[136]

18.112   His Lordship went on to suggest that generally local authorities would:

> ... only be justified in seeking a without notice order for the removal of an incapacitated or vulnerable adult in the kind of circumstances which in the case of a child would justify a without notice application for an emergency protection order.[137]

The range of potential declarations

18.113   In the *Newham LBC* decision, Wall J made a declaration authorising the local authority to continue with the care home arrangement (with defined contact between the father and daughter). Additionally he declared that the authority was to consult her father about any future medical treatment/care arrangements she might require, and that she be provided with an independent advocate.

18.114   Declarations can also be sought concerning future situations, provided they are rooted in a serious 'justiciable issue' and are not overly hypothetical.[138] In *Re S (Adult patient) (inherent jurisdiction: family life)*[139] the local authority was concerned that it might have to return to the court – repeatedly – for additional declarations, given the difficult relationship that existed between it and the incapacitated person's father. The authority accordingly asked the court to declare that it had – in effect – proxy decision-making power on a range of social welfare questions. Munby J (as he then was) held that the court 'has jurisdiction to grant whatever relief in declaratory form is necessary to safeguard and promote the incapable adult's welfare and interests'.

---

135 [2006] EWHC 2584 (Fam), (2006) 9 CCLR 596 at [37].
136 [2010] EWHC 978 (Fam), (2010) 13 CCLR 404 at [99].
137 [2010] EWHC 978 (Fam), (2010) 13 CCLR 404, referring to *X council v B (emergency protection orders)* [2004] EWHC 2015 (Fam) and *Re X (emergency protection orders)* [2006] EWHC 510 (Fam). These cases stressed that ex parte notices would only be appropriate if the case is genuinely one of emergency or other great urgency or if there are compelling reasons to believe that the child's welfare will be compromised if the parents are alerted in advance to what is going on.
138 See eg *R v Portsmouth Hospitals NHS Trust ex p Glass* (1999) 2 FLR 905, (1999) 50 BMLR 269 where the court held a future treatment decision to be too hypothetical.
139 [2002] EWHC 2278 (Fam), [2003] 1 FLR 292.

Criminal offences

18.115 While it is debatable how far the possibility of being charged with a criminal offence deters people from abusing adults, over the last few years there has been an increase in the number of offences which are specific to adults who are in vulnerable situations or may be vulnerable to abuse.[140] These include provisions set out below.

Mental Health Act 1983 s127

18.116 MHA 1983 s127 makes it an offence for managers of hospitals or care homes, or their staff, to ill-treat or wilfully neglect a patient (whether detained or not) who is receiving treatment for his or her mental disorder in that hospital or care home. This offence also applies to individuals receiving treatment for mental disorder when they are on the premises of the hospital or care home. In addition, it is an offence for any individual to ill-treat or wilfully neglect a mentally disordered person who is subject to the individual's guardianship under MHA 1983, or otherwise in his or her custody or care.

18.117 While this is potentially a wide-ranging provision, it is limited procedurally since proceedings can only be instigated by or with the permission of the Director of Public Prosecutions.

Sexual Offences Act 2003 ss30–41

18.118 The Sexual Offences Act (SOA) 2003 contains a range of provisions relating to people with mental disorder (bearing the same meaning as in the MHA 1983). SOA 2003 ss30–33 create offences that rely on the inability of the person to refuse the sexual activity on account of lack of capacity or where the person is unable to communicate refusal. Sections 34–37 relate to situations where the person suffering from a mental disorder is induced, threatened or deceived into sexual activity where the perpetrator knows or could reasonably be expected to know that the person suffered a mental disorder. Sections 38–41 relate to care workers where the assumption is that the worker must have known or reasonably expected to have known that the person had a mental disorder and do not rely on the inability of the victim to refuse.

Domestic Violence, Crime and Victims Act 2004 s5

18.119 Domestic Violence, Crime and Victims Act 2004 s5 makes it an offence to cause or allow the death of a child or vulnerable adult, and is designed to address the evidential problem of proving who in a household was actually responsible for causing or allowing the death to occur. In such circumstances a person is guilty of an offence if there was significant risk of serious physical harm, and the person either caused the victim's death, or was or ought to have been aware of the risk and failed to take steps to protect

140 See also J Williams, *Protection of older people in Wales: a guide to the law*, chapter 5: The criminal justice system, Older People's Commissioner for Wales, 2011.

the victim, and the act occurred in circumstances that the person foresaw or ought to have foreseen. The definition of household includes people who do not live in the property but whose visits are sufficiently frequent for them to be counted as a member of such.[141]

Mental Capacity Act 2005 s44

18.120 MCA 2005 s44 makes it an offence for anyone caring for, or who is an attorney under a LPA or EPA, or is a deputy for a person who lacks capacity, to ill-treat or wilfully neglect that person. The provision is limited to people who lack capacity (and accordingly narrower in scope than MHA 1983 s127 above) but is not restricted by a requirement to obtain leave before charges are laid. However, the Law Commission noted that at consultation events with police officers on its review of adult social care law, 'it was suggested that prosecutions were being dropped in practice because doctors cannot confirm or have not documented that the person lacks capacity'.[142]

18.121   In the case of *R v Dunn*[143] the Court of Appeal considered the relationship between section 44 and the test for capacity as set out in sections 2 and 3 of the Act. The appellant had been convicted for ill-treating three elderly residents of a care home, all of whom had dementia. She appealed on the basis that the recorder's direction to the jury had failed to focus sufficiently on the capacity of each of the complainants to make decisions at the time at which the alleged ill-treatment took place. It was argued that the lack of reference to '"the specific decision test of capacity" and "the specific time of decision requirement" resulted in a direction that was flawed because it was incomplete'.[144]

18.122   While acknowledging that the 'convoluted and complex' tests involved in sections 2 and 3 'do not appear to be entirely appropriate to defining the constituent elements of the criminal offence', the Court of Appeal considered that the purpose of section 44 was also significant: that everyone, who can no longer live an independent life and 'is a vulnerable individual living in a residential home, is entitled to be protected from ill-treatment if he or she lacks "capacity" as defined in the Act'. In rejecting the appellant's argument, the Court of Appeal held that:

> ... it was open to the jury to conclude that the decisions about the care of each of these residents at the time when they were subjected to ill-treatment were being made for them by others, including the appellant, just because they lacked the capacity to make these decisions for themselves. For the purposes of section 2, this was 'the matter' envisaged in the legislation. On this basis the Recorder's direction properly expressed the issues which the jury was required to address and resolve by putting the direction clearly within the ambit of the language used in section 2.

141 For further information see Home Office circular 9/2005.
142 See Law Commission, *Adult social care*, Law Com No 326 HC 941, 2011, para 9.144 and Recommendation 46.
143 [2010] EWCA Crim 2935.
144 The recorder had summarised the test for incapacity under section 2, but had not mentioned that this was to be assessed at the 'material time', nor had he included the test for determining whether a person is unable to make a decision as set out in section 3.

... In the context of long-term residential care, and on the facts of this particular case, it was unnecessary for the Recorder further to amplify his directions and complicate the position for the jury by referring in this part of his summing-up to any of the provisions of section 3, or for them to be incorporated into his directions. Therefore, the omission to incorporate them or to refer to the material contained in section 3 does not lead us to doubt the safety of the conviction of offences contrary to section 44 of the 2005 Act.

Fraud Act 2006 s4

18.123 Fraud Act 200 s4 concerns 'fraud by abuse of position' and makes it an offence for a person who occupies a position where he or she is required to safeguard (or not act against) the financial interests of another person, to dishonestly abuse that position, with the intent of self-benefit or to benefit others.

Crime and Security Act 2010 s24

18.124 Crime and Security Act 2010 s24 empowers a senior police officer to issue a domestic violence protection notice prohibiting a named adult from molesting someone where the authorising officer has reasonable grounds for believing that the named party has: (a) been violent towards, or has threatened violence towards, an associated person; and (b) the issue of the notice is necessary to protect that person from violence or a threat of violence by the named party. The notice triggers an obligation on the police to apply for a magistrates' court hearing within 48 hours for application for a domestic violence protection order, providing judicial backing for the prohibitions placed on the alleged perpetrator for 14 to 28 days. It is a criminal offence to breach the notice or the order.

Vulnerable witnesses

18.125 Many victims of crime, whose mental capacity is impaired, experience considerable difficulties in delivering their evidence. The report Speaking up for justice[145] made a number of recommendations aimed at encouraging and supporting vulnerable or intimidated witnesses to give their best evidence in criminal cases, many of which were enacted in Youth Justice and Criminal Evidence Act 1999 Part 2. This included the right of vulnerable witnesses to have the assistance of an intermediary when being interviewed or giving evidence (section 29). The Ministry of Justice has issued guidance concerning the procedures.[146]

145 Home Office, 1998.
146 Home Office, *Achieving best evidence in criminal proceedings: guidance for vulnerable or intimidated witnesses (including children)*, 2011.

CHAPTER 19

Information, data protection and confidentiality

Introduction

19.1   This chapter considers the duty on social services authorities to provide information concerning adult social care entitlements; the right of access to personal information; and the right to have one's personal information kept confidential. Clearly there is potential for these rights to conflict, and this chapter explores how the law regulates such situations.

The general duty to inform

Background

19.2   This section reviews the obligations that local authorities have to inform adults in need and carers of their rights. It is essentially a proactive obligation – to disseminate information regardless of an individual request – as well as a duty to provide specific information when asked, or when the authority considers it appropriate.

19.3   The community care reforms of the 1990s led to the effective privatisation of social care provision. The Care Act (CA) 2014 builds on this by enabling the assessment function to be outsourced (see para 1.25) and by requiring that all care and support needs be commodified (see para 10.4 above). Social care becomes, therefore, a business which relies on the existence of a functioning market of care services[1] (see para 1.70) which – economic theory stipulates – requires that individuals exercise choice (see para 2.28). Rational choice theories require that individuals have full information about the choices available and are able to rank these in order to make the best choices. Of course the application of this theory to social care is contested, but it is the underpinning ethos of the CA 2014, and accordingly the duty to provide information is one of the 'essential building blocks to all of the [CA 2014] reforms' (statutory guidance to the CA 2014 para 3.7).

19.4   Although the duty on social services to provide general information is primarily statutory (and in particular under CA 2014 s4) all public bodies have general public law obligations to provide information in certain situations. As discussed at para 20.211 below, there is a developing duty to provide reasons for certain decisions. In addition, the European Court of Human Rights has held that Article 8 of the European Convention on Human Rights (ECHR) may oblige state authorities to provide information – particularly when that information will enable individuals to make crucial decisions about the extent of a physical risk they may face.[2]

---

1   Described variously by the statutory guidance to the CA 2014 as 'efficient', 'effective', 'vibrant', 'responsive', 'diverse' and 'healthy': Department of Health, *Care and support statutory guidance* to support implementation of Part 1 of the CA 2014 by local authorities, 2016 ('the statutory guidance').

2   See *McGinley and Egan v UK* (1998) 27 EHRR 1; and *KH v Slovakia* (Application no 32881/04), 28 April 2009.

19.5   CA 2014 s4 places a more specific duty on local authorities to provide information and advice than operated under the previous legislation.[3] Section 4(1) requires each authority to 'establish and maintain a service for providing people in its area with information and advice relating to care and support for adults and support for carers.' Section 4(2) then specifies as follows:

> (2) The service must provide information and advice on the following matters in particular–
> (a) the system provided for by this Part and how the system operates in the authority's area,
> (b) the choice of types of care and support, and the choice of providers, available to those who are in the authority's area,
> (c) how to access the care and support that is available,
> (d) how to access independent financial advice on matters relevant to the meeting of needs for care and support, and
> (e) how to raise concerns about the safety or well-being of an adult who has needs for care and support.

Accessibility

19.6   In 2013 the joint committee that scrutinised the draft Care and Support Bill[4] noted that more than 5 million households were without internet access, and expressed concern that 'the Government had given the impression that digital was their preferred channel for information services'. Their report recorded the reassurance given by the secretary of state that 'we will make sure there is provision for people who are not IT literate, because they are some of the most vulnerable people whom we need to help'.

19.7   In 2012, 71 per cent of adults aged 75 years and over had never used the internet[5] and for disabled adults the figure was 3.91 million: individuals with a disability were three times more likely never to have used the internet than individuals with no disability.[6]

19.8   CA 2014 s4(4) requires that information and advice 'must be accessible to, and proportionate to the needs of, those for whom it is being provided'. The statutory guidance stresses that advice, information and materials should be 'as accessible as possible for all potential users' (para 3.27) and reminds authorities that their obligations under the Equality Act (EqA) 2010 to make reasonable adjustments extends to ensuring that their information and advice services are accessible (para 3.28). Importantly, it states that the information and advice 'duty in the Care Act will not be

---

3 National Assistance Act 1948 s29(1)(a) empowered authorities to make arrangements for informing' disabled adults of the services available for them; and Chronically Sick and Disabled Persons Act 1970 s1(2) required that authorities published 'from time to time at such times and in such manner as they consider appropriate general information as to the services' – for further information see the 5th edition of this book at para 2.42.

4 Joint Committee on the Draft Care and Support Bill, *Draft Care and Support Bill*, HL Paper 143 HC 822, The Stationery Office, 2013, para 87.

5 Office for National Statistics, *Internet access quarterly update, 2012 Q2*, 15 August 2012, p2.

6 Office for National Statistics, *Internet access quarterly update, 2012 Q2*, 15 August 2012, p4.

met through the use of digital channels alone, and information and advice channels are likely to include ... face-to-face contact ...' (para 3.29).

The scope of the duty

19.9   The duty to provide advice and information extends to the whole of the local population and not just those who are in receipt of funded care or support (statutory guidance, para 3.11) and is 'distinct from the duty to meet eligible needs' (para 3.4), although it is clear that a person's eligible needs may be met by the provision of information and advice (see para 7.6 above).

19.10   A 2016 ombudsman report[7] illustrates the interaction between the two duties. It concerned a disabled person whose support plan included as an outcome being able to 'manage financial matters and assist with correspondence and communication as necessary'. His support plan stated he was to have a specified number of hours of advocacy available each year to help with all finances, bills and paperwork. The CA 2014 advocacy service did not feel the advocate should be doing anything other than advocacy, and therefore declined to provide the service. In finding maladministration, the ombudsman considered that the plan was insufficiently clear: it failed to specify that the need was not for advocacy but reading and help with finances and bills.

19.11   The duty to provide information and advice extends to 'more than just basic information about care and support' and must 'cover the wide range of care and support related areas ... [including] prevention of care and support needs, finances, health, housing, employment, what to do in cases of abuse or neglect of an adult and other areas where required (statutory guidance para 3.5).

19.12   A significant number of local government ombudsman complaints concern the failure of local authorities to provide appropriate and accurate advice, and the extensive reference in chapter 3 of the statutory guidance to the need for high quality and timely information is likely to be cited in many future local government ombudsman reports. For instance, it is stressed that the advice and information duty is a continuing one, and will arise, for example (para 3.25):

- at first point of contact with the local authority
- as part of a needs or carer's assessment, including joint continuing healthcare assessments
- during a period of reablement
- around and following financial assessment
- when considering a financial commitment such as a deferred payment agreement or top-up agreement
- during or following an adult safeguarding enquiry
- when considering take up of a personal budget and/or direct payment
- during the care and support planning process
- during the review of a person's care and support plan
- when a person may be considering a move to another local authority area
- at points in transition, for example when people needing care or carers under 18 become adults and the systems for support may change

7   Complaint no 14 013 726 against Surrey CC, 3 June 2016.

Independent advice

19.13 As noted below, the CA 2014 requires that local authorities ensure that independent financial advice and information is available – but the requirement for independence in relation to other advice and information is only located in the statutory guidance. It states that local authorities do not have to provide the information service themselves (para 3.14) and that there are 'some circumstances where it is particularly important for information and advice to be impartially provided', adding (para 3.22):

> Local authorities should consider when this might most effectively be provided by an independent source rather than by the local authority itself. This is particularly likely to be the case when people need advice about how and whether to question or challenge the decisions of the local authority ...

19.14 It appears, however, that this guidance has not always been heeded: at least one local authority has used the CA 2014 s4 duty as a pretext for withdrawing funding from the only Citizens Advice Bureau in its area.[8] Given the significant concerns voiced by the local government ombudsman concerning the operation of the adult social care system (see para 20.90 below), the CA 2014's failure to require independent advice for non-financial disputes is troubling.

Financial advice[9]

19.15 The joint committee that scrutinised the draft Care and Support Bill[10] considered that the 'need for advice to be impartial is particularly acute in the case of financial advice' and regretted that a duty in relation to 'financial advice' did not appear in the draft bill. This concern was taken on board by the government. CA 2014 s4(3) requires that in discharge of their information and advice duty, local authorities must 'in particular':

    (a) have regard to the importance of identifying adults in the authority's area who would be likely to benefit from financial advice on matters relevant to the meeting of needs for care and support, and

    (b) seek to ensure that what it provides is sufficient to enable adults–

        (i) to identify matters that are or might be relevant to their personal financial position that could be affected by the system provided for by this Part,

        (ii) to make plans for meeting needs for care and support that might arise, and

        (iii) to understand the different ways in which they may access independent financial advice on matters relevant to the meeting of needs for care and support.

19.16 CA 2014 s4(5) defines 'Independent financial advice' as 'financial advice provided by a person who is independent of the local authority in question'; and the statutory guidance notes that when it refers to 'regulated' financial advice it means 'advice from an organisation regulated by the Financial Conduct Authority' (para 3.10).

---

8 *Herefordshire CAB to close in June 2016* (www.ilegal.org.uk/thread/8937/herefordshire-cab-close-june-2016).

9 See further paras 8.13–8.19 above.

10 Joint Committee on the Draft Care and Support Bill, *Draft Care and Support Bill*, HL Paper 143 HC 822, The Stationery Office, 2013, paras 88–93.

19.17   It would appear that one of the reasons for the emphasis given to financial advice in the CA 2014 is that, at the time it received royal assent, it was
expected that it would cover large numbers of 'self-funders' affected by the
'cap on care costs' provisions.[11] Many such individuals would have had to
make complex financial decisions based on the probability of their care
costs reaching the 'cap'.

19.18   The statutory guidance requires that financial advice (as with general
advice and information) is provided for individuals 'at different points in
their journey to enable them to make sustainable plans to pay for their
care' and that it covers 'the full spectrum of financial information and
advice – from basic budgeting tips to regulated advice – to ensure that
people within its area who would benefit can access it' (para 3.40). Classically this will include advice on 'the availability of different ways to pay for
care including through income and assets (for example, pension or housing wealth), a deferred payment agreement[12] ..., a financial product or a
combination of these things' (para 3.44).

19.19   Importantly, the duty to provide financial advice is something that
extends to all people, regardless of wealth. The statutory guidance advises
that it will also cover people who need (para 3.45):

> ... basic information and support to help them rebalance their finances in
> light of their changing circumstances. Topics may include welfare benefits,
> advice on good money management, help with basic budgeting and pos-
> sibly on debt management. The local authority may be able to provide some
> of this information itself, for example on welfare benefits, but where it can-
> not, it should help people access it.

Information strategies

19.20 The statutory guidance requires that authorities 'develop and implement
a plan regarding their information and advice services that matches their
circumstances and meets the needs of its population' – and provides
detailed advice on what this should contain (paras 3.56–3.70).

Freedom of information duties

19.21 Access to non-confidential publicly-held information is presently regu-
lated by a variety of statutory and non-statutory provisions, including the
Local Government Act (LGA) 1972 and the Freedom of Information Act
(FOIA) 2000.

Local Government Act 1972

19.22 Prior to the coming into force of the FOIA 2000 (below) the principal statute
governing access to local authority information was the LGA 1972. The relevant provisions of this Act (sections 100A–100K), which remain in force,
are concerned primarily with the public's right of access to meetings, and

---

11 CA 2014, ss15, 16, 28 and 29. These provisions are not scheduled to come into force
until 2020 – at the earliest – and are not therefore covered in this book.

12 See para 8.282 above.

the papers considered at these meetings, including 'background papers' relating to reports considered at the meetings. Papers, agendas and minutes of meetings must generally be available three clear days prior to the date of the meeting. With the advent of the internet, many authorities (and government bodies) argue that they comply with this obligation by placing the information on their websites.

Freedom of Information Act 2000

19.23 The FOIA 2000 gives any person (which includes not only individuals but also companies, other organisations and other public authorities) the general right of access to all types of 'recorded' information[13] held by public authorities (and those providing services for them), sets out exemptions from that right, and places a number of obligations on public authorities. A 'public authority' is widely defined and includes parliament, government departments and local authorities, National Health Service (NHS) bodies, GPs etc. Authorities must comply with a request within 20 working days – although if a 'conditional exemption' (see below) applies – the timescale is then such period as is reasonable in the circumstances.

19.24 The FOIA 2000 places two main responsibilities on public authorities, namely:

1) the adoption and maintenance of a 'publication scheme'; and
2) the provision of information in response to requests from the public.

19.25 A publication scheme must specify the types of information the authority publishes, the form in which that information is published and details of any charges for accessing that information. The scheme must be approved by the information commissioner,[14] who is additionally responsible for enforcing and overseeing the Data Protection Act (DPA) 1998.

19.26 The FOIA 2000 provides that anyone requesting information from a public authority is entitled to be informed in writing whether it holds information, and if so to have that information communicated to him or her. The application must, however, (1) be in writing, (2) state the applicant's name and address, and (3) describe the information requested. There is therefore no special form or precedent[15] to use for such requests, although it is wise to describe as precisely as possible what information is sought (as otherwise the authority might refuse to provide it on costs grounds) and to state that the request is being made under 'the Freedom of Information Act 2000'.

19.27 Regulations[16] made under the FOIA 2000 stipulate that requests for information below a ceiling of £600 staff time for central government or £450 for other authorities must be provided free of charge: it has been suggested that this equates to 2.5 days of staff time. Where the fee would exceed this limit, the public body can refuse to supply the information, or

---

13 This is widely defined: there is no time limit for when the material was compiled and it may include photos, plans etc.
14 See www.ico.org.uk.
15 See appendix B for a FOIA 2000 precedent letter.
16 Freedom of Information and Data Protection (Appropriate Limit and Fees) Regulations 2004 SI No 3244.

decide to supply it subject to payment of the full costs of doing so. Authorities are, however, entitled to be paid for disbursements, such as the cost
of photocopying/printing and postage etc.

19.28   Authorities are exempted from providing the information in certain
situations – depending upon whether an 'absolute' or 'conditional' exemption applies. Where an absolute exemption applies, the authority is not
even under a duty to confirm or deny the existence of the information.
All that is required is a letter, within 20 working days, explaining that the
exemption is being invoked and advising the applicant of his or her right
to appeal or complain about the decision. Absolute exemptions include
information otherwise accessible; information concerning security matters; information in court records; parliamentary privileged material; personal information (that relates to the applicant); information provided in
confidence; and information whose disclosure is restricted by law.

19.29   Conditional exemptions apply where it may be in the public interest
not to have disclosure. In some cases there is a presumption that disclosure will be against the public interest, whereas in others the authority is
required to provide credible evidence of the particular prejudice, before
it can use the ground as a reason for withholding disclosure. Those
cases where no prejudice need be established include information that is
intended for future publication as well as information that concerns public inquiries, government policy formulation, and legal professional privilege. Those cases where prejudice needs to be established include such
matters as: national security; law enforcement; audit functions; effective
conduct of public affairs; and health and safety.

19.30   Where a request concerns personal information, the FOIA 2000 defers
to the DPA 1998 and in general the information should be sought under
the DPA 1998. Sometimes it will not be clear which Act is relevant – for
instance, a request for information concerning the salary paid to a public
officer. The information commissioner has advised that in general, where
information is sought concerning someone acting in an official capacity,
it should be provided under the FOIA 2000.[17] The data protection regime
regulating the retention and accessibility of personal information is considered further below.

19.31   Anyone dissatisfied with a response to his or her request has a number
of options, including a right to have the refusal reviewed by the authority,
and a right of appeal to the information commissioner and thence to the
first-tier tribunal (general regulatory chamber).

Data protection and confidentiality

Background

19.32   Crucial to any analysis of the law of confidentiality is an appreciation
that the right is not an 'absolute' one. It is qualified and, like all qualified
rights, requires a balance to be struck between competing interests and

17 See the Information Commissioner's guidance, *Requests for personal data about public
authority employees*, 2013.

principles. In certain situations therefore the state is entitled to interfere with a person's 'privacy' provided the interference pursues a legitimate aim (for instance, the protection of the person or another) and the interference is not disproportionate. Therefore, an understanding of the law requires an understanding of ECHR Article 8 – the right (among other things) to respect for one's private life. At times, the right can only be 'respected' by a disclosure of confidential information – for instance, where a vulnerable person lacking capacity has been abused and the police need to be informed of this fact.

19.33   In 2012, the government commissioned *The information governance review* ('the 2013 IGR review'),[18] led by Dame Fiona Caldicott. The review focused on both the health and social care sector in England[19] to consider the balance between information sharing and confidentiality when making decisions for the benefit of the individual service-user. The review report set out its context (at para 1.5):

> There is a perception that too much information is being disclosed inadvertently[20] as well as too little being shared deliberately. Furthermore there is uncertainty among many patients and users of services, who are unaware of how personal confidential data about them is collected and shared. If people do not know how their data will be used, it is wrong to assume they have given their implied consent[21] to sharing.

19.34   Following the 2013 IGR review, in 2013 the Health and Social Care Information Centre (HSCIC) published *A guide to confidentiality in health and social care*[22] (referred to as the '2013 HSCIC guide') to provide clarity about

18 F Caldicott (chair), *Information: to share or not to share? The information governance review*, Department of Health, 2013. The 2013 IGR review considered (among other things) Dame Fiona Caldicott's earlier report, The Caldicott Committee, *Review of the users of patient-identifiable information*, Department of Health, 1997, which devised six principles of information governance for NHS organisations with access to patient identifiable information (see para 19.78 below).

19 The 2013 IGR review notes that, while the issues relating to England formed the basis of the 2013 IGR review, much of the report 'should prove useful in all the jurisdictions of the United Kingdom' (p7).

20 In 2013 the Information Commissioner's Office (ICO) audited 16 local authorities' compliance with the Data Protection Act (DPA) 1998 and found *clear room for improvement* overall, with the ICO has also imposed fines of £2.3 million upon local authorities. The breaches were most commonly personal information being disclosed in error and lost or stolen paperwork and hardware: ICO, *Findings from ICO audits of 16 local authorities January to December 2013*, 2014. Examples of local authorities failing to comply with the DPA 1998 are: a council fined £80,000 when a unencrypted USB stick was lost which contained 286 records of sensitive data relating to children with special educational needs; and a council served with an enforcement notice after a social worker disclosed a report to a former service-user about their time in care but failed to remove sensitive information about the recipient's sister – see ICO, 'Action we have taken', North East Lincolnshire Council, 29 October 2013; and Wolverhampton Council, 29 May 2014 respectively.

21 'Implied consent' is considered in the 2013 IGR review at paras 3.2: it broadly allows professionals to disclose certain information about individuals to others when it would be impractical to do otherwise eg when a social worker refers a person to an occupational therapist. It requires the professional to respond appropriately to the person's needs and also to keep their personal information confidential.

22 Health and Social Care Information Centre (HSCIC), *A guide to confidentiality in health and social care. Treating confidential information with respect*, version 1.1, September 2013.

the processing of confidential information relating to a person's care. The intention is that it be used and understood by all those involved in giving and receiving personal information, including service-users, patients, carers, family members and staff.[23] It is also accompanied by a reference document,[24] which provides a further explanation of the law as well as examples of good practice; it is referred to in this chapter as the '2013 HSCIC reference guide'.

19.35   The 2013 HSCIC guide notes the changing context of the health and social care and, in particular, that 'For too long, people have hidden behind the obscurity of the Data Protection Act 1998 or alleged rules of information governance in order to avoid taking decisions that benefit the service user or patient'.[25] It focuses on the approach to be taken when sharing an individual's personal information, noting starkly that 'Lives may be lost if information is not shared as it should be'.[26] Almost two decades after the passing of the DPA 1998, there is as much concern about the need to share information in an appropriate way as there is about ensuring that the privacy of the individual is maintained.[27]

19.36   The 2013 HSCIC guide has been issued through the powers of the HSCIC to provide advice and guidance on matters relating to the use of information.[28] It therefore applies to health and social care bodies and any organisation funded by them to provide such care (eg independent care providers), all of whom must 'have regard' to it.[29]

19.37   The statutory guidance to the CA 2014 reflects the work of the 2013 IGR review in the context of safeguarding.[30] It is also noted that the provisions of the CA 2014 – for example, in the context of greater integration with the NHS (section 3) and the duties of co-operation between a range of public sector bodies, including local authorities and the NHS (sections 6 and 7)[31] – will require appropriate data and information sharing agreements, and processes to be implemented for the benefit of those persons using health and social care services.[32]

---

23 A concise leaflet version has also been published: Department of Health, *Confidentiality and information sharing for direct care guidance for health and care professionals*, 2014.

24 HSCIC, *A guide to confidentiality in health and social care: references. Treating confidential information with respect*, version 1.1, September 2013.

25 See 2013 HSCIC guide, p4.

26 See 2013 HSCIC guide, p8.

27 As the 2013 IGR review noted: 'The issue of whether professionals shared information effectively and safely was not regarded as a problem at the time' of the DPA 1998 (p9).

28 Under Health and Social Care Act 2012 s256.

29 See 2013 HSCIC guide p7.

30 See the statutory guidance to the CA 2014, in particular para 14.187: it gives guidance on how 'Agencies should draw up a common agreement relating to confidentiality and setting out the principles governing the sharing of information, based on the welfare of the adult or of other potentially affected adults'.

31 See the statutory guidance to the CA 2014 at chapter 15 'Integration, cooperation and partnerships'.

32 The *Data sharing code of practice* (ICO, 2011) sets out that any data sharing agreement must address a number of issues, including the purpose of the agreement; the types of data which is intended to be shared as well as ensuring that a clear procedure exists to deal with an individual's right of access to the shared data.

The legal framework

Overview

19.38 The striking of the balance between access and confidentiality has not been eased by the legal framework that has developed to regulate this important function, as the 2013 IGR review noted.[33] In essence there are three domains of the law that bear upon such decisions, namely:

- the DPA 1998;
- the Human Rights Act (HRA) 1998; and
- the common law.

19.39 The relevant provisions of the DPA 1998, the HRA 1998 and the common law are reviewed below. However, the interplay between them was considered in *R (S) v Plymouth City Council*.[34] The case concerned C, a 27-year-old man with learning and behavioural difficulties who had been assessed as lacking mental capacity to consent to the disclosure of information in his health and social services files to his mother (his nearest relative for the purposes of Mental Health Act (MHA) 1983 s11). The local authority obtained a guardianship order in relation to C, since it believed that it was not in his best interests to live with his mother. The mother expressed concern about this action and, in order to decide whether or not to object, she asked to see the relevant papers in his social services and healthcare files. The local authority refused, initially asserting that it could not disclose the information because it was confidential. Subsequently it shifted its position, accepting that it had power to disclose, but that this could not occur without very good reasons (and it considered that none existed). The Court of Appeal disagreed with this approach. Reviewing the DPA 1998, it noted that although all the information that the mother was seeking was 'sensitive personal data' within the meaning of DPA 1998 s2(e), this did not mean that it could not be disclosed to third parties – since the Act permitted this in various situations, including:[35]

> ... where it is necessary in order to protect the vital interests of the data subject or another person in a case where consent cannot be given by or on behalf of the data (Sched 3, para 3); or for the purpose of, or in connection with, any legal proceedings (including prospective legal proceedings) or for the purpose of obtaining legal advice, or where it is otherwise necessary for the purposes of establishing, exercising or defending legal rights (para 6); or where it is necessary for the administration of justice, or for the exercise of any functions conferred on any person by or under an enactment (at [7]).

33 The following extract from the 2013 IGR review gives a flavour of its findings: '[A] culture of anxiety permeates the health and social care sector. Managers, who are fearful that their organisations may be fined for breaching data protection laws, are inclined to set unduly restrictive rules for information governance.' See also para 9.4.2 which referred to 'little consistency in the competence and experience of information governance' and to 'few people understanding the professional regulatory or legal framework or other legislation such as the common law duty of confidentiality and Human Rights Act'.

34 [2002] EWCA Civ 388, [2002] 1 WLR 2583, (2002) 5 CCLR 251.

35 [2002] EWCA Civ 388, [2002] 1 WLR 2583, (2002) 5 CCLR 251 at [27].

19.40   In the circumstances, therefore, it considered that the Act provided little assistance and that the final decision on the disclosure of the confidential information[36] depended upon a careful analysis of the relevant common law and HRA 1998 principles – which required that 'a balance be struck between the public and private interests in maintaining the confidentiality of this information and the public and private interests in permitting, indeed requiring, its disclosure for certain purposes'.

19.41   Following a detailed analysis the court concluded as follows:

> 48. Hence both the common law and the Convention require that a balance be struck between the various interests involved. These are the confidentiality of the information sought; the proper administration of justice; the mother's right of access to legal advice to enable her to decide whether or not to exercise a right which is likely to lead to legal proceedings against her if she does so; the rights of both C and his mother to respect for their family life and adequate involvement in decision-making processes about it; C's right to respect for his private life; and the protection of C's health and welfare. In some cases there might also be an interest in the protection of other people, but that has not been seriously suggested here.

> 49. C's interest in protecting the confidentiality of personal information about himself must not be under-estimated. It is all too easy for professionals and parents to regard children and incapacitated adults as having no independent interests of their own: as objects rather than subjects. But we are not concerned here with the publication of information to the whole wide world. There is a clear distinction between disclosure to the media with a view to publication to all and sundry and disclosure in confidence to those with a proper interest in having the information in question. We are concerned here only with the latter. The issue is only whether the circle should be widened from those professionals with whom this information has already been shared (possibly without much conscious thought being given to the balance of interests involved) to include the person who is probably closest to him in fact as well as in law and who has a statutory role in his future and to those professionally advising her. C also has an interest in having his own wishes and feelings respected. It would be different in this case if he had the capacity to give or withhold consent to the disclosure: any objection from him would have to be weighed in the balance against the other interests, although as *W v Egdell*[37] shows, it would not be decisive. C also has an interest in being protected from a risk of harm to his health or welfare which would stem from disclosure; but it is important not to confuse a possible risk of harm to his health or welfare from being discharged from guardianship with a possible risk of harm from disclosing the information sought. As *Re D*[38] shows, he also has an interest in decisions about his future being properly informed.

> 50. That balance would not lead in every case to the disclosure of all the information a relative might possibly want, still less to a fishing exercise amongst the local authority's files. But in most cases it would lead to the disclosure of the basic statutory guardianship documentation. In this case it must also lead to the particular disclosure sought. There is no suggestion

---

36   The court was of the view that it was overly simplistic to consider that all the information in the file was confidential, commenting at [33], 'some of it may not be confidential at all: straightforward descriptions of everyday life are not normally thought confidential'.

37   [1990] 2 WLR 471, CA – see para 19.82 below.

38   *Re D (minors) (adoption reports: confidentiality)* [1995] 3 WLR 483, HL.

that C has any objection to his mother and her advisers being properly informed about his health and welfare. There is no suggestion of any risk to his health and welfare arising from this. The mother and her advisers have sought access to the information which her own psychiatric and social work experts need in order properly to advise her. That limits both the context and the content of disclosure in a way which strikes a proper balance between the competing interests.

19.42   In such cases, public bodies should analyse precisely why they are asserting 'confidentiality' and ask themselves whether this does indeed promote the best interests of the third party: is confidentiality being claimed to protect themselves rather than the disabled person? The statutory guidance to the CA 2014 gives emphasis to this point, stating (para 14.190):

> Principles of confidentiality designed to safeguard and promote the interests of service users and patients should not be confused with those designed to protect the management interests of an organisation. These have a legitimate role but must never be allowed to conflict with the interests of service users and parents.[39]

Data Protection Act 1998

Overview

19.43   All social services and health records are covered by the DPA 1998. It is not the most accessible of Acts, and where possible courts tend to try to articulate the law using other reference points – principally the common law and ECHR Article 8 (as did the Court of Appeal in the *Plymouth City Council* case above). Indeed, a former Lord Chancellor has observed that:

> The problem about the Data Protection Act is that it is almost incomprehensible. It is very difficult to understand. The precise limits of it are problematic. There are constant difficulties about what information you are allowed to share between departments for instance. I just think it needs to be looked at again at some stage to make it more simple.

19.44   Legal guidance on the DPA 1998 has been issued by the information commissioner,[40] in addition to which specific NHS[41] and social services guidance has been issued by the Department of Health: *Data Protection Act 1998 – guidance to social services.*[42] In the following section, paragraph references are to the social services guidance ('the 2000 DPA guidance') unless the context indicates otherwise.

19.45   The DPA 1998 applies to all 'accessible public records', no matter when they were compiled, and includes electronic and manual data. An accessible public record is a record which contains any personal information held by the health body or social services department for the purposes of their health/social services functions, irrespective of when the information

---

39 The statutory guidance has replaced *No Secrets: guidance on developing and implementing multi-agency policies and procedures to protect vulnerable adults from abuse* (Department of Health and the Home Office, 2000) (see para 18.13 above).

40 ICO, *Guide to data protection*, 2009. The Commissioner's website (www.ico.gov.uk) contains has extensive list of subject-specific guidance on the DPA 1998.

41 See eg Department of Health, *Guidance for access to health records requests*, 2010.

42 Department of Health, 2000. Although archived, the guidance appears to remain valid guidance about the DPA 1998 for social services departments.

was recorded (DPA 1998 s68). The information held may include factual material as well as 'any expressions of opinion, and the intentions of the authority in relation to the individual' (2000 DPA guidance, para 5.4).

19.46   The DPA 1998 applies eight basic principles to the disclosure of information. These essentially require data to be processed fairly, legally, accurately and that the information be retained no longer than necessary;[43] they restrict the transfer of data as well as unnecessary reprocessing of data; and require organisations holding such information to take appropriate measures to restrict unauthorised access to it.

19.47   Where joint records are held, for example, by social services and an NHS trust in a community mental health team, a request for access to that information can be made to either body – the guidance stating that (2000 DPA guidance, para 5.2):

> Authorities and their partners in joint record holding will therefore need to have procedures in place to ensure that the data subject is aware that he/she is not obliged to apply to all partners for access and to inform each other that access has been given.

19.48 The DPA 1998 gives a right of access by individuals to any personal information held by the authority about them. Where the information concerns other individuals (for instance, a local authority file on an entire family) one member is not in general entitled to see information about another member without that person's consent (2000 DPA guidance, paras 5.5–5.7).

19.49   The DPA 1998 permits the disclosure of information notwithstanding that it has been provided by a third party and that party has not consented to the disclosure.[44] This is considered further below at para 19.68.

Access to information by or on behalf of children

19.50 The 2000 DPA guidance (at para 5.8 and following) makes clear that where a person under 18 years seeks access to their records, the authority must decide whether or not they have 'sufficient understanding to do so', which means 'does he or she understand the nature of the request?'[45] If the requisite capacity exists, the authority should then comply with the request for access to their personal information. If, however, insufficient understanding exists, the request may be made by a person with parental responsibility who can make the request on the child's behalf. Disclosure to parents in such cases should only occur after the authority has satisfied itself:

1) that the child lacks capacity to make a valid application, or has capacity and has authorised the parent to make the application; and
2) (where the child does not have capacity) that the request made by the parent on the child's behalf is in that child's interest (guidance para 5.9).

---

43 For further information about data retention, see the decision of the Supreme Court in *Catt and R (T) v Commissioner of the Police of the Metropolis* [2015] UKSC 9.
44 DPA 1998 s7(4)(b).
45 For a review of the law concerning children's capacity to consent, see generally, S Broach, L Clements and J Read, *Disabled children: a legal handbook*, 2nd edn, Legal Action Group, 2016.

19.51   The advice accurately reflects the statutory and common law position. Mental Capacity Act (MCA) 2005 s1 creates a presumption that all persons aged 16 or older have capacity to make decisions. The definition of parental responsibility in Children Act 1989 s3(1) includes the right of parents to consent on the child's behalf to a wide range of matters, including medical treatment.[46] In *Gillick v West Norfolk and Wisbech Area Health Authority*[47] the House of Lords had to consider when the parental right to make decisions on a child's behalf ended – for example, when the child achieved sufficient intelligence and understanding to make its own decision. The court held that it did, and cited with approval comments of Lord Denning,[48] namely:

> ... the legal right of a parent to the custody of a child ends at the 18th birthday: and even up till then, it is a dwindling right which the courts will hesitate to enforce against the wishes of the child, and the more so the older he is. It starts with a right of control and ends with little more than advice.

Requests made through another person (an agent)

19.52   Individuals with sufficient mental capacity are entitled to make their request for information via an agent. The guidance states that agents should provide evidence (normally in writing) of their authority and confirm their identity and relationship to the individual; and that authorities (if satisfied that the agent is duly authorised) must treat the request as if it had been made by the individual concerned (2000 DPA guidance, para 5.13). The guidance accepts that some persons with profound physical impairments may not be able to give written consent to their agents and that in such cases the local authority should give the individual as much assistance as possible and ultimately need not always insist on permission in writing (2000 DPA guidance, para 5.14).

Access to information on behalf of an adult lacking mental capacity

19.53   A general outline of the law concerning adults who lack mental capacity is contained at chapter 13 above.

19.54   The DPA 1998 is silent on the subject of requests for access made on behalf of an adult who lacks sufficient understanding to make the request in his or her own name.[49] The 2000 DPA guidance, however, states that (at para 5.11):

> ... if a person lacks capacity to manage their affairs, a person acting under an order of the Court of Protection or acting within the terms of a registered Enduring Power of Attorney can request access on her or his behalf.

19.55   The absence of provisions relating to those who lack capacity have been ameliorated to a degree by the approach taken by the courts, by utilising the powers available under the common law and those implemented by

---

46   See also Family Law Reform Act 1969 s8 and *Re W (a minor) (medical treatment)* [1992] 3 WLR 758.
47   [1985] 3 WLR 830.
48   *Hewer v Bryant* [1970] 1 QB 357 at 369.
49   It is noted that the DPA 1998 and the guidance were written before the introduction of the MCA 2005, which probably accounts at least in part for the unhelpful absence of appropriate information on this subject.

the HRA 1998 (as evidenced in *R (S) v Plymouth City Council*[50] – see paras 19.39–19.42 above).

19.56   In addition, the code of practice to the MCA 2005 (see para 13.7 above) contains useful information on the principles applicable to disclosure. It considers and gives examples of the situations where local authorities and health bodies are empowered to disclose information to third parties (even when these persons are not empowered by an enduring power of attorney, a lasting power of attorney or a deputyship) and includes:

> 16.19 Healthcare and social care staff may disclose information about somebody who lacks capacity only when it is in the best interests of the person concerned to do so, or when there is some other, lawful reason for them to do so.

> 16.20 The Act's requirement to consult relevant people when working out the best interests of a person who lacks capacity will encourage people to share the information that makes a consultation meaningful. But people who release information should be sure that they are acting lawfully and that they can justify releasing the information. They need to balance the person's right to privacy with what is in their best interests or the wider public interest ...

> 16.21 Sometimes it will be fairly obvious that staff should disclose information. For example, a doctor would need to tell a new care worker about what drugs a person needs or what allergies the person has. This is clearly in the person's best interests.

> 16.22 Other information may need to be disclosed as part of the process of working out someone's best interests. A social worker might decide to reveal information about someone's past when discussing their best interests with a close family member. But staff should always bear in mind that the Act requires them to consider the wishes and feelings of the person who lacks capacity.

> 16.23 In both these cases, staff should only disclose as much information as is relevant to the decision to be made.

19.57   The principles of the MCA 2005 are reflected in the 2013 HSCIC guide in that, where a person lacks capacity to give valid consent to the sharing of personal information with family members and/or carers, the decision about information sharing is to be made in the person's 'best interests'.[51]

19.58   The CA 2014 broadens the availability of independent advocacy services to individuals in the social care system, including persons without capacity.[52] The statutory guidance to the CA 2014 states (para 7.47):

> Where a person does not have capacity to decide whether an advocate should look at their relevant records or talk to their family and friends, then the advocate should consult the records and the family and others as appropriate, but consulting the family and others only where the advocate considers this is in the person's best interests. The Care Act allows advocates

---

50 [2002] EWCA Civ 388, [2002] 1 WLR 2583, (2002) 5 CCLR 251.
51 See 2013 HSCIC guide at p14 and further guidance is provided in the 2013 HSCIC reference guide at p23.
52 See the guidance 2014 para 7.4 for the conditions which apply when a local authority must provide a person with an independent advocate and para 13.81 above.

to examine and take copies of relevant records in certain circumstances.[53] This mirrors the powers of an Independent Mental Capacity Advocate.

19.59   MCA 2005 s35(6) entitles independent mental capacity advocates (see para 13.81 above) to examine and take copies of (i) any health record, (ii) any record of, or held by, a local authority and compiled in connection with a social services function, and (iii) any record held by a person registered under the Care Standards Act 2000 Part 2 or the Health and Social Care Act 2008 Part 1 Chapter 2 which the person holding the record considers may be relevant to the independent mental capacity advocate's investigation.

19.60   Research has suggested that some professionals use 'confidentiality smokescreens' as a way of withholding information from carers.[54] This occurs in situations where good practice requires that professionals anticipate such problems and (for instance) negotiate advance agreements when the disabled person has the capacity to consent and insight into their needs.[55] The 2013 HSCIC guide[56] states that (p23):

> Those involved in the direct care of a patient/service user should establish with them what information they wish to be shared, with whom, and in what circumstances. This will be particularly important if the patient has fluctuating or diminished capacity or is likely to lose capacity, even temporarily. Early discussions of this nature can help to avoid disclosures to which patients would object. They can also help to avoid misunderstandings with, or causing offence to, anyone with whom the patient/service user would want information to be shared.

19.61   The local government ombudsman has indicated that 'confidentiality' should not be used as a reason for not disclosing relevant information in such cases. In criticising a council for not sharing information with the parents of a 24-year-old man with serious learning difficulties, she commented:

> I accept that this would not be regular practice when the Council is looking after an adult: the privacy of the individual demands that the parents be kept at some distance. But [the user] had such a high level of dependency that the Council should have been willing to reconsider its approach to parental involvement in this case.[57]

Access procedures

19.62   DPA 1998 s7(2)(a) requires all requests for access to information to be in writing, and section 7(8) requires the information to be disclosed 'promptly' and in any event within 40 days. All information must be disclosed,

53   See CA 2014 s67(7)(f) and s67(9); and also the Care and Support (Independent Advocacy) (No 2) Regulations 2014 SI No 2889.
54   B Gray, C Robinson, D Seddon and A Roberts, '"Confidentiality smokescreens" and carers for people with mental health problems: the perspectives of professionals' in *Health and Social Care in the Community* (2008) 16(4), 378–387.
55   B Gray, C Robinson, D Seddon and A Roberts, '"Confidentiality smokescreens" and carers for people with mental health problems: the perspectives of professionals' in *Health and Social Care in the Community* (2008) 16(4), 378–387.
56   This approach is also endorsed by the General Medical Council (GMC) in *Confidentiality*, 2009, para 64.
57   Complaint no 97/C/4618 against Cheshire, 19 May 1999.

unless subject to any of the exceptions detailed below (most notably where the data includes information about another person).

19.63 The information should not be altered in any way (2000 DPA guidance, para 5.20) and should be the information which the authority held at the time of the request. Any amendment or deletion made between the time of request and supply should, however, be noted (if the changes would have occurred regardless of the request) (2000 DPA guidance, para 5.21). The DPA 1998 contains further procedures by which applicants can apply to have inaccurate information corrected.[58]

19.64 DPA 1998 s8(2) stipulates that the information should generally be provided in the form of a permanent copy, although a copy need not be provided if it is not possible, or if it would involve disproportionate effort, or if the applicant has agreed otherwise.

19.65 The 40-day period for disclosure is subject to certain restrictions, namely:

1) **Sufficient description of information sought.** The applicant must provide the authority with sufficient information to enable it to identify the person about whom the information is sought and where that information is likely to be held. Authorities are permitted to provide a standard request form for this purpose but are not permitted to insist on its use (2000 DPA guidance, para 5.16).

2) **Payment of the appropriate fee.** Authorities are permitted to charge a fee for the provision of information, which must not, however, exceed the statutory maximum of £10,[59] including the cost of supplying copies (special rules apply for access to manual health records for which the maximum fee is currently £50[60]). The guidance requires authorities to advise applicants promptly of the need to pay a fee (if one is charged) and advises that procedures should exist for waiving the fee where the applicant's means or any other circumstances dictate such a course (2000 DPA guidance, para 5.17). Since the 40-day period only commences when the fee has been paid, it may be appropriate to include payment in the initial letter of request.[61]

   The guidance advises that where authorities do not have the requested information, applicants should be informed as quickly as possible, and a decision then made as to whether the fee should be returned (2000 DPA guidance, para 2.18). In so deciding, it should consider the applicant's circumstances, the effort involved in discovering that there was no data, and its own policy on charging.

3) **Repeated requests.** DPA 1998 s8(3) provides that access can be refused where the authority has previously complied with an identical or similar request from the applicant, unless a reasonable interval separates the requests.[62]

58 DPA 1998 s14; see also 2000 DPA guidance, paras 5.31 and following.
59 Data Protection (Subject Access) (Fees and Miscellaneous Provisions) Regulations 2000 SI No 191 reg 3.
60 Data Protection (Subject Access) (Fees and Miscellaneous Provisions) (Amendment) Regulations 2001 SI No 3223.
61 See appendix B for a DPA 1998 precedent letter.
62 2000 DPA guidance, para 5.19 gives advice on what amounts to a 'reasonable interval'.

19.66 Not infrequently, social services authorities suggest that the individual first view the data (eg files) in the presence of a social worker, before providing such copies as are required. It is very doubtful whether it is lawful for an authority to refuse to copy a file to an individual without their prior attendance to view it in the company of a social worker, since this imposes an extra non-statutory hurdle to access. Attendance at a social services office may be physically difficult for many service users, and may be particularly daunting for the unassertive. The arrangements for prior attendance should not significantly delay the provision of copies and proper consideration must be given to any difficulties service users may have in attending any such appointment. In such circumstances, prior attendance requirement may be acceptable as good practice if its purpose is to explain confusing or unclear aspects of the information and how it has been recorded.[63]

Third party information

19.67 DPA 1998 s7(4) states that where an authority is unable to comply with a request for information without disclosing information relating to another individual (who can be identified from that information), it is not obliged to comply with the request, unless, either:

a) the other individual has consented to the disclosure; or

b) it is reasonable in all the circumstances to comply with the request without the consent.

19.68 In deciding whether or not it is reasonable to make a disclosure without the third party's consent, DPA 1998 s7(6) requires the authority to have particular regard to the following factors:

a) any duty of confidentiality owed to that other individual;

b) any steps taken by the authority with a view to seeking the consent of the other individual;

c) whether the other individual is capable of giving consent;

d) any express refusal of consent by the other individual.

19.69 The 2000 DPA guidance makes the following observations:

5.24 Section 7(6) is likely to be of particular relevance when a request is received for access to very old files and the possibility of tracing any third party is remote.

5.25 An authority should set itself a sensible timescale, within the 40 days allowed, in which to seek any third party consent. The 40 day period does not commence until the authority has received the written request, the appropriate fee, and if necessary, the further information required to satisfy itself as to the identity of the person making the request, and to locate the information sought.

5.26 If consent is not given by a third party within 40 days, an authority should give as much information as possible without identifying the third party (see DPA section 7(5)). An authority should explain why some of the information requested has not been given. Where the other person's consent is not or cannot be given, and the authority considers it reasonable to comply with the request without consent, then it may do so. However, it

---

63 See also the 2000 DPA guidance, paras 5.29 and 5.30 on 'presenting the information'.

may later be required to justify its actions if the [third party] later says the particular disclosure was a breach of their rights under the DPA ...

5.27 Where the authority is satisfied that the data subject will not be able to identify the [third party source] from the information to be disclosed, taking into account any other information which the authority reasonably believes is likely to be in or to come into the possession of the [applicant], then the authority must provide the information.

19.70   In addition to the above factors, the statutory exemptions detailed below also apply to decisions about disclosure, most importantly where it is considered that disclosure could result in serious harm to the third party. However, where the third party is a social worker, access cannot be refused unless the 'serious harm test' applies (see the 2000 DPA guidance, para 5.37(ii) and appendix 2).

Statutory exemptions justifying a refusal of access to information

19.71   DPA 1998 Part IV provides that authorities do not have to disclose information in certain situations. The principal grounds of relevance for the purposes of social care are (in summary):

1) **Information about physical or mental health conditions (DPA 1998 s30(1)).** Social services are prohibited from disclosing any information without first consulting an appropriate health professional (normally this will be the person responsible for the person's current clinical care, eg a GP or psychiatrist) in connection with the matters to which the information relates. The relevant exemption order in relation to health information specifically permits the refusal of disclosure to the extent to which it would be likely to cause serious harm to the physical or mental health or condition of the data subject or any other person.[64]

2) **Where disclosure is prevented by another enactment.** This category includes such examples as adoption records and reports, parental order records and reports under Human Fertilisation and Embryology Act 1990 s30.[65]

3) **Specific social services exemptions.** Information held for the purposes of social work is exempt from disclosure if it would be likely to prejudice the carrying out of social work, by causing serious harm to the physical or mental health (or condition) of the applicant or another person.[66]

19.72   If any of these exemptions are to be relied upon, the applicant must be notified as soon as practicable and in writing, even where the decision has also been given in person; reasons should also be given (2000 DPA guidance, para 5.39).

---

64 As defined in the relevant order, namely the Data Protection (Subject Access Modification) (Health) Order 2000 SI No 413 (as amended); see also the 2000 DPA guidance, para 5.37(iii).

65 These exemptions are listed in the Data Protection (Miscellaneous Subject Access Exemptions) Order 2000 SI No 419 (as amended); see also the 2000 DPA guidance, para 5.37(iv).

66 Data Protection (Subject Access Modification) (Social Work) Order 2000 SI No 415 (as amended); see also the 2000 DPA guidance, para 5.37(ii).

Disclosure of personal information without consent

19.73　The DPA 1998 provides for the disclosure of a person's confidential information without consent, and also without informing the person of the disclosure, where it is necessary to achieve a prescribed purpose. For example, a local authority may disclose personal information to the police where that information is needed to prevent or detect crime or to catch and prosecute a suspect (DPA 1998 s29). It does not allow for disclosure of all the personal information about that person, but requires the authority to consider the release of the minimum amount of information which would enable the police (or others) to carry out their investigation. Furthermore, the authority may only disclose the person's confidential information where it considers that not disclosing it would be likely to prejudice (ie significantly harm) the stated purpose (eg the criminal investigation or crime prevention).[67]

Appeals procedure

19.74　If disclosure is refused, the applicant may apply either to the information commissioner or to the courts; the choice of remedy is up to the applicant (2000 DPA guidance, para 5.41).

Caldicott reviews – information management and sharing

19.75　In the 1990s, considerable concern had been expressed about the way the NHS and other statutory bodies respected the confidential information they stored. As a result of this concern, in 1996/1997, a review was commissioned by the Chief Medical Officer of England into the use of patient-identifiable information by the NHS in England and Wales with the aim of ensuring that confidentiality was not being compromised.[68] The review was chaired by Dame Fiona Caldicott.

19.76　　Her subsequent report[69] made a number of recommendations, including the need to raise awareness of confidentiality and information security requirements among all staff within the NHS; the need to track all dataflows within the NHS and the need for protocols to protect the exchange of patient-identifiable information between NHS and non-NHS bodies.

19.77　　It also recommended the appointment of a senior person, in every health organisation, to act as a guardian, responsible for safeguarding the confidentiality of patient information. This person is known as a 'Caldicott guardian'[70] and the role of the Caldicott guardian was subsequently extended to cover all English social services departments.[71]

67　See also ICO guidance note: *Releasing information to prevent or detect crime (section 29).*

68　2013 IGR review.

69　The Caldicott Committee, *Report on the review of patient-identifiable information,* Department of Health, 1997.

70　The description of a 'Caldicott guardian' in the 2013 HSCIC guide is a 'senior person responsible for protecting the confidentiality of patient and service user information and enabling appropriate information sharing' (p28 fn 40).

71　Department of Health, *Implementing the Caldicott standard in social care* HSC 2002/003: LAC (2002)2, 2002.

19.78   The 1997 review also provided for six principles, which were extended to seven principles following the further work by Dame Fiona Caldicott in 2013.[72] These are:

I.   Justify the purpose(s) for the use or transfer of the person's confidential information;

II.   Do not use personal confidential information unless it is absolutely necessary;

III.   Use the minimum necessary personal confidential information;

IV.   Access to personal confidential information should be on a strict need-to-know basis;

V.   Everyone with access to personal confidential information should be aware of their responsibilities;

VI.   Every use of personal confidential information must be lawful;

VII.   The duty to share information can be as important as the duty to protect a person's confidentiality.

19.79   These principles have been distilled into five 'confidentiality rules' which the public is entitled to expect will be followed in care settings run by the NHS or in publicly funded adult social care services.[73] These are of benefit to the public in providing some clarity about an individual's rights to the use of their confidential information, as well as to those professionals who have to made decisions on a daily basis about using and sharing personal information. In brief, the five rules are as follows:

1)   Confidential information about service users or patients should be treated confidentially and respectfully.

2)   Members of a care team should share confidential information when it is needed for the safe and effective care of an individual.

3)   Information that is shared for the benefit of the community should be anonymised.

4)   An individual's right to object to the sharing of confidential information about him or her should be respected.

5)   Organisations should put policies, procedures and systems in place to ensure the confidentiality rules are followed.

The common law and the Human Rights Act 1998

19.80   As has been noted above, the DPA 1998 is only one part of our domestic legal framework that seeks to both protect confidentiality and promote the right of access to personal information. The common law and HRA 1998 also play an important role in this respect, particularly in clarifying the principles that are relevant in the exercise of discretion to (or not to) disclose and/or share personal information.

The common law

19.81   The common law has long recognised the concept of a person's right to confidentiality,[74] a right that arises 'when confidential information comes to the knowledge of the person (the confidant) in circumstances where he

---

72   See paras 19.33–19.36 above.

73   See 2013 HSCIC guide at p9.

74   *Prince Albert v Strange* (1849) 1 Mac and G 25.

has notice or is held to have agreed that the information is confidential with the effect that it would be just in all the circumstances that he should be precluded from disclosing the information to others'.[75] The common law of confidentiality is based upon a presumption against disclosure to third parties.[76]

19.82   *W v Egdell*[77] concerned a doctor who disclosed a medical report commissioned from him by solicitors acting for a patient who was held in a secure hospital having killed a number of people. The patient applied to a tribunal with the eventual purpose of being discharged from detention. The doctor considered that the patient still posed a danger and although he stated this in his report, the solicitors decided not to disclose it. The doctor was so concerned about the potential risk that he gave a copy of the report to the hospital, which then copied it to the tribunal. The patient sued the doctor for breach of confidence.

19.83   In his judgment, Bingham LJ accepted that the doctor owed a duty of confidence:

> He could not lawfully sell the contents of his report to a newspaper. Nor could he, without a breach of the law as well as professional etiquette, discuss the case in a learned article, or in his memoirs, or in gossiping with friends, unless he took the appropriate steps to conceal the identity of W.

19.84   However, the Court of Appeal concluded that the 'public interest' justified Dr Egdell's limited disclosure – his limited breach of the obligation of confidentiality.

19.85   In *Woolgar v Chief Constable of Sussex Police and the UKCC*[78] the Court of Appeal considered the extent of the 'public interest' defence and concluded that the disclosure of confidential information to a regulatory body (the UK Central Council for Nursing, Midwifery and Health Visiting) to assist it in its investigation of a matter which might affect the safety of patients, was sufficiently serious as to justify this action. The court came to a similar conclusion in *Brent LBC v SK and HK*[79] where it was held that an authority was entitled to disclose to another local authority confidential information about a care worker's assault on one of her children as there was a real risk of harm to vulnerable adults if this information was not disclosed. Likewise, in *Maddock v Devon CC*[80] which concerned the disclosure of confidential information from the applicant's social services file to a university at which the applicant had obtained a place to study to become a social worker: the essence of the information being that she was potentially unsuited to that role.

---

75 *Attorney-General v Guardian Newspapers* [1988] 3 WLR 776, HL, per Lord Goff.
76 *R v Mid Glamorgan FHSA ex p Martin* [1995] 1 WLR 110.
77 [1990] 2 WLR 471, CA.
78 [2000] 1 WLR 25, CA and see also *R v Chief Constable of North Wales ex p AB* [1997] 3 WLR 724, (2000) 3 CCLR 25.
79 [2007] EWHC 1250 (Fam).
80 [2004] EWHC 3494 (QB).

Human Rights Act 1998

19.86 In *A Health Authority v X*[81] the court had to determine whether it was permissible to order the disclosure of personal health records held by a GP practice to a health authority (investigating various alleged irregularities in the way the practice had been run). The court held that since the proposed disclosure of the records did amount to an interference with that patient's rights under ECHR Article 8, it could only be justified where:

1) the authority reasonably required them for its regulatory or administrative functions;
2) there was a compelling public interest in their disclosure; and
3) there was in place effective and adequate safeguards against abuse including safeguards of the particular patient's confidentiality and anonymity.

19.87 The demands of Article 8 were again considered in *H and L v A City Council and B City Council*[82] where a service user challenged a local authority decision to disclose information about him (including that he had been convicted of the indecent assault of a child) to a number of disabled people's organisations in which he had a role, and to his personal care assistants. The court undertook a proportionality review[83] and adopted the applicant's argument that there had to be a 'pressing need' for disclosure. In this case the local authority argued that this was a 'pressing need to protect children' – but the evidence was that the service user was not coming into contact with children and so this factor could not justify disclosure. The court also considered that in most cases, the local authority would only be acting proportionately if, before making its decision (as to disclosure), it had given the person an opportunity to comment on what it was proposing to do.

19.88   HRA 1998 s6 requires public authorities to act in conformity with ECHR rights, including Article 8, which protects privacy. In a number of cases, the European Court of Human Rights has confirmed that Article 8 is concerned both with the duty on the state to protect individuals from the unreasonable disclosure of publicly held confidential information[84] as well as with the right of individuals to access such information.

19.89   In *Gaskin v UK*[85] the applicant sought access to his social services records. The request was refused in part on the ground that some of the information had originally been given in confidence and certain of the informants had not consented to their material being disclosed. The information was important to Mr Gaskin as he had spent almost all his life in care and he wanted it in order to understand his early childhood: essentially for his own sense of identity. His was a legitimate claim, as indeed was the refusal to divulge the information, which had been given

---

81 [2001] 2 FLR 673; upheld on appeal [2001] EWCA Civ 2014, [2002] 2 All ER 780, [2002] 1 FLR 1045.
82 [2011] EWCA Civ 403.
83 Relying heavily upon the approach adopted in *R (L) v Commissioner of Police of the Metropolis* [2009] UKSC 3, [2010] 1 AC 410, [2009] 3 WLR 1056.
84 See eg *Z v Finland* (1997) 25 EHRR 371; and *MS v Sweden* (1997) 3 BHRC 248.
85 (1989) 12 EHRR 36. See also *MG v UK* (2003) 36 EHRR 3, (2002) 5 CCLR 525.

to the local authority in confidence. The court concluded that Article 8 required a balancing of the conflicting interests in such a situation; and that this required an independent adjudication system to decide whether the papers should be disclosed. As no such system existed, it found a violation of Article 8.

19.90   In 2012, the European Court of Human Rights in *MM V UK*[86] found a violation of the applicant's right to privacy under Article 8. The case concerned the law in Northern Ireland and the court held that a criminal-record check to a prospective employer contained inappropriately extensive disclosure. In the court's opinion the relevant law lacked the necessary safeguards – including (for example) the ability to distinguish between the seriousness or circumstances of the offence, the time which had elapsed since its commission and the continuing risk posed by the individual.

19.91   In subsequent (2014) conjoined proceedings, the Supreme Court[87] held that there was no requirement that 'spent' cautions be disclosed.[88] In broad terms, the Police Act (PA) 1997 provided for enhanced criminal record certificates where a person sought employment working with children and vulnerable adults. This required that every 'relevant matter' recorded on the Police National Computer, including any otherwise spent conviction or caution, was to be disclosed to a prospective employer.

19.92   The Supreme Court cases concerned police cautions/warnings issued for minor offences of dishonesty which were then disclosed many years later when the relevant parties applied for work which might involve contact with children or vulnerable adults. The Supreme Court held that the disclosures violated Article 8 and made declarations that the relevant provisions of the PA 1997 were incompatible with that Article.

19.93   The Protection of Freedoms Act 2012 seeks to address the shortcomings in the PA 1997. It created the Disclosure and Barring Service (DBS)[89] which amalgamated the functions of the Criminal Records Bureau and the Independent Safeguarding Authority. The Act and associated regulations[90] make provision for the DBS to 'filter' old and minor cautions and convictions so that they are no longer disclosed on criminal record checks. However, all cautions and convictions for specified offences of relevance for posts concerned with safeguarding children and vulnerable adults will remain subject to disclosure. Convictions that resulted in a custodial sentence (whether or not suspended) will remain subject to disclosure, as will all convictions where more than one conviction is recorded.

19.94   The broad effect of these changes is to prevent the wholesale disclosure of a person's criminal record to an employer without attempting, albeit in a fairly mechanistic way, to find a balance between, on the one hand, the

---

86   *MM v UK* 24029/07, judgment 13.11.2012.

87   *R (T and another) v. Secretary of State for the Home Department and another* [2014] UKSC 35.

88   It also applies to reprimands and warnings, which are spent as soon as they are given (see para 76 of the judgment). The relevant law at that time was the Rehabilitation of Offenders Act 1974 (Exceptions) Order 1975 SI No 1023 and Police Act 1974 ss113A and 113B, Part V.

89   For more information about the DBS see para 18.51 above.

90   Rehabilitation of Offenders Act 1974 (Exceptions) Order 1975 (Amendment) (England and Wales) Order 2013 SI No 1198.

need to disclose information for the protection of others without, on the other hand, infringing the person's right to privacy under Article 8. Where a person is to be barred from working with children and/or vulnerable adults, the arrangements provided for by the DBS require (other than for the most serious offences) that a person must be given the opportunity to make representations before any final decision is made.

19.95   The subject of disclosure of information, including criminal records, in the context of safeguarding, is too wide for this book. However, it is noted that the broad principles set out by the courts above in the context of human rights law are mirrored by the considerations in the DPA 1998 as well as under the common law. The issues which were under scrutiny in the Strasbourg and Supreme Court cases, when considered in the context of the DPA 1998, would arguably produce a similar result, ie that the wholesale disclosure of a person's criminal record to a third party (the prospective employer) would not be lawful. The issues are summarised as follows:

- The information was not being disclosed fairly, ie there was no consideration of the seriousness or the circumstances of the offence.
- There was no review of the time which had elapsed since the commission of the offence and whether the caution was spent. In the language of the DPA 1998, the information must only be retained for as long as necessary and any subsequent disclosure should recognise the need to consider the effect of the passage of time.[91]
- There was no assessment at any stage in the disclosure process of the relevance the caution to the employment sought or of the extent to which the person could be perceived as continuing to pose a risk. In other words, there was no consideration of the purpose of the disclosure and whether any potential disclosure of personal data (ie criminal records) was in fact being made in accordance with the law (ie the 'public interest' defence in common law terms).

---

91 For further information about data retention, see the decision of the Supreme Court in *Catt and R (T) v Commissioner of the Police of the Metropolis* [2015] UKSC 9.

CHAPTER 20

Remedies

continued

Introduction

20.1   There is no straightforward judicial appeal route for resolving a social care dispute, where informal negotiation has failed. This contrasts with some other areas of social welfare law where there is access to the tribunal system where both the merits and the legality of a decision can be tested.

20.2   There are currently six procedures for challenging community care decisions. These are:

1) a complaint via the local authority or National Health Service (NHS) complaints procedures;
2) a complaint via the relevant ombudsman;
3) an application to the High Court for judicial review;

and, less commonly:

4) a complaint to the local authority monitoring officer;
5) an application to the Secretary of State for Health or the Welsh Assembly to use their default powers;
6) an ordinary court application under Human Rights Act (HRA) 1998 s7.

20.3   Stand-alone human rights claims are rare in the social care context (see para 2.64 above): most judicial involvement is through public law claims made by way of judicial review. These are considered in detail below, but in essence an application for judicial review is appropriate where the challenge is to the legality of the public authority's action or inaction, and where there is a current issue to be resolved. It is not a forum for considering the factual merits of a case, or for apportioning blame for past actions. An application for judicial review must usually be made after any alternative remedies have been exhausted, and generally it must also be brought within at most three months of the decision under review. This creates a potential catch-22 situation, in that consideration always needs to be given to using the statutory complaints procedure, but there will not usually be time to complete the process prior to issuing judicial review proceedings (see para 20.159 for a more detailed analysis).

20.4   The complaints procedure will generally be the first port of call for anyone who is dissatisfied with his or her treatment at the hands of the NHS or a local authority. If this fails to resolve the problem, then it may be possible to make a complaint to the appropriate ombudsmen or to make an application for judicial review. These are mutually exclusive remedies: the legislation establishing the ombudsmen schemes precludes an investigation of a complaint that is subject to legal proceedings (see para 20.107).

20.5   If the issue complained about has been resolved, but the person concerned feels that he or she has suffered as a result of the conduct of the public body and wants (a) to try to ensure that no one else has to undergo a similar experience, and/or (b) some sort of recompense to be made, then the appropriate ombudsmen schemes are likely to be the most appropriate route. If, on the other hand, there is a current issue, which is underpinned by a disagreement about whether or not the public body is acting lawfully, then judicial review may be the appropriate remedy. For instance, a complainant may argue that the local authority has made an unlawful decision about his or her personal budget because they have applied a local policy which is at odds with the legal requirements under the Care Act (CA) 2014. Judicial review would provide a legal resolution determining the lawfulness of the particular policy and could quash the particular personal budget decision.

20.6   This chapter describes the first four remedies outlined above, and considers aspects that may influence which remedy is chosen, including the important issue of funding.

Local authority and NHS complaints in England

Background

20.7   The Health and Social Care (Community Health and Standards) Act (HSC(CHS)A) 2003 authorises the secretary of state in England to make regulations concerning the handling of NHS[1] and adult social services complaints.[2]

20.8   Until 2009, the NHS and the local authorities had separate complaints procedures, involving various stages with rigid time limits for those stages.[3] However, research commissioned by the Department of Health in 2005 found that the complaints processes for both health and social care were not easy to understand.[4] In brief, the complaints processes were seen as:

- too prescriptive and inflexible, not meeting the needs of the person making the complaint;
- fragmented, with different procedures to follow depending on what the problem is and with whom; and
- lacking the proper emphasis on resolving problems locally, quickly and effectively.[5]

The 2009 complaints process

20.9   As a consequence of these concerns, in 2009 a common approach to handling NHS complaints and complaints about adult social care was introduced by way of regulations: the Local Authority Social Services and National Health Service Complaints (England) Regulations 2009 SI No 309[6] (referred to in this chapter as the '2009 complaints regulations'). In

---

1   HSC(CHS)A 2003 s114.
2   HSC(CHS)A 2003 s113.
3   The relevant regulations for local authority and NHS complaints were: Local Authority Social Services Complaints (England) Regulations 2006 SI No 1681 and National Health Service (Complaints) Regulations 2004 SI No 1768, as amended by the National Health Service (Complaints) Amendment Regulations 2006 SI No 2084.
4   Department of Health, *Making experiences count: the proposed new arrangement for handling health and social care complaints, response to consultation*, 2008, p5.
5   Department of Health, *Making experiences count: the proposed new arrangement for handling health and social care complaints, response to consultation*, 2008, p5.
6   Amended by the Local Authority Social Services and National Health Service Complaints (England) (Amendment) Regulations 2009 SI No 1768, issued under HSC(CHS)A 2003 ss113 and 114.

2009 the Department of Health also issued best practice guidance on the scheme – *Listening, improving, responding: a guide to better customer care* (referred to as 'the guide' below) – together with a series of 'advice sheets' aimed at complaints professionals: *Advice sheet 1: investigating complaints*; *Advice sheet 2: joint working on complaints*; and *Advice sheet 3: dealing with serious complaints.*

20.10   The current system lacks the various stages and specific timescales that characterised the previous arrangements. Instead, it requires the 'responsible body'[7] to make arrangements for the handling and consideration of complaints[8]. These arrangements must be carried out in accordance with the 2009 complaints regulations, but these do not prescribe any particular process for doing so. The intention was to enable organisations to develop more flexible and responsive complaints handling systems, focussing on the specific needs of the complainant with the aim of seeking a speedy local resolution. How complaints must be handled and considered is further explored below.

20.11   The process is based on the six principles of good complaints handling, published by the parliamentary and health service ombudsman and endorsed by the local government ombudsman, namely:

- getting it right;
- being customer focused;
- being open and accountable;
- acting fairly and proportionately;
- putting things right;
- seeking continuous improvement.[9]

What can be complained about?

20.12   In relation to local authorities, complaints may be made about the exercise of their social care functions[10] (which include those under partnership arrangements made between the local authority and the NHS[11]). Complaints relate not only to the actions of the local authority – but also of their agents, for example, when the authority has made arrangements with another person or body (such as a care home or domiciliary care agency) to discharge its functions.[12]

20.13   In relation to the NHS, complaints may be made about the exercise of the functions of an NHS body[13] including those under partnership arrangements with the local authority.[14] The 2009 complaints regulations

---

7   Reg 2(3) states that the 'responsible body' means a local authority, NHS body, primary care provider or independent provider.
8   See 2009 complaints regulations reg 3(1).
9   Quoted in the Department of Health letter of 26 February 2009, introducing *Listening, improving, responding: a guide to better customer care.*
10 2009 complaints regulations reg 6(1)(a)(i).
11 See 2009 complaints regulations reg 6(1)(a)(ii); and see generally para 1.3 above.
12 2009 complaints regulations reg 6(1A), inserted by Local Authority Social Services and National Health Service Complaints (England) (Amendment) Regulations 2009 SI No 1768.
13 2009 complaints regulations reg 6(1)(b)(i).
14 2009 complaints regulations reg 6(1)(b)(ii).

also apply to complaints about the provision of services by primary care providers and independent providers, where those services have been commissioned by an NHS body.[15]

Who may complain?

20.14   There are two categories of persons who may make a complaint under the regulations. The first is a person who receives or who has received services from a responsible body (eg NHS patient or someone receiving social care services from the local authority).[16]

20.15   The second is described as someone 'who is affected, or likely to be affected, by the action, omission or decision of the responsible body which is the subject of the complaint'.[17] This latter category may therefore include, for example, carers or family of those receiving services from the NHS or the local authority, who would be able to make a complaint in their own right.

Representatives

20.16   However, representatives may also complain on behalf of a person in certain, specified circumstances. These include where the person:

- has died;
- is a child;
- is unable to make the complaint themselves because of a physical disability or a lack of capacity within the meaning of the Mental Capacity Act (MCA) 2005; or
- has appointed a representative to act on their behalf (this may or may not be a professional representative).

20.17   Where a representative makes a complaint on behalf of a child, the responsible body must not consider the complaint unless it is satisfied that there are reasonable grounds for the representative, rather than the child, making the complaint. If it is not satisfied, it must notify the representative in writing and state the reason(s) for its decision.[18] Such a situation might arise if, for example, the child is considered to have sufficient capacity to complain[19] and is not in agreement with the complaint being made.

20.18   Where the responsible body is satisfied that the representative is not conducting the complaint in the best interests of the child or of a person lacking capacity under the MCA 2005, they must cease consideration of the complaint. The representative must be notified by the responsible body in writing, with reason(s) for its decision.[20] There is no requirement in the regulations for the representative to be acting under a lasting power

---

15 2009 complaints regulations reg 6(1)(c) and (d).
16 2009 complaints regulations reg 5(1)(a).
17 2009 complaints regulations reg 5(1)(b).
18 2009 complaints regulations reg 5(3).
19 The capacity of people 16 and over to make decisions is considered at chapter 13 – however, this book does not consider the law concerning the capacity of people under that age. For a detailed analysis of this question see S Broach, L Clements and J Read, *Disabled children: a legal handbook*, 2nd edn, Legal Action Group, 2016, chapter 7.
20 2009 complaints regulations reg 5(4) and (5).

of attorney (LPA) or deputyship and there is, therefore, no legal basis for the respondent body imposing any such conditions.

20.19   Where the complainant or representative disagrees with the decision not to investigate, the remedy would lie by way of an ombudsman complaint, or conceivably a judicial review challenge to the rationality or legal basis of the decision. The NHS ombudsman has upheld a complaint[21] (under the previous complaints system), which concerned a NHS trust's refusal to respond to a complaint made by a friend of a patient with dementia. The trust had cited 'patient confidentiality'; 'the Data Protection Act'; and had agreed to 'take up the matters' with the patient's sister. The ombudsman held that:

> ... while patient confidentiality is a legitimate consideration when deciding whether a representative is a suitable complainant, the Trust did not adequately explain to Mr P why it should not respond to his complaints. Nor did it demonstrate that it had adequately considered the NHS Complaints Regulations or the relevant legislation in reaching its decision. We found no evidence that the Trust had established whether Mr T was capable of providing consent for the release of confidential information to Mr P, or considered if Mr T had given implied consent to release. There was no evidence that the Trust had considered whether there was any overriding public interest reason for disclosing information to Mr P, or if any aspects of his complaint could be responded to without releasing confidential information.

Reluctance to complain

20.20   An inquiry into the home care of older people by the Equality and Human Rights Commission[22] reported that almost a quarter of respondents said they would not have the confidence to complain. They cited a number of reasons, including: not wanting to upset care staff; unwillingness to make a fuss; fear of retribution including being put into residential care or losing their care; thinking complaining would not improve care, and previous negative experience of complaints. Some reported needing support to make a complaint.

20.21   Given these difficulties, authorities should be slow to question the good faith or 'standing' of a representative, particularly if the issue raised is one of importance.

Time limits for making a complaint

20.22   Complaints should usually be made within 12 months of the date of the incident which is the subject of a complaint or, alternatively, from the date the complainant first became aware of the matter which is the subject of the complaint.[23]

21 Parliamentary and Health Service Ombudsman, *Annual Report 2007–08* 2008, Complaint against Bedfordshire and Luton Mental Health and Social Care Partnership NHS Trust Case Study 15 p37.

22 Equality and Human Rights Commission, *Close to home: an inquiry into older people and human rights in home care*, 2011, pp82–83.

23 2009 complaints regulations reg 12(1)(a) and (b).

20.23   The 12-month time limit may be extended where the responsible body is satisfied that the complainant had good reasons for not making the complaint within the time limit,[24] provided it is still possible to investigate the complaint effectively and fairly. Where a decision is made not to investigate, the complainant has the opportunity to approach the relevant ombudsman.[25]

20.24   Although the current guidance is silent as to the circumstances which might justify an extension, similar provisions existed in the previous complaints regulations and the earlier guidance[26] addressed this question. It advised, for instance, that it might not be appropriate to apply the time limit where 'it would not be reasonable to expect the complainant to have made the complaint earlier and it would still be possible to consider the complaint in a way that would be effective and fair to those involved'. It gave as possible examples (among others) 'if a service user was particularly vulnerable and did not complain due to fear of reprisal' or 'where there is likely to be sufficient access to information or individuals involved at the time, to enable an effective and fair investigation to be carried out'.

Responsibility for the complaints arrangements

20.25   The local authority or NHS body must designate a 'responsible person', whose function is to ensure compliance with the 2009 complaints regulations and, in particular, that action is taken if necessary in the light of an outcome of a complaint.[27] This would involve, for example, ensuring that any training needs identified as being required during the investigation of the complaint would be provided, as well as ensuring that any undertakings given to the complainant are honoured.

20.26   The 2009 complaints regulations also specify who may be the 'responsible person', although their functions may be performed by any person authorised by the responsible body to act on their behalf.[28] In the case of a local authority or NHS body, the responsible person must be the chief executive officer. In other types of organisation, the responsible person must be, in broad terms, someone with decision-making powers within the organisation (eg chief executive, sole proprietor, partner, director).[29]

20.27   A 'complaints manager' must also be designated by the responsible body. His or her role is to be responsible for managing the procedures for handling and considering complaints, in accordance with the procedures made under the 2009 complaints regulations.[30]

---

24 2009 complaints regulations reg 12(2)(a).
25 Department of Health, *Making experiences count: the proposed new arrangement for handling health and social care complaints, response to consultation*, 2008, at pp13 and 14.
26 Department of Health, *Learning from complaints: social services complaints procedure for adults*, 2006, see paras 3.3.2–3.3.3.
27 2009 complaints regulations reg 4(1)(b).
28 2009 complaints regulations reg 4(2).
29 2009 complaints regulations reg 4(4).
30 2009 complaints regulations reg 4(1)(b).

20.28 The functions of the complaints manager may be performed by any person authorised by the responsible person to act on behalf of the complaints manager.[31]

20.29 The complaints manager may be the same person as the responsible person, which is perhaps more likely to be the case in smaller organisations. Alternatively, they may be someone who is not an employee of the organisation, which would allow for the appointment of an external organisation to deal with complaints. A designated complaints manager from another responsible body may also act as the complaints manager for that organisation.[32] The local government ombudsman has expressed the view that a complaints system of this type can only function properly if the manager is of sufficient seniority to ensure that complaints are addressed with adequate commitment[33] and has commented as follows:

> In my view the Council's procedures for dealing with complaints are seriously flawed. There seems to be no officer of sufficient seniority to run the complaints system and to ensure that complaints are dealt with, not only within the statutory times, but also with sufficient commitment.[34]

Complaints excluded under the 2009 complaints regulations

20.30 There are a number of exclusions from the regulations. Some are 'technical' in nature,[35] whereas others are more relevant to service users and their families. A complaint is excluded where it has been made orally and is resolved to the complainant's satisfaction no later than the next working day after it was made.[36] Complaints which have previously been investigated are also excluded[37] (ie repeat complaints raising the same issues).

20.31 Where a responsible body makes a decision that a complaint is excluded, it must 'as soon as reasonably practicable notify the complainant in writing of its decision and the reasons for its decision'.[38] However, this requirement does not apply if the reason for the exclusion falls under regulation 8(c) (an oral complaint resolved by the next working day.

20.32 The 2009 complaints regulations specify that where a complaint contains an element excluded for a reason listed in regulation 8, there is nothing to prevent the remainder of the complaint being investigated.[39]

20.33 The 2009 complaints regulations do not, unlike their predecessors, specifically exclude complaints, where the complainant has stated in writing that they intend to take legal proceedings. The Department of Health

31 2009 complaints regulations reg 4(3).
32 2009 complaints regulations reg 4(5).
33 Complaint no 92/A/3725 against Haringey LBC 1993.
34 Report no 94/C/2659 against Nottingham CC.
35 2009 complaints regulations reg 8(1) – eg a complaint made by a responsible body; a complaint by an NHS or local authority employee about any matter relating to their employment or where a responsible body has allegedly failed to disclose information under its Freedom of Information Act 2000 obligations.
36 2009 complaints regulations reg 8(1)(c).
37 2009 complaints regulations reg 8(1)(e).
38 2009 complaints regulations reg 8(2), inserted by Local Authority Social Services and National Health Service Complaints (England) Amendment Regulations 2009 SI No 1768.
39 2009 complaints regulations reg 8(3).

has advised[40] that in such cases (or where there is a police investigation) good practice requires that discussions take place with the relevant legal advisers to establish whether the progression of the complaint may prejudice any subsequent legal action. If so, the complaint may be put on hold – with the complainant being advised of this and given reasons for the decision. The Department of Health's view, however, is that:

> ... the default position in cases where the complainant has expressed an intention to take legal proceedings would be to seek to continue to resolve the complaint unless there are clear legal reasons not to do so.[41]

20.34   In a similar vein, there is no longer an exclusion relating to the investigation of complaints where disciplinary action is being considered or taken against a member of staff – provided the organisation has regard to good practice in respect of restrictions in supplying confidential/personal information to the complainant. However, although the complaints handling arrangements will operate alongside the disciplinary arrangements, the two arrangements will remain separate. Both of the above changes are justified on the basis that:

> In all cases, it will be important to ensure the potential implications for patient safety and/or organisational learning are investigated as quickly as possible, to allow urgent action to be taken to prevent similar incidents arising.[42]

20.35   Although direct payments and personal budgets do not form part of the complaints procedure, both would be covered by the 2009 complaints regulations where the complaint is about the process of allocating a direct payment or a personal budget, including the calculation of the amount. The Department of Health's explanation for the exclusion is that 'the authority hands over money to the service user, and so decisions made by the service user are outside the [complaints] procedure'.[43]

Complaints handling and consideration

20.36   The process established by the responsible body must ensure that:

- complaints are dealt with efficiently;
- complaints are properly investigated;
- complainants are treated with respect and courtesy;
- complainants receive, so far as is reasonably practical, assistance to enable them to understand the complaints procedure or advice on where they may obtain such assistance;
- complainants receive a timely and appropriate response;
- complainants are told the outcome of the investigation of their complaint; and

---

40 See Department of Health, *Clarification of the complaints regulations 2009*, 2010.
41 Department of Health, *Clarification of the complaints regulations 2009*, 2010.
42 Department of Health, *Clarification of the complaints regulations 2009*, 2010.
43 Department of Health, *Reform of the complaints system:* 2009, Letter to NHS Chief Executives and Directors of Adult Social Care, with Key Messages. Gateway reference: 11380: 25 February 2009.

- action is taken if necessary in the light of the outcome of the complaint.[44]

Publicity

20.37 In addition, the responsible body must make information available to the public about its arrangements for dealing with complaints and how further information about those arrangements may be obtained.[45]

The form of a complaint, and its acknowledgement

20.38 Although the 2009 complaints regulations do not prescribe how the complaints process itself must work, they set out in some detail the process to be followed by responsible bodies on receipt of a complaint. A person may make a complaint orally, in writing or electronically.[46] Where the complaint is made orally, the responsible body to which the complaint is made must make a written record of the complaint and send a copy of that written record to the complainant.[47] The usual timescale for the responsible body to acknowledge the complaint is within three working days after the day it received the complaint.[48] The acknowledgement of the complaint may be made orally or in writing.[49]

20.39 It is advisable to put a complaint in writing to avoid any subsequent dispute about the precise nature of the complaint. A template complaint letter can be found in appendix B below.

Complaints made to another body

20.40 Regulation 6 sets out the procedure to be followed where a person makes a complaint but inadvertently directs it to the wrong body, for example, the complaint is directed to a local authority but the substance relates to an NHS body or an independent provider.

20.41 In this situation, where it appears to the body (the first body) who receives the complaint that it relates to another responsible body (the second body), the first body sends the complaint to the second, and the complainant is deemed to have made the complaint to the second body.[50] It is then the responsibility of the second body to acknowledge the complaint within three working days after the date on which it receives the complaint from the first body.[51] The regulations do not require the consent of the complainant when the first body decides to send the complaint to the second body.

---

44 2009 complaints regulations reg 3(2).
45 2009 complaints regulations reg 16(a) and (b).
46 2009 complaints regulations reg 13(1).
47 2009 complaints regulations reg 13(2).
48 2009 complaints regulations reg 13(3).
49 2009 complaints regulations reg 13(6).
50 2009 complaints regulations reg 6(5) and (6).
51 2009 complaints regulations reg 13(4).

Duty to co-operate

20.42   In 2007, the local government ombudsman published a special report[52] on the problems caused by the lack of a unified system to enable joint investigations into complaints that straddle (amongst other bodies) health and social services. This difficulty of complainants having to make multiple complaints was recognised during the consultation process[53] and is addressed in the 2009 complaints regulations, which create a formal 'duty to co-operate'.[54] The duty applies where a responsible body is considering a complaint, which contains material relating to a second responsible body. Where the complaint would fall to be handled by that second body, had the complaint be made directly to that second body, there is a duty to co-operate imposed upon both the first and second responsible bodies.

20.43   The bodies must co-operate for the purposes of co-ordinating the handling of the complaint and ensuring that the complainant receives a co-ordinated response to the complaint. In particular, each responsible body must agree which of the two bodies should take the lead in co-ordinating the handling of the complaint and communicating with the complainant. They must also provide each other with information relevant to the consideration of the complaint, which is 'reasonably' requested by the other body and attend or ensure adequate representation at any meeting required in connection with the consideration of the complaint.[55]

Complaints involving other 'providers' or commissioners

20.44   The 2009 complaints regulations deal with the procedures to be adopted where the responsible body considers that a complaint (or part of it) concerns another local authority or health body or relates to services provided by a third party. In this respect, the regulations are detailed, requiring the responsible body to keep the complainant fully informed as to what it is doing (and providing for time limits).[56]

Investigation of complaints

20.45   When the responsible body acknowledges the complaint, it must give the complainant the opportunity to discuss how it is to be handled.[57] However, the 2009 complaints regulations are silent as to how complaints must be conducted, other than to state that the responsible body 'must investigate the complaint in a manner appropriate to resolve it speedily and

---

52 Local Government Ombudsman, *Special report: handling complaints about local partnerships*, 2007.
53 Department of Health, *Reform of health and social care complaints: proposed changes to the legislative framework*, 2008.
54 2009 complaints regulations reg 9.
55 2009 complaints regulations reg 9.
56 2009 complaints regulations regs 7, 11 and 13.
57 2009 complaints regulations reg 13(7).

efficiently'.[58] It also provides that the complainant must be kept informed, 'as far as reasonably practicable, as to the progress of the investigation'.[59]

20.46 The regulations, unlike the previous complaints system, do not provide for a rigid timetable. Instead, they allow for the complainant and the responsible body to discuss a 'response period' for the completion of the investigation and for the sending of a full response to the complaint. Where such a discussion does not take place, the responsible body is able to determine the response period itself and notify the complainant accordingly.[60]

20.47 The only prescribed time limit is for a maximum response period of six months from the date of the receipt of the complaint. Even then, time may be extended, with the agreement of the complainant and the responsible body, where the agreement to extend the response period is made before the expiry of the six-month period.[61] However, where the response period is not met, the responsible body must notify the complainant in writing as to the reasons why, and it must send a full response 'as soon as is reasonably practicable' after the expiry of the response period.[62] A failure to comply with the six-month time limit, without good reason and without following the notification requirements, could be taken up with the relevant ombudsman.

20.48 Once the investigation is concluded, the complainant must be sent a response 'as soon as is reasonably practicable', signed by the responsible person, which includes a report giving an explanation of how the complaint was investigated and its conclusions reached, including any matters where remedial action is needed. The response should also confirm whether such remedial action has been taken or is proposed to be taken and, further, advise the complainant of their right to take the matter to the relevant local government or health service ombudsman.[63]

20.49 The Department of Health's 2009 best practice guidance *Listening, responding, improving: a guide to better customer care* ('the guide') states that 'the new approach ends the bureaucracy of the old system' and that 'organisations will be encouraged to ask people what they think of their care, to sort out problems more effectively and to use the opportunities to learn'.[64]

20.50 As part of the process of the investigation, the guide makes it clear that the organisation should, when the complaint is first received, categorise the complaint, reviewing that category as the investigation proceeds. The seriousness of the complaint is to be assessed using a three-step process to gauge the impact of the complaint(s) on those involved, the potential risks to the organisation (including the risk of litigation and adverse publicity) and the response required. The guide cautions, 'It is also important to remember that a complaint can have a very different effect on an organisation compared with an individual', acknowledging that this is particularly

---

58 2009 complaints regulations reg 14(1)(a).
59 2009 complaints regulations reg 14(1)(b).
60 2009 complaints regulations reg 13(7) and (8).
61 2009 complaints regulations reg 14(3).
62 2009 complaints regulations reg 14(4).
63 2009 complaints regulations reg 14(2).
64 Department of Health, *Listening, responding, improving*, 2009, pp4–5.

important where the person is vulnerable for any reason.[65] In the context of health and social care, it is difficult to envisage a situation where a person using such services is not vulnerable for one reason or another.

20.51   The guide provides examples of different types of incidents,[66] categorising as 'low' what it describes as 'simple, non-complex issues', for example, an 'event resulting in minor harm (eg. cut, strain)' as well as issues such as a lack of cleanliness, lost property, transport problems or missing medical records. Examples in the 'moderate' category are an event 'resulting in moderate harm (eg fracture)', as well as incorrect treatment, delayed discharge and medical errors.[67] Such incidents are often of enormous importance to the individuals concerned: it is difficult to envisage how the likely assessment of the incident by the organisation is not going to be at odds with the view of the complainant. An example in the 'high' category is an event 'resulting in serious harm (eg damage to internal organs)'; and the 'extreme' category would include events 'resulting in serious harm or death'.

20.52   In 2009 the Department of Health also produced a series of 'advice sheets' (see para 20.9 above). The first one is called *Investigating complaints*. It makes it clear that most complaints will be considered by someone from the organisation involved, who should be appropriately trained and independent of the service which is the subject of the complaint. It also notes that, for serious complaints, it may be necessary to involve an independent investigator.[68]

20.53   The advice sheet advises that complaints investigators must be clear about what they are investigating, 'A key question to ask yourself before beginning any investigation is whether you will be able to reach any robust conclusions', citing as an example a scenario where the complaint is solely about something said in conversation where there is no record of it or any witnesses. In this situation, the advice sheet makes it clear that reaching a robust conclusion is unlikely and it suggests that mediation may be an appropriate, alternative route to resolving this complaint.[69] The guide recommends the use of mediation where there is a risk of a relationship or communication breaking down.[70]

20.54   The advice sheet also recommends that 'the key to a good investigation is a good plan',[71] giving three key questions to define the investigation, as follows:

- What happened?
- What should have happened?
- What are the differences between those two things?[72]

20.55   The advice sheet also makes it clear that the investigator will need to understand the background information to the complaint, both from the complainant and also from the organisation (eg legal or policy require-

---

65 Department of Health, *Listening, responding, improving*, 2009, pp16–17.
66 Department of Health, *Listening, responding, improving*, 2009, pp 18–19.
67 Department of Health, *Listening, responding, improving*, 2009.
68 Department of Health, *Advice sheet 1: investigating complaints*, 2009, *Advice* at p1.
69 Department of Health, *Advice sheet 1: investigating complaints*, 2009, *Advice* at p2.
70 See Department of Health, *Listening, responding, improving*, 2009, pp26–27.
71 Department of Health, *Advice sheet 1: investigating complaints*, 2009, p3.
72 Department of Health, *Listening, responding, improving*, 2009.

ments).[73] It also provides tips on obtaining evidence, including documentary evidence, interviews and, where appropriate, site inspections.[74]

The final response to the complaint

20.56 The advice sheet advises that both parties should have the chance to provide feedback, particularly to correct any factual inaccuracies before publication of the final response. It also notes that the 'purpose of the report is to record and explain the conclusions' reached by the complaint investigator and, further, that a good report is likely to be complete, relevant, logical, balanced and robust. It also makes it clear that a good report should not come as a surprise to anyone, recommending that it is a good idea to be open with both parties during the investigation.[75]

Remedies following a complaint

20.57 The guide recognises that complainants will seek a range of remedies following a complaint and advises that 'complaints can be resolved more effectively if [it] is clear from the outset what the person complaining expects as an outcome'.[76] Furthermore, the complainant has a right to a response which explains how their concerns have been resolved and what action has been taken.[77] A range of responses are of course possible and any remedy needs to be proportionate to the circumstances.

20.58 The guide quotes the advice of the local government ombudsman (at pp28–29):

> There are some simple principles you can follow when you want to put things right. Whenever possible: put someone in the position they would have been if the fault had not occurred, make the remedy appropriate and proportionate to the harm suffered, take specific action if it's needed, offer compensation if appropriate and always apologise if you are at fault. Also consider whether any practices, procedures or policies should be reviewed.

Compensation

20.59 One of the defects of many early local authority complaints procedures was their disinclination to award compensation. Historically, this stemmed from a belief that this was not permitted by law. However, as a result of pressure from the ombudsman,[78] the government legislated to put this point beyond doubt: Local Government Act (LGA) 2000 s92 provides that:

> (1) Where a relevant authority consider–
>   (a) that action taken by or on behalf of the authority in the exercise of their functions amounts to, or may amount to, maladministration, and

---

73 Department of Health, *Listening, responding, improving*, 2009.
74 Department of Health, *Advice sheet 1: investigating complaints*, 2009 at p4.
75 Department of Health, *Advice sheet 1: investigating complaints*, 2009 at p6.
76 Department of Health, *Listening, responding, improving*, 2009 at pp28–29.
77 Department of Health, *Listening, responding, improving*, 2009 at pp28–29.
78 *Annual report 1998/99*, p7.

(b) that a person has been, or may have been, adversely affected by that action,

the authority may, if they think appropriate, make a payment to, or provide some other benefit for, that person.

...

(3) In this section–

'action' includes failure to act,

'relevant authority' has the same meaning as in Part III of this Act.

20.60   The guide says almost nothing about financial recompense, simply referring to good practice guidance issued by the local government ombudsman (LGO) – *Guidance on good practice: remedies* – which was updated in 2014 (referred to in this section as 'the LGO remedies guidance').[79] The approach is broadly one of restorative justice; proportionate, appropriate and reasonable remedies. The restorative principle means that financial recompense will focus on quantifiable financial loss, for instance costs of care funded by the complainant where those costs should have been met by the local authority. The LGO will not, however, recommend payment to recover 'avoidable expenses'; these include legal fees unless there are exceptional circumstances, for instance a highly complex case. Even then the recommended fees would be limited to those which 'directly and necessarily flow from the fault identified' and are proportionate. See also para 20.120 below when the approach of the LGO to awards is further considered.

20.61   Financial redress may also be recommended to acknowledge distress, harm, risk or other unfair impact. This may include, for example, the time and trouble of bringing a complaint. The amount will depend on the circumstances of the case, but is described as a 'symbolic amount'.

20.62   The LGO guidance is useful in helping a complainant to clarify and evidence what remedies are feasible and what the complainant wants to achieve from a complaint.

Record keeping and reporting

20.63   The responsible body is required to maintain a record of each complaint received, including the subject matter and outcome of each complaint. In addition, where the responsible body agreed the response period (or any amended period) with the complainant, the monitored information will also include whether or not the report of the outcome of the investigation was sent within the required response time.[80]

20.64   In addition, the responsible body is required to produce an annual report, including the following information:

- the number of complaints received;
- the number of complaints which the responsible body decided were well founded;
- the number of complaints referred to the relevant ombudsman;
- a summary of the subject matter of complaints, including any matters of general importance arising out of those complaints, or the way in which the complaints were handled;

79 LGO, 2014.
80 2009 complaints regulations reg 17.

- a summary of any matters where action has been or is to be taken to improve services as a consequence of those complaints.[81]

Overlap with other local authority functions

20.65 In the context of local authorities, it is important to note that the Regulations relate to complaints about adult social care. They are therefore not applicable to complaints concerning education or housing (or indeed any other local authority function). Good administration requires, however, that any complaints process must incorporate the principles outlined in the LGO guidance on the operation of complaints procedures.[82]

20.66 A practical example of the consequences of these separate remedies can be seen in a 2009 complaint against the London Borough of Croydon, where the LGO's expressed concern about the need for separate complaints in a social services and a special educational needs (SEN) matter, commenting that 'the legislation does not provide a single route of appeal where a child's inseparable social care and educational needs have not been adequately assessed or met'.[83]

20.67 Not infrequently, it may be unclear whether a complaint relates to a housing or social services function: for instance, a dispute concerning adaptations funded via a disabled facilities grant – or the provision of a house identified as needed in a care plan. The LGO has considered a number of such cases. In a complaint against Kirklees Metropolitan Council[84] she concluded:

> There was confusion within the Council as to whether [the] complaint should be considered by the Housing or Social Services Department. From [the complainants'] point of view this was irrelevant, they simply wanted the complaint to be considered thoroughly and promptly. The Council should have been able to do that. Although officers say they made internal changes as a result of the complaint no remedy was offered to [the complainants] for the Council's acknowledged failings.

20.68 Likewise in a complaint against Sunderland City Council[85] she concluded:

> I consider that [the complainant's] complaint about the failure to rehouse his family should also have been dealt with under the Social Services Statutory Complaints Procedure as the application arose out of a stated need in a Care Plan. The failure to consider the complaint under the statutory procedure was maladministration. This has caused injustice as it denied [the

---

81 2009 complaints regulations reg 18(1).
82 LGO, *Good practice 1: devising a complaints system*, 1992; see also Complaint no 94/C/2959 against Nottingham CC, 28 November 1994; Complaint no 97/C/1614 against Bury MBC, 1999, where the ombudsman accepted that part of the complaint lay outside the statutory complaints process but nevertheless warranted investigation, and commented, 'it is hard to identify any aspect of the Council's handling of Mr Redfern's complaints which was in the proper manner or in full accordance with the statutory complaints procedure and/or the Council's own written complaints procedure'.
83 Complaint nos 07B 04696 and 07B 10996 against Croydon LBC, 16 September 2009.
84 Complaint no 01/C/00627 against Kirklees MC, 28 January 2003, para 68.
85 Complaint nos 00/C/12118 and 00/C/12621 against Sunderland CC, 21 August 2002, para 252.

complainant] the opportunity of having his complaints properly addresses at an earlier date.

Children procedures

20.69   For social care, there is a separate and distinct complaints procedure for children and young people, as required by the Representations Procedure (England) Regulations 2006 SI No 1738; and the accompanying statutory guidance issued by the Department for Education and Skills in 2006, *Getting the best from complaints: social care complaints and representations for children, young people and others.* These are not covered in this book – but see S Broach, L Clements and J Read *Disabled children: a legal handbook,* 2nd edn, Legal Action Group, 2016.

Independent and private sector providers

20.70   In England, although all health and adult social care providers must be registered with the Care Quality Commission (CQC) to ensure that they meet the 'fundamental standards',[86] the CQC as a regulatory body does not investigate complaints by individuals. The role of the CQC and the regulation of care provisions in general is considered further at chapter 17.

20.71   Under the 2009 complaints regulations anyone whose health or social care is arranged or funded by a local authority or by the NHS is entitled to make a complaint to the commissioning body, as well as utilising the provider's complaints procedures. Additionally, self-funders have the right to take their complaint to the LGO, if it has not been possible to resolve it directly with the provider (see para 20.91 below).

Patient advice and liaison service

20.72   *The NHS Plan: a plan for investment, a plan for reform,* published in 2000, announced the commitment to establish a patient advice and liaison service (PALS) in every English NHS trust by 2002.[87] PALS are a non-statutory advice service that:

> ... do not replace existing specialist advocacy services, such as mental health and learning disability advocacy. Rather, they are complementary to existing services. Providing information and on the spot help for patients, their families and carers, they are powerful lever for change and improvement.[88]

20.73   PALS are regulated by a Department of Health standards and evaluation framework[89] and their core functions include:

- being accessible to patients, their carers, friends and families;
- providing on-the-spot help in every trust with the power to negotiate immediate solutions or speedy resolutions of problems. PALS will listen and provide the relevant information and support to help resolve service users' concerns quickly and efficiently. It will liaise with staff

---

86 See paras 7.102 and 9.20.
87 Department of Health, *The NHS Plan,* 2000, Cm 4818-I, para 10.17.
88 See www.gov.uk/government/organisations/department-of-health.
89 Department of Health, *PALS core national standards and evaluation framework,* 2003.

and managers, and, where appropriate, with other PALS services, health and related organisations, to facilitate a resolution;

• acting as a gateway to appropriate independent advice and advocacy services, including the independent complaints advocacy services;

• providing accurate information to patients, carers and families.

Patient and public involvement and independent advocacy

20.74 The Local Government and Public Involvement in Health Act (LGPIHA) 2007 required local authorities to make arrangements to promote patient and public involvement in health and social care[90] and to do so by way of contracting with local Healthwatch bodies,[91] whose role is to act as a voice of local people.

20.75 The LGPIHA 2007, as amended, also requires local authorities to arrange a separate independent advocacy service for a range of health and/ or social care complaints, including complaints to the health service or local government ombudsmen.[92] These are provided by third sector organisations commissioned by local authorities. In some areas they are still known as ICAS (Independent Complaints Advocacy Service), although that earlier advocacy provision was officially replaced from April 2013 by the NHS Complaints Advocacy Service.

Challenging discharge and continuing care decisions

20.76 The procedures for challenging hospital discharge and NHS continuing healthcare decisions are considered separately in chapters 5 and 12 above.

The need for reform of complaints

Background

20.77 The focus of this chapter has been on complaint mechanisms for those in need of care and support and their carers. There are other statutory complaints procedures which are not covered here – for instance, complaints about public health functions, which are contained in Part 5 of the NHS Bodies and Local Authorities (Partnership Arrangements, Care Trusts, Public Health and Local Healthwatch) Regulations SI No 3094. The complexity and inaccessibility of differing procedures has been one of the many criticisms made of current arrangements.

20.78 Arrangements for handling complaints, especially but not exclusively in the NHS, have come in for attack from a number of sources. The Health Select Committee reported on complaints in 2011 saying:

---

90 LGPIHA 2007 s221, as amended by the Health and Social Care Act 2012.
91 LGPIHA 2007 s222.
92 LGPIHA 2007 s223.

There are unwarranted variations in how the complaints system works across England, some elements of the system are ineffective, and the cultures that exist often do not support effective resolution and redress.[93]

20.79   The recommended government review of the NHS complaints system was overtaken by scandalous treatment of patients at the Mid Staffordshire NHS Foundation Trust, which sparked a flurry of inquiries and reports, some of which focused specifically on complaints handling. Following his public inquiry into events in Mid Staffordshire, Robert Francis QC published his final report in February 2013. Several of his recommendations addressed complaints handling, and as a result the government commissioned Ann Clwyd MP and Professor Tricia Hart to review the operation of the complaints system in hospital trusts. Their core recommendations included improvements in the way complaints are handled and greater perceived and actual independence in the complaints process.[94]

20.80   In 2015 the Health Select Committee stressed the need for better co-ordinated complaints handling in both the NHS and social care, including that:

> People should not be forced to search out the most appropriate way to raise concerns. We recommend that the complaints system be simplified and streamlined by establishing a single 'branded' complaints gateway across all NHS providers ...

> On the evidence we have heard there is a strong case for working towards the integration of social care complaints into a single complaints system. As a first step we consider there should be a single health and social care ombudsman.[95]

Proposals under the Care Act 2014

20.81   The Law Commission, in its initial scoping report on adult social care reform in 2008,[96] proposed that their review should consider the 'efficacy of the legal structures in place for complaining about, and seeking redress for failures in decision-making and service provision by local authorities'. This was to have included the possibility of introducing a tribunal to provide an independent review of the merits of local authority decision making. The proposal was not pursued as the government took the view that it fell outside the remit of the Law Commission's work.

20.82   However, throughout the Law Commission's consultation and during the parliamentary process of the Care Bill, there was support for an independent appeal procedure. This call was reiterated by the Joint Committee reporting on the draft bill, which recommended setting up a care and support tribunal to provide independent merits reviews of local authority

---

93 Health Committee, Sixth Report of Session 2010–12, *Complaints and litigation*, HC 786-I, para 4.

94 Clwyd and Hart, *A review of the NHS hospital complaints system: putting patients back in the picture*, Department of Health, October 2013.

95 Health Committee, *Second Report of Session 2014–2015, Complaints and Raising Concerns*, HC 350, pp37–38. In its report the Committee welcomed 2014 guidance ('My expectations – for raising concerns and complaints') published by the NHS Ombudsman, the LGO and Healthwatch England as 'an important first step towards an over- arching, single access-point complaints system'.

96 Law Commission, *Scoping report*, November 2008, para 4.348.

decisions and to resolve NHS continuing healthcare disputes.[97] As a result, section 72 of the CA 2014 was added as a government amendment, providing a regulation making power to introduce an appeals system.

20.83   In 2015, a preliminary consultation on structure and functions of the new system was issued by the Department of Health,[98] which was far removed from the effective independent appeal structure the Law Commission and Joint Committee had in mind. In broad terms it set out a three-stage process:

1) Early resolution – to try to resolve the appeal internally and early.
2) The independent review stage – a review by a local authority appointed independent reviewer.
3) The local authority decision – where a senior local authority officer decides whether or not to implement the recommendations of the independent reviewer.

20.84   The proposed system would have given the local authority the power to decide if an expression of dissatisfaction was a complaint (referred to as an 'appeal')[99] and the system would have been limited to nine narrowly defined CA 2014 functions. For example, the only area of appeal in relation to the carrying out of an assessment would have been 'the local authority's decision as to the format of the needs or carers assessment e.g. should it be face-to-face compared with a phone assessment'.[100] Extraordinarily, the substance of an assessment – for instance, the failure to consider a material fact – could not have been the subject of a complaint.

20.85   In June 2015[101] the government announced that it has decided to defer the introduction of the new appeals system 'to enable it to be considered as part of the wider Spending Review that will launch shortly'. At the time of writing (January 2017) no further proposals for the reform of the complaints process have been published.

The ombudsman process

20.86   There are a number of different ombudsmen in England whose task is to investigate complaints made against a range of government organisations. The role of each of the following ombudsmen is considered separately below:

- local government ombudsman (LGO);
- parliamentary and health services ombudsman (PHSO);
- housing ombudsman service (HOS).

---

97 Joint Committee on the draft Care and Support Bill, *Report*, Session 2012–2013, HL Paper 143 HC 222, paras 257–264.

98 *Care Act 2014: Consultation on draft regulations and guidance to implement the cap on care costs and policy proposals for a new appeals system for care and support*, Department of Health, February 2015.

99 'A written notification should be sent from the local authority to a person expressing dissatisfaction within 3 working days notifying them if their dissatisfaction is an appeal' – see Consultation, para 16.24.

100 Consultation, para 15.17.

101 Written Statement of 17 July 2015 the Parliamentary Under Secretary of State, Department of Health, Lord Prior of Brampton.

Local government ombudsman

Introduction

20.87   The powers of the Commissioners for Local Administration in England and Wales (generally known as the LGO) are defined by the Local Government Act (LGA) 1974 as amended by the LGPIHA 2007. The LGO may investigate complaints of maladministration or service failure causing injustice, once the local authority or provider has been given an opportunity to respond to the initial complaint. These concepts are considered further below.

20.88   The LGO website[102] is a useful starting point for would be complainants. It contains an electronic complaint form, advice on complaining, previous decisions and reports, publications and guidance. The LGO publishes helpful factsheets on a range of different types of social care complaints, available on its website.[103] Copies of all the LGO investigation reports in England published since 2006 and of all decisions since 2013 are also available from the LGO website.

20.89   In a commendable spirit of transparency, the LGO website also provides access to internal policy and staff guidance.[104] The internal guidance is in the form of a set of three useful manuals, describing the approach to each stage of the investigation:

> **Intake** – our front-line support to accessing our service, handling all new enquiries and re-submitted complaints.
> **Assessment** – making early decisions on complaints that: can be resolved quickly, warrant further detailed investigation or are out of our jurisdiction.
> **Investigation** – making decisions on complaints referred from assessment and identifying learning from cases of public interest.

20.90   The latest published adult social care complaints review (2015/2016)[105] shows a continuation of the steady rise in complaints to the LGO in this area – 2,969 received during the period of the report, an increase of 6 per cent on the previous year. The highest incidence of complaints concerned assessment and care planning, with 70 per cent of those complaints upheld. The Ombudsman's approach is proactive:

> We know there are significant funding and organisational pressures on the care sector and councils. However, these pressures do not excuse poor practice and we operate a zero tolerance approach to what, in isolation, may appear to be 'small' issues. Respect for individual preferences around food and drink, what to wear and when to get up and go to bed are important to any individual and become emphasised when a person is not able to do these things independently. We are clear that care and support should maintain the dignity of the person being supported at all times.[106]

---

102 See www.lgo.org.uk.
103 See www.lgo.org.uk/make-a-complaint/fact-sheets/social-care/.
104 www.lgo.org.uk/information-centre/staff-guidance /.
105 Review of Adult Social Care Complaints, 2015/2016, published November 2016: www.lgo.org.uk/information-centre/reports/annual-review-reports/adult-social-care-reviews/.
106 Review, page 5.

Scope of complaints considered

20.91   The LGO considers complaints about local authority services, those commissioned by local authorities, and privately funded providers. Self-funders
and their families had, until October 2010, experienced difficulties in making complaints about their care providers as they could rarely make use of
either the local authority complaints procedure or the LGO. The role of the
LGO was extended in 2010, to provide an independent complaints review
service for people who arrange and fund their own adult social care.[107]
This includes both those who are paying privately and those whose care is
funded by means of personal budgets.

20.92   This extension of the LGO jurisdiction is growing. The Ombudsman
reported an increase in 2015/16 by 21 per cent on the previous year to 386
individual complaints. For instance the LGO identifies common faults in
the provision of domiciliary care, including:

- failure to provide a service, including being late, not staying long
  enough or cancelling visits;
- receiving care from too many different care workers;
- inaccurate invoicing and record keeping; and
- poor communication between the home care provider and the commissioning council.

Who can complain?

20.93   Any member of the public who has suffered injustice can complain, or a
person authorised by him or her in writing. Where authorisation is not
possible, a personal representative or anyone the LGO considers suitable
can bring the complaint.

20.94   Complainants may come from a wide range of aggrieved parties – for
example, in 2013 a company providing care had its complaint upheld. It
had continued to provide services, but had not received payment for several clients because of the failure by the local authority to assess needs in a
timely and adequate way and to provide direct payments. The LGO recommended back payments of direct payments to the nine affected individuals and £10,000 to the company for its time and trouble in bringing the
complaint.[108]

Definition of maladministration

20.95   The LGO cannot question whether a decision is right or wrong simply
because he disagrees with it. He must consider whether there was fault in
the way the decision was reached. [109] The meaning of maladministration[110]
has been considered by the Court of Appeal. In *R v Commissioner for Local
Administration ex p Eastleigh BC*[111] Lord Donaldson MR commented:

---

107 LGA 1974, Part III A, inserted by Health Act 2009 s35.
108 Complaint no 08 017 525 against Birmingham City Council, 13 March 2013.
109 LGA 1974 s34(3).
110 LGA 1974 s26(1)(a).
111 [1988] 3 WLR 113, CA.

Maladministration is not defined in the 1974 Act, but its meaning was considered in *R v Local Comr for Administration for the North and East Area of England, ex p Bradford MCC* [1979] 2 All ER 881. All three judges (Lord Denning MR, Eveleigh LJ and Sir David Cairns) expressed themselves differently, but in substance each was saying the same thing, namely that administration and maladministration, in the context of a local authority, is concerned with the manner in which decisions by the authority are reached and the manner in which they are or are not implemented.

20.96   The HSO in his annual report for 1993/94 commented on the nature of maladministration in the following terms (para 1.4):

The terms given by Mr Richard Crossman in 1966 were 'bias, neglect, inattention, delay, incompetence, ineptitude, perversity, turpitude, arbitrariness and so on'. I have added:

- rudeness (though that is a matter of degree);
- unwillingness to treat the complainant as a person with rights; refusal to answer reasonable questions;
- neglecting to inform a complainant on request of his or her rights or entitlement;
- knowingly giving advice which is misleading or inadequate;
- ignoring valid advice or overruling considerations which would produce an uncomfortable result for the overruler;
- offering no redress or manifestly disproportionate redress;
- showing bias whether because of colour, sex or any other grounds;
- omission to notify those who thereby lose a right of appeal;
- refusal to inform adequately of the right of appeal;
- faulty procedures; failure by management to monitor compliance with adequate procedures;
- cavalier disregard of guidance which is intended to be followed in the interest of equitable treatment of those who use the service;
- partiality; and
- failure to mitigate the effects of rigid adherence to the letter of the law where that produces manifestly inequitable treatment.

Definition of service failure

20.97   The LGO can investigate 'an alleged or apparent failure in a service which it was the authority's function to provide'[112] and also 'an alleged or apparent failure to provide such a service'.[113]

20.98   In most cases, the failure of a service provided by the authority or the failure to provide a service at all will also lead to a finding of maladministration against the authority. However, this is not always the case and, in some circumstances, maladministration will not be found or it is not necessary to invest resources in finding maladministration because the outcome of the investigation has provided an appropriate remedy to resolve the complaint.

112 LGA 1974 s26(1)(a).
113 LGA 1974 s26(1)(b).

Injustice

20.99 In order for the LGO to investigate a complaint, there must be some injustice caused to the complainant.[114] In other words, an authority may be responsible for potentially appalling maladministration or service failure but, in the absence of it causing injustice, the LGO is unable to investigate the issue.

20.100 There is no statutory definition of 'injustice', but the LGO appears to be requiring that it is progressively more serious. Whereas hurt feelings, distress, worry or inconvenience were previously considered sufficient, the LGO's 2016 guidance *Assessment code*[115] refers to the complainant having 'suffered serious loss, harm, or distress as a direct result of faults or failures by the service provider' or that there has been 'continuous and ongoing instances of a lower level injustice that remain unresolved over a long period of time'. In the exercise of her discretion the LGO is unlikely to pursue an investigation unless the initial complaint sets out allegations both of maladministration or service failure and records the injustice suffered.

LGO procedures

20.101 Complaints must in general be made in writing to the LGO within 12 months from the date on which the person aggrieved first had notice of the matters alleged in the complaint, although the LGO has an overall discretion to extend time if it is considered reasonable to do so (LGA 1974 s26B). The internal guidance on jurisdiction advises:

> In *R v Local Commissioner for Administration ex p Bradford Metropolitan City Council* (1979) QB 287 in the Court of Appeal, Lord Denning said: 'time bars are not to be enforced rigidly against a complainant where justice requires that the time be extended and his complaint heard'.
>
> It may not have been reasonable for the complainant to have come to us within 12 months if s/he:
> - was ill or through some other incapacity was unable to act in time;
> - was taking the complaint through the body's complaints procedure;
> - believed that action was being taken on the complaint by the council or its contractors;
> - believed a solicitor or other adviser was taking up the complaint on his/her behalf;
> - has not at any time allowed the matter to rest for more than a few months.
>
> The above is not an exhaustive list ... It may also be relevant to consider whether there might be a wider injustice caused if we do not investigate.

20.102 The LGO cannot investigate a complaint unless it has first been drawn to the attention of the local authority in question, and that authority has been afforded an opportunity to investigate and reply to the complaint (LGA 1974 s26(5)(a)). In general, the LGO requires complainants to use the authority's complaints procedures before being prepared to investigate the matter.

---

114 LGA 1974 s26A.
115 Available at www.lgo.org.uk/information-centre/staff-guidance/assessment-code#injustice.

20.103   By virtue of LGA 1974 s26(5)(b) where the LGO is satisfied that 'in the particular circumstances' it is not reasonable to expect the matter to be brought to the notice of the authority or, alternatively, for the authority to be allowed the opportunity to investigate the matter, the matter may be investigated by the LGO without the complaint having traversed the local authority's entire complaints process.

20.104   Again, the LGO internal guidance on jurisdiction sets out some parameters. Although the LGO's starting point is that there is a rebuttable presumption against investigating late complaints, he advises that discretion may be exercised where the local authority or service provider has been notified of a complaint but failed to respond within a reasonable time; refused to consider the complaint or progress it to the next stage in its procedure; where the substance of the complaint has already been the subject of a independent appeal or review procedure and nothing would be gained by undergoing the complaints procedure, or where a viable complaint has been received which may merit joint working and one but not both complaints procedures have been exhausted.

20.105   The LGO has also stated in the past that that investigations will be undertaken before the statutory complaints process has been exhausted 'where there has been a breakdown of trust between the complainant and the authority, or where both sides agree that there is no point in completing a process which is unlikely to satisfy the complainant'.[116] Although not specifically referred to in the current guidance, this still appears to be a relevant ground for the exercise of the LGO's discretion in suitable cases.

20.106   The LGO helpline can advise on difficult cases. For instance, if there is a strong arguable case of maladministration, which has led, say, to the loss of a critical service, and a complaint has been lodged but the local authority in question will not consider reinstating the service pending their investigation, the LGO has indicated willingness to intervene in order to try and procure the continuation of the service during the local authority investigation.

The availability of an alternative remedy

20.107   Unless the LGO is satisfied that, in the particular circumstances, it is not reasonable to expect the aggrieved person to resort to such a remedy, complaints cannot be entertained where there is an alternative remedy, for instance a right of appeal to a tribunal or to a minister of the Crown or a remedy by way of court proceedings.[117]

20.108   The LGO's internal guidance on jurisdiction includes extensive advice on alternative remedies. The issue is less acute in adult social care cases than in other areas of the LGO's jurisdiction, because the absence of any statutory appeals procedure means that generally the only alternative remedy is judicial review. In this respect the Ombudsman refers to the judgment of Lord Justice Henry in *R v Commission for Local Administration ex p Liverpool City Council*.[118] He goes on to provide a list of relevant factors to

---

116   J White, 'Community care and the local government ombudsman for England' (2006) 9 CCLR 8.
117   LGA 1974 s26(6).
118   [2000] All ER (D) 235.

be considered in the exercise of his discretion as to whether judicial review may be available:

- the allegation can be best investigated by the resources and powers of the LGO;
- the LGO is in a position to get to the bottom of the prima facie case of maladministration and the complainants would be unlikely to reach that goal 'having regards to the weaknesses of the coercive fact finding potential of judicial review ... it would be very difficult, if not impossible, for the complainants to obtain the necessary evidence in judicial review proceedings';
- the complainants are unlikely to have the means to pursue a remedy through the courts;
- the LGO's investigation and report can provide a just remedy when judicial review might fail to do so.

20.109 Although not specifically referred to in the *Liverpool City Council* case, the LGO also advises that other matters, such as whether it would have been reasonable to expect the complainant to make an application for judicial review within the required time limit, uncertainty as to whether there is a remedy by means of judicial review and the availability for legal aid funding for judicial review, are relevant when exercising his discretion under LGA 1974 s26(6)(c). The LGO has previously indicated that 'in general' judicial review is not considered to provide a remedy 'that is reasonable for most complainants to resort to'.[119]

Judicial review and the LGO procedures

20.110 As complaints to the LGO are only (in general) accepted if no effective legal remedy is available, the judicial review and ombudsman procedures are distinct and not 'alternative options'.[120] In *R v Commissioner for Local Administration ex p PH*,[121] an applicant had commenced judicial review proceedings against a local authority on the grounds that it had delayed undertaking a special educational needs assessment. As a consequence, such an assessment took place. Subsequently she complained to the LGO seeking compensation for the effect of the council's delay. The LGO decided, under LGA 1974 s26(6), that the complaint was outside his jurisdiction because the complainant had already sought a judicial review of the council's actions. In upholding the LGO's decision, Turner J held:

> It can hardly have been the intention of Parliament to have provided two remedies, one substantive by way of judicial review and one compensatory by was of the Local Commissioner ... where a party has ventilated a grievance by way of judicial review it was not contemplated that they should enjoy and alternative, let alone an additional right by way of complaint to a local commissioner.

119 J White, 'Community care and the local government ombudsman for England' (2006) 9 CCLR 8 at 9.

120 Ombudsman decisions are, however, susceptible to judicial review; see, eg *R v Parliamentary Commissioner ex p Bachin* (1999) EGCS 78.

121 [1999] COD 382, as cited in the *Annual report 1998/99*, p7.

20.111   Prior judicial review proceedings will not, however, always be a bar to a subsequent LGO investigation. In *R (Goldsmith) v Wandsworth LBC*[122] the Court of Appeal quashed a local authority decision to require a resident to move to a nursing home (from her residential care home of many years). In order to avoid the contested move (pending the court decision) the resident's daughter had paid a private agency to provide her mother's nursing needs. On the Court of Appeal ruling that the local authority's decision making was irrational, the daughter complained to the LGO seeking to recover her expenditure on the nursing costs amounting to over £27,000 plus interest. The LGO upheld her complaint and recommended the compensation be paid in that sum.[123]

20.112   The fact that lawyers are involved and threatening legal action does not of itself make the LGO process unavailable. A 2001 report concerned a council that delayed the provision of (assessed) services until threatened with a judicial review. A subsequent complaint concerning the delay was upheld and a compensation recommendation made by the LGO.[124]

The pros and cons of using the LGO

20.113   There are advantages to using the LGO procedures. They are free to the complainant; they can result in the award of significant sums in compensation; and the authority is required to publicise the LGO's report (LGA 1974 s30). The LGO has access to all the relevant files and other records; can require the authority to furnish additional information; and has the same powers as the High Court in respect of the attendance and examination of witnesses and the production of documents (LGA 1974 s29). Complaints to the LGO are not subject to such short time limits as judicial review applications.

20.114   The LGO is concerned with the factual basis of local authority decisions – whereas in judicial review the court is largely confined to a review of the decision's legality. The LGO is capable of undertaking a very detailed review of the relevant documentation, of interviewing all the participants to a decision (eg the director of social services, councillors as well as the staff in actual contact with service user/carers). This analysis frequently sees through protestations by an authority that its decision was not 'resource led'. Examples of this type of review can be found at paras 4.117 and 4.161 above.

20.115   The disadvantages include the apparent reluctance of the LGO to accept many complaints, although there is some evidence that this is changing. In 2015/16 2,969 complaints were received, 1274 of which were referred back for local resolution, while 1,756 were considered and 58 per cent upheld. The LGO currently completes most investigations with 26 weeks, with complicated cases taking longer.[125] More significantly, the LGO cannot determine the legality or otherwise of local authority conduct and his recommendations are not binding on local authorities.

---

122 [2004] EWCA Civ 1170, (2004) 7 CCLR 472.
123 Complaint no 05/B/02414 against Wandsworth, 27 September 2006.
124 Complaint no 99/B/04621 against Cambridgeshire, 29 January 2001.
125 See www.lgo.org.uk/make-a-complaint/faqs.

20.116　　In *R (Gallagher) v Basildon DC*[126] the court held that the LGO's *findings* are binding on the local authority unless the authority successfully challenges the findings by way of judicial review; *recommendations*, however, are not binding and do not require 'cogent reasons' for non-compliance, but a failure to follow them can be challenged on public law grounds. In *Gallagher* Kenneth Parker J held that the refusal by the council to pay low level compensation to travellers, whose personal details had been made public, unlawfully failed to take account of relevant factors, took irrelevant factors into account and that the council had asked itself the wrong question.

20.117　　Each year, a small number of recommendations are not accepted by respondents (or, even more occasionally, a council fails to implement an agreed settlement[127]). LGA 1967 s31 requires the LGO to produce a further report if he is not satisfied with the local authority's response to his recommendations. In a complaint against Shropshire, the council accepted two of the recommendations, but refused to compensate a carer who had been prevented from working because of the council's maladministration – the recommendation was to pay £61,270 'in recognition of the care he had provided which the Council had not funded'. The LGO published a further report nine months later, in which he asked the council to reconsider, concluding:[128]

> My report highlighted the Council poorly handled Mrs Ryan's complaint when it began in 2010, a conclusion it accepts. It compounds that poor handling now by seeking to re-open points it has made before, making untested allegations against Mrs Ryan and introducing arguments irrelevant to my investigation. I trust the Council will now recognise that I have given careful consideration to all that it has said.

20.118　Similar, though not identical, provisions exist under LGA 1974 s34I, to enable the LGO to produce an adverse findings notice when private providers fail to follow recommendations. The LGO in 2014 used this power when she issued an adverse notice against a care home that had failed either to refund overpaid fees of £4,403.26 following (double funding by the complainant and the local authority) or to apologise.[129] Clearly when such a deadlock occurs (and it is not limited to English cases[130]) it is profoundly unsatisfactory for the complainant and evidence of the limitations of the process (compared to that of judicial review).

20.119　　Another key factor in deciding whether or not the LGO is an appropriate remedy in a particular case is the nature of the relief sought, as well as the urgency. The LGO has no power to offer injunctive relief. Although she may ask the respondent to, for instance, maintain services pending the outcome of a complaint into their withdrawal, he cannot order it. In general, the time scales involved in investigations and the lack of enforce-

---

126 [2010] EWHC 2824 (Admin).
127 See eg Complaint no 08 004 517 against Corby BC, 17 September 2009.
128 Further Report on an investigation into complaint ref no 12 007 311 against Shropshire Council, 13 January 2014
129 LGO, Adverse Findings Notice Rooks (Care Homes) Ltd and Green Hill Care Home No. 12 008 756, 4 November 2014.
130 See eg the comments of the Public Service Ombudsman for Wales in his *Annual report 2006/07* (p22) concerning the failure of Gwynedd Council.

ability of recommendations mean that the LGO is the appropriate route to take where what is sought is an 'after-the-event' review, not where the wrong is continuing and needs to be put right. This is particularly the case where there is a significant dispute about the interpretation of the law. The LGO cannot give a definitive interpretation of the law; only the administrative court can do that through judicial review.

Compensation/other recommendations

20.120 The LGO will often recommend action in addition to an apology and compensation.[131] By way of example, a 2006 complaint against Blackpool BC[132] included a recommendation that (among other things) the council should:

- offer Mrs Lloyd an appropriate form of tribute or memorial to her aunt (whose death had prompted the complaint) and bring that into effect within six months;
- formally adopt at member level a policy that ensures that risks to individual service users will be assessed as an integral part of the response to both individual complaints and a known failure in home care services;
- ensure that there are adequate resources available to the contracts unit so that it can fulfil its role in monitoring contract performance;
- review complaint procedures and staff training to ensure the development of an appropriate customer care culture which recognises the difficulty and fears that vulnerable service users may have in making complaints.

20.121 Other examples include cases where the LGO has recommended that a council:

- commission and consider a report from its chief executive about the capacity of senior managers in the relevant services to provide leadership and a working environment that supports, values and responds effectively to 'front line' concerns about service failures and pressures;[133]
- create a fund of £5,000 to be spent on items or activities chosen by the other children in the family, in recognition of the effect on them of the strain caused to their mother, their restricted living space and witnessing their brothers' distress and indignity;[134]
- pay for a two-week UK summer holiday for the family.[135]

20.122 LGO awards can be very substantial. In 2012, over £100,000 in compensation was recommended (and paid) in a case where the local authority had given incorrect information to the Independent Living Fund (ILF): the sum comprising lost past and future payments. The award was to be

---

131 Compensation may be significant: see Complaint no 09 014 026 against City of London, where a carer was awarded £50,880, representing the value of the respite care to which she had been entitled but which the council had failed to provide to her.

132 Complaint no 03/C/17141 against Blackpool BC, 23 February 2006.

133 Complaint no 07C03887 against Bury MBC, 14 October 2009, para 49.

134 Complaint no 07C03887 against Bury MBC, 14 October 2009, para 49.

135 Complaint no 04/C/16622 against Leeds CC, 4 May 2006, para 38.

'administered ... in such a way as to ensure [that the complainant did] not lose any of his welfare benefits'.[136]

Overlap with the Health Service Ombudsman

20.123 Concern about the difficulty of investigating complains that straddled both health and social care failures[137] resulted in the introduction of the Regulatory Reform (Collaboration etc between Ombudsmen) Order 2007 which enabled joint investigations.

20.124 The first investigation[138] under the regulatory reform order is illustrative. The parents of a severely disabled adult with high needs for 1:1 care complained about his care in a residential home run jointly by the council and the health trust. His needs were not properly assessed, and there were significant failings in his care and in the complaints handling.

20.125 In the opinion of both ombudsmen in their joint report, 'the greater a person's disability or communication difficulties, the greater the need for proper consideration to ensure the protection of basic rights such as human dignity' and that Articles 3, 8 and 14 of the European Convention on Human Rights were engaged. In consequence of the maladministration compensation totalling £32,000 was recommended to be paid, apportioned equally between the two bodies.

20.126 A subsequent (2009) report on a joint investigation by the LGO and the health service ombudsman concerned complaints brought by Mencap on behalf of the families of six people with learning disabilities who died whilst in NHS or local authority care.[139] The ombudsmen's overview summary was:

> The investigation reports illustrate some significant and distressing failures in service across both health and social care. They show the devastating impact of organisational behaviour which does not adapt to individual needs, or even consistently follow procedures designed to maintain a basic quality of service for everyone. They identify a lack of leadership and a failure to understand the law in relation to disability discrimination and human rights. This led to situations in which people with learning disabilities were treated less favourably than others, resulting in prolonged suffering and inappropriate care.

Parliamentary and health service ombudsman

20.127 The health service ombudsman (HSO) also fulfils the role of parliamentary service ombudsman (PSO). The HSO has wide powers to investigate complaints concerning NHS bodies, health service providers, such as GPs and dentists, and independent providers of NHS services. These powers

---

136 Complaint no 08 020 110 against Bradford MDC, 27 July 2012 para 42.
137 Cabinet Office, *Consultation paper: reform of public sector ombudsmen services in England*, 2005.
138 Complaint nos 03/A/04618 and HS-2608 against Buckinghamshire CC and Oxfordshire and Buckinghamshire Mental Health Partnership Trust (respectively), 17 March 2008.
139 *Six lives: the provision of public services to people with learning difficulties* was laid before parliament on 23 March 2009. See www.gov.uk/government/publications/six-lives-the-provision-of-public-services-to-people-with-learning-difficulties-2008-to-2009.

derive from the Health Service Commissioners Act (HSCA) 1993 (as amended[140]) and provide (at section 3) for the commissioner to investigate complaints made:

> ... by or on behalf of a person that he has sustained injustice or hardship in consequence of–
> (a) a failure in a service provided by a health service body,
> (b) a failure of such a body to provide a service which it was a function of the body to provide, or
> (c) maladministration connected with any other action taken by or on behalf of such a body.

20.128 HSCA 1993 s5 originally contained a general inhibition on the investigation of matters of clinical judgment, but this was repealed by Health Service Commissioners (Amendment) Act 1996 s6. Accordingly, the potential scope of the HSO's powers is wide. There are, however, limits, including that she should restrict her investigations to the complaints that have been made and not (for instance) widen the scope of the investigation beyond the statutory purpose of the investigation..[141]

20.129 Broadly the scheme mirrors that outlined above in respect of the LGO. Complaints must concern issues of maladministration and/or service failure, including matters of clinical judgment, leading to hardship or injustice. It must also be made in writing within one year of the date when the action complained about occurred. In general, the HSO cannot consider a complaint until the relevant NHS complaints procedures have been exhausted. Details of the complaints procedures and past reports are accessible at the HSO's website.[142]

20.130 Since the joint health and social care complaints procedure came into effect in 2009 (see above), a complainant who remains dissatisfied at the outcome of the NHS investigation into his or her complaint is able to take the matter directly to the HSO. This has resulted in a substantial increase in the number of inquiries being made (from 6,780 in 2008/09[143] to 20,109 in the year 2014/15[144]).

20.131 In the 2013/14 report, the HSO summarised the findings from three pieces of HSO research[145] into NHS complaints, noting that:

> We have identified a 'toxic cocktail' of patients' and carers' reluctance to complain, coupled with a culture of defensiveness by NHS organisations.[146]

20.132 The PHSO has published *The ombudsman's principles*,[147] which outline the approach the ombudsman believes public bodies should adopt when delivering good administration and customer service, including how to

---

140 By the Health Service Commissioners (Amendment) Act 1996 and HSC(CHS)A 2003 Part 2 chapter 9.
141 *Cavanagh and others v Health Service Commissioner* [2005] EWCA Civ 1578, [2006] 1 WLR 1229.
142 See www.ombudsman.org.uk.
143 *Annual report 2009/2010*, published 15 July 2010.
144 PHSO, *The Ombudsman's Annual Report and Accounts 2014–15*, HC 570, p17.
145 *The NHS hospital complaints system: a case for urgent treatment?*, 2013; *NHS governance of complaints handling*; and *Designing good together: transforming hospital complaints handling*, 2013.
146 *Annual report 2013/2014*, p 24
147 See www.ombudsman.org.uk/improving-public-service/ombudsmansprinciples.

respond when things go wrong. The principles make clear that they are not a checklist, and that the each complaint will be decided on its merits. Given the current time of financial austerity across all publicly funded services, the PHSO also provides some guidance on the question of limited resources:

> We also understand that the actions of public bodies are limited by their resources and all public bodies must spend money with care. There is often a balance between being sensitive to the needs of a customer and yet acting proportionately within available resources. Public bodies have to take decisions bearing in mind all the circumstances; delivering good service often means taking a broad and balanced view of all of the individuals or organisations that may be affected by decisions. However, finite resources should not be used as an excuse for poor service, poor administration, poor complaint handling or failing to provide a fair remedy.[148]

20.133 The HSO has also issued a number of highly influential reports concerning the provision of NHS continuing care, and these are considered separately at chapter 12 above.

Housing ombudsman service

20.134 The HOS was established under the Housing Act (HA) 1996,[149] which requires all social housing providers, including local housing authorities to belong to the HOS. Managing agents and private landlords may also join. This provides tenants of a housing association or local authority with the right to complain to the housing ombudsman, rather than the LGO. The current scheme replaced the independent housing ombudsman scheme in April 2013, when local authorities were brought within the jurisdiction.

20.135 In common with the other ombudsman schemes, the HOS will consider complaints brought by a dissatisfied tenant after the final stage of the landlord's own complaint process has been completed. However, this scheme differs in a number of details, in particular it is a membership scheme and, under HA 1996 Sch 2, which sets out the detail of the scheme, the housing ombudsman can order landlords to pay compensation or that certain contract terms are not required or performed.[150] Subject to the complainant's consent, the housing ombudsman can investigate jointly with the LGO.[151]

20.136 The housing ombudsman *Scheme*, published by the HOS in 2013, provides a detailed guide to the post-2013 regime.[152] All HOS decisions involving housing cases are collated in a single website.[153] There have been a number of decisions in respect of delays in the provision of disabled facilities grants (see, for example, paras 7.63 and 14.109).

---

148 See 'Ombudsman's introduction to the principles'.
149 Amended by the Housing and Regeneration Act 2008 and the Localism Act 2011.
150 HA 1996 Sch 2 para 7.
151 HA 1996 Sch 2 para 10A.
152 Available at www.housing-ombudsman.org.uk/media/13142/hos-final-scheme.pdf.
153 See www.housemark.co.uk/hmkb2.nsf/cdhp?openform.

Complaint to local authority monitoring officer

20.137 The duties of the monitoring officer are set out in Local Government and Housing Act 1989 s5.[154] Section 5(2) provides that, if it at any time it appears to the monitoring officer that 'any proposal, decision or omission by the authority' (or any officer or committee of the authority) is likely to contravene 'any enactment or rule of law or of any code of practice made or approved by or under any enactment', then the monitoring officer must investigate this and prepare a report on the issue in question. Formerly, this obligation also applied to allegations that the authority's actions amounted to maladministration. The situation now, however, is that in such cases the monitoring officer has a power to investigate (which presumably it would be wise to do if the evidence provided were substantial) but not a duty – until such time as the LGO/PSO has 'conducted an investigation' in relation to the alleged maladministration.[155] Given that the duty to investigate and prepare a report is triggered by the monitoring officer receiving credible evidence that the law or a 'rule of law' has been (or will be) contravened, letters seeking the involvement of the monitoring officer should (if it be the case) be phrased in these terms.

20.138   Where there appear to be grounds for judicial review, but it is not a feasible route, for instance because of financial constraints or a reluctance to litigate, a complaint to the monitoring officer, should be considered. It may also be a useful route where there appears to be a systemic problem, such as unlawful use of a funding panel, and cases have been settled without any change in the policy and practice. The post of monitoring officer will usually be filled by the most senior legal officer in the local authority. Structurally this may tend to compromise independence.

Judicial review

The nature of judicial review

20.139 'The basis of judicial review rests in the free-standing principle that every action of a public body must be justified by law.'[156] Judicial review is a procedure by which the High Court reviews the lawfulness of decisions made by public bodies, such as the departments of state, local authorities and NHS bodies. 'Public law is not at base about rights, even though abuses of power may and often do invade private rights; it is about wrongs – that is to say misuses of public power.'[157] This means that there must be a current material wrong to be put right. It is not the procedure for those seeking an after the event remedy; in those circumstances a complaint to the relevant

---

154 As amended by LGA 2003 s113.
155 Local Government and Housing Act 1989 s2A.
156 Laws LJ in *R (Beeson) v Dorset CC* [2003] UKHRR 353 at [17].
157 Sedley J in *R v Somerset CC ex p Dixon[1998] ELR 111 at* [121] and applied by the Court of Appeal in *R (Corner House research) v Secretary of State for Trade and Industry* [2005] EWCA Civ 192 [2005] 1WLR 2600 at [145].

ombudsman is the appropriate route. The courts 'exist to resolve real problems and not disputes of merely academic significance'.[158]

20.140   Judicial review is primarily concerned with lawful process in public administration. As such, it is neither a mechanism for determining the merits of a case, nor of resolving factual disputes. As Collins J observed in *Gunter v South Western Staffordshire PCT*:

> Judicial review is an unsatisfactory means of dealing with cases ... where there are judgments to be made and factual issues may be in dispute. At best, it can identify failures to have regard to material considerations and a need for a reconsideration. Very rarely if ever will it result in mandatory orders to the body which has the responsibility to reach the relevant decision.[159]

20.141   In general, the law allows private individuals or businesses to behave unreasonably or make capricious decisions – public bodies, however, have no such freedom. Their duties and the extent of their powers are set out in primary and secondary legislation (Acts of parliament and regulations made under such Acts). Thus it follows that public bodies must act lawfully. In very broad terms this means that they must act legally, rationally and procedurally fairly, or risk being challenged by way of judicial review. The grounds for judicial review are set out in more detail below. The process is two-staged: a claimant must obtain the permission of the court before their case can proceed to a hearing. The procedure is described in more detail below.

Time limits

20.142   Applications for a judicial review must generally be made promptly, and in any event within three months of when the claim first arose.[160] The time limits cannot be extended by the agreement of the parties.[161] The court can extend time, but in practice almost never does and tends to take a strict view when considering time limits.[162] This means that time is of the essence and it is vital that advisors weigh up at a very early stage whether a referral to a specialist solicitor is appropriate. This applies whether or not the case is being dealt with under the complaints procedure as time runs from the decision complained about and any delays in complaints handling are likely to lead to a case for judicial review being time-barred.

---

158 *R (Smeaton) v Secretary of State for Health* [2002] EWHC 886 (Admin), [2002] 2 FLR 146 at [420].
159 [2005] EWHC 1894 (Admin), (2006) 9 CCLR 121 at [19].
160 Civil Procedure Rules (CPR) 54.5.
161 CPR 54.5(2).
162 See the decision in *R (Enfield LBC) v Secretary of State for Health, Barnet PCT, Enfield PCT and Haringey Teaching PCT* [2009] EWHC 743 (Admin) where, in an unusual case, the court refused the claimant's permission to bring judicial review proceedings where the authority had delayed making the judicial review application to allow the secretary of state's scrutiny procedure to be completed.

What is a public body?

20.143   In the context of social care, it is established law that decisions made by public bodies, such as a local authority or by the NHS, will be subject to judicial review. But what of decisions made by private or voluntary providers (such as independent nursing homes or voluntary sector day centres, etc)? In general terms, such decisions would not be susceptible to judicial review, but the law is changing in this area.

20.144   The requirement not to interfere with human rights set out in Human Rights Act (HRA) 1998 s6(1) also applies only to public authorities, which includes organisations 'certain of whose functions are functions of a public nature'.[163] In the case of *R (Weaver) v London and Quadrant Housing Trust*[164] the Court of Appeal decided that, although a registered social landlord, the trust had acted as a public authority for the purposes of HRA 1998 s6(3)(b) in respect of the function of management and allocation of its housing stock. As such, its decision to terminate a tenancy was therefore amenable to judicial review. The Court of Appeal commented that being a 'public authority' under the HRA 1998 was not necessarily the same as being subject to judicial review, but in this case the two functions were the same. The CA 2014 s73 extends the meaning of a public authority to include all registered care providers (see para 17.6 above) who provide care funded by a local authority.

20.145   As *Weaver* demonstrates, a non-statutory organisation will often carry out both public and private functions, so decisions are made on a case-by-case basis depending on their facts. As a general principle, a decision by a private or voluntary provider is more likely to be subject to judicial review where the decision is authorised by an Act of parliament; where the organisation is carrying out a 'public function' which would otherwise have to be performed by a public authority, or where the decision is 'adopted' by the relevant public body.

The funding and costs of judicial review proceedings

20.146   In general, this will require either legal aid funding (and obtaining this can take not inconsiderable time) or access to significant resources. There is nothing in the court rules to stop an individual seeking to take a judicial review without lawyers.[165] It is, however, a complex and legalistic procedure.

20.147   In general terms, legal aid for judicial review claims in social care cases will be granted only where the Legal Aid Agency (LAA) assesses the case as having sufficient merits and, further, where the individual has satisfied a means test and is found to be eligible on financial grounds.

20.148   The extent to which judicial review is able to fulfil its constitutional purpose of acting as a check on the use of executive power has been weakened

---

163 HRA 1998 s6(3)(b).
164 [2009] EWCA Civ 587.
165 The procedure is detailed in CPR Part 54. A useful guide to the process is J Manning, S Salmon and R Brown, *Judicial review proceedings: a practitioner's guide*, 3rd edn, Legal Action Group, 2013. Although High Court fees are substantial, procedures exist for these to be reduced or waived for applicants on low incomes.

by recent government actions, not least in relation to funding and costs issues. Legal aid regulations[166] removing entitlement to payment for legal services up to and including the permission decision unless permission is granted were overturned in the High Court.[167] Further regulations are now in force,[168] so that the principles allowing legal aid costs to be met at or pre-permission can be summarised as:

- when the court gives permission to bring judicial review proceedings;
- when the defendant withdraws proceedings;
- when the court orders an oral permission hearing;
- when the court orders a 'rolled-up' hearing (ie one in which both the application for permission and the substantive hearing of the judicial review application are heard at the same time); and
- when the court neither refuses nor gives permission – payment of costs in this circumstance is at the discretion of the Lord Chancellor, subject to considerations set out in the regulations.

20.149 Judicial review proceedings usually follow the general costs principle that the 'losing' party pays the costs of the 'winning' party. Therefore, for those claimants who undertake judicial review proceedings (particularly those without the benefit of costs protection afforded by legal aid funding), a significant consideration is the risk, if unsuccessful, of having to pay the costs of the other party.

20.150 However, costs decisions are, subject to the legal framework, at the court's discretion so that, for instance where the claimant is successful the courts may not make an order for costs in a legally aided case on the basis that it simply shifts public money form one public body to another or on the basis of the conduct of a party.[169] However, the courts have, in recent years, acknowledged that 'the consequences for solicitors who do publicly funded work must be taken into account'[170] and, even in a case that settles without a hearing, that the culture in which no order for costs is made at this stage 'is no longer acceptable'.[171]

20.151 In certain situations, the court is prepared to consider limiting the sum an unsuccessful party may have to pay by making what was, until recently, known as a 'protective costs order' (PCO). This is only considered in relation to cases that are brought in the wider public interest, to establish a legal principle, rather than for personal reasons. In *R (Corner House Research) v Secretary of State for Trade and Industry*,[172] the Court of Appeal set out the guidance to be considered by the courts when determining an application for a PCO. This includes matters such as where: the issues are of general public importance; public interest requires that those issues should be resolved; the claimant has no private interest in the outcome of the case; having regard to the financial resources of the parties and the

166 Civil Legal Aid (Remuneration) (Amendment) No 3 Regulations 2014 SI No 607.
167 *R (Ben Hoare Bell and others) v The Lord Chancellor* [2015] EWHC 523 (Admin).
168 Civil Legal Aid (Remuneration) (Amendment) Regulations 2015 SI No 898, amending Civil Legal Aid (Remuneration) Regulations 2103 SI No 422.
169 For example, *R (TH) v East Sussex* [2013] EWCA Civ 1027.
170 *In re appeals by Governing Body of JFS* [2009] UKSC 1, [2009] 1 WLR 2353 at [24]–[25].
171 *R (Bahta) v Secretary of State for the Home Department* [2011] EWCA Civ 895 at [49].
172 [2005] EWCA Civ 192.

amount of costs likely to be involved, it is fair and just to make the order; if the order is not made, the claimant will probably discontinue the proceedings, and will be acting reasonably in so doing.

20.152   PCOs have now been replaced by 'cost capping orders', the terms of which are set out in the Criminal Justice and Courts Act (CJCA) 2015 (ss88–90). The statutory framework applies similar, though more rigorous, principles to the making of a cost capping order. Such an order can only be made following the grant of permission and subject to detailed financial information concerning the applicant's circumstances, the court must be satisfied that the applicant would otherwise withdraw from the proceedings. CJCA 2015 s88(7) defines proceedings as being in the public interest only if:

- the issue is of general public importance;
- the public interest requires the issue to be resolved; and
- the proceedings are likely to provide an appropriate means of resolving it.

In making this determination the court must have regard to the scale of the likely impact, notably the number of people likely to be affected, the significance of that effect and whether the proceedings involve consideration of a point of law that is of general public importance.[173]

Sufficient standing

20.153 In order to apply for judicial review, an applicant must have a 'sufficient interest' in the matter to which the application relates and the courts have generally given this phrase a liberal interpretation. For instance in *R v Gloucestershire CC ex p RADAR*,[174] Carnwath J considered an application by the Royal Association for Disability and Rehabilitation (RADAR) for judicial review of a decision made by Gloucestershire CC, relating to a general procedure which the council had adopted for the reassessment of the community care needs of disabled people. RADAR wished to challenge this general procedure and Carnwath J found that this procedure was:

> ... one which can, in my view, properly and conveniently be asserted by a body such as RADAR. It cannot be in anyone's interests that it should be left to each individual separately to assert that right. No doubt other individual test cases can be bought, but there is always a risk that if the particular individual loses his direct interest, either because his circumstances change or because the Authority carry out a reassessment, then the proceedings will prove abortive. In my view, RADAR has a sufficient interest to entitle it to a declaration as to the position as I have outlined it.

An alternative remedy?

20.154 Judicial review is not available where the claimant has failed to pursue an equally convenient, expeditious and effective remedy. This will mean that, in the absence of cogent reasons, a claimant should first use the complaints procedures or (less commonly) seek to invoke an available 'default'

173 CJCA 2015 s88(8).
174 (1997–98) 1 CCLR 476, QBD.

remedy (see para 20.215 below). As a general rule, disputes which are primarily factual are best suited to the complaints process and disputes which concern the interpretation of directions or guidance may be suited to resolution via the default procedures.[175]

20.155 The court may be prepared to consider a judicial review, notwithstanding that the applicant has not attempted to use the complaints or default procedures, if it can be shown that there are substantial reasons for believing that these remedies are not 'equally convenient, expeditious and effective'. Frequently this will be the case where:

- the matter in issue is a clear-cut dispute over a legal definition/statutory construction;
- what is in issue is an unlawful policy adopted by the local authority;
- there is an urgent need for the service (ie a requirement for interim relief by way of an injunction) This might not be the case if the local authority were willing to provide the interim relief of its own volition pending consideration of a complaint.

20.156 Unless the legal issues come into the above categories or are otherwise novel and important,[176] the courts will generally adopt a relatively strict approach in deciding whether or not the complaints procedure should be followed. In *Cowl and others v Plymouth CC*,[177] the Court of Appeal, finding that there was no point of legal principle in the case, spoke of the heavy obligation on lawyers in such disputes to resort to litigation only where it is unavoidable, stating:

> The parties do not today, under the CPR, have a right to have a resolution of their respective contentions by judicial review in the absence of an alternative procedure which would cover exactly the same ground as judicial review. The courts should not permit, except for good reason, proceedings for judicial review to proceed if a significant part of the issues between the parties could be resolved outside the litigation process ... If subsequently it becomes apparent that there is a legal issue to be resolved, that can thereafter be examined by the courts which may be considerably assisted by the findings made by the complaints panel.[178]

20.157 It is clear that judicial review is not a mechanism for dealing with the factual minutiae of the social care process. For instance, in *R (Lloyd) v Barking and Dagenham LBC*,[179] the Court of Appeal held that it was not the appropriate forum to prescribe the degree of detail that should go into a care plan or the amount of consultation to be carried out with a patient's advisers.

---

175 *R v Westminster CC ex p P and others* (1997–98) 1 CCLR 486, CA; and see also *R v Kirklees MBC ex p Good* (1997–98) 1 CCLR 506, QBD.

176 See, for example, *R v Devon CC ex p Baker and others* [1995] 1 All ER 73.

177 [2001] EWCA Civ 1935, [2002] 1 WLR 803, (2002) 5 CCLR 42 at [27]. These views were reiterated by Maurice Kay J in *R (Dudley, Whitbread and others) v East Sussex CC* [2003] EWHC 1093 (Admin).

178 At [14].

179 [2001] EWCA Civ 533, (2001) 4 CCLR 196 at 205G; and also the comments of McCombe J in *R (F, J, S, R and others) v Wirral BC* [2009] EWHC 1626 (Admin) at [75] and following.

20.158   However, in *R (JL) v Islington LBC*[180] in response to the respondent's contention that the claimant should have exhausted the complaints process before pursuing a claim for judicial review, the judge usefully set out the parameters of a complaint and judicial review, observing:

> The claimants are indeed using the local authority complaints process to address the detailed issues that they wish to raise concerning the assessment and the care plan. Had they attempted to raise those matters in the judicial review proceedings, they would validly have met with the answer that they should first exhaust the complaints process as it constitutes a remedy which is not only available but also more appropriate to resolve such issues. However, if they are correct in arguing that the local authority has confined its consideration of how to meet JL's needs (or at least some aspects of them) to applying its eligibility criteria rather than identifying JL's actual needs and how they might be met for him, whatever progress may be made through the complaints process in relation to detail will not alter the fundamental parameters of the core assessment. Real change to the outcome in JL's case could only be achieved by a successful challenge to the eligibility criteria. As it is at least arguable that the assessment *was* confined by the eligibility criteria, the existence of the complaints procedure is not, in my view, a reason to refuse permission to bring the judicial review proceedings.

20.159 Tactically, potential claimants can face difficulties in determining which is the appropriate remedy to pursue. In *Cowl* the Court of Appeal recommended the resolution of the factual dispute (was there a promise to care home residents of a 'home for life') should be by way of a complaint and then the ensuing question of whether the decision to close the care home in question was lawful could, if necessary, be resolved through judicial review. However, the risk inherent in waiting for the outcome of a complaint prior to embarking on a judicial review is that the claimant is then very likely to be time-barred by the three-month time limitation period, unless the complaints procedure itself throws up a fresh ground for judicial review. If it is clear from the outset that judicial review is the only or most appropriate way of resolving a case, then judicial review should be pursued promptly.[181] In appropriate cases it may be advisable to pursue both the complaints procedure and judicial review in order to preserve the time limit. In these circumstances the judicial review letter before claim can double as a formal complaint.

20.160   The proliferation of judicial review applications and the desire of the government to limit this tendency has led to a requirement that the court not only considers alternative remedies, but also possible outcomes at an early stage. CJCA 2015 s84(2) enables the court to consider whether the outcome for the applicant would be substantially different if the conduct complained of had not occurred. This consideration is mandatory at the defendant's request. If the outcome would not, in the court's view, be substantially different, permission must be refused unless it is appropriate to grant leave for reasons of 'exceptional public interest'.

---

180 [2009] EWHC 458 (Admin) at [31].
181 See, for instance, *R (Enfield LBC) v Secretary of State for Health* [2009] EWHC 743 (Admin) at [48].

Judicial review procedure

20.161 The procedure for judicial review applications to the High Court is set out in the Civil Procedure Rules (CPR) Part 54 and the relevant practice direction.[182]

20.162   Most applications for judicial review start with the claimant sending a 'Judicial Review Pre-action Protocol' letter to the defendant, known as a 'letter before claim' setting out the details of the decision being challenged, the factual background, the relevant law and the remedy sought. The defendant is allowed a period of 14 days to provide a 'letter of response', although this timescale may be shortened in very urgent cases. If this matter is extremely urgent, proceedings may be issued without the need to undertake the pre-action protocol procedure. This may be necessary, for instance, in cases involving destitute asylum-seekers, but in community care matters, such circumstances are likely to be rare.

20.163   If this process does not resolve the matter, the claimant may proceed to the issue of an application for judicial review in the High Court in which written evidence and full grounds for judicial review will be included. However, at this stage, the application is for permission to proceed to a full hearing for judicial review. This stage acts as a filter for wholly unmeritorious cases. A single judge will grant permission if there is an arguable case. Such decisions are usually made by consideration of the papers, although oral hearings may be held in certain circumstances.

20.164   If permission is granted, a full hearing of the case will consist of oral arguments in respect of the substantive issues in the case after the submission of further written evidence and legal arguments. Witnesses are almost never called to give evidence and, as such cases do not involve the determination of factual matters, there is usually no order for disclosure of documents.

Remedies

20.165 In judicial review cases, remedies are discretionary: in other words, even where the court finds that the decision is unlawful, it is not obliged to grant any remedy to the successful claimant. For instance, it may not do so where there has been delay in bringing proceedings or where the court considers that the granting of relief would 'be likely to cause substantial hardship to, or substantially prejudice the rights of, any person or would be detrimental to good administration'.[183]

20.166   In *R (LH) v Shropshire Council*[184] the Court of Appeal made a declaration that the council had, in breach of the common law duty, failed to consult the users of a day centre and their carers before deciding to close it. By the time the case reached the Court of Appeal, the centre had been closed for some time and the claimants had not sought an injunction to keep it open

---

182 The relevant rules and practice direction are available on the Ministry of Justice website.

183 Senior Courts Act 1981 s31(6) and (7).

184 [2014] EWCA Civ 404, (2014) 17 CCLR 216.

pending the appeal. The court held that it would not be consonant with good administration to quash the earlier decision and order consultation.

20.167   There are a range of orders which the court may make in judicial review proceedings and the court may make more than one order, depending on the case. These are as follows:

- **Quashing order:** This makes the decision being challenged completely invalid; the court will usually send the case back to the public body for the decision to be made again.
- **Prohibiting order:** Such an order prevents a public body from doing something which it was intending to do which would be in breach of its powers (eg deport someone).
- **Mandatory order:** This order requires the public body to do something which it was obliged to do (eg carry out an assessment of a person's needs under CA 2014 s9.)
- **Declaration:** This is not an order as such, as it does not tell the parties what they should do, but it does advise the respective parties of their rights and obligations (eg that a proposed rule was unlawful). If either party then fails to comply with the declaration, it would be possible for the court to make other orders in any subsequent proceedings.
- **Injunction:** Such an order may be made by the court to stop a public body from acting in an unlawful way or, alternatively, it may compel a public body to do something. These orders are often made by way of interim relief at an early stage in proceedings.
- **Damages:** The award of damages is possible, though unusual, in judicial review proceedings.[185]

20.168   The court cannot substitute its own decision for that of the public authority, unless there is – in reality – only one possible outcome as a result of the court's judgment. This is rare in practice. Thus the outcome of a successful judicial review is more likely to require the public body to make a fresh decision lawfully in compliance with the judgment of the court. It is often described as giving rise to a procedural remedy, rather than a substantive one. Public bodies may make the same decision again, simply correcting the unlawful procedure, for instance a failure to consult.

20.169   CJCA 2015 s84(1) prevents the court from granting relief to a successful applicant 'if it appears to the court to be highly likely that the outcome for the applicant would not have been substantially different if the conduct complained of had not occurred'. The court can only disregard this test for reasons of exceptional public interest (see para 20.160 above).

20.170   It is essential that prospective claimants understand these limiting factors when they consider pursuing a judicial review, as well as the relatively low success rate for such applications. For example, of the 7,500 cases considered for permission in 2012 only about 1,400 succeeded.[186] However, despite its shortcomings, judicial review is a vital tool in ensuring that the decisions of public bodies are made in accordance with the law and in holding the executive to account. Where a public body has failed to comply

---

185 Useful information and guides on various aspects of judicial review are available to the public at www.publiclawproject.org.uk.

186 Statistics cited by the Ministry of Justice in *Proposals for further reform: the government's response*, February 2014.

with the law, notification of an intention to apply for judicial review in the form of a letter before claim is often enough to settle a case without the need for court proceedings.

Grounds for judicial review

Introduction

20.171 As noted above, judicial review generally concerns a challenge to the decision-making process (ie the procedure followed in coming to the decision) rather than to the decision itself. In such 'procedural' challenges, applicants are required to show some material flaw in the process by which the public body reached its decision. In certain cases, though rarely, the court will entertain a 'substantive' challenge to the actual decision itself; for instance, on the basis that (given the process followed) the decision is so absurd that in reaching it, the local authority must 'have taken leave of [its] senses'.[187]

20.172 Although the three 'classic' grounds for judicial review are (1) illegality, (2) irrationality (*Wednesbury* unreasonableness) and (3) procedural impropriety, the underlying principles are complex and multi-faceted; they are continually being refined and developed by the judiciary. Thus, when in *Kruse v Johnson*[188] the High Court indicated that it would be prepared to set aside local authority decisions which were 'manifestly unjust, partial, made in bad faith or so gratuitous and oppressive that no reasonable person could think them justified', it was merely outlining the type of situation which might provoke judicial intervention, not making any definitive statement of the potential grounds for review. Likewise, 50 years later, in *Associated Provincial Picture Houses v Wednesbury Corporation*[189] when Lord Greene described what are now the classic '*Wednesbury*' principles, he was again only sketching out examples of administrative behaviour which might attract judicial censure, not seeking to compile an exhaustive list. In his judgment, he instanced the following behaviour as being potentially justiciable:

- contravention of the law;
- a fettering of a discretion;
- unreasonableness in the sense of bad faith or dishonesty;
- failing to consider 'matters which he is bound to consider';
- failing to exclude matters which are irrelevant;
- reaching a decision that is 'so absurd that no sensible person could even dream that it lay within the powers of the authority'.

20.173 With the enactment of the HRA 1998, the courts accepted that their traditional approach to administrative scrutiny needed reconsideration. In *R (Daly) v Secretary of State for the Home Department*,[190] Lord Steyn contrasted the traditional *Wednesbury* approach with the requirements of

---

187 *R v Secretary of State for the Environment ex p Nottinghamshire CC* [1986] AC 240 at 247, HL.
188 [1898] 2 QB 91.
189 [1948] 1 KB 223.
190 [2001] UKHL 26, [2001] 2 WLR 1622 at [27]–[28].

'proportionality', in circumstances where a decision potentially engaged considerations of whether interference with a fundamental human right was justifiable. In his view although there was considerable overlap between the two approaches, they differed: not least that the doctrine of proportionality required courts to be more involved in assessing the evidence and determining the relative weight that should accorded to the competing interests and considerations, characterised as 'anxious scrutiny' – and that this had to be done in a broader range of cases, than merely ones involving extreme facts or situations.

20.174   The following subsections list some of the main principles which are used by the courts today, to test the validity of public law decisions. As indicated above, the labelling of these principles is not a taxonomic science, but merely an attempt to illustrate some of the more obvious characteristics of the jurisprudence in this field.

Illegality

20.175   A judicial review challenge on the grounds of illegality is based upon the notion that a 'decision-maker must understand correctly the law that regulates his decision-making power and give effect to it'.[191] Illegality may present itself in a number of guises, for instance, action by an authority which although within its power, has an ulterior and improper motive, such as action designed to frustrate the purpose of a statute. Common examples are outlined below.

Ultra vires[192]

20.176   Local authorities and NHS bodies are statutory creatures and only able to act in accordance with the powers they have been given by statute. Accordingly, it is unlawful for a public body to act beyond its powers (ultra vires). As noted above (para 1.65) although local authorities now have very wide powers, these are not unlimited.

20.177   By way of example, certain actions are well established as being in general outside social services authority powers: for instance, the provision of nursing care by a registered nurse (see para 11.111 above) or the provision of care and support to people entitled to NHS continuing healthcare (see para 12.19 above).

20.178   In *R (Evans) v The Lord Chancellor and another*,[193] the claimant challenged new legal aid rules which prevented the granting of legal aid funding where the case was being brought 'in the public interest'. Evidence was adduced that part of the reason for the decision by the Lord Chancellor was founded in concerns expressed by the Ministry of Defence that adverse judgments in publicly funded cases concerning matters in Iraq or Afghanistan may damage the government's policy interests. The court held (at [25]–[29]):

> For the State to inhibit litigation by the denial of legal aid because the court's judgment might be unwelcome or apparently damaging would constitute

191 *Council of Civil Service Unions v Minister for the Civil Service* [1985] AC 374 at 410, HL.
192 Action which is outside the public body's legal powers.
193 [2011] EWHC 1146 (Admin).

an attempt to influence the incidence of judicial decisions in the interests of government. It would therefore be frankly inimical to the rule of law ... [and] ... In those circumstances a legally inadmissible consideration was taken into account, and in my judgment the amendments must be quashed for that reason.

Misdirection of law

20.179 A decision may be challenged by way of judicial review if the authority can be shown to have misunderstood the relevant law in reaching its decision,[194] although the mere existence of a mistake of law is generally insufficient unless it 'is a relevant error of law, ie, an error in the actual making of the decision which affected the decision itself'.

20.180   In *AJ v Calderdale BC and others*[195] the court held that the council had made such a mistake when it excluded service users and their carers from panels evaluating competing bids to provide supported living services in the mistaken belief that this would breach procurement law. In similar terms, social care service provision decisions that are made on the basis of financial considerations without a lawful assessment of the needs of the individual have been struck down by the court.[196]

20.181   An authority may make an error of law by misunderstanding the nature of its statutory obligation; it may, for instance, consider its obligation to be discretionary when it is in fact mandatory.

Decision not made in accordance with the facts

20.182 The decision made by the authority must be in accordance with (and supported by) the evidence. Authorities cannot simply 'go through the motions' by paying lip service to the evidence but in reality having no regard to the individual merits of the case.[197] Accordingly in *R v Avon CC ex p M*[198] Henry J overruled a decision by the social services authority which directly conflicted with a recommendation made by the panel. In so doing, he stated:

> The evidence before [the panel] had, as to the practicalities, been largely one way. The panel had directed themselves properly at law, and had arrived at a decision in line with the strength of the evidence before them ... the strength, coherence and apparent persuasiveness of that decision had to be addressed head-on if it were to be set aside and not followed. These difficulties were not faced either by the Respondent's officers in their paper to the Social Services committee or by the Social Services committee themselves. Not to face them was either unintentional perversity on their part or showed a wrong appreciation of the legal standing of that decision. It seems

194 *R v Hull University Visitor ex p Page* [1993] AC 682 at 701–702, HL.

195 *AJ v Calderdale BC and Calderdale Primary Care Trust (Interested party)* [2012] EWHC 3552 (Admin), (2013) 16 CCLR 50.

196 See, for instance, *In the matter of an application by DM acting by his next friend, Kathleen McCollum* [2012] NIQB 98, (2013) 16 CCLR 39.

197 *Hemns v Wheller* [1948] 2 KB 61 and *Sagnata Investments v Norwich Corporation* [1971] 2 QB 614, CA.

198 (1999) 2 CCLR 185, QBD; and see also complaint no 15 019 312 against Barking & Dagenham LBC, 08 June 2016.

to me that you do not properly reconsider a decision when, on the evidence, it is not seen that the decision was given the weight it deserved.

Relevant and irrelevant considerations

20.183   'It is a basic and long-standing principle of judicial review that a public body should take in to account all relevant considerations and no irrelevant ones. A material failure to do so is a common ground on which the court will intervene'.[199] This ground arises not infrequently in the social care context.

20.184   In *R v Avon CC ex p M* (above), the court found that the authority, in deciding which residential placement to support, had ignored the applicant's psychological needs. In so doing, it failed to take account of a relevant (and in the court's view a 'crucial') consideration. In addition, the authority had decided that the applicant's preferred home should not be funded because (among other reasons) such a funding decision would 'set a precedent'. In this context the judge held that this was a misleading consideration; essentially whether or not the decision set a precedent was irrelevant. In *R (Clue) v Birmingham City Council* the council decided not to provide support for a destitute mother and child. The mother had overstayed her leave to remain in the UK, but had made a further application for leave on human rights grounds, which was very likely to succeed. The court held, (among other things) that the 'assessment did not ... take account of the application for leave to remain', and for this reason it was unlawful.[200]

20.185   As these cases illustrate, the failure to take account of relevant considerations (and/or taking irrelevant ones into account) undermines the legality of the decision – the relevant material must be *material* to the decision.

Fettering of discretion

20.186   As noted above, public law duties cannot be frustrated by fixed or 'blanket' policies. The same holds true, even when the obligation is expressed as a 'power' rather than a 'duty'. Although an authority 'is entitled to promulgate a policy or guidelines as an indication of a norm which is intended to be followed',[201] it is not entitled to fetter its discretion by approaching a decision with a predetermined policy as to how all cases falling within a particular class will be treated. Accordingly, in *R v Ealing LBC ex p Leaman*[202] Mann J held that where a disabled person had applied to a local authority for financial assistance in taking a privately arranged holiday,[203] it was an error of law for the authority to decline to consider the application on the ground that it would only grant such assistance for holidays which it itself had arranged or sponsored (as the legislation specifically

---

199 M Fordham QC, *Judicial review handbook*, 6th edn, Hart Publishing, 2012.
200 [2010] EWCA Civ 460, (2010) 13 CLR 276 at [77]–[78].
201 See *R v Eastleigh BC ex p Betts* [1983] 2 AC 613, HL.
202 (1984) *Times* 10 February.
203 Under the (then) Chronically Sick and Disabled Persons Act (CSDPA) 1970 s2(1)(f).

allowed for the support of holidays 'provided under arrangements made by the authority or otherwise').

20.187   In *R v North West Lancashire Health Authority ex p A*,[204] the Court of Appeal held that the respondent's policy of not providing treatment for gender reassignment 'save in cases of overriding clinical need' was 'nonsense' since the authority considered that there was no effective treatment for the condition and, accordingly, an 'overriding clinical need' could not arise. Auld, LJ held:

> ... the stance of the authority, coupled with the near uniformity of its reasons for rejecting each of the respondent's requests for funding was not a genuine application of a policy subject to individually determined exceptions of the sort considered acceptable by Lord Scarman in *Findlay*.[205] It is similar to the over-rigid application of the near 'blanket policy' questioned by Judge J in *R v Warwickshire County Council ex p Collymore* [1995] ELR 217, at 224 *et seq*:
>
> > 'which while in theory admitting exceptions, may not, in reality result in the proper consideration of each individual case on its merits'.

20.188   The current financial constraints faced by local authorities inevitably result in policies to find ways of managing to meet legal obligations within shrinking budgets. For instance, local authorities commonly limit or cap expenditure on domiciliary care to the cost of a residential care placement. As Leggatt LJ held in *R v Bexley LBC ex p Jones*[206] in a different context:

> It is ... legitimate for a statutory body ... to adopt a policy designed to ensure a rational and consistent approach to the exercise of a statutory discretion in particular types of case. But it can only do so provided that the policy fairly admits of exceptions to it. In my judgment, the respondents effectively disabled themselves from considering individual cases and there has been no convincing evidence that at any material time they had an exceptions procedure worth the name. There is no indication that there was a genuine willingness to consider individual cases.

Unlawful delegation or dictation

20.189   Decision makers cannot avoid their duties by allowing themselves to be dictated to by, or simply accepting the decision of, another body.[207] Decision makers may not delegate their decisions to others unless they have specific power to do so and have done so properly. Local authorities are however able to delegate decision making functions to officers and where this occurs, the allocation of functions should be a clear and comprehensible.[208] Relatively complex rules also exist in relation to delegation arrangements under the Public Contracts Regulations 2006 SI No 5.[209]

---

204 (1999) *Times*, 24 August.

205 *In re Findlay* [1985] 1 AC 316.

206 [1995] ELR 42, p55.

207 J Manning, S Salmon and R Brown, *Judicial review proceedings: a practitioner's guide*, 3rd edn, Legal Action Group, 2013.

208 *R (Pemberton International Ltd) v Lambeth LBC* [2014] EWHC 1998 (Admin).

209 Delegation is permitted in such cases under what is termed the '*Teckal* exemption' (*Teckal Srl v Comune di Viano* (C-107/98) [1999] ECR I-8121) for example, where a local authority creates a separate company over which it has effective control – see, for example, *Tachie v Welwyn Hatfield BC* [2013] EWHC 3972 (QB).

20.190   In the context of adult social care, delegation of many of the key local authority functions, including assessments, is now permissible under CA 2014 s79 (see para 1.25 above). However, such delegation must adhere to the terms of the power as set out in section 79, for instance any authorisation must be for a specified term rather than open-ended (section 79(5)(a)).

Procedural impropriety

20.191 Procedural impropriety embraces a number of issues of natural justice.

The duty to act fairly

20.192 Decision makers must act fairly; must not be biased; must allow a party time to prepare his or her case; must ensure that a party has a proper opportunity to be heard; and, in appropriate situations, must give reasons for their decisions.

20.193   In *R (Montgomery) v Hertfordshire CC*,[210] for instance, the court held that the local authority had acted unlawfully because it had:

> ... failed manifestly and flagrantly to comply with the fundamental principles of fairness. They had given no notice of their action, they did not explain the grounds of their action, they have not explained the basis of future fears based upon the past complaints and they have not given the claimant any opportunity before this decision was taken to respond to any such matters with effective representations.

Procedural and substantive legitimate expectation

20.194 The courts, initially, developed the notion of 'legitimate expectation' as a facet of 'procedural impropriety' or the requirement of administrative fairness. A legitimate expectation can arise from past conduct by the authority, giving rise to an expectation of procedural fairness. Learning disabled young adults and their families having been consulted over the establishment of a charging scheme, could legitimately expect to be consulted over subsequent changes to the scheme, which were significant and would have a detrimental effect on them through increased charges.[211]

20.195   The courts have extended the doctrine's reach to encompass substantive challenges. In *R v North and East Devon Health Authority ex p Coughlan*[212] the Court of Appeal reviewed the development of the doctrine. In doing so, it noted that courts might adopt different approaches to public bodies that seek to change or withdraw from a policy or representation that created a 'legitimate expectation'. The court gave three contrasting examples. In the first case, the court might decide that the public body was only required to bear in mind its previous policy or representation, giving it the weight it sees fit, in which case it would only be reviewable on *Wednesbury* grounds of reasonableness. The second situation was where the circumstances give rise to a procedural legitimate expectation (see above). The third was a case where the nature of the promise or previous

210 [2005] EWHC 2026 (Admin) at [34].
211 *R (Carton) v Coventry City Council* (2001) 4 CCLR 41.
212 [2000] 2 WLR 622, (1999) 2 CCLR 285, CA.

practice gave rise to a substantive legitimate expectation, the breach of which would amount to an abuse of power.

20.196   In *Coughlan* the Health Authority had given patients a written promise of a home for life in the nursing home which it subsequently decided to close. It did so without making arrangements for the future care of the patients, which it regarded (wrongly) as the responsibility of the local authority. The Court of Appeal held:

> We have no hesitation in concluding that the decision to move Miss Coughlan against her will and in breach of the Health Authority's own promise was in the circumstances unfair. It was unfair because it frustrated her legitimate expectation of having a home for life in Mardon House. There was no overriding public interest which justified it ....We cannot prejudge what would be the result if there was on offer accommodation which could be said to be reasonably equivalent to Mardon House and the Health Authority made a properly considered decision in favour of closure in the light of that offer. However, absent such an offer, here there was unfairness amounting to an abuse of power by the Health Authority.[213]

20.197   Thus, as a general principle, such cases will only concern statements which were 'clear, unambiguous and devoid of relevant qualification'.[214] In *R v Secretary of State for the Home Department ex p Nadarajah*[215] Laws LJ held that the 'requirement of good administration' by public bodies meant that:

> Where a public authority has issued a promise or adopted a practice which represents how it proposes to act in a given area, the law will require the promise or practice to be honoured unless there is good reason not to do so.

20.198   In determining whether good reasons exist for not complying with its general practice/undertaking, Laws LJ considered that a number of factors came into play – including the respective force of the competing interests arising in the case and whether there was detrimental reliance. He considered that denial of promises made to an individual or specific group would generally be 'harder to justify as a proportionate measure' than those 'where the government decision-maker is concerned to raise wide-ranging or "macro-political" issues of policy'. In relation to promises made to individuals, Laws LJ subsequently observed[216] that holding public bodies to promises in such cases was essentially a condemnation of an abuse of power.

20.199   An authority may be released of its obligation to meet a person's legitimate expectation where the circumstances have changed after it gave its undertaking – *R (Lindley) v Tameside MBC*.[217]

---

213 *Coughlan* at [89].

214 *R v IRC Ex p MFK Underwriting* [1990]1 WLR1545, 1569G per Bingham LJ.

215 [2005] EWCA Civ 1363 at [68]–[69].

216 In *R v Secretary of State for Education and Employment, ex p Begbie* [2000] 1 WLR 1115, 1130–1131, citing with approval comments made by Wade and Forsyth, *Administrative law*, 7th edn, 1994, p404.

217 [2006] EWHC 2296 (Admin).

The duty to consult

20.200 A duty to consult can arise on the basis of a legitimate expectation or because procedural fairness demands it. It may also arise because of a statutory or contractual requirement.

20.201   In *R (Moseley) v Haringey LBC*[218] the Supreme Court considered the components of this duty and agreed with the classic formulation put forward by Sedley J in *R v Brent LBC ex p Gunning*[219] where the duty to consult was formulated as consisting of four parts, the requirements being:

> First that the consultation must be at a time when proposals are still at a formative stage. Second that the proposer must give sufficient reasons for any proposal to permit of intelligent consideration and response. Third ... that adequate time must be given for consideration and response and, finally ... that the product of consultation must be conscientiously taken into account in finalising any statutory proposals.[220]

20.202 The Supreme Court in *Moseley* approved two further general points from earlier authorities (at [16]):

> First, the degree of specificity with which, in fairness, the public authority should conduct its consultation exercise may be influenced by the identity of those whom it is consulting ... Second, in the words of Simon Brown LJ in the Baker case, at p 91, "the demands of fairness are likely to be somewhat higher when an authority contemplates depriving someone of an existing benefit or advantage than when the claimant is a bare applicant for a future benefit".

These two considerations are likely to be significant factors in any consultation exercise involving cuts to services used by disabled people, particularly where the users have any degree of cognitive impairment.

20.203   The Supreme Court also considered the extent to which a public authority may be required to include alternative options in the consultation process (at [27]):

> Sometimes, particularly when statute does not limit the subject of the requisite consultation to the preferred option, fairness will require that interested persons be consulted not only upon the preferred option but also upon arguable yet discarded alternative options.

20.204 In *R (Eisai Ltd) v NICE*,[221] the High Court considered that for a consultation exercise to be carried out fairly it was under an obligation:

> ... to let those who have a potential interest in the subject matter know in clear terms what the proposal is and exactly why it is under positive consideration, telling them enough (which may be a good deal) to enable them to make an intelligent response. The obligation, although it may be quite onerous, goes no further than this.

20.205 The NHS has a duty under National Health Service Act (NHSA) 2006 s242[222] to consult and involve users and carers in the planning and

218 [2014] UKSC 56.
219 (1986) 84 LGR 168.
220 [1995] 1 All ER 89 at 91.
221 [2007] EWHC 1941 (Admin), (2007) 10 CCLR 638.
222 As amended by Local Government and Public Involvement in Health Act 2007 s233 (formerly Health and Social Care Act 2001 s11).

provision of services, as well as in the development and consideration of proposals to reconfigure such services.

20.206 Even if aspects of the consultation process are 'unfortunate', the court may exercise its discretion not to intervene where the overall process is fair and not fundamentally erroneous.[223]

20.207 In 2000 the government issued a code of practice on consultation which has been repeatedly revised – most recently to become considerably less prescriptive. The 2016 version[224] expressly does not have legal force (though it would be a relevant consideration in the performance of a consultation exercise).

20.208 While earlier guidance specified 12 weeks as a standard minimum period for consultations, the 2016 guidance merely requires that they 'last for a proportionate amount of time' noting that 'consulting for too long will unnecessarily delay policy development. Consulting too quickly will not give enough time for consideration and will reduce the quality of responses.' It also notes that some organisations may need more time to respond than others and that account needs to be taken if the consultation spans a holiday period. The 2016 guidance also requires (among other things) that consultations:

- should be clear and concise and avoid acronyms: for example, by being clear what questions you are asking and limit the number of questions to those that are necessary;
- should have enough information for the issues to be comprehensible and include 'validated assessments of the costs and benefits of the options being considered when possible';
- should not be undertaken simply 'for the sake of it': they should take place at a formative stage and not when the department already has a final view. They should also be 'only part of a process of engagement';
- should be targeted – accordingly departments should consider 'how to tailor consultation to the needs and preferences of particular groups, such as older people, younger people or people with disabilities that may not respond to traditional consultation methods';
- should be published within 12 weeks of the consultation if possible, and all relevant materials should be available on the GOV.UK website – such as the original consultation, responses from consultees and how these have informed the policy.

Equality duty

20.209 The public sector equality duty (PSED) under Equality Act 2010 s149 imposes (among other things) considerable consultation obligations on public bodies – and this is considered further at para 2.59 above. Where the section 149 duty arises it requires that an 'impact assessment' be produced. There is, however, no requirement to produce such an assessment before a consultation is undertaken, as one purpose of the consultation is to provide material to inform the PSED impact assessment.[225] The interplay

---

223 *Easyjet v Civil Aviation Authority* [2009] EWHC 1422 (Admin).
224 Cabinet Office, *Consultation principles*, 2016.
225 *R (Bracking and others) v Secretary of State for Work and Pensions* [2013] EWHC 897 (Admin), (2013) 16 CCLR 479 para 36.

between the duty to consult and the subsequent obligation (if required) to produce PSED impact assessment is illustrated by a 2012 ombudsman report which found maladministration where a council had decided to out-source the provision of care services provision without first: (a) consulting on the proposal; and (b) completing a PSED impact assessment.[226]

The duty to act in accordance with mandatory or directory requirements

20.210 A further requirement of the duty to act fairly is that the decision maker must comply with procedures laid down by parliament. This is some-times known as the duty to act in accordance with 'mandatory or direc-tory requirements'. In *R v North Yorkshire CC ex p Hargreaves*,[227] it was accepted that the respondent authority, in assessing the applicant's sister's needs, failed to take into account the preferences of the sister, contrary to the mandatory (or directory) requirements set out in the relevant statutory guidance.[228] See also *Secretary of State for Trade and Industry v Langridge*[229] where guidance was given on the principles to be applied in deciding whether a particular duty is mandatory or directory.

The duty to give reasons

20.211 Although there is no general duty on authorities to give reasons for their decisions, the courts will often find that procedural fairness requires a public authority to explain itself, if, for instance, the decision would other-wise be unintelligible, or would contravene the minimum standards of fairness.[230] In some situations the relevant statute, regulation or direction stipulates that reasons should be given. For instance, CA 2014 s24 (2)(a) requires written reasons to be given when a local authority decides that an individual is ineligible for support.

20.212   Where reasons are required, they must be 'proper, adequate and intelli-gible' and must deal with the substantial points raised by the complainant. An unparticularised assertion that 'on the evidence' the decision maker makes certain findings 'and recommends' will be considered, in general, to be inadequate.[231]

20.213   In *R (Savva) v Kensington and Chelsea RLBC*,[232] the Court of Appeal held that fairness required the respondent authority to explain how it had reached its final figure when calculating the amount of the appellant's personal budget. Although it was not a case where the relevant regula-tions imposed a duty to provide reasons for the decision, the Court of Appeal held that it was one in which the common law required reasons

226 Public Services Ombudsman for Wales, Complaint no 201100412 against Wrexham County BC, 4 October 2012, paras 80–81.
227 (1994) 30 September, QBD, CO/878/94.
228 Department of Health, *Community care in the next decade and beyond: policy guidance*, 1990, paras 3.16 and 3.25: the equivalent guidance is now the revised statutory guidance to the Care Act 2014, although the duty to consider an adult's preferences is now located in CA 2014 s1(3)(b).
229 [1991] 2 WLR 1343.
230 *R v Secretary of State for Home Department ex p Doody* [1993] 3 WLR 154, HL.
231 *R v Secretary of State for Transport ex p Cumbria CC* [1983] RTR 129, QBD.
232 [2010] EWCA Civ 1209.

to be given[233] and cited *Stefan v The General Medical Council (Medical Act 1983)*,[234] which sets out a helpful consideration of the developing law of the duty upon public bodies to give reasons for their decisions (at [21]–[24]). In that case, the court held (at [32]):

> The extent and substance of the reasons must depend upon the circumstances. They need not be elaborate or lengthy, but should be such as to tell the parties in broad terms why the decision was reached.

20.214 In reviewing the authorities, the Privy Council in *Stefan* considered that the common law duty to give reasons may be becoming the norm:

> There is certainly a strong argument for the view that what were once seen as exceptions to a rule may now be becoming examples of the norm, and the cases where reasons are not required may be taking on the appearance of exceptions.[235]

Default procedures

20.215 Local Authority Social Services Act (LASSA) 1970 s7D[236] provides:

(1) If the secretary of state is satisfied that any local authority have failed without reasonable excuse, to comply with any of their duties which are social services functions . . . he may make an order declaring that authority to be in default with respect to the duty in question.

(2) An order under subsection (1) may contain such directions for the purpose of ensuring that the duty is complied with within such period as may be specified in the order as appear to the secretary of state to be necessary.

(3) Any such direction shall, on the application of the secretary of state, be enforceable by mandamus.

A similar power to 'direct' is found in the NHSA 2006, see para 11.10 above.

20.216　On the face of it, a person aggrieved by a local authority decision may seek redress by making formal request to the secretary of state that he or she use this default power to remedy the particular injustice. In reality, such executive powers are rarely if ever exercised. The power under LASSA 1970 s7D is no exception; it appears that it has never been used, and it is highly unlikely that, in anything but the most extreme of situations, it would be so exercised. The power can only be used where the authority has failed to exercise a 'duty' (rather than a 'power'); it only arises if the local authority has 'no reasonable excuse' for its failure; the secretary of state has to be 'satisfied' about the lack of any reasonable excuse; and even then he or she has wide discretion whether or not to take any such action.

20.217　In the 1997 document *Correspondence on social services matters*[237] the Department of Health set out its policy on responding to correspondence

---

233 [2010] EWCA Civ 1209 at [19].

234 [1999] UKPC 10.

235 At [22]. See also M Fordham QC, *Judicial review handbook*, 6th edn, Hart Publishing, 2012 at 62.1 for a summary of the arguments as to whether the duty can yet be said to be generally applicable.

236 Inserted by National Health Service and Community Care Act 1990 s50 and replacing an equivalent provision under National Assistance Act 1948 s36(1). The default procedures available under section 7D are unaffected by the enactment of the CA 2014.

237 Department of Health, *Correspondence on social services matters* LASSL 96(12), 1997.

received from the public (as well as from MPs and corporate bodies). In general the department copies the correspondence to the relevant authority, but (at para 10):

> ... where the letter seems strongly to suggest that SSD policy or practice may be inconsistent in some significant respect with the law or Departmental guidance we will normally expect to reply substantively ourselves, but will refer the letter to the SSD for their observations before doing so.

20.218   In practice such an exchange, where the local authority is required to explain its position to the department, can prove to be an effective lever. There is some evidence that this action has, in the past at least, led to a resolution of various problems.[238]

20.219   In *R v Kent CC ex p Bruce*[239] it was held that the secretary of state was not a 'tribunal of fact' and in considering whether to exercise the default procedure 'must properly be concerned with whether the local authority had misdirected itself in law or formed an irrational view of the facts'. In *R v Devon CC ex p Baker and others*[240] an argument that the existence of the default procedure constituted an alternative remedy which thereby excluded the use of judicial review was, in this particular case, rejected (see para 20.154 above).[241]

20.220   In *R v Westminster CC ex p P and others*[242] four destitute asylum-seekers challenged the policy of various London boroughs to accommodate them outside London. Simon Brown LJ, in rejecting the application (on grounds that there was an alternative remedy) held as follows in a very fact-specific context:

> For my part I have reached the clear conclusion that the more 'convenient, expeditious and effective' course here is indeed that of applying to the secretary of state to exercise his default powers under s7D. This is par excellence an area of administration in which the Secretary of State rather than the courts should be closely involved. In the first place it is the secretary of state who funds the housing of asylum seekers under s21 of the 1948 Act. Secondly, it is the proper construction and application of his own directions and guidance which lie at the heart of the dispute. Thirdly, it was at the secretary of state's insistence that the appeal form the Court of Appeal's decision in *R v Westminster CC ex p M*,[243] which was to be heard by the House of Lords last month, was adjourned, specifically because the government are currently conducting a review of the treatment of asylum seekers and did not wish to risk a final judgment depriving asylum seekers of all protection until a decision had been made as to what (if any) alternative arrangements should be made.

---

238 See RADAR, *Putting teeth into the Act*, 2001, eg pp5 and following, a report produced by RADAR on attempts made between 1970–81 to enforce CSDPA 1970 s2.

239 (1986) *Times* 8 February.

240 [1995] 1 All ER 73.

241 See also the case of *R (Enfield LBC) v Secretary of State for Health* [2009] EWHC 743 (Admin), where the claimant's decision to wait until the NHS default procedure was completed was criticised by the court (at [48]).

242 (1997–98) 1 CCLR 486, CA and see also *R v Kirklees MBC ex p Good* (1997–98) 1 CCLR 506, QBD.

243 *R v Westminster CC ex p M* (1997–98) 1 CCLR 85, CA.

APPENDICES

Legislation[1]

CARE ACT 2014 Part 1, Schs 1–4

PART 1: CARE AND SUPPORT
General responsibilities of local authorities
Promoting individual well-being
1 (1) The general duty of a local authority, in exercising a function under this Part in the case of an individual, is to promote that individual's well-being.

(2) 'Well-being', in relation to an individual, means that individual's well-being so far as relating to any of the following–
  (a) personal dignity (including treatment of the individual with respect);
  (b) physical and mental health and emotional well-being;
  (c) protection from abuse and neglect;
  (d) control by the individual over day-to-day life (including over care and support, or support, provided to the individual and the way in which it is provided);
  (e) participation in work, education, training or recreation;
  (f) social and economic well-being;
  (g) domestic, family and personal relationships;
  (h) suitability of living accommodation;
  (i) the individual's contribution to society.

(3) In exercising a function under this Part in the case of an individual, a local authority must have regard to the following matters in particular–
  (a) the importance of beginning with the assumption that the individual is best-placed to judge the individual's well-being;
  (b) the individual's views, wishes, feelings and beliefs;
  (c) the importance of preventing or delaying the development of needs for care and support or needs for support and the importance of reducing needs of either kind that already exist;
  (d) the need to ensure that decisions about the individual are made having regard to all the individual's circumstances (and are not based only on the individual's age or appearance or any condition of the individual's or aspect of the individual's behaviour which might lead others to make unjustified assumptions about the individual's well-being);
  (e) the importance of the individual participating as fully as possible in decisions relating to the exercise of the function concerned and being provided with the information and support necessary to enable the individual to participate;
  (f) the importance of achieving a balance between the individual's well-being and that of any friends or relatives who are involved in caring for the individual;
  (g) the need to protect people from abuse and neglect;
  (h) the need to ensure that any restriction on the individual's rights or freedom of action that is involved in the exercise of the function is kept to the minimum necessary for achieving the purpose for which the function is being exercised.

(4) 'Local authority' means–
  (a) a county council in England,
  (b) a district council for an area in England for which there is no county council,
  (c) a London borough council, or
  (d) the Common Council of the City of London.

Preventing needs for care and support

2 (1) A local authority must provide or arrange for the provision of services, facilities or resources, or take other steps, which it considers will–

    (a) contribute towards preventing or delaying the development by adults in its area of needs for care and support;

    (b) contribute towards preventing or delaying the development by carers in its area of needs for support;

    (c) reduce the needs for care and support of adults in its area;

    (d) reduce the needs for support of carers in its area.

(2) In performing that duty, a local authority must have regard to–

    (a) the importance of identifying services, facilities and resources already available in the authority's area and the extent to which the authority could involve or make use of them in performing that duty;

    (b) the importance of identifying adults in the authority's area with needs for care and support which are not being met (by the authority or otherwise);

    (c) the importance of identifying carers in the authority's area with needs for support which are not being met (by the authority or otherwise).

(3) Regulations may–

    (a) permit a local authority to make a charge for providing or arranging for the provision of services, facilities or resources, or for taking other steps, under this section;

    (b) prohibit a local authority from making a charge it would otherwise be permitted to make by virtue of paragraph (a).

(4) The regulations may in particular (in reliance on section 125(7)) make provision by reference to services, facilities or resources which–

    (a) are of a specified type;

    (b) are provided in specified circumstances;

    (c) are provided to an adult of a specified description;

    (d) are provided for a specified period only.

(5) A charge under the regulations may cover only the cost that the local authority incurs in providing or arranging for the provision of the service, facility or resource or for taking the other step.

(6) In cases where a local authority performs the duty under subsection (1) jointly with one or more other local authorities in relation to the authorities' combined area–

    (a) references in this section to a local authority are to be read as references to the authorities acting jointly, and

    (b) references in this section to a local authority's area are to be read as references to the combined area.

(7) Sections 21 (exception for persons subject to immigration control), 22 (exception for provision of health services) and 23 (exception for provision of housing etc) apply in relation to the duty under subsection (1), but with the modifications set out in those sections.

(8) 'Adult' means a person aged 18 or over.

Promoting integration of care and support with health services etc

3 (1) A local authority must exercise its functions under this Part with a view to ensuring the integration of care and support provision with health provision and health-related provision where it considers that this would–

    (a) promote the well-being of adults in its area with needs for care and support and the well-being of carers in its area,

    (b) contribute to the prevention or delay of the development by adults in its area of needs for care and support or the development by carers in its area of needs for support, or

    (c) improve the quality of care and support for adults, and of support for carers, provided in its area (including the outcomes that are achieved from such provision).

(2) 'Care and support provision' means–

    (a) provision to meet adults' needs for care and support,

    (b) provision to meet carers' needs for support, and

    (c) provision of services, facilities or resources, or the taking of other steps, under section 2.

(3) 'Health provision' means provision of health services as part of the health service.

(4) 'Health-related provision' means provision of services which may have an effect on the health of individuals but which are not–

    (a) health services provided as part of the health service, or

    (b) services provided in the exercise of social services functions (as defined by section 1A of the Local Authority Social Services Act 1970).

(5) For the purposes of this section, the provision of housing is health-related provision.

(6) In section 13N of the National Health Service Act 2006 (duty of NHS Commissioning Board to promote integration), at the end insert–

'(5) For the purposes of this section, the provision of housing accommodation is a health-related service.'

(7) In section 14Z1 of that Act (duty of clinical commissioning groups to promote integration), at the end insert–

'(4) For the purposes of this section, the provision of housing accommodation is a health-related service.'

Providing information and advice

4 (1) A local authority must establish and maintain a service for providing people in its area with information and advice relating to care and support for adults and support for carers.

(2) The service must provide information and advice on the following matters in particular–

    (a) the system provided for by this Part and how the system operates in the authority's area,

    (b) the choice of types of care and support, and the choice of providers, available to those who are in the authority's area,

    (c) how to access the care and support that is available,

    (d) how to access independent financial advice on matters relevant to the meeting of needs for care and support, and

    (e) how to raise concerns about the safety or well-being of an adult who has needs for care and support.

(3) In providing information and advice under this section, a local authority must in particular–

    (a) have regard to the importance of identifying adults in the authority's area who would be likely to benefit from financial advice on matters relevant to the meeting of needs for care and support, and

    (b) seek to ensure that what it provides is sufficient to enable adults–

        (i) to identify matters that are or might be relevant to their personal financial position that could be affected by the system provided for by this Part,

        (ii) to make plans for meeting needs for care and support that might arise, and

        (iii) to understand the different ways in which they may access independent financial advice on matters relevant to the meeting of needs for care and support.

(4) Information and advice provided under this section must be accessible to, and proportionate to the needs of, those for whom it is being provided.

(5) 'Independent financial advice' means financial advice provided by a person who is independent of the local authority in question.

(6) In cases where a local authority performs the duty under subsection (1) jointly with one or more other local authorities by establishing and maintaining a service for their combined area–

    (a) references in this section to a local authority are to be read as references to the authorities acting jointly, and

    (b) references in this section to a local authority's area are to be read as references to the combined area.

Promoting diversity and quality in provision of services

5 (1) A local authority must promote the efficient and effective operation of a market in services for meeting care and support needs with a view to ensuring that any person in its area wishing to access services in the market–

(a) has a variety of providers to choose from who (taken together) provide a variety of services;

(b) has a variety of high quality services to choose from;

(c) has sufficient information to make an informed decision about how to meet the needs in question.

(2) In performing that duty, a local authority must have regard to the following matters in particular–

(a) the need to ensure that the authority has, and makes available, information about the providers of services for meeting care and support needs and the types of services they provide;

(b) the need to ensure that it is aware of current and likely future demand for such services and to consider how providers might meet that demand;

(c) the importance of enabling adults with needs for care and support, and carers with needs for support, who wish to do so to participate in work, education or training;

(d) the importance of ensuring the sustainability of the market (in circumstances where it is operating effectively as well as in circumstances where it is not);

(e) the importance of fostering continuous improvement in the quality of such services and the efficiency and effectiveness with which such services are provided and of encouraging innovation in their provision;

(f) the importance of fostering a workforce whose members are able to ensure the delivery of high quality services (because, for example, they have relevant skills and appropriate working conditions).

(3) In having regard to the matters mentioned in subsection (2)(b), a local authority must also have regard to the need to ensure that sufficient services are available for meeting the needs for care and support of adults in its area and the needs for support of carers in its area.

(4) In arranging for the provision by persons other than it of services for meeting care and support needs, a local authority must have regard to the importance of promoting the well-being of adults in its area with needs for care and support and the well-being of carers in its area.

(5) In meeting an adult's needs for care and support or a carer's needs for support, a local authority must have regard to its duty under subsection (1).

(6) In cases where a local authority performs the duty under subsection (1) jointly with one or more other local authorities in relation to persons who are in the authorities' combined area–

(a) references in this section to a local authority are to be read as references to the authorities acting jointly, and

(b) references in this section to a local authority's area are to be read as references to the combined area.

(7) 'Services for meeting care and support needs' means–

(a) services for meeting adults' needs for care and support, and

(b) services for meeting carers' needs for support.

(8) The references in subsection (7) to services for meeting needs include a reference to services, facilities or resources the purpose of which is to contribute towards preventing or delaying the development of those needs.

Co-operating generally

6 (1) A local authority must co-operate with each of its relevant partners, and each relevant partner must co-operate with the authority, in the exercise of–

(a) their respective functions relating to adults with needs for care and support,

(b) their respective functions relating to carers, and

(c) functions of theirs the exercise of which is relevant to functions referred to in paragraph (a) or (b).

(2) A local authority must co-operate, in the exercise of its functions under this Part, with such other persons as it considers appropriate who exercise functions, or are engaged in activities, in the authority's area relating to adults with needs for care and support or relating to carers.

(3) The following are examples of persons with whom a local authority may consider it appropriate to co-operate for the purposes of subsection (2)–
  (a) a person who provides services to meet adults' needs for care and support, services to meet carers' needs for support or services, facilities or resources of the kind referred to in section 2(1);
  (b) a person who provides primary medical services, primary dental services, primary ophthalmic services, pharmaceutical services or local pharmaceutical services under the National Health Service Act 2006;
  (c) a person in whom a hospital in England is vested which is not a health service hospital as defined by that Act;
  (d) a private registered provider of social housing.

(4) A local authority must make arrangements for ensuring co-operation between–
  (a) the officers of the authority who exercise the authority's functions relating to adults with needs for care and support or its functions relating to carers,
  (b) the officers of the authority who exercise the authority's functions relating to housing (in so far as the exercise of those functions is relevant to functions referred to in paragraph (a)),
  (c) the Director of Children's Services at the authority (in so far as the exercise of functions by that officer is relevant to the functions referred to in paragraph (a)), and
  (d) the authority's director of public health (see section 73A of the National Health Service Act 2006).

(5) The references in subsections (1) and (4)(a) to a local authority's functions include a reference to the authority's functions under sections 58 to 65 (transition for children with needs etc).

(6) The duties under subsections (1) to (4) are to be performed for the following purposes in particular–
  (a) promoting the well-being of adults with needs for care and support and of carers in the authority's area,
  (b) improving the quality of care and support for adults and support for carers provided in the authority's area (including the outcomes that are achieved from such provision),
  (c) smoothing the transition to the system provided for by this Part for persons in relation to whom functions under sections 58 to 65 are exercisable,
  (d) protecting adults with needs for care and support who are experiencing, or are at risk of, abuse or neglect, and
  (e) identifying lessons to be learned from cases where adults with needs for care and support have experienced serious abuse or neglect and applying those lessons to future cases.

(7) Each of the following is a relevant partner of a local authority–
  (a) where the authority is a county council for an area for which there are district councils, each district council;
  (b) any local authority, or district council for an area in England for which there is a county council, with which the authority agrees it would be appropriate to co-operate under this section;
  (c) each NHS body in the authority's area;
  (d) the Minister of the Crown exercising functions in relation to social security, employment and training, so far as those functions are exercisable in relation to England;
  (e) the chief officer of police for a police area the whole or part of which is in the authority's area;
  (f) the Minister of the Crown exercising functions in relation to prisons, so far as those functions are exercisable in relation to England;
  (g) a relevant provider of probation services in the authority's area;

(h) such person, or a person of such description, as regulations may specify.
(8) The reference to an NHS body in a local authority's area is a reference to–
    (a) the National Health Service Commissioning Board, so far as its functions are exercisable in relation to the authority's area,
    (b) a clinical commissioning group the whole or part of whose area is in the authority's area, or
    (c) an NHS trust or NHS foundation trust which provides services in the authority's area.
(9) 'Prison' has the same meaning as in the Prison Act 1952 (see section 53(1) of that Act).
(10) 'Relevant provider of probation services' has the meaning given by section 325 of the Criminal Justice Act 2003.

Co-operating in specific cases

7 (1) Where a local authority requests the co-operation of a relevant partner, or of a local authority which is not one of its relevant partners, in the exercise of a function under this Part in the case of an individual with needs for care and support or in the case of a carer, a carer of a child or a young carer, the partner or authority must comply with the request unless it considers that doing so–
    (a) would be incompatible with its own duties, or
    (b) would otherwise have an adverse effect on the exercise of its functions.
(2) Where a relevant partner of a local authority, or a local authority which is not one of its relevant partners, requests the co-operation of the local authority in its exercise of a function in the case of an individual with needs for care and support or in the case of a carer, a carer of a child or a young carer, the local authority must comply with the request unless it considers that doing so–
    (a) would be incompatible with its own duties, or
    (b) would otherwise have an adverse effect on the exercise of its functions.
(3) A person who decides not to comply with a request under subsection (1) or (2) must give the person who made the request written reasons for the decision.
(4) 'Relevant partner', in relation to a local authority, has the same meaning as in section 6.
(5) 'Carer of a child' means a person who is a carer for the purposes of section 60.

Meeting needs for care etc

How to meet needs

8 (1) The following are examples of what may be provided to meet needs under sections 18 to 20–
    (a) accommodation in a care home or in premises of some other type;
    (b) care and support at home or in the community;
    (c) counselling and other types of social work;
    (d) goods and facilities;
    (e) information, advice and advocacy.
(2) The following are examples of the ways in which a local authority may meet needs under sections 18 to 20–
    (a) by arranging for a person other than it to provide a service;
    (b) by itself providing a service;
    (c) by making direct payments.
(3) 'Care home' has the meaning given by section 3 of the Care Standards Act 2000.

Assessing needs

Assessment of an adult's needs for care and support

9 (1) Where it appears to a local authority that an adult may have needs for care and support, the authority must assess–
    (a) whether the adult does have needs for care and support, and
    (b) if the adult does, what those needs are.
(2) An assessment under subsection (1) is referred to in this Part as a 'needs assessment'.

(3) The duty to carry out a needs assessment applies regardless of the authority's view of–

    (a) the level of the adult's needs for care and support, or

    (b) the level of the adult's financial resources.

(4) A needs assessment must include an assessment of–

    (a) the impact of the adult's needs for care and support on the matters specified in section 1(2),

    (b) the outcomes that the adult wishes to achieve in day-to-day life, and

    (c) whether, and if so to what extent, the provision of care and support could contribute to the achievement of those outcomes.

(5) A local authority, in carrying out a needs assessment, must involve–

    (a) the adult,

    (b) any carer that the adult has, and

    (c) any person whom the adult asks the authority to involve or, where the adult lacks capacity to ask the authority to do that, any person who appears to the authority to be interested in the adult's welfare.

(6) When carrying out a needs assessment, a local authority must also consider–

    (a) whether, and if so to what extent, matters other than the provision of care and support could contribute to the achievement of the outcomes that the adult wishes to achieve in day-to-day life, and

    (b) whether the adult would benefit from the provision of anything under section 2 or 4 or of anything which might be available in the community.

(7) This section is subject to section 11(1) to (4) (refusal by adult of assessment).

Assessment of a carer's needs for support

10 (1) Where it appears to a local authority that a carer may have needs for support (whether currently or in the future), the authority must assess–

    (a) whether the carer does have needs for support (or is likely to do so in the future), and

    (b) if the carer does, what those needs are (or are likely to be in the future).

(2) An assessment under subsection (1) is referred to in this Part as a 'carer's assessment'.

(3) 'Carer' means an adult who provides or intends to provide care for another adult (an 'adult needing care'); but see subsections (9) and (10).

(4) The duty to carry out a carer's assessment applies regardless of the authority's view of–

    (a) the level of the carer's needs for support, or

    (b) the level of the carer's financial resources or of those of the adult needing care.

(5) A carer's assessment must include an assessment of–

    (a) whether the carer is able, and is likely to continue to be able, to provide care for the adult needing care,

    (b) whether the carer is willing, and is likely to continue to be willing, to do so,

    (c) the impact of the carer's needs for support on the matters specified in section 1(2),

    (d) the outcomes that the carer wishes to achieve in day-to-day life, and

    (e) whether, and if so to what extent, the provision of support could contribute to the achievement of those outcomes.

(6) A local authority, in carrying out a carer's assessment, must have regard to–

    (a) whether the carer works or wishes to do so, and

    (b) whether the carer is participating in or wishes to participate in education, training or recreation.

(7) A local authority, in carrying out a carer's assessment, must involve–

    (a) the carer, and

    (b) any person whom the carer asks the authority to involve.

(8) When carrying out a carer's assessment, a local authority must also consider–

    (a) whether, and if so to what extent, matters other than the provision of support could contribute to the achievement of the outcomes that the carer wishes to achieve in day-to-day life, and

(b) whether the carer would benefit from the provision of anything under section 2 or 4 or of anything which might be available in the community.

(9) An adult is not to be regarded as a carer if the adult provides or intends to provide care–

(a) under or by virtue of a contract, or

(b) as voluntary work.

(10) But in a case where the local authority considers that the relationship between the adult needing care and the adult providing or intending to provide care is such that it would be appropriate for the latter to be regarded as a carer, that adult is to be regarded as such (and subsection (9) is therefore to be ignored in that case).

(11) The references in this section to providing care include a reference to providing practical or emotional support.

(12) This section is subject to section 11(5) to (7) (refusal by carer of assessment).

Refusal of assessment

11 (1) Where an adult refuses a needs assessment, the local authority concerned is not required to carry out the assessment (and section 9(1) does not apply in the adult's case).

(2) But the local authority may not rely on subsection (1) (and so must carry out a needs assessment) if–

(a) the adult lacks capacity to refuse the assessment and the authority is satisfied that carrying out the assessment would be in the adult's best interests, or

(b) the adult is experiencing, or is at risk of, abuse or neglect.

(3) Where, having refused a needs assessment, an adult requests the assessment, section 9(1) applies in the adult's case (and subsection (1) above does not).

(4) Where an adult has refused a needs assessment and the local authority concerned thinks that the adult's needs or circumstances have changed, section 9(1) applies in the adult's case (but subject to further refusal as mentioned in subsection (1) above).

(5) Where a carer refuses a carer's assessment, the local authority concerned is not required to carry out the assessment (and section 10(1) does not apply in the carer's case).

(6) Where, having refused a carer's assessment, a carer requests the assessment, section 10(1) applies in the carer's case (and subsection (5) above does not).

(7) Where a carer has refused a carer's assessment and the local authority concerned thinks that the needs or circumstances of the carer or the adult needing care have changed, section 10(1) applies in the carer's case (but subject to further refusal as mentioned in subsection (5) above).

Assessments under sections 9 and 10: further provision

12 (1) Regulations must make further provision about carrying out a needs or carer's assessment; the regulations may, in particular–

(a) require the local authority, in carrying out the assessment, to have regard to the needs of the family of the adult to whom the assessment relates;

(b) specify other matters to which the local authority must have regard in carrying out the assessment (including, in particular, the matters to which it must have regard in seeking to ensure that the assessment is carried out in an appropriate and proportionate manner);

(c) specify steps that the local authority must take for the purpose of ensuring that the assessment is carried out in an appropriate and proportionate manner;

(d) specify circumstances in which the assessment may or must be carried out by a person (whether or not an officer of the authority) who has expertise in a specified matter or is of such other description as is specified, jointly with or on behalf of the local authority;

(e) specify circumstances in which the adult to whom the assessment relates may carry out the assessment jointly with the local authority;

(f) specify circumstances in which the local authority must, before carrying out the assessment or when doing so, consult a person who has expertise in a specified matter or is of such other description as is specified;

(g) specify circumstances in which the local authority must refer the adult concerned for an assessment of eligibility for NHS continuing healthcare.

(2) The regulations may include provision for facilitating the carrying out of a needs or carer's assessment in circumstances specified under subsection (1)(d) or (e); they may, for example, give the local authority power to provide the person carrying out the assessment–

   (a) in the case of a needs assessment, with information about the adult to whom the assessment relates;

   (b) in the case of a carer's assessment, with information about the carer to whom the assessment relates and about the adult needing care;

   (c) in either case, with whatever resources, or with access to whatever facilities, the authority thinks will be required to carry out the assessment.

(3) The local authority must give a written record of a needs assessment to–

   (a) the adult to whom the assessment relates,

   (b) any carer that the adult has, if the adult asks the authority to do so, and

   (c) any other person to whom the adult asks the authority to give a copy.

(4) The local authority must give a written record of a carer's assessment to–

   (a) the carer to whom the assessment relates,

   (b) the adult needing care, if the carer asks the authority to do so, and

   (c) any other person to whom the carer asks the authority to give a copy.

(5) A local authority may combine a needs or carer's assessment with an assessment it is carrying out (whether or not under this Part) in relation to another person only if the adult to whom the needs or carer's assessment relates agrees and–

   (a) where the combination would include an assessment relating to another adult, that other adult agrees;

   (b) where the combination would include an assessment relating to a child (including a young carer), the consent condition is met in relation to the child.

(6) The consent condition is met in relation to a child if–

   (a) the child has capacity or is competent to agree to the assessments being combined and does so agree, or

   (b) the child lacks capacity or is not competent so to agree but the local authority is satisfied that combining the assessments would be in the child's best interests.

(7) Where a local authority is carrying out a needs or carer's assessment, and there is some other assessment being or about to be carried out in relation to the adult to whom the assessment relates or in relation to a relevant person, the local authority may carry out that other assessment–

   (a) on behalf of or jointly with the body responsible for carrying it out, or

   (b) if that body has arranged to carry out the other assessment jointly with another person, jointly with that body and the other person.

(8) A reference to a needs or carer's assessment includes a reference to a needs or carer's assessment (as the case may be) which forms part of a combined assessment under subsection (5).

(9) A reference to an assessment includes a reference to part of an assessment.

(10) 'NHS continuing health care' is to be construed in accordance with standing rules under section 6E of the National Health Service Act 2006.

(11) A person is a 'relevant person', in relation to a needs or carer's assessment, if it would be reasonable to combine an assessment relating to that person with the needs or carer's assessment (as mentioned in subsection (5)).

The eligibility criteria

13 (1) Where a local authority is satisfied on the basis of a needs or carer's assessment that an adult has needs for care and support or that a carer has needs for support, it must determine whether any of the needs meet the eligibility criteria (see subsection (7)).

(2) Having made a determination under subsection (1), the local authority must give the adult concerned a written record of the determination and the reasons for it.

(3) Where at least some of an adult's needs for care and support meet the eligibility

criteria, the local authority must–

(a) consider what could be done to meet those needs that do,

(b) ascertain whether the adult wants to have those needs met by the local authority in accordance with this Part, and

(c) establish whether the adult is ordinarily resident in the local authority's area.

(4) Where at least some of a carer's needs for support meet the eligibility criteria, the local authority must–

(a) consider what could be done to meet those needs that do, and

(b) establish whether the adult needing care is ordinarily resident in the local authority's area.

(5) Where none of the needs of the adult concerned meet the eligibility criteria, the local authority must give him or her written advice and information about–

(a) what can be done to meet or reduce the needs;

(b) what can be done to prevent or delay the development of needs for care and support, or the development of needs for support, in the future.

(6) Regulations may make provision about the making of the determination under subsection (1).

(7) Needs meet the eligibility criteria if–

(a) they are of a description specified in regulations, or

(b) they form part of a combination of needs of a description so specified.

(8) The regulations may, in particular, describe needs by reference to–

(a) the effect that the needs have on the adult concerned;

(b) the adult's circumstances.

Charging and assessing financial resources

Power of local authority to charge

14 (1) A local authority–

(a) may make a charge for meeting needs under sections 18 to 20, and

(b) where it is meeting needs because Condition 2 in section 18 or Condition 2 or 4 in section 20 is met, may make a charge (in addition to the charge it makes under paragraph (a)) for putting in place the arrangements for meeting those needs.

(2) The power to make a charge under subsection (1) for meeting needs under section 18 is subject to section 15.

(3) The power to make a charge under subsection (1) for meeting a carer's needs for support under section 20 by providing care and support to the adult needing care may not be exercised so as to charge the carer.

(4) A charge under subsection (1)(a) may cover only the cost that the local authority incurs in meeting the needs to which the charge applies.

(5) Regulations may make provision about the exercise of the power to make a charge under subsection (1).

(6) Regulations may prohibit a local authority from making a charge under subsection (1); and the regulations may (in reliance on section 125(7)) prohibit a local authority from doing so where, for example, the care and support or the support–

(a) is of a specified type;

(b) is provided in specified circumstances;

(c) is provided to an adult of a specified description;

(d) is provided for a specified period only.

(7) A local authority may not make a charge under subsection (1) if the income of the adult concerned would, after deduction of the amount of the charge, fall below such amount as is specified in regulations; and the regulations may in particular (in reliance on section 125(7)) specify–

(a) different amounts for different descriptions of care and support;

(b) different amounts for different descriptions of support.

(8) Regulations under subsection (7) may make provision as to cases or circumstances in which an adult is to be treated as having income that would, or as having income that would not, fall below the amount specified in the regulations if a charge were to be made.

Cap on care costs

15 (1) A local authority may not make a charge under section 14 for meeting an adult's needs under section 18 if the total of the costs accrued in meeting the adult's eligible needs after the commencement of this section exceeds the cap on care costs.

(2) The reference to costs accrued in meeting eligible needs is a reference–

(a) in so far as the local authority met those needs, to the cost to the local authority of having done so (as reckoned from the costs specified in the personal budget for meeting those needs (see section 26));

(b) in so far as another local authority met the needs, to the cost to that other local authority of having done so (as reckoned from the costs so specified for meeting those needs);

(c) in so far as a person other than a local authority met the needs, to what the cost of doing so would have been to the local authority which would otherwise have done so (as reckoned from the costs specified in the independent personal budget for meeting those needs (see section 28).

(3) An adult's needs are 'eligible needs' if, at the time they were met–

(a) they met the eligibility criteria,

(b) they were not being met by a carer, and

(c) the adult was ordinarily resident or present in the area of a local authority.

(4) The 'cap on care costs' is the amount specified as such in regulations; and the regulations may in particular (in reliance on section 125(7))–

(a) specify different amounts for persons of different age groups;

(b) specify zero as the amount for persons of a specified description.

(5) The total of the costs accrued in meeting an adult's eligible needs after the commencement of this section (as referred to in subsection (1)) is referred to in this Part as the adult's 'accrued costs'.

(6) Where the costs accrued include daily living costs, the amount attributable to the daily living costs is to be disregarded in working out for the purposes of subsection (1) the total of the costs accrued in meeting an adult's eligible needs after the commencement of this section.

(7) Where the cost to a local authority of meeting an adult's needs under section 18 includes daily living costs, and the accrued costs exceed the cap on care costs (with the result that subsection (1) applies), the local authority may nonetheless make a charge to cover the amount attributable to those daily living costs.

(8) For the purposes of this Part, the amount attributable to an adult's daily living costs is the amount specified in, or determined in accordance with, regulations.

Cap on care costs: annual adjustment

16 (1) Where it appears to the Secretary of State that the level of average earnings in England is different at the end of a review period from what it was at the beginning of that period, the Secretary of State must make regulations under section 15(4) to vary the cap on care costs by the percentage increase or decrease by which that level has changed.

(2) If a variation is made under subsection (1), each adult's accrued costs are to be varied by the same percentage with effect from when the variation itself takes effect (and local authorities must accordingly ensure that care accounts and other records reflect the variation).

(3) The 'level of average earnings in England' means the amount which represents the average annual earnings in England estimated in such manner as the Secretary of State thinks fit.

(4) 'Review period' means–

(a) the period of 12 months beginning with the day on which section 15 comes into force, and

(b) each subsequent period of 12 months.

(5) The duty under subsection (1) does not restrict the exercise of the power to make regulations under section 15(4).

Assessment of financial resources

17 (1) Where a local authority, having made a determination under section 13(1), thinks that, if it were to meet an adult's needs for care and support, it would charge the adult under section 14(1) for meeting at least some of the needs, it must assess–
  (a) the level of the adult's financial resources, and
  (b) the amount (if any) which the adult would be likely to be able to pay towards the cost of meeting the needs for care and support.

(2) Where a local authority thinks that, in meeting an adult's needs for care and support, it would make a charge under section 15(7), it must assess–
  (a) the level of the adult's financial resources, and
  (b) the amount (if any) which the adult would be likely to be able to pay towards the amount attributable to the adult's daily living costs.

(3) Where a local authority, having made a determination under section 13(1), thinks that, if it were to meet a carer's needs for support, it would charge the carer under section 14(1) for meeting at least some of the needs, it must assess–
  (a) the level of the carer's financial resources, and
  (b) the amount (if any) which the carer would be likely to be able to pay towards the cost of meeting the needs for support.

(4) Where a local authority, having made a determination under section 13(1), thinks that, if it were to meet a carer's needs for support, it would charge the adult needing care under section 14(1) for meeting at least some of the needs, it must assess–
  (a) the level of the financial resources of the adult needing care, and
  (b) the amount (if any) which the adult needing care would be likely to be able to pay towards the cost of meeting the carer's needs for support.

(5) An assessment under this section is referred to in this Part as a 'financial assessment'.

(6) A local authority, having carried out a financial assessment, must give a written record of the assessment to the adult to whom it relates.

(7) Regulations must make provision about the carrying out of a financial assessment.

(8) The regulations must make provision as to cases or circumstances in which, if the financial resources of an adult who has needs for care and support (whether in terms of income, capital or a combination of both) exceed a specified level, a local authority is not permitted to, or may (but need not)–
  (a) in a case where the adult's accrued costs do not exceed the cap on care costs, pay towards the cost of the provision of care and support for the adult;
  (b) in a case where the adult's accrued costs exceed the cap on care costs, pay towards the amount attributable to the adult's daily living costs.

(9) The regulations must make provision as to cases or circumstances in which, if the financial resources of a carer who has needs for support or of the adult needing care (whether in terms of income, capital or a combination of both) exceed a specified level, a local authority is not permitted to, or may (but need not), pay towards the cost of the provision of support for the carer.

(10) The level specified for the purposes of subsections (8) and (9) is referred to in this Part as 'the financial limit'; and the regulations may in particular (in reliance on section 125(7)) specify–
  (a) different levels for different descriptions of care and support;
  (b) different levels for different descriptions of support.

(11) The regulations must make provision for–
  (a) calculating income;
  (b) calculating capital.

(12) The regulations may make provision–
  (a) for treating, or not treating, amounts of a specified type as income or as capital;
  (b) as to cases or circumstances in which an adult is to be treated as having, or as not having, financial resources above the financial limit.

(13) The regulations may make provision as to cases or circumstances in which a local authority is to be treated as–

(a) having carried out a financial assessment in an adult's case, and

(b) being satisfied on that basis that the adult's financial resources exceed, or that they do not exceed, the financial limit.

Duties and powers to meet needs

Duty to meet needs for care and support

18 (1) A local authority, having made a determination under section 13(1), must meet the adult's needs for care and support which meet the eligibility criteria if–

(a) the adult is ordinarily resident in the authority's area or is present in its area but of no settled residence,

(b) the adult's accrued costs do not exceed the cap on care costs, and

(c) there is no charge under section 14 for meeting the needs or, in so far as there is, condition 1, 2 or 3 is met.

(2) Condition 1 is met if the local authority is satisfied on the basis of the financial assessment it carried out that the adult's financial resources are at or below the financial limit.

(3) Condition 2 is met if–

(a) the local authority is satisfied on the basis of the financial assessment it carried out that the adult's financial resources are above the financial limit, but

(b) the adult nonetheless asks the authority to meet the adult's needs.

(4) Condition 3 is met if–

(a) the adult lacks capacity to arrange for the provision of care and support, but

(b) there is no person authorised to do so under the Mental Capacity Act 2005 or otherwise in a position to do so on the adult's behalf.

(5) A local authority, having made a determination under section 13(1), must meet the adult's needs for care and support which meet the eligibility criteria if–

(a) the adult is ordinarily resident in the authority's area or is present in its area but of no settled residence, and

(b) the adult's accrued costs exceed the cap on care costs.

(6) The reference in subsection (1) to there being no charge under section 14 for meeting an adult's needs for care and support is a reference to there being no such charge because–

(a) the authority is prohibited by regulations under section 14 from making such a charge, or

(b) the authority is entitled to make such a charge but decides not to do so.

(7) The duties under subsections (1) and (5) do not apply to such of the adult's needs as are being met by a carer.

Power to meet needs for care and support

19 (1) A local authority, having carried out a needs assessment and (if required to do so) a financial assessment, may meet an adult's needs for care and support if–

(a) the adult is ordinarily resident in the authority's area or is present in its area but of no settled residence, and

(b) the authority is satisfied that it is not required to meet the adult's needs under section 18.

(2) A local authority, having made a determination under section 13(1), may meet an adult's needs for care and support which meet the eligibility criteria if–

(a) the adult is ordinarily resident in the area of another local authority,

(b) there is no charge under section 14 for meeting the needs or, in so far as there is such a charge, condition 1, 2 or 3 in section 18 is met, and

(c) the authority has notified the other local authority of its intention to meet the needs.

(3) A local authority may meet an adult's needs for care and support which appear to it to be urgent (regardless of whether the adult is ordinarily resident in its area) without having yet–

(a) carried out a needs assessment or a financial assessment, or

(b) made a determination under section 13(1).

(4) A local authority may meet an adult's needs under subsection (3) where, for

example, the adult is terminally ill (within the meaning given in section 82(4) of the Welfare Reform Act 2012).

(5) The reference in subsection (2) to there being no charge under section 14 for meeting an adult's needs is to be construed in accordance with section 18(6).

Duty and power to meet a carer's needs for support

20 (1) A local authority, having made a determination under section 13(1), must meet a carer's needs for support which meet the eligibility criteria if–

    (a) the adult needing care is ordinarily resident in the local authority's area or is present in its area but of no settled residence,

    (b) in so far as meeting the carer's needs involves the provision of support to the carer, there is no charge under section 14 for meeting the needs or, in so far as there is, condition 1 or 2 is met, and

    (c) in so far as meeting the carer's needs involves the provision of care and support to the adult needing care–

        (i) there is no charge under section 14 for meeting the needs and the adult needing care agrees to the needs being met in that way, or

        (ii) in so far as there is such a charge, condition 3 or 4 is met.

(2) Condition 1 is met if the local authority is satisfied on the basis of the financial assessment it carried out that the carer's financial resources are at or below the financial limit.

(3) Condition 2 is met if–

    (a) the local authority is satisfied on the basis of the financial assessment it carried out that the carer's financial resources are above the financial limit, but

    (b) the carer nonetheless asks the authority to meet the needs in question.

(4) Condition 3 is met if–

    (a) the local authority is satisfied on the basis of the financial assessment it carried out that the financial resources of the adult needing care are at or below the financial limit, and

    (b) the adult needing care agrees to the authority meeting the needs in question by providing care and support to him or her.

(5) Condition 4 is met if–

    (a) the local authority is satisfied on the basis of the financial assessment it carried out that the financial resources of the adult needing care are above the financial limit, but

    (b) the adult needing care nonetheless asks the authority to meet the needs in question by providing care and support to him or her.

(6) A local authority may meet a carer's needs for support if it is satisfied that it is not required to meet the carer's needs under this section; but, in so far as meeting the carer's needs involves the provision of care and support to the adult needing care, it may do so only if the adult needing care agrees to the needs being met in that way.

(7) A local authority may meet some or all of a carer's needs for support in a way which involves the provision of care and support to the adult needing care, even if the authority would not be required to meet the adult's needs for care and support under section 18.

(8) Where a local authority is required by this section to meet some or all of a carer's needs for support but it does not prove feasible for it to do so by providing care and support to the adult needing care, it must, so far as it is feasible to do so, identify some other way in which to do so.

(9) The reference in subsection (1)(b) to there being no charge under section 14 for meeting a carer's needs for support is a reference to there being no such charge because–

    (a) the authority is prohibited by regulations under section 14 from making such a charge, or

    (b) the authority is entitled to make such a charge but decides not to do so.

(10) The reference in subsection (1)(c) to there being no charge under section 14 for meeting an adult's needs for care and support is to be construed in accordance with section 18(6).

Exception for persons subject to immigration control

21 (1) A local authority may not meet the needs for care and support of an adult to whom
section 115 of the Immigration and Asylum Act 1999 ('the 1999 Act') (exclusion
from benefits) applies and whose needs for care and support have arisen solely–

(a) because the adult is destitute, or

(b) because of the physical effects, or anticipated physical effects, of being
destitute.

[(2) For the purposes of subsection (1), section 95(2) to (7) of the 1999 Act applies but
with the references in section 95(4) and (5) to the Secretary of State being read as
references to the local authority in question.

(3) But, until the commencement of section 44(6) of the Nationality, Immigration and
Asylum Act 2002, subsection (2) is to have effect as if it read as follows–

(2) For the purposes of subsection (1), section 95(3) and (5) to (8) of, and paragraph 2
of Schedule 8 to, the 1999 Act apply but with references in section 95(5) and (7) and
that paragraph to the Secretary of State being read as references to the local authority in question.]

*(2) For the purposes of subsection (1), section 95(3) and (5) to (8) of, and paragraph 2
of Schedule 8 to, the 1999 Act apply but with references in section 95(5) and (7) and
that paragraph to the Secretary of State being read as references to the local authority
in question.*[2]

(4) The reference in subsection (1) to meeting an adult's needs for care and support
includes a reference to providing care and support to the adult in order to meet a
carer's needs for support.

(5) For the purposes of its application in relation to the duty in section 2(1) (preventing
needs for care and support), this section is to be read as if–

(a) for subsection (1) there were substituted–

'(1) A local authority may not perform the duty under section 2(1) in relation
to an adult to whom section 115 of the Immigration and Asylum Act 1999
('the 1999 Act') (exclusion from benefits) applies and whose needs for care
and support have arisen, or for whom such needs may in the future arise,
solely–

(a) because the adult is destitute, or

(b) because of the physical effects, or anticipated physical effects, of being
destitute.', and

(b) subsection (4) were omitted.

Exception for provision of health services

22 (1) A local authority may not meet needs under sections 18 to 20 by providing or
arranging for the provision of a service or facility that is required to be provided
under the National Health Service Act 2006 unless–

(a) doing so would be merely incidental or ancillary to doing something else to
meet needs under those sections, and

(b) the service or facility in question would be of a nature that the local authority
could be expected to provide.

(2) Regulations may specify–

(a) types of services or facilities which, despite subsection (1), may be provided or
the provision of which may be arranged by a local authority, or circumstances
in which such services or facilities may be so provided or the provision of which
may be so arranged;

(b) types of services or facilities which may not be provided or the provision of
which may not be arranged by a local authority, or circumstances in which such
services or facilities may not be so provided or the provision of which may not
be so arranged;

(c) services or facilities, or a method for determining services or facilities, the provision of which is, or is not, to be treated as meeting the conditions in subsection (1)(a) and (b).

2   Subss (2), (3) in square brackets have been substituted by the Immigration Act s66, Sch 11
Pt 1 para 44. This is not yet in force.

(3) A local authority may not meet needs under sections 18 to 20 by providing or arranging for the provision of nursing care by a registered nurse.

(4) But a local authority may, despite the prohibitions in subsections (1) and (3), arrange for the provision of accommodation together with the provision of nursing care by a registered nurse if–

(a) the authority has obtained consent for it to arrange for the provision of the nursing care from whichever clinical commissioning group regulations require, or

(b) the case is urgent and the arrangements for accommodation are only temporary.

(5) In a case to which subsection (4)(b) applies, as soon as is feasible after the temporary arrangements are made, the local authority must seek to obtain the consent mentioned in subsection (4)(a).

(6) Regulations may require a local authority–

(a) to be involved in the specified manner in processes for assessing a person's needs for health care and for deciding how those needs should be met;

(b) to make arrangements for determining disputes between the authority and a clinical commissioning group or the National Health Service Commissioning Board about whether or not a service or facility is required to be provided under the National Health Service Act 2006.

(7) Nothing in this section affects what a local authority may do under the National Health Service Act 2006, including entering into arrangements under regulations under section 75 of that Act (arrangements with NHS bodies).

(8) A reference to the provision of nursing care by a registered nurse is a reference to the provision by a registered nurse of a service involving–

(a) the provision of care, or

(b) the planning, supervision or delegation of the provision of care,

other than a service which, having regard to its nature and the circumstances in which it is provided, does not need to be provided by a registered nurse.

(9) Where, in a case within subsection (4), the National Health Service Commissioning Board has responsibility for arranging for the provision of the nursing care, the reference in paragraph (a) of that subsection to a clinical commissioning group is to be read as a reference to the Board.

(10) For the purposes of its application in relation to the duty in section 2(1) (preventing needs for care and support), this section is to be read as if references to meeting needs under sections 18 to 20 were references to performing the duty under section 2(1).

Exception for provision of housing etc

23 (1) A local authority may not meet needs under sections 18 to 20 by doing anything which it or another local authority is required to do under–

(a) the Housing Act 1996, or

(b) any other enactment specified in regulations.

(2) 'Another local authority' includes a district council for an area in England for which there is also a county council.

(3) For the purposes of its application in relation to the duty in section 2(1) (preventing needs for care and support), this section is to be read as if, in subsection (1), for 'meet needs under sections 18 to 20' there were substituted 'perform the duty under section 2(1)'.

Next steps after assessments

The steps for the local authority to take

24 (1) Where a local authority is required to meet needs under section 18 or 20(1), or decides to do so under section 19(1) or (2) or 20(6), it must–

(a) prepare a care and support plan or a support plan for the adult concerned,

(b) tell the adult which (if any) of the needs that it is going to meet may be met by direct payments, and

(c) help the adult with deciding how to have the needs met.

(2) Where a local authority has carried out a needs or carer's assessment but is not

required to meet needs under section 18 or 20(1), and does not decide to do so under section 19(1) or (2) or 20(6), it must give the adult concerned–
(a) its written reasons for not meeting the needs, and
(b) (unless it has already done so under section 13(5)) advice and information about–
    (i) what can be done to meet or reduce the needs;
    (ii) what can be done to prevent or delay the development by the adult concerned of needs for care and support or of needs for support in the future.
(3) Where a local authority is not going to meet an adult's needs for care and support, it must nonetheless prepare an independent personal budget for the adult (see section 28) if–
(a) the needs meet the eligibility criteria,
(b) at least some of the needs are not being met by a carer, and
(c) the adult is ordinarily resident in the authority's area or is present in its area but of no settled residence.

Care and support plan, support plan

25 (1) A care and support plan or, in the case of a carer, a support plan is a document prepared by a local authority which–
(a) specifies the needs identified by the needs assessment or carer's assessment,
(b) specifies whether, and if so to what extent, the needs meet the eligibility criteria,
(c) specifies the needs that the local authority is going to meet and how it is going to meet them,
(d) specifies to which of the matters referred to in section 9(4) the provision of care and support could be relevant or to which of the matters referred to in section 10(5) and (6) the provision of support could be relevant,
(e) includes the personal budget for the adult concerned (see section 26), and
(f) includes advice and information about–
    (i) what can be done to meet or reduce the needs in question;
    (ii) what can be done to prevent or delay the development of needs for care and support or of needs for support in the future.
(2) Where some or all of the needs are to be met by making direct payments, the plan must also specify–
(a) the needs which are to be so met, and
(b) the amount and frequency of the direct payments.
(3) In preparing a care and support plan, the local authority must involve–
(a) the adult for whom it is being prepared,
(b) any carer that the adult has, and
(c) any person whom the adult asks the authority to involve or, where the adult lacks capacity to ask the authority to do that, any person who appears to the authority to be interested in the adult's welfare.
(4) In preparing a support plan, the local authority must involve–
(a) the carer for whom it is being prepared,
(b) the adult needing care, if the carer asks the authority to do so, and
(c) any other person whom the carer asks the authority to involve.
(5) In performing the duty under subsection (3)(a) or (4)(a), the local authority must take all reasonable steps to reach agreement with the adult or carer for whom the plan is being prepared about how the authority should meet the needs in question.
(6) In seeking to ensure that the plan is proportionate to the needs to be met, the local authority must have regard in particular–
(a) in the case of a care and support plan, to the matters referred to in section 9(4);
(b) in the case of a support plan, to the matters referred to in section 10(5) and (6).
(7) The local authority may authorise a person (including the person for whom the plan is to be prepared) to prepare the plan jointly with the authority.

(8) The local authority may do things to facilitate the preparation of the plan in a case within subsection (7); it may, for example, provide a person authorised under that subsection with–

    (a) in the case of a care and support plan, information about the adult for whom the plan is being prepared;

    (b) in the case of a support plan, information about the carer and the adult needing care;

    (c) in either case, whatever resources, or access to whatever facilities, the authority thinks are required to prepare the plan.

(9) The local authority must give a copy of a care and support plan to–

    (a) the adult for whom it has been prepared,

    (b) any carer that the adult has, if the adult asks the authority to do so, and

    (c) any other person to whom the adult asks the authority to give a copy.

(10) The local authority must give a copy of a support plan to–

    (a) the carer for whom it has been prepared,

    (b) the adult needing care, if the carer asks the authority to do so, and

    (c) any other person to whom the carer asks the authority to give a copy.

(11) A local authority may combine a care and support plan or a support plan with a plan (whether or not prepared by it and whether or not under this Part) relating to another person only if the adult for whom the care and support plan or the support plan is being prepared agrees and–

    (a) where the combination would include a plan prepared for another adult, that other adult agrees;

    (b) where the combination would include a plan prepared for a child (including a young carer), the consent condition is met in relation to the child.

(12) The consent condition is met in relation to a child if–

    (a) the child has capacity or is competent to agree to the plans being combined and does so agree, or

    (b) the child lacks capacity or is not competent so to agree but the local authority is satisfied that the combining the plans would be in the child's best interests.

(13) Regulations may specify cases or circumstances in which such of paragraphs (a) to (f) of subsection (1) and paragraphs (a) and (b) of subsection (2) as are specified do not apply.

(14) The regulations may in particular specify that the paragraphs in question do not apply as regards specified needs or matters.

Personal budget

26 (1) A personal budget for an adult is a statement which specifies–

    (a) the cost to the local authority of meeting those of the adult's needs which it is required or decides to meet as mentioned in section 24(1),

    (b) the amount which, on the basis of the financial assessment, the adult must pay towards that cost, and

    (c) if on that basis the local authority must itself pay towards that cost, the amount which it must pay.

(2) In the case of an adult with needs for care and support which the local authority is required to meet under section 18, the personal budget must also specify–

    (a) the cost to the local authority of meeting the adult's needs under that section, and

    (b) where that cost includes daily living costs–

        (i) the amount attributable to those daily living costs, and

        (ii) the balance of the cost referred to in paragraph (a).

(3) A personal budget for an adult may also specify other amounts of public money that are available in the adult's case including, for example, amounts available for spending on matters relating to housing, health care or welfare.

(4) Regulations may make provision for excluding costs to a local authority from a personal budget if the costs are incurred in meeting needs for which the authority–

    (a) does not make a charge, or

    (b) is not permitted to make a charge.

Review of care and support plan or of support plan

27 (1) A local authority must–

    (a) keep under review generally care and support plans, and support plans, that it has prepared, and

    (b) on a reasonable request by or on behalf of the adult to whom a care and support plan relates or the carer to whom a support plan relates, review the plan.

(2) A local authority may revise a care and support plan; and in deciding whether or how to do so, it–

    (a) must have regard in particular to the matters referred to in section 9(4) (and specified in the plan under section 25(1)(d)), and

    (b) must involve–

        (i)   the adult to whom the plan relates,

        (ii) any carer that the adult has, and

        (iii) any person whom the adult asks the authority to involve or, where the adult lacks capacity to ask the authority to do that, any person who appears to the authority to be interested in the adult's welfare.

(3) A local authority may revise a support plan; and in deciding whether or how to do so, it–

    (a) must have regard in particular to the matters referred to in section 10(5) and (6) (and specified in the plan under section 25(1)(d)), and

    (b) must involve–

        (i)   the carer to whom the plan relates,

        (ii) the adult needing care, if the carer asks the authority to do so, and

        (iii) any other person whom the carer asks the authority to involve.

(4) Where a local authority is satisfied that circumstances have changed in a way that affects a care and support plan or a support plan, the authority must–

    (a) to the extent it thinks appropriate, carry out a needs or carer's assessment, carry out a financial assessment and make a determination under section 13(1), and

    (b) revise the care and support plan or support plan accordingly.

(5) Where, in a case within subsection (4), the local authority is proposing to change how it meets the needs in question, it must, in performing the duty under subsection (2)(b)(i) or (3)(b)(i), take all reasonable steps to reach agreement with the adult concerned about how it should meet those needs.

Independent personal budget

28 (1) An independent personal budget is a statement which specifies what the cost would be to the local authority concerned (see section 24(3)) of meeting the adult's eligible needs for care and support.

(2) Where the amount referred to in subsection (1) includes daily living costs, the independent personal budget for the adult must specify–

    (a) the amount attributable to those daily living costs, and

    (b) the balance of the amount referred to in subsection (1).

(3) An adult's needs are 'eligible needs' if, at the time they were met–

    (a) they met the eligibility criteria,

    (b) they were not being met by a carer, and

    (c) the adult was ordinarily resident or present in the area of the local authority.

(4) A local authority must–

    (a) keep under review generally independent personal budgets that it has prepared, and

    (b) on a reasonable request by or on behalf of the adult to whom an independent personal budget relates, review the independent personal budget.

(5) A local authority may revise an independent personal budget; and in deciding whether or how to do so, it must, in so far as it is feasible to do so, involve–

    (a) the adult to whom the independent personal budget relates,

    (b) any carer that the adult has, and

    (c) any other person whom the adult asks the authority to involve or, where the adult lacks capacity to ask the authority to do that, any person who appears to the authority to be interested in the adult's welfare.

(6) Where a local authority is satisfied that the circumstances of the adult to whom an independent personal budget applies have changed in a way that affects the independent personal budget, the authority must–

    (a) to the extent it thinks appropriate, carry out a needs assessment and make a determination under section 13(1), and

    (b) revise the independent personal budget accordingly.

(7) Where, in a case within subsection (6), an adult refuses a needs assessment and the local authority thinks that the adult's refusal is unreasonable, it need no longer keep an up-to-date care account in the adult's case.

(8) Having reviewed an independent personal budget, a local authority must–

    (a) if it revises the independent personal budget, notify the adult to whom the independent personal budget relates of the revisions and provide an explanation of the effect of each revision, or

    (b) if it does not revise the independent personal budget, notify the adult accordingly.

Care account

29 (1) Where an adult has needs for care and support which meet the eligibility criteria, the local authority in whose area the adult is ordinarily resident or, if the adult is of no settled residence, in whose area the adult is present–

    (a) must keep an up-to-date record of the adult's accrued costs (a 'care account'), and

    (b) once those costs exceed the cap on care costs, must inform the adult.

(2) Where a local authority which has been keeping a care account is no longer required to do so, it must nonetheless retain the account that it has kept so far until–

    (a) the end of the period of 99 years beginning with the day on which it last updated the account, or

    (b) where the adult dies, the local authority becomes aware of the death.

(3) A care account must specify such amount as is attributable to the adult's daily living costs.

(4) A local authority which is keeping a care account must, at such times as regulations may specify, provide the adult concerned with a statement which–

    (a) sets out the adult's accrued costs, and

    (b) includes such other matters as regulations may specify.

(5) Regulations may specify circumstances in which the duty under subsection (4) does not apply.

Cases where adult expresses preference for particular accommodation

30 (1) Regulations may provide that where–

    (a) a local authority is going to meet needs under sections 18 to 20 by providing or arranging for the provision of accommodation of a specified type,

    (b) the adult for whom the accommodation is going to be provided expresses a preference for particular accommodation of that type, and

    (c) specified conditions are met,

the local authority must provide or arrange for the provision of the preferred accommodation.

(2) The regulations may provide for the adult or a person of a specified description to pay for some or all of the additional cost in specified cases or circumstances.

(3) 'Additional cost' means the cost of providing or arranging for the provision of the preferred accommodation less that part of the amount specified in the personal budget for the purposes of section 26(1)(a) that relates to the provision of accommodation of that type.

Direct payments

Adults with capacity to request direct payments

31 (1) This section applies where–

    (a) a personal budget for an adult specifies an amount which the local authority must pay towards the cost of meeting the needs to which the personal budget relates, and

(b) the adult requests the local authority to meet some or all of those needs by making payments to the adult or a person nominated by the adult.

(2) If conditions 1 to 4 are met, the local authority must, subject to regulations under section 33, make the payments to which the request relates to the adult or nominated person.

(3) A payment under this section is referred to in this Part as a 'direct payment'.

(4) Condition 1 is that–
  (a) the adult has capacity to make the request, and
  (b) where there is a nominated person, that person agrees to receive the payments.

(5) Condition 2 is that–
  (a) the local authority is not prohibited by regulations under section 33 from meeting the adult's needs by making direct payments to the adult or nominated person, and
  (b) if regulations under that section give the local authority discretion to decide not to meet the adult's needs by making direct payments to the adult or nominated person, it does not exercise that discretion.

(6) Condition 3 is that the local authority is satisfied that the adult or nominated person is capable of managing direct payments–
  (a) by himself or herself, or
  (b) with whatever help the authority thinks the adult or nominated person will be able to access.

(7) Condition 4 is that the local authority is satisfied that making direct payments to the adult or nominated person is an appropriate way to meet the needs in question.

Adults without capacity to request direct payments

32 (1) This section applies where–
  (a) a personal budget for an adult specifies an amount which the local authority must pay towards the cost of meeting the needs to which the personal budget relates, and
  (b) the adult lacks capacity to request the local authority to meet any of those needs by making payments to the adult, but
  (c) an authorised person requests the local authority to meet some or all of those needs by making payments to the authorised person.

(2) If conditions 1 to 5 are met, the local authority must, subject to regulations under section 33, make the payments to which the request relates to the authorised person.

(3) A payment under this section is referred to in this Part as a 'direct payment'.

(4) A person is authorised for the purposes of this section if–
  (a) the person is authorised under the Mental Capacity Act 2005 to make decisions about the adult's needs for care and support,
  (b) where the person is not authorised as mentioned in paragraph (a), a person who is so authorised agrees with the local authority that the person is a suitable person to whom to make direct payments, or
  (c) where the person is not authorised as mentioned in paragraph (a) and there is no person who is so authorised, the local authority considers that the person is a suitable person to whom to make direct payments.

(5) Condition 1 is that, where the authorised person is not authorised as mentioned in subsection (4)(a) but there is at least one person who is so authorised, a person who is so authorised supports the authorised person's request.

(6) Condition 2 is that–
  (a) the local authority is not prohibited by regulations under section 33 from meeting the adult's needs by making direct payments to the authorised person, and
  (b) if regulations under that section give the local authority discretion to decide not to meet the adult's needs by making direct payments to the authorised person, it does not exercise that discretion.

(7) Condition 3 is that the local authority is satisfied that the authorised person will act in the adult's best interests in arranging for the provision of the care and support for which the direct payments under this section would be used.

(8) Condition 4 is that the local authority is satisfied that the authorised person is capable of managing direct payments–
  (a) by himself or herself, or
  (b) with whatever help the authority thinks the authorised person will be able to access.
(9) Condition 5 is that the local authority is satisfied that making direct payments to the authorised person is an appropriate way to meet the needs in question.

Direct payments: further provision
33 (1) Regulations must make further provision about direct payments.
  (2) The regulations may, in particular, specify–
    (a) cases or circumstances in which a local authority must not, or cases or circumstances in which it has the discretion to decide not to, meet needs by making direct payments;
    (b) conditions which a local authority may or must attach to the making of direct payments;
    (c) matters to which a local authority may or must have regard when making a decision of a specified type in relation to direct payments;
    (d) steps which a local authority may or must take before, or after, making a decision of a specified type in relation to direct payments;
    (e) cases or circumstances in which an adult who lacks capacity to request the making of direct payments must or may nonetheless be regarded for the purposes of this Part or the regulations as having capacity to do so;
    (f) cases or circumstances in which an adult who no longer lacks capacity to make such a request must or may nonetheless be regarded for any of those purposes as lacking capacity to do so;
    (g) cases or circumstances in which a local authority making direct payments must review the making of those payments.
  (3) A direct payment is made on condition that it be used only to pay for arrangements under which the needs specified under section 25(2)(a) in the care and support plan or (as the case may be) the support plan are met.
  (4) In a case where one or more of conditions 1 to 4 in section 31 is no longer met or one or more of conditions 1 to 5 in section 32 is no longer met, the local authority must terminate the making of direct payments.
  (5) In a case where a condition specified under subsection (2)(b) or the condition mentioned in subsection (3) is breached, the local authority–
    (a) may terminate the making of direct payments, and
    (b) may require repayment of the whole or part of a direct payment (with section 69 accordingly applying to sums which the local authority requires to be repaid).

Deferred payment agreements, etc
Deferred payment agreements and loans
34 (1) Regulations may, in such cases or circumstances and subject to such conditions as may be specified, require or permit a local authority to enter into a deferred payment agreement with an adult.
  (2) A 'deferred payment agreement' is an agreement under which a local authority agrees not to require until the specified time either or both of the following–
    (a) the payment of the specified part of the amounts due from an adult to the authority under such provision of this Part or of regulations under this Part as is specified in regulations;
    (b) the repayment of the specified part of a loan made under the agreement by the authority to an adult for the purpose of assisting the adult to obtain the provision of care and support for the adult.
  (3) The care and support mentioned in subsection (2)(b) includes care and support the provision of which–
    (a) the authority does not consider to be necessary to meet the adult's needs;
    (b) is in addition to care and support which is being provided, arranged for, or paid for (in whole or in part) by the authority.

(4) Regulations under subsection (1) may, in particular, prohibit a local authority from entering into, or permit it to refuse to enter into, a deferred payment agreement unless it obtains adequate security for the payment of the adult's deferred amount.

(5) Regulations may specify what constitutes adequate security for the purposes of subsection (4); they may, for example, specify–

(a) an obligation on the adult to give the authority a charge over the adult's legal or beneficial interest in the property which the adult occupies as his or her only or main residence (or in a property which the adult used to occupy as such) to secure payment of the adult's deferred amount;

(b) a guarantee from another person to pay the adult's deferred amount.

(6) A reference in this section or section 35 to an adult's deferred amount, in relation to a deferred payment agreement, is a reference to the amount of which the local authority agrees not to require payment or repayment until the specified time.

(7) 'Specified', in relation to a time or a part of an amount or loan, means specified in or determined in accordance with regulations; and the specified part of an amount or loan may be 100%.

(8) This section applies in relation to an agreement under which a local authority agrees to make a loan to an adult for the purpose of assisting the adult to obtain the provision of care and support for the adult as it applies in relation to a deferred payment agreement; and for that purpose–

(a) the reference in subsection (3) to subsection (2)(b) is to be read as a reference to this subsection; and

(b) the references in subsections (4) and (5) to payment of the adult's deferred amount are to be read as references to repayment of the loan.

Deferred payment agreements and loans: further provision

35 (1) Regulations may require or permit a local authority to charge–

(a) interest on an adult's deferred amount;

(b) such amount relating to the authority's administrative costs as is specified in or determined in accordance with the regulations;

(c) interest on an amount charged under paragraph (b).

(2) The regulations may specify costs which are, or which are not, to be regarded as administrative costs for the purposes of subsection (1)(b).

(3) The regulations may–

(a) require or permit adequate security to be obtained for the payment of any interest or other amount referred to in subsection (1);

(b) require or permit any such interest or other amount to be treated in the same way as the adult's deferred amount;

(c) specify what constitutes adequate security for the purposes of paragraph (a).

(4) The authority may not charge interest under regulations made under subsection (1) or under a deferred payment agreement at a rate that exceeds the rate specified in or determined in accordance with the regulations; the regulations may, for example, provide for a rate to be determined by reference to a specified interest rate or other specified criterion.

(5) The regulations must enable the adult to terminate a deferred payment agreement by–

(a) giving the authority notice, and

(b) paying the authority the full amount for which the adult is liable with respect to the adult's deferred amount and any interest or other amount charged under regulations made under subsection (1) or under the agreement.

(6) The regulations may make other provision about the duration of a deferred payment agreement and for its termination by either party.

(7) The regulations may make provision as to the rights and obligations of the authority and the adult where the adult disposes of any legal or beneficial interest in a property to which a deferred payment agreement relates and acquires a legal or beneficial interest in another property (whether or not it is in the area of that authority); they may, for example, make provision–

    (a) for the authority not to require payment of the amounts referred to in subsection (5)(b) until the time specified in or determined in accordance with the regulations;

    (b) for the adult to give the authority a charge over the adult's legal or beneficial interest in the other property.

(8) The regulations may–

    (a) require or permit terms or conditions of a specified description, or in a specified form, to be included in a deferred payment agreement;

    (b) permit such other terms or conditions as the authority considers appropriate to be included in such an agreement;

    (c) require statements or other information relating to specified matters, or in a specified form, to be included in such an agreement.

(9) The regulations may make provision for the purpose of enabling local authorities to protect (for example, by registration) or enforce security obtained for the payment of the adult's deferred amount or the payment of any interest or other amount referred to in subsection (1); and, for that purpose, the regulations may amend, repeal, or revoke an enactment, or provide for an enactment to apply with specified modifications.

(10) This section applies in relation to an agreement of the kind mentioned in section 34(8) as it applies in relation to a deferred payment agreement; and for that purpose–

    (a) the references in subsections (1), (3) and (5) to the adult's deferred amount are to be read as references to the loan; and

    (b) the reference in subsection (9) to payment of the adult's deferred amount is to be read as a reference to repayment of the loan.

Alternative financial arrangements

36 (1) Regulations may, in such cases or circumstances and subject to such conditions as may be specified, require or permit a local authority to enter into alternative financial arrangements of a specified description with an adult.

(2) 'Alternative financial arrangements' means arrangements which in the Secretary of State's opinion–

    (a) equate in substance to a deferred payment agreement or an agreement of the kind mentioned in section 34(8), but

    (b) achieve a similar effect to an agreement of the kind in question without including provision for the payment of interest.

(3) The regulations may make provision in connection with alternative financial arrangements to which they apply, including, in particular, provision of the kind that may (or must) be made in regulations under section 34 or 35 (apart from provision for the payment of interest).

Continuity of care and support when adult moves

Notification, assessment, etc

37 (1) This section applies where–

    (a) an adult's needs for care and support are being met by a local authority ('the first authority') under section 18 or 19,

    (b) the adult notifies another local authority ('the second authority') (or that authority is notified on the adult's behalf) that the adult intends to move to the area of the second authority, and

    (c) the second authority is satisfied that the adult's intention is genuine.

(2) This section also applies where–

    (a) an adult is not having needs for care and support met under either of those sections but a local authority ('the first authority') is nonetheless keeping a care account in the adult's case,

    (b) the adult notifies another local authority ('the second authority') (or that authority is notified on the adult's behalf) that the adult intends to move to the area of the second authority, and

    (c) the second authority is satisfied that the adult's intention is genuine.

(3) This section also applies where–

    (a) an adult's needs for care and support are being met by a local authority ('the first authority') under section 18 or 19 by the first authority arranging for the provision of accommodation in the area of another local authority ('the second authority'),

    (b) the adult notifies the second authority (or that authority is notified on the adult's behalf) that the adult intends to move out of that accommodation but to remain, and be provided with care and support at home or in the community, in its area, and

    (c) the second authority is satisfied that the adult's intention is genuine.

(4) The second authority must–

    (a) provide the adult and, if the adult has or is proposing to have a carer, the carer with such information as it considers appropriate (in so far as it would not do so under section 4), and

    (b) notify the first authority that it is satisfied as mentioned in subsection (1)(c), (2)(c) or (3)(c).

(5) The first authority, having received the notification under subsection (4)(b), must provide the second authority with–

    (a) a copy of any care and support plan prepared for the adult,

    (b) a copy of any independent personal budget prepared for the adult,

    (c) in a case within subsection (2), a copy of the most recent needs assessment in the adult's case,

    (d) if the first authority has been keeping a care account in the adult's case, a copy of that account,

    (e) if the adult has a carer and that carer is to continue as the adult's carer after the move, a copy of any support plan prepared for the carer, and

    (f) such other information relating to the adult and, if the adult has a carer (whether or not one with needs for support), such other information relating to the carer as the second authority may request.

(6) The second authority must–

    (a) assess whether the adult has needs for care and support and, if the adult does, what those needs are, and

    (b) where the adult has or is proposing to have a carer and it is appropriate to do so, assess whether the carer has or is likely to have needs for support and, if the carer does or is likely to, what those needs are or are likely to be.

(7) In carrying out an assessment under subsection (6)(a) or (b), the second authority must have regard to the care and support plan provided under subsection (5)(a) or (as the case may be) the support plan provided under subsection (5)(e).

(8) This Part–

    (a) applies to an assessment under subsection (6)(a) as it applies to a needs assessment, and

    (b) applies to an assessment under subsection (6)(b) as it applies to a carer's assessment.

(9) Pending the adult's move, the first authority must keep in contact with the second authority in order to ascertain the progress that the second authority is making in preparing to meet–

    (a) any needs for care and support under section 18 or 19 in the adult's case, and

    (b) where the adult is proposing to have a carer immediately after the move, any needs for support under section 20 in the carer's case.

(10) The first authority must keep the adult (and, where applicable, the carer) informed about its contact under subsection (9) with the second authority and must involve the adult (and, where applicable, the carer) in the contact.

(11) Where the needs identified by an assessment under subsection (6)(a) carried out by the second authority are different from those specified in the care and support plan provided under subsection (5)(a), the second authority must provide a written explanation of the difference to–

    (a) the adult,

    (b) any carer that the adult has, if the adult asks the authority to do so, and

(c) any other person to whom the adult asks the authority to provide the explanation.

(12) Where the cost to the second authority of meeting the adult's eligible needs is different from the cost to the first authority of doing so, the second authority must provide a written explanation of the difference to–

(a) the adult,

(b) any carer that the adult has, if the adult asks the authority to do so, and

(c) any other person to whom the adult asks the authority to provide the explanation.

(13) Where the needs identified by an assessment under subsection (6)(b) carried out by the second authority are different from those in the support plan provided under subsection (5)(e), the second authority must provide a written explanation of the difference to–

(a) the carer,

(b) the adult needing care, if the carer asks the authority to do so, and

(c) any other person to whom the carer asks the authority to provide an explanation.

(14) Regulations may specify steps which a local authority must take for the purpose of being satisfied as mentioned in subsection (1)(c), (2)(c) or (3)(c).

(15) In this section–

(a) an adult's needs are 'eligible needs' if they meet the eligibility criteria and are not being met by a carer,

(b) a reference to moving to an area is a reference to moving to that area with a view to becoming ordinarily resident there, and

(c) a reference to remaining in an area is a reference to remaining ordinarily resident there.

Case where assessments not complete on day of move

38 (1) If, on the day of the intended move as mentioned in section 37(1)(b), (2)(b) or (3)(b), the second authority has yet to carry out the assessment or assessments under section 37(6), or has done so but has yet to take the other steps required under this Part in the adult's case, it must–

(a) meet the adult's needs for care and support, and the needs for support of any carer who is continuing as the adult's carer, which the first authority has been meeting, and

(b) where the first authority has been keeping a care account in the adult's case, itself keep that account on the same basis as the first authority has been keeping it.

(2) The second authority is subject to the duty under subsection (1) until it has–

(a) carried out the assessment or assessments under section 37(6), and

(b) taken the other steps required under this Part in the adult's case.

(3) In deciding how to meet the adult's needs for care and support under subsection (1), the second authority must involve–

(a) the adult,

(b) any carer who is continuing as the adult's carer, and

(c) any person whom the adult asks the authority to involve or, where the adult lacks capacity to ask the authority to do that, any person who appears to the authority to be interested in the adult's welfare.

(4) In deciding how to meet the needs for support of any carer who is continuing as the adult's carer, the second authority must involve–

(a) the carer,

(b) the adult needing care, if the carer asks the authority to do so, and

(c) any other person whom the carer asks the authority to involve.

(5) In performing the duty under subsection (3)(a) or (4)(a), the second authority must take all reasonable steps to reach agreement with the adult or carer about how it should meet the needs in question.

(6) The first authority is not required to meet the adult's needs for care and support or, if the adult has a carer, such needs for support as the carer has, for so long as the second authority is subject to the duty under subsection (1).

(7) Where, having complied with the duty under subsection (1), the second authority is not required to meet the adult's needs for care and support under section 18 because the adult is still ordinarily resident in the area of the first authority, the second authority may recover from the first authority the costs it incurs in complying with the duty under subsection (1).

(8) Regulations may specify matters to which the second authority must have regard in deciding how to perform the duty under subsection (1).

Establishing where a person lives, etc

Where a person's ordinary residence is

39 (1) Where an adult has needs for care and support which can be met only if the adult is living in accommodation of a type specified in regulations, and the adult is living in accommodation in England of a type so specified, the adult is to be treated for the purposes of this Part as ordinarily resident–

(a) in the area in which the adult was ordinarily resident immediately before the adult began to live in accommodation of a type specified in the regulations, or

(b) if the adult was of no settled residence immediately before the adult began to live in accommodation of a type so specified, in the area in which the adult was present at that time.

(2) Where, before beginning to live in his or her current accommodation, the adult was living in accommodation of a type so specified (whether or not of the same type as the current accommodation), the reference in subsection (1)(a) to when the adult began to live in accommodation of a type so specified is a reference to the beginning of the period during which the adult has been living in accommodation of one or more of the specified types for consecutive periods.

(3) The regulations may make provision for determining for the purposes of subsection (1) whether an adult has needs for care and support which can be met only if the adult is living in accommodation of a type specified in the regulations.

(4) An adult who is being provided with accommodation under section 117 of the Mental Health Act 1983 (after-care) is to be treated for the purposes of this Part as ordinarily resident in the area of the local authority in England or the local authority in Wales on which the duty to provide the adult with services under that section is imposed; and for that purpose–

(a) 'local authority in England' means a local authority for the purposes of this Part, and

(b) 'local authority in Wales' means a local authority for the purposes of the Social Services and Well-being (Wales) Act 2014.

(5) An adult who is being provided with NHS accommodation is to be treated for the purposes of this Part as ordinarily resident–

(a) in the area in which the adult was ordinarily resident immediately before the accommodation was provided, or

(b) if the adult was of no settled residence immediately before the accommodation was provided, in the area in which the adult was present at that time.

(6) 'NHS accommodation' means accommodation under–

(a) the National Health Service Act 2006,

(b) the National Health Service (Wales) Act 2006,

(c) the National Health Service (Scotland) Act 1978, or

(d) Article 5(1) of the Health and Personal Social Services (Northern Ireland) Order 1972.

(7) The reference in subsection (1) to this Part does not include a reference to section 28 (independent personal budget).

(8) Schedule 1 (which makes provision about cross-border placements to and from Wales, Scotland or Northern Ireland) has effect.

Disputes about ordinary residence or continuity of care

40 (1) Any dispute about where an adult is ordinarily resident for the purposes of this Part, or any dispute between local authorities under section 37 about the application of that section, is to be determined by–

(a) the Secretary of State, or

(b) where the Secretary of State appoints a person for that purpose (the 'appointed person'), that person.

(2) The Secretary of State or appointed person may review a determination under subsection (1), provided that the review begins within 3 months of the date of the determination.

(3) Having carried out a review under subsection (2), the Secretary of State or appointed person must—

(a) confirm the original determination, or

(b) substitute a different determination.

(4) Regulations may make further provision about resolution of disputes of the type mentioned in subsection (1); the regulations may, for example, include—

(a) provision for ensuring that care and support is provided to the adult while the dispute is unresolved;

(b) provision requiring the local authorities in dispute to take specified steps before referring the dispute to the Secretary of State or (as the case may be) the appointed person;

(c) provision about the procedure for referring the dispute to the Secretary of State or appointed person;

(d) where a review of a determination has been carried out under subsection (2) and a different determination substituted, provision requiring a local authority to take specified steps (including paying specified amounts) in relation to the period before the determination was substituted.

Financial adjustments between local authorities

41 (1) This section applies where—

(a) a local authority has been meeting an adult's needs for care and support, but

(b) it transpires (whether following the determination of a dispute under section 40 or otherwise) that the adult was, for some or all of the time that the authority has been meeting the adult's needs, ordinarily resident in the area of another local authority.

(2) This section also applies where—

(a) a local authority has been meeting a carer's needs for support, but

(b) it transpires (whether following the determination of a dispute under section 40 or otherwise) that the adult needing care was, for some or all of the time that the authority has been meeting the carer's needs, ordinarily resident in the area of another local authority.

(3) The local authority concerned may recover from the other local authority the amount of any payments it made towards meeting the needs in question at a time when the other local authority was instead liable to meet them under section 18 or 20(1) (as the case may be).

(4) Subsection (3) does not apply to payments which are the subject of a deferred payment agreement entered into by the local authority in question, unless it agrees with the other local authority to assign its rights and obligations under the deferred payment agreement to that other authority.

(5) Any period during which a local authority was meeting the needs in question under section 19 or 20(6) is to be disregarded for the purposes of this section.

Safeguarding adults at risk of abuse or neglect

Enquiry by local authority

42 (1) This section applies where a local authority has reasonable cause to suspect that an adult in its area (whether or not ordinarily resident there)—

(a) has needs for care and support (whether or not the authority is meeting any of those needs),

(b) is experiencing, or is at risk of, abuse or neglect, and

(c) as a result of those needs is unable to protect himself or herself against the abuse or neglect or the risk of it.

(2) The local authority must make (or cause to be made) whatever enquiries it thinks

necessary to enable it to decide whether any action should be taken in the adult's case (whether under this Part or otherwise) and, if so, what and by whom.

(3) 'Abuse' includes financial abuse; and for that purpose 'financial abuse' includes–
   (a) having money or other property stolen,
   (b) being defrauded,
   (c) being put under pressure in relation to money or other property, and
   (d) having money or other property misused.

Safeguarding Adults Boards

43 (1) Each local authority must establish a Safeguarding Adults Board (an 'SAB') for its area.
   (2) The objective of an SAB is to help and protect adults in its area in cases of the kind described in section 42(1).
   (3) The way in which an SAB must seek to achieve its objective is by co-ordinating and ensuring the effectiveness of what each of its members does.
   (4) An SAB may do anything which appears to it to be necessary or desirable for the purpose of achieving its objective.
   (5) Schedule 2 (which includes provision about the membership, funding and other resources, strategy and annual report of an SAB) has effect.
   (6) Where two or more local authorities exercise their respective duties under subsection (1) by establishing an SAB for their combined area–
   (a) a reference in this section, section 44 or Schedule 2 to the authority establishing the SAB is to be read as a reference to the authorities establishing it, and
   (b) a reference in this section, that section or that Schedule to the SAB's area is to be read as a reference to the combined area.

Safeguarding adults reviews

44 (1) An SAB must arrange for there to be a review of a case involving an adult in its area with needs for care and support (whether or not the local authority has been meeting any of those needs) if–
   (a) there is reasonable cause for concern about how the SAB, members of it or other persons with relevant functions worked together to safeguard the adult, and
   (b) condition 1 or 2 is met.
   (2) Condition 1 is met if–
   (a) the adult has died, and
   (b) the SAB knows or suspects that the death resulted from abuse or neglect (whether or not it knew about or suspected the abuse or neglect before the adult died).
   (3) Condition 2 is met if–
   (a) the adult is still alive, and
   (b) the SAB knows or suspects that the adult has experienced serious abuse or neglect.
   (4) An SAB may arrange for there to be a review of any other case involving an adult in its area with needs for care and support (whether or not the local authority has been meeting any of those needs).
   (5) Each member of the SAB must co-operate in and contribute to the carrying out of a review under this section with a view to–
   (a) identifying the lessons to be learnt from the adult's case, and
   (b) applying those lessons to future cases.

Supply of information

45 (1) If an SAB requests a person to supply information to it, or to some other person specified in the request, the person to whom the request is made must comply with the request if–
   (a) conditions 1 and 2 are met, and
   (b) condition 3 or 4 is met.
   (2) Condition 1 is that the request is made for the purpose of enabling or assisting the SAB to exercise its functions.

(3) Condition 2 is that the request is made to a person whose functions or activities the SAB considers to be such that the person is likely to have information relevant to the exercise of a function by the SAB.

(4) Condition 3 is that the information relates to–
    (a) the person to whom the request is made,
    (b) a function or activity of that person, or
    (c) a person in respect of whom that person exercises a function or engages in an activity.

(5) Condition 4 is that the information–
    (a) is information requested by the SAB from a person to whom information was supplied in compliance with another request under this section, and
    (b) is the same as, or is derived from, information so supplied.

(6) Information may be used by the SAB, or other person to whom it is supplied under subsection (1), only for the purpose of enabling or assisting the SAB to exercise its functions.

Abolition of local authority's power to remove persons in need of care

46   Section 47 of the National Assistance Act 1948 (which gives a local authority power to remove a person in need of care from home) ceases to apply to persons in England.

Protecting property of adults being cared for away from home

47 (1) This section applies where–
    (a) an adult is having needs for care and support met under section 18 or 19 in a way that involves the provision of accommodation, or is admitted to hospital (or both), and
    (b) it appears to a local authority that there is a danger of loss or damage to movable property of the adult's in the authority's area because–
        (i) the adult is unable (whether permanently or temporarily) to protect or deal with the property, and
        (ii) no suitable arrangements have been or are being made.

(2) The local authority must take reasonable steps to prevent or mitigate the loss or damage.

(3) For the purpose of performing that duty, the local authority–
    (a) may at all reasonable times and on reasonable notice enter any premises which the adult was living in immediately before being provided with accommodation or admitted to hospital, and
    (b) may deal with any of the adult's movable property in any way which is reasonably necessary for preventing or mitigating loss or damage.

(4) A local authority may not exercise the power under subsection (3)(a) unless–
    (a) it has obtained the consent of the adult concerned or, where the adult lacks capacity to give consent, the consent of a person authorised under the Mental Capacity Act 2005 to give it on the adult's behalf, or
    (b) where the adult lacks capacity to give consent and there is no person so authorised, the local authority is satisfied that exercising the power would be in the adult's best interests.

(5) Where a local authority is proposing to exercise the power under subsection (3)(a), the officer it authorises to do so must, if required, produce valid documentation setting out the authorisation to do so.

(6) A person who, without reasonable excuse, obstructs the exercise of the power under subsection (3)(a)–
    (a) commits an offence, and
    (b) is liable on summary conviction to a fine not exceeding level 4 on the standard scale.

(7) A local authority may recover from an adult whatever reasonable expenses the authority incurs under this section in the adult's case.

Provider failure

Temporary duty on local authority

48 (1) This section applies where a person registered under Chapter 2 of Part 1 of the Health and Social Care Act 2008 (a 'registered care provider') in respect of the carrying on of a regulated activity (within the meaning of that Part) becomes unable to carry on that activity because of business failure.

(2) A local authority must for so long as it considers necessary (and in so far as it is not already required to do so) meet those of an adult's needs for care and support and those of a carer's needs for support which were, immediately before the registered care provider became unable to carry on the regulated activity, being met by the carrying on of that activity in the authority's area by the provider.

(3) A local authority is accordingly required to meet needs under subsection (2) regardless of–

(a) whether the relevant adult is ordinarily resident in its area;

(b) whether the authority has carried out a needs assessment, a carer's assessment or a financial assessment;

(c) whether any of the needs meet the eligibility criteria.

(4) Where a local authority is meeting needs under subsection (2), it is not required to carry out a needs assessment, a carer's assessment or a financial assessment or to determine whether any of the needs meet the eligibility criteria.

(5) A local authority may make a charge for meeting needs under subsection (2) (except in so far as doing so involves the provision of information or advice); and a charge under this subsection may cover only the cost that the local authority incurs in meeting the needs to which the charge applies.

(6) Subsection (5) does not apply if section 49 (cross-border cases) applies (see subsection (3) of that section).

(7) If the relevant adult is not ordinarily resident in the area of the local authority which is required to meet needs under subsection (2), that authority–

(a) must, in meeting needs under that subsection which were being met under arrangements made by another local authority, co-operate with that authority (in so far as it is not already required to do so by section 6);

(b) must, in meeting needs under that subsection which were being met under arrangements all or part of the cost of which was paid for by another local authority by means of direct payments, co-operate with that authority (in so far as it is not already required to do so by section 6);

(c) may recover from the other local authority mentioned in paragraph (a) or (b) (as the case may be) the cost it incurs in meeting those of the adult's or carer's needs referred to in the paragraph in question.

(8) Any dispute between local authorities about the application of this section is to be determined under section 40 as if it were a dispute of the type mentioned in subsection (1) of that section.

(9) 'The relevant adult' means–

(a) in a case involving an adult's needs for care and support, that adult;

(b) in a case involving a carer's needs for support, the adult needing care.

Section 48: cross-border cases

49 (1) This section applies where, in a case within section 48, immediately before the registered care provider became unable to carry on the regulated activity, some or all of the adult's needs for care and support or the carer's needs for support were being met by the carrying on of that activity by the provider under arrangements made–

(a) by a local authority in Wales discharging its duty under section 35 or 40, or exercising its power under section 36 or 45, of the Social Services and Well-being (Wales) Act 2014,

(b) by a local authority in Scotland discharging its duty under section 12 or 13A of the Social Work (Scotland) Act 1968 or section 25 of the Mental Health (Care and Treatment) (Scotland) Act 2003, or

(c) by a Health and Social Care trust under Article 15 of the Health and Personal

Social Services (Northern Ireland) Order 1972 or section 2 of the Carers and Direct Payments Act (Northern Ireland) 2002.

(2) This section also applies where, in a case within section 48–

   (a) immediately before the registered care provider became unable to carry on the regulated activity, some or all of the adult's needs for care and support or the carer's needs for support were being met by the carrying on of that activity by the provider, and

   (b) all or part of the cost of the accommodation or other services provided by the provider to meet those needs was paid for by means of direct payments made–

     (i) under section 50 or 52 of the Social Services and Well-being (Wales) Act 2014,

     (ii) as a result of a choice made by the adult pursuant to section 5 of the Social Care (Self-directed Support) (Scotland) Act 2013, or

     (iii) by virtue of section 8 of the Carers and Direct Payments Act (Northern Ireland) 2002.

(3) The local authority which is required to meet needs under section 48(2)–

   (a) must, in meeting needs under section 48(2) which were being met by the authority which made the arrangements referred to in subsection (1), co-operate with that authority;

   (b) must, in meeting needs under section 48(2) which were being met by the provision of accommodation or other services all or part of the cost of which was paid for by an authority by means of direct payments as referred to in subsection (2), co-operate with that authority;

   (c) may recover from the authority referred to in paragraph (a) or (b) (as the case may be) the cost it incurs in meeting those of the adult's or carer's needs referred to in the paragraph in question;

   (d) may recover from the adult or carer the cost it incurs in meeting those of the adult's or carer's needs other than those referred to in paragraph (a) or (b) (as the case may be).

(4) Any dispute between a local authority and a local authority in Wales, a local authority in Scotland or a Health and Social Care trust about the application of section 48 or of this section is to be resolved in accordance with paragraph 5 of Schedule 1.

(5) 'Local authority in Wales' and 'local authority in Scotland' each have the meaning given in paragraph 12 of Schedule 1.

(6) The references in paragraphs (a) and (b) of subsection (3) to an authority are references to a local authority in Wales, a local authority in Scotland or a Health and Social Care trust (as the case may be).

Temporary duty on local authority in Wales

50 (1) This section applies where a person registered under Part 2 of the Care Standards Act 2000 in respect of an establishment or agency–

   (a) becomes unable to carry on or manage the establishment or agency because of business failure, and

   (b) immediately before becoming unable to do so, was providing an adult with accommodation or other services in Wales under arrangements made–

     (i) by a local authority meeting an adult's needs for care and support or a carer's needs for support under this Part,

     (ii) by a local authority in Scotland discharging its duty under section 12 or 13A of the Social Work (Scotland) Act 1968 or section 25 of the Mental Health (Care and Treatment) (Scotland) Act 2003, or

     (iii) by a Health and Social Care trust under Article 15 of the Health and Personal Social Services (Northern Ireland) Order 1972 or section 2 of the Carers and Direct Payments Act (Northern Ireland) 2002.

(2) This section also applies where a person registered under Part 2 of the Care Standards Act 2000 in respect of an establishment or agency–

   (a) becomes unable to carry on or manage the establishment or agency because of business failure, and

   (b) immediately before becoming unable to do so, was providing an adult with accommodation or other services in Wales all or part of the cost of which was paid for by means of direct payments made–

    (i)   under this Part of this Act,

    (ii) as a result of a choice made by the adult pursuant to section 5 of the Social Care (Self-directed Support) (Scotland) Act 2013, or

    (iii) by virtue of section 8 of the Carers and Direct Payments Act (Northern Ireland) 2002.

(3) The local authority in Wales in whose area the accommodation is situated or the services were provided must for so long as it considers necessary meet those of the adult's needs for care and support or the carer's needs for support which were being met by the registered person by the provision of the accommodation or other services.

(4) A local authority in Wales which is required to meet needs under subsection (3)–

    (a) must, in meeting needs under that subsection which were being met by the authority which made the arrangements referred to in subsection (1)(b), co-operate with that authority;

    (b) must, in meeting needs under subsection (3) which were being met by the provision of accommodation or other services all or part of the cost of which was paid for by an authority by means of direct payments as referred to in subsection (2)(b), co-operate with that authority;

    (c) may recover from the authority referred to in paragraph (a) or (b) (as the case may be) the cost it incurs in meeting those of the adult's or carer's needs referred to in the paragraph in question.

(5) Any dispute about the application of this section is to be resolved in accordance with paragraph 5 of Schedule 1.

(6) 'Local authority in Wales' and 'local authority in Scotland' each have the meaning given in paragraph 12 of Schedule 1.

(7) The references in paragraphs (a) and (b) of subsection (4) to an authority are references to a local authority, a local authority in Scotland or a Health and Social Care trust (as the case may be).

Temporary duty on Health and Social Care trust in Northern Ireland

51 (1) This section applies where a person registered under Part 3 of the Health and Social Services (Quality, Improvement and Regulation) (Northern Ireland) Order 2003 in respect of an establishment or agency–

    (a) becomes unable to carry on or manage the establishment or agency because of business failure, and

    (b) immediately before becoming unable to do so, was providing an adult with accommodation or other services in Northern Ireland under arrangements made–

        (i)   by a local authority meeting an adult's needs for care and support or a carer's needs for support under this Part,

        (ii) by a local authority in Wales discharging its duty under section 35 or 40, or exercising its power under section 36 or 45, of the Social Services and Well-being (Wales) Act 2014, or

        (iii) by a local authority in Scotland discharging its duty under section 12 or 13A of the Social Work (Scotland) Act 1968 or section 25 of the Mental Health (Care and Treatment) (Scotland) Act 2003.

(2) This section also applies where a person registered under Part 3 of the Health and Personal Social Services (Quality, Improvement and Regulation) (Northern Ireland) Order 2003 in respect of an establishment or agency–

    (a) becomes unable to carry on or manage the establishment or agency because of business failure, and

    (b) immediately before becoming unable to do so, was providing an adult with accommodation or other services in Northern Ireland, all or part of the cost of which was paid for by means of direct payments made–

        (i)   under this Part of this Act,

        (ii) under section 50 or 52 of the Social Services and Well-being (Wales) Act 2014, or

    (iii) as a result of a choice made by the adult pursuant to section 5 of the Social
        Care (Self-directed Support) (Scotland) Act 2013.

(3) The Health and Social Care trust in whose area the accommodation is situated or
the services were provided must for so long as it considers necessary meet those of
the adult's needs for care and support or the carer's needs for support which were
being met by the registered person by the provision of the accommodation or other
services.

(4) A Health and Social Care trust which is required to meet needs under
subsection (3)–

   (a) must, in meeting needs under that subsection which were being met by the
authority which made the arrangements referred to in subsection (1)(b), co-
operate with that authority;

   (b) must, in meeting needs under subsection (3) which were being met by the provision of accommodation or other services all or part of the cost of which was
paid for by an authority by means of direct payments as referred to in subsection (2)(b), co-operate with that authority;

   (c) may recover from the authority referred to in paragraph (a) or (b) (as the case
may be) the cost it incurs in meeting those of the adult's or carer's needs
referred to in the paragraph in question.

(5) Any dispute about the application of this section is to be resolved in accordance
with paragraph 5 of Schedule 1.

(6) 'Local authority in Wales' and 'local authority in Scotland' each have the meaning
given in paragraph 12 of Schedule 1.

(7) The references in paragraphs (a) and (b) of subsection (4) to an authority are references to a local authority, a local authority in Wales or a local authority in Scotland
(as the case may be).

Sections 48 to 51: supplementary

52 (1) An authority becomes subject to the duty under section 48(2), 50(3) or 51(3) as soon
as it becomes aware of the business failure.

(2) Section 8 (how to meet needs) applies to meeting needs under section 48(2) as it
applies to meeting needs under section 18.

(3) Section 34 of the Social Services and Well-being (Wales) Act 2014 (how to meet
needs) applies to meeting needs under section 50(3) as it applies to meeting needs
under section 35 of that Act.

(4) In deciding how to meet an adult's needs for care and support under section 48(2),
50(3) or 51(3), an authority must involve–

   (a) the adult,

   (b) any carer that the adult has, and

   (c) any person whom the adult asks the authority to involve or, where the adult
lacks capacity to ask the authority to do that, any person who appears to the
authority to be interested in the adult's welfare.

(5) In deciding how to meet a carer's needs for support under section 48(2), 50(3) or
51(3), an authority must involve–

   (a) the carer, and

   (b) any person whom the carer asks the authority to involve.

(6) In carrying out the duty under subsection (4)(a) or (5)(a), an authority must take
all reasonable steps to reach agreement with the adult or carer about how it should
meet the needs in question.

(7) Sections 21 to 23 (exceptions to duty to meet needs) apply to meeting needs under
section 48(2) as they apply to meeting needs under section 18.

(8) Sections 46 to 49 of the Social Services and Well-being (Wales) Act 2014 (exceptions to, and restrictions on, duty to meet needs) apply to meeting needs under
section 50(3) as they apply to meeting needs under section 35 of that Act.

(9) Where an adult whose case comes within section 48 is being provided with NHS
continuing healthcare under arrangements made by a clinical commissioning
group no part of whose area is in the local authority's area, the group is to be treated
as a relevant partner of the authority for the purposes of sections 6 and 7.

(10) 'NHS continuing healthcare' is to be construed in accordance with standing rules under section 6E of the National Health Service Act 2006.

(11) Where a local authority considers it necessary to do so for the purpose of carrying out its duty under section 48(2), it may request the registered care provider, or such other person involved in the provider's business as it considers appropriate, to provide it with specified information.

(12) Regulations must make provision as to the interpretation for the purposes of sections 48, 50 and 51 and this section of references to business failure or to being unable to do something because of business failure; and the regulations may, in particular, specify circumstances in which a person is to be treated as unable to do something because of business failure.

(13) Pending the commencement of Part 4 of the Social Services and Well-being (Wales) Act 2014–

  (a) a reference in section 49 or 51 to making arrangements to meet needs under section 35 or 36 of that Act is to be read as a reference to making arrangements or providing services under–
    (i)   Part 3 of the National Assistance Act 1948,
    (ii) section 45 of the Health Services and Public Health Act 1968,
    (iii) section 117 of the Mental Health Act 1983, or
    (iv) Schedule 15 to the National Health Service (Wales) Act 2006;

  (b) a reference in section 49 or 51 to making arrangements to meet needs under section 40 or 45 of that Act is to be read as a reference to providing services as referred to in section 2 of the Carers and Disabled Children Act 2000;

  (c) a reference in section 49 or 51 to making direct payments under section 50 or 52 of that Act is to be read as a reference to making direct payments by virtue of section 57 of the Health and Social Care Act 2001;

  (d) subsection (8) is to be read as if there were substituted for it–
    '(8) Sections 21(1A) and (8) and 29(6) of the National Assistance Act 1948 apply to meeting needs under section 50(3) as they apply to the exercise of functions under sections 21 and 29 of that Act by a local authority in Wales (within the meaning given in paragraph 12 of Schedule 1).'

(14) Pending the commencement of section 5 of the Social Care (Self-directed Support) (Scotland) Act 2013–

  (a) sections 49(2)(b)(ii) and 50(2)(b)(ii) are to be read as if there were substituted for each of them–
    '(ii) under section 12B of the Social Work (Scotland) Act 1968,', and

  (b) section 51(2)(b)(iii) is to be read as if there were substituted for it–
    '(iii) under section 12B of the Social Work (Scotland) Act 1968.'.

Market oversight

Specifying criteria for application of market oversight regime

53 (1) Regulations must specify criteria for determining whether (subject to regulations under subsection (4)) section 55 (financial sustainability assessment) applies to a registered care provider who is registered in respect of the carrying on of a regulated activity relating to the provision of social care for adults.

  (2) In specifying the criteria, the Secretary of State must have regard to the following in particular–
    (a) the amount of social care provided by a registered care provider,
    (b) the geographical concentration of a registered care provider's business,
    (c) the extent to which a registered care provider specialises in the provision of particular types of care.

  (3) The Secretary of State must–
    (a) at such times as the Secretary of State considers appropriate, review the criteria for the time being specified in the regulations, and
    (b) publish information about how the matters mentioned in subsection (2), and any other matters to which the Secretary of State has regard in specifying the criteria, are to be measured.

  (4) Regulations may provide that section 55 does not apply, or applies only to the extent

specified, to a specified registered care provider or to a registered care provider of a specified description, regardless of whether that provider or a provider of that description would satisfy the criteria.

(5) Regulations may provide that section 55 applies, or applies to the extent specified, to a specified registered care provider or to a registered care provider of a specified description, regardless of whether that provider or a provider of that description would satisfy the criteria.

(6) The circumstances in which regulations may be made under subsection (4) include those in which the Secretary of State is satisfied that certain registered care providers are already subject to a regulatory regime comparable to that provided for by sections 55 and 56; and regulations made in such circumstances may, for example, make provision requiring specified persons to co-operate or to share information of a specified description.

(7) 'Social care' has the same meaning as in Part 1 of the Health and Social Care Act 2008.

Determining whether criteria apply to care provider

54 (1) The Care Quality Commission must determine, in the case of each registered care provider, whether the provider satisfies one or more of the criteria specified in regulations under section 53.

(2) If the Commission determines that the provider satisfies one or more of the criteria, section 55 applies to that provider unless, or except in so far as, regulations under section 53(4) provide that it does not apply.

(3) Where section 55 applies to a registered care provider (whether as a result of subsection (2) or as a result of regulations under section 53(5)), the Commission must inform the provider accordingly.

Assessment of financial sustainability of care provider

55 (1) Where this section applies to a registered care provider, the Care Quality Commission must assess the financial sustainability of the provider's business of carrying on the regulated activity in respect of which it is registered.

(2) Where the Commission, in light of an assessment under subsection (1), considers that there is a significant risk to the financial sustainability of the provider's business, it may–
   (a) require the provider to develop a plan for how to mitigate or eliminate the risk;
   (b) arrange for, or require the provider to arrange for, a person with appropriate professional expertise to carry out an independent review of the business.

(3) Where the Commission imposes a requirement on a care provider under subsection (2)(a), it may also require the provider–
   (a) to co-operate with it in developing the plan, and
   (b) to obtain its approval of the finalised plan.

(4) Where the Commission arranges for a review under subsection (2)(b), it may recover from the provider such costs as the Commission incurs in connection with the arrangements (other than its administrative costs in making the arrangements).

(5) Regulations may make provision for enabling the Commission to obtain from such persons as it considers appropriate information which the Commission believes will assist it to assess the financial sustainability of a registered care provider to which this section applies.

(6) Regulations may make provision about the making of the assessment required by subsection (1).

(7) The Commission may consult such persons as it considers appropriate on the method for assessing the financial sustainability of a registered care provider's business; and, having done so, it must publish guidance on the method it expects to apply in making the assessment.

Informing local authorities where failure of care provider likely

56 (1) This section applies where the Care Quality Commission is satisfied that a registered care provider to which section 55 applies is likely to become unable to carry

on the regulated activity in respect of which it is registered because of business failure as mentioned in section 48.

(2) The Commission must inform the local authorities which it thinks will be required to carry out the duty under section 48(2) if the provider becomes unable to carry on the regulated activity in question.

(3) Where the Commission considers it necessary to do so for the purpose of assisting a local authority to carry out the duty under section 48(2), it may request the provider, or such other person involved in the provider's business as the Commission considers appropriate, to provide it with specified information.

(4) Where (as a result of subsection (3) or otherwise) the Commission has information about the provider's business that it considers may assist a local authority in carrying out the duty under section 48(2), the Commission must give the information to the local authority.

(5) Regulations may make provision as to the circumstances in which the Commission is entitled to be satisfied for the purposes of subsection (1) that a registered care provider is likely to become unable to carry on a regulated activity.

(6) The Commission may consult such persons as it considers appropriate on the methods to apply in assessing likelihood for the purposes of subsection (1); and, having carried out that consultation, it must publish guidance on the methods it expects to apply in making the assessment.

Sections 54 to 56: supplementary

57 (1) For the purposes of Part 1 of the Health and Social Care Act 2008, the duties imposed on the Care Quality Commission under sections 54(1) and 55(1) are to be treated as regulatory functions of the Commission.

(2) For the purposes of that Part of that Act, the doing by the Commission of anything for the purpose of assisting a local authority to carry out the duty under section 48(2) is to be treated as one of the Commission's regulatory functions.

(3) For the purposes of sections 17 and 18 of that Act (cancellation or suspension of registration under Part 1 of that Act), a requirement imposed on a registered care provider under or by virtue of any of sections 54 to 56 (or by virtue of subsection (1) or (2)) is to be treated as a requirement imposed by or under Chapter 6 of Part 1 of that Act.

(4) The Commission must, in exercising any of its functions under sections 54 to 56, have regard to the need to minimise the burdens it imposes on others.

Transition for children to adult care and support, etc

Assessment of a child's needs for care and support

58 (1) Where it appears to a local authority that a child is likely to have needs for care and support after becoming 18, the authority must, if it is satisfied that it would be of significant benefit to the child to do so and if the consent condition is met, assess–

(a) whether the child has needs for care and support and, if so, what those needs are, and

(b) whether the child is likely to have needs for care and support after becoming 18 and, if so, what those needs are likely to be.

(2) An assessment under subsection (1) is referred to in this Part as a 'child's needs assessment'.

(3) The consent condition is met if–

(a) the child has capacity or is competent to consent to a child's needs assessment being carried out and the child does so consent, or

(b) the child lacks capacity or is not competent so to consent but the authority is satisfied that carrying out a child's needs assessment would be in the child's best interests.

(4) Where a child refuses a child's needs assessment and the consent condition is accordingly not met, the local authority must nonetheless carry out the assessment if the child is experiencing, or is at risk of, abuse or neglect.

(5) Where a local authority, having received a request to carry out a child's assessment

from the child concerned or a parent or carer of the child, decides not to comply with the request, it must give the person who made the request–

   (a) written reasons for its decision, and

   (b) information and advice about what can be done to prevent or delay the development by the child of needs for care and support in the future.

(6) 'Parent', in relation to a child, includes–

   (a) a parent of the child who does not have parental responsibility for the child, and

   (b) a person who is not a parent of the child but who has parental responsibility for the child.

(7) 'Carer', in relation to a child, means a person, other than a parent, who is providing care for the child, whether or not under or by virtue of a contract or as voluntary work.

(8) The reference to providing care includes a reference to providing practical or emotional support.

Child's needs assessment: requirements etc

59 (1) A child's needs assessment must include an assessment of–

   (a) the impact on the matters specified in section 1(2) of what the child's needs for care and support are likely to be after the child becomes 18,

   (b) the outcomes that the child wishes to achieve in day-to-day life, and

   (c) whether, and if so to what extent, the provision of care and support could contribute to the achievement of those outcomes.

(2) A local authority, in carrying out a child's needs assessment, must involve–

   (a) the child,

   (b) the child's parents and any carer that the child has, and

   (c) any person whom the child or a parent or carer of the child requests the local authority to involve.

(3) When carrying out a child's needs assessment, a local authority must also consider whether, and if so to what extent, matters other than the provision of care and support could contribute to the achievement of the outcomes that the child wishes to achieve in day-to-day life.

(4) Having carried out a child's needs assessment, a local authority must give the child–

   (a) an indication as to whether any of the needs for care and support which it thinks the child is likely to have after becoming 18 are likely to meet the eligibility criteria (and, if so, which ones are likely to do so), and

   (b) advice and information about–

      (i) what can be done to meet or reduce the needs which it thinks the child is likely to have after becoming 18;

      (ii) what can be done to prevent or delay the development by the child of needs for care and support in the future.

(5) But in a case where the child is not competent or lacks capacity to understand the things which the local authority is required to give under subsection (4), that subsection is to have effect as if for 'must give the child' there were substituted 'must give the child's parents'.

(6) Where a person to whom a child's needs assessment relates becomes 18, the local authority must decide whether to treat the assessment as a needs assessment; and if the authority decides to do so, this Part applies to the child's needs assessment as if it were a needs assessment that had been carried out after the person had become 18.

(7) In considering what to decide under subsection (6), a local authority must have regard to–

   (a) when the child's needs assessment was carried out, and

   (b) whether it appears to the authority that the circumstances of the person to whom the child's needs assessment relates have changed in a way that might affect the assessment.

(8) 'Carer' has the same meaning as in section 58.

Assessment of a child's carer's needs for support

60 (1) Where it appears to a local authority that a carer of a child is likely to have needs for support after the child becomes 18, the authority must, if it is satisfied that it would be of significant benefit to the carer to do so, assess–
   (a) whether the carer has needs for support and, if so, what those needs are, and
   (b) whether the carer is likely to have needs for support after the child becomes 18 and, if so, what those needs are likely to be.

(2) An assessment under subsection (1) is referred to in this Part as a 'child's carer's assessment'.

(3) Where a child's carer refuses a child's carer's assessment, the local authority is not required to carry out the assessment (and subsection (1) does not apply in the carer's case).

(4) Where, having refused a child's carer's assessment, a child's carer requests the assessment, subsection (1) applies in the carer's case (and subsection (3) does not).

(5) Where a child's carer has refused a child's carer's assessment and the local authority concerned thinks that the carer's needs or circumstances have changed, subsection (1) applies in the carer's case (but subject to further refusal as mentioned in subsection (3)).

(6) Where a local authority, having received a request to carry out a child's carer's assessment from the carer concerned, decides not to comply with the request, it must give the carer–
   (a) written reasons for its decision, and
   (b) information and advice about what can be done to prevent or delay the development by the carer of needs for support in the future.

(7) 'Carer', in relation to a child, means an adult (including one who is a parent of the child) who provides or intends to provide care for the child (but see subsection (8)).

(8) An adult is not a carer for the purposes of this section if the adult provides or intends to provide care–
   (a) under or by virtue of a contract, or
   (b) as voluntary work.

(9) But in a case where the local authority considers that the relationship between the child and the adult providing or intending to provide care is such that it would be appropriate for the adult to be regarded as a carer, the adult is to be regarded as such (and subsection (8) is therefore to be ignored in that case).

(10) The references to providing care include a reference to providing practical or emotional support.

Child's carer's assessment: requirements etc

61 (1) A child's carer's assessment must include an assessment of–
   (a) whether the carer is able to provide care for the child and is likely to continue to be able to do so after the child becomes 18,
   (b) whether the carer is willing to do so and is likely to continue to be willing to do so after the child becomes 18,
   (c) the impact on the matters specified in section 1(2) of what the carer's needs for support are likely to be after the child becomes 18,
   (d) the outcomes that the carer wishes to achieve in day-to-day life, and
   (e) whether, and if so to what extent, the provision of support could contribute to the achievement of those outcomes.

(2) A local authority, in carrying out a child's carer's assessment, must have regard to–
   (a) whether the carer works or wishes to do so, and
   (b) whether the carer is participating in or wishes to participate in education, training or recreation.

(3) A local authority, in carrying out a child's carer's assessment, must involve–
   (a) the carer, and
   (b) any person whom the carer asks the local authority to involve.

(4) When carrying out a child's carer's assessment, a local authority must also consider whether, and if so to what extent, matters other than the provision of support could contribute to the achievement of the outcomes that the carer wishes to achieve in day-to-day life.

(5) Having carried out a child's carer's assessment, a local authority must give the carer–

 (a) an indication as to whether any of the needs for support which it thinks the carer is likely to have after the child becomes 18 are likely to meet the eligibility criteria (and, if so, which ones are likely to do so), and

 (b) advice and information about–

 (i) what can be done to meet or reduce the needs which it thinks the carer is likely to have after the child becomes 18;

 (ii) what can be done to prevent or delay the development by the carer of needs for support in the future.

(6) Where, in the case of a carer to whom a child's carer's assessment relates, the child becomes 18, the local authority must decide whether to treat the assessment as a carer's assessment; and if the authority decides to do so, this Part applies to the child's carer's assessment as if it were a carer's assessment that had been carried out after the child had become 18.

(7) In considering what to decide under subsection (6), a local authority must have regard to–

 (a) when the child's carer's assessment was carried out, and

 (b) whether it appears to the authority that the circumstances of the carer to whom the child's carer's assessment relates have changed in a way that might affect the assessment.

(8) 'Carer' has the same meaning as in section 60.

Power to meet child's carer's needs for support

62 (1) Where a local authority, having carried out a child's carer's assessment, is satisfied that the carer has needs for support, it may meet such of those needs as it considers appropriate.

(2) Regulations may make provision in connection with the exercise of the power under subsection (1); the regulations may, in particular, provide for provisions of this Part to apply with such modifications as may be specified.

(3) In deciding whether or how to exercise the power under subsection (1), a local authority must have regard to any services being provided to the carer under–

 (a) section 17 of the Children Act 1989, or

 (b) sections 37 to 39 of the Social Services and Well-being (Wales) Act 2014.

(4) 'Carer' has the same meaning as in section 60.

Assessment of a young carer's needs for support

63 (1) Where it appears to a local authority that a young carer is likely to have needs for support after becoming 18, the authority must, if it is satisfied that it would be of significant benefit to the young carer to do so and if the consent condition is met, assess–

 (a) whether the young carer has needs for support and, if so, what those needs are, and

 (b) whether the young carer is likely to have needs for support after becoming 18 and, if so, what those needs are likely to be.

(2) An assessment under subsection (1) is referred to in this Part as a 'young carer's assessment'.

(3) The consent condition is met if–

 (a) the young carer has capacity or is competent to consent to a young carer's assessment being carried out and the young carer does so consent, or

 (b) the young carer lacks capacity or is not competent so to consent but the authority is satisfied that carrying out a young carer's assessment would be in the young carer's best interests.

(4) Where a young carer refuses a young carer's assessment and the consent condition is accordingly not met, the local authority must nonetheless carry out the

assessment if the young carer is experiencing, or is at risk of, abuse or neglect.

(5) Where a local authority, having received a request to carry out a young carer's assessment from the young carer concerned or a parent of the young carer, decides not to comply with the request, it must give the person who made the request–
  (a) written reasons for its decision, and
  (b) advice and information about what can be done to prevent or delay the development by the young carer of needs for support in the future.

(6) 'Young carer' means a person under 18 who provides or intends to provide care for an adult (but see subsection (7)).

(7) A person is not a young carer for the purposes of this section if the person provides or intends to provide care–
  (a) under or by virtue of a contract, or
  (b) as voluntary work.

(8) But in a case where the local authority considers that the relationship between the adult and the person under 18 providing or intending to provide care is such that it would be appropriate for the person under 18 to be regarded as a young carer, that person is to be regarded as such (and subsection (7) is therefore to be ignored in that case).

(9) The references to providing care include a reference to providing practical or emotional support.

Young carer's assessment: requirements etc

64 (1) A young carer's assessment must include an assessment of–
  (a) whether the young carer is able to provide care for the person in question and is likely to continue to be able to do so after becoming 18,
  (b) whether the young carer is willing to do so and is likely to continue to be willing to do so after becoming 18,
  (c) the impact on the matters specified in section 1(2) of what the young carer's needs for support are likely to be after the young carer becomes 18,
  (d) the outcomes that the young carer wishes to achieve in day-to-day life, and
  (e) whether, and if so to what extent, the provision of support could contribute to the achievement of those outcomes.

(2) A local authority, in carrying out a young carer's assessment, must have regard to–
  (a) the extent to which the young carer works or wishes to work (or is likely to wish to do so after becoming 18),
  (b) the extent to which the young carer is participating in or wishes to participate in education, training or recreation (or is likely to wish to do so after becoming 18).

(3) A local authority, in carrying out a young carer's assessment, must involve–
  (a) the young carer,
  (b) the young carer's parents, and
  (c) any person whom the young carer or a parent of the young carer requests the authority to involve.

(4) When carrying out a young carer's assessment, a local authority must also consider whether, and if so to what extent, matters other than the provision of support could contribute to the achievement of the outcomes that the young carer wishes to achieve in day-to-day life.

(5) Having carried out a young carer's assessment, a local authority must give the young carer–
  (a) an indication as to whether any of the needs for support which it thinks the young carer is likely to have after becoming 18 are likely to meet the eligibility criteria (and, if so, which ones are likely to do so), and
  (b) advice and information about–
    (i) what can be done to meet or reduce the needs for support which it thinks the young carer is likely to have after becoming 18;
    (ii) what can be done to prevent or delay the development by the young carer of needs for support in the future.

(6) But in a case where the young carer is not competent or lacks capacity to understand the things which the local authority is required to give under subsection (5), that subsection is to have effect as if for 'must give the young carer' there were substituted 'must give the young carer's parents'.

(7) Where a person to whom a young carer's assessment relates becomes 18, the local authority must decide whether to treat the assessment as a carer's assessment; and if the authority decides to do so, this Part applies to the young carer's assessment as if it were a carer's assessment that had been carried out after the person had become 18.

(8) In considering what to decide under subsection (7), a local authority must have regard to—
   (a) when the young carer's assessment was carried out, and
   (b) whether it appears to the authority that the circumstances of the person to whom the young carer's assessment relates have changed in a way that might affect the assessment.

Assessments under sections 58 to 64: further provision

65 (1) Regulations under section 12—
   (a) may make such provision about carrying out a child's needs assessment as they may make about carrying out a needs assessment;
   (b) may make such provision about carrying out a child's carer's assessment or a young carer's assessment as they may make about carrying out a carer's assessment.

(2) A local authority may combine a child's needs assessment or young carer's assessment with an assessment it is carrying out (whether or not under this Part) in relation to another person only if the consent condition is met in relation to the child to whom the child's needs or young carer's assessment relates and—
   (a) where the combination would include an assessment relating to another child, the consent condition is met in relation to that other child;
   (b) where the combination would include an assessment relating to an adult, the adult agrees.

(3) A local authority may combine a child's carer's assessment with an assessment it is carrying out (whether or not under this Part) in relation to another person only if the adult to whom the child's carer's assessment relates agrees and—
   (a) where the combination would include an assessment relating to another adult, that other adult agrees, and
   (b) where the combination would include an assessment relating to a child, the consent condition is met in relation to that child.

(4) The consent condition is met in relation to a child if—
   (a) the child has capacity or is competent to agree to the assessments being combined and does so agree, or
   (b) the child lacks capacity or is not competent so to agree but the local authority is satisfied that combining the assessments would be in the child's best interests.

(5) Where a local authority is carrying out a child's needs assessment, a child's carer's assessment or a young carer's assessment, and there is some other assessment being or about to be carried out in relation to the person to whom the assessment relates or in relation to a relevant person, the local authority may carry out that other assessment—
   (a) on behalf of or jointly with the body responsible for carrying it out, or
   (b) if that body has arranged to carry out the other assessment jointly with another person, jointly with that body and the other person.

(6) A reference to an assessment includes a reference to part of an assessment.

(7) A person is a 'relevant person', in relation to a child's needs, child's carer's or young carer's assessment, if it would be reasonable to combine an assessment relating to that person with the child's needs, child's carer's or young carer's assessment (as mentioned in subsections (2) and (3)).

Continuity of services under other legislation

66 (1) Before section 17A of the Children Act 1989 insert–

'**Section 17 services: transition for children to adult care and support**

17ZH(1) Subsections (2) to (4) apply where a local authority in England providing services for a child in need in the exercise of functions conferred by section 17–

   (a) are required by section 58(1) or 63(1) of the Care Act 2014 to carry out a child's needs assessment or young carer's assessment in relation to the child, or

   (b) are required by section 60(1) of that Act to carry out a child's carer's assessment in relation to a carer of the child.

  (2) If the local authority carry out the assessment before the child reaches the age of 18 and decide to treat it as a needs or carer's assessment in accordance with section 59(6), 61(6) or 64(7) of the Care Act 2014 (with Part 1 of that Act applying to the assessment as a result), the authority must continue to comply with section 17 after the child reaches the age of 18 until they reach a conclusion in his case.

  (3) If the local authority carry out the assessment before the child reaches the age of 18 but decide not to treat it as a needs or carer's assessment in accordance with section 59(6), 61(6) or 64(7) of the Care Act 2014–

   (a) they must carry out a needs or carer's assessment (as the case may be) after the child reaches the age of 18, and

   (b) they must continue to comply with section 17 after he reaches that age until they reach a conclusion in his case.

  (4) If the local authority do not carry out the assessment before the child reaches the age of 18, they must continue to comply with section 17 after he reaches that age until–

   (a) they decide that the duty under section 9 or 10 of the Care Act 2014 (needs or carer's assessment) does not apply, or

   (b) having decided that the duty applies and having discharged it, they reach a conclusion in his case.

  (5) Subsection (6) applies where a local authority in England providing services for a child in need in the exercise of functions conferred by section 17–

   (a) receive a request for a child's needs assessment or young carer's assessment to be carried out in relation to the child or for a child's carer's assessment to be carried out in relation to a carer of the child, but

   (b) have yet to be required by section 58(1), 60(1) or 63(1) of the Care Act 2014 to carry out the assessment.

  (6) If the local authority do not decide, before the child reaches the age of 18, whether or not to comply with the request, they must continue to comply with section 17 after he reaches that age until–

   (a) they decide that the duty under section 9 or 10 of the Care Act 2014 does not apply, or

   (b) having decided that the duty applies and having discharged it, they reach a conclusion in his case.

  (7) A local authority reach a conclusion in a person's case when–

   (a) they conclude that he does not have needs for care and support or for support (as the case may be), or

   (b) having concluded that he has such needs and that they are going to meet some or all of them, they begin to do so, or

   (c) having concluded that he has such needs, they conclude that they are not going to meet any of those needs (whether because those needs do not meet the eligibility criteria or for some other reason).

  (8) In this section, 'child's needs assessment', 'child's carer's assessment', 'young carer's assessment', 'needs assessment', 'carer's assessment' and 'eligibility criteria' each have the same meaning as in Part 1 of the Care Act 2014.

Section 17 services: provision after EHC plan no longer maintained

17ZI(1) This section applies where a local authority in England providing services for a person in the exercise, by virtue of section 17ZG, of functions conferred by section 17 are required to carry out a needs assessment in that person's case.

(2) If the EHC plan for the person ceases to be maintained before the local authority reach a conclusion in the person's case, they must continue to comply with section 17 until they do reach a conclusion in his case.

(3) The references to the local authority reaching a conclusion in a person's case are to be read with section 17ZH(7).

(4) In this section, 'needs assessment' has the same meaning as in Part 1 of the Care Act 2014.'

(2) In section 17ZG of that Act (continued provision of services under section 17 where EHC plan maintained), in subsection (2), after 'after the EHC plan has ceased to be maintained' insert ', except in so far as the authority is required to do so under section 17ZH or 17ZI'.

(3) After section 2 of the Chronically Sick and Disabled Persons Act 1970 insert–

'Welfare services: transition for children to adult care and support

2A(1) Subsections (2) to (4) apply where a local authority in England making arrangements for a disabled child under section 2 are required by section 58(1) of the Care Act 2014 to carry out a child's needs assessment in relation to the child.

(2) If the local authority carry out the assessment before the child reaches the age of 18 and decide to treat it as a needs assessment in accordance with section 59(6) of the Care Act 2014 (with Part 1 of that Act applying to the assessment as a result), the authority must continue to comply with section 2 after the child reaches the age of 18 until they reach a conclusion in his case.

(3) If the local authority carry out the assessment before the child reaches the age of 18 but decide not to treat it as a needs assessment in accordance with section 59(6) of that Act–
   (a) they must carry out a needs assessment after the child reaches the age of 18, and
   (b) they must continue to comply with section 2 after he reaches that age until they reach a conclusion in his case.

(4) If the local authority do not carry out the assessment before the child reaches the age of 18, they must continue to comply with section 2 after he reaches that age until–
   (a) they decide that the duty under section 9 of the Care Act 2014 (needs assessment) does not apply, or
   (b) having decided that the duty applies and having discharged it, they reach a conclusion in his case.

(5) Subsection (6) applies where a local authority in England making arrangements for a disabled child under section 2–
   (a) receive a request for a child's needs assessment to be carried out in relation to the child, but
   (b) have yet to be required by section 58(1) of the Care Act 2014 to carry out the assessment.

(6) If the local authority do not decide, before the child reaches the age of 18, whether or not to comply with the request, they must continue to comply with section 2 after he reaches that age until–
   (a) they decide that the duty under section 9 of the Care Act 2014 does not apply, or
   (b) having decided that the duty applies and having discharged it, they reach a conclusion in his case.

(7) A local authority reach a conclusion in a person's case when–
   (a) they conclude that he does not have needs for care and support,
   (b) having concluded that he has such needs and that they are going to meet some or all of them, they begin to do so, or

(c) having concluded that he has such needs, they conclude that they are not going to meet any of those needs (whether because those needs do not meet the eligibility criteria or for some other reason).

(8) In this section, 'child's needs assessment', 'needs assessment' and 'eligibility criteria' each have the same meaning as in Part 1 of the Care Act 2014.'

Independent advocacy support

Involvement in assessments, plans etc

67 (1) This section applies where a local authority is required by a relevant provision to involve an individual in its exercise of a function.

(2) The authority must, if the condition in subsection (4) is met, arrange for a person who is independent of the authority (an 'independent advocate') to be available to represent and support the individual for the purpose of facilitating the individual's involvement; but see subsection (5).

(3) The relevant provisions are–
  (a) section 9(5)(a) and (b) (carrying out needs assessment);
  (b) section 10(7)(a) (carrying out carer's assessment);
  (c) section 25(3)(a) and (b) (preparing care and support plan);
  (d) section 25(4)(a) and (b) (preparing support plan);
  (e) section 27(2)(b)(i) and (ii) (revising care and support plan);
  (f) section 27(3)(b)(i) and (ii) (revising support plan);
  (g) section 59(2)(a) and (b) (carrying out child's needs assessment);
  (h) section 61(3)(a) (carrying out child's carer's assessment);
  (i) section 64(3)(a) and (b) (carrying out young carer's assessment).

(4) The condition is that the local authority considers that, were an independent advocate not to be available, the individual would experience substantial difficulty in doing one or more of the following–
  (a) understanding relevant information;
  (b) retaining that information;
  (c) using or weighing that information as part of the process of being involved;
  (d) communicating the individual's views, wishes or feelings (whether by talking, using sign language or any other means).

(5) The duty under subsection (2) does not apply if the local authority is satisfied that there is a person–
  (a) who would be an appropriate person to represent and support the individual for the purpose of facilitating the individual's involvement, and
  (b) who is not engaged in providing care or treatment for the individual in a professional capacity or for remuneration.

(6) For the purposes of subsection (5), a person is not to be regarded as an appropriate person unless–
  (a) where the individual has capacity or is competent to consent to being represented and supported by that person, the individual does so consent, or
  (b) where the individual lacks capacity or is not competent so to consent, the local authority is satisfied that being represented and supported by that person would be in the individual's best interests.

(7) Regulations may make provision in connection with the making of arrangements under subsection (2); the regulations may in particular–
  (a) specify requirements that must be met for a person to be independent for the purposes of subsection (2);
  (b) specify matters to which a local authority must have regard in deciding whether an individual would experience substantial difficulty of the kind mentioned in subsection (4);
  (c) specify circumstances in which the exception in subsection (5) does not apply;
  (d) make provision as to the manner in which independent advocates are to perform their functions;
  (e) specify circumstances in which, if an assessment under this Part is combined with an assessment under this Part that relates to another person, each person

may or must be represented and supported by the same independent advocate or by different independent advocates;

    (f) provide that an independent advocate may, in such circumstances or subject to such conditions as may be specified, examine and take copies of relevant records relating to the individual.

(8) This section does not restrict the provision that may be made under any other provision of this Act.

(9) 'Relevant record' means–

    (a) a health record (within the meaning given in section 68 of the Data Protection Act 1998 (as read with section 69 of that Act)),

    (b) a record of, or held by, a local authority and compiled in connection with a function under this Part or a social services function (within the meaning given in section 1A of the Local Authority Social Services Act 1970),

    (c) a record held by a person registered under Part 2 of the Care Standards Act 2000 or Chapter 2 of Part 1 of the Health and Social Care Act 2008, or

    (d) a record of such other description as may be specified in the regulations.

Safeguarding enquiries and reviews

68 (1) This section applies where there is to be–

    (a) an enquiry under section 42(2),

    (b) a review under section 44(1) of a case in which condition 2 in section 44(3) is met or a review under section 44(4).

(2) The relevant local authority must, if the condition in subsection (3) is met, arrange for a person who is independent of the authority (an 'independent advocate') to be available to represent and support the adult to whose case the enquiry or review relates for the purpose of facilitating his or her involvement in the enquiry or review; but see subsections (4) and (6).

(3) The condition is that the local authority considers that, were an independent advocate not to be available, the individual would experience substantial difficulty in doing one or more of the following–

    (a) understanding relevant information;

    (b) retaining that information;

    (c) using or weighing that information as part of the process of being involved;

    (d) communicating the individual's views, wishes or feelings (whether by talking, using sign language or any other means).

(4) The duty under subsection (2) does not apply if the local authority is satisfied that there is a person–

    (a) who would be an appropriate person to represent and support the adult for the purpose of facilitating the adult's involvement, and

    (b) who is not engaged in providing care or treatment for the adult in a professional capacity or for remuneration.

(5) For the purposes of subsection (4), a person is not to be regarded as an appropriate person unless–

    (a) where the adult has capacity to consent to being represented and supported by that person, the adult does so consent, or

    (b) where the adult lacks capacity so to consent, the local authority is satisfied that being represented and supported by that person would be in the adult's best interests.

(6) If the enquiry or review needs to begin as a matter of urgency, it may do so even if the authority has not yet been able to comply with the duty under subsection (2) (and the authority continues to be subject to the duty).

(7) 'Relevant local authority' means–

    (a) in a case within subsection (1)(a), the authority making the enquiry or causing it to be made;

    (b) in a case within subsection (1)(b), the authority which established the SAB arranging the review.

Enforcement of debts

Recovery of charges, interest etc

69 (1) Any sum due to a local authority under this Part is recoverable by the authority as a debt due to it.

(2) But subsection (1) does not apply in a case where a deferred payment agreement could, in accordance with regulations under section 34(1), be entered into, unless–

(a) the local authority has sought to enter into such an agreement with the adult from whom the sum is due, and

(b) the adult has refused.

(3) A sum is recoverable under this section–

(a) in a case in which the sum becomes due to the local authority on or after the commencement of this section, within six years of the date the sum becomes due;

(b) in any other case, within three years of the date on which it becomes due.

(4) Where a person misrepresents or fails to disclose (whether fraudulently or otherwise) to a local authority any material fact in connection with the provisions of this Part, the following sums are due to the authority from the person–

(a) any expenditure incurred by the authority as a result of the misrepresentation or failure, and

(b) any sum recoverable under this section which the authority has not recovered as a result of the misrepresentation or failure.

(5) The costs incurred by a local authority in recovering or seeking to recover a sum due to it under this Part are recoverable by the authority as a debt due to it.

(6) Regulations may–

(a) make provision for determining the date on which a sum becomes due to a local authority for the purposes of this section;

(b) specify cases or circumstances in which a sum due to a local authority under this Part is not recoverable by it under this section;

(c) specify cases or circumstances in which a local authority may charge interest on a sum due to it under this Part;

(d) where interest is chargeable, provide that it–

(i) must be charged at a rate specified in or determined in accordance with the regulations, or

(ii) may not be charged at a rate that exceeds the rate specified in or determined in accordance with the regulations.

Transfer of assets to avoid charges

70 (1) This section applies in a case where an adult's needs have been or are being met by a local authority under sections 18 to 20 and where–

(a) the adult has transferred an asset to another person (a 'transferee'),

(b) the transfer was undertaken with the intention of avoiding charges for having the adult's needs met, and

(c) either the consideration for the transfer was less than the value of the asset or there was no consideration for the transfer.

(2) The transferee is liable to pay to the local authority an amount equal to the difference between–

(a) the amount the authority would have charged the adult were it not for the transfer of the asset, and

(b) the amount it did in fact charge the adult.

(3) But the transferee is not liable to pay to the authority an amount which exceeds the benefit accruing to the transferee from the transfer.

(4) Where an asset has been transferred to more than one transferee, the liability of each transferee is in proportion to the benefit accruing to that transferee from the transfer.

(5) 'Asset' means anything which may be taken into account for the purposes of a financial assessment.

(6) The value of an asset (other than cash) is the amount which would have been

realised if it had been sold on the open market by a willing seller at the time of the transfer, with a deduction for–
  (a) the amount of any incumbrance on the asset, and
  (b) a reasonable amount in respect of the expenses of the sale.
  (7) Regulations may specify cases or circumstances in which liability under subsection (2) does not arise.

Review of funding provisions

Five-yearly review by Secretary of State
71 (1) The Secretary of State must review–
  (a) the level at which the cap on care costs is for the time being set under regulations under section 15(4),
  (b) the level at which the amount attributable to an adult's daily living costs is for the time being set under regulations under section 15(8), and
  (c) the level at which the financial limit is for the time being set under regulations under section 17(8).
  (2) In carrying out the review, the Secretary of State must have regard to–
  (a) the financial burden on the state of each of those matters being at the level in question,
  (b) the financial burden on local authorities of each of those matters being at the level in question,
  (c) the financial burden on adults who have needs for care and support of each of those matters being at the level in question,
  (d) the length of time for which people can reasonably be expected to live in good health,
  (e) changes in the ways or circumstances in which adults' needs for care and support are being or are likely to be met,
  (f) changes in the prevalence of conditions for which the provision of care and support is or is likely to be required, and
  (g) such other factors as the Secretary of State considers relevant.
  (3) The Secretary of State must prepare and publish a report on the outcome of the review.
  (4) The first report must be published before the end of the period of five years beginning with the day on which section 15 comes into force.
  (5) Each subsequent report must be published before the end of the period of five years beginning with the day on which the previous report was published.
  (6) The Secretary of State may arrange for some other person to carry out the whole or part of a review under this section on the Secretary of State's behalf.
  (7) The Secretary of State must lay before Parliament a report prepared under this section.

Appeals

Part 1 appeals
72 (1) Regulations may make provision for appeals against decisions taken by a local authority in the exercise of functions under this Part in respect of an individual (including decisions taken before the coming into force of the first regulations made under this subsection).
  (2) The regulations may in particular make provision about–
  (a) who may (and may not) bring an appeal;
  (b) grounds on which an appeal may be brought;
  (c) pre-conditions for bringing an appeal;
  (d) how an appeal is to be brought and dealt with (including time limits);
  (e) who is to consider an appeal;
  (f) matters to be taken into account (and disregarded) by the person or body considering an appeal;
  (g) powers of the person or body deciding an appeal;
  (h) what action is to be taken by a local authority as a result of an appeal decision;
  (i) providing information about the right to bring an appeal, appeal procedures

and other sources of information and advice;

    (j) representation and support for an individual bringing or otherwise involved in an appeal;

    (k) investigations into things done or not done by a person or body with power to consider an appeal.

(3) Provision about pre-conditions for bringing an appeal may require specified steps to have been taken before an appeal is brought.

(4) Provision about how an appeal is to be dealt with may include provision for–

    (a) the appeal to be treated as, or as part of, an appeal brought or complaint made under another procedure;

    (b) the appeal to be considered with any such appeal or complaint.

(5) Provision about who is to consider an appeal may include provision–

    (a) establishing, or requiring or permitting the establishment of, a panel or other body to consider an appeal;

    (b) requiring an appeal to be considered by, or by persons who include, persons with a specified description of expertise or experience.

(6) Provision about representation and support for an individual may include provision applying any provision of or made under section 67, with or without modifications.

(7) The regulations may make provision for–

    (a) an appeal brought or complaint made under another procedure to be treated as, or as part of, an appeal brought under the regulations;

    (b) an appeal brought or complaint made under another procedure to be considered with an appeal brought under the regulations;

    (c) matters raised in an appeal brought under the regulations to be taken into account by the person or body considering an appeal brought or complaint made under another procedure.

(8) The regulations may include provision conferring functions on a person or body established by or under an Act (including an Act passed after the passing of this Act); for that purpose, the regulations may amend, repeal, or revoke an enactment, or provide for an enactment to apply with specified modifications.

(9) Regulations may make provision, in relation to a case where an appeal is brought under regulations under subsection (1)–

    (a) for any provision of this Part to apply, for a specified period, as if a decision ('the interim decision') differing from the decision appealed against had been made;

    (b) as to what the terms of the interim decision are, or as to how and by whom they are to be determined;

    (c) for financial adjustments to be made following a decision on the appeal.

(10) The period specified under subsection (9)(a) may not begin earlier than the date on which the decision appealed against was made, or end later than the date on which the decision on the appeal takes effect.

Miscellaneous

Human Rights Act 1998: provision of regulated care or support etc a public function

73 (1) This section applies where–

    (a) in England, a registered care provider provides care and support to an adult or support to a carer, in the course of providing–

        (i) personal care in a place where the adult receiving the personal care is living when the personal care is provided, or

        (ii) residential accommodation together with nursing or personal care;

    (b) in Wales, a person registered under Part 2 of the Care Standards Act 2000 provides care and support to an adult, or support to a carer, in the course of providing–

        (i) personal care in a place where the adult receiving the personal care is living when the personal care is provided, or

        (ii) residential accommodation together with nursing or personal care;

(c) in Scotland, a person provides advice, guidance or assistance to an adult or support to a carer, in the course of providing a care service which is registered under section 59 of the Public Services Reform (Scotland) Act 2010 and which consists of the provision of–

    (i) personal care in a place where the adult receiving the personal care is living when the personal care is provided, or

    (ii) residential accommodation together with nursing or personal care;

(d) in Northern Ireland, a person registered under Part 3 of the Health and Personal Social Services (Quality, Improvement and Regulation) (Northern Ireland) Order 2003 provides advice, guidance or assistance to an adult or services to a carer, in the course of providing–

    (i) personal care in a place where the adult receiving the personal care is living when the personal care is provided, or

    (ii) residential accommodation together with nursing or personal care.

In this section 'the care or support' means the care and support, support, advice, guidance, assistance or services provided as mentioned above, and 'the provider' means the person who provides the care or support.

(2) The provider is to be taken for the purposes of section 6(3)(b) of the Human Rights Act 1998 (acts of public authorities) to be exercising a function of a public nature in providing the care or support, if the requirements of subsection (3) are met.

(3) The requirements are that–

(a) the care or support is arranged by an authority listed in column 1 of the Table below, or paid for (directly or indirectly, and in whole or in part) by such an authority, and

(b) the authority arranges or pays for the care or support under a provision listed in the corresponding entry in column 2 of the Table.

TABLE	
Authority	*Provisions imposing duty or conferring power to meet needs*
Local authority in England	Sections 2, 18, 19, 20, 38 and 48 of this Act.
Local authority in Wales	Part 4 and section 189 of the Social Services and Well-being (Wales) Act 2014.
	Section 50 of this Act.
Local authority in Scotland	Sections 12, 13A, 13B and 14 of the Social Work (Scotland) Act 1968.
	Section 3 of the Social Care (Self-directed Support) (Scotland) Act 2013.
Health and Social Care trust	Article 15 of the Health and Personal Social Services (Northern Ireland) Order 1972.
	Section 51 of this Act.
Authority (within the meaning of section 10 of the Carers and Direct Payments Act (Northern Ireland) 2002)	Section 2 of the Carers and Direct Payments Act (Northern Ireland) 2002.

(4) In this section–

'local authority in England' means a local authority for the purposes of this Part;

'local authority in Wales' means a local authority for the purposes of the Social Services and Well-being (Wales) Act 2014;

'local authority in Scotland' means a council constituted under section 2 of the Local Government etc (Scotland) Act 1994;

'nursing care', for England, Wales and Northern Ireland, has the same meaning as in the Health and Social Care Act 2008 (Regulated Activities) Regulations 2010, as amended from time to time;

'personal care'–

(a) for England, Wales and Northern Ireland, has the same meaning as in the Health and Social Care Act 2008 (Regulated Activities) Regulations 2010, as amended from time to time;

(b) for Scotland, has the same meaning as in Part 5 of the Public Services Reform (Scotland) Act 2010, as amended from time to time.

Discharge of hospital patients with care and support needs

74 Schedule 3 (which includes provision about the discharge of hospital patients with care and support needs) has effect.

After-care under the Mental Health Act 1983

75 (1) In section 117 of the Mental Health Act 1983 (after-care), in subsection (2), after 'to provide' insert 'or arrange for the provision of'.

(2) In subsection (2D) of that section, for the words from 'as if' to the end substitute 'as if the words 'provide or' were omitted.'

(3) In subsection (3) of that section, after 'means the local social services authority' insert

'–

(a) if, immediately before being detained, the person concerned was ordinarily resident in England, for the area in England in which he was ordinarily resident;

(b) if, immediately before being detained, the person concerned was ordinarily resident in Wales, for the area in Wales in which he was ordinarily resident; or

(c) in any other case'.

(4) After that subsection insert–

'(4) Where there is a dispute about where a person was ordinarily resident for the purposes of subsection (3) above–

(a) if the dispute is between local social services authorities in England, section 40 of the Care Act 2014 applies to the dispute as it applies to a dispute about where a person was ordinarily resident for the purposes of Part 1 of that Act;

(b) if the dispute is between local social services authorities in Wales, section 195 of the Social Services and Well-being (Wales) Act 2014 applies to the dispute as it applies to a dispute about where a person was ordinarily resident for the purposes of that Act;

(c) if the dispute is between a local social services authority in England and a local social services authority in Wales, it is to be determined by the Secretary of State or the Welsh Ministers.

(5) The Secretary of State and the Welsh Ministers shall make and publish arrangements for determining which of them is to determine a dispute under subsection (4)(c); and the arrangements may, in particular, provide for the dispute to be determined by whichever of them they agree is to do so.'

(5) After subsection (5) insert–

'(6) In this section, 'after-care services', in relation to a person, means services which have both of the following purposes–

(a) meeting a need arising from or related to the person's mental disorder; and

(b) reducing the risk of a deterioration of the person's mental condition (and, accordingly, reducing the risk of the person requiring admission to a hospital again for treatment for mental disorder).'

(6) After section 117 of that Act insert–

'117A After-care: preference for particular accommodation

(1) The Secretary of State may by regulations provide that where–

(a) the local social services authority under section 117 is, in discharging its duty under subsection (2) of that section, providing or arranging for the provision of accommodation for the person concerned;

(b) the person concerned expresses a preference for particular accommodation;

and

(c) any prescribed conditions are met,

the local social services authority must provide or arrange for the provision of the person's preferred accommodation.

(2) Regulations under this section may provide for the person concerned, or a person of a prescribed description, to pay for some or all of the additional cost in prescribed cases.

(3) In subsection (2), 'additional cost' means the cost of providing or arranging for the provision of the person's preferred accommodation less the amount that the local social services authority would expect to be the usual cost of providing or arranging for the provision of accommodation of that kind.

(4) The power to make regulations under this section–

(a) is exercisable only in relation to local social services authorities in England;

(b) includes power to make different provision for different cases or areas.'

(7) The ways in which a local authority may discharge its duty under section 117 of the Mental Health Act 1983 include by making direct payments; and for that purpose Part 1 of Schedule 4 (which includes modifications of the provisions of this Part relating to direct payments) has effect.

(8) In section 53 of the Social Services and Well-being (Wales) Act 2014 (direct payments: further provision), at the end insert–

'(11) The ways in which a local authority may discharge its duty under section 117 of the Mental Health Act 1983 include by making direct payments; and for that purpose Schedule A1 (which includes modifications of sections 50 and 51 and this section) has effect.'

(9) Before Schedule 1 to that Act insert the Schedule A1 contained in Part 2 of Schedule 4 to this Act.

(10) In section 194 of that Act (ordinary residence), after subsection (4) insert–

'(4A) A person who is being provided with accommodation under section 117 of the Mental Health Act 1983 (after-care) is to be treated for the purposes of this Act as ordinarily resident in the area of the local authority, or the local authority in England, on which the duty to provide that person with services under that section is imposed.'

(11) In consequence of subsections (7) to (9), in subsection (2C) of section 117 of the Mental Health Act 1983–

(a) in paragraph (a), for 'regulations under section 57 of the Health and Social Care Act 2001 or' substitute

'–

(i) sections 31 to 33 of the Care Act 2014 (as applied by Schedule 4 to that Act),

(ii) sections 50, 51 and 53 of the Social Services and Well-being (Wales) Act 2014 (as applied by Schedule A1 to that Act), or

(iii) regulations under',

(b) in paragraph (b), after 'apart from' insert 'those sections (as so applied) or'.

(12) In the case of a person who, immediately before the commencement of subsections (3) and (4), is being provided with after-care services under section 117 of the Mental Health Act 1983, the amendments made by those subsections do not apply while those services are continuing to be provided to that person.

(13) In section 145 of the Mental Health Act 1983 (interpretation), for the definition of 'local social services authority' substitute–

''local social services authority' means–

(a) an authority in England which is a local authority for the purposes of Part 1 of the Care Act 2014, or

(b) an authority in Wales which is a local authority for the purposes of the Social Services and Well-being (Wales) Act 2014.'

Prisoners and persons in approved premises etc

76 (1) In its application to an adult who is detained in prison, this Part has effect as if

references to being ordinarily resident in an area were references to being detained in prison in that area.

(2) In its application to an adult who is residing in approved premises, this Part has effect as if references to being ordinarily resident in an area were references to being resident in approved premises in that area.

(3) In its application to an adult who is residing in any other premises because a requirement to do so has been imposed on the adult as a condition of the grant of bail in criminal proceedings, this Part has effect as if references to being ordinarily resident in an area were references to being resident in premises in that area for that reason.

(4) The power under section 30 (preference for particular accommodation) may not be exercised in the case of an adult who is detained in prison or residing in approved premises except for the purpose of making provision with respect to accommodation for the adult–
(a) on his or her release from prison (including temporary release), or
(b) on ceasing to reside in approved premises.

(5) Sections 31 to 33 (direct payments) do not apply in the case of an adult who, having been convicted of an offence, is–
(a) detained in prison, or
(b) residing in approved premises.

(6) Sections 37 and 38 (continuity of care), in their application to an adult who is detained in prison or residing in approved premises, also apply where it is decided that the adult is to be detained in prison, or is to reside in approved premises, in the area of another local authority; and accordingly–
(a) references to the adult's intention to move are to be read as references to that decision, and
(b) references to carers are to be ignored.

(7) Sections 42 and 47 (safeguarding: enquiry by local authority and protection of property) do not apply in the case of an adult who is–
(a) detained in prison, or
(b) residing in approved premises.

(8) An SAB's objective under section 43(2) does not include helping and protecting adults who are detained in prison or residing in approved premises; but an SAB may nonetheless provide advice or assistance to any person for the purpose of helping and protecting such adults in its area in cases of the kind described in section 42(1) (adults with needs for care and support who are at risk of abuse or neglect).

(9) Section 44 (safeguarding adults reviews) does not apply to any case involving an adult in so far as the case relates to any period during which the adult was–
(a) detained in prison, or
(b) residing in approved premises.

(10) Regulations under paragraph 1(1)(d) of Schedule 2 (membership of Safeguarding Adults Boards) may not specify the governor, director or controller of a prison or a prison officer or prisoner custody officer.

(11) 'Prison' has the same meaning as in the Prison Act 1952 (see section 53(1) of that Act); and–
(a) a reference to a prison includes a reference to a young offender institution, secure training centre or secure children's home,
(b) the reference in subsection (10) to the governor, director or controller of a prison includes a reference to the governor, director or controller of a young offender institution, to the governor, director or monitor of a secure training centre and to the manager of a secure children's home, and
(c) the reference in that subsection to a prison officer or prisoner custody officer includes a reference to a prison officer or prisoner custody officer at a young offender institution, to an officer or custody officer at a secure training centre and to a member of staff at a secure children's home.

(12) 'Approved premises' has the meaning given in section 13 of the Offender Management Act 2007.

(13) 'Bail in criminal proceedings' has the meaning given in section 1 of the Bail Act 1976.

(14) For the purposes of this section–

    (a) a person who is temporarily absent from prison is to be treated as detained in prison for the period of absence;

    (b) a person who is temporarily absent from approved premises is to be treated as residing in approved premises for the period of absence;

    (c) a person who is temporarily absent from other premises in which the person is required to reside as a condition of the grant of bail in criminal proceedings is to be treated as residing in the premises for the period of absence.

Registers of sight-impaired adults, disabled adults, etc

77 (1) A local authority must establish and maintain a register of sight-impaired and severely sight-impaired adults who are ordinarily resident in its area.

  (2) Regulations may specify descriptions of persons who are, or are not, to be treated as being sight-impaired or severely sight-impaired for the purposes of this section.

  (3) A local authority may establish and maintain one or more registers of adults to whom subsection (4) applies, and who are ordinarily resident in the local authority's area, for the purposes in particular of–

    (a) planning the provision by the authority of services to meet needs for care and support, and

    (b) monitoring changes over time in the number of adults in the authority's area with needs for care and support and the types of needs they have.

  (4) This subsection applies to an adult who–

    (a) has a disability,

    (b) has a physical or mental impairment which is not a disability but which gives rise, or which the authority considers may in the future give rise, to needs for care and support, or

    (c) comes within any other category of persons the authority considers appropriate to include in a register of persons who have, or the authority considers may in the future have, needs for care and support.

  (5) 'Disability' has the meaning given by section 6 of the Equality Act 2010.

Guidance, etc

78 (1) A local authority must act under the general guidance of the Secretary of State in the exercise of functions given to it by this Part or by regulations under this Part.

  (2) Before issuing any guidance for the purposes of subsection (1), the Secretary of State must consult such persons as the Secretary of State considers appropriate.

  (3) The Secretary of State must have regard to the general duty of local authorities under section 1(1) (promotion of individual well-being)–

    (a) in issuing guidance for the purposes of subsection (1);

    (b) in making regulations under this Part.

Delegation of local authority functions

79 (1) A local authority may authorise a person to exercise on its behalf a function it has under–

    (a) this Part or regulations under this Part (but see subsection (2)), or

    (b) section 117 of the Mental Health Act 1983 (after-care services).

  (2) The references in subsection (1)(a) to this Part do not include a reference to–

    (a) section 3 (promoting integration with health services etc),

    (b) sections 6 and 7 (co-operating),

    (c) section 14 (charges),

    (d) sections 42 to 47 (safeguarding adults at risk of abuse or neglect), or

    (e) this section.

  (3) An authorisation under this section may authorise an employee of the authorised person to exercise the function to which the authorisation relates; and for that purpose, where the authorised person is a body corporate, 'employee' includes a director or officer of the body.

(4) An authorisation under this section may authorise the exercise of the function to which it relates–
  (a) either wholly or to the extent specified in the authorisation;
  (b) either generally or in cases, circumstances or areas so specified;
  (c) either unconditionally or subject to conditions so specified.
(5) An authorisation under this section–
  (a) is for the period specified in the authorisation;
  (b) may be revoked by the local authority;
  (c) does not prevent the local authority from exercising the function to which the authorisation relates.
(6) Anything done or omitted to be done by or in relation to a person authorised under this section in, or in connection with, the exercise or purported exercise of the function to which the authorisation relates is to be treated for all purposes as done or omitted to be done by or in relation to the local authority.
(7) But subsection (6) does not apply–
  (a) for the purposes of the terms of any contract between the authorised person and the local authority which relate to the function, or
  (b) for the purposes of any criminal proceedings brought in respect of anything done or omitted to be done by the authorised person.
(8) Schedule 15 to the Deregulation and Contracting Out Act 1994 (which permits disclosure of information between local authorities and contractors where that is necessary for the exercise of the functions concerned, even if that would otherwise be unlawful) applies to an authorisation under this section as it applies to an authorisation by virtue of an order under section 70(2) of that Act.
(9) The Secretary of State may by order–
  (a) amend subsection (2) so as to add to or remove from the list a provision of this Part;
  (b) amend subsection (1) so as to add to or remove from the list a provision relating to care and support for adults or support for carers;
  (c) impose conditions or other restrictions on the exercise of the power under subsection (1), whether by amending this section or otherwise.
(10) The provision which may be made in an order under subsection (9) in reliance on section 125(8) (supplementary etc provision in orders under this Act) includes, in particular, provision as to the rights and obligations of local authorities and persons authorised under this section in light of the provision made by the order.
(11) 'Function' includes a power to do anything that is calculated to facilitate, or is conducive or incidental to, the exercise of a function.

General

Part 1: interpretation

80 (1) For the purposes of this Part, an expression in the first column of the following table is defined or otherwise explained by the provision of this Act specified in the second column.

Expression	Provision
Abuse	Section 42(3)
Accrued costs	Section 15(5)
Adult	Section 2(8)
Adult needing care	Section 10(3)
Authority under the Mental Capacity Act 2005	Subsection (3) below
Best interests	Subsection (2) below
Cap on care costs	Section 15(4)
Capacity, having or lacking	Subsection (2) below
Care and support plan	Section 25
Care account	Section 29

Carer (other than in sections 58 to 62)	Section 10(3)
Carer's assessment	Sections 10(2) and 12(8) and (9)
Child's carer's assessment	Section 60(2)
Child's needs assessment	Section 58(2)
Daily living costs, amount attributable to	Section 15(8)
Deferred payment agreement	Section 34
Direct payment	Sections 31 and 32
Eligibility criteria	Section 13
Financial assessment	Section 17(5)
Financial limit	Section 17(10)
Financial year	Section 126
The health service	Section 126
Independent personal budget	Section 28
Local authority	Section 1(4)
Needs assessment	Sections 9(2) and 12(8) and (9)
Parent	Section 58(6)
Personal budget	Section 26
Registered care provider	Section 48
Support plan	Section 25
Well-being	Section 1(2)
Young carer	Section 63(6)
Young carer's assessment	Section 63(2)

(2) A reference in this Part to having or lacking capacity, or to a person's best interests, is to be interpreted in accordance with the Mental Capacity Act 2005.

(3) A reference in this Part to being authorised under the Mental Capacity Act 2005 is a reference to being authorised (whether in general or specific terms) as–

   (a) a donee of a lasting power of attorney granted under that Act, or

   (b) a deputy appointed by the Court of Protection under section 16(2)(b) of that Act.

SCHEDULE 1: CROSS-BORDER PLACEMENTS

Section 39

Placements from England to Wales, Scotland or Northern Ireland

1 (1) Where a local authority in England is meeting an adult's needs for care and support by arranging for the provision of accommodation in Wales, the adult–

   (a) is to be treated for the purposes of this Part as ordinarily resident in the local authority's area, and

   (b) is accordingly not to be treated for the purposes of the Social Services and Well-being (Wales) Act 2014 as ordinarily resident anywhere in Wales.

(2) Where a local authority in England, in reliance on section 22(4), is making arrangements which include the provision of accommodation in Wales, section 22(4) is to have effect as if for paragraph (a) there were substituted–

   '(a) the authority has obtained consent for it to arrange for the provision of the nursing care from the Local Health Board for the area in which the accommodation is provided,'.

(3) Where a local authority in England is meeting an adult's needs for care and support by arranging for the provision of accommodation in Scotland–

   (a) the adult is to be treated for the purposes of this Part as ordinarily resident in the local authority's area, and

(b) no duty under Part 2 of the Social Work (Scotland) Act 1968 or sections 25 to 27 of the Mental Health (Care and Treatment) (Scotland) Act 2003 applies in the adult's case.

(4) Where a local authority in England is meeting an adult's needs for care and support by arranging for the provision of accommodation in Northern Ireland–

   (a) the adult is to be treated for the purposes of this Part as ordinarily resident in the local authority's area, and

   (b) no duty under the Health and Personal Social Services (Northern Ireland) Order 1972 or the Health and Social Care (Reform) Act (Northern Ireland) 2009 to provide or secure the provision of accommodation or other facilities applies in the adult's case.

(5) Section 22 (prohibition on provision of health services) is to have effect–

   (a) in its application to a case within sub-paragraph (1)–

      (i) as if the references in subsections (1) and (6) to the National Health Service Act 2006 included a reference to the National Health Service (Wales) Act 2006, and

      (ii) as if the reference in subsection (6) to a clinical commissioning group or the National Health Service Commissioning Board included a reference to a Local Health Board;

   (b) in its application to a case within sub-paragraph (3)–

      (i) as if the references in subsections (1) and (6) to the National Health Service Act 2006 included a reference to the National Health Service (Scotland) Act 1978, and

      (ii) as if the reference in subsection (6) to a clinical commissioning group or the National Health Service Commissioning Board included a reference to a Health Board or Special Health Board;

   (c) in its application to a case within sub-paragraph (4)–

      (i) as if the references in subsections (1) and (6) to a service or facility provided under the National Health Service Act 2006 included a reference to health care provided under the Health and Personal Social Services (Northern Ireland) Order 1972 or the Health and Social Care (Reform) Act (Northern Ireland) 2009, and

      (ii) as if the reference in subsection (6) to a clinical commissioning group or the National Health Service Commissioning Board included a reference to a Health and Social Care trust.

(6) Regulations may make further provision in relation to arrangements of the kind referred to in this paragraph.

(7) The regulations may specify circumstances in which, in a case within sub-paragraph (3), specified duties under Part 2 of the Social Work (Scotland) Act 1968 are nonetheless to apply in the case of the adult concerned (and paragraph (b) of that sub-paragraph is to be read accordingly).

Placements from Wales to England, Scotland or Northern Ireland

2 (1) Where a local authority in Wales is discharging its duty under section 35 of the Social Services and Well-being (Wales) Act 2014 by arranging for the provision of accommodation in England, the adult concerned–

   (a) is to be treated for the purposes of that Act as ordinarily resident in the local authority's area, and

   (b) is accordingly not to be treated for the purposes of this Part of this Act as ordinarily resident anywhere in England.

(2) Where a local authority in Wales is arranging for the provision of accommodation in England in the exercise of its power under section 36 of the Social Services and Well-being (Wales) Act 2014–

   (a) the adult concerned is to be treated for the purposes of that Act–

      (i) in a case where the adult was within the local authority's area immediately before being provided by the local authority with accommodation in England, as remaining within that area;

      (ii) in a case where the adult was outside but ordinarily resident in the local authority's area immediately before being provided by the local authority with accommodation in England, as remaining outside but ordinarily resident in that area, and

(b) the adult concerned is not to be treated for the purposes of this Part of this Act as ordinarily resident anywhere in England (unless the adult was so ordinarily resident immediately before being provided by the local authority with accommodation in England).

(3) Where a local authority in Wales is discharging its duty under section 35 of the Social Services and Well-being (Wales) Act 2014 by arranging for the provision of accommodation in Scotland–

(a) the adult is to be treated for the purposes of that Act as ordinarily resident in the local authority's area, and

(b) no duty under Part 2 of the Social Work (Scotland) Act 1968 or sections 25 to 27 of the Mental Health (Care and Treatment) (Scotland) Act 2003 applies in the adult's case.

(4) Where a local authority in Wales is arranging for the provision of accommodation in Scotland in the exercise of its power under section 36 of the Social Services and Well-being (Wales) Act 2014–

(a) the adult concerned is to be treated for the purposes of that Act–

(i) in a case where the adult was within the local authority's area immediately before being provided by the local authority with accommodation in Scotland, as remaining within that area;

(ii) in a case where the adult was outside but ordinarily resident in the local authority's area immediately before being provided by the local authority with accommodation in Scotland, as remaining outside but ordinarily resident in that area, and

(b) no duty under Part 2 of the Social Work (Scotland) Act 1968 or sections 25 to 27 of the Mental Health (Care and Treatment) (Scotland) Act 2003 applies in the adult's case.

(5) But paragraph (b) of sub-paragraph (4) does not prevent a duty mentioned in that paragraph from applying in the case of an adult who was ordinarily resident in Scotland immediately before being provided by the local authority with accommodation in Scotland.

(6) Where a local authority in Wales is discharging its duty under section 35 of the Social Services and Well-being (Wales) Act 2014 by arranging for the provision of accommodation in Northern Ireland–

(a) the adult is to be treated for the purposes of that Act as ordinarily resident in the local authority's area, and

(b) no duty under the Health and Personal Social Services (Northern Ireland) Order 1972 or the Health and Social Care (Reform) Act (Northern Ireland) 2009 to provide or secure the provision of accommodation or other facilities applies in the adult's case.

(7) Where a local authority in Wales is arranging for the provision of accommodation in Northern Ireland in the exercise of its power under section 36 of the Social Services and Well-being (Wales) Act 2014–

(a) the adult concerned is to be treated for the purposes of that Act–

(i) in a case where the adult was within the local authority's area immediately before being provided by the local authority with accommodation in Northern Ireland, as remaining within that area;

(ii) in a case where the adult was outside but ordinarily resident in the local authority's area immediately before being provided by the local authority with accommodation in Northern Ireland, as remaining outside but ordinarily resident in that area, and

(b) no duty under the Health and Personal Social Services (Northern Ireland) Order 1972 or the Health and Social Care (Reform) Act (Northern Ireland) 2009 to provide or secure the provision of accommodation or other facilities applies in the adult's case.

(8) But paragraph (b) of sub-paragraph (7) does not prevent a duty mentioned in that

paragraph from applying in the case of an adult who was ordinarily resident in Northern Ireland immediately before being provided by the local authority with accommodation in Northern Ireland.

(9) Regulations may make further provision in relation to arrangements of the kind referred to in this paragraph.

(10) The regulations may specify circumstances in which, in a case within sub-paragraph (3) or (4), specified duties under Part 2 of the Social Work (Scotland) Act 1968 are nonetheless to apply in the case of the adult concerned (and paragraph (b) of each of those sub-paragraphs is to be read accordingly).

Placements from Scotland to England, Wales or Northern Ireland

3 (1) Where a local authority in Scotland is discharging its duty under section 12 or 13A of the Social Work (Scotland) Act 1968 or section 25 of the Mental Health (Care and Treatment) (Scotland) Act 2003 by securing the provision of accommodation in England, the adult in question is not to be treated for the purposes of this Part of this Act as ordinarily resident anywhere in England.

(2) Where a local authority in Scotland is discharging its duty under a provision referred to in sub-paragraph (1) by securing the provision of accommodation in Wales, the adult in question is not to be treated for the purposes of the Social Services and Well-being (Wales) Act 2014 as ordinarily resident anywhere in Wales.

(3) Where a local authority in Scotland is discharging its duty under a provision referred to in sub-paragraph (1) by securing the provision of accommodation in Northern Ireland, no duty under the Health and Personal Social Services (Northern Ireland) Order 1972 or the Health and Social Care (Reform) Act (Northern Ireland) 2009 to provide or secure the provision of accommodation or other facilities applies in the case of the adult in question.

(4) In section 5 of the Community Care and Health (Scotland) Act 2002 (local authority arrangements for residential accommodation outside Scotland)–
  (a) in subsection (1), after 'the 1968 Act' insert 'or under section 25 of the Mental Health (Care and Treatment) (Scotland) Act 2003 (care and support)',
  (b) in subsection (2), for 'such arrangements' substitute 'persons for whom such arrangements are made', and
  (c) for subsections (5) and (6) substitute–
    '(5) In subsections (1) and (3) above, 'appropriate establishment' means an establishment of such description or conforming to such requirements as may be specified in regulations under subsection (1).'

(5) Regulations may make further provision in relation to arrangements of the kind referred to in this paragraph.

Placements from Northern Ireland to England, Wales or Scotland

4 (1) Where there are arrangements under Article 15 of the Health and Personal Social Services (Northern Ireland) Order 1972 for the provision of accommodation in England, the adult in question–
  (a) is to be treated for the purposes of that Order and the Health and Social Care (Reform) Act (Northern Ireland) 2009 as ordinarily resident in the area of the relevant Health and Social Care trust, and
  (b) is accordingly not to be treated for the purposes of this Part of this Act as ordinarily resident anywhere in England.

(2) Where there are arrangements under Article 15 of the Health and Personal Social Services (Northern Ireland) Order 1972 for the provision of accommodation in Wales, the adult in question–
  (a) is to be treated for the purposes of that Order and the Health and Social Care (Reform) Act (Northern Ireland) 2009 as ordinarily resident in the area of the relevant Health and Social Care trust, and
  (b) is accordingly not to be treated for the purposes of the Social Services and Well-being (Wales) Act 2014 as ordinarily resident anywhere in Wales.

(3) Where there are arrangements under Article 15 of the Health and Personal Social Services (Northern Ireland) Order 1972 for the provision of accommodation in Scotland–

(a) the adult in question is to be treated for the purposes of that Order and the Health and Social Care (Reform) Act (Northern Ireland) 2009 as ordinarily resident in the area of the relevant Health and Social Care trust, and

(b) no duty under Part 2 of the Social Work (Scotland) Act 1968 or sections 25 to 27 of the Mental Health (Care and Treatment) (Scotland) Act 2003 applies in the adult's case.

(4) The reference to the relevant Health and Social Care trust is a reference to the Health and Social Care trust in whose area the adult in question was ordinarily resident immediately before the making of arrangements of the kind referred to in this paragraph.

(5) Regulations may make further provision in relation to arrangements of the kind referred to in this paragraph.

(6) The regulations may specify circumstances in which, in a case within sub-paragraph (3), specified duties under Part 2 of the Social Work (Scotland) Act 1968 are nonetheless to apply in the case of the adult concerned (and paragraph (b) of that sub-paragraph is to be read accordingly).

Dispute resolution

5 (1) Any dispute about the application of any of paragraphs 1 to 4 to an adult's case is to be determined in accordance with this paragraph.

(2) If the dispute is between a local authority in England and a local authority in Wales, it is to be determined by the Secretary of State or the Welsh Ministers.

(3) If the dispute is between a local authority in England and a local authority in Scotland, it is to be determined by the Secretary of State or the Scottish Ministers.

(4) If the dispute is between a local authority in England and a Health and Social Care trust, it is to be determined by the Secretary of State or the Northern Ireland Department.

(5) If the dispute is between a local authority in Wales and a local authority in Scotland, it is to be determined by the Welsh Ministers or the Scottish Ministers.

(6) If the dispute is between a local authority in Wales and a Health and Social Care trust, it is to be determined by the Welsh Ministers or the Northern Ireland Department.

(7) If the dispute is between a local authority in Scotland and a Health and Social Care trust, it is to be determined by the Scottish Ministers or the Northern Ireland Department.

(8) In Article 36 of the Health and Personal Social Services (Northern Ireland) Order 1972, after paragraph (2) insert–

'(2A) Any question under this Order as to the ordinary residence of a person is to be determined by the Department.'

(9) Regulations must make provision for determining which of the persons concerned is to determine the dispute; and the regulations may, in particular, provide for the dispute to be determined by whichever of them they agree is to do so.

(10) Regulations may make provision for the determination of disputes between more than two parties.

(11) Regulations may make further provision about determination of disputes under this paragraph or under regulations under sub-paragraph (10); the regulations may, for example, include–

(a) provision requiring parties to a dispute to take specified steps before referring the dispute for determination under this paragraph;

(b) provision about the procedure for referring the dispute under this paragraph.

Financial adjustments

6 (1) This paragraph applies where–

(a) an adult has been provided with accommodation in England, Wales, Scotland or Northern Ireland, and

(b) it transpires (whether following the determination of a dispute under paragraph 5 or otherwise) that an authority in another of the territories was, for some or all of the time that the accommodation was being provided, liable to provide the adult with accommodation.

(2) The authority which made the arrangements may recover from the authority in the other territory the amount of any payments it made towards the making of the arrangements at a time when the other authority was liable to provide the adult with accommodation.

(3) A reference to an authority is a reference to a local authority in England, Wales or Scotland or a Health and Social Care trust in Northern Ireland.

7 (1) In section 86 of the Social Work (Scotland) Act 1968 (adjustments between authorities providing accommodation), in subsections (1) and (10), after 'a local authority in England or Wales' insert 'and to a Health and Social Care trust in Northern Ireland'.

(2) In subsection (2) of that section, after 'the ordinary residence of a person shall' insert ', in a case where there is a dispute about the application of any of paragraphs 1 to 4 of Schedule 1 to the Care Act 2014 (cross-border placements), be determined in accordance with paragraph 5 of that Schedule; and in any other case, the question shall'.

(3) After subsection (10) of that section insert–

'(10A) A person who, as a result of Schedule 1 to the Care Act 2014 (cross-border placements), is treated as ordinarily resident in an area in England, Wales or Northern Ireland (as the case may be) is to be treated as ordinarily resident in that area for the purposes of this section.

(10B) A person who, as a result of that Schedule, is not treated as ordinarily resident anywhere in England or Wales (as the case may be) is not to be treated as ordinarily resident there for the purposes of this section.'

(4) In section 97 of that Act (extent)–

(a) in subsection (1), for 'sections 86 and 87' substitute 'section 87', and

(b) after that subsection insert–

'(1A) Section 86 of this Act shall extend to England and Wales and to Northern Ireland.'

Provision of NHS accommodation not to affect deemed ordinary residence etc

8 (1) In a case where, as a result of this Schedule, an adult is treated as ordinarily resident in an area in England, Wales or Northern Ireland (as the case may be), the adult does not cease to be so treated merely because the adult is provided with NHS accommodation.

(2) In a case where, as a result of this Schedule, an adult is not treated as ordinarily resident anywhere in England or Wales (as the case may be), the adult continues not to be so treated even if the adult is provided with NHS accommodation.

(3) In a case where, as a result of this Schedule, no duty under a relevant enactment applies, the duty does not apply merely because the adult in question is provided with NHS accommodation; and for this purpose 'relevant enactment' means–

(a) Part 2 of the Social Work (Scotland) Act 1968,

(b) sections 25 to 27 of the Mental Health (Care and Treatment) (Scotland) Act 2003,

(c) the Health and Personal Social Services (Northern Ireland) Order 1972, or

(d) the Health and Social Care (Reform) Act (Northern Ireland) 2009.

(4) In a case where, as a result of paragraph 2(2), (4) or (7), an adult is treated as remaining within, or as remaining outside but ordinarily resident in, an area in Wales, the adult does not cease to be so treated merely because the adult is provided with NHS accommodation.

Direct payments

9 (1) Regulations may provide for this Schedule to apply, with such modifications as may be specified, to a case where accommodation in England, Wales, Scotland or Northern Ireland is provided for an adult by means of direct payments made by an authority in another of the territories.

(2) The reference in sub-paragraph (1) to direct payments accordingly includes a reference to direct payments made–

(a) under section 50 or 52 of the Social Services and Well-being (Wales) Act 2014,

(b) as a result of a choice made by the adult pursuant to section 5 of the Social Care (Self-directed Support) (Scotland) Act 2013, or

(c) by virtue of section 8 of the Carers and Direct Payments Act (Northern Ireland) 2002.

Particular types of accommodation

10 (1) Regulations may provide for this Schedule to apply, with such modifications as may be specified, to a case where–

(a) an adult has needs for care and support which can be met only if the adult is living in accommodation of a type specified in the regulations,

(b) the adult is living in accommodation in England, Wales, Scotland or Northern Ireland that is of a type so specified, and

(c) the adult's needs for care and support are being met by an authority in another of the territories providing or arranging for the provision of services other than the accommodation.

(2) In section 5 of the Community Care and Health (Scotland) Act 2002 (the title to which becomes 'Local authority arrangements for residential accommodation etc outwith Scotland'), in subsection (1), at the end insert 'or for the provision in England and Wales or in Northern Ireland of a service or facility of such other description as may be specified in the regulations'.

Regulations

11 Regulations under this Schedule–

(a) if they include provision relating to Wales, may not be made without the consent of the Welsh Ministers;

(b) if they include provision relating to Scotland, may not be made without the consent of the Scottish Ministers;

(c) if they include provision relating to Northern Ireland, may not be made without the consent of the Northern Ireland Department.

Interpretation

12 (1) This paragraph applies for the purposes of this Schedule.

(2) 'Accommodation in England' means accommodation in England of a type specified in regulations under section 39 but not of a type specified in regulations under this paragraph.

(3) 'Accommodation in Wales' means accommodation in Wales of a type specified in regulations under section 194 of the Social Services and Well-being (Wales) Act 2014 but not of a type specified in regulations under this paragraph.

(4) 'Accommodation in Scotland' means residential accommodation in Scotland of a type which may be provided under or by virtue of section 12 or 13A of the Social Work (Scotland) Act 1968, or section 25 of the Mental Health (Care and Treatment) (Scotland) Act 2003, but not of a type specified in regulations under this paragraph.

(5) 'Accommodation in Northern Ireland' means residential or other accommodation in Northern Ireland of a type which may be provided under Article 15 of the Health and Personal Social Services (Northern Ireland) Order 1972.

(6) 'Local authority in England' means a local authority for the purposes of this Part.

(7) 'Local authority in Wales' means a local authority for the purposes of the Social Services and Well-being (Wales) Act 2014.

(8) 'Local authority in Scotland' means a council constituted under section 2 of the Local Government etc (Scotland) Act 1994.

(9) 'The Northern Ireland Department' means the Department of Health, Social Services and Public Safety in Northern Ireland.

(10) 'NHS accommodation' has the meaning given in section 39(6).

Consequential provision

13   In section 194 of the Social Services and Well-being (Wales) Act 2014 (ordinary residence), at the end insert–

'(8) For provision about cross-border placements to and from England, Scotland or Northern Ireland, see Schedule 1 to the Care Act 2014.

(8) Am ddarpariaeth ynghylch lleoliadau trawsffiniol i Loegr, yr Alban neu Ogledd Iwerddon neu o Loegr, yr Alban neu Ogledd Iwerddon, gweler Atodlen 1 i Ddeddf Gofal 2014.'

Transitory provision

14 (1) Pending the commencement of Part 4 of the Social Services and Well-being (Wales) Act 2014, this Schedule is to have effect with the modifications set out in this paragraph.

(2) A reference to that Act in paragraphs 1, 3 and 4 is to be read as a reference to Part 3 of the National Assistance Act 1948.

(3) In paragraph 2–
  (a) the references in sub-paragraphs (1), (3) and (6) to discharging a duty under section 35 of the Social Services and Well-being (Wales) Act 2014 by arranging for the provision of accommodation are to be read as references to providing residential accommodation under Part 3 of the National Assistance Act 1948;
  (b) the references in paragraph (a) of each of those sub-paragraphs to the Social Services and Well-being (Wales) Act 2014 are to be read as references to Part 3 of the National Assistance Act 1948;
  (c) sub-paragraphs (2), (4) and (7) are to be ignored; and
  (d) in sub-paragraph (10), the references to sub-paragraph (4) and paragraph (b) of sub-paragraph (4) are to be ignored.

(4) In paragraph 9, the reference to sections 50 and 52 of the Social Services and Well-being (Wales) Act 2014 is to be read as a reference to section 57 of the Health and Social Care Act 2001.

(5) In paragraph 12, sub-paragraph (3) is to be read as if the following were substituted for it–
  '(3) Accommodation in Wales' means residential accommodation in Wales of a type that may be provided under Part 3 of the National Assistance Act 1948 but not of a type specified in regulations under this paragraph.'

(6) In that paragraph, sub-paragraph (7) is to be read as if the following were substituted for it–
  '(7) Local authority in Wales' means a local authority in Wales for the purposes of Part 3 of the National Assistance Act 1948.'

(7) This paragraph does not affect the generality of section 124(2).

SCHEDULE 2: SAFEGUARDING ADULTS BOARDS

Section 43

Membership, etc

1 (1) The members of an SAB are–
  (a) the local authority which established it,
  (b) a clinical commissioning group the whole or part of whose area is in the local authority's area,
  (c) the chief officer of police for a police area the whole or part of which is in the local authority's area, and
  (d) such persons, or persons of such description, as may be specified in regulations.

(2) The membership of an SAB may also include such other persons as the local authority which established it, having consulted the other members listed in sub-paragraph (1), considers appropriate.

(3) A local authority, having consulted the other members of its SAB, must appoint as the chair a person whom the authority considers to have the required skills and experience.

(4) Each member of an SAB must appoint a person to represent it on the SAB; and the representative must be a person whom the member considers to have the required skills and experience.

(5) Where more than one clinical commissioning group or more than one chief officer of police comes within sub-paragraph (1), a person may represent more than one of the clinical commissioning groups or chief officers of police.

(6) The members of an SAB (other than the local authority which established it) must, in acting as such, have regard to such guidance as the Secretary of State may issue.

(7) Guidance for the local authority on acting as a member of the SAB is to be included in the guidance issued for the purposes of section 78(1).

(8) An SAB may regulate its own procedure.

Funding and other resources

2 (1) A member of an SAB listed in paragraph 1(1) may make payments towards expenditure incurred by, or for purposes connected with, the SAB–
  (a) by making the payments directly, or
  (b) by contributing to a fund out of which the payments may be made.

(2) A member of an SAB listed in paragraph 1(1) may provide staff, goods, services, accommodation or other resources for purposes connected with the SAB.

Strategic plan

3 (1) An SAB must publish for each financial year a plan (its 'strategic plan') which sets out–
  (a) its strategy for achieving its objective (see section 43), and
  (b) what each member is to do to implement that strategy.

(2) In preparing its strategic plan, the SAB must–
  (a) consult the Local Healthwatch organisation for its area, and
  (b) involve the community in its area.

(3) In this paragraph and paragraph 4, 'financial year', in relation to an SAB, includes the period–
  (a) beginning with the day on which the SAB is established, and
  (b) ending with the following 31 March or, if the period ending with that date is 3 months or less, ending with the 31 March following that date.

Annual report

4 (1) As soon as is feasible after the end of each financial year, an SAB must publish a report on–
  (a) what it has done during that year to achieve its objective,
  (b) what it has done during that year to implement its strategy,
  (c) what each member has done during that year to implement the strategy,
  (d) the findings of the reviews arranged by it under section 44 (safeguarding adults reviews) which have concluded in that year (whether or not they began in that year),
  (e) the reviews arranged by it under that section which are ongoing at the end of that year (whether or not they began in that year),
  (f) what it has done during that year to implement the findings of reviews arranged by it under that section, and
  (g) where it decides during that year not to implement a finding of a review arranged by it under that section, the reasons for its decision.

(2) The SAB must send a copy of the report to–
  (a) the chief executive and the leader of the local authority which established the SAB,
  (b) the local policing body the whole or part of whose area is in the local authority's area,
  (c) the Local Healthwatch organisation for the local authority's area, and
  (d) the chair of the Health and Wellbeing Board for that area.

(3) 'Local policing body' has the meaning given by section 101 of the Police Act 1996.

SCHEDULE 3: DISCHARGE OF HOSPITAL PATIENTS WITH CARE AND SUPPORT NEEDS

Section 74

Cases where hospital patient is likely to have care and support needs after discharge

1 (1) Where the NHS body responsible for a hospital patient considers that it is not likely to be safe to discharge the patient unless arrangements for meeting the patient's needs for care and support are in place, the body must give notice to–
(a) the local authority in whose area the patient is ordinarily resident, or
(b) if it appears to the body that the patient is of no settled residence, the local authority in whose area the hospital is situated.

(2) A notice under sub-paragraph (1) is referred to in this Schedule as an 'assessment notice'; and the local authority to which an assessment notice is given is referred to in this Schedule as 'the relevant authority'.

(3) An assessment notice–
(a) must describe itself as such, and
(b) may not be given more than seven days before the day on which the patient is expected to be admitted to hospital.

(4) Before giving an assessment notice, the NHS body responsible for the patient must consult–
(a) the patient, and
(b) where it is feasible to do so, any carer that the patient has.

(5) An assessment notice remains in force until–
(a) the patient is discharged (whether by the NHS body responsible for the patient or by the patient himself or herself),
(b) the patient dies, or
(c) the NHS body responsible for the patient withdraws the notice by giving a notice (a 'withdrawal notice') to the relevant authority.

(6) A reference in this paragraph to a hospital patient includes a reference to a person who it is reasonable to expect is about to become one.

Assessment notice given by responsible NHS body to local authority

2 (1) The NHS body responsible for a hospital patient, having given the relevant authority an assessment notice, must–
(a) consult the authority before deciding what it will do for the patient in order for discharge to be safe, and
(b) give the authority notice of the day on which it proposes to discharge the patient.

(2) A notice under sub-paragraph (1)(b) is referred to in this Schedule as a 'discharge notice'.

(3) A discharge notice must specify–
(a) whether the NHS body responsible for the patient will be providing or arranging for the provision of services under the National Health Service Act 2006 to the patient after discharge, and
(b) if it will, what those services are.

(4) A discharge notice remains in force until–
(a) the end of the relevant day, or
(b) the NHS body responsible for the patient withdraws the notice by giving a withdrawal notice to the relevant authority.

(5) The 'relevant day' is the later of–
(a) the day specified in the discharge notice, and
(b) the last day of such period as regulations may specify.

(6) A period specified under sub-paragraph (5)(b) must–
(a) begin with the day after that on which the assessment notice is given, and
(b) last for a period of at least two days.

3 (1) The relevant authority, having received an assessment notice and having in light of it carried out a needs assessment and (where applicable) a carer's assessment,

must inform the NHS body responsible for the patient–
  (a) whether the patient has needs for care and support,
  (b) (where applicable) whether a carer has needs for support,
  (c) whether any of the needs referred to in paragraphs (a) and (b) meet the eligibility criteria, and
  (d) how the authority plans to meet such of those needs as meet the eligibility criteria.
 (2) Where, having carried out a needs assessment or carer's assessment in a case within section 27(4), the relevant authority considers that the patient's needs for care and support or (as the case may be) the carer's needs for support have changed, it must inform the NHS body responsible for the patient of the change.

Cases where discharge of the patient is delayed

4 (1) If the relevant authority, having received an assessment notice and a discharge notice, has not carried out a needs or (where applicable) carer's assessment and the patient has not been discharged by the end of the relevant day, the NHS body responsible for the patient may require the relevant authority to pay the specified amount for each day of the specified period.
 (2) If the relevant authority has not put in place arrangements for meeting some or all of those of the needs under sections 18 to 20 that it proposes to meet in the case of the patient or (where applicable) a carer, and the patient has for that reason alone not been discharged by the end of the relevant day, the NHS body responsible for the patient may require the relevant authority to pay the specified amount for each day of the specified period.
 (3) If, in a case within sub-paragraph (1) or (2), the assessment notice ceases to be in force, any liability arising under that sub-paragraph before it ceased to be in force is unaffected.
 (4) A payment under sub-paragraph (1) or (2) must be made to–
  (a) the NHS body responsible for the patient, or
  (b) in such a case as regulations may specify, the person specified.
 (5) The 'relevant day' has the meaning given by paragraph 2(5).
 (6) A reference to a requirement to pay the specified amount is a reference to a requirement to pay the amount specified in regulations; and the reference to the specified period is a reference to the period specified in or determined in accordance with regulations.
 (7) In specifying the amount of a payment, the Secretary of State must have regard in particular to either or both of–
  (a) costs to NHS bodies of providing accommodation and personal care to patients ready to be discharged, and
  (b) costs to local authorities of meeting needs under sections 18 to 20 in the case of persons who have been discharged.

Delegation to management of independent hospital

5 (1) An NHS body may make arrangements with any person connected with the management of an independent hospital for that person (or an employee of that person) to do, on behalf of the NHS body and in accordance with the arrangements, anything which is required or authorised to be done by the NHS body by or under this Schedule in relation to hospital patients accommodated in that hospital.
 (2) Anything done or omitted to be done by or in relation to the authorised person (or an employee of that person) under such arrangements is to be treated as done or omitted to be done by or in relation to the NHS body.
 (3) Nothing in this paragraph prevents anything being done by or in relation to the NHS body.

Adjustments between local authorities

6 (1) Regulations may modify, or otherwise make provision about, the application of a provision of this Schedule in a case where it appears to the NHS body responsible for a hospital patient that the patient is ordinarily resident in the area of another local authority.

(2) The regulations may, in particular, authorise or require a local authority–
  (a) to accept an assessment notice given to it even though it may wish to dispute that it was the correct authority to which to give the notice;
  (b) to become the relevant authority in the patient's case;
  (c) to recover expenditure incurred–
    (i) in the exercise of functions under this Schedule;
    (ii) in meeting needs under sections 18 to 20 in a case under this Schedule.

Meaning of 'hospital patient', 'NHS hospital', 'NHS body', etc

7 (1) A hospital patient is a person ordinarily resident in England who–
  (a) is being accommodated at an NHS hospital, or at an independent hospital as a result of arrangements made by an NHS body, and
  (b) is receiving (or has received or can reasonably be expected to receive) acute care.
(2) 'NHS hospital' means a health service hospital (as defined by the National Health Service Act 2006) in England.
(3) 'Independent hospital' means a hospital (as defined by that Act) in the United Kingdom which is not–
  (a) an NHS hospital,
  (b) a health service hospital as defined by section 206 of the National Health Service (Wales) Act 2006,
  (c) a health service hospital as defined by section 108 of the National Health Service (Scotland) Act 1978, or
  (d) a hospital vested in the Department of Health, Social Services and Public Safety in Northern Ireland or managed by a Health and Social Care trust.
(4) 'NHS body' means–
  (a) an NHS trust established under section 25 of the National Health Service Act 2006,
  (b) an NHS foundation trust,
  (c) the National Health Service Commissioning Board, or
  (d) a clinical commissioning group.
(5) A reference to the NHS body responsible for a hospital patient is–
  (a) if the hospital is an NHS hospital, a reference to the NHS body managing it, or
  (b) if the hospital is an independent hospital, a reference to the NHS body that arranged for the patient to be accommodated in it.
(6) 'Acute care' means intensive medical treatment provided by or under the supervision of a consultant, that lasts for a limited period after which the person receiving the treatment no longer benefits from it.
(7) Care is not 'acute care' if the patient has given an undertaking (or one has been given on the patient's behalf) to pay for it; nor is any of the following 'acute care'–
  (a) care of an expectant or nursing mother;
  (b) mental health care;
  (c) palliative care;
  (d) a structured programme of care provided for a limited period to help a person maintain or regain the ability to live at home;
  (e) care provided for recuperation or rehabilitation.
(8) 'Mental health care' means psychiatric services, or other services provided for the purpose of preventing, diagnosing or treating illness, the arrangements for which are the primary responsibility of a consultant psychiatrist.

Further provision about assessment notices, discharge notices, etc

8 Regulations may–
  (a) specify the form and content of an assessment notice, a discharge notice or a withdrawal notice;
  (b) specify the manner in which an assessment notice, a discharge notice or a withdrawal notice may be given;
  (c) specify when a discharge notice may be given;
  (d) specify circumstances in which a withdrawal notice must be given;

(e) make provision for determining the day on which an assessment notice, a discharge notice or a withdrawal notice is to be regarded as given.

SCHEDULE 4: DIRECT PAYMENTS: AFTER-CARE UNDER THE MENTAL HEALTH ACT 1983

Section 75

Part 1: After-care Under the Mental Health Act 1983: Direct Payments

1 (1) Sections 31 (adults with capacity to request direct payments), 32 (adults without capacity to request direct payments) and 33 (direct payments: further provision) apply in relation to section 117 of the Mental Health Act 1983 but as if the following modifications were made to those sections.

(2) For subsection (1) of section 31, substitute–

'(1) This section applies where an adult to whom section 117 of the Mental Health Act 1983 (after-care) applies requests the local authority to make payments to the adult or a person nominated by the adult that are equivalent to the cost of providing or arranging for the provision of after-care services for the adult under that section.'

(3) In subsection (5) of that section–

(a) in paragraph (a), for 'meeting the adult's needs' substitute 'discharging its duty under section 117 of the Mental Health Act 1983', and

(b) in paragraph (b), for 'to meet the adult's needs' substitute 'to discharge its duty under that section'.

(4) In subsection (7) of that section, for 'to meet the needs in question' substitute 'to discharge its duty under section 117 of the Mental Health Act 1983'.

(5) For subsection (1) of section 32, substitute–

'(1) This section applies where–

(a) an adult to whom section 117 of the Mental Health Act 1983 (after-care) applies lacks capacity to request the local authority to make payments equivalent to the cost of providing or arranging for the provision of after-care services for the adult under that section, and

(b) an authorised person requests the local authority to make such payments to the authorised person.'

(6) In subsection (4)(a) of that section, for 'the adult's needs for care and support' substitute 'the provision to the adult of after-care services under section 117 of the Mental Health Act 1983'.

(7) In subsection (6) of that section–

(a) in paragraph (a), for 'meeting the adult's needs' substitute 'discharging its duty under section 117 of the Mental Health Act 1983', and

(b) in paragraph (b), for 'to meet the adult's needs' substitute 'to discharge its duty under that section'.

(8) In subsection (7) of that section, for 'the provision of the care and support' substitute 'the provision of after-care services under section 117 of the Mental Health Act 1983'.

(9) In subsection (9) of that section, for 'to meet the needs in question' substitute 'to discharge its duty under section 117 of the Mental Health Act 1983'.

(10) In subsection (2)(a) of section 33, for 'meet needs' substitute 'discharge its duty under section 117 of the Mental Health Act 1983'.

(11) For subsection (3) of that section, substitute–

'(3) A direct payment is made on condition that it be used only to pay for arrangements under which after-care services for the adult are provided under section 117 of the Mental Health Act 1983.'

Part 2: Provision to be inserted in Social Services and Well-being (Wales) Act 2014

'SCHEDULE A1: DIRECT PAYMENTS: AFTER-CARE UNDER THE MENTAL HEALTH ACT 1983

General

1 Sections 50 (direct payments to meet an adult's needs), 51 (direct payments to meet a child's needs) and 53 (direct payments: further provision) apply in relation to section 117 of the Mental Health Act 1983 but as if the following modifications were made to those sections.

Modifications to section 50

2 For subsection (1) of section 50 substitute–
'(1) Regulations may require or allow a local authority to make payments to an adult to whom section 117 of the Mental Health Act 1983 (after-care) applies that are equivalent to the cost of providing or arranging for the provision of after-care services for the adult under that section.'

3 In subsection (3) of that section–
(a) in paragraph (a), for 'who has needs for care and support ('A')' substitute 'in respect of the provision to the adult ('A') of after-care services under section 117 of the Mental Health Act 1983', and
(b) in paragraph (c)(i), for 'of meeting A's needs' substitute 'of discharging its duty towards A under section 117 of the Mental Health Act 1983'.

4 In subsection (4) of that section–
(a) in paragraph (a), for 'who has needs for care and support ('A')' substitute 'to whom section 117 of the Mental Health Act 1983 applies ('A')', and
(b) in paragraph (d)(i), for 'meeting A's needs' substitute 'discharging its duty towards A under section 117 of the Mental Health Act 1983'.

5 In subsection (5) of that section–
(a) in paragraph (a), for 'A's needs for care and support' substitute 'the provision to A of after-care services under section 117 of the Mental Health Act 1983', and
(b) in paragraph (b), for 'towards the cost of meeting A's needs for care and support' substitute 'equivalent to the cost of providing or arranging the provision to A of after-care services under section 117 of the Mental Health Act 1983'.

6 In subsection (6)(b) of that section, for 'A's needs for care and support' substitute 'the provision to A of after-care services under section 117 of the Mental Health Act 1983'.

Modifications to section 51

7 For subsection (1) of section 51 substitute–
'(1) Regulations may require or allow a local authority to make payments to a person in respect of a child to whom section 117 of the Mental Health Act 1983 (after-care) applies that are equivalent to the cost of providing or arranging the provision of after-care services for the child under that section.'

8 In subsection (3)(a) and (b) of that section, for 'who has needs for care and support' (in each place it occurs) substitute 'to whom section 117 of the Mental Health Act 1983 applies'.

9 In subsection (5)(a) of that section, for 'meeting the child's needs' substitute 'discharging its duty towards the child under section 117 of the Mental Health Act 1983'.

Modifications to section 53

10 In subsection (1) of section 53–
(a) in the opening words, for '50, 51 or 52' substitute '50 or 51',
(b) omit paragraphs (a), (b) and (c),
(c) in paragraph (i), for 'a local authority's duty or power to meet a person's needs for care and support or a carer's needs for support is displaced'

substitute 'a local authority's duty under section 117 of the Mental Health Act 1983 (after-care) is discharged', and

(d) in paragraph (k), for '50 to 52' substitute '50 and 51'.

11 Omit subsections (2) to (8) of that section.

12 After subsection (8) of that section insert–

'(8A)Regulations under sections 50 and 51 must specify that direct payments to meet the cost of providing or arranging for the provision of after-care services under section 117 of the Mental Health Act 1983 (after-care) must be made at a rate that the local authority estimates to be equivalent to the reasonable cost of securing the provision of those services to meet those needs.'

13 In subsection (9) of that section–

(a) for ', 51 or 52' substitute 'or 51', and

(b) for 'care and support (or, in the case of a carer, support)' substitute 'after-care services'.

14 In subsection (10) of that section, for 'care and support (or, in the case of a carer, support) to meet needs' substitute 'after-care services'.'

HOUSING GRANTS, CONSTRUCTION AND REGENERATION ACT 1996 ss23, 24

Grants: purposes for which grant must or may be given

23 (1) The purposes for which an application for a grant must be approved, subject to the provisions of this Chapter, are the following–

(a) facilitating access by the disabled occupant to and from–
(i) the dwelling, qualifying houseboat or caravan, or
(ii) the dwelling or the building in which the dwelling or, as the case may be, flat is situated;

(b) making–
(i) the dwelling, qualifying houseboat or caravan, or
(ii) the building,
safe for the disabled occupant and other persons residing with him;

(c) facilitating access by the disabled occupant to a room used or usable as the principal family room;

(d) facilitating access by the disabled occupant to, or providing for the disabled occupant, a room used or usable for sleeping;

(e) facilitating access by the disabled occupant to, or providing for the disabled occupant, a room in which there is a lavatory, or facilitating the use by the disabled occupant of such a facility;

(f) facilitating access by the disabled occupant to, or providing for the disabled occupant, a room in which there is a bath or shower (or both), or facilitating the use by the disabled occupant of such a facility;

(g) facilitating access by the disabled occupant to, or providing for the disabled occupant, a room in which there is a washhand basin, or facilitating the use by the disabled occupant of such a facility;

(h) facilitating the preparation and cooking of food by the disabled occupant;

(i) improving any heating system in the dwelling, qualifying houseboat or caravan to meet the needs of the disabled occupant or, if there is no existing heating system in the dwelling or any such system is unsuitable for use by the disabled occupant, providing a heating system there suitable to meet his needs;

(j) facilitating the use by the disabled occupant of a source of power, light or heat by altering the position of one or more means of access to or control of that source or by providing additional means of control;

(k) facilitating access and movement by the disabled occupant around the dwelling, qualifying houseboat or caravan in order to enable him to care for a person who is normally resident there and is in need of such care;

(l) such other purposes as may be specified by order of the Secretary of State.

(2) ...

(3) If in the opinion of the local housing authority the relevant works are more or less extensive than is necessary to achieve any of the purposes set out in subsection (1), they may, with the consent of the applicant, treat the application as varied so that the relevant works are limited to or, as the case may be, include such works as seem to the authority to be necessary for that purpose.

Grants: approval of application

24 (1) The local housing authority shall approve an application for a grant for purposes within section 23(1) subject to the following provisions.

(2) Where an authority entertain an owner's application for a grant made by a person who proposes to acquire a qualifying owner's interest, they shall not approve the application until they are satisfied that he has done so.

(3) A local housing authority shall not approve an application for a grant unless they are satisfied–

(a) that the relevant works are necessary and appropriate to meet the needs of the disabled occupant, and

(b) that it is reasonable and practicable to carry out the relevant works having regard to the age and condition of –

(i) the dwelling, qualifying houseboat or caravan, or

(ii) the building.

In considering the matters mentioned in paragraph (a) a local housing authority which is not itself a social services authority shall consult the social services authority.

(4) ...

(5) A local housing authority shall not approve a common parts application for a grant unless they are satisfied that the applicant has a power or is under a duty to carry out the relevant works.

MENTAL HEALTH ACT 1983 ss17, 17A, 17B

After-care

117 (1) This section applies to persons who are detained under section 3 above, or admitted to a hospital in pursuance of a hospital order made under section 37 above, or transferred to a hospital in pursuance of a hospital direction made under section 45A above or a transfer direction made under section 47 or 48 above, and then cease to be detained and (whether or not immediately after so ceasing) leave hospital.

(2) It shall be the duty of the clinical commissioning group or Local Health Board and of the local social services authority to provide or arrange for the provision of, in co-operation with relevant voluntary agencies, after-care services for any person to whom this section applies until such time as the clinical commissioning group or Local Health Board and the local social services authority are satisfied that the person concerned is no longer in need of such services; but they shall not be so satisfied in the case of a community patient while he remains such a patient.

(2A) ...

(2B) Section 32 above shall apply for the purposes of this section as it applies for the purposes of Part II of this Act.

(2C) References in this Act to after-care services provided for a patient under this section include references to services provided for the patient

    (a) in respect of which direct payments are made under

        (i) sections 31 to 33 of the Care Act 2014 (as applied by Schedule 4 to that Act),

        (ii) sections 50, 51 and 53 of the Social Services and Well-being (Wales) Act 2014 (as applied by Schedule A1 to that Act), or

        (iii) regulations under section 12A(4) of the National Health Service Act 2006, and

    (b) which would be provided under this section apart from those sections (as so applied) or the regulations.

(2D) Subsection (2), in its application to the clinical commissioning group, has effect as if the words 'provide or' were omitted.

(2E) The Secretary of State may by regulations provide that the duty imposed on the clinical commissioning group by subsection (2) is, in the circumstances or to the extent prescribed by the regulations, to be imposed instead on another clinical commissioning group or the National Health Service Commissioning Board.

(2F) Where regulations under subsection (2E) provide that the duty imposed by subsection (2) is to be imposed on the National Health Service Commissioning Board, subsection (2D) has effect as if the reference to the clinical commissioning group were a reference to the National Health Service Commissioning Board.

(2G) Section 272(7) and (8) of the National Health Service Act 2006 applies to the power to make regulations under subsection (2E) as it applies to a power to make regulations under that Act.

(3) In this section 'the Clinical commissioning group or Local Health Board' means the Clinical commissioning group or Local Health Board, and 'the local social services authority' means the local social services authority, for the area in which the person concerned is resident or to which he is sent on discharge by the hospital in which he was detained.

(4) Where there is a dispute about where a person was ordinarily resident for the purposes of subsection (3) above

    (a) if the dispute is between local social services authorities in England, section 40 of the Care Act 2014 applies to the dispute as it applies to a dispute about where a person was ordinarily resident for the purposes of Part 1 of that Act;

    (b) if the dispute is between local social services authorities in Wales, section 195 of the Social Services and Well-being (Wales) Act 2014 applies to the dispute as it applies to a dispute about where a person was ordinarily resident for the purposes of that Act;

    (c) if the dispute is between a local social services authority in England and a local social services authority in Wales, it is to be determined by the Secretary of State or the Welsh Ministers.

(5) The Secretary of State and the Welsh Ministers shall make and publish arrangements for determining which of them is to determine a dispute under subsection (4)(c); and the arrangements may, in particular, provide for the dispute to be determined by whichever of them they agree is to do so.

(6) In this section, 'after-care services', in relation to a person, means services which have both of the following purposes
   (a) meeting a need arising from or related to the person's mental disorder; and
   (b) reducing the risk of a deterioration of the person's mental condition (and, accordingly, reducing the risk of the person requiring admission to a hospital again for treatment for mental disorder).

After-care: preference for particular accommodation

117A(1)The Secretary of State may by regulations provide that where
   (a) the local social services authority under section 117 is, in discharging its duty under subsection (2) of that section, providing or arranging for the provision of accommodation for the person concerned;
   (b) the person concerned expresses a preference for particular accommodation; and
   (c) any prescribed conditions are met,
   the local social services authority must provide or arrange for the provision of the person's preferred accommodation.

(2) Regulations under this section may provide for the person concerned, or a person of a prescribed description, to pay for some or all of the additional cost in prescribed cases.

(3) In subsection (2), 'additional cost' means the cost of providing or arranging for the provision of the person's preferred accommodation less the amount that the local social services authority would expect to be the usual cost of providing or arranging for the provision of accommodation of that kind.

(4) The power to make regulations under this section
   (a) is exercisable only in relation to local social services authorities in England;
   (b) includes power to make different provision for different cases or areas.

After-care: exception for provision of nursing care

117B(1)Section 117 does not authorise or require a local social services authority . . ., in or in connection with the provision of services under that section, to provide or arrange for the provision of nursing care by a registered nurse.

(2) In this section 'nursing care by a registered nurse' means a service provided by a registered nurse involving
   (a) the provision of care, or
   (b) the planning, supervision or delegation of the provision of care,
   other than a service which, having regard to its nature and the circumstances in which it is provided, does not need to be provided by a registered nurse.

LOCAL AUTHORITY SOCIAL SERVICES ACT 1970 ss6, 7, 7A–7E

The director of social services

6(A1) A local authority in England shall appoint an officer, to be known as the director of adult social services, for the purposes of their social services functions, other than those for which the authority's director of children's services is responsible under section 18 of the Children Act 2004.

(1) ...

(2) Two or more local authorities may, if they consider that the same person can efficiently discharge, for both or all of them, the functions of director of adult social services, concur in the appointment of a person as director of adult social services for both or all of those authorities.

(3), (5) ...

(6) A local authority which have appointed, or concurred in the appointment of, a person under this section, shall secure the provision of adequate staff for assisting him in the exercise of his functions.

(7) ...

(8) ...

Local authorities to exercise social services functions under guidance of Secretary of State

7 (1) Local authorities shall, in the exercise of their social services functions, including the exercise of any discretion conferred by any relevant enactment, act under the general guidance of the Secretary of State.

(1A) Section 78 of the Care Act 2014 applies instead of this section in relation to functions given by Part 1 of that Act or by regulations under that Part.

(2), (3) ...

Directions by the Secretary of State as to exercise of social services functions

7A(1) Without prejudice to section 7 of this Act, every local authority shall exercise their social services functions in accordance with such directions as may be given to them under this section by the Secretary of State.

(2) Directions under this section–
  (a) shall be given in writing; and
  (b) may be given to a particular authority, or to authorities of a particular class, or to authorities generally.

7B ...

Inquiries

7C(1) The Secretary of State may cause an inquiry to be held in any case where, whether on representations made to him or otherwise, he considers it advisable to do so in connection with the exercise by any local authority of any of their social services functions (except in so far as those functions relate to persons under the age of eighteen).

(2) Subsections (2) to (5) of section 250 of the Local Government Act 1972 (powers in relation to local inquiries) shall apply in relation to an inquiry under this section as they apply in relation to an inquiry under that section.

Default powers of Secretary of State as respects social services functions of local authorities

7D(1) If the Secretary of State is satisfied that any local authority have failed, without reasonable excuse to comply with any of their duties which are social services functions (other than a duty imposed by or under the Children Act 1989, section 1 or 2(4) of the Adoption (Intercountry Aspects) Act 1999 or the Adoption and Children Act 2002), he may make an order declaring that authority to be in default with respect to the duty in question.

(2) An order under subsection(1) may contain such directions for the purpose of ensuring that the duty is complied with within such period as may be specified in the order as appear to the Secretary of State to be necessary.

(3) Any such direction shall, on the application of the Secretary of State, be enforceable by mandamus.

Grants to local authorities in respect of social services for the mentally ill

7E The Secretary of State may, with the approval of the Treasury, make grants out of money provided by Parliament towards any expenses of local authorities incurred in connection with the exercise of their social services functions in relation to persons suffering from mental illness.

Precedents

In addition to the precedents in this section a larger range of precedent/template letters (and other social care resources) can be accessed at: www.lukeclements. co.uk/resources/.

PRECEDENT 1   Social care assessment request: adult in need

To: Director of Adult Social Services

[*address*]

From: *Applicant's name*

[*address*]

Date:

Dear Director of Adult Social Services,

Care Act 2014 Assessment:
Mr Albert Smith 10 Red Street, Middlemarch – DOB 01/01/1940

I am the [*solicitor/carer/agent/advocate*] for the above named who has asked that I assist him in obtaining an assessment of his needs for social care and support under section 9 of the Care Act 2014.

Mr Smith is [*insert*] years of age and is a [*disabled/elderly/ill*] person, in that he

[*here detail as precisely as possible the illness / impairments which have resulted in the applicant needing social care support*].

The help that Mr Smith currently envisages as being necessary, is

[*here detail if possible the services which are required*].

I understand that your care manager will wish to contact Mr Smith in order to undertake the assessment. He suggests that this be done by [*here give a telephone contact number and the time/days that Mr Smith is normally available or some other convenient way that contact can be made*].

Please confirm receipt of this request.

Yours faithfully,

[*sign*]

PRECEDENT 2   Social care assessment request: carer

To: Director of Adult Social Services

[address]

From: Applicant's name

[address]

Date:

Dear Director of Adult Social Services

Care Act 2014 Assessment:
Mrs Alice Smith 10 Red Street, Middlemarch – DOB 02/03/1944

I am the [*solicitor/carer/agent/advocate*] for the above named who has asked that I assist her in obtaining an assessment of her needs as a carer for social care support under section 10 of the Care Act 2014.

Mrs Smith is [*insert*] years of age and cares for [*name of person(s) she cares for and the nature of their needs and the nature and the extent of the care she provides*].

The support that Mrs Smith currently envisages as being necessary, is

[*here detail what she would like to happen as a result of the assessment –ie that she can go back to work / college etc; that Mr Smith have a proper support package so that she does not have to provide care / provide the same amount of care etc*].

I understand that your care manager will wish to contact Mrs Smith in order to undertake the assessment. She suggests that this be done by [*here give a telephone contact number and the time/days that Mrs Smith is normally available or some other convenient way that contact can be made*].

Please confirm receipt of this request.

Yours faithfully,

[*sign*]

PRECEDENT 3   Access to information letter

To: Director of Adult Social Services / CCG / NHS Trust etc

[*address*]

From: Applicant's name

[*address*]

Date:

Reference:

Dear

Access to personal information: Data Protection Act 1998 s7

I formally request that you give me access to the personal information held by your authority relating to my personal circumstances, by copying the relevant information to [*me*] [*my agent, namely . . .*] at [*insert address*].

The information I require to be disclosed is all personal information which your authority holds which relates to myself. [*If possible describe as precisely as possible the information that is sought, including for instance where the information is likely to be located, the nature of the information and the dates between which it was collected*].

I understand that I am entitled to receive this information within 40 days.

If you need further information from me, or a fee,[1] please let me know as soon as possible. If you do not normally handle these requests for your organisation, please pass this letter to your Data Protection Officer or another appropriate officer.

Please confirm receipt of this request.

Yours faithfully,

[*sign*]

---

1   The 40-day period runs from the date of receipt of the request and any necessary fee (see para 19.65 above). Accordingly, provision should be expedited if the fee is actually enclosed.

PRECEDENT 4   Formal complaint letter[2]

To: Director of Adult Social Services

[*address*]

From: Applicant's name

[*address*]

Date:

Dear Director of Adult Social Services,

Formal complaint

I ask that you treat this letter as a formal complaint concerning the discharge by your authority of its functions in respect of [*myself*] [*the person for whom I care, Mr/Mrs/Ms etc. . .*]. I require the complaint to be investigated at the earliest opportunity

My complaint is:

[*here set out as precisely as possible*

(a) what it is that is being complained about

(b) the names of the key social workers who the complaints investigator will need to speak to;

(c) the dates of the relevant acts / omissions;

If possible also enclose copies of any relevant papers]

What I want to achieve by making this complaint is

[*here set out as precisely as possible what you want to be the result of your complaint: ie an apology, a changed service provision, an alteration to practice, compensation, etc*]

I understand that your Complaints Manager will wish to contact me in order to investigate this complaint. I suggest that this be done by [*here give a telephone contact number and the time/days you are normally available or some other convenient way you can be contacted*]

I also understand that in investigating this complaint you may need to share information with other relevant parties /agencies and also to access my records. I confirm that I am in agreement to you taking this action – so far as it is strictly necessary, and accordingly give my consent to this, under the Data Protection Act 1998. [*if the complaint is in a representative capacity, then either attach a letter signed & dated by the person on whose behalf the complaint is made (agreeing for the information to be disclosed) or state that you believe the person lacks sufficient mental capacity to consent to this disclosure and you are of the opinion that such disclosure would be in his or her best interests*]

Please confirm receipt of this letter of complaint.

Signed:

2   See generally para 20.7 above.

PRECEDENT 5   Request under Care Act 2014 s7 letter[3]

To: District Council / CCG / Chief of Police / Probation Officer

[*address*]

From: Director of Adult Social Services (or senior officer etc).

[*address*]

Date:

Dear

Formal request for cooperation under Care Act 2014 s7
Mr Albert Smith, 10 Red Street, Middlemarch – DOB 01/01/1940

I ask that you treat this letter as a formal request for specific cooperation in relation to Mr Albert Smith under section 7 of the Care Act 2014.

My authority has undertaken an 'adult in need' assessment [*or alternatively a 'carers assessment*] of Mr Smith's needs for social care support under the Care Act 2014. The assessment has identified a need for [*specify what it is that is needed*] that my authority is unable to meet and for this reason I request specific cooperation from your [*name of authority / organisation*].

[*Here specify the support that is required – ie health care services (see para 12.202 above) or housing services (see para 14.16 above) etc.*]

[*Here specify why it is not possible for the social services authority to meet this need – eg it is health related and prohibited by virtue section 22 of the Care Act 2014 (see para 12.13 above) or it is housing and prohibited by virtue section 23 of the Care Act 2014 (see para 14.12 above) etc.*]

We have endeavoured to liaise with your [*name of authority/organisation*] but unfortunately [*here explain why the degree of co-operation required has not been provided*]. It is for this reason that I now make a formal request for specific cooperation by your [*name of authorit /organisation*].

The co-operation my authority seeks is that you:

[*Specify as precisely as possible what it is you require the other party to do*];

[*Specify the date(s) by which you require this to be done*].

Please confirm receipt of this formal letter seeking cooperation.

Yours faithfully,

Signed:

---

3 A formal request can be made by a social services authority to any 'relevant partner' (see paras 3.116 and 11.44 above): 'relevant partner' is defined in Care Act 2014 s6(7). It will include a housing department of a district council, any NHS body, probation service, chief police officer etc.

Index